AA

GUIDE TO GOLF COURSES

OVER 2500 ENTRIES FOR BRITAIN AND IRELAND

COLOUR PHOTOGRAPHS THROUGHOUT

Produced by AA Publishing

Maps prepared by the Cartographic Department of
The Automobile Association

Directory generated by the AA Establishment Database,
Information Research, Hotel and Touring Services

Editor: David Hancock

Design by Design Directions, Twyford, Berkshire

The Automobile Association would like to thank the following photographers and libraries for their assistance in the preparation of this book.

The Automobile Association would like to thank the following photographers and libraries for their assistance in the preparation of this book.

AA Photo Library 12 (R Victor), 13 (P Baker), 14 (K Paterson), 23 (S Day),
317 (Ellington), 392 (H Williams);
Allsport U.K. Ltd 4;
Peter Dazeley Front & back cover;
K Ferguson 388;
Derek George Photography 413;
Jim Long 14/15b, 15;
Phil Sheldon 3, 5, 6, 7a, 7b, 8, 10, 14/15a;

Editorial contributors: John Ingham, writer for Golf Monthly and Charlie Mulqueen of the Cork Examiner

Head of Advertisement Sales
Christopher Heard: Tel 01256 491544

Advertisement Production
Karen Weeks: Tel 01256 491545

Typeset/Repro by Avonset, 1 Palace Yard Mews, Monmouth Place, Bath BA1 2NH

Printed in Italy by Rotolito, Lambarda

The contents of this book are believed correct at the time of printing. Nevertheless, the Publisher cannot be held responsible for any errors or omissions or for changes in the details given in this guide or for the consequences of any reliance on the information provided in the same. Although every effort has been made to ensure accuracy we always welcome any information from readers to assist in such efforts and to keep the book up to date.

A CIP catalogue record for this book is available from
the British Library

Published by AA Publishing, which is a trading name of Automobile Association Developments Limited whose registered office is Norfolk House, Priestley Road, Basingstoke, Hampshire RG24 9NY, Registered number 1878835.

ISBN 0 7495 1936 3

AA Ref 10170

CONTENTS

WHY PACKAGE GOLF MAKES SUCH GOOD SENSE

The sun never sets on the small white ball flying, bouncing and rolling towards flagsticks or hazards somewhere in our huge golfing empire where people from all nationalities play to win little more than a 19th-hole celebration.

Cannes Open, Royal Mougins, France 1996

In the last fifty years, writes John Ingham, I've seen wondrous changes to the game, not only in equipment, but in the quality of layouts in far-flung places. Who could have imagined our royal (and ancient) hobby could ever return to China, or begin to take deep roots in Russia, or indeed be played over summer-time green fairways in Iceland? Today, they are incredible golfing holiday locations.

When I started, with a 1930's wooden-shafted driver, Ryder Cup teams sailed to America, the prize for winning the Open was £300 and golfing holidays were exclusively for the rich, who motored to Gleneagles, or the South of France, with clubs in leather bags firmly strapped in place, and they enjoyed hotels boasting giant potted plants and an in-house orchestra to brighten après golf evenings.

My favourite memory of the early 1960's was driving a French car from the Martinez Hotel, Cannes, with our fourball to play the elegant Mougins, and meeting with the then professional there, Henry Cotton. Soon afterwards came the revolution called package holidays which, quite suddenly, brought the world closer together.

The jet aircraft must take the credit for the improvement in most golfers who now tee up to hit shots over crocodiles in Florida, lily ponds in Fanling, or cork trees near Faro. And the famous Thomas Cook travel people, who have been going for years, suddenly faced fierce competition from hundreds of experts catering to the wishes of 45 million worldwide golfers keen to swing on foreign fairways. Americans come here, we go there, groups from Japan can be found swinging in Africa and in all my travels in a career surrounding golf, I have seldom failed to meet someone I know, at some club. Obviously we all have favourite locations but let me embark on an objective look because the fun is worth every penny and lifetime memories lie in wait.

Why Europe Delivers all its Promises

Package trips for golfers are now well regarded and represent one of the world's great bargains. The reason is the competition for travellers is so fierce, profit margins have been slashed. Add to this the currency advantages, and you are rightly on your way. And of all places, Europe delivers.

However, if you want testing links of the severe kind, well that's fine, too. It means you go to Carnoustie, Scotland and, maybe, find your teeth blown out. Or you can fly to Stornaway, where the green fee is £10, although the risk of gale-force winds is greater.

But I prefer to cross the Irish Sea or the Channel, and taking the car is good, too. But on a package trip, the hard work evaporates and you let the experts take the strain.

Vale do Lobo, Portugal

Ireland

Alongside the oceans edge, Ballybunion, on the West Coast, epitomises what's best in Ireland. Raw and wild nature, it is the stuff dreams are made of, and everyone wants to return – particularly as there are now two courses there. However, playing both in a day, could prove exhausting, as well as a financial strain – one day green fee is £65 which is more than most in the Emerald Isle, although the now famous K Club, a hotel complex eighteen miles west of Dublin, charge £85.

Golf can still be low budget but the great tests, like Royal County Down in the north, or Royal Portrush (one of the world's best) still require serious money from the visitor.

Christy O'Connor Jnr tells me his favourite is Ceann Sibeal (Dingle) which is Europe's most westerly course. In County Kerry, near Ballyferriter, they charge £18 for the day. "I take my wife there" says Christy "And there's nothing better." Interesting, because most tournament players usually only play newer venues, keen on publicity. Travellers must learn to search out what Nick Faldo called "The hidden gems"

Ireland has almost 260 courses, and two are placed among the world's experts – Ballybunion and Royal County Down, 30 miles south of Belfast. However, those in Dublin will claim Portmarnock is great, as indeed it is if you can hit your drive 270 yards in strong winds.

Many wax lyrical about Killarney, in County Kerry and the views are spectacular, as indeed is the modern clubhouse. And many maintain that the Jack Nicklaus designed Mount Juliet, all of a whopping 7143 yards, 10 miles from Kilkenny, is worth a visit. Faldo thinks highly of it, at least he did after shooting a course record 65 in 1993!

There are some brilliant package trips in Ireland (Eire Golf Ltd 00 353 643 1638; Bill Goff Golf Tours 0191 427 5003; Leisure Golf 0151 734 5200; JD Golf Tours 0800 626 324), and, if the weather's good, there is nothing to touch the place... "There's one place I'll never forget" a friend tells me. "It's Waterville, in the Ring of Kerry – I intend to go back."

France

France has much to offer. You must try Le Touquet which, years ago, had a cachet with well-off folk who played a morning round, then took an excellent lunch at Le Manoir before a snooze, and then some time at the casino. Now it has become, how shall we say, somewhat more popular and my tip would be to go the extra mile or so to Hardelot, half an hour south of Boulogne. It's totally excellent, even though comparatively new, having opened in 1991. It has two fine courses, and a wonderful clubhouse serving elegant meals, and you can get there with the help of French Golf Holidays (01277 374374), and 3D Golf plc (0800 333 323).

Hardelot Les Pins, France

Aloha, Spain

However, northern France is not my personal favourite area in a country which has 340 golf courses, some pre-war and mature, and some smart new ones. The picturesque places I know include Biarritz and Pau in the south west and the scenic fairways there were laid more than 100 years ago.

However, French golf has caught the attention with more northern courses such as Chantilly, 35 miles north of Paris, and Fontainebleau, south-east of the capital. And you cannot forget St Germain, further south, although it is very up-market and jeans, however well-cut and expensive, will rightly be frowned on! But the way of life, and golf, is very different in France which is good, and why we travel. Don't expect British food, or tea, or fish and chips. Look for other things. What I like is that in the golf clubs there, you are served red wine in proper cut glass, and the whole atmosphere is very civilised. Anyway, let's look at more possible ideas to explore.

The gems in France include such courses as St Cloud, a splendid course designed by Harry Colt – but I still take the view that if you head south, then take aim at Cannes, and play the famous Mougins course which was originally built in 1925 and was 'modernised' later. The area, however, remains absolutely stunning, and, can you believe it, they've just built a course at Grasse, just north of Cannes. Incidentally, the professionals play at Royal Mougins designed by American Robert von Hagge. But play Cannes-Mougins, on the Route d'Antibes because it is delightful.

Some years ago I watched Seve Ballesteros play Pont Royal, south-east of Avignon on

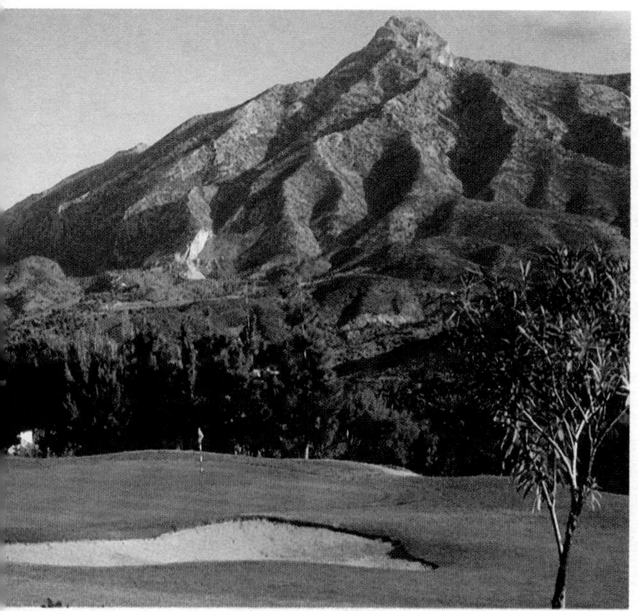

Quinta do Logo and Vale do Lobo were both fun, and Sunsport Algarve out there can give you prices, if you call them on (351) 89393244.

Ashfield is another company that can help you to Portugal, or other places where groups are welcome. Call in the afternoon on 01789 262977 because the team, probably, are sharpening their own game in the morning! If you want a free brochure on Portugal, try Exclusive Golf Tours who say they can obtain reduced, or even free, green fees out

the N7. Go there if you can because the course, and the area, is the stuff of artists, as you would expect in Provence and the Côte d'Azur. What I would look for is a travel company to deliver me to either these top French courses, or I'd take a firm aim at the Bordeaux area and attempt to play Chantaco, St Jean-de-Luz which I recall from my youth.

If, like me, you fancy the south of France, then talk with Cresta either on 0181 944 1260 or by calling Thomas Cook direct on 0990 666 222. And if you're planning to go to Marseille, or Aix-en-Provence then include me in, as well!

Portugal and Spain

The most popular holiday locations in Europe now are Portugal and Spain. Since my honeymoon at Penina, in the Algarve, thousands have streamed into this Portuguese playground where companies like KB Golf of Bournemouth (01202 768272) offer a grand service, but not necessarily to the expensive hotels. I found Penina a tough 18-holes, and preferred Vilamoura, down the coast. But

there. They're onto something, and on 0181 882 7153. There are dozens of companies that can get you to Portugal, and other places. Lotus Supertravel say one in six go free which is great, assuming there are six of you. Anyway, try your luck on 0171 962 9494 if only to ask for a brochure.

Quinta do Logo, Portugal

Why, you cry, call anyone. Why not buy a ticket and just book yourself in? Well, years ago that was a good idea in Europe, but these travel people get such discounts that, frankly, few can do this today – so the package trip is in. And you are not required to room with strangers, or play golf with them!

Those in Spain who love the Costa del Sol will hear nothing against it. They speak English out there, Brits buy villas and such as Sean Connery and others even have hideaway's there. In Marbella you can walk

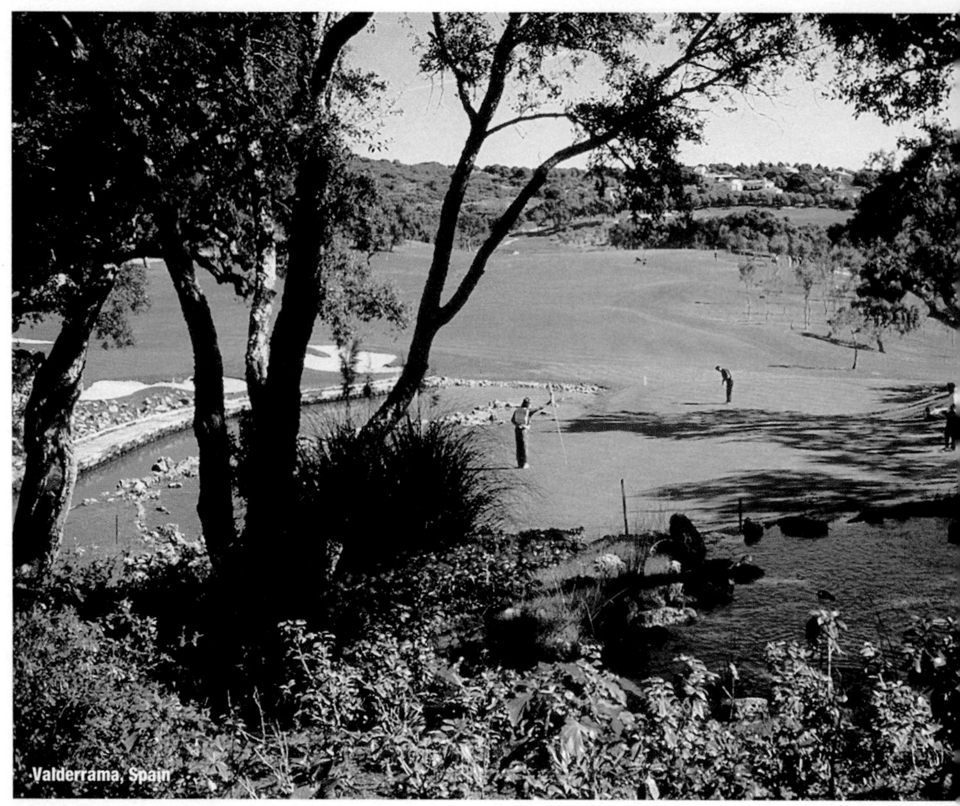
Valderrama, Spain

round the smart harbour, take in a bullfight, play on a whole stretch of courses as we did, or drive up into the hills and find parts of Spain that remain Spanish!

Most courses in the heart of the Nueva Andalucia Valley deliver the promises, too. They are aimed not only at the tourist tripper to Spain, but also at those wishing to rent, or buy, apartments along this 'golden' coastline which boasts distant views of the mountains to the east. The Los Naranjos course, designed by an American and decorated with imported palm trees, offers eighteen fine golf holes, and 100 new apartments nearby. There are views of the sea and, more often than not, sunshine all the way.

Back in London, Steve, who kindly straightened my dented car, tells me he has a holiday villa in Marbella. "For golfers" he said, pushing the dreaded invoice across his portacabin desk, "It's the place to be...." And I notice Hamptons International (0171 823 3222) think the same way, sending blurb through the post claiming the area is the "fairway to heaven." In certain cases, I fear, this could be true – and slow play on crowded courses just might be the killer!

I played the old Sotogrande some years ago now, but recall even then that we were obliged to take our time. The course has huge greens and if approach shots are not spot on, you can be left with a 40-foot putt over switch-back slopes. But it's a good test, and the 1000 members are happy. Since you can see Gibraltar in the distance, it might be a good idea to check which is the best airport to fly into, Gib or Malaga and Jim Long of Golf Links International (01494 563935) will

give sound advice, and then sell you a ticket.

That neck of the woods includes 5-star Valderrama, famous for the Ryder Cup, and a European victory. The course, even nearer the Rock, is highly rated by everyone who has played it – even Tiger Woods who failed, surprisingly, in the big International.

The course I enjoyed most on this coastline was Aloha, about six miles from Marbella and its smart port Puerto Banus. But Alcaidesa Links, designed by the mighty Peter Alliss, is good, while Atalaya and Las Brisas are established and, in a sense, are the senior courses. Interesting because they were built not so long ago in 1968, and even the oldest courses on the coast, such as Guadalmina (1959), Sotogrande (1964) and Rio Real (1965) are still comparative newcomers. Since they were opened, more than a dozen other courses have gone into business and they all have fabulous clubhouses, and service to match. In this regard, some British clubs could learn a lot from the Costa golfing playground.

Other areas in Spain I know include San Sebastian, where there is a real classic course about ten miles north-east of the town centre. In Madrid I got diverted to a motor race instead of sampling the famous Puerta de Hierro (built 1904) or the Villa de Madrid, some 67 years old. The splendid city has a dozen courses in this part of real Spain which is what you find when you visit Toledo – the real thing, if you feel compelled, as I did, to explore the stunning cathedral instead of playing yet another round of golf!

Foolishly, I didn't take clubs to La Manga when I was invited to its grand opening, back in 1971. It was so grand, in fact, that I sank beneath one red wine too many, but I well recall they had bulldozed in 3000 palm trees which, later, had to be replaced. Money is no object here, and a trip there is worthwhile.

Finally, don't miss two possibly unusual places. The Basque region, despite local rumblings, has some wonderful scenes and golf well worth playing. While I realise St Jean de Luz is just over the border in South West France, if you can get into the area, the Chantaco course is delightful.

Technically, of course, this isn't Spain and, in some regards, the Canary Isles isn't – although the Golfer's Handbook rightly tells you it is! Anyway, go there as I did. There are six courses, the oldest being Real Golf Las Palmas, on the Gran Canaria since 1891 and designed by a Scot. The islands there make a super package holiday.

Italy

Massimo Mannelli, an Italian pro, told me that the game has still not "caught on" in Italy in the same way as in some other countries, although I believe that in Germany, despite Bernhard Langer, golf is still played only by the very rich, or by caddies who get on – into the pro ranks.

Either way there are pickings for the visitor to Italy. With about 100 courses to choose from in Italy, I would again advise travellers to aim at beauty spots which, in the case of this country, could mean almost everywhere, except big, industrial cities such as Milan. For a choice of package deals contact The Magic of Italy (0990 462 442), Page & Moy (0116 250 7676), Timescape Holidays (0181 980 7244) or Crystal Italy (0181 390 5554.)

Fly to Rome with Alitalia and then switch aircraft for the hop across to Sardinia where two courses, both a revelation, await your pleasure. They've already played tournaments at Is Molas, in the south of the island, but in the north – well Pevero, Costa Smeralda was blasted through rocks and hills and is a golfing wonder. Back in the 1970's, at a grand opening, I competed and won a Pevero prize, presented by the owner who paid a fortune to have created a course fit for a king, in this case the Aga Khan, better known for horses than golf.

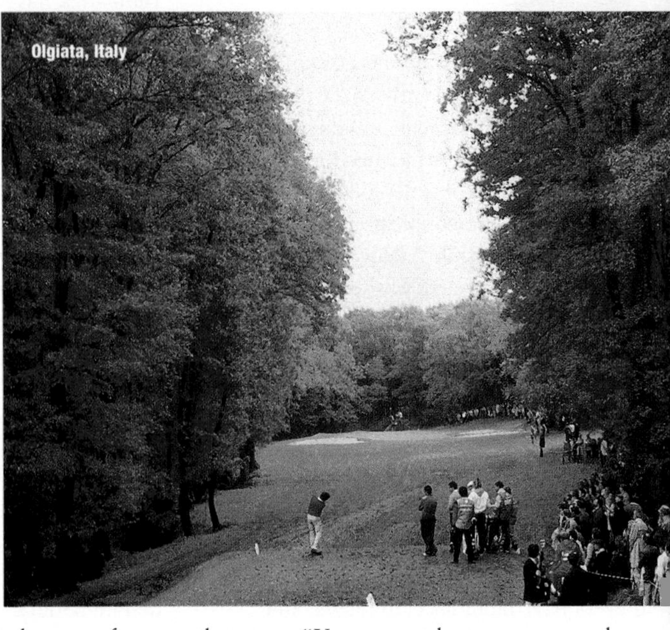
Olgiata, Italy

Search around for a package deal which, for Sardinia, is not easy. Green fees here range from £20 to £90 which is somewhat daunting. But the island has so much to offer, and our waterside hotel, the Cali di Volpe, was stunning – but costly.

I wanted to go to Elba for our honeymoon, but Henry Cotton persuaded me to take my new wife to Portugal. However, there is a 9-hole layout there in Elba, but I imagine the fairways to be steep, although the green fee, at 45,000 lire, isn't.

But the great and famous courses in Italy are such as Villa d'Este at Montorfano, Como and Alitalia can help, and tell of the other diversions for the traveller, like looking over the old Italian empire, or boar and chamois hunting at Citizzano. While golf courses maybe not as fine as the art treasures on view, they need exploring. But as I've already said, I'll take Pevero, on the island of Sardinia and enjoy the magical views of the Mediterranean, looking from the 10th tee over the Bay of Foxes. This emerald coast has everything, but getting a special deal there, with a package company, may require persistence.

Sweden

Of all the countries in Europe, tournament golfer Fredrik Lindgren reckons Sweden is where the game is enjoying the fastest growth. Playing eighteen holes with him, he waxed lyrical about the Swedish attitude to the game, "Young people are encouraged, and big business backs those who want to play in tournaments, or make a career in golf" he said. "We Swedes don't differentiate between amateur and professional – you would call it open golf, like we have in tennis."

The result: ordinary beginners can start with a handicap of 54, everyone is given the opportunity to play and now the top events are being won by Swedes. Now they are adding new courses to existing classic ones like Falsterbo which was opened back in

1909 and Halmstad, also on sandy soil, but with pine trees as well.

Falsterbo is on the south western tip, 300 miles from the capital Stockholm and in wild, remote country. Although there are Baltic breezes which can sweep across this seaside links, the excitement and challenge of the place never lets up, with sea inlets, and a beautiful old lighthouse, making it a memorable experience.

The sea, of course, plays a great part in golf with many links situated on land left by receeding oceans. And ships deposit holiday-makers and golfers at Gothenburg, with Scandinavian Seaways actually laying on a 5-course golfing 'feast' that starts with a round at Stenungsbaden-Spekerod, and going through to Orust, in the north west. Those interested in joining this golf tour should call 0990 333 222. Sailings are available from Newcastle and Harwich.

Sweden now has 234 courses so it is little wonder their players have registered in world-wide events, both amateur and professional. Great players like Anders Forsbrand, Matts Lanner and Ryder Cup star Per Ulrik Johansson have emerged from great courses which, admittedly are sometimes viewed under a midnight sun, or under snow at which time the golfers follow a trend set by wild geese, and fly south!

Almost every week new courses spring up, but Goteburg, eight miles from Gothenburg, dates from 1902 so you can still find elderly members, and traditions, in a country which admits it has gone golf crazy.

If you're interested in Sweden, you can also fly to there with Maersk Air from Gatwick. This route to Copenhagen, Denmark, is good because you could first look at Copenhagen, before taking the ferry across to Oresund, to Sweden. Alternatively, you could fly direct to Malmo from City Airport, with two flights a day. July, August and September are popular. Green fees are reasonable, with top-ranked Falsterbo about £30 a round. They even welcome the not-so-young in Sweden, so call Airtours on 01235 824428 and learn about the Golden Years break!

Nick Faldo's Gem

Established venues elsewhere in Europe include Baden-Baden in Germany. The course boasts some incredible holes, and is near the Black Forest, and tumbling mountain streams. The whole place was immaculate, and the members charming. Belgium gave us a huge welcome at the Knokke La Zoute course, praised by Nick Faldo who described the links there as a "hidden gem". It's no longer out of sight as tournaments are now held there, partly thanks to Faldo's praise. I stayed in the clubhouse itself, in a dormie-house situation, and ate staggering meals. They know how to cook and the club is what I call a proper one, with a family atmosphere.

Sunshine, and the Stuff of Dreams

While European trips represent astonishing value, with Portugal, Spain, France and Italy high on the list of favourites, my golfing expeditions have led me to play some excellent courses just beyond European shores, yet only a few hours flying time from London .

My first trip, in a turbo prop Viscount, was to Malta where, believe it or not, they have a golf course built, I believe, by the military. It can be found three miles from

Valetta and it's been there for more than 100 years. While most trippers head for the beach, £10 in Malta money can buy 18 holes, on a par 68 stretch. My problem, on that visit, was sunstroke, achieved at midday when even mad dogs hide from the August glare!

It was a dangerous mistake, never repeated. But a trip to Malta is a super bargain. As was our flight to Morocco where we found Casablanca never had a Rik's bar with or without Humphry Bogart, that most people spoke fluent Arabic, with a Berber accent – and that business in currency conversion to Dirhams was brisk. We heard great stories of golf at Dar-es-Salaam, but chose instead to drive to Marrakesh where there are two royal clubs, and a newly-built one, put in place after they diverted the local river.

The thing about Morocco is that it's another world, and just three and a half hours by plane from London. When you've hit the shots in sub-tropical warmth, head for the Atlas Mountains and try for lunch at La Roserie. The flight out by Royal Air Maroc is fun, and they'll tell you to visit Fez, which one day I hope to do, and will rattle off towns and places to evoke the mystic eastern culture. We hired a guide, it cost a bit, but for a luxury holiday with golf, and the astonishing extras, Morocco is hard to beat.

British Airways (01293 732131) put together packages for golfers to most places and Tunisia, friends tell me, is also worth looking into with the Citrus Club boasting two 18-hole courses, and a nine-holer as well as the Yasmine, with 27-holes available. Whopping hotels at Hammamet may not be to everyone's taste, but the prices look right with Premier Iberian on 01327 350394.

However, one of the finest of my golfing excursions was to Jerusalem where I played the course at Caesarea, built out of the desert, not far from the holy city. Few associate this struggling nation with golf – but they're wrong. I found the course a super test and if your drive wanders off the much-watered green fairways, it slows to a halt in the most vast bunker. This golfing oasis would be dead in a day if the water was switched off. But it isn't and a holiday here includes sight-seeing – essential for a mixed group of golfers.

Far-flung destinations for the golfing nomad

Manchester Course, Mandeville in Jamaica

The list of superb courses, where package trips are a speciality, must take in several unexpected locations on more exotic shores and here, in no particular order, are trips I've been on, and thoroughly recommend. Fax for travel documents to British Airways on 01293 722702 and you'll find that youngsters between 2-15 can have organised activities, sometimes free of charge, while the grown-ups golf.

British Airways flew us direct to Bermuda which is a jewel and, for the golfer, a wonderful place – providing you can handle the stiff Atlantic winds that sometimes blow. We stayed at the Castle Harbour and had a fine time, but their hotel course is just one of several, the most famous and wondrous being Mid-Ocean which is played through magical garden-like scenes with bluebirds whistling at you almost all the way. So attractive is Bermuda that it is almost impossible to pay attention to the shot-making. The après golf attractions include swimming from pink-sanded beaches, wandering around Hamilton and shopping for old pirate maps, and trinkets. The trip there is not low budget, but totally worthwhile and almost anywhere on the island is great.

My ambition is to explore the Caribbean more fully. I already rate Eleuthera, a slim island about 250 miles off the coast of Florida. We flew in, and were driven to the Cotton Bay Club, a proper old establishment where you can sit with a rum punch after your game, and look out into the ocean. It is a dream place, and although we were told there was another course, the Cotton Bay one stays in my mind, despite the excessive 19th hole activity!

You'll notice that an increasing number of tour operators are serving the island of Jamaica, where the golf ranges from very good, to fairly basic. Either way, I found the place quite wonderful and have been several times, playing the Tryall course, walking over the Half Moon course and going down by car to Runaway Bay, beyond Falmouth and hard against the foaming ocean.

Jamaica Tourist Board in London (0171 224 0505) tell me what I already knew, that their island in the sun has a special welcome for golfers, particularly in the Montego Bay area. Call Kuoni on their special number in Surrey (England) on 01306 742222 and they'll tell you about beachside accommodation at Sandels, or at the incredible Hotel Jamaica-Jamaica where I had a Red Stripe, but left fairly quickly, alarmed at the almost not dressed guests. For the golfing fanatic, Jamaica boasts a David Leadbetter Golf Academy, at the Half Moon, Tennis and Beach Resort and for 25 dollars you can have a one-hour group lesson. Call Kevin Cunningham on (876) 953 9767. Frankly, if you want to come close to paradise, then Jamaica, with its colonial architecture and plantation feel is the place.

My expeditions across the Atlantic have also included playing American courses like Pebble Beach in California, the Desert Inn, Arizona, Pinehurst in North Carolina and Harbour Town, not to mention the huge stretch in Florida where almost wall-to-wall they have great spots like Turnberry Isle. Florida, of course, is huge when it comes to golf, and you can rent rooms (fax 0115 976 1722) or phone free to Paraclete Realty Inc (after 2pm) on 0800 897576. The trick is to rent a car because prices are sensible, and fuel cheap. Avis on 0181 848 8733, or Hertz on 0181 679 1799 will steer you right. I played Bay Hill, near Orlando, and loved it and I'm told there's a whole new ball game opened up at Daytona Beach – and you can get details in Britain, from 0171 935 7756.

There are a 1000 different golf courses in Florida and Delta Airline (0171 731 3979) can tell you about how mind-blowing golf overlooking the Gulf of Mexico can be!

Also, high on your list of 'must go there' places must be the Far East. The Royal

Mt Irvine Bay, Tobago

Selangor in Malaysia is terrific if you can handle the different types of grass, and the sun. Singapore has provided me with great times, and the most famous Island Country Club is totally 5-star, as is the nearby Sentosa club. And take a trip to Hong Kong where the course at Fanling is just one of several excellent stretches for the tripper as, I'm told, is Thailand. For expeditions to the Far East, Kuoni have a hot-line on 01306 740500.

China? Yes. I played at the Chung Shan Hot Springs course in street shoes, and with borrowed clubs. Never do that. Always take your own gear, and feel more comfortable. But it's a great place, with lifetime memories of a different culture.

It's obvious the choice of holiday trips is overwhelming, and the trick is to decide what you want. The best golf is in the United Kingdom, but many trippers want the bonus of sight-seeing in foreign parts. If you compel me to say where I would wish to go, again, I'd find the answer simple: I'd first aim at Ireland, then take in Jamaica. But first I'd want to decide how much to spend and in this regard would find Europe hard to beat.

Fraens Hill, Malaysia

MR TRAVEL NAMES HIS TOP THREE LOCATIONS

We asked Jim Long, of Golf Links International (01494 563935) to tell us about his three favourite locations for a holiday. As a former professional golfer, Jim is now one of the world's most experienced travellers.

Writes Jim: For the last 25 years I've organised golf tournaments in many places. There's been the midnight sun in Finland, the old Iron Curtain country of Estonia and in the South, I've enjoyed golf around the sand dunes of Cape Town beneath Table Mountain. The Far East offers so much, too. You can be charmed by Thailand, or go to the West for volcanic courses in Hawaii. All are spectacular. However, let me tell you of my three top locations.

Arizona, USA

Dubai

The Emirates Golf Course is cut out of the sand deserts of the United Arab Emirates and irrigated by sea water – after it's been de-salinated. The incredible cost and hard work has produced a lush oasis and the course is now an absolute treat to play. Splendid hotels line the nearby sandy beaches not far from the

clubhouse and only half an hours drive away is the city of Dubai, with its own Dubai Creek Golf and Yacht Club, voted tops by all who go there. Nearby you can find Nad Al Shiba Golf Course set around the famous race course. Explore Dubai at night, with arcades and Gold Souk with brilliant eating places.

Sun City, South Africa

Two and a half hours drive north of Johannesburg, through bush and inhospitable landscape, and you'll find the fabulous Sun City rising up out of an old and extinct volcano! It boasts superb hotels, entertainment and two world-class golf courses – the Gary Player Course and the fantastic Lost City Golf Course with an amazing hole – the short 13th over a crocodile pit which cuts right into the green. I recommend you take along your golf rules book to check on how best to deal with this hazard when looking into the eyes of a 16-foot crocodile.

Scottsdale, Arizona

It is understandable why this area is the playground for North Americans in the winter-time. Golf is booming. The latest technology and skills are used to build magnificent golf courses. They are landscaped out of the rough desert and major championships are played within only a year or so from the first digging of the dirt. Hard to believe, but true. Courses in Arizona are not rated on how mature they are but how new they are and the newest in town is the 'one to play'!

Dubai, United Arab Emirates

Just imagine playing in this Wild West territory around huge saguro cactus and boulders. You half expect a wagon train to appear around the corner! There is nothing better than finishing the last few holes in the Arizona dusk as the sun sets with the sound of coyotes howling up in the mountains. This is Arizona at its best. Once the golf is over, Scottsdale/Phoenix City is one of the fastest growing cities in America where entertainment abounds, from the Old West shoot out fun towns to sophisticated town nightlife.

HOW TO USE THIS GUIDE

This guide contains about 2800 golf courses in Britain and Ireland most of which welcome visiting golfers. This includes many newly-built courses.

All You Need to Know

We have endeavoured to supply all the information you need to know before your visit by telling you what kind of course you can expect, what club facilities are available, including catering, any leisure facilities and the green fees you can expect to pay. We have also included AA-recommended accommodation – whether it be at the course itself or slightly further away.

Arranging a Visit

Some courses want advance notice of any visit, and possibly a letter of introduction from your own club. They may also require a handicap certificate. If this is the case the directory will include this information. However, it is always a good idea to check with any course in advance as details in the directory can change, particularly green fees, during the currency of the guide.

Course Notes

Courses that are considered to be of particular merit or interest have been placed within a shaded box. They may be very historic clubs or they may have been chosen because their courses are particularly testing or enjoyable to play. Some have been included because they are in holiday areas and have proved popular with visiting golfers. Such a selection cannot be either exhaustive or totally objective, and these courses do not represent any formal category on quality or other grounds.

Major Championship courses have special treatment with a full page entry, including a selection of places at which to eat as well as to stay.

The Directory

The directory is arranged in countries: England, Northern Ireland and the Republic of Ireland are listed in alphabetical location within each country. Scotland and Wales are listed in alphabetical location within regions – the counties that comprise each region are listed below the region heading. If you are not sure where your chosen course may be, there is an alphabetical index of courses at the end of the directory. The maps at the end of the book will also help to locate any golf course.

Map References

Should you be travelling in an unfamiliar part of the country and want to know the choice of courses available to you, consult the atlas at the end of the book. In its directory entry, each course has a map number and National Grid reference and there are directions to the course giving the nearest place located on the map.The grid references for the Irish Republic are unique to the atlas at the back of this book.

Symbols and Abbreviations

In order to maximise the space available, we have used certain symbols and abbreviations within the directory entries and these are explained in the panel below.

04 TQ21	atlas page and National Grid reference
☎	telephone number
IR£	Irish Punts (Republic only – the rates of exchange between Punts and pounds sterling are liable to fluctuate)
⊗	lunch
ⅲ	dinner
♨	bar snacks
☕	tea/coffee
🍷	bar open midday and evenings
🛏	accommodation at club
⚲	changing rooms
⌂	well-stocked shop
⛳	clubs for hire
↘	motorised cart/trolley for hire
🚗	Buggies for hire
⚐	Trolley for hire
⟟	driving range
★	hotel classification
❁	Restaurant classification (applicable to championship course entry only)
Q	Guest house classification
B	AA Branded group hotels
TH	Town House hotels

Entries in Bold Italics

NB Although we make every effort to obtain up-to-date information from golf clubs, in some cases we have been unable to verify details with the club's management. Where this is the case the course name is shown in bold italics and you would be strongly advised to check with the club in advance of your visit

Telephone Codes

The area codes shown against telephone numbers under Republic of Ireland courses are applicable within the Republic only. Similarly the area codes shown for entries in Great Britain and Northern Ireland cannot be used direct from the Republic. Check your telephone directory for details.

Accommodation

For each course listed, we recommend a nearby AA-appointed hotel, giving its classification, full name and address, telephone number and total number of bedrooms, including the number with private bath or shower. In some cases the hotel will be within the grounds of the golf course itself. The hotels recommended in the Golf Guide are mostly in the ★★, ★★★, and ★★★★ star categories. Where there is no AA-appointed hotel nearby, we have recommended an AA-inspected Listed Establishment These are classified by a quality assessment, or Q rating, of 1-5 Q's.

Club Accommodation

🛏 Some courses offer accommodation at their club. Where this facility exists, the 'bed' symbol (🛏) will appear in the entry under club facilities. This has been listed as a further option for those who might wish to stay at the course. However, unless the club accommodation has an AA star-rating, the only accommodation recommended by the AA is the star-rated hotel that appears at the foot of each entry.

HOW THE AA CLASSIFIES HOTELS

In the 1990s the hotel guest can expect to find the following minimum standards at all star levels:

- clean, comfortable, secure bedrooms equipped with modern amenities.
- beds, bedding and other bedroom furniture and appointments in good condition
- proper attention to hygiene in bathrooms and WCs
- all bedrooms with en suite bath/shower rooms at all except the one star level, where some may not be fully en suite
- adequate heating and independent temperature controls
- a sufficient hot water supply at reasonable times.
- unless there is 24-hour room service, tea and coffee making facilities in the room
- amenities such as an iron and ironing board available on request
- at all but the one star level, TV and/or radio should be standard in every room
- from the three star level upward, direct dial telephones should be standard
- well prepared, wholesome meals presented in an appetising manner

★ What the star classification denotes

Star classification is a quality scheme at five levels. The assessment rises from one star, denoting hotels with the simplest range of facilities, to five stars, denoting large, luxury hotels with a range of services and facilities that meet the best international standards.

In addition to the star classification, the AA also makes two further quality assessments to help intending guests in their choice of hotel: Red Star awards and the Quality Percentage Score, explained below.

★ Red Star Awards

AA star classifications are usually depicted in black on signs and in the AA's guides and electronic products. However, at each of the five classification levels, the AA recognises exceptional quality of accommodation and hospitality by awarding Red Stars for excellence.

A hotel with Red Stars, therefore, has been judged to be the best in its star classification and recognises that the hotel offers outstanding levels of comfort, hospitality and customer care.

Quality Percentage Score

When they visit an hotel, AA inspectors supplement their general report with a subjective assessment of the quality of everything the hotel offers, including hospitality, based on what they experience as the 'mystery guest'. This enables them to award a percentage score for overall quality.

A one star hotel may receive as high a quality percentage score within its classification as a four or five star hotel, because the percentage score offers a comparison of quality within the star classification.

An intending guest, therefore, can see at a glance that a two star hotel, for example, with a percentage score of 69, offers a higher quality experience within its star classification than a two star hotel with a percentage score of 59.

To gain AA recognition in the first place, a hotel must achieve a minimum quality score of 50 per cent. If it achieves more than 80 per cent, it is almost certain to qualify for Red Stars. The percentage score for hotels with Red Stars is not shown in our guides.

Effectively, therefore, the quality percentage score for the ordinary star classification runs between 50 and 80 per cent, and Red Star hotels, as a general rule, achieve from 81 to 100 per cent.

Minimum Requirements for AA Recognition

★ One Star Hotels

Hotels in this classification are likely to be small and independently owned, with a family atmosphere. Services may be provided by the owner and family on an informal basis. There may be a limited range of facilities and meals may be fairly simple. Lunch, for example, may not be served. Some bedrooms may not have en suite bath/shower rooms. Maintenance, cleanliness and comfort should, however, always be of an acceptable standard.

★★ Two Star Hotels

In this classification hotels will typically be small to medium sized and offer more extensive facilities than at the one star level. Some business hotels come into the two star classification and guests can expect comfortable, well equipped, overnight accommodation, usually with an en-suite bath/shower room. Reception and other staff will aim for a more professional presentation that at the one star level, and offer a wider range of straightforward services, including food and drink.

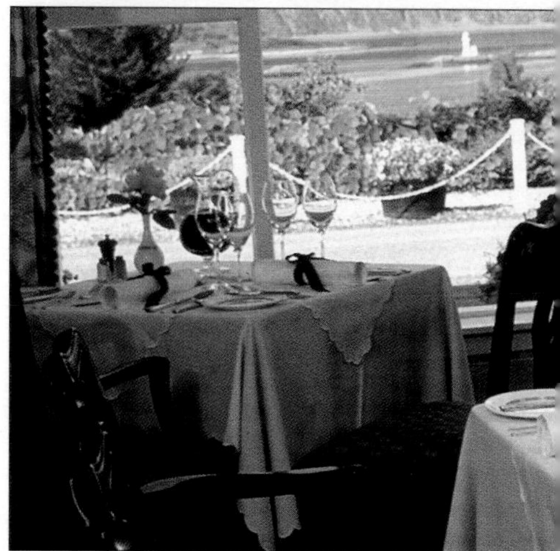

★★★ Three Star Hotels

At this level, hotels are usually of a size to support higher staffing levels, and a significantly greater quality and range of facilities than at the lower star classifications. Reception and the other public rooms will be more spacious and the restaurant will normally also cater for non-residents. All bedrooms will have fully en suite bath and shower rooms and offer a good standard of comfort and equipment, such as a hair dryer, direct dial telephone, toiletries in the bathroom. Some room service can be expected, and some provision for business travellers.

★★★★ Four Star Hotels

Expectations at this level include a degree of luxury as well as quality in the furnishings, decor and equipment, in every area of the hotel. Bedrooms will also usually offer more space than at the lower star levels, and well designed, co-ordinated furnishings and decor. The en-suite bathrooms will have both bath and fixed shower. There will be a high enough ratio of staff to guests to provide services like porterage, 24-hour room service, laundry and dry-cleaning. The restaurant will demonstrate a serious approach to its cuisine.

★★★★★ Five Star Hotels

Here you should find spacious and luxurious accommodation throughout the hotel, matching the best international standards. Interior design should impress with its quality and attention to detail, comfort and elegance. Furnishings should be immaculate. Services should be formal, well supervised and flawless in attention to guests' needs, without being intrusive. The restaurant will demonstrate a high level of technical skill, producing dishes to the highest international

standards. Staff will be knowledgeable, helpful, well versed in all aspects of customer care, combining efficiency with courtesy.

HOW THE AA ASSESSES RESTAURANTS FOR ROSETTE AWARDS

The AA's rosette award scheme is the only home-grown, nation-wide scheme for assessing the quality of food served by restaurants and hotels. The rosette scheme is an award scheme, not a classification scheme and although there is necessarily an element of subjectivity when it comes to assessing taste, we aim for a consistent approach to our awards throughout the UK. It is important, however, to remember that many places serve enjoyable food but do not qualify for an AA award.

Our awards are made solely on the basis of a meal visit or visits by one or more of our hotel and restaurant inspectors who have an unrivalled breadth and depth of experience in assessing quality. They award rosettes annually on a rising scale of one to five.

Recommendations from users of the guides are always welcome and will be passed on to the inspectors on merit for their consideration, but we do not guarantee a meal visit or an entry in the guide. Rosette awards are made or withdrawn only on the basis of our own inspectors' meal visits.

SO WHAT MAKES A RESTAURANT WORTHY OF A ROSETTE AWARD?

For our inspectors, frequently eating alone, the top and bottom line is the food. They are not swayed by a fashionable or luxurious setting, by the friendliness or immaculate uniforms of the staff, by fussy, over-elaborate presentation, or even by the size of the bill. The taste of the food is what counts for them, and whether the dish successfully delivers to the diner what the menu promises. A restaurant is only as good as its worst meal.

Although presentation and competent service should be appropriate to the style of the restaurant and the quality of the food, they cannot affect the rosette assessment as such, either up or down.

The following summaries attempt to explain what our inspectors look for, but are intended only as guidelines. The AA is constantly reviewing its award criteria and competition usually results in an all-round improvement in standards, so it becomes increasingly difficult for restaurants to reach award level.

❀ One rosette

At the simplest level, one rosette, the chef should display a mastery of basic techniques and be able to produce dishes of sound quality and clarity of flavours, using good, fresh ingredients:

❀❀ Two rosettes

To gain two rosettes, the chef must show greater technical skill, more consistency and judgement in combining and balancing ingredients and a clear ambition to achieve high standards. Inspectors will look for evidence of innovation to test the dedication of the kitchen brigade, and the use of seasonal ingredients sourced from quality suppliers.

❀❀❀ Three rosettes

This award takes a restaurant into the big league, and, in a typical year, fewer than 10 per cent of restaurants in our scheme achieve this distinction. Expectations of the kitchen are high, and inspectors find little room for inconsistencies. Exact technique, flair and imagination will come through in every dish, and balance and depth of flavour are all-important.

❀❀❀❀ Four rosettes

This is an exciting award because, at this level, not only should all technical skills be exemplary, but there should also be daring ideas, and they must work. There is no room for disappointment. Flavours should be accurate and vibrant.

❀❀❀❀❀ Five rosettes

This award is the ultimate, awarded only when the cooking is at the pinnacle of achievement. Technique should be of such perfection that flavours, combinations and textures show a faultless sense of balance, giving each dish an extra dimension. The sort of cooking that never falters and always strives to give diners a truly memorable taste experience.

ENGLAND

John Ingham writes: Although I detest most of them, motorways have made our world seem a smaller place. And, for golfers, the construction of these speeds traps altered attitudes to those who now find an away-day, with eighteen holes included, a realistic possibility. In short, our range is increased, with targets galore!

World travellers, coming here, are astonished at the variety of English courses, particularly in and around the major cities. Near Manchester you have the finest stretches of coastal links anywhere, with places like Formby and Hillside, not to mention Southport and Ainsdale, supporting the more famous championship tests at Birkdale, and Lytham. And thirty miles around London are wondrous courses which, if planted anywhere on this planet, would be worthy of a book in themselves.

Go to Birmingham, or Wolverhampton and not far away are Lindrick, and Woodhall Spa, my two favourites, and such courses as Hollinwell (Notts) and the much under-rated Sherwood Forest. And up in Yorkshire, they are rightly proud of Ganton while I have vivid memories of Moortown having played, and failed to win, the English championship when in my twenties.

People ask which, of all the courses in all of England, is my favourite. It's an absurd question, like asking which is your favourite wine, or ice-cream! But when pushed, I mention that I like a course that doesn't make golfers feel inadequate, that doesn't require them to hit the ball 200 yards over artificial duckponds, and won't tolerate rounds of four hours. On that score I name my home course of Royal Wimbledon - and might mention the world's finest nine-holer at Royal Worlington, although I haven't been there since I played Leonard Crawley, so cannot vouch for the quality of the lunches - most important!

But most writers of things golf will say that Sunningdale Old, or New, tops their list of favourites with, maybe, the Berkshire or Royal St George's (Sandwich) added for good measure. The golfing menu in England is totally remarkable, and nobody will argue with that.

ENGLAND

BEDFORDSHIRE

ASPLEY GUISE Map 04 SP93

Aspley Guise & Woburn Sands West Hill MK17 8DX
☎ 01908 583596 Fax 01908 582974 (Pro Shop)
A fine undulating course in expansive heathland interspersed with many attractive clumps of gorse, broom and bracken. Some well-established silver birch are a feature. The 7th, 8th and 9th are really tough holes to complete the first half.
18 holes, 6135yds, Par 71, SSS 70, Course record 67.
Club membership 560.
Visitors with member only at weekends.
Societies normally booked 6 mths ahead.
Green Fees £23 per round; £29 per day.
Cards
Prof David Marsden
Designer Sandy Herd
Facilities
Location 2m W of M1 junc 13

Hotel ★★★ 71% Moore Place Hotel, The Square, ASPLEY GUISE
☎ 01908 282000 39 Annexe15

BEDFORD Map 04 TL04

Bedford & County Green Ln, Clapham MK41 6ET
☎ 01234 352617 Fax 01234 357195
A mature parkland course established in 1912 with views over Bedford and surrounding countryside. Beware of the brook that discreetly meanders through the 7th, 10th, 11th and 15th holes. The testing par 4 15th is one of the most challenging holes in the area.
18 holes, 6347yds, Par 70, SSS 70.
Club membership 600.
Visitors handicap certificate required, weekends with member only.
Societies welcome Mon,Tue,Thu & Fri, telephone in advance.
Green Fees not confirmed.
Prof E Bullock
Facilities
Location 2m N off A6

Hotel ★★★ 74% Woodlands Manor Hotel, Green Ln, Clapham, BEDFORD
☎ 01234 363281 30 Annexe3

Bedfordshire Bromham Rd, Biddenham MK40 4AF
☎ 01234 261669 Fax 01234 261669
An attractive and easy walking parkland course with plenty of trees providing a problem for 'off-line' golfers.
18 holes, 6305yds, Par 70, SSS 70, Course record 63.
Club membership 700.
Visitors may not play at weekends except with member.
Societies must telephone in advance/confirm in writing.
Green Fees £20 per round; £26 for 36 holes.
Prof Peter Saunders
Facilities
Location 1m W on A428

Hotel ★★★ 74% Woodlands Manor Hotel, Green Ln, Clapham, BEDFORD
☎ 01234 363281 30 Annexe3

Mowsbury Cleat Hill, Kimbolton Rd MK41 8DQ
☎ 01234 771041 & 216374 (prof)
Parkland municipal course in rural surroundings. Long and testing 14-bay driving range and squash facilities.
18 holes, 6514yds, Par 72, SSS 71, Course record 66.
Club membership 800.
Visitors no restrictions.
Societies apply in writing.
Green Fees on application.
Prof Malcolm Summers
Designer Hawtree
Facilities
& Leisure squash.
Location 2m N of town centre on B660

Hotel ★★★ 74% Woodlands Manor Hotel, Green Ln, Clapham, BEDFORD
☎ 01234 363281 30 Annexe3

CHALGRAVE Map 04 TL02

Chalgrave Manor Dunstable Rd LU5 6JN
☎ 01525 876556 Fax 01525 876556
Undulating course constructed in 1994 offering a good test of golf for all standards of golfer. Feature holes include the short 10th (150 yards) that requires an accurate shot across water to a splendid sloping green, and the Par 4 11th which incorporates an elevated tee, a ditch, several bunkers, a pond and perilously close out of bounds.
18 holes, 6382yds, Par 72, SSS 70, Course record 69.
Club membership 450.
Visitors welcome, dress code smart casual, after 11am at weekends.
Societies apply in writing or telephone, in advance.
Green Fees £15 per round (£30 weekends).
Prof Martin Brewer
Designer M Palmer
Facilities by prior arrangement
Location From M1 junct 12 take A5120 through Toddington, entrance about 1m out, well signposted

Hotel ★★★ 68% Old Palace Lodge Hotel, Church St, DUNSTABLE ☎ 01582 662201 68

COLMWORTH Map 04 TL15

Colmworth & North Bedfordshire New Rd MK44 2BY
☎ 01234 378181
An easy walking course with well-bunkered greens, opened in 1991. The course is often windy and plays longer than the yardage suggests. Water comes into play on 3 holes.
18 holes, 6459yds, Par 71, SSS 71, Course record 69.
Club membership 230.
Visitors advisable to contact in advance, tee reserved for members Sat & Sun until 9.30 am & between 12.30 & 2pm.
Societies telephone in advance.
Green Fees £10 per 18 holes (£17 weekends and bank holidays).
Designer John Glasgow

Facilities & Leisure fishing.
Location 7m NE of Bedford, off B660

Hotel ★★★ 72% The Barns Hotel, Cardington Rd, BEDFORD ☎ 01234 270044 48

DUNSTABLE Map 04 TL02

Dunstable Downs Whipsnade Rd LU6 2NB
☎ 01582 604472 Fax 01582 478700
A fine downland course set on two levels with far-reaching views and frequent sightings of graceful gliders. The 9th hole is one of the best short holes in the country. There is a modernised clubhouse.
18 holes, 6255yds, Par 70, SSS 70, Course record 64.
Club membership 600.

Visitors weekends with member only. Handicap certificate required.
Societies apply in advance.
Green Fees £30 per day; £20 per round.
Prof Michael Weldon
Designer James Braid
Facilities
Location 2m S off B4541

Hotel ★★★ 68% Old Palace Lodge Hotel, Church St, DUNSTABLE ☎ 01582 662201 68

Griffin Chaul End Rd, Caddington LU1 4AX
☎ 01582 415573 Fax 01582 415314
A challenging 18-hole course with ponds, lakes and a SSS of 69.
18 holes, 6161yds, Par 71, SSS 69.
Club membership 480.

Visitors welcome Mon-Fri & after 2pm weekends no need to book.
Societies welcome midweek book by telephone.
Green Fees £11-£13 per 18 holes (£16 weekends & bank holidays).
Facilities
Location Off A505 Luton/Dunstable

Hotel ★★★ 58% Luton Gateway, 641 Dunstable Rd, LUTON ☎ 01582 575955 109

FLITWICK Map 04 TL03

See advertisment above

LEIGHTON BUZZARD Map 04 SP92

Leighton Buzzard Plantation Rd LU7 7JF
☎ 01525 373811 Fax 01525 373843
Parkland course with easy walking. The 17th and 18th holes are challenging tree-lined finishing holes with tight fairways. 11th par 3 is signature hole.
18 holes, 5945yds, Par 71, SSS 70, Course record 66.
Club membership 700.

Visitors may play yellow tees, may not play Tue (Ladies Day). May only play with member weekends and bank holidays. Handicap certificate required unless playing with member.
Societies prior booking required.

Green Fees £30 per day; £22 per round.
Prof Lee Scarbrow
Facilities
Location 1.5m N of town centre off A4146

Hotel ★★★ 55% Swan Hotel, High St, LEIGHTON BUZZARD ☎ 01525 372148 38

LOWER STONDON Map 04 TL13

Mount Pleasant Station Rd SG16 6JL
☎ 01462 850999
A 9-hole course which, when played over 18 totals some 6003 yards. The course is undulating meadowland with mature hedges and trees and also 10,000 new trees. Two small ponds are crossed and there is a significant ditch in play on 2,7,8,9,11,16,17,18th holes. The 9,11 14th holes are all 400yds and play long into the prevailing West wind. Visitors consider the greens some of the best conditioned in the area and with good drainage the course rarely has to close.
9 holes, 6003yds, Par 70, SSS 69.
Club membership 300.

Visitors no restrictions, can book 2 days in advance, booking advisable weekends & evenings May-Sep.
Societies telephone or apply in writing.
Green Fees £10.50 per 18 holes; £6 per 9 holes (£14.50/£8 weekends).
Cards
Prof Mike Roberts
Designer Derek Young

Facilities
Location 0.75m W of A600

Hotel ★★★ 75% Flitwick Manor Hotel, Church Rd, FLITWICK ☎ 01525 712242 15

LUTON — Map 04 TL02

South Beds Warden Hill LU2 7AA
☎ 01582 591500 Fax 01582 495381
27-hole downland course, slightly undulating.
Galley Course: 18 holes, 6389yds, Par 71, SSS 71, Course record 64.
Warden Course: 9 holes, 2424yds, Par 32, SSS 32.
Club membership 1000.
Visitors must contact in advance.
Societies telephone for details.
Green Fees Galley Course: £19 per round (£26 weekends & bank holidays). Warden Course: £5 (£6 weekends & bank holidays).
Prof Eddie Cogle
Facilities by prior arrangement
Location 2m N of Luton on A6

Hotel ★★★ 71% Strathmore Thistle, Arndale Centre, LUTON ☎ 01582 734199 150

Stockwood Park London Rd LU1 4LX ☎ 01582 413704
Well laid out municipal parkland course with established trees and several challenging holes.
18 holes, 6049yds, Par 69, SSS 69, Course record 67.
Club membership 800.
Visitors no restrictions.
Societies Mon, Tue & Thu only, telephone for application.
Green Fees not confirmed.
Prof Glyn McCarthy
Facilities
Location 1m S

Hotel ★★★ 58% The Chiltern, Waller Av, Dunstable Rd, LUTON ☎ 01582 575911 91

MILLBROOK — Map 04 TL03

Lyshott Heath Millbrook Village MK45 2JB
☎ 01525 840252 Fax 01525 406249
Long parkland course, on rolling countryside high above the Bedfordshire plains, with several water hazards. Laid out on well-drained sandy soil with many fairways lined with silver birch, pine and larch.
18 holes, 7100yds, Par 74, SSS 73.
Club membership 550.
Visitors must contact in advance, may not play after 11am on Thu.
Societies telephone for details.
Green Fees £30 per day; £18 per round (£30 per round after 2.30pm weekends & bank holidays).
Prof David Armor
Designer William Sutherland
Facilities
Location E side of village off A507

Hotel ★★★ 75% Flitwick Manor Hotel, Church Rd, FLITWICK ☎ 01525 712242 15

PAVENHAM — Map 04 SP95

Pavenham Park MK43 7PE
☎ 01234 822202 Fax 01234 826602
Mature, undulating parkland course with fast contoured greens.
18 holes, 6353yds, Par 71, SSS 70, Course record 63.
Club membership 790.
Visitors welcome weekdays, weekends as members guests only.
Societies telephone in advance.
Green Fees £15 per round weekdays.
Cards
Prof Zac Thompson
Designer Zac Thompson
Facilities
Location 1.5m from A6, N of Bedford

Hotel ★★ 62% The Laws Hotel, High St, TURVEY ☎ 01234 881213 & 881655 Fax 01234 888864 23rm(20)

SANDY — Map 04 TL14

John O'Gaunt Sutton Park SG19 2LY
☎ 01767 260360 Fax 01767 261381
Two magnificent parkland courses - John O'Gaunt and Carthagena - covering a gently undulating and tree-lined terrain. The John O'Gaunt course makes the most of numerous natural features, notably a river which crosses the fairways of four holes. The Carthagena course has larger greens, longer tees and from the back tees is a challenging course. Fine clubhouse.
John O'Gaunt Course: 18 holes, 6513yds, Par 71, SSS 71, Course record 64.
Carthagena Course: 18 holes, 5869yds, Par 69, SSS 69, Course record 62.
Club membership 1500.
Visitors must contact in advance.
Societies must pre-book.
Green Fees £45 per day/round (£50 weekends & bank holidays).
Cards
Prof Peter Round
Designer John O'Gaunt/Others
Facilities
Location 3m NE of Biggleswade on B1040

Hotel ★★ 64% Abbotsley Golf Hotel, Potton Rd, Eynesbury Hardwicke, ST NEOTS ☎ 01480 474000 17

SHEFFORD — Map 04 TL13

Beadlow Manor Hotel & Golf & Country Club SG17 5PH
☎ 01525 860800 Fax 01525 861345
A 36-hole golf and leisure complex. The Baroness Manhattan and the Baron Manhattan golf courses are undulating with water hazards on numerous holes. These are good challenging courses for both the beginner and low handicap player.
Baroness Course: 18 holes, 6072yds, Par 71, SSS 69, Course record 67.
Baron Course: 18 holes, 6619yds, Par 73, SSS 72.
Club membership 600.
Visitors book in advance & must adhere to dress code.

Societies apply in writing or telephone in advance.
Green Fees not confirmed.
Prof Phil Bradley/G Dixon
Facilities
& Leisure sauna, solarium, gymnasium.
Location 2m W on A507

Hotel ★★★ 61% Beadlow Manor, Beadlow, SHEFFORD ☎ 01525 860800 33

TILSWORTH Map 04 SP92

Tilsworth Dunstable Rd LU7 9PU
☎ 01525 210721/2 Fax 01525 210465
An undulating parkland course upgraded from 9 to 18 holes in 1992. 30-bay floodlit driving range.
18 holes, 5306yds, Par 69, SSS 66, Course record 66.
Club membership 400.
Visitors may book up to 7 days in advance. May not play before 10am Sundays.
Societies welcome weekdays, apply in advance.
Green Fees £10 per 18 holes; £6.50 per 9 holes (£12/£7.50 weekends).
Cards
Prof Darren Charlton
Facilities
Location 0.5m NE off A5

Hotel ★★★ 68% Old Palace Lodge Hotel, Church St, DUNSTABLE ☎ 01582 662201 68

WHIPSNADE Map 04 TL01

Whipsnade Park Studham Ln, Dagnall HP4 1RH
☎ 01442 842330 Fax 01442 842090
Parkland course situated on downs overlooking the Chilterns adjoining Whipsnade Zoo. Easy walking, good views.
18 holes, 6800yds, Par 73, SSS 72, Course record 66.
Club membership 600.
Visitors welcome weekdays, with member only at weekends. Must contact in advance.
Societies by prior arrangement.
Green Fees £33 per 36 holes; £23 per 18 holes.
Cards
Prof Michael Lewendon
Facilities
Location 1m E off B4506

Hotel ★★★ 68% Old Palace Lodge Hotel, Church St, DUNSTABLE ☎ 01582 662201 68

WOBURN Map 04 SP93

For Woburn Golf Course see Bow Brickhill, Buckinghamshire. See page 35.

WYBOSTON Map 04 TL15

Wyboston Lakes MK44 3AL
☎ 01480 223004 Fax 01480 407330
Parkland course, with narrow fairways, small greens, set around four lakes and a river which provide the biggest challenge on this very scenic course.
18 holes, 5803yds, Par 70, SSS 69, Course record 65.
Club membership 300.
Visitors a booking system is in operation at weekends, book no more than 8 days in advance.
Societies telephone in advance.
Green Fees £11 per 18 holes; £6 per 9 holes (£15/£7 weekends & bank holidays) Twilight round £7.
Prof Paul Ashwell
Designer N Oakden
Facilities
& Leisure fishing, sauna, solarium, gymnasium.
Location 1m S of St Neots off A1/A428

Hotel ★★★ 74% Woodlands Manor Hotel, Green Ln, Clapham, BEDFORD ☎ 01234 363281 30 Annexe3

BERKSHIRE

ASCOT Map 04 SU96

Berkshire Swinley Rd SL5 8AY ☎ 01344 621496
Two heathland courses with splendid tree-lined fairways.
Red Course: 18 holes, 6369yds, Par 72, SSS 71.
Blue Course: 18 holes, 6260yds, Par 71, SSS 71.
Club membership 1000.
Visitors weekdays only on application to secretary.
Societies applications in writing only.
Green Fees £70 per day; £50 per round.
Prof P Anderson
Designer H Fowler
Facilities
Location 2.5m NW of M3 jct 3 on A332

Hotel ★★★★ 68% The Berystede, Bagshot Rd, Sunninghill, ASCOT ☎ 01344 2331 91

Lavender Park Swinley Rd SL5 8BD
☎ 01344 890940 & 886096
Public parkland course, ideal for the short game featuring challenging narrow fairways. Driving range with 9-hole par 3 course, floodlit until 22.30 hrs.
9 holes, 1102yds, Par 27, SSS 28.
Visitors no restrictions.
Societies welcome, notice prefered.
Green Fees not confirmed.
Prof Wayne Ower/Andy Piper
Facilities
Location 3.5m SW of Ascot, on A332

Hotel ★★★★ 68% The Berystede, Bagshot Rd, Sunninghill, ASCOT ☎ 01344 2331 91

Mill Ride Mill Ride SL5 8LT
☎ 01344 886777 Fax 01344 886820
Opened for play in 1991, this 18-hole course combines links and parkland styles. The holes require as much thinking as playing.
18 holes, 6752yds, Par 72, SSS 72, Course record 64.
Club membership 400.
Visitors must contact in advance, limited access at weekends.
Societies apply in advance.

Green Fees prices on application.
Cards
Prof Mark Palmer
Designer Donald Steel
Facilities
& Leisure sauna, steamroom.
Location 2m W of Ascot

Hotel ★★★★ 68% The Berystede, Bagshot Rd, Sunninghill, ASCOT ☎ 01344 23311 91

Royal Ascot Winkfield Rd SL5 7LJ
☎ 01344 625175 Fax 01344 872330
Heathland course inside Ascot racecourse and exposed to weather.
18 holes, 5716yds, Par 68, SSS 68, Course record 65.
Club membership 620.
Visitors must be guest of member or contact secretary in advance. Not weekends.
Societies telephone for provisional booking.
Green Fees not confirmed.
Prof Alistair White
Designer J H Taylor
Facilities
Location 0.5m N on A330

Hotel ★★★★ 68% The Berystede, Bagshot Rd, Sunninghill, ASCOT ☎ 01344 23311 91

Swinley Forest Coronation Rd SL5 9LE
☎ 01344 874979 (Secretary) Fax 01344 874733
An attractive and immaculate course of heather and pine situated in the heart of Swinley Forest. The 17th is as good a short hole as will be found, with a bunkered plateau green and the 12th hole is one of the most challenging par 4's.
18 holes, 6100yds, Par 69, SSS 70, Course record 62.
Club membership 325.
Visitors on introduction of a member or by invitation only.
Societies must contact in writing.
Green Fees £65 per day.
Prof R C Parker
Designer Harry Colt
Facilities
Location 1.5m S, off A330

Hotel ★★★★ 68% The Berystede, Bagshot Rd, Sunninghill, ASCOT ☎ 01344 23311 91

BINFIELD Map 04 SU87

Blue Mountain Golf Centre Wood Ln RG42 4EX
☎ 01344 300200 Fax 01344 360960
An 18-hole Pay and Play course with many testing holes with water hazards. Greens are large, undulating and strategically placed bunkers provide a fair challenge.
18 holes, 6097yds, Par 70, SSS 70, Course record 61.
Club membership 1250.
Visitors tee times bookable in person at the Golf Shop up to 9 days in advance.
Societies must contact in advance.
Green Fees £16 per 18 holes; £9 per 9 holes (£20/£12 weekends).
Cards
Prof Neil Dainton
Facilities
Location 2m from junct 10 of the M4

Hotel ★★★★ 76% Coppid Beech, John Nike Way, BRACKNELL ☎ 01344 303333 205

CHADDLEWORTH Map 04 SU47

West Berkshire RG20 7DU
☎ 01488 638574 & 638851 Fax 01488 638781
Challenging and interesting downland course with testing 635 yds 5th hole, one of the longest par 5's in southern England. Bunkers are well placed from tees and around the greens to catch any wayward shots.
18 holes, 7059yds, Par 73, SSS 74.
Club membership 650.
Visitors must contact in advance, may play weekends pm only.
Societies telephone in advance
Green Fees £18 per round (£22 weekends).
Cards
Prof Paul Simpson
Designer Robin Stagg
Facilities
Location 1m S of village off A338

Hotel ★★★ 63% The Chequers, Oxford St, NEWBURY
☎ 01635 38000 45 Annexe11

COOKHAM Map 04 SU88

Winter Hill Grange Ln SL6 9RP
☎ 01628 527613 (Secretary)
Parkland course set in a curve of the Thames with wonderful views across the river to Cliveden.
18 holes, 6408yds, Par 72, SSS 71, Course record 63.
Club membership 850.
Visitors not permitted weekends.
Societies welcome Wed & Fri, telephone initially.
Green Fees not confirmed.
Prof Mark Booth
Designer Charles Lawrie
Facilities
Location 1m NW off B4447

Hotel ★★★★ 69% The Compleat Angler, Marlow Bridge, MARLOW
☎ 01628 484444 62

CROWTHORNE Map 04 SU86

East Berkshire Ravenswood Ave RG45 6BD
☎ 01344 772041 Fax 01344 777378
An attractive heathland course with an abundance of heather and pine trees. Walking is easy and the greens are exceptionally good. Some fairways become tight where the heather encroaches on the line of play. The course is testing and demands great accuracy.
18 holes, 6344yds, Par 69, SSS 70.
Club membership 766.

Visitors must contact in advance and have a handicap certificate; must play with member at weekends & bank holidays.
Societies telephone for availability.
Green Fees £37 per day.
Prof Arthur Roe
Designer P Paxton
Facilities ⊗ ⅏ 🍽 ☕ 🍸 🏌 🏠 ⛳ 🛒
Location W side of town centre off B3348

Hotel ★★★★ Pennyhill Park Hotel, London Rd, BAGSHOT ☎ 01276 471774 22 Annexe67

DATCHET — Map 04 SU97

Datchet Buccleuch Rd SL3 9BP
☎ 01753 543887 & 541872 Fax 01753 541872
Meadowland course, easy walking.
9 holes, 5978yds, Par 70, SSS 69, Course record 63.
Club membership 430.
Visitors may play weekdays before 3pm.
Societies Tue only. (Other times by prior arrangement)
Green Fees £24 per day; £16 per round.
Facilities
Location NW side of Datchet off B470

Hotel ★★★ 72% The Castle Hotel, High St, WINDSOR ☎ 01753 851011 104

MAIDENHEAD — Map 04 SU88

Bird Hills Drift Rd, Hawthorn Hill SL6 3ST
☎ 01628 771030 Fax 01628 631023
A gently undulating course with easy walking and many water hazards. Some challenging holes are the Par 5 6th dogleg, Par 3 9th surrounded by water and bunkers, and the 16th which is a long uphill Par 4 and a two-tier green.
18 holes, 6176yds, Par 72, SSS 69, Course record 65.
Club membership 400.
Visitors to book ring 7 days in advance.
Societies write or telephone in advance.
Green Fees £11 per 18 holes; £7.50 per 9 holes (£16/£9.50 weekends & bank holidays).
Cards
Prof Nick Slimming
Facilities
Location 4m SW of Bray on A330

Hotel ★★★ 73% Stirrups Country House, Maidens Green, BRACKNELL ☎ 01344 882284 24

Castle Royle Golf & Country Club Bath Rd, Knowl Hill RG10 9XA ☎ 01628 829252 Fax 01628 829299
Designed to championship standard, Castle Royle has six lakes and is well drained and irrigated. In attractive countryside with views of Windsor Castle, this gently undulating parkland course is very well bunkered with wide fairways and there are Par 3's with all four aspects to the prevailing wind as each faces a different direction.
18 holes, 6828yds, Par 72, SSS 73.
Club membership 500.
Visitors weekdays only. Handicap certificate required.
Societies must telephone in advance.
Green Fees £40 (£50 weekends).
Cards
Prof Paul Stanwick
Designer Neil Coles
Facilities
Location Bath road A4

Hotel ★★★★ 80% Fredrick's Hotel, Shoppenhangers Rd, MAIDENHEAD ☎ 01628 635934 37

Maidenhead Shoppenhangers Rd SL6 2PZ
☎ 01628 624693 Fax 01628 624693
A pleasant parkland course on level ground with easy walking to good greens. Perhaps a little short but there are many natural features and some first-rate short holes.
18 holes, 6364yds, Par 70, SSS 70.
Club membership 650.
Visitors may not play after noon on Fri or at weekends. Must contact in advance and have a handicap certificate.
Societies must contact in writing.
Green Fees not confirmed.
Prof Steve Geary
Designer Alex Simpson
Facilities
Location S side of town centre off A308

Hotel ★★★★ 80% Fredrick's Hotel, Shoppenhangers Rd, MAIDENHEAD ☎ 01628 635934 37

Temple Henley Rd, Hurley SL6 5LH
☎ 01628 824795 Fax 01628 828119
An open parkland course with many excellent, fast greens relying on natural slopes rather than heavy bunkering. On one 'blind' punchbowl hole there is actually a bunker on the green. Good drainage assures play when many other courses are closed.
18 holes, 6207yds, Par 70, SSS 70, Course record 63.
Club membership 480.
Visitors must contact in advance, limited weekend access.
Societies apply in writing for formal bookings.
Green Fees £40 per 36 holes; £25 per 18 holes (£40/£30 weekends).
Cards
Prof James Whiteley
Designer Willie Park (Jnr)
Facilities by prior arrangement
Location Exit M4 jct 8/9 take A404M then A4130,or M40 exit jct 4 take A404 then A4130,signposted Henley

Hotel ★★★★ 69% The Compleat Angler, Marlow Bridge, MARLOW ☎ 01628 484444 62

NEWBURY — Map 04 SU46

Donnington Valley Old Oxford Rd, Donnington RG14 3AG
☎ 01635 551199
Undulating, short, but testing course with mature trees and elevated greens, some protected by water.

18 holes, 4000yds, Par 61, SSS 60, Course record 59.
Club membership 500.
Visitors booking system up to 7 days in advance, members have priority weekends.
Societies write or telephone in advance.
Green Fees not confirmed.
Prof Nick Mitchell
Designer Cox family
Facilities
& Leisure hard tennis courts.
Location 2m N of Newbury

Hotel ★★★★ 79% Donnington Valley Hotel & Golf Course, Old Oxford Rd, Donnington, NEWBURY ☎ 01635 551199 58

Newbury & Crookham Bury's Bank Rd, Greenham RG19 8BZ ☎ 01635 40035 Fax 01635 40045
A well-laid out, attractive course running mostly through woodland, and giving more of a challenge than its length suggests.
18 holes, 5940yds, Par 69, SSS 68.
Club membership 800.
Visitors must play with member on weekends & bank holidays. Handicap certificate required.
Societies must contact in advance.
Green Fees not confirmed.
Prof David Harris
Facilities
Location 2m SE off A34

Hotel ★★★ 63% The Chequers, Oxford St, NEWBURY ☎ 01635 38000 45 Annexe11

READING Map 04 SU77

Calcot Park Bath Rd, Calcot RG31 7RN
☎ 0118 942 7124 Fax 0118 945 3373
A delightfully sporting parkland course just outside the town. Hazards include a lake and many trees. The 6th is the longest, 507 yard par 5, with the tee-shot hit downhill over cross-bunkers to a well-guarded green. The 13th (194 yards) requires a big carry over a gully to a plateau green.
18 holes, 6283yds, Par 70, SSS 70, Course record 65.
Club membership 730.
Visitors must have handicap certificate or letter of introduction from club. May play weekdays only, excluding bank holidays.
Societies must apply in writing.
Green Fees £36 per day/round; £22 after noon winter and after 4pm summer.
Prof Ian Campbell
Designer H S Colt
Facilities
& Leisure fishing.
Location 1.5m from M4 junct 4 on A4 towards Reading

Hotel ★★★ 77% The Copper Inn, Church Rd, PANGBOURNE ☎ 0118 984 2244 14 Annexe8

Hennerton Crazies Hill Rd, Wargrave RG10 8LT
☎ 0118 940 1000 Fax 0118 940 1042
Overlooking the Thames Valley, this Par 68 course has many of existing natural features and an good number of hazards such as bunker, mature trees and two small lakes. The most memorable hole is probably the 7th which is a par 3, 183 yards crossing a sharp valley to the green from which there are spectacular views of the whole course.
9 holes, 5460yds, Par 68, SSS 67, Course record 66.
Club membership 430.
Visitors telephone in advance.
Societies telephone or write for information.
Green Fees £15 per 18 holes; £10 per 9 holes (£18/£14 weekends).
Cards
Prof William Farrow
Designer Col D Beard
Facilities
Location Follow signs from A321 Wargrave High Street

Hotel ★★★ 70% Red Lion Hotel, Hart St, HENLEY-ON-THAMES ☎ 01491 572161 26rm(23)

Mapledurham Chazey Heath, Mapledurham RG4 7UD
☎ 0118 946 3353 Fax 0118 946 3363
18-hole course designed by Bob Sandow. Flanked by hedgerows and mature woods, it is testing for players of all levels.
18 holes, 5750yds, Par 69, SSS 68, Course record 66 or 57 holes.
Club membership 340.
Visitors dress code and advanced booking required
Societies must contact in advance.
Green Fees £14 per 18 holes; £8.50 per 9 holes (£17/£10 weekends).
Cards
Prof Symon O'Keefe
Designer Bob Sandow
Facilities
Location On A4074 to Oxford

Hotel ★★★★ 59% Holiday Inn, Caversham Bridge, Richfield Av, READING ☎ 0118 925 9988 111

Reading 17 Kidmore End Rd, Emmer Green RG4 8SG
☎ 0118 947 2909 (Manager)
Pleasant tree-lined parkland course, part hilly and part flat with interesting views and several challenging par 3's.
18 holes, 6212yds, Par 70, SSS 70, Course record 67.
Club membership 700.
Visitors contact the professional. Welcome weekdays, with member only weekends.
Societies apply by telephone.
Green Fees not confirmed.
Prof Andrew Wild
Facilities
Location 2m N off B481

Hotel ★★★ 65% Ship Hotel, 4-8 Duke St, READING ☎ 0118 958 3455 32

SUNNINGDALE

SUNNINGDALE *Berks* ☎ 01344 621681
Fax 01344 624154 Map 04 SU96

John Ingham writes: Many famous golfers maintain that Sunningdale, on the borders of Berkshire, is the most attractive inland course in Britain. The great Bobby Jones once played the 'perfect' round of 66 made up of threes and fours on the Old Course. Later, Norman von Nida of Australia shot a 63 while the then professional at the club, Arthur Lees, scored a 62 to win a huge wager.

To become a member of this club takes years of waiting. Maybe it is the quality of the courses, maybe the clubhouse atmosphere and perhaps the excellence of the professionals shop has something to do with it; but added up, it has to be the most desirable place to spend a day.

Founded in 1900, the Old Course was designed by Willie Park, while H.S. Colt created the New Course in 1923. Most golfers will agree that there isn't one indifferent hole on either course. While the Old Course, with silver birch, heather and perfect turf, is lovely to behold, the New Course alongside is considered by many to be its equal. But just as golfers want to play the Old Course at St Andrews, and miss the redesigned Jubilee, so visitors to Sunningdale opt for the Old, and fail to realise what they are overlooking by not playing the New.

The classic Old Course is not long, measuring just 6341 yards, and because the greens are normally in excellent condition, anyone with a 'hot' putter can have an exciting day, providing they keep teeshots on the fairway and don't stray into the gorse and the pine trees that lie in wait. On a sunny day, if you had to be anywhere in the world playing well, then we opt for the elevated 10th tee on the Old. What bliss!

Visitors May not play Fri, Sat, Sun or public holidays. Must contact in advance and have a handicap certificate and letter of introduction
Societies Tue, Wed, Thu by arrangement.
Green fees Old Course £100 per day, New Course £75; Combined £125.
Facilities
Professional Keith Maxwell
Location Ridgemount Rd Sunningdale, Ascot SL5 9RR (1m S of Sunningdale, off A30)

36 holes. Old Course: 18 holes, 6341yds, Par 70, SSS 70
New Course: 18 holes 6433yds, Par 71, SSS 71

WHERE TO STAY AND EAT NEARBY

HOTELS:

ASCOT

★★★★ 68% The Berystede, Bagshot Rd, Sunninghill. ☎ 01344 23311. 91 (1 90)

★★★★ 69% The Royal Berkshire, London Rd, Sunninghill. ☎ 01344 23322. 63

★★ 74% Highclere, 19 Kings Rd, Sunninghill. ☎ 01344 25220. 11

BAGSHOT

★★★★ Pennyhill Park, London Rd. ☎ 01276 471774 22 Annexe 67

RESTAURANTS:

BRAY

Waterside Inn, River Cottage, Ferry Road. ☎ 01628 620691.

SINDLESHAM — Map 04 SU76

Bearwood Mole Rd RG41 5DB ☎ 0118 976 0060
Flat parkland course with one water hazard, the 40 acre lake which features on the challenging 6th and 7th holes. Also driving range.
9 holes, 5610yds, Par 70, SSS 68, Course record 66.
Club membership 500.

Visitors welcome weekdays and weekend afternoons.
Societies apply in writing.
Green Fees £15 per 18 holes; £10 per 9 holes (£20/£14 weekends).
Cards
Prof Barry Tustin
Designer Barry Tustin
Facilities
Location 1m SW on B3030

Hotel ★★★★ 64% Reading Moat House, Mill Ln, Sindlesham, WOKINGHAM
☎ 0118 949 9988 96

SONNING — Map 04 SU77

Sonning Duffield Rd RG4 6GJ
☎ 0118 969 3332 Fax 0118 944 8409
A quality parkland course and the scene of many county championships. Wide fairways, not overbunkered, and very good greens. Holes of changing character through wooded belts.
18 holes, 6366yds, Par 70, SSS 70, Course record 65.

Visitors weekdays only. Handicap certificate or proof of membership of another club required.
Societies must apply in writing.
Green Fees on application.
Prof R McDougall
Designer Hawtree
Facilities
Location 1m S off A4

Hotel ★★★ 72% The French Horn, SONNING
☎ 0118 969 2204 12 Annexe8

STREATLEY — Map 04 SU58

Goring & Streatley RG8 9QA
☎ 01491 873229 Fax 01491 875224
A parkland/moorland course that requires 'negotiating'. Four well-known first holes lead up to the heights of the 5th tee, to which there is a 300ft climb. Wide fairways, not overbunkered, with nice rewards on the way home down the last few holes. A delightful course that commands magnificent views of the Ridgeway and the River Thames.
18 holes, 6320yds, Par 71, SSS 70, Course record 65.
Club membership 740.

Visitors must contact in advance, with member only at weekends.
Societies apply in writing.
Green Fees £30 per day; £22 per round.
Prof Roy Mason
Facilities
Location N of village off A417

Hotel ★★★★ 67% The Swan Diplomat Hotel, High St, STREATLEY
☎ 01491 873737 46

SUNNINGDALE — Map 04 SU96

SUNNINGDALE See page 31

Sunningdale Ladies Cross Rd SL5 9RX ☎ 01344 620507
A short 18-hole course with a typical Surrey heathland layout. A very tight course, making for a challenging game.
18 holes, 3616yds, Par 60, SSS 60.
Club membership 350.

Visitors telephone in advance.
Societies Ladies societies only.
Green Fees not confirmed.
Facilities
Location 1m S off A30

Hotel ★★★★ 68% The Berystede, Bagshot Rd, Sunninghill, ASCOT ☎ 01344 23311 91

WOKINGHAM — Map 04 SU86

Downshire Easthampstead Park RG40 3DH
☎ 01344 302030 Fax 01344 301020
Beautiful municipal parkland course with mature trees. Water hazards come into play on the 14th and 18th holes, and especially on the short 7th, a testing downhill 169 yards over the lake. Pleasant easy walking. Challenging holes: 7th (par 4), 15th (par 4), 16th (par 3).
18 holes, 6416yds, Par 73, SSS 71.
Club membership 1000.

Visitors must book six days in advance by telephone or seven days in person, weekend times available.
Societies must telephone in advance.
Green Fees £13.50 (£16.50 weekends).
Prof Wayne Owers
Facilities
& Leisure 9 hole pitch & putt.
Location 3m SW of Bracknell

Hotel ★★★★ 76% Coppid Beech, John Nike Way, BRACKNELL ☎ 01344 303333 205

Sand Martins Finchampstead Rd RG40 3RQ
☎ 0118 977 0265 Fax 0118 977 0282
Two different 9-hole loops: the front nine is mostly tree-lined with ponds and the back nine is similar to a links course.
18 holes, 6204yards, Par 70, SSS 70, Course record 65.
Club membership 800.

Visitors no restrictions, but with member only at weekends.
Societies prior arrangement by telephone.
Green Fees £37 per day; £22 per 18 holes.
Cards
Prof Andrew Hall
Designer Edward Fox
Facilities
Location 1m S of Wokingham

Hotel ★★★★ 64% Reading Moat House, Mill Ln, Sindlesham, WOKINGHAM
☎ 0118 949 9988 96

BRISTOL

BRISTOL Map 03 ST57

Bristol and Clifton Beggar Bush Ln, Failand BS8 3TH
☎ 01275 393474 Fax 01275 394611
A downland course with splendid turf and fine tree-lined fairways. The 222-yard (par 3) 13th with the green well below, and the par 4 16th, with its second shot across an old quarry, are outstanding. There are splendid views over the Bristol Channel towards Wales.
18 holes, 6316yds, Par 70, SSS 70, Course record 65.
Club membership 950.
Visitors must have a handicap certificate. Weekends restricted.
Societies telephone to enquire.
Green Fees £30 per day (£35 weekends).
Prof Peter Mawson
Designer Peter McEvoy
Facilities ⊗ by prior arrangement
Location 4m W on B3129 off A369

Hotel ★★★ 69% Redwood Lodge Hotel, Beggar Bush Ln, Failand, BRISTOL
☎ 01275 393901 108

Filton Golf Course Ln, Filton BS31 7QS
☎ 0117 969 4169 Fax 0117 931 4359
Challenging parkland course situated on high ground in a pleasant suburb to the north of the city. Extensive views can be enjoyed from the course, especially from the second tee and the clubhouse, where on a clear day the Cotswold Hills and the Brecon Beacons can be seen. Good par 4 testing hole 'dog-leg' 383 yds.
18 holes, 6310yds, Par 70, SSS 70, Course record 68.
Club membership 730.
Visitors advisable to contact in advance for availability, may not play at weekends unless with member.
Societies apply in writing/phone for details.
Green Fees £25 per day; £20 per round.
Prof J C N Lumb
Facilities ⊗
Location 5m NW off A38

Hotel B Forte Posthouse Bristol, Filton Rd, Hambrook, BRISTOL
☎ 0117 956 4242 197

Henbury Henbury Hill, Westbury-on-Trym BS10 7QB
☎ 0117 950 0044 & 950 2121 (Prof) Fax 0117 959 1928
A parkland course tree-lined and on two levels. The River Trym comes into play on the 7th drop-hole with its green set just over the stream. The last nine holes have the beautiful Blaise Castle woods for company.
18 holes, 6039yds, Par 70, SSS 70, Course record 62.
Club membership 760.
Visitors with member only weekends. Advisable to contact in advance for availability.
Societies apply in writing or telephone well in advance. Tue & Fri only.
Green Fees not confirmed.
Prof Nick Riley
Facilities ⊗
Location 3m NW of city centre on B4055 off A4018

Hotel ★★★ 62% Henbury Lodge Hotel, Station Rd, Henbury, BRISTOL
☎ 0117 950 2615 11 Annexe8

Knowle West Town Ln, Brislington BS4 5DF
☎ 0117 977 0660 Fax 0117 972 0615
A parkland course with nice turf. The first five holes climb up and down hill but the remainder are on a more even plane.

18 holes, 6016yds, Par 69, SSS 69, Course record 61.
Club membership 700.
Visitors must have handicap certificate, must telephone professional 01179 779193 for weekends.
Societies Thu only, apply in writing.
Green Fees £27 per day; £22 per 18 holes (£32/£27 weekends).
Prof Gordon Brand Snr
Designer Hawtree/J H Taylor
Facilities ⊗
Location 3m SE of city centre off A37

Hotel ★★★ Hunstrete House Hotel, Chelwood, HUNSTRETE
☎ 01761 490490 23

Mangotsfield Carsons Rd, Mangotsfield BS17 3LW
☎ 0117 956 5501
An easy hilly parkland course. Caravan site.
18 holes, 5337yds, Par 68, SSS 66, Course record 61.
Club membership 400.
Visitors no restrictions.
Societies bookings in advance to Craig Trewin.
Green Fees not confirmed.
Prof Craig Trewin
Designer John Day
Facilities ⊗
& Leisure sauna.
Location 6m NE of city centre off B4465

Hotel B Forte Posthouse Bristol, Filton Rd, Hambrook, BRISTOL
☎ 0117 956 4242 197

Shirehampton Park Park Hill, Shirehampton BS11 0UL
☎ 0117 982 3059 Fax 0117 982 2083
A lovely parkland course with views across the Avon Gorge.
18 holes, 5430yds, Par 67, SSS 66.
Club membership 600.
Visitors with member only at weekends. Must have a handicap certificate.
Societies Thu (book through Secretary)
Green Fees £18 per round (weekdays).
Prof Brent Ellis
Facilities ⊗
Location 2m E of junct 18 M5 on B4054

Hotel ★★★ 69% Redwood Lodge Hotel, Beggar Bush Ln, Failand, BRISTOL
☎ 01275 393901 108

Woodlands Woodlands Ln, Almondsbury BS12 4JZ
☎ 01454 619319 Fax 01454 619397
Situated on the edge of the Severn Valley, bordered by Hortham Brook and Shepherds Wood this interesting parkland course, features five testing par 3's set around the course's five lakes, notably the 206 yd 5th hole which extends over water.
18 holes, 6068yds, Par 69, SSS 67.
Club membership 101.

Visitors no restrictions.
Societies telephone in advance.
Green Fees £11 per round (£13 weekends & bank holidays).
Designer Cliff Chapman
Facilities
& Leisure fishing.
Location N of Bristol off A38

Hotel B Forte Posthouse Bristol, Filton Rd, Hambrook, BRISTOL
☎ 0117 956 4242 197

BUCKINGHAMSHIRE

AYLESBURY Map 04 SP81

Aylesbury Golf Centre Hulcott Ln, Bierton HP22 5GA
☎ 01296 393644
A parkland course with magnificent views to the Chiltern Hills. The course is tight with out of bounds coming into play on the 1st, 2nd, 6th 7th and 8th.
18 holes, 5965yds, Par 71, SSS 69.
Club membership 200.

Visitors no restrictions, but booking advisable.
Societies telephone for details.
Green Fees £9 per round (£10 weekends & bank holidays).
Cards
Prof Mitch Kierstenson
Designer T S Benwell
Facilities
Location 1m N of Aylesbury on A418

Hotel B Forte Posthouse Aylesbury, Aston Clinton Rd, AYLESBURY ☎ 01296 393388 94

Aylesbury Park Oxford Rd HP17 8QQ
☎ 01296 399196 Fax 01296 399196
Parkland course with mature trees, located just south-west of Aylesbury.
18 holes, 6148yds, Par 70, SSS 69, Course record 69.
Club membership 380.

Visitors may book up to 1 week in advance.
Societies telephone for Society Pack
Green Fees £12 per round (£16 weekends).
Cards
Prof David Boot
Designer H Hawtree
Facilities
Location 0.5m SW of Aylesbury, on the A418

Hotel ★★★ 63% Holiday Inn Garden Court, Buckingham Rd, Watermead, AYLESBURY
☎ 01296 398839 40

Ellesborough Butlers Cross HP17 0TZ
☎ 01296 622114 Fax 01296 622114
Once part of the property of Chequers, and under the shadow of the famous monument at the Wendover end of the Chilterns. A downland course, it is rather hilly with most holes enhanced by far-ranging views over the Aylesbury countryside.
18 holes, 6283yds, Par 71, SSS 71, Course record 64.
Club membership 700.

Visitors welcome on weekdays, handicap certificate required.
Societies Wed & Thu only, by prior arrangement with General Manager.
Green Fees £40 per day; £25 per round.
Prof Mark Squire
Designer James Braid
Facilities
Location 1m E of Ellesborough on B4010

Hotel ★★★ 73% The Bell Inn, ASTON CLINTON ☎ 01296 630252 5 Annexe15

BEACONSFIELD Map 04 SU99

Beaconsfield Seer Green HP9 2UR
☎ 01494 676545 Fax 01494 681148
An interesting and, at times, testing tree-lined and parkland course which frequently plays longer than appears on the card! Each hole differs to a considerable degree and here lies the charm. Walking is easy, except perhaps to the 6th and 8th. Well bunkered.
18 holes, 6493yds, Par 72, SSS 71, Course record 63.
Club membership 850.

Visitors must contact in advance and have a handicap certificate. May not play weekends.
Societies phone for details
Green Fees £40 per day; £30 per round.
Prof Michael Brothers
Designer H S Colt
Facilities
Location 2m E,S of Seer Green

WOBURN

BOW BRICKHILL *Bucks* ☎ 01908 370756
Fax 01908 378436 Map O4 SP93

John Ingham writes: Come off the M1 motorway at Junction 13 and you are quickly at Woburn, with its magnificent stately home, wildlife safari park and surrounding echoes of Henry VIII and the Dukes of Bedford. Within the last 25 years two new attractions have been added - two golf courses designed by the famed Charles Lawrie of Cotton Pennink.

To create these beautiful courses, the bulldozers got among pine and chestnut and literally cut fairways through some of the most picturesque country in all England - but it had been country seen by very few. From the very back tees, both courses are somewhat long for the weekend amateur. The Duke's measures 6961 yards and makes for a stiff test for any class of golfer, while the 'easier' Duchess, measuring a very respectable 6651 yards, requires a high degree of skill on its fairways guarded by towering pines.

Today, under the direction of Alex Hay, a Scottish TV golf commentator, the Dukes course has become the home of the increasingly popular Weetabix Women'sBritish Open. It has been held at Woburn since 1990.

The town of Woburn and the Abbey are both within Bedfordshire, while the golf and country club actually lie over the border in Buckinghamshire. Although just 45 miles from London, you will feel very much in the wilds and the local pubs and people, plus some wonderful countryside, make this area an excellent place to stay for a few days.

And, if you can hit the ball straight, you might get near the course record of 63 achieved by Peter Baker and Ian Woosnam!

Visitors must play with a member at weekends. Midweek by prior arrangement
Societies must telephone in advance on application.
Green fees All credit & charge cards.
Facilities Professional (Luther Blacklock),
Leisure hard tennis court, outdoor swimming pool (heated)
Location Bow Brickhill, Milton Keynes MK17 9LJ. (SE of Bow Brickhill 4m W of J13 M1 off A5130

**36 holes. Dukes Course: 18 holes, 6961 yds, Par 72 , SSS 74.
Duchess Course: 18 holes, 6651yds, Par 72, SSS 72.**

WHERE TO STAY AND EAT NEARBY

HOTELS:

ASPLEY GUISE
★★★ 71% Moore Place, The Square ☎ 01908 282000, 39 Annexe 15

FLITWICK
★★★ 75% Flitwick Manor, Church Rd. ☎ 01525 712242. 15 (2 . 12 1)

WOBURN
★★★ 70% Bedford Arms, George St. ☎ 01525 290441 53

RESTAURANTS:

WOBURN
Paris House, Woburn Park ☎ 01525 290692.

Hotel ★★★★ 65% Bellhouse Hotel, Oxford Rd, BEACONSFIELD ☎ 01753 887211 136

BLETCHLEY Map 04 SP83

Windmill Hill Tattenhoe Ln MK3 7RB
☎ 01908 631113 Fax 01908 630034
Long, open-parkland course, the first championship course designed by Henry Cotton, opened in 1972. Proprietary Pay & Play. No winter greens.
18 holes, 6720yds, Par 73, SSS 72, Course record 68.
Club membership 400.

Visitors booking system in operation up to 7 days in advance.
Societies packages available, contact for details.
Green Fees £10.50 per 18 holes (£13.60 weekends).
Cards
Prof Colin Clingan
Designer Henry Cotton
Facilities
Location W side of town centre on A421

Hotel ★★ 70% Shenley Church Inn, Burchard Crescent, Shenley Church End, MILTON KEYNES ☎ 01908 505467 50

BOW BRICKHILL Map 04 SP93

BOW BRICKHILL See page 35

BUCKINGHAM Map 04 SP63

Buckingham Tingewick Rd MK18 4AE
☎ 01280 815566 Fax 01280 821812
Undulating parkland course with a stream and river affecting 8 holes.
18 holes, 6082yds, Par 70, SSS 69, Course record 67.
Club membership 690.

Visitors welcome Mon-Fri, with member only at weekends.
Societies by prior arrangement.
Green Fees not confirmed.
Prof Tom Gates
Facilities
Location 1.5m W on A421

Hotel ★★★ 66% Buckingham Four Pillars Hotel, Buckingham Ring Rd South, BUCKINGHAM ☎ 01280 822622 70

BURNHAM Map 04 SU98

Burnham Beeches Green Ln SL1 8EG
☎ 01628 661448 Fax 01628 668968
In the centre of the lovely Burnham Beeches countryside. Wide fairways, carefully maintained greens, some hills, and some devious routes to a few holes. A good finish.
18 holes, 6449yds, Par 70, SSS 71.
Club membership 670.

Visitors must contact in advance. May play on weekdays only.
Societies welcome Apr-Oct, write or telephone for information.
Green Fees £42 per day; £30 per round.
Prof Ronnie Bolton
Facilities
Location 0.5m NE of Burnham

Hotel ★★★ 69% Burnham Beeches Hotel, Grove Rd, BURNHAM ☎ 01628 429955 75

Lambourne Dropmore Rd SL1 8NF
☎ 01628 666755 Fax 01628 663301
A championship standard 18-hole parkland course. Undulating terrain with many trees and several lakes, notably on the tricky 7th hole which has a tightly guarded green reached via a shot over a lake.
18 holes, 6771yds, Par 72, SSS 73, Course record 67.
Club membership 670.

Visitors must contact in advance & have a handicap certificate. May not play at weekends.
Green Fees £36.
Cards
Prof David Hart
Designer Donald Steel
Facilities
& Leisure sauna.
Location Access via M4 junct 7 towards Burnham or M40 junct 2 towards Slough/Burnham

Hotel ★★★ 69% Burnham Beeches Hotel, Grove Rd, BURNHAM ☎ 01628 429955 75

CHALFONT ST GILES Map 04 SU99

Harewood Downs Cokes Ln HP8 4TA ☎ 01494 762308
A testing undulating parkland course with sloping greens and plenty of trees.
18 holes, 5958yds, Par 69, SSS 69, Course record 64.

Visitors must contact in advance.
Societies apply in writing or telephone.
Green Fees £25 per round (£30 weekends & bank holidays).
Cards
Prof G C Morris
Facilities
Location 2m E of Amersham on A413

Hotel ★★★★ 65% Bellhouse Hotel, Oxford Rd, BEACONSFIELD ☎ 01753 887211 136

CHARTRIDGE Map 04 SP90

Chartridge Park HP5 2TF ☎ 01494 791772
A family run, easy walking parkland course set high in the beautiful Chiltern Hills, affording breathtaking views.
18 holes, 5516yds, Par 69, SSS 67, Course record 67.
Club membership 600.

Visitors may not play before 10.30am weekends.
Societies must telephone in advance.
Green Fees not confirmed.
Cards
Prof Peter Gibbins
Designer John Jacobs
Facilities
Location 3m NW of Chesham

Hotel ★★★ 65% The Crown, High St, AMERSHAM ☎ 01494 721541 19 Annexe4

CHESHAM Map 04 SP90

Chesham & Ley Hill Ley Hill Common HP5 1UZ
☎ 01494 784541 Fax 01494 785506
Wooded parkland course on hilltop with easy walking. Subject to wind.
9 holes, 5296yds, Par 66, SSS 65, Course record 62.
Club membership 400.

Visitors may play Mon & Thu all day, Wed after noon, Fri up to 4pm.
Societies subject to approval, Thu only.
Green Fees £20 per day; £12 per round.
Facilities
Location 2m E of Chesham

Hotel ★★★ 65% The Crown, High St, AMERSHAM ☎ 01494 721541 19 Annexe4

DENHAM Map 04 TQ08

Buckinghamshire Denham Court Dr UB9 5BG
☎ 01895 835777 Fax 01895 835210
A John Jacobs designed championship-standard course. Visitors only welcome as guests of members to this beautiful course in 269 acres of lovely grounds including mature trees, five lakes and two rivers. The testing 7th hole requires a 185 yd carry over a stream, followed by a second shot over a river to a green guarded by a lake.
18 holes, 6880yds, Par 72, SSS 73, Course record 70.
Club membership 500.

Visitors with member only or introduced by member. Weekdays only.
Societies must contact in advance.
Green Fees £70 (£80 weekends & bank holidays).
Cards
Prof John O'Leary
Designer John Jacobs
Facilities by prior arrangement by prior arrangement
& Leisure sauna.
Location Just beyond junct 1 on M40

Hotel ★★★★ 65% Bellhouse Hotel, Oxford Rd, BEACONSFIELD ☎ 01753 887211 136

Denham Tilehouse Ln UB9 5DE ☎ 01895 832022 Fax 01895 835340
A beautifully maintained parkland/heathland course, home of many county champions. Slightly hilly and calling for good judgement of distance in the wooded areas.
18 holes, 6456yds, Par 70, SSS 71, Course record 66.
Club membership 790.

Visitors must contact in advance & have handicap certificate. Must play with member Fri-Sun.
Societies Tue-Thu. Must book in advance.
Green Fees £50 per day; £35 per round.
Prof Stuart Campbell
Designer H S Colt
Facilities by prior arrangement by prior arrangement
Location 0.5m N of North Orbital Road, 2m from Uxbridge

Hotel ★★★★ 65% Bellhouse Hotel, Oxford Rd, BEACONSFIELD ☎ 01753 887211 136

FLACKWELL HEATH Map 04 SU89

Flackwell Heath Treadaway Rd, High Wycombe HP10 9PE
☎ 01628 520929 Fax 01628 530040
Open sloping heath and tree-lined course on hills overlooking Loudwater and the M40. Some good challenging par 3's and a several testing small greens.
18 holes, 6207yds, Par 71, SSS 70, Course record 63.
Club membership 800.

Visitors with member only at weekends.
Societies Wed & Thu only, by prior booking.
Green Fees not confirmed.
Prof Paul Watson
Facilities
Location NE side of town centre

Hotel ★★★★ 65% Bellhouse Hotel, Oxford Rd, BEACONSFIELD ☎ 01753 887211 136

GERRARDS CROSS Map 04 TQ08

Gerrards Cross Chalfont Park SL9 0QA
☎ 01753 883263 Fax 01753 883593
A wooded parkland course which has been modernised in recent years and is now a very pleasant circuit with infinite variety. The best part lies on the plateau above the clubhouse where there are some testing holes.
18 holes, 6295yds, Par 69, SSS 70, Course record 64.
Club membership 773.

Visitors must contact professional in advance, a handicap certificate is required, may not play Tuesday, weekends or public holidays.
Societies booking well in advance necessary, handicap certicates required, packages to suit.
Green Fees £44 per day; £32 per 18 holes.
Prof Matthew Barr
Designer Bill Pedlar
Facilities by prior arrangement
Location NE side of town centre off A413

Hotel ★★★★ 65% Bellhouse Hotel, Oxford Rd, BEACONSFIELD ☎ 01753 887211 136

HALTON Map 04 SP81

Chiltern Forest Aston Hill HP22 5NQ
☎ 01296 631267 Fax 01296 631267
Extended to 18 holes in 1992, this very hilly wooded parkland course is on two levels. It is a true test of skill to the low handicap golfer, as well as being a fair challenge to higher handicap golfers. The surrounding woodland makes the course very scenic.

18 holes, 5765yds, Par 70, SSS 70, Course record 69.
Club membership 600.

Visitors welcome weekdays, must play with member at weekends.
Societies contact in advance for booking form.
Green Fees £23 per day; £18 per round.
Prof C Skeet
Facilities
Location 1m NE off A4011

Hotel ★★★ 64% Rose & Crown Hotel & Restaurant, High St, TRING ☎ 01442 824071 27

HIGH WYCOMBE — Map 04 SU89

Hazlemere Golf & Country Club Penn Rd, Hazlemere HP15 7LR ☎ 01494 714722 Fax 01494 713914
Undulating parkland course in beautiful countryside with water hazards in play on some holes. Two long par 5s and a fine par 4 closing hole.
18 holes, 5873yds, Par 70, SSS 68, Course record 62.
Club membership 700.

Visitors weekdays all day. Weekends by prior arrangement through Pro. shop telephone 01494 718298.
Societies by prior telephone arrangement.
Green Fees on application.
Prof Alistair McKay/Paul Harrison
Designer Terry Murray
Facilities
Location 2m NE, A404 towards Amersham

Hotel ★★★ 65% The Crown, High St, AMERSHAM ☎ 01494 721541 19 Annexe4

IVER — Map 04 TQ08

Iver Hollow Hill Ln, Langley Park Rd SL0 0JJ
☎ 01753 655615 Fax 01753 654225
Fairly flat, pay and play parkland course with challenging par 5s, plenty of hazards - water and ditches - and strong crosswinds to contend with.
9 holes, 6288yds, Par 72, SSS 72, Course record 68.
Club membership 200.

Visitors competitions at weekends, telephone to pre book tee times.
Societies telephone in advance.
Green Fees £10 per 18 holes; £5.50 per 9 holes (£13.50/£7 weekends and bank holidays.
Cards
Prof Karl Teschner
Facilities
Location 1.5m SW off B470

Hotel ★★★★ 66% Heathrow Marriott, Ditton Rd, Langley, SLOUGH ☎ 01753 544244 380

Richings Park Golf & Country Club North Park SL0 9DL
☎ 01753 655370 Fax 01753 655409
Set amongst mature trees and attractive lakes, this testing par 70 parkland course provides a suitable challenge to golfers of all abilities. Well irrigated greens and abundant wildlife.
18 holes, 6144yds, Par 70, SSS 69.
Club membership 620.

Visitors welcome but may not play until after 12 noon at weekends.
Societies apply in writing or telephone.
Green Fees £20 per 18 holes (£30 at weekends).
Cards
Prof Martin Heys
Designer Alan Higgins
Facilities
& Leisure 5 hole academy course.
Location Junct 5 on M4, A4 towards Heathrow, left at lights, Sutton Lane, right at next lights North Park

Hotel ★★★ 68% Courtyard by Marriott Slough/Windsor, Church St, Chalvey, SLOUGH ☎ 01753 551551 148

IVINGHOE — Map 04 SP91

Ivinghoe Wellcroft LU7 9EF ☎ 01296 668696
Testing parkland course with water on three holes. Easy walking on rolling countryside.
9 holes, 4508yds, Par 62, SSS 62, Course record 57.
Club membership 250.

Visitors may only play after 8am.
Societies must contact in advance.
Green Fees not confirmed.
Prof Bill Garrad
Facilities
Location N side of village

Hotel ★★★ 73% The Bell Inn, ASTON CLINTON ☎ 01296 630252 5 Annexe15

LITTLE CHALFONT — Map 04 SU99

Little Chalfont Lodge Ln HP8 4AJ
☎ 01494 764877 Fax 01494 762860
Gently undulating flat course surrounded by woods.
9 holes, 5852yds, Par 68, SSS 68, Course record 66.
Club membership 300.

Visitors no restrictions, please phone to ensure there are no competitions in progress. Must contact for weekend play.
Societies please telephone in advance.
Green Fees £10 per 18 holes (£12 weekends).
Cards
Prof M Dunne
Facilities
& Leisure one motorised cart for hire by arrangement.
Location Between Little Chalfont & Chorleywood

Hotel ★★★ 65% The Crown, High St, AMERSHAM ☎ 01494 721541 19 Annexe4

LOUDWATER — Map 04 SU89

Wycombe Heights Golf Centre Rayners Ave HP10 9SW
☎ 01494 816686 Fax 01494 816728
Opened in 1991 and designed by the John Jacobs Partnership. The golf centre includes a 24-bay driving range.
18 holes, 6253yds, Par 70, SSS 72, Course record 69.
Club membership 950.

Visitors booking advisable 6 days in advance.
Societies telephone in advance & confirm in writing.
Green Fees £10.45 (£15.45 weekends).

Cards
Prof Adam Bishop
Designer John Jacobs
Facilities
Hotel B Forte Posthouse High Wycombe, Handy Cross, HIGH WYCOMBE 01494 442100 106

Marlow Map 04 SU88

Harleyford Harleyford Estate, Henley Rd SL7 2SP
01628 402300 Fax 01628 478434
Set in 160 acres, this Donald Steel designed course, founded in 1996, makes the most of the natural rolling contours of the beautiful parkland of the historic Harleyford Estate. A challenging course to golfers of all handicaps. Stunning views across the Thames Valley.
18 holes, 6604yds, Par 72.
Club membership 800.
Visitors soft spikes only, preferable to contact in advance.
Societies handicap cert required, Tel 01628 402344 Groups co-ordinator.
Green Fees £40 (£60 weekends & bank holidays).
Cards
Prof Alasdair Barr
Designer Donald Steel
Facilities
& Leisure chipping green.
Location S side A4156 Marlow/Henley road, close to A404 Marlow bypass linking junct 4 M40/junct 8/9 M4

Hotel ★★★★ 74% Danesfield House, Henley Rd, MARLOW-ON-THAMES 01628 891010 87

Mentmore Map 04 SP91

Mentmore Golf & Country Club LU7 0UA
01296 662020 Fax 01296 662592
Two 18-hole courses - Rosebery and Rothschild - set within the wooded estate grounds of Mentmore Towers. Gently rolling parkland course with mature trees and lakes and two interesting feature holes; the long par 5 (606 yds) 9th on the Rosebery course with fine views of the Chilterns and the par 4 (340yd) 5th on the Rothschild course, in front of the hall.
Rosebery Course: 18 holes, 6777yds, Par 72, SSS 72.
Rothschild Course: 18 holes, 6791yds, Par 72, SSS 72.
Club membership 1100.
Visitors must contact in advance, may not play weekends before 11am.
Societies by prior arrangement.
Green Fees not confirmed.
Cards
Prof Pip Elson
Designer Bob Sandow
Facilities
& Leisure hard tennis courts, heated indoor swimming pool, fishing, sauna, gymnasium.
Location 4m S of Leighton Buzzard

Hotel ★★★ 55% Swan Hotel, High St, LEIGHTON BUZZARD 01525 372148 38

Milton Keynes Map 04 SP83

Abbey Hill Two Mile Ash MK8 8AA 01908 563845
Undulating municipal course within the new city. Tight fairways and well-placed bunkers. Stream comes into play on five holes. Also Par 3 course.
18 holes, 6177yds, Par 68, SSS 69.
Club membership 600.
Visitors no restrictions.
Societies must telephone (01908) 562408 in advance.
Green Fees not confirmed.
Prof Gary George
Facilities
Location 2m W of new town centre off A5

Hotel ★★★ 63% Quality Friendly Hotel, Monks Way, Two Mile Ash, MILTON KEYNES 01908 561666 88

Three Locks Great Brickhill MK17 9BH
01525 270470 & 270050
Parkland course offering a challenge to beginners and experienced golfers, with water coming into play on ten holes. Magnificent views.
18 holes, 5850yds, Par 69, SSS 68, Course record 69.
Club membership 350.
Visitors telephone 01525 270050 to book tee times.
Societies write or telephone for details.
Green Fees not confirmed.
Facilities
& Leisure fishing.
Location A4146 between Leighton Buzzard/Bletchley

Hotel ★★ 70% Shenley Church Inn, Burchard Crescent, Shenley Church End, MILTON KEYNES 01908 505467 50

Princes Risborough Map 04 SP80

Whiteleaf Upper Icknield Way, Whiteleaf HP27 0LY
01844 274058
Short, hilly and tricky 9-hole parkland course, requiring great accuracy, set high in the Chilterns with beautiful views.
9 holes, 5391yds, Par 66, SSS 66, Course record 64.
Club membership 400.
Visitors advisable to contact in advance, with member only at weekends.
Societies on Thu only, must contact the secretary in advance.
Green Fees £18 per round.
Prof Ken Ward
Facilities
Location 1m NE off A4010

Hotel ★★★ 73% The Bell Inn, ASTON CLINTON 01296 630252 5 Annexe15

Stoke Poges Map 04 SU98

Farnham Park Park Rd SL2 4PJ
01753 643332 & 647065 Fax 01753 643332
Fine, public parkland course in pleasing setting.
18 holes, 6172yds, Par 71, SSS 70, Course record 68.
Club membership 600.
Visitors telephone in advance for tee times.
Societies apply in writing.

Green Fees £9 per round (£12 weekends & bank holidays).
Cards
Prof Paul Warner
Designer Hawtree
Facilities
Location W side of village off B416

Hotel ★★★★ 66% Heathrow Marriott, Ditton Rd, Langley, SLOUGH
☎ 01753 544244 380

Stoke Poges Stoke Park, North Dr SL2 4PG
☎ 01753 717171 Fax 01753 717181
Judgement of the distance from the tee is all important on this first-class parkland course. There are 8 outstanding par 4's of around 440 yards, several calling for much thought. Fairways are wide and the challenge seemingly innocuous. The 7th hole being the model for the well known 12th hole at Augusta. A further 9 holes are due to be playable in August '98.
18 holes, 6654yds, Par 71, SSS 72, Course record 65.
Club membership 600.
Visitors must contact in advance. Tuesday morning Ladies Day no visitors.
Societies apply in writing or telephone in advance.
Green Fees not confirmed.
Cards
Prof Tim Morrison
Designer Harry Shapland Colt
Facilities
& Leisure hard tennis courts, fishing.
Location 2m N of Slough

Hotel ★★★★ 66% Heathrow Marriott, Ditton Rd, Langley, SLOUGH
☎ 01753 544244 380

WAVENDON Map 04 SP93

Wavendon Golf Centre Lower End Rd MK17 8DA
☎ 01908 281811 Fax 01908 281257
Pleasant parkland course set within mature oak and lime trees and incorporating several small lakes as water hazards. Easy walking.
18 holes, 5540yds, Par 68, SSS 68.
Club membership 300.
Visitors must book 3 days in advance.
Societies must contact in advance by telephone.
Green Fees £10 per 18 holes; £4 per 9 holes (£14/£5 weekends).
Cards
Prof Greg Iron
Designer J Drake/N Elmer
Facilities
Location Just off A421

Hotel ★★★ 71% Moore Place Hotel, The Square, ASPLEY GUISE
☎ 01908 282000 39 Annexe15

WESTON TURVILLE Map 04 SP81

Weston Turville Golf & Squash Club New Rd HP22 5QT
☎ 01296 424084
Parkland course situated at the foot of the Chiltern Hills and providing an excellent challenge for the accomplished golfer, yet not too daunting for the higher handicap player. Flat easy walking with water hazards and many interesting holes, notably the testing dog-leg 5th (418yds).
18 holes, 6008yds, Par 69, SSS 69, Course record 71.
Club membership 600.
Visitors no restrictions.
Societies must contact in advance.
Green Fees £15 (£20 weekends).
Cards
Prof Gary George
Facilities
& Leisure squash.
Location 2m SE of Aylesbury, off A41

Hotel ★★★ 73% The Bell Inn, ASTON CLINTON
☎ 01296 630252 5 Annexe15

WEXHAM STREET Map 04 SU98

Wexham Park SL3 6ND
☎ 01753 663271 Fax 01753 663318
Gently undulating parkland course. Three courses. One 18 hole, one challenging 9 hole and another 9 hole suitable for beginners.
Blue: 18 holes, 5346yds, Par 68, SSS 66.
Red: 9 holes, 2822yds, Par 34, SSS 68.
Green: 9 holes, 2283yds, Par 32, SSS 32.
Club membership 800.
Visitors no restrictions
Societies must contact in advance.
Green Fees on application.
Cards
Prof David Morgan
Facilities
Location 0.5m S

Hotel ★★★★ 66% Heathrow Marriott, Ditton Rd, Langley, SLOUGH
☎ 01753 544244 380

WING Map 04 SP82

Aylesbury Vale Stewkley Rd LU7 0UJ
☎ 01525 240196
The course set in quiet countryside is gently undulating, it was opened in the autumn of 1991. There are five ponds to add interest, notably on the par 4 420 yd 13th - unlucky for some - where the second shot is all downhill with an inviting pond spanning the approach to the green. In addition there is a 10-bay driving range and practice putting green.
18 holes, 6612yds, Par 72, SSS 72, Course record 69.
Club membership 545.
Visitors must adhere to dress regulations. Must contact in advance.
Societies telephone to book in advance.
Green Fees £10 per 18 holes; £6 per 9 holes (£21/£11 weekends & bank holidays, £14/£7 after 2pm).
Cards
Prof Chris Skeet
Designer D Wright
Facilities
Location 2m NW on unclassified Stewkley road, between Wing/Stewkley

Hotel ★★★ 55% Swan Hotel, High St, LEIGHTON BUZZARD ☎ 01525 372148 38

CAMBRIDGESHIRE

BAR HILL Map 05 TL36

Cambridgeshire Moat House Moat House Hotel CB3 8EU ☎ 01954 780098 & 249988 Fax 01954 780010
Undulating parkland course with lake and water hazards, easy walking. Many leisure facilities.
18 holes, 6734yds, Par 72, SSS 72, Course record 73.
Club membership 700.

Visitors must book in advance.
Societies must telephone in advance.
Green Fees £22 per round (£30 per round weekends & bank holidays).
Cards
Prof David Vernon
Facilities
& Leisure hard tennis courts, heated indoor swimming pool, gymnasium, beauty salon.
Location 5m NW of Cambridge on A604

Hotel ★★★ 66% Cambridgeshire Moat House, BAR HILL ☎ 01954 249988 99

BRAMPTON Map 04 TL27

Brampton Park Buckden Rd PE18 8NF
☎ 01480 434700 Fax 01480 411145
Set in truly attractive countryside, bounded by the River Great Ouse and bisected by the River Lane. Great variety with mature trees, lakes and water hazards. One of the most difficult holes is the 4th, a Par 3 island green, 175 yards in length.
18 holes, 6300yds, Par 71, SSS 72, Course record 69.
Club membership 700.

Visitors must contact in advance.
Societies apply in advance.
Green Fees £25 (£35 weekends & bank holidays).
Prof Alisdair Currie
Designer Simon Gidman
Facilities
Hotel ★★ 64% Grange Hotel, 115 High St, Brampton, HUNTINGDON ☎ 01480 459516 9rm(1 7)

CAMBRIDGE Map 05 TL45

Gog Magog Shelford Bottom CB2 4AB
☎ 01223 247626 Fax 01223 414990
Situated just outside the centre of the university town, Gog Magog, established in 1901, is known as the nursery of Cambridge undergraduate golf. The courses are on high ground, and it is said that if you stand on the highest point and could see far enough to the east the next highest ground would be the Ural Mountains! The courses are open but there are enough trees and other hazards to provide plenty of problems. Views from the high parts are superb. The nature of the ground ensures good winter golf.
Old Course: 18 holes, 6400yds, Par 70, SSS 70, Course record 60.
Wandlebury: 18 holes, 6754yds, Par 72, SSS 73.
Club membership 1280.

Visitors must contact in advance.
Societies Mon, Tue, Thu & Fri by reservation.
Green Fees £37.50 per day; £30 per round.
Prof Ian Bamborough
Designer Hawtree Ltd
Facilities
Location 3m SE on A1307

Hotel ★★★ 70% Gonville Hotel, Gonville Place, CAMBRIDGE ☎ 01223 366611 64

ELY Map 05 TL58

Ely City Cambridge Rd CB7 4HX
☎ 01353 662751 (Office) Fax 01353 668636
Parkland course slightly undulating with water hazards formed by lakes and natural dykes. Demanding par 4 5th hole (467yds), often into a headwind, and a testing par 3 2nd hole (160yds) played over 2 ponds Magnificent views of Cathedral. Lee Trevino is the professional record holder.
18 holes, 6627yds, Par 72, SSS 72, Course record 66.
Club membership 850.

Visitors advisable to contact the club in advance.
Societies Tue to Fri, advisable to contact club well in advance.
Green Fees £28 per day (£34 weekends & bank holidays).
Prof Andrew George
Designer Sir Henry Cotton
Facilities
Location S of city on A10

Hotel ★ 64% The Nyton Hotel, 7 Barton Rd, ELY ☎ 01353 662459 10

GIRTON Map 05 TL46

Girton Dodford Ln CB3 0QE
☎ 01223 276169 Fax 01223 277150
Flat, open parkland course with many trees and ditches. Easy walking.
18 holes, 6085yds, Par 69, SSS 69, Course record 66.
Club membership 800.

Visitors with member only at weekends. Contact professional in advance (01223 276991).
Societies apply writing.
Green Fees £16 per day.
Prof Scott Thomson
Designer Allan Gow
Facilities
Location NW side of village

Hotel B Forte Posthouse Cambridge, Lakeview, Bridge Rd, Impington, CAMBRIDGE ☎ 01223 237000 118

HEMINGFORD ABBOTS Map 04 TL27

Hemingford Abbots Cambridge Rd PE18 9HQ
☎ 01480 495000 & 493900 Fax 01480 4960000
Interesting 9-hole course featuring a par 5 dog-leg 4th with a testing tapering fairway, two ponds at the entrance to the 8th green and an island green on the 9th.
9 holes, 5468yds, Par 68, SSS 68, Course record 69.
Club membership 170.

Visitors advisable to phone in advance, particularly for weekends.
Societies advise in writing or telephone.
Green Fees £11.50 per 18 holes; £7.50 per 9 holes (£17/£10.50weekends).
Prof Craig Watson
Designer Ray Paton
Facilities
Location A14 Hemingford Abbots turning

Hotel ★★★ 75% The Old Bridge Hotel, HUNTINGDON ☎ 01480 452681 26

MARCH Map 05 TL49

March Frogs Abbey, Grange Rd PE15 0YH
☎ 01354 652364
Nine-hole parkland course with a particularly challenging par 3 9th hole, with out of bounds on the right and high hedges to the right.
9 holes, 6204yds, Par 70, SSS 70, Course record 65.
Club membership 413.
Visitors contact in advance, with member only at weekends.
Societies apply in writing.
Green Fees £15 per round.
Cards
Prof Jason Hadland
Facilities by prior arrangement by prior arrangement by prior arrangement
Location 0.5m off A141, March bypass

Hotel ★★ 66% Olde Griffin Hotel, High St, MARCH ☎ 01354 652517 20rm(19)

PETERBOROUGH Map 04 TL19

Elton Furze Bullock Rd, Haddon PE7 3TT
☎ 01832 280189 Fax 01832 280299
A new course opened in 1993. Wooded parkland 18-hole course in lovely surroundings.
18 holes, 6289yds, Par 70, SSS 70, Course record 67.
Visitors welcome, preferably Tue & Thu, weekends only with prior permission.
Societies by prior arrangement telephone for details.
Green Fees £22 per round (£32 per round weekends).
Cards
Prof Frank Kiddie
Designer Roger Fitton
Facilities
Location 4m SW of Peterborough, off A605

Hotel ★★★★ 64% Swallow Hotel, Peterborough Business Park, Lynchwood, PETERBOROUGH ☎ 01733 371111 163

Orton Meadows Ham Ln, Orton Waterville PE2 0UU
☎ 01733 237478
Pretty public parkland course set within the Nene Valley Country Park with large lakes and water hazards. Challenging 3rd hole (616yards from white tee) incorporating lots of water and 'out of bounds' areas. Also 12-hole pitch and putt course.
18 holes, 5269yds, Par 67, SSS 68, Course record 69.
Club membership 650.
Visitors no restrictions.
Societies apply in advance.
Green Fees £9.80 per round (£12.50 weekends & bank holidays).
Cards
Prof N Grant/J Mitchell
Designer D & R Fitton
Facilities
& Leisure 12 hole pitch & putt.
Location 3m W of town on A605

Hotel ★★★ 69% Orton Hall Hotel, Orton Longueville, PETERBOROUGH ☎ 01733 391111 49

Peterborough Milton Milton Ferry PE6 7AG
☎ 01733 380489 Fax 01733 380489
Designed by James Braid, this well-bunkered parkland course is set in the grounds of the Milton Estate, many of the holes being played in full view of Milton Hall. Challenging holes are the difficult dog-leg 10th and 15th. Easy walking.
18 holes, 6198yds, Par 71, SSS 70, Course record 66.
Club membership 800.
Visitors must contact in advance.
Societies bookings in writing to secretary.
Green Fees £30 per day; £20 per round (£25 per round weekends & bank holidays).
Prof Michael Gallagher
Designer James Braid
Facilities
Location 2m W of Peterborough on A47

Hotel ★★★ 66% Butterfly Hotel, Thorpe Meadows, Longthorpe Parkway, PETERBOROUGH ☎ 01733 64240 70

Thorpe Wood Thorpe Wood, Nene Parkway PE3 6SE
☎ 01733 267701
Gently undulating, parkland course designed by Peter Alliss and Dave Thomas. Challenging holes include the 5th, the longest hole usually played with prevailing wind and the 14th, entailing a difficult approach shot over water to a two-tier green.
18 holes, 7086yds, Par 73, SSS 74, Course record 71.
Club membership 750.
Visitors phone for reservations 7 days in advance.
Societies must telephone in advance, society bookings taken up to year ahead.
Green Fees £9.80 per round (£12.50 weekends & bank holidays).
Cards
Prof Dennis & Roger Fitton
Designer Peter Allis/Dave Thomas
Facilities
Location 3m W of city centre on A47

Hotel ★★★ 67% Peterborough Moat House, Thorpe Wood, PETERBOROUGH ☎ 01733 289988 125

PIDLEY Map 05 TL37

Lakeside Lodge Fen Rd PE17 3DD
☎ 01487 740540 Fax 01487 740852
A well designed, spacious course incorporating eight lakes, 12,000 trees and a modern clubhouse. The 9th and 18th holes both finish dramatically alongside a lake in front of the

clubhouse. Also 9-hole Par 3 and 25-bay driving range. The Manor provides an interseting contrast with its undulating fairways and angular greens.
Lodge Course: 18 holes, 6821yds, Par 72, SSS 73, Course record 72.
The Manor: 9 holes, 2501yds.
Club membership 500.
Visitors no restrictions.
Societies must telephone in advance.
Green Fees £10 per 18 holes (£16 weekends).
Cards
Prof Scott Waterman
Designer A W Headley
Facilities
& Leisure fishing.
Hotel ★★★ 67% Slepe Hall Hotel, Ramsey Rd, ST IVES ☎ 01480 463122 16

RAMSEY Map 04 TL28

Old Nene Golf & Country Club Muchwood Ln, Bodsey PE17 1XQ ☎ 01487 813519 & 815622
A flat well-drained course with water hazards. There are excellent greens and the 3rd, 4th, 7th, 8th and 9th holes are challenging across water in either a head wind or cross wind. Eastern Area Environmental Winner 1996.
9 holes, 2788yds, Par 68, SSS 68, Course record 66.
Club membership 200.
Visitors book in advance especially evenings & weekends. Dress code must be adhered to.
Societies arrange in advance with Secretary.
Green Fees £10 per 18 holes; £7 per 9 holes (£14/£9 weekends & bank holidays).
Prof Stewart Mills
Designer R Edrich
Facilities by prior arrangement
& Leisure fishing, practice area.
Location 0.75m N of Ramsey towards Ramsey Mereside

Hotel ★★★ 75% The Old Bridge Hotel, HUNTINGDON ☎ 01480 452681 26

Ramsey 4 Abbey Ter PE17 1DD
☎ 01487 812600 Fax 01487 815746
Flat, parkland course with water hazards and well irrigated greens, mature tees and fairways, assuring a good surface whatever the conditions. It gives the impression of wide open spaces, but the wayward shot is soon punished.
18 holes, 5830yds, Par 71, SSS 68, Course record 65.
Club membership 750.
Visitors contact professional in advance 01487 813022, may only play with member at weekends & bank holidays.
Societies apply in writing.
Green Fees £25 per day.
Prof Stuart Scott
Designer J Hamilton Stutt
Facilities
& Leisure snooker tables,6 rink bowls green.
Location 12m SE of Peterborough on B1040

Hotel ★★★ 75% The Old Bridge Hotel, HUNTINGDON ☎ 01480 452681 26

ST IVES Map 05 TL37

St Ives (Cambs) Westwood Rd PE17 4RS
☎ 01480 468392 Fax 01480 468392
Picturesque parkland course.
9 holes, 6100yds, Par 70, SSS 69, Course record 68.
Club membership 500.
Visitors may not play weekends.
Societies welcome Wednesday & Fridays.
Green Fees £20 per day.
Prof Darren Glasby
Facilities
Location W side of town centre off A1123

Hotel ★★★ 67% Slepe Hall Hotel, Ramsey Rd, ST IVES ☎ 01480 463122 16

ST NEOTS Map 04 TL16

Abbotsley Golf & Squash Club PE19 4XN
☎ 01480 474000 & 215153 Fax 01480 471018
Two courses - main Abbotsley course featuring mature parkland with tree-lined fairways, plenty of water hazards and a particularly testing par 3 2nd hole - the 'Mousehole'. Cromwell course, opened in 1991, is less demanding with tricky driving holes and sloping greens. Courses surround moated country house and hotel. Residential golf schools 30 weeks of the year plus floodlit, covered driving range.
Abbotsley Course: 18 holes, 6311yds, Par 73, SSS 72, Course record 69.
Cromwell Course: 18 holes, 6087yds, Par 70, SSS 69.
Club membership 550.
Visitors welcome all times. Necessary to book weekends.
Societies prior booking essential.
Green Fees Abbotsley: £25 per round (£20 weekends). Cromwell: £11 per round (£15 weekends).
Cards
Prof Vivien Saunders
Designer D Young/V Saunders
Facilities
& Leisure squash, gymnasium.
Location 2m SE off B1046

Hotel ★★ 64% Abbotsley Golf Hotel, Potton Rd, Eynesbury Hardwicke, ST NEOTS ☎ 01480 474000 17

St Neots Crosshall Rd PE19 4AE ☎ 01480 472363
Undulating and very picturesque parkland course with lake and water hazards and exceptional greens, close to the Kym and Great Ouse rivers. Easy, level walking.
18 holes, 6074yds, Par 69, SSS 69, Course record 64.
Club membership 630.
Visitors must book in advance. with member only at weekends.
Societies must contact in advance.
Green Fees not confirmed.
Prof Graham Bithrey
Designer H Vardon
Facilities
& Leisure putting green, practice area.
Location Just off the A1 with the jct B1048 heading into St Neots

Hotel ★★ 64% Grange Hotel, 115 High St, Brampton, HUNTINGDON
☎ 01480 459516 9rm(1 ⇌7 ⛿)

THORNEY Map 04 TF20

Thorney English Drove, Thorney PE6 0TJ
☎ 01733 270570
The 18-hole Fen course is ideal for the beginner, while the Lakes course, opened in June 1995, has a challenging links-style layout with eight holes around water.
Fen Course: 18 holes, 6104yds, Par 70, SSS 69, Course record 66.
Lakes Course: 18 holes, 6402yds, Par 71, SSS 70, Course record 69.
Club membership 400.
Visitors book in advance for Fen course, limited weekend play Lakes course.
Societies contact in advance.
Green Fees not confirmed.
Prof Mark Templeman
Designer A Dow
Facilities
Location Off A47, 7m NE of Peterborough

Hotel ★★★ 66% Butterfly Hotel, Thorpe Meadows, Longthorpe Parkway, PETERBOROUGH
☎ 01733 64240 70 ⇌ ⛿

TOFT Map 05 TL35

Cambridge Meridian Comberton Rd CB3 7RY
☎ 01223 264700 Fax 01223 264701
Opened in 1993. Set in 207 acres to a Peter Allis/Clive Clark design with sweeping fairways, lakes and well bunkered greens. The 4th hole has bunker complexes, a sharp dog-leg and a river with the green heavily guarded by bunkers. The 9th and 10th holes challenge the golfer with river crossings.
18 holes, 6651yds, Par 73, SSS 72, Course record 72.
Club membership 600.
Visitors must contact in advance.
Societies telephone for provisional booking
Green Fees not confirmed.
Prof Michael Clemons
Designer Peter Allis/Clive Clark
Facilities
Location 3m W of Cambridge, on B1046

Hotel ★★ 64% Abbotsley Golf Hotel, Potton Rd, Eynesbury Hardwicke, ST NEOTS
☎ 01480 474000 17 ⇌ ⛿

CHESHIRE

ALDERLEY EDGE Map 07 SJ87

Alderley Edge Brook Ln SK9 7RU ☎ 01625 585583
Well-wooded, undulating pastureland course. A stream crosses 7 of the 9 holes.
9 holes, 5823yds, Par 68, SSS 68, Course record 62.
Club membership 400.
Visitors by arrangement on Thu.
Societies Thu only, apply in writing or telephone.
Green Fees £18 per round; (£22 weekends).
Prof Peter Bowring
Facilities
Location 1m NW on B5085

Hotel ★★★ 70% Alderley Edge Hotel, Macclesfield Rd, ALDERLEY EDGE
☎ 01625 583033 32 ⇌ ⛿

ALSAGER Map 07 SJ75

Alsager Golf & Country Club Audley Rd ST7 2UR
☎ 01270 875700 Fax 01270 882207
An 18-hole parkland course situated in rolling Cheshire countryside and offering a challenge to all golfers whatever their standard. Clubhouse is well appointed with good facilities and a friendly atmosphere.
18 holes, 6200yds, Par 70, SSS 70.
Club membership 640.
Visitors must contact in advance, can only play with member at weekends.
Societies must contact in advance.
Green Fees £22 per day.
Prof Richard Brown
Facilities
Location 2m NE of M6 junct 16

Hotel ★★★ 68% Manor House Hotel, Audley Rd, ALSAGER
☎ 01270 884000 57 ⇌ ⛿

CHESTER Map 07 SJ46

Carden Park Hotel Carden Park CH3 9DQ
☎ 01829 731000 Fax 01829 731032
A superb golf resort set in 75 acres of beautiful Cheshire countryside. Facilities include the mature parkland Cheshire Course, the new Nicklaus Course, the 9 hole par 3 Azalea Course, Europe's first Jack Nicklaus Residential Golf School and a luxurious clubhouse.

Cheshire: 18 holes, 6891yds, Par 72, SSS 71.
Nicklaus: 18 holes, 5294yds, Par 72, SSS 71.
Club membership 250.
Visitors must contact in advance, handicap certificate required for the Nicklaus Course.
Societies contact for details.
Green Fees not confirmed.
Cards
Prof David Williams

Facilities & Leisure hard tennis courts, heated indoor swimming pool, sauna, solarium, gymnasium, golf school, treatment rooms.
Location Off A534

Hotel ★★★★ 71% Carden Park Hotel Golf Resort & Spa, Carden Park, BROXTON
☎ 01829 731000 44 Annexe81

Chester Curzon Park CH4 8AR
☎ 01244 677760 Fax 01244 676667
Meadowland course on two levels contained within a loop of the River Dee. The car park overlooks the racecourse across the river.
18 holes, 6508yds, Par 72, SSS 71, Course record 66.
Club membership 820.
Visitors must contact in advance.
Societies must telephone or write in advance.
Green Fees £23 per day (£26 weekends).
Prof George Parton
Facilities
Location 1m W of city centre

Hotel ★★★★ 66% Chester Moat House, Trinity St, CHESTER ☎ 01244 899988 152

Upton-by-Chester Upton Ln, Upton-by-Chester CH2 1EE
☎ 01244 381183
Pleasant, tree-lined, parkland course. Not easy for low-handicap players to score well. Testing holes are 2nd (par 4), 14th (par 4) and 15th (par 3).
18 holes, 5808yds, Par 69, SSS 68, Course record 63.
Club membership 800.
Visitors must contact in advance.
Societies apply in writing.
Green Fees not confirmed.
Prof P A Gardner
Facilities
Location N side off A5116

Hotel ★★★★ 66% Mollington Banastre Hotel, Parkgate Rd, CHESTER
☎ 01244 851471 63

Vicars Cross Tarvin Rd, Great Barrow CH3 7HN
☎ 01244 335174 Fax 01244 335686
Tree-lined parkland course, with undulating terrain.
18 holes, 6243yds, Par 72, SSS 70, Course record 64.
Club membership 750.
Visitors advisable to contact in advance, visitors may not play competition days or Wed.
Societies Tue & Thu only. Must book in advance.
Green Fees £22 per day.
Prof J A Forsythe
Designer J Richardson
Facilities
Location 4m E on A51

Hotel ★★★ 66% Rowton Hall Hotel, Whitchurch Rd, Rowton, CHESTER
☎ 01244 335262 42

CONGLETON Map 07 SJ86

Astbury Peel Ln, Astbury CW12 4RE
☎ 01260 272772 & 279139
Parkland course in open countryside, bisected by a canal. The testing 12th hole involves a long carry over a tree-filled ravine. Large practice area.
18 holes, 6296yds, Par 71, SSS 70, Course record 61.
Club membership 720.
Visitors weekdays ring for availability 01260 298663, with member only at weekends, contact for further details.
Societies contact for details.
Green Fees £25 per day.
Prof Ashley Salt
Facilities
Location 1.5m S between A34 and A527

Hotel ★★★ 63% Lion & Swan Hotel, Swan Bank, CONGLETON
☎ 01260 273115 21

Congleton Biddulph Rd CW12 3LZ ☎ 01260 273540
Superbly-manicured parkland course with views over three counties from the balcony of the clubhouse.
9 holes, 5103yds, Par 68, SSS 65.
Club membership 400.
Visitors may not play during competitions. Must contact in advance.
Societies must apply in writing to Secretary.
Green Fees £20 per day (£30 weekends).
Prof John Colclough
Facilities
Location 1.5m SE on A527

Hotel ★★★ 63% Lion & Swan Hotel, Swan Bank, CONGLETON
☎ 01260 273115 21

CREWE Map 07 SJ75

Crewe Fields Rd, Haslington CW1 5TB
☎ 01270 584099 Fax 01270 584099
Undulating parkland course.
18 holes, 6424yds, Par 71, SSS 71, Course record 67.
Club membership 674.
Visitors contact for details.
Societies Tue only, prior arrangement with the secretary.
Green Fees Summer: £27 per day (£22 after 1pm). Winter: £17 per day.
Prof Mike Booker
Facilities
Location 2.25m NE off A534

Hotel ★★★ 62% Hunters Lodge Hotel, Sydney Rd, Sydney, CREWE
☎ 01270 583440 47

Queen's Park Queen's Park Dr CW2 7SB
☎ 01270 666724 Fax 01270 569902
A short but testing municipal course, the 9 holes are highlighted by the tight dogleg 4th holes and 450yard Par 4 7th hole. There is a testing Par 4 on finishing hole with a bomb crater on left and outerbounds on the right.
9 holes, 4920yds, Par 68, SSS 64, Course record 67.
Club membership 400.
Visitors booking for weekends, cannot play Wed or Sun before 10.30am.
Societies must book at least 2 weeks in advance.
Green Fees £5 per 18 holes; £4 per 9 holes (£7/£5 weekends & bank holidays).
Cards
Prof David Evanson
Facilities
& Leisure hard tennis courts, bowling green.
Location Located behind Queen's Park. Well signposted

Hotel ★★★ 62% Hunters Lodge Hotel, Sydney Rd, Sydney, CREWE
☎ 01270 583440 47

DELAMERE Map 07 SJ56

Delamere Forest Station Rd CW8 2JE
☎ 01606 883264 Fax 01606 883800
Played mostly on undulating open heath there is great charm in the way this course drops down into the occasional pine sheltered valley. Six of the first testing nine hole are between 420 and 455 yards in length.
18 holes, 6305yds, Par 69, SSS 70, Course record 63.
Club membership 500.
Visitors must contact in advance.
Societies apply in writing.
Green Fees not confirmed.
Prof Ellis B Jones
Designer H Fowler
Facilities by prior arrangement
Location 1.5m NE, off B5152

Hotel ★★★ Nunsmere Hall Country House Hotel, Tarporley Rd, Oakmere, SANDIWAY ☎ 01606 889100 32

DISLEY Map 07 SJ98

Disley Stanley Hall Ln, Jacksons Edge SK12 2JX
☎ 01663 762071
Straddling a hilltop site above Lyme Park, this undulating parkland/moorland course affords good views and requires accuracy of approach to almost all the greens which lie on either a ledge or plateau. Testing holes are the 3rd and 4th.
18 holes, 6015yds, Par 71, SSS 69, Course record 63.
Club membership 500.
Visitors contact in advance, may not normally play at weekends.
Societies by prior arrangement.
Green Fees £25 per day (£30 weekends).
Prof Andrew Esplin
Facilities
Location NW side of village off A6

Hotel ★★★ 66% County Hotel Bramhall, Bramhall Ln South, BRAMHALL
☎ 0161 439 8116 & 455 9988 Fax 0161 440 80 71 65

ELLESMERE PORT Map 07 SJ47

Ellesmere Port Chester Rd, Childer Thornton L66 1QF
☎ 0151 339 7689 Fax 0151 339 7689
Municipal parkland course with natural hazards of woods, brook and ponds.
18 holes, 6432yds, Par 71, SSS 71, Course record 70.
Club membership 300.
Visitors must book with professional & send a deposit.
Societies by arrangement with professional.
Green Fees not confirmed.
Prof David Yates
Designer Cotton, Pennick & Lawrie
Facilities
& Leisure squash, golf simulator for hire with professional.
Location NW side of town centre on A41

Hotel ★★★ 67% Woodhey Hotel, Welsh Rd, Little Sutton, WIRRAL
☎ 0151 339 5121 53

FRODSHAM Map 07 SJ57

Frodsham Simons Ln WA6 6HE
☎ 01928 732159 Fax 01928 734070
Undulating parkland course with pleasant views from all parts. Emphasis on accuracy over the whole course, the long

and difficult par 5 18th necessitating a drive across water to the green. Crossed by two footpaths so extreme care needed.
18 holes, 6298yds, Par 70, SSS 70.
Club membership 600.

Visitors must contact in advance. May not play at weekends.
Societies telephone for bookings.
Green Fees £30 per round.
Cards
Prof Graham Tonge
Designer John Day
Facilities
& Leisure snooker room.
Location 1.5m SW

Hotel ★★★ 66% Forest Hills Hotel & Leisure Complex, Bellemonte Rd, Overton Hill, FRODSHAM ☎ 01928 735255 57

HELSBY Map 07 SJ47

Helsby Towers Ln WA6 0JB
☎ 01928 722021 Fax 01928 725384
Parkland course with several tree plantations and natural pits as water hazards. Total of 46 bunkers.
18 holes, 6229yds, Par 70, SSS 70, Course record 69.
Club membership 590.

Visitors must contact in advance. Weekends and bank holidays with member only.
Societies Tue & Thu. Booking through Hon Secretary.
Green Fees £22 per round.
Prof Matthew Jones
Designer James Braid (part)
Facilities
Location 1m S off A56

Hotel ★★★★★ 75% The Chester Grosvenor Hotel, Eastgate, CHESTER ☎ 01244 324024 85

KNUTSFORD Map 07 SJ77

Heyrose Budworth Rd, Tabley WA16 0HZ
☎ 01565 733664 Fax 01565 734267
An 18-hole course in wooded and gently undulating terrain. The par 3 16th (237yrds), bounded by a small river in a wooded valley, is an interesting and testing hole - one of the toughest par 3s in Cheshire. Both the course and the comfortable clubhouse have attractive views.
18 holes, 6515yds, Par 73, SSS 71, Course record 66.
Club membership 600.

Visitors not before 3pm Sat, ladies priority Wed and seniors priority Thu am.
Societies must contact in advance.
Green Fees £24 per day; £19 per round (£29/£24 weekends & bank holidays).
Prof Martin Redrup
Designer C N Bridge
Facilities
Location 1.5m from junc 19 on M6

Hotel ★★★★ 69% Cottons Hotel, Manchester Rd, KNUTSFORD ☎ 01565 650333 99

Knutsford Mereheath Ln WA16 6HS ☎ 01565 633355
Parkland course set in a beautiful old deer park. It demands some precise iron play.
9 holes, 6288yds, Par 70, SSS 70.
Club membership 230.

Visitors are not permitted weekends and restricted Wed. Must contact in advance.
Societies Thursday only by prior arrangement.
Green Fees £18 per round (£24 weekends & bank holidays).
Prof A Gillies
Facilities
Location N side of town centre off A50

Hotel ★★★★ 69% Cottons Hotel, Manchester Rd, KNUTSFORD ☎ 01565 650333 99

Mere Golf & Country Club Chester Rd, Mere WA16 6LJ ☎ 01565 830155 Fax 01565 830713
A gracious parkland championship course designed by James Braid in the Cheshire sand belt, with several holes close to a lake. The round has a tight finish with four testing holes.
18 holes, 6817yds, Par 71, SSS 73, Course record 64.
Club membership 540.

Visitors by prior arrangement only, not able to play Wed, Fri, Sat & Sun.
Societies Mon,Tue & Thu only by prior arrangement.
Green Fees £70 per round.
Cards
Prof Peter Eyre
Designer James Braid
Facilities
& Leisure hard tennis courts, heated indoor swimming pool, squash, fishing, sauna, solarium, gymnasium.
Location 1m E of junc 19 of M6

Hotel ★★★★ 69% Cottons Hotel, Manchester Rd, KNUTSFORD ☎ 01565 650333 99

LYMM Map 07 SJ68

Lymm Whitbarrow Rd WA13 9AN
☎ 01925 752177 & 755020
Fax 01925 755020
First ten holes are gently undulating with the Manchester Ship Canal running alongside the 9th hole. The remaining holes are comparatively flat.
18 holes, 6304yds, Par 71, SSS 70.
Club membership 650.

Visitors may not play at weekends except with member.
Societies Wed only, must contact in advance.
Green Fees not confirmed.

Prof Steve McCarthy
Facilities
Location 0.5m N off A6144

Hotel ★★★ 65% Lymm Hotel, Whitbarrow Rd, LYMM ☎ 01925 752233 15 Annexe47

MACCLESFIELD Map 07 SJ97

Macclesfield The Hollins SK11 7EA
☎ 01625 615845 (Secretary) Fax 01625 260061
Hillside heathland course situated on the edge of the Pennines with excellent views across the Cheshire Plain. A pleasant course providing a good test for players of all abilities.
18 holes, 5769yds, Par 70, SSS 68, Course record 66.
Club membership 620.
Visitors apply in advance.
Societies telephone initially.
Green Fees £20 per day/round (£25 weekends & bank holidays).
Prof Tony Taylor
Designer Hawtree & Son
Facilities
Location SE side of town centre off A523

Hotel ★★★ 65% Belgrade Hotel & Restaurant, Jackson Ln, Kerridge, Bollington, MACCLESFIELD ☎ 01625 573246 54

Shrigley Hall Hotel Shrigley Park, Pott Shrigley SK10 5SB
☎ 01625 575757 Fax 01625 573323
Parkland course set in 262-acre estate with breathtaking views over the Peak District and Cheshire Plain. Designed by Donald Steel, this championship standard course provides a real sporting challenge while the magnificent hotel provides a wealth of sporting facilities as well as accommodation and food.

18 holes, 6281yds, Par 71, SSS 71, Course record 68.
Club membership 400.
Visitors must contact in advance by telephone.
Societies contact in advance.
Green Fees £28 per round Mon-Thu (£35 Fri-Sun & bank holidays).
Cards
Prof Granville Ogden
Designer Donald Steel
Facilities
& Leisure hard tennis courts, heated indoor swimming pool, fishing, sauna, solarium, gymnasium.
Hotel ★★★★ 63% Shrigley Hall Hotel Golf & Country Club, Shrigley Park, Pott Shrigley, MACCLESFIELD ☎ 01625 575757 150

Tytherington Dorchester Way, Tytherington SK10 2JP
☎ 01625 434562 Fax 01625 430882
Modern championship course in beautiful, mature parkland setting with numerous water features. Testing holes, notably the signature 12th hole (par 5), played from an elevated tee with adjacent snaking ditch and a lake guarding the green. Headquarters of the Women's European Tour and venue of the WPGET English Open and County matches. Country club facilities.
18 holes, 6750yds, Par 72, SSS 74.
Club membership 3100.
Visitors advisable to contact in advance and be of handicap standard.
Societies weekdays only by prior arrangement.
Green Fees £35 per day; £28 per 18 hole (£45/£34 weekends).
Cards
Prof Gordon McLeod
Designer Dave Thomas/Patrick Dawson
Facilities
Location 1m N of Macclesfield off A523

Hotel ★★★★ 63% Shrigley Hall Hotel Golf & Country Club, Shrigley Park, Pott Shrigley, MACCLESFIELD ☎ 01625 575757 150

NANTWICH Map 07 SJ65

Reaseheath Reaseheath College CW5 6DF
☎ 01270 625131
The course at Reaseheath is attached to Reaseheath College, which is one of the major centres of greenkeeper training in the UK. It is a short 9-hole which can only be played with a member.
9 holes, 1766yds, Par 62, SSS 58.
Club membership 350.
Visitors with member only.
Societies by prior arrangement, apply in writing.
Green Fees £5 per 18 holes.
Designer D Mortram
Location 1.5m NE of Nantwich, off A51

OSCROFT Map 07 SJ56

Pryors Hayes Willington Rd CH3 8NL
☎ 01829 741250 Fax 01829 741250
Picturesque 18-hole parkland course set in the heart of Cheshire. Gently undulating fairways demand accurate drives, and numerous trees and water hazards make the course a challenging test of golf.
18 holes, 6074yds, Par 69, SSS 69.
Club membership 625.
Visitors no restrictions.
Societies apply for application form.
Green Fees £20 per round (£25 weekends).
Prof Colin Iddon
Designer John Day
Facilities
Location Between A54 & A51 roads, approx 6m E of Chester, village of Oscroft near Tarvin

Hotel ★★★ 63% Willington Hall Hotel, Willington, TARPORLEY ☎ 01829 752321 10

POYNTON Map 07 SJ98

Davenport Worth Hall, Middlewood Rd SK12 1TS
☎ 01625 876951 Fax 01625 876951
Undulating parkland course. Extensive view over Cheshire Plain from elevated 5th tee. Testing 17th hole, par 4.
18 holes, 6027yds, Par 69, SSS 69, Course record 64.
Club membership 700.

Visitors contact professional in advance, 01625 858387. May not play Wed or Sat.
Societies Tue and Thu only. Must apply in advance.
Green Fees £25 per day (£30 weekends & bank holidays).
Prof Wyn Harris
Facilities
Location 1m E off A523

Hotel ★★★ 66% County Hotel Bramhall, Bramhall Ln South, BRAMHALL
☎ 0161 439 8116 & 455 9988 Fax 0161 440 80 71 65

PRESTBURY Map 07 SJ97

Prestbury Macclesfield Rd SK10 4BJ
☎ 01625 828241 Fax 01625 828241
Rather strenuous parkland course, undulating hills, with many plateau greens looked after by one of only 7 Master Greenkeepers in the world. The 9th hole has a challenging uphill 3-tier green and the 17th is over a valley. Host to county and inter-county championships as well as England v USA competitions.
18 holes, 6359yds, Par 71, SSS 71, Course record 64.
Club membership 702.

Visitors must contact in advance and have an introduction from own club, with member only at weekends.
Societies apply in writing, Thu only.
Green Fees £38 per day.

Prof Nick Summerfield
Designer Harry S Colt
Facilities
Location S side of village off A538

Hotel ★★★★ 67% Mottram Hall Hotel, Wilmslow Rd, Mottram St Andrew, Prestbury ☎ 01625 828135 132

RUNCORN Map 07 SJ58

Runcorn Clifton Rd WA7 4SU
☎ 01928 574214
Parkland course with tree-lined fairways and easy walking. Fine views over Mersey and Weaver valleys. Testing holes: 7th par 5; 14th par 5; 17th par 4.
18 holes, 6035yds, Par 69, SSS 69, Course record 58.
Club membership 570.

Visitors weekends restricted to playing with member only.
Societies telephone in advance.
Green Fees £18 per day.
Facilities
Location 1.25m S of Runcorn Station

Hotel B Forte Posthouse Warrington/Runcorn, Wood Ln, Beechwood, RUNCORN
☎ 01928 714000 135

SANDBACH Map 07 SJ76

Malkins Bank Betchton Rd, Malkins Bank CW11 4XN
☎ 01270 765931 Fax 01270 764730
Parkland course. Tight 13th hole with stream running through.
18 holes, 6071yds, Par 70, SSS 69, Course record 65.
Club membership 500.

Visitors no restrictions. Advisable to book in advance.
Societies apply for booking form to course professional
Green Fees £7.50 per round (£8.50 weekends).
Cards
Prof David Wheeler
Designer Hawtree
Facilities
Location 1.5m SE off A533

Hotel ★★★ 63% Saxon Cross Hotel, Holmes Chapel Rd, SANDBACH
☎ 01270 763281 52

Sandbach Middlewich Rd CW11 9BT ☎ 01270 762117
Meadowland, undulating course with easy walking. Limited facilities.
9 holes, 5598yds, Par 68, SSS 67.
Club membership 570.

Visitors weekdays except Tue, and with member only weekends & bank holidays. Must contact in advance.
Societies apply by letter.
Green Fees not confirmed.
Facilities
Location 0.5m W on A533

Hotel ★★★ 63% Saxon Cross Hotel, Holmes Chapel Rd, SANDBACH ☎ 01270 763281 52

SANDIWAY Map 07 SJ67

Sandiway Chester Rd CW8 2DJ
☎ 01606 883247 (Secretary) Fax 01606 888548
Delightful undulating wood and heathland course with long hills up to the 8th, 16th and 17th holes. Many dog-legged and tree-lined holes give opportunities for the deliberate fade or draw.

▶

18 holes, 6404yds, Par 70, SSS 72, Course record 67. Club membership 700.

Visitors book through secretary, members have reserved tees 8.30-9.30 and 12.30-1.30 (11.30-12.30 winter).
Societies book in advance through Secretary/Manager.
Green Fees £40 per day; £35 per round (£45/£40 weekends & bank holidays).
Prof William Laird
Designer Ted Ray
Facilities by prior arrangement
Location 2m W of Northwich on A556

Hotel ★★ 64% Wincham Hall, Hall Ln, Wincham, NORTHWICH ☎ 01606 43453 10rm(9)

TARPORLEY Map 07 SJ56

Portal Golf & Country Club Cobbler's Cross Ln CW6 0DJ
☎ 01829 733933 Fax 01829 733928
Opened in 1991, there are two 18-hole courses here - Championship and Premier - and one 9-hole course - Arderne. They are set in mature, wooded parkland. There are fine views over the Cheshire Plain and numerous water hazards. The Championship 14th is just a short iron through trees, but its green is virtually an island surrounded by water.
Championship Course: 18 holes, 7037yds, Par 73, SSS 74, Course record 64.
Premier Course: 18 holes, 6508yds, Par 71, SSS 72, Course record 67.
Arderne Course: 9 holes, 1724yds, Par 30, Course record 26. Club membership 250.

Visitors must contact in advance.
Societies must pre-book.
Green Fees Championship: £40 per round. Premier: £30 per round. Arderne £10 per round.
Cards
Prof David Clare
Designer Donald Steel
Facilities
& Leisure hard tennis courts, Indoor Golf Academy.
Location Off A49

Hotel ★★★ 67% The Wild Boar, Whitchurch Rd, Beeston, TARPORLEY ☎ 01829 260309 37

WARRINGTON Map 07 SJ68

Birchwood Kelvin Close, Science Park North, Birchwood WA3 7PB
☎ 01925 818819 (Club) & 816574 (Pro) Fax 01925 822403
Very testing parkland course with many natural water hazards and the prevailing wind creating a problem on each hole. The 11th hole is particularly challenging.
18 holes, 6727yds, Par 71, SSS 73, Course record 66. Club membership 720.

Visitors advisable to check with the professional to determine if course is being used.
Societies Mon, Wed & Thu. Apply in writing, or telephone.
Green Fees £26 per day; £18 per round (£34 Sat & bank holidays).
Cards
Prof Paul McEwan
Designer T J A Macauley
Facilities
& Leisure sauna.
Location 4m NE on A574

Hotel B Forte Posthouse Haydock, Lodge Ln, HAYDOCK ☎ 01942 717878 136

Leigh Kenyon Hall, Broseley Ln, Culcheth WA3 4BG
☎ 01925 762943 (Secretary) Fax 01925 765097
A pleasant, well-wooded parkland course. Any discrepancy in length is compensated by the wide variety of golf offered here. The course is well maintained and there is a comfortable clubhouse.
18 holes, 5853yds, Par 69, SSS 68, Course record 64. Club membership 550.

Visitors contact professional for details.

Societies Mon (ex bank hols) & Tue, apply by telephone.
Green Fees not confirmed.
Prof Andrew Baguley
Designer James Braid
Facilities ⊗ 🍴 🍺 ☕ 🍷 👤 🏠 🏌
Location 5m NE off A579

Hotel ★★★ 66% Fir Grove Hotel, Knutsford Old Rd, WARRINGTON ☎ 01925 267471 40 🛁 🚿

Poulton Park Dig Ln, Cinnamon Brow, Padgate WA2 0SH
☎ 01925 822802 Fax 01925 822802
Tight, flat parkland course with good greens and many trees. A straight drive off each tee is important. The 4/13th has a fairway curving to the left with water and out-of-bounds on left and trees on right.
9 holes, 4978metres, Par 68, SSS 66, Course record 66.
Club membership 350.
Visitors midweek only. Contact professional for details 01925 825220.
Societies apply in advance.
Green Fees £17.
Prof Darren Newing
Facilities ⊗ 🍴 🍺 ☕ 🍷 👤 🏠
Location 3m from Warrington on A574

Hotel ★★★ 66% Fir Grove Hotel, Knutsford Old Rd, WARRINGTON ☎ 01925 267471 40 🛁 🚿

Walton Hall Warrington Rd, Higher Walton WA4 5LU
☎ 01925 263061 (bookings)
A quiet, wooded, municipal parkland course on Walton Hall estate.
18 holes, 6801yds, Par 72, SSS 73, Course record 70.
Club membership 250.
Visitors must book 6 days in advance.
Societies must contact in writing.
Green Fees £8 per round (£9.80 weekends).
Prof John Jackson
Facilities ⊗ 🍴 🍺 ☕ 🍷 👤 🏠 🏌 🏌
Location 2m from junct 11 of M56

Hotel ★★★ 66% Fir Grove Hotel, Knutsford Old Rd, WARRINGTON ☎ 01925 267471 40 🛁 🚿

Warrington Hill Warren, London Rd, Appleton WA4 5HR
☎ 01925 261775 (Secretary) Fax 01925 265933
Meadowland, with varied terrain and natural hazards. Major work has recently been carried out on both the clubhouse and the course to ensure high standards. The course is a constant challenge with with ponds, trees and bunkers threatening the errant shot!
18 holes, 6305yds, Par 72, SSS 70, Course record 61.
Club membership 840.
Visitors contact in advance.
Societies by prior arrangement with Secretary.
Green Fees £25 per day (£30 weekends & bank holidays).
Prof Reay Mackay
Designer James Braid
Facilities ⊗ 🍴 🍺 ☕ 🍷 👤 🏠 🏌 🏌
Location 1.5m N of junct 10 of M56 on A49

Hotel ★★ 74% Rockfield Hotel, Alexandra Rd, Grappenhall, WARRINGTON
☎ 01925 262898 6 🛁 🚿 Annexe6 🛁 🚿

Waverton — Map 07 SJ46

Eaton Guy Ln CH3 7PH
☎ 01244 335885 & 335826 Fax 01244 335782
Eaton Golf Club has moved to a new course. Designed by Donald Steel, the course was opened in 1993 and is parkland with a liberal covering of both mature trees and new planting enhanced by natural water hazards. The old course at Eccleston has been returned to nature.
18 holes, 6562yds, Par 72, SSS 71, Course record 69.
Club membership 550.
Visitors must contact in advance particularly for weekends.
Societies must contact in advance. May not play weekends or Wednesdays.
Green Fees £25 weekdays (£30 weekends & bank holidays).
Prof Neil Dunroe
Designer Donald Steel
Facilities ⊗ 🍴 🍺 ☕ 🍷 👤 🏠 🏌 🏌 🏌 🏌
Location 3m SE of Chester off A41

Hotel ★★★★★ 75% The Chester Grosvenor Hotel, Eastgate, CHESTER
☎ 01244 324024 85 🛁 🚿

Widnes — Map 07 SJ58

St Michael Jubilee Dundalk Rd WA8 8BS
☎ 0151 424 6230 Fax 0151 495 2124
Municipal parkland course dominated by the 'Stewards Brook'. It is divided into two sections which are split by the main road and joined by an underpass.
18 holes, 5925yds, Par 69, SSS 67.
Visitors welcome.
Societies must contact in writing.
Green Fees not confirmed.
Prof Darren Chapman
Facilities ⊗ 🍺 ☕ 🍷 👤 🏠 🏌
Location W side of town centre off A562

Hotel ★★★ 64% Everglades Park Hotel, Derby Rd, WIDNES ☎ 0151 495 2040 67 🛁 🚿

Widnes Highfield Rd WA8 7DT
☎ 0151 424 2440 Fax 0151 495 2849
Parkland course, easy walking.
18 holes, 5719yds, Par 69, SSS 68.
Visitors may play after 9am & after 4pm on competition days. Must contact in advance.
Societies must contact in writing.
Green Fees not confirmed.
Prof J O'Brien
Facilities 🍷 👤 🏠
Hotel ★★★ 64% Everglades Park Hotel, Derby Rd, WIDNES ☎ 0151 495 2040 67 🛁 🚿

Wilmslow — Map 07 SJ88

Mottram Hall Wilmslow Rd, Mottram St Andrew SK10 4QT
☎ 01625 828135
Championship standard course with flat meadowland on the front nine and undulating woodland on the back with well guarded greens. The course was designed in 1989 and opened in May 1991. The course is unusual as each half opens and closes with Par 5's. The hotel offers many leisure facilities.
▶

18 holes, 7006yds, Par 72, SSS 74, Course record 65.
Club membership 500.
Visitors must contact in advance.
Societies must contact in advance.
Green Fees not confirmed.
Prof Tim Rastall
Designer Dave Thomas
Facilities
& Leisure hard tennis courts, heated indoor swimming pool, squash, sauna, solarium, gymnasium.
Location On A538 between Wilmslow and Preston

Hotel ★★★★ 67% Mottram Hall Hotel, Wilmslow Rd, Mottram St Andrew, Prestbury
☎ 01625 828135 132

Styal Station Rd, Styal SK9 4JN
☎ 01625 531359 Fax 01625 530063
Well designed flat parkland course with testing bunkers and water hazards. Boasts the longest hole in Cheshire!
18 holes, 6301yds, Par 71, SSS 70.
Club membership 700.
Visitors contact to reserve tee time.
Societies telephone in advance.
Green Fees £18 per day; £12 per round (£24/£16 weekends).
Cards
Prof Simon Forrest
Designer Tony Holmes
Facilities
Hotel ★★★★ 63% Belfry Hotel, Stanley Rd, HANDFORTH
☎ 0161 437 0511 80

Wilmslow Great Warford, Mobberley WA16 7AY
☎ 01565 872148 Fax 01565 872172
A fine parkland championship course, of middle length, fair to all classes of player and almost in perfect condition.
18 holes, 6607yds, Par 72, SSS 72, Course record 62.
Club membership 800.
Visitors must contact in advance.
Societies Tue & Thu only application in writing.
Green Fees £40 per day; £30 per round (£50/£40 weekends).
Prof John Nowicki
Facilities
Location 2m SW off B5058

Hotel ★★★ 70% Alderley Edge Hotel, Macclesfield Rd, ALDERLEY EDGE
☎ 01625 583033 32

WINSFORD Map 07 SJ66

Knights Grange Grange Ln CW7 2PT
☎ 01606 552780
Attractive, well maintained municipal parkland course with water hazards. Within a large recreation complex including a public house and childrens' play area.
9 holes, 2719yds, Par 33, SSS 68.
Visitors 24 hr booking system for weekly play, after 10am Wed for weekend bookings.
Societies apply in writing.
Green Fees not confirmed.
Prof Graham Moore
Facilities
& Leisure hard and grass tennis courts.
Location N side of town off A54

Hotel ★★ 64% Wincham Hall, Hall Ln, Wincham, NORTHWICH
☎ 01606 43453 10rm(9)

CORNWALL & ISLES OF SCILLY

BODMIN Map 02 SX06

Lanhydrock Lostwithiel Rd, Lanhydrock PL30 5AQ
☎ 01208 73600 Fax 01208 77325
Championship standard parkland/moorland course adjacent to the National Trust property Lanhydrock house. Nestling in a picturesque wooded valley of oak and birch, this undulating course provides an exciting and enjoyable challenge to all abilities with discreet use of water and bunkers.
18 holes, 6100yds, Par 70, SSS 70, Course record 66.
Club membership 300.
Visitors no restrictions.
Societies please telephone in advance.
Green Fees £34 per day; £26 per 18 holes.
Cards
Prof Jason Broadway
Designer Hamilton Ştutt
Facilities
Location 1m S of Bodmin from B3268

Hotel ★★★ 66% Restormel Lodge Hotel, Hillside Gardens, LOSTWITHIEL
☎ 01208 872223 21 Annexe12

BUDE Map 02 SS20

Bude & North Cornwall Burn View EX23 8DA
☎ 01288 352006 Fax 01288 356855
Seaside links course with natural sand bunkers, superb greens and breathtaking views. Club established in 1893.
18 holes, 6205yds, Par 71, SSS 70.
Club membership 1000.
Visitors book by telephone 6 days in advance for starting time - or before 6 days with a deposit.
Societies apply in writing or by telephone/fax.
Green Fees £20 per round; £8 per additional round (£25/£8 weekends & bank holidays).
Prof John Yeo
Facilities
Location N side of town

Hotel ★★ 68% Camelot Hotel, Downs View, BUDE
☎ 01288 352361 21

BUDOCK VEAN Map 02 SW73

Budock Vean Golf & Country House Hotel Mawnan Smith TR11 5LG ☎ 01326 250288
Set in 65 acres of mature grounds with a private foreshore to the Helford River, this undulating parkland course has a

tough par 4 5th hole (456yds) which dog-legs at halfway around an oak tree.
9 holes, 2657yds, Par 68, SSS 65, Course record 61.
Club membership 200.
Visitors must contact in advance.
Societies apply in writing or telephone in advance.
Green Fees £16 per day (£20 Sun & bank holidays).
Cards
Designer James Braid
Facilities
& Leisure hard tennis courts, heated indoor swimming pool.
Location 1.5m SW

Hotel ★★★ 75% Budock Vean Golf & Country House Hotel, MAWNAN SMITH
☎ 01326 250288 & 250230
Fax 01326 250892 58

CAMBORNE Map 02 SW64

Tehidy Park TR14 0HH
☎ 01209 842208 Fax 01209 843680
A well-maintained parkland course providing good holiday golf.
18 holes, 6241yds, Par 72, SSS 71, Course record 65.
Club membership 850.
Visitors must contact in advance and have a handicap certificate.
Societies telephone followed by letter.
Green Fees £28 per day; £22 per round (£33/£27 weekends).
Prof James Dumbreck
Facilities
Location On Portreath/Pool road, 2m S of Camborne

Hotel ★★★ 66% Penventon Hotel, REDRUTH
☎ 01209 214141 50

CAMELFORD Map 02 SX18

Bowood Park Lanteglos PL32 9RF
☎ 01840 213017 Fax 01840 212622
A testing parkland course situated in Bowood Park, formerly the largest deer park in Cornwall. The first nine holes are designed around rolling hills; the back nine being played through the River Allen Valley. Plenty of wildlife, water and trees.
18 holes, 6692yds, Par 72, SSS 72.
Visitors booking system in operation
Societies contact for details.
Green Fees £35 per day; £25 per round.
Cards
Prof Tony Moore
Designer Sandow
Facilities
Location Through Camelford, 0.5m turn right Tintagel/Boscastle B3266, 1st left at garage

Hotel ★★ 78% Trebrea Lodge, Trenale, TINTAGEL
☎ 01840 770410 6 Annexe1

CARLYON BAY Map 02 SX05

Carlyon Bay Hotel Sea Rd PL25 3RD
☎ 01726 814250
Championship-length, cliff-top course moving into parkland. Magnificent views surpassed only by the quality of the course. The 230-yard (par 3) 18th with railway and road out-of-bounds, holds the player's interest to the end.
18 holes, 6549yds, Par 72, SSS 71, Course record 66.
Club membership 500.
Visitors must contact in advance.
Societies must contact in advance.
Green Fees £22-29 per round.
Cards
Prof Mark Rowe
Facilities
& Leisure hard tennis courts, outdoor and indoor heated swimming pools, sauna, solarium, 9 hole approach course.
Hotel ★★★★ 73% Carlyon Bay Hotel, Sea Rd, Carlyon Bay, ST AUSTELL
☎ 01726 812304 73

CONSTANTINE BAY Map 02 SW87

Trevose PL28 8JB
☎ 01841 520208 Fax 01841 521057
Well known links course with early holes close to the sea on excellent springy turf. A championship course affording varying degrees of difficulty appealing to both the professional and higher handicap player. It is a good test with well-positioned bunkers, and a meandering stream, and the wind playing a decisive role in preventing low scoring. Self-catering accommodation is available at the club.
Championship Course: 18 holes, 6461yds, Par 71, SSS 71, Course record 67.
Short Course: 9 holes, 1360yds, Par 29, SSS 29.
New Course: 9 holes, 3031yds, Par 35, SSS 35.
Club membership 1500.
Visitors subject to reservations, handicap certificate required for championship course. Advisable to contact in advance.
Societies telephone or write to the secretary.
Green Fees £22-£33 per round.
Cards
Prof Gary Alliss
Designer H S Colt
Facilities by prior arrangement
& Leisure hard tennis courts, heated outdoor swimming pool, snooker & games room, boutique.
Location N of Constantine Bay, off B3276

Hotel ★★★ 77% Treglos Hotel, CONSTANTINE BAY ☎ 01841 520727 44

FALMOUTH Map 02 SW83

Falmouth Swanpool Rd TR11 5BQ
☎ 01326 311262 & 01326 314296 Fax 01326 317783
Seaside/parkland course with outstanding coastal views. Sufficiently bunkered to punish any inaccurate shots. Five acres of practice grounds.

18 holes, 6129yds, Par 72, SSS 70.
Club membership 500.

Visitors please book for tee time.
Societies must contact in advance.
Green Fees £26 per 36 holes; £20 per 18 holes.
Cards
Prof Bryan Patterson
Facilities
Location SW side of town centre

Hotel ★★★★ 71% Royal Duchy Hotel, Cliff Rd, FALMOUTH ☎ 01326 313042 43

HOLYWELL BAY Map 02 SW75

Holywell Bay TR8 5PW
☎ 01637 830095 Fax 01637 831000
Holywell Golf Club is situated beside a family fun park with many amenities. The course is an 18 hole Par 3 with excellent sea views. Fresh Atlantic winds make the course hard to play and there are several tricky holes, particularly the 18th over the trout pond. The site also has and excellent 18 hole Pitch & Putt course for the whole family.
18 holes, 2784yds, Par 61, Course record 58.
Club membership 100.
Visitors no restrictions.
Societies telephone in advance.
Green Fees £7.50 per round.
Designer Hartley
Facilities
& Leisure hard tennis courts, heated outdoor swimming pool, fishing.
Location Off A3075 Newquay/Perranporth road

Hotel ★★ 69% Crantock Bay Hotel, West Pentire, CRANTOCK ☎ 01637 830229 34

LAUNCESTON Map 02 SX38

Launceston St Stephens PL15 8HF
☎ 01566 773442 Fax 01566 777506
Undulating parkland course with views over Tamar Valley to Dartmoor and Bodmin Moor. Dominated by the 'The Hill' up which the 8th and 11th fairways rise, and on which the 8th, 9th, 11th and 12th greens sit.
18 holes, 6407yds, Par 70, SSS 71, Course record 65.
Club membership 800.
Visitors must contact in advance, may not play weekends Apr-Oct.
Societies telephone in first instance.
Green Fees £25 per day.
Prof John Tozer
Facilities
Location NW side of town centre on B3254

Hotel ★★ 61% Eagle House, Castle St, LAUNCESTON ☎ 01566 772036 14

Trethorne Kennards House PL15 8QE
☎ 01566 86324 Fax 01566 86903
Rolling parkland course with well maintained fairways and computer irrigated greens. Plenty of trees and natural water hazards make this well respected course a good challenge.
18 holes, 6432yds, Par 71, SSS 71.
Club membership 630.
Visitors must contact in advance.
Societies write or telephone Colin Willis.
Green Fees £17 per round; £8.50 per 9 holes.
Prof Chris Kaminski
Designer Frank Frayne
Facilities
Location Just off the A30, 3m W of Launceston, on junct with the A395 (Camelford)

Hotel ★★ 77% Penhallow Manor Country House Hotel, ALTARNUN ☎ 01566 86206 7

LELANT Map 02 SW53

West Cornwall TR26 3DZ ☎ 01736 753319
A seaside links with sandhills and lovely turf adjacent to the Hayle estuary and St Ives Bay. A real test of the player's skill, especially 'Calamity Corner' starting at the 5th on the lower land by the River Hayle. A small (3 hole) course is available for practice.
18 holes, 5884yds, Par 69, SSS 69, Course record 63.
Club membership 748.
Visitors must prove handicap certificate, be a member of a club affiliated to the EGU, advisable to contact in advance.
Societies must apply in writing.
Green Fees £20 per day (£25 weekends & bank holidays); 5 Day ticket £60, 7 Day ticket £80.
Prof Paul Atherton
Designer Reverend Tyack
Facilities
Location N side of village off A3074

Hotel ★★ 68% Pedn-Olva Hotel, The Warren, ST IVES ☎ 01736 796222 28 Annexe7rm(4)

LOOE Map 02 SX25

Looe Widegates PL13 1PX ☎ 01503 240239
Designed by Harry Vardon in 1935, this downland/parkland course commands panoramic views over south-east Cornwall and the coast. Easy walking.
18 holes, 5940yds, Par 70, SSS 68, Course record 64.
Club membership 600.
Visitors booking in advance recommended, no limitations subject to availability.
Societies telephone in advance, booking to be confirmed in writing.
Green Fees £26 per day; £20 per round.
Cards
Prof Alistair Macdonald

Designer Harry Vardon
Facilities
Location 3.5m NE off B3253

Hotel ★★ 68% Commonwood Manor Hotel, St Martin's Rd, LOOE ☎ 01503 262929 11

LOSTWITHIEL Map 02 SX15

Lostwithiel Hotel, Golf & Country Club Lower Polscoe PL22 0HQ ☎ 01208 873550 Fax 01208 87479
An undulating, parkland course with water hazards. Overlooked by Restormel Castle and the River Fowey flows alongside the course. Driving range.
18 holes, 5984yds, Par 72, SSS 71.
Club membership 500.
Visitors must contact in advance.
Societies contact in advance.
Green Fees £20 per round (£23 weekends & bank holidays) Twilight rates available.
Cards
Prof Tony Nash
Designer S Wood
Facilities
& Leisure hard tennis courts, heated indoor swimming pool, fishing, gymnasium, snooker.
Location 1m outside Lostwithiel off A390

Hotel ★★ 68% Lostwithiel Hotel Golf & Country Club, Lower Polscoe, LOSTWITHIEL ☎ 01208 873550 18

MAWGAN PORTH Map 02 SW86

Merlin TR8 4DN ☎ 01841 540222 Fax 01841 541031
A heathland course. The most challenging hole is the Par 5 12th with out of bounds along the lefthand side.
18 holes, 5227yds, Par 67, SSS 67.
Club membership 300.
Visitors no restrictions, except during club competitions.
Societies telephone in advance.
Green Fees £10 per day.
Designer Ross Oliver
Facilities
Hotel ★★ 67% Tredragon Hotel, MAWGAN PORTH ☎ 01637 860213 27

MAWNAN SMITH Map 02 SW72

See **Budock Vean**

MULLION Map 02 SW61

Mullion Cury TR12 7BP ☎ 01326 240685
Founded in 1895, a clifftop and links course with panoramic views over Mounts Bay. A steep downhill slope on 6th and the 10th descends to the beach with a deep ravine alongside the green. Most southerly course in the British Isles.
18 holes, 6037yds, Par 70, SSS 70.
Club membership 654.
Visitors preferable to contact in advance, restricted during club competitions.
Societies must contact in advance.

Green Fees £20 per day.
Prof Phil Blundell
Designer W Sich
Facilities
Location 1.5m NW of Mullion, off A3083

Hotel ★★★ 74% Polurrian Hotel, MULLION ☎ 01326 240421 39

NEWQUAY Map 02 SW86

Newquay Tower Rd TR7 1LT
☎ 01637 874354 & 872091
Fax 01637 874066
Gently undulating seaside course running parallel to the beach and open to wind. Breathtaking views.
18 holes, 6140yds, Par 69, SSS 69, Course record 63.
Club membership 700.
Visitors please telephone in advance.
Societies apply in writing or telephone.
Green Fees £25 per day; £20 per round.
Cards
Prof Andrew J Cullen
Designer H Colt
Facilities
& Leisure hard tennis courts.
Location W side of town

Hotel ★★★ 69% Hotel Bristol, Narrowcliff, NEWQUAY ☎ 01637 875181 74

Treloy TR8 4JN ☎ 01637 878554 Fax 01637 871710
An Executive course constructed in 1991 to American specifications with large contoured and mounded greens. Offers an interesting round for all categories of player.
9 holes, 2143yds, Par 32, SSS 31, Course record 63.
Visitors no restrictions.
Societies telephone in advance.
Green Fees £16 per day; £12.50 per 18 holes, £8 per 9 holes.
Cards
Designer M R M Sandow
Facilities
Location On A3059 Newquay to St Columb Major Road

Hotel ★★ 71% Whipsiderry Hotel, Trevelgue Rd, Porth, NEWQUAY
☎ 01637 874777 24rm(5 14)

PADSTOW Map 02 SW97

See **Constantine Bay**

PERRANPORTH Map 02 SW75

Perranporth Budnick Hill TR6 0AB
☎ 01872 573701 Fax 01872 573701
There are three testing par 5 holes on the links course (2nd, 5th, 11th) and a fine view over Perranporth Beach from all holes.
18 holes, 6288yds, Par 72, SSS 72, Course record 62.
Club membership 832.
Visitors no reserved tee times.
Societies by prior arrangement.
Green Fees £20 per day (£25 weekends & bank holidays).
Cards
Prof D Michell
Designer James Braid
Facilities
Location 0.75m NE on B3285

Hotel ★★ 63% Beach Dunes Hotel, Ramoth Way, Reen Sands, PERRANPORTH
☎ 01872 572263 6rm(5) Annexe3

PRAA SANDS Map 02 SW52

Praa Sands Germoe Cross Roads TR20 9TQ
☎ 01736 763445 Fax 01736 763399
A beautiful parkland course, overlooking Mount's Bay with outstanding sea views from every tee and green.
9 holes, 4122yds, Par 62, SSS 60, Course record 59.
Club membership 220.
Visitors restricted Sun 8-12.30pm, no need to phone.
Societies telephone for details.
Green Fees £20 per day; £14.50 per 18 holes; £10 per 9 holes.
Designer R Hamilton
Facilities
Location A394 midway between Penzance/Helston

Hotel ★★ 76% Nansloe Manor Hotel, Meneage Rd, HELSTON
☎ 01326 574691 7rm(6)

ROCK Map 02 SW97

St Enodoc PL27 6LD
☎ 01208 863216 Fax 01208 862976
Classic links courses with huge sand hills and rolling fairways. James Braid laid out the original 18 holes in 1907 and changes were made in 1922 and 1935. English County Final and English Ladies Closed Amateur Championships held recently. On the Church, the 10th is the toughest par 4 on the course and on the 6th is a truly enormous sand hill known as the Himalayas.
Church Course: 18 holes, 6207yds, Par 69, SSS 70, Course record 65.
Holywell Course: 18 holes, 4103yds, Par 63, SSS 61.
Club membership 1500.
Visitors may not play on bank holidays. Must have a handicap certificate of 24 or below for Church Course. Must contact in advance.
Societies must contact in writing.
Green Fees Church: £50 per day; £35 per round (£55/£40 weekends). Holywell: £21 per day; £15 per round.
Prof Nick Williams
Designer James Braid
Facilities
Location W side of village

Hotel ★★ 74% Cornish Cottage Hotel & Restaurant, New Polzeath, POLZEATH
☎ 01208 862213 14rm(3 10)

ST AUSTELL Map 02 SX05

Porthpean Porthpean PL26 6AY ☎ 01726 64613
A challenging 9-hole course which plays out at over 6500 yards. There are spectacular views over St Austell Bay. There is also an 8-bay covered and floodlit driving range.
18 holes, 5184yds, Par 67, SSS 67.
Club membership 300.
Visitors no restrictions
Societies telephone in advance.
Green Fees not confirmed.
Facilities
Location 1.5m from St Austell by-pass

Hotel ★★ 66% The Pier House, Harbour Front, Charlestown, ST AUSTELL
☎ 01726 67955 25

St Austell Tregongeeves Ln PL26 7DS
☎ 01726 72649 Fax 01726 74756
Very interesting inland parkland course designed by James Braid and offering glorious views of the surrounding countryside. Undulating, well-covered with tree plantations and well-bunkered. Notable holes are 8th (par 4) and 16th (par 3).
18 holes, 6089yds, Par 69, SSS 69, Course record 67.
Club membership 700.
Visitors advisable to contact in advance, weekend play is limited. Must be a member of a recognised golf club and hold a handicap certificate.
Societies must apply in writing.
Green Fees £18 per day (£20 weekends).
Prof Tony Pitts
Facilities
Location 1m W of St Austell on A390 ▶

Hotel ★★★ 65% Porth Avallen Hotel, Sea Rd, Carlyon Bay, ST AUSTELL ☎ 01726 812802 24

ST IVES Map 02 SW54

Tregenna Castle Hotel, Golf & Country Club TR26 2DE
☎ 01736 797381 Fax 01736 796066
Parkland course surrounding a castellated hotel and overlooking St Ives Bay and harbour.
18 holes, 3260yds, Par 60, SSS 58.
Club membership 140.

Visitors no booking needed. Dress code in operation.
Societies telephone for details.
Green Fees £17.50 per day; £12.50 per round.
Cards
Designer Abercrombie
Facilities & Leisure hard tennis courts, outdoor and indoor heated swimming pools, squash, sauna, solarium, gymnasium, snooker, steam room, jaccuzzi, beauty treatment.
Location From A30 Penzance road turn off just past Hayle onto A3074

Hotel ★★★ 71% Carbis Bay Hotel, Carbis Bay, ST IVES ☎ 01736 795311 30

ST JUST (NEAR LAND'S END) Map 02 SW33

Cape Cornwall Golf & Country Club Cape Cornwall TR19 7NL ☎ 01736 788611 Fax 01736 788611
Coastal parkland, walled course. The walls are an integral part of its design. Country club facilities.
18 holes, 5650yds, Par 70, SSS 68, Course record 69.
Club membership 630.

Visitors may not play before 11.30am at weekends.
Societies must contact in advance.
Green Fees not confirmed.
Cards
Prof Paul Atherton
Designer Bob Hamilton
Facilities & Leisure heated indoor swimming pool, sauna, solarium, gymnasium.
Location 1m W of St Just

Hotel ★★★ 65% Higher Faugan Hotel, Newlyn, PENZANCE ☎ 01736 362076 11

ST MARY'S Map 02

Isles of Scilly TR21 0NF ☎ 01720 422692
Links course, glorious views.
9 holes, 6001yds, Par 73, SSS 69.
Club membership 300.

Visitors only with member on Sun.
Societies must apply in writing
Green Fees not confirmed.
Facilities
Location 1m N of Hugh Town

Hotel ★★ 74% Tregarthens Hotel, Hugh Town, ST MARY'S
☎ 01720 422540 32 Annexe1

ST MELLION Map 02 SX36

ST MELLION See page 59

ST MINVER Map 02 SW97

Roserrow Golf & Country Club Roserrow PL27 6QT
☎ 01208 863000
Picturesque course in an undulating wooded valley with automated irrigation system. Testing 5th hole requiring a tight drive across a meandering stream with little margin for a wayward tee shot.
18 holes, 6507yds, Par 71, SSS 71.
Club membership 261.

Visitors by arrangement weekdays or weekends, must pre book tee times.
Societies apply in writing or telephone in advance.
Green Fees £30 per day; £24 per round.
Cards
Prof Hywel Roberts
Facilities & Leisure hard tennis courts, heated indoor swimming pool, sauna, gymnasium.
Location Between Polzeath and St Minver off the B3314

Hotel ★★ 64% The Molesworth Arms Hotel, Molesworth St, WADEBRIDGE
☎ 01208 812055 16rm(14)

SALTASH Map 02 SX45

China Fleet Country Club PL12 6LJ
☎ 01752 848668 Fax 01752 848456
A parkland course with river views. The 14th tee shot has to carry a lake of approximately 150yards.
18 holes, 6551yds, Par 72, SSS 72, Course record 69.
Club membership 550.

Visitors may play anytime and can book up to 7 days in advance.
Societies telephone for provisional booking.
Green Fees £20 per day (£25 weekends).
Cards
Prof Robert Moore
Designer Hawtree
Facilities & Leisure hard tennis courts, heated indoor swimming pool, squash, sauna, solarium, gymnasium.
Location 1m from the Tamar Bridge

ST MELLION

ST MELLION *Cornwall* ☎ 01579 351351
Fax 01579 350537 Map 02 SX36

John Ingham writes: Five miles north west of Saltash, St Mellion is set in Sherlock Holmes country, not far from the famous moor. Opened in 1976, the big course was created by two farming brothers, Martin and Hermon Bond who decided the Tamar Valley, not far from Plymouth, deserved a golf course – and they were prepared to sacrifice their farm to achieve that end.

The first problem was to get hold of an architect who would not be overwhelmed by the problem of converting the rugged countryside into eighteen holes. They had set their hearts on a Jack Nicklaus layout and to ensure he would take on the task, they sent him a letter and a cheque, said to be for £1 million and their determination concentrated the mind of Nicklaus comprehensively!

I have known Tony Moore, the one-time tournament professional (now living locally), for thirty odd years and he suggested I play the course, with his long-hitting son Bobby. But first we were to enjoy a dinner at the heart of this St Mellion International Golf & Country Club, which they thought, would be the ideal preparation for the task of facing a course with four holes in excess of 500 yards!

Tony's son Bobby was one of those strapping lads who lashed the ball miles. But in the first few holes he was missing the fairway, and lost four balls fairly quickly, putting me in what I thought was an unbeatable position. But his erratic play did not last, neither did my lead despite a birdie two at the short 11th, a delightful hole across water from a tee almost overlooked by the ancient church in the background. The two courses (the Old Course was designed by H. J Stutt) are both rugged tests, and St Mellion has staged several top-flight tournaments.

When Jack Nicklaus played here he said: 'I knew it was going to be good, but not this good – it's everything I had hoped for and more ... St Mellion is potentially the finest course in Europe'.This may be true. But it is a tough one, and for some it's too severe a challenge.

Visitors telephone in advance 01579 352002
Societies please apply in writing or telephone.
Green fees Nicklaus Course £35 per round. Old Course £25 per round. All major credit/debit cards
Facilities Professionals Andrew Milton/David Moon
Leisure hard tennis courts, indoor swimming (heated), squash, health spa
Location Saltash PL12 6SD (0.5m NW off A388)

36 holes. Nicklaus Course: 18 holes, 6651yds, Par72 SSS 72 Course record 63
The Old Course: 18 holes, 5782yds, Par 68 SSS 68

WHERE TO STAY AND EAT NEARBY

HOTELS:

ST MELLION
★★★ 73% St Mellion Hotel, ☎ 01579 351351. Annexe 38

LISKEARD
★★ Well House, St Keyne ☎ 01579 342001. 9

RESTAURANTS:

CALSTOCK
Danescombe Valley, Lower Kelly ☎ 01822 832414

Hotel B Travelodge, Callington Rd, Carkeel, SALTASH ☎ Central Res 0800 850950 Fax 01752 849028 32

TORPOINT Map 02 SX45

Whitsand Bay Hotel Golf & Country Club Portwrinkle PL11 3BU ☎ 01503 230276 Fax 01503 230329
Testing seaside course laid-out on cliffs overlooking Whitsand Bay. Easy walking after 1st hole. The par 3 (3rd) hole is acknowledged as one of the most attractive holes in Cornwall.
18 holes, 5998yds, Par 69, SSS 68, Course record 62.
Club membership 400.
Visitors visitors welcome.
Societies must contact in advance.
Green Fees £17.50 per day; (£20 weekends).
Cards
Prof Stephen Poole
Designer Fernie
Facilities
& Leisure heated indoor swimming pool, sauna, solarium, gymnasium.
Location 5m W off B3247

Hotel ★★ 66% Whitsand Bay Hotel, Golf & Country Club, Poerwrinkle, TORPOINT ☎ 01503 230276 34rm(32)

TRURO Map 02 SW84

Killiow Park Killiow, Kea TR3 6AG ☎ 01872 270246 Fax 01872 240915
Picturesque parkland course with mature oaks and woodland and five holes played across or around water hazards. Floodlit, all-weather driving range and practice facilities.
18 holes, 3829yds, Par 61.
Club membership 500.
Visitors may not play until after 9.30am at weekends.
Societies apply in writing, limited catering facilities at present.
Green Fees £12 per 18 holes under review.
Designer Ross Oliver
Facilities
Location 3m SW of Truro, off A39

Hotel ★★★ 68% Brookdale Hotel, Tregolls Rd, TRURO ☎ 01872 273513 & 279305 Fax 01872 272400 22

Truro Treliske TR1 3LG
☎ 01872 278684 Fax 01872 278684
Picturesque and gently undulating parkland course with small greens requiring accurate play. Lovely views over the cathedral city of Truro.
18 holes, 5306yds, Par 66, SSS 66, Course record 60.
Club membership 900.
Visitors must have handicap certificate, advisable to ring for availability although casual fees welcome.
Societies telephone for details.
Green Fees £18 per day (£22 weekends & bank holidays).
Prof Nigel Bicknell
Designer Colt, Alison & Morrison
Facilities
Location 1.5m W on A390 towards Redruth, adjacent to Treliske Hospital

Hotel ★★★ 68% Brookdale Hotel, Tregolls Rd, TRURO ☎ 01872 273513 & 279305 Fax 01872 272400 22

WADEBRIDGE Map 02 SW97

St Kew St Kew Highway PL30 3EF
☎ 01208 841500 Fax 01208 841500
An interesting, well-laid out 9-hole parkland course with 6 holes with water and 15 bunkers. In a picturesque setting there are 10 par 4s and 8 par 3s. No handicap certificate required but some experience of the game is essential. 9 extra tees have now been provided allowing a different teeing area for the back nine.
9 holes, 4543yds, Par 64, SSS 62.
Club membership 240.
Visitors no restrictions. Start time system in operation allowing prebooking.
Societies apply in writing, telephone or fax (same as phone number).
Green Fees £13 per 18 holes; £8.50 per 9 holes.
Cards
Prof Nick Rogers
Designer David Derry
Facilities
& Leisure fishing.
Location 2m N, main A39

Hotel ★★ 69% Port Gaverne Hotel, PORT GAVERNE ☎ 01208 880244 17

CUMBRIA

ALSTON Map 12 NY74

Alston Moor The Hermitage, Middleton in Teesdale Rd CA9 3DB ☎ 01434 381675
Parkland course with lush fairways and naturally interesting greens.
10 holes, 5518yds, Par 68, SSS 66, Course record 67.
Club membership 170.
Visitors usually turn up and play but some weekends busy with competitions.
Societies telephone or write in advance.
Green Fees £9 per day (£11 weekends & bank holidays).
Facilities
Location 1 S of Alston on B6277

Hotel ★★ 68% Lowbyer Manor Country House Hotel, ALSTON ☎ 01434 381230 8 Annexe4

APPLEBY-IN-WESTMORLAND Map 12 NY62

Appleby Brackenber Moor CA16 6LP
☎ 017683 51432
This remotely situated heather and moorland course offers interesting golf with the rewarding bonus of several long par-4 holes that will be remembered. There are superb views of the Pennines and the Lakeland hills.
18 holes, 5901yds, Par 68, SSS 68, Course record 63.
Club membership 800.

Visitors phone for details.
Societies must contact in advance by letter.
Green Fees £14 per day (£18 weekends & bank holidays).
Prof Paul Jenkinson
Designer Willie Fernie
Facilities ⊗ ⅲ 🍴 ☕ 🍸 ⛳ 🏠 🚗 ✓
Location 2m E of Appleby 0.5m off A66

Hotel ★★★ 75% Appleby Manor Country House Hotel, Roman Rd, APPLEBY-IN-WESTMORLAND
☎ 017683 51571 23 ⇌ ⌐ Annexe7 ⇌ ⌐

Askam-in-Furness Map 07 SD27

Dunnerholme Duddon Rd LA16 7AW
☎ 01229 462675
Unique 10-hole (18 tee) links course with view of the Cumbrian mountains and a stream running through.
10 holes, 6154yds, Par 72, SSS 70.
Club membership 450.
Visitors restricted times on Sun.
Societies apply in writing to the secretary.
Green Fees not confirmed.
Facilities 🍴 ☕ 🍸 ⛳
Location 1m N on A595

Hotel ★★ 64% Lisdoonie Hotel, 307/309 Abbey Rd, BARROW-IN-FURNESS
☎ 01229 827312 12 ⇌ ⌐

Barrow-in-Furness Map 07 SD26

Barrow Rakesmoor Ln, Hawcoat LA14 4QB
☎ 01229 825444 & 832121 (Prof)
Pleasant course laid out two levels on meadowland with extensive views of the nearby Lakeland fells. Upper level is affected by easterly winds.
18 holes, 6209yds, Par 71, SSS 70, Course record 66.
Club membership 620.
Visitors must be a member of a recognised golf club, advisable to contact the professional regarding tee time.
Societies small groups ring professional for details, groups over 12 apply to the secretary in advance.
Green Fees £15 per day.
Prof Jim McLeod
Facilities ⊗ ⅲ by prior arrangement 🍴 ☕ 🍸 ⛳ 🏠 🚗 ✓
Location 2m N off A590

Hotel ★★ 64% Lisdoonie Hotel, 307/309 Abbey Rd, BARROW-IN-FURNESS
☎ 01229 827312 12 ⇌ ⌐

Furness Central Dr LA14 3LN ☎ 01229 471232
Links golf with a fairly flat first half but a much sterner second nine played across subtle sloping ground. There are good views of the Lakes, North Wales and the Isle of Man.
18 holes, 6363yds, Par 71, SSS 71, Course record 65.
Club membership 630.
Visitors must contact the secretary in advance.
Societies apply in writing, must be member of recognised club with handicap certificate.
Green Fees £17 per day. ▶

Facilities
Location 1.75 W of town centre off A590

Hotel ★★ 64% Lisdoonie Hotel, 307/309 Abbey Rd, BARROW-IN-FURNESS
☎ 01229 827312 12

BOWNESS-ON-WINDERMERE Map 07 SD49

Windermere Clearbarrow LA23 3NB
☎ 015394 43123 Fax 015394 43123
Enjoyable holiday golf on a short, slightly hilly but sporting course in this delightful area of the Lake District National Park, with superb views of the mountains as the backcloth to the lake and the course.
18 holes, 5122yds, Par 67, SSS 65, Course record 58. Club membership 1043.

Visitors contact pro shop 7 days before day of play, 10-12 & 2-4.30 or before 9am by arrangement.
Societies by arrangement contact the secretary.
Green Fees £23 per day (£28 weekends & bank holidays).
Prof W S M Rooke
Designer G Lowe
Facilities
Location B5284 1.5m from Bowness

Hotel ★★★ 73% Wild Boar Hotel, Crook, WINDERMERE
☎ 015394 45225 36
See advertisement on page 61.

BRAMPTON Map 12 NY56

Brampton Talkin Tarn CA8 1HN
☎ 016977 2255 & 2000
Challenging golf across glorious rolling fell country demanding solid driving and many long second shots. A number of particularly fine holes, the pick of which may arguably be, the 3rd and 11th. The course offers unrivalled panoramic views from its hilly position.
18 holes, 6407yds, Par 72, SSS 71, Course record 64. Club membership 800.

Visitors visitors intending to play at weekends are recommended to telephone in advance.
Societies apply in writing to M Ogilvie (Hon Commercial Sec), 3 Warwick St, Carlisle, Cumbria CA3 8QW or telephone 01228 401996.
Green Fees Apr-Oct '98; £22 (£28 weekends & bank holidays).
Prof Stewart Wilkinson
Designer James Braid
Facilities
Location 1.5m SE of Brampton on B6413

Hotel ★★ 65% The Tarn End House Hotel, Talkin Tarn, BRAMPTON
☎ 016977 2340 7

CARLISLE Map 11 NY35

Carlisle Aglionby CA4 8AG
☎ 01228 513029 & 513241 (Pro) Fax 01228 513303
Majestic looking parkland course with great appeal. A complete but not too severe test of golf, with fine turf, natural hazards, a stream and many beautiful trees. A qualifying course for the Open Championship.

18 holes, 6278yds, Par 71, SSS 70, Course record 63.
Club membership 800.

Visitors may not play before 9am and between 12-1.30 and when tee is reserved. Very limited play Sunday and with member only Saturday and Tuesday.
Societies Mon, Wed & Fri, contact in advance for details.
Green Fees £33 per day; £22 per round (Sun £40/£30).
Prof John Smith More
Designer Mackenzie Ross
Facilities
Location On A69 0.5m E of M6 junc 43

Hotel ★★★ 74% Crown Hotel, Wetheral, CARLISLE ☎ 01228 561888 49 Annexe2

Stony Holme Municipal St Aidans Rd CA1 1LS
☎ 01228 34856
Municipal parkland course, bounded on three sides by the River Eden.
18 holes, 5783yds, Par 69, SSS 68, Course record 68.
Club membership 350.

Visitors advance booking recommended at weekends.
Societies must telephone pro shop 01228 34856 in advance.
Green Fees not confirmed.
Prof S Ling
Facilities
Location 2m W of M6 (junct 43) and A69

Hotel B Forte Posthouse Carlisle, Parkhouse Rd, CARLISLE ☎ 01228 31201 93

COCKERMOUTH Map 11 NY13

Cockermouth Embleton CA13 9SG
☎ 017687 76223 & 76941 Fax 017687 76941
Fell-land course, fenced, with exceptional views and a hard climb on the 3rd and 11th holes. Testing holes: 10th and 16th (rearranged by James Braid).
18 holes, 5496yds, Par 69, SSS 67, Course record 62.
Club membership 600.

Visitors restricted Wed, Sat & Sun.
Societies apply in writing to the secretary.
Green Fees £15 per day/round (£20 weekends & bank holidays).
Designer J Braid
Facilities
Location 3m E off A66

Hotel ★★★ 68% The Trout Hotel, Crown St, COCKERMOUTH ☎ 01900 823591 30

CROSBY-ON-EDEN Map 12 NY45

Eden CA6 4RA ☎ 01228 573003 Fax 01228 818435
Open, championship-length parkland course following the River Eden. A large number of water hazards, including the river on certain holes, demands acuracy, as do the well designed raised greens. Flood-lit driving range and excellent clubhouse facilities.
18 holes, 6368yds, Par 72, SSS 72, Course record 64.
Club membership 500.

Visitors must contact in advance.
Societies telephone to check availability.
Green Fees £23 per day; £18 per round (£28/£23 weekends & bank holidays).
Cards
Prof Steve Harrison
Facilities
& Leisure hard tennis courts.
Location 5m from M6 junc 44,on A689 towards Brampton & Newcastle-Upon-Tyne

Hotel ★★★ 76% Crosby Lodge Country House Hotel, High Crosby, Crosby-on-Eden, CARLISLE ☎ 01228 573618 9 Annexe2

GRANGE-OVER-SANDS Map 07 SD47

Grange Fell Fell Rd LA11 6HB
☎ 015395 32536 Fax 015395 35357
Hillside course with magnificent views over Morecambe Bay and the surrounding Lakeland mountains.
9 holes, 5278yds, Par 70, SSS 66, Course record 65.
Club membership 400.

Visitors may normally play Mon-Sat.
Green Fees £12 per day (£17 weekends & bank holidays).
Facilities
Location 1m W on Grange-Over-Sands/Cartmel

Hotel ★★★ 67% Netherwood Hotel, Lindale Rd, GRANGE-OVER-SANDS ☎ 015395 32552 29
See advertisement on page 64.

Grange-over-Sands Meathop Rd LA11 6QX
☎ 015395 33180 or 33754 Fax 015395 33754
Interesting parkland course with well sited tree plantations, ditches and water features. The four par 3s are considered to be some of the best in the area.
18 holes, 5958yds, Par 70, SSS 69, Course record 68.
Club membership 650.

Visitors advisable to contact in advance for play at weekends.
Societies apply in writing but very limited availability at weekends and bank holidays.
Green Fees £24 per day; £18 per round (£28/£24 weekends & bank holidays).
Prof Steve Sumner-Roberts
Facilities
Location NE of town centre off B5277

Hotel ★★★ 68% Grange Hotel, Station Square, GRANGE-OVER-SANDS ☎ 015395 33666 41

KENDAL Map 07 SD59

Carus Green Burneside Rd LA9 6EB
☎ 01539 721097 Fax 01539 721097
Bounded by the Kent and Sprint rivers (brought into play on 5 holes), this flat course enjoys open views to the Lakeland Fells.
18 holes, 5691yds, Par 70, SSS 68.
Club membership 400.

Visitors no restrictions except during Club competitions at weekend, check by phone.
Societies telephone for details.
Green Fees £10 (£12 weekends).
Designer W Adamson
Facilities
Location From rdbt N end of Kendal (A591) proceed to Burnside then to Kendal, course entrance at 30mph sign

Hotel ★★ 70% Garden House Hotel, Fowl-ing Ln, KENDAL ☎ 01539 731131 11

Kendal The Heights LA9 4PQ ☎ 01539 723499
Elevated parkland/fell course affording breathtaking views of Lakeland fells and surrounding district.
18 holes, 5515yds, Par 66, SSS 67, Course record 60.
Club membership 737.

Visitors must have a handicap certificate, weekends subject to availability. Telephone to reserve tee-off time.
Societies must contact in advance.
Green Fees £20 per day (£25 weekends & bank holidays).
Prof D J Turner
Facilities
Location 1m W of town centre

Hotel ★★ 70% Garden House Hotel, Fowl-ing Ln, KENDAL ☎ 01539 731131 11

KESWICK Map 11 NY22

Keswick Threlkeld Hall CA12 4SX ☎ 017687 79324
Varied fell and tree-lined course with commanding views of Lakeland scenery.
18 holes, 6225yds, Par 71, SSS 72, Course record 68.
Club membership 900.

Visitors booking up to 7 days in advance 017687 79010. Restricted on competition days.
Societies apply in writing to secretary.
Green Fees £17 per day (£22 weekends & bank holidays).
Prof Craig Hamilton
Designer Eric Brown
Facilities
& Leisure fishing, bowling green.
Location 4m E of Keswick, off A66

Hotel ★★★★ 64% Keswick Country House Hotel, Station Rd, KESWICK ☎ 017687 72020 66

KIRKBY LONSDALE Map 07 SD67

Kirkby Lonsdale Scaleber Ln, Barbon LA6 2LJ
☎ 015242 76365
Parkland course on the east bank of the River Lune and crossed by Barbon Beck. Mainly following the lie of the land, the gently undulating course uses the beck to provide water hazards.
18 holes, 6472yds, Par 72, SSS 71, Course record 68.
Club membership 600.

Visitors restricted on Sunday, must telephone in advance or call in at pro shop.
Societies apply in writing for society package.
Green Fees £18 per day (£22 weekends).
Prof Chris Barrett
Designer Bill Squires
Facilities
Location 6m S of Sedbergh on A683

Hotel ★★ 68% Pheasant Inn, CASTERTON ☎ 015242 71230 10

Maryport Map 11 NY03

Maryport Bankend CA15 6PA ☎ 01900 812605
A tight seaside links course exposed to Solway breezes. Fine views across Solway Firth. Course comprises 9 holes links and 9 holes parkland and small streams can be hazardous on several holes.
18 holes, 6088yds, Par 70, SSS 69, Course record 65.
Club membership 400.

Visitors contact club in advance. Dress code must be observed.
Societies must apply in writing.
Green Fees £15 per day/round (£20 weekends & bank hols).
Facilities
Location 1m N on B5300

Hotel ★★★ 63% Broughton Craggs Hotel, Great Broughton, COCKERMOUTH ☎ 01900 824400 14

Penrith Map 12 NY53

Penrith Salkeld Rd CA11 8SG
☎ 01768 891919 Fax 01768 891919
A beautiful and well-balanced course, always changing direction, and demanding good length from the tee. It is set on rolling moorland with occasional pine trees and some fine views.
18 holes, 6047yds, Par 69, SSS 69, Course record 63.
Club membership 850.

Visitors contact in advance. Handicap certificate required.
Societies telephone in advance.
Green Fees £25 for 2 rounds; £20 per round (£30/£25 weekends).
Prof Garry Key
Facilities
Location 0.75m N off A6

Hotel ★★ 71% George Hotel, Devonshire St, PENRITH ☎ 01768 862696 31

St Bees Map 11 NX91

St Bees CA27 0EJ ☎ 01946 824300
Links course, down hill and dale, with sea views.
9 holes, 5082yds, Par 64, SSS 65.
Club membership 275.

Visitors no restrictions.
Green Fees not confirmed.
Location 0.5m W of village off B5345

Hotel ★★★ 78% Ennerdale Country House Hotel, CLEATOR ☎ 01946 813907 30

Seascale Map 06 NY00

Seascale The Banks CA20 1QL
☎ 019467 28202 Fax 019467 28202
A tough links requiring length and control. The natural terrain is used to give a variety of holes and considerable character. Undulating greens add to the challenge. Fine views over the Western Fells, the Irish Sea and Isle of Man.
18 holes, 6416yds, Par 71, SSS 71, Course record 65.
Club membership 670.

Visitors no restrictions, but advisable to contact for tee reservation times.
Societies telephone to make provisional booking.
Green Fees £25 per day; £20 per round (£30/£25 weekends & bank holidays).
Designer Willie Campbell
Facilities
Location NW side of village off B5344

Hotel ★★ 69% Westlakes Hotel, GOSFORTH ☎ 019467 25221 9

Sedbergh Map 07 SD69

Sedbergh Catholes, Abbot Holme LA10 5SS
☎ 015396 21551 (Club) & 20993 (Sec)
A tree-lined grassland course with superb scenery in the Yorkshire Dales National Park. Feature hole is the par 3 2nd (110yds) where the River Dee separates the tee from the green.
9 holes, 5624yds, Par 70, SSS 68, Course record 66.
Club membership 250.

Visitors must book to play on weekends & bank hols.
Societies must contact in advance.
Green Fees £18 per day; £14 per round (£21/£16 weekends).
Designer W G Squires
Facilities
Location 1m S off A683, 5m junct 37 M6

Hotel ★★ 70% Garden House Hotel, Fowl-ing Ln, KENDAL ☎ 01539 731131 11

Silecroft Map 06 SD18

Silecroft LA18 4PQ ☎ 01229 774250
Seaside links course parallel to the coast of the Irish Sea. Often windy. Easy walking. Spectacular views inland of Lakeland hills.
9 holes, 5877yds, Par 68, SSS 68, Course record 66.
Club membership 300.

Visitors may be restricted competition days & bank holidays
Societies must contact in writing.
Green Fees £15 per day.
Facilities
Location 1m SW

Silloth Map 11 NY15

Silloth on Solway CA5 4BL
☎ 016973 31304 & 32404 Fax 016973 31782
Billowing dunes, narrow fairways, heather and gorse and the constant subtle problems of tactics and judgement make these superb links on the Solway an exhilarating and searching test. The 13th is a good long hole. Superb views.
18 holes, 6614yds, Par 72, SSS 73, Course record 65.
Club membership 700.

Visitors must contact in advance.
Societies telephone for times available.
Green Fees £25 per day (£30 per round weekends).
Cards
Prof Carl Weatherhead
Designer Willie Park Jnr
Facilities
Location S side of village off B5300

▶

Hotel ★★ 64% Golf Hotel, Criffel St, SILLOTH
☎ 016973 31438 22

ULVERSTON Map 07 SD27

Ulverston Bardsea Park LA12 9QJ
☎ 01229 582824
Inland golf with many medium length holes on undulating parkland. The 17th is a testing par 4. Overlooking Morecambe Bay the course offers extensive views to the Lakeland Fells.
18 holes, 6201yds, Par 71, SSS 70, Course record 67.
Club membership 750.

Visitors must contact in advance, be a member of an accredited golf club with a handicap certificate. May not play on Sat competition days or on Tue Ladies day.
Societies by arrangement in writing.
Green Fees £30 per day; £25 per round (£35/£30 weekends & bank holidays).
Prof M R Smith
Facilities
Location 2m S off A5087

Hotel ★★★ 65% Whitewater Hotel, The Lakeland Village, NEWBY BRIDGE
☎ 015395 31133 35

WINDERMERE

See **Bowness-on-Windermere**

WORKINGTON Map 11 NX92

Workington Branthwaite Rd CA14 4SS ☎ 01900 67828
Meadowland course, undulating, with natural hazards created by stream and trees. Good views of Solway Firth and Lakeland Hills. 10th, 13th and 15th holes are particularly testing.
18 holes, 6217yds, Par 72, SSS 70.
Club membership 735.

Visitors advisable to contact pro for weekday, weekends are generally very busy & Tue is Ladies Day.
Societies booking required for over 8 people.
Green Fees Summer: £19 per day; £15 per round (£25/£18 weekends & bank holidays).
Prof Aidrian Drabble
Designer James Braid
Facilities
Location 1.75m E off A596

Hotel ★★★ 73% Washington Central Hotel, Washington St, WORKINGTON
☎ 01900 65772 47

DERBYSHIRE

ALFRETON Map 08 SK45

Alfreton Wingfield Rd, Oakerthorpe DE66 7LH
☎ 01773 832070
A small parkland course with tight fairways and many natural hazards.
11 holes, 5393yds, Par 67, SSS 66.
Club membership 300.

Visitors must contact in advance.
Societies apply in writing or telephone in advance.
Green Fees not confirmed.
Prof Julian Mellor
Facilities by prior arrangement by prior arrangement
Location 1m W on A615

Hotel ★★★★ 67% Swallow Hotel, Carter Ln East, SOUTH NORMANTON
☎ 01773 812000 160

ASHBOURNE Map 07 SK14

Ashbourne Clifton DE6 2GJ ☎ 01335 342078
Undulating parkland course.
9 holes, 5359yds, Par 66, SSS 66.
Club membership 400.

Visitors may not play on competition days. With member only at weekends.
Societies telephone in advance.
Green Fees £14 per day (£20 weekends).
Designer F Penninck
Facilities
Location 1.5m SW on A515

Hotel ★★★ 75% Callow Hall, Mappleton Rd, ASHBOURNE ☎ 01335 343403 & 342412
Fax 01335 343624 16

BAKEWELL Map 08 SK26

Bakewell Station Rd DE45 1GB ☎ 01629 812307
Parkland course, hilly, with plenty of natural hazards to test the golfer. Magnificent views across the Wye Valley.
9 holes, 5240yds, Par 68, SSS 66.
Club membership 325.

Visitors with members only weekends.
Societies apply in writing.
Green Fees £15 per day (£20 weekends & bank holidays).
Facilities
Location E side of town off A6

Hotel ★★ 67% Milford House Hotel, Mill St, BAKEWELL
☎ 01629 812130 12

BAMFORD Map 08 SK28

Sickleholme Saltergate Ln S33 0BN
☎ 01433 651306
Undulating downland course in the lovely Peak District, with rivers and ravines and spectacular scenery.
18 holes, 6064yds, Par 69, SSS 69, Course record 62.
Club membership 700.

Visitors must contact in advance, restricted weekends.
Societies telephone in advance.
Green Fees £27 per day.
Prof P H Taylor
Facilities
Location 0.75m S on A6013

Hotel ★★ 66% Yorkshire Bridge Inn, Ashopton Rd, Yorkshire Bridge, BAMFORD ☎ 01433 651361 10

BREADSALL Map 08 SK33

Marriot Breadsall Priory Hotel & Country Club Moor Rd, Morley DE7 6DL ☎ 01332 832235 Fax 01332 833509
Set in 200 acres of mature parkland, the Old Course is built on the site of a 13th-century priory. Full use had been made of natural features and fine old trees. In contrast the Moorland Course, opened in Spring 1992, designed by Donald Steel and built by Brian Piersen, features Derbyshire stone walls and open moors heavily affected by winds.
Priory Course: 18 holes, 6100yds, Par 72, SSS 69, Course record 63.
Moorland Course: 18 holes, 6087yds, Par 70, SSS 69.
Club membership 900.

Visitors must contact in advance.
Societies telephone in advance.
Green Fees Priory: £55 per day; £40 per round (£45 per round weekends & bank holidays). Moorland: £55 per day; £35 per round (£40 per round weekends & bank holidays).
Cards
Prof Andrew Smith
Facilities
& Leisure hard tennis courts, heated indoor swimming pool, sauna, solarium, gymnasium.
Location 0.75m W

Hotel ★★★★ 66% Marriott Breadsall Priory, Moor Rd, MORLEY ☎ 01332 832235 12 Annexe100

BUXTON Map 07 SK07

Buxton & High Peak Townend, Waterswallows Rd SK17 7EN ☎ 01298 23453
Bracing, well-drained meadowland course; the highest in Derbyshire. Challenging course where wind direction is a major factor on some holes; others require blind shots to sloping greens.
18 holes, 5966yds, Par 69, SSS 69, Course record 65.
Club membership 670.

Visitors contact Mrs S Arnfield.
Societies apply in writing to Mrs S Arnfield.
Green Fees not confirmed.
Prof Gary Brown
Designer J Morris
Facilities
Location 1m NE off A6

Hotel ★★★ 64% Palace Hotel, Palace Rd, BUXTON ☎ 01298 22001 122

Cavendish Gadley Ln SK17 6XD
☎ 01298 25052 Fax 01298 79708
This parkland/moorland course with its comfortable clubhouse nestles below the rising hills. Generally open to the prevailing west wind, it is noted for its excellent surfaced greens which contain many deceptive subtleties. Designed by Dr Alastair McKenzie, good holes include the 8th, 9th and 18th.
18 holes, 5833yds, Par 68, SSS 68, Course record 61.
Club membership 650.

Visitors must contact in advance, weekends are restricted by competitions.
Societies telephone professional on 01298 25052.
Green Fees not confirmed.
Prof Paul Hunstone
Designer Dr Mackenzie
Facilities
Location 0.75m W of town centre off A53

Hotel ★★★ 73% Lee Wood Hotel, 13 Manchester Rd, BUXTON ☎ 01298 23002 36 Annexe2

CHAPEL-EN-LE-FRITH Map 07 SK08

Chapel-en-le-Frith The Cockyard, Manchester Rd SK23 9UH ☎ 01298 812118 & 813943 (sec) Fax 01298 813943
Scenic parkland course, with testing holes at the 14th (par 4) and 18th (517 yds), par 5. Good views.
18 holes, 6054yds, Par 70, SSS 69, Course record 67.
Club membership 676.

Visitors must contact professional or secretary in advance.
Societies apply in advance to Secretary.
Green Fees £20 per day (£30 weekends & bank holidays).
Cards
Prof David J Cullen
Facilities
Location On B5470

Hotel ★★★ 73% Lee Wood Hotel, 13 Manchester Rd, BUXTON ☎ 01298 23002 36 Annexe2

CHESTERFIELD Map 08 SK37

Chesterfield Walton S42 7LA
☎ 01246 279256 Fax 01246 276622
A varied and interesting, undulating parkland course with trees picturesquely adding to the holes and the outlook alike. Stream hazard on back nine. Views over four counties.
18 holes, 6326yds, Par 71, SSS 70, Course record 65.
Club membership 600.

Visitors must contact in advance and must play with member at weekends and bank holidays. A handicap certificate is generally required.
Societies apply in writing.
Green Fees £34 per day; £25 per round.
Prof Mike McLean
Facilities
Location 2m SW off A632

Hotel ★★★ 59% The Chesterfield Hotel, Malkin St, CHESTERFIELD ☎ 01246 271141 73

Grassmoor Golf Centre North Wingfield Rd, Grassmoor S41 5EA ☎ 01246 856044
An 18-hole heathland course with interesting and challenging water features. 26-bay floodlit driving range, practice bunkers and putting area.
18 holes, 5723yds, Par 69, SSS 69, Course record 67.
Club membership 420.

Visitors contact Manager in advance.
Societies telephone in Manager in advance.
Green Fees not confirmed.
Prof Peter Goldthorpe
Designer Hawtree

Facilities
& Leisure sauna.
Location Between Chesterfield & Grassmoor, off B6038

Hotel ★★★ 59% The Chesterfield Hotel, Malkin St, CHESTERFIELD ☎ 01246 271141 73

Stanedge Walton Hay Farm S45 0LW ☎ 01246 566156
Moorland course in hilly situation open to strong winds. Some tricky short holes with narrow fairways, so accuracy is paramount. Magnificent views over four counties. Extended course now open.
9 holes, 5786yds, SSS 69.
Club membership 310.
Visitors with member only Sat & Sun, and may not play after 2pm weekdays.
Societies apply in writing.
Green Fees £15 per round (18 holes).
Facilities
Location 5m SW off B5057 nr Red Lion public house

Hotel ★★★ 59% The Chesterfield Hotel, Malkin St, CHESTERFIELD ☎ 01246 271141 73

Tapton Park Municipal Tapton Park, Tapton S41 0EQ
☎ 01246 239500
Municipal parkland course with some fairly hard walking. The 620 yd (par 5) 5th is a testing hole.
Tapton Main: 18 holes, 6013yds, Par 71, SSS 69.
Dobbin Clough: 9 holes, 2613yds, Par 34.
Club membership 750.
Visitors must contact in advance. No caddies allowed.
Societies apply in writing.
Green Fees not confirmed.
Prof Fraser Scott
Facilities
Location 0.5m E of Chesterfield Station

Hotel ★★★ 59% The Chesterfield Hotel, Malkin St, CHESTERFIELD ☎ 01246 271141 73

CODNOR Map 08 SK44

Ormonde Fields Golf & Country Club Nottingham Rd DE5 9RG ☎ 01773 570043 (Secretary) & 742987 (Pro)
Parkland course with undulating fairways and natural hazards. There is a practice area.
18 holes, 6502yds, Par 71, SSS 72, Course record 68.
Club membership 500.
Visitors must contact in advance.
Societies telephone in advance.
Green Fees £17.50 per day (£22.50 per round weekends).
Cards
Prof Peter Buttifant
Designer W Hawtree
Facilities
Location 1m SE on A610

Hotel ★★★ 74% Makeney Hall Country House Hotel, Makeney, Milford, BELPER ☎ 01332 842999 27 Annexe18

DERBY Map 08 SK33

Allestree Park Allestree Hall, Duffield Rd, Allestree DE22 2EU ☎ 01332 550616 Fax 01332 541195
Municipal course, picturesque and undulating set in 300 acre park with views across Derbyshire.
18 holes, 5806yds, Par 68, SSS 68.
Visitors start times may be booked in advance by telephone, visitors welcome any day.
Societies apply in writing or by telephone in advance.
Green Fees £10.30.
Prof John Siddons
Facilities
& Leisure fishing.
Location N of Derby, from A38 take A6 towards north, course in 1.5m on left

Hotel ★★ 69% Kedleston Country House Hotel, Kedleston Rd, DERBY ☎ 01332 559202 & 556507 Fax 01332 558822 14

Mickleover Uttoxeter Rd, Mickleover DE3 5AD
☎ 01332 518662 Fax 01332 512092
Undulating parkland course in pleasant setting, affording splendid country views. Some attractive par 3s and a number of elevated greens..
18 holes, 5708yds, Par 68, SSS 68, Course record 64.
Club membership 800.
Visitors must contact in advance.
Societies apply in writing.
Green Fees not confirmed.
Prof Tim Coxon
Designer J Pennink
Facilities
Location 3m W off A516/B5020

Hotel ★★★★ 75% Mickleover Court Hotel, Etwall Rd, Mickleover, DERBY ☎ 01332 521234 80

Sinfin Wilmore Rd, Sinfin DE24 9HD
☎ 01332 766462 Fax 01332 769004
Municipal parkland course with tree lined fairways an excellent test of golf. Generally a flat course it is suitable for golfers of all ages.
18 holes, 6163yds, Par 70, SSS 69.
Visitors starting time must be booked in advance by telephone, visitors welcome any day.
Societies apply in writing or by telephone in advance.
Green Fees £10.30 per round.
Prof Steven Lamb
Facilities
Location 3.5m S of city centre

Hotel ★★★ 65% International Hotel, 288 Burton Rd, DERBY ☎ 01332 369321 41 Annexe21

DRONFIELD Map 08 SK37

Hallowes Hallowes Ln S18 6UA
☎ 01246 413734 Fax 01246 411196
Attractive moorland/meadowland course set in the Derbyshire hills. Several testing par 4's and splendid views.
18 holes, 6342yds, Par 71, SSS 71, Course record 64.
Club membership 630.

Visitors may only play with member at weekends. Must contact in advance.
Societies must contact in advance.
Green Fees not confirmed.
Prof Philip Dunn
Facilities ⊗ 🍴 ⛳ ☕ 🍷 ⛱ 🛒 🏌
Location S side of town

Hotel ★★ 65% Chantry Hotel, Church St, DRONFIELD ☎ 01246 413014 7 🛏

Duffield Map 08 SK34

Chevin Golf Ln DE56 4EE
☎ 01332 841864 Fax 01332 841864
A mixture of parkland and moorland, this course is rather hilly which makes for some hard walking, but with most rewarding views of the surrounding countryside. The 8th hole, aptly named "Tribulation", requires an accurate tee shot, and is one of the most difficult holes in the country.
18 holes, 6057yds, Par 69, SSS 69, Course record 64.
Club membership 750.
Visitors not before 9.30am or off first tee between 12.30 and 2pm. Proof of handicap required.
Societies contact in advance.
Green Fees £28 per day/round.
Prof Willie Bird
Facilities ⊗ 🍴 ⛳ ☕ 🍷 ⛱ 🛒 🏌
Location N side of town off A6

Hotel ★★ 69% Kedleston Country House Hotel, Kedleston Rd, DERBY ☎ 01332 559202 & 556507 Fax 01332 558822 14 🛏

Glossop Map 07 SK09

Glossop and District Hurst Ln, off Sheffield Rd SK13 7PU
☎ 01457 865247
Moorland course in good position, excellent natural hazards. Difficult closing hole (9th & 18th).
11 holes, 5800yds, Par 68, SSS 68.
Club membership 250.
Visitors may not play on bank holidays or Sat (Apr-Nov).
Societies must apply in writing to professional.
Green Fees not confirmed.
Prof Daniel Marsh
Facilities ⊗ 🍴 ⛳ ☕ 🍷 ⛱ 🛒 🏌
Location 1m E off A57

Hotel ★★ 70% York House Hotel, York Place, Richmond St, ASHTON-UNDER-LYNE ☎ 0161 330 9000 24 🛏 Annexe10 🛏

Horsley Map 08 SK34

Horsley Lodge Smalley Mill Rd DE21 5BL
☎ 01332 780838 Fax 01332 781118
This lush meadowland course, opened in 1991 and set in 100 acres of Derbyshire countryside, has some challenging holes. Also Par 3 course and floodlit driving range. Recently installed USGA world class greens designed by former World Champion Peter McEvoy.
18 holes, 6400yds, Par 72, SSS 71, Course record 72.
Club membership 650.
Visitors must contact professional in advance and have handicap. May not play weekends.
Societies must telephone in advance.
Green Fees not confirmed.
Prof Paul Kent
Designer Bill White
Facilities ⊗ 🍴 ⛳ ☕ 🍷 ⛱ 🛒 🏌
& Leisure fishing, sauna, solarium.
Location 4m NE of Derby, off A38

Hotel ★★★★ 66% Marriott Breadsall Priory, Moor Rd, MORLEY ☎ 01332 832235 12 🛏 Annexe100 🛏

Kedleston Map 08 SK34

Kedleston Park DE22 5JD
☎ 01332 840035 Fax 01332 842329
The course is laid out in flat mature parkland with fine trees and background views of historic Kedleston Hall (National Trust). Many testing holes are included in each nine and there is an excellent modern clubhouse.
18 holes, 6583yds, Par 71, SSS 72, Course record 63.
Club membership 868.
Visitors must contact in advance. With member only at weekends.
Societies weekdays only, apply in writing.
Green Fees £36 per day; £28 per round.
Cards
Prof David J Russell
Designer James Braid
Facilities ⊗ 🍴 ⛳ ☕ 🍷 ⛱ 🛒 🏌
& Leisure sauna.
Location Signposted Kedleston Hall from A38

Hotel ★★ 69% Kedleston Country House Hotel, Kedleston Rd, DERBY ☎ 01332 559202 & 556507 Fax 01332 558822 14 🛏

Matlock Map 08 SK36

Matlock Chesterfield Rd, Matlock Moor DE4 5LZ
☎ 01629 582191
Moorland course with fine views of the beautiful Peak District.
18 holes, 5804yds, Par 70, SSS 68, Course record 64.
Club membership 700.
Visitors with member only weekends & bank holidays. Members only weekdays 12.30-1.30pm.
Societies prior arrangement with Secretary.
Green Fees £30 per day; £25 per round.
Prof M A Whithorn
Designer Tom Williamson
Facilities ⊗ by prior arrangement 🍴 by prior arrangement ⛳ ☕ 🍷 ⛱ 🛒 🏌
Location 1.5m NE of Matlock on A632

Hotel ★★★ 67% New Bath Hotel, New Bath Rd, MATLOCK ☎ 01629 583275 55 🛏

Mickleover Map 08 SK33

Pastures Pastures Hospital DE3 5DQ ☎ 01332 521074
Small course laid-out on undulating meadowland in the grounds of a psychiatric hospital, with good views across the Trent valley. Fishing and snooker.
9 holes, 5095yds, Par 64, SSS 65, Course record 67.
Club membership 320.
▶

Visitors must be accompanied by a member, may not play on Sun & between noon-4pm Sun.
Societies Mon & Tue, must contact in advance.
Green Fees not confirmed.
Designer J F Pennik
Facilities by prior arrangement by prior arrangement
Location 1m SW off A516

Hotel ★★★ 65% International Hotel, 288 Burton Rd, DERBY
01332 369321 41 Annexe21

Morley Map 08 SK34

Morley Hayes Main Rd DE7 6DG
01332 780480 Fax 01332 781094
Peaceful pay and play course set in a splendid valley and incorporating charming water features and woodland. Floodlit driving range.
Manor Course: 18 holes, 6744yds, Par 72.
Visitors welcome. Tower 9 hole course now open.
Societies booking essential telephone for details.
Green Fees £25 per day; £15 per 18 holes; £10 per 9 holes (£30/£20/£12.50 weekends & bank holidays).
Cards
Prof Mark Whithorn
Facilities
Location A608

Hotel ★★★★ 66% Marriott Breadsall Priory, Moor Rd, MORLEY
01332 832235 12 Annexe100

New Mills Map 07 SK08

New Mills Shaw Marsh SK12 4QE 01663 743485
Moorland course with panoramic views and first-class greens.
9 holes, 5633yds, Par 68, SSS 67.
Club membership 350.
Visitors must play with member on Sunday & special days.
Societies must contact in advance.
Green Fees not confirmed.
Facilities
Location 0.5m N off B6101

Hotel ★★ 68% Red Lion Inn, 112 Buxton Rd, High Ln, STOCKPORT 01663 765227 6

Renishaw Map 08 SK47

Renishaw Park Club House, Mill Ln S21 3UZ
01246 432044 & 435484
Part parkland and part meadowland with easy walking.
18 holes, 6262yds, Par 71, SSS 70, Course record 65.
Club membership 750.
Visitors must contact in advance. Visitors not allowed Thu, weekends or competition days.
Societies by arrangement.
Green Fees not confirmed.
Prof John Oates
Designer Sir George Sitwell
Facilities
Location 1.5m W of junct 30 M1

Hotel ★★★ 58% Sitwell Arms Hotel, Station Rd, RENISHAW
01246 435226 30

Risley Map 08 SK43

Maywood Rushy Ln DE72 3ST
0115 939 2306
Wooded parkland course with numerous water hazards.
18 holes, 6424yds, Par 72, SSS 71, Course record 70.
Club membership 450.
Visitors advisable to contact in advance during summer, may not play during competitions. Standard dress code applies.
Societies by prior arrangement.
Green Fees not confirmed.
Prof Colin Henderson
Designer P Moon
Facilities
Location Near junct 25 on M1

Hotel ★★★ 71% Risley Hall Hotel, Derby Rd, RISLEY 0115 9399000 16

Shirland Map 08 SK45

Shirland Lower Delves DE55 6AU
01773 834935
Rolling parkland and tree-lined course with extensive views of Derbyshire countryside.
18 holes, 6072yds, Par 71, SSS 70, Course record 70.
Club membership 600.
Visitors contact professional in advance.
Societies contact Professional.
Green Fees £15 per round (£20 weekends).
Prof Neville Hallam
Facilities
Location S side of village off A61

Hotel ★★★★ 67% Swallow Hotel, Carter Ln East, SOUTH NORMANTON
01773 812000 160

Stanton-by-Dale Map 08 SK43

Erewash Valley DE7 4QR
0115 932 3258 Fax 0115 932 2984
Parkland/meadowland course overlooking valley and M1. Unique 4th and 5th in Victorian quarry bottom: 5th-testing par 3.
18 holes, 6557yds, Par 72, SSS 71, Course record 67.
Club membership 750.
Visitors no restrictions
Societies contact in advance.
Green Fees £27.50 per day; £22.50 per round (£27 per round weekends).
Prof M J Ronan
Designer Hawtree
Facilities
& Leisure snooker tables.
Location 1m W, 2m from junct 25 on M1

Hotel ★★★ 71% Risley Hall Hotel, Derby Rd, RISLEY 0115 9399000 16

UNSTONE Map 08 SK37

Birch Hall Sheffield Rd S18 4DB ☎ 01246 291979
Very testing woodland course demanding respect and a good straight game if one is to walk away with a respectable card. Sloping fairways gather wayward drives into thick gorse and deep ditches. Signature holes are the tough 6th and scenic 13th, the latter begs a big-hitter to go for a shot to the green.
18 holes, 6409yds, Par 73, SSS 71, Course record 74.
Club membership 320.

Visitors welcome at all times except before noon at weekends, midweek medals held regularly telephone for details.
Societies apply in writing to secretary or telephone course.
Green Fees not confirmed.
Designer D Tucker
Facilities
Location Turn off A61 between Sheffield and Chesterfield, outskirts of Unstone village

Hotel ★★ 65% Chantry Hotel, Church St, DRONFIELD ☎ 01246 413014 7

DEVON

AXMOUTH Map 03 SY29

Axe Cliff EX12 4AB
☎ 01297 21754 & 24371 Fax 01297 24371
Undulating links course with coastal views.
18 holes, 6000yds, Par 70, SSS 70, Course record 70.
Club membership 400.

Visitors may only play after 11am on Wed & Sun.
Societies must contact in advance.
Green Fees £19 per day (£21 weekends).
Prof Mark Dack
Facilities
Location 0.75m S on B3172

Hotel ★★ 68% Anchor Inn, BEER ☎ 01297 20386 8rm(5)

BIGBURY-ON-SEA Map 03 SX64

Bigbury TQ7 4BB ☎ 01548 810207
Clifftop, heathland course with easy walking. Exposed to winds, but with fine views over the sea and River Avon. 7th hole particularly tricky.
18 holes, 6048yds, Par 70, SSS 69, Course record 65.
Club membership 850.

Visitors must have handicap certificate.
Societies must apply in writing.
Green Fees £24 per day (£26 weekends & bank holidays).
Prof Simon Lloyd
Designer J H Taylor
Facilities by prior arrangement
Location 1m S on B3392

Hotel ★ 69% Henley Hotel, BIGBURY-ON-SEA ☎ 01548 810240 8

BLACKAWTON Map 03 SX85

Dartmouth Golf & Country Club TQ9 7DQ
☎ 01803 712686 & 712650
The 9-hole Club course and the 18-hole Championship course are both worth a visit and not just for the beautiful views. The Championship is one of the most challenging courses in the West Country with a 4th hole visitors will always remember.
Championship Course: 18 holes, 6663yds, Par 72, SSS 72.
Club Course: 9 holes, 5166yds, Par 66, SSS 65.
Club membership 800.

Visitors must contact in advance, visitors welcome subject to availability.
Societies telephone in advance.
Green Fees not confirmed.
Prof Peter Laugher
Designer Jeremy Pern
Facilities
& Leisure heated indoor swimming pool, sauna, solarium, gymnasium.
Location On A3122 Totnes/Dartmouth road

Hotel ★★★ 65% Stoke Lodge Hotel, Stoke Fleming, DARTMOUTH ☎ 01803 770523 24

BUDLEIGH SALTERTON Map 03 SY08

East Devon North View Rd EX9 6DQ
☎ 01395 443370 Fax 01395 445547
An interesting course with downland turf, much heather and gorse, and superb views over the bay. The early holes climb to the cliff edge. The downhill 17th has a heather section in the fairway, leaving a good second to the green.
18 holes, 6239yds, Par 70, SSS 70, Course record 64.
Club membership 850.

Visitors no visitors before 10am and between 12.30-2pm. Visitors must be member of a recognised club and must produce proof of handicap.
Societies must contact in advance. Large parties 16+ only on Thu.
Green Fees £35 per day; £27 per round (£42/£35 weekends & bank holidays).
Cards
Prof Trevor Underwood
Facilities
Location W side of town centre

Hotel ★★★ 64% The Imperial, The Esplanade, EXMOUTH ☎ 01395 274761 57

CHITTLEHAMHOLT Map 03 SS62

Highbullen Hotel EX37 9HD
☎ 01769 540561 Fax 01769 540492
Mature parkland course with water hazards and outstanding scenic views to Exmoor and Dartmoor. Excellent facilities offered by the hotel.
18 holes, 5755yds, Par 68, SSS 67.
Club membership 100.

Visitors to book tee time telephone 01769 540530 daytime, 01769 540561 evenings.
Societies must contact in advance.
Green Fees from £14 per round (from £18 weekends). ▶

Cards
Prof Paul Weston
Designer M Neil/ J Hamilton
Facilities
& Leisure hard tennis courts, outdoor and indoor heated swimming pools, squash, fishing, sauna, solarium, gymnasium.
Location 0.5m S of village

Hotel ★★★ 68% Highbullen Hotel, CHITTLEHAMHOLT ☎ 01769 540561 12 Annexe25

CHRISTOW Map 03 SX88

Teign Valley EX6 7PA
☎ 01647 253026 Fax 01647 253026
A scenically spectacular 18 hole course set beside the River Teign in the Dartmoor National Park. Offering a good challenge to both low and high handicap golfers, it features two lakeside holes, rolling fairways and fine views.
18 holes, 5913yds, Par 70, SSS 68.
Club membership 300.

Visitors no restrictions, but need to book by telephone.
Societies write or telephone for bookings.
Green Fees £12 per round (£18 weekends).
Prof Richard Stephenson
Designer P Nicholson
Facilities
Location Take Teignvalley exit off A38, Exeter/Plymouth Expressway and follow GC signs up valley on B3193

Hotel ★★ 74% The White Hart Hotel, The Square, MORETONHAMPSTEAD ☎ 01647 440406 17 Annexe3

CHULMLEIGH Map 03 SS61

Chulmleigh Leigh Rd EX18 7BL
☎ 01769 580519 Fax 01769 580519
Situated in a scenic area with views to distant Dartmoor, this undulating meadowland course offers a good test for the most experienced golfer and is enjoyable for newcomers to the game. Short 18 hole summer course with a tricky 1st hole; in winter the course is changed to 9 holes and made longer for players to extend their game.
Summer Short Course: 18 holes, 1450yds, Par 54, SSS 54, Course record 51.
Winter Course: 9 holes, 2310yds, Par 54, SSS 54, Course record 62.
Club membership 77.

Visitors welcome anytime, closed on Mon from Oct-1 Apr.
Societies telephone in advance.
Green Fees £11.50 per day; £9.50 per 36 holes; £6.50 per 18 holes.
Designer John Goodban
Facilities
Location SW side of village just off A377

Hotel ★★★ 72% Northcote Manor, BURRINGTON ☎ 01769 560501 12

CHURSTON FERRERS Map 03 SX95

Churston Dartmouth Rd TQ5 0LA
☎ 01803 842751 & 842218 Fax 01803 845738
A cliff-top downland course with splendid views over Brixham harbour and Tor Bay. There is some gorse with a wooded area inland. A variety of shot is called for, with particularly testing holes at the 3rd, 9th and 15th, all par 4. A new clubhouse opens in 1998 and will offer conference facilities and a well equipped shop.
18 holes, 6219yds, Par 70, SSS 70, Course record 64.
Club membership 700.
Visitors must telephone in advance and be a member of recognised golf club with a handicap certificate.
Societies apply in writing or telephone.
Green Fees £22 per round (£27 weekends).
Cards
Prof Neil Holman
Facilities
Location NW side of village on A379

Hotel ★★ 65% Dainton Hotel, 95 Dartmouth Rd, Three Beaches, Goodrington, PAIGNTON ☎ 01803 550067 11

CREDITON Map 03 SS80

Downes Crediton Hookway EX17 3PT
☎ 01363 773025 & 774464 Fax 01363 775060
Recently refurbished and extended clubhouse. Parkland course with water features. Flat front nine. Hilly and wooded back nine.
18 holes, 5934yds, Par 70, SSS 68.
Club membership 700.
Visitors handicap certificate required, must contact in advance, restricted at weekends.
Societies must contact in advance.
Green Fees £25 per day; £18 per round (£22 per round weekends).
Cards
Prof Howard Finch
Facilities
Location 1.5m SE off A377

Hotel ★★★ 73% Barton Cross Hotel & Restaurant, Huxham, Stoke Canon, EXETER ☎ 01392 841245 7

A comprehensive list of driving ranges is given at the back of this guide. See page 479

Cullompton Map 03 ST00

Padbrook Park EX15 1RU
☎ 01884 38286 Fax 01884 34359
A 9-hole, 18 tee parkland course with many water and woodland hazards and spectacular views. The dog-leg 2nd and pulpit 7th are of particular challenge to golfers of all standards.
9 holes, 6108yds, Par 70, SSS 70.
Club membership 250.
Visitors welcome at all times, tee must be reserved by telephoning in advance.
Societies apply in writing or telephone.
Green Fees pay as you play.
Prof Stewart Adwick
Designer Bob Sandow
Facilities
& Leisure fishing, gymnasium.
Location Southern edge of Cullompton on B3181

Hotel ★★★ 61% The Tiverton Hotel, Blundells Rd, TIVERTON ☎ 01884 256120 74

Dawlish Warren Map 03 SX97

Warren EX7 0NF
☎ 01626 862255 & 864002 Fax 01626 888005
Typical flat, genuine links course lying on spit between sea and Exe estuary. Picturesque scenery, a few trees but much gorse. Testing in windy conditions. The 7th hole provides the opportunity to go for the green across a bay on the estuary.
18 holes, 5965yds, Par 69, SSS 69.
Club membership 600.
Visitors must contact in advance & have handicap certificate.
Societies prior arrangement essential.
Green Fees £21.50 per day (£24.50 weekends & bank holidays).
Cards
Prof Andrew Naldrett
Facilities
Location E side of village

Hotel ★★★ 67% Langstone Cliff Hotel, Dawlish Warren, DAWLISH
☎ 01626 865155 64 Annexe4

Down St Mary Map 03 SS70

Waterbridge EX17 5LG ☎ 01363 85111
A testing course of 9-holes set in a gently sloping valley. The Par of 32 will not be easily gained with 1 par 5, 3 par 4's and 5 par 3's, although the course record holder has Par 29! The 3rd hole which is a raised green is surrounded by water and the 4th (439 yards) is demanding for beginners.
9 holes, 3910yds, Par 64, SSS 64.
Visitors no restrictions.
Societies no restrictions.
Green Fees £10 per 18 holes; £6 per 9 holes (£12/£7 weekends & bank holidays).
Prof David Ridyard
Designer D Taylor
Facilities
Location From Exeter on A377 towards Barnstaple

Hotel ★★★ 72% Northcote Manor, BURRINGTON
☎ 01769 560501 12

Exeter Map 03 SX99

Exeter Golf & Country Club Topsham Rd, Countess Wear EX2 7AE ☎ 01392 874139 Fax 01392 874139
A sheltered parkland course with some very old trees and known as the flattest course in Devon. 15th & 17th are testing par 4 holes. Small, well guarded greens.
18 holes, 6000yds, Par 69, SSS 69, Course record 62.
Club membership 800.
Visitors welcome but may not play during match or competitions, very busy pre booking needed up to 1 week in advance. Must have handicap certificate.
Societies welcome Thu only, booking available by telephone to manager tel 01392 874139.
Green Fees £26 per day.
Cards
Prof Mike Rowett
Designer J Braid
Facilities
& Leisure hard tennis courts, heated indoor plus outdoor swimming pool, squash, sauna, solarium, gymnasium.
Location SE side of city centre off A379

Hotel B Travel Inn, 398 Topsham Rd, Countess Wear Roundabout, Exeter Bypass, EXETER
☎ 01392 875441 44

Woodbury Park Woodbury Castle, Woodbury EX5 1JJ
☎ 01395 233382 Fax 01395 233384
Two courses set in the lovely wooded parkland of Woodbury Castle.
Oaks: 18 holes, 6870yds, Par 72, SSS 72.
Acorn: 9 holes, 2350yds, Par 33, SSS 62.
Club membership 750.
Visitors welcome, please reserve tee times in advance.
Societies contact in advance.
Green Fees £25 per round.
Cards
Prof Alan Richards
Designer J Hamilton-Stutt
Facilities
& Leisure hard tennis courts, heated indoor swimming pool, squash, fishing, sauna, gymnasium.
Hotel ★★★ 68% Ebford House Hotel, Exmouth Rd, EBFORD ☎ 01392 877658 16

High Bickington Map 02 SS52

Libbaton EX37 9BS
☎ 01769 560269 & 560167 Fax 01769 560342
Parkland course on undulating land with no steep slopes. Floodlit driving range.
18 holes, 6494yds, Par 73, SSS 72, Course record 72.
Club membership 500.
Visitors book in advance.
Societies telephone to book in advance.
Green Fees £18 per day; £15 per 18 holes (£22/£18 bank holidays & weekends).
Cards
Prof John Phillips
Designer H Col Badham
Facilities
& Leisure fishing, gymnasium.
Hotel ★★★ 68% Highbullen Hotel, CHITTLEHAMHOLT
☎ 01769 540561 12 Annexe25

HOLSWORTHY Map 02 SS30

Holsworthy Killatree EX22 6LP
☎ 01409 253177 Fax 01409 253177
Pleasant parkland course with gentle slopes and numerous trees.
18 holes, 6062yds, Par 70, SSS 69, Course record 64.
Club membership 600.

Visitors may not play Sun am.
Societies by arrangement with secretary or professional.
Green Fees £20 per day/round (£25 weekends & bank holidays).
Cards
Prof Simon Chapman
Facilities
Location 1.5m W on A3072

Hotel ★★ 73% Court Barn Country House Hotel, Clawton, HOLSWORTHY
☎ 01409 271219 8rm(7)

HONITON Map 03 ST10

Honiton Middlehills EX14 8TR ☎ 01404 44422 & 42943
Level parkland course on a plateau 850ft above sea level. Easy walking and good views. The 4th hole is a testing par 3. The club was founded in 1896.
18 holes, 5902yds, Par 69, SSS 68.
Club membership 800.

Visitors must contact in advance.
Societies society bookings on Thursdays.
Green Fees not confirmed.
Prof Adrian Cave
Facilities
Location 1.25m SE of Honiton

Hotel ★★ 74% Home Farm Hotel, Wilmington, HONITON
☎ 01404 831278 831246 Fax 01404 831411 6 Annexe7

ILFRACOMBE Map 02 SS54

Ilfracombe Hele Bay EX34 9RT
☎ 01271 862176 Fax 01271 867731
A sporting, clifftop, heathland course with views over the Bristol Channel and moors from every tee and green.
18 holes, 5893yds, Par 69, SSS 69, Course record 66.
Club membership 642.

Visitors recommended to make tee reservation prior to visit, member only 12-2 daily and before 10 am on weekends.
Societies telephone in advance.
Green Fees not confirmed.
Prof David Hoare
Designer T K Weir
Facilities
Location 1.5m E off A399

Hotel ★★ 71% Elmfield Hotel, Torrs Park, ILFRACOMBE
☎ 01271 863377 11 Annexe2

IPPLEPEN Map 03 SX86

Dainton Park Totnes Rd, Ipplepen TQ12 5TN
☎ 01803 813812
A challenging parkland type course in typical Devon countryside, with gentle contours, tree-lined fairways and raised tees. Water hazards make the two opening holes particularly testing. The 8th, a dramatic 180yard drop hole totally surrounded by sand, is one of four tough Par 3's on the course. It is advisable to book start times.
18 holes, 6207yds, Par 71, SSS 70, Course record 70.
Club membership 500.

Visitors prior booking by phone advisable to guarantee start time.
Societies apply in writing.
Green Fees £14.50 per round (£17 weekends & bank holidays).
Cards
Prof Martin Tyson
Designer Adrian Stiff
Facilities
Location 2m S of Newton Abbot on A381

Hotel ★★ 65% Old Church House Inn, Torbryan, IPPLEPEN ☎ 01803 812372 12

IVYBRIDGE Map 02 SX65

Dinnaton Sporting & Country Club Blachford Rd PL21 9HU ☎ 01752 892512 & 892452 Fax 01752 698334
Challenging 9-hole moorland course overlooking the South Hams. With 5 par 4 and 4 par 3 holes, three lakes and tight fairways; excellent for improving the short game. Floodlit practice area.

9 holes, 4089yds, Par 64, SSS 60.
Club membership 275.

Visitors no restrictions.
Societies telephone in advance.
Green Fees £10 per day (£12.50 weekends & bank holidays).
Prof David Ridyard
Designer Cotton & Pink
Facilities
& Leisure hard tennis courts, heated indoor swimming pool, squash, sauna, solarium, gymnasium.
Location Leave A38 at Ivybridge junct and continue towards town centre. At first rdbt follow signs for club

Hotel ★★ 74% Glazebrook House Hotel & Restaurant, SOUTH BRENT
01364 73322 10

MORETONHAMPSTEAD Map 03 SX78

Manor House Hotel TQ13 8RE 01647 440998
This enjoyable parkland course has enough hazards to make any golfer think. Most hazards are natural such as the Rivers Bowden and Bovey which meander through the first eight holes.
18 holes, 6016yds, Par 69, SSS 69, Course record 65.
Club membership 120.

Visitors must contact in advance and pre-arrange starting times.
Societies must telephone for reservation in advance.
Green Fees £30 per day; £24 per round (£37/£30 weekends).
Cards
Prof Richard Lewis
Designer J Abercrombie
Facilities
& Leisure hard tennis courts, fishing.
Location 3m W of Moretonhampstead, off B3212

Hotel ★★★★ 62% Manor House Hotel, MORETONHAMPSTEAD
01647 440355 89

MORTEHOE Map 02 SS44

Mortehoe & Woolacombe EX34 7EH
01271 870225
Attached to a camping and caravan site, this 9-hole course has 2 par 3s and 7 par 4s. The gently sloping clifftop course has spectacular views across Morte Bay.
9 holes, 4690yds, Par 66, SSS 63, Course record 66.
Club membership 245.

Visitors no restrictions.
Societies must telephone or write in advance.
Green Fees £10 per 18 holes; £6 per 9 holes.
Cards
Designer D Hoare
Facilities
& Leisure heated indoor swimming pool, indoor bowls, skittles, table tennis.
Location 0.25m before Mortehoe on station road

Hotel ★★★ 77% Watersmeet Hotel, Mortehoe, WOOLACOMBE
01271 870333 23

NEWTON ABBOT Map 03 SX87

Newton Abbot (Stover) Bovey Rd TQ12 6QQ
01626 352460 (Secretary) Fax 01626 330210
Wooded parkland course with a stream coming into play on eight holes. Fairly flat.
18 holes, 5862yds, Par 69, SSS 68, Course record 63.
Club membership 800.

Visitors must have proof of membership of recognised club or current handicap certificate.
Societies by arrangement on Thu only.
Green Fees £22 per day/round.
Prof Malcolm Craig
Designer James Braid
Facilities
Location 3m N on A382

Hotel ★★ 65% Queens Hotel, Queen St, NEWTON ABBOT 01626 63133 & 54106
Fax 01626 64922 22rm(20)

OKEHAMPTON Map 02 SX59

Okehampton Tors Rd EX20 1EF
01837 52113 Fax 01837 52734
A good combination of moorland, woodland and river make this one of the prettiest, yet testing courses in Devon.
18 holes, 5243yds, Par 68, SSS 67, Course record 66.
Club membership 600.

Visitors advance booking recommended, limited times available at weekends.
Societies by prior arrangement.
Green Fees £17 per day (£22 Sat, £19 Sun).
Prof Simon Jefferies
Designer J F Taylor
Facilities
Location 1m S off A30

Hotel ★★ 67% Oxenham Arms, SOUTH ZEAL
01837 840244 & 840577
Fax 01837 840791 8rm(7)

PLYMOUTH Map 02 SX45

Elfordleigh Plympton PL7 5EB
01752 336428 Fax 01752 344581
Charming, saucer-shaped parkland course with alternate tees for 18 holes. Tree-lined fairways and three lakes. Fairly hard walking.
9 holes, 5664yds, Par 68, SSS 67, Course record 66.
Club membership 450.

Visitors must contact in advance and hold a handicap certificate.
Societies by arrangement.
Green Fees £15 per day (£20 weekend & bank holidays).
Prof C Rendell
Designer J H Taylor
Facilities
& Leisure hard tennis courts, heated outdoor swimming pool, squash, gymnasium.
Location 8m NE off B3416

Hotel ★★★ 68% Elfordleigh Hotel, Colebrook, Plympton, PLYMOUTH
01752 336428 18

Staddon Heights Plymstock PL9 9SP
☎ 01752 402475 Fax 01752 401998
Seaside course affording spectacular views across Plymouth Sound, Dartmoor and Bodmin Moor. Testing holes include the par 3 17th with its green cut into a hillside and the par 4 14th across a road. Easy walking.
18 holes, 5869yds, Par 68, SSS 70, Course record 66.
Club membership 750.

Visitors must have handicap certificate and contact the pro or secretary in advance.
Societies apply by telephone in advance.
Green Fees £18 (£22 weekends).
Prof Ian Marshall
Designer Hamilton Stutt
Facilities
Location 5m SW of city centre

Hotel B Forte Posthouse Plymouth, Cliff Rd, The Hoe, PLYMOUTH
☎ 01752 662828 106

SAUNTON Map 02 SS43

Saunton EX33 1LG
☎ 01271 812436 Fax 01271 814241
Two traditional championship links courses. Windy, with natural hazards.
East Course: 18 holes, 6729yds, Par 71, SSS 73, Course record 65.
West Course: 18 holes, 6403yds, Par 71, SSS 72, Course record 67.
Club membership 1100.

Visitors prior booking recommended and must have handicap certificate.
Societies must apply in advance, handicap certificates required.
Green Fees £30 per round (£40 weekends & bank holidays).
Prof A T MacKenzie
Designer F Pennick
Facilities
Location S side of village off B3231

Hotel ★★★★ 69% Saunton Sands Hotel, SAUNTON ☎ 01271 890212 92
Additional hotel ★★ 73% Kittiwell House Hotel & Restaurant, St Mary's Rd, CROYDE
☎ 01271 890247
Fax 01271 890469 12

SIDMOUTH Map 03 SY18

Sidmouth Cotmaton Rd, Peak Hill EX10 8SX
☎ 01395 513451 & 516407 Fax 01395 514661
Situated on the side of Peak Hill, offering beautiful coastal views. Club founded in 1889.
18 holes, 5100yds, Par 66, SSS 65, Course record 59.
Club membership 700.

Visitors by prior arrangement.
Societies by prior arrangement with the secretary.
Green Fees £20 per day/round.
Cards
Prof Gaele Tapper
Designer J H Taylor
Facilities
Location W side of town centre

Hotel ★★★★ 72% Victoria Hotel, Esplanade, SIDMOUTH ☎ 01395 512651 61

SOUTH BRENT Map 03 SX66

Wrangaton (S Devon) Golf Links Rd, Wrangaton TQ10 9HJ ☎ 01364 73229 Fax 01364 73229
Unique 18 hole course with 9 holes on moorland and 9 holes on parkland. The course lies within Dartmoor National Park. Spectacular views towards sea and rugged terrain. Natural fairways and hazards include bracken, sheep and ponies.
18 holes, 6083yds, Par 70, SSS 69, Course record 66.
Club membership 700.

Visitors play any time. Must have a handicap certificate and contact in advance.
Societies write or telephone.
Green Fees £17 per day (£23 weekends & bank holidays).
Prof Adrian Whitehead
Designer D M A Steel
Facilities
Location 2.25 m SW off A38

Hotel ★★ 74% Glazebrook House Hotel & Restaurant, SOUTH BRENT
☎ 01364 73322 10

SPARKWELL Map 02 SX55

Welbeck Manor & Sparkwell Golf Course Blacklands PL7 5DF ☎ 01752 837219
A mature parkland course with several challenging holes, it features fairway and greenside bunkers, mature trees and streams. The house on the site, now the hotel, was built by Isambard Kingdom Brunel. Several of the holes have been named to commemorate some of his famous works - the 6th

being The Great Western. This is a very challenging Par 5 tee which is out of bounds all the way up the left.
9 holes, 2886yds, Par 68, SSS 68, Course record 68.
Club membership 200.

Visitors no restrictions
Societies telephone in advance.
Green Fees £10 per 18 holes; £6 per 9 holes (£12/£7 weekends).
Cards
Designer John Gabb
Facilities
Location 1m N of A38 Plymouth/Ivybridge road

Hotel ★★★ 68% Boringdon Hall, Colebrook, Plympton, PLYMOUTH
☎ 01752 344455 41

TAVISTOCK Map 02 SX47

Hurdwick Tavistock Hamlets PL19 8PZ ☎ 01822 612746
This Executive parkland course with many bunkers and fine views opened in 1990. The idea of Executive golf originated in America and the concept is that a round should take no longer than 3 hours whilst offering solid challenge, thus suiting the busy business person.
18 holes, 5200yds, Par 68, SSS 67.
Club membership 180.

Visitors no restrictions.
Societies must contact in advance.
Green Fees £14 per day.
Designer Hawtree
Facilities
Location 1m N of Tavistock

Hotel ★★★ 62% Bedford Hotel, Plymouth Rd, TAVISTOCK
☎ 01822 613221 31rm(30)

Tavistock Down Rd PL19 9AQ
☎ 01822 612344 Fax 01822 612344
Set on Whitchurch Down in south-west Dartmoor with easy walking and magnificent views over rolling countryside into Cornwall. Downland turf with some heather, and interesting holes on undulating ground.
18 holes, 6250yds, Par 70, SSS 70, Course record 64.
Club membership 700.

Visitors advisable to contact in advance.
Societies by arrangement with secretary.
Green Fees £18 (£23 weekends).
Prof D Rehaag
Designer H Fowler
Facilities
Location 1m SE of town centre, on Whitchurch Down

Hotel ★★★ 62% Bedford Hotel, Plymouth Rd, TAVISTOCK
☎ 01822 613221 31rm(30)

TEDBURN ST MARY Map 03 SX89

Fingle Glen EX6 6AF ☎ 01647 61817
9-hole course containing six par 4's and three par 3's set in 52 acres of rolling countryside. Testing 4th, 5th and 9th holes. 12-bay floodlit driving range.
9 holes, 4818yds, Par 66, SSS 63, Course record 63.
Club membership 400.

Visitors must contact in advance.
Societies write or telephone in advance.
Green Fees not confirmed.
Prof Stephen Gould
Designer Bill Pilz
Facilities
Location 5m W of Exeter, off A30

Hotel ★★ 64% Fingle Glen Hotel, Golf & Country Club, Old Tedburn Rd, TEDBURN ST MARY
☎ 01647 61817 7

TEIGNMOUTH Map 03 SX97

Teignmouth Haldon Moor TQ14 9NY
☎ 01626 777070 Fax 01626 777070
This fairly flat heathland course is high up with a fine panoramic views of sea, moors and river valley. Good springy turf with some heather and an interesting layout makes for very enjoyable holiday golf. Designed by Dr Alister MacKenzie, the world famous architect who also designed Augusta GC USA.
18 holes, 6200yds, Par 71, SSS 70, Course record 65.
Club membership 900.

Visitors handicap certificate required, groups must contact in advance, restricted tee off times at weekends.
Societies telephone in advance and confirm in writing.
Green Fees £22 per day (£25 weekends).
Prof Peter Ward
Designer Dr Alister Mackenzie
Facilities
Location 2m NW off B3192

Hotel ★★ 70% Ness House Hotel, Marine Dr, Shaldon, TEIGNMOUTH
☎ 01626 873480 7 Annexe5

THURLESTONE Map 03 SX64

Thurlestone TQ7 3NZ
☎ 01548 560405 Fax 01548 560405
Situated on the edge of the cliffs with typical downland turf and good greens. The course, after an interesting opening hole, rises to higher land with fine seaviews, and finishes with an excellent 502-yard downhill hole to the clubhouse.
18 holes, 6340yds, Par 71, SSS 70, Course record 65.
Club membership 770.

Visitors must contact in advance & have handicap certificate from a recognised club.
Green Fees £26 per day.
Prof Peter Laugher
Designer Harry S Colt
Facilities by prior arrangement
& Leisure hard and grass tennis courts.
Location S side of village

Hotel ★★★★ 71% Thurlestone Hotel, THURLESTONE
☎ 01548 560382 65

TIVERTON Map 03 SS91

Tiverton Post Hill EX16 4NE ☎ 01884 252187
A parkland course where the many different species of tree are a feature and where the lush pastures ensure some of the finest fairways in the south-west. There are a number of interesting holes which visitors will find a real challenge.
18 holes, 6236yds, Par 71, SSS 71, Course record 65.
Club membership 725.

Visitors must have a current handicap certificate.
Societies apply in writing or telephone.
Green Fees not confirmed.
Prof David Sheppard
Designer Braid
Facilities
Hotel ★★ 63% Hartnoll Hotel, Bolham, TIVERTON ☎ 01884 252777 11 Annexe5

TORQUAY Map 03 SX96

Torquay 30 Petitor Rd, St Marychurch TQ1 4QF
☎ 01803 329113 Fax 01803 316116
Unusual combination of cliff and parkland golf, with wonderful views over the sea and Dartmoor.
18 holes, 6175yds, Par 69, SSS 70, Course record 65.
Club membership 700.

Visitors must contact in advance.
Societies must apply in writing.
Green Fees £24 per day/round (£28 weekends & bank holidays).
Prof Martin Ruth
Facilities
Location 1.25m N

Hotel ★★ 60% Norcliffe Hotel, 7 Babbacombe Downs Rd, Babbacombe, TORQUAY ☎ 01803 328456 27

TORRINGTON Map 02 SS41

Torrington Weare Trees, Great Torrington EX38 7EZ
☎ 01805 622229
Hard walking on hilly commonland 9 hole course. Challenging par 3 4th hole with a sloping green and difficult crosswinds. Small greens and outstanding views.
9 holes, 4419yds, Par 64, SSS 62, Course record 58.
Club membership 420.

Visitors cannot play Sat & Sun before noon.
Societies by arrangement.
Green Fees not confirmed.
Facilities by prior arrangement
Location 1m W of Torringdon

Hotel ★★ 63% Beaconside Hotel, Landcross, BIDEFORD ☎ 01237 477205 8rm(6)

UPOTTERY Map 03 ST20

Otter Valley Golf Centre
☎ 01404 861266, Fax 01404 861266 (5m NW of H oniton off A30, on Upottery Rd) This Golf School set in beautiful Devon countryside was established in 19 89. There are practice facilities with driving range, ap proach green, chipping green with bunkers and 8 prac tice holes. Weekend and 5 day courses are available a nd there is self catering accommodation, telephone fo r details. All coaching is given personally by Andrew Thompson P.G.A.

WESTWARD HO! Map 02 SS42

Royal North Devon Golf Links Rd EX39 1HD
☎ 01237 473817 Fax 01237 423456
Oldest links course in England with traditional links features and a museum in the clubhouse.
18 holes, 6644yds, Par 71, SSS 72, Course record 68.
Club membership 1000.

Visitors advisable to telephone and book tee time, must have handicap certificate or letter of introduction from club.
Societies apply in writing or telephone.
Green Fees £34 per day; £28 per round (£36/£30 weekends & bank holidays).
Cards
Prof Iain Higgins
Designer Old Tom Morris
Facilities
& Leisure snooker.
Location N side of village off B3236

Hotel ★★ 64% Culloden House Hotel, Fosketh Hill, WESTWARD HO! ☎ 01237 479421 9rm(2 5)

WOOLFARDISWORTHY Map 02 SS32

Hartland Forest Woolsery, Bideford EX39 5RA
☎ 01237 431442
This course is affected by winds and can be very windy at times.
18 holes, 6015yds, Par 71, SSS 69.
Club membership 240.

Visitors no restrictions.
Societies apply in writing.
Green Fees not confirmed.
Facilities
& Leisure hard tennis courts, heated indoor swimming pool, fishing, sauna, solarium, gymnasium.
Location 4m E of A39

Hotel ★★★ 73% Penhaven Country House, PARKHAM ☎ 01237 451388 & 451711 Fax 01237 451878 12

YELVERTON Map 02 SX56

Yelverton Golf Links Rd PL20 6BN
☎ 01822 852824 Fax 01822 852824
An excellent course on Dartmoor with plenty of gorse and heather. Tight lies in the fairways, fast greens and challenging hazards. Boasts 3 of the best holes in Devon (12th, 13th & 16th). Outstanding views.
18 holes, 6363yds, Par 71, SSS 72, Course record 68.
Club membership 650.

Visitors must have handicap certificate and subject to availability, advisable to contact in advance.
Societies must be booked in advance, by telephone initially.
Green Fees £30 per day (£40 weekends & bank holidays).
Prof Tim McSherry
Designer Herbert Fowler
Facilities
Location 1m S of Yelverton, off A386

Hotel ★★★ 70% Moorland Links Hotel, YELVERTON ☎ 01822 852245 45

DORSET

BEAMINSTER Map 03 ST40

Chedington Court South Perrott DT8 3HU
☎ 01935 891413
At present 9 holes, though due to be extended to 18, this course is laid out in parkland using the natural features of the rolling countryside. The Par 5 4th is 596yards and looks daunting but it is downhill from the tee to the green. The Par 4 9th is a tricky final hole with its hidden small lake waiting for the errant second shot. Preservation of wildlife and the natural flora are of prime concern in manging the course.
9 holes, 6754yds, Par 74, SSS 72, Course record 72.
Club membership 260.

Visitors must book tee time.
Societies apply in writing or telephone.
Green Fees not confirmed.
Designer David Hemstock
Facilities
Location 5m NE of Beaminster

Hotel ★★★ 71% Bridge House Hotel, 3 Prout Bridge, BEAMINSTER ☎ 01308 862200 9 Annexe4

BELCHALWELL Map 03 ST70

Dorset Heights DT11 0EG
☎ 01258 861386 Fax 01258 860900
Set in an area of outstanding natural beauty, rich in wildlife, which provides a picturesque backdrop to this stimulating, undulating course. Modern clubhouse with magnificent views.
18 holes, 6138yds, Par 70, SSS 70, Course record 74.
Club membership 270.

Visitors must contact in advance, dress restrictions.
Societies must telephone in advance.
Green Fees £12 (£15 weekends).
Cards
Prof Andy Stuart
Designer David Astill
Facilities
Hotel ★★★ 67% Crown Hotel, West St, BLANDFORD FORUM ☎ 01258 456626 33

BERE REGIS Map 03 SY89

East Dorset BH20 7NT
☎ 01929 472244 Fax 01929 471294
Lakeland is a long 18-hole parkland course with natural water features. The Woodland is a second 9-hole, 18-tee course is set amongst trees and rhododendrons. Floodlit 22-bay driving range, golf shop.
Lakeland Course: 18 holes, 6580yds, Par 72, SSS 73, Course record 68.
Woodland Course: 9 holes, 4887yards, Par 66, SSS 64, Course record 60.
Club membership 550.

Visitors must contact in advance and handicap certificate required for Lakeland course.
Societies apply in advance.

▶

Green Fees Lakeland: £32 per day; £27 per round (£37/£30 weekends). Woodland: £20 per day; £18 per round (£24/£22 weekends).
Cards
Prof Derwynne Honan
Designer Martin Hawtree
Facilities
Location 5m NW off A352

Hotel ★★ 68% Kemps Country House Hotel, East Stoke, WAREHAM ☎ 01929 462563 5rm(4) Annexe10

Blandford Forum — Map 03 ST80

Ashley Wood Wimborne Rd DT11 9HN
☎ 01258 452253 Fax 01258 450190
Undulating and well drained downland course with superb views over the Tarrant and Stour Valleys.
18 holes, 6276yds, Par 70, SSS 70, Course record 65.
Club membership 700.
Visitors phone in advance. Handicap certificate required weekends unless with member.
Societies apply to Secretary.
Green Fees £20 per day (£25 weekends).
Prof Spencer Taylor
Designer P Tallack
Facilities
Location 2m E on B3082

Hotel ★★★ 67% Crown Hotel, West St, BLANDFORD FORUM ☎ 01258 456626 33

Bournemouth — Map 04 SZ09

Bournemouth & Meyrick Central Dr, Meyrick Park BH2 6LH ☎ 01202 292425
Picturesque muncipal parkland course founded in 1890.
18 holes, 5852yds, Par 70, SSS 69, Course record 64.
Club membership 500.
Visitors advance booking is essential.
Societies telephone in advance.
Green Fees not confirmed.
Prof Lee Thompson
Facilities
& Leisure squash.
Hotel ★★★ 64% Burley Court Hotel, Bath Rd, BOURNEMOUTH ☎ 01202 552824 & 556704 Fax 01202 298514 38

Knighton Heath Francis Av, West Howe BH11 8NX
☎ 01202 572633 Fax 01202 590774
Undulating heathland course on high ground inland from Poole.
18 holes, 6084yds, Par 70, SSS 69.
Club membership 700.
Visitors may not play weekend. Phone for availability.
Societies must book in advance.
Green Fees £25 per day; £20 per round.
Prof Jane Miles
Facilities
Location N side of town centre off A348

Hotel ★★★ 65% Bridge House Hotel, 2 Ringwood Rd, Longham, FERNDOWN ☎ 01202 578828 37

Queen's Park Queens Park Dr West BH8 9BY
☎ 01202 396198 & 302611 Fax 01202 302611
Undulating parkland course of pine and heather, with narrow, tree-lined fairways. Public course played over by 'Boscombe Golf Club' and 'Bournemouth Artisans Golf Club'.
18 holes, 6305yds, Par 72, SSS 70, Course record 69.
Visitors Thu (ladies day)
Societies must contact in advance.
Green Fees £12.85 per round.
Cards
Prof Richard Hill
Facilities
Location 2m NE of town centre off A338

Hotel ★★ 67% Hotel Riviera, West Cliff Gardens, BOURNEMOUTH ☎ 01202 552845 34

Bridport — Map 03 SY49

Bridport & West Dorset East Cliff, West Bay DT6 4EP
☎ 01308 421491 & 421095 Fax 01308 421095
Seaside links course on the top of the east cliff, with fine views over Lyme Bay and surrounding countryside. A popular feature is the pretty and deceptive 14th hole, its sunken green lying 90 feet below the tee and guarded by natural hazards and bunkers.
18 holes, 6343yds, Par 73, SSS 70.
Club membership 700.
Visitors must contact in advance.
Societies must contact in writing in advance.
Green Fees £22 per day (£16 after 2pm, £10 after 5pm).
Prof David Parsons
Designer Hawtree
Facilities
& Leisure pitch & putt (holiday season).
Location 2m S of Bridport

Hotel ★★ 67% Ullswater Hotel, West Cliff Gardens, BOURNEMOUTH ☎ 01202 555181 42

Additional hotel ★ 60% Bridport Arms Hotel, West Bay, BRIDPORT ☎ 01308 422994 Fax 01308 425141 8rm(1 5) Annexe5rm

BROADSTONE Map 04 SZ09

Broadstone (Dorset) Wentworth Dr BH18 8DQ
☎ 01202 692595 Fax 01202 692595
Undulating and demanding heathland course with the 2nd, 7th, 13th and 16th being particularly challenging holes.
18 holes, 6315yds, Par 70, SSS 70, Course record 66.
Club membership 700.
Visitors restricted at weekends & bank holidays. Must contact in advance.
Societies contact in advance.
Green Fees £37 per day; £28 per round (£40 per round weekends & bank holidays).
Prof Nigel Tokely
Designer Colt/Dunn
Facilities
Location N side of village off B3074

Hotel ★★★ 58% King's Head Hotel, The Square, WIMBORNE ☎ 01202 880101 27

CERNE ABBAS Map 03 ST60

Lyons Gate Lyons Gate Farm, Lyons Gate DT2 7AZ
☎ 01300 345239
Since this course was opened in 1990, it has gained a reputation as 'the toughest 9-hole course in English golf' and the most spectacular.
9 holes, 4000yds, Par 30, SSS 30, Course record 32.
Club membership 200.
Visitors no restrictions.
Societies telephone for details.
Green Fees not confirmed.
Facilities
Location On A352, 11m N of Dorchester

Inn QQQ The Poachers Inn, PIDDLETRENTHIDE ☎ 01300 348358 3 Annexe9

CHRISTCHURCH Map 04 SZ19

Dudmoor Farm Dudmoor Farm Rd BH23 6AQ
☎ 01202 483980
A non-membership golf course with tree-lined par 3 and 4 fairways.
9 holes, 1428mtrs, Par 31.
Visitors no restrictions.
Societies telephone in advance.
Green Fees not confirmed.
Facilities
& Leisure squash, fishing.
Hotel ★★★ 76% Waterford Lodge Hotel, 87 Bure Ln, Friars Cliff, Mudeford, CHRISTCHURCH ☎ 01425 272948 17

Iford Bridge Barrack Rd BH23 2BA ☎ 01202 473817
Parkland course with the River Stour running through. Driving range.
9 holes, 2165yds, Par 34, SSS 32.
Club membership 350.
Visitors must contact in advance.
Societies must contact in advance.
Green Fees £6.25 (£7 weekends).
Prof Peter Troth
Facilities
& Leisure hard and grass tennis courts.
Location W side of town centre on A35

Hotel ★★★ 76% Waterford Lodge Hotel, 87 Bure Ln, Friars Cliff, Mudeford, CHRISTCHURCH ☎ 01425 272948 17

DORCHESTER Map 03 SY69

Came Down Came Down DT2 8NR ☎ 01305 813494
Scene of the West of England Championships on several occasions, this fine course lies on a high plateau commanding glorious views over Portland. Three par 5 holes add interest to a round. The turf is of the springy, downland type.
18 holes, 6244yds, Par 70, SSS 71.
Club membership 750.
Visitors advisable to phone in advance, must have handicap certificate. May play after 9am weekdays & after noon Sun.
Societies by arrangement on Wed only.
Green Fees not confirmed.
Prof Robert Preston
Designer J H Taylor
Facilities
Location 2m S off A354

Guest house QQQQQ Yalbury Cottage Hotel & Restaurant, Lower Bockhampton, DORCHESTER ☎ 01305 262382 8

FERNDOWN Map 04 SU00

Dudsbury Christchurch Rd BH22 8ST
☎ 01202 593499 Fax 01202 594555
Set in 150 acres of beautiful Dorset countryside rolling down to the River Stour. Wide variety of interesting and challenging hazards, notably water which comes into play on 14 holes.
Championship Course: 18 holes, 6763yds, Par 71, SSS 73, Course record 64.
Club membership 700.
Visitors welcome by arrangement with secretary or golf professional.
Societies telephone in advance.
Green Fees not confirmed.
Prof Roger Tuddenham
Designer Donald Steel
Facilities
& Leisure fishing.
Location 3m N of Bournemouth on B3073, between Parley and Longham

Hotel ★★★★ 69% The Dormy, New Rd, FERNDOWN ☎ 01202 872121 115

Ferndown 119 Golf Links Rd BH22 8BU
☎ 01202 874602 Fax 01202 873926
Fairways are gently undulating amongst heather, gorse and pine trees giving the course a most attractive appearance. There are a number of dog-leg holes, and, on a clear day, there are views across to the Isle of Wight.
Championship Course: 18 holes, 6452yds, Par 71, SSS 71, Course record 65.
Presidents Course: 9 holes, 5604yds, Par 70, SSS 68, Course record 65.
Club membership 700.
Visitors must contact in advance & have handicap certificate, no visitors on Thursdays except on Presidents course, numbers restricted at weekends.
Societies welcome Tue & Fri only, telephone in advance.
Green Fees Championship: £47 per day; £42 per round (£50 weekends). Presidents: £15 per day (£20 weekends).
Prof Iain Parker
Designer Harold Hilton
Facilities
Location S side of town centre off A347

Hotel ★★★★ 69% The Dormy, New Rd, FERNDOWN ☎ 01202 872121 115

Ferndown Forest Forest Links Rd BH22 9QE
☎ 01202 876096 Fax 01202 894095
Flat parkland course dotted with mature oak trees, several interesting water features, and some tight fairways.
18 holes, 4920yds, Par 67, SSS 65.
Club membership 700.
Visitors advisable to contact in advance,
Societies apply in writing.
Green Fees £18 per day/round (£10 weekends and bank holidays).
Cards
Prof Kevin Spurgeon
Designer Guy Hunt/Richard Graham
Facilities
& Leisure fishing.
Location From London M3 then A31, end of dual carriageway Dolmans Crossing rdbt right exit Forest Links Rd

Hotel ★★★ 65% Bridge House Hotel, 2 Ringwood Rd, Longham, FERNDOWN ☎ 01202 578828 37

HALSTOCK Map 03 ST50

Halstock Common Ln BA22 9SF
☎ 01935 891689 Fax 01935 891839
Halstock is a short tight course, but presents an interesting challenge to players of all abilities. The terrain is gently undulating in places and there are plenty of trees and water hazards.
18 holes, 4351yds, Par 65, SSS 61, Course record 61.
Club membership 160.
Visitors no restrictions, telephone first.
Societies telephone in advance.
Green Fees £10 per 18 holes; £5.50 per 9 holes (£12/£7 weekends).
Cards
Facilities
Location 6m S of Yeovil

Hotel ★★★ Summer Lodge, EVERSHOT ☎ 01935 83424 11 Annexe6

HIGHCLIFFE Map 04 SZ29

Highcliffe Castle 107 Lymington Rd BH23 4LA
☎ 01425 272210 Fax 01425 272210
Picturesque parkland course with easy walking.
18 holes, 4776yds, Par 64, SSS 63, Course record 58.
Club membership 500.
Visitors must have handicap certificate or be a member of recognised club. Telephone in advance.
Societies write or telephone in advance.
Green Fees £25 per day (£30 weekends & bank holidays 9.30am-noon); £15 any day after 4pm.
Facilities
Location SW side of town on A337

Hotel ★★★ 76% Waterford Lodge Hotel, 87 Bure Ln, Friars Cliff, Mudeford, CHRISTCHURCH ☎ 01425 272948 17

HURN Map 04 SZ19

Parley Parley Green Ln BH23 6BB ☎ 01202 591600
Flat parkland course with few hazards and only one Par 5. Friendly atmosphere.
9 holes, 4584yds, Par 66, SSS 64, Course record 69.
Club membership 238.
Visitors good standard of dress expected.
Societies write or telephone.
Green Fees not confirmed.
Prof Ken Gilhespy
Designer P Goodfellow
Facilities
Location Opposite Bournemouth airport

Hotel ★★ 67% Fisherman's Haunt Hotel, Sailsbury Rd, Winkton, CHRISTCHURCH ☎ 01202 477283 & 484071 Fax 01202 478883 4 Annexe14

LYME REGIS Map 03 SY39

Lyme Regis Timber Hill DT7 3HQ ☎ 01297 442963
Undulating cliff-top course with magnificent views of Golden Cap and Lyme Bay.
18 holes, 6283yds, Par 71, SSS 70, Course record 67.
Club membership 575.
Visitors must contact in advance & have handicap certificate or be a member of recognised golf club. No play on Thu & Sun mornings.
Societies Tue, Wed & Fri; must contact in writing.
Green Fees £24 per day; £20 mornings; £17 after 2pm.
Prof Andrew Black
Designer Donald Steel
Facilities
Location 1.5m N on A3052

Hotel ★★★ 69% Alexandra Hotel, Pound St, LYME REGIS ☎ 01297 442010 27

Lytchett Matravers Map 03 SY99

Bulbury Woods Bulbury Ln BH16 6HR
☎ 01929 459574 Fax 01929 459000
Parkland course amidst ancient woodland, with a mixture of American and traditional style greens and extensive views over the Purbecks and Poole Harbour.
18 holes, 6065yds, Par 72, SSS 70, Course record 68.
Club membership 700.

Visitors must contact in advance.
Societies must contact in advance.
Green Fees £20 (£25 weekends).
Cards
Prof Nigel Gravelle
Facilities
Location A35 Poole to Dorchester, 3m from Poole centre

Hotel ★★★ Priory Hotel, Church Green, WAREHAM
☎ 01929 551666 15 Annexe4

Poole Map 04 SZ09

Parkstone Links Rd, Parkstone BH14 9QS
☎ 01202 707138 Fax 01202 796027
Very scenic heathland course with views of Poole Bay. Club founded in 1910.
18 holes, 6250yds, Par 72, SSS 70, Course record 63.
Club membership 700.

Visitors must contact in advance and have handicap certificate.
Societies apply in writing.
Green Fees £40 per day; £30 per round (£50/£40 weekends & bank holidays).
Designer Willie Park Jnr
Facilities
Location E side of town centre off A35

Hotel ★★★ 81% Salterns Hotel, 38 Salterns Way, Lilliput, POOLE
☎ 01202 707321 20

Sherborne Map 03 ST61

Sherborne Higher Clatcombe DT9 4RN
☎ 01935 814431 Fax 01935 814218
A sporting course of first-class fairways with far-reaching views over the lovely Blackmore Vale and the Vale of Sparkford. Parkland in character, the course has many well-placed bunkers. The dog-leg 2nd calls for an accurately placed tee shot, and another testing hole is the 7th, a 194-yard, par 3. There is a practice area.
18 holes, 5882yds, Par 70, SSS 68, Course record 63.
Club membership 900.

Visitors must contact in advance & have handicap certificate.
Societies prior booking only.
Green Fees £30 per day (£40 weekends & bank holidays).
Prof Stewart Wright
Designer James Braid (part)
Facilities
Location 2m N off B3145

Hotel ★★★ 62% The Sherborne Hotel, Horsecastles Ln, SHERBORNE
☎ 01935 813191 59

Sturminster Marshall Map 03 ST90

Sturminster Marshall Moor Ln BH21 4AH
☎ 01258 858444 Fax 01258 858262
Privately owned club with pay & play facilities set in beautiful Dorset countryside. Played off 18 different tees the course is ideal for golfers of all standards.
9 holes, 4882yds, Par 68, SSS 64.
Club membership 350.

Visitors no restrictions.
Societies must contact in advance.
Green Fees £10 per 18 holes; £7 per 9 holes.
Cards
Prof Graham Howell
Designer John Sharkey/David Holdsworth
Facilities
Location On A350. Signposted from village

Hotel ★★★ 67% Crown Hotel, West St, BLANDFORD FORUM
☎ 01258 456626 33

Swanage Map 04 SZ07

Isle of Purbeck BH19 3AB
☎ 01929 450361 & 450354 Fax 01929 450501
A heathland course sited on the Purbeck Hills with grand views across Swanage, the Channel and Poole Harbour. Holes of note include the 5th, 8th, 14th, 15th, and 16th where trees, gorse and heather assert themselves. The very attractive clubhouse is built of the local stone.
Purbeck Course: 18 holes, 6295yds, Par 70, SSS 71, Course record 66. ▶

Dene Course: 9 holes, 4014yds, Par 60.
Club membership 500.
Visitors advisable to telephone.
Societies must contact in advance.
Green Fees Purbeck: £35 per day; £26 per round (£40/£32 weekends). Dene: £12 per day.
Cards
Prof Ian Brake
Designer H Colt
Facilities
Location 2.5m N on B3351

Hotel ★★★ 68% The Pines Hotel, Burlington Rd, SWANAGE ☎ 01929 425211 51rm(49)

VERWOOD Map 04 SU00

Crane Valley BH31 7LE
☎ 01202 814088 Fax 01202 813407
Two secluded parkland courses set amid rolling Dorset countryside and mature woodland - a 9-hole Pay and Play and an 18-hole Valley course for golfers holding a handicap certificate.The 6th nestles in the bend of the River Crane and there are 4 long Par 5's ranging from 499 to 545 yards.
Valley: 18 holes, 6445yds, Par 72, SSS 71, Course record 66.
Woodland: 9 holes, 2020yds, Par 33, SSS 60.
Club membership 700.
Visitors must have handicap certificate for Valley course.
Societies telephone in advance.
Green Fees Valley, £20 per weekday (£30 per round weekends). Woodland, £5.50 per 9 holes (£6.50 weekends).
Cards
Prof Paul Cannings
Designer Donald Steel
Facilities
Location 6m N of Ferndown on B3081

Hotel ★★★★ 69% The Dormy, New Rd, FERNDOWN ☎ 01202 872121 115

WAREHAM Map 03 SY98

Wareham Sandford Rd BH20 4DH
☎ 01929 554147 & 554156 Fax 01929 554147
At the entrance to the Purbecks with splendid views over poole Harbour and Wareham Forest. A mixture of undulating parkland and heathland fairways. A challenge for golfers of all abilities.
18 holes, 5603yds, Par 69, SSS 67, Course record 66.
Club membership 500.
Visitors must contact the club in advance and hold a handicap certificate. Must be accompanied by a member at weekends & bank holidays.
Societies weekdays only. Must contact in advance.
Green Fees £20 per day; £15 per round.
Prof Richard Emery
Facilities
Location Adjacent to A351, nr Wareham railway station

Hotel ★★★ 71% Springfield Country Hotel & Leisure Club, Grange Rd, WAREHAM ☎ 01929 552177 48

WEYMOUTH Map 03 SY67

Weymouth Links Rd DT4 0PF
☎ 01305 773981 (Secretary) & 773997 (Prof) Fax 01305 78 8029
Seaside parkland course. The 5th is played off an elevated tee over copse.
18 holes, 5976yds, Par 70, SSS 69, Course record 63.
Club membership 750.
Visitors advisable to contact in advance.
Societies apply in writing.
Green Fees £22 per day/round (£28 weekends & bank holidays).
Prof Des Lochrie
Designer James Braid
Facilities by prior arrangement
Location N side of town centre off B3157

Hotel ★★ 67% Hotel Rex, 29 The Esplanade, WEYMOUTH ☎ 01305 760400 31

CO DURHAM

BARNARD CASTLE Map 12 NZ01

Barnard Castle Harmire Rd DL12 8QN
☎ 01833 638355 & 631980
Perched high on the steep bank of the River Tees, the extensive remains of Barnard Castle with its splendid round tower dates back to the 12th and 13th centuries. The parkland course is flat and lies in open coutryside.
18 holes, 6406yds, Par 73, SSS 71.
Club membership 650.
Visitors must contact in advance, restricted at weekends. Handicap certificate required.
Societies apply in writing.
Green Fees £18 per 18 holes (£25 weekends).
Prof Darren Pearce
Designer A Watson
Facilities
Location 1m N of town centre on B6278

Hotel ★★ 74% Rose & Crown Hotel, ROMALDKIRK ☎ 01833 650213 7 Annexe5

BEAMISH Map 12 NZ25

Beamish Park DH9 0RH
☎ 0191 370 1382 Fax 0191 370 2937
Parkland course. Designed by Henry Cotton and W Woodend.
18 holes, 6204yds, Par 71, SSS 70, Course record 64.
Club membership 630.
Visitors must contact in advance and may only play weekdays.
Societies telephone in advance.
Green Fees £20 per day; £16 per round.
Prof Chris Cole
Designer H Cotton
Facilities
Location 1m NW off A693

Hotel ★★★ 66% Beamish Park Hotel, Beamish Burn Rd, MARLEY HILL
☎ 01207 230666 47

BILLINGHAM Map 08 NZ42

Billingham Sandy Ln TS22 5NA
☎ 01642 533816 & 554494 Fax 01642 533816
Parkland course on edge of urban-rural district, with hard walking and water hazards.
18 holes, 6404yds, Par 73, SSS 71, Course record 63.
Club membership 1050.
Visitors contact professional in advance.
Societies apply in writing to Secretary/Manager.
Green Fees £20 per day (£33 weekends).
Prof Michael Ure
Designer F Pennick
Facilities
Location 1m W of town centre E of A19

Hotel ★★★ 60% Billingham Arms Hotel, The Causeway, Billingham, STOCKTON-ON-TEES ☎ 01642 553661 & 360880
Fax 01642 552104 69

BISHOP AUCKLAND Map 08 NZ22

Bishop Auckland High Plains, Durham Rd DL14 8DL
☎ 01388 663648
A rather hilly parkland course with many well-established trees offering a challenging round. A small ravine adds interest to several holes including the short 7th, from a raised tee to a green surrounded by a stream, gorse and bushes. Pleasant views down the Wear Valley and over the residence of the Bishop of Durham.
18 holes, 6420yds, Par 72, SSS 71, Course record 64.
Club membership 950.
Visitors must contact in advance. Handicap certificate advisable. Dress rules apply.
Societies weekdays only; must contact in advance.
Green Fees £24 per day; £20 per round.
Prof David Skiffington
Designer James Kay
Facilities
& Leisure snooker tables.
Location 1m NE on A689

Hotel ★★ 59% The Postchaise Hotel, 36 Market Place, BISHOP AUCKLAND
☎ 01388 661296 & 606312
Fax 01388 606312 12

BURNOPFIELD Map 12 NZ15

Hobson Municipal Hobson NE16 6BZ
☎ 01207 271605 Fax 01207 271069
Meadowland course opened in 1981. Very easy walking.
18 holes, 6403yds, Par 69, SSS 68, Course record 65.
Club membership 700.
Visitors no restrictions. Must book in advance at weekends.
Societies must contact in advance.
Green Fees £12 per round (£15 weekends & bank holidays).
Prof Jack Ord
Facilities
Location 0.75m S on A692

Hotel ★★★ 68% Swallow Hotel, High West St, GATESHEAD
☎ 0191 477 1105 103

CHESTER-LE-STREET Map 12 NZ25

Chester-le-Street Lumley Park DH3 4NS
☎ 0191 388 3218 (Secretary) Fax 0191 388 1220
Parkland course in castle grounds, good views, easy walking.
18 holes, 6437yds, Par 71, SSS 71, Course record 71.
Club membership 650.
Visitors must contact in advance and have an introduction from own club or handicap certificate.
Societies must apply in writing.
Green Fees £20 per day (£25 weekends & bank holidays).
Prof David Fletcher
Designer J H Taylor
Facilities
Location 0.5m E off B1284

Hotel ★★★ 72% Ramside Hall Hotel, Carrville, DURHAM ☎ 0191 386 5282 82

Roseberry Grange Grange Villa DH2 3NF
☎ 0191 370 0670 Fax 0191 370 0660
Testing holes on this parkland course include the uphill par 3 12th (147yds) and the par 4 8th (438yds) with a ditch crossing the fairway.
18 holes, 5628yds, Par 70, SSS 69.
Club membership 550.
Visitors after 11.30am Sun & 10.30am Sat in summer, pay and play Mon-Fri.
Societies booking form available on request.
Green Fees not confirmed.
Cards
Prof Alan Hartley
Facilities
Hotel ★★★ 67% George Washington County Hotel, Stone Cellar Rd, District 12, High Usworth, WASHINGTON
☎ 0191 402 9988 105

CONSETT Map 12 NZ15

Consett & District Elmfield Rd DH8 5NN
☎ 01207 502186 Fax 01207 505060
Undulating parkland/moorland course with views across the Derwent Valley to the Cheviot Hills.
18 holes, 6023yds, Par 71, SSS 69, Course record 63.
Club membership 900.
Visitors advised to contact Professional in advance on 01207 580210.
Societies apply in writing.
Green Fees £17 per day (£25 weekends).
Prof Craig Dilley
Facilities
& Leisure snooker room.
Location N side of town on A691

Hotel ★★ 69% Lord Crewe Arms Hotel, BLANCHLAND
☎ 01434 675251 10 Annexe10

CROOK Map 12 NZ13

Crook Low Jobs Hill DL15 9AA
☎ 01388 762429 & 767926
Meadowland/parkland course in elevated position with natural hazards, varied holes and terrain. Panoramic views over Durham and Cleveland Hills.
18 holes, 6102yds, Par 70, SSS 69, Course record 64.
Club membership 660.
Visitors must contact Secretary for weekend play, limited availability.
Societies apply in writing to Secretary.
Green Fees £16 per day (£23 per round weekends).
Facilities
Location 0.5m E off A690

Hotel ★★ 66% Kensington Hall Hotel, Kensington Ter, WILLINGTON
☎ 01388 745071 10

DARLINGTON Map 08 NZ21

Blackwell Grange Briar Close, Blackwell DL3 8QX
☎ 01325 464458
Pleasant parkland course with good views, easy walking.
18 holes, 5621yds, Par 68, SSS 67, Course record 63.
Club membership 700.
Visitors restricted Wed & weekends.
Societies welcome weekdays except Wed (Ladies Day).
Green Fees £22 per day; £16 per round.
Prof Ralph Givens
Designer F Pennink
Facilities
Location 1m SW off A66, turn into Blackwell, signposted

Hotel ★★★★ 59% Blackwell Grange Hotel, Blackwell Grange, DARLINGTON
☎ 01325 509955 99

Darlington Haughton Grange DL1 3JD
☎ 01325 355324 Fax 01325 488126
Fairly flat parkland course with tree-lined fairways, and large first-class greens. Championship standard.
18 holes, 6271yds, Par 71, SSS 70, Course record 64.
Club membership 850.
Visitors may not play weekends unless accompanied by member.
Societies by prior arrangement with the Secretary but not at weekends.
Green Fees £20 per round.
Prof Mark Rogers
Designer McKenzie (part)
Facilities
Location N side of town centre off A1150

Hotel ★★★ 68% Headlam Hall Hotel, Headlam, Gainford, DARLINGTON
☎ 01325 730238 19 Annexe9

Hall Garth Golf & Country Club Hotel Coatham Mundeville DL1 3LU ☎ 01325 300400
A 6900yard course with mature trees and Victorian deer folly. Three greens have been newly laid. The challenging 165 yard Par 3 3rd requires teeing over water, whilst the 500 yard Par 5 6th hole features the picturesque River Swale running alongside the fairway and the green.
9 holes, 6621yds, Par 72, SSS 72.
Visitors advisable to book at least 1 week in advance.
Societies prior booking by telephone.
Green Fees not confirmed.
Designer Brian Moore
Facilities
& Leisure grass tennis courts, heated indoor swimming pool, sauna, solarium, gymnasium.
Location 0.5m from A1(M) off A167

Hotel ★★★ 70% Hall Garth Golf and Country Club Hotel, Coatham Mundeville, DARLINGTON
☎ 01325 300400 30 Annexe11

Stressholme Snipe Ln DL2 2SA ☎ 01325 461002
Picturesque municipal parkland course, long but wide, with 98 bunkers and a par 3 hole played over a river.
18 holes, 6511yds, Par 71, SSS 71.
Club membership 650.
Visitors must contact in advance.
Societies apply to the steward or professional.
Green Fees not confirmed.
Prof Tim Jenkins
Facilities
Location SW side of town centre on A67

Hotel ★★★ 70% King's Head Hotel, Priestgate, DARLINGTON ☎ 01325 380222 85

DURHAM Map 12 NZ24

Brancepeth Castle Brancepeth Village DH7 8EA
☎ 0191 378 0075 Fax 0191 3783835
Parkland course overlooked at the 9th hole by beautiful Brancepeth Castle.
18 holes, 6300yds, Par 70, SSS 70, Course record 64.
Club membership 780.
Visitors must contact in advance, restricted weekends.
Societies must contact in advance.
Green Fees £29 per day (£35 weekends & bank holidays).
Cards
Prof David Howdon
Designer H S Holt
Facilities
Location 4m from Durham A690 towards Crook, left at xrds in Brancepath, left turn at Castle Gates,400yds

Hotel ★★★★ 67% Royal County Hotel, Old Elvet, DURHAM ☎ 0191 386 6821 150

Durham City Littleburn, Langley Moor DH7 8HL
☎ 0191 378 0806 & 378 0029
Undulating parkland course bordered on several holes by the River Browney.
18 holes, 6321yds, Par 71, SSS 70, Course record 67.
Club membership 750.
Visitors restricted on competition days.
Societies apply in writing or telephone the club professional.
Green Fees £22 per day/round; £14 per round winter weekdays (£30 weekends & bank holidays).
Prof Steve Corbally
Designer C Stanton
Facilities
& Leisure practice bunker & driving nets.
Location 2m W of Durham City, turn left off A690into Littleburn Ind Est

Hotel ★★★ 70% Three Tuns Hotel, New Elvet, DURHAM ☎ 0191 386 4326 47

Mount Oswald South Rd DH1 3TQ
☎ 0191 386 7527 Fax 0191 386 0975
Flat, wooded parkland course with a Georgian clubhouse and good views of Durham cathedral on the back nine.
18 holes, 6101yds, Par 71, SSS 69.
Club membership 120.

Visitors must contact in advance for weekends but may not play before 10am on Sun.
Societies must telephone in advance.
Green Fees £10 per round (£12 weekends & bank holidays).
Cards
Facilities
Location On A177, 1m SW og city centre

Hotel ★★ 67% Bridge Toby Hotel, Croxdale, DURHAM ☎ 0191 378 0524 46

Ramside Hall Carrville DH1 1TD
☎ 0191 386 9514 Fax 0191 386 9519
Three recently constructed 9-hole parkland courses - Princes, Bishops, Cathedral - with 14 lakes and panoramic views surrounding an impressive hotel. Excellent golf academy and driving range.
Princes: 9 holes, 3235yds, Par 36, SSS 36.
Bishops: 9 holes, 3285yds, Par 36.
Cathedral: 9 holes, 2874yds, Par 34.
Club membership 400.

Visitors open at all times subject to tee availability.
Societies telephone in advance.
Green Fees not confirmed.
Designer Johnathan Gaunt
Facilities
Location 500m from A1/A690 interchange

Hotel ★★★ 72% Ramside Hall Hotel, Carrville, DURHAM ☎ 0191 386 5282 82

EAGLESCLIFFE Map 08 NZ41

Eaglescliffe and District Yarm Rd TS16 0DQ
☎ 01642 780098 Fax 01642 780238
This hilly course offers both pleasant and interesting golf to all classes of player. It lies in a delightful setting on a rolling plateau, shelving to the River Tees. There are fine views to the Cleveland Hills.
18 holes, 6275yds, Par 72, SSS 70, Course record 60.
Club membership 550.

Visitors restricted Tue, Thu, Fri & weekends.
Societies must contact in advance, apply to secretary on 01642 780238
Green Fees £24 per day (£30 weekends & bank holidays).
Prof Paul Bradley
Designer J Braid/H Cotton
Facilities
Location E side of village off A135

Hotel ★★★★ 66% Swallow Hotel, John Walker Square, STOCKTON-ON-TEES ☎ 01642 679721 125

HARTLEPOOL Map 08 NZ53

Castle Eden & Peterlee Castle Eden TS27 4SS
☎ 01429 836510
Beautiful parkland course alongside a nature reserve. Hard walking but trees provide wind shelter.
18 holes, 6262yds, Par 70, SSS 69, Course record 65.
Club membership 750.

Visitors with member only during 12-1.30pm & 4-6.30pm. Must contact in advance.
Societies must contact in advance tel: 01429 836689.
Green Fees £22 per day/round (£30 weekends & bank hols).
Prof Graham J Laidlaw
Designer Henry Cotton
Facilities
Location 2m S of Peterlee on B1281 off A19

Hotel ★★ 69% Hardwicke Hall Manor Hotel, HESLEDEN ☎ 01429 836326 15

Hartlepool Hart Warren TS24 9QF
☎ 01429 274398 Fax 01429 274129
A seaside course, half links, overlooking the North Sea. A good test and equally enjoyable to all handicap players. The 10th, par 4, demands a precise second shot over a ridge and between sand dunes to a green down near the edge of the beach, alongside which several holes are played.
18 holes, 6215yds, Par 70, SSS 70, Course record 64.
Club membership 700.

Visitors with member only on Sun.
Societies must apply in writing in advance.
Green Fees £20 per day (£30 weekends).
Prof Malcolm E Cole
Designer Partly Braid
Facilities
Location N of Hartlepool, off A1086

Hotel ★★ 66% Ryedale Moor, 3 Beaconsfield St, Headland, HARTLEPOOL ☎ 01429 231436 14

MIDDLETON ST GEORGE Map 08 NZ31

Dinsdale Spa Neasham Rd DL2 1DW
☎ 01325 332297
A mainly flat, parkland course on high land above the River Tees with views of the Cleveland Hills. Water hazards in front 10th tee and green, the prevailing west wind affects the later holes. There is a practice area by the clubhouse.
18 holes, 6090yds, Par 71, SSS 69, Course record 65.
Club membership 870.
Visitors welcome Mon & Wed-Fri, contact for further details.
Societies bookings through office, no weekends or Tue. Apply in writing or telephone.
Green Fees £20 per day.
Facilities
Location 1.5m SW

Hotel ★★★ 63% St George Hotel, Middleton St George, TEES-SIDE AIRPORT
☎ 01325 332631 59

NEWTON AYCLIFFE Map 08 NZ22

Aycliffe School Aycliffe Ln DL5 4EF
☎ 01325 312994
A parkland course in a country setting.
18 holes, 5430yds, Par 68, SSS 66, Course record 63.
Club membership 100.
Visitors must contact in advance (01325 310820).
Societies apply in writing.
Green Fees not confirmed.
Prof Clive Burgess
Facilities
& Leisure squash.
Location 6m N of Darlington, off A6072

Hotel ★★★★ 72% Redworth Hall Hotel & Country Club, REDWORTH
☎ 01388 772442 100

Woodham Golf & Country Club Burnhill Way DL5 4PN
☎ 01325 320574 Fax 01325 315254
Beautiful parkland course offering golfers a full and varied challenge with plenty of trees, numerous lakes and meandering streams.
18 holes, 6771yds, Par 73, SSS 72, Course record 68.
Club membership 694.
Visitors must book in advance for weekends.
Societies telephone or write in advance.
Green Fees £20 per day; £15 per 9/18 holes (£24 per 9/18 holes weekends).
Cards
Prof Ernie Wilson
Designer James Hamilton Stutt
Facilities
Location Off A167

Hotel ★★★ 69% Eden Arms Swallow Hotel, RUSHYFORD
☎ 01388 720541 46

SEAHAM Map 12 NZ44

Seaham Dawdon SR7 7RD
☎ 0191 581 2354 & 581 1268 (Sec)
Heathland links course with several holes affected by strong prevailing winds.
18 holes, 6017yds, Par 70, SSS 69, Course record 64.
Club membership 600.
Visitors contact professional at all times, with member only weekends until 3.30pm. must apply in advance.
Green Fees £15 per day/round (£18 weekends).
Prof Glyn Jones
Facilities by prior arrangement by prior arrangement
Location 3m E of A19, exit for Seaham

Hotel ★★★★ 64% Swallow Hotel, Queen's Pde, Seaburn, SUNDERLAND
☎ 0191 529 2041 65

SEATON CAREW Map 08 NZ52

Seaton Carew Tees Rd TS25 1DE
☎ 01429 261040 & 266249
A championship links course taking full advantage of its dunes, bents, whins and gorse. Renowned for its par 4 (17th); just enough fairway for an accurate drive followed by another precise shot to a pear-shaped, sloping green that is severely trapped.
The Old Course: 18 holes, 6604yds, Par 72, SSS 72.
Brabazon Course: 18 holes, 6849yds, Par 73, SSS 73.
Club membership 650.
Visitors restricted until after 10am at weekends & bank holidays.
Societies must apply in writing.
Green Fees £29 per day (£40 weekends & bank holidays).
Prof W Hector
Designer McKenzie
Facilities
Location SE side of village off A178

Hotel ★★ 66% Ryedale Moor, 3 Beaconsfield St, Headland, HARTLEPOOL
☎ 01429 231436 14

SEDGEFIELD Map 08 NZ32

Knotty Hill Golf Centre TS21 2BB ☎ 01740 620320 Fax 01740 622227
The 18-hole Princes course is set in rolling parkland with many holes routed through shallow valleys. Several holes are set wholly or partially within woodland and water hazards abound. Bishops Course, a new, challenging 18-hole course, is currently under construction; 9 holes were playable at time of going to press.
Princes Course: 18 holes, 6577yds, Par 72, SSS 71.
Visitors must telephone in advance.
Societies package available on request.
Green Fees £12 per 18 holes; £8 per 9 holes.
Prof Nick Walton
Designer C Stanton
Facilities
& Leisure practice bunker, target golf.

Location 1m N of Sedgefield on A177, 2m from junct 60 on A1(M)

Hotel ★★★ 64% Hardwick Hall Hotel, SEDGEFIELD
☎ 01740 620253 17

STANLEY Map 12 NZ15

South Moor The Middles, Craghead DH9 6AG
☎ 01207 232848 Fax 01207 284616
Moorland course with natural hazards designed by Dr Alistair McKenzie in 1926 and remains on of the most challenging of its type in north east England. Out of bounds features on 11 holes from the tee and the testing par 5 12th hole is uphill and usually against a strong headwind.
18 holes, 6445yds, Par 72, SSS 71, Course record 66.
Club membership 650.
Visitors must contact in advance but may only play Sun with member. Handicap certificate required.
Societies apply in writing to Secretary.
Green Fees £22 per day; £15 per round (£26 per day/round weekends & bank holidays).
Prof Shaun Cowell
Designer Dr Alistair Mackenzie
Facilities ⊗
Location 1.5m SE on B6313

Hotel ★★★ 66% Beamish Park Hotel, Beamish Burn Rd, MARLEY HILL
☎ 01207 230666 47

STOCKTON-ON-TEES Map 08 NZ41

Norton Norton TS20 1SU ☎ 01642 676385
An interesting parkland course with long drives from the 7th and 17th tees. Several water hazards.
18 holes, 5855yds, Par 70.
Visitors no restrictions.
Societies apply in advance.
Green Fees not confirmed.
Prof Terry Myles
Facilities ⊗
Location At Norton 2m N off A19

Hotel ★★★ 60% Billingham Arms Hotel, The Causeway, Billingham, STOCKTON-ON-TEES ☎ 01642 553661 & 360880
Fax 01642 552104 69

Teesside Acklam Rd, Thornaby TS17 7JS
☎ 01642 676249
Flat parkland course, easy walking.
18 holes, 6472yds, Par 72, SSS 71.
Club membership 600.
Visitors with member only weekdays after 4.30pm, weekends after 11am.
Societies must contact in writing.
Green Fees not confirmed.
Facilities
Location 1.5m SE on A1130

Hotel B Forte Posthouse Teeside, low Ln, Stainton Village, Thornaby, STOCKTON-ON-TEES
☎ 01642 591213 135

ESSEX

ABRIDGE Map 05 TQ49

Abridge Golf and Country Club Epping Ln, Stapleford Tawney RM4 1ST
☎ 01708 688396 Fax 01708 688550
A parkland course with easy walking. The quick drying course is by no means easy to play. This has been the venue of several professional tournaments. Abridge is a Golf and Country Club and has all the attendant facilities.
18 holes, 6692yds, Par 72, SSS 72, Course record 67.
Club membership 650.
Visitors must have current handicap certificate, contact in advance. Play with member only at weekends.
Societies telephone in advance.
Green Fees not confirmed.
Prof Stuart Layton
Designer Henry Cotton
Facilities ⊗ by prior arrangement
& Leisure heated outdoor swimming pool, sauna.
Location 1.75m NE

Hotel B Forte Posthouse Epping, High Rd, Bell Common, EPPING
☎ 01992 573137 Annexe79

BASILDON Map 05 TQ78

Basildon Clay Hill Ln, Kingswood SS16 5JP
☎ 01268 533297 Fax 01268 533849
Undulating municipal parkland course. Testing 13th hole (par 4).
18 holes, 6236yds, Par 72, SSS 70.
Club membership 300.
Visitors contact professional in advance 01268 533532.
Societies may contact for details.
Green Fees not confirmed.
Prof W Paterson
Designer A Cotton
Facilities ⊗
Location 1m S off A176

Hotel B Forte Posthouse Basildon, Cranes Farm Rd, BASILDON ☎ 01268 533955 110

BENFLEET Map 05 TQ78

Boyce Hill Vicarage Hill, South Benfleet SS7 1PD
☎ 01268 793625 & 752565
Hilly parkland course with good views.
18 holes, 5956yds, Par 68, SSS 68, Course record 61.
Club membership 700.
Visitors must have a handicap certificate, must contact 24hrs in advance, may not play at weekends.
Societies Thu only, book well in advance by telephone.
Green Fees not confirmed.
Prof Graham Burroughs
Designer James Braid
Facilities ⊗
Location 0.75m NE of Benfleet Station

Hotel B Forte Posthouse Basildon, Cranes Farm Rd, BASILDON ☎ 01268 533955 110

BILLERICAY Map 05 TQ69

The Burstead Tye Common Rd, Little Burstead CM12 9SS
☎ 01277 631171 Fax 01277 632766
The Burstead is an attractive parkland course set amidst some of the most attractive countryside in south Essex. It is an excellent test of golf to players of all standards with the greens showing maturity beyond their years. Challenging holes include the Par 4 16th hole which at 348yds requires an accurate tee shot to leave a second shot played over a lake protecting an attractive contoured green. The 18th is the longest hole on the course.
18 holes, 6275yds, Par 71, SSS 70, Course record 67.
Club membership 900.

Visitors must have handicap certificate and may only play weekdays.
Societies apply in writing and/or telephone for reservation.
Green Fees £19 per round.
Cards
Prof Keith Bridges
Designer Patrick Tallack
Facilities
Hotel ★★★ 66% Chichester Hotel, Old London Rd, Wickford, BASILDON ☎ 01268 560555 2 Annexe32

Stock Brook Manor Golf & Country Club Queens Park Av, Stock CM12 0SP
☎ 01277 653616 Fax 01277 633063
Set in 250 acres of picturesque countryside the 27 holes comprise three undulating 9's, offering the challenge of water on a large number of holes. Any combination can be played, but the Stock and Brook courses make the 18-hole, 6750 yard championship course. There are extensive clubhouse facilities.
Stock & Brook Courses: 18 holes, 6728yds, Par 72, SSS 72, Course record 66.
Manor Course: 9 holes, 2997yds, Par 35.
Club membership 750.

Visitors handicap certificate required, must contact 24hrs in advance.
Societies apply in writing or telephone.
Green Fees £25 per day (incl £2.50 towards lunch) (£30 per round weekends).
Cards
Prof Kevin Merry
Designer Martin Gillet
Facilities
& Leisure sauna.

Hotel ★★★ 65% The Heybridge Hotel, Roman Rd, INGATESTONE ☎ 01277 355355 22

BRAINTREE Map 05 TL72

Braintree Kings Ln, Stisted CM7 8DA
☎ 01376 346079 Fax 01376 330216
Parkland course with many unique mature trees. Good par 3s with the 14th -'Devils Lair'-regarded as one of the best in the county.
18 holes, 6199yds, Par 70, SSS 69, Course record 65.
Club membership 850.

Visitors weekdays only, contact the pro shop in advance 01376 343465.
Societies society days Wed & Thu early booking advised.
Green Fees £25 per day; £18 per round.
Cards
Prof Tony Parcell
Designer Hawtree
Facilities
Location 1m E, off A120

Hotel ★★★ 62% White Hart Hotel, Bocking End, BRAINTREE ☎ 01376 321401 31

Towerlands Panfield Rd CM7 5BJ
☎ 01376 326802 Fax 01376 552487
Undulating, grassland course. Driving range and sports hall.
9 holes, 2749yds, Par 34, SSS 66.
Club membership 300.

Visitors must not play before 12.30pm weekends. Correct dress at all times.
Societies must contact in advance by telephone.
Green Fees not confirmed.
Designer G Shiels
Facilities
& Leisure squash.
Location On B1053

Hotel ★★★ 62% White Hart Hotel, Bocking End, BRAINTREE ☎ 01376 321401 31

BRENTWOOD Map 05 TQ59

Bentley Ongar Rd CM15 9SS
☎ 01277 373179 Fax 01277 375097
Parkland course with water hazards.
18 holes, 6709yds, Par 72, SSS 72.
Club membership 600.

Visitors should contact in advance, may not play at weekends.
Societies must write or telephone in advance.
Green Fees prices not confirmed.
Prof Nick Garrett
Designer Alec Swann
Facilities
Location 3m NW on A128

Hotel B Forte Posthouse Brentwood, Brook St, BRENTWOOD ☎ 01277 260260 145

Hartswood King George's Playing Fields, Ingrave Rd CM14 5AE ☎ 01277 218850 & 214830
Municipal parkland course, easy walking.
18 holes, 6160yds, Par 70, SSS 69.
Club membership 500.

Visitors pre-booking usually essential am.
Societies must contact in advance.
Green Fees £9 (£13 weekends).
Prof Stephan Cole
Facilities
Location 0.75m SE on A128

Hotel B Forte Posthouse Brentwood, Brook St, BRENTWOOD ☎ 01277 260260 145

Warley Park Magpie Ln, Little Warley CM13 3DX
☎ 01277 224891 Fax 01277 200679
Parkland course with reasonable walking. Numerous water hazards. There is also a golf-practice ground.
1st & 2nd: 18 holes, 5967yds, Par 69, SSS 68, Course record 67.
1st & 3rd: 18 holes, 6232yds, Par 71, SSS 69, Course record 65.
2nd & 3rd: 18 holes, 6223yds, Par 70, SSS 69, Course record 70.
Club membership 800.
Visitors must have handicap certificate and contact in advance. May not play at weekends.
Societies telephone in advance for provisional booking.
Green Fees £36 per day; £25 per round.
Cards
Prof Jason Groat
Designer Reg Plumbridge
Facilities
Location 0.5m N off junct 29 of M25/A127

Hotel B Forte Posthouse Brentwood, Brook St, BRENTWOOD ☎ 01277 260260 145

Weald Park Coxtie Green Rd, South Weald CM14 5RJ
☎ 01277 375101
Tranquil parkland course with many mature oak trees, lakes, ponds and plentiful wildlife. The undulating terrain and the numerous hedges and ponds make this par 71 course a fair test of golf for all abilities.
18 holes, 6285yds, Par 71, SSS 70, Course record 65.
Club membership 570.
Visitors telephone booking preferable, no weekday restrictions, after 12 noon only at weekends and bank holidays.
Societies apply in writing or telephone for package.
Green Fees £20 per round (£25 weekends).
Cards
Prof Paul Barham
Designer Reg Plumbridge
Facilities
& Leisure Hard court tennis from Spring 1999.
Location 3m from M25

Hotel ★★★★ 70% Marygreen Manor, London Rd, BRENTWOOD
☎ 01277 225252 3 Annexe30

BULPHAN Map 05 TQ68

Langdon Hills Golf Centre Lower Dunton Rd RM14 3TY
☎ 01268 548444 Fax 01268 490084
Well situated with the Langdon Hills on one side and dramatic views across London on the other, the Centre offers an interchangeable 27 hole course, a floodlit 22-bay driving range and three academy holes.
Langdon Course: 9 holes, 3132yds, Par 35, SSS 71.
Horndon Course: 9 holes, 3054yds, Par 36, SSS 70.
Bulpman Course: 9 holes, 3054yds, Par 36, SSS 70.
Club membership 600.
Visitors preference given to members on weekend mornings.
Societies apply in writing or telephone.
Green Fees not confirmed.
Facilities
Location Between A13 & A127 N of A128 S of Basildon

Hotel ★★★★ 70% Marygreen Manor, London Rd, BRENTWOOD
☎ 01277 225252 3 Annexe30

BURNHAM-ON-CROUCH Map 05 TQ99

Burnham-on-Crouch Ferry Rd, Creeksea CM0 8PQ
☎ 01621 782282 Fax 01621 782282
Undulating meadowland course, easy walking, windy.
18 holes, 6056yds, Par 70, SSS 69, Course record 66.
Club membership 586.
Visitors welcome weekdays. Must play with member at weekends.
Societies apply in writing or telephone.
Green Fees £22 per day (weekdays only).
Cards
Designer Swan
Facilities
Location 1.25m W off B1010

Hotel ★★ 64% Blue Boar Hotel, Silver St, MALDON
☎ 01621 852681 20 Annexe8

CANEWDON Map 05 TQ99

Ballards Gore Gore Rd SS4 2DA ☎ 01702 258917
A parkland course with several lakes.
18 holes, 7062yds, Par 73, SSS 74, Course record 69.
Club membership 500.
Visitors may not play at weekends.
Societies weekdays only, apply in advance.
Green Fees not confirmed.
Prof Andrew Curry
Facilities by prior arrangement
Location 2m NE of Rochford

Hotel ★★★ 68% Hotel Renouf, Bradley Way, ROCHFORD ☎ 01702 541334 24

CANVEY ISLAND Map 05 TQ78

Castle Point Somnes Av SS8 9FG ☎ 01268 510830
A flat seaside links and part parkland course with water hazards on 13 holes and views of the estuary and Hadleigh Castle. Always a test for any golfer when the wind starts to blow.
18 holes, 6176yds, Par 71, SSS 69, Course record 69.
Club membership 275.
Visitors must book for weekends.
Societies phone or write for details.
Green Fees not confirmed.
Prof Paul Joiner
Facilities
Location SE of Basildon, A130 to Canvey Island

Hotel ★★★ 66% Chichester Hotel, Old London Rd, Wickford, BASILDON
☎ 01268 560555 2 Annexe32

A comprehensive list of driving ranges is given at the back of this guide. See page 479

CHELMSFORD Map 05 TL70

Channels Belstead Farm Ln, Little Waltham CM3 3PT
☎ 01245 440005 Fax 01245 442032
The Channels course is built on land from reclaimed gravel pits, 18 very exciting holes with plenty of lakes providing an excellent test of golf. Belsteads a nine hole course is mainly flat but has 3 holes where water has to be negotiated.
Channels Course: 18 holes, 6272yds, Par 71, SSS 71.
Belsteads: 9 holes, 4779yds, Par 67, SSS 63.
Club membership 650.

Visitors Channels Course; must contact in advance and may only play with member at weekends. Belsteads Course; available anytime.
Societies telephone starter on 01245 443311.
Green Fees Channels: £20 per round. Belsteads: £18 per 18 holes; £12 per 9 holes.
Prof Ian Sinclair
Designer Cotton & Swan
Facilities
& Leisure fishing.
Location 2m NE on A130

Hotel ★★★ 60% South Lodge Hotel, 196 New London Rd, CHELMSFORD
☎ 01245 264564 25 Annexe16

Chelmsford Widford Rd CM2 9AP
☎ 01245 256483 Fax 01245 256483
An undulating parkland course, hilly in parts, with 3 holes in woods and four difficult par 4's. From the reconstructed clubhouse there are fine views over the course and the wooded hills beyond.
18 holes, 5981yds, Par 68, SSS 69, Course record 66.
Club membership 650.

Visitors must contact in advance. Society days Wed/Thu, Ladies Day Tue. With member only at weekends.
Societies must contact in advance.
Green Fees not confirmed.
Prof Dennis Bailey
Designer Tom Dunn
Facilities
Location 1.5m S of town centre off A12

Hotel ★★★ 60% South Lodge Hotel, 196 New London Rd, CHELMSFORD
☎ 01245 264564 25 Annexe16

CHIGWELL Map 05 TQ49

Chigwell High Rd IG7 5BH
☎ 0181 500 2059 Fax 0181 501 3410
A course of high quality, mixing meadowland with parkland. For those who believe 'all Essex is flat' the undulating nature of Chigwell will be a refreshing surprise. The greens are excellent and the fairways tight with mature trees.
18 holes, 6279yds, Par 71, SSS 70, Course record 66.
Club membership 670.

Visitors must contact in advance & have handicap certificate, but must be accompanied by member at weekends.
Societies recognised societies welcome by prior arrangement.
Green Fees £40 per day; £30 per round.
Prof Ray Beard
Designer Hawtree/Taylor
Facilities by prior arrangement
Location 0.5m S on A113

Hotel ★★ 62% Roebuck Hotel, North End, BUCKHURST HILL
☎ 0181 505 4636 29

CHIGWELL ROW Map 05 TQ49

Hainault Forest Romford Rd, Chigwell Row IG7 4QW
☎ 0181 500 2131 Fax 0181 501 5196
Club playing over Borough of Redbridge public courses; hilly parkland subject to wind. Two courses, driving range.
No 1 Course: 18 holes, 5687yds, Par 70, SSS 67, Course record 65.
No 2 Course: 18 holes, 6238yds, Par 71, SSS 71.
Club membership 600.

Visitors no restrictions.
Societies must contact in writing.
Green Fees not confirmed.
Prof Chris Hope
Designer Taylor & Hawtree
Facilities
Location 0.5m S on A1112

Hotel ★★★ 66% County Hotel Epping Forest, Oak Hill, WOODFORD GREEN
☎ 0181 787 9988 99

CLACTON-ON-SEA Map 05 TM11

Clacton West Rd CO15 1AJ
☎ 01255 421919 Fax 01255 424602
Windy, seaside course.
18 holes, 6494yds, Par 71, SSS 69.
Club membership 650.

Visitors must contact in advance.
Societies must contact in writing.
Green Fees not confirmed.
Prof S J Levermore
Facilities
Location 1.25m SW of town centre

Hotel ★★ 70% Maplin Hotel, Esplanade, FRINTON-ON-SEA
☎ 01255 673832 12rm(10)

COLCHESTER Map 05 TL92

Birch Grove Layer Rd, Kingsford CO2 0HS
☎ 01206 734276
A pretty, undulating course surrounded by woodland - small but challenging with excellent greens. Challenging 6th hole cut through woodland with water hazards and out of bounds.
9 holes, 4038yds, Par 62, SSS 60, Course record 58.
Club membership 250.

Visitors restricted Sun mornings.
Societies apply in writing or telephone.
Green Fees £10 per day; £7 per 9 holes.
Facilities
Location 2.5m S on B1026

Hotel ★★★ 70% George Hotel, 116 High St, COLCHESTER ☎ 01206 578494 45

Colchester Braiswick CO4 5AU
☎ 01206 853396 Fax 01206 852698
A fairly flat, yet scenic, parkland course with tree-lined fairways and small copses. Mainly level walking.
18 holes, 6307yds, Par 70, SSS 70, Course record 64.
Club membership 700.

Visitors by prior arrangement.
Societies apply in writing or by telephone, Mon, Thu & Fri only.
Green Fees £25 per day; £20 per round (£30 per round weekends).
Prof Mark Angel
Designer James Braid
Facilities & Leisure indoor practice nets.
Location 1.5m NW of town centre on B1508

Hotel ★★★ 70% George Hotel, 116 High St, COLCHESTER ☎ 01206 578494 45

Colchester & Lexden Golf Centre Bakers Ln CD3 4AU
☎ 01206 843333 Fax 01206 854775
New 18-hole course within easy reach of the town centre. Also a 9-hole pitch and putt course, and a floodlit driving range.
18 holes, 5500yds, Par 67.
Club membership 500.

Visitors welcome.
Societies telephone for details.
Green Fees £18 per day; £15 per 18 holes.
Cards
Prof Stephen Hall
Designer J Johnson
Facilities & Leisure 9 hole pitch & putt.
Location Adjacent to A12. Take Colchester Central from A12 and then follow tourist signs

Hotel ★★★ 68% Marks Tey Hotel, London Rd, Marks Tey, COLCHESTER ☎ 01206 210001 110

Stoke-by-Nayland Keepers Ln, Leavenheath CO6 4PZ
☎ 01206 262836 Fax 01206 263356
Two undulating courses (Gainsborough and Constable) situated in Dedham Vale. Some water hazards and hedges. On Gainsborough the 10th (par 4) takes 2 shots over a lake; very testing par 3 at 11th.
Gainsborough Course: 18 holes, 6581yds, Par 72, SSS 71, Course record 63.
Constable Course: 18 holes, 6544yds, Par 72, SSS 71, Course record 67.
Club membership 1360.

Visitors write or telephone for details.
Societies write or telephone for brochures and booking forms.
Green Fees not confirmed.
Prof Kevin Lovelock
Facilities & Leisure fishing.
Location 1.5m NW of Stoke-by-Nayland on B1068

Hotel ★★★ Maison Talbooth, Stratford Rd, DEDHAM ☎ 01206 322367 10

Earls Colne — Map 05 TL82

Colne Valley Station Rd CO6 2LT
☎ 01787 224233 Fax 01787 224126
An 18-hole course along the valley of the River Colne. Opened in 1991.
18 holes, 6301yds, Par 70, SSS 70, Course record 68.
Club membership 600.

Visitors only after 10am at weekends, must dress correctly, no sharing of clubs. Must contact in advance.
Societies apply in writing, minimum of 12 persons.
Green Fees £17 per round (£22 weekends).
Cards
Prof Scott Clark
Designer Howard Swan
Facilities & Leisure sauna.
Location Off A604

Hotel ★★★ 68% Marks Tey Hotel, London Rd, Marks Tey, COLCHESTER ☎ 01206 210001 110

Essex Golf & Country Club CO6 2NS
☎ 01787 224466 Fax 01787 224410
Created on the site of a World War II airfield, this challenging course contains 12 lakes. Also 9-hole course as well as a variety of leisure facilities.
County Course: 18 holes, 6800yds, Par 73, SSS 73, Course record 67.
Garden Course: 9 holes, 2190yds, Par 34.
Club membership 600.

Visitors contact golf reception.
Societies apply in writing to the Society Secretary.
Green Fees Country Course £20 (£25 weekends); Garden Course £15 per 18 holes; £10 per 9 holes.
Cards
Prof Mark Spooner
Designer Reg Plumbridge
Facilities & Leisure hard tennis courts, heated indoor swimming pool, fishing, sauna, solarium, gymnasium, indoor practice bunker, video teaching studio, injury clinic.
Location Off the A120 onto the B1024

Hotel ★★★ 68% Marks Tey Hotel, London Rd, Marks Tey, COLCHESTER ☎ 01206 210001 110

Epping — Map 05 TL40

Nazeing Middle St, Nazeing EN9 2LW
☎ 01992 893798 Fax 01992 893882
Parkland course built with American sand based greens and tees and five strategically placed lakes. One of the most notable holes is the difficult par 3 13th with out of bounds and a large lake coming into play.
18 holes, 6598yds, Par 72, SSS 71, Course record 68.
Club membership 400.

Visitors not compulsory to contact except for weekends when pm only available.
Societies prior arrangement required in writing.
Green Fees £20 weekdays after 8.30am (£28 weekends after 1pm).
Cards

Prof Robert Green
Designer M Gillete
Facilities
Location Just outside Waltham Abbey

Hotel ★★★ 64% Harlow Moat House, Southern Way, HARLOW ☎ 01279 829988 119

FRINTON-ON-SEA Map 05 TM22

Frinton 1 The Esplanade CO13 9EP
☎ 01255 674618 Fax 01255 674618
Deceptive, flat seaside links course providing fast, firm and undulating greens that will test the best putters and tidal ditches that cross many of the fairways, requiring careful placement of shots. Its open character means that every shot has to be evaluated with both wind strength and direction in mind. Easy walking.
Long Course: 18 holes, 6265yds, Par 71, SSS 70, Course record 64.
Short Course: 9 holes, 1367yds, Par 58.
Club membership 850.
Visitors must contact in advance.
Societies by arrangement, apply in writing to the secretary, Wed, Thu and some Fri.
Green Fees £30 per day; £25 per round; short course £10 per day; £7.50 per round.
Prof Peter Taggart
Designer Willy Park Jnr
Facilities by prior arrangement
& Leisure snooker table.
Location SW side of town centre

Hotel ★★ 70% Maplin Hotel, Esplanade, FRINTON-ON-SEA ☎ 01255 673832 12rm(10)

GOSFIELD Map 05 TL72

Gosfield Lake The Manor House, Hall Dr CO9 1SE
☎ 01787 474747 Fax 01787 476044
Parkland course with bunkers, lakes and water hazards. Designed by Sir Henry Cotton/Mr Howard Swan and opened in 1988. Also 9-hole course; ideal for beginners and improvers.
Lakes Course: 18 holes, 6615yds, Par 72, SSS 72.
Meadows Course: 9 holes, 4180yds, Par 66, SSS 63.
Club membership 650.
Visitors Lakes Course: must contact in advance, handicap certificate required, Sat & Sun from noon only. Meadows Course: restricted during competitions, handicap certificate not required, advisable to contact.
Societies welcome Mon-Fri by arrangement, telephone or write.
Green Fees Lakes: £25 per day; £20 per round. Meadows: £12 per day; £10 per round.
Prof Richard Wheeler
Designer Henry Cotton/Howard Swan
Facilities
& Leisure sauna.
Location 1m W of Gosfield off B1017

Hotel ★★★ 62% White Hart Hotel, Bocking End, BRAINTREE ☎ 01376 321401 31

HARLOW Map 05 TL40

Canons Brook Elizabeth Way CM19 5BE
☎ 01279 421482 Fax 01279 626393
Challenging parkland course designed by Henry Cotton in 1963. Accuracy is the key requiring straight driving from the tees, especially on the par 5 11th to fly a gap with out of bounds left and right before setting up the shot to the green.
18 holes, 6800yds, Par 73, SSS 72, Course record 65.
Club membership 850.
Visitors must contact in advance, may not play at weekends.
Societies welcome Mon, Wed and Fri, must book in advance by telephone.
Green Fees £27 per day; £20 per round.
Prof Alan McGinn
Designer Henry Cotton
Facilities
Location 3m NW of junct 7 on M11

Hotel ★★★ 72% Churchgate Manor Hotel, Churchgate St Village, Old Harlow, HARLOW ☎ 01279 420246 85

North Weald Rayley Ln, North Weald CM16 6AR
☎ 01992 522118 Fax 01992 522881
Although only opened in November 1995, the blend of lakes and meadowland give this testing course an air of maturity.
18 holes, 6052yds, Par 71, SSS 70, Course record 66.
Club membership 780.
Visitors must contact in advance, limited at weekends.
Societies contact in advance.
Green Fees £17.50 (£25 weekends & bank holidays).
Cards
Prof Michael Janes
Facilities
Location M11 exit 7,off A414 towards Chipping Ongar

Hotel ★★★ 64% Harlow Moat House, Southern Way, HARLOW ☎ 01279 829988 119

HARWICH Map 05 TM23

Harwich & Dovercourt Station Rd, Parkeston CO12 4NZ
☎ 01255 503616 Fax 01255 503323
Flat moorland course with easy walking.
9 holes, 5900yds, Par 70, SSS 69, Course record 58.
Club membership 420.
Visitors visitors with handicap certificate may play by prior arrangement, with member only at weekends.
Societies prior arrangement essential.
Green Fees £17 per 18 holes; £8.50 per 9 holes.
Facilities
& Leisure practice net, practice bunker.
Location Off A120 near Ferry Terminal

Hotel ★★ 72% The Pier at Harwich, The Quay, HARWICH ☎ 01255 241212 6

INGRAVE Map 05 TQ69

Thorndon Park CM13 3RH
☎ 01277 811666 Fax 01277 810645
Among the best of the Essex courses with a fine new purpose-built clubhouse and a lake. The springy turf is easy on the feet. Many newly planted young trees now replace the famous old oaks that were such a feature of this course.
18 holes, 6492yds, Par 71, SSS 71.
Club membership 670.
Visitors must contact in advance, at weekends with member only.
Societies welcome Tue and Fri but must apply in writing.
Green Fees £50 per day; £35 per round.
Prof Brian White
Designer Colt/Alison
Facilities
Location W side of village off A128

Hotel B Forte Posthouse Brentwood, Brook St, BRENTWOOD
☎ 01277 260260 145

LOUGHTON Map 05 TQ49

High Beech Wellington Hill IG10 4AH ☎ 0181 508 7323
Short 9-hole course set in Epping Forest.
9 holes, 1477, Par 27, Course record 25 or 9 holes, 847, Par 27.
Visitors welcome.
Green Fees £2.80-£3.25.
Prof Clark Baker
Facilities
Location Close to M25 Waltham Abbey junct

Loughton Clays Ln, Debden Green IG10 2RZ
☎ 0181 502 2923
Hilly 9-hole parkland course on the edge of Epping Forest.
9 holes, 4652yds, Par 66, SSS 63, Course record 65.
Club membership 180.
Visitors must contact in advance.
Societies telephone in advance.
Green Fees £9 per 18 holes; £6 per 9 holes (£10.50/£7 weekends & bank holidays).
Prof Richard Layton
Facilities
Location 1.5m SE of Theydon Bois

Hotel B Forte Posthouse Epping, High Rd, Bell Common, EPPING
☎ 01992 573137 Annexe79

MALDON Map 05 TL80

Forrester Park Beckingham Rd, Great Totham CM9 8EA
☎ 01621 891406 Fax 01621 891406
Tight, undulating parkland course with tree-lined fairways and good views over the Blackwater estuary. Easy walking. Attractive 16th-century clubhouse.
18 holes, 6073yds, Par 71, SSS 69, Course record 69.
Club membership 1000.
Visitors must contact in advance but may not play before noon weekends & bank holidays.
Societies must apply in advance.
Green Fees £18 per round (£20 weekends).
Cards
Prof Gary Pike
Designer T R Forrester-Muir
Facilities by prior arrangement
& Leisure hard tennis courts.
Location 3m NE of Maldon off B1022

Hotel ★★ 64% Blue Boar Hotel, Silver St, MALDON
☎ 01621 852681 20 Annexe8

Maldon Beeleigh, Langford CM9 6LL ☎ 01621 853212
Flat, parkland course in a triangle of land bounded by the River Chelmer, the Blackwater Canal and an old railway embankment. Alternate tees on 2nd nine holes. Testing par 3 14th (166yds) demanding particular accuracy to narrow green guarded by bunkers and large trees.
9 holes, 6253yds, Par 71, SSS 70, Course record 71.
Club membership 380.
Visitors telephone to check availability, may only play with member at weekends. Handicap certificate required.
Societies intially telephone then confirm in writing.
Green Fees £20 per day; £15 per round (Mon-Fri).
Designer Thompson of Felixstowe
Facilities
Location 1m NW off B1019

Hotel ★★ 64% Blue Boar Hotel, Silver St, MALDON ☎ 01621 852681 20 Annexe8

ORSETT Map 05 TQ68

Orsett Brentwood Rd RM16 3DS
☎ 01375 891352 Fax 01375 892471
A very good test of golf - this heathland course with its sandy soil is quick drying and provides easy walking. Close to the Thames estuary it is seldom calm and the main hazards are the prevailing wind and thick gorse. Any slight deviation can be exaggerated by the wind and a lost ball in the gorse results. The clubhouse has been modernised.
18 holes, 6614yds, Par 72, SSS 72, Course record 68.
Club membership 750.
Visitors restricted weekends & bank holidays. Must contact in advance and have a handicap certificate.
Societies must contact in advance.
Green Fees £32.50 per day; £22.50 per round after 1pm.
Prof Paul Joiner
Designer James Braid
Facilities
Location At junct of A13 off A128

Hotel B Forte Posthouse Basildon, Cranes Farm Rd, BASILDON
☎ 01268 533955 110

PURLEIGH Map 05 TL80

Three Rivers Stow Rd CM3 6RR
☎ 01621 828631 Fax 01621 828060
Set in 265 acres of landscaped wooded parkland, Three Rivers is a fully matured 18-hole course affording good valley views over the Crouch, Blackwater and Roach rivers ▶

that give the course its name. With ponds and dog-legs among the challenges it is ideal for beginners and seasoned golfers who have the opportunity to improve their short game.
Kings Course: 18 holes, 6536yds, Par 73, SSS 71.
Jubilee Course: 18 holes, 4800yds, Par 65.
Club membership 800.
Visitors telephone before visit.
Societies apply in writing or telephone.
Green Fees £25.
Cards
Prof Pat O'Connor
Designer Hawtree
Facilities
& Leisure hard tennis courts, squash.
Location 1m from Purleigh on B1012

Hotel ★★ 64% Blue Boar Hotel, Silver St, MALDON ☎ 01621 852681 20 Annexe8

ROCHFORD Map 05 TQ89

Rochford Hundred Hall Rd SS4 1NW
☎ 01702 544302 Fax 01702 541343
Parkland course with ponds and ditches as natural hazards.
18 holes, 6292yds, Par 72, SSS 70, Course record 64.
Club membership 800.
Visitors must have handicap certificate. Visitors may not play Tue morning (Ladies) or Sun without a member.
Societies must contact in writing.
Green Fees not confirmed.
Prof Graham Hill
Designer James Braid
Facilities
Location W on B1013

Hotel ★★★ 68% Hotel Renouf, Bradley Way, ROCHFORD ☎ 01702 541334 24

SAFFRON WALDEN Map 05 TL53

Saffron Walden Windmill Hill CB10 1BX
☎ 01799 522786 Fax 01799 522786
Undulating parkland course, beautiful views.
18 holes, 6606yds, Par 72, SSS 72.
Club membership 950.
Visitors must contact in advance and have a handicap certificate. With member only at weekends.
Societies must contact in advance.
Green Fees £30 per day/round.
Prof Philip Davis
Facilities
Location NW side of town centre off B184

Hotel ★★ 67% The Crown House, GREAT CHESTERFORD ☎ 01799 530515 8 Annexe10

SOUTHEND-ON-SEA Map 05 TQ88

Belfairs Eastwood Rd North, Leigh on Sea SS9 4LR
☎ 01702 525345
Municipal parkland course run by the Borough Council. Tight second half through thick woods, easy walking.
18 holes, 5840yds, Par 70, SSS 68, Course record 68.
Club membership 350.
Visitors contact for booking, correct dress code must be adhered to.
Societies contact 01702 610455.
Green Fees not confirmed.
Prof Martin Foreman
Designer H S Colt
Facilities
& Leisure hard tennis courts.
Location 3m W, N of A13

Hotel ★★★ 64% Balmoral Hotel, 34 Valkyrie Rd, Westcliffe-on-Sea, SOUTHEND-ON-SEA ☎ 01702 342947 29

Thorpe Hall Thorpe Hall Av, Thorpe Bay SS1 3AT
☎ 01702 582205
Parkland course with narrow fairways where placement rather than length is essential.
18 holes, 6286yds, Par 71, SSS 71, Course record 64.
Club membership 995.
Visitors must contact in advance, with member only weekends & bank holidays.
Societies apply in writing, only a certain number a year.
Green Fees not confirmed.
Prof Bill McColl
Facilities
& Leisure squash, sauna.
Location 2m E off A13

Hotel ★★★ 64% Balmoral Hotel, 34 Valkyrie Rd, Westcliffe-on-Sea, SOUTHEND-ON-SEA ☎ 01702 342947 29

SOUTH OCKENDON Map 05 TQ58

Belhus Park Belhus Park RM15 4PX
☎ 01708 854260 Fax 01708 851952
A well established 18 hole course set in beautiful parkland.
18 holes, 5255yds, Par 68, SSS 68, Course record 63.
Club membership 200.
Visitors no restrictions. Must have proper golf shoes and shirts to be worn at all times. Booking advisable at weekends.
Societies contact in writing or telephone
Green Fees £8.50-£9 per round (£13-£13.50 weekends).
Prof Gary Lunn
Designer Capability Brown
Facilities
& Leisure heated indoor swimming pool, solarium, gymnasium.
Location Off the B1335, 10mins from Lakeside Shopping Centre

Hotel ★★★ 67% Stifford Moat House, High Rd, North Stifford, GRAYS ☎ 01708 719988 96

Top Meadow Fen Ln, North Ockendon RM14 3PR
☎ 01708 852239
Set in the Essex countryside with a panoramic view of the area. Some holes are very difficult with the variable wind directions, especially 1st, 6th, 7th and 13th.
Top Meadow: 18 holes, 6348yds, Par 72, SSS 71, Course record 68.
Club membership 600.
Visitors welcome Mon-Fri.
Societies telephone in advance.

Green Fees not confirmed.
Prof Paul King/Kevin Smith
Designer Burns/Stock
Facilities
& Leisure fishing.
Hotel B Travelodge, EAST HORNDON
☎ 01277 810819 22

STANFORD-LE-HOPE Map 05 TQ68

St Clere's Hall London Rd SS17 0LX
☎ 01375 361565 Fax 01375 361565
All year round golf with views of the Thames, with several challenging par 3's, notably the 223 yard 13th.
18 holes, 6474yds, Par 72, SSS 71, Course record 71.
Club membership 460.
Visitors welcome after 9.30am Mon-Sun, telephone for times.
Societies welcome Mon, Tue and Thu, telephone for details.
Green Fees £15 per 18 holes; £7.50 per 9 holes (£20/£10 weekends).
Prof David Wood
Designer A Stiff
Facilities
Location 5m from M25 E of London on A13, take Stanford turn off in direction Linford, St Clere on the left

Hotel ★★★ 67% Stifford Moat House, High Rd, North Stifford, GRAYS
☎ 01708 719988 96

STAPLEFORD ABBOTTS Map 05 TQ59

Stapleford Abbotts Horsemanside, Tysea Hill RM4 1JU
☎ 01708 381108 Fax 01708 386345
Abbotts course, provides a challenging test for players of all abilities as mature trees, large greenside bunkers and many lakes are all brought into play.
Abbotts Course: 18 holes, 6501yds, Par 72, SSS 71.
Priors Course: 18 holes, 5720yds, Par 69, SSS 69.
Friars Course: 9 holes, 1140yds, Par 27, SSS 27.
Club membership 800.
Visitors Abbotts Course midweek only. Priors and Friars, 7 days per week. Advisable to telephone starter on 01277 373344 for Priors and 01277 381108 for Abbotts and Friars.
Societies must be pre booked.
Green Fees Abbots £30; Priors £11 (£15 weekends); Friars £5 (£8 weekends).
Cards
Prof Dominic Eagle
Designer Henry Cotton/Howard Swan
Facilities
& Leisure sauna.
Location 1m E of Stapleford Abbotts, off B175

Hotel ★★★★ 70% Marygreen Manor, London Rd, BRENTWOOD
☎ 01277 225252 3 Annexe30

A comprehensive list of driving ranges is given at the back of this guide. See page 479

THEYDON BOIS Map 05 TQ49

Theydon Bois Theydon Rd CM16 4EH
☎ 01992 812460 & 813054 Fax 01992 813054
The course was originally nine-holes built into Epping Forest. It was later extendend to 18-holes which were well-planned and well-bunkered but in keeping with the 'forest tradition. The old nine in the Forest are short and have two bunkers between them, but even so a wayward shot can be among the trees. The autumn colours here are truly magnificent.
18 holes, 5480yds, Par 68, SSS 68, Course record 64.
Club membership 600.
Visitors may not play Wed, Thu, Sat & Sun mornings, ring 01992 812460 in advance to be sure tee is available.
Societies book through the secretary.
Green Fees £23 per round.
Prof R Hall
Designer James Braid
Facilities by prior arrangement
Location 2m from junct 26 on M25

Hotel B Forte Posthouse Epping, High Rd, Bell Common, EPPING
☎ 01992 573137 Annexe79

TOLLESHUNT KNIGHTS Map 05 TL91

Five Lakes Hotel Golf & Country Club Colchester Rd CM9 8HX ☎ 01621 868888
Two 18-hole courses. The Links is a seaside course with a number of greenside ponds and strategically placed bunkers, while the Lakes is a championship course with large water features and mounding between fairways.
Links Course: 18 holes, 6250yds, Par 71, SSS 70, Course record 67.
Lakes Course: 18 holes, 6767yds, Par 72, SSS 72, Course record 63.
Club membership 600.
Visitors must contact in advance.
Societies must contact in advance.
Green Fees Links: £20 per round (£25 weekends & bank holidays). Lakes: £25 per round (£33 weekends & bank holidays).
Cards
Prof Gary Carter
Designer Lakes Neil Cole
Facilities
& Leisure hard tennis courts, heated indoor swimming pool, squash, sauna, solarium, gymnasium, putting green.
Location 1.75m NE on B1026

Hotel ★★★★ 74% Five Lakes Hotel, Golf & Country Club, Colchester Rd, TOLLESHUNT KNIGHTS ☎ 01621 868888 114

TOOT HILL Map 05 TL50

Toot Hill School Rd CM5 9PU
☎ 01277 365523 Fax 01277 364509
Pleasant course with several water hazards and sand greens.
18 holes, 6053yds, Par 70, SSS 69, Course record 65.
Club membership 400.

Visitors welcome Mon-Fri by prior arrangement, handicap certificate may be required.
Societies Tue & Thu contact in advance.
Green Fees £35 per day; £25 per round.
Prof Mark Bishop
Designer Martin Gillett
Facilities
Location 7m SE of Harlow, off A414

Hotel B Forte Posthouse Epping, High Rd, Bell Common, EPPING
01992 573137 Annexe79

WITHAM Map 05 TL81

Benton Hall Wickham Hill CM8 3LH
01376 502454 Fax 01376 521050
Set in rolling countryside and surrounded by dense woodland, this challenging course provides a severe test even to the very best golfers. The River Blackwater dominates the front nine and natural lakes come into play on five other holes. 20-bay driving range.
18 holes, 6500yds, Par 72, SSS 72, Course record 64.
Club membership 470.
Visitors no restrictions.
Societies telephone in advance.
Green Fees £20 per round (£25 weekends).
Cards
Prof John Hudson/Peter McBride
Facilities
Location Witham turn off on A12, signposted

Hotel ★★★ 62% White Hart Hotel, Bocking End, BRAINTREE 01376 321401 31

Braxted Park Braxted Park Estate CM8 3EN
01376 572372 Fax 01621 892840
A Pay and Play course in ancient parkland, surrounded by lakes and extremely pretty countryside. Suitable for beginners and experienced players.
9 holes, 2940yds, Par 35, SSS 34.
Club membership 83.
Visitors welcome weekdays from 7.30am onwards.
Societies telephone to arrange.
Green Fees £12 per 18 holes; £9 per 9 holes.
Prof Tony Parcell
Designer Sir Allen Clark
Facilities
& Leisure fishing.
Location 2m from A12 near Kelvedon/Witham, at Gt Braxted

Hotel ★★★ 62% White Hart Hotel, Bocking End, BRAINTREE 01376 321401 31

WOODHAM WALTER Map 05 TL80

Bunsay Downs Little Baddow Rd CM9 6RW
01245 222648 Fax 01245 223989
Attractive 9-hole public course. Also Par 3 course.
9 holes, 2932yds, Par 70, SSS 68.
Badgers: 9 holes, 1319yds, Par 54.
Club membership 400.
Visitors no restrictions.
Societies Mon-Fri only. Must contact in advance.
Green Fees not confirmed.
Prof Mickey Walker
Facilities by prior arrangement
Hotel ★★ 64% Blue Boar Hotel, Silver St, MALDON
01621 852681 20 Annexe8

Warren CM9 6RW 01245 223258 Fax 01245 223989
Attractive parkland course with natural hazards and good views.
18 holes, 6229yds, Par 70, SSS 70, Course record 65.
Club membership 765.
Visitors contact in advance, weekend pm only, Wed pm only.
Societies arrange by telephone, confirm in writing, weekdays ex Wed.
Green Fees not confirmed.
Prof Mickey Walker
Facilities by prior arrangement
Location 0.5m SW

Hotel ★★ 64% Blue Boar Hotel, Silver St, MALDON
01621 852681 20 Annexe8

GLOUCESTERSHIRE

CHELTENHAM Map 03 SO92

Cotswold Hills Ullenwood GL53 9QT
01242 515264 Fax 01242 515263/4
A gently undulating course with open aspects and views of the Cotswolds.
18 holes, 6889yds, Par 71, SSS 74.
Club membership 750.
Visitors telephone in advance, handicap certificate preferred.
Societies must apply in writing or telephone.
Green Fees £30 per day: £24 per round (£36/£30 Sundays).
Cards
Prof Noel Boland
Designer M D Little
Facilities
Location 3m SE on A435 and A436

Hotel B Forte Posthouse Gloucester, Crest Way, Barnwood, GLOUCESTER
01452 613311 123

Lilley Brook Cirencester Rd, Charlton Kings GL53 8EG
01242 526785 Fax 01242 256880
Undulating parkland course. Magnificent views over Cheltenham and surrounding coutryside.
18 holes, 6212yds, Par 69, SSS 70, Course record 61.
Club membership 800.
Visitors advisable to enquire of availability.
Societies apply in writing.
Green Fees £30 per day; £25 round (£35/£30 weekends).
Prof Forbes Hadden
Designer Mackenzie
Facilities
Location 2m S of Cheltenham on A435

Hotel ★★★★ 66% Cheltenham Park Hotel, Cirencester Rd, Charlton Kings, CHELTENHAM
☎ 01242 222021 144

Shipton Shipton Oliffe, Andoverford GL54 4HT
☎ 01242 890237 Fax 01242 820336
Deceptive, easy walking course situated in the heart of the Cotswolds and providing a fair challenge and panoramic views.
9 holes, 2516yds, Par 34, Course record 33.
Visitors pay & play course no bookings taken.
Societies welcome.
Green Fees £6 per 9 holes, 2nd round £3 (£7 weekends; 2nd round £3).
Facilities
Location On A436, south of junct with A40

Hotel ★★★ 62% The Frogmill, Shipton Oliffe, Andoversford, CHELTENHAM
☎ 01242 820547 11 Annexe5

CHIPPING SODBURY Map 03 ST78

Chipping Sodbury BS17 6PU ☎ 01454 319042
Parkland courses of Championship proportions. The old course may be seen from the large opening tee by the clubhouse at the top of the hill. Two huge drainage dykes cut through the course and form a distinctive hazard on eleven holes.
New Course: 18 holes, 6912yds, Par 73, SSS 73, Course record 65.
Old Course: 9 holes, 6184yds, Par 70, SSS 69.
Club membership 800.
Visitors no restriction on Old Course, must have a handicap certificate and may only play until after noon at weekends on New Course.
Societies must contact in writing.
Green Fees not confirmed.
Prof Mike Watts
Designer Hawtree
Facilities
Location 0.5m N

Hotel ★★ 61% Cross Hands Hotel, OLD SODBURY
☎ 01454 313000 24rm(3 17)

CIRENCESTER Map 04 SP00

Cirencester Cheltenham Rd, Bagendon GL7 7BH
☎ 01285 653939 Fax 01285 650665
Undulating Cotswold course.
18 holes, 6020yds, Par 70, SSS 69.
Club membership 800.
Visitors restricted play at weekends, contact professional shop in advance.
Societies telephone Secretary/Manager.
Green Fees £25 per day; £20 per round (£30/£25 weekends & bank holidays).
Prof Peter Garratt
Designer J Braid
Facilities
Location 2 N on A435

Hotel ★★★ 69% Stratton House Hotel, Gloucester Rd, CIRENCESTER ☎ 01285 651761 41

CLEEVE HILL Map 03 SO92

Cleeve Hill GL52 3PW ☎ 01242 672025
Undulating and open heathland course affected by crosswinds.
18 holes, 6411yds, Par 72, SSS 71, Course record 69.
Club membership 450.
Visitors bookings taken 7 days in advance. Limited play weekends.
Societies telephone in advance.
Green Fees £10 per day (£12 weekends & bank holidays).
Prof Richard Jenkins
Facilities
Location 1m NE on B4632

Hotel ★★★ 65% Rising Sun Hotel, CLEEVE HILL
☎ 01242 676281 24

COLEFORD Map 03 SO51

Forest Hills Mile End Rd GL16 7BY ☎ 01594 810620
A parkland course on a plateau with panoramic views of Coleford and Forest of Dean. Some testing holes with the par-5 13th hole sitting tight on a water hazard, and the challenging 18th with 2nd shot over large pond to a green protected by another pond and bunker - all in front of the clubhouse.
18 holes, 6740yds, Par 68, SSS 68, Course record 64.
Visitors no restrictions.
Societies contact in advance.
Green Fees £13 per round (£15 weekends).
Cards
Prof J Nicholl
Designer A Stiff ▶

Facilities
Hotel ★★★ 65% The Speech House, Forest Of Dean, COLEFORD ☎ 01594 822607 14

Forest of Dean Lords Hill GL16 8BD
☎ 01594 832583 Fax 01594 832584
Established in 1973 and now matured into an extremely pleasant parkland course. Well bunkered with light rough, a few blind tee shots and water in play on several holes.
18 holes, 6033yds, Par 70, SSS 69.
Club membership 500.
Visitors are required to book tee-off times.
Societies must telephone in advance.
Green Fees £16.50 per round (£18.50 weekends & bank holidays).
Cards
Prof Philip Worthing
Designer John Day
Facilities
& Leisure hard tennis courts.
Location 0.25m from Coleford town centre on B4431 Coleford to Parkend road

Hotel ★★★ 65% The Speech House, Forest Of Dean, COLEFORD ☎ 01594 822607 14

DURSLEY Map 03 ST79

Stinchcombe Hill Stinchcombe Hill GL11 6AQ
☎ 01453 542015 Fax 01453 549545
High on the hill with splendid views of the Cotswolds, the River Severn and the Welsh hills. A downland course with good turf, some trees and an interesting variety of greens. Protected greens make this a challenging course in windy conditions.
18 holes, 5734yds, Par 68, SSS 68, Course record 63.
Club membership 550.
Visitors restricted at weekends. Must contact professional in advance 01453 543878.
Societies must apply in advance.
Green Fees not confirmed.
Prof Paul Bushell
Designer Arthur Hoare
Facilities
Location 1m W off A4135

Hotel ★★★ 61% Prince Of Wales Hotel, BERKELEY ☎ 01453 810474 43

GLOUCESTER Map 03 SO81

Brickhampton Court Cheltenham Rd, Churchdown GL2 9QF ☎ 01452 859444 Fax 01452 859333
27 holes, including the county's first intermediate course (9-hole par 31) for the new and developing golfer, set in undulating parkland. The Spa course offers a good golfing challenge, featuring lakes, streams and well placed bunkers.
Spa: 18 holes, 6449yds, Par 71, SSS 71.
Glevum: 9 holes, 1859yds, Par 31.
Club membership 650.
Visitors advance booking recommended, recognised golfing attire to be worn and evidence of golfing ability preferred.
Societies contact for information and booking form.
Green Fees Spa: £25 per day; £16 per round (£30/£22.50 weekends). Glevum: £10 per 18 holes; £6.50 per 9 holes (£12/£8 weekends).
Cards
Prof David Finch
Designer Simon Gidman
Facilities
Location Junct 11 M5, A40 towards Gloucester, at Elmbridge Court rdbt B4063 signed Churchdown, approx 2m

Hotel ★★★ 62% Hatherley Manor Hotel, Down Hatherley Ln, GLOUCESTER ☎ 01452 730217 56

Jarvis Gloucester Hotel & Country Club Matson Ln, Robinswood Hill GL4 6EA ☎ 01452 411331
Undulating, wooded course, built around a hill with superb views over Gloucester and the Cotswolds. The 12th is a drive straight up a hill, nicknamed 'Coronary Hill'.
18 holes, 6170yds, Par 70, SSS 69, Course record 65.
Club membership 600.
Visitors can book up to 7 days in advance.
Societies telephone in advance.
Green Fees not confirmed.
Prof Peter Darnell
Facilities
& Leisure hard tennis courts, heated indoor swimming pool, squash, sauna, solarium, gymnasium.
Location 2.5m SE of Gloucester, off B4073

Hotel ★★★ 76% Hatton Court, Upton Hill, Upton St Leonards, GLOUCESTER ☎ 01452 617412 17 Annexe28

Rodway Hill Newent Rd, Highnam GL2 8DN
☎ 01452 384222
A challenging 18-hole course with superb panoramic views. Testing front 5 holes and the par 3 13th and par 5 16th being affected by strong croswinds off the River Severn.
18 holes, 5860yds, Par 70, SSS 68, Course record 69.
Club membership 400.
Visitors no restrictions.
Societies telephone in advance.
Green Fees £15 per day; £9 per 18 holes; £7 per 9 holes (£12 per 18 holes/£8 per 9 holes).
Cards
Prof Tony Grubb
Designer John Gabb
Facilities
Location 2m outside Gloucester on B4215

Hotel ★★★ 62% Hatherley Manor Hotel, Down Hatherley Ln, GLOUCESTER ☎ 01452 730217 56

LYDNEY Map 03 SO60

Lydney Lakeside Av GL15 5QA ☎ 01594 842614
Flat parkland/meadowland course with prevailing wind along fairways.
9 holes, 5298yds, Par 66, SSS 66, Course record 63.
Club membership 350.
Visitors with member only at weekends & bank holidays.
Societies apply in writing to the Secretary.
Green Fees £10 per day.

Facilities
Location SE side of town centre

Hotel ★★★ 65% The Speech House, Forest Of Dean, COLEFORD ☎ 01594 822607 14

MINCHINHAMPTON Map 03 SO80

Minchinhampton (New Course) New Course GL6 9BE
☎ 01453 833866 Fax 01453 833860
The Cherington course is set in undulating upland. Large contoured greens, pot bunkers, and, at times, a stiff breeze present a very fair test of skill. The Avening course has a variety of holes including water on the 10th and 13th.
Avening: 18 holes, 6279yds, Par 70, SSS 70, Course record 65.
Cherington: 18 holes, 6320yds, Par 71, SSS 70.
Club membership 1200.

Visitors must contact in advance.
Societies must contact by telephone.
Green Fees £25 per day; (£30 weekends & bank holidays).
Prof Chris Steele
Designer Hawtree & Son
Facilities
Location 2m SE

Hotel ★★★ 67% Burleigh Court, Minchinhampton, STROUD
☎ 01453 883804 11 Annexe6

Minchinhampton (Old Course) Old Course GL6 9AQ
☎ 01453 832642 & 836382
An open grassland course 600 feet above sea level. The numerous humps and hollows around the greens tests the golfer's ability to play a variety of shots - often in difficult windy conditions. Panoramic Cotswold views.
18 holes, 6019yds, Par 71, SSS 69.
Club membership 700.

Visitors must contact in advance.
Societies must contact by telephone.
Green Fees £10 weekdays (£13 weekends & bank holdays).
Facilities
Location 1m NW

Hotel ★★★ 67% Burleigh Court, Minchinhampton, STROUD ☎ 01453 883804 11 Annexe6

NAUNTON Map 04 SP12

Naunton Downs GL54 3AE ☎ 01451 850090
New in 1993, Naunton Downs course plays over beautiful Cotswold countryside. A valley running through the course is one of the main features, creating 1 par 3 hole that crosses over it. The prevailing wind adds extra challenge to the par 5's (which play into the wind), combined with small undulating greens.
18 holes, 6078yds, Par 71, SSS 69, Course record 73.
Club membership 900.

Visitors must contact in advance.
Societies telephone for details.
Green Fees £19.95 per round (£25 weekends).
Prof Martin Seddon
Designer J Pott
Facilities
& Leisure hard tennis courts.
Location B4068 Stow/Cheltenham

Hotel ★★★ 77% Lords of the Manor, UPPER SLAUGHTER
☎ 01451 820243 28

PAINSWICK Map 03 SO80

Painswick GL6 6TL ☎ 01452 812180
Downland course set on Cotswold Hills at Painswick Beacon, with fine views. Short course more than compensated by natural hazards and tight fairways.
18 holes, 4895yds, Par 67, SSS 65, Course record 61.
Club membership 480.

Visitors member only on Sun.
Societies must apply in advance.
Green Fees £20 per day; £15 per round.
Cards
Facilities
Location 1m N on A46

Hotel ★★★ 75% Painswick Hotel, Kemps Ln, PAINSWICK ☎ 01452 812160 19

TEWKESBURY Map 03 SO83

Stakis Puckrup Hall Hotel Puckrup GL20 6EL
☎ 01684 296200 Fax 01684 850788
Set in 140 acres of undulating parkland with lakes, existing trees and marvellous views of the Malvern hills. There are water hazards at the 5th and a cluster of bunkers on the long 14th before the challenging tee shot across the water to the par-3 18th.
18 holes, 6189yds, Par 70, SSS 70.
Club membership 500.

Visitors must be a regular golfer familiar with rules and etiquette, must book a tee time, may book up to 5 days in advance.
Societies telephone in advance.
Green Fees £30 per day; £25 per round (£35/£30 weekends).
Cards
Prof Kevin Pickett

Designer Simon Gidman
Facilities
& Leisure heated indoor swimming pool, sauna, solarium, gymnasium.
Location 4m N, on main A38

Hotel ★★★ 71% Old Schoolhouse Hotel & Restaurant, SEVERN STOKE ☎ 01905 371368 & 371464 Fax 01905 371591 13

Tewkesbury Park Hotel Golf & Country Club Lincoln Green Ln GL20 7DN
☎ 01684 295405 Fax 01684 292386
A parkland course overlooking the Abbey and rivers Avon and Severn. The par 3, 5th is an exciting hole calling for accurate distance judgment. The hotel and country club offer many sports and club facilities including a well equipped gym with cardio theatre.
18 holes, 6533yds, Par 73, SSS 72, Course record 66.
Club membership 650.

Visitors must book in advance via pro shop/hotel reservations.
Societies telephone initially.
Green Fees £20 per round (£25 weekend).
Cards
Prof Robert Taylor
Facilities
& Leisure hard tennis courts, heated indoor swimming pool, squash, sauna, solarium, gymnasium.
Location 1m SW off A38

Hotel ★★★ 68% Tewkesbury Park Hotel, Lincoln Green Ln, TEWKESBURY ☎ 01684 295405 78

THORNBURY Map 03 ST69

Thornbury Golf Centre Bristol Rd BS35 3XL
☎ 01454 281144 Fax 01454 281177
Two 18 hole pay & play courses designed by Hawtree and set in undulating terrain with estensive views towards the Severn estuary. The Low 18 is a Par 3 with holes ranging from 80 to 207 yards and is ideal for beginners. The High course puts to test the more experienced golfer. Excellent 25 bay floodlit driving range.
High Course: 18 holes, 6154yds, Par 71, SSS 69.
Low Course: 18 holes, 2195yds, Par 54.
Club membership 420.
Visitors must contact in advance.
Societies apply in writing for brochure.
Green Fees £23 per day; £14 per round £8.30 (£26/£16/£9 weekends).
Cards

Prof Simon Hubbard
Designer Hawtree
Facilities
& Leisure putting green.
Location Off A38

Hotel ★★★ Thornbury Castle, Castle St, THORNBURY ☎ 01454 281182 18

WESTONBIRT Map 03 ST88

Westonbirt Westonbirt School GL8 8QG ☎ 01666 880242
A parkland course with good views.
9 holes, 4504yds, Par 64, SSS 64.
Club membership 150.
Visitors no restrictions.
Societies no reserved tees.
Green Fees £7.50 per round.
Facilities
Location E side of village off A433

Hotel ★★★ 67% Hare & Hounds Hotel, Westonbirt, TETBURY
☎ 01666 880233 22 Annexe8

WICK Map 03 ST77

Tracy Park Tracy Park, Bath Rd BS30 5RN
☎ 0117 937 2251 Fax 0117 937 4288
Three undulating 9-hole parkland courses situated on the south-western escarpment of the Cotswolds, affording fine views. Whichever 18-hole combination is played, the variety of holes will ensure an enjoyable and

interesting challenge to all levels of handicap. Natural water hazards affect a number of holes. The clubhouse dates back to 1600 and is a building of great beauty and elegance, set in the 220 acre estate of this golf and country club.
Avon Course: 9 holes, 3091yds, Par 35, SSS 35.
Bristol Course: 9 holes, 3332yds, Par 35, SSS 35.
Cotswold Course: 9 holes, 3098yds, Par 35, SSS 35.
Club membership 900.

Visitors no restrictions.
Societies must telephone or write to Graham Packer.
Green Fees £24 per day/round (£30 weekends).
Cards
Prof Richard Berry
Designer Grant Aitken
Facilities
& Leisure hard tennis courts, squash.
Location S side of village off A420

Hotel ★★★ The Queensberry Hotel, Russel St, BATH ☎ 01225 447928 22

WOTTON-UNDER-EDGE Map 03 ST79

Cotswold Edge Upper Rushmire GL12 7PT
☎ 01453 844167 Fax 01453 845120
Meadowland course situated in a quiet Cotswold valley with magnificent views. First half flat and open, second half more varied.
18 holes, 6170yds, Par 71, SSS 71.
Club membership 800.

Visitors preferable to contact in advance, at weekends may only play with member.
Societies must contact in writing or telephone in advance.
Green Fees £15 per day/round.
Prof David Gosling
Facilities
Location N of town on B4058 Wotton-Tetbury road

Hotel ★★ 70% Egypt Mill Hotel, NAILSWORTH ☎ 01453 833449 8 Annexe10

GREATER LONDON

Those courses which fall within the confines of the London Postal District area (ie have London postcodes - W1, SW1 etc) are listed under the county heading of **London** in the gazetteer (see page 180).

ADDINGTON Map 05 TQ36

The Addington 205 Shirley Church Rd CR0 5AB
☎ 0181 777 1055
A world of heather, bracken, silver birch and pine referred to by Henry Longhurst as his favourite inland course. It is one where thought is required at every hole.
18 holes, 6242yds, Par 71, SSS 71, Course record 66.

Visitors may not play weekends. Must belong to recognised club.
Societies weekdays only, telephone for prior arrangement.
Green Fees £35 per day weekdays only.
Designer Abercromby
Facilities
& Leisure practice area.
Hotel ★★★★ 69% Croydon Park Hotel, 7 Altyre Rd, CROYDON ☎ 0181 680 9200 211

Addington Court Featherbed Ln CR0 9AA
☎ 0181 657 0281 Fax 0181 651 0282
Challenging, well-drained courses designed by F. Hawtree. Two 18-hole courses, 9-hole course and a pitch-and-putt course designed to suit all standards.
Championship Course: 18 holes, 5577yds, Par 68, SSS 67, Course record 60.
Falconwood: 18 holes, 5360yds, Par 68, SSS 67, Course record 62.
9 Hole: 9 holes, 1733yds, Par 31.
Club membership 350.

Visitors no restrictions. Advisable to phone in advance to play on Old Course.
Societies must telephone in advance.
Green Fees Championship: £14 (£15 weekends); Falconwood: £11 (£13 weekends); 9 hole £6; Pitch & putt £3.
Cards
Prof Russ Critcher
Designer Hawtree Snr
Facilities
Location 1m S off A2022

Hotel ★★★★ 70% Selsdon Park Hotel, Addington Rd, Sanderstead, CROYDON ☎ 0181 657 8811 170

Addington Palace Addington Park, Gravel Hill CR0 5BB
☎ 0181 654 3061 Fax 0181 655 3632
Hard-walking parkland course, with two (par 4) testing holes (2nd and 10th).
18 holes, 6286yds, Par 71, SSS 71, Course record 63.
Club membership 700.

Visitors telephone in advance, must play with member at weekends & bank holidays.
Societies Tue, Wed & Fri only, telephone in advance.
Green Fees not confirmed.
Prof Roger Williams ▶

Designer	J H Taylor
Facilities	⊗
Location	0.5m SW on A212

Hotel ★★★★ 70% Selsdon Park Hotel, Addington Rd, Sanderstead, CROYDON ☎ 0181 657 8811 170

BARNEHURST — Map 05 TQ57

Barnehurst Mayplace Rd East DA7 6JU
☎ 01322 523746 Fax 01322 554612
Public parkland course with well matured greens. Easy walking.
9 holes, 5320yds, Par 66, SSS 66.
Club membership 300.

Visitors	restricted Tue, Thu, Sat (pm) & Sun.
Societies	by arrangement.
Green Fees	£7.50 per 9 holes (£10.20 weekends & bank holidays).
Facilities	⊗
Location	0.75m NW of Crayford off A2000

Hotel B Forte Posthouse Bexley, Black Prince Interchange, Southwold Rd, BEXLEY ☎ 01322 526900 103

BARNET — Map 04 TQ29

Arkley Rowley Green Rd EN5 3HL
☎ 0181 449 0394 Fax 0181 440 5214
Wooded parkland course situated on highest spot in Hertfordshire with fine views.
18 holes, 6117yds, Par 69, SSS 69.
Club membership 450.

Visitors	may play weekdays only (ex Tue).
Societies	must contact in advance.
Green Fees	£20 per day/round.
Prof	Martin Porter
Designer	Braid
Facilities	⊗
Location	Off A1 at Arkley sign

Hotel ★★★ 73% Edgwarebury Hotel, Barnet Ln, ELSTREE ☎ 0181 953 8227 47

Dyrham Park Country Club Galley Ln EN5 4RA
☎ 0181 440 3361 Fax 0181 441 9836
Parkland course.
18 holes, 6369yds, Par 71, SSS 70, Course record 65.
Club membership 1200.

Visitors	must be guest of member.
Societies	Wed only, must book in advance.
Green Fees	not confirmed.
Prof	Bill Large
Facilities	⊗ (all day)
& Leisure	hard tennis courts, heated outdoor swimming pool, fishing, caddies available.
Location	3m NW off A1081

Hotel B Forte Posthouse South Mimms, SOUTH MIMMS ☎ 01707 643311 120

Old Fold Manor Old Fold Ln, Hadley Green EN5 4QN
☎ 0181 440 9185 Fax 0181 441 4863
Heathland course, good test of golf.
18 holes, 6481yds, Par 71, SSS 71, Course record 66.
Club membership 520.

Visitors	with member only weekends & bank holidays.
Societies	must apply in writing.
Green Fees	£27 per 36 holes; £20 per 18 holes; Public Days Mon/Wed £11 per round.
Prof	Garry Potter
Facilities	⊗ (ex Mon & Wed)
& Leisure	snooker.
Location	Off A1000 between Barnet/Potters Bar

Hotel ★★★★ 69% West Lodge Park Hotel, Cockfosters Rd, HADLEY WOOD ☎ 0181 440 8311 44 Annexe2

BECKENHAM — Map 05 TQ36

Beckenham Place Park The Mansion, Beckenham Place Park BR3 2BP ☎ 0181 650 2292 Fax 0181 663 1201
Picturesque course in the grounds of a public park. The course varies from open to tight surroundings with the back nine providing a challenge for both the novice and low handicapper. A water-filled ditch comes into play on several holes.
18 holes, 5722yds, Par 68, SSS 68.

Visitors	booked tee times operate contact for details.
Societies	apply in writing or telephone for Society pack.
Green Fees	not confirmed.
Prof	How Davis-Thomas
Facilities	⊗
& Leisure	hard tennis courts.
Location	Main Catford/Beckenham road, just off A21

Hotel ★★★ 69% Bromley Court Hotel, Bromley Hill, BROMLEY ☎ 0181 464 5011 116

Langley Park Barnfield Wood Rd BR3 6SZ
☎ 0181 658 6849
This is a pleasant, but difficult, well-wooded, parkland course with natural hazards including a lake at the 18th hole.
18 holes, 6488yds, Par 69, SSS 71, Course record 65.
Club membership 700.

Visitors	must contact in advance and may not play weekends.
Societies	Wed & Thu only, telephone to book.
Green Fees	£25-£35 per day/round.
Prof	Colin Staff
Designer	J H Taylor
Facilities	⊗ by prior arrangement
Location	0.5 N on B2015

Hotel ★★★ 69% Bromley Court Hotel, Bromley Hill, BROMLEY ☎ 0181 464 5011 116

BEXLEYHEATH — Map 05 TQ47

Bexleyheath Mount Rd DA6 8JS
☎ 0181 303 6951
Undulating course.
9 holes, 5162yds, Par 66, SSS 66, Course record 65.
Club membership 330.

Visitors	must contact Secretary in advance, may not play weekends.
Societies	telephone in advance.

Green Fees not confirmed.
Facilities
Location 1m SW

Hotel B Forte Posthouse Bexley, Black Prince Interchange, Southwold Rd, BEXLEY ☎ 01322 526900 103

BIGGIN HILL Map 05 TQ45

Cherry Lodge Jail Ln TN16 3AX
☎ 01959 572250 Fax 01959 540672
Undulating parkland course set 600feet above sea level with panoramic views of the surrounding Kent countryside. An enjoyable test of golf for all standards. The 14th is 434 yards across a valley and uphill, requiring two good shots to reach the green.
18 holes, 6652yds, Par 72, SSS 73, Course record 69.
Club membership 700.
Visitors must contact in advance but may not play at weekends.
Societies must telephone in advance.
Green Fees £30 per day; £25 per round.
Prof Nigel Child
Designer John Day
Facilities
& Leisure sauna.
Location 1m E

Hotel ★★★ 68% Kings Arms Hotel, Market Square, WESTERHAM ☎ 01959 562990 17

BROMLEY Map 05 TQ46

Bromley Magpie Hall Ln BR2 8JF ☎ 0181 462 7014
Flat course, ideal for beginners.
9 holes, 2745yds, Par 70, SSS 67.
Visitors no restrictions.
Societies apply in writing.
Green Fees £5 per 9 holes (£6.50 weekends & bank holidays).
Prof Danny Williams
Facilities
Location 2m SE off A21

Hotel ★★★ 69% Bromley Court Hotel, Bromley Hill, BROMLEY ☎ 0181 464 5011 116

Shortlands Meadow Rd, Shortlands BR2 0PB
☎ 0181 460 8828
Easy walking parkland course with a brook as a natural hazard.
9 holes, 5261yds, Par 65, SSS 66, Course record 59.
Club membership 410.
Visitors must be guest of member.
Green Fees not confirmed.
Prof John Murray
Facilities
Location 0.75m W off A222

Hotel ★★★ 69% Bromley Court Hotel, Bromley Hill, BROMLEY ☎ 0181 464 5011 116

A comprehensive list of driving ranges is given at the back of this guide. See page 479

Sundridge Park Garden Rd BR1 3NE
☎ 0181 460 0278 Fax 0181 289 3050
The East course is longer than the West but many think the shorter of the two courses is the more difficult. The East is surrounded by trees while the West is more hilly, with good views. Both are certainly a good test of golf.
East Course: 18 holes, 6516yds, Par 71, SSS 71, Course record 63.
West Course: 18 holes, 6019yds, Par 69, SSS 69, Course record 65.
Club membership 1200.
Visitors may only play on weekdays. Must contact in advance and must have a handicap certificate. No advance booking necessary.
Societies must contact well in advance.
Green Fees £40 per day.
Prof Bob Cameron
Designer Willie Park
Facilities
Location N side of town centre off A2212

Hotel ★★★ 69% Bromley Court Hotel, Bromley Hill, BROMLEY ☎ 0181 464 5011 116

CARSHALTON Map 04 TQ26

Oaks Sports Centre Woodmansterne Rd SM5 4AN
☎ 0181 643 8363 Fax 0181 770 7303
Public parkland course with floodlit, covered driving range.
18 Holes: 18 holes, 6025yds, Par 70, SSS 69, Course record 65.
The Oaks: 9 holes, 1443yds, Par 28, SSS 28.
Club membership 864.

Visitors no restrictions.
Societies must apply in writing.
Green Fees 18 Hole: £12 per round (£14 weekends). The Oaks: £5.65 per round (£6.60 weekends).
Prof Horley/Russell/Pilkington
Facilities
& Leisure squash.
Location 0.5m S on B278

Hotel B Forte Posthouse Croydon, Purley Way, CROYDON ☎ 0181 688 5185 83

CHESSINGTON Map 04 TQ16

Chessington Garrison Ln KT9 2LW
☎ 0181 391 0948 Fax 0181 397 2068
Tree-lined parkland course designed by Patrick Tallack. ▶

9 holes, 1400yds, Par 27, SSS 28.
Club membership 100.
Visitors must book 7.30am-noon weekends only.
Societies must telephone 1 month in advance.
Green Fees not confirmed.
Designer Patrick Tallack
Facilities
Location Opposite Chessington South Station nr Zoo

Hotel ★★ 65% Haven Hotel, Portsmouth Rd, ESHER
☎ 0181 398 0023 16 Annexe4

CHISLEHURST Map 05 TQ47

Chislehurst Camden Park Rd BR7 5HJ
☎ 0181 467 2782 Fax 0181 295 0974
Pleasantly wooded undulating parkland/heathland course. Magnificent clubhouse with historical associations.
18 holes, 5106yds, Par 66, SSS 65, Course record 61.
Club membership 800.
Visitors with member only weekends.
Societies weekdays only.
Green Fees £25 per round/day.
Prof Mark Lawrence
Designer Park
Facilities by prior arrangement
Hotel ★★★ 69% Bromley Court Hotel, Bromley Hill, BROMLEY ☎ 0181 464 5011 116

COULSDON Map 04 TQ25

Coulsdon Manor Hotel Coulsdon Court Rd CR5 2LL
☎ 0181 660 6083 Fax 0181 668 3118
Set in its own 140 acres of landscaped parkland.
18 holes, 6037yds, Par 70, SSS 68.
Visitors must telephone up to 5 days in advance.
Societies by arrangement.
Green Fees £14 per round (£17 weekends & bank holidays).
Cards
Prof David Copsey
Designer Harry Colt
Facilities
& Leisure hard tennis courts, squash, sauna, solarium, gymnasium.
Location 0.75m E off A23 on B2030

Hotel ★★★★ 77% Coulsdon Manor Hotel, Coulsdon Court Rd, Coulsdon, CROYDON
☎ 0181 668 0414 35

Woodcote Park Meadow Hill, Bridle Way CR5 2QQ
☎ 0181 668 2788 Fax 0181 668 2788
Slightly undulating parkland course.
18 holes, 6669yds, Par 71, SSS 72, Course record 66.
Club membership 650.
Visitors handicap certificate required, contact professional for details. Visitors may not play weekends.
Societies must contact Secretary in advance.
Green Fees £40 per day; £30 per round.
Prof D Hudspith
Facilities
Location 1m N of town centre off A237

Hotel B Forte Posthouse Croydon, Purley Way, CROYDON ☎ 0181 688 5185 83

CROYDON Map 04 TQ36

Croham Hurst Croham Rd CR2 7HJ
☎ 0181 657 5581 Fax 0181 657 3229
Parkland course with tree-lined fairways and bounded by wooded hills. Easy walking.
18 holes, 6290yds, Par 70, SSS 70.
Club membership 800.
Visitors must contact in advance & have handicap certificate. With member only weekends & bank holidays.
Societies must book 1 year in advance.
Green Fees £33 per 18 holes (£42 weekends & bank holidays).
Prof Eric Stillwell
Facilities
Location 1.5m SE, between South Croydon and Selsdon on B269

Hotel ★★★★ 70% Selsdon Park Hotel, Addington Rd, Sanderstead, CROYDON
☎ 0181 657 8811 170

Selsdon Park Addington Rd, Sanderstead CR2 8YA
☎ 0181 657 8811 Fax 0181 651 6171
Parkland course. Full use of hotel's sporting facilities by residents.
18 holes, 6473yds, Par 73, SSS 71.
Visitors welcome, booking advisable, booking 1 week in advance for weekends.
Societies telephone in advance.
Green Fees £25 (£30 weekends).
Cards
Prof Malcolm Churchill
Designer J H Taylor
Facilities
& Leisure hard and grass tennis courts, outdoor and indoor heated swimming pools, squash, sauna, solarium, gymnasium.
Location 3m S on A2022

Hotel ★★★★ 70% Selsdon Park Hotel, Addington Rd, Sanderstead, CROYDON
☎ 0181 657 8811 170

Shirley Park 194 Addiscombe Rd CR0 7LB
☎ 0181 654 1143
This parkland course lies amid fine woodland with good views of Shirley Hills. The more testing holes come in the middle section of the course. The remarkable 7th hole calls for a 187-yard iron or wood shot diagonally across a narrow valley to a shelved green set right-handed into a ridge. The redesigned 13th hole, 160yds, is considered to be one of the finest short holes in the county.
18 holes, 6210yds, Par 71, SSS 70, Course record 66.
Club membership 600.
Visitors should contact in advance. With member only at weekends.
Societies by arrangement.
Green Fees £30 per day/round weekdays (£20 winter).
Prof Paul Webb
Facilities by prior arrangement
Location E side of town centre on A232

Hotel	★★★★ 69% Croydon Park Hotel, 7 Altyre Rd, CROYDON ☎ 0181 680 9200 211

DOWNE Map 05 TQ46

High Elms High Elms Rd BR6 7JL
☎ 01689 853232 & 858175 bookings
Municipal parkland course. Very tight 13th, 230 yds (par 3).
18 holes, 6210yds, Par 71, SSS 70, Course record 68.
Club membership 450.

Visitors no restrictions.
Societies telephone to book. Tel 01689 861813.
Green Fees £10 per 18 holes (£13 weekends & bank holidays).
Prof Peter Remy
Designer Hawthorn
Facilities
& Leisure putting green, practice area.
Location 1.5m NE

Hotel ★★★ 69% Bromley Court Hotel, Bromley Hill, BROMLEY ☎ 0181 464 5011 116

West Kent West Hill BR6 7JJ ☎ 01689 851323
Fax 01689 858693
Partly hilly downland course.
18 holes, 6399yds, Par 70, SSS 70.
Club membership 700.

Visitors with member only at weekends. Must contact in advance.
Societies must apply in writing.
Green Fees £26 per round.
Prof Roger Fidler
Facilities
& Leisure practice area.
Location 0.75m SW

Hotel ★★★ 69% Bromley Court Hotel, Bromley Hill, BROMLEY ☎ 0181 464 5011 116

ENFIELD Map 04 TQ39

Crews Hill Cattlegate Rd, Crews Hill EN2 8AZ
☎ 0181 363 6674 Fax 0181 364 5641
Parkland course in country surroundings.
18 holes, 6250yds, Par 70, SSS 70, Course record 65.
Club membership 600.

Visitors must play with member at weekends. Handicap certificate required.
Societies Wed-Fri; must apply in writing.

Green Fees on application.
Prof Neil Wichelow
Designer Harry Colt
Facilities
Location 3m NW off A1005

Hotel ★★ 70% Oak Lodge Hotel, 80 Village Rd, Bush Hill Park, ENFIELD ☎ 0181 360 7082 5

Enfield Old Park Rd South EN2 7DA
☎ 0181 363 3970 Fax 0181 342 0381
Parkland course. Salmons Brook crosses 7 holes.
18 holes, 6154yds, Par 72, SSS 70, Course record 61.
Club membership 700.

Visitors Mon & Wed-Fri only, must contact in advance & have handicap certificate from an approved golf club.
Societies must contact the secretary in advance.
Green Fees £35 per day; £25 per round (under review).
Prof Lee Fickling
Designer James Braid
Facilities
Location M25 jnct 24, A1005 to Enfield to rdbt with church on left, right down Slades Hill, 1st left to end

Hotel ★★ 70% Oak Lodge Hotel, 80 Village Rd, Bush Hill Park, ENFIELD ☎ 0181 360 7082 5

Whitewebbs Municipal Beggars Hollow, Clay Hill EN2 9JN
☎ 0181 363 4454
Flat wooded parkland course. 9th hole is a left-hand dog-leg with second shot over a brook.
18 holes, 5863yds, Par 68, SSS 68, Course record 61.
Club membership 350.

Visitors can play all times, can book in advance
Societies must apply in writing to Course Manager
Green Fees not confirmed.
Prof Peter Garlick
Facilities
Location N side of town centre

Hotel ★★ 70% Oak Lodge Hotel, 80 Village Rd, Bush Hill Park, ENFIELD ☎ 0181 360 7082 5

GREENFORD Map 04 TQ18

C & L Golf & Country Club Westend Rd, Northolt UB5 6RD ☎ 0181 845 5662
Parkland course.
18 holes, 4438yds, Par 64, SSS 63.
Club membership 150.

Visitors welcome, but may not play Sun mornings.
Societies contact for details.
Green Fees not confirmed.
Prof Richard Kelly
Designer Patrick Tallack
Facilities
& Leisure hard tennis courts, outdoor swimming pool, squash, sauna, solarium, gymnasium.
Location Junct Westend Road/A40

Hotel ★★★ 71% The Bridge Hotel, Western Av, GREENFORD ☎ 0181 566 6246 68

Ealing Perivale Ln UB6 8SS
☎ 0181 997 0937 Fax 0181 998 0756
Flat, parkland course relying on natural hazards; trees, tight fairways, and the River Brent which affects 9 holes.
18 holes, 6216yds, Par 70, SSS 70, Course record 64.
Club membership 700.

Visitors Mon-Fri only on application to pro shop.
Societies Mon, Wed & Thu only by arrangement.
Green Fees on application.
Prof Ian Parsons
Designer H S Colt
Facilities
Location Off A40 travelling W from London

Hotel ★★★ 71% The Bridge Hotel, Western Av, GREENFORD ☎ 0181 566 6246 68

Horsenden Hill Whitten Av, Woodland Rise UB6 0RD
☎ 0181 902 4555
A well-kept, tree-lined short course.
9 holes, 1632yds, Par 28, SSS 28.
Club membership 135.

Visitors no restrictions.
Societies telephone for details.
Green Fees not confirmed.
Prof Simon Hoffman
Facilities
Location 3m NE on A4090

Hotel ★★★ 71% The Bridge Hotel, Western Av, GREENFORD ☎ 0181 566 6246 68

Lime Trees Park Ruislip Rd, Northolt UB5 6QZ
☎ 0181 842 0442
Parkland course.
9 holes, 5836yds, Par 71, SSS 69.
Club membership 300.

Visitors no restrictions, but advisable to book for weekends.
Societies contact for details.
Green Fees not confirmed.
Prof Ian Godleman
Facilities
Location 300yds off A40 at Polish War Memorial/A4180 towards Hayes

Hotel ★★★ 71% The Bridge Hotel, Western Av, GREENFORD ☎ 0181 566 6246 68

Perivale Park Stockdove Way UB6 8TJ ☎ 0181 575 7116
Parkland course.
9 holes, 2667yds, Par 68, SSS 67.
Club membership 250.

Visitors no restrictions.
Societies one weeks notice required.
Green Fees not confirmed.
Prof Peter Bryant
Facilities
Location E side of town centre, off A40

Hotel B Hilton National Wembley, Empire Way, WEMBLEY ☎ 0181 902 8839 306

Hadley Wood — Map 04 TQ29

Hadley Wood Beech Hill EN4 0JJ
☎ 0181 449 4328 & 4486 Fax 0181 364 8633
A parkland course on the northwest edge of London. The gently undulating fairways have a friendly width inviting the player to open his shoulders, though the thick rough can be very punishing to the unwary. The course is pleasantly wooded and there are some admirable views.
18 holes, 6457yds, Par 72, SSS 71, Course record 66.
Club membership 600.

Visitors handicap certificate required, may not play Tue mornings & Sat. Must contact in advance.
Societies must contact in advance.
Green Fees on application.
Prof Peter Jones
Designer Alistair Mackenzie
Facilities
Location E side of village

Hotel ★★★★ 69% West Lodge Park Hotel, Cockfosters Rd, HADLEY WOOD ☎ 0181 440 8311 44 Annexe2

Hampton — Map 04 TQ17

Fulwell Wellington Rd, Hampton Hill TW12 1JY
☎ 0181 977 3844 & 0181-977 2733
Championship-length parkland course with easy walking. The 575-yd, 17th, is notable.
18 holes, 6544yds, Par 71, SSS 71.
Club membership 750.

Visitors may not play Tue & weekends. Must contact in advance and have a handicap certificate.
Societies must apply in writing.
Green Fees not confirmed.
Prof Nigel Turner
Facilities
Location 1.5m N on A311

Hotel ★★★ 66% Richmond Hill, Richmond Hill, RICHMOND UPON THAMES ☎ 0181 940 2247 & 0181 940 5466 Fax 0181 9 40 5424 138

Hampton Wick — Map 04 TQ16

Home Park KT1 4AD ☎ 0181 977 2423
Flat, parkland course with easy walking.
18 holes, 6611yds, Par 71, SSS 71.
Club membership 550.

Visitors welcome all week subject to club competitions.
Societies apply in writing.
Green Fees not confirmed.
Prof Len Roberts
Facilities
Location Off A308 on W side of Kingston Bridge

Hotel ★★★ 66% Richmond Hill, Richmond Hill, RICHMOND UPON THAMES ☎ 0181 940 2247 & 0181 940 5466 Fax 0181 9 40 5424 138

HILLINGDON Map 04 TQ08

Hillingdon 18 Dorset Way UB10 0JR
01895 233956 & 239810 Fax 01895 233956
Parkland course west of London.
9 holes, 5490yds, Par 68, SSS 67.
Club membership 400.

Visitors must contact in advance. May not play Thu, weekends, or bank holidays. Handicap certificate required.
Societies must apply in writing.
Green Fees £15 per round.
Prof Neil Wichelow
Facilities
Location W side of town off A4020

Hotel ★★★ 63% Master Brewer Hotel, Freezeland Way, HILLINGDON
01895 251199 106

HOUNSLOW Map 04 TQ17

Airlinks Southall Ln TW5 9PE 0181 561 1418
Meadowland/parkland course designed by P. Allis and D. Thomas.
18 holes, 6000yds, Par 72, SSS 68, Course record 63.
Club membership 500.

Visitors may not play before noon at weekends.
Societies must apply in writing.
Green Fees not confirmed.
Prof Chris Woodcocks
Facilities
Location W of Hounslow off M4 junc 3

Hotel ★★★ 64% Master Robert Hotel, Great West Rd, HOUNSLOW 0181 570 6261 94

Hounslow Heath Municipal Staines Rd TW4 5DS
0181 570 5271
Heathland course in a conservation area, planted with an attractive variety of trees. The 15th hole lies between the fork of two rivers.
18 holes, 5901yds, Par 69, SSS 68, Course record 62.
Club membership 300.

Visitors pay & play, bookings taken for weekends & bank holidays seven days in advance.
Societies must telephone and confirm at least 14 days in advance.
Green Fees not confirmed.
Designer Fraser M Middleton
Facilities
Hotel ★★★★ 67% Forte Crest Heathrow, Sipson Rd, WEST DRAYTON
0181 759 2323 569

ILFORD Map 05 TQ48

Ilford Wanstead Park Rd IG1 3TR
0181 554 2930 Fax 0181 554 0822
Fairly flat parkland course intersected five times by a river.
18 holes, 5297yds, Par 67, SSS 66, Course record 61.
Club membership 600.

Visitors must contact in advance, book with pro on 0181 554 0094.
Societies telephone for provisional date and booking form.
Green Fees £15 per round (£20 weekends).
Cards
Prof S Dowsett
Facilities noon-10pm
Location NW side of town centre off A12

Hotel ★★★ 66% County Hotel Epping Forest, Oak Hill, WOODFORD GREEN
0181 787 9988 99

ISLEWORTH Map 04 TQ17

Wyke Green Syon Ln TW7 5PT
0181 847 0685 (Prof) Fax 0181 569 8392
Fairly flat parkland course.
18 holes, 6211yds, Par 69, SSS 70, Course record 64.
Club membership 650.

Visitors may not play before 3pm weekends and bank holidays, must have a handicap certificate or equivalent.
Societies must apply in writing or telephone in advance.
Green Fees per round Mon-Thu prior 3.30pm. £20. after 3.30pm £15; Day ticket Mon-Fri £25 (weekends and bank holidays after 4pm £20 per round.
Prof Neil Smith
Facilities
Location 1.5m N on B454 off A4

Hotel ★★★ 64% Master Robert Hotel, Great West Rd, HOUNSLOW 0181 570 6261 94

KINGSTON UPON THAMES Map 04 TQ16

Coombe Hill Golf Club Dr, Coombe Ln West KT2 7DF
0181 942 2284 Fax 0181 336 7601
A splendid course in wooded terrain. The undulations and trees make it an especially interesting course of great charm. And there is a lovely display of rhododendrons in May and June.
18 holes, 6293yds, Par 71, SSS 71, Course record 67.
Club membership 600.

Visitors must contact in advance. With member only at weekends.
Societies must book in advance.
Green Fees £65 per day/round.
Cards
Prof Craig Defoy
Designer J F Abercromby
Facilities
& Leisure sauna.
Location 1.75m E on A238

Hotel ★★★ 69% Kingston Lodge Hotel, Kingston Hill, KINGSTON UPON THAMES 0181 541 4481 62

Coombe Wood George Rd, Kingston Hill KT2 7NS
0181 942 0388 Fax 0181 942 0388
Mature parkland course with seven varied and challenging par 3's.
18 holes, 5210yds, Par 66, SSS 66, Course record 61.
Club membership 640.

Visitors must play with member at weekends.
Societies Wed, Thu & Fri; must contact in advance.

Green Fees £35 per day; £23 per round. £15 after 6pm.
Prof David Butler
Designer Tom Williamson
Facilities by prior arrangement
Location 1.25m NE on A308

Hotel ★★★ 69% Kingston Lodge Hotel, Kingston Hill, KINGSTON UPON THAMES 0181 541 4481 62

MITCHAM Map 04 TQ26

Mitcham Carshalton Rd CR4 4HN
0181 648 4280 Fax 0181 647 4197
A wooded heathland course on a gravel base.
18 holes, 5935yds, Par 69, SSS 68, Course record 65.
Club membership 500.
Visitors must telephone & book in advance, restricted play at weekends.
Societies must phone in advance.
Green Fees £13.
Prof Jeff Godfrey
Designer T Scott/T Morris
Facilities
Location 1m S

Hotel B Forte Posthouse Croydon, Purley Way, CROYDON 0181 688 5185 83

NEW MALDEN Map 04 TQ26

Malden Traps Ln KT3 4RS
0181 942 0654 Fax 0181 336 2219
Parkland course with the hazard of the Beverley Brook which affects 4 holes (3rd, 7th, 8th and 12th).
18 holes, 6295yds, Par 71, SSS 70.
Club membership 800.
Visitors restricted weekends and bank holidays. Advisable to telephone.
Societies must apply in writing.
Green Fees on application.
Prof Robert Hunter
Facilities
Location N side of town centre off B283

Hotel ★★★ 69% Kingston Lodge Hotel, Kingston Hill, KINGSTON UPON THAMES 0181 541 4481 62

NORTHWOOD Map 04 TQ09

Haste Hill The Drive HA6 1HN 01923 822877
Parkland course with stream running through. Excellent views.
18 holes, 5787yds, Par 68, SSS 68, Course record 67.
Club membership 250.
Visitors no restrictions.
Societies must apply in advance.
Green Fees not confirmed.
Cards
Facilities
Location 0.5m S off A404

Hotel ★★★ 66% Quality Harrow Hotel, Roxborough Bridge, 12-22 Pinner Rd, HARROW 0181 427 3435 54 Annexe23

Northwood Rickmansworth Rd HA6 2QW
01923 821384 Fax 01923 840150
A very old club to which, it is said, golfers used to drive from London by horse-carriage. They would find their golf interesting as present-day players do. The course is relatively flat although there are some undulations, and trees and whins add not only to the beauty of the course but also to the test of golf.
18 holes, 6553yds, Par 71, SSS 71, Course record 67.
Club membership 650.
Visitors must contact in advance. May not play weekends.
Societies must apply in writing.
Green Fees not confirmed.
Prof C J Holdsworth
Facilities
Location On main A404

Hotel ★★★ 66% Quality Harrow Hotel, Roxborough Bridge, 12-22 Pinner Rd, HARROW 0181 427 3435 54 Annexe23

Sandy Lodge Sandy Lodge Ln HA6 2JD
01923 825429 Fax 01923 824319
A links-type, very sandy, heathland course.
18 holes, 6347yds, Par 71, SSS 71, Course record 64.
Club membership 780.
Visitors must contact in advance, may not play at weekends. Handicap certificate required.
Societies must telephone in advance.
Green Fees £31.
Prof Jeff Pinsent
Designer H Vardon
Facilities
Location N side of town centre off A4125

Hotel ★★★ 64% The White House, Upton Rd, WATFORD 01923 237316 60 Annexe26

ORPINGTON Map 05 TQ46

Chelsfield Lakes Golf Centre Court Rd BR6 9BX
01689 896266 Fax 01689 824577
A downland course but some holes are played through the orchards which used to occupy the site. The 9th and 18th holes are separated by a hazardous lake.
18 holes, 6077yds, Par 71, SSS 69, Course record 64.
Club membership 438.
Visitors must book in advance.
Societies telephone in advance.
Green Fees not confirmed.
Prof N Lee/B Hodkin/D Clark
Designer M Sandow
Facilities
Location Exit M25 junct 4, on A224 Court Rd

Hotel ★★★ 69% Bromley Court Hotel, Bromley Hill, BROMLEY 0181 464 5011 116

Cray Valley Sandy Ln BR5 3HY
01689 837909 & 871490 Fax 01689 891428
An easy walking open parkland course with two man-made lakes and open ditches.

18 holes, 5669yds, Par 70, SSS 67.
Club membership 640.

Visitors no restrictions.
Societies by arrangement.
Green Fees £6-£13 per 18 holes; £5.50.per 9 holes (£9-£19/£8.20 weekends).
Cards
Prof Andy Langdon
Facilities
Location 1m off A20

Hotel ★★★ 69% Bromley Court Hotel, Bromley Hill, BROMLEY ☎ 0181 464 5011 116

Lullingstone Park Parkgate, Chelsfield BR6 7PX
☎ 01959 533793
Popular 27-hole public course set in 690 acres of undulating parkland. Championship length 18-holes, plus 9-hole course and a further 9-hole pitch and putt.
Main Course: 18 holes, 6759yds, Par 72, SSS 72, Course record 71 or 9 holes, 2432yds, Par 33, SSS 33.

Visitors telephone for details.
Societies must telephone in advance.
Green Fees not confirmed.
Prof Alan Hodgson
Facilities
Location Leave M25 junct 4 and take Well Hill turn

Hotel ★★★ 69% Bromley Court Hotel, Bromley Hill, BROMLEY ☎ 0181 464 5011 116

Ruxley Park Golf Centre Sandy Ln, St Paul's Cray BR5 3HY ☎ 01689 871490 Fax 01689 891428
Undulating parkland course with public, floodlit driving range. Difficult 6th hole, par 4. Easy walking and good views.
18 holes, 5703yds, Par 70, SSS 68, Course record 63.
Club membership 450.

Visitors may book 7 days in advance and regular dress code expected.
Societies telephone for details 01689 839677.
Green Fees £5-£11 per round (£8-£18 weekends); Par3 £3.50 at all times.
Cards
Prof Andy Langdon
Facilities
Location 2m NE on A223

Hotel ★★★ 69% Bromley Court Hotel, Bromley Hill, BROMLEY ☎ 0181 464 5011 116

PINNER Map 04 TQ18

Grims Dyke Oxhey Ln, Hatch End HA5 4AL
☎ 0181 428 4539 Fax 0181 421 5494
Pleasant, undulating parkland course.
18 holes, 5600yds, Par 69, SSS 67, Course record 61.
Club membership 580.

Visitors must contact in advance, may not play weekends.
Societies by arrangement, booked in advance.
Green Fees not confirmed.
Prof John Rule
Designer Braid
Facilities
Location 3m N of Harrow on A4008

Hotel ★★★ 66% Quality Harrow Hotel, Roxborough Bridge, 12-22 Pinner Rd, HARROW ☎ 0181 427 3435 54 Annexe23

Pinner Hill Southview Rd, Pinner Hill HA5 3YA
☎ 0181 866 0963 Fax 0181 868 4817
A hilly, wooded parkland course.
18 holes, 6086yds, Par 71, SSS 69.
Club membership 770.

Visitors are required to have handicap certificate on Mon, Tue & Fri. Public days Wed & Thu. Contact in advance.
Societies Mon, Tue & Fri only, by arrangement.
Green Fees £25 per day Mon, Tue & Fri; £12 per round Wed & Thu. (£32 per day weekends on application).
Prof Mark Grieve
Designer J H Taylor
Facilities
Location 2m NW off A404

Hotel ★★★ 66% Quality Harrow Hotel, Roxborough Bridge, 12-22 Pinner Rd, HARROW ☎ 0181 427 3435 54 Annexe23

PURLEY Map 05 TQ36

Purley Downs 106 Purley Downs Rd CR2 0RB
☎ 0181 657 8347 Fax 0181 651 5044
Hilly downland course which is a good test for golfers.
18 holes, 6200yds, Par 70, SSS 70, Course record 64.
Club membership 650.

Visitors must contact in advance & play on weekends only with member.
Societies must contact in advance.
Green Fees £30 per day; £24 per round.
Prof Graham Wilson
Designer J Taylor/H S Colt
Facilities
Location E side of town centre off A235

Hotel B Forte Posthouse Croydon, Purley Way, CROYDON ☎ 0181 688 5185 83

RICHMOND UPON THAMES Map 04 TQ17

Richmond Sudbrook Park, Petersham TW10 7AS
☎ 0181 940 4351
A beautiful and historic wooded, parkland course on the edge of Richmond Park, with six par-3 holes. The 4th is often described as the best short hole in the south of England. Low scores are uncommon because cunningly sited trees call for great accuracy. The clubhouse is one of the most distinguished small Georgian mansions in England.
18 holes, 6007yds, Par 70, SSS 69.
Club membership 700.

Visitors may not play weekends.
Societies must apply in writing.
Green Fees not confirmed.
Prof Nick Job
Facilities
Location 1.5m S off A307

Hotel ★★★ 66% Richmond Hill, Richmond Hill, RICHMOND UPON THAMES ☎ 0181 940 2247 & 0181 940 5466 Fax 0181 940 5424 138

Royal Mid-Surrey Old Deer Park TW9 2SB
☎ 0181 940 1894 Fax 0181 332 2957
A long playing parkland course. The flat fairways are cleverly bunkered. The 18th provides an exceptionally good par 4 finish with a huge bunker before the green to catch the not quite perfect long second.
Outer Course: 18 holes, 6343yds, Par 69, SSS 70.
Inner Course: 18 holes, 5544yds, Par 68, SSS 67.
Club membership 1250.

Visitors may not play at weekends. Must contact in advance and bring a handicap certificate.
Societies must apply in writing.
Green Fees £40-£60.
Prof David Talbot
Designer J H Taylor
Facilities
Location 0.5m N of Richmond upon Thames off A316

Hotel ★★★ 66% Richmond Hill, Richmond Hill, RICHMOND UPON THAMES ☎ 0181 940 2247 & 0181 940 5466 Fax 01 81 940 5424 138

ROMFORD Map 05 TQ58

Maylands Golf Club & Country Park Colchester Rd, Harold Park RM3 0AZ
☎ 01708 346466 Fax 01708 373080
Picturesque undulating parkland course.
18 holes, 6351yds, Par 71, SSS 70, Course record 65.
Club membership 700.

Visitors handicap certificate required.
Societies Mon, Wed & Fri only, by arrangement.
Green Fees £30 per day; £20 per 18 holes; £10 per 9 holes (£40/£30/£15 weekends and bank holidays). 5% surcharge for credit cards..
Cards
Prof John Hopkin/Robert Coles
Designer H S Colt
Facilities
& Leisure pitching/chipping green.
Hotel B Forte Posthouse Brentwood, Brook St, BRENTWOOD ☎ 01277 260260 145

Risebridge Golf Centre Risebridge Chase, Lower Bedfords Rd RM1 4DG ☎ 01708 741429 Fax 01708 741429
A well matured parkland golf course, with many challenging holes especially the long 12th, the Par 4 13th and Par 5 14th with water and a two tiered green.
18 holes: 18 holes, 6000yds, Par 71, SSS 70, Course record 66.
9 holes: 9 holes, 459yds, Par 27, SSS 27.
Club membership 300.

Visitors no restrictions.
Societies must telephone in advance.
Green Fees £10.50 per round (£13 weekends & bank holidays).
Prof Paul Jennings
Designer Hawtree
Facilities
& Leisure pitch & putt.
Location Between Colier Row and Harold Hill

Hotel ★★★ 61% Palms Hotel, Southend Arterial Rd, HORNCHURCH ☎ 01708 346789 137

Romford Heath Dr, Gidea Park RM2 5QB
☎ 01708 749393
A many-bunkered parkland course with easy walking. It is said there are as many bunkers as there are days in the year. The ground is quick drying making a good course for winter play when other courses might be too wet.
18 holes, 6374yds, Par 72, SSS 70.
Club membership 693.

Visitors with member only weekends & bank holidays. Must contact in advance & have handicap certificate.
Societies must telephone in advance.
Green Fees not confirmed.
Prof Harry Flatman
Facilities
Location 1m NE on A118

Hotel B Forte Posthouse Brentwood, Brook St, BRENTWOOD ☎ 01277 260260 145

RUISLIP Map 04 TQ08

Ruislip Ickenham Rd HA4 7DQ
☎ 01895 638081 & 638835 Fax 01895 635780
Municipal parkland course. Many trees.
18 holes, 5700yds, Par 69, SSS 68, Course record 65.
Club membership 500.

Visitors telephone in advance.
Societies must contact in advance.
Green Fees not confirmed.
Prof Paul Glozier/Stephen Bryan
Designer Sand Herd
Facilities
Location 0.5m SW on B466

Hotel ★★★ 63% Master Brewer Hotel, Freezeland Way, HILLINGDON ☎ 01895 251199 106

SIDCUP Map 05 TQ47

Sidcup 7 Hurst Rd DA15 9AE ☎ 0181 300 2150
Easy walking parkland course with natural water hazards.
9 holes, 5722yds, Par 68, SSS 68.
Club membership 370.

Visitors contact in advance and may not play weekends.
Societies must contact in advance.
Green Fees not confirmed.
Designer James Braid
Facilities
Location N side of town centre off A222

Hotel ★★★★ 71% Swallow Hotel, 1 Broadway, BEXLEYHEATH ☎ 0181 298 1000 142

SOUTHALL Map 04 TQ17

West Middlesex Greenford Rd UB1 3EE
☎ 0181 574 3450
Gently undulating parkland course.
18 holes, 6242yds, Par 69, SSS 69, Course record 64.
Club membership 700.

Visitors must contact in advance and may not play at weekends.

Societies must apply in advance.
Green Fees not confirmed.
Prof I P Harris
Facilities
& Leisure squash.
Location W side of town centre on A4127 off A4020

Hotel ★★★ 64% Master Robert Hotel, Great West Rd, HOUNSLOW ☎ 0181 570 6261 94

STANMORE Map 04 TQ19

Stanmore 29 Gordon Av HA7 2RL ☎ 0181 954 2599
North London parkland course.
18 holes, 5860yds, Par 68, SSS 68, Course record 61.
Club membership 560.
Visitors may not play weekends. Contact professional 0181 954 2646.
Societies phone in advance for booking sheet.
Green Fees £15 per day; £12 per round Mon & Fri; £32 per day £25 per round Tue-Thu.
Prof V Law
Facilities
Location S side of town centre, between Stanmore & Belmont

Hotel ★★★ 66% Quality Harrow Hotel, Roxborough Bridge, 12-22 Pinner Rd, HARROW ☎ 0181 427 3435 54 Annexe23

SURBITON Map 04 TQ16

Surbiton Woodstock Ln KT9 1UG
☎ 0181 398 3101 (Secretary) & 398 6619 (Pro)
Fax 0181 339 0992
Parkland course with easy walking.
18 holes, 6055yds, Par 70, SSS 69, Course record 63.
Club membership 700.
Visitors with member only at weekends & bank holidays. No visitors Tue am (Ladies Day).
Societies Mon & Fri only. Apply year in advance.
Green Fees £30 per round.
Prof Paul Milton
Designer Tom Dunn
Facilities
Location 2m S off A3, take A309 from Hook junct of A3,turn left into Woodstock Lane

Hotel ★★ 65% Haven Hotel, Portsmouth Rd, ESHER ☎ 0181 398 0023 16 Annexe4

TWICKENHAM Map 04 TQ17

Strawberry Hill Wellesley Rd, Strawberry Hill TW2 5SD
☎ 0181 894 0165
Parkland course with easy walking.
9 holes, 4762yds, Par 64, SSS 62, Course record 59.
Club membership 300.
Visitors must contact in advance, with member only at weekends.
Societies must apply in writing.
Green Fees £20 per weekday.
Prof Peter Buchan
Designer J H Taylor
Facilities
Location S side of town centre off A311

Hotel ★★★ 66% Richmond Hill, Richmond Hill, RICHMOND UPON THAMES ☎ 0181 940 2247 & 0181 940 5466 Fax 0181 9 40 5424 138

Twickenham Staines Rd TW2 5JD
☎ 0181 783 1748 & 1698 Fax 0181 941 9134
Interesting tree lined parkland course with water feature.
9 holes, 3180yds, Par 36, SSS 69.
Visitors must book in advance for weekends & bank holidays.
Societies apply in advance
Green Fees £6 per 9 holes (£7 weekends & bank holidays).
Cards
Prof Suzy Watt
Facilities
& Leisure putting green.
Location 2m W on A305

Hotel ★★★ 66% Richmond Hill, Richmond Hill, RICHMOND UPON THAMES ☎ 0181 940 2247 & 0181 940 5466 Fax 0181 940 5424 138

UPMINSTER Map 05 TQ58

Upminster 114 Hall Ln RM14 1AU
☎ 01708 222788 (Secretary) 220000 (Pro)
Fax 01708 222788
The meandering River Ingrebourne features on several holes of this partly undulating parkland course situated on one side of the river valley. It provides a challenge for golfers of all abilities. The clubhouse is a beautiful Grade II listed building.
18 holes, 6076yds, Par 69, SSS 69, Course record 66.
Club membership 1000.
Visitors contact in advance, may not play at weekends.
Societies telephone initially.
Green Fees £30 per day; £25 per round.
Prof Neil Carr
Designer W G Key
Facilities
Location 2m W from A127 junct with M25

Hotel ★★★ 61% Palms Hotel, Southend Arterial Rd, HORNCHURCH ☎ 01708 346789 137

UXBRIDGE Map 04 TQ08

Stockley Park Stockley Park UB11 1AQ
☎ 0181 813 5700 561 6339 (tee times) Fax 0181 813 5655
Hilly and challenging parkland championship course designed by Trent Jones in 1993 and situated within two miles of Heathrow Airport.
18 holes, 6548yds, Par 72, SSS 71.
Visitors 6 day in advance reservation facility.
Societies please telephone for details.
Green Fees £23 (£33 weekends).
Cards
Prof Alex Knox
Designer Robert Trent Jones Snr
Facilities
Location 2m N of junct4 M4

Hotel ★★★★ 73% Holiday Inn Crowne Plaza, Stockley Rd, WEST DRAYTON ☎ 01895 445555 374

Uxbridge The Drive, Harefield Place UB10 8AQ
☎ 01895 237287 Fax 01895 813539
Municipal parkland course, undulating and tricky.
18 holes, 5750yds, Par 68, SSS 68, Course record 66.
Club membership 400.
Visitors no restrictions.
Societies by arrangment.
Green Fees £11.85 (£16.85 weekends & bank holidays).
Cards
Prof Phil Howard
Facilities
Location 2m N off B467

Hotel ★★★★ 73% Holiday Inn Crowne Plaza, Stockley Rd, WEST DRAYTON ☎ 01895 445555 374

WEMBLEY — Map 04 TQ18

Sudbury Bridgewater Rd HA0 1AL
☎ 0181 902 3713 Fax 0181 903 2966
Undulating parkland course very near centre of London.
18 holes, 6282yds, Par 69, SSS 70.
Club membership 650.
Visitors must have handicap certificate. With member only at weekends.
Societies must apply in writing.
Green Fees not confirmed.
Prof Neil Jordan
Facilities
Location SW side of town centre on A4090

Hotel ★★★ 71% The Bridge Hotel, Western Av, GREENFORD ☎ 0181 566 6246 68

WEST DRAYTON — Map 04 TQ07

Heathpark Stockley Rd UB7 9BW ☎ 01895 444232
Fairly large, testing, hilly par 4 course suitable both for beginners and scratch players.
9 holes, 2032yds, Par 64, Course record 50.
Club membership 80.
Visitors no restrictions.
Societies by arrangement.
Green Fees not confirmed.
Designer Niel Coles
Facilities
& Leisure heated indoor swimming pool, sauna, solarium, gymnasium.
Location 1m SE off A408 via junct 4 on M4

Hotel ★★★★ 73% Holiday Inn Crowne Plaza, Stockley Rd, WEST DRAYTON ☎ 01895 445555 374

WOODFORD GREEN — Map 05 TQ49

Woodford Sunset Av IG8 0ST
☎ 0181 504 3330 & 504 0553
Forest land course on the edge of Epping Forest. Views over the Lea Valley to the London skyline.
9 holes, 5806yds, Par 70, SSS 68, Course record 66.
Club membership 420.
Visitors advisable to contact in advance. May not play Sat or Sun afternoon.
Societies telephone for details.
Green Fees not confirmed.
Prof Ashley Johns
Designer Tom Dunn
Facilities
Location NW side of town centre off A104

Hotel ★★★ 66% County Hotel Epping Forest, Oak Hill, WOODFORD GREEN ☎ 0181 787 9988 99

GREATER MANCHESTER

ALTRINCHAM — Map 07 SJ78

Altrincham Stockport Rd WA15 7LP ☎ 0161 928 0761
Municipal parkland course with easy walking, water on many holes, rolling contours and many trees. Driving range in grounds.
18 holes, 6162yds, Par 71, SSS 69.
Club membership 350.
Visitors must book in advance.
Societies by prior arrangement.
Green Fees £8.50 per round (£9.50 weekends & bank holidays).
Prof Scott Partington
Facilities
Location 0.75 E of Altrincham on A560

Hotel ★★★ 66% Cresta Court Hotel, Church St, ALTRINCHAM ☎ 0161 927 7272 138

Dunham Forest Oldfield Ln WA14 4TY
☎ 0161 928 2605 Fax 0161 929 8975
Attractive parkland course cut through magnificent beech woods.
18 holes, 6636yds, Par 72, SSS 72.
Club membership 680.
Visitors by prior arrangement. May not play weekends & bank holidays.
Societies apply in writing or telephone in advance.
Green Fees £40 per round; £45 per 27 holes.
Prof Ian Wrigley
Designer Dave Thomas
Facilities
& Leisure hard tennis courts, squash.
Location 1.5m W off A56

Hotel ★★★ 67% Bowdon Hotel, Langham Rd, Bowdon, ALTRINCHAM ☎ 0161 928 7121 89

Ringway Hale Mount, Hale Barns WA15 8SW
☎ 0161 980 8432 (pro) & 0161 904 9609
Parkland course, with interesting natural hazards. Easy walking, good views.
18 holes, 6494yds, Par 71, SSS 71, Course record 67.
Club membership 700.
Visitors may not play before 9.30am or between 1-2pm, play restricted Tue, Fri & Sat.
Societies Thu only May-Sep.
Green Fees not confirmed.
Prof Nick Ryan
Designer Colt

Facilities ⊗)Ⅲ ♨ ☕ ♀ ⛺ ⌂ ♈ ♂
Location M56 junct 6, take A538 signposted Hale & Altrincham

Hotel ★★★ 66% Cresta Court Hotel, Church St, ALTRINCHAM ☎ 0161 927 7272 138 ⇄ ↱

ASHTON-IN-MAKERFIELD Map 07 SJ59

Ashton-in-Makerfield Garswood Park, Liverpool Rd WN4 0YT ☎ 01942 727267 & 719330
Well-wooded parkland course. Easy walking.
18 holes, 6250yds, Par 70, SSS 70.
Club membership 800.
Visitors with member only weekends & bank holidays. No visitors Wed.
Societies apply in writing.
Green Fees £30 per day; £25 per round.
Prof Peter Allan
Facilities ⊗)Ⅲ ♨ ☕ ♀ ⛺ ⌂ ♈ ♂
Location 0.5m W of M6 (junc 24) on A58

Hotel B Forte Posthouse Haydock, Lodge Ln, HAYDOCK ☎ 01942 717878 136 ⇄ ↱

ASHTON-UNDER-LYNE Map 07 SJ99

Ashton-under-Lyne Gorsey Way, Higher Hurst OL6 9HT ☎ 0161 330 1537 Fax 0161 330 1537
A testing, varied moorland course, with large greens. Easy walking. Three new holes have improved the course.
18 holes, 6209yds, Par 70, SSS 70, Course record 67.
Club membership 550.
Visitors must contact in advance, with member only weekends & bank holidays.
Societies apply in advance.
Green Fees £25 per day/round.
Prof Colin Boyle
Facilities ⊗)Ⅲ ♨ ☕ ♀ ⛺ ⌂ 🛒 ♂
& Leisure snooker table.
Location N off B6194

Hotel ★★ 70% York House Hotel, York Place, Richmond St, ASHTON-UNDER-LYNE ☎ 0161 330 9000 24 ⇄ ↱ Annexe10 ⇄ ↱

Dukinfield Lyne Edge, Yew Tree Ln SK16 5DF ☎ 0161 338 2340
Recently extended, tricky hillside course with several difficult Par 3s and a very long par 5.
18 holes, 5303yds, Par 67, SSS 66.
Club membership 400.
Visitors may not play on Wed afternoons & must play with member at weekends, advisable to contact in advance.
Societies apply in writing or telephone.
Green Fees not confirmed.
Prof Jason Peel
Facilities ⊗)Ⅲ ♨ ☕ ♀ ⛺ ⌂ ♂
Location S off B6175

Hotel ★★ 70% York House Hotel, York Place, Richmond St, ASHTON-UNDER-LYNE ☎ 0161 330 9000 24 ⇄ ↱ Annexe10 ⇄ ↱

BOLTON Map 07 SD70

Bolton Lostock Park, Chorley New Rd BL6 4AJ ☎ 01204 843067 & 843278 Fax 01204 843067
This well maintained heathland course is always a pleasure to visit. The 12th hole should be treated with respect and so too should the final four holes which have ruined many a card.
18 holes, 6237yds, Par 70, SSS 70, Course record 66.
Club membership 612.

Visitors not able to play Tue before 2.30pm or on competition days, before 10am and between 12-2pm.
Societies write or telephone in advance, not accepted Tue, Sat or Sun.
Green Fees £36 per day; £29 per round (£40/£33 weekends & bank holidays).
Prof R Longworth
Facilities ⊗)Ⅲ ♨ ☕ ♀ ⛺ ⌂ ♂
Location 3m W of Bolton, on A673

Hotel ★★★★ 63% Georgian House Hotel, Manchester Rd, Blackrod, BOLTON ☎ 01942 814598 100 ⇄ ↱

Breightmet Red Bridge, Ainsworth BL2 5PA ☎ 01204 527381
Long parkland course.
9 holes, 6416yds, Par 72, SSS 71, Course record 68.
Club membership 350.
Visitors may not play Wed or weekends.
Societies welcome Mon, Tue, Thu & Fri only, apply in advance in writing.
Green Fees £15 per round (£18 weekends & bank holidays).
Facilities ⊗)Ⅲ ♨ ☕ ♀ ⛺
Location E side of town centre off A58

Hotel ★★★ 66% Egerton House Hotel, Blackburn Rd, Egerton, BOLTON ☎ 01204 307171 32 ⇄ ↱

Deane Broadford Rd, Deane BL3 4NS ☎ 01204 61944 Fax 01204 651808
Undulating parkland course with small ravines on approaches to some holes.
18 holes, 5652yds, Par 68, SSS 67, Course record 64.
Club membership 470.
Visitors must be a member of a golf club or member's guest. Restricted weekends.
Societies must telephone in advance and confirm in writing.

▶

Green Fees £20 per day (£25 weekends & bank holidays).
Prof David Martindale
Facilities
Location 1m from exit 5 on M61 towards Bolton

Hotel ★★★ 63% The Beaumont Hotel, Beaumont Rd, BOLTON ☎ 01204 651511 101

Dunscar Longworth Ln, Bromley Cross BL7 9QY
☎ 01204 303321
A scenic moorland course with panoramic views. A warm friendly club.
18 holes, 6085yds, Par 71, SSS 69, Course record 65.
Club membership 600.
Visitors must telephone 01204 592992 in advance and have a handicap certificate.
Societies must apply in writing.
Green Fees £20 per round (£30 weekends & bank holidays).
Prof Gary Treadgold
Facilities
Location 2m N off A666

Hotel ★★★ 66% Egerton House Hotel, Blackburn Rd, Egerton, BOLTON ☎ 01204 307171 32

Great Lever & Farnworth Plodder Ln, Farnworth BL4 0LQ ☎ 01204 656137 Fax 01204 656137
Downland course with easy walking.
18 holes, 6064yds, Par 70, SSS 69, Course record 67.
Club membership 600.
Visitors must contact in advance, weekend by prior arrangement.
Societies must contact in advance.
Green Fees £16.50 per day (£27 weekends & bank holidays).
Prof Tony Howarth
Facilities
Location 1m junct 4 M61

Hotel ★★★ 63% The Beaumont Hotel, Beaumont Rd, BOLTON ☎ 01204 651511 101

Harwood Springfield, Roading Brook Rd, Harwood BL2 4JD ☎ 01204 522878 & 524233 (Sec)
Mainly flat parkland course.
18 holes, 5778yds, Par 70, SSS 69.
Club membership 524.
Visitors must be members of a golf club and hold a current handicap certificate. May not play at weekends.
Societies contact in writing to the Secretary.
Green Fees £20 per round.
Prof M Dance
Facilities
Location 2.5m NE off B6196

Hotel ★★★ 66% Egerton House Hotel, Blackburn Rd, Egerton, BOLTON ☎ 01204 307171 32

Old Links Chorley Old Rd, Montserrat BL1 5SU
☎ 01204 842307 Fax 01204 842307
Championship moorland course.
18 holes, 6406yds, Par 72, SSS 72.
Club membership 600.
Visitors must contact in advance and may only play weekends with member.
Societies apply by letter or telephone.
Green Fees £27 per day/round (£40 weekends & bank holidays).
Prof Paul Horridge
Designer Dr Alistair MacKenzie
Facilities
Location NW of town centre on B6226

Hotel ★★★★ 63% Georgian House Hotel, Manchester Rd, Blackrod, BOLTON ☎ 01942 814598 100

Regent Park Links Rd, Chorley New Rd BL2 9XX
☎ 01204 844170
Parkland course.
18 holes, 6130yds, Par 70, SSS 69, Course record 67.
Club membership 200.
Visitors must book 6 days in advance.
Societies must telephone 01204 495421 in advance.
Green Fees not confirmed.
Prof Bob Longworth
Facilities
Location 3.5m W off A673

Hotel ★★★ 63% The Beaumont Hotel, Beaumont Rd, BOLTON ☎ 01204 651511 101

BRAMHALL Map 07 SJ88

Bramall Park 20 Manor Rd SK7 3LY
☎ 0161 485 3119 & 7101 (secretary) Fax 0161 485 7101
Well-wooded parkland course with splendid views of the Pennines.
18 holes, 6043yds, Par 70, SSS 69.
Club membership 600.
Visitors must contact in advance.
Societies apply in writing.
Green Fees £25 per day/round (£35 weekends & bank holidays).
Prof M Proffitt
Facilities
Location NW side of town centre off B5149

Hotel ★★★ 66% County Hotel Bramhall, Bramhall Ln South, BRAMHALL ☎ 0161 439 8116 & 455 9988 Fax 0161 440 8071 65

Bramhall Ladythorn Rd SK7 2EY
☎ 0161 439 6092 Fax 0161 439 0264
Undulating parkland course, easy walking.
18 holes, 6340yds, Par 70, SSS 70.
Club membership 700.
Visitors must contact in advance.
Societies apply in writing.
Green Fees £24 per round (£31 weekends & bank holidays).
Prof Richard Green
Facilities
Location E side of town centre off A5102

Hotel ★★★ 66% County Hotel Bramhall, Bramhall Ln South, BRAMHALL ☎ 0161 439 8116 & 455 9988 Fax 0161 440 8071 65

BROMLEY CROSS Map 07 SD71

Turton Wood End Farm, Chapeltown Rd BL7 9QH
☎ 01204 852235
Moorland course with panoramic views. A wide variety of holes which challenge any golfer's technique.
18 holes, 6159yds, Par 70, SSS 70, Course record 70.
Club membership 450.

Visitors avoid 11.30-2pm Wed Ladies day. Sat tee available after last competition. Restricted Sun.
Societies must contact in writing.
Green Fees £16 per day (£20 per round weekends & bank holidays).
Designer Alex Herd
Facilities ⊗)Ⅲ ⛾ ☕ ♀ ⌂
Location 3m N on A666

Hotel ★★★ 66% Egerton House Hotel, Blackburn Rd, Egerton, BOLTON
☎ 01204 307171 32

BURY Map 07 SD81

Bury Unsworth Hall, Blackford Bridge, Manchester Rd BL9 9TJ ☎ 0161 766 4897 Fax 0161 796 3480
Moorland course, difficult in part. Tight and good test of golf.
18 holes, 5961yds, Par 69, SSS 68, Course record 64.
Club membership 650.

Visitors may not normally play at weekends. Must contact in advance.
Societies telephone 0161 766 4897.
Green Fees £26 weekdays..
Prof S Crake
Designer Mackenzie
Facilities ⊗)Ⅲ ⛾ ☕ ♀ ⌂
Location 2m S on A56

Hotel ★★★ 65% Bolholt Country Park Hotel, Walshaw Rd, BURY
☎ 0161 764 3888 Freephone 0800 174141 Fax 0161 763 1789 59

Lowes Park Hilltop, Lowes Rd BL9 6SU
☎ 0161 764 1231 Fax 0161 763 9503
Moorland course, with easy walking. Usually windy.
9 holes, 6009yds, Par 70, SSS 69, Course record 65.
Club membership 400.

Visitors may not play Wed & Sat, by appointment Sun. Must contact in advance.
Societies apply in writing.
Green Fees £17 per day (£23 Sun & bank holidays).
Facilities ⊗)Ⅲ ⛾ ☕ ♀ ⌂
Location N side of town centre off A56

Hotel ★★★ 65% Bolholt Country Park Hotel, Walshaw Rd, BURY
☎ 0161 764 3888 Freephone 0800 174141 Fax 0161 763 1789 59

Walmersley Garretts Close, Walmersley BL9 6TE
☎ 0161 764 1429 & 0161 764 7770 Fax 01706 827618
Moorland hillside course, with wide fairways, large greens and extensive views. Testing holes: 2nd (484 yds) par 5; 5th par 4 with severe dogleg and various hazards.
18 holes, 5341yds, Par 69, SSS 67.
Club membership 475.

Visitors welcome by arrangement with secretary. May only play with member at weekend,
Societies must apply in writing.
Green Fees £20 per day.
Prof S Crake
Designer S Marnoch
Facilities ⊗)Ⅲ ⛾ ☕ ♀ ⌂
& Leisure snooker.
Location 2m N off A56

Hotel ★★★ 62% Old Mill Hotel, Springwood, RAMSBOTTOM ☎ 01706 822991 36

CHEADLE Map 07 SJ88

Cheadle Cheadle Rd SK8 1HW ☎ 0161 491 4452
Parkland course with hazards on every hole, from sand bunkers and copses to a stream across six of the fairways.
9 holes, 5006yds, Par 64, SSS 65.
Club membership 425.

Visitors may not play Tue & Sat, & restricted Sun. Must contact in advance and have a handicap certificate and be member of a bona-fide golf club.
Societies apply in writing to secretary
Green Fees not confirmed.
Prof S Booth
Designer T Renouf
Facilities ⊗)Ⅲ ⛾ ☕ ♀ ⌂
Location S side of village off A5149

Hotel ★★ 67% The Wycliffe Hotel, 74 Edgeley Rd, Edgeley, STOCKPORT
☎ 0161 477 5395 20

DENTON Map 07 SJ99

Denton Manchester Rd M34 2NU ☎ 0161 336 3218
Easy, flat parkland course with brook running through. Notable hole is one called 'Death and Glory'.
18 holes, 6541yds, Par 72, SSS 71, Course record 66.
Club membership 585.

Visitors must contact in advance & may not play summer weekends.
Societies apply in advance.
Green Fees not confirmed.
Prof M Hollingworth
Designer T McCauley
Facilities ⊗)Ⅲ ⛾ ☕ ♀ ⌂
Location 1.5m W on A57

Hotel ★★ 70% York House Hotel, York Place, Richmond St, ASHTON-UNDER-LYNE
☎ 0161 330 9000 24 Annexe10

FAILSWORTH Map 07 SD80

Brookdale Medlock Rd M35 9WQ
☎ 0161 681 4534 Fax 0161 681 4534
Undulating parkland course, with river crossed 5 times in play. Hard walking.
18 holes, 5841yds, Par 68, SSS 68, Course record 64.
Club membership 600.

Visitors advisable to contact in advance. May only play as guest of member at weekends.
Societies must contact in advance.
Green Fees £20 per round. ▶

Prof Tony Cuppello
Facilities
Location N side of Manchester

Hotel ★★ 70% York House Hotel, York Place, Richmond St, ASHTON-UNDER-LYNE ☎ 0161 330 9000 24 Annexe10

FLIXTON — Map 07 SJ79

William Wroe Municipal Pennybridge Ln, Flixton Rd M41 5DX ☎ 0161 748 8680
Parkland course, with easy walking.
18 holes, 4395yds, Par 68, SSS 65.
Visitors must book in advance.
Societies contact for details.
Green Fees not confirmed.
Prof Scott Partington
Facilities
Location E side of village off B5158

Hotel ★★★ 60% Trafford Hall Hotel, 23 Talbot Rd, Old Trafford, MANCHESTER ☎ 0161 848 7791 31 Annexe3

GATLEY — Map 07 SJ88

Gatley Waterfall Farm, Styal Rd, Heald Green SK8 3TW ☎ 0161 437 2091
Parkland course. Moderately testing.
9 holes, 5934yds, Par 68, SSS 68.
Club membership 400.
Visitors may not play Tue & Sat. With member only weekends. Handicap certificate required.
Societies apply in writing.
Green Fees £20 per round.
Prof Simon Reeves
Facilities by prior arrangement by prior arrangement
& Leisure squash.
Location S side of village off B5166

Hotel ★★★★ 63% Belfry Hotel, Stanley Rd, HANDFORTH ☎ 0161 437 0511 80

HALE — Map 07 SJ78

Hale Rappax Rd WA15 0NU ☎ 0161 980 4225
Beautiful, undulating parkland course, with the River Bollin winding round fairways.
9 holes, 5780yds, Par 70, SSS 68, Course record 65.
Club membership 300.
Visitors may not play before 4.30pm Thu; with member only weekends.
Societies apply in writing
Green Fees £20 per day/round.
Prof Mike Grantham
Facilities by prior arrangement
Location Off Bankhall Lane close to Altrincham Priory Hospital

Hotel ★★★ 67% Bowdon Hotel, Langham Rd, Bowdon, ALTRINCHAM ☎ 0161 928 7121 89

HAZEL GROVE — Map 07 SJ98

Hazel Grove Buxton Rd SK7 6LU ☎ 0161 483 3978
Testing parkland course with tricky greens and water hazards coming into play on several holes.
18 holes, 6310yds, Par 71, SSS 71.
Club membership 600.
Visitors must contact in advance tel: 0161 483 7272.
Societies must apply in writing, Thu & Fri only.
Green Fees £25 per round (£35 weekends).
Prof M E Hill
Facilities
Location 1m E off A6

Hotel ★★★ 66% County Hotel Bramhall, Bramhall Ln South, BRAMHALL ☎ 0161 439 8116 & 455 9988 Fax 0161 440 8071 65

HINDLEY — Map 07 SD60

Hindley Hall Hall Ln WN2 2SQ ☎ 01942 255131
Parkland course with mostly easy walking.
18 holes, 5913yds, Par 69, SSS 68, Course record 64.
Club membership 430.
Visitors must contact in advance and may not play weekends.
Societies apply in advance to Secretary
Green Fees £20 per round.
Prof Neil Brazell
Facilities
Location 1m N off A58

Hotel ★★★ 65% Oak Hotel, Riverway, WIGAN ☎ 01942 826888 88

HYDE — Map 07 SJ99

Werneth Low Werneth Low Rd, Gee Cross SK14 3AF ☎ 0161 368 2503
Hard walking but good views from this moorland course. Exposed to wind.
11 holes, 6113yds, Par 70, SSS 70, Course record 69.
Club membership 375.
Visitors may not play Tue mornings or Sun and by prior arrangement on Sat.
Societies must contact in at least 14 days in advance.
Green Fees not confirmed.
Prof Tony Bacchus
Facilities
Location 2m S of town centre

Hotel ★★ 68% Red Lion Inn, 112 Buxton Rd, High Ln, STOCKPORT ☎ 01663 765227 6

LEIGH — Map 07 SD60

Pennington St Helen's Rd WN7 4HW ☎ 01942 682852
Municipal parkland course, with natural hazards of brooks, ponds and trees, and easy walking.
9 holes, 2919yds, Par 35, SSS 34.
Club membership 200.
Visitors no restrictions.
Societies must contact in advance.
Green Fees not confirmed.
Prof Tim Kershaw

Facilities
Location SW side of town centre off A572

Hotel ★★ 62% Kirkfield Hotel, 2/4 Church St, NEWTON LE WILLOWS
01925 228196 14

LITTLEBOROUGH Map 07 SD91

Whittaker Whittaker Ln OL15 0LH 01706 378310
Moorland 9-hole course with outstanding views of Hollingworth Lake Countryside Park and the Pennine Hills.
9 holes, 5632yds, Par 68, SSS 67, Course record 61.
Club membership 190.
Visitors welcome except for Tue pm and Sun.
Societies apply to Secretary.
Green Fees £12 per day (£16 weekends).
Facilities
Location 1.5m out of Littleborough off A58

Hotel ★★★ 68% Norton Grange Hotel, Manchester Rd, Castleton, ROCHDALE
01706 30788 51

MANCHESTER Map 07 SJ89

Blackley Victoria Ave East, Blackley M9 6HW
0161 643 2980 & 654 7770
Parkland course. Course crossed by footpath.
18 holes, 6237yds, Par 70, SSS 70.
Club membership 760.
Visitors with member only Thu, weekends and bank holidays.
Societies apply in advance.
Green Fees £24 per day.
Prof Andrew Cory
Facilities
Location 4m N of city centre, on Rochdale Rd

Hotel ★★★ 63% Bower Hotel, Hollinwood Av, Chadderton, OLDHAM
0161 682 7254 63

Chorlton-cum-Hardy Barlow Hall, Barlow Hall Rd, Chorlton-cum-Hardy M21 7JJ
0161 881 5830 Fax 0161 881 5830
Meadowland course with trees, stream and several ditches.
18 holes, 5980yds, Par 70, SSS 69, Course record 64.
Club membership 802.
Visitors handicap certificate required.
Societies on Thu only by prior booking.
Green Fees £22 per day (£27 weekends & bank holidays).
Prof David Screeton
Facilities
Location 4m S of Manchester A5103/A5145

Hotel ★★★ 61% Willow Bank Hotel, 340-342 Wilmslow Rd, Fallowfield, MANCHESTER
0161 224 0461 116

Davyhulme Park Gleneagles Rd, Davyhulme M41 8SA
0161 748 2260
Parkland course.
18 holes, 6237yds, Par 72, SSS 70, Course record 67.
Club membership 680.
Visitors must contact in advance, may not play Wed, weekends by prior notice.
Societies telephone in advance.
Green Fees not confirmed.
Prof Dean Butler
Facilities
Location 8m S adj to Trafford General Hospital

Hotel ★★★ 60% Trafford Hall Hotel, 23 Talbot Rd, Old Trafford, MANCHESTER
0161 848 7791 31 Annexe3

Didsbury Ford Ln, Northenden M22 4NQ
0161 998 9278 Fax 0161 998 9278
Parkland course.
18 holes, 6273yds, Par 70, SSS 70, Course record 63.
Club membership 750.
Visitors advised to check dates/times with manager or professional.
Societies Thu & Fri, must contact in advance.
Green Fees £26 per day (£30 weekends & bank holidays).
Cards
Prof Peter Barber
Facilities
Location 6m S of city centre off A5145

Hotel B Forte Posthouse Manchester, Palatine Rd, Northenden, MANCHESTER
0161 998 7090 190

Fairfield "Boothdale", Booth Rd, Audenshaw M34 5GA
0161 370 1641 & 370 2292
Parkland course set around a reservoir. Course demands particularly accurate placing of shots.
18 holes, 4956yds, Par 68, SSS 68, Course record 65.
Club membership 450.
Visitors may not play mornings at weekends & may be restricted on Wed & Thu.
Societies prior booking through Secretary.
Green Fees £17 per round (£23 weekends & bank holidays).
Prof Stephen Pownell
Facilities by prior arrangement by prior arrangement
Location 5m E of Manchester, off A635

Hotel ★★ 70% York House Hotel, York Place, Richmond St, ASHTON-UNDER-LYNE
0161 330 9000 24 Annexe10

Northenden Palatine Rd, Northenden M22 4FR
0161 998 4738 Fax 0161 5592
Parkland course surrounded by the River Mersey.
18 holes, 6503yds, Par 72, SSS 71, Course record 64.
Club membership 800.
Visitors Must contact in advance.
Societies Tue & Fri only, apply in advance to Secretary.
Green Fees £25 per day (£30 weekends & bank holidays).
Prof P A Scott
Designer Renouf
Facilities
Location 6.5m S of city centre on B1567 off A5103

Hotel B Forte Posthouse Manchester, Palatine Rd, Northenden, MANCHESTER
0161 998 7090 190

Pike Fold Cooper Ln, Victoria Av, Blackley M9 6QQ
0161 740 1136
Picturesque, hilly course. Good test of golf.
9 holes, 5785yds, Par 70, SSS 68, Course record 66. ▶

Club membership 200.
Visitors may not play Sun. Must be with member Sat & bank holidays.
Societies apply in writing.
Green Fees not confirmed.
Facilities
Location 4m N of city centre off Rochdale Rd

Hotel ★★★ 63% Bower Hotel, Hollinwood Av, Chadderton, OLDHAM ☎ 0161 682 7254 63

Withington 243 Palatine Rd, West Didsbury M20 2UE
☎ 0161 445 9544
Flat parkland course bordering the river Mersey. Easy walking with an extremely tough finish.
18 holes, 6410yds, Par 71, SSS 71.
Club membership 600.
Visitors welcome except Thu, must contact in advance, restricted at weekends.
Societies telephone in advance, welcome except Thu, Sat & Sun.
Green Fees £30 per day; £25 per round (£35/£30 weekends).
Prof R J Ling
Facilities
Location 4m SW of city centre off B5167

Hotel B Forte Posthouse Manchester, Palatine Rd, Northenden, MANCHESTER ☎ 0161 998 7090 190

Worsley Stableford Av, Worsley M30 8AP
☎ 0161 789 4202 Fax 0161 789 3200
Well-wooded parkland course.
18 holes, 6252yds, Par 72, SSS 70, Course record 65.
Club membership 600.
Visitors must contact professional in advance restricted during club competitions.
Societies apply in advance.
Green Fees £20 per round (£30 per day weekends & bank holidays).
Prof Ceri Cousins
Designer James Braid
Facilities
Location 6.5m NW of city centre off A572

Hotel ★★★ 65% Novotel, Worsley Brow, WORSLEY ☎ 0161 799 3535 119

MELLOR Map 07 SJ98

Mellor & Townscliffe Gibb Ln, Tarden SK6 5NA
☎ 0161 427 2208 (secretary) & 427 5759 (pro)
Scenic parkland and moorland course, undulating with some hard walking. Good views. Testing 200 yd, 9th hole, par 3.
18 holes, 5925yds, Par 70, SSS 69.
Club membership 650.
Visitors with member only Sun.
Societies apply by letter.
Green Fees £20 per day (£27.50 weekends & bank holidays).
Prof Gary R Broadley
Facilities
Location 7m SE of Stockport off A626

Hotel ★ 74% Springfield Hotel, Station Rd, MARPLE ☎ 0161 449 0721 7

MIDDLETON Map 07 SD80

Manchester Hopwood Cottage, Rochdale Rd M24 2QP
☎ 0161 643 3202 Fax 0161 643 9174
Moorland golf of unique character over a spaciously laid out course with generous fairways sweeping along to large greens. A wide variety of holes will challenge the golfer's technique, particularly the testing last three holes.
18 holes, 6519yds, Par 72, SSS 70, Course record 65.
Club membership 650.
Visitors must contact in advance, limited play weekends and Wed.
Societies telephone in advance.
Green Fees £40 per day; £30 per round (£45 per round weekends & bank holidays).
Cards
Prof Brian Connor
Designer Shapland Colt
Facilities
Location 2.5m N off A664

Hotel ★★ 59% Midway Hotel, Manchester Rd, Castleton, ROCHDALE ☎ 01706 32881 24

North Manchester Rhodes House, Manchester Old Rd M24 4PE ☎ 0161 643 9033
A long, tight heathland course with natural water hazards. Excellent views of the Yorkshire Wolds.
18 holes, 6527yds, Par 72, SSS 72, Course record 66.
Club membership 750.
Visitors no restrictions.
Societies telephone in advance.
Green Fees not confirmed.
Prof Frank Accleton
Designer J Braid
Facilities
Location W side of town centre off A576

Hotel ★★★ 63% Bower Hotel, Hollinwood Av, Chadderton, OLDHAM ☎ 0161 682 7254 63

MILNROW Map 07 SD91

Tunshill Kiln Ln OL16 3TS ☎ 01706 342095
Testing moorland course, particularly 6th and 15th (par 5's).
9 holes, 5804yds, Par 70, SSS 68.
Club membership 275.
Visitors must contact in advance, restricted weekends & evenings.
Societies apply in writing.
Green Fees not confirmed.
Facilities
Location 1m NE M62 exit junc 21 off B6225

Hotel ★★★ 68% Norton Grange Hotel, Manchester Rd, Castleton, ROCHDALE ☎ 01706 30788 51

Oldham Map 07 SD90

Crompton & Royton Highbarn OL2 6RW
☎ 0161 624 0986 Fax 0161 624 0986
Undulating moorland course.
18 holes, 6214yds, Par 70, SSS 70, Course record 65.
Club membership 500.

Visitors must contact in advance and may not play Tue or Sat, limited play Sun pm and Wed.
Societies apply in advance
Green Fees £24 (£30 weekends & bank holidays).
Prof David Melling
Facilities
Location 0.5m NE of Royton

Hotel ★★★ 63% Bower Hotel, Hollinwood Av, Chadderton, OLDHAM
☎ 0161 682 7254 63

Oldham Lees New Rd OL4 5PN ☎ 0161 624 4986
Moorland course, with hard walking.
18 holes, 5122yds, Par 66, SSS 65, Course record 62.
Club membership 370.

Visitors no restrictions.
Societies must contact in advance.
Green Fees £16 (£22 weekends & bank holidays).
Prof Jason Peel
Facilities by prior arrangement
Location 2.5m E off A669

Hotel ★★ 70% York House Hotel, York Place, Richmond St, ASHTON-UNDER-LYNE
☎ 0161 330 9000 24 Annexe10

Werneth Green Ln, Garden Suburb OL8 3AZ
☎ 0161 624 1190
Semi-moorland course, with a deep gulley and stream crossing eight fairways. Testing hole: 3rd (par 3).
18 holes, 5363yds, Par 68, SSS 66.
Club membership 460.

Visitors may not play on Tue or Thu and weekends. Must contact in advance.
Societies must contact in advance.
Green Fees £18.50 per day.
Prof Roy Pennet
Facilities
Location S side of town centre off A627

Hotel ★★ 70% York House Hotel, York Place, Richmond St, ASHTON-UNDER-LYNE
☎ 0161 330 9000 24 Annexe10

Prestwich Map 07 SD80

Heaton Park Municipal Heaton Park, Middleton Rd M25 2SW ☎ 0161 654 9899 Fax 0161 653 2003
A parkland style course in historic Heaton Park with rolling hills and lakes, boasting some spectacular holes. A good test of skill for golfers of all abilities.
18 holes, 5815yds, Par 70, SSS 70.
Club membership 190.

Visitors restricted to club members only between 8-10am Sat & Sun.
Societies apply in writing or by telephone to Matthew Riley
Green Fees £9 (£10 weekends & bank holidays).
Cards
Prof Dennis Durnian
Designer J H Taylor
Facilities
Location N of Manchester near junct 18 of M62

Hotel ★★★★ 63% Bolton Moat House, 1 Higher Bridge St, BOLTON
☎ 01204 879988 128

Prestwich Hilton Ln M25 9XB
☎ 0161 773 2544 Fax 0161 773 1404
Parkland course, near to Manchester city centre.
18 holes, 4806yds, Par 64, SSS 63, Course record 60.
Club membership 507.

Visitors handicap certificate, weekdays by arrangement, restricted at weekends.
Societies apply in writing or telephone.
Green Fees £19.50 Mon-Fri.
Prof Simon Wakefield
Facilities
Location N side of town centre on A6044

Hotel ★★★ 65% Novotel, Worsley Brow, WORSLEY
☎ 0161 799 3535 119

Rochdale Map 07 SD81

Castle Hawk Chadwick Ln, Castleton OL11 3BY
☎ 01706 40841 Fax 01706 860587
Two parkland courses, with challenging par 3s, and a driving range.
New Course: 9 holes, 2699yds, Par 34, SSS 34, Course record 30.
Old Course: 18 holes, 3276yds, Par 55, SSS 55.
Club membership 220.

Visitors no restrictions.
Societies must contact in advance.
Green Fees not confirmed.
Prof Mike Vipond
Designer T Wilson
Facilities
& Leisure fishing.
Location S of Rochdale, nr junc 20 (M62)

Hotel ★★★ 68% Norton Grange Hotel, Manchester Rd, Castleton, ROCHDALE
☎ 01706 30788 51

Rochdale Edenfield Rd OL11 5YR
☎ 01706 43818 Fax 01706 43818
Parkland course with enjoyable golf and easy walking.
18 holes, 6050yds, Par 71, SSS 69, Course record 65.
Club membership 750.

Visitors must telephone in advance.
Societies apply in writing or telephone
Green Fees £25 per day/round (£30 weekends & bank holidays).
Prof Andrew Laverty
Designer George Lowe
Facilities
Location 1.75m W on A680

Hotel ★★ 59% Midway Hotel, Manchester Rd, Castleton, ROCHDALE
☎ 01706 32881 24

Springfield Park Springfield Park, Bolton Rd OL11 4RE
☎ 01706 56401 (weekend only)
Parkland-moorland course situated in a valley. The River Roch adds an extra hazard to the course.
18 holes, 5237yds, Par 67, SSS 66, Course record 64.
Club membership 300.

Visitors must contact professional in advance.
Societies telephone in advance.
Green Fees not confirmed.
Prof David Wills
Facilities
Location 1.5m SW off A58

Hotel ★★ 59% Midway Hotel, Manchester Rd, Castleton, ROCHDALE
☎ 01706 32881 24

ROMILEY Map 07 SJ99

Romiley Goose House Green SK6 4LJ
☎ 0161 430 2392 Fax 0161 430 7258
Semi-parkland course on the edge of the Derbyshire Hills, providing a good test of golf with a number of outstanding holes, notably the 6th, 9th, 14th and 16th. The latter enjoys magnificent views from the tee.
18 holes, 6454yds, Par 70, SSS 71, Course record 66.
Club membership 700.

Visitors are advised to contact in advance, may not play Thu or Sat before 4pm.
Societies Tue & Wed, must book in advance.
Green Fees not confirmed.
Prof Gary Butler
Facilities by prior arrangement
Location E side of town centre off B6104

Hotel ★★ 68% Red Lion Inn, 112 Buxton Rd, High Ln, STOCKPORT
☎ 01663 765227 6

SALE Map 07 SJ79

Ashton on Mersey Church Ln M33 5QQ
☎ 0161 976 4390 & 962 3727 Fax 0161 976 4390
Parkland course with easy walking alongside the River Mersey.
9 holes, 6146yds, Par 71, SSS 69, Course record 66.
Club membership 485.

Visitors with member only Sun & bank holidays, not Sat or Tue.
Societies Thu only. Apply in writing.
Green Fees £18 per day.
Prof Mike Williams
Facilities
& Leisure sauna.
Location 1m W of M63 junc 7, off Glebelands Road

Hotel ★★★ 66% Cresta Court Hotel, Church St, ALTRINCHAM
☎ 0161 927 7272 138

Sale Golf Rd M33 2XU
☎ 0161 973 1638 (Gen Man) Fax 0161 962 4217
Tree-lined parkland course. Feature holes are the 13th - Watery Gap - and the par 3 (117yd) 17th.
18 holes, 6352yds, Par 71, SSS 70.
Club membership 700.

Visitors contact professional in advance.
Societies apply by letter.
Green Fees not confirmed.
Prof Mike Stewart
Facilities
Location NW side of town centre off A6144

Hotel ★★★ 66% Cresta Court Hotel, Church St, ALTRINCHAM
☎ 0161 927 7272 138

SHEVINGTON Map 07 SD50

Gathurst 62 Miles Ln WN6 8EW
☎ 01257 255235 (Secretary) & 254909 (Pro)
Testing parkland course, slightly hilly.
18 holes, 6016yds, Par 70, SSS 69, Course record 65.
Club membership 575.

Visitors may play anytime except competition days.
Societies welcome Mon, Tue, Thu & Fri. Apply in writing to Secretary.
Green Fees £22 per day.
Prof David Clarke
Designer N Pearson
Facilities
Location W side of village B5375 off junc 27 of M6

Hotel ★★★ 65% Wigan/Standish Moat House, Almond Brook Rd, Standish, WIGAN
☎ 01257 499988 124

STALYBRIDGE Map 07 SJ99

Stamford Oakfield House, Huddersfield Rd SK15 3PY
☎ 01457 832126 & 834829
Undulating moorland course.
18 holes, 5701yds, Par 70, SSS 68, Course record 62.
Club membership 600.

Visitors limited play at weekends.
Societies apply in writing.
Green Fees £20 per day/round (£25 weekends).
Facilities
Location 2m NE off A635

Hotel ★★ 70% York House Hotel, York Place, Richmond St, ASHTON-UNDER-LYNE
☎ 0161 330 9000 24 Annexe10

STANDISH Map 07 SD51

Standish Court Rectory Ln WN6 0XD
☎ 01257 425777 Fax 01257 425888
Undulating 18 hole parkland course, not overly long but provides a good test for all level of players. Front nine more open with room for errors, back nine very scenic through woodland, a number of tight driving holes. Greens in excellent condition.
18 holes, 5625yds, Par 68, SSS 66.
Club membership 500.

Visitors can play anytime, phone in advance for tee time, standard golfing dress required.
Societies telephone in advance.
Green Fees £20 per day; £11 per round (£30/£16 weekends).
Cards
Prof J Kershaw
Designer P Dawson
Facilities

Location Off M6 junct 27, just through traffic lights in Standish village

Hotel ★★★★ 67% Kilhey Court Hotel, Chorley Rd, Standish, WIGAN ☎ 01257 472100 63

STOCKPORT Map 07 SJ89

Heaton Moor Heaton Mersey SK4 3NX
☎ 0161 432 0846
Parkland course, easy walking.
18 holes, 5968, Par 70, SSS 69, Course record 66.
Club membership 400.
Visitors restricted Tue, bank holidays & Sat (summer).
Societies apply in writing.
Green Fees £23 per day (£31 weekends & bank holidays).
Prof Simon Marsh
Facilities
Location N of town centre off B5169

Hotel ★★ 67% Saxon Holme Hotel, 230 Wellington Rd, STOCKPORT ☎ 0161 432 2335 33

Houldsworth Houldsworth Park, Reddish SK5 6BN
☎ 0161 442 9611 & 0161 442 1712
Flat parkland course, tree-lined and with water hazards. Testing holes 9th (par 5) and 13th (par 5).
18 holes, 6209yds, Par 71, SSS 70.
Club membership 680.
Visitors may not play weekends & bank holidays unless by prior arrangement with professional.
Societies by prior arrangement.
Green Fees not confirmed.
Prof David Naylor
Facilities
Location 4m SE of city centre off A6

Hotel ★★★ 61% Willow Bank Hotel, 340-342 Wilmslow Rd, Fallowfield, MANCHESTER ☎ 0161 224 0461 116

Marple Barnsfold Rd, Hawk Green, Marple SK6 7EL
☎ 0161 427 2311 Fax 0161 427 1125
Parkland course.
18 holes, 5552yds, Par 68, SSS 67, Course record 66.
Club membership 640.
Visitors restricted Thu afternoon & weekend competition days.
Societies apply in writing to professional.
Green Fees £20 per day (£30 weekends & bank holidays).
Prof David Myers
Facilities
Location S side of town centre

Hotel ★★ 68% Red Lion Inn, 112 Buxton Rd, High Ln, STOCKPORT ☎ 01663 765227 6

Reddish Vale Southcliffe Rd, Reddish SK5 7EE
☎ 0161 480 2359 Fax 0161 477 8242
Undulating heathland course designed by Dr. A Mackenzie and situated in the River Tame valley.
18 holes, 6100yds, Par 69, SSS 69, Course record 64.
Club membership 550.
Visitors must play with member at weekends.
Societies must contact in writing.
Green Fees £22 per day.
Prof Bob Freeman
Designer Dr A Mackenzie
Facilities
Location 1.5m N off Sandy Lane

Hotel ★★ 67% The Wycliffe Hotel, 74 Edgeley Rd, Edgeley, STOCKPORT ☎ 0161 477 5395 20

Stockport Offerton Rd, Offerton SK2 5HL
☎ 0161 427 8369 (Secretary) & 427 2421 (Pro) Fax 0161 4 49 8293
A beautifully situated course in wide open countryside with views of the Cheshire and Derbyshire hills. It is not too long but requires that the player plays all the shots, to excellent greens. Demanding holes include the dog-leg 3rd, 12th, and 18th and the 460 yard opening hole is among the toughest in Cheshire.
18 holes, 6326yds, Par 71, SSS 71, Course record 66.
Club membership 500.
Visitors must contact professional in advance, limited play weekends.
Societies Wed & Thu only, apply in writing to Secretary.
Green Fees £35 per round (£45 weekends & bank holidays).
Prof Mike Peel
Designer P Barrie/A Herd
Facilities
Location 4m SE on A627

Hotel ★★ 68% Red Lion Inn, 112 Buxton Rd, High Ln, STOCKPORT ☎ 01663 765227 6

SWINTON Map 07 SD70

Swinton Park East Lancashire Rd M27 5LX
☎ 0161 794 0861
One of Lancashire's longest inland courses.
18 holes, 6726yds, Par 73, SSS 72, Course record 66.
Club membership 600.
Visitors may not play weekends or Thu. Must contact in advance and have handicap certificate.
Societies apply by letter.
Green Fees not confirmed.
Prof James Wilson
Designer James Braid
Facilities
Location 1m W off A580

Hotel ★★★ 65% Novotel, Worsley Brow, WORSLEY ☎ 0161 799 3535 119

UPPERMILL Map 07 SD90

Saddleworth Mountain Ash OL3 6LT ☎ 01457 873653
Moorland course, with superb views of Pennines.
18 holes, 5976yds, Par 71, SSS 69, Course record 65.
Club membership 800.
Visitors must contact in advance, restricted at weekends.
Societies contact in advance.
Green Fees £23 per day (£30 weekends & bank holidays).
Prof Tom Shard
Designer George Lowe/Dr McKenzie
Facilities
Location E side of town centre off A670

Hotel ★★★ 70% Hotel Smokies Park, Ashton Rd, Bardsley, OLDHAM
☎ 0161 624 3405 47

URMSTON Map 07 SJ79

Flixton Church Rd, Flixton M41 6EP
☎ 0161 748 2116
Meadowland course bounded by River Mersey.
9 holes, 6410yds, Par 71, SSS 71.
Club membership 430.

Visitors contact professional in advance, with member only weekends & bank holidays.
Societies apply in writing.
Green Fees £16 per day.
Prof Daniel Procter
Facilities
& Leisure snooker.
Location S side of town centre on B5213

Hotel ★★★★ 64% Copthorne Manchester, Clippers Quay, Salford Quays, MANCHESTER
☎ 0161 873 7321 166

WALKDEN Map 07 SD70

Brackley Municipal M38 9TR ☎ 0161 790 6076
Mostly flat course.
9 holes, 3003yds, Par 35, SSS 69.

Visitors no restrictions.
Green Fees not confirmed.
Facilities
Location 2m NW on A6

Hotel ★★★ 65% Novotel, Worsley Brow, WORSLEY ☎ 0161 799 3535 119

WESTHOUGHTON Map 07 SD60

Westhoughton Long Island, School St BL5 2BR
☎ 01942 811085 Fax 01942 608958
Compact downland course.
9 holes, 2886yds, Par 70, SSS 68, Course record 64.
Club membership 280.

Visitors with member only at weekends.
Societies telephone in advance or apply in writing.
Green Fees not confirmed.
Prof Jason Seed
Facilities
Location 0.5m NW off A58

Hotel ★★★ 63% The Beaumont Hotel, Beaumont Rd, BOLTON ☎ 01204 651511 101

WHITEFIELD Map 07 SD80

Stand The Dales, Ashbourne Grove M45 7NL
☎ 0161 766 3197 Fax 0161 796 3234
A semi-parkland course with five moorland holes. A fine test of golf with a very demanding finish.
18 holes, 6411yds, Par 72, SSS 71, Course record 67.
Club membership 500.

Visitors must contact professional in advance.
Societies Wed & Fri, apply by telephone.
Green Fees £25 per day (£30 weekends).
Prof Mark Dance
Designer G Lowe/A Herd
Facilities
Location 1m W off A667

Hotel ★★★ 65% Bolholt Country Park Hotel, Walshaw Rd, BURY
☎ 0161 764 3888 Freephone 0800 174141
Fax 0161 763 1789 59

Whitefield Higher Ln M45 7EZ ☎ 0161 766 2904 & 2728
Fine sporting parkland course with well-watered greens.
18 holes, 6045yds, Par 69, SSS 69, Course record 64.

Visitors must contact in advance, play restricted weekends.
Societies must contact in advance.
Green Fees £25 per day Mon-Fri.
Prof Paul Reeves
Facilities
& Leisure hard tennis courts.
Location N side of town centre on A665

Hotel ★★★★ 60% The Portland Thistle, 3/5 Portland St, Piccadilly Gardens, MANCHESTER
☎ 0161 228 3400 205

WIGAN Map 07 SD50

Haigh Hall Haigh Country Park, Aspull WN2 1PE
☎ 01942 831107
Municipal parkland course, with hard walking, and a canal forms the west boundary. Adjacent to 'Haigh Country Park' with many facilities.
18 holes, 6423yds, Par 70, SSS 71, Course record 65.
Club membership 250.

Visitors must contact professional in advance.
Societies apply in writing to professional.
Green Fees £7 per 18 holes (£9.50 weekends).
Prof Ian Lee
Designer Frank Pennink
Facilities
Location 2m NE off B5238

Hotel ★★ 64% Bel-Air Hotel, 236 Wigan Ln, WIGAN ☎ 01942 241410 12

Wigan Arley Hall, Haigh WN1 2UH ☎ 01257 421360
Among the best of Lancashire's 9-hole courses. The fine old clubhouse is the original Arley Hall, and is surrounded by a 12th century moat.
9 holes, 6036yds, Par 70, SSS 69.
Club membership 200.

Visitors must contact in advance. May not play Tue or Sat.
Societies apply by telephone.
Green Fees not confirmed.
Facilities
Location 3m NE off B5238

Hotel ★★★ 65% Wigan/Standish Moat House, Almond Brook Rd, Standish, WIGAN
☎ 01257 499988 124

WOODFORD Map 07 SJ88

Avro Old Hall Ln SK7 1QR ☎ 0161 439 2709
An attractive, tight and challenging 9-hole course.
9 holes, 5735yds, Par 69, SSS 68.
Club membership 400.
Visitors restricted weekends and competition days. not able to take societies.
Green Fees not confirmed.
Facilities
Location W side of village on A5102

Hotel ★★★ 66% County Hotel Bramhall, Bramhall Ln South, BRAMHALL
☎ 0161 439 8116 & 455 9988 Fax 0161 440 80 71 65

WORSLEY Map 07 SD70

Ellesmere Old Clough Ln M28 7HZ
☎ 0161 799 0554 & 790 8591
Parkland course with natural hazards. Testing holes: 3rd (par 5), 9th (par 3), 15th (par 5). Hard walking.
18 holes, 6248yds, Par 70, SSS 70, Course record 67.
Club membership 700.
Visitors welcome except club competition days & bank holidays.
Societies apply in advance.
Green Fees £25 per day; £19 per round (£26 per day/round weekends & bank holidays).
Prof Terry Morley
Facilities
Location N side of village off A580

Hotel ★★★ 65% Novotel, Worsley Brow, WORSLEY ☎ 0161 799 3535 119

HAMPSHIRE

ALDERSHOT Map 04 SU85

Army Laffans Rd GU11 2HF
☎ 01252 337272 Fax 01252 337562
The second oldest course in Hampshire. Picturesque heathland course with three par 3's, over 200 yds.
18 holes, 6550yds, Par 71, SSS 71, Course record 67.
Club membership 715.
Visitors may not play weekends.
Societies apply in writing.
Green Fees £24 per round.
Prof Graham Cowley
Facilities
Location 1.5m N of town centre off A323/A325

Hotel ★★★ 69% Potters International Hotel, 1 Fleet Rd, ALDERSHOT
☎ 01252 344000 97

ALRESFORD Map 04 SU53

Alresford Cheriton Rd, Tichborne Down SO24 0PN
☎ 01962 733746 Fax 01962 736040
A testing downland course on well drained chalk.Now expanded to 18 holes, incorporating the original 12, but changing direction of play to give two starting points and two closing greens near clubhouse.
18 holes, 5905yds, Par 69, SSS 68, Course record 64.
Club membership 720.
Visitors must contact in advance.
Societies must telephone in advance.
Green Fees £23 per round (£41 weekends & bank holidays).
Prof Malcolm Scott
Designer Scott Webb Young
Facilities
Location 1m S on B3046

Hotel ★★ 59% Swan Hotel, 11 West St, ALRESFORD ☎ 01962 732302 & 734427 Fax 01962 735274 23rm(10)

ALTON Map 04 SU73

Alton Old Odiham Rd GU34 4BU
☎ 01420 82042 & 86518
Undulating meadowland course.
9 holes, 5744yds, Par 68, SSS 68, Course record 64.
Club membership 350.
Visitors must contact in advance and must have a handicap certificate to play at weekends.
Societies must contact in advance.
Green Fees £12 per 18 holes; £8 per 9 holes (£15 per 18 holes weekends & bank holidays).
Prof Paul Brown
Designer James Braid
Facilities
Location 2m N off A32

Hotel ★★★ 66% Alton House Hotel, Normandy St, ALTON ☎ 01420 80033 39

Worldham Park Cakers Ln, East Worldham GU34 3BF
☎ 01420 543151 Fax 01420 84124
The course is in a picturesque woodland setting with an abundance of challenging holes (doglegs, water and sand). Increased to 18-holes in the summer of 1995.
18 holes, 5800yds, Par 71, SSS 68.
Club membership 500.
Visitors are advised to book in advance at weekends.
Societies Mon-Fri only. Must contact in advance.
Green Fees £11 per round (£13 weekends).
Cards
Prof Jon Le Roux
Designer F J Whidborne
Facilities
Location B3004, 2mins from Alton

Hotel ★★★ 67% Alton Grange Hotel, London Rd, ALTON
☎ 01420 86565 26 Annexe4

AMPFIELD Map 04 SU42

Ampfield Par Three Winchester Rd SO51 9BQ
☎ 01794 368480
Pretty parkland course designed by Henry Cotton in 1963. Well-bunkered greens.
18 holes, 2478yds, Par 54, SSS 53, Course record 49.
Club membership 470.

Visitors must contact in advance & have a handicap certificate to play at weekends & bank holidays.
Societies must contact in advance.
Green Fees £15 per day; £9 per round (£15.50 per round weekends & bank holidays).
Prof Richard Benfield
Designer Henry Cotton
Facilities by prior arrangement
Location 4m NE of Romsey on A31

Hotel ★★★ 68% Potters Heron Hotel, Winchester Rd, Ampfield, ROMSEY ☎ 01703 266611 54

ANDOVER Map 04 SU34

Andover 51 Winchester Rd SP10 2EF ☎ 01264 358040
Undulating downland course combining a good test of golf for all abilities with breathtaking views across Hampshire countryside. Well guarded greens and a notable par 3, 9th (225yds) with the tee perched on top of a hill, 100ft above the green.
9 holes, 6096yds, Par 70, SSS 69, Course record 66.
Club membership 450.

Visitors must contact professional in advance tel: 01264 324151.
Societies Mon-Wed only. Must contact in advance.
Green Fees £10 per 18 holes; (£22 weekends & bank holidays).
Prof D Lawrence
Designer J H Taylor
Facilities by prior arrangement by prior arrangement
Location 0.5m S on A3057

Hotel ★★★ 62% Ashley Court Hotel, Micheldever Rd, ANDOVER ☎ 01264 357344 9 Annexe26

ASHLEY HEATH Map 04 SU10

Moors Valley Moors Valley Country Park, Horton Rd BH24 2ET ☎ 01425 479776 Fax 01425 472057
This municipal course is set in the beautiful surroundings of a country park. It offers a test for all standards. It is gently undulating, with water hazards on six holes.
18 holes, 6200yds, Par 72, SSS 70.
Club membership 250.

Visitors must contact in advance.
Societies telephone for availability.
Green Fees £10 per 18 holes; £7 per 11 holes (£12.50/£8 weekends).
Cards
Prof Michael Torrens
Designer Hawtree & Son
Facilities
Location Signposted from A31 Ashley Heath roundabout

Hotel ★★★ 66% St Leonards Hotel, ST LEONARDS ☎ 01425 471220 34

BARTON-ON-SEA Map 04 SZ29

Barton-on-Sea Milford Rd BH25 5PP
☎ 01425 615308 Fax 01425 621457
Though not strictly a links course, it is right on a cliff edge with views over the Isle of Wight and Christchurch Bay. On a still day there is nothing much to it - but when it blows the course undergoes a complete change in character. Recently reconstructed to create 27 holes.
Becton-Needles: 18 holes, 6505yds, Par 72, SSS 71.
Needles-Stroller: 18 holes, 6453yds, Par 72, SSS 71.
Stroller-Becton: 18 holes, 6296yds, Par 72, SSS 70.
Club membership 940.

Visitors must contact in advance and have a handicap certificate.
Societies must telephone in advance.
Green Fees £27.50 per day (£32.50 weekends & bank holidays).
Prof Pat Coombs
Designer Hamilton Stutt
Facilities & Leisure snooker.
Location B3058 SE side of town

Hotel ★★★★★ Chewton Glen Hotel, Christchurch Rd, NEW MILTON ☎ 01425 275341 50 Annexe2

BASINGSTOKE Map 04 SU65

Basingstoke Kempshott Park RG23 7LL
☎ 01256 465990 Fax 01256 331793
A well-maintained parkland course with wide and inviting fairways. You are inclined to expect longer drives than are actually achieved - partly on account of the trees. There are many two-hundred-year-old beech trees, since the course was built on an old deer park.
18 holes, 6350yds, Par 70, SSS 70, Course record 66.
Club membership 700.

Visitors must contact in advance and play Mon-Fri only (ex bank holidays).
Societies must contact in advance.
Green Fees £35 per day; £25 per round.
Cards
Prof Ian Hayes
Designer James Braid
Facilities
Location 3.5m SW on A30 M3 exit 7

Hotel B Forte Posthouse Basingstoke, Grove Rd, BASINGSTOKE ☎ 01256 468181 84

Dummer Dummer RG25 2AR
☎ 01256 397888 Fax 01256 397889
Opened in July 1993 and designed by Peter Alliss/Clive Clark with several water hazards. Gentle terrain makes the course suitable for players of all ages.
18 holes, 6427yds, Par 72.
Club membership 750.

Visitors must contact in advance, handicap required, limited at weekends.
Societies contact in advance.

Green Fees £30 per day; £20 per round.
Cards
Prof Gary Stubbington
Designer Peter Allis
Facilities
& Leisure sauna, practice range.
Location Off junc 7 of M3 towards Dummer village

Hotel ★★★ 70% Centrecourt Hotel, Tennis & Health Club, Centre Dr, Chineham, BASINGSTOKE
☎ 01256 816664 50

Weybrook Park Rooksdown Ln RG24 9NT
☎ 01256 320347 Fax 01256 812973
A course designed to be enjoyable for all standards of player. Easy walking with fablous views.
18 holes, 6468yds, Par 71, SSS 71.
Club membership 600.
Visitors telephone for availability.
Societies telephone in advance for availability and confirm in writing.
Green Fees £15 (£20 weekends).
Prof Anthony Dillon
Facilities
Location 2m W of town centre, entrance via A339

Hotel ★★★ 61% Ringway Hotel, Popley Way, Aldermaston Roundabout, Ringway North (A339), BASINGSTOKE
☎ 01256 320212 134

BORDON Map 04 SU73

Blackmoor Firgrove Rd, Whitehill GU35 9EH
☎ 01420 472775 Fax 01420 487666
A first-class moorland course with a great variety of holes. Fine greens and wide pine tree-lined fairways are a distinguishing feature. The ground is mainly flat and walking easy.
18 holes, 6164yds, Par 69, SSS 69, Course record 65.
Club membership 750.
Visitors must contact in advance and may not play at weekends.
Societies must telephone in advance.
Green Fees £30 per round; £40 per 36 holes.
Prof Stephen Clay
Designer H S Colt
Facilities
Location Travelling S on A325, 6m beyond Farnham, pass through Whitehill and turn right at crossroads

Hotel ★★★ 60% Swan Hotel, High St, ALTON
☎ 01420 83777 36

BOTLEY Map 04 SU51

Botley Park Hotel, Golf & Country Club Winchester Rd, Boorley Green SO32 2UA
☎ 01489 796000 Fax 01489 789242
Pleasantly undulating course with water hazards. Driving range and country club facilities.
18 holes, 6341yds, Par 70, SSS 70, Course record 67.
Club membership 750.
Visitors must play with member. Must contact in advance & have handicap certificate.
Societies contact in advance.
Green Fees £30 per round.
Cards
Prof Tim Barter
Designer Ewan Murray
Facilities
& Leisure hard tennis courts, heated indoor swimming pool, squash, sauna, solarium, gymnasium, extensive leisure club.
Location 1m NW of Botley on B3354

Hotel ★★★★ 68% Botley Park Hotel Golf & Country Club, Winchester Rd, Boorley Green, BOTLEY
☎ 01489 780888 100

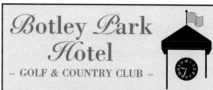

BROCKENHURST Map 04 SU20

Brokenhurst Manor Sway Rd SO42 7SG
☎ 01590 623332 (Secretary) Fax 01590 624140
An attractive woodland/heathland course set at the edge of the New Forest, with the unusual feature of three loops of six holes each to complete the round. Fascinating holes include the short 5th and 12th, and the 4th and 17th, both dog-legged. A stream also features on seven of the holes.
18 holes, 6222yds, Par 70, SSS 70, Course record 63.
Club membership 700.

Visitors must contact in advance, numbers limited. Must have a handicap certificate.
Societies Thu only, apply in writing.
Green Fees £40 per day; £30 per round (£55 weekends & bank holidays).
Prof John Lovell
Designer H S Colt
Facilities ⊗)Ⅲ ℡ ☕ 🍸 ⛺ 🏠 ✓
Location 1m S on B3055

Hotel ★★★ 65% Balmer Lawn Hotel, Lyndhurst Rd, BROCKENHURST ☎ 01590 623116 55 ⇄ ↱
Additional hotel ★★ 68% Watersplash Hotel, The Rise, BROCKENHURST ☎ 01590 622344 Fax 01590 624047 23 ⇄ ↱

BURLEY Map 04 SU20

Burley Cott Ln BH24 4BB
☎ 01425 402431 & 403737 Fax 01425 402431
Undulating heather and gorseland. The 7th requires an accurately placed tee shot to obtain par 4. Played off different tees on second nine.
9 holes, 6149yds, Par 71, SSS 69, Course record 68.
Club membership 520.

Visitors must contact in advance & preferably have a handicap certificate or be a member of a recognised golf club. May not play before 4pm Sat.
Societies parties up to 14 only.
Green Fees £14 per round/day (£16 weekends & bank holidays).
Facilities ⊗ by prior arrangement ℡ ☕ 🍸 ⛺ ✓
Location E side of village

Hotel ★★★ 63% Moorhill House, BURLEY ☎ 01425 403285 24 ⇄ ↱

CORHAMPTON Map 04 SU62

Corhampton Sheep's Pond Ln SO32 3LP ☎ 01489 877279
Free draining downland course situated in the heart of the picturesque Meon Valley.
18 holes, 6444yds, Par 71, SSS 71.
Club membership 800.

Visitors weekdays only and must contact in advance.
Societies Mon & Thu only, contact in writing or telephone.
Green Fees not confirmed.
Prof Ian Roper
Facilities ⊗)Ⅲ ℡ ☕ ⛺ 🏠 ✓
Location 1m W of Corhampton, off B3035

Hotel ★★ 75% Old House Hotel, The Square, WICKHAM ☎ 01329 833049 9 Annexe3

CRONDALL Map 04 SU74

Oak Park Heath Ln GU10 5PB
☎ 01252 850880 & 850850 Fax 01252 850851
Village: Gently undulating parkland course overlooking pretty village. 16-bay floodlit driving range, practice green and practice bunker. Woodland: Undulating on holes 10 to 13. Panoramic views, mature trees, very challenging.
Woodland: 18 holes, 6240yds, Par 70, SSS 70.
Village: 9 holes, 3279yds, Par 36, SSS 71.
Club membership 600.

Visitors no restrictions for Village Course. Must book in advance and have a handicap certificate for Woodland Course.
Societies must telephone in advance.
Green Fees not confirmed.
Prof Simon Coaker
Designer Patrick Dawson
Facilities
& Leisure gymnasium.
Location 0.5m E of village off A287 Farnham-Odiham

Hotel ★★★ 60% Farnham House Hotel, Alton Rd, FARNHAM ☎ 01252 716908 20

DIBDEN Map 04 SU40

Dibden Main Rd SO45 5TB ☎ 01703 207508
Municipal parkland course with views over Southampton Water. A pond guards the green at the par 5, 3rd hole. Twenty-bay driving range.
Course 1: 18 holes, 5900yds, Par 70, SSS 69, Course record 63.
Course 2: 9 holes, 1520yds, Par 29.
Club membership 600.

Visitors must book in advance.
Societies must contact in writing.
Green Fees £10 per 18 holes, £4.50 per 9 holes (£12/£5.50 weekends).
Prof Alan Bridge
Designer Hamilton Stutt
Facilities
Location 2m NW of Dibden Purlieu, off A326 to Hythe

Hotel ★★★ 65% Forest Lodge Hotel, Pikes Hill, Romsey Rd, LYNDHURST ☎ 01703 283677 23

EASTLEIGH Map 04 SU41

Fleming Park Magpie Ln SO50 9LS ☎ 01703 612797
Parkland course with stream-'Monks Brook'-running through.
18 holes, 4436yds, Par 65, SSS 62.
Club membership 300.

Visitors no restrictions.
Societies must contact in advance.
Green Fees not confirmed.
Prof Chris Strickett
Facilities
Location E side of town centre

Hotel B Forte Posthouse Eastleigh/Southampton, Leigh Rd, EASTLEIGH ☎ 01703 619700 116

EAST WELLOW Map 04 SU32

Wellow Ryedown Ln SO51 6BD
☎ 01794 323833 & 322872
Three 9-hole courses set in 217 acres of parkland surrounding Embley Park, former home of Florence Nightingale.
Ryedown & Embley: 18 holes, 5966yds, Par 70, SSS 69.
Embley & Blackwater: 18 holes, 6295yds, Par 72, SSS 70.
Blackwater & Ryedown: 18 holes, 5819yds, Par 70, SSS 68.
Club membership 500.

Visitors advisable to contact in advance weekdays.
Societies apply in writing or telephone, Mon-Fri not bank holidays.
Green Fees £20 per day; £16 per 18 holes.
Prof Neil Bratley
Designer W Wiltshire
Facilities
Location Exit2 of M27, then A36 to Salisbury then 1m right

Hotel ★★★ 63% The White Horse, Market Place, ROMSEY ☎ 01794 512431 33

FAREHAM Map 04 SU50

Cams Hall Porchester Rd PO16 8UP
☎ 01329 827222 Fax 01329 827111
Two Peter Alliss/Clive Clark designed golf courses opened in 1993. The Creek Course is coastal and has salt and fresh water lakes and the fairways are lined with undulating hills. The Park Course is designed in the grounds of Cams Hall.
Creek Course: 18 holes, 6244yds, Par 71, SSS 71, Course record 69.
Park Course: 9 holes, 3247yds, Par 36, SSS 36.
Club membership 950.

Visitors must contact in advance, tee times available any time.
Societies telephone for details and society golf day pack.
Green Fees £30 per day; £19 per round (£35/£25 weekends).
Cards
Prof Jason Neve
Designer Peter Alliss
Facilities
& Leisure sauna.
Location M27 exit 11 to A27

Hotel ★★★ 65% Lysses House Hotel, 51 High St, FAREHAM ☎ 01329 822622 21

FARNBOROUGH Map 04 SU85

Southwood Ively Rd, Cove GU14 0LJ
☎ 01252 548700 Fax 01252 515855
Municipal parkland course with stream running through.
18 holes, 5738yds, Par 69, SSS 68, Course record 61.
Club membership 650.

Visitors must book in advance.
Societies must contact in advance.
Green Fees £12.50 (£15 weekends).
Cards
Prof Bob Hammond
Designer Hawtree & Son

Facilities
Location 0.5m W

Hotel B Forte Posthouse Farnborough, Lynchford Rd, FARNBOROUGH ☎ 01252 545051 143

FLEET Map 04 SU85

North Hants Minley Rd GU13 8RE
☎ 01252 616443 Fax 01252 811627

Picturesque tree-lined course with much heather and gorse close to the fairways. A comparatively easy par-4 first hole may lull the golfer into a false sense of security, only to be rudely awakened at the testing holes which follow. The ground is rather undulating and, though not tiring, does offer some excellent 'blind' shots, and more than a few surprises in judging distance.
18 holes, 6257yds, Par 69, SSS 70, Course record 65.
Club membership 600.

Visitors must contact at least 48 hours in advance. Must play with member at weekends.
Societies Tue & Wed only. Must telephone in advance.
Green Fees £30 per round; £37 two rounds.
Prof Steve Porter
Designer James Braid
Facilities
Location 0.25m N of Fleet station on B3013

Hotel ★★★ 62% Lismoyne Hotel, Church Rd, FLEET ☎ 01252 628555 44

GOSPORT Map 04 SZ69

Gosport & Stokes Bay Off Fort Rd, Haslar PO12 2AT
☎ 01705 527941 Fax 01705 527941
A testing links course overlooking the Solent, with plenty of gorse and short rough. Changing winds.
9 holes, 5999yds, Par 70, SSS 69, Course record 65.
Club membership 499.
Visitors may not play Sun and Thu.
Societies must contact in writing.
Green Fees £20 per day; £15 per round (£20 per round weekends).
Facilities
Location A32 S from Fareham, E on Fort rd to Haslar

Hotel ★★★ 61% Belle Vue Hotel, 39 Marine Pde East, LEE-ON-THE-SOLENT
☎ 01705 550258 24 Annexe3

Hartley Wintney Map 04 SU75

Hartley Wintney London Rd RG27 8PT
☎ 01252 844211 (Sec) 843779 (Prof) Fax 01252 844211
Easy walking, parkland course in pleasant countryside. Played off different tees on back nine, with testing par 4s at 4th and 13th.
9 holes, 6096yds, Par 70, SSS 69.
Club membership 475.
Visitors must contact in advance.
Societies Tue & Thu only by prior arrangement.
Green Fees on application.
Prof Martin Smith
Facilities ⊗ 🍺 ♨ 🏠 ✓
Location NE side of village on A30

Hotel ★★★ 62% Lismoyne Hotel, Church Rd, FLEET ☎ 01252 628555 44 ⇌ ↱

Hayling Island Map 04 SU70

Hayling Links Ln PO11 0BX
☎ 01705 464446 Fax 01705 464446
A delightful links course among the dunes offering fine sea-scapes and views across to the Isle of Wight. Varying sea breezes and sometimes strong winds ensure that the course seldom plays the same two days running. Testing holes at the 12th and 13th, both par 4. Club selection is important.
18 holes, 5521yds, Par 71, SSS 71, Course record 65.
Club membership 800.
Visitors must contact in advance and have a handicap certificate, no jeans or denims allowed.
Societies welcome Tue & Wed, or half days Mon & Thu, apply in writing or telephone.
Green Fees £33 per day; £27 per round (£44/£35 weekends).
Prof Raymond Gadd
Designer Taylor 1905, Simpson 1933
Facilities ⊗))) by prior arrangement 🍺 ☕ ♨ 🏠 ↱ ✓
Location SW side of island at West Town

Hotel B Forte Posthouse Havant, Northney Rd, HAYLING ISLAND
☎ 01705 465011 92 ⇌ ↱

Kingsclere Map 04 SU55

Sandford Springs Wolverton RG26 5RT
☎ 01635 297883 & 297881 Fax 01635 298065
The course has unique variety in beautiful surroundings and offers three distinctive loops of 9 holes. There are water hazards, woodlands and gradients to negotiate, providing a challenge for all playing categories. From its highest point there are extensive views.
The Park: 9 holes, 2963yds, Par 34.
The Lakes: 9 holes, 3042yds, Par 35.
The Wood: 9 holes, 3180yds, Par 36.
Club membership 650.
Visitors must contact in advance. Restricted at weekends.
Societies must contact in advance.
Green Fees £29 per day; £23 per 18 holes; £15 per 9 holes.
Cards [card symbols]
Prof Gary Edmunds/Kim Brake
Designer Hawtree & Son
Facilities ⊗))) 🍺 ☕ ♀ ♨ 🏠 ↱ 🚗 ✓
Location On A339

Hotel ★★★ 61% Millwaters Hotel & Restaurant, London Rd, NEWBURY
☎ 01635 528838 30 ⇌ ↱

Kingsley Map 04 SU73

Dean Farm GU35 9NG ☎ 01420 489478 & 472313
Undulating downland course.
9 holes, 1500yds, Par 29.
Visitors no restrictions.
Societies must contact in writing.
Green Fees £6 per 18 holes; £4 per 9 holes.
Facilities 🍺 ☕ ♀ 🏠 ↱
& Leisure hard tennis courts.
Location W side of village off B3004

Hotel ★★★ 67% Alton Grange Hotel, London Rd, ALTON
☎ 01420 86565 26 ⇌ ↱ Annexe4 ⇌ ↱

Leckford Map 04 SU33

Leckford SO20 6JG ☎ 01264 810320
A testing downland course with good views.
9 holes, 6444yds, Par 70, SSS 71.
Club membership 200.
Green Fees not confirmed.
Facilities ♨
Location 1m SW off A3057

Hotel ★★★ 62% Grosvenor Hotel, High St, STOCKBRIDGE
☎ 01264 810606 25 ⇌ ↱

Lee-on-the-Solent Map 04 SU50

Lee-on-Solent Brune Ln PO13 9PB
☎ 01705 551170 Fax 01705 554233
A modest parkland/heathland course, yet a testing one. The five short holes always demand a high standard of play and the 13th is rated one of the best in the country. A new clubhouse completed in 1997.
18 holes, 5755yds, Par 69, SSS 69, Course record 64.
Club membership 750.
Visitors may not play before 9am. Handicap certificate required.
Societies must contact in advance.
Green Fees £30 per day/round (£35 weekends).
Prof John Richardson
Facilities ⊗))) 🍺 ☕ ♀ ♨ 🏠 ✓ ⟨
Location 1m N off B3385

Hotel ★★★ 61% Belle Vue Hotel, 39 Marine Pde East, LEE-ON-THE-SOLENT
☎ 01705 550258 24 ⇌ ↱ Annexe3 ⇌ ↱

A comprehensive list of driving ranges is given at the back of this guide. See page 479.

LIPHOOK Map 04 SU83

Liphook Wheatsheaf Enclosure GU30 7EH
☎ 01428 723271 & 723785 Fax 01428 724853
Heathland course with easy walking and fine views.
18 holes, 6167yds, Par 70, SSS 69, Course record 67.
Club membership 800.

Visitors must contact in advance; may not play Tue, competition days etc.
Societies Wed-Fri only. Must contact in advance.
Green Fees £40 per day; £30 per round (£50/£40 weekends).
Prof Ian Large
Designer A C Croome
Facilities
Location 1m S on B2030 (old A3)

Hotel ★★★★ 71% Lythe Hill Hotel, Petworth Rd, HASLEMERE
☎ 01428 651251 40

Old Thorns Griggs Green GU30 7PE
☎ 01428 724555
A challenging 18-hole championship-standard course designed around magnificent oaks, beeches and Scots pine.
18 holes, 6041yds, Par 72, SSS 70.

Visitors no restrictions.
Societies must telephone in advance.
Green Fees £50 per day; £35 per round (£65/£45 weekends).
Cards
Prof P Loxley
Designer Peter Allis/Dave Thomay
Facilities
& Leisure hard tennis courts, heated indoor swimming pool, sauna, solarium.
Location Leave A3 at Griggs Green, S of Liphook, signposted 'Old Thorns'

Hotel ★★★ 73% Old Thorns Golf Course Hotel & Restaurants, Longmoor Rd, Griggs Green, LIPHOOK
☎ 01428 724555 28 Annexe5

LYNDHURST Map 04 SU20

Bramshaw Brook SO43 7HE
☎ 01703 813433 Fax 01703 813958
Two 18-hole courses. The Manor Course is landscaped parkland with excellent greens, and features mature trees and streams. The Forest course is set amidst beautiful open forest. Easy walking. The Bell Inn Hotel, attached to the club, provides fine accommodation just a wedge shot from the first tee, and reserved tee times for its guests.
Manor Course: 18 holes, 6517yds, Par 71, SSS 71, Course record 66.
Forest Course: 18 holes, 5774yds, Par 69, SSS 68, Course record 65.
Club membership 950.

Visitors must be accompanied by member at weekends and bank holidays.
Societies apply in writing or telephone in advance.
Green Fees £40 per day; Manor: £27 per round; Forest: £21 per round.

Prof Clive Bonner
Facilities
& Leisure golfing rates at Bell Inn.
Location On B3079 1m W of M27 junc 1

Hotel ★★★ 67% Bell Inn, BROOK
☎ 01703 812214 25

New Forest Southampton Rd SO43 7BU
☎ 01703 282752
This picturesque heathland course is laid out in a typical stretch of the New Forest on high ground a little above the village of Lyndhurst. Natural hazards include the inevitable forest ponies. The first two holes are somewhat teasing, as is the 485-yard (par 5) 9th. Walking is easy.
18 holes, 5742yds, Par 69, SSS 68.
Club membership 850.
Visitors must contact in advance.
Societies must contact in advance.
Green Fees £16 per day; £12 per round.
Prof Danny Harris
Facilities
Location 0.5m NE off A35

Hotel ★★★ 71% Crown Hotel, High St, LYNDHURST ☎ 01703 282922 39

NEW MILTON Map 04 SZ29

Chewton Glen Hotel Christchurch Rd BH25 6QS
☎ 01425 275341 Fax 01425 272310
A 9-hole, Par 3 course with the hotel grounds plus a practice area. ONLY open to residents of the hotel or as a guest of a member of the club.
9 holes, 854yds, Par 27.
Club membership 150.
Visitors non residents must play with member.
Societies must contact in advance.
Green Fees not confirmed.
Cards
Facilities
& Leisure hard tennis courts, outdoor and indoor heated swimming pools, sauna, gymnasium.
Hotel ★★★★★ Chewton Glen Hotel, Christchurch Rd, NEW MILTON
☎ 01425 275341 50 Annexe2

OVERTON Map 04 SU54

Test Valley Micheldever Rd RG25 3DS ☎ 01256 771737
A downland course with prominent bunker features and lakes. Teeing variations at most holes enabling the course to be played from 5000 to 7000yds. Free drainage for consistent all-year play. The 2nd, 4th, 12th and 17th holes are particularly challenging but every hole has its own appealing individual character. Has hosted Hampshire Open and many PGA events.
18 holes, 6811yds, Par 72, SSS 73, Course record 66.
Club membership 500.
Visitors advisable to ring in advance. Must play after 11am weekends & bank holidays.
Societies apply in writing or telephone in advance.
Green Fees phone for details.
Cards

Prof Alastair Briggs
Designer Don Wright
Facilities
Location 1.5m N of A303

Hotel ★★★ 70% Centrecourt Hotel, Tennis & Health Club, Centre Dr, Chineham, BASINGSTOKE
☎ 01256 816664 50

OWER Map 04 SU31

Paultons Golf Centre Old Salisbury Rd SO51 6AN
☎ 01703 813992
A Pay and Play 18-hole course built within the original Paultons parkland which was laid out by 'Capability' Brown. There is also a 9-hole academy course, ideal fo beginners or players wishing to improve their short games as well as a 20-bay floodlit driving range.
18 holes, 6238yds, Par 71, SSS 70, Course record 72.
Academy: 9 holes, 1324yds, Par 27, SSS 27, Course record 24.
Club membership 500.
Visitors pay & play.
Societies telephone for details.
Green Fees not confirmed.
Prof John Cave & Heath Teschner
Designer J R Smith
Facilities
Hotel ★★★ 67% Bartley Lodge, Lyndhurst Rd, CADNAM ☎ 01703 812248 31

PETERSFIELD Map 04 SU72

Petersfield (New Course) Tankerdale Ln, Liss GU33 7QY
☎ 01730 895165 Fax 01730 894713
A new course designed by Martin Hawtree in an area of outstanding natural beauty with magnificent panoramic views.
18 holes, 6400yds, Par 72, SSS 71.
Club membership 800.
Visitors anytime during week no start times required, although telephone call prior to play advisable, no visitors before noon weekends.
Societies booking forms and deposit required.
Green Fees £30 per day; £25 per round (£30 per round weekends).
Prof Greg Hughes
Facilities
Location Off the A3 Petersfield by pass, between the Midhurst/Petersfield & Liss exit

Hotel ★★★ 73% Spread Eagle Hotel, South St, MIDHURST
☎ 01730 816911 35 Annexe4

Petersfield (Old Course) Sussex Rd GU31 4EJ
☎ 01730 267732 Fax 01730 894713
9 hole parkland course on level ground in an area of outstanding natural beauty. Numerous trees and water features.
9 holes, 3005yds, Par 72, SSS 69.
Visitors starting times required, pay & play at all times.
Societies booking form must be completed & deposit paid.
Green Fees £10 per 18 holes; £6 per 9 holes (£12/£10 weekends & bank holidays).
Prof Greg Hughes
Facilities

Location Off Sussex Road , B214

Hotel ★★★ 73% Spread Eagle Hotel, South St, MIDHURST
☎ 01730 816911 35 Annexe4

PORTSMOUTH & SOUTHSEA Map 04 SU60

Great Salterns Public Course Burrfields Rd PO3 5HH
☎ 01705 664549 Fax 01705 650525
Easy walking, seaside course with open fairways and testing shots onto well-guarded, small greens. Testing 13th hole, par 4, requiring 130yd shot across a lake.
18 holes, 5610yds, Par 69, SSS 66, Course record 64.
Club membership 700.
Visitors no restrictions.
Societies must contact in advance.
Green Fees £11 summer; £8.80 winter.
Cards
Prof Terry Healy
Facilities
Location NE of town centre on A2030

Hotel ★★★ 66% Innlodge Hotel, Burrfields Rd, PORTSMOUTH ☎ 01705 650510 73

Southsea The Clubhouse, Burrfields Rd PO3 5JJ
☎ 01705 664549
Municipal, meadowland course.
18 holes, 5800yds, Par 71, SSS 68, Course record 64.
Club membership 440.
Visitors no restrictions. Booking advisable.
Societies must contact in advance, tel: 01705 664549.
Green Fees £10.60 per round.
Cards
Prof Terry Healy
Facilities
Location 0.5m off M27

Hotel ★★★ 66% Innlodge Hotel, Burrfields Rd, PORTSMOUTH ☎ 01705 650510 73

ROMSEY Map 04 SU32

Dunwood Manor Shootash Hill SO51 0GF
☎ 01794 340549 Fax 01794 34215
Undulating parkland course with fine views. Recently redesigned with fine holes running through mature woodland.
18 holes, 5771yds, Par 68, SSS 68, Course record 61.
Club membership 720.
Visitors always welcome advisable to contact in advance; essential for weekends after 11am.
Societies must contact in advance.
Green Fees £22 per round (£30 weekends).
Prof Heath Teschner
Facilities
Location 4m W off A27

Hotel ★★★ 67% Bell Inn, BROOK
☎ 01703 812214 25

Romsey Romsey Rd, Nursling SO16 0XW
☎ 01703 734637 Fax 01703 741036
Parkland/woodland course with narrow tree-lined fairways. Six holes are undulating, rest are sloping. There are superb views over the Test valley.
18 holes, 5851yds, Par 69, SSS 68.
Club membership 900.
Visitors welcome Mon-Fri, must play with member weekends and bank holidays.
Societies Mon, Tue & Thu, must contact in advance.
Green Fees not confirmed.
Prof Mark Desmond
Facilities
Location 3m S on A3057

Hotel ★★★ 63% The White Horse, Market Place, ROMSEY ☎ 01794 512431 33

ROTHERWICK Map 04 SU75

Tylney Park RG27 9AY
☎ 01256 762079 Fax 01256 763079
Parkland course. Practice area.
18 holes, 6109yds, Par 70, SSS 69, Course record 67.
Club membership 730.
Visitors must be with member at weekends or have a handicap certificate.
Societies must apply by phone in advance.
Green Fees £21 per day/round (£28 per weekends).
Prof Chris de Bruin
Designer W Wiltshire
Facilities
Location 0.5m SW of Rotherwick, 2m NW of Hook, 2.5m from M3 junct 5 via Newnham

Hotel ★★★★ Tylney Hall Hotel, ROTHERWICK
☎ 01256 764881 35 Annexe75

ROWLANDS CASTLE Map 04 SU71

Rowlands Castle 31 Links Ln PO9 6AE
☎ 01705 412784 Fax 01705 413649
Reasonably dry in winter, the flat parkland course is a testing one with a number of tricky dog-legs and bunkers much in evidence. The Par 4 13th is a signature hole necessitating a drive to a narrow fairway and a second shot to a two-tiered green. The 7th, at 522yds, is the longest hole on the course and leads to a well-guarded armchair green.
18 holes, 6612yds, Par 72, SSS 72, Course record 69.
Club membership 800.
Visitors may not play Sat; must contact in advance and hold a handicap certificate.
Societies Tue & Thu only; must contact in writing.
Green Fees £25 per day (£30 weekends).
Cards
Prof Peter Klepacz
Designer Colt
Facilities by prior arrangement
Location W side of village off B2149

Hotel ★★★ 69% Brookfield Hotel, Havant Rd, EMSWORTH
☎ 01243 373363 & 376383 Fax 01243 376 342 40

Entries with a shaded background identify courses that are considered to be particularly interesting

SHEDFIELD Map 04 SU51

Marriott Meon Valley Hotel & Country Club Sandy Ln SO32 2HQ ☎ 01329 833455 Fax 01329 834411
It has been said that a golf course architect is as good as the ground on which he has to work. Here Hamilton Stutt had magnificent terrain at his disposal and a very good and lovely parkland course is the result. There are three holes over water. The hotel provides many sports facilities.
Meon Course: 18 holes, 6519yds, Par 71, SSS 71, Course record 67.
Valley Course: 9 holes, 5770yds, Par 70, SSS 68.
Club membership 910.

Visitors may book up to seven days in advance, not available at weekends and bank holidays.
Societies telephone in advance, written confirmation.
Green Fees not confirmed.
Cards
Prof Jason O'Malley
Designer Hamilton Stutt
Facilities
& Leisure hard tennis courts, heated indoor swimming pool, sauna, solarium, gymnasium, Health & beauty treatment area.
Location Off A334 between Botley and Wickham. Access via junct 7 M27

Hotel ★★★★ 65% Meon Valley Hotel, Sandy Ln, SHEDFIELD ☎ 01329 833455 83

SOUTHAMPTON Map 04 SU41

Chilworth Main Rd, Chilworth SO16 7JP ☎ 01703 740544
A course with two loops of nine holes, with a restricted booking system to allow undisturbed play. The first nine are fairly long and undulating and include water hazards. The remaining nine are flatter, but still quite a stiff test.
Manor Golf Course: 18 holes, 5740yds, Par 69, SSS 69, Course record 68.
Club membership 600.

Visitors must book in advance.
Societies telephone in advance and complete booking form, various packages available.
Green Fees not confirmed.
Prof M Butcher/Jon Barnes/Andy Vass
Designer J Garner
Facilities
Location A27 towards Romsey

Hotel ★★★ 60% County Hotel Southampton, Highfield Ln, Portswood, SOUTHAMPTON ☎ 01703 359955 66

Southampton Golf Course Rd, Bassett SO16 7LE ☎ 01703 760478
This beautiful municipal parkland course always ensures a good game, fast in summer, slow in winter. Three par 4's over 450 yds.
18 holes, 6213yds, Par 69, SSS 70.
Club membership 500.

Visitors no restrictions.
Societies welcome.
Green Fees not confirmed.
Facilities
Location 4m N of city centre off A33

Hotel ★★ 58% The Star Hotel & Restaurant, 26 High St, SOUTHAMPTON ☎ 01703 339939 43rm(37)

Stoneham Monks Wood Close, Bassett SO16 3TT ☎ 01703 769272 Fax 01703 766320
A hilly, heather course with sand or peat sub-soil; the fairways are separated by belts of woodland and heather to present a varied terrain. The interesting 4th is a difficult par 4 and the fine 11th has cross-bunkers about 150 yards from the tee.
18 holes, 6310yds, Par 72, SSS 70, Course record 63.
Club membership 800.

Visitors advisable to contact in advance.
Societies Mon, Thu & Fri only. Must telephone in advance.
Green Fees £22/£29 per round (£29/£40 weekends & bank holidays).
Cards
Prof Ian Young
Designer Willie Park
Facilities
Location 4m N of city centre off A27

Hotel ★★★ 60% County Hotel Southampton, Highfield Ln, Portswood, SOUTHAMPTON ☎ 01703 359955 66

SOUTHWICK Map 04 SU60

Southwick Park Naval Recreation Centre Pinsley Dr PO17 6EL ☎ 01705 380131
Set in 100 acres of parkland.
18 holes, 5972yds, Par 69, SSS 69.
Club membership 700.

Visitors must contact in advance and may play weekday mornings only.
Societies Tue only, telephone in advance.
Green Fees not confirmed.
Prof John Green
Facilities
Location 0.5m SE off B2177

Hotel ★★ 75% Old House Hotel, The Square, WICKHAM ☎ 01329 833049 9 Annexe3

TADLEY Map 04 SU66

Bishopswood Bishopswood Ln RG26 4AT ☎ 0118 9812200 Fax 0118 9815213
Wooded course, fairly tight, with stream and natural water hazards.
9 holes, 6474yds, Par 72, SSS 71, Course record 66.
Club membership 485.

Visitors must contact in advance. No play weekends or bank holidays.
Societies must contact by telephone.
Green Fees £9 per 9 holes, £14 per 18 holes.
Cards
Prof Steve Ward
Designer M W Phillips/G Blake
Facilities ▶

Location 1m W off A340

Hotel ★★★ 74% Romans Hotel, Little London Rd, SILCHESTER
☎ 0118 970 0421 11 Annexe14

WATERLOOVILLE Map 04 SU60

Portsmouth Crookhorn Ln, Purbrook PO7 5QL
☎ 01705 372210 Fax 01705 200766
Hilly, challenging course with good views of Portsmouth Harbour. Rarely free from the wind and the picturesque 6th, 17th and 18th holes can test the best.
18 holes, 6139yds, Par 69, SSS 70, Course record 64.
Club membership 700.
Visitors must book in advance.
Societies must book in advance, in writing or by telephone.
Green Fees £18.50 per day; £11.50 per round.
Cards
Prof Jason Banting
Designer Hawtree
Facilities
Location 2m S, off A3

Hotel ★★★ 63% The Bear Hotel, East St, HAVANT
☎ 01705 486501 42

Waterlooville Cherry Tree Av, Cowplain PO8 8AP
☎ 01705 263388 Fax 01705 347513
Parkland course, easy walking. Challenging course with 5 par 5's over 500 yards and featuring 4 ponds and a stream running through.
18 holes, 6602yds, Par 72, SSS 72, Course record 64.
Club membership 800.
Visitors must contact in advance & may only play on weekdays.
Societies Thu only; apply by letter or telephone.
Green Fees £30 per day; £25 per round.
Prof John Hay
Designer Henry Cotton
Facilities
Location NE side of town centre off A3

Hotel B Forte Posthouse Havant, Northney Rd, HAYLING ISLAND
☎ 01705 465011 92

WINCHESTER Map 04 SU42

Hockley Twyford SO21 1PL
☎ 01962 713165 Fax 01962 713612
High downland course with good views.
18 holes, 6296yds, Par 71, SSS 70, Course record 64.
Club membership 750.
Visitors are advised to phone in advance. Handicap certificate required.
Societies must telephone in advance and confirm in writing with deposit.
Green Fees £30 per day.
Prof Terry Lane
Designer James Braid
Facilities
Location Jct 11 M3, follow sign to Twyford

Hotel ★★★★ 66% The Wessex, Paternoster Row, WINCHESTER ☎ 01962 861611 94

Royal Winchester Sarum Rd SO22 5QE
☎ 01962 852462 Fax 01962 865048
The Royal Winchester course is a sporting downland course centred on a rolling valley, so the course is hilly in places. After a disastrous fire in 1994, a new clubhouse was built (opened August 1995). Royal Winchester must be included in any list of notable clubs, because of its age (it dates from 1888) and also because the club was involved in one of the very first professional matches.
18 holes, 6204yds, Par 71, SSS 70, Course record 65.
Club membership 800.

Visitors must play with member at weekends. Must contact in advance and have a handicap certificate.
Societies must contact in writing or by telephone.
Green Fees not confirmed.
Cards
Prof Steven Hunter
Facilities
Location 1.5m W off A3090

Hotel ★★★★ 78% Lainston House Hotel, Sparsholt, WINCHESTER ☎ 01962 863588 38

South Winchester Pitt SO22 5QW
☎ 01962 877800 Fax 01962 877900
Opened in September 1993, this Peter Alliss/Dave Thomas designed course incorporates downland, meadows and seven lakes. Visitors are only welcome if playing with a member. Home of the Hampshire PGA and the venue for European Ladies Tour Pro-Ams.
18 holes, 7086yds, Par 72, SSS 74, Course record 68.
Club membership 750.

Visitors members guests only.
Societies must contact in advance.
Green Fees not confirmed.
Cards
Prof Richard Adams
Designer Dave Thomas/Peter Allis
Facilities
Location On A3090 Romsey road

Hotel ★★★ 67% Royal Hotel, Saint Peter St, WINCHESTER ☎ 01962 840840 75

HEREFORDSHIRE

Hereford Map 03 SO53

Belmont Lodge Belmont HR2 9SA
☎ 01432 352666 Fax 01432 358090
Parkland course designed in two loops of nine. The first nine take the higher ground, offering magnificent views over Herefordshire. The second nine run alongside the river Wye with five holes in play against the river.
18 holes, 6511yds, Par 72, SSS 71, Course record 66.
Club membership 450.

Visitors advised to contact in advance at weekends. Tel: 01432 352666.
Societies must telephone in advance.
Green Fees on application.
Cards
Prof Mike Welsh
Designer Bob Sandow
Facilities
& Leisure hard tennis courts, fishing, snooker room.
Location 2m S off A465

Hotel ★★★ 61% Belmont Lodge & Golf Course, Belmont, HEREFORD ☎ 01432 352666 30

Burghill Valley Tillington Rd, Burghill HR4 7RW
☎ 01432 760456 Fax 01432 761654
The course is situated in typically beautiful Herefordshire countryside. The walking is easy on gently rolling fairways with a background of hills and woods and in the distnce, the Welsh mountains. Some holes have been constructed through mature cider orchards and there are two lakes to negotiate. A fair but interesting test for players of all abilities.
18 holes, 6239yds, Par 71, SSS 70, Course record 69.
Club membership 700.

Visitors contact in advance.
Societies apply in writing or telephone in advance.
Green Fees £25 per day; £17 per round (£30/£21 weekends & bank holidays).
Cards
Prof Nigel Clarke
Designer M Barnett
Facilities
Location 4m NW of Hereford

Hotel ★★★ 65% The Green Dragon, Broad St, HEREFORD ☎ 01432 272506 87

Hereford Municipal Hereford Leisure Centre, Holmer Rd HR4 9UD ☎ 01432 344376
This municipal parkland course is more challenging than first appearance. The well-drained greens are open all year round with good drainage for excellent winter golf.
9 holes, 3060yds, Par 35, SSS 69.
Club membership 160.

Visitors restrictions on race days.
Societies telephone in advance.
Green Fees £6 per 18 holes; £4 per 9 holes (£7.50/£5 weekends).
Cards
Prof Philip Brookes
Facilities
& Leisure squash, sauna, gymnasium.
Location Adjacent to race course & leisure centre

Hotel ★★ 66% The Merton Hotel & Governors Restaurant, 28 Commercial Rd, HEREFORD ☎ 01432 265925 19

Kington Map 03 SO25

Kington Bradnor Hill HR5 3RE
☎ 01544 230340 & 231320
The highest 18-hole course in England, with magnificent views over seven counties. A natural heathland course with easy walking on mountain turf cropped by sheep. There is bracken to catch any really bad shots but no sand traps.
18 holes, 5980yds, Par 70, SSS 68, Course record 65.
Club membership 640.

Visitors contact the professional.
Societies must book in advance through the Hon Secretary.
Green Fees not confirmed.
Prof Dean Oliver
Designer Major Hutchison
Facilities ⊗)Ⅲ ⛳ ☕ ♀ ⛺ ⌂ ⛿ ✓ ⟟
Location 0.5m N of Kington, off B4355

Hotel ★★ 66% Talbot Hotel, West St, LEOMINSTER ☎ 01568 616347 20 ⇨ ↱

LEOMINSTER Map 03 SO45

Leominster Ford Bridge HR6 0LE ☎ 01568 611402 (Prof) & 610055 (Sec) Fax 01568 610055
On undulating parkland with the lower holes running alongside the River Lugg and others on the higher part of the course affording fine panoramic views over the surrounding countryside.
18 holes, 6029yds, Par 70, SSS 69.
Club membership 550.
Visitors must contact in advance.
Societies must telephone in advance.
Green Fees Tue-Fri: £18 per day; £14.50 per round; Mon: £15 per day; £8 per round (£21 per day weekends & bank holidays).
Prof Andrew Ferriday
Designer Bob Sandow
Facilities ⊗)Ⅲ ⛳ ☕ ♀ ⛺ ⌂ ⛿ ✓ ⟟
& Leisure fishing.
Location 3m S on A49. Clearly signposted from Leominster by-pass

Hotel ★★ 66% Talbot Hotel, West St, LEOMINSTER ☎ 01568 616347 20 ⇨ ↱

ROSS-ON-WYE Map 03 SO62

Ross-on-Wye Two Park, Gorsley HR9 7UT
☎ 01989 720267 Fax 01989 720212
The undulating, parkland course has been cut out of a silver birch forest; the fairways being well-screened from each other. The fairways are tight, the greens good and the bunkers have recently been re-structured.
18 holes, 6451yds, Par 72, SSS 73, Course record 68.
Club membership 760.
Visitors must contact professional in advance 01989 720439.
Societies must telephone in advance.
Green Fees £45 day; £35 per 18 holes.
Prof Nick Catchpole
Facilities ⊗)Ⅲ ⛳ ☕ ♀ ⛺ ⌂ ✓ ⟟
Location On B4221 N side of M50 junc 3

Hotel ★★★ 77% Pengethley Manor, Pengethley Park, ROSS-ON-WYE ☎ 01989 730211 11 ⇨ ↱ Annexe14 ⇨ ↱

UPPER SAPEY Map 03 SO66

Sapey WR6 6XT
☎ 01886 853288 & 853567 Fax 01886 853485
Parkland course with views of the Malvern Hills. Trees, lakes and water hazards. Not too strenuous a walk.
18 holes, 5935yds, Par 69, SSS 68, Course record 63.
Club membership 520.
Visitors must contact in advance.
Societies must contact in advance.

Green Fees £24 per day; £16 per round (£30/£22 weekends & bank holidays).
Prof Chris Knowles
Designer R McMurray
Facilities
& Leisure bowling green.
Location B4203 Bromyard/Whitley Rd

Hotel ★★★ 78% The Elms, ABBERLEY 01299 896666 16

WORMSLEY Map 03 SO44

Herefordshire Ravens Causeway HR4 8LY
01432 830219
Undulating parkland course with expansive views.
18 holes, 6036yds, Par 70, SSS 69, Course record 61.
Club membership 800.
Visitors must contact in advance.
Societies must apply in advance.
Green Fees £22 per day; £17 per round (£28/£20 weekends & bank holidays).
Prof David Hemming
Facilities
Location E side of village

Hotel ★★★ 65% The Green Dragon, Broad St, HEREFORD 01432 272506 87

HERTFORDSHIRE

ALDBURY Map 04 SP91

Stocks Hotel Golf & Country Club Stocks Rd HP23 5RX
01442 851341 Fax 01442 851253
An 18-hole parkland course is one of the many facilities at this country club. The course plays off blue, white (6,804 yards), yellow and red tees. There is also a driving range.
18 holes, 6804yds, Par 72, SSS 73, Course record 65.
Visitors must contact in advance and have a handicap certificate. May not play before 2pm at weekends.
Societies must contact well in advance.
Green Fees £30 per round (£40 weekends by arrangement).
Cards
Prof Peter Lane
Designer Mike Billcliffe
Facilities
& Leisure hard tennis courts, heated outdoor swimming pool, sauna, solarium, gymnasium, snooker, croquet, jacuzzi.
Location 2m from A41 at Tring

Hotel ★★★★ 60% Pendley Manor, Cow Ln, TRING 01442 891891 71

ALDENHAM Map 04 TQ19

Aldenham Golf and Country Club Church Ln WD2 8AL
01923 853929 Fax 01923 858472
Undulating parkland course.
Old Course: 18 holes, 6480yds, Par 70, SSS 71.
New Course: 9 holes, 2350yds, Par 33, SSS 66.
Club membership 550.
Visitors Old Course restricted weekends before noon. New Course no restrictions.
Societies must contact in advance.
Green Fees Old Course: £25 per day (£32 weekends & bank holidays). New Course: not confirmed.
Cards
Prof Pat Winston
Facilities
Location W side of village

Hotel ★★★ 63% Watford Moat House, 30-40 St Albans Rd, WATFORD 01923 429988 90

BERKHAMSTED Map 04 SP90

Berkhamsted The Common HP4 2QB
01442 865832 Fax 01442 863730
There are no sand bunkers on this Championship heathland course but this does not make it any easier to play. The natural hazards will test the skill of the most able players, with a particularly testing hole at the 11th, 568 yards, par 5. Fine Greens, long carries and heather and gorse. The clubhouse is very comfortable.
18 holes, 6605yds, Par 71, SSS 72, Course record 65.
Club membership 700.
Visitors must contact in advance.
Societies must contact in advance.
Green Fees £35 per day; £24 per round (£35 weekends after 11.30am).
Prof Basil Proudfoot
Designer Colt/Braid
Facilities by prior arrangement
Location 1.5m E

Hotel ★★★★ 60% Pendley Manor, Cow Ln, TRING 01442 891891 71

BISHOP'S STORTFORD Map 05 TL42

Bishop's Stortford Dunmow Rd CM23 5HP
01279 654715 Fax 01279 655215
Parkland course, fairly flat.
18 holes, 6404yds, Par 71, SSS 71.
Club membership 900.
Visitors must have a valid handicap certificate, must play with member at weekends. Must contact in advance in writing.
Societies must contact in writing.
Green Fees £30 per day; £20 per 18 holes.
Cards
Prof Vince Duncan
Designer James Braid
Facilities
Location 0.5m W of M11 junc 8 on A1250

Hotel ★★★★ 67% Down Hall Country House Hotel, Hatfield Heath, BISHOP'S STORTFORD 01279 731441 103

Great Hadham Great Hadham Rd, Much Hadham SG10 6JE 01279 843558 Fax 01279 842122
An undulating open meadowland/links course offering excellent country views and a challenge with its ever present breeze.
18 holes, 6854yds, Par 72, SSS 73, Course record 67.
Club membership 700.

Visitors welcome all times except am Mon, Wed, Sat & Sun.
Societies by advance booking in writing.
Green Fees £28 per day; £16 per round (£23 weekends & bank holidays).
Cards
Prof Kevin Lunt
Designer Iain Roberts
Facilities
Location On the B1004, 3m SW of Bishop's Stortford

Hotel ★★★★ 67% Down Hall Country House Hotel, Hatfield Heath, BISHOP'S STORTFORD ☎ 01279 731441 103

BRICKENDON Map 05 TL30

Brickendon Grange SG13 8PD
☎ 01992 511258 Fax 01992 511258
Undulating parkland course with some fine par 4's. 17th hole reputed to be best in the county.
18 holes, 6395yds, Par 71, SSS 70, Course record 66.
Club membership 680.
Visitors must have handicap certificate. With member only at weekends & bank holidays.
Societies by arrangement.
Green Fees £33 per day; £27 per round.
Prof John Hamilton
Designer C K Cotton
Facilities
Location W side of village

Hotel ★★★ 65% The White Horse, Hertingfordbury, HERTFORD ☎ 01992 586791 42

BROOKMANS PARK Map 04 TL20

Brookmans Park Golf Club Rd AL9 7AT
☎ 01707 652487
Brookman's Park is an undulating parkland course, with several cleverly constructed holes. But it is a fair course, although it can play long. The 11th, par 3, is a testing hole which plays across a lake.
18 holes, 6460yds, Par 71, SSS 71, Course record 66.
Club membership 750.
Visitors must contact professional in advance 01707 652468 and have a handicap certificate; must play with member at weekends & bank holidays.
Societies must telephone in advance.
Green Fees not confirmed.
Prof Ian Jelley
Facilities
Location N side of village off A1000

Hotel B Forte Posthouse South Mimms, SOUTH MIMMS ☎ 01707 643311 120

BUNTINGFORD Map 05 TL32

East Herts Hamels Park SG9 9NA ☎ 01920 821922 (Pro)
An attractive undulating parkland course with magnificent specimen trees.
18 holes, 6456yds, Par 71, SSS 71.
Club membership 750.
Visitors must contact in advance & have handicap certificate, but may not play on Wed & weekends.
Societies apply in writing.
Green Fees £33 per day; £26 per round.
Prof S Bryan
Facilities by prior arrangement
Location 1m N of Puckeridge off A10

Hotel ★★★ 64% Vintage Court Hotel, Vintage Corner, PUCKERIDGE ☎ 01920 822722 25

BUSHEY Map 04 TQ19

Bushey Golf & Country Club High St WD2 1BJ
☎ 0181 950 2283 Fax 0181 386 1181
Undulating parkland with challenging 2nd and 9th holes. The latter has a sweeping dolgleg left, playing to a green in front of the club house. For the rather too enthusiatic golfer, Bushey offers its own physiotherapist!
9 holes, 6000yds, Par 70, SSS 69, Course record 67.
Club membership 411.
Visitors must contact in advance.
Societies apply in writing or by telephone.
Green Fees £12 per 18 holes; £7 per 9 holes.
Cards
Prof Michael Lovegrove
Facilities
& Leisure sauna, solarium, gymnasium.
Hotel ★★★ 73% Edgwarebury Hotel, Barnet Ln, ELSTREE ☎ 0181 953 8227 47

Bushey Hall Bushey Hall Dr WD2 2EP
☎ 01923 225802 & 222253 Fax 01923 229759
Parkland course.
18 holes, 6099yds, Par 70, SSS 69.
Club membership 500.
Visitors may book 7 days in advance.
Societies must contact in writing.
Green Fees not confirmed.
Cards
Prof Ken Wickham
Facilities
Location 1.5m NW on A4008

Hotel ★★★ 63% Watford Moat House, 30-40 St Albans Rd, WATFORD ☎ 01923 429988 90

Hartsbourne Golf & Country Club Hartsbourne Ave WD2 1JW ☎ 0181 950 1133
Parkland course with good views.
18 holes, 6305yds, Par 71, SSS 70, Course record 62.
Club membership 750.
Visitors must be guest of a member.
Societies phone for details.
Green Fees not confirmed.
Prof Geoff Hunt
Facilities
Location 5m SE of Watford

Hotel ★★★ 63% Watford Moat House, 30-40 St Albans Rd, WATFORD ☎ 01923 429988 90

CHESHUNT Map 05 TL30

Cheshunt Cheshunt Park, Park Ln EN7 6QD
☎ 01992 629777 & 624009
Municipal parkland course, well-bunkered with ponds, easy walking.
18 holes, 6613yds, Par 71, SSS 71.
Club membership 350.
Visitors must book Tee-times through Pro shop.
Societies must apply in writing.
Green Fees not confirmed.
Prof Chris Newton
Facilities
Location 1.5m NW off B156

Hotel ★★★★ 65% Cheshunt Marriott Hotel, Halfhide Ln, Turnford, BROXBOURNE ☎ 01992 451245 142

CHORLEYWOOD Map 04 TQ09

Chorleywood Common Rd WD3 5LN ☎ 01923 282009
Heathland course with natural hazards and good views.
9 holes, 5676yds, Par 68, SSS 67.
Club membership 300.
Visitors must contact in advance, restricted weekends.
Societies must apply in writing.
Green Fees £16 per day; £20 weekends & bank holidays.
Facilities
Location E side of village off A404

Hotel ★★★ 72% The Bedford Arms Hotel, CHENIES ☎ 01923 283301 10

ELSTREE Map 04 TQ19

Elstree Watling St WD6 3AA
☎ 0181 953 6115 Fax 0181 207 6390
Parkland course.
18 holes, 6556yds, Par 73, SSS 72.
Club membership 650.
Visitors advisable to contact in advance, no restrictions weekdays, may not play until after 2pm weekends unless tee time available day prior.
Societies telephone in advance.
Green Fees £30 per day; £20 per round (£25 per 18 holes weekends & bank holidays).
Cards
Prof Marc Warwick
Designer Donald Steel
Facilities
Location A5183 between Radlett and Elstree

Hotel ★★★ 73% Edgwarebury Hotel, Barnet Ln, ELSTREE ☎ 0181 953 8227 47

ESSENDON Map 04 TL20

Hatfield London Country Club Bedwell Park AL9 6JA
☎ 01707 642624 Fax 01707 646187
Parkland course with many varied hazards, including ponds, a stream and a ditch. 19th-century manor clubhouse. 9-hole pitch and putt.
18 holes, 6880yds, Par 72, SSS 72.
Club membership 250.
Visitors must contact in advance.
Societies must contact in advance.
Green Fees not confirmed.
Cards
Prof Norman Greer
Designer Fred Hawtry
Facilities
& Leisure hard tennis courts.
Location On B158 1m S

Hotel ★★★ 65% Hatfield Oak Hotel, Roehyde Way, HATFIELD ☎ 01707 266033 76

GRAVELEY Map 04 TL22

Chesfield Downs Jack's Hill SG4 7EQ
☎ 01462 482929 Fax 01462 482930
A revolutionary new golf course with the emphasis on facilities for the entire family. Its undulating, open downland course has an inland links feel. There is a 25-bay floodlit, covered driving range, a 9-hole Par 3 and many other facilities.
18 holes, 6648yds, Par 71, SSS 72.
Club membership 500.
Visitors no restrictions.
Societies must telephone in advance.
Green Fees £14.75 per round (£21 weekends).
Cards
Prof Jane Fernley
Designer J Gaunt
Facilities
& Leisure putting green, practice area.
Location Jct 8 of A1, B197 to Graveley

Hotel ★★★ 60% Hertfordpark Hotel, Danestrete, STEVENAGE ☎ 01438 779955 98

HARPENDEN Map 04 TL11

Aldwickbury Park Piggottshill Ln AL5 1AB
☎ 01582 760112 Fax 01582 760113
Attractive parkland course with large areas of mature woodland and good views across the Lee Valley.
Park: 18 holes, 6352yds, Par 71, SSS 70, Course record 66.
Club membership 700.
Visitors telephone in advance.
Societies telephone for brochure, various packages available.
Green Fees Park: £20 (£26 weekends). Manor 9 hole par3 £4.50 (£5.50 weekends).
Cards
Prof Sean Clark
Designer Ken Brown/Martin Fillett
Facilities
Location Located just off Wheathampstead Road, between Harpenden/Wheathampstead, 10mins from junct 9 of M1

Hotel ★★★ 64% Harpenden House Hotel, 18 Southdown Rd, HARPENDEN ☎ 01582 449955 18 Annexe35

Harpenden Hammonds End, Redbourn Ln AL5 2AX
☎ 01582 712580 Fax 01582 712725
Gently undulating parkland course, easy walking.
18 holes, 6381yds, Par 70, SSS 70, Course record 67.
Club membership 800.

Visitors must contact in advance. May not play Thu & weekends.
Societies must apply in writing.
Green Fees £34 per day; £24 per round.
Prof Peter Cherry
Designer Hawtree & Taylor
Facilities
Location 1m S on B487

Hotel ★★★ 64% Harpenden House Hotel, 18 Southdown Rd, HARPENDEN ☎ 01582 449955 18 Annexe35

Harpenden Common Cravells Rd, East Common AL5 1BL ☎ 01582 715959 Fax 01582 715959
Flat, easy walking, good greens, typical common course.
18 holes, 6214yds, Par 70, SSS 70, Course record 67.
Club membership 710.
Visitors must contact in advance.
Societies Thu & Fri only. Must apply in writing.
Green Fees £28 per day; £23 per round.
Prof Danny Fitzsimmons
Facilities
Location 1m S on A1081

Hotel ★★★ 73% Glen Eagle Hotel, 1 Luton Rd, HARPENDEN ☎ 01582 760271 60

HEMEL HEMPSTEAD Map 04 TL00

Boxmoor 18 Box Ln, Boxmoor HP3 0DJ ☎ 01442 242434
Challenging, very hilly, moorland course with sloping fairways divided by trees. Fine views. Testing holes: 3rd (par 3), 4th (par 4).
9 holes, 4812yds, Par 64, SSS 63, Course record 62.
Club membership 280.
Visitors may not play on Sun & bank holidays. Restricted some Sat.
Societies must contact in advance.
Green Fees not confirmed.
Facilities
Location 2m SW on B4505

Hotel ★★★ 61% The Two Brewers, The Common, CHIPPERFIELD ☎ 01923 265266 20

Little Hay Box Ln, Bovingdon HP3 0DQ ☎ 01442 833798
Semi-parkland, inland links.
18 holes, 6678yds, Par 72, SSS 72.
Visitors advisable to contact in advance.
Societies telephone for details.
Green Fees not confirmed.
Cards
Prof D Johnson/S Proudfoot
Designer Hawtree
Facilities
Location 1.5m SW on B4505 off A41

Hotel B Forte Posthouse Hemel Hempstead, Breakspear Way, HEMEL HEMPSTEAD ☎ 01442 251122 146

Shendish Manor London Rd, Apsley HP3 0AA ☎ 01442 251806 Fax 01442 230683
A hilly course with plenty of trees and good greens. A tough course for any golfer.
18 holes, 5660yds, Par 70, SSS 67.
Club membership 100.
Visitors no restrictions but advisable to book in advance
Societies must contact in advance.
Green Fees £25 per day; £15 per round (£35/£20 weekends).
Cards
Prof Murray White
Designer D Steel
Facilities by prior arrangement
& Leisure sauna, solarium, gymnasium.
Location Just off A4251

Hotel ★★★★ 60% Pendley Manor, Cow Ln, TRING ☎ 01442 891891 71

KNEBWORTH Map 04 TL22

Knebworth Deards End Ln SG3 6NL ☎ 01438 812752 Fax 01438 815216
Parkland course, easy walking.
18 holes, 6492yds, Par 71, SSS 71, Course record 66.
Club membership 900.
Visitors must have handicap certificate , but must play with member at weekends.
Societies Mon, Tue & Thu. Must contact in advance.
Green Fees £30 per day/round.
Cards
Prof Garry Parker
Designer W Park (Jun)
Facilities
Location N side of village off B197

Hotel B Forte Posthouse Stevenage, Old London Rd, Broadwater, STEVENAGE ☎ 01438 365444 54

LETCHWORTH Map 04 TL23

Letchworth Letchworth Ln SG6 3NQ ☎ 01462 683203 Fax 01462 484567
Planned more than 50 years ago by Harry Vardon, this adventurous, parkland course is set in a peaceful corner of 'Norman' England. To its variety of natural and artificial hazards is added an unpredictable wind.
18 holes, 6181yds, Par 70, SSS 69, Course record 65.
Club membership 750.
Visitors with member only at weekends. Must contact in advance and have a handicap certificate.
Societies Wed, Thu & Fri only, must telephone in advance.
Green Fees £33 per day; £24 per round.
Prof J Mutimer
Designer Harry Vardon
Facilities
Location S side of town centre off A505

Hotel ★★★ 64% Blakemore Thistle, Blakemore End Rd, Little Wymondley, HITCHIN ☎ 01438 355821 82

LITTLE GADDESDEN Map 04 SP91

Ashridge HP4 1LY ☎ 01442 842244 Fax 01442 843770
Good parkland course, challenging but fair. Good clubhouse facilities.
18 holes, 6547yds, Par 72, SSS 71, Course record 63.
Club membership 720.

Visitors must contact in advance , be a member of a recognised club & have handicap certificate, may not play weekends & bank holidays.
Societies must apply in writing and complete booking form.
Green Fees on application.
Prof Andrew Ainsworth
Designer Sir G Campbell/C Hutchinson/N Hutchinson
Facilities ⊗)Ⅲ ⛾ ☕ ♀ ⛺ 🏠 ⛳ ✓
Location 5m N of Berkhamsted on the B4506

Hotel ★★★ 73% The Bell Inn, ASTON CLINTON ☎ 01296 630252 5 ⇌ ↱ Annexe15 ⇌ ↱

MUCH HADHAM Map 05 TL41

Much Hadham Little Hadham Rd SG10 6HD
☎ 01279 843253 Fax 01920 468686
Naturally undulating course with good views extending to Canary Wharf in London on a clear day.
18 holes, 6516yds, Par 71, Course record 71.
Visitors no restrictions.
Societies telephone in advance.
Green Fees £7.50 per round before 2pm, £5 after 2pm (£10/£7.50 weekends).
Designer Martin Gillett
Facilities ⛾ ☕ ♀ ⛺ 🏠
Location 1.5m S of A120 fom Little Hadham traffic lights

Hotel ★★★ 64% Vintage Court Hotel, Vintage Corner, PUCKERIDGE ☎ 01920 822722 25 ⇌ ↱

POTTERS BAR Map 04 TL20

Potters Bar Darkes Ln EN6 1DE ☎ 01707 652020
Undulating parkland course with water in play on many holes.
18 holes, 6279yds, Par 71, SSS 70.
Club membership 500.
Visitors with member only at weekends, Ladies Day Wed morning.
Societies Mon-Fri & Wed (pm only) by arrangement with Secretary.
Green Fees £30 per day; £20 per round.
Prof Gary A'Ris
Designer James Braid
Facilities ⊗)Ⅲ ⛾ ☕ ♀ ⛺ 🏠 ⛳ ✓
Location 1m N of M25 junct 24

Hotel B Forte Posthouse South Mimms, SOUTH MIMMS ☎ 01707 643311 120 ⇌ ↱

RADLETT Map 04 TL10

Porters Park Shenley Hill WD7 7AZ ☎ 01923 854127
A splendid, undulating parkland course with fine trees and lush grass. The holes are all different and interesting - on many accuracy of shot to the green is of paramount importance.
18 holes, 6313yds, Par 70, SSS 70, Course record 64.
Club membership 820.
Visitors must book 24hrs in advance. With member only weekends.
Societies Wed & Thu only, must apply in writing.
Green Fees not confirmed.
Prof David Gleeson
Designer Braid
Facilities ⊗ ⛾ ☕ ♀ ⛺ 🏠 ⛳ ✓
Location NE side of village off A5183

Hotel ★★★★ 71% The Noke Thistle, Watford Rd, ST ALBANS ☎ 01727 854252 111 ⇌ ↱

REDBOURN Map 04 TL11

Redbourn Kinsbourne Green Ln AL3 7QA
☎ 01582 793493 Fax 01582 794362
Testing parkland course (Five par 4's over 400 yds). Also 9-hole par 3 course.
Ver Course: 18 holes, 6506yds, Par 70, SSS 71, Course record 67.
Kingsbourne Course: 9 holes, 1361yds, Par 27.
Club membership 850.
Visitors must contact up to 3 days in advance for Ver Course. No restrictions for Par 3.
Societies must telephone in advance.
Green Fees £18 (£24 weekends).
Cards
Prof Mike Varney
Facilities ⊗)Ⅲ ⛾ ☕ ♀ ⛺ 🏠 ⛳ ✓
Location 1m N off A5183

Hotel ★★★ 64% Harpenden House Hotel, 18 Southdown Rd, HARPENDEN ☎ 01582 449955 18 ⇌ ↱ Annexe35 ⇌ ↱

RICKMANSWORTH Map 04 TQ09

Moor Park WD3 1QN
☎ 01923 773146 Fax 01923 777109
Two parkland courses.
High Golf Course: 18 holes, 6713yds, Par 72, SSS 72, Course record 63.
West Golf Course: 18 holes, 5815yds, Par 69, SSS 68, Course record 63.
Club membership 1700.
Visitors must contact in advance but may not play at weekends, bank holidays or before 1pm on Tue & Thu.
Societies must contact in advance.
Green Fees High: £50 per round. West: £30 per round.
Prof Lawrence Farmer
Designer H S Colt
Facilities ⊗ ⛾ ☕ ♀ ⛺ 🏠 ⛳ ✓
& Leisure hard and grass tennis courts.
Location 1.5m SE off A4145

Hotel ★★★ 63% Watford Moat House, 30-40 St Albans Rd, WATFORD ☎ 01923 429988 90 ⇌ ↱

Rickmansworth Public Course Moor Ln WD3 1QL
☎ 01923 775278
Undulating, municipal parkland course.
18 holes, 4469yds, Par 63, SSS 62.
Club membership 240.
Visitors must contact the club in advance.
Societies must contact in advance.
Green Fees £9.30/£13.50 per round.
Cards
Prof Alan Dobbins ▶

Designer Colt
Facilities
Location 2m S of town off A4145

Hotel ★★★ 63% Watford Moat House, 30-40 St Albans Rd, WATFORD
☎ 01923 429988 90

ROYSTON Map 05 TL34

Barkway Park Nuthampstead Rd, Barkway SG8 8EN
☎ 01763 849070 & 848215
An undulating course criss-crossed by ditches which come into play on several holes. The challenging par 3 7th features a long, narrow green with out of bounds close to the right edge of the green.
18 holes, 6997yds, Par 74, SSS 74.
Club membership 410.
Visitors telephone for tee times, weekends after 11.30am only.
Societies apply for booking form.
Green Fees not confirmed.
Prof Jamie Bates
Designer Vivien Saunders
Facilities
Location Off B1368 from A10

Hotel ★★★ 70% Duxford Lodge Hotel, Ickleton Rd, DUXFORD
☎ 01223 836444 11 Annexe4

Heydon Grange Golf & Country Club Heydon SG8 7NS
☎ 01763 208988 Fax 01763 208926
Three 9-hole parkland courses - the Essex, Cambridgeshire and Hertfordshire - situated in gently rolling countryside.
Essex: 9 holes, 3138yds, Par 36, SSS 35, Course record 67.
Cambridgeshire: 9 holes, 3374yds, Par 36, SSS 36.
Hertfordshire: 9 holes, 3249yds, Par 36, SSS 36.
Club membership 250.
Visitors must contact to book tee times, welcome all times weekends included.
Societies telephone in advance for booking form.
Green Fees £15 per 18 holes; £10 per 9 holes (£20/£12.50 weekends).
Cards
Prof Stuart Smith
Designer Cameron Sinclair
Facilities
Location A505 between Royston/Duxford, off junct 10 on M11

Hotel ★★★ 70% Duxford Lodge Hotel, Ickleton Rd, DUXFORD
☎ 01223 836444 11 Annexe4

Kingsway Cambridge Rd, Melbourn SG8 6EY
☎ 01763 262727 Fax 01763 263298
Short and deceptively tricky 9-hole course providing a good test for both beginners and experienced golfers. Out of bounds and strategically placed bunkers come into play on several holes, in particular the tough par 3 7th.
9 holes, 2455yds, Par 33, SSS 32.
Club membership 150.
Visitors welcome.
Societies telephone for details.
Green Fees £9 per 18 holes; £6 per 9 holes (£11/£7 weekends & bank holidays).
Prof Denise Hastings/Richard Jessop
Facilities
Location Off the A10

Hotel ★★★ 70% Duxford Lodge Hotel, Ickleton Rd, DUXFORD
☎ 01223 836444 11 Annexe4

Royston Baldock Rd SG8 5BG
☎ 01763 242696 Fax 01763 242696
Heathland course on undulating terrain and fine fairways.The 8th, 9th and 18th are the most notable holes.
18 holes, 6052yds, Par 70, SSS 69, Course record 65.
Club membership 550.
Visitors Mon-Fri only subject to availability. Must contact in advance.
Societies by arrangement Mon-Fri.
Green Fees not confirmed.
Prof Mark Hatcher
Facilities
Location 0.5m W of town centre

Hotel ★★★ 70% Duxford Lodge Hotel, Ickleton Rd, DUXFORD
☎ 01223 836444 11 Annexe4

ST ALBANS Map 04 TL10

Abbey View Westminster Lodge Leisure Ctr, Hollywell Hill AL1 2DL ☎ 01727 868227
Abbey View is a public golf course designed for beginners, but is sufficiently challenging for experienced golfers who only have time for a short game. There is a resident professional for assistance and lessons.
9 holes, 1388yds, Par 29.
Visitors welcome but no sharing clubs, suitable footwear & wide wheel trolleys.
Green Fees £4.25 per 9 holes; £6.75 per 18 holes.
Prof Mark Sibley
Facilities
& Leisure heated indoor swimming pool, sauna, solarium, gymnasium, leisure centre adjacent to course.
Hotel ★★★ 66% Hertfordshire Moat House, London Rd, Markyate, ST ALBANS
☎ 01582 449988 89

Batchwood Hall Batchwood Dr AL3 5XA
☎ 01727 844250 Fax 01727 858506
Municipal parkland course designed by J H Taylor and opened in 1935.
18 holes, 6487yds, Par 71, SSS 71.
Club membership 200.
Visitors must contact in advance, in person.
Societies must contact in advance.
Green Fees not confirmed.
Cards
Prof Mark Flitton
Facilities
& Leisure hard tennis courts, squash, solarium, gymnasium.
Location 1m NW off A5183

Hotel ★★★ 75% The Manor St Michael's Village, Fishpool St, ST ALBANS
☎ 01727 864444 23

Verulam London Rd AL1 1JG
☎ 01727 853327 Fax 01727 812201
Parkland course with fourteen holes having out-of-bounds. Water affects the 12th, 13th and 14th holes. Samuel Ryder was Captain here in 1927 when he began the now celebrated Ryder Cup Competition.
18 holes, 6448yds, Par 72, SSS 71, Course record 65.
Club membership 650.

Visitors must contact in advance. With member only at weekends.
Societies must contact advance.
Green Fees £22-£35 per day; £13-£25 per round.
Cards
Prof Nick Burch
Designer Braid
Facilities
Location 1m from junc 22 of M25 off A1081

Hotel ★★★★ 76% Sopwell House Hotel & Country Club, Cottonmill Ln, Sopwell, ST ALBANS
☎ 01727 864477 92

SAWBRIDGEWORTH Map 05 TL41

Manor of Groves Golf & Country Club High Wych CM21 0LA ☎ 01279 722333
The course is set out over 150 acres of established parkland and rolling countryside and is a true test of golf for the club golfer.
18 holes, 6280yds, Par 71, SSS 70, Course record 65.
Club membership 450.

Visitors telephone bookings preferred, may not play until after 12 noon at weekends.
Societies Mon-Fri by prior arrangement, telephone in advance.
Green Fees not confirmed.
Prof Craig Laurence
Facilities
& Leisure hard tennis courts, outdoor swimming pool, gymnasium.
Location 1.5m on west side of town

Hotel ★★★ 72% Churchgate Manor Hotel, Churchgate St Village, Old Harlow, HARLOW
☎ 01279 420246 85

STANSTEAD ABBOTS Map 05 TL31

Briggens House Hotel Briggens Park, Stanstead Rd SG12 8LD ☎ 01279 793742 Fax 01279 793685
An attractive 9-hole course set in the grounds of a 80 acres of countryside.
9 holes, 2793yds, Par 36, SSS 69, Course record 31.
Club membership 180.

Visitors may not play Thu 5-6pm and Sun am. No jeans. Must have own clubs and golf shoes.
Societies must contact in advance.
Green Fees not confirmed.
Cards
Prof Alan McGinn
Facilities
& Leisure hard tennis courts, heated outdoor swimming pool, fishing.
Location Off Stanstead road A414

Hotel ★★★★ 63% Briggens House, Stanstead Rd, STANSTEAD ABBOTS
☎ 01279 829955 54

STEVENAGE Map 04 TL22

Stevenage Golf Centre Aston Ln SG2 7EL
☎ 01438 880424 & 880223 Fax 01438 880040
Municipal course designed by John Jacobs, with natural water hazards and some wooded areas.
18 holes, 6451yds, Par 72, SSS 71.
Club membership 600.

Visitors no restrictions.
Societies must contact 1 week in advance. Deposit required.
Green Fees £13.80 (£10.40 weekends).
Prof Keith Bond
Designer John Jacobs
Facilities
Location 4m SE off B5169

Hotel B Forte Posthouse Stevenage, Old London Rd, Broadwater, STEVENAGE
☎ 01438 365444 54

WARE Map 05 TL31

Chadwell Springs Hertford Rd SG12 9LE
☎ 01920 461447
Quick drying moorland course on high plateau subject to wind. The first two holes are par 5 and notable.
9 holes, 6418yds, Par 72, SSS 71, Course record 68.
Club membership 650.

Visitors with member only at weekends.
Societies bookings accepted, Mon, Wed & Fri only.
Green Fees not confirmed.
Prof Mark Wall
Facilities
Location 0.75m W on A119

Hotel ★★★ 64% County Hotel Ware, Baldock St, WARE ☎ 01920 409955 50

Hanbury Manor Golf & Country Club SG12 0SD
☎ 01920 487722 Fax 01920 487692
Superb parkland course designed by Jack Nicklaus II. Large oval tees, watered fairways and undulating greens make up the first 9 holes. Attractive lakes and deep-faced bunkers are strategically sited. Second 9 holes offer open panoramas and challenging holes and are based on the original Harry Vardon 9 hole design.
18 holes, 6622yds, Par 72, SSS 72, Course record 70.
Club membership 800.

Visitors with handicap certificate, members guest and hotel residents welcome. Must contact in advance.
Societies must be booked in advance.
Green Fees £60 per round.
Cards
Prof Peter Blaze
Designer Jack Nicklaus II
Facilities
& Leisure hard tennis courts, heated indoor swimming pool, sauna, solarium, gymnasium, croquet lawn, health/dance studio, beauty treatment, hairdresser, spa bath.

Location Adjacent to A10. From the N just past the Thunderidge sign

Hotel ★★★★★ 77% Marriott Hanbury Manor, WARE ☎ 01920 487722 69 Annexe27

Whitehill Dane End SG12 0JS ☎ 01920 438495
Undulating course providing a good test for both the average golfer and the low handicapper. Several lakes in challenging positions.
18 holes, 6681yds, Par 72, SSS 72.
Club membership 600.

Visitors handicap certificate must be produced or competence test taken (free), appropriate clothing must be worn.
Societies telephone or write for booking form.
Green Fees not confirmed.
Prof David Ling
Facilities
Hotel ★★★ 64% County Hotel Ware, Baldock St, WARE ☎ 01920 409955 50

WATFORD Map 04 TQ19

West Herts Cassiobury Park WD1 7SL
☎ 01923 236484
Another of the many clubs that were inaugurated in the 1890's when the game of golf was being given a tremendous boost by the the performances of the first star professionals, Braid, Vardon and Taylor. The West Herts course is close to Watford but its tree-lined setting is beautiful and tranquil. Set out on a plateau the course is exceedingly dry. It also has a very severe finish with the 17th, a hole of 378 yards, the toughest on the course. The last hole measures over 480 yards.
18 holes, 6400yds, Par 72, SSS 71, Course record 66.
Club membership 700.

Visitors must contact in advance.
Societies must telephone in advance and confirm in writing.
Green Fees not confirmed.
Prof Charles Gough
Designer Tom Morris
Facilities
Location W side of town centre off A412

Hotel ★★★ 63% Watford Moat House, 30-40 St Albans Rd, WATFORD ☎ 01923 429988 90

WELWYN GARDEN CITY Map 04 TL21

Mill Green Gypsy Ln AL6 4TY
☎ 01707 276900 & 279542 (Pro shop) Fax 01707 276898
The course plays over the front 9 holes around the lakes and sweeps back through the woods. The final 9 holes are subject to the prevailing winds. The par 3 9-hole gives a good test for improving the short game.
18 holes, 6615yds, Par 72, SSS 72, Course record 68.
Club membership 700.

Visitors must contact in advance by telephone.
Societies apply in writing for details.
Green Fees not confirmed.
Cards
Prof Alan Hall
Designer Alliss & Clark
Facilities
Location Exit 4 of A1(M), A414 to Mill Green

Hotel ★★★ 61% Quality Clock Hotel, The Link, WELWYN ☎ 01438 716911 96

Panshanger Golf & Squash Complex Old Herns Ln AL7 2ED ☎ 01707 333350 & 333312 Fax 01707 390010
Picturesque, mature course overlooking Mimram Valley.
18 holes, 6347yds, Par 72, SSS 70, Course record 65.
Club membership 600.

Visitors no restrictions.
Societies telephone for details.
Green Fees £11.50 per round (£15.75 weekends & bank holidays).
Cards
Prof Bryan Lewis/Mick Corlass
Designer Peter Kirkham
Facilities
& Leisure squash, Par 3 course.
Location N side of town centre signposted off B1000

Hotel ★★★ 61% Quality Clock Hotel, The Link, WELWYN ☎ 01438 716911 96

Welwyn Garden City Mannicotts, High Oaks Rd AL8 7BP
☎ 01707 325243 Fax 01707 393213
Undulating parkland course with a ravine. A former course record holder is Nick Faldo.
18 holes, 6074yds, Par 70, SSS 69, Course record 64.
Club membership 975.

Visitors must contact in advance but may not play Sun am.
Societies must contact in advance.
Green Fees £25 (£35 weekends).
Prof Richard May
Facilities
Location W side of city, exit 6 off A1

Hotel ★★★ 61% Quality Clock Hotel, The Link, WELWYN ☎ 01438 716911 96

WHEATHAMPSTEAD Map 04 TL11

Mid Herts Lamer Ln, Gustard Wood AL4 8RS
☎ 01582 832242 Fax 01582 832242
Commonland, wooded with heather and gorse-lined fairways.
18 holes, 6060yds, Par 69, SSS 69.
Club membership 760.

Visitors may not play Tue, Wed afternoons & weekends.
Societies must contact in writing.
Green Fees not confirmed.
Prof Nick Brown
Facilities
Location 1m N on B651

Hotel ★★★ 64% Harpenden House Hotel, 18 Southdown Rd, HARPENDEN ☎ 01582 449955 18 Annexe35

KENT

ADDINGTON — Map 05 TQ65

West Malling London Rd ME19 5AR
☎ 01732 844785 Fax 01732 844795
Two 18-hole parkland courses.
Spitfire Course: 18 holes, 6142yds, Par 70, SSS 70, Course record 67.
Hurricane Course: 18 holes, 6324yds, Par 70, SSS 70, Course record 68.

Visitors must contact in advance, may not play weekends until 2pm.
Societies prior booking required.
Green Fees £30 per day; £20 per round (£30 per round after noon weekends & bank holidays).
Cards
Prof Duncan Lambert
Designer Max Falkner
Facilities
Location 1m S off A20

Hotel ★★★ 64% Larkfield Priory Hotel, London Rd, Larkfield, MAIDSTONE
☎ 01732 846858 51

ASH — Map 05 TQ66

The London South Ash Manor Estate TN15 7EN
☎ 01474 879899 Fax 01474 879912
Visitors may only play the courses at LGC as guests of members or prospective members by invitation.The courses, the Heritage and the International were designed by Jack Nicklaus: both include a number of lakes, generous fairways framed with native grasses and many challenging holes. A state-of-the-art drainage system ensures continuous play.
Heritage Course: 18 holes, 6771yds, Par 72, SSS 73, Course record 68.
International Course: 18 holes, 6574yds, Par 72, SSS 72, Course record 66.
Club membership 400.

Visitors guest of member & prospective members invited by the membership office only.
Green Fees Guest of member. Heritage: £50 per round; International £40 per round (£60/£45 weekends).
Cards
Prof Keith Morgan
Designer Jack Nicklaus
Facilities
& Leisure sauna.
Location A20, 2m from Brands Hatch

Hotel ★★★ 64% Larkfield Priory Hotel, London Rd, Larkfield, MAIDSTONE
☎ 01732 846858 51

ASHFORD — Map 05 TR04

Ashford Sandyhurst Ln TN25 4NT
☎ 01233 622655 Fax 01233 622655
Parkland course with good views and easy walking. Narrow fairways and tightly bunkered greens ensure a challenging game.
18 holes, 6263yds, Par 71, SSS 70, Course record 65.
Club membership 650.

Visitors must contact in advance & have handicap certificate.
Societies Tue & Thu only, by arrangement.
Green Fees £30 per day; £20 per round (£42 per round weekends).
Prof Hugh Sherman
Designer Cotton
Facilities by prior arrangement
Location 1.5m NW off A20

Hotel ★★★★ 62% Ashford International, Simone Weil Av, ASHFORD
☎ 01233 219988 200
Additional Farmhouse Elvey Farm Country Hotel, PLUCKLEY
☎ 01233 840442
Fax 01233 840726 10

Homelands Bettergolf Centre Ashford Rd, Kingsnorth TN26 1NJ ☎ 01233 661620 Fax 01233 720934
Challenging 9-hole course designed by Donald Steel to provide a stern test for experienced golfers and for others to develop their game. With 4 par 3s and 5 par 4s it demands accuracy rather than length. Floodlit driving range.
9 holes, 2205yds, Par 32, SSS 31.
Club membership 200.

Visitors no restrictions, but booking essential for weekend and summer evenings.
Societies prior arrangements are essential.
Green Fees £10.50 per 18 holes; £7 per 9 holes (£14/£8 weekends & bank holidays).
Cards
Prof Tony Bowers
Designer Donald Steel
Facilities
& Leisure 4 hole Academy Course.
Hotel ★★★ 64% Master Spearpoint Hotel, Canterbury Rd, Kennington, ASHFORD
☎ 01233 636863 34

BARHAM Map 05 TR25

Broome Park The Broome Park Estate CT4 6QX
☎ 01227 831701 Fax 01227 831973
Championship standard parkland course in a valley, with a 350-year-old mansion clubhouse.
18 holes, 6610yds, Par 72, SSS 72, Course record 66.
Club membership 700.

Visitors advisable to contact in advance, must have handicap certificate, but may not play Sat/Sun mornings.
Societies Mon-Fri and Sat-Sun after 12 only, apply in writing or by telephone.
Green Fees £26 per round (£32 weekends).
Cards
Prof Tienne Britz
Designer Donald Steel
Facilities
& Leisure hard tennis courts, heated outdoor swimming pool, squash, sauna, solarium.
Location 1.5m SE on A260

Hotel ★★★ 64% The Chaucer, Ivy Ln, CANTERBURY
☎ 01227 464427 42

BEARSTED Map 05 TQ85

Bearsted Ware St ME14 4PQ
☎ 01622 738198 Fax 01622 738198
Parkland course with fine views of the North Downs.
18 holes, 6437yds, Par 72, SSS 71.
Club membership 780.

Visitors must have handicap certificate and may not play weekends unless with member. Must contact in advance.
Societies write for reservation forms.
Green Fees £36 per day; £27 per round (£33 per round weekends).
Prof Tim Simpson
Facilities
Location 2.5m E of Maidstone off A20

Hotel ★★★★ 68% Marriott Tudor Park, Ashford Rd, Bearsted, MAIDSTONE
☎ 01622 734334 118

BIDDENDEN Map 05 TQ83

Chart Hills Weeks Ln TN27 8JX
☎ 01580 292222 Fax 01580 292233
Created by Nick Faldo and completed in 1993, this huge course of grand design measures 7,000 yards from the back tees. Facilities include a David Leadbetter Golf Academy.
18 holes, 7086yds, Par 72, SSS 74.
Club membership 335.

Visitors contact for details.
Societies telephone for details.
Green Fees not confirmed.
Prof William Easdale
Designer Nick Faldo
Facilities
& Leisure sauna, solarium, gymnasium.
Location 1m N of Biddenden off A274

Hotel ★★ Kennel Holt Hotel, Goudhurst Rd, CRANBROOK ☎ 01580 712032 10

BOROUGH GREEN Map 05 TQ65

Wrotham Heath Seven Mile Ln TN15 8QZ
☎ 01732 884800 Fax 01732 887370
Heathland woodland course with magnificent views of North Downs.
18 holes, 5954yds, Par 70, SSS 69.
Club membership 550.

Visitors must contact in advance, weekends with member only.
Societies Thu & Fri only, by arrangement.
Green Fees £25 per round.
Prof Harry Dearden
Designer Donald Steel (part)
Facilities
Location 2.25m E on B2016

Hotel B Forte Posthouse Maidstone/Sevenoaks, London Rd, Wrotham Heath, WROTHAM
☎ 01732 883311 106

BRENCHLEY Map 05 TQ64

Moatlands Watermans Ln TN12 6ND
☎ 01892 724400 Fax 01892 723300
A rolling parkland course with dramatic views over the Weald of Kent. The challenging holes are the Par 4 8th with its tough dogleg, the 10th where there is a wooded copse with a Victorian bath-house to be avoided and the 14th where the approach to the green is guarded by oak trees.

18 holes, 6693yds, Par 72, SSS 72, Course record 71.
Club membership 560.
Visitors must book in advance.
Societies apply in writing or telephone.
Green Fees £29 per round (£39 weekends).
Cards
Prof Simon Wood
Designer H Sugio
Facilities by prior arrangement
& Leisure hard tennis courts, heated indoor swimming pool, sauna, gymnasium.
Location 3m N of Brenchley off B2160

Hotel ★★ 65% Russell Hotel, 80 London Rd, TUNBRIDGE WELLS
01892 544833 19 Annexe5

BROADSTAIRS Map 05 TR36

North Foreland Convent Rd, Kingsgate CT10 3PU
01843 862140 Fax 01843 862663
A picturesque course situated where the Thames Estuary widens towards the sea. North Foreland always seems to have a breath of tradition of golf's earlier days about it. Perhaps the ghost of one of its earlier professionals, the famous Abe Mitchell, still haunts the lovely turf of the fairways. Walking is easy and the wind is deceptive. The 8th and 17th, both par 4, are testing holes. There is also an 18 hole approach and putting course.
18 holes, 6430yds, Par 71, SSS 71, Course record 65.
Club membership 1100.
Visitors for Main course are required to book in advance & have handicap certificate. May play afternoons only Mon and Tue, weekends restricted and no visitors Sun morning. Short course has no restrictions.
Societies Wed & Fri only, by arrangement.
Green Fees not confirmed.
Prof Neil Hansen
Designer Fowler & Simpson
Facilities by prior arrangement
& Leisure hard tennis courts.
Location 1.5m N off B2052

Hotel ★★★ 58% Royal Albion Hotel, Albion St, BROADSTAIRS
01843 868071 19

CANTERBURY Map 05 TR15

Canterbury Scotland Hills, Littlebourne Rd CT1 1TW
01227 453532
Undulating parkland course, densely wooded in places, with elevated trees and difficult drives on several holes.
18 holes, 6249yds, Par 70, SSS 70, Course record 64.
Club membership 650.
Visitors may only play after 3pm weekends & bank holidays. Must have a handicap certificate.
Societies by arrangement.
Green Fees £36 per 36 holes; £27 per 18 holes.
Prof Paul Everard
Designer Harry Colt
Facilities
Location 1.5m E on A257

Hotel ★★★ 64% The Chaucer, Ivy Ln, CANTERBURY 01227 464427 42

CHART SUTTON Map 05 TQ84

The Ridge Chartway St, East Sutton ME17 3DL
01622 844382
Opened in 1993, this flat parkland course was designed by Patrick Dawson around mature orchards to challenge all levels of player. The par 5, 18th has two lakes to negotiate.
18 holes, 6254yds, Par 71, SSS 70, Course record 68.
Club membership 650.
Visitors weekdays only, must have handicap certificate.
Societies Tue & Thu, by arrangement.
Green Fees £25.
Cards
Prof Matthew Rackham
Designer Tyton Design
Facilities
& Leisure solarium, gymnasium.
Location 5m S of Bearsted, off A274

Hotel ★★★★ 68% Marriott Tudor Park, Ashford Rd, Bearsted, MAIDSTONE
01622 734334 118

CRANBROOK Map 05 TQ73

Executive Golf Club at Cranbrook Golford Rd TN17 4AL
01580 712833 Fax 01580 714274
Scenic, parkland course with easy terrain, backed by Hemstead Forest and close to Sissinghurst Castle (1m) and Bodiam Castle (6m). The course has been transformed over recent years with the introduction of over 5,000 mature pine trees. Keeping the ball straight is paramount, a challenging test of golf for all levels.
18 holes, 6305yds, Par 70, SSS 71.
Club membership 700.
Visitors welcome weekdays after 8.30 am. weekends after 11.30 am. Tee reservations may be booked up to 1 calendar month in advance.
Societies minimum of 12 write or telephone to book.
Green Fees £23 per 18 holes (£30 weekends).
Cards
Prof Alan Gillard
Designer Commander J Harris
Facilities
Location 2m E

Hotel ★★ 69% Hartley Mount Country House, Hartley Rd, CRANBROOK
01580 712230 6

DARTFORD Map 05 TQ57

Birchwood Park Birchwood Rd, Wilmington DA2 7HJ
01322 662038 & 660554 Fax 01322 667283
The main course offers highly challenging play and will test golfers of all abilities. Beginners and those requiring a quick game or golfers wishing to improve their short game will appreciate the 9 hole course where holes range from 96 to 258yards.
18 holes, 6364yds, Par 71, SSS 70, Course record 64 or 9 holes, 1259yds, Par 28.
Club membership 500.
Visitors must contact in advance.
Societies telephone for details.

Green Fees £14.50 per round (£18.50 weekends). 9 hole course £4.20 (£5.20 weekends).
Cards
Prof Cranfield Golf Academy
Designer Howard Swann
Facilities
& Leisure health & fitness suite opening winter 1998.
Location B258 between Dartford & Swanley

Hotel ★★★★ 71% Swallow Hotel, 1 Broadway, BEXLEYHEATH ☎ 0181 298 1000 142

Dartford Upper Heath Ln, Dartford Heath DA1 2TN
☎ 01322 226455
Heathland course.
18 holes, 5914yds, Par 69, SSS 69, Course record 63.
Club membership 700.
Visitors may not play at weekends. Must have a handicap certificate.
Societies Mon & Fri only by prior arrangement with Secretary.
Green Fees £28 per day; £20 per round.
Designer James Braid
Facilities
Hotel B Forte Posthouse Bexley, Black Prince Interchange, Southwold Rd, BEXLEY ☎ 01322 526900 103

DEAL Map 05 TR35

Royal Cinque Ports Golf Rd CT14 6RF
☎ 01304 374007 Fax 01304 379530
Famous championship seaside links, windy but with easy walking. Outward nine is generally considered the easier, inward nine is longer and includes the renowned 16th, perhaps the most difficult hole. On a fine day there are wonderful views across the Channel.
18 holes, 6785yds, Par 72, SSS 72.
Club membership 850.
Visitors restricted Wed mornings, weekends & bank holidays. Must contact in advance and have a handicap certificate.
Societies must contact in advance.
Green Fees £50 per day/round; £40 per round after 1pm..
Cards
Prof Andrew Reynolds
Designer James Braid
Facilities
Location Along seafront at N end of Deal

Hotel B Forte Posthouse Dover, Singledge Ln, Whitfield, DOVER ☎ 01304 821222 67

EDENBRIDGE Map 05 TQ44

Edenbridge Golf & Country Club Crouch House Rd TN8 5LQ ☎ 01732 865097 & 867381 Fax 01732 867029
Parkland course with water on many holes, quiet with excellent views of rural Kent.
Old Course: 18 holes, 6646yds, Par 73.
Skeynes Course: 18 holes, 5600yds, Par 67.
Club membership 1100.
Visitors must contact in advance for Old Course. All tee times bookable 7 days in advance.
Societies contact in advance.
Green Fees Old Course: £17.50 (£23.50 weekends). Skeynes Course: £12 (£16 weekends).
Prof Keith Burkin
Facilities
& Leisure hard tennis courts, gymnasium.
Location 0.75m W of town centre, signposted 'Golf Course'

Hotel ★★★ Gravetye Manor Hotel, EAST GRINSTEAD ☎ 01342 810567 18

Sweetwoods Park Cowden TN8 7JN
☎ 01342 850729 (Pro shop) & 850942 (Secretary) Fax 013 42 850866
An undulating and mature parkland course with fast greens, testing water hazards and fine views across the Weald from four holes. A good challenge off the back tees. Signature holes include the 2nd, 4th and 14th.
18 holes, 6512yds, Par 71, SSS 71, Course record 67.
Club membership 800.
Visitors no restrictions.
Societies Mon-Fri after 9am, contact for details.
Green Fees £20 (£30 weekends).
Cards
Prof Bob Wynn/Ben Clover
Designer P Strand
Facilities
Location 5m E of East Grinstead on the A264

Hotel ★★★ 65% Woodbury House Hotel, Lewes Rd, EAST GRINSTEAD ☎ 01342 313657 14

EYNSFORD Map 05 TQ56

Austin Lodge Eynsford Station DA4 0HU
☎ 01322 863000 Fax 01322 862406
A well drained course designed to lie naturally in three secluded valleys in rolling countryside. Over 7000 yds from the medal tees. Practice ground, nets and a putting green add to the features.
18 holes, 6600yds, Par 73, SSS 71.
Club membership 600.
Visitors must contact in advance, may not play until after 1pm on weekends and bank holidays.
Societies telephone for bookings.
Green Fees £16 per round (£25 weekends & bank holidays).
Cards
Prof Paul Edwards
Designer P Bevan
Facilities
Location 6m S of Dartford

Hotel ★★★★ 63% The Brands Hatch Thistle Hotel, BRANDS HATCH ☎ 01474 854900 137

FAVERSHAM Map 05 TR06

Boughton Brickfield Ln ME13 9AJ
☎ 01227 752277 Fax 01227 752361
Rolling parkland/downland course set in 160 acres of Kent countryside, providing a good test of golf, even for the more accomplished players.
18 holes, 6452yds, Par 72, SSS 71, Course record 70.
Club membership 325.
Visitors booking by telephone advisable.
Societies telephone for details.

Green Fees £15 per 18 holes (£20 weekends; £15 after 12 noon).
Cards
Prof Trevor Dungate
Designer P Sparks
Facilities
Location Off junct 7 of M2 - Brenley Corner

Hotel ★★★★★ 77% Eastwell Manor, Eastwell Park, Boughton Lees, ASHFORD
☎ 01233 219955 23

Faversham Belmont Park ME13 0HB
☎ 01795 890561
A beautiful inland course laid out over part of a large estate with pheasants walking the fairways quite tamely. Play follows two heavily wooded valleys but the trees affect only the loose shots going out of bounds. Fine views.
18 holes, 6030yds, Par 70, SSS 69.
Club membership 800.
Visitors must have handicap certificate. With member only at weekends. Contacting the club in advance is advisable.
Societies must contact in advance.
Green Fees not confirmed.
Prof Stuart Rokes
Facilities
Location 3.5m S

Hotel ★★★★★ 77% Eastwell Manor, Eastwell Park, Boughton Lees, ASHFORD
☎ 01233 219955 23

FOLKESTONE Map 05 TR23

Etchinghill Canterbury Rd, Etchinghill CT18 8FA
☎ 01303 863863 Fax 01303 863210
A varied course incorporating parkland on the outward 9 holes and an interesting downland landscape with many challenging holes on the back 9.
18 holes, 6121yds, Par 70, SSS 69, Course record 67.
Club membership 600.

Visitors advisable to reserve tee time in advance.
Societies telephone or write, packages available.
Green Fees £15 per round (£20 weekends).
Cards
Prof Chris Hodgson
Designer John Sturdy
Facilities
& Leisure 9 hole par3.
Location N of M20, access from junct 11 or 12

Hotel ★★★ 62% Wards Restaurant & Hotel, 39 Earls Ave, FOLKESTONE
☎ 01303 245166 10

GILLINGHAM Map 05 TQ76

Gillingham Woodlands Rd ME7 2AP ☎ 01634 853017
Parkland course.
18 holes, 5347yds, Par 67, SSS 65.
Club membership 800.
Visitors contact in advance, weekends only with member.
Societies must apply in writing.
Green Fees not confirmed.
Prof Brian Impett
Designer James Braid
Facilities
Location 1.5m SE on A2

Hotel B Forte Posthouse Rochester, Maidstone Rd, ROCHESTER
☎ 01634 687111 105

GRAVESEND Map 05 TQ67

Mid Kent Singlewell Rd DA11 7RB
☎ 01474 568035 Fax 01474 564218
A well-maintained downland course with some easy walking and some excellent greens. The first hole is short, but nonetheless a real challenge. The slightest hook and the ball is out of bounds or lost.
18 holes, 6199yds, Par 69, SSS 69, Course record 60.
Club membership 900.
Visitors must contact in advance & have handicap certificate. May not play weekends.
Societies Tue only, apply in writing.
Green Fees not confirmed.
Prof Mark Foreman
Designer Frank Pennick
Facilities
Location S side of town centre off A227

Hotel ★★★ 57% Overcliffe Hotel, 15-16 The Overcliffe, GRAVESEND
☎ 01474 322131 19 Annexe10

HALSTEAD Map 05 TQ46

Broke Hill Sevenoaks Rd TN14 7HR
☎ 01959 533225 Fax 01959 532680
Testing downland course featuring 80 bumkers, strategically placed water hazards and good views.
18 holes, 6454yds, Par 72, SSS 71, Course record 69.
Club membership 650.
Visitors weekdays only.
Societies telephone for details.
Green Fees £50 per day; £30 per round.
Cards
Prof Chris West
Designer David Williams
Facilities
& Leisure sauna.
Location 5m S of Bromley off A21

Hotel ★★★ 68% Kings Arms Hotel, Market Square, WESTERHAM ☎ 01959 562990 17

HAWKHURST Map 05 TQ73

Hawkhurst High St TN18 4JS
☎ 01580 754074 & 752396 Fax 01580 754074
Undulating parkland course.
9 holes, 5751yds, Par 70, SSS 68, Course record 69.
Club membership 508.

Visitors may play weekdays, weekends with member only.
Societies must apply in advance.
Green Fees £20 per day, £15 per round.
Cards
Prof Tony Collins
Designer W A Baldock
Facilities
& Leisure squash.
Location W side of village off A268

Hotel ★★★ 66% Tudor Court Hotel, Rye Rd, HAWKHURST ☎ 01580 752312 18

HEADCORN Map 05 TQ84

Weald of Kent Maidstone Rd TN27 9PT
☎ 01622 891671 Fax 01622 891793
Enjoying delightful views over the Weald of Kent, this pay and play course features a range of natural hazards, including lakes, trees, ditches and undulating fairways. A good test to golfers of every standard.
18 holes, 6240yds, Par 70, SSS 70, Course record 64.
Club membership 450.

Visitors can book 3 days in advance, smart casual dress no jeans.
Societies apply in writing or by telephone.
Green Fees £15 per round (£19 weekends).
Designer John Millen
Facilities
Location Through Leeds village take A274 towards Headcorn, golf course on left

Hotel ★★ 75% Tanyard Hotel, Wierton Hill, Boughton Monchelsea, MAIDSTONE ☎ 01622 744705 6

HERNE BAY Map 05 TR16

Herne Bay Eddington CT6 7PG ☎ 01227 373964
Parkland course with bracing air.
18 holes, 4966yds, Par 65, SSS 64.
Club membership 500.

Visitors may not play mornings at weekends. Temporary course pending road works.
Societies apply in advance.
Green Fees not confirmed.
Prof S Dordoyt
Designer James Braid
Facilities
Location 1m S on A291

Hotel ★★★ 70% Falstaff Hotel, St Dunstans St, Westgate, CANTERBURY ☎ 01227 462138 24

HEVER Map 05 TQ44

Hever Edenbridge TN8 7NG
☎ 01732 700771 Fax 01732 700775
The newly established Hever course has recently been voted one of the top ten developments in the British Isles. The 18-hole parkland course is set in 210 acres with water hazards and outstanding holes like the Par 3 12th which is similar to the 12th at Augusta. A further 9-holes are due to open in June 1998.
18 holes, 7002yds, Par 72, SSS 75, Course record 69.
Club membership 620.

Visitors must book tee times Mon-Fri.
Societies telephone for details.
Green Fees £35 per 18 holes (£55 weekends & bank holidays).
Cards
Prof Richard Tinworth
Designer Dr Nicholas
Facilities
& Leisure hard tennis courts, heated indoor swimming pool, fishing, sauna, solarium, gymnasium.
Location 10mins from M25

Hotel ★★★ 76% The Spa Hotel, Mount Ephraim, TUNBRIDGE WELLS ☎ 01892 520331 74

HILDENBOROUGH Map 05 TQ54

Nizels Nizels Ln TN11 9LU
☎ 01732 838926 (Bookings) Fax 01732 833764

Woodland course with many mature trees, wildlife and lakes that come into play on several holes. The 2nd hole is a 553yd Par 5, the green being guarded by bunkers hidden by a range of hillocks. The Par 4 7th has water on both sides of the fairway and a pitch over water to the green. The 10th is

539yd Par 5 with a sharp dogleg to the right, followed by a very narrow entry between trees for the 2nd shot.
18 holes, 6408yds, Par 72, SSS 71, Course record 66.
Club membership 650.

Visitors telephone professional shop for tee reservation 01732 838926 at least 4 days in advance.
Societies weekdays only, telephone initially.
Green Fees £45 per day; £30 per round.
Cards
Prof Sue Hodge
Designer Donaldson/Edwards Partnership
Facilities
Location Off B245

Hotel ★★★ 59% Rose & Crown Hotel, 125 High St, TONBRIDGE ☎ 01732 357966 48

Hoo — Map 05 TQ77

Deangate Ridge ME3 8RZ ☎ 01634 251180
Parkland, municipal course designed by Fred Hawtree. 18-hole pitch and putt.
18 holes, 6300yds, Par 71, SSS 70.
Club membership 700.

Visitors no restrictions.
Societies must apply in writing.
Green Fees not confirmed.
Prof Richard Fox
Facilities
& Leisure hard tennis courts.
Location 4m NE of Rochester off A228

Hotel B Forte Posthouse Rochester, Maidstone Rd, ROCHESTER ☎ 01634 687111 105

Hythe — Map 05 TR13

Hythe Imperial Princes Pde CT21 6AE
☎ 01303 267441 Fax 01303 264610
A 9-hole links course played off alternative tees on the second nine. Flat but interesting and testing. Hotel provides many leisure and sports facilities.
9 holes, 5560yds, Par 68, SSS 66, Course record 61.
Club membership 300.

Visitors course closed some Sun until 11am.
Societies must apply in writing.
Green Fees not confirmed.
Prof Gordon Ritchie
Facilities
& Leisure hard and grass tennis courts, heated indoor swimming pool, squash, sauna, solarium, gymnasium, steam room, croquet, snooker, hair & beauty salon.
Location SE side of town

Hotel ★★★★ 76% The Hythe Imperial Hotel, Princes Pde, HYTHE ☎ 01303 267441 100
Additional hotel ★★★ 74% Stade Court Hotel, West Pde, HYTHE ☎ 01303 268263 Fax 01303 261803 42

Sene Valley Sene CT18 8BL
☎ 01303 268513 (Manager) & 268514 (Pro)
A two-level downland course which provides interesting golf over an undulating landscape with sea views.
18 holes, 6196yds, Par 71, SSS 69, Course record 61.
Club membership 650.

Visitors must contact professional in advance.
Societies telephone in advance.
Green Fees £20 per round (£25 weekends).
Prof Nick Watson
Designer Henry Cotton
Facilities
Location 1m NE off B2065

Hotel ★★★★ 76% The Hythe Imperial Hotel, Princes Pde, HYTHE ☎ 01303 267441 100

Kingsdown — Map 05 TR34

Walmer & Kingsdown The Leas CT14 8EP
☎ 01304 373256 Fax 01304 363017
This course near Deal has through the years been overshadowed by its neighbours at Deal and Sandwich, yet it is a testing circuit with many undulations. The course is famous as being the one on which, in 1964, Assistant Professional, Roger Game became the first golfer in Britain to hole out in one at two successive holes; the 7th and 8th. The course is situated on top of the cliffs, with fine views.
18 holes, 6437yds, Par 72, SSS 71, Course record 66.
Club membership 600.

Visitors must contact in advance. Not before 9.30am weekdays and noon weekends & bank holidays.
Societies apply in writing.
Green Fees £28 per day; £22 per round (£30/£24 weekends & bank holidays).
Prof Matthew Paget
Designer James Braid
Facilities
Location 0.5m S off B2057

Hotel B Forte Posthouse Dover, Singledge Ln, Whitfield, DOVER ☎ 01304 821222 67

Lamberhurst — Map 05 TQ63

Lamberhurst Church Rd TN3 8DT
☎ 01892 890591 Fax 01892 891140
Parkland course crossing river twice. Fine views.
18 holes, 6345yds, Par 72, SSS 70, Course record 65.
Club membership 700.

Visitors may only play after noon weekends unless with member, handicap certificate required.
Societies Tue, Wed & Thu only from Apr-Oct, by arrangement.
Green Fees £33 per day; £22 per round (£36 weekends pm). Credit cards accepted in pro shop.
Prof Mike Travers
Facilities by prior arrangement
Location N side of village on B2162

Hotel ★★★ 76% The Spa Hotel, Mount Ephraim, TUNBRIDGE WELLS ☎ 01892 520331 74

Littlestone
Map 05 TR02

Littlestone St Andrew's Rd TN28 8RB
☎ 01797 363355 Fax 01797 362740
Located in the Romney Marshes, this flattish seaside links course calls for every variety of shot. The 8th, 15th, 16th and 17th are regarded as classics by international golfers. Allowance for wind must always be made. Extensive practice area.
18 holes, 6460yds, Par 71, SSS 72, Course record 67.
Club membership 550.
Visitors must contact in advance, no visitors before 3pm weekends and bank holidays.
Societies must apply in advance.
Green Fees £42 per day; £30 per round (£50/£45 weekends and bank holidays).
Cards
Prof Stephen Watkins
Designer Laidlaw Purves
Facilities
Location N side of village

Hotel ★★★★ 76% The Hythe Imperial Hotel, Princes Pde, HYTHE
☎ 01303 267441 100

Romney Warren St Andrews Rd TN28 8RB
☎ 01797 362231 Fax 01797 362740
A traditional links course, newly developed alongside the 9-hole course at Littlestone. Flat providing easy walking and play challenged by sea breezes.
18 holes, 5126yds, Par 67, SSS 65, Course record 69.
Club membership 300.
Visitors contact professional in advance.
Societies contact in advance.
Green Fees £22 per day; £12 per round (£29/£17 weekend & bank holidays).
Cards
Prof Stephen Watkins
Facilities
Location N side of Littlestone

Hotel ★★★★ 76% The Hythe Imperial Hotel, Princes Pde, HYTHE
☎ 01303 267441 100

Lydd
Map 05 TR02

Lydd Romney Rd TN29 9LS
☎ 01797 320808 Fax 01797 321482
A links-type course offering some interesting challenges, including a number of eye-catching water hazards, wide fairways and plenty of semi-rough. A good test for experienced golfers and appealing to the complete novice.
18 holes, 6517yds, Par 71, Course record 65.
Club membership 415.
Visitors contact in advance on 01797 321201.
Societies telephone in advance.
Green Fees £14 per round (£18 weekends).
Cards
Prof Andrew Jones
Designer Mike Smith
Facilities
Location B2075

Hotel ★★★ 62% The George, High St, RYE
☎ 01797 222114 22

Maidstone
Map 05 TQ75

Cobtree Manor Park Chatham Rd, Sandling ME14 3AZ
☎ 01622 753276
An undulating parkland course with some water hazards.
18 holes, 5716yds, Par 69, SSS 68, Course record 66.
Club membership 500.
Visitors no restrictions.
Societies Mon-Fri only, by arrangement tel: 01622 751881.
Green Fees ring and book on day of play.
Cards
Prof Paul Foston
Facilities
Location On A229 0.25m N of M20 junc 6

Hotel ★★ 67% Russell Hotel, 136 Boxley Rd, MAIDSTONE ☎ 01622 692221 42

Leeds Castle Ashford Rd ME17 1PL
☎ 01622 880467
Situated around Leeds Castle, this is one of the most picturesque courses in Britain. Re-designed in the 1980s by Neil Coles, it is a challenging 9-hole course with the added hazard of the Castle moat. 18-holes may be played on weekdays.
9 holes, 2880yds, Par 34, SSS 34, Course record 32.

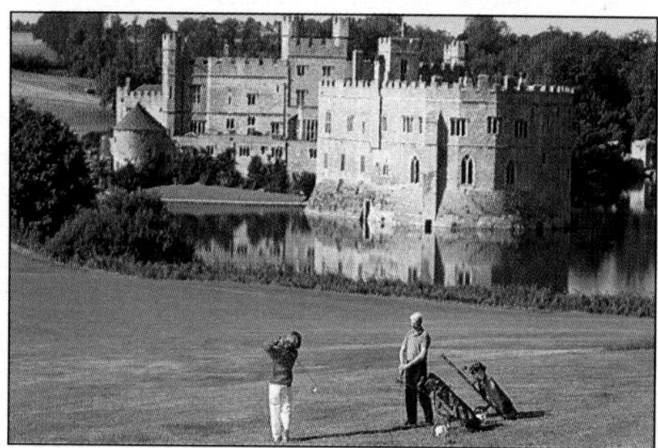

Visitors booking must be made. Bookings taken from 6 days in advance.
Societies apply in advance.
Green Fees not confirmed.
Designer Neil Coles
Facilities
Location On A20, 4m E of Maidstone

Hotel ★★★★ 68% Marriott Tudor Park, Ashford Rd, Bearsted, MAIDSTONE
☎ 01622 734334 118

Marriott Tudor Park Hotel & Country Club Ashford Rd, Bearsted ME14 4NQ ☎ 01622 734334 Fax 01622 735360
The course is set in a 220 acre former deerpark with the pleasant undulating Kent countyside as a backdrop. The natural features of the land have been incorporated into this picturesque course to form a challenge for those of both high and intermediate standard. The Par 5 14th is particularly interesting. It can alter your score dramatically should you gamble with a drive to a narrow fairway. This hole has to be carefully thoughtout from tee to green depending on the wind direction. ▶

ROYAL ST. GEORGE'S

SANDWICH ***Kent*** **☎ 01304 613090**
Fax 01304 611245 **Map 05 TR35**

John Ingham writes: Sandwich is one of the most beautiful and unspoiled towns in southern England. Driving to this part of Kent is much like stepping back into history. The big golf course here, Royal St George's, is where Sandy Lyle won the Open Championship in 1985 by one shot from that colourful American, Payne Stewart.

Like the region, the clubhouse is old-fashioned and the seats near the window in the bar seem to have been there forever. The bar staff may know as much about fishing or lifeboats as they know about beer, and make a visit there a delight, providing you are not looking for modern sophistication.

The course itself is the truest links you will find in all England and the Royal & Ancient, in its wisdom, choose Royal St George's (designed by Dr Laidlaw Purves in 1887) for major championships knowing it will find the pedigree player at the end of a week. Close to the sea, overlooking Pegwell Bay, any kind of wind can make this man-size test even tougher. The sweeping rough at the 1st can be daunting, so can the bunkers and the huge sandhills. But there are classic shots here.

Off-sea breezes can turn to incredible gales, and it is possible to find the course virtually unplayable. A smooth swing can be blown inside out and stories of three good woods to reach certain greens, into wind, are commonplace. Often the problem in high winds is simply to stand up and address the ball. Putting, too, can be almost impossible, with the ball blown off the surface and maybe into the sand.

Visitors	must contact in advance and have a handicap certificate. May not play at weekends or BHs
Societies	must apply in writing
Green fees	Midweek only £85 per day, £60 per round.
Facilities	⊗ (by arrangement) Professional (Andrew Brooks)
Location	Sandwich CT13 9PB (1.5m E of town)

18 holes, 6565yds, Par 70, SSS 72.
Course record 63

WHERE TO STAY AND EAT NEARBY

HOTELS:

CANTERBURY
★★★ 70% Falstaff, St Dunstans St. ☎ 01227 462138. 24 (2 22)
★★★ 61% Chaucer, Ivy Lane ☎ 01227 464427. 42 (1 41)

DOVER
★★★70% Churchill, Dover Waterfront. ☎ 01304 203633. 68 (52 15
★★★ 63% County, Townwall St. ☎ 01304 509955. 79

ST MARGARET'S AT CLIFFE
★★ Wallets Court, West Cliffe ☎ 01304 852424 3 Annexe 9

RESTAURANTS:

CANTERBURY
Ristorante Tuo e Mio, 16 The Borough. ☎ 01227 761471

18 holes, 6041yds, Par 70, SSS 69, Course record 64.
Club membership 750.
Visitors may not play Sat & Sun before noon. Contact pro shop 01622 739412 for bookings.
Societies please call the Golf Manager.
Green Fees not confirmed.
Designer Donald Steel
Facilities
& Leisure hard tennis courts, heated indoor swimming pool, sauna, solarium, gymnasium.
Location On A20, 1.25m W of M20 junct 8

Hotel ★★★★ 68% Marriott Tudor Park, Ashford Rd, Bearsted, MAIDSTONE
☎ 01622 734334 118

RAMSGATE Map 05 TR36

St Augustine's Cottington Rd, Cliffsend CT12 5JN
☎ 01843 590333 Fax 01843 590444
A comfortably flat course in this famous bracing Championship area of Kent. Neither as long nor as difficult as its lordly neighbours, St Augustine's will nonetheless extend most golfers. Dykes run across the course.
18 holes, 5197yds, Par 69, SSS 65, Course record 61.
Club membership 670.
Visitors must contact in advance.
Societies must contact in advance.
Green Fees £21.50 per day; £14 after 12 noon (£23.50/£16 weekends & bank holidays).
Prof Derek Scott
Designer Tom Vardon
Facilities
Hotel ★★★ 65% San Clu Hotel, Victoria Pde, East Cliff, RAMSGATE
☎ 01843 592345 44

ROCHESTER Map 05 TQ76

Rochester & Cobham Park Park Pale ME2 3UL
☎ 01474 823411 Fax 01474 824446
A first-rate course of challenging dimensions in undulating parkland. All holes differ and each requires accurate drive placing to derive the best advantage. The clubhouse and course are situated a quarter of a mile from the western end of the M2. The club was formed in 1891 and the course was redesigned by Donald Steel in 1995.
18 holes, 6596yds, Par 71, SSS 71, Course record 67.
Club membership 720.
Visitors must contact in advance & have handicap certificate. No visitors weekends.
Societies apply in advance.
Green Fees £36 per day; £26 per round.
Cards
Prof Joe Blair
Designer Donald Steel
Facilities
Location 2.5m W on A2

Hotel ★★★★ 77% Bridgewood Manor Hotel, Bridgewood Roundabout, Maidstone Rd, CHATHAM ☎ 01634 201333 100

SANDWICH Map 05 TR35

Prince's Prince's Dr, Sandwich Bay CT13 9QB
☎ 01304 611118 Fax 01304 612000
With 27 championship holes, Prince's Golf Club enjoys a world wide reputation as a traditional links of the finest quality and is a venue that provides all that is best in modern links golf. The purpose built clubhouse, located at the centre of the three loops of nine, can seat 200 diners and offers panoramic views over Sandwich Bay and the course.
Dunes: 9 holes, 3343yds, Par 36, SSS 36.
Himalayas: 9 holes, 3163yds, Par 35, SSS 35.
Shore: 9 holes, 3347yds, Par 36, SSS 35.
Club membership 200.
Visitors available all week, must contact in advance.
Societies welcome all week, please contact in advance.
Green Fees £45 per day; £40 per round (£51/£42 Sat, £48/£42 Sun) Winter packages from £25.
Cards
Prof Chris Evans
Designer Sir H Mallaby-Deeley/P M Lucas
Facilities
Location 2m E via toll road, follow signs from Sandwich

Hotel ★★★ 65% San Clu Hotel, Victoria Pde, East Cliff, RAMSGATE
☎ 01843 592345 44

SANDWICH Map 05 TR35

ROYAL ST GEORGES See page 155

SEVENOAKS Map 05 TQ55

Knole Park Seal Hollow Rd TN15 0HJ
☎ 01732 452150 Fax 01732 463159
The course is set in a majestic park with many fine trees and deer running loose. It has a wiry turf seemingly impervious to rain. Certainly a pleasure to play on. Excellent views of Knole House and the North Downs. Outstanding greens.
18 holes, 6266yds, Par 70, SSS 70, Course record 64.
Club membership 800.
Visitors may not play at weekends or bank holidays. Must contact Secretary in advance.
Societies telephone initially.
Green Fees £42 per 36 holes; £32 per 18 holes.
Prof P E Gill
Designer J A Abercromby
Facilities
& Leisure squash.
Location SE side of town centre off B2019

Hotel ★★★ 60% Royal Oak Hotel, Upper High St, SEVENOAKS ☎ 01732 451109
21 Annexe16

SHEERNESS Map 05 TQ97

Sheerness Power Station Rd ME12 3AE
☎ 01795 662585 Fax 01795 666840
Marshland course, few bunkers, but many ditches and water hazards. Often windy.
18 holes, 6460yds, Par 72, SSS 71, Course record 66.
Club membership 750.

Visitors with member only at weekends.
Societies Tue-Thu only, telephone in advance.
Green Fees £20 per day; £15 per round.
Prof R Tattersall
Facilities
Location 1.5m E off A249

Hotel ★★★★ 77% Bridgewood Manor Hotel, Bridgewood Roundabout, Maidstone Rd, CHATHAM ☎ 01634 201333 100

SHOREHAM Map 05 TQ56

Darenth Valley Station Rd TN14 7SA
☎ 01959 522944 & 522922 Fax 01959 525089
Easy walking parkland course in beautiful valley. Testing 12th hole, par 4.
18 holes, 6327yds, Par 72, SSS 71, Course record 64.

Visitors must book in advance.
Societies contact in advance.
Green Fees not confirmed.
Prof Scott Fotheringham
Facilities
& Leisure fishing.
Location 1m E on A225

Hotel ★★★ 60% Royal Oak Hotel, Upper High St, SEVENOAKS ☎ 01732 451109 21 Annexe16

SITTINGBOURNE Map 05 TQ96

The Oast Golf Centre Church Rd, Tonge ME9 9AR
☎ 01795 473527
A Par 3 Approach course of 9 holes with 18 tees augmented by a 17-bay floodlit driving range and a putting green.
9 holes, 1664yds, Par 54, SSS 54.

Visitors no restrictions.
Societies telephone in advance.
Green Fees £6 per 18 holes; £4 per 9 holes.
Designer D Chambers
Facilities
Location 2m NE

Hotel ★★★★ 77% Bridgewood Manor Hotel, Bridgewood Roundabout, Maidstone Rd, CHATHAM ☎ 01634 201333 100

Sittingbourne & Milton Regis Wormdale, Newington ME9 7PX ☎ 01795 842261 Fax 01795 844117
A downland course with pleasant vistas. There are a few uphill climbs, but the course is far from difficult. The new back line holes are very testing.
18 holes, 6291yds, Par 71, SSS 70, Course record 64.
Club membership 670.

Visitors by prior arrangement or letter of introduction. Must contact in advance, may not play at weekends.
Societies Tue & Thu, apply in advance.
Green Fees £32 per 36 holes; £20 per 18 holes.
Prof John Hearn
Designer Donald Steel
Facilities
Location Turn off Chestnut Street (old A249) at Dalaway

Hotel ★★★★ 77% Bridgewood Manor Hotel, Bridgewood Roundabout, Maidstone Rd, CHATHAM ☎ 01634 201333 100

Upchurch River Valley Golf Centre Oak Ln, Upchurch ME9 7AY ☎ 01634 379592 Fax 01634 387784
Undulating parkland course set in picturesque countryside. Testing water hazards on several holes. Excellent winter course. The 9-hole course is ideal for beginners and for those keen to sharpen up their short game.
18 holes, 6237yds, Par 70, SSS 70.
Club membership 421.

Visitors can play anytime, book for weekend 5 days in advance, weekdays 2 days in advance.
Societies telephone 01634 360626 for details.
Green Fees not confirmed.
Prof Roger Cornwell
Designer David Smart
Facilities
& Leisure heated outdoor swimming pool.
Location A2 between Rainham and Newington

Hotel ★★ 67% Russell Hotel, 136 Boxley Rd, MAIDSTONE ☎ 01622 692221 42

SNODLAND Map 05 TQ76

Oastpark Malling Rd ME6 5LG
☎ 01634 242661 Fax 01634 240744
A challenging parkland course for golfers of all abilities. The course has water hazards, orchards and views across the Valley of Dean.
18 holes, 6173yds, Par 69, SSS 69, Course record 71.
Club membership 300.

Visitors may book 7 days in advance.
Societies early booking with deposits required.
Green Fees £8.50 per 18 holes; £6 per 9 holes (£14/£7 weekends) to be reviewed.
Prof John Gregory
Designer J D Banks
Facilities
Location Access via junct 4 on M20

Hotel ★★★ 64% Larkfield Priory Hotel, London Rd, Larkfield, MAIDSTONE ☎ 01732 846858 51

TENTERDEN Map 05 TQ83

Tenterden Woodchurch Rd TN30 7DR
☎ 01580 763987 Fax 01580 763987
Set in tranquil undulating parkland with beautiful views, the course is challenging with several difficult holes.
18 holes, 6071yds, Par 70, SSS 69, Course record 65.
Club membership 600.

Visitors contact professional shop. May only play with member weekends and bank holidays.
Societies must apply in writing.
Green Fees contact for details.
Prof Andrew Scullion

▶

Facilities ⊗)|((⛳ ☕ 🍷 ♨ 🏠 🚜 ✓
Location 0.75m E on B2067

Hotel ★★ 69% Hartley Mount Country House, Hartley Rd, CRANBROOK
☎ 01580 712230 6

TONBRIDGE Map 05 TQ54

Poultwood Higham Ln TN11 9QR
☎ 01732 364039 Fax 01732 353781
With the opening of a 9-hole course in the summer of 1994 there are now two public 'pay and play' parkland courses in an idyllic woodland setting. The courses are ecologically designed, offering varied walking, water hazards, natural and interesting playing opportunities for all standards of golfer.
18 holes, 5569yds, Par 68, SSS 67 or 9 holes, 1281yds, Par 28.

Visitors non registered golfers may book up to 2 days in advance for 18 hole course, or take available tee times, pay and play system on 9 hole.
Societies apply in advance to the clubhouse manager.
Green Fees £11 (£16 weekends). 9 hole course; £4.90 per 9 holes (£6.20 weekends).
Prof Chris Miller
Facilities ⊗)|((⛳ ☕ 🍷 ♨ 🏠 ✓
& Leisure squash.
Location Off A227, 3m N of Tonbridge

Hotel ★★★ 59% Rose & Crown Hotel, 125 High St, TONBRIDGE ☎ 01732 357966 48

TUNBRIDGE WELLS (ROYAL) Map 05 TQ53

Nevill Benhall Mill Rd TN2 5JW
☎ 01892 525818 Fax 01892 517861
Just within Sussex, the county boundary with Kent runs along the northern perimeter of the course. Open undulating ground, well-wooded with some heather and gorse for the first half. The second nine holes slope away from the clubhouse to a valley where a narrow stream hazards two holes.
18 holes, 6349yds, Par 71, SSS 70, Course record 66.
Club membership 900.

Visitors must contact 48 hours in advance, handicap certificate required, permission from secretary for weekends play.
Societies must apply in writing one month in advance.
Green Fees £33 per day; £25 per round (£46 per round weekends & bank holidays).
Prof Paul Huggett
Designer Henry Cotton
Facilities ⊗)|((⛳ ☕ 🍷 ♨ 🏠 🚜 ✓
Location S of Tunbridge Wells, off forest road

Hotel ★★★ 76% The Spa Hotel, Mount Ephraim, TUNBRIDGE WELLS
☎ 01892 520331 74

Tunbridge Wells Langton Rd TN4 8XH
☎ 01892 523034
Somewhat hilly, well-bunkered parkland course with lake; trees form natural hazards.
9 holes, 4725yds, Par 65, SSS 62, Course record 59.
Club membership 450.

Visitors must contact in advance, limited availability weekends.
Societies weekdays, apply in advance.
Green Fees £20 per day; £15 per 18 holes (£25 per round weekends).
Prof Mike Barton
Facilities ⊗)|((⛳ ☕ 🍷 ♨ 🏠 ✓
Location 1m W on A264

Hotel ★★★ 76% The Spa Hotel, Mount Ephraim, TUNBRIDGE WELLS
☎ 01892 520331 74

WESTGATE ON SEA Map 05 TR37

Westgate and Birchington 176 Canterbury Rd CT8 8LT
☎ 01843 831115
Seaside course.
18 holes, 4926yds, Par 64, SSS 64, Course record 60.
Club membership 310.

Visitors Mon-Sat after 10am, Sun and bank holidays after 11am, must contact in advance & have handicap certificate, restricted at weekends.
Societies must contact three months in advance.
Green Fees £13 (£15 weekends & bank holidays).
Prof Roger Game
Facilities ☕ 🍷 ♨ 🏠 ✓
Location E side of town centre off A28

Hotel ★★★ 58% Royal Albion Hotel, Albion St, BROADSTAIRS
☎ 01843 868071 19

WEST KINGSDOWN Map 05 TQ56

Woodlands Manor Woodlands TN15 6AB
☎ 01959 523806 & 524161
Interesting, challenging & undulating parkland course with testing 1st, 9th and 15th holes. Set in a designated area of outstanding natural beauty.
18 holes, 6100yds, Par 69, SSS 68, Course record 64.
Club membership 650.

Visitors welcome, at weekends by arrangement.
Societies apply in advance.
Green Fees on application.
Cards
Prof Philip Womack
Designer Lyons/Coles
Facilities ⊗)|((⛳ ☕ 🍷 ♨ 🏠 🚜 ✓
& Leisure hard tennis courts.
Location 2m S off A20

Hotel ★★★★ 63% The Brands Hatch Thistle Hotel, BRANDS HATCH
☎ 01474 854900 137

WHITSTABLE Map 05 TR16

Chestfield (Whitstable) 103 Chestfield Rd CT5 3LU
☎ 01227 794411 & 792243 Fax 01227 794454
Gently undulating parkland course with sea views. The Par 3 3rd is generally played into the wind and the Par 4th has a difficult lefthand dogleg.
18 holes, 5834yds, Par 69, SSS 68, Course record 65.
Club membership 650.

Visitors with member weekends.
Societies must apply in writing.

Green Fees £24 per day; £15 per round.
Prof John Brotherton
Facilities
Location 2m SE off A299

Hotel ★★★ 64% The Chaucer, Ivy Ln, CANTERBURY
☎ 01227 464427 42

Whitstable & Seasalter Collingwood Rd CT5 1EB
☎ 01227 272020
Links course.
9 holes, 5314yds, Par 66, SSS 63, Course record 62.
Club membership 300.
Visitors must contact in advance. Weekend play by prior arrangement.
Green Fees £16 per 18 holes.
Facilities
Location W side of town centre off B2205

Hotel ★★★ 64% The Chaucer, Ivy Ln, CANTERBURY
☎ 01227 464427 42

LANCASHIRE

ACCRINGTON Map 07 SD72

Accrington & District Devon Av, Oswaldtwistle BB5 4LS
☎ 01254 381614 Fax 01254 381614
Moorland course with pleasant views of the Pennines and surrounding areas.
18 holes, 6044yds, Par 70, SSS 69, Course record 63.
Club membership 600.
Visitors must contact in advance.
Societies contact in advance.
Green Fees £20 Mon-Thu; £25 Fri-Sat.
Prof Bill Harling
Designer J Braid
Facilities
Location Mid way between Accrington & Blackburn

Hotel ★★★ 70% Dunkenhalgh Hotel, Blackburn Rd, Clayton le Moors, ACCRINGTON
☎ 01254 398021 37 Annexe42

Baxenden & District Top o' th' Meadow, Baxenden BB5 2EA ☎ 01254 234555
Moorland course with a long par 3 to start.
9 holes, 5740yds, Par 70, SSS 68, Course record 67.
Club membership 340.
Visitors may not play Sat, Sun and bank holidays except with member.
Societies must contact in advance.
Green Fees £15 per round.
Facilities
Location 1.5m SE off A680

Hotel ★★★ 70% Dunkenhalgh Hotel, Blackburn Rd, Clayton le Moors, ACCRINGTON
☎ 01254 398021 37 Annexe42

Green Haworth Green Haworth BB5 3SL
☎ 01254 237580
Moorland course dominated by quarries and difficult in windy conditions.
9 holes, 5556yds, Par 68, SSS 67, Course record 65.
Club membership 360.
Visitors may not play Sun, Mar-Oct.
Societies apply in writing. Weekdays only before 5pm. Or contact secretary on above telephone number.
Green Fees £15 (£20 weekends & bank holidays).
Facilities
Location 2m S off A680

Hotel ★★★ 59% County Hotel Blackburn, Preston New Rd, BLACKBURN
☎ 01254 899988 98

BACUP Map 07 SD82

Bacup Maden Rd OL13 8HY ☎ 01706 873170
Moorland course, predominantly flat except climbs to 1st and 10th holes.
9 holes, 6008yds, Par 70, SSS 69.
Club membership 350.
Visitors no restrictions.
Societies must contact in writing.
Green Fees not confirmed.
Facilities
Location W side of town off A671

Hotel ★★ 62% Comfort Friendly Inn, Keirby Walk, BURNLEY ☎ 01282 427611 50

BARNOLDSWICK Map 07 SD84

Ghyll Skipton Rd BB18 6JH ☎ 01282 842466
Excellent, parkland course with outstanding views, especially from the 8th tee where you can see the Three Peaks. Testing 3rd hole is an uphill par 4.
9 holes, 5790yds, Par 68, SSS 66, Course record 62.
Club membership 345.
Visitors may not play Tue, Fri after 4.30pm & Sun.
Societies must contact in writing.
Green Fees not confirmed.
Facilities by prior arrangement by prior arrangement by prior arrangement evenings only
Location 1m NE on B6252

Hotel ★★★ 66% Stirk House Hotel, GISBURN
☎ 01200 445581 36 Annexe10

BLACKBURN Map 07 SD62

Blackburn Beardwood Brow BB2 7AX
☎ 01254 51122 Fax 01254 665578
Parkland course on a high plateau with stream and hills. Superb views of Lancashire coast and the Pennines.
18 holes, 6144yds, Par 71, SSS 70.
Club membership 550.
Visitors must contact professional in advance.
Societies must contact in advance.
Green Fees £24 per day (£28 weekends).
Prof Alan Rodwell
Facilities
Location 1.25m NW of town centre off A677

Hotel ★★★ 59% County Hotel Blackburn, Preston New Rd, BLACKBURN ☎ 01254 899988 98

BLACKPOOL Map 07 SD33

Blackpool North Shore Devonshire Rd FY2 0RD
☎ 01253 352054 Fax 01253 591240
Undulating parkland course.
18 holes, 6432yds, Par 71, SSS 71, Course record 63.
Club membership 900.

Visitors may not play Thu & Sat. Advisable to contact in advance.
Societies must contact in advance.
Green Fees £27.50 per day (£32.50 weekends & bank holidays).
Prof Brendan Ward
Facilities
Location On A587 N of town centre

Hotel ★★ 70% Brabyns Hotel, 1-3 Shaftesbury Av, North Shore, BLACKPOOL ☎ 01253 354263 22 Annexe3

De Vere Blackpool (Herons Reach) East Park Blackpool FY3 8LL ☎ 01253 766156 & 838866 Fax 01253 798800
The course was designed by Peter Alliss and Clive Clarke. There are 10 man-made lakes and several existing ponds. Built to a links design, well mounded but fairly easy walking. Water comes into play on 9 holes, better players can go for the carry or shorter hitters can take the safe route. The course provides an excellent and interesting challenge for golfers of all standards.
18 holes, 6461yds, Par 72, SSS 71, Course record 64.
Club membership 550.

Visitors may book up to 4 days in advance tel 01253 766156, (hotel guest/visiting society no limit to how far in advance bookings can be made). Handicap essential, etiquette and dress rules must be adhered to.
Societies telephone or write to golf sales office 01253 838866 ext 573.
Green Fees not confirmed.
Cards
Prof Dominik Naughton
Designer Peter Alliss/Clive Clark
Facilities
& Leisure hard tennis courts, heated indoor swimming pool, squash, sauna, solarium, gymnasium.
Location Off A587 adjacent to Stanley Park & Zoo

Hotel ★★★★ 64% De Vere Hotel, East Park Dr, BLACKPOOL ☎ 01253 838866 164

Stanley Park Municipal North Park Dr FY3 8LS
☎ 01253 397916 Fax 01253 397916
The golf course, situated in Stanley Park is municipal. The golf club (Blackpool Park) is private but golfers may use the clubhouse facilities if playing the course. An abundance of grassy pits, ponds and open dykes.
18 holes, 6087yds, Par 70, SSS 69, Course record 64.
Club membership 600.

Visitors must apply to Mrs A Hirst, Town Hall, Talbot Square, Blackpool.
Societies must apply in writing to Mrs A Hirst, Blackpool Borough Council, Town Hall, Talbot Square, Blackpool.
Green Fees £10.50 (£12.50 weekends & bank holidays).
Prof Brian Purdie
Designer Mckenzie
Facilities by prior arrangement
Location 1m E of Blackpool Tower

Hotel ★★★ 57% Clifton Hotel, Talbot Square, BLACKPOOL ☎ 01253 21481 77

BURNLEY Map 07 SD83

Burnley Glen View BB11 3RW
☎ 01282 421045 & 451281
Moorland course with hilly surrounds.
18 holes, 5911yds, Par 69, SSS 69, Course record 65.
Club membership 750.

Visitors must contact in advance. May not play on Saturdays.
Societies must apply in writing.
Green Fees £20 per day (£25 weekends & bank holidays).
Prof William Tye
Facilities
Location 1.5m S off A646

Hotel ★★ 62% Comfort Friendly Inn, Keirby Walk, BURNLEY ☎ 01282 427611 50

Towneley Towneley Park, Todmorden Rd BB11 3ED
☎ 01282 438473
Parkland course, with other sporting facilities.
18 holes, 5811yds, Par 70, SSS 68, Course record 67.
Club membership 290.

Visitors must contact in advance.
Societies must contact in advance in writing.
Green Fees not confirmed.
Cards
Facilities
Location 1m SE of town centre on A671

Hotel ★★★ 73% Oaks Hotel, Colne Rd, Reedley, BURNLEY ☎ 01282 414141 53

CHORLEY Map 07 SD51

Charnock Richard Preston Rd, Charnock Richard PR7 5LE
☎ 01257 470707 Fax 01257 794343
Flat parkland course, established in 1994, with plenty of water hazards.
18 holes, 6234yds, Par 71, SSS 70, Course record 68.
Club membership 550.

Visitors strict full dress code, members time 8.30-9.30pm and 12.00-1.00pm weekdays, telephone for weekend play.
Societies contact club secretary in writing.
Green Fees £15 per round (£20 weekends).
Cards
Designer Chris Cart
Facilities
Location On the main A49, 0.25m from Camelot Theme Park

Hotel ★★★ 69% Park Hall Hotel, Charnock Richard, CHORLEY ☎ 01257 452090 54 Annexe86

Chorley Hall o' th' Hill, Heath Charnock PR6 9HX
☎ 01257 480263 Fax 01257 480722
A splendid moorland course with plenty of fresh air. The well-sited clubhouse affords some good views of the Lancashire coast and of Angelzarke, a local beauty spot. Beware of the short 3rd hole with its menacing out-of-bounds.
18 holes, 6307yds, Par 71, SSS 70, Course record 63.
Club membership 550.

Visitors must contact in advance and may not play weekends or bank holidays.
Societies must contact in advance. Tue-Fri only.
Green Fees £27 day/round Mon-Fri.
Prof Gavin Mutch
Designer J A Steer
Facilities
Location 2.5m SE on A673

Hotel ★★★ 65% Pines Hotel, Clayton le Woods, CHORLEY ☎ 01772 338551 38

Duxbury Jubilee Park Duxbury Hall Rd PR7 4AS
☎ 01257 265380 & 241634
Municipal parkland course.
18 holes, 6390yds, Par 71, SSS 70.
Club membership 250.

Visitors must contact 6 days in advance via Pro shop.
Societies must contact in advance by letter.
Green Fees £7.25 per day (£10.50 weekends & bank holidays).
Prof S Middelman
Designer Hawtree & Sons
Facilities
Location 2.5m S off A6

Hotel B Welcome Lodge, Mill Ln, Charnock Richard, CHORLEY ☎ 01257 791746 100

Shaw Hill Hotel Golf & Country Club Preston Rd, Whittle-Le-Woods PR6 7PP
☎ 01257 269221 Fax 01257 261223
A fine course designed by one of Europe's most prominent golf architects and offering a considerable challenge as well as tranquillity and scenic charm. Seven lakes guard par 5 and long par 4 holes.
18 holes, 6405yds, Par 72, SSS 71, Course record 65.
Club membership 500.

Visitors must contact in advance, denims and trainers not allowed on course or in clubhouse. Jacket and tie required in restaurant.
Societies must telephone in advance.
Green Fees not confirmed.
Prof David Clark
Facilities
Location On A6 1.5m N

Hotel ★★★ 68% Shaw Hill Hotel Golf & Country Club, Preston Rd, Whittle-le-Woods, CHORLEY ☎ 01257 269221 26 Annexe4

CLITHEROE Map 07 SD74

Clitheroe Whalley Rd, Pendleton BB7 1PP
☎ 01200 422292 Fax 01200 422292
One of the best inland courses in the country. Clitheroe is a parkland-type course with water hazards and good scenic views, particularly on towards Longridge, and Pendle Hill. The Club has been the venue for the Lancashire Amateur Championships, the 1991 County Championships Tournament and the English Ladies (Intermediate) Championship.
18 holes, 6326yds, Par 71, SSS 71, Course record 67.
Club membership 725.

Visitors must contact in advance.
Societies must contact in advance.
Green Fees £33 per day (£39 weekends & bank holidays).
Prof John Twissell
Designer James Braid
Facilities
Location 2m S of Clitheroe on A671

Hotel ★★ 68% Shireburn Arms Hotel, HURST GREEN ☎ 01254 826518 18

COLNE Map 07 SD84

Colne Law Farm, Skipton Old Rd BB8 7EB
☎ 01282 863391
Moorland course with scenic surroundings.
9 holes, 5961yds, Par 70, SSS 69, Course record 63.
Club membership 356.

Visitors restricted Thu. Must contact in advance.
Societies must contact in advance.
Green Fees £16 per day (£20 weekends & bank holidays).
Facilities
Location 1m E off A56

▶

Hotel ★★★ 66% Stirk House Hotel, GISBURN ☎ 01200 445581 36 Annexe10

DARWEN Map 07 SD62

Darwen Winter Hill BB3 0LB ☎ 01254 701287
First 9 holes on parkland, the second 9 on moorland.
18 holes, 5863yds, Par 69, SSS 68, Course record 63.
Club membership 600.
Visitors may not play on Tue or Sat.
Societies must contact in advance.
Green Fees £20/£25 (£25/£35 weekends).
Prof Wayne Lennon
Facilities
Location 1m NW

Hotel ★★★ 66% Whitehall Hotel, Springbank, Whitehall, DARWEN ☎ 01254 701595 15

FLEETWOOD Map 07 SD34

Fleetwood Princes Way FY7 8AF
☎ 01253 873661 Fax 01253 773573
Championship length, flat seaside links where the player must always be alert to changes of direction or strength of the wind.
18 holes, 6723yds, Par 72, SSS 72.
Club membership 600.
Visitors may not play on competition days or Tue.
Societies must contact in advance. A deposit of £5 per player is required.
Green Fees £24 per day (£30 weekends & bank holidays).
Prof S McLaughlin
Designer J A Steer
Facilities
Location W side of town centre

Hotel ★★ 70% Brabyns Hotel, 1-3 Shaftesbury Av, North Shore, BLACKPOOL ☎ 01253 354263 22 Annexe3

GARSTANG Map 07 SD44

Garstang Country Hotel & Golf Club Garstang Rd, Bowgreave PR3 1YE ☎ 01995 600100 Fax 01995 600950
Fairly flat parkland course following the contours of the Rivers Wyre and Calder and providing a steady test of ability, especially over the longer back nine. Exceptional drainage makes the course playable all year round.
18 holes, 6050yds, Par 68, SSS 68.
Visitors tee times bookable 6 days in advance.
Societies telephone for availability and confirm in writing.
Green Fees £12 per round (£14 weekends & bank holidays).
Cards
Prof Robert Head
Designer Richard Bradbeer
Facilities
Location Situated on B6430 1m S of Garstang

Hotel ★★★ 64% Garstang Country Hotel & Golf Club, Garstang Rd, Bowgreave, GARSTANG ☎ 01995 600100 32

GREAT HARWOOD Map 07 SD73

Great Harwood Harwood Bar, Whalley Rd BB6 7TE
☎ 01254 884391
Flat parkland course with fine views of the Pendle region.
9 holes, 6415yds, Par 73, SSS 71, Course record 68.
Club membership 320.
Visitors must contact in advance.
Societies welcome mid-week only, apply in writing.
Green Fees £16 per day (£22 weeeknds & bank holidays).
Facilities
Location E side of town centre on A680

Hotel ★★★ 70% Dunkenhalgh Hotel, Blackburn Rd, Clayton le Moors, ACCRINGTON ☎ 01254 398021 37 Annexe42

HASLINGDEN Map 07 SD72

Rossendale Ewood Ln Head BB4 6LH
☎ 01706 831339 Fax 01706 228669
Testing meadowland course, mainly flat, situated on a plateau with panoramic views.
18 holes, 6293yds, Par 72, SSS 70, Course record 64.
Club membership 700.
Visitors must contact in advance. Must play with member on Sat.
Societies must telephone in advance & confirm in writing.
Green Fees £22.50 per day (£27.50 weekends & bank holidays).
Cards
Prof Stephen Nicholls
Facilities (ex Mon)
Location 0.5m S off A56

Hotel ★★★ 62% Old Mill Hotel, Springwood, RAMSBOTTOM ☎ 01706 822991 36

HEYSHAM Map 07 SD46

Heysham Trumacar Park, Middleton Rd LA3 3JH
☎ 01524 851011 Fax 10524 853030
Seaside parkland course, partly wooded. The 15th is a 459 yard Par 4 hole nearly always played into the prevailing south west wind.
18 holes, 6258yds, Par 69, SSS 70, Course record 64.
Club membership 1100.
Visitors book in advance via the professional, restricted at weekends.
Societies must contact in advance.
Green Fees £22 per day; £17 per round (£27 weekends & bank holidays).
Prof Ryan Done
Designer Alex Herd
Facilities
Location 0.75m S off A589

Hotel ★★ 62% Clarendon Hotel, Marine Rd West, West End Promenade, MORECAMBE ☎ 01524 410180 31rm(28)

KNOTT END-ON-SEA Map 07 SD34

Knott End Wyreside FY6 0AA
☎ 01253 810576 Fax 01253 810576
Pleasant, undulating parkland course on banks of River

Wyre. Open to sea breezes.
18 holes, 5789yds, Par 69, SSS 68, Course record 63.
Club membership 500.

Visitors book via professional up to 7 days in advance.
Societies must contact in advance.
Green Fees £21 per round (£23 weekends).
Prof Paul Walker
Designer Braid
Facilities
Location W side of village off B5377

Hotel ★★ 70% Brabyns Hotel, 1-3 Shaftesbury Av, North Shore, BLACKPOOL ☎ 01253 354263 22 Annexe3

Lancaster Map 07 SD46

Lancaster Golf Club Ashton Hall, Ashton-with-Stodday LA2 0AJ ☎ 01524 751247 Fax 01524 752742
This course is unusual for parkland golf as it is exposed to the winds coming off the Irish Sea. It is situated on the Lune estuary and has some natural hazards and easy walking. There are however several fine holes among woods near the old clubhouse.
18 holes, 6282yds, Par 71, SSS 71.
Club membership 925.

Visitors residential visitors only at weekends. Must contact in advance and have a handicap certificate.
Societies Mon-Fri only. Must contact in advance. Handicap certificate required.
Green Fees £32 per day/round.
Prof David Sutcliffe
Designer James Braid
Facilities
Location 3m S on A588

Hotel ★★★★ 69% Lancaster House Hotel, Green Ln, Ellel, LANCASTER ☎ 01524 844822 80

Lansil Caton Rd LA1 3PE ☎ 01524 61233
Parkland course.
9 holes, 5608yds, Par 70, SSS 67, Course record 68.
Club membership 375.

Visitors may not play before 1pm on Sunday.
Societies weekdays only; must contact in writing.
Green Fees £12 per day.
Designer 1947
Facilities by prior arrangement by prior arrangement by prior arrangement
Location N side of town centre on A683

Hotel B Forte Posthouse Lancaster, Waterside Park, Caton Rd, LANCASTER ☎ 01524 65999 115

Langho Map 07 SD73

Mytton Fold Farm Hotel Whalley Rd BB6 8AB
☎ 01254 240662 Fax 01254 248119
The course has panoramic views across the Ribble Valley and Pendle Hill. Tight fairways and water hazards are designed to make this a challenging course for any golfer.
Mytton Fold Farm Hotel: 18 holes, 6217yds, Par 72, SSS 70.
Club membership 200.

Visitors must contact in advance.
Societies telephone in advance.
Green Fees not confirmed.
Prof Gary P Coope
Designer Frank Hargreaves
Facilities
Location On A59 between Langho and Whalley

Hotel ★★★ 72% Northcote Manor, Northcote Rd, LANGHO ☎ 01254 240555 14

Leyland Map 07 SD52

Leyland Wigan Rd PR5 2UD
☎ 01772 436457 Fax 01772 436457
Parkland course, fairly flat and usually breezy.
18 holes, 6123yds, Par 69, SSS 70, Course record 64.
Club membership 650.

Visitors must contact in advance. Welcome weekdays, with member only at weekends.
Societies must contact in advance.
Green Fees £25 per weekday.
Prof Colin Burgess
Facilities
Location E side of town centre on A49

Hotel ★★★ 65% Pines Hotel, Clayton le Woods, CHORLEY ☎ 01772 338551 38

Longridge Map 07 SD63

Longridge Fell Barn, Jeffrey Hill PR3 2TU
☎ 01772 783291
One of the oldest courses in England. A moorland course with panoramic views of the Ribble Valley, Trough of Bowland, The Fylde and Welsh Mountains.
18 holes, 5975yds, Par 70, SSS 69, Course record 65.
Club membership 700.

Visitors welcome. Must contact in advance weekends May-Aug.
Societies welcome by prior arrangement.
Green Fees £20 per day, £15 per round (£25 per day weekends & bank holidays).
Prof Stephen Taylor
Facilities
Location 8m NE of Preston off B6243

Hotel ★★ 68% Shireburn Arms Hotel, HURST GREEN ☎ 01254 826518 18

Lytham St Annes Map 07 SD32

Fairhaven Lytham Hall Park, Ansdell FY8 4JU
☎ 01253 736741 (Secretary) 736976 (Pro)
A flat, but interesting parkland links course of good standard. There are natural hazards as well as numerous bunkers and players need to produce particularly accurate second shots.
18 holes, 6883yds, Par 74, SSS 73, Course record 66.
Club membership 750.

Visitors telephone professional in advance.
Societies must contact in advance.
Green Fees not confirmed.
Prof Brian Plucknett
Designer J A Steer
Facilities
Location E side of town centre off B5261

Hotel ★★★ 65% Bedford Hotel, 307-311 Clifton Dr South, LYTHAM ST ANNES
☎ 01253 724636 36

Lytham Green Drive Ballam Rd FY8 4LE
☎ 01253 737390 Fax 01253 731350
Pleasant parkland course, ideal for holidaymakers.
18 holes, 6163yds, Par 70, SSS 69, Course record 64.
Club membership 740.

Visitors must contact in advance. May not play at weekends.
Societies must apply in writing.
Green Fees £35 per day; £25 per round (£35 per round Sun & bank holidays).
Prof Andrew Lancaster
Designer Steer
Facilities
Location E side of town centre off B5259

Hotel ★★★★ 62% Clifton Arms, West Beach, Lytham, LYTHAM ST ANNES
☎ 01253 739898 44

Royal Lytham St Annes See page 165

St Annes Old Links Highbury Rd FY8 2LD
☎ 01253 723597
Seaside links, qualifying course for Open Championship; compact and of very high standard, particularly greens. Windy, very long 5th, 17th and 18th holes. Famous hole: 9th (171 yds), par 3. Excellent club facilities.
18 holes, 6616yds, Par 72, SSS 72.
Club membership 950.

Visitors may not play on Sat or before 9.15am & between noon-2pm weekdays. Sundays by prior arrangement only. Handicap certificate requested.
Societies must contact in advance.
Green Fees £35 per day/round (£45 weekends).
Prof G Hardiman
Designer George Lowe
Facilities
Location N side of town centre

Hotel ★★★ 65% Bedford Hotel, 307-311 Clifton Dr South, LYTHAM ST ANNES
☎ 01253 724636 36

Morecambe Map 07 SD46

Morecambe Bare LA4 6AJ
☎ 01524 412841 Fax 01524 412841
Holiday golf at its most enjoyable. The well-maintained, wind-affected seaside parkland course is not long but full of character. Even so the panoramic views across Morecambe Bay and to the Lake District and Pennines make concentration difficult. The 4th is a testing hole.
18 holes, 5770yds, Par 67, SSS 68, Course record 63.
Club membership 850.

Visitors must contact in advance.
Societies must contact in advance.
Green Fees not confirmed.
Prof Simon Fletcher
Designer Dr Alister Mackenzie
Facilities
Location N side of town centre on A5105

Hotel ★★★ 66% Elms Hotel, Bare Village, MORECAMBE
☎ 01524 411501 40

Nelson Map 07 SD83

Marsden Park Townhouse Rd BB9 8DG ☎ 01282 661912
Hilly, parkland course open to the wind and suitable for golfers of all abilities.
18 holes, 5813yds, Par 70, SSS 68, Course record 66.
Club membership 298.

Visitors must telephone in advance at weekends.
Societies Must contact in writing.
Green Fees £8 per day (£9 weekends & bank holidays).
Cards
Facilities
Location E side of town centre off A56

Hotel ★ 61% Smuggler's Haunt Hotel & Restaurant, Church Hill East, BRIXHAM
☎ 01803 853050 & 859416 Fax 01803 858738
14rm(4) Annexe2rm

Nelson King's Causeway, Brierfield BB9 0EU
☎ 01282 611834 & 617000 Fax 01282 606226
Moorland course, usually windy, with good views. Testing 8th hole, par 4.
18 holes, 5967yds, Par 70, SSS 69, Course record 63.
Club membership 500.

Visitors must telephone 01282 617000 in advance, may not play before 9.30am or between 12.30-1.30pm.
Societies must contact in writing.
Green Fees £25 per day (£30 weekends & bank holidays).
Prof Nigel Sumner
Designer Dr Mackenzie
Facilities
Location 1.5m SE

Hotel ★★★ 73% Oaks Hotel, Colne Rd, Reedley, BURNLEY ☎ 01282 414141 53

Ormskirk Map 07 SD40

Hurlston Hall Hurlston Ln, Southport Rd, Scarisbrick L40 8JD ☎ 01704 840400 & 841120 Fax 01704 841404
Designed by Donald Steel and opened in 1994, this gently undulating course offers fine views across the Pennines and Bowland Fells. With generous fairways, large tees and greens, two streams and seven lakes, it provides a good test of golf for players of all standards. Luxurious colonial-style clubhouse.
18 holes, 6746yds, Par 72, SSS 72, Course record 66.

Visitors welcome, but may be asked for handicap certificate or letter of introduction from own club. Preferable to book in advance.
Societies registered Golf Societies and others approved by club, write or telephone for details.
Green Fees £25 per 18 holes (£30 weekends and bank holidays).
Cards
Prof Gerry Bond ▶

ROYAL LYTHAM AND ST ANNES

LYTHAM ST ANNES *Lancs* ☎ 01253 724206
Fax 01253 780946 Map 07 SD32

John Ingham writes: Venue for many Open Championships, the most famous winner here was amateur Bobby Jones who, in 1926, put together a four-round total of 291 using wooden clubs and the old-fashioned ball. In the last round, when level with Al Watrous with two to play, Jones bunkered his teeshot at the 17th while Watrous hit a perfect drive and then a fine second on to the green. Jones climbed into the bunker, decided a 175-yard shot was needed if he had any chance, and hit a club similar to today's 4-iron. The shot was brilliant and finished, not only on the green, but nearer than his rival. Shaken, Watrous 3-putted, Jones got his four and finished with a perfect par while Watrous, rattled, had taken six. The club placed a plaque by the famous bunker and it's there to this day.

Since that time the course, which runs close to the railway but slightly inland from the sea, has staged other historic Opens. Bob Charles of New Zealand became the only left-hander to win the title while Tony Jacklin, in 1969, signalled the re-awakening of British golf by winning.

This huge links, founded in 1886 not far from Blackpool, is not easy. When the wind gets up it can be a nightmare. And not everyone approves a championship course that starts with a par 3 hole and it is, in fact, a rare thing in Britain. Some object to the close proximity of red-bricked houses, and aren't keen on trains that rattle past. Now there is an additional nine-hole course and a driving range.

But it's a test full of history and deserves to be played.

Visitors	weekdays only (unless guest at Dormy House). Must contact in advance, and have a handicap certificate
Societies	must apply to Secretary (large groups Mon & Thur only)
Green fees	£80 per round (includes lunch)
Facilities	⊗ Professional (E.Birchenough)
Leisure	snooker
Location	Links Gate, Lytham FY8 3LQ (0.5m E of St Annes town)

18 holes, 6334 yds, Par 71, SSS 71,

WHERE TO STAY AND EAT NEARBY

HOTELS:

LYTHAM ST ANNES

★★★★ Clifton Arms, West Beach, Lytham ☎ 01253 739898 44

★★★ 66% Bedford, 307-311 Clifton Drive South. ☎ 01253 724636. 36 (14 22)

★★★ 67% Chadwick, South Promenade. ☎ 01253 720061. 72 (7 65)

★★ 67% Glendower, North Promenade. ☎ 01253 723241. 60

★★ 66% St Ives, 7-9 South Promenade. ☎ 01253 720011. 70 (3 60)

RESTAURANT:

THORNTON

The Victorian House, ☎ 01253 860619

Designer Donald Steel
Facilities ⊗ ☾ ⊾ ☕ ♀ ⛀ ⌂ ⛳ ✂
& Leisure fishing.
Location Situated 6m from Southpark and 2m from Ormskirk along A570

Hotel ★★★ 64% Beaufort, High Ln, Burscough, ORMSKIRK ☎ 01704 892655 21 ⇨ ↱

Ormskirk Cranes Ln, Lathom L40 5UJ
☎ 01695 572112 Fax 01695 572112
A pleasantly secluded, fairly flat, parkland course with much heath and silver birch. Accuracy from the tees will provide an interesting variety of second shots.
18 holes, 6358yds, Par 70, SSS 70, Course record 63.
Club membership 300.
Visitors restricted Sat.
Societies must contact in writing.
Green Fees not confirmed.
Prof Jack Hammond
Facilities ⛀ ⌂ ✂
Location 1.5m NE

Hotel ★★★ 66% Holland Hall Hotel, 6 Lafford Ln, UPHOLLAND
☎ 01695 624426 28 ⇨ ↱ Annexe6 ⇨ ↱

PLEASINGTON Map 07 SD62

Pleasington BB2 5JF
☎ 01254 202177 Fax 01254 201028
Plunging and rising across lovely moorland turf this course tests judgement of distance through the air to greens of widely differing levels. The 11th and 17th are testing holes.
18 holes, 6417yds, Par 71, SSS 71.
Club membership 700.
Visitors may play Mon & Wed-Fri only.
Societies must contact in advance.
Green Fees £36 (£42 weekends & bank holidays).
Prof Ged Furey
Facilities ⊗ ☾ ⊾ ☕ ♀ ⛀ ⌂ ✂
Location W side of village

Hotel ★★★ 59% County Hotel Blackburn, Preston New Rd, BLACKBURN
☎ 01254 899988 98 ⇨ ↱

POULTON-LE-FYLDE Map 07 SD33

Poulton-le-Fylde Breck Rd FY6 7HJ ☎ 01253 892444
Municipal parkland course, with easy walking.
9 holes, 3028yds, Par 70, SSS 68.
Club membership 200.
Visitors no restrictions.
Societies contact in advance by telephone or in writing.
Green Fees not confirmed.
Prof Lewis Ware
Designer E Astbury
Facilities ⊗ ⊾ ☕ ♀ ⛀ ⌂ ↟ ✂
& Leisure heated indoor swimming pool.
Location N side of town

Hotel ★★ 70% Brabyns Hotel, 1-3 Shaftesbury Av, North Shore, BLACKPOOL
☎ 01253 354263 22 ⇨ ↱ Annexe3 ⇨ ↱

PRESTON Map 07 SD52

Ashton & Lea Tudor Av, Lea PR4 0XA
☎ 01772 726480 & 735282 Fax 01772 735762
Heathland/parkland course with pond and streams, offering pleasant walks and some testing holes.
18 holes, 6346yds, Par 71, SSS 70, Course record 65.
Club membership 650.
Visitors must contact professional on 01772 724370 or secretary on 01772 735282.
Societies must contact in writing or by telephone.
Green Fees £20 per day (£23 weekends & bank holidays).
Cards ▬
Prof M Greenough
Designer J Steer
Facilities ⊗ ☾ ⊾ ☕ ♀ ⛀ ⌂ ✂
Location 3m W on A5085

Hotel B Forte Posthouse Preston, Ringway, PRESTON ☎ 01772 259411 121 ⇨ ↱

Fishwick Hall Glenluce Dr, Farringdon Park PR1 5TD
☎ 01772 798300 & 795870
Meadowland course overlooking River Ribble. Natural hazards.
18 holes, 6045yds, Par 70, SSS 69, Course record 66.
Club membership 750.
Visitors advisable to contact in advance.
Societies must contact in advance.
Green Fees £22 per day (£27 weekends & bank holidays).
Prof Mike Hadfield
Facilities ⊗ ☾ ⊾ ☕ ♀ ⛀ ⌂ ✂
Hotel B Forte Posthouse Preston, Ringway, PRESTON ☎ 01772 259411 121 ⇨ ↱

Ingol Tanterton Hall Rd, Ingol PR2 7BY ☎ 01772 734556
Long, high course with natural water hazards.
18 holes, 6296yds, Par 72, SSS 70, Course record 67.
Club membership 800.
Visitors must contact in advance but may not play on competition days.
Societies must contact in writing.
Green Fees not confirmed.
Facilities ♀ ⛀ ⌂
& Leisure squash.
Location 2m NW junc 32 of M55 off B5411

Hotel B Forte Posthouse Preston, Ringway, PRESTON ☎ 01772 259411 121 ⇨ ↱

Penwortham Blundell Ln, Penwortham PR1 0AX
☎ 01772 744630 Fax 01772 744630
A progressive golf club set close to the banks of the River Ribble. The course has tree-lined fairways, excellent greens, and provides easy walking. Testing holes include the 178-yd, par 3 third, the 480-yd, par 5 sixth, and the 398-yd par 4 sixteenth.
18 holes, 6056yds, Par 69, SSS 69.
Club membership 975.
Visitors must contact in advance; restricted Sun.
Societies must apply in writing.

Green Fees £25 per day; £22 per round (£28 weekends).
Prof Norman Marshall
Facilities ⊗ 🍴 🍽 ☕ 🍷 ⛺ 🏠 ✓
Location 1.5m W of town centre off A59

Hotel ★★★ 68% Tickled Trout, Preston New Rd, Samlesbury, PRESTON
☎ 01772 877671 72 ⇌ ↱

Preston Fulwood Hall Ln, Fulwood PR2 8DD
☎ 01772 700011 Fax 01772 794234
Pleasant inland golf at this course set in very agreeable parkland. There is a well-balanced selection of holes, undulating amongst groups of trees, and not requiring great length.
18 holes, 6254yds, Par 71, SSS 70.
Club membership 800.
Visitors may play midweek only. Must contact in advance and have a handicap certificate.
Societies must contact in writing/telephone.
Green Fees £30 per day; £25 per round.
Prof Andrew Greenbank
Designer James Braid
Facilities ⊗ 🍴 🍽 ☕ 🍷 ⛺ 🏠 ✓
Location N side of town centre

Hotel ★★★★ 69% Preston Marriott, Garstang Rd, Broughton, PRESTON
☎ 01772 864087 98 ⇌ ↱

Rishton Map 07 SD73

Rishton Eachill Links, Hawthorn Dr BB1 4HG
☎ 01254 884442
Undulating moorland course.
9 holes, 6097yds, Par 70, SSS 69, Course record 68.
Club membership 270.
Visitors must play with member on weekends and bank holidays.
Societies must contact in writing.
Green Fees not confirmed.
Facilities ⊗ 🍴 🍽 ☕ 🍷 by arrangement ⛺
Location S side of town off A678

Hotel ★★★ 70% Dunkenhalgh Hotel, Blackburn Rd, Clayton le Moors, ACCRINGTON
☎ 01254 398021 37 ⇌ ↱ Annexe42 ⇌ ↱

Silverdale Map 07 SD47

Silverdale Redbridge Ln LA5 0SP
☎ 01524 701300 Fax 01524 702074
Difficult heathland course with rock outcrops. Excellent views.
12 holes, 5463yds, Par 69, SSS 67.
Club membership 500.
Visitors may only play on Sun in summer if accompanied by a member.
Societies must contact in writing.
Green Fees £15 per day (£18 weekends & bank holidays).
Facilities ⊗ 🍽 ☕ 🍷 ⛺
Location Opposite Silverdale Station

Hotel ★★ 61% Royal Station Hotel, Market St, CARNFORTH ☎ 01524 732033 & 733636 Fax 01524 720267 12 ⇌ ↱

Upholland Map 07 SD50

Beacon Park Beacon Ln WN8 7RU
☎ 01695 622700 Fax 01695 633066
Undulating/hilly parkland course, designed by Donald Steel, with magnificent view of the Welsh hills. Twenty-four-bay floodlit driving range open 9am-9pm in summer.
18 holes, 6000yds, Par 72, SSS 69, Course record 68.
Club membership 200.
Visitors may book 6 days in advance.
Societies must contact in advance.
Green Fees £6.50 (£9 weekends & bank holidays).
Prof Ray Peters
Designer Donald Steel
Facilities ⊗ 🍴 by prior arrangement 🍽 by prior arrangement ☕ 🍷 ⛺ 🏠 ⛳ ✓ 🏌
Location S of Ashurst Beacon Hill

Hotel ★★★ 66% Holland Hall Hotel, 6 Lafford Ln, UPHOLLAND
☎ 01695 624426 28 ⇌ ↱ Annexe6 ⇌ ↱

Dean Wood Lafford Ln WN8 0QZ
☎ 01695 622219 Fax 01695 622245
This parkland course has a varied terrain - flat front nine, undulating back nine. Beware the par 4, 11th and 17th holes, which has ruined many a card. If there were a prize for the best maintained course in Lancashire, Dean Wood would be a strong contender.
18 holes, 6179yds, Par 71, SSS 71, Course record 66.
Club membership 800.
Visitors must play with member Tue, Wed & weekends.
Societies must contact in advance.
Green Fees £27 per day (£30 weekends).
Prof Tony Coop
Designer James Braid
Facilities ⊗ 🍴 🍽 ⛺ 🏠 ✓
Location 1m from junct 26 of M6

Hotel ★★★ 66% Holland Hall Hotel, 6 Lafford Ln, UPHOLLAND
☎ 01695 624426 28 ⇌ ↱ Annexe6 ⇌ ↱

Whalley Map 07 SD73

Whalley Long Leese Barn, Portfield Ln BB7 9DR
☎ 01254 822236
Parkland course near Pendle Hill, overlooking the Ribble Valley. Superb views. Ninth hole over pond.
9 holes, 6258yds, Par 72, SSS 70.
Club membership 400.
Visitors must telephone 01254 824766 in advance.
Societies must apply in writing.
Green Fees £15 per day (£20 weekends & bank holidays).
Prof H Smith
Facilities ⊗ 🍴 🍽 ☕ 🍷 ⛺ 🏠 ✓
Location 1m SE off A671

Hotel ★★★★ 64% Foxfields Country Hotel & Restaurant, Whalley Rd, Billington, BLACKBURN
☎ 01254 822556 28 ⇌ ↱ Annexe16 ⇌ ↱

WHITWORTH Map 07 SD81

Lobden Lobden Moor OL12 8XJ
☎ 01706 343228 Fax 01706 343228
Moorland course, with hard walking. Windy.
9 holes, 5697yds, Par 70, SSS 68, Course record 66.
Club membership 250.

Visitors must contact in advance. May not play Sat.
Societies must apply in writing to Secretary.
Green Fees £10 per day (£15 weekends & bank holidays).
Facilities
Location E side of town centre off A671

Hotel ★★ 59% Midway Hotel, Manchester Rd, Castleton, ROCHDALE
☎ 01706 32881 24

WILPSHIRE Map 07 SD63

Wilpshire Whalley Rd BB1 9LF
☎ 01254 248260 Fax 01254 248260
Parkland/moorland course with varied and interesting holes. Magnificent views of Ribble Valley, the coast and the Yorkshire Dales.
18 holes, 5921yds, Par 69, SSS 66, Course record 68.
Club membership 500.

Visitors must contact in advance.
Societies must contact by telephone and confirm in writing.
Green Fees £25.50 per day/round (£30.50 weekends & bank holidays).
Prof Walter Slaven
Designer James Braid
Facilities
Location 2m NE of Blackburn, on A666 towards Clitheroe

Hotel ★★★ 59% County Hotel Blackburn, Preston New Rd, BLACKBURN
☎ 01254 899988 98

LEICESTERSHIRE

ASHBY-DE-LA-ZOUCH Map 08 SK31

Willesley Park Measham Rd LE65 2PF
☎ 01530 414596 Fax 01530 414596
Undulating heathland and parkland course with quick draining sandy sub-soil.
18 holes, 6304yds, Par 70, SSS 70, Course record 64.
Club membership 600.

Visitors Must contact in advance. Restricted weekends. Handicap certificate required.
Societies Wed-Fri only. Must apply in writing.
Green Fees £30.
Prof C J Hancock
Facilities by prior arrangement
Location SW side of town centre on A453

Hotel ★★★ 65% The Fallen Knight, Kilwardby St, ASHBY-DE-LA ZOUCH
☎ 01530 412230 24

BIRSTALL Map 04 SK50

Birstall Station Rd LE4 3BB
☎ 0116 267 4322 Fax 0116 267 4322
Parkland course with trees, shrubs, ponds and ditches.
18 holes, 6222yds, Par 70, SSS 70.
Club membership 650.

Visitors with member only weekends; may not play Tue.
Societies apply in writing.
Green Fees not confirmed.
Prof David Clarke
Facilities
Location 3m N of Leicester on A6

Hotel ★★★ 60% Hotel Saint James, Abbey St, LEICESTER ☎ 0116 251 0666 73

BOTCHESTON Map 04 SK40

Forest Hill Markfield Ln LE9 9FJ
☎ 01455 824800 Fax 01455 828522
Parkland course with many trees, four Par 4s, but no steep gradients.
18 holes, 6039yds, Par 72, SSS 69.
Club membership 450.

Visitors must contact in advance for weekends.
Societies Mon-Fri, must telephone in advance.
Green Fees not confirmed.
Prof Philip Harness
Facilities
Hotel ★★★ 65% Field Head Hotel, Markfield Ln, MARKFIELD ☎ 01530 245454 28

COSBY Map 04 SP59

Cosby Chapel Ln, Broughton Rd LE9 1RG
☎ 0116 286 4759 Fax 0116 286 4484
Undulating parkland course with a number of tricky, tight driving holes.
18 holes, 6410yds, Par 71, SSS 71, Course record 68.
Club membership 750.

Visitors restricted weekdays before 4pm. May not play at weekends. Recommended to telephone in advance. Handicap certificate required.
Societies book with secretary.
Green Fees £26 per day; £16 per round.
Prof Martin Wing
Designer Hawtrees
Facilities
Location S side of village

Hotel B Forte Posthouse Leicester, Braunstone Ln East, LEICESTER
☎ 0116 263 0500 164

EAST GOSCOTE Map 08 SK61

Beedles Lake 170 Broome Ln LE7 3WQ ☎ 0116 260 6759
Fairly flat parkland course, founded in 1992, with an adjoining lake and well maintained greens.
18 holes, 6625yds, Par 72, SSS 72, Course record 71.
Club membership 400.

Visitors telephone booking required for weekends.
Societies welcome Mon-Fri
Green Fees £9 (£12 weekends).
Prof Sean Byrne

Designer D Tucker
Facilities & Leisure fishing.
Location Off A46, just N of Leicester through village of Ratcliffe on the Wreake

Hotel ★★★ 65% Rothley Court, Westfield Ln, ROTHLEY
0116 237 4141 13 Annexe21

ENDERBY Map 04 SP59

Enderby Mill Ln LE9 5HL
0116 284 9388 Fax 0116 284 9388
A gently undulating 9-hole course at which beginners are especially welcome. The longest hole is the 2nd at 407 yards and there are 5 Par 3's.
9 holes, 2133yds, Par 31, SSS 31, Course record 27.
Club membership 150.
Visitors no restrictions.
Societies must telephone in advance.
Green Fees £4.50 per 9 holes; £5.50 per 18 holes (£5.50/£7.50 weekends).
Prof Chris D'Araujo
Designer David Lowe
Facilities
& Leisure heated indoor swimming pool, squash, sauna, solarium, gymnasium.
Location 2m S, M1 junct21 on Narborough road. Right turn off roundabout at Foxhunter pub, 0.5m on left

Hotel ★★ 63% Charnwood Hotel, 48 Leicester Rd, Narborough, LEICESTER
0116 286 2218 20

HINCKLEY Map 04 SP49

Hinckley Leicester Rd LE10 3DR 01455 615124
Rolling parkland with lake features, and lined fairways.
18 holes, 6517yds, Par 71, SSS 71.
Club membership 1000.
Visitors with member only weekends and bank holidays. Must contact in advance and have a handicap certificate.
Societies apply by letter.
Green Fees not confirmed.
Prof Richard Jones
Facilities
Location 1.5m NE on A47

Hotel ★★ 67% Longshoot Toby Hotel, Watling St, NUNEATON
01203 329711 Annexe47

KETTON Map 04 SK90

Luffenham Heath PE9 3UU 01780 720205
This undulating heathland course with low bushes, much gorse and many trees, lies in a conservation area for flora and fauna. From the higher part of the course there is a magnificent view across the Chater Valley.
18 holes, 6273yds, Par 70, SSS 70, Course record 64.
Club membership 550.
Visitors must contact in advance.
Societies write or telephone in advance.
Green Fees £35 per day/round (£40 weekends & bank holidays).
Prof Ian Burnett
Designer James Braid
Facilities by prior arrangement by prior arrangement
Location 1.5m SW of Ketton by Fosters Railway Bridge on A6121

Hotel ★★★ 75% George of Stamford Hotel, St Martins, STAMFORD
01780 755171 47

KIBWORTH Map 04 SP69

Kibworth Weir Rd, Beauchamp LE8 0LP
0116 279 2301 Fax 0116 279 2301
Parkland course with easy walking. A brook affects a number of fairways
18 holes, 6333yds, Par 71, SSS 70, Course record 65.
Club membership 700.
Visitors must contact in advance. With member only weekends.
Societies must contact in advance.
Green Fees £22 weekdays only.
Prof Bob Larratt
Facilities
Location S side of village off A6

Hotel ★★★ 68% Three Swans Hotel, 21 High St, MARKET HARBOROUGH
01858 466644 20 Annexe16

KIRBY MUXLOE Map 04 SK50

Kirby Muxloe Station Rd LE9 2EP
0116 239 3457 Fax 0116 239 3457
Pleasant parkland course with a lake in front of the 17th green and a short 18th.
18 holes, 6351yds, Par 70, SSS 70, Course record 65.
Club membership 890.
Visitors must contact in advance and a handicap certificate is required. No visitors on Tue or at weekends.
Societies must contact in advance.
Green Fees £28 per day; £22 per round.
Prof Bruce Whipham
Facilities
Location S side of village off B5380

Hotel ★★★★ 61% Holiday Inn, St Nicholas Circle, LEICESTER 0116 253 1161 188

LEICESTER Map 04 SK50

Humberstone Heights Gypsy Ln LE5 0TB
0116 276 3680 & 276 467(Pro Shop)
Municipal parkland course with 9 hole pitch and putt and 30 bay driving range.
18 holes, 6343yds, Par 70, SSS 70, Course record 66.
Club membership 400.
Visitors must telephone in advance at weekends.
Societies must telephone in advance.
Green Fees Summer: £6.75-£10.25; Winter: £5.75-£9.25.
Prof Philip Highfield ▶

Designer Hawtry & Sons
Facilities
& Leisure pitch & putt.
Location 2.5m NE of city centre

Hotel ★★★ 72% Belmont House Hotel, De Montfort St, LEICESTER ☎ 0116 254 4773 75

Leicestershire Evington Ln LE5 6DJ
☎ 0116 273 8825 Fax 0116 273 8825
Pleasantly undulating parkland course.
18 holes, 6326yds, Par 68, SSS 70, Course record 63.
Club membership 800.
Visitors must contact in advance. May not play Sat. Must hold a handicap certificate.
Societies must contact in advance.
Green Fees £29 per day; £24 per round (£35/£30 weekends & bank holidays).
Prof John R Turnbull
Designer Hawtree
Facilities
Location 2m E of city off A6030

Hotel ★★★ 64% Hermitage Hotel, Wigston Rd, Oadby, LEICESTER
☎ 0116 256 9955 57

Western Scudamore Rd, Braunstone Frith LE3 1UQ
☎ 0116 287 2339 & 287 6158
Pleasant, undulating parkland course with open aspect fairways in two loops of nine holes.Not too difficult but a good test of golf off the back tees.
18 holes, 6518yds, Par 72, SSS 71.
Club membership 400.
Visitors must contact in advance.
Societies must contact the professional in advance.
Green Fees £10 per round.
Prof Dave Butler
Facilities
Location 1.5m W of city centre off A47

Hotel B Forte Posthouse Leicester, Braunstone Ln East, LEICESTER
☎ 0116 263 0500 164

LOUGHBOROUGH Map 08 SK51

Longcliffe Snell's Nook Ln, Nanpantan LE11 3YA
☎ 01509 239129 Fax 01509 231286
A re-designed course of natural heathland with outcrops of granite forming natural hazards especially on the 1st and 15th. The course is heavily wooded and has much bracken and gorse. There are a number of tight fairways and one blind hole.
18 holes, 6611yds, Par 72, SSS 72.
Club membership 660.
Visitors must contact in advance. With member only at weekends.
Societies telephone for availability, handicap certificate required.
Green Fees £32 per day; £25 per round.
Prof Ian D Bailey
Designer Williamson
Facilities
Location 3m SW off B5350

Hotel ★★★ 63% Quality Friendly Hotel, New Ashby Rd, LOUGHBOROUGH
☎ 01509 211800 94

LUTTERWORTH Map 04 SP58

Kilworth Springs South Kilworth Rd, North Kilworth LE17 6HJ ☎ 01858 575082 & 575974
An 18-hole course of two loops of 9: the front 9 are links style while the back 9 are in parkland with 4 lakes. On a windy day it is a very challenging course and the 6th hole is well deserving of its nickname 'the Devil's Toenail'.
18 holes, 6543yds, Par 72, SSS 71, Course record 66.
Club membership 800.
Visitors welcome subject to availability.
Societies contact in advance.
Green Fees not confirmed.
Prof N Melvin
Facilities
Location 4m E of M1 junc 20, A427 to Mkt Harborough

Hotel ★★★ 63% Denbigh Arms Hotel, High St, LUTTERWORTH ☎ 01455 553537 31

Lutterworth Rugby Rd LE17 4HN
☎ 01455 552532 Fax 01455 553586
Hilly course with River Swift running through.
18 holes, 6226yds, Par 70, SSS 70.
Club membership 700.
Visitors must play with member at weekends.
Societies must contact in advance.
Green Fees not confirmed.
Prof Roland Tisdall
Facilities
Location 0.5m S on A426

Hotel ★★★ 63% Denbigh Arms Hotel, High St, LUTTERWORTH ☎ 01455 553537 31

MARKET HARBOROUGH Map 04 SP78

Market Harborough Oxendon Rd LE16 8NF
☎ 01858 463684
A parkland course situated close to the town. There are wide-ranging views over the surrounding countryside. Lakes a feature on 4 holes; challenging last 3 holes.
18 holes, 6022yds, Par 70, SSS 69, Course record 63.
Club membership 600.
Visitors must play with member at weekends.
Societies must apply in writing.
Green Fees £25 per day; £20 per round.
Prof Frazer Baxter
Designer H Swan
Facilities
Location 1m S on A508

Hotel ★★★ 68% Three Swans Hotel, 21 High St, MARKET HARBOROUGH
☎ 01858 466644 20 Annexe16

Stoke Albany Ashley Rd, Stoke Albany LE16 8PL
☎ 01858 535208 Fax 01858 535505
Parkland course tucked away in the picturesque Welland Valley. Affording good views, the course should appeal to the mid-handicap golfer, and provide an interesting test to the more experienced player.

18 holes, 6132yds, Par 71, SSS 69.
Club membership 400.

Visitors welcoome at all times.
Societies please telephone secretary.
Green Fees £12 per 18 holes (£16 weekends and bank holidays).
Prof Adrian Clifford
Designer Hawtree
Facilities
Location Located N off A427 Market Harborough/Corby Road, follow Stoke Albany 500m towards Ashley village

Hotel ★★★ 68% Three Swans Hotel, 21 High St, MARKET HARBOROUGH ☎ 01858 466644 20 Annexe16

MELTON MOWBRAY Map 08 SK71

Melton Mowbray Waltham Rd, Thorpe Arnold LE14 4SD ☎ 01664 562118 Fax 01664 562118
Downland but flat course providing easy walking.
18 holes, 6222yds, Par 70, SSS 70.
Club membership 600.

Visitors must contact professional on 01664 569629.
Societies must contact in advance.
Green Fees £17 (£20 weekends).
Prof James Hetherington
Facilities by prior arrangement
Location 2m NE on A607

Hotel ★★★ 63% Sysonby Knoll Hotel, Asfordby Rd, MELTON MOWBRAY ☎ 01664 63563 23 Annexe1

OADBY Map 04 SK60

Glen Gorse Glen Rd LE2 4RF ☎ 0116 271 4159 Fax 0116 271 4159
Fairly flat 18-hole parkland course with some strategically placed mature trees, new saplings and ponds affecting play on 6 holes. Ridge and furrow is a feature of 5 holes.
18 holes, 6648yds, Par 72, SSS 72, Course record 67.
Club membership 600.

Visitors must contact in advance. Must play with member at weekends.
Societies must telephone secretary in advance.
Green Fees £28.50 per day; £24 per round.
Prof Dominic Fitzpatrick
Facilities
& Leisure snooker.
Location On A6 trunk road between Oadby/Great Glen

Hotel ★★★ 64% Hermitage Hotel, Wigston Rd, Oadby, LEICESTER ☎ 0116 256 9955 57

Oadby Leicester Rd LE2 4AJ ☎ 0116 270 9052
Municipal parkland course.
18 holes, 6376yds, Par 72, SSS 70, Course record 60.
Club membership 500.

Visitors no restrictions.
Societies by arrangement contact pro shop.
Green Fees not confirmed.
Prof Alan Kershaw
Facilities
Location West of Oadby, off A6

Hotel ★★★ 64% Hermitage Hotel, Wigston Rd, Oadby, LEICESTER ☎ 0116 256 9955 57

ROTHLEY Map 08 SK51

Rothley Park Westfield Ln LE7 7LH ☎ 0116 230 2809 Fax 0116 230 2809
Parkland course in picturesque situation.
18 holes, 6477yds, Par 71, SSS 71, Course record 67.
Club membership 600.

Visitors must contact professional on 0116 230 3023.
Societies apply in writing to secretary.
Green Fees £30 per day; £25 per round.
Prof Andrew Collins
Facilities
Location 0.75m W on B5328

Hotel ★★★ 65% Rothley Court, Westfield Ln, ROTHLEY ☎ 0116 237 4141 13 Annexe21

SCRAPTOFT Map 04 SK60

Scraptoft Beeby Rd LE7 9SJ ☎ 0116 241 8863
Pleasant, inland country course.
18 holes, 6166yds, Par 69, SSS 69.
Club membership 550.

Visitors with member only weekends. Handicap certificate required.
Societies apply in writing.
Green Fees not confirmed.
Facilities
Location 1m NE

Hotel ★★★ 64% Hermitage Hotel, Wigston Rd, Oadby, LEICESTER ☎ 0116 256 9955 57

SEAGRAVE Map 08 SK61

Park Hill Park Hill LE12 7NG ☎ 01509 815454 & 815775 (pro) Fax 01509 816062

A new rolling parkland course with tree lined fairways and views over Charnwood Forest. The opening hole is 420yards with a forced water carry 100yards short of the green. The 10th is a 610yard Par 5 against the prevailing wind and there are 2 Par 5's to finish.
18 holes, 7219yds, Par 73, SSS 74, Course record 71.
Club membership 500.

Visitors must contact in advance. ▶

Societies apply in advance.
Green Fees £20 per round (£24 weekends & bank holidays).
Prof David C Mee
Facilities
Location 6m N of Leicester on A46

Hotel ★★★ 63% Quality Friendly Hotel, New Ashby Rd, LOUGHBOROUGH
☎ 01509 211800 94

ULLESTHORPE Map 04 SP58

Ullesthorpe Frolesworth Rd LE17 5BZ ☎ 01455 209023
Set in 130 acres of parkland surrounding a 17th-century manor house, this championship length course can be very demanding and offers a challenge to both beginners and professionals. Excellent leisure facilities.
18 holes, 6650yds, Par 72, SSS 72, Course record 67.
Club membership 650.
Visitors must contact in advance.
Societies contact well in advance.
Green Fees not confirmed.
Prof David Bowring
Facilities
& Leisure hard tennis courts, heated indoor swimming pool, sauna, solarium, gymnasium.
Location 0.5m N off B577

Hotel ★★★ 63% Denbigh Arms Hotel, High St, LUTTERWORTH ☎ 01455 553537 31

WHETSTONE Map 04 SP59

Whetstone Cambridge Rd, Cosby LE9 1SJ
☎ 0116 286 1424
Small and very flat parkland course adjacent to motorway.
18 holes, 5795yds, Par 68, SSS 68.
Club membership 500.
Visitors limited times at weekends
Societies must contact in advance.
Green Fees not confirmed.
Prof David Raitt
Facilities
Location 1m S of village

Hotel ★★★ 66% Time Out Hotel & Leisure, Enderby Rd, Blaby, LEICESTER
☎ 0116 278 7898 25

WILSON Map 08 SK42

Breedon Priory Green Ln DE73 1AT ☎ 01332 863081
A relatively short and forgiving course set in undulating countryside with magnificent views from several holes.
18 holes, 5530yds, Par 70, SSS 67, Course record 67.
Club membership 779.
Visitors may play any time if tee available, must book for weekends.
Societies apply in writing or telephone for booking form.
Green Fees not confirmed.
Prof Ben Hill
Designer David Snell
Facilities
Location 4m W of A42/M1 junct 24

Hotel ★★★ 69% The Priest House on the River, Kings Mills, CASTLE DONINGTON
☎ 01332 810649 25 Annexe20

WOODHOUSE EAVES Map 08 SK51

Charnwood Forest Breakback Ln LE12 8TA
☎ 01509 890259 Fax 01509 890925
Hilly heathland course with hard walking, but no bunkers.
9 holes, 5960yds, Par 69, SSS 69, Course record 64.
Club membership 210.
Visitors must contact in advance.
Societies Wed & Thu only. Must contact in advance. Mon & Fri by special arrangement.
Green Fees £15-£25 (£25 per round weekdays & bank holidays).
Designer James Braid
Facilities
Location 0.75m NW off B591

Hotel ★★★★ 71% Quorn Country Hotel, Charnwood House, Leicester Rd, QUORN
☎ 01509 415050 20

Lingdale Joe Moore's Ln LE12 8TF ☎ 01509 890703
Parkland course located in Charnwood Forest with some hard walking at some holes. The par 3, (3rd) and par 5, (8th) are testing holes. Several holes have water hazards.
18 holes, 6545yds, Par 71, SSS 71, Course record 68.
Club membership 610.
Visitors must telephone professional in advance for weekend play.
Societies must contact in advance.
Green Fees £23 per day; £20 per round (£25 weekends).
Prof Peter Sellears
Designer David Tucker
Facilities
Location 1.5m S off B5330

Hotel ★★★★ 71% Quorn Country Hotel, Charnwood House, Leicester Rd, QUORN
☎ 01509 415050 20

LINCOLNSHIRE

BELTON Map 08 SK93

Belton Woods Hotel NG32 2LN
☎ 01476 593200 Fax 01476 574547
Two challenging 18-hole courses, a 9-hole Par 3 and a driving range. The Lakes Course has 13 lakes, while The Woodside boasts the third longest hole in Europe at 613 yards. Many leisure facilities.
The Lakes Course: 18 holes, 6808yds, Par 72, SSS 73, Course record 68.
The Woodside Course: 18 holes, 6834yds, Par 73, SSS 73.
Spitfire Course: 9 holes, 1164yds, Par 27.
Club membership 500.
Visitors available at all times, for further informatiom or reservation telephone the sales office.
Societies welcome all week, reservations to be made by telephone or letter.

Green Fees Lakes or Woodside: Apr-Oct, £40 per day; £27 per round (£50/£30 weekends). Nov-Mar, £40 per day; £25 per round. Spitfire £5 per round all year.
Cards
Prof Tony Roberts
Facilities
& Leisure hard tennis courts, heated indoor swimming pool, squash, sauna, solarium, gymnasium.
Location On A607, 2m N of Grantham

Hotel ★★★★ 73% Belton Woods Hotel, BELTON ☎ 01476 593200 136

BLANKNEY Map 08 TF06

Blankney LN4 3AZ
☎ 01526 320263 Fax 01526 322521
Open parkland course with mature trees; fairly flat.
18 holes, 6634yds, Par 72, SSS 73, Course record 69.
Club membership 640.
Visitors must contact in advance, may not play Wed mornings, restricted at weekends.
Societies not Wed mornings, booking required.
Green Fees £30 per day; £20 per round (£35/£30 weekends & bank holidays).
Prof Graham Bradley
Designer C Sinclair
Facilities
& Leisure squash, snooker.
Location 1m SW on B1188

Hotel ★★★ 65% Moor Lodge Hotel, Sleaford Rd, BRANSTON ☎ 01522 791366 24

BOSTON Map 08 TF34

Boston Cowbridge, Horncastle Rd PE22 7EL
☎ 01205 350589 Fax 01205 350589
Parkland course many water hazards in play on ten holes.
18 holes, 6490yds, Par 72, SSS 71, Course record 69.
Club membership 650.
Visitors contact in advance for tee time.
Societies apply in writing.
Green Fees £24 per day; £18 per round (£30/£24 weekends & bank holidays).
Prof Terry Squires
Facilities
Location 2m N of Boston on B1183

Hotel ★★★ 61% New England, 49 Wide Bargate, BOSTON ☎ 01205 365255 25

Kirton Holme Holme Rd, Kirton Holme PE20 1SY
☎ 01205 290669
A young parkland course designed for mid to high handicappers. It is flat but has 2500 young trees, two natural water course plus water hazards. The 2nd is a challenging, 386yard Par 4 dogleg.
9 holes, 5778yds, Par 70, SSS 68, Course record 71.
Club membership 350.
Visitors no restrictions but booking advisable for weekends & summer evenings.
Societies by prior arrangement.
Green Fees £8 per day; £4.50 per 9 holes (£9/£5.50 weekends & bank holidays).
Designer D W Welberry
Facilities
Location 4m W of Boston off A52

Hotel ★★ 67% Comfort Friendly Inn, Donnington Rd, Bicker Bar, BOSTON ☎ 01205 820118 55

BOURNE Map 08 TF02

Toft Hotel Toft PE10 0JT
☎ 01778 590614 Fax 01778 590264
Parkland course on the verge of the Lincoln Edge. Includes lake and uses contours of the hills to full effect.
18 holes, 6486yds, Par 72, SSS 71, Course record 63.
Club membership 450.
Visitors advisable to book for weekends.
Societies apply in advance by telephone.
Green Fees £16 per round (£20 weekends).
Cards
Prof Mark Jackson
Designer Roger Fitton
Facilities
Location On A6121 Bourne/Stamford road

Hotel ★★ 59% Angel Hotel, Market Place, BOURNE ☎ 01778 422346 14

CLEETHORPES Map 08 TA30

Cleethorpes Kings Rd DN35 0PN
☎ 01472 814060
Flat meadowland seaside course intersected by large dykes.
18 holes, 6349yds, Par 70, SSS 69, Course record 64.
Club membership 720.
Visitors restricted Wed afternoons, handicap certificate preferred.
Societies Tue,Thu or Fri only. Must contact in advance.
Green Fees £25 per day; £20 per round.
Prof Paul Davies
Facilities
Location 1.5m S off A1031

Hotel ★★★ 70% Kingsway Hotel, Kingsway, CLEETHORPES ☎ 01472 601122 50

Tetney Station Rd, Tetney DN36 5HY
☎ 01472 211644 & 811344 Fax 01472 211644
18-hole parkland course set at the foot of the Linclolnshire Wolds. Noted for its challenging water features.
18 holes, 6100yds, Par 71, SSS 69.
Club membership 450.
Visitors contact in advance.
Societies apply in writing.
Green Fees £10 per 18 holes; £6 per 11 holes; £4 per 7 holes.
Cards
Prof Jason Abrams
Designer J S Grant
Facilities
Location 1m off A16 Louth/Grimsby road

Hotel ★★★ 70% Kingsway Hotel, Kingsway, CLEETHORPES ☎ 01472 601122 50

ELSHAM Map 08 TA01

Elsham Barton Rd DN20 0LS ☎ 01652 680291
Parkland course in country surroundings. Easy walking.
18 holes, 6429yds, Par 71, SSS 71, Course record 67.
Club membership 650.

Visitors with member only weekends & bank holidays. Must contact in advance.
Societies must apply in writing.
Green Fees £24 per round.
Prof Stuart Brewer
Facilities
Location 2m SW on B1206

Hotel ★★★ 65% Wortley House Hotel, Rowland Rd, SCUNTHORPE ☎ 01724 842223 38

GAINSBOROUGH Map 08 SK88

Gainsborough Thonock DN21 1PZ
☎ 01427 613088 Fax 01427 810172
Thonock Park course, founded in 1894 and redesigned in 1987, is an attractive parkland course with many deciduous trees. Karsten Lakes course is a new championship course designed by Neil Coles and opened in April 1997. Set in rolling countryside the lakes and well bunkered greens provide a true test of golf. Floodlit driving range.
Thonock Park: 18 holes, 6266yds, Par 72, SSS 70, Course record 63.
Karsten Lakes: 18 holes, 6721yds, Par 72, SSS 72, Course record 66.
Club membership 600.

Visitors Thonock Park: welcome weekdays. Ladies Day Thu morning. Karsten Lakes: welcome 7 days, advance booking available.
Societies must telephone in advance.
Green Fees Thonock Park £25 per day, £18 per round. Karsten Lakes £35 per day, £25 per round.
Cards
Prof Stephen Cooper
Facilities
Location 1m N off A159. Signposted off A631

Hotel ★★★ 65% West Retford Hotel, 24 North Rd, RETFORD ☎ 01777 706333 Annexe60

GEDNEY HILL Map 08 TF31

Gedney Hill West Drove PE12 0NT
☎ 01406 330922 Fax 01406 330323
Flat parkland course similar to a links course. Made testing by Fen winds and small greens. Also a 10-bay driving range.
18 holes, 5493yds, Par 70, SSS 66, Course record 67.
Club membership 300.

Visitors no restrictions.
Societies telephone in advance.
Green Fees £6.25 (£10.50 weekends).
Cards
Prof David Hutton
Designer Monkwise Ltd
Facilities
Location 5m SE of Spalding

Hotel ★★ 63% Rose & Crown Hotel, Market Place, WISBECH ☎ 01945 589800 20

GRANTHAM Map 08 SK93

Belton Park Belton Ln, Londonthorpe Rd NG31 9SH
☎ 01476 567399 Fax 01476 592078
Three 9-hole courses set in classic mature parkland of Lord Brownlow's country seat, Belton House. Gently undulating with streams, ponds, plenty of trees and beautiful scenery, including a deer park. Famous holes: 5th, 12th, 16th and 18th. Combine any of the three courses for a testing 18-hole round.
Brownlow: 18 holes, 6420yds, Par 71, SSS 71, Course record 65.
Ancaster: 18 holes, 6252yds, Par 70, SSS 70.
Belmont: 18 holes, 6016yds, Par 69, SSS 69.
Club membership 850.

Visitors contact for tee booking.
Societies apply in advance.
Green Fees £27.50 per day; £22 per round (£33/£29 weekends & bank holidays, £20/£15 Mondays).
Prof Brian McKee
Designer Williams/Allis
Facilities
Location 1.5m NE of Grantham

Hotel ★★★ 68% Kings Hotel, North Pde, GRANTHAM ☎ 01476 590800 21

Sudbrook Moor Charity St, Carlton Scroop NG32 3AT
☎ 01400 250796 Fax 01400 250796
A testing 9-hole parkland/meadowland course in a picturesque valley setting with easy walking.
9 holes, 4811yds, Par 66, SSS 64, Course record 69.

Visitors telephone in advance.
Green Fees £5 per day (£7 weekends & bank holidays).
Cards
Prof Tim Hutton
Designer Tim Hutton
Facilities
Location 6m NE of Grantham on A607

Hotel ★★★ 68% Kings Hotel, North Pde, GRANTHAM ☎ 01476 590800 21

GRIMSBY Map 08 TA21

Grimsby Littlecoates Rd DN34 4LU
☎ 01472 342630 Fax 01472 342630
Undulating parkland course.
18 holes, 6098yds, Par 70, SSS 69, Course record 66.
Club membership 730.

Visitors contact in advance.
Societies by prior arrangement with secretary.
Green Fees £25 per day; £20 per round (£25 per round weekends).
Prof Richard Smith
Designer Colt
Facilities
Location 1m from A180 & 1m from A46

Hotel B Forte Posthouse Grimsby, Littlecoates Rd, GRIMSBY ☎ 01472 350295 52

HORNCASTLE Map 08 TF26

Horncastle West Ashby LN9 5PP ☎ 01507 526800
Heathland course with many water hazards and bunkers; very challenging. There is a 25-bay floodlit driving range.
18 holes, 5717yds, Par 70, SSS 70, Course record 71.
Club membership 200.

Visitors dress code must be adhered to, welcome anytime, may contact in advance.
Societies apply in writing or telephone in advance.
Green Fees £15 per day; £10 per round.
Cards
Prof E C Wright
Designer E C Wright
Facilities
& Leisure fishing, large ballroom.
Location Off A158 Lincoln/Skegness road at Edlington, off A153 at West Ashby

Hotel ★★ 67% Admiral Rodney Hotel, North St, HORNCASTLE ☎ 01507 523131 31

IMMINGHAM Map 08 TA11

Immingham St Andrews Ln, off Church Ln DN40 2EU
☎ 01469 575298 Fax 01469 577636
An excellent, flat parkland course noted for its numerous dykes which come into play on most holes.
18 holes, 6215yds, Par 71, SSS 70, Course record 69.
Club membership 700.

Visitors telephone in advance.
Societies telephone (am) to arrange date.
Green Fees £22 per day; £15 per round (£22 per round weekends & bank holidays).
Cards
Prof Nick Harding
Designer Hawtree & Son
Facilities
Location 7m NW off Grimsby

Hotel ★★ 64% Old Chapel Hotel & Restaurant, 50 Station Rd, Habrough, IMMINGHAM
☎ 01469 572377 14

LACEBY Map 08 TA20

Manor Barton St, Laceby Manor DN37 7EA
☎ 01472 873468 Fax 01472 276706
Upgraded to 18 holes in the summer of 1995. The first nine holes as a parkland course, all the fairways lined with young trees. The newly created second nine are mainly open fairways. The 18th hole green is surrounded by water.
18 holes, 6354yds, Par 71, SSS 70.
Club membership 500.

Visitors welcome but requested to book tee times.
Societies telephone in advance.
Green Fees £20 per day; £15 per 18 holes.
Cards
Facilities
& Leisure fishing, solarium.
Location A18 Barton St - Laceby/Louth

Hotel ★★★ 57% St James, St James's Square, GRIMSBY ☎ 01472 359771 125

LINCOLN Map 08 SK97

Canwick Park Canwick Park, Washingborough Rd
LN4 1EF ☎ 01522 522166 & 542912
Parkland course with views of Lincoln Cathedral. Testing 5th hole (200 yd par 3).
18 holes, 6160yds, Par 70, SSS 69, Course record 65.
Club membership 650.

Visitors with member only Sat also Sun before 3pm.
Societies weekdays only by prior arrangement in writing.
Green Fees £19 per day; £15 per round (£25/£19 weekends).
Prof S Williamson
Designer Hawtree & Sons
Facilities
Location 1m E of Lincoln

Hotel B Forte Posthouse Lincoln, Eastgate, LINCOLN
☎ 01522 520341 70

Carholme Carholme Rd LN1 1SE
☎ 01522 523725 Fax 01522 533733
Parkland course where prevailing west winds can add interest. Good views. 1st hole out of bounds left and right of fairway, pond in front of bunkered green at 5th, lateral water hazards across several fairways. ▶

18 holes, 6243yds, Par 71, SSS 70, Course record 69.
Club membership 625.

Visitors must contact in advance. Weekends may not play before 2.30pm.
Societies apply in writing.
Green Fees £18 per day; £14 per round (£17 per round weekends).
Prof Gary Leslie
Facilities
Location 1m W of city centre on A57

Hotel ★★★★ 62% The White Hart, Bailgate, LINCOLN ☎ 01522 526222 48

LOUTH Map 08 TF38

Louth Crowtree Ln LN11 9LJ
☎ 01507 603681 Fax 01507 603681
Undulating parkland course, fine views in an area of outstanding natural beauty.
18 holes, 6424yds, Par 72, SSS 71, Course record 64.
Club membership 700.

Visitors must contact in advance to make sure tee is not reserved for competition.
Societies a booking form will be sent on request.
Green Fees £22 day; £16 per round (£30/£25 weekends & bank holidays).
Prof A Blundell
Facilities
& Leisure squash.
Location W side of Louth between A157/A153

Hotel ★★★ 68% Beaumont Hotel, 66 Victoria Rd, LOUTH ☎ 01507 605005 16

MARKET RASEN Map 08 TF18

Market Rasen & District Legsby Rd LN8 3DZ
☎ 01673 842319
Picturesque, well-wooded heathland course, easy walking, breezy with becks forming natural hazards. Good views of Lincolnshire Wolds.
18 holes, 6045yds, Par 70, SSS 69, Course record 66.
Club membership 600.

Visitors must play with member at weekends and must contact in advance.
Societies Tue & Fri only; must contact in advance.
Green Fees £25 per day; £18 per round.
Prof A M Chester
Facilities
Location 1m E, off A46

Hotel ★★★ 68% Beaumont Hotel, 66 Victoria Rd, LOUTH ☎ 01507 605005 16

Market Rasen Race Course (Golf Course) Legsby Rd LN8 3EA ☎ 01673 843434 Fax 01673 844532
This is a public course set within the bounds of Market Rasen race course - the entire racing area is out of bounds. The longest hole is the 4th at 454yards with the race course providing a hazard over the whole length of the drive.
9 holes, 2532yds, Par 32.

Visitors closed racedays apart from evening meetings when open until noon.
Societies telephone in advance to arrange.
Green Fees £6 per 18 holes; £4 per 9 holes (£8/£5 weekends & bank holidays).
Designer Edward Stenton
Facilities
Location 2m E of Market Rasen

Hotel ★★★ 68% Beaumont Hotel, 66 Victoria Rd, LOUTH ☎ 01507 605005 16

NORMANBY Map 08 SE81

Normanby Hall Normanby Park DN15 9HU
☎ 01724 720226
Parkland course.
18 holes, 6561yds, Par 72, SSS 71, Course record 68.
Club membership 770.

Visitors book in advance by contacting professional.
Societies must contact in advance: Rachael Lennox, 01724 297860.
Green Fees £18 per day; £11.50 per round (£13 per round weekends & bank holidays).
Prof Christopher Mann
Designer Hawtree & Son
Facilities by prior arrangement
Location 3m N of Scunthorpe adj to Normanby Hall on B1130

Hotel ★★★ 64% Royal Hotel, Doncaster Rd, SCUNTHORPE ☎ 01724 282233 33

SCUNTHORPE Map 08 SE81

Ashby Decoy Burringham Rd DN17 2AB
☎ 01724 866561 Fax 01724 271708
Pleasant, flat parkland course to satisfy all tastes, yet test the experienced golfer.
18 holes, 6281yds, Par 71, SSS 71, Course record 66.
Club membership 650.

Visitors may not play Sun, Tue or bank holidays. Sat with member only.
Societies apply in advance.
Green Fees £18 per 18 holes; £24 per 36 holes.
Prof A Miller
Facilities
Location 2.5m SW on B1450 near Asda Superstore

Hotel ★★★ 64% Royal Hotel, Doncaster Rd, SCUNTHORPE ☎ 01724 282233 33

Forest Pines - Briggate Lodge Inn Hotel Ermine St, Broughton DN20 0AQ
☎ 01652 650770 & 650756 Fax 01652 650495
Set in 185 acres of mature parkland and open heathland and constructed in a similar design to that of Wentworth or Sunningdale, Forest Pines offers three challenging 9-hole courses - Forest, Pines and Beeches. Any combination can be played. Facilities include a 17-bay driving range and a spacious clubhouse. Has been voted best new golf club in England by Golf World magazine.
Forest Course: 9 holes, 3291yds, Par 36, SSS 36.
Pines Course: 9 holes, 3591yds, Par 37, SSS 37.
Beeches: 9 holes, 3102yds, Par 35, SSS 35.
Club membership 330.

Visitors must contact in advance.
Societies telephone in advance.
Green Fees £35 per day; £30 per round (£30 per round weekends & bank holidays).
Cards

Prof David Edwards
Designer John Morgan
Facilities
& Leisure cycle hire, jogging track.
Location 200yds from junct 4 M180

Hotel ★★★ 70% Briggate Lodge Inn, Ermine St, Broughton, SCUNTHORPE ☎ 01652 650770 86

Holme Hall Holme Ln, Bottesford DN16 3RF
☎ 01724 862078 Fax 01724 862078
Heathland course with sandy subsoil. Easy walking.
18 holes, 6404yds, Par 71, SSS 71, Course record 65.
Club membership 724.
Visitors must play with member at weekends & bank holidays. Must contact in advance.
Societies must contact in advance.
Green Fees £22 per day; £20 per round.
Prof Richard McKiernan
Facilities
Location 3m SE

Hotel ★★★ 64% Royal Hotel, Doncaster Rd, SCUNTHORPE ☎ 01724 282233 33

Kingsway Kingsway DN15 7ER ☎ 01724 840945
Parkland course with many par 3's.
9 holes, 1915yds, Par 29, Course record 28.
Visitors no restrictions.
Green Fees not confirmed.
Prof Chris Mann
Facilities
Location W side of town centre off A18

Hotel ★★★ 64% Royal Hotel, Doncaster Rd, SCUNTHORPE ☎ 01724 282233 33

SKEGNESS Map 09 TF56

North Shore Hotel & Golf Club North Shore Rd PE25 1DN
☎ 01754 763298 Fax 01754 761902
A half-links, half-parkland course designed by James Braid in 1910. Easy walking and good sea views.
18 holes, 6200yds, Par 71, SSS 71, Course record 67.
Club membership 450.
Visitors tee times must be booked if possible.
Societies write or telephone in advance.
Green Fees £29 per day; £19 per round (£39/£29 weekdays).
Cards
Prof J Cornelius
Designer James Braid
Facilities
Location 1m N of town centre off A52

Hotel ★★ 63% North Shore Hotel, North Shore Rd, SKEGNESS ☎ 01754 763298 30 Annexe3

Seacroft Drummond Rd, Seacroft PE25 3AU
☎ 01754 763020 Fax 01754 763020
A typical seaside links with flattish fairways separated by low ridges and good greens. Easy to walk round. To the east are sandhills leading to the shore. Southward lies 'Gibraltar Point Nature Reserve'.
18 holes, 6479yds, Par 71, SSS 71, Course record 67.
Club membership 590.
Visitors must be a member of an affiliated golf club.
Societies contact in advance.
Green Fees not confirmed.
Prof Robin Lawie
Designer Tom Dunn
Facilities
Location S side of town centre

Hotel ★★★ 62% Crown Hotel, Drummond Rd, Seacroft, SKEGNESS ☎ 01754 610760 28

SLEAFORD Map 08 TF04

Sleaford Willoughby Rd, South Rauceby NG34 8PL
☎ 01529 488273 Fax 01529 488326
Inland links-type course, moderately wooded and fairly flat.
18 holes, 6443yds, Par 72, SSS 71, Course record 64.
Club membership 650.
Visitors may not play Sun in winter.
Societies telephone enquiry to fixture secretary or professional.
Green Fees £18 per day; £14 per round (£28 weekends & bank holidays).
Prof James Wilson

Designer T Williamson
Facilities
Location 2m W of Sleaford, off A153

Hotel ★★★ 60% Angel & Royal Hotel, High St, GRANTHAM ☎ 01476 565816 29

SOUTH KYME Map 08 TF14

South Kyme Skinners Ln LN4 4AT
☎ 01526 861113 Fax 01526 861113
A challenging fenland course described as an 'Inland links'. More water hazards, trees and fairway hazards added during 1995 so the course is improving all the time.
18 holes, 6597yds, Par 71, SSS 71, Course record 67 or 6 holes, 895yds.
Club membership 300.
Visitors must telephone in advance for tee times.
Societies telephone for booking form.
Green Fees £10 per round (£12 weekends).
Prof Peter Chamberlain
Designer G Bradley
Facilities
Location Off B1395 in South Kyme village

Hotel B Travelodge, Holdingham, SLEAFORD ☎ 01529 414752 40

SPALDING Map 08 TF22

Spalding Surfleet PE11 4EA
☎ 01775 680988 (office) & 680474 (pro)
Fax 01775 680988
A pretty, well laid-out course in a fenland area. The River Glen runs beside the 1st, 2nd and 4th holes, and ponds and lakes are very much in play on the 9th, 10th and 11th holes. Challenging holes include the river dominated 2nd and the 10th which involves a tight drive and dog-leg left to reach a raised three-tier green.
18 holes, 6478yds, Par 72, SSS 71, Course record 62.
Club membership 750.
Visitors must contact in advance. Handicap certificate required.
Societies write to the secretary, Societies on Thu all day and Tue pm.
Green Fees £25 per day (£30 weekends & bank holidays, £20 after 2pm Sun).
Prof John Spencer
Designer Price/ Spencer/Ward
Facilities
Location 4m N of Spalding adjacent to A16

Hotel ★★ 64% Cley Hall Hotel, 22 High St, SPALDING ☎ 01775 725157 4 Annexe8

STAMFORD Map 08 TF00

Burghley Park St Martins PE9 3JX
☎ 01780 762100 & 753789 Fax 01780 753789
Open parkland course with superb greens, many new trees, ponds and bunkers. Situated in the grounds of Burghley House.
18 holes, 6236yds, Par 70, SSS 70, Course record 64.
Club membership 805.
Visitors with member only weekends. Must contact in advance & have handicap certificate.
Societies prior arrangement in writing, preferably by 1st Dec previous year.
Green Fees £21 per day weekdays only; Twilight round £13.50.
Prof Glenn Davies
Designer Rev J Davy (1938)
Facilities by prior arrangement
Location 1m S of town on B1081

Hotel ★★★ 75% George of Stamford Hotel, St Martins, STAMFORD ☎ 01780 755171 47

STOKE ROCHFORD Map 08 SK92

Stoke Rochford NG33 5EW ☎ 01476 530275
Parkland course designed by C. Turner and extended in 1936 to 18 holes by Major Hotchkin.
18 holes, 6252yds, Par 70, SSS 70, Course record 65.
Club membership 525.
Visitors must contact in advance, restricted to 9am weekdays, 10.30am weekends & bank holidays.
Societies contact one year in advance, in writing.
Green Fees £27 per day; £20 per round (£40/£28 weekends & bank holidays).
Prof Angus Dow
Designer Major Hotchkin
Facilities
Location Off A1 5m S of Grantham

Hotel ★★★ 68% Kings Hotel, North Pde, GRANTHAM ☎ 01476 590800 21

SUTTON BRIDGE Map 09 TF42

Sutton Bridge New Rd PE12 9RQ
☎ 01406 350323
Parkland course built around Victorian dock basin, near river Nene.
9 holes, 5724yds, Par 70, SSS 68.
Club membership 350.
Visitors may not play competition days, weekends & bank holidays, must contact in advance. Must have handicap certificate.
Societies write or telephone in advance.
Green Fees £17 per day/round.
Prof D Hawkins
Facilities
Location E side of village off A17

Hotel ★★★ 66% The Duke's Head, Tuesday Market Place, KING'S LYNN ☎ 01553 774996 71

SUTTON ON SEA Map 09 TF58

Sandilands Roman Bank LN12 2RJ ☎ 01507 441432
Flat links course on the sea shore.
18 holes, 5995yds, Par 70, SSS 69.
Club membership 230.
Visitors no restrictions.
Societies telephone in advance.
Green Fees £18 per day; £12 per round (£18 per round weekends & bank holidays).
Cards

WOODHALL SPA

WOODHALL SPA ***Lincs*** **☎ 01526 352511**
Fax 01526 352778 **Map 08 TF16**

John Ingham writes: Opened in 1905 and regarded as the finest inland course in the British Isles, it has been purchased for £8 million by the English Golf Union to use as a headquarters. Many miles from the nearest towns, the heathland course is covered with silver birch and the fairways are made up of dry, springy turf and several big competitions have been played here.

In the 1960s I played in the Central England Mixed Foursomes and enjoyed the hospitality of the then owner, Neil Hotchkin, who had somehow helped create a wonderful clubhouse atmosphere, with country people behind the bar, giving the place a friendly glow. It remains the same today.

Although 18 miles south-east of Lincoln, I now understand it is wise to telephone to see whether the course can receive visitors for the day. If the answer is 'yes' then be prepared for a treat. Tony Jacklin brought his friend Tom Weiskopf to play and the American was thrilled with the shot-making that is required.

Designed by the Col. S.V. Hotchkin, the course is a pleasant and fairly flat walk but because of the clever shaping of the holes, and the delightful isolation of almost each hole, hidden like a corridor through a stately home, the course becomes a most private place for a friendly four-ball. Measuring 6942 yards, it doesn't appear that long because of the fast-running fairways. The club don't like men visitors to have a handicap above 20 or the women above 30 and since the course is renowned for its huge bunkers, it is to the advantage of players to know how to escape from sand traps. In many ways, Woodhall Spa is like Sunningdale and as those who know that course would readily admit, there is no greater compliment.

Visitors must be a member of a golf club affiliated to the appropriate Golf Union. Handicap certificate must be produced
Societies apply by telephone
Green fees £65 per day, £40 per round.
Facilities Professional (C C Elliot)
Location The Broadway LN10 6PU (NE side of village B1191)

18 holes, 6921yards, Par 73 SSS 73
Course record 68

WHERE TO STAY NEARBY

HOTELS:

WOODHALL SPA

★★★ 66% Petwood House Hotel, Stixwould Rd ☎ 01526 352411. 47

★★★ 64% Golf Hotel, The Broadway ☎ 01526 353535. 50 (14 36)

Facilities ⊗)|||(🍴 ☕ 🍷 ⛺ 🏠 🎯 🛏 🏌
& Leisure grass tennis courts.
Location 1.5m S off A52

Hotel ★★★ 68% Grange & Links Hotel, Sea Ln, Sandilands, MABLETHORPE ☎ 01507 441334 23 ⇨ ↱

TORKSEY Map 08 SK87

Lincoln LN1 2EG ☎ 01427 718721 Fax 01427 718721
A mature testing inland course with automated underground fairway irrigation to maintain first class condition.
18 holes, 6438yds, Par 71, SSS 71, Course record 67.
Club membership 650.
Visitors welcome on non event days.
Societies apply in writing or telephone.
Green Fees £28 per day; £22 per round.
Prof Ashley Carter
Facilities ⊗)|||(🍴 ☕ 🍷 ⛺ 🏠 🏌
Location NE side of village, off A156 midway between Lincoln & Gainsborough

Hotel ★★★★ 62% The White Hart, Bailgate, LINCOLN ☎ 01522 526222 48 ⇨

Millfield Sandfield Farm, Laughterton LN1 2LB
☎ 01427 718255
There is an unusual set-up at Millfield with a 15 hole 4,201 yard Family course on which anyone can play, as well as a 9-hole Par 3 and an 18-hole course of nearly 6,000 yards. Due to its location in flat Lincolnshire the courses are affected by winds, which change every day.
18 holes, 5974yds, Par 72, SSS 69.
Family 15: 18 holes, 4201yds, Par 56.
Visitors 18 hole; shoes must be worn, no jeans etc. Family 18 hole no restrictions.
Green Fees not confirmed.
Facilities ⊗)|||(🍴 ☕ 🍷 🏠 🛏 🏌
Location On A1133 1m N of A57

Hotel ★★★★ 62% The White Hart, Bailgate, LINCOLN ☎ 01522 526222 48 ⇨

WOODHALL SPA See page 179

WOODTHORPE Map 09 TF48

Woodthorpe Hall LN13 0DD ☎ 01507 463664
Parkland course.
18 holes, 5010yds, Par 66, SSS 65.
Club membership 400.
Visitors contact in advance for weekends.
Societies Mon-Fri, telephone in first instance at least one month prior to visit.
Green Fees not confirmed.
Facilities ⊗)|||(🍴 ☕ 🍷 🏠 🎯 🛏 🏌
& Leisure fishing.
Location 3m NNW of Alford on B1373

Hotel ★★★ 68% Grange & Links Hotel, Sea Ln, Sandilands, MABLETHORPE ☎ 01507 441334 23 ⇨ ↱

LONDON

Courses within the London Postal District area (ie those that have London Postcodes - W1, SW1 etc) are listed here in postal district order commencing East then North, South and West. Courses outside the London Postal area, but within Greater London are to be found listed under the county of **Greater London** in the gazetteer (see page 103).

E4 CHINGFORD

Royal Epping Forest Forest Approach, Chingford E4 7AZ
☎ 0181 529 2195
Woodland course. 'Red' garments must be worn.
18 holes, 6342yds, Par 71, SSS 70.
Club membership 400.
Visitors booking system in operation.
Societies must contact secretary in advance.
Green Fees £10.10 (£13.80 weekends).
Prof R Gowers/J Francis
Facilities ☕ 🏠 🎯 🏌
Location 300 yds S of Chingford station

Hotel ★★★ 66% County Hotel Epping Forest, Oak Hill, WOODFORD GREEN ☎ 0181 787 9988 99 ⇨ ↱

West Essex Bury Rd, Sewardstonebury, Chingford E4 7QL
☎ 0181 529 7558 Fax 0181 524 7870
Testing parkland course within Epping Forest. Notable holes are 8th (par 4), 16th (par 4), 18th (par 5).
18 holes, 6289yds, Par 71, SSS 70.
Club membership 645.
Visitors must have handicap certificate but may not play on Tue morning, Thu afternoon & weekends.
Societies must contact in advance.
Green Fees £30 per day; £25 per round.
Prof Robert Joyce
Designer James Braid
Facilities ⊗)|||(🍴 ☕ 🍷 ⛺ 🏠 🚜 🏌 ⛳
Location 1.5m N of Chingford station. Access via M25 junct 26

Hotel ★★ 62% Roebuck Hotel, North End, BUCKHURST HILL ☎ 0181 505 4636 29 ⇨ ↱

E11 LEYTONSTONE & WANSTEAD

Wanstead Overton Dr, Wanstead E11 2LW
☎ 0181 989 3938 Fax 0181 532 9138
A flat, picturesque parkland course with many trees and shrubs and providing easy walking. The par 3, 16th, involves driving across a lake.
18 holes, 6004yds, Par 69, SSS 69, Course record 62.
Club membership 600.
Visitors must contact in advance and may only play Mon, Tue & Fri.
Societies by prior arrangement.
Green Fees £25 per day.
Prof David Hawkins
Designer James Braid
Facilities ⊗)|||(🍴 ☕ 🍷 ⛺ 🏠 🎯 🏌
& Leisure fishing.
Location From central London A12 NE to Wanstead

Hotel ★★★ 66% County Hotel Epping Forest, Oak Hill, WOODFORD GREEN
☎ 0181 787 9988 99

N2 East Finchley

Hampstead Winnington Rd N2 0TU
☎ 0181 455 0203 Fax 0181 731 6194
Undulating parkland course.
18 holes, 5822yds, Par 68, SSS 68, Course record 65.
Club membership 526.
Visitors restricted Tue and weekends. Contact Professional in advance on 0181 455 7089.
Societies small societies by prior arrangement.
Green Fees £30 per round (£35 weekends).
Prof Peter Brown
Designer Tom Dunn
Facilities
Location Off Hampstead Lane

Hotel B Forte Posthouse Hampstead, 215 Haverstock Hill, LONDON ☎ 0171 794 8121 140

N6 Highgate

Highgate Denewood Rd N6 4AH
☎ 0181 340 1906 Fax 0181 348 9152
Parkland course.
18 holes, 5985yds, Par 69, SSS 69, Course record 66.
Club membership 800.
Visitors may not play Wed & weekends.
Societies by arrangement.
Green Fees not confirmed.
Prof Robin Turner
Facilities
Hotel ★★★★ 68% Regents Park Marriott, 128 King Henry's Rd, LONDON
☎ 0171 722 7711 303

N9 Lower Edmonton

Lee Valley Leisure Picketts Lock Sports Centre, Meridian Way, Edmonton N9 0AS ☎ 0181 803 3611
Tricky municipal parkland course with some narrow fairways and the River Lea providing a natural hazard.
18 holes, 4902yds, Par 66, SSS 64, Course record 66.
Club membership 200.
Visitors may telephone for advance bookings.
Societies must telephone in advance.
Green Fees not confirmed.
Prof R Gerken
Facilities
& Leisure heated indoor swimming pool, squash, sauna, solarium, gymnasium.
Hotel ★★ 70% Oak Lodge Hotel, 80 Village Rd, Bush Hill Park, ENFIELD
☎ 0181 360 7082 5

N14 Southgate

Trent Park Bramley Rd, Oakwood N14 4UW
☎ 0181 366 7432
Parkland course set in 150 acres of green belt area. Seven holes played across Merryhills brook. Testing holes are 2nd (423 yds) over brook, 190 yds from the tee, and up to plateau green; 7th (463 yds) dog-leg, over brook, par 4.
18 holes, 6085yds, Par 70, SSS 69, Course record 68.
Club membership 1200.
Visitors must contact 7 days in advance.
Societies must telephone in advance.
Green Fees not confirmed.
Prof Mike Plumbridge
Designer D McGibbon
Facilities
Location Opposite Oakwood underground station

Hotel ★★★★ 69% West Lodge Park Hotel, Cockfosters Rd, HADLEY WOOD
☎ 0181 440 8311 44 Annexe2

N20 Whetstone

North Middlesex The Manor House, Friern Barnet Ln, Whetstone N20 0NL ☎ 0181 445 1604 & 0181 445 3060
Short parkland course renowned for its tricky greens.
18 holes, 5625yds, Par 69, SSS 67, Course record 64.
Club membership 580.
Visitors advisable to contact in advance, contact professional shop.
Societies bookings in advance, winter offers & summer packages by prior arrangement.
Green Fees not confirmed.
Prof Steve Roberts
Designer Willie Park Jnr
Facilities
Hotel ★★★ 73% Edgwarebury Hotel, Barnet Ln, ELSTREE ☎ 0181 953 8227 47

South Herts Links Dr, Totteridge N20 8QU
☎ 0181 445 2035 Fax 0181 445 7569
An open undulating parkland course officially in Hertfordshire, but now in a London postal area. It is, perhaps, most famous for the fact that two of the greatest of all British professionals, Harry Vardon and Dai Rees, CBE were professionals at the club. The course is testing, over rolling fairways, especially in the prevailing south-west wind.
18 holes, 6432yds, Par 72, SSS 71, Course record 65.
Club membership 850.
Visitors must be members of recognised golf club & have handicap certificate of 24 or less. May not play at weekends.
Societies Wed-Fri only, must apply in writing.
Green Fees £35 per day; £25 per round.
Prof Bobby Mitchell
Designer Harry Vardon
Facilities
Location 2m E of A1 at Apex Corner

Hotel B Forte Posthouse South Mimms, SOUTH MIMMS ☎ 01707 643311 120

N21 Winchmore Hill

Bush Hill Park Bush Hill, Winchmore Hill N21 2BU
☎ 0181 360 5738 Fax 0181 360 5583
Pleasant parkland course surrounded by trees. Contains a large number of both fairway sandtraps and green side bunkers. Undulating, but not too harsh.
18 holes, 5809yds, Par 70, SSS 68.
Club membership 700.
▶

Visitors may not play Wed mornings or weekends & bank holidays.
Societies by arrangement.
Green Fees not confirmed.
Prof Adrian Andrews
Facilities
Hotel ★★ 70% Oak Lodge Hotel, 80 Village Rd, Bush Hill Park, ENFIELD ☎ 0181 360 7082 5

N22 Wood green

Muswell Hill Rhodes Av, Wood Green N22 4UT
☎ 0181 888 1764 Fax 0181 889 9380
Narrow parkland course featuring numerous water hazards.
18 holes, 6438yds, Par 71, SSS 71, Course record 65.
Club membership 560.
Visitors must contact in advance, restricted weekends.
Societies apply in writing or telephone.
Green Fees not confirmed.
Prof David Wilton
Facilities
Location Off N Circular Rd at Bounds Green

Hotel ★★★ 67% Raglan Hall Hotel, 8-12 Queens Ave, Muswell Hill, LONDON ☎ 0181 883 9836 46

Nw4 Hendon Map 04 TQ28

The Metro Golf Centre Barnet Copthall Sports Centre, Gt North Way NW4 1PF 0181 202 1202 Fax 0181 203 1203
Located just seven miles from London's West End, the Metro Golf Centre represents a new generation of golf facility dedicated to the development of all standards of golfer. Facilities include a 48 bay two-tiered driving range, a testing 9-hole par 3 course with water hazards, pot bunkers and postage stamp greens, a short game practice area, and a Golf Academy offering unique teaching methods.
9 holes, 898yds, Par 27, SSS 27, Course record 24.
Club membership 500.
Visitors welcome any time between 8am-10pm all week for lessons, to play on the course or use driving range.
Societies telephone in advance.
Green Fees £9 per 18 holes; £5 per 9 holes.
Cards
Prof Barney Puttick
Designer Cousells
Facilities
& Leisure comprehensive teaching academy.
Location Just off A41 and A1 at junct 2 of the M1, within the Barnet Copthall Sporting Complex

Hotel ★★★ 70% Holiday Inn Garden Court, Tilling Rd, Brent Cross, LONDON ☎ 0181 455 4777 Res & 0181 201 8686 Fax 0181 455 4660 153

Nw7 Mill hill

Finchley Nether Court, Frith Ln, Mill Hill NW7 1PU
☎ 0181 346 2436 & 346 5086 Fax 0181 343 4205
Easy walking on wooded parkland course.
18 holes, 6411yds, Par 72, SSS 71.
Club membership 500.
Visitors must contact in advance.
Societies must apply in writing.
Green Fees £30 per day; £24 per round (£36/£30 weekends & bank holidays).
Cards
Prof David Brown
Designer James Braid
Facilities by prior arrangement
Location Near Mill Hill East Tube Station

Hotel ★★★ 73% Edgwarebury Hotel, Barnet Ln, ELSTREE ☎ 0181 953 8227 47

Hendon Ashley Walk, Devonshire Rd, Mill Hill NW7 1DG
☎ 0181 346 6023 Fax 0181 343 1974
Easy walking, parkland course with a good variety of trees, and providing testing golf.
18 holes, 6266yds, Par 70, SSS 70.
Club membership 540.
Visitors must contact in advance. Restricted weekends & bank holidays.
Societies Tue-Fri. Must contact in advance.
Green Fees not confirmed.
Prof Stuart Murray
Designer H S Colt
Facilities
Location 10 mins from junc 2 of M1 southbound

Hotel ★★★ 73% Edgwarebury Hotel, Barnet Ln, ELSTREE ☎ 0181 953 8227 47

Mill Hill 100 Barnet Way, Mill Hill NW7 3AL
☎ 0181 959 2339 Fax 0181 906 0731
Undulating parkland course with tree and shrub lined fairways, water features strongly on holes 2,10 and 17.
18 holes, 6247yds, Par 70, SSS 70, Course record 65.
Club membership 550.

Visitors restricted weekends & bank holidays. Must contact in advance.
Societies must contact in advance.
Green Fees on application.
Prof Gary Harvey
Designer J F Abercrombie/H S Colt
Facilities
Location On A1 S bound carriageway

Hotel ★★★ 73% Edgwarebury Hotel, Barnet Ln, ELSTREE ☎ 0181 953 8227 47

Se9 Eltham

Eltham Warren Bexley Rd, Eltham SE9 2PE
☎ 0181 850 4477 & 850 1166

Parkland course with narrow fairways and small greens. The course is bounded by the A210 on one side and Eltham Park on the other.
9 holes, 5840yds, Par 69, SSS 68, Course record 66.
Club membership 440.

Visitors may not play at weekends. Must contact in advance and have a handicap certificate.
Societies Thu only. Must book in advance. Deposit required.
Green Fees £25 per day.
Prof Gary Brett
Facilities
& Leisure snooker tables.
Location 0.5m from Eltham station on A210

Hotel ★★★ 69% Bromley Court Hotel, Bromley Hill, BROMLEY ☎ 0181 464 5011 116

Royal Blackheath Court Rd SE9 5AF
☎ 0181 850 1795 Fax 0181 859 0150
A pleasant, parkland course of great character as befits the antiquity of the Club; the clubhouse dates from the 17th century. Many great trees survive and there are two ponds. The 18th requires a pitch to the green over a thick clipped hedge, which also crosses the front of the 1st tee.
18 holes, 6219yds, Par 70, SSS 70.
Club membership 720.

Visitors must contact in advance but may play mid-week only, handicap certificate is required.
Societies must apply in writing.
Green Fees £40 per day; £30 per round.
Cards
Prof Ian McGregor
Designer James Braid
Facilities by prior arrangement
& Leisure golf museum.
Location From M25 junct 3 take A20 towards London. Turn right at 2nd traffic lights to club 500yds on right

Hotel ★★★ 69% Bromley Court Hotel, Bromley Hill, BROMLEY ☎ 0181 464 5011 116

SE18 WOOLWICH Map 05 TQ47

Shooters Hill Eaglesfield Rd, Shooters Hill SE18 3DA
☎ 0181 854 6368 Fax 0181 854 0469
Hilly and wooded parkland course with good view and natural hazards.
18 holes, 5721 yds, Par 69, SSS 68, Course record 63.
Club membership 900.

Visitors must have handicap certificate and be a member of a recognised golf club but may not play at weekends.
Societies Tue & Thu only, by arrangement.
Green Fees £27 per day; £22 per round.
Prof Michael Ridge
Designer Willie Park
Facilities
Location Shooters Hill Rd from Blackheath

Hotel B Forte Posthouse Bexley, Black Prince Interchange, Southwold Rd, BEXLEY ☎ 01322 526900 103

SE21 DULWICH

Dulwich & Sydenham Hill Grange Ln, College Rd SE21 7LH ☎ 0181 693 3961 & 693 8491
Parkland course overlooking London. Hilly with narrow fairways.
18 holes, 6008yds, Par 69, SSS 69, Course record 63.
Club membership 850.

Visitors must contact in advance and have a handicap certificate. May not play weekends or bank holidays.
Societies must telephone in advance & confirm in writing.
Green Fees not confirmed.
Prof David Baillie
Facilities
Hotel ★★★ 69% Bromley Court Hotel, Bromley Hill, BROMLEY ☎ 0181 464 5011 116

SE22 EAST DULWICH

Aquarius Marmora Rd, Honor Oak, Off Forest Hill Rd SE22 0RY ☎ 0181 693 1626
Course laid-out on two levels around and over covered reservoir; hazards include vents and bollards.
9 holes, 5246yds, Par 66, SSS 66, Course record 66.
Club membership 350.

Visitors must be accompanied by member and have a handicap certificate.
Green Fees £10 per day/round.
Prof Frederick Private
Facilities
Hotel ★★★ 69% Bromley Court Hotel, Bromley Hill, BROMLEY ☎ 0181 464 5011 116

SE28 WOOLWICH

Riverside Summerton Way, Thamesmead SE28 8PP
☎ 0181 310 7975
A delightful undulating course with a mix of mature trees, new trees and water hazards. The 4th hole is a challenging 515yards down a narrow fairway.
9 holes, 5462yds, Par 70, SSS 66.
Club membership 150.

Visitors no restrictions.
Societies book by telephone or in writing.
Green Fees not confirmed.
Prof Paul Jolner
Designer Heffernan
Facilities
Hotel ★★★ 65% Bardon Lodge Hotel, 15-17 Stratheden Rd, LONDON ☎ 0181 853 4051 31

SW15 PUTNEY

Richmond Park Roehampton Gate, Priory Ln SW15 5JR ☎ 0181 876 1795 Fax 0181 878 1354
Two public parkland courses.
Princes Course: 18 holes, 5868yds, Par 69, SSS 68, Course record 64.
Dukes Course: 18 holes, 6036yds, Par 68, SSS 67.

Visitors must contact in advance or pay and play.
Societies must contact in advance.
Green Fees £13 per round (£16 weekends & bank holidays).
Cards

Prof Stuart Hill & David Bown
Designer Fred Hawtree
Facilities
Hotel ★★★ 66% Richmond Hill, Richmond Hill, RICHMOND UPON THAMES ☎ 0181 940 2247 & 0181 940 5466 Fax 0181 940 5424 138

SW18 WANDSORTH

Central London Golf Centre Burntwood Ln, Wandsworth SW17 0AT ☎ 0181 871 2468 Fax 0181 874 7447
Attractive flat parkland course in the middle of London. The longest drive is the 430 yard 3rd to one of the course's superb greens. Well placed bunkers trap the careless shot and the course rewards the accurate player.
9 holes, 2250yds, Par 62, SSS 62.
Club membership 100.
Visitors must contact in advance.
Societies telephone or write to the secretary.
Green Fees £12 per 18 holes; £7 per 9 holes (£14/£9 weekends & bank holidays).
Cards
Prof Jeremy Robson
Designer Patrick Tallock
Facilities
& Leisure putting green, practice area.
Location Between Garatt Lane and Trinity Road

Hotel ★★★★ 76% Cannizaro House, West Side, Wimbledon Common, LONDON ☎ 0181 879 1464 46

SW19 WIMBLEDON

Royal Wimbledon 29 Camp Rd SW19 4UW
☎ 0181 946 2125 Fax 0181 944 8652
A club steeped in the history of the game, it is also of great age, dating back to 1865. Of sand and heather like so many of the Surrey courses its 12th hole (par 4) is rated as the best on the course.
18 holes, 6300yds, Par 70, SSS 70, Course record 66.
Club membership 1050.
Visitors must be guests of current club member.
Societies welcome Wed-Thu. Must apply in writing.
Green Fees £21 per round.
Prof Hugh Boyle
Designer H Colt
Facilities
Hotel ★★★★ 76% Cannizaro House, West Side, Wimbledon Common, LONDON ☎ 0181 879 1464 46

Wimbledon Common Camp Rd SW19 4UW
☎ 0181 946 0294 Fax 0181 946 7571
Quick-drying course on Wimbledon Common. Well wooded, with tight fairways, challenging short holes but no bunkers.The course is also played over by London Scottish Golf Club (0181 788 0135). All players must wear plain red upper garments.
18 holes, 5438yds, Par 68, SSS 66.
Club membership 250.
Visitors with member only at weekends.
Societies must telephone in advance.
Green Fees not confirmed.
Prof J S Jukes
Facilities
Hotel ★★★★ 76% Cannizaro House, West Side, Wimbledon Common, LONDON ☎ 0181 879 1464 46

Wimbledon Park Home Park Rd, Wimbledon SW19 7HR
☎ 0181 946 1250
Easy walking on parkland course. Sheltered lake provides hazard on 3 holes.
18 holes, 5465yds, Par 66, SSS 66.
Club membership 700.
Visitors restricted weekends & bank holidays. Must contact in advance and have handicap certificate or letter of introduction.
Societies must apply in writing.
Green Fees not confirmed.
Prof Dean Wingrove
Designer Willie Park Jnr
Facilities
Location 400 yds from Wimbledon Park Station

Hotel ★★★ 66% Richmond Hill, Richmond Hill, RICHMOND UPON THAMES ☎ 0181 940 2247 & 0181 940 5466 Fax 0181 940 5424 138

W7 HANWELL

Brent Valley 138 Church Rd, Hanwell W7 3BE
☎ 0181 567 1287
Municipal parkland course with easy walking. The River Brent winds through the course.
18 holes, 5426yds, Par 67, SSS 66.
Club membership 350.
Visitors no restrictions.
Societies one month's notice required.
Green Fees £15 per day; £9.50 (£14 weekends & bank holidays).
Cards
Prof Peter Bryant
Facilities
Hotel ★★★ 64% Master Robert Hotel, Great West Rd, HOUNSLOW ☎ 0181 570 6261 94

MERSEYSIDE

BEBINGTON Map 07 SJ38

Brackenwood Brackenwood Golf Course, Bracken Ln L63 2LY ☎ 0151 608 3093
Municipal parkland course with easy walking, a very testing but fair course in a fine rural setting, usually in very good condition..
18 holes, 6285yds, Par 70, SSS 70, Course record 66.
Club membership 320.
Visitors must book for weekends one week in advance.
Societies must apply in advance.
Green Fees £6.50 per round.
Prof Ken Lamb
Facilities
Location 0.75m N of M53 junc 4 on B5151

Hotel ★★★ 68% Thornton Hall Hotel, Neston Rd, THORNTON HOUGH ☎ 0151 336 3938 5 Annexe58

Birkenhead — Map 07 SJ38

Arrowe Park Woodchurch L49 5LW ☎ 0151 677 1527
Pleasant municipal parkland course.
18 holes, 6435yds, Par 72, SSS 71, Course record 68.
Club membership 220.
Visitors no restrictions.
Societies must telephone in advance.
Green Fees not confirmed.
Prof Clive Scanlon
Facilities
Location 1m from M53 junc 3 on A551

Hotel ★★★ 68% Bowler Hat Hotel, 2 Talbot Rd, Oxton, BIRKENHEAD ☎ 0151 652 4931 32

Prenton Golf Links Rd, Prenton L42 8LW
☎ 0151 608 1053 Fax 0151 609 1580
Parkland course with easy walking and views of the Welsh Hills.
18 holes, 6429yds, Par 71, SSS 71.
Club membership 610.
Visitors no restrictions.
Societies must telephone in advance and confirm in writing.
Green Fees £30 per day (£35 weekends & bank holidays).
Prof Robin Thompson
Designer James Braid
Facilities
Location M53 junct 3 off A552 towards Birkenhead

Hotel ★★ 66% Riverhill Hotel, Talbot Rd, Oxton, BIRKENHEAD ☎ 0151 653 3773 16

Wirral Ladies 93 Bidston Rd, Oxton L43 6TS
☎ 0151 652 1255 Fax 0151 653 4323
Heathland course with heather and birch.
18 holes, 4948yds, Par 69, SSS 69.
Club membership 430.
Visitors may not play before 11am weekends or over Christmas and Easter holidays.
Societies must telephone in advance. Weekdays only.
Green Fees £20.50 per round.
Prof Angus Law
Facilities
Location W side of town centre on B5151

Hotel ★★★ 68% Bowler Hat Hotel, 2 Talbot Rd, Oxton, BIRKENHEAD ☎ 0151 652 4931 32

Blundellsands — Map 07 SJ39

West Lancashire Hall Rd West L23 8SZ
☎ 0151 924 1076 Fax 0151 931 4448
Challenging, traditional links with sandy subsoil overlooking the Mersey Estuary. The course provides excellent golf throughout the year. The four short holes are very fine.
18 holes, 6763yds, Par 72, SSS 73, Course record 66.
Club membership 650.
Visitors may not play on competition days until 3.30pm, must have a handicap certificate.
Societies must contact in advance.
Green Fees £50 per day; £35 per round (£60 per day weekends & bank holidays).
Prof Tim Hastings
Designer C K Cotton
Facilities
Location N side of village

Hotel ★★★ 65% Blundellsands Hotel, The Serpentine, BLUNDELLSANDS ☎ 0151 924 6515 37

Bootle — Map 07 SJ39

Bootle 2 Dunnings Bridge Rd L30 2PP ☎ 0151 928 6196
Municipal seaside course, with prevailing north-westerly wind. Testing holes: 5th (200 yds) par 3; 7th (415 yds) par 4.
18 holes, 6362yds, Par 70, SSS 70, Course record 64.
Club membership 380.
Visitors must contact in advance.
Societies must apply in writing.
Green Fees not confirmed.
Prof Alan Bradshaw
Facilities
& Leisure hard tennis courts.
Location 2m NE on A5036

Hotel ★★★ 65% Blundellsands Hotel, The Serpentine, BLUNDELLSANDS ☎ 0151 924 6515 37

Bromborough — Map 07 SJ38

Bromborough Raby Hall Rd L63 0NW
☎ 0151 334 2155 Fax 0151 334 0303
Parkland course.
18 holes, 6650yds, Par 72, SSS 73, Course record 67.
Club membership 800.
Visitors are advised to contact professional on 0151 334 4499 in advance.
Societies normal society day Wed ; must apply in advance.
Green Fees £28 per day.
Prof Geoff Berry
Designer J Hassall
Facilities
Location 0.5m W of Station

Hotel B Travel Inn, High St, Bromborough Cross, BROMBOROUGH ☎ 0151 334 2917 31

Caldy — Map 07 SJ28

Caldy Links Hey Rd L48 1NB
☎ 0151 625 5660 Fax 0151 6257394
A parkland course situated on the estuary of the River Dee with many of the fairways running parallel to the river. Of Championship length, the course offers excellent golf all year, but is subject to variable winds that noticeably alter the day to day playing of each hole. There are excellent views of North Wales and Snowdonia.
18 holes, 6668yds, Par 72, SSS 73, Course record 68.
Club membership 800.
▶

Visitors may play on weekdays only.
Societies must telephone in advance.
Green Fees £40 per day, £35 per round.
Prof K Jones
Facilities by prior arrangement by prior arrangement
Location SE side of village, from Caldy rdbt on A540 follow signs to Caldy and golf club

Hotel ★★★ 68% Thornton Hall Hotel, Neston Rd, THORNTON HOUGH 0151 336 3938 5 Annexe58

EASTHAM — Map 07 SJ38

Eastham Lodge 117 Ferry Rd L62 0AP
0151 327 3003 Fax 0151 327 3003
A parkland course with many mature trees, recently upgraded to 18 holes.
18 holes, 5706yds, Par 68, SSS 68.
Club membership 800.
Visitors advisable to telephone in advance to check availability, tel 0151 327 3008 professionals shop, with member only at weekends.
Societies welcome Tue. Must apply in writing.
Green Fees not confirmed.
Prof R Boobyer
Designer Hawtree/D Hemstock
Facilities
& Leisure snooker.
Location 1.5m N

Hotel B Travel Inn, High St, Bromborough Cross, BROMBOROUGH 0151 334 2917 31

FORMBY — Map 07 SD30

Formby Golf Rd L37 1LQ
01704 872164 Fax 01704 833028
Championship seaside links through sandhills and partly through pine trees. Sheltered from the wind by high dunes it features firm, springy turf, fast seaside greens and natural sandy bunkers. Well drained it plays well throughout the year.
18 holes, 6496yds, Par 72, SSS 72, Course record 65.
Club membership 680.
Visitors must contact in advance, very limited on Sat & Wed.
Societies must contact well in advance.
Green Fees £50 per day/round.
Prof Clive Harrison
Designer Park/Colt
Facilities
Location N side of town

Hotel ★★★ 65% Blundellsands Hotel, The Serpentine, BLUNDELLSANDS 0151 924 6515 37

Formby Ladies Golf Rd L37 1YH
01704 873493 Fax 01704 873493
Seaside links - one of the few independent ladies clubs in the country. The course has contrasting hard-hitting holes in flat country and tricky holes in sandhills and woods.
18 holes, 5374yds, Par 71, SSS 71.
Club membership 423.
Visitors must contact in advance and may not play Thu or before noon Sat & Sun.
Societies must apply in advance.
Green Fees £30 per day (£35 weekends & bank holidays).
Prof Clive Harrison
Facilities by prior arrangement by prior arrangement
Location N side of town

Hotel ★★★ 65% Blundellsands Hotel, The Serpentine, BLUNDELLSANDS 0151 924 6515 37

HESWALL — Map 07 SJ28

Heswall Cottage Ln L60 8PB
0151 342 1237 Fax 0151 342 1237
A pleasant parkland course in soft undulating country over-looking the estuary of the River Dee. There are excellent views of the Welsh hills and coastline, and a good test of golf. The clubhouse is modern and well-appointed with good facilities.
18 holes, 6492yds, Par 72, SSS 72, Course record 62.
Club membership 940.
Visitors must contact in advance.
Societies must apply in advance.
Green Fees £35 per day/round (£40 weekends).
Prof Alan Thompson
Facilities
Location 1m S off A540

Hotel ★★★ 68% Thornton Hall Hotel, Neston Rd, THORNTON HOUGH 0151 336 3938 5 Annexe58

HOYLAKE — Map 07 SJ28

Hoylake Carr Ln, Municipal Links L47 4BG
0151 632 2956
Flat, generally windy semi-links course. Tricky fairways.
18 holes, 6313yds, Par 70, SSS 70, Course record 67.
Club membership 303.
Societies must telephone 0151 632 4883 club steward or 0151 632 2956 club professional.
Green Fees not confirmed.
Prof Simon Hooton
Facilities (ex Fri)
Location SW side of town off A540

Hotel ★★★ 66% Leasowe Castle Hotel, Leasowe Rd, MORETON 0151 606 9191 47

Royal Liverpool Meols Dr L47 4AL
0151 632 3101 & 632 3102 Fax 0151 632 6737
A world famous, windswept seaside links course, venue for ten Open Championships and 17 Amateur Championships.
18 holes, 6199yds, Par 72, SSS 71.
Club membership 650.
Visitors must contact in advance & have a handicap certificate. Restricted before 9.30am & between 1-2pm. No play Thu am (ladies day). Limited play weekends (pm only).
Societies must contact in advance.

Green Fees £80 per day; £55/£75 per round (£70/£100 weekends).
Cards
Prof John Heggarty
Designer R Chambers/G Morris
Facilities
Location SW side of town on A540

Hotel ★★★ 66% Leasowe Castle Hotel, Leasowe Rd, MORETON
☎ 0151 606 9191 47

Huyton Map 07 SJ49

Bowring Bowring Park, Roby Rd L36 4HD
☎ 0151 489 1901
Flat parkland course.
18 holes, 5651yds, Par 70.
Club membership 200.
Visitors no restrictions.
Green Fees not confirmed.
Facilities
Location On A5080 adjacent M62 junc 5

Hotel ★ 61% Rockland Hotel, View Rd, RAINHILL
☎ 0151 426 4603 11rm(9 1)

Huyton & Prescot Hurst Park, Huyton Ln L36 1UA
☎ 0151 489 3948 Fax 0151 489 0797
An easy walking, parkland course providing excellent golf.
18 holes, 5839yds, Par 68, SSS 68, Course record 66.
Club membership 700.
Visitors must contact in advance. Must play with member at weekends.
Societies must apply in writing.
Green Fees £22.50 per round.
Facilities
Location 1.5m NE off B5199

Hotel ★ 61% Rockland Hotel, View Rd, RAINHILL
☎ 0151 426 4603 11rm(9 1)

Liverpool Map 07 SJ39

Allerton Park Allerton Manor Golf Estate, Allerton Rd L18 3JT ☎ 0151 428 1046
Parkland course.
18 holes, 5459yds, Par 67, SSS 67.
Club membership 300.
Visitors must book with professional in advance.
Green Fees not confirmed.
Prof Barry Large
Facilities
Location 5.5m SE of city centre off A562 and B5180

Hotel ★★★★ 59% Atlantic Tower Thistle, Chapel St, LIVERPOOL ☎ 0151 227 4444 226

The Childwall Naylors Rd, Gateacre L27 2YB
☎ 0151 487 0654 Fax 0151 487 0882
Parkland golf is played here over a testing course, where accuracy from the tee is well-rewarded. The course is very popular with visiting societies for the clubhouse has many amenities. Course designed by James Braid.
18 holes, 6425yds, Par 72, SSS 71, Course record 66.
Club membership 650.
Visitors must contact in advance.
Societies must apply in writing.
Green Fees £26 per day (£35 weekends).
Prof Nigel M Parr
Designer James Braid
Facilities
Location 7m E of city centre off B5178

Hotel ★ 61% Rockland Hotel, View Rd, RAINHILL
☎ 0151 426 4603 11rm(9 1)

Kirkby-Liverpool Municipal Ingoe Ln, Kirkby L32 4SS
☎ 0151 546 5435
Flat, easy course.
18 holes, 6704yds, Par 72, SSS 72, Course record 68.
Club membership 150.
Societies must contact 1 week in advance.
Green Fees not confirmed.
Prof Dave Weston
Facilities
Location 7.5m NE of city centre on A506

Hotel ★★★★ 57% Liverpool Moat House Hotel, Paradise St, LIVERPOOL
☎ 0151 471 9988 251

Lee Park Childwall Valley Rd L27 3YA ☎ 0151 487 3882
Flat course with ponds in places.
18 holes, 5508mtrs, Par 71, SSS 69.
Club membership 600.
Visitors must dress acceptably.
Societies must contact in advance.
Green Fees not confirmed.
Facilities
Location 7m E of city centre off B5178

Hotel ★★★★ 57% Liverpool Moat House Hotel, Paradise St, LIVERPOOL
☎ 0151 471 9988 251

West Derby Yew Tree Ln, West Derby L12 9HQ
☎ 0151 228 1540 Fax 0151 259 0505
A parkland course always in first-class condition, and so giving easy walking. The fairways are well-wooded. Care must be taken on the first nine holes to avoid the brook which guards many of the greens. A modern well-designed clubhouse with many amenities, overlooks the course.
18 holes, 6257yds, Par 72, SSS 70, Course record 67.
Club membership 550.
Visitors may not play before 9.30am. May not play weekends and bank holidays.
Societies may not play on Sat, Sun & bank holidays; must contact in advance.
Green Fees £27 per day; £25 per round.
Prof Andrew Witherup
Facilities
Location 4.5m E of city centre off A57

Hotel ★★★★ 59% Atlantic Tower Thistle, Chapel St, LIVERPOOL
☎ 0151 227 4444 226

Woolton Speke Rd, Woolton L25 7TZ
☎ 0151 486 2298 Fax 0151 486 1664
Parkland course providing a good round of golf for all standards.
18 holes, 5717yds, Par 69, SSS 68.
Club membership 700.

Visitors must contact in advance. Restricted at weekends.
Societies must contact in advance.
Green Fees £20 per day (£30 weekends).
Prof Alan Gibson
Facilities
Location 7m SE of city centre off A562

Hotel ★★★★ 59% Atlantic Tower Thistle, Chapel St, LIVERPOOL ☎ 0151 227 4444 226

NEWTON-LE-WILLOWS Map 07 SJ59

Haydock Park Newton Ln WA12 0HX
☎ 01925 228525 Fax 01925 228525
A well-wooded parkland course, close to the well-known racecourse, and always in excellent condition. The pleasant undulating fairways offer some very interesting golf and the 6th, 9th, 11th and 13th holes are particularly testing. The clubhouse is very comfortable.
18 holes, 6043yds, Par 70, SSS 69, Course record 65.
Club membership 560.

Visitors welcome weekdays except Tue, with member only weekends & bank holidays. Must contact in advance.
Societies must contact in advance.
Green Fees £25 per day.
Prof Peter Kenwright
Designer James Braid
Facilities
Location 0.75m NE off A49

Hotel B Forte Posthouse Haydock, Lodge Ln, HAYDOCK ☎ 01942 717878 136

RAINHILL Map 07 SJ49

Blundells Hill Blundells Ln L35 6NA
☎ 01744 24892 Fax 01744 28861
Blundells Hill Club: 18 holes, 6256yds, Par 71, SSS 70.
Club membership 600.

Visitors may not play off white tees.
Societies telephone for prices and availability.
Green Fees £25 per day, £20 per round (£40/£30 weekends & bank holidays).
Cards
Prof Richard Leach
Designer Steve Marnoch
Facilities
Location 3 mins from junct 7 (eastbound M62)

Hotel ★ 61% Rockland Hotel, View Rd, RAINHILL ☎ 0151 426 4603 11rm(9 1)

ST HELENS Map 07 SJ59

Grange Park Prescot Rd WA10 3AD
☎ 01744 26318 Fax 01744 26318
A course of Championship length set in plesant country surroundings - playing the course it is hard to believe that industrial St Helens lies so close at hand. The course is a fine test of golf and there are many attractive holes liable to challenge all grades.
18 holes, 6422yds, Par 72, SSS 71, Course record 65.
Club membership 730.

Visitors play allowed any day except public holidays. Advisable to contact professional in advance (01744 28785)
Societies apply in writing
Green Fees £24 per 18 holes (£36 weekends).
Prof Paul Roberts
Designer James Braid
Facilities
Location 1.5m SW on A58

Hotel ★★ 62% Kirkfield Hotel, 2/4 Church St, NEWTON LE WILLOWS ☎ 01925 228196 14

Sherdley Park Sherdley Rd WA9 5DE ☎ 01744 813149
Fairly hilly course with ponds in places.
18 holes, 5941yds, Par 70, SSS 69.
Club membership 160.

Visitors no restrictions.
Green Fees not confirmed.
Facilities
Location 2m S off A570

Hotel ★★ 62% Kirkfield Hotel, 2/4 Church St, NEWTON LE WILLOWS ☎ 01925 228196 14

SOUTHPORT Map 07 SD31

The Hesketh Cockle Dick's Ln, off Cambridge Rd PR9 9QQ ☎ 01704 536897 Fax 01704 539250
The Hesketh is the oldest of the six clubs in Southport, founded in 1885. The 'Links' are of Championship standard having hosted the Lancashire County Championship in 1995, the British Senior Amateur and British Girls Amateur. Used as a final qualifying course for the Open Championship.
18 holes, 6522yds, Par 72, SSS 72, Course record 66.
Club membership 600.

Visitors welcome, with handicap certificate, at all time other than Tues am (Ladies) and 12.30-2pm daily. Must contact in advance.
Societies please contact Martyn G Senior in advance.
Green Fees £40 per day; £35 per round (£50 weekends).
Prof John Donoghue
Designer J F Morris
Facilities
Location 1m NE of town centre off A565

Hotel ★★★ 66% Stutelea Hotel & Leisure Club, Alexandra Rd, SOUTHPORT ☎ 01704 544220 20

THE ROYAL BIRKDALE

SOUTHPORT *Merseyside* ☎ 01704 567920
Fax 01704 562327 **Map 07 SD31**

John Ingham writes: There are few seaside links in the world that can be described as 'great', but Royal Birkdale, with its expanse of towering sandhills and willow scrub, is one of them. There have been some changes since the club (designed by George Lowe) was founded in 1889 and they have hosted everything that matters here, including the Open and the Ryder Cup. Some changes have been made even since Arnold Palmer hit that wondrous recovery shot that helped him win an Open in the early sixties, and led to a plaque being erected at the spot from which the divot was taken.

Well bunkered, the sandhills run along the edges of the fairways and make ideal platforms from which to view the Open Championship - played frequently here because the examination is supreme in the United Kingdom.

The links, in a wind, may be too difficult for the weekender. Certainly it found out Dai Rees in 1961 when he was chasing Palmer for the title. In the last round the course struck at the very first hole. Rees had hit his teeshot a might to the left, and then had to wait for the players to hole out on the green ahead, before attempting a powerful shot with a lofted wood from the fairway. The ball smacked into the back of a bunker, and fell back into sand. Rees took an awful seven and Palmer beat him for the trophy - by one shot. The Welshman had stormed back in 31 but his chance to win an Open had gone forever. But Rees still touched his hat to the links, and held it in great respect as, indeed, does Arnold Palmer.

But for the amateur, another problem is simply hitting the ball far enough. If you play this terrific course from the Open Championship back tees, it measures 6726 yards and par 72 takes some getting, even with your handicap allowance!

Visitors must contact in advance, and have a handicap certificate. Normally not Fri & Sat, and restricted on Sun

Societies must apply in advance.

Green fees £110 per day, £90 per round (£110 per round Sun). Fee includes 3-course lunch or high tea.

Facilities ⊗ Ⅲ ♿ ☕ 🍸 ⛺ 🏠 ⛳ Professional (Richard Bradbeer)

Location Waterloo Road, Birkdale, Southport PR8 2LX (2m S of town on A565)

18 holes, 6726yds, Par 72, SSS 73, Course record 63

WHERE TO STAY AND EAT NEARBY

HOTELS:

SOUTHPORT

★★★ ❀ 69% Royal Clifton, Promenade. ☎ 01704 533771. 106 (6 ⛳ 100 ⇄ ⛳)

★★★ 69% Scarisbrick, Lord St. ☎ 01704 543000. 77 (1 ⛳ 76 ⇄ ⛳)

★★ 70% Balmoral Lodge, 41 Queens Rd. ☎ 01704 544298. 15 ⇄ ⛳

★★★ 66% Stutelea Hotel & Leisure Club, Alexandra Rd. ☎ 01704 544220. 20 ⇄ ⛳

RESTAURANT:

WRIGHTINGTON

❀❀ High Moor Inn, Highmoor Ln (jct 27 off M6, take B5239). ☎ 01257 252364

Hillside Hastings Rd, Hillside PR8 2LU
☎ 01704 567169 Fax 01704 563192
Championship links course with natural hazards open to strong wind.
18 holes, 6850yds, Par 72, SSS 74, Course record 66.
Club membership 700.
Visitors must contact in advance through secretary.
Societies must apply to secretary in advance.
Green Fees £50 per day; £40 per round (£50 per round Sun).
Prof Brian Seddon
Designer Hawtree
Facilities
Location 3m S of town centre on A565

Hotel ★★★ 69% Royal Clifton Hotel, Promenade, SOUTHPORT ☎ 01704 533771 106

SOUTHPORT See page 189

Southport & Ainsdale Bradshaws Ln, Ainsdale PR8 3LG ☎ 01704 578000 Fax 01704 570896
'S and A', as it is known in the North is another of the fine Championship courses for which this part of the country is famed. This Club has staged many important events and offers golf of the highest order.
18 holes, 6603yds, Par 72, SSS 73, Course record 62.
Club membership 815.
Visitors welcome except Thu am, weekends & bank holidays. Must contact club in advance & have handicap certificate.
Societies must apply in advance.
Green Fees £45 per day; £35 per round.
Prof M Houghton
Designer James Braid
Facilities
Location 3m S off A565

Hotel ★★★ 69% Royal Clifton Hotel, Promenade, SOUTHPORT ☎ 01704 533771 106

Southport Municipal Park Rd West PR9 0JR
☎ 01704 535286
Municipal seaside links course. Played over by Southport Municipal, Alt and Park golf clubs.
18 holes, 6400yds, Par 70, SSS 69, Course record 66.
Club membership 750.
Visitors no restrictions.
Societies must telephone 6 days in advance.
Green Fees not confirmed.
Prof Bill Fletcher
Facilities
Location N side of town centre off A565

Hotel ★★★ 69% Royal Clifton Hotel, Promenade, SOUTHPORT ☎ 01704 533771 106

Southport Old Links Moss Ln, Churchtown PR9 7QS
☎ 01704 228207
Seaside course with tree-lined fairways and easy walking. One of the oldest courses in Southport, Henry Vardon won the 'Leeds Cup' here in 1922.
9 holes, 6244yds, Par 72, SSS 71, Course record 68.
Club membership 450.
Visitors advisable to contact in advance.
Societies apply in writing.
Green Fees £25.50 per day; £18.50 per round (£25.50 per round weekends).
Facilities
& Leisure snooker, pool table, darts.
Location NW side of town centre off A5267

Hotel ★★ 65% Bold Hotel, 585 Lord St, SOUTHPORT ☎ 01704 532578 23

WALLASEY Map 07 SJ29

Bidston Bidston Link Rd L44 2HR ☎ 0151 638 3412
Parkland course, with westerly winds.
18 holes, 6140yds, Par 70, SSS 71, Course record 66.
Club membership 650.
Visitors must contact in advance, restricted weekends.
Societies must apply in writing.
Green Fees not confirmed.
Prof J Law
Facilities
Location 0.5m W of M53 junc 1 entrance off A551

Hotel ★★★ 66% Leasowe Castle Hotel, Leasowe Rd, MORETON ☎ 0151 606 9191 47

Leasowe Moreton L46 3RD ☎ 0151 677 5852
Rather flat, semi-links, seaside course.
18 holes, 6227yds, Par 71, SSS 71.
Club membership 602.
Visitors telephone professional (0151 678 5460). Handicap certificate required.
Societies contact in advance.
Green Fees not confirmed.
Prof Neil Sweeney
Designer John Ball Jnr
Facilities
Location 2m W on A551

Hotel ★★★ 66% Leasowe Castle Hotel, Leasowe Rd, MORETON ☎ 0151 606 9191 47

Wallasey Bayswater Rd L45 8LA
☎ 0151 691 1024 Fax 0151 638 8988
A well-established sporting links, adjacent to the Irish Sea, with huge sandhills and many classic holes where the player's skills are often combined with good fortune. Large, firm greens and fine views but not for the faint-hearted.
18 holes, 6607yds, Par 72.
Club membership 605.
Visitors must contact one month in advance.
Societies must apply in writing or telephone.
Green Fees £40 per day; £35 per round (£45 weekends & bank holidays).
Prof Mike Adams
Designer Tom Morris

Facilities
Location N side of town centre off A554

Hotel ★★★ 66% Leasowe Castle Hotel, Leasowe Rd, MORETON
☎ 0151 606 9191 47

Warren Grove Rd L45 0JA ☎ 0151 639 8323
Short, undulating links course with first-class greens and prevailing winds off the sea.
9 holes, 5854yds, Par 72, SSS 68.
Club membership 150.

Visitors welcome except Sun 7-11am.
Green Fees not confirmed.
Prof Steve Konrad
Facilities
Location N side of town centre off A554

Hotel ★★★ 66% Leasowe Castle Hotel, Leasowe Rd, MORETON ☎ 0151 606 9191 47

NORFOLK

Barnham Broom Map 05 TG00

Barnham Broom Hotel,Golf,Conference,Leisure
Honingham Rd NR9 4DD ☎ 01603 759393 Fax 01603 758224
Attractive river valley courses with modern hotel and leisure complex.
Valley Course: 18 holes, 6603yds, Par 72, SSS 72.
Hill Course: 18 holes, 6650yds, Par 71, SSS 71.
Club membership 500.

Visitors must contact in advance. With member only at weekends.
Societies must contact in advance.
Green Fees Valley £50 per day; £35 per round. Hill £35 per day; £30 per round.
Cards
Prof S Beckham/P Ballingall
Designer Frank Pennink
Facilities
& Leisure hard tennis courts, heated indoor swimming pool, squash, sauna, solarium, gymnasium, snooker table.
Location 1m N, S of A47

Hotel ★★★ 72% Barnham Broom Hotel, BARNHAM BROOM
☎ 01603 759393 53
See advertisement on page 195.

Bawburgh Map 05 TG10

Bawburgh Glen Lodge, Marlingford Rd NR9 3LU
☎ 01603 740404 Fax 01603 740403
Undulating course, mixture of parkland & heathland. Excellent 18th hole to finish.
18 holes, 6224yds, Par 70, SSS 70.
Club membership 700.

Visitors must contact in advance, limited play at weekends.
Societies must contact in advance.
Green Fees £18 per weekday (£22 weekends).
Cards
Prof Chris Potter
Designer Shaun Mansell
Facilities
Location S of Royal Norfolk Showground, on A47

Hotel ★★★ 70% Hotel Norwich, 121-131 Boundary Rd, NORWICH
☎ 01603 787260 106

Brancaster Map 09 TF74

Royal West Norfolk PE31 8AX
☎ 01485 210223 Fax 01485 210087
If you want to see what golf courses were like years ago, then go to the Royal West Norfolk where tradition exudes from both clubhouse and course. Close by the sea, the links are laid out in the grand manner and are characterised by sleepered greens, superb cross-bunkering and salt marshes.
18 holes, 6428yds, Par 71, SSS 71, Course record 66.
Club membership 740.

Visitors must contact well in advance. Restrictions at weekends and in Aug.
Societies must contact Secretary in advance.
Green Fees £43 (£53 weekends).
Cards
Prof R E Kimber
Designer Holcombe-Ingleby
Facilities
Location 7m E of Hunstanton. In Brancaster village turn N at the beach/Broad Lane junct with A149 for 1m

Hotel ★★ 72% Titchwell Manor Hotel, TITCHWELL ☎ 01485 210221 11rm(7) Annexe4

Cromer Map 09 TG24

Royal Cromer 145 Overstrand Rd NR27 0JH
☎ 01263 512884 Fax 01263 512884
Seaside course set out on cliff edge, hilly and subject to wind.
18 holes, 6447yds, Par 72, SSS 71, Course record 67.
Club membership 650.

Visitors must contact in advance & have handicap certificate. Restricted at weekends.
Societies must contact in advance.
Green Fees £30 per day (£36 weekends & bank holidays).
Prof Robin Page
Designer J H Taylor
Facilities
Location 1m E on B1159

Hotel ★★ 70% Red Lion, Brook St, CROMER
☎ 01263 514964 12

Denver
Map 05 TF60

Ryston Park PE38 0HH ☎ 01366 382133
Parkland course.
9 holes, 6310yds, Par 70, SSS 70, Course record 66.
Club membership 330.
Visitors must contact in advance. May not play weekends or bank holidays.
Societies must apply in writing.
Green Fees £20 per day; £15 per round.
Designer James Braid
Facilities
Location 0.5m S on A10

Hotel ★★ 69% Castle Hotel, High St, DOWNHAM MARKET ☎ 01366 384311 12rm(9)

Dereham
Map 09 TF91

Dereham Quebec Rd NR19 2DS
☎ 01362 695900 & 695904 Fax 01362 695904
Parkland course.
9 holes, 6225yds, Par 71, SSS 70, Course record 64.
Club membership 400.
Visitors must contact in advance and have a handicap certificate; must play with member at weekends.
Societies must apply in writing.
Green Fees not confirmed.
Prof Robert Curtis
Facilities
Location N side of town centre off B1110

Hotel ★★★ 72% Barnham Broom Hotel, BARNHAM BROOM
☎ 01603 759393 53

Reymerston Hingham Rd, Reymerston NR9 4QQ
☎ 01362 850297 Fax 01362 850614
The course was opened in June 1993 with large tees and greens which drain very well. Created from open farmland, it has many ditches and hedges and room for the 18th green to be over 1000sq.yds. The 17th green is protected by two large trees in front.
18 holes, 6609yds, Par 72, SSS 72, Course record 74.
Club membership 400.
Visitors must book tee times.
Societies telephone or write to arrange tee times.
Green Fees not confirmed.
Prof Alison Sheard
Designer Adas
Facilities
Location 12m W of Norwich, off B1135

Hotel ★★★ 72% Barnham Broom Hotel, BARNHAM BROOM
☎ 01603 759393 53

Diss
Map 05 TM18

Diss Stuston IP22 3JB ☎ 01379 641025 Fax 01379 641025
Commonland course with natural hazards.
18 holes, 6238yds, Par 73, SSS 70.
Club membership 650.
Visitors must contact in advance but may not play weekends & bank holidays.
Societies by arrangement.
Green Fees not confirmed.
Facilities
Location 1.5m SE on B1118

Hotel ★★★ 70% Cornwallis Arms, BROME
☎ 01379 870326 11

Fakenham
Map 09 TF92

Fakenham Gallow Sports Centre, The Race Course N21 7NY ☎ 01328 863534
A well-wooded 9-hole course.
9 holes, 6174yds, Par 71, SSS 70, Course record 65.
Club membership 460.
Visitors any time with member, restricted until after noon weekends and bank holidays.
Societies apply in writing or telephone.
Green Fees £18 per day (£24 weekends & bank holidays).
Prof Colin Williams
Facilities
& Leisure hard tennis courts, squash.
Hotel ★★ 65% Crown Hotel, Market Place, FAKENHAM ☎ 01328 851418 11

Gorleston-on-Sea
Map 05 TG50

Gorleston Warren Rd NR31 6JT
☎ 01493 661911 & 662103
Seaside course.
18 holes, 6391yds, Par 71, SSS 71, Course record 68.
Club membership 860.
Visitors advisable to contact in advance, must have handicap.
Societies must apply in writing.
Green Fees £21 per day/round (£25 weekends & bank holidays).
Prof Nick Brown
Designer J H Taylor
Facilities
Location S side of town centre

Hotel ★★★ 74% Cliff Hotel, Gorleston, GREAT YARMOUTH ☎ 01493 662179 39

Great Yarmouth
Map 05 TG50

Caldecott Hall Golf & Leisure Caldecott Hall, Beccles Rd, Fritton NR31 9EY ☎ 01493 488488 Fax 01493 488561
Facilities at Caldecott Hall include an 18-hole course with testing dog-leg fairways, a short par 3 9-hole course, a floodlit driving range, and good practising areas.
Club membership 500.

Societies arrangements in advance.
Prof Mark Snazell
Facilities
& Leisure equestrian centre with tuition and 400 acres of woodland hacking.
Location On the A143 Beccles/Gt Yarmouth road at Fritton

Hotel ★★★ 74% Cliff Hotel, Gorleston, GREAT YARMOUTH ☎ 01493 662179 39

Great Yarmouth & Caister Beach House, Caister-on-Sea NR30 5TD ☎ 01493 728699
This great old club, which celebrated its centenary in 1982, has played its part in the development of the game. It is a fine old-fashioned links where not many golfers have bettered the SSS in competitions. The 468-yard 8th (par 4), is a testing hole and the 7th is an extremely fine short hole.
18 holes, 6330yds, Par 70, SSS 70, Course record 66.
Club membership 720.
Visitors must contact in advance. Restricted weekends.
Societies must apply in writing or telephone.
Green Fees £27 per day (£30 weekends & bank holidays).
Prof James Hill
Designer H Colt
Facilities
& Leisure snooker.
Location 0.5m N off A149

Hotel ★★★ 66% Imperial Hotel, North Dr, GREAT YARMOUTH ☎ 01493 851113 39

HUNSTANTON Map 09 TF64

Hunstanton Golf Course Rd PE36 6JQ
☎ 01485 532811 Fax 01485 532319
A championship links course set among some of the most natural golfing country in East Anglia. Keep out of the numerous bunkers and master the fast greens to play your handicap - then you only have the wind to contend with! Good playing conditions all year round.
18 holes, 6735yds, Par 72, SSS 72, Course record 65.
Club membership 675.
Visitors must contact in advance and be a club member with current handicap certificate. Restricted at weekends & may not play bank holiday weekends. Play in two ball format ie singles or foursomes.
Societies apply in advance.
Green Fees £45 per day (£55 weekends). £30 after 4pm weekdays.
Prof John Carter
Designer James Braid
Facilities by prior arrangement
Location Off A149 in Old Hunstanton Village signposted

Hotel ★★ 71% Caley Hall Motel, Old Hunstanton Rd, HUNSTANTON ☎ 01485 533486 Annexe33

KING'S LYNN Map 09 TF62

Eagles 39 School Rd, Tilney All Saints PE34 4RS
☎ 01553 827147 Fax 01553 829777
Parkland course with plenty of water hazards and bunkers. Also Par-3 course and floodlit, covered driving range.
9 holes, 4284yds, Par 64, SSS 61, Course record 64.
Club membership 300.
Visitors no restrictions.
Societies must contact in advance.
Green Fees £12 per 18 holes, £6 per 9 holes (£14/£7 weekends & bank holidays).
Cards
Prof Nigel Pickerell
Designer D W Horn
Facilities
Location Off A47 at roundabout to Tilney All Saints

Hotel ★★★ 66% The Duke's Head, Tuesday Market Place, KING'S LYNN ☎ 01553 774996 71

King's Lynn Castle Rising PE31 6BD
☎ 01553 631654
Challenging, wooded parkland course.
18 holes, 6609yds, Par 72, SSS 72.
Club membership 1000.
Visitors must contact in advance.
Societies must contact in advance.
Green Fees not confirmed.
Prof Chris Hanlon
Designer Thomas & Allis
Facilities
Location 4m NE off A149

Hotel ★★★ 66% The Duke's Head, Tuesday Market Place, KING'S LYNN ☎ 01553 774996 71

MATTISHALL Map 09 TG01

Mattishall South Green NR20 3JZ
☎ 01362 850111
Mattishall has the distinction of having the longest hole in Norfolk at a very demanding 615yds.
9 holes, 3109yds, Par 35, SSS 69.
Club membership 120.
Visitors no restrictions.
Societies welcome.
Green Fees £10 per 18 holes; £6 per 9 holes.
Designer B Todd
Facilities
Hotel ★★★ 72% Barnham Broom Hotel, BARNHAM BROOM ☎ 01603 759393 53

MIDDLETON Map 09 TF61

Middleton Hall PE32 1RH ☎ 01553 841800
The 9-hole King's course (played off 18 tees) is a pleasant parkland course constructed with conservation in mind around numerous mature trees, pond and reservoir. Additional Par 3 pitch and putt course.
9 holes, 5570yds, Par 68, SSS 67, Course record 69.
Club membership 300.

Visitors no restrictions.
Societies must contact in advance.
Green Fees not confirmed.
Prof Brian McKee
Facilities
Location 4m from King's Lynn off A47

Hotel ★★★ 65% Butterfly Hotel, Beveridge Way, Hardwick Narrows, KING'S LYNN ☎ 01553 771707 50

MUNDESLEY Map 09 TG33

Mundesley Links Rd NR11 8ES
☎ 01263 720279 & 720095 Fax 01263 720279
Seaside course, undulating with panoramic views, short but competitive.
9 holes, 5410yds, Par 68, SSS 66, Course record 64.
Club membership 400.
Visitors restricted Wed & weekends, also Tue 4-6pm, dress regulations, no sharing clubs, golf shoes must be worn.
Societies must contact one month in advance.
Green Fees £17 per day; £12 per round; £7.50 per 9 holes (£20 per round weekends & bank holidays).
Prof T G Symmons
Facilities
Location W side of village off B1159

Hotel ★★ 70% Red Lion, Brook St, CROMER ☎ 01263 514964 12

NORWICH Map 05 TG20

Costessy Park Old Costessy NR8 5AL
☎ 01603 746333 & 747085 Fax 01603 746185
The course lies in the gently contoured Two River valley, providing players with a number of holes that bring the river and man-made lakes into play.
18 holes, 5820yds, Par 71, SSS 68.
Club membership 600.
Visitors may not play competition days, prior booking required for weekends.
Societies welcome by prior arrangement.
Green Fees £21 per day; £17 per round (£22 day/round weekends).
Cards
Prof Simon Cook
Facilities
Hotel ★★★ 64% Norwich Sport Village Hotel, Drayton High Rd, Hellesdon, NORWICH ☎ 01603 789469 55

Eaton Newmarket Rd NR4 6SF
☎ 01603 451686 & 452881 Fax 01603 451686
An undulating, tree-lined parkland course with excellent trees. Easy opening par 5 followed by an intimidating par 3 that is well bunkered with deep rough on both sides. The challenging 17th hole is uphill to a small hidden green and always needs more club than expected.
18 holes, 6114yds, Par 70, SSS 69, Course record 64.
Club membership 800.
Visitors restricted before 11.30am weekends. Advised to contact in advance.
Societies must contact in advance.
Green Fees £28 per day; £17 per round (£35/£22 weekends).
Prof Mark Allen
Facilities by prior arrangement
Location 1.5m SW of city centre off A11

Hotel ★★★ 64% Norwich Sport Village Hotel, Drayton High Rd, Hellesdon, NORWICH ☎ 01603 789469 55

Royal Norwich Drayton High Rd, Hellesdon NR6 5AH
☎ 01603 429928
Undulating mature parkland course complimented with gorse, the 5th-11th holes being in open parkland with newly planted trees.
18 holes, 6603yds, Par 72, SSS 72, Course record 67.
Club membership 700.
Visitors must contact in advance. Restricted weekends & bank holidays.
Societies must contact in advance.
Green Fees £30 per day (£36 weekends & bank holidays). Reduced fees after 2pm.
Prof Dean Futter
Designer James Braid
Facilities by prior arrangement
Location 2.5m NW of city centre on A1067

Hotel ★★★ 70% Hotel Norwich, 121-131 Boundary Rd, NORWICH ☎ 01603 787260 106

Sprowston Park Wroxham Rd NR7 8RP
☎ 01603 410657 Fax 01603 788884
A Pay & Play course set in 100 acres of parkland. A very tight course, so accuracy is required for good golf. The facilities include a 27-bay driving range, a practice area and tuition from a team of professionals.
18 holes, 5843yds, Par 70, SSS 68, Course record 63.
Club membership 640.
Visitors no restrictions.
Societies must contact in advance.
Green Fees £17 per round (£21 weekends & bank holidays).
Cards
Prof Philip J Grice
Facilities
Location 4m NE from city centre on A1151

Hotel ★★★★ 70% Sprowston Manor, Sprowston Park, Wroxham Rd, Sprowston, NORWICH ☎ 01603 410871 94

Wensum Valley Beech Av, Taverham NR8 6HP
☎ 01603 261012 Fax 01603 261664
An undulating, picturesque golf course situated on the side of a valley. The greens in particular are very undulating and always give the average golfer a testing time. The 12th hole from a raised tee provides a blind and windy tee shot and a very slopey green.
Valley Course: 18 holes, 6059yds, Par 71, SSS 69, Course record 67.
Wensum Course: 9 holes, 2906yds, Par 70, SSS 68.
Club membership 900.
Visitors no restrictions but advisable to book tee times at weekends.
Societies apply in writing or by telephone.
Green Fees £18 day ticket including bar meal. Twilight £10.
Cards
Prof Tony Varney
Designer B Todd
Facilities
& Leisure fishing.
Location 5m NE of Norwich

Hotel ★★★ 70% Hotel Norwich, 121-131 Boundary Rd, NORWICH ☎ 01603 787260 106

SHERINGHAM — Map 09 TG14

Sheringham Weybourne Rd NR26 8HG
☎ 01263 823488 & 822038 Fax 01263 825189
Splendid cliff-top links with gorse, good 'seaside turf' and plenty of space. Straight driving is essential for a low score. The course is close to the shore and can be very windswept, but offers magnificent views.
18 holes, 6464yds, Par 70, SSS 71, Course record 65.
Club membership 680.

Visitors must contact in advance & have handicap certificate. Restricted weekends.
Societies must apply in writing.
Green Fees £35 (£40 weekends & bank holidays).
Prof M W Jubb
Designer Tom Dunn
Facilities ⊗
Location W side of town centre on A149

Hotel ★★ 69% Beaumaris Hotel, South St, SHERINGHAM ☎ 01263 822370 22

SWAFFHAM — Map 05 TF80

Swaffham Cley Rd PE37 8AE ☎ 01760 721611
Heathland course and designated wildlife site.
9 holes, 6252yds, Par 72, SSS 70.
Club membership 385.

Visitors must contact in advance. With member only at weekends.
Societies must contact in advance.
Green Fees not confirmed.
Prof Peter Field
Facilities ⊗
Location 1.5m SW

Hotel ★★★ 64% George Hotel, Station Rd, SWAFFHAM ☎ 01760 721238 27

THETFORD — Map 05 TL88

Feltwell Thor Ave, Feltwell IP26 4AY ☎ 01842 827644
In spite of being an inland links, this 9-hole course is still open and windy.
9 holes, 6256yds, Par 70, SSS 70, Course record 68.
Club membership 400.

Visitors dress restriction, no jeans,tracksuits or collarless shirts, golf shoes to be worn.
Societies apply in writing or telephone in advance.
Green Fees £14 per day (£22 weekends & bank holidays). Winter 9 holes after 2pm £6 (£8 weekends). Summer 18 holes after 4pm £12.
Prof Peter Field
Facilities ⊗ (closed Mon)
Location On B1112

Hotel ★★★ 62% The Bell, King St, THETFORD ☎ 01842 754455 47

Thetford Brandon Rd IP24 3NE
☎ 01842 752169 Fax 01842 766212
This is a course with a good pedigree. It was laid-out by a fine golfer, C.H. Mayo, later altered by James Braid and then again altered by another famous course designer, Mackenzie Ross. It is a testing heathland course with a particularly stiff finish.
18 holes, 6879yds, Par 72, SSS 73, Course record 66.
Club membership 850.

Visitors pre booking advisable, may not play weekends or bank holidays except with member. Handicap certificate required.
Societies must contact in advance, Wed-Fri only.
Green Fees £32 per day/round.
Prof Gary Kitley
Facilities ⊗
Location 2m W of Thetford on B1107

Hotel ★★★ 62% The Bell, King St, THETFORD ☎ 01842 754455 47

WATTON — Map 05 TF90

Richmond Park Saham Rd IP25 6EA
☎ 01953 881803 Fax 01953 881817
Meadowland course dotted with newly planted trees and set on either side of the Little Wissey River.
18 holes, 6289yds, Par 71, SSS 70, Course record 69.
Club membership 600.

Visitors must contact in advance.
Societies must contact in advance.
Green Fees £24 per day; £18 per round (£24 per day/round weekends).
Prof Alan Hemsley
Designer D Jessup/D Scott ▶

Facilities
& Leisure gymnasium.
Location 500yds NW of town centre

Hotel ★★★ 64% George Hotel, Station Rd, SWAFFHAM ☎ 01760 721238 27

WESTON LONGVILLE Map 09 TG11

Weston Park NR9 5JW
☎ 01603 872363 Fax 01603 873040
Testing course set in 200 acres of mature parkland with specimen trees.
18 holes, 6603yds, Par 72, SSS 72.
Club membership 400.

Visitors must telephone for tee times on 01603 872998
Societies must telephone for prices and tee times.
Green Fees £35 per day; £24 per 18 holes (£39/£29 weekends).
Prof Michael Few
Facilities
& Leisure hard tennis courts, croquet lawn.
Location Off the A1067 Norwich/Fakenham road

Hotel ★★★ 66% Quality Friendly Hotel, 2 Barnard Rd, Bowthorpe, NORWICH ☎ 01603 741161 80

WEST RUNTON Map 09 TG14

Links Country Park Hotel & Golf Club NR27 9QH
☎ 01263 838215 Fax 01263 38264
Parkland course 500 yds from the sea, with superb views overlooking West Runton. The hotel offers extensive leisure facilities.
9 holes, 4814yds, Par 66, SSS 64.
Club membership 250.

Visitors must have a handicap certificate.
Societies must telephone in advance.
Green Fees £20 per day (£25 weekends & bank holidays).
Cards
Prof Lee Patterson
Facilities
& Leisure hard tennis courts, heated indoor swimming pool, sauna, solarium.
Location S side of village off A149

Hotel ★★ 69% Beaumaris Hotel, South St, SHERINGHAM ☎ 01263 822370 22

NORTHAMPTONSHIRE

CHACOMBE Map 04 SP44

Cherwell Edge OX17 2EN
☎ 01295 711591 Fax 01295 712404
Parkland course open since 1980. The front nine is short and tight with mature trees. The back nine is longer and more open.
18 holes, 5947yds, Par 70, SSS 68, Course record 64.
Club membership 650.
Visitors no restrictions but golf shoes to be worn (can be hired) and tidy appearance expected.
Societies must apply in advance.
Green Fees £12 per round (£16 weekends).
Cards
Prof Joe Kingston
Designer R Davies
Facilities
Location Exit M40 junct 11, 0.5m S off B4525

Hotel ★★★ 68% Whately Hall, Banbury Cross, BANBURY ☎ 01295 263451 73

COLD ASHBY Map 04 SP67

Cold Ashby Stanford Rd NN6 6EP
☎ 01604 740548 Fax 01604 740548
Undulating parkland course, nicely matured, with superb views. The 27 holes consist of three loops of nine which can be interlinked with each other. All three loops have their own challenge and any combination of two loops will give an excellent course. The start of the Elkington loop offers 5 holes of scenic beauty and testing golf and the 3rd on the Winwick loop is a 200-yard par 3 from a magnificent plateau tee.
Ashby-Elkington: 18 holes, 6308yds, Par 72, SSS 70, Course record 69.
Winwick-Ashby: 18 holes, 6004yds, Par 70, SSS 69, Course record 67.
Elkington-Winwick: 18 holes, 6250yds, Par 70, SSS 70, Course record 69.
Club membership 700.
Visitors start time must be reserved at weekends.
Societies must contact in advance.
Green Fees £23 per day; £15 per round (£17 per round weekends).
Cards
Prof Shane Rose
Designer David Croxton

Facilities
Location Close to junct 1 A14 & junct 18 M1 midway between Rugby, Leicester & Northampton

Hotel B Forte Posthouse Northampton/Rugby, CRICK ☎ 01788 822101 88

COLLINGTREE Map 04 SP75

Collingtree Park Windingbrook Ln NN4 0XN
☎ 01604 700000 Fax 01604 702600
Superb 18-hole resort course designed by former U.S. and British Open champion Johnny Miller. Stunning island green at the 18th hole. The Golf Academy includes a driving range, practice holes, indoor video teaching room.
18 holes, 6695yds, Par 72, SSS 72, Course record 66.
Visitors must contact in advance & have handicap certificate.
Societies contact in advance.
Green Fees not confirmed.
Prof Geoff Pook
Designer Johnny Miller
Facilities
& Leisure fishing.
Location M1-junc 15 on A508 to Northampton

Hotel ★★★★ 68% Swallow Hotel, Eagle Dr, NORTHAMPTON ☎ 01604 768700 120

CORBY Map 04 SP88

Corby Public Stamford Rd, Weldon NN17 3JH
☎ 01536 260756
Municipal course laid out on made-up quarry ground and open to prevailing wind. Wet in winter. Played over by Priors Hall Club.
18 holes, 6677yds, Par 72, SSS 72.
Club membership 600.
Visitors are advised to book in advance.
Societies must contact in advance.
Green Fees not confirmed.
Facilities by prior arrangement
Location 4m NE on A43

Hotel ★★★ 68% The Talbot, New St, OUNDLE ☎ 01832 273621 39

DAVENTRY Map 04 SP56

Daventry & District Norton Rd NN11 5LS
☎ 01327 702829
A hilly course with hard walking.
9 holes, 5555yds, Par 69, SSS 67, Course record 68.
Club membership 360.
Visitors restricted Sun mornings & weekends (Oct-Mar).
Societies contact the club secretary.
Green Fees £10 (£12 weekends & bank holidays).
Facilities by prior arrangement by prior arrangement by prior arrangement
Location 1m NE

Hotel ★★★★ 62% Hanover International Hotel & Club Daventry, Sedgemoor Way, Ashby Rd, DAVENTRY ☎ 01327 301777 138

FARTHINGSTONE Map 04 SP65

Farthingstone Hotel & Golf Course NN12 8AH
☎ 01327 361533 & 361291 Fax 01327 361645
Pleasant rambling course with open aspect and widespread views.
18 holes, 6299yds, Par 70, SSS 70, Course record 68.
Club membership 500.
Visitors must contact in advance.
Societies must contact in advance.
Green Fees £13-£25.
Cards
Prof Garry Buckle
Designer Don Donaldson
Facilities
& Leisure squash.
Location 1m W

Hotel ★★ 65% Globe Hotel, High St, WEEDON ☎ 01327 340336 15 Annexe3

HELLIDON Map 04 SP55

Hellidon Lakes Hotel & Country Club NN11 6LN
☎ 01327 262550 Fax 01327 262559
Spectacular parkland course designed by David Snell.
18 holes, 6691yds, Par 72, SSS 72 or 9 holes, 2791yds, Par 70, SSS 67.
Club membership 500.
Visitors 18 hole course; must contact in advance & have handicap certificate at weekends. 9 hole; open to beginners.
Societies must telephone in advance.
Green Fees not confirmed.
Prof Gary Wills
Designer D Snell
Facilities
& Leisure hard tennis courts, heated indoor swimming pool, fishing, sauna, solarium, gymnasium.
Hotel ★★★★ 70% Hellidon Lakes Hotel & Country Club, HELLIDON ☎ 01327 262550 45

KETTERING Map 04 SP87

Kettering Headlands NN15 6XA
☎ 01536 511104
A very pleasant, mainly flat meadowland course with easy walking.
18 holes, 6081yds, Par 69, SSS 69, Course record 64.
Club membership 700.
Visitors welcome but with member only weekends & bank holidays.
Societies Wed & Fri only, apply in writing.
Green Fees £22 per day; £15 per round.
Prof Kevin Theobald
Designer Tom Morris
Facilities
Location S side of town centre

Hotel ★★★★ 74% Kettering Park Hotel, Kettering Parkway, KETTERING ☎ 01536 416666 90

NORTHAMPTON Map 04 SP76

Brampton Heath Sandy Ln, Church Brampton NN6 8AX
☎ 01604 843939 Fax 01604 843885
Appealing to both the novice and experienced golfer, this beautiful, well drained heathland course affords panoramic views over Northampton.
18 holes, 6233yds, Par 71, SSS 70, Course record 67.
Club membership 500.

Visitors advisable to book especially for weekends, may book up to 8 days in advance.
Societies write or telephone for details.
Green Fees £19.20 per day; £12 per 18 holes; £7.20 per 9 holes (£28/£16/£9.60 weekends).
Cards
Prof Richard Hudson
Designer D Snell
Facilities
& Leisure short course par 3.
Location Signposted off old A50 Kingsthorpe to Welford road, 2m N of Kingsthorpe

Hotel ★★★ 69% Lime Trees Hotel, 8 Langham Place, Barrack Rd, NORTHAMPTON
☎ 01604 32188 27

Delapre Golf Complex Eagle Dr, Nene Valley Way NN4 7DU ☎ 01604 764036 Fax 01604 706378
Rolling parkland course, part of municipal golf complex, which includes two 9-hole, par 3 courses, pitch-and-putt and 33 bay driving-range.
Main Course: 18 holes, 6269yds, Par 70, SSS 70, Course record 66.
Hardingstone Course: 9 holes, 2109yds, Par 32, SSS 32.
Club membership 900.

Visitors no restrictions but advance booking advised for weekends.
Societies must book and pay full green fees 2 weeks in advance.
Green Fees £8.50 per 18 holes; £5.75 per 9 holes (£12/£7.25 weekends & bank holidays).
Prof John Corby
Designer John Jacobs/John Corby
Facilities
Location 2m SE

Hotel ★★★ 64% Westone Hotel, Ashley Way, Weston Favell, NORTHAMPTON
☎ 01604 739955 31 Annexe35

Kingsthorpe Kingsley Rd NN2 7BU
☎ 01604 710610 Fax 01604 710610
A compact, undulating parkland course set within the town boundary. Not a long course but testing enough to attract a competitive membership that boasts several County players.
18 holes, 5918yds, Par 69, SSS 69, Course record 63.
Club membership 630.

Visitors must contact in advance and have handicap certificate. With member only weekends.
Societies must contact in advance.
Green Fees £25 per day/round.
Prof Paul Armstrong
Designer Mr Alison
Facilities
Location N side of town centre on A5095 between the Racecourse and Kingsthorpe

Hotel ★★★ 64% Westone Hotel, Ashley Way, Weston Favell, NORTHAMPTON
☎ 01604 739955 31 Annexe35

Northampton Harlestone NN7 4EF
☎ 01604 845155 Fax 01604 820262
Parkland course with water in play on three holes.
18 holes, 6615yds, Par 72, SSS 72, Course record 67.
Club membership 750.

Visitors must contact in advance and have handicap certificate. With member only at weekends.
Societies must contact in advance.
Green Fees Weekdays: £30 per day/round.
Prof Kevin Dickens
Designer Sinclair Steel
Facilities
Location NW of town centre on A428

Hotel ★★★ 66% Northampton Moat House, Silver St, NORTHAMPTON
☎ 01604 739988 141

Northamptonshire County Golf Ln, Church Brampton NN6 8AZ ☎ 01604 843025 Fax 01604 843025
A fine, traditional course situated on undulating heathland with areas of gorse, heather and extensive coniferous and deciduous woodland. A river and a railway line pass through the course.
18 holes, 6503yds, Par 70, SSS 71, Course record 65.
Club membership 650.

Visitors restricted weekends. May not play on bank holidays. Must contact in advance and have a handicap certificate.
Societies Wed/Thu only, must contact in advance.
Green Fees £37 per day.
Prof Tim Rouse
Designer H S Colt
Facilities
Location 5m NW of Northampton, off A50

Hotel ★★★ 64% Westone Hotel, Ashley Way, Weston Favell, NORTHAMPTON
☎ 01604 739955 31 Annexe35

OUNDLE Map 04 TL08

Oundle Benefield Rd PE8 5AF
☎ 01832 273267 (Gen Manager) Fax 01832 273267
Undulating parkland course, shortish but difficult. A small brook affects some of the approaches to the greens.
18 holes, 6235yds, Par 71, SSS 70, Course record 72.
Club membership 600.

Visitors may not play Tue (Ladies Day) or before 10.30am weekends unless with member.
Societies must apply in advance.
Green Fees £22 per day (£30 weekends); weekdays £12 after 3pm.
Prof Richard Keys
Facilities
Location 1m W on A427

Hotel ★★★ 68% The Talbot, New St, OUNDLE
☎ 01832 273621 39

Staverton Map 04 SP56

Staverton Park NN11 6JT ☎ 01327 302000
Open course, fairly testing with good views.
18 holes, 6661yds, Par 71, SSS 72, Course record 65.
Club membership 300.

Visitors restricted weekends. Must contact in advance. Handicap certificates preferred.
Societies must contact in advance.
Green Fees not confirmed.
Prof Richard Mudge
Designer Cmdr John Harris
Facilities
& Leisure sauna, gymnasium.
Location 0.75m NE of Staverton on A425

Hotel ★★★★ 62% Hanover International Hotel & Club Daventry, Sedgemoor Way, Ashby Rd, DAVENTRY ☎ 01327 301777 138

Wellingborough Map 04 SP86

Rushden Kimbolton Rd, Chelveston NN9 6AN
☎ 01933 418511
Parkland course with brook running through the middle.
10 holes, 6335yds, Par 71, SSS 70, Course record 68.
Club membership 400.

Visitors may not play Wed afternoon. With member only weekends.
Societies must apply in writing.
Green Fees £18 per day/round.
Facilities
Location 2m E of Higham Ferrers on Kimbolton Rd

Hotel ★★★ 66% Hind Hotel, Sheep St, WELLINGBOROUGH ☎ 01933 222827 34

Wellingborough Great Harrowden Hall NN9 5AD
☎ 01933 677234 Fax 01933 679379
An undulating parkland course with many trees. The 514-yd, 14th is a testing hole. The clubhouse is a stately home.
18 holes, 6617yds, Par 72, SSS 72, Course record 68.
Club membership 820.

Visitors may not play at weekends & bank holidays or Tue between 10am and 2.30pm.
Societies must apply in writing.
Green Fees £35 per day/round.
Prof David Clifford
Designer Hawtree
Facilities
& Leisure outdoor swimming pool, snooker.
Location 2m N on A509

Hotel ★★★ 66% Hind Hotel, Sheep St, WELLINGBOROUGH ☎ 01933 222827 34

Whittlebury Map 04 SP64

Whittlebury Park Golf & Country Club NN12 8XW
☎ 01327 858092 Fax 01327 858009
The 36 holes incorporate three loops of tournament-standard nines plus a short course. The 1905 Course is a reconstruction of the original parkland course built at the turn of the century, the Royal Whittlewood is a lakeland course playing around copses and the Grand Prix, next to Silverstone Motor Racing circuit has a strong links feel playing over gently undulating grassland with challenging lake features.
Grand Prix: 9 holes, 3339yds, Par 36, SSS 36.
Royal Whittlewood: 9 holes, 3323yds, Par 36, SSS 36.
1905: 9 holes, 3256yds, Par 36, SSS 36.
Club membership 450.

Visitors must contact in advance.
Societies telephone 01327 857509 in advance.
Green Fees £20 Tue-Fri; £10 Mon (£30 weekends & bank holidays).
Cards
Prof Martin Leung
Designer Cameron Sinclair
Facilities by prior arrangement
Location A413 Buckingham Road

Hotel ★★ 64% The Saracens Head, 219 Watling St, TOWCESTER ☎ 01327 350414 21

NORTHUMBERLAND

Allendale Map 12 NY85

Allendale High Studdon, Allenheads Rd NE47 9DH
☎ 01434 683926
Challenging and hilly parkland course set 1000 feet above sea level with superb views of Allendale. Holes with interesting features include the 3rd, 7th and 8th. An additional 7 tees have recently been added and a new club house is operational.
16 holes, 4541yds, Par 66, SSS 62, Course record 70.
Club membership 215.

Visitors may not play Aug bank holiday.
Societies must apply in writing to Secretary.
Green Fees £10 per day.
Facilities by prior arrangement
Location 1.5m S on B6295

Hotel ★★ 62% County Hotel, Priestpopple, HEXHAM ☎ 01434 602030 9

Alnmouth Map 12 NU21

Alnmouth Foxton Hall NE66 3BE
☎ 01665 830231 Fax 01665 830922
Coastal course with pleasant views.
18 holes, 6429yds, Par 69, SSS 69, Course record 64.
Club membership 850.

Visitors may not play Wed, Fri, weekends & bank holidays.
Societies Mon, Tue or Thu only.
Green Fees £27 per day.
Cards
Designer H S Colt
Facilities
& Leisure snooker.
Location 1m NE

Hotel ★★★ 63% White Swan Hotel, Bondgate Within, ALNWICK ☎ 01665 602109 58

Alnmouth Village Marine Rd NE66 2RZ ☎ 01665 830370
Seaside course with part coastal view.
9 holes, 6078yds, Par 70, SSS 70, Course record 63.
Club membership 480.
Visitors may not play before 11am on competition days.
Societies must contact in advance.
Green Fees not confirmed.
Facilities
Location E side of village

Hotel ★★★ 63% White Swan Hotel, Bondgate Within, ALNWICK ☎ 01665 602109 58

ALNWICK Map 12 NU11

Alnwick Swansfield Park NE66 2AT ☎ 01665 602632
Parkland course offering a fair test of golfing skills.
18 holes, 6284yds, Par 70, SSS 70, Course record 66.
Club membership 550.
Visitors no restrictions.
Societies must contact secretary in advance.
Green Fees £16 per day; £12 per round (£20/£16 weekends & bank holidays).
Designer Rochester
Facilities
Location S side of town

Hotel ★★★ 63% White Swan Hotel, Bondgate Within, ALNWICK ☎ 01665 602109 58

BAMBURGH Map 12 NU13

Bamburgh Castle NE69 7DE
☎ 01668 214378 (club) & 24321 (sec)
Superb coastal course with excellent greens that are both fast and true, natural hazards of heather and whin bushes abound. Magnificent views of Farne Islands, Holy Island, Lindisfarne Castle, Bamburgh Castle and Cheviot Hils.
18 holes, 5621yds, Par 68, SSS 67, Course record 64.
Club membership 665.
Visitors must contact in advance. Restricted weekends, bank holidays and competition days.
Societies apply in writing. Weekdays only.
Green Fees £25 per day/round (£35 per day;£30 per round weekends & bank holidays).
Designer George Rochester
Facilities
Location 6m E of A1 via B1341 or B1342

Hotel ★★ 67% Lord Crewe Arms, Front St, BAMBURGH ☎ 01668 214243 24rm(21)

BEDLINGTON Map 12 NZ28

Bedlingtonshire Acorn Bank NE22 6AA ☎ 01670 822087
Meadowland/parkland course with easy walking. Under certain conditions the wind can be a distinct hazard.
18 holes, 6813mtrs, Par 73, SSS 73, Course record 68.
Club membership 960.
Visitors must contact in advance.
Societies must apply in writing.
Green Fees £15 per day (£20 weekends).
Prof Marcus Webb
Designer Frank Pennink
Facilities
Location 1m SW on A1068

Hotel ★★★★ 61% Holiday Inn, Great North Rd, SEATON BURN ☎ 0191 201 9988 150

BELFORD Map 12 NU13

Belford South Rd NE70 7DP
☎ 01668 213433 Fax 01668 213919
An east coast parkland course. Crosswinds affect the 4th but the compensation is spectacular views over Holy Island.
9 holes, 3152yds, Par 72, SSS 70, Course record 72.
Club membership 200.
Visitors no restrictions.
Societies must contact in advance.
Green Fees not confirmed.
Designer Nigel Williams
Facilities
Location Off A1, midway between Alnwick & Berwick on Tweed

Hotel ★★★ 67% Blue Bell Hotel, Market Place, BELFORD ☎ 01668 213543 17

BELLINGHAM Map 12 NY88

Bellingham Boggle Hole NE48 2DT
☎ 01434 220530 (Secretary) Fax 01434 220160
This highly regarded 18-hole golf course is situated between Hadrian's Wall and the Scottish Border. A rolling parkland course with many natural hazards. There is a mixture of testing par threes, long par fives and tricky par fours.
18 holes, 6077yds, Par 70, SSS 70, Course record 68.
Club membership 650.
Visitors advisable to contact in advance as starting sheet in operation.
Societies must contact in advance.
Green Fees £17.50 per day/round (£22.50 weekends & bank holidays).
Designer E Johnson/I Wilson
Facilities
Location N side of village on B6320

Hotel ★★ 69% Riverdale Hall Hotel, BELLINGHAM ☎ 01434 220254 20

BERWICK-UPON-TWEED Map 12 NT95

Berwick-upon-Tweed (Goswick) Goswick TD15 2RW
☎ 01289 387256
Natural seaside links course, with undulating fairways, elevated tees and good greens.
18 holes, 6465yds, Par 72, SSS 71, Course record 69.
Club membership 600.
Visitors must contact in advance for weekends, advisable at other times.
Societies must telephone in advance (apply in writing Apr-Sep).
Green Fees £25 per day; £20 per round (£32/£25 weekends).
Prof Paul Terras

Designer James Braid
Facilities
Location 6m S off A1

Hotel ★★★ 67% Blue Bell Hotel, Market Place, BELFORD ☎ 01668 213543 17

Magdalene Fields Magdalene Fields TD15 1NE
☎ 01289 306384 & 306130 Fax 01289 306384
Seaside course with natural hazards formed by sea bays. All holes open to winds. Testing 8th hole over bay (par 3).
18 holes, 6407yds, Par 72, SSS 71, Course record 65.
Club membership 400.
Visitors must contact in advance for weekend play.
Societies must contact in advance.
Green Fees £47 per day(7 days per week); £16 per round (£18 weekends).
Designer Willie Park
Facilities
Location 0.5m on E side of town centre

Hotel ★★★ 72% Tillmouth Park Hotel, CORNHILL-ON-TWEED ☎ 01890 882255 12 Annexe2

BLYTH Map 12 NZ38

Blyth New Delaval, Newsham NE24 4DB
☎ 01670 367728
Course built over old colliery. Parkland with water hazards.
18 holes, 6456yds, Par 72, SSS 71, Course record 65.
Club membership 820.
Visitors with member only after 3pm & at weekends. Must contact in advance.
Societies apply in writing.
Green Fees £20 per day; £18 per round.
Prof Andrew Brown
Designer Hamilton Stutt
Facilities
Location 6m N of Whitley Bay

Hotel ★★★ 64% Windsor Hotel, South Pde, WHITLEY BAY ☎ 0191 251 8888 63

CRAMLINGTON Map 12 NZ27

Arcot Hall NE23 7QP
☎ 0191 236 2794 Fax 0191 217 0370
A wooded parkland course, reasonably flat.
18 holes, 6380yds, Par 70, SSS 70, Course record 65.
Club membership 660.
Visitors must contact in advance. May not play weekends.
Societies must contact in advance.
Green Fees £26 per day; £21 per round (£30 weekends).
Prof Graham Cant
Designer James Braid
Facilities
Location 2m SW off A1

Hotel ★★★★ 61% Holiday Inn, Great North Rd, SEATON BURN ☎ 0191 201 9988 150

EMBLETON Map 12 NU22

Dunstanburgh Castle NE66 3XQ
☎ 01665 576562 Fax 01665 576562
Rolling links designed by James Braid, adjacent to the beautiful Embleton Bay. Historic Dunstansburgh Castle is at one end of the course and a Nationasl Trust lake and bird sanctuary at the other. Superb views.
18 holes, 6298yds, Par 70, SSS 69, Course record 69.
Club membership 376.
Visitors advisable to contact in advance at weekends and holiday periods.
Societies must contact in advance.
Green Fees £15 per day (£25 per day; £20 per round weekends & bank holidays).
Designer James Braid
Facilities
Location 7m NE of Alnwick off A1

Hotel ★★ 70% Beach House Hotel, Sea Front, SEAHOUSES ☎ 01665 720337 14

GREENHEAD Map 12 NY66

Haltwhistle Banktop CA6 7HL
☎ 016977 47367 & 01434 344000 (sec) Fax 01434 344311
Interesting course with panoramic views of Northumberland National Park. The 515yard Par 5 8th hole is a real test of golf skill, played from the highest point of the course through an undulating fairway to a viciously sloping green. The 188yard Par 3 10th hole, played uphill, is particularly difficult playing into the prevailing west wind.
18 holes, 5532yds, Par 69, SSS 67, Course record 70.
Club membership 300.
Visitors no visitors Sun mornings.
Societies apply in writing to: Hon Secretary, John Gilbertson, Parkhead Farmhouse, Bardon Mill, Northumberland NE47 7JS.
Green Fees £12 per day (£15 weekends).
Facilities
Location N on A69 past Haltwhistle on Gilsland Road ▶

Hotel ★★ 68% Kirby Moor Country House Hotel, Longtown Rd, BRAMPTON
☎ 016977 3893 6rm(5)

HEXHAM Map 12 NY96

Hexham Spital Park NE46 3RZ
☎ 01434 603072 Fax 01434 601865
A very pretty undulating parkland course with interesting natural contours. From parts of the course, particularly the elevated 6th tee, there are the most exquisite views of the valley below. As good a parkland course as any in the North of England.
18 holes, 6000yds, Par 70, SSS 68, Course record 64.
Club membership 700.

Visitors advance booking advisable.
Societies welcome weekdays, contact in advance.
Green Fees £35 per day; £27 per round (£35 per round weekends & bank holidays).
Cards
Prof Martin Forster
Designer G K Cotton
Facilities
& Leisure squash.
Location 1m NW on B6531

Hotel ★★★ 67% Beaumont Hotel, Beaumont St, HEXHAM
☎ 01434 602331 23

Slaley Hall Slaley NE47 OBY
☎ 01434 673350 (hotel) & 673154 (pro) Fax 01434 673152
Measuring 7073yds from the championship tees, this Dave Thomas designed course incorporates forest, parkland and moorland with an abundance of lakes and streams. The challenging par 4 9th (452yds) is played over water through a narrow avenue of towering trees and dense rhododendrons. An official PGA European Tour venue and hosts the COMPAQ European Grand Prix. A second championship standard course, designed by Neil Coles, is due to open during 1999.
18 holes, 6809yds, Par 72, SSS 73, Course record 65.
Club membership 350.

Visitors must contact in advance, times subject to availability. May not play weekends or public holidays. Must provide proof of official handicap Gentlemen max28, Ladies max36.
Societies apply in writing to bookings co-ordinator, small groups 8 or less may book through pro shop.
Green Fees £80 per 36 holes; £50 per 18 holes (Discounts for hotel residents etc).
Cards
Prof Mark Stancer
Designer Dave Thomas
Facilities
& Leisure heated indoor swimming pool, fishing, sauna, solarium, gymnasium.
Location 8m S of Hexham off A68

Tynedale Tyne Green NE46 3HQ ☎ 01434 608154
Flat, easy moorland course. Bounded by river and railway.
9 holes, 5643yds, Par 69, SSS 67, Course record 67.
Club membership 421.

Visitors may not play Sun mornings.
Societies must contact in advance.
Green Fees not confirmed.

Prof Claire Brown
Facilities
Location N side of town

Hotel ★★★ 67% Beaumont Hotel, Beaumont St, HEXHAM ☎ 01434 602331 23

LONGHORSLEY Map 12 NZ19

Linden Hall NE65 8XF
☎ 01670 788050 Fax 01670 788544
Set within the picturesque Linden Hall Estate, with views of the Cheviot Hills and the Northumberland coast, this newly established course features mature woodland and several burns and lakes.
18 holes, 6809yds, Par 72, SSS 73.
Club membership 220.

Visitors must book in advance.
Societies must be of reasonable standard of play, observe dress code & etiquette, preferably have handicap certificate.
Green Fees £22.50 per round (£25 weekends).
Cards
Prof David Curry
Designer Jonathan Gaunt
Facilities
& Leisure hard tennis courts, heated indoor swimming pool, sauna, solarium, gymnasium, ballooning, rallycarting, clay pigeon shooting, cycling, jogging track.
Location From A1 N/S take A697 to Coldstream, approx 4m to Longhorsley, Linden Hall 0.5m past village

Hotel ★★★★ 70% Linden Hall Hotel and Health Spa, LONGHORSLEY ☎ 01670 516611 50

MATFEN Map 12 NZ07

Matfen Hall NE20 0RQ
☎ 01661 886500 Fax 01661 886055
An 18-hole parkland course set in beautiful countryside with many natural and man-made hazards. Also a challenging 9-hole par 3 course and a driving range.
18 holes, 6744yds, Par 72, SSS 72, Course record 67.
Club membership 450.

Visitors contact in advance, restricted on weekends between 8-10am.
Societies telephone for details.
Green Fees £25 per day; £19 per round (£29/£23 weekends).
Prof John Harrison
Facilities
& Leisure 9 hole par3.
Location Just off B6318 Military road 15m W of Newcastle

Hotel ★★ 68% Angel Inn, Main St, CORBRIDGE ☎ 01434 632119 5

MORPETH Map 12 NZ28

Morpeth The Common NE61 2BT
☎ 01670 504942
Parkland course with views of the Cheviots.
18 holes, 6206yds, Par 71, SSS 69, Course record 65.
Club membership 700.

Visitors restricted weekends & bank holidays. Must contact in advance and have a handicap certificate.
Societies apply in writing.
Green Fees £25 per day; £20 per round (£33/£25 weekends & bank holidays).
Prof Martin Jackson
Designer Harry Vardon
Facilities
Location S side of town centre on A197

Hotel ★★★★ 63% Longhirst Hall, Longhirst, MORPETH ☎ 01670 791348 75

NEWBIGGIN-BY-THE-SEA Map 12 NZ38

Newbiggin-by-the-Sea Prospect Place NE64 6DW
☎ 01670 817344 Fax 01670 520236
Seaside-links course.
18 holes, 6452yds, Par 72, SSS 71, Course record 65.
Club membership 570.

Visitors must contact professional on arrival and may not play before 10am.
Societies must apply in writing.
Green Fees not confirmed.
Prof Marcus Webb
Facilities
& Leisure snooker.
Location N side of town

Hotel ★★★★ 63% Longhirst Hall, Longhirst, MORPETH
☎ 01670 791348 75

PONTELAND Map 12 NZ17

Ponteland 53 Bell Villas NE20 9BD ☎ 01661 822689
Open parkland course offering testing golf and good views.
18 holes, 6524yds, Par 72, SSS 71, Course record 66.
Club membership 720.

Visitors with member only Fri, weekends & bank holidays.
Societies welcome Tue & Thu only. Must contact in advance.
Green Fees not confirmed.
Prof Alan Crosby
Facilities
Location 0.5m E on A696

Hotel ★★★ 64% Newcastle Airport Moat House, Woolsington, NEWCASTLE UPON TYNE AIRPORT ☎ 0191 401 9988 100

PRUDHOE Map 12 NZ06

Prudhoe Eastwood Park NE42 5DX
☎ 01661 832466 Fax 01661 830710
Parkland course with natural hazards and easy walking along undulating fairways.
18 holes, 5812yds, Par 69, SSS 68, Course record 60.
Club membership 700.

Visitors must contact in advance. Weekends after 4.30pm
Societies must contact in writing.
Green Fees not confirmed.
Prof John Crawford
Facilities
Location E side of town centre off A695

Hotel ★★ 62% County Hotel, Priestpopple, HEXHAM ☎ 01434 602030 9

ROTHBURY Map 12 NU00

Rothbury Old Race Course NE65 7TR
☎ 01669 620718 & 621271
Very flat parkland course alongside the River Coquet.
9 holes, 5681yds, Par 68, SSS 67, Course record 65.
Club membership 400.

Visitors may play at weekends by arrangement only.
Societies Must contact secretary in advance.
Green Fees £11 per day (£16 weekends).
Designer J Radcliffe
Facilities by prior arrangement
Location S side of town off B6342

Hotel ★★★ 63% White Swan Hotel, Bondgate Within, ALNWICK
☎ 01665 602109 58

SEAHOUSES Map 12 NU23

Seahouses Beadnell Rd NE68 7XT ☎ 01665 720794
Typical links course with many hazards, including the famous 10th, 'Logans Loch', water hole.
18 holes, 5516yds, Par 67, SSS 67, Course record 63.
Club membership 750.

Visitors must contact in advance.
Societies must contact in advance. May not play Sun.
Green Fees £16 per day (£20 weekends). ▶

Facilities
Location S side of village on B1340

Hotel ★★ 73% Olde Ship Hotel, SEAHOUSES 01665 720200 12 Annexe4

Stocksfield — Map 12 NZ06

Stocksfield New Ridley Rd NE43 7RE
01661 843041 Fax 01661 843046
Challenging course: parkland (9 holes), woodland (9 holes). Some elevated greens and water hazards.
18 holes, 5978yds, Par 70, SSS 70, Course record 63.
Club membership 900.
Visitors welcome except Wed am & weekends until 4pm.
Societies must contact in advance.
Green Fees £24 per day; £18 per round (£24 per round weekends & bank holidays).
Designer Pennick
Facilities
Location 2.5m SE off A695

Hotel ★★★ 67% Beaumont Hotel, Beaumont St, HEXHAM 01434 602331 23

Swarland — Map 12 NU10

Swarland Hall Coast View NE65 9JG
01670 787010
Parkland course set in mature woodland. There are seven Par 4 holes in excess of 400 yards.
18 holes, 6628yds, Par 72, SSS 72.
Club membership 400.
Visitors restricted on competition days. Advisable to contact in advance.
Societies apply in advance.
Green Fees £18 per day; £14 per round (£25/£18 weekends & bank holidays).
Cards
Prof David Fletcher/Linzi Hardy
Facilities
Location Approx 1m W of A1

Hotel ★★★★ 70% Linden Hall Hotel and Health Spa, LONGHORSLEY 01670 516611 50

Warkworth — Map 12 NU20

Warkworth The Links NE65 0SW
01665 711596
Seaside links course, with good views and alternative tees for the back nine.
9 holes, 5870yds, Par 70, SSS 68, Course record 66.
Club membership 470.
Visitors welcome except Tue & Sat.
Societies must contact in advance.
Green Fees £12 per day (£20 Sun & bank holidays).
Designer T Morris
Facilities
Location 0.5m E of village off A1068

Hotel ★★★ 63% White Swan Hotel, Bondgate Within, ALNWICK 01665 602109 58

Wooler — Map 12 NT92

Wooler Dod Law, Doddington NE71 6EA
01668 281137
Hilltop, moorland course with spectacular views over the Glendale valley. Nine greens played from 18 tees. A very challenging course when windy with one Par 5 of 580 yards. The course is much under used during the week so is always available.
9 holes, 6358yds, Par 72, SSS 70.
Club membership 300.
Visitors normally no restrictions.
Societies by prior arrangement with secretary.
Green Fees £10 (£15 weekends & bank holidays).
Facilities by prior arrangement
Location At Doddington on B6525 Wooler/Berwick Rd

Hotel ★★ 64% Tankerville Arms Hotel, Cottage Rd, WOOLER 01668 281581 16

NOTTINGHAMSHIRE

Calverton — Map 08 SK64

Ramsdale Park Golf Centre Oxton Rd NG14 6NU
0115 965 5600 Fax 0115 965 4105
The High course is a challenging and comprehensive test for any standard ofgolfer. A relatively flat front nine is followed by an undulating back nine that is renowned as one of the best 9 holes of golf in the county. The Low course comprises contoured and bunkered greens that is ideal for both beginner and established golfer who wants to improve his iron and shot play.
High Course: 18 holes, 6546yds, Par 71, SSS 71, Course record 70.
Low Course: 18 holes, 2844yds.
Club membership 400.
Visitors may book up to 6 days in advance with credit card.
Societies welcome midweek, apply in writing or telephone.
Green Fees Low Course: £7.50 per round; High Course: £14 per round.
Cards
Prof Robert Macey
Designer Hawtree
Facilities
Location 8m NE of Nottingham, off B6386

Hotel ★★★ 63% Saracen's Head, Market Place, SOUTHWELL 01636 812701 27

Springwater Moor Ln NG14 6FZ 0115 965 2129
1998 will see this attracive golf course, set in rolling countryside close to Nottingham, extended to 18 holes. It offers an interesting and challenging game of golf to players of all handicaps, as well as fine views over the Trent Valley.
18 holes, 6224yds, Par 71, SSS 70.
Visitors 5 day advance booking by telephone, booking available all week subject to competitions and Society/Corporate reservations.
Societies apply in writing or telephone for Society Pack.
Green Fees £15 per round (£20 weekends).

Prof Paul Wharmsby
Designer Neil Footitty/Paul Wharmsby
Facilities
& Leisure short game academy.
Location 300yds on the left from the turning to Calverton off A6097

Hotel ★★★ 63% Saracen's Head, Market Place, SOUTHWELL ☎ 01636 812701 27

EAST LEAKE Map 08 SK52

Rushcliffe Stocking Ln LE12 5RL
☎ 01509 852959
Hilly, tree-lined and picturesque parkland course.
18 holes, 6013yds, Par 70, SSS 69, Course record 63.
Club membership 700.
Visitors welcome but may not play Tue and restricted weekends & bank holidays 9.30-11am & 3-4.30pm.
Societies must apply in advance.
Green Fees £22 per day (£25 weekends).
Prof Chris Hall
Facilities
Location 1m N

Hotel ★★★ 66% Yew Lodge, 33 Packington Hill, KEGWORTH
☎ 01509 672518 64

HUCKNALL Map 08 SK54

Leen Valley Golf Centre Wigwam Ln NG15 7TA
☎ 0115 964 2037 Fax 0115 964 2724
An interesting and challenging parkland course, featuring several lakes, the River Leen and the Baker Brook. Suitable for all standards of golfers.
18 holes, 6233yds, Par 72, SSS 70.
Club membership 750.
Visitors tee times can be booked in advance and are advisable for Fri, Sat & Sun.
Societies by arrangement.
Green Fees £8.50 per 18 holes; £4.25 per 9 holes (£9.50/£4.75 weekends).
Cards
Prof Shaun Smith
Designer Tom Hodgetts
Facilities
Location 0.5m from Hucknall Town Centre, follow signs for railway station and turn left into Wigwam Lane

Hotel ★★★ 65% Bestwood Lodge, Bestwood Country park, Arnold, NOTTINGHAM
☎ 0115 920 3011 40

KEYWORTH Map 08 SK63

Stanton on the Wolds Golf Rd, Stanton-on-the-Wolds NG12 5BH ☎ 0115 937 2044 & 937 4885
Parkland course, fairly flat with stream running through four holes.
18 holes, 6437yds, Par 73, SSS 71, Course record 67.
Club membership 705.
Visitors Must contact in advance. Must play with member at weekends and may not play Tue.
Societies must apply in writing.
Green Fees £ 20 per day/round.
Prof Nick Hernon
Designer Tom Williamson
Facilities
Location E side of village

Hotel ★★ 65% Rufford Hotel, 53 Melton Rd, West Bridgford, NOTTINGHAM
☎ 0115 981 4202 34

KIRKBY IN ASHFIELD Map 08 SK55

Notts Derby Rd NG17 7QR
☎ 01623 753225 Fax 01623 753655
Undulating heathland Championship course.
18 holes, 7030yds, Par 72, SSS 74, Course record 64.
Club membership 500.
Visitors must contact in advance & have handicap certificate. With member only weekends & bank holidays.
Societies must apply in advance.
Green Fees £55 per day; £40 per round.
Prof Alasdair Thomas
Designer Willie Park
Facilities
Location 1.5m SE off A611

Hotel ★★★★ 67% Swallow Hotel, Carter Ln East, SOUTH NORMANTON
☎ 01773 812000 160

LONG EATON Map 08 SK43

Trent Lock Golf Centre Lock Ln, Sawley NG10 2FY
☎ 0115 9464398 Fax 01159 461183
Parkland course.
18 holes, 6211yds, Par 73, SSS 70, Course record 73.
Club membership 400.
Visitors no restriction Mon-Fri am but booking system 12pm Fri-closing Sun.
Societies apply in writing or telephone in advance.
Green Fees not confirmed.
Prof M Taylor/E McCausland
Designer E McCausland
Facilities
& Leisure fishing.
Hotel ★★★ 65% Novotel, Bostock Ln, LONG EATON ☎ 0115 946 5111 105

MANSFIELD Map 08 SK56

Sherwood Forest Eakring Rd NG18 3EW
☎ 01623 626689 Fax 01623 420412
As the name suggests, the Forest is the main feature of this natural heathland course with its heather, silver birch and pine trees. The homeward nine holes are particularly testing. The 11th to the 14th are notable par 4 holes on this well-bunkered course designed by the great James Braid.
18 holes, 6698yds, Par 71, SSS 73, Course record 68.
Club membership 750.
Visitors weekdays only by prior arrangement with the Secretary.
Societies by arrangement with the Secretary.
Green Fees on application.
Prof Ken Hall ▶

Designer W S Colt/James Braid
Facilities ⊗ 𝄃 ⛾ ☕ 🍸 ⛹ 🏠 🚗 ✐
& Leisure snooker.
Location E of Mansfield

Hotel ★★ 67% Pine Lodge Hotel, 281-283 Nottingham Rd, MANSFIELD ☎ 01623 22308 20 ⇌ 🛁

MANSFIELD WOODHOUSE Map 08 SK56

Mansfield Woodhouse Leeming Ln North NG19 9EU
☎ 01623 23521
Easy walking on heathland.
9 holes, 2446yds, Par 68, SSS 64.
Club membership 130.
Visitors no restrictions.
Societies must contact by telephone.
Green Fees £3.30 (9 holes); £5 (18 holes).
Prof Leslie Highfield
Designer A Highfield & F Horfman
Facilities ⊗ 𝄃 ⛾ ☕ 🍸 🏠 🏌
Location N side of town centre off A60

Hotel ★★ 67% Pine Lodge Hotel, 281-283 Nottingham Rd, MANSFIELD ☎ 01623 22308 20 ⇌ 🛁

NEWARK-ON-TRENT Map 08 SK75

Newark Coddington NG24 2QX
☎ 01636 626282 Fax 01636 626497
Wooded, parkland course in secluded situation with easy walking.
18 holes, 6421yds, Par 71, SSS 71, Course record 66.
Club membership 600.
Visitors must contact in advance and have handicap certificate. May not play Tue (Ladies Day).
Societies must contact in advance.
Green Fees £27 per day; £22 per round.
Prof P A Lockley
Facilities ⊗ 𝄃 ⛾ ☕ 🍸 ⛹ 🏠 ✐
& Leisure snooker.
Location 4m E on A17

Hotel ★★ 71% Grange Hotel, 73 London Rd, NEWARK ☎ 01636 703399 10 ⇌ 🛁 Annexe5 ⇌ 🛁

NOTTINGHAM Map 08 SK53

Beeston Fields Old Dr, Wollaton Rd, Beeston NG9 3DD
☎ 0115 925 7062 Fax 0115 925 4280
Parkland course with sandy subsoil and wide, tree-lined fairways. The par 3, 14th has elevated tee and small bunker-guarded green.
18 holes, 6402yds, Par 71, SSS 71, Course record 64.
Club membership 800.
Visitors must contact in advance.
Societies must apply in advance.
Green Fees £35 per 36 holes; £25 per round (£30 per round weekends).
Prof Alun Wardle
Designer Tom Williamson
Facilities ⊗ 𝄃 by prior arrangement ⛾ ☕ 🍸 ⛹ 🏠 🏌 ✐
Location 400mtrs SW off A52 Nottingham/Derby road

Hotel B Forte Posthouse Nottingham/Derby, Bostocks Ln, SANDIACRE ☎ 0115 9397800 91 ⇌ 🛁

Bramcote Hills Thoresby Rd, off Derby Rd, Bramcote NG9 3EP ☎ 0115 928 1880
A Pay and Play, 18-hole Par 3 course with challenging greens.
18 holes, 1500yds, Par 54.
Visitors no restrictions.
Societies telephone in advance.
Green Fees not confirmed.
Facilities 🏌
Location Off A52 Derby rd

Hotel ★★ 65% Priory Hotel, Derby Rd, Wollaton Vale, NOTTINGHAM ☎ 0115 922 1691 31 ⇌ 🛁

Bulwell Forest Hucknall Rd, Bulwell NG6 9LQ
☎ 0115 977 0576
Municipal heathland course with many natural hazards. Very tight fairways and subject to wind.
18 holes, 5606yds, Par 68, SSS 67, Course record 62.
Club membership 350.
Visitors restricted weekends. Must contact in advance.
Societies must apply in advance.
Green Fees £16 per day; £10 per round.
Prof Lee Rawlings
Facilities ⊗ 𝄃 by prior arrangement ⛾ ☕ 🍸 ⛹ 🏠 🏌 ✐
& Leisure hard tennis courts, flat green bowls, childrens playground.
Location 4m NW of city centre on A611

Hotel ★★★ 66% Nottingham Moat House, Mansfield Rd, NOTTINGHAM ☎ 0115 935 9988 172 ⇌ 🛁

Chilwell Manor Meadow Ln, Chilwell NG9 5AE
☎ 0115 925 8958 Fax 0115 922 0575
Flat parkland course.
18 holes, 6379yds, Par 70, SSS 70.
Club membership 750.
Visitors with member only weekends. Must contact in advance and have a handicap certificate.
Societies welcome Mon, must apply in advance.
Green Fees not confirmed.
Prof Paul Wilson
Facilities ⊗ 𝄃 ⛾ ☕ 🍸 ⛹ 🏠 ✐
Location 4m SW on A6005

Hotel ★★ 61% Europa Hotel, 20-22 Derby Rd, LONG EATON ☎ 0115 972 8481 13 ⇌ 🛁

Edwalton Municipal Wellin Ln, Edwalton NG12 4AS
☎ 0115 923 4775
Gently sloping, 9-hole parkland course. Also 9-hole Par 3 and large practice ground.
9 holes, 3336yds, Par 72, SSS 72, Course record 71.
Club membership 900.
Visitors booking system in operation.
Societies prior booking necessary.
Green Fees not confirmed.
Prof John Staples
Facilities ⊗ 𝄃 ⛾ ☕ 🍸 ⛹ 🏠 🏌 ✐
Location S of Nottingham, off A606

Hotel ★★ 65% Rufford Hotel, 53 Melton Rd, West Bridgford, NOTTINGHAM
☎ 0115 981 4202 34

Mapperley Central Av, Plains Rd, Mapperley NG3 5RH
☎ 0115 955 6672
Hilly meadowland course but with easy walking.
18 holes, 6283yds, Par 71, SSS 70, Course record 68.
Club membership 650.

Visitors must contact in advance. May not play Tue or Sat.
Societies must telephone in advance.
Green Fees £20 per day (£25 weekends & bank holidays).
Prof Malcolm Allen
Designer John Mason
Facilities
Location 3m NE of city centre off B684

Hotel B Forte Posthouse Nottingham City, St James's St, NOTTINGHAM
☎ 0115 947 0131 130

Nottingham City Lawton Dr, Bulwell NG6 8BL
☎ 0115 927 6916 & 927 2767 Fax 0115 927 6916
A pleasant municipal parkland course on the city outskirts.
18 holes, 6218yds, Par 69, SSS 70, Course record 65.
Club membership 425.

Visitors restricted Sat 7am-3pm.
Societies welcome except weekends.
Green Fees not confirmed.
Prof Cyril Jepson
Designer H Braid
Facilities
Location 4m NW of city centre off A6002

Hotel ★★★ 66% Nottingham Moat House, Mansfield Rd, NOTTINGHAM
☎ 0115 935 9988 172

Wollaton Park Limetree Av, Wollaton Park NG8 1BT
☎ 0115 978 7574 Fax 0115 978 7574
A pleasant, fairly level course set in a park close to the centre of Nottingham, with red and fallow deer herds. The fairways are tree-lined. The 502-yd dog-leg 15th is a notable hole. The stately home - Wollaton Hall - is situated in the park.
18 holes, 6445yds, Par 71, SSS 71, Course record 64.
Club membership 650.

Visitors may not play Wed or competition days.
Societies must apply in advance.
Green Fees £35 per day; £25 per round (£40/£30 weekends).
Prof John Lower
Designer W Williamson
Facilities
Location 2.5m W of city centre off A52

Hotel ★★★ 61% Swans Hotel & Restaurant, 84-90 Radcliffe Rd, West Bridgeford, NOTTINGHAM
☎ 0115 981 4042 30

A comprehensive list of driving ranges is given at the back of this guide. See page 479

Ollerton Map 08 SK66

Rufford Park Golf Centre Rufford Ln, Rufford NG22 9DG
☎ 01623 825253 Fax 01623 825254
Rufford Park is noted for its pictuesque 18 holes with its especially challenging Par 3's. From the unique 173yard Par 3 17th over water to the riverside 596yard 13th, the course offers everything the golfer needs from beginner to professional.
18 holes, 6155yds, Par 70, SSS 69.
Club membership 550.

Visitors are advised to book in advance.
Societies society packages on request, need to be booked in advance.
Green Fees £20 per day; £14 per round (£18 per round weekends).
Cards
Prof John Vaughan/James Thompson
Designer David Hemstock
Facilities
Location S Of Ollerton off A614. Take the 'Rufford Mill' turn

Hotel ★★ 66% Hop Pole Hotel, Main St, OLLERTON
☎ 01623 822573 11rm(10)

Oxton Map 08 SK65

Oakmere Park Oaks Ln NG25 0RH
☎ 0115 965 3545 Fax 0115 965 5628
Set in rolling parkland in the heart of picturesque Robin Hood country. The par 4 (16th) and par 5 (1st) are notable. Thirty-bay floodlit driving range.
Admirals: 18 holes, 6617yds, Par 72, SSS 72.
Commanders: 9 holes, 6573yds, Par 72, SSS 72.
Club membership 450.

Visitors correct golf attire required, please book for weekends.
Societies please apply in writing or telephone.
Green Fees Admirals: £16 per round (£20 weekends). Commanders: £12 per 18 holes (£16 weekends).
Prof Daryl St-John Jones
Designer Frank Pennick
Facilities
Location 1m NW off A6097

Hotel ★★★ 63% Saracen's Head, Market Place, SOUTHWELL ☎ 01636 812701 27

Radcliffe-on-Trent Map 08 SK63

Cotgrave Place Golf & Country Club Main Rd, Stragglethorpe NG12 3HB ☎ 0115 933 3344 & 933 4686
The course has been designed in three nines to play in three separate and self-contained styles. The first nine holes are dotted around a beautiful lake, man-made ponds and a canal. Water comes into play at every hole, but many are hidden from the tee waiting to catch the wayward drive. The second nine are in magnificent parkland with wide, lush fairways and with huge bunkers. The 13th is protected by enourmous tiers.The final nine are set amidst hedgerows and coppices requiring well-placed tee shots.
Lakeside: 9 holes, 3186yds, Par 36.
Parkland: 9 holes, 3117yds, Par 35.
Fox Coverts: 9 holes, 2755yds, Par 33.
Club membership 700.

Visitors must contact in advance.
Societies telephone in advance.
Green Fees not confirmed.
Prof Greg Towne
Facilities
Location Off A52, 6miles from Nottingham

Hotel ★★★ 71% Langar Hall, LANGAR ☎ 01949 860559 11

Radcliffe-on-Trent Dewberry Ln, Cropwell Rd NG12 2JH
☎ 0115 933 3000 Fax 0115 9116991
Fairly flat, parkland course with three good finishing holes: 16th (427 yds) par 4; 17th (180 yds) through spinney, par 3; 18th (331 yds) dog-leg par 4. Excellent views.
18 holes, 6381yds, Par 70, SSS 71, Course record 64.
Club membership 670.
Visitors must contact in advance.
Societies welcome Wed. Must contact in advance.
Green Fees £23 per day/round (£28 weekends).
Prof Robert Ellis
Designer Tom Williamson
Facilities
Location 1m SE off A52

Hotel ★★★ 61% Swans Hotel & Restaurant, 84-90 Radcliffe Rd, West Bridgeford, NOTTINGHAM ☎ 0115 981 4042 30

RETFORD Map 08 SK78

Retford Brecks Rd, Ordsall DN22 7UA
☎ 01777 860682 (Secretary) & 703733 (Pro)
A wooded, parkland course.
18 holes, 6411yds, Par 71, SSS 71, Course record 67.
Club membership 700.
Visitors advisable to contact in advance, with member only at weekends and holidays.
Societies apply in writing or telephone. Not welcome Tue morning or bank holidays, limited availability weekends.
Green Fees £23 per day; £19 per round.
Prof Stuart Betteridge
Designer Tom Williamson
Facilities
Location 1.5m S A620, between Worksop & Gainsborough

Hotel ★★★ 65% West Retford Hotel, 24 North Rd, RETFORD ☎ 01777 706333 Annexe60

RUDDINGTON Map 08 SK53

Ruddington Grange Wilford Rd NG11 6NB
☎ 0115 984 6141
Undulating parkland course with water hazards on 12 holes.
18 holes, 6543yds, Par 72, SSS 72, Course record 69.
Club membership 650.
Visitors a handicap certificate is required, contact in advance if possible. Play may be restricted Sat & Wed mornings.
Societies must contact in advance.
Green Fees £15 per day (£22.50 weekends).
Cards
Prof Robert Simpson
Facilities
Location 5m S of Nottingham, A60 to Ruddington

Hotel ★★★ 61% Swans Hotel & Restaurant, 84-90 Radcliffe Rd, West Bridgeford, NOTTINGHAM ☎ 0115 981 4042 30

SERLBY Map 08 SK68

Serlby Park DN10 6BA
☎ 01777 818268 Fax 01302 536336
Parkland course.
11 holes, 5325yds, Par 66, SSS 66, Course record 63.
Club membership 250.
Visitors must be introduced by and play with member.
Societies apply in writing before 31 Dec for following year.
Green Fees £10 (£11 weekends).
Designer Galway
Facilities
Location E side of village off A638

Hotel ★★★ 66% Charnwood Hotel, Sheffield Rd, BLYTH ☎ 01909 591610 34

SUTTON IN ASHFIELD Map 08 SK45

Coxmoor Coxmoor Rd NG17 5LF
☎ 01623 557359 Fax 01623 557359
Undulating moorland/heathland course with easy walking and excellent views. The clubhouse is modern with a well-equipped games room. The course lies adjacent to Forestry Commission land over which there are several footpaths and extensive views.
18 holes, 6571yds, Par 73, SSS 72, Course record 64.
Club membership 700.
Visitors must play with member weekends & bank holidays. Must contact in advance.
Societies must apply in advance.
Green Fees £28 per 18 holes; £36 per 27 holes; £40 per 36 holes.
Prof David Ridley
Facilities
Location 2m SE off A611. 4m from junct 27 on M1

Hotel ★★★★ 67% Swallow Hotel, Carter Ln East, SOUTH NORMANTON ☎ 01773 812000 160

WORKSOP Map 08 SK57

Bondhay Golf & Country Club Bondhay Ln, Whitwell S80 3EH ☎ 01909 724709 & 723608 Fax 01909 720226
The wind usually plays quite an active role in making this pleasantly undulating course testing. Signatures holes are the 1st which requires a 2nd shot over water into a basin of trees; the 2nd comes back over the same expanse of water and requires a mid to short iron to a long, narrow green; the 18th is a Par 5 with a lake right in lay up distance - the dilemma is whether to lay up short or go for the carry.
Devonshire Course: 18 holes, 6720yds, Par 72, SSS 71, Course record 67.
Family Course: 9 holes, 1118yds, Par 27, Course record 24.
Club membership 400.
Visitors must contact in advance.
Societies must telephone in advance.
Green Fees on application.
Cards

Prof Martin Bell
Designer Donald Steel
Facilities
& Leisure fishing.
Location 5m W of Worksop, off A619

Hotel ★★ 62% Regancy Hotel, Carlton Rd, WORKSOP ☎ 01909 474108 13rm(7)

Kilton Forest Blyth Rd S81 0TL
☎ 01909 485994 & 486563
Slightly undulating, parkland course on the north edge of Sherwood Forest. Includes three ponds.
18 holes, 6424yds, Par 72, SSS 71, Course record 69.
Club membership 350.
Visitors must contact in advance.
Societies must contact in advance.
Green Fees not confirmed.
Prof Peter W Foster
Facilities
Location 1m NE of town centre on B6045

Hotel ★★ 72% Lion Hotel, 112 Bridge St, WORKSOP ☎ 01909 477925 32

Lindrick Lindrick Common S81 8BH
☎ 01909 475282 Fax 01909 488685
Heathland course with some trees and masses of gorse.
18 holes, 6486yds, Par 71, SSS 72, Course record 65.
Club membership 490.
Visitors must contact in advance. Restricted Tue & weekends. Handicap certificate required.
Societies welcome except Tue (am) & weekends by prior arrangement with the Secretary.
Green Fees £45 per day (any day).
Prof Peter Cowen
Facilities
Location 4m NW on A57

Hotel ★★ 72% Lion Hotel, 112 Bridge St, WORKSOP ☎ 01909 477925 32

Worksop Windmill Ln S80 2SQ
☎ 01909 472696 & 477731 Fax 01909 477731
Adjacent to Clumber Park this course has a heathland-type terrain, with gorse, broom, oak and birch trees. Fast, true greens, dry all year round.
18 holes, 6660yds, Par 72, SSS 73.
Club membership 500.
Visitors by arrangement with professional tel: 01909 477732.
Societies must apply in advance.
Green Fees £32 per day; £24 per round (£32 weekends & bank holidays).
Prof J R King
Facilities by prior arrangement by prior arrangement
Location Off A57 Ringroad

Hotel ★★★ 70% Clumber Park Hotel, Clumber Park, WORKSOP ☎ 01623 835333 48

OXFORDSHIRE

ABINGDON Map 04 SU49

Drayton Park Steventon Rd, Drayton Village OX14 2RR
☎ 01235 550607 Fax 01235 525731
Set in the heart of the Oxfordshire countryside, an 18-hole parkland course designed by Hawtree. Five lakes and sand based greens.
18 holes, 5500yds, Par 67, SSS 67.
Club membership 500.
Visitors may phone to book, must have golf shoes, no jeans or tracksuits.
Societies contact in advance.
Green Fees £20 per day; £12 per round (£15 per round weekends & bank holidays).
Prof Dinah Masey
Designer Hawtree
Facilities by prior arrangement
& Leisure 9 hole par 3 course.
Location Between Oxford & Newbury,off A34 at Didcot

Hotel ★★★ 67% The Upper Reaches, Thames St, ABINGDON ☎ 01235 522311 19 Annexe6

BANBURY Map 04 SP44

Rye Hill Milcombe OX15 4RU
☎ 01295 721818 Fax 01295 720911
Constructed in 1993, this well drained course features wide fairways, large undulating greens, water hazards on the 7th, and fine views.
18 holes, 6692yds, Par 71, SSS 72.
Club membership 400.
Visitors no restrictions.
Societies telephone for details of Packages available.
Green Fees £13 (£15 weekends and bank holidays).
Cards
Facilities
& Leisure fishing.
Location Junct 11 M40. A361 towards Chipping Norton, signed 1m out of Bloxham

Hotel ★★★ 67% Banbury House, Oxford Rd, BANBURY ☎ 01295 259361 63

BURFORD Map 04 SP21

Burford Swindon Rd OX18 4JG
☎ 01993 822583
Created out of open-farmland, this parkland course has high quality fairways and greens.
18 holes, 6414yds, Par 71, SSS 71, Course record 64.
Club membership 830.
Visitors must contact in advance. May not play weekends.
Societies apply in writing.
Green Fees not confirmed.
Prof Norman Allen
Designer John H Turner
Facilities
Location 0.5m S off A361

Hotel ★★ 64% Golden Pheasant Hotel, 91 High St, BURFORD 01993 823223 12rm(11)

CHESTERTON Map 04 SP52

Chesterton Golf & Country Club OX6 8TE
01869 242023
Laid out over one-time farmland. Well-bunkered, and water hazards increase the difficulty of the course.
18 holes, 6229yds, Par 71, SSS 70, Course record 68.
Club membership 500.

Visitors must pre-book upto 4 days ahead.
Societies must contact in advance.
Green Fees not confirmed.
Prof J Wilkshire
Designer R Stagg
Facilities
Location 0.5m W off A4095, 1m E of B430 at Weston-on-the-Green

Hotel ★★ 69% Jersey Arms Hotel, MIDDLETON STONEY 01869 343234 & 343505 Fax 01869 343565 6 Annexe10

CHIPPING NORTON Map 04 SP32

Chipping Norton Southcombe OX7 5QH
01608 642383 Fax 01608 645422
Pleasant downland course open to winds.
18 holes, 6241yds, Par 71, SSS 70, Course record 62.
Club membership 900.

Visitors with member only at weekends & bank holidays.
Societies telephone in advance.
Green Fees not confirmed.
Prof Derek Craik
Facilities
Location 1.5m E on A44

Hotel ★★ 64% The White Hart Hotel, 16 High St, CHIPPING NORTON 01608 642572 14 Annexe5

Lyneham Lyneham OX7 6QQ
01993 831841 Fax 01993 831775
Lyneham was designed to use the natural features. It is set in 170 acres on the fringe of the Costwolds and bleds superbly with its surroundings. Lakes and streams enhance the challenge of the course with water coming into play on 8 of the 18 holes. All greens are sand based, built to USGA specification.
18 holes, 6669yds, Par 72, SSS 72.
Club membership 680.

Visitors must contact in advance.
Societies apply in advance.
Green Fees £22 per day; £15 per round (£29/£22 weekends).
Prof Richard Jeffries
Designer D G Carpenter
Facilities
Location Off A361, between Burford/Chipping Norton

Hotel ★★ 65% Shaven Crown Hotel, SHIPTON-UNDER-WYCHWOOD 01993 830330 9rm(8)

DIDCOT Map 04 SU59

Hadden Hill Wallingford Rd OX11 9BJ
01235 510410 Fax 01235 510410
A challenging course on undulating terrain with excellent drainage so visitors can be sure of playing no matter what the weather conditions have been. Two loops of nine holes.
18 holes, 6563yds, Par 71, SSS 71, Course record 65.
Club membership 400.

Visitors telephone to book tee times.
Societies telephone to arrange times & dates & receive booking form.
Green Fees £12.50 per 18 holes; £7.50 per 9 holes (£17/£9 weekends).
Prof Dean Halford/Adrian Waters
Designer Michael V Morley
Facilities
Location On A4130 1m E of Didcot

Hotel ★★★ 68% Abingdon Four Pillars Hotel, Marcham Rd, ABINGDON 01235 553456 63

FARINGDON Map 04 SU29

Carswell Carswell Home Farm, Carswell SN7 8PU
01367 870422 Fax 01367 870592
An attractive course set in undulating wooded countryside close to Faringdon. Mature trees, five lakes and well placed bunkers add interest to the course. Floodlit driving range.
18 holes, 6133yds, Par 72, SSS 70.

Visitors book in advance to avoid dissapointment.
Societies at weekends only telephone to check availability, deposit required,
Green Fees £13 per round (£18 weekends & bank holidays).
Prof Geoff Robbins
Facilities
Location Just off the A420 between Oxford and Swindon

Hotel ★★★ 72% Sudbury House Hotel & Conference Centre, London St, FARINGDON 01367 241272 49

FRILFORD Map 04 SU49

Frilford Heath OX13 5NW
01865 390864 Fax 01865 390823
54 holes in three distinctive layouts of significantly differing character. The Green course is a fully mature heathland course of some 6000 yards. The Red course is of championship length at 6800 yards with a parkland flavour and a marked degree of challenge. The Blue course is of modern design, opened in 1994 at 6728 yards, it incorporates water hazards and large shallow sand traps.
Red Course: 18 holes, 6884yds, Par 73, SSS 73, Course record 68.
Green Course: 18 holes, 6006yds, Par 69, SSS 69, Course record 63.
Blue Course: 18 holes, 6728yds, Par 72, SSS 72, Course record 68.
Club membership 1300.

Visitors contact in advance. Handicap certificates required.
Societies apply in advance.
Green Fees £45 per day (£60 weekends).

Cards
Prof Derek Craik
Designer J Taylor/D Cotton/S Gidman
Facilities
Location 3m W of Abingdon off A338 Oxford-Wantage road

Hotel ★★★ 68% Abingdon Four Pillars Hotel, Marcham Rd, ABINGDON
☎ 01235 553456 63

HENLEY-ON-THAMES Map 04 SU78

Aspect Park Remenham Hill RG9 3EH
☎ 01491 577562 & 578306
Parkland course.
18 holes, 6643yds, Par 72, SSS 72.
Club membership 500.
Visitors must contact in advance, suitable golf attire required on course, no jeans in the clubhouse.
Societies must contact in advance.
Green Fees not confirmed.
Prof Terry Notley
Designer Tim Winsland
Facilities
Hotel ★★★ 70% Red Lion Hotel, Hart St, HENLEY-ON-THAMES
☎ 01491 572161 26rm(23)

Badgemore Park RG9 4NR
☎ 01491 573667 Fax 01491 576899
Mature parkland course with easy walking. The 13th is a very difficult par 3 hole played over a valley to a narrow green and accuracy off the tee is essential.
18 holes, 6112yds, Par 69, SSS 69, Course record 65.
Club membership 600.
Visitors contact professional shop on 01491 574175. Tuesday morning Ladies only, bookings to be made for all other times.
Societies contact General Manager to book.
Green Fees £17 (£25 weekends).
Cards
Prof Jonathon Dunn
Designer Robert Sandow
Facilities
Location 1m W

Hotel ★★★ 70% Red Lion Hotel, Hart St, HENLEY-ON-THAMES
☎ 01491 572161 26rm(23)

Henley Harpsden RG9 4HG
☎ 01491 575742 Fax 01491 412179
Undulating parkland course. 6th hole, blind (par 4), with steep hill.
18 holes, 6329yds, Par 70, SSS 70, Course record 65.
Club membership 800.
Visitors must contact in advance. Weekend only with a member.
Societies Wed & Thu, apply in writing.
Green Fees £30 per day.
Prof Mark Howell
Designer James Braid
Facilities
Location 1.25m S off A4155

Hotel ★★★ 70% Red Lion Hotel, Hart St, HENLEY-ON-THAMES
☎ 01491 572161 26rm(23)

HORTON-CUM-STUDLEY Map 04 SP51

Studley Wood The Straight Mile OX33 1BF
☎ 01865 351122 & 351144 Fax 01865 351166
Woodland course set in a former deer park with five lakes and specimen oak trees providing challenging natural hazards on almost all the holes.
18 holes, 6811yds, Par 73, SSS 73, Course record 65.
Club membership 700.
Visitors must play to handicap standard, tee times booked up to 4 days in advance.
Societies contact secretary for details.
Green Fees £32 per day; £21 per 18 holes (£45/£30 weekends & bank holidays).
Cards
Prof Tony Williams
Designer Simon Gidman
Facilities
Location 4m from Oxford follow signs for Horton-cum-Studley from Headington rdbt on Oxford ringroad

Hotel ★★★ 77% Studley Priory Hotel, HORTON-CUM-STUDLEY
☎ 01865 351203 351254
Fax 01865 351613 19

MILTON COMMON Map 04 SP60

The Oxfordshire Rycote Ln OX9 2PU
☎ 01844 278300 Fax 01844 278003
Designed by Rees Jones, The Oxfordshire is considered to be one of the most exciting courses in the country. With four man-made lakes and 135 bunkers, it is a magnificent test of shot-making where almost every hole deserves special mention. Unfortunately it is only open to members and their guests.
18 holes, 6856yds, Par 72, SSS 75, Course record 65.
Club membership 750.
Visitors members guests only.
Green Fees on application.
Cards
Prof Ian Mosey
Designer Rees Jones
Facilities
Location 1.5m from junct 7, M40 on A329

Hotel ★★★ 75% Spread Eagle Hotel, Cornmarket, THAME
☎ 01844 213661 33

NUFFIELD Map 04 SU68

Huntercombe RG9 5SL
☎ 01491 641207 Fax 01491 642060
This heathland/woodland course overlooks the Oxfordshire plain and has many attractive and interesting fairways and greens. Walking is easy after the 3rd which is a notable hole. The course is subject to wind and grass pot bunkers are interesting hazards.
18 holes, 6301yds, Par 70, SSS 70, Course record 63.
Club membership 800. ▶

Visitors must contact in advance and have a handicap certificate.
Societies must contact in advance.
Green Fees not confirmed.
Prof John B Draycott
Designer Willy Park
Facilities
Location N off A423

Hotel ★★★ 65% Shillingford Bridge Hotel, Shillingford, WALLINGFORD
01865 858567 34 Annexe8

OXFORD Map 04 SP50

North Oxford Banbury Rd OX2 8EZ
01865 554924 Fax 01865 515921
Gently undulating parkland course.
18 holes, 5736yds, Par 67, SSS 67, Course record 62.
Club membership 700.
Visitors at weekends & bank holidays may only play after 4pm.
Societies must contact in advance.
Green Fees £25 per day; £18 per round.
Cards
Prof Robert Harris
Facilities
& Leisure putting green.
Location 3m N of city centre on A423

Hotel ★★★ 66% Oxford Moat House, Godstow Rd, Wolvercote Roundabout, OXFORD
01865 489988 155

Southfield Hill Top Rd OX4 1PF
01865 242158 Fax 01865 242158
Home of the City, University and Ladies Clubs, and well-known to graduates throughout the world. A challenging course, in varied parkland setting, providing a real test for players.
18 holes, 6328yds, Par 70, SSS 70, Course record 61.
Club membership 850.
Visitors with member only at weekends.
Societies must apply in writing.
Green Fees £24 per day; £18 per round.
Cards
Prof Tony Rees
Designer H S Colt
Facilities
Location 1.5m SE of city centre off B480

Hotel ★★★ 64% Eastgate Hotel, The High, Merton St, OXFORD
01865 248244 43

SHRIVENHAM Map 04 SU28

Shrivenham Park Penny Hooks SN6 8EX
01793 783853 Fax 01793 782999
Parkland course with easy walking. The par 5, 17th is a difficult dog-leg.
18 holes, 5713yds, Par 69, SSS 69, Course record 64.
Club membership 450.
Visitors phone in advance.
Societies phone for details.
Green Fees £14 per round (£16 weekends & bank holidays).
Cards
Prof Barry Randall
Facilities
Location 0.5m NE of town centre

Hotel ★★★ 63% The Regal Hotel, Oxford Rd, Stratton St Margaret, SWINDON
01793 831333 91

TADMARTON Map 04 SP33

Tadmarton Heath OX15 5HL
01608 737278 Fax 01608 730548
A mixture of heath and sandy land, the course, which is open to strong winds, incorporates the site of an old Roman encampment. The clubhouse is an old farm building with a 'holy well' from which the greens are watered. The 7th is a testing hole over water.
18 holes, 5917yds, Par 69, SSS 69, Course record 63.
Club membership 600.
Visitors weekday by appointment, with member only at weekends.
Societies by arrangement with club office.
Green Fees Summer: £28 per round; Winter: £18 per round.
Prof Tom Jones
Designer Col Hutchinson
Facilities
& Leisure fishing.
Location 1m SW of Lower Tadmarton off B4035, 4m from Banbury

Hotel ★★★ 67% Banbury House, Oxford Rd, BANBURY 01295 259361 63

WATERSTOCK Map 04 SP60

Waterstock Thame Rd OX33 1HT
01844 338093 Fax 01844 338036
A 6,500yard course designed by Donald Steel with USGA greens and tees fully computer irrigated. Four Par 3's facing North, South, East and West. A brook and hidden lake affect six holes, with doglegs being 4th and 10th holes. Five Par 5's on the course, making it a challenge for players of all standards.
18 holes, 6535yds, Par 73, SSS 71, Course record 70.
Club membership 500.
Visitors no restrictions.
Societies apply in writing or telephone.
Green Fees £14 per 18 holes; £7.50 per 9 holes (£17/£9.50 weekends & bank holidays).
Cards
Prof Julian Goodman
Designer Donald Steel
Facilities
& Leisure fishing, archery, clay pigeon shooting.
Location On junc 8 of M40

Hotel ★★★ 75% Spread Eagle Hotel, Cornmarket, THAME 01844 213661 33

RUTLAND

GREAT CASTERTON Map 08 TF00

Rutland County PE9 4AQ
☎ 01780 460330 Fax 01780 460437
Inland links-style course with gently rolling fairways, large tees and greens. Playable all year round due to good drainage.
18 holes, 6401yds, Par 71, SSS 71.
Club membership 530.

Visitors must book in advance at the shop, tel 01780 460239.
Societies contact office by phone, must be booked in advance.
Green Fees £30 per day; £20 per 18 holes (£35/£30 weekends).
Cards
Prof James Darroch
Designer Cameron Sinclair
Facilities
Location 2m N of Stamford on A1

Hotel ★★★ 65% Garden House Hotel, St Martin's, STAMFORD ☎ 01780 763359 20

GREETHAM Map 08 SK91

Greetham Valley Wood Ln LE15 7NP
☎ 01780 460004 Fax 01780 460623
Set in 200 acres, including mature woodland and water hazards, Greetham Valley was opened in spring 1992. The complex comprises 27 holes providing 3 x 18 combinations, a clubhouse, 9-hole Par 3 and a 21-bay floodlit driving range. A further 9 holes due to open during 1999.
A + B: 18 holes, 6351yds, Par 71, SSS 71, Course record 64.
B + C: 18 holes, 5879yds, Par 68, SSS 68.
C + A: 18 holes, 5890yds, Par 69, SSS 68.
Club membership 850.

Visitors must contact in advance.
Societies must contact in advance.
Green Fees £26 per day; £22 per round (£30/£25 weekends).
Cards
Prof John Pengelly
Designer F E Hinch
Facilities
& Leisure bowls green.
Location Off B668 in Greetham

Hotel ★★★ 72% Barnsdale Lodge, The Avenue, Rutland Water, OAKHAM ☎ 01572 724678 29

SHROPSHIRE

BRIDGNORTH Map 07 SO79

Bridgnorth Stanley Ln WV16 4SF
☎ 01746 763315 Fax 01746 761381
A pleasant course laid-out on parkland on the bank of the River Severn.
18 holes, 6673yds, Par 73, SSS 73, Course record 65.
Club membership 725.

Visitors must contact in advance but may not play on Wed. Restricted weekends.
Societies must contact in writing.
Green Fees £30 per 36 holes; £18 per 18 holes (£36/£28 weekends & bank holidays).
Prof Paul Hinton
Facilities
& Leisure fishing.
Location 1m N off B4373, 0.5m from town centre

Hotel ★★ 61% Falcon Hotel, Saint John St, Lowtown, BRIDGNORTH ☎ 01746 763134 15rm(5 7)

CHURCH STRETTON Map 07 SO49

Church Stretton Trevor Hill SY6 6JH ☎ 01694 722281
Hillside course designed by James Braid on the lower slopes of the Long Mynd.
18 holes, 5020yds, Par 66, SSS 65, Course record 63.
Club membership 400.

Visitors Tee reserved for members Sat 9-10.30 & 1-2.30, Sun prior to 10.30 & 1-2.30.
Societies must contact in advance.
Green Fees £12 (£18 weekends & bank holidays).
Prof P Seal (wknds only)
Designer James Braid
Facilities
Location W of the town. From Cardington Valley drive up Trevor Hill, a steep, winding road

Hotel ★★ 72% Mynd House Hotel, Little Stretton, CHURCH STRETTON ☎ 01694 722212 7

CLEOBURY MORTIMER

Cleobury Mortimer Wyre Common DY14 8HQ
☎ 01299 271112 Fax 01299 271628
Well designed 27-hole parkland course set in undulating countryside with fine views from all holes, and offering an interesting challenge to golfers of all abilities.
Foxes Run: 9 holes, 2942yds, Par 34, SSS 34.
Badgers Sett: 9 holes, 3271yds, Par 36, SSS 36.
Deer Park: 9 holes, 3167yds, Par 35, SSS 35.
Club membership 650.

Visitors advisable to book in advance, handicap certificate may be required at weekends.
Societies write or telephone in advance.
Green Fees £17 per 18 holes, £8 per 9 holes (£20/£10 weekends & bank holidays.
Cards
Prof Graham Farr
Facilities
& Leisure fishing.
Location 10m W of Kidderminster on A4117 1m N of Cleobury Mortimer, off B4201

Hotel ★★ 73% Redfern Hotel, CLEOBURY MORTIMER ☎ 01299 270395 5 Annexe6

HIGHLEY Map 07 SO78

Severn Meadows ***WV16 6HZ*** ☎ 01746 862212
Picturesque course set alongside the River Severn and providing a tight test of golf with much of the course bordered by mature trees.
9 holes, 5258yds, Par 68, SSS 67.
Club membership 170.
Visitors booking advisable for weekends.
Societies advance booking necessary.
Green Fees not confirmed.
Facilities
Hotel ★★★★ 66% Mill Hotel & Restaurant, ALVELEY ☎ 01746 780437 21

LILLESHALL Map 07 SJ71

Lilleshall Hall TF10 9AS ☎ 01952 603840
Heavily-wooded parkland course. Easy walking.
18 holes, 5906yds, Par 68, SSS 68.
Club membership 650.
Visitors must contact in advance and play with member at weekends.
Societies must apply in writing by Dec for the following year.
Green Fees £20 weekdays.
Prof Nigel Bramall
Designer H S Colt
Facilities
Location 3m SE

Hotel ★★ 67% White House Hotel, Wellington Rd, Muxton, TELFORD
☎ 01952 604276 & 603603
Fax 01952 670336 30

LUDLOW Map 07 SO57

Ludlow Bromfield SY8 2BT ☎ 01584 856285
A long-established heathland course in the middle of the racecourse. Very flat, quick drying, with broom and gorse-lined fairways.
18 holes, 6277yds, Par 70, SSS 70, Course record 65.
Club membership 700.
Visitors advisable to contact in advance.
Societies apply in advance.
Green Fees £18 per day (£24 weekends & bank holidays).
Prof Russell Price
Facilities
Location 1m N of Ludlow, off A49

Hotel ★★★ 70% The Feathers at Ludlow, Bull Ring, LUDLOW ☎ 01584 875261 39

MARKET DRAYTON Map 07 SJ63

Market Drayton Sutton TF9 2HX
☎ 01630 652266 Fax 01630 652266
Parkland course in quiet, picturesque surroundings providing a good test of golf. Bungalow on course is made available for golfing holidays.
18 holes, 6290yds, Par 71, SSS 71, Course record 69.
Club membership 550.
Visitors may not play on Sun; must play with member on Sat. Must contact in advance.
Societies welcome Mon,Wed,Thu & Fri, must contact in advance.
Green Fees £44 per day; £33 per 27 holes; £22 per 18 holes.
Prof Russell Clewes
Facilities
Location 1m SW

Hotel ★★★ 70% Goldstone Hall, Goldstone, MARKET DRAYTON
☎ 01630 661202 & 661487
Fax 01630 661585 8

MEOLE BRACE Map 07 SJ41

Meole Brace SY2 6QQ ☎ 01743 364050
Pleasant municipal course.
9 holes, 5830yds, Par 68, SSS 68, Course record 66.
Club membership 300.
Visitors may not play Wed and must book in advance for weekends & bank holidays.
Societies must contact Mr R Wootton, Shrewsbury & Atcham Borough Council on 01743 231456.
Green Fees not confirmed.
Prof Ian Doran
Facilities
Location NE side of village off A49

Hotel ★★★ 63% The Lion, Wyle Cop, SHREWSBURY
☎ 01743 353107 59

OSWESTRY Map 07 SJ22

Mile End Mile End, Old Shrewsbury Rd SY11 4JE
☎ 01691 671246 Fax 01691 670580
A gently undulating parkland-type course boasting challenging holes for all standards of golfing ability. Longest hole is par 5 14th at 540yds. A number of water features need to be negotiated including two large ponds on the 3rd and 17th. The course is set in 140 acres, ensuring all holes are sufficiently isolated.
18 holes, 6194yds, Par 71, SSS 69, Course record 69.
Club membership 550.
Visitors welcome at all times please telephone in advance to check availability.
Societies must contact in advance, information available.
Green Fees £20 per day; £14 per round (£25/£18 weekends & bank holidays).
Prof Scott Carpenter
Designer Price/Gough
Facilities
Location 1m SE of Oswestry, just off A5

Hotel ★★★ 70% Wynnstay Hotel, Church St, OSWESTRY ☎ 01691 655261 27

Oswestry Aston Park SY11 4JJ
☎ 01691 610535 Fax 01691 610535
Parkland course laid-out on undulating ground.
18 holes, 6024yds, Par 70, SSS 69, Course record 62.
Club membership 960.
Visitors must contact in advance. Must have a handicap certificate or play with member.
Societies must contact in advance.
Green Fees £20 per day (£28 weekends & bank holidays).
Prof David Skelton
Designer James Braid

Facilities ⊗ ⅢI ℡ ☕ ⅀ ⚲ ⌂ ✓
Location 2m SE on A5

Hotel ★★★ 70% Wynnstay Hotel, Church St, OSWESTRY ☎ 01691 655261 27 ⇌ ↱

Pant Map 07 SJ22

Llanymynech SY10 8LB ☎ 01691 830983
Upland course on the site of an early Iron Age/Roman hillfort with far-reaching views. 15 holes in Wales 3 holes in England, drive off in Wales putt out in England.
18 holes, 6114yds, Par 70, SSS 69, Course record 65.
Club membership 700.

Visitors must contact in advance, some weekends restricted.
Societies must contact Secretary.
Green Fees not confirmed.
Prof Andrew P Griffiths
Facilities ⊗ ⅢI ℡ ☕ ⅀ ⚲ ⌂ ✓
Location 6m S of Oswestry on A483. Turn at Cross Guns Inn

Hotel ★★★ 70% Wynnstay Hotel, Church St, OSWESTRY ☎ 01691 655261 27 ⇌ ↱

Shifnal Map 07 SJ70

Shifnal Decker Hill TF11 8QL
☎ 01952 460330 Fax 01952 460330
Well-wooded parkland course. Walking is easy and an attractive country mansion serves as the clubhouse.
18 holes, 6468yds, Par 71, SSS 71, Course record 65.
Club membership 600.

Visitors must contact in advance, may not play at weekends.
Societies must contact in advance.
Green Fees £30 per day; £22 per round.
Prof Justin Flanagan
Designer Pennick
Facilities ⊗ ⅢI ℡ ☕ ⅀ ⚲ ⌂ ✓
Location 1m N of Shifnal, off B4379

Hotel ★★★★ 60% Park House Hotel, Park St, SHIFNAL ☎ 01952 460128 38 ⇌ ↱ Annexe16 ⇌ ↱

Shrewsbury Map 07 SJ41

Arscott Arscott, Pontesbury SY5 0XP
☎ 01743 860114 Fax 01743 860114
At 365feet above sea level, the views from Arscott Golf Club of the hills of south Shropshire and Wales are superb. Arscott is a new course, set in parkland with water features and holes demanding all sorts of club choice. A challenge to all golfers both high and low handicap.
18 holes, 6178yds, Par 70, SSS 69, Course record 68.
Club membership 550.

Visitors most times available by prior arrangement.
Societies apply in writing for tee reservation.
Green Fees £18 per day/round (£21 weekends).
Prof Ian Doran
Designer M Hamer
Facilities ⊗ ⅢI ℡ ☕ ⅀ ⚲ ⌂ ✓
& Leisure fishing.
Location Off A488, S of Shrewsbury 3m from A5

Hotel ★★★ 63% The Lion, Wyle Cop, SHREWSBURY ☎ 01743 353107 59 ⇌ ↱

Shrewsbury Condover SY5 7BL
☎ 01743 872976 Fax 01743 874647
Parkland course. First nine flat, second undulating with good views of the Long Mynd Range. Several holes with water features. Fast putting surfaces.
18 holes, 6300yds, Par 70, SSS 70.
Club membership 872.

Visitors must contact in advance and have a handicap certificate.
Societies must contact in writing.
Green Fees £23 per day; £19 per round (£23 weekends & bank holidays).
Prof Peter Seal
Facilities ⊗ ⅢI ℡ ☕ ⅀ ⚲ ⌂ ✓
Location 4m S off A49

Hotel ★★★ 63% Prince Rupert Hotel, Butcher Row, SHREWSBURY ☎ 01743 499955 65 ⇌ ↱

Telford Map 07 SJ60

County Hotel Telford Golf & Country Club Great Hay Dr, Sutton Hill TF7 4DT
☎ 01952 429977 Fax 01952 586602
Rolling parkland course with easy walking. Five lakes and large sand traps are hazards to the fine greens.
18 holes, 6761yds, Par 72, SSS 72, Course record 66.
Club membership 450.

Visitors must contact in advance, be a competent golfer and abide by dress regulations.
Societies must book in advance 01952 429977
Green Fees £35 per day; £25 per round (£30 per round weekends).
Cards
Prof Ian Doran
Designer Allis/Dromas
Facilities ⊗ ⅢI ℡ ☕ ⅀ ⚲ ⌂ ✓
& Leisure heated indoor swimming pool, squash, sauna, solarium, gymnasium, 6 hole par 3 course.
Location 4m S of town centre off A442

Hotel ★★★ 67% County Hotel Telford Golf & Country Club, Great Hay Dr, Sutton Hill, TELFORD ☎ 01952 429977 86 ⇌ ↱

The Shropshire Muxton Ln, Muxton TF2 8PQ
☎ 01952 677800 Fax 01952 677622
Designed by Martin Hawtree this 27 hole course comprises 3 loops of 9. Each course has an abundance of lakes and water hazards making club selection a vital part of the round. Championship tees are available by pre-arrangement for the low handicap player.
Blue/Silver: 18 holes, 6589yds, Par 71, SSS 71.
Silver/Gold: 18 holes, 6637yds, Par 72, SSS 72.
Blue/Gold: 18 holes, 6620yds, Par 71, SSS 71.
Club membership 400.

Visitors recommended to book in advance.
Societies must book in advance.
Green Fees £15 per 18 holes; £9 per 9 holes (£20/£11 weekends).
Cards
Prof Daniel Bateman
Designer Martin Hawtree

Facilities
& Leisure 12 hole par 3 course.
Location From M54/A5 take B5060 towards Donnington. Take 3rd exit at Granville rdbt and continue

Hotel ★★★ 69% Holiday Inn, St Quentin Gate, TELFORD ☎ 01952 292500 100

WELLINGTON Map 07 SJ61

Wrekin Ercall Woods, Golf Links Ln TF6 5BX
☎ 01952 244032 Fax 01952 252906
Downland course with some hard walking but rewarding views.
18 holes, 5699yds, Par 67, SSS 66, Course record 64.
Club membership 681.

Visitors must contact in advance. Limited weekends & bank holidays.
Societies must apply in writing.
Green Fees £20 per round (£28 weekends & bank holidays).
Prof K Housden
Facilities
Location 1.25m S off B5061

Hotel ★★★ 67% Buckatree Hall Hotel, The Wrekin, Wellington, TELFORD
☎ 01952 641821 60

WESTON-UNDER-REDCASTLE Map 07 SJ52

Hawkstone Park Hotel SY4 5UY
☎ 01939 200611 Fax 01939 200335
The Hawkstone Course plays through the English Heritage designated Grade I landscape of the historic park and follies providing a beautiful, tranquil yet dramatic back drop to a round of golf. The Windmill Course, re-designed and opened in 1995, utilises many American style features and extensive water hazards and is a challenging alternative.
Hawkstone Course: 18 holes, 6491yds, Par 72, SSS 72.
Windmill Course: 18 holes, 6476yds, Par 72, SSS 72.
Academy Course: 6 holes, 741yds, Par 18.
Club membership 750.
Visitors must book and pay in advance.
Societies must contact in advance by telephone.
Green Fees £28 per round (£23.50/£36 weekends).
Cards
Prof Paul Brown & Paul Wesseling
Designer B Huggett
Facilities
Location N side of village 0.75m E of A49

WHITCHURCH Map 07 SJ54

Hill Valley Terrick Rd SY13 4JZ
☎ 01948 663584 & 667788 Fax 01948 665927
Two testing parkland courses ideally suited to the club and scratch golfer alike. The West Course, cleverly designed by Peter Alliss and Dave Thomas, has fairways that thread their way through 160 acres of trees, lakes and streams to American-style greens trapped by sand and water. Shorter East Course with smaller greens requiring accurate approach shots.
West Course: 18 holes, 6240yds, Par 73, SSS 70, Course record 64.
East Course: 18 holes, 4973yds, Par 66, SSS 65.
Club membership 600.
Visitors must contact in advance, deposit required
Societies must contact in advance; a deposit will be required.
Green Fees West: £18 (£21 weekends); East £8 (£11 weekends).
Cards
Prof A R Minshall
Designer Peter Alliss/Dave Thomas
Facilities
& Leisure hard tennis courts, sauna, solarium, gymnasium.
Location 1m N. Follow signs from Bypass

Hotel ★★ 62% Redbrook Hunting Lodge Hotel, Wrexham Rd, REDBROOK MAELOR
☎ 01948 780204 13

WORFIELD Map 07 SO79

Worfield Roughton WV15 5HE
☎ 01746 716372 Fax 01746 716302
Opened in 1991, this undulating course with good-sized greens, well placed bunkers and 2 lakes, rated highly in a golf magazine survey.

Entries with a shaded background identify courses that are considered to be particularly interesting

Call the AA Hotel Booking Service on 0990 050505 to book at AA recognised hotels and B & Bs in the UK and Ireland, or through our Internet site: http://www.theaa.co.uk/hotels

18 holes, 6801yds, Par 73, SSS 73, Course record 68.
Club membership 400.
Visitors must contact in advance, weekends only after 12am (not Sat).
Societies contact in advance.
Green Fees £22 per day; £16 per round (£25 per round weekends).
Cards
Prof Steve Russell
Designer T Williams
Facilities
Location 3m W of Bridgenorth, off A454

Hotel ★★★ 78% Old Vicarage Hotel, WORFIELD
☎ 01746 716497 10 Annexe4

SOMERSET

BACKWELL Map 03 ST46

Tall Pines Cooks Bridle Path, Downside BS19 3DJ
☎ 01275 472076 Fax 01275 474869
Parkland course with views over the Bristol Channel.
18 holes, 6049yds, Par 70, SSS 69.
Club membership 500.
Visitors must book in advance at weekends.
Societies prior arrangement by telephone for details.
Green Fees £14 per round (£16 weekends).
Prof Alex Murray
Designer T Murray
Facilities
Location Adjacent to Bristol Airport, 1m off A38

Hotel ★★★ 65% Walton Park Hotel, Wellington Ter, CLEVEDON ☎ 01275 874253 40

BATH Map 03 ST76

Bath Sham Castle, North Rd BA2 6JG
☎ 01225 463834 Fax 01225 331027
Considered to be one of the finest courses in the west, this is the site of Bath's oldest golf club. An interesting course situated on high ground overlooking the city and with splendid views over the surrounding countryside. The rocky ground supports good quality turf and there are many good holes. The 17th is a dog-leg right past, or over the corner of an out-of-bounds wall, and thence on to an undulating green.
18 holes, 6438yds, Par 71, SSS 71, Course record 66.
Club membership 750.
Visitors advisable to contact in advance. Handicap certificates required.
Societies Wed & Fri by prior arrangement.
Green Fees £30 per day; £25 per round (£35/£30 weekends & bank holidays).
Prof Peter J Hancox
Designer Colt & others
Facilities
Location 1.5m SE city centre off A36

Hotel ★★★ 68% The Francis, Queen Square, BATH ☎ 01225 424257 94

Entry Hill BA2 5NA ☎ 01225 834248
9 holes, 2065yds, Par 33, SSS 30.
Club membership 650.
Visitors advisable to book in advance, must wear golf shoes or training shoes.
Societies bookings required in advance.
Green Fees £18 per 18 holes; £5 per 9 hole (£9.25/£6 weekends & bank holidays before 2pm).
Prof Tim Tapley
Facilities
Location Off A367

Lansdown Lansdown BA1 9BT
☎ 01225 422138 Fax 01225 339252
A flat parkland course situated 800 feet above sea level, providing a challenge to both low and high handicap golfers.
18 holes, 6316yds, Par 71, SSS 70, Course record 65.
Club membership 700.
Visitors must contact in advance to ascertain availability and have a handicap certificate.
Societies apply in writing or telephone in advance.
Green Fees £18 per day.
Cards
Prof Terry Mercer
Designer C A Whitcombe
Facilities
Location 6m SW of exit 18 of M4

Hotel ★★★ 64% Pratt's Hotel, South Pde, BATH
☎ 01225 460441 46

BRIDGWATER Map 03 ST23

Cannington Cannington College, Cannington TA5 2LS
☎ 01278 652394
Nine hole golf course of 'links-like' appearance, designed by Martin Hawtree of Oxford. The 4th hole is a challenging 464yard Par 4, slightly up hill and into the prevailing wind.
9 holes, 2929yds, Par 34, SSS 34.
Club membership 200.
Visitors pay & play anytime ex Wed evening.
Societies apply in writing.
Green Fees £10 per 18 holes (£12 weekends). Economy 9 holes £6.50 after 2.30pm winter, 6.30pm summer.
Prof Ron Macrow
Designer Martin Hawtree
Facilities
& Leisure hard tennis courts.
Location 4m NW of Bridgwater of A39

Hotel ★★ 67% Friarn Court Hotel, 37 St Mary St, BRIDGWATER
☎ 01278 452859 16

BURNHAM-ON-SEA Map 03 ST34

Brean Coast Rd, Brean Sands TA8 2QY
☎ 01278 752111 Fax 01278 752111
Level and open moorland course with water hazards. Facilities of 'Brean Leisure Park' adjoining.
18 holes, 5715yds, Par 69, SSS 68, Course record 66.
Club membership 350.
Visitors may not play on Sat & Sun before 11.30am. Book in advance through professional.
Societies contact office or professional in advance.

Green Fees £20 per day; £15 per round (£18 per round weekends).
Cards
Prof Ms S Spencer
Facilities
& Leisure heated indoor swimming pool, fishing, sauna.
Location 4m from junct 22 M5 on coast road

Hotel ★★ 65% Batch Country Hotel, LYMPSHAM
☎ 01934 750371 8

Burnham & Berrow St Christopher's Way TA8 2PE
☎ 01278 785760 Fax 01278 795440
Links championship course with large sandhills.
Championship Course: 18 holes, 6447yds, Par 71, SSS 72, Course record 66.
9 Hole Course: 9 holes, 6332yds, Par 72, SSS 70.
Club membership 900.
Visitors must contact in advance & have handicap certificate (22 or under gentlemen, 30 or under ladies) to play on the Championship course.
Societies telephone in advance.
Green Fees £36 per day/round (£50 weekends & bank holidays); 9 hole £10 per day/round.
Prof Mark Crowther-Smith
Facilities
Location 1m N of town on B3140

Hotel ★★ 74% Woodlands Hotel, Hill Ln, BRENT KNOLL
☎ 01278 760232 6
Additional hotel ★★ 65% Batch Country Hotel, LYMPSHAM
☎ 01934 750371 Fax 01934 750501 8

CHARD Map 03 ST30

Windwhistle Golf, Squash & Country Club Cricket St Thomas TA20 4DG ☎ 01460 30231 Fax 01460 30055
Parkland course at 735 ft above sea level with outstanding views over the Somerset Levels to the Bristol Channel and South Wales.
East/West Course: 18 holes, 5812yds, Par 71, SSS 68, Course record 69.
Club membership 600.
Visitors must contact in advance.
Societies by prior arrangement.
Green Fees £16 per day; £14per round (£20/£18 weekends & bank holidays).
Cards
Prof Duncan Driver
Designer Braid & Taylor
Facilities
& Leisure squash.
Location 3m E on A30

Hotel ★★★ 65% Shrubbery Hotel, ILMINSTER
☎ 01460 52108 14

CLEVEDON Map 03 ST47

Clevedon Castle Rd, Walton St Mary BS21 7AA
☎ 01275 874057
Situated on the cliff-top overlooking the Severn estuary and with distant views of the Welsh coast. Excellent parkland course in first-class condition overlooking the Severn estuary. Magnificent scenery and some tremendous 'drop' holes. Strong winds.
18 holes, 6117yds, Par 70, SSS 69, Course record 65.
Club membership 640.
Visitors must contact in advance. No play Wed morning.
Societies not Fri or bank holidays, telephone or apply in writing.
Green Fees £25 per day; £20 per round (£30 per day/round weekends & bank holidays).
Cards
Prof Martin Heggie
Designer S Herd
Facilities
Location 1m NE of town centre

Hotel ★★★ 65% Walton Park Hotel, Wellington Ter, CLEVEDON
☎ 01275 874253 40

CONGRESBURY Map 03 ST46

Mendip Spring Honeyhall Ln BS19 5JT
☎ 01934 852322 Fax 01934 853021
Set in peaceful countryside with the Mendip Hills as a backdrop, this 18-hole course includes lakes and numerous water hazards covering some 12 acres of the course. The 12th is an island green surrounded by water and there are long drives on the 7th and 13th. The 9-hole Lakeside course is an easy walking course, mainly par 4. Floodlit driving range.
Brinsea Course: 18 holes, 6334yds, Par 71, SSS 70, Course record 64.
Lakeside: 9 holes, 4520yds, Par 68, SSS 68.
Club membership 445.
Visitors must contact in advance for Brinsea course and handicap certificate required for weekends. Lakeside is play & pay anytime.
Societies booking in advance by arrangement.

Green Fees Brinsea £27 per day; £21 per round (£30/£24 weekends & bank holidays). Lakeside £7 per 9 holes (£7.50 weekends & bank holidays).
Cards
Prof John Blackburn
Facilities
Location 8m E of Weston-Super-Mare between A370 and A38

Hotel ★★★ 71% Daneswood House Hotel, Cuck Hill, SHIPHAM ☎ 01934 843145 & 843945 Fax 01934 843824 9 Annexe3

ENMORE Map 03 ST23

Enmore Park TA5 2AN
☎ 01278 671481 Fax 01278 671481
Hilly, parkland course with water features on foothills of Quantocks. Wooded countryside and views of Quantocks and Mendips. 1st and 10th are testing holes.
18 holes, 6406yds, Par 71, SSS 71, Course record 64.
Club membership 750.
Visitors phone professional for details. Restricted
Societies must apply in writing.
Green Fees £25 per day; £18 per round (£25 per round).
Prof Nigel Wixon
Designer Hawtree
Facilities
Location A39 to Minehead, at first set of lights turn left to Spaxton, then 1.5m to reservoir and turn left

Hotel ★★★ 72% Walnut Tree Hotel, North Petherton, BRIDGWATER ☎ 01278 662255 32

FARRINGTON GURNEY Map 03 ST65

Farrington Marsh Ln BS18 5TS
☎ 01761 241274 (office) & 214274 (pro)
Fax 01761 241274
USGA spec greens on both challenging 9 and 18 hole courses. Newly completed 18 hole course with computerised irrigation, six lakes, four tees per hole and excellent views. Testing holes include the 12th (282yds) with the green set behind a lake at the base of a 100ft drop, and the 17th which is played between two lakes.
Executive Course: 9 holes, 3022yds, Par 54, SSS 53, Course record 56.
Main Course: 18 holes, 6693yds, Par 72, SSS 72, Course record 68.
Club membership 750.
Visitors must book starting times at weekends.
Societies welcome except for weekends & bank holidays, telephone or write in advance.
Green Fees Main course; £27.50 per day; £20 per round (£36/£30 weekends & bank holidays). Executive course; £12 per day; £7 per 9 holes (£14/£9 weekends & bank holidays).
Prof Peter Thompson
Designer Peter Thompson
Facilities
& Leisure sauna, video teaching studio.
Hotel ★★ 71% Country Ways Hotel, Marsh Ln, FARRINGTON GURNEY ☎ 01761 452449 6

FROME Map 03 ST74

Frome Golf Centre Critchill Manor BA11 4LJ
☎ 01373 453410 Fax 01373 453410
Attractive parkland course, founded in 1993, situated in a picturesque valley just outside the town, complete with practice areas and a driving range.
18 holes, 4890yds, Par 66, SSS 64, Course record 62.
Club membership 330.
Visitors no restrictions.
Societies telephone in advance.
Green Fees £14 per day; £10 per 18 holes; £7 per 9 holes (£16/£12/£8 weekends & bank holidays).
Prof Adrian Wright
Designer R Flower
Facilities
Location A361 Frome/Shepton Mallet, at Nunney Catch rdbt through Nunney, course on left before Frome

Hotel ★★ 68% The George at Nunney, 11 Church St, NUNNEY ☎ 01373 836458 9

Orchardleigh BA11 2PH
☎ 01373 454200 Fax 01373 454202
Originally designed by Ryder Cup golfer, Brian Huggett, as two returning nines through mature parkland. Five new lakes bring water into play on seven holes.
18 holes, 6831yds, Par 72, SSS 73.
Club membership 500.
Visitors no visitors before 11am at weekends and bank holidays.
Societies apply in writing or telephone in advance.
Green Fees £30 per round, £35 per 27/36 holes (£40 weekends).
Cards
Prof Peter Green
Designer Brian Huggett
Facilities
& Leisure fishing.
Location 1m W of Frome on the A362

Hotel ★★ 68% The George at Nunney, 11 Church St, NUNNEY ☎ 01373 836458 9

GURNEY SLADE Map 03 ST64

Mendip BA3 4UT ☎ 01749 840570 Fax 01749 841439
Undulating downland course offering an interesting test of golf on superb fairways and extensive views over the surrounding countryside.
18 holes, 6330yds, Par 71, SSS 70, Course record 65.
Club membership 900.
Visitors must contact in advance. Handicap certificates required for play at weekends and bank holidays.
Societies by arrangement with secretary.
Green Fees £25 per day; £20 per round (£30 per day weekends & bank holidays).
Prof Ron Lee
Facilities
Location 1.5m S off A37

Hotel ★★★ 71% Centurion Hotel, Charlton Ln, MIDSOMER NORTON ☎ 01761 417711 44

KEYNSHAM Map 03 ST66

Stockwood Vale Stockwood Ln BS18 2ER
☎ 0117 986 6505 Fax 0117 986 0509
Undulating and challenging public course in a beautiful setting with interesting well bunkered holes, in particular the superb par 5 556 yrd 7th hole. Good views.
18 holes, 6031yds, Par 71, SSS 69.
Club membership 600.

Visitors no restrictions, but must reserve a start time.
Societies telephone in advance.
Green Fees £12 per 18 holes (£14 weekends).
Cards
Prof John Richards
Facilities
Hotel ★★ 64% Chelwood House Hotel, CHELWOOD
☎ 01761 490730 12

LANGPORT Map 03 ST42

Long Sutton Long Sutton TA10 9JU
☎ 01458 241017 Fax 01458 241022
Gentle, undulating, Pay and Play course.
18 holes, 6367yds, Par 71, SSS 70, Course record 71.
Club membership 500.

Visitors advisable to phone in advance.
Societies telephone in advance.
Green Fees £20 per day; £14 per round (£25/£17 weekends).
Cards
Prof Michael Blackwell
Designer Patrick Dawson
Facilities
Location 5m NW of Yeovil off A372

Hotel ★★★ 68% The Hollies, Bower Hinton, MARTOCK
☎ 01935 822232 Annexe30

LONG ASHTON Map 03 ST57

Long Ashton The Clubhouse, Clarken Coombe BS41 9DW
☎ 01275 392316 Fax 01275 394395
Wooded parkland course with nice turf, wonderful views of Bristol and surrounding areas and a spacious practice area. Good testing holes, especially the back nine, in prevailing south-west winds. The short second hole (126yds) cut from an old quarry and played over a road can ruin many a card! Good drainage ensures pleasant winter golf.
18 holes, 6077yds, Par 70, SSS 70, Course record 66.
Club membership 700.

Visitors recommended to telephone the professional.
Societies must contact the secretary in advance.
Green Fees £32 per day; £28 per day (£35 per round weekends & bank holidays).
Prof Denis Scanlan
Designer J H Taylor
Facilities
Location 0.5m N on B3128

Hotel ★★★ 69% Redwood Lodge Hotel, Beggar Bush Ln, Failand, BRISTOL
☎ 01275 393901 108

Woodspring Golf & Country Club Yanley Ln BS18 9LR
☎ 01275 394378 Fax 01275 394473
Set in 180 acres of undulating heathland featuring superb natural water hazards, protected greens and a rising landscape. Designed by Peter Alliss and Clive Clark and laid out by Donald Steel, the course has three individual 9-hole courses, the Avon, Severn & Brunel. The 9th hole on the Brunel course is a feature hole here, with an elevated tee shot over a natural gorge. In undulating hills south of Bristol, long carries to tight fairways, elevated island tees and difficult approaches to greens make the most of the 27 holes.
Avon Course: 9 holes, 2960yds, Par 35, SSS 34.
Brunel Course: 9 holes, 3320yds, Par 37, SSS 35.
Severn Course: 9 holes, 3267yds, Par 36, SSS 35.
Club membership 960.

Visitors must contact in advance, weekends may be limited to play after midday. Dress codes must be adhered to.
Societies must contact Kevin Pitts in advance.
Green Fees £25 per 18 holes (£28.50 weekends & bank holidays).
Cards
Prof Nigel Beer
Designer Clarke/Alliss/Steel
Facilities
& Leisure sauna.
Location Off A38 Bridgewater Road

Hotel ★★★ 69% Redwood Lodge Hotel, Beggar Bush Ln, Failand, BRISTOL
☎ 01275 393901 108

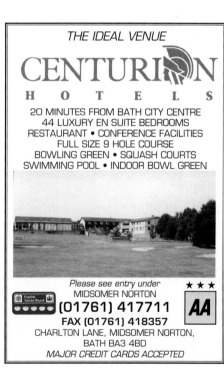

Midsomer Norton Map 03 ST65

Fosseway Country Club Charlton Ln BA3 4BD
☎ 01761 412214 Fax 01761 418357
Very attractive tree-lined parkland course, not demanding but with lovely views towards the Mendip Hills.
9 holes, 4278yds, Par 68, SSS 65.
Club membership 200.

Visitors may not play on Wed evenings, Sun mornings & competitions days.
Societies apply in writing or telephone.
Green Fees £9 per day (£11 weekends & bank holidays).
Cards
Designer C K Cotton/F Pennink
Facilities
& Leisure heated indoor swimming pool, squash, bowls.
Location SE of town centre off A367

Hotel ★★★ 71% Centurion Hotel, Charlton Ln, MIDSOMER NORTON
☎ 01761 417711 44

Minehead Map 03 SS94

Minehead & West Somerset The Warren TA24 5SJ
☎ 01643 702057 Fax 01643 705095
Flat seaside links, very exposed to wind, with good turf set on a shingle bank. The last five holes adjacent to the beach are testing. The 215-yard 18th is wedged between the beach and the club buildings and provides a good finish.
18 holes, 6228yds, Par 71, SSS 71, Course record 65.
Club membership 620.

Visitors must contact secretary in advance.
Societies telephone in advance.
Green Fees £22 per day (£25 weekends & bank holidays). Reductions most afternoons.
Prof Ian Read
Facilities
Location E end of esplanade

Hotel ★★★ 68% Northfield Hotel, Northfield Rd, MINEHEAD
☎ 01643 705155 25

Saltford Map 03 ST66

Saltford Golf Club Ln BS18 3AA
☎ 01225 873220 & 872043
Parkland course with easy walking and panoramic views over the Avon Valley. The par 4, 2nd and 13th are notable.
18 holes, 6081yds, Par 69, SSS 69.
Club membership 800.

Visitors must contact in advance & have handicap certificate.
Societies must telephone in advance.
Green Fees not confirmed.
Prof Dudley Millinstead
Facilities
Location S side of village

Hotel ★★★ Hunstrete House Hotel, Chelwood, HUNSTRETE
☎ 01761 490490 23

Somerton Map 03 ST42

Wheathill Wheathill TA11 7HG
☎ 01963 240667 Fax 01963 240230
A Par 68 parkland course with nice views in quiet countryside. It is flat lying with the 13th hole along the river. There is an Academy 4-hole course and a massive practice area.
18 holes, 5362yds, Par 68, SSS 66.
Club membership 350.

Visitors no restrictions.
Societies telephone to arrange.
Green Fees £15 per day; £10 per round (£20/£15 weekends).
Prof A England
Designer J Pain
Facilities
Location 5m E of Somerton off B3153

Hotel ★★★ 60% Wessex Hotel, High St, STREET
☎ 01458 443383 50

Taunton Map 03 ST22

Oake Manor Oake TA4 1BA
☎ 01823 461993 Fax 01823 461995
A parkland/lakeland course situated in breathtaking Somerset countryside with views of the Quantock, Blackdown and Brendon Hills. Ten holes feature water hazards such as lakes, cascades and a trout stream. The 15th hole (Par 5, 476yds) is bounded by water all down the left with a carry over another lake on to an island green. The course is challenging yet great fun for all standards of golfer.
18 holes, 6109yds, Par 70, SSS 69.
Club membership 600.

Visitors no restrictions but visitors must book in advance.
Societies contact Russell Gardner by telephone.
Green Fees not confirmed.
Prof Russell Gardner
Designer Adrian Stiff
Facilities
Location Exit M5 junct 26, take A38 towards Taunton and follow signs to Oake

Hotel ★★★ 71% Rumwell Manor Hotel, Rumwell, TAUNTON
☎ 01823 461902 10 Annexe10

Taunton & Pickeridge Corfe TA3 7BY
☎ 01823 421537
Downland course with extensive views.
18 holes, 5927yds, Par 69, SSS 68, Course record 61.
Club membership 600.

Visitors must have a handicap certificate
Societies must telephone in advance.
Green Fees not confirmed.
Prof Gary Milne
Facilities
Location 4m S off B3170

Hotel ★★★ 71% The Mount Somerset Hotel, Henlade, TAUNTON
☎ 01823 442500 11

Taunton Vale Creech Heathfield TA3 5EY
☎ 01823 412220 Fax 01823 413583
An 18 hole and a 9 hole golf course in a parkland complex occupying 156 acres in the Vale of Taunton. Complex includes a floodlit driving range.
Charlton Course: 18 holes, 6142yds, Par 70, SSS 69, Course record 66.
Durston Course: 9 holes, 2004yds, Par 64, SSS 60.
Club membership 670.
Visitors telephone booking essential.
Societies must book in advance.
Green Fees 18 holes: £15 per round (£19 weekends & bank holidays). 9 holes: £7.50 per round (£9.50 weekends & bank holidays).
Prof Martin Keitch
Designer John Payne
Facilities by prior arrangement
Location Off A361 between juncts 24 & 25 on M5

Hotel ★★★ 71% The Mount Somerset Hotel, Henlade, TAUNTON
☎ 01823 442500 11

Vivary Park Municipal Fons George TA1 3JU
☎ 01823 333875
A parkland course, tight and narrow with ponds.
18 holes, 4620yds, Par 63, SSS 63, Course record 59.
Club membership 700.
Visitors may play anytime except weekends before 10.30, bookings can be made 8 days in advance.
Societies apply in writing.
Green Fees £7.80 per round.
Prof Mike Steadman
Designer W H Fowler
Facilities
& Leisure hard tennis courts.
Location S side of town centre off A38

Hotel ★★ 61% Falcon Hotel, Henlade, TAUNTON
☎ 01823 442502 11

WEDMORE — Map 03 ST44

Isle of Wedmore Lineage BS28 4QT
☎ 01934 713649 (Office)
Gentle undulating course designed to maintain natural environment. Existing woodland and hedgerow enhanced by new planting. Magnificent panoramic views of Cheddar Valley and Glastonbury Tor.
18 holes, 6006yds, Par 70, SSS 69, Course record 70.
Club membership 560.
Visitors phone professional in advance.
Societies weekdays only, telephone in advance.
Green Fees £22 per day; £18 per round (£25/£22 weekends).
Prof Graham Coombe
Designer Terry Murray
Facilities
Location Off B3139 between Wells & Burnham-on-Sea

Hotel ★★★ 68% Swan Hotel, Sadler St, WELLS
☎ 01749 678877 38

WELLS — Map 03 ST54

Wells (Somerset) East Horrington Rd BA5 3DS
☎ 01749 675005 Fax 01749 675005
Beautiful wooded course with wonderful views. The prevailing SW wind complicates the 448-yd, 3rd.
18 holes, 6015yds, Par 70, SSS 69, Course record 66.
Club membership 775.
Visitors must contact in advance & have handicap certificate weekends. Tee times restricted at weekends to after 9.30pm
Societies must apply in advance.
Green Fees £18 per round (£22 weekends & bank holidays).
Prof Adrian Bishop
Facilities by prior arrangement
Location 1.5m E off B3139

Hotel ★★★ 68% Swan Hotel, Sadler St, WELLS
☎ 01749 678877 38

WESTON-SUPER-MARE — Map 03 ST36

Puxton Park Puxton Ln, Hewish BS24 6TA
☎ 01934 876942
A Pay and Play course built on flat moorland dissected by a network of waterways.
18 holes, 6636yds, Par 72, SSS 71.
Club membership 250.
Visitors must contact in advance.
Societies apply in advance.
Green Fees not confirmed.
Prof Mike Smedley
Facilities
Location 2m junc 21 of M5 on A370

Hotel ★★★ 71% Commodore Hotel, Beach Rd, Sand Bay, Kewstoke, WESTON-SUPER-MARE
☎ 01934 415778 12 Annexe6

Weston-super-Mare Uphill Rd North BS23 4NQ
☎ 01934 626968 & 633360 Fax 01934 626968
A compact and interesting layout with the opening hole adjacent to the beach. The sandy, links-type course is slightly undulating and has beautifully maintained turf and greens. The 15th is a testing 455-yard, par 4.
18 holes, 6300yds, Par 70, SSS 70, Course record 65.
Club membership 778.
Visitors must have handicap certificate to play at weekends.
Societies apply in writing or telephone.
Green Fees £24 per day (£35 per day weekends & bank holidays).
Prof Mike Laband
Designer T Dunne/Dr Mackenzie
Facilities
Location S side of town centre off A370

Hotel ★★ 66% Beachlands Hotel, 17 Uphill Rd North, WESTON-SUPER-MARE
☎ 01934 621401 23

Worlebury Monks Hill BS22 9SX
☎ 01934 625789 Fax 01934 625789
Situated on the ridge of Worlebury Hill, this seaside course offers fairly easy walking and extensive views of the Severn estuary and Wales.
18 holes, 5963yds, Par 70, SSS 69, Course record 66.
Club membership 590.

Visitors must be recognised golfers, handicap certificate or proof of club membership may be required
Societies apply in writing or telephone in advance.
Green Fees £20 (£30 weekends).
Prof Gary Marks
Designer A Hawtree
Facilities ⊗ ☕ 🍸
& Leisure snooker table.
Location 5m NE off A370

Hotel ★★★ 71% Commodore Hotel, Beach Rd, Sand Bay, Kewstoke, WESTON-SUPER-MARE ☎ 01934 415778 12 Annexe6

YEOVIL Map 03 ST51

Yeovil Sherborne Rd BA21 5BW
☎ 01935 422965 Fax 01935 411283
On the Old Course the opener lies by the River Yeo before the gentle climb to high downs with good views. The outstanding 14th and 15th holes present a challenge, being below the player with a deep railway cutting on the left of the green. The 1st on the Newton Course is played over the river which then leads to a challenging but scenic golf course.
Old Course: 18 holes, 6144yds, Par 72, SSS 70, Course record 64.
Newton Course: 9 holes, 4891yds, Par 68, SSS 65.
Club membership 1000.

Visitors must contact in advance. Members only before 9.30am and 12.30-2.
Societies telephone in advance.
Green Fees Old Course: £30 per day; £25 per round (£40/£30 weekends). Newton Course: £15 per day/round (£18 weekends).
Cards
Prof Geoff Kite
Designer Fowler & Allison
Facilities ⊗ ☕ 🍸
Location 1m E on A30

Hotel ★★★ 72% Yeovil Court Hotel, West Coker Rd, YEOVIL ☎ 01935 863746 15 Annexe11

STAFFORDSHIRE

BROCTON Map 07 SJ91

Brocton Hall ST17 0TH
☎ 01785 661901 Fax 01785 661591
Parkland course with gentle slopes in places, easy walking.
18 holes, 6095yds, Par 69, SSS 69, Course record 67.
Club membership 665.

Visitors not competition days. Must contact in advance.
Societies must apply in advance.
Green Fees £28 per day (£33 weekends & bank holidays).

▶

Prof R G Johnson
Designer Harry Vardon
Facilities
Location NW side of village off A34

Hotel ★★★ 65% Garth Hotel, Wolverhampton Rd, Moss Pit, STAFFORD
☎ 01785 256124 60

BURTON-UPON-TRENT Map 07 SK22

Branston Burton Rd, Branston DE14 3DP
☎ 01283 512211 Fax 01283 566984
Flat semi-parkland course, adjacent to River Trent, on undulating ground with natural water hazards on 13 holes.
18 holes, 6647yds, Par 72, SSS 72, Course record 67.
Club membership 800.
Visitors may not play before noon or at weekends. Must contact in advance.
Societies must telephone in advance.
Green Fees £35 per day; £25 per round (£35 per round weekends & bank holidays).
Cards
Prof Sean Stiff
Designer G Ramshall
Facilities
& Leisure heated indoor swimming pool, sauna, solarium, gymnasium.
Location 1.5m SW on A5121

Hotel ★★★ 69% Riverside Hotel, Riverside Dr, Branston, BURTON UPON TRENT
☎ 01283 511234 22

Burton-upon-Trent 43 Ashby Rd East DE15 0PS
☎ 01283 544551 Fax 01283 544551
Undulating parkland course with trees a major feature. There are testing par 3s at 10th and 12th. The 18th has a lake on the approach to the green.
18 holes, 6579yds, Par 71, SSS 71, Course record 63.
Club membership 600.
Visitors must contact in advance and have a handicap certificate.
Societies must contact in advance.
Green Fees £32 per day; £27 per round (£35 per day; £30 per round weekends & bank holidays).
Prof Gary Stafford
Designer H S Colt
Facilities
Location 3m E on A50

Hotel ★★★ 69% Riverside Hotel, Riverside Dr, Branston, BURTON UPON TRENT
☎ 01283 511234 22

Craythorne Craythorne Rd, Stretton DE13 0AZ
☎ 01283 564329 Fax 01283 511908
A relatively short and challenging parkland course with tight fairways and views of the Trent Valley. Excellent greens. Suits all standards but particularly good for society players. Tees and greens recently renovated.
18 holes, 5365yds, Par 68, SSS 67, Course record 66.
Club membership 500.
Visitors must contact in advance.
Societies apply in writing or telephone for details.
Green Fees £18 per round (£23 weekends).
Cards
Prof Steve Hadfield
Facilities
Location Off A38 through Stretton village

Hotel ★★★ 69% Riverside Hotel, Riverside Dr, Branston, BURTON UPON TRENT
☎ 01283 511234 22

Hoar Cross Hall Health Spa Golf Academy Hoar Cross DE13 8QS ☎ 01283 575671
Newly constructed golf academy located in the grounds of a stately home, now a well appointed health spa resort and hotel. Driving range, bunker and practice areas.
Club membership 300.
Visitors day guests & residents.
Societies golfing societies that are resident only.
Green Fees on application.
Prof Gary Prince
Designer Geoffrey Collins
Facilities
& Leisure hard tennis courts, heated indoor swimming pool, sauna, solarium, gymnasium.
Hotel ★★★★ 69% Hoar Cross Hall Health Spa, Hoar Cross, BURTON UPON TRENT
☎ 01283 575671 86

CANNOCK Map 07 SJ91

Beau Desert Rugeley Rd, Hazelslade WS12 5PJ
☎ 01543 422626 Fax 01543 451137
Heathland course surrounded by a forest.
18 holes, 6310yds, Par 70, SSS 71, Course record 64.
Club membership 500.
Visitors are advised to contact in advance.
Societies must contact in advance.
Green Fees £35 per day (£45 weekends & bank holidays).
Prof Barrie Stevens
Designer Herbert Fowler
Facilities
Location 0.5m NE of village

Hotel ★★★ 66% Roman Way Hotel, Watling St, Hatherton, CANNOCK
☎ 01543 572121 56

Cannock Park Stafford Rd WS11 2AL ☎ 01543 578850
Part of a large leisure centre, this parkland-type course plays alongside Cannock Chase. Good drainage, open most of year.
18 holes, 5149yds, Par 67, SSS 65.
Club membership 250.
Visitors must book in advance.
Societies must contact in advance.
Green Fees not confirmed.
Prof David Dunk
Designer John Mainland
Facilities
& Leisure hard tennis courts, heated indoor swimming pool, sauna, solarium, gymnasium.
Location 4m S of Brocton

Hotel ★★★ 66% Roman Way Hotel, Watling St, Hatherton, CANNOCK
☎ 01543 572121 56

ENVILLE — Map 07 SO88

Enville Highgate Common DY7 5BN
☎ 01384 872074 (Office) Fax 01384 873396
Easy walking on two fairly flat parkland/moorland courses - the 'Highgate' and the 'Lodge'.
Highgate Course: 18 holes, 6556yds, Par 72, SSS 72, Course record 65.
Lodge Course: 18 holes, 6275yds, Par 70, SSS 70.
Club membership 900.
Visitors must play with member at weekends.
Societies phone initially for details.
Green Fees £38 per 36 holes; £32 per 27 holes; £28 per 18 holes.
Prof Sean Power
Facilities
Location Take A458 towards Bridgnorth, after 4.5m turn right. Golf club signposted

Hotel ★★★ 62% Talbot Hotel, High St, STOURBRIDGE ☎ 01384 394350 25

GOLDENHILL — Map 07 SJ85

Goldenhill Mobberley Rd ST6 5SS
☎ 01782 234200 Fax 01782 234303
Rolling parkland course with water features on six of the back nine holes.
18 holes, 5957yds, Par 71, SSS 69.
Club membership 400.
Visitors contact in advance for weekend play.
Societies must apply in writing or telephone.
Green Fees Summer: £10 per round; Winter £5 per round.
Facilities
Location On A50, 4m N of Stoke

Hotel ★★★ 68% Manor House Hotel, Audley Rd, ALSAGER ☎ 01270 884000 57

HIMLEY — Map 07 SO89

Himley Hall Golf Centre Log Cabin, Himley Hall Park DY3 4DF ☎ 01902 895207
Parkland course set in grounds of Himley Hall Park, with lovely views. Large practice area including a pitch-and-putt.
9 holes, 6215yds, Par 72, SSS 70, Course record 65.
Club membership 200.
Visitors restricted weekends.
Green Fees not confirmed.
Prof Jeremy Nichols
Designer A Baker
Facilities
& Leisure 9 hole pitch & putt.
Location 0.5m E on B4176

Hotel ★★★ 62% Himley Country Hotel, School Rd, HIMLEY ☎ 01902 896716 73

LEEK — Map 07 SJ95

Leek Birchall, Cheddleton Rd ST13 5RE ☎ 01538 384779
Undulating, challenging mainly parkland course, reputedly one of the best in the area.
18 holes, 6240yds, Par 70, SSS 70, Course record 63.
Club membership 750.
Visitors must contact Professional in advance.
Societies must apply in advance.
Green Fees £24 per day (£30 weekends & bank holidays).
Prof Peter A Stubbs
Facilities
& Leisure snooker.
Location 0.75m S on A520

Hotel ★★★ 69% George Hotel, Swan Square, Burslem, STOKE-ON-TRENT ☎ 01782 577544 39

Westwood (Leek) Newcastle Rd ST13 7AA
☎ 01538 398385 & 398897 (Prof) Fax 01538 382485
A challenging moorland/parkland course.
18 holes, 6207yds, Par 70, SSS 69.
Club membership 700.
Visitors must book inadvance.
Societies apply by phone or in writing.
Green Fees £18 per round.
Cards
Prof Neale Hyde
Facilities
Location On A53, S of Leek

Hotel ★★★ 69% George Hotel, Swan Square, Burslem, STOKE-ON-TRENT ☎ 01782 577544 39

LICHFIELD — Map 07 SK10

Seedy Mill Elmhurst WS13 8HE
☎ 01543 417333 Fax 01543 418098
New, gently-rolling parkland course in picturesque rural setting. Lakes and streams are abundant, and there are four challenging Par 3s. Well contoured green, good bunkering. Also a superb 9-hole Par 3 course.
18 holes, 6308yds, Par 72, SSS 70, Course record 68.
Club membership 800.
Visitors must contact in advance.
Societies apply in writing.
Green Fees not confirmed.
Cards
Prof Richard O'Hanlon
Designer Hawtree & Son
Facilities
Location At Elmhurst, 2m N of Lichfield, off A515

Hotel ★★★ 65% Little Barrow Hotel, Beacon St, LICHFIELD ☎ 01543 414500 24

Whittington Heath Tamworth Rd WS14 9PW
☎ 01543 432317 Fax 01543 432317
18 magnificent holes winding their way through heathland and trees, presenting a good test for the serious golfer. Leaving the fairway can be severely punished. The dog-legs are most tempting, inviting the golfer to chance his arm. Local knowledge is a definite advantage. Clear views of the famous three spires of Lichfield Cathedral.
18 holes, 6490yds, Par 70, SSS 71, Course record 65.
Club membership 660.
Visitors must contact in advance. May not play at weekends. Handicap certificate required.
Societies welcome Wed & Thu, must apply in writing.
Green Fees £32 per day; £24 per round. ▶

Prof Adrian Sadler
Designer Colt
Facilities
Location 2.5m SE on A51 Litchfield-Tamworth road

Hotel ★★★ 65% Little Barrow Hotel, Beacon St, LICHFIELD ☎ 01543 414500 24

NEWCASTLE-UNDER-LYME Map 07 SJ84

Newcastle Municipal Newcastle Rd, Keele ST5 5AB
☎ 01782 627596
Open course on the side of a hill without mature trees.
18 holes, 6396yds, Par 71, SSS 70, Course record 64.
Club membership 280.
Visitors must contact in advance.
Societies by prior arrangement to Newcastle-Under-Lyme Borough Council, Civic Offices, Merrial St, Newcastle-Under-Lyme, Staffs.
Green Fees not confirmed.
Prof Colin Smith
Facilities
Location 2m W on A525

Hotel B Forte Posthouse Stoke on Trent, Clayton Rd, NEWCASTLE-UNDER-LYME
☎ 01782 717171 119

Newcastle-Under-Lyme Whitmore Rd ST5 2QB
☎ 01782 617006
Parkland course.
18 holes, 6404yds, Par 72, SSS 71.
Club membership 600.
Visitors must contact in advance. With member only weekends.
Societies must contact in advance.
Green Fees not confirmed.
Prof Paul Symonds
Facilities
Location 1m SW on A53

Hotel ★★ 64% Comfort Friendly Inn, Liverpool Rd, NEWCASTLE-UNDER-LYME
☎ 01782 717000 45 Annexe23

Wolstanton Dimsdale Old Hall, Hassam Pde, Wolstanton ST5 9DR ☎ 01782 622413 (Sec) & 616995
A challenging undulating suburban course incorporating 6 difficult Par 3 holes. The 6th hole (Par 3) is 233yds from the Medal Tee.
18 holes, 5807yds, Par 68, SSS 68, Course record 63.
Club membership 700.
Visitors must contact in advance. May not play Tue (Ladies Day). With member only at weekends & bank holidays.
Societies must contact in advance.
Green Fees £20 per day/round.
Prof Simon Arnold
Facilities by prior arrangement
& Leisure snooker tables.
Location 1.5m from town centre. Turn off A34 at The Sportsman Inn

Hotel B Forte Posthouse Stoke on Trent, Clayton Rd, NEWCASTLE-UNDER-LYME
☎ 01782 717171 119

ONNELEY Map 07 SJ74

Onneley CW3 9QF ☎ 01782 750577
A tight, picturesque, hillside parkland course. An ideal test for the short game
9 holes, 5584yds, Par 70, SSS 67, Course record 67.
Club membership 480.
Visitors welcome except during competitions, but may not play on Sun and with member only Sat and bank holidays.
Societies packages available apply in writing to secretary.
Green Fees £15 per 18 holes.
Facilities by prior arrangement
Location 2m from Woore on A525

Hotel ★★ 69% Wheatsheaf Inn at Onneley, Barhill Rd, ONNELEY ☎ 01782 751581 5

PATTINGHAM Map 07 SO89

Patshull Park Hotel Golf & Country Club WV6 7HR
☎ 01902 700100 Fax 01902 700874
Picturesque course set in 280 acres of glorious Capability Brown landscaped parkland. Designed by John Jacobs, the course meanders alongside trout fishing lakes. Many leisure facilities.
18 holes, 6400yds, Par 72, SSS 71, Course record 63.
Club membership 400.
Visitors must contact in advance.
Societies must contact in advance.
Green Fees £22.50 per round (£27.50 weekends).
Cards
Prof Joe Higgins/Richard Bissell

Designer John Jacobs
Facilities ⊗ 🍴 🍺 ☕ 🍷 👜 🏠 🏌 🛏 🚗 🏌 🛒
& Leisure heated indoor swimming pool, fishing, sauna, solarium, gymnasium.
Location Off A464

Hotel ★★★ 66% Patshull Park Hotel Golf & Country Club, Patshull Park, PATTINGHAM
☎ 01902 700100 49 ⇌ ↱

PERTON Map 07 SO89

Perton Park Wrottesley Park Rd WV6 7HL
☎ 01902 380103 & 380073 Fax 01902 326219
Flat meadowland course set in open countryside.
18 holes, 6620yds, Par 72, SSS 72.
Club membership 300.
Visitors must book in advance.
Societies must telephone in advance.
Green Fees £20 per day; £10 per round (£30/£15 weekends & bank holidays).
Cards
Prof Jeremy Harrold
Facilities
& Leisure hard tennis courts, snooker, pool table.
Location 6m W of Wolverhampton, off A454

Hotel ★★ 69% Ely House Hotel, 53 Tettenhall Rd, WOLVERHAMPTON
☎ 01902 311311 18 ⇌ ↱

STAFFORD Map 07 SJ92

Stafford Castle Newport Rd ST16 1BP ☎ 01785 223821
Parkland type course built around Stafford Castle.
9 holes, 6382yds, Par 71, SSS 70, Course record 68.
Club membership 400.
Visitors must contact in advance. May not play at weekends.
Societies must apply in writing.
Green Fees £14 per day (£18 weekends & bank holidays).
Facilities ⊗ by prior arrangement 🍴 by prior arrangement 🍺 by prior arrangement
Location SW side of town centre off A518

Hotel ★★★ 64% Tillington Hall Hotel, Eccleshall Rd, STAFFORD ☎ 01785 253531 90 ⇌ ↱

STOKE-ON-TRENT Map 07 SJ84

Burslem Wood Farm, High Ln, Tunstall ST6 7JT
☎ 01782 837006
On the outskirts of Tunstall, a moorland course with hard walking.
9 holes, 5354yds, Par 66, SSS 66, Course record 66.
Club membership 250.
Visitors except Sun & with member only Sat & bank holidays.
Societies must telephone in advance.
Green Fees £16 per day.
Facilities ⊗ by prior arrangement 🍴 by prior arrangement 🍺 by prior arrangement
Location 4m N of city centre on B5049

Hotel ★★★ 69% George Hotel, Swan Square, Burslem, STOKE-ON-TRENT
☎ 01782 577544 39 ⇌ ↱

Greenway Hall Stanley Rd, Stockton Brook ST9 9LJ
☎ 01782 503158
Moorland course with fine views of the Pennines.
18 holes, 5678yds, Par 68, SSS 67.
Club membership 560.
Visitors may play weekdays only.
Societies must apply in writing.
Green Fees not confirmed.
Facilities ⊗ 🍴 by prior arrangement
Location 5m NE off A53

Hotel ★★★ 69% George Hotel, Swan Square, Burslem, STOKE-ON-TRENT
☎ 01782 577544 39 ⇌ ↱

Trentham 14 Barlaston Old Rd, Trentham ST4 8HB
☎ 01782 658109 Fax 01782 644024
Parkland course. The par 3, 4th is a testing hole reached over a copse of trees.
18 holes, 6644yds, Par 72, SSS 72, Course record 63.
Club membership 600.
Visitors must contact in advance. Must play with member at weekends.
Societies must contact in advance.
Green Fees £25 per 18 holes (£35 weekends & bank holidays).
Prof Sandy Wilson
Designer Colt & Alison
Facilities
& Leisure squash, putting green, practice area.
Location 3m S off A5035

Hotel ★★★ 65% Haydon House Hotel, 1-13 Haydon St, Basford, STOKE-ON-TRENT
☎ 01782 711311 17 ⇌ ↱ Annexe14 ⇌ ↱

Trentham Park Trentham Park ST4 8AE
☎ 01782 658800 Fax 01782 658800
Fine woodland course.
18 holes, 6425yds, Par 71, SSS 71, Course record 67.
Club membership 850.
Visitors must contact in advance.
Societies Wed & Fri, must apply in advance.
Green Fees not confirmed.
Prof Brian Rimmer
Facilities
Location Adjacent to Trentham Gardens, off A34 3m S of Newcastle-under-Lyme

Hotel B Forte Posthouse Stoke on Trent, Clayton Rd, NEWCASTLE-UNDER-LYME
☎ 01782 717171 119 ⇌ ↱

STONE Map 07 SJ93

Barlaston Meaford Rd ST15 8UX
☎ 01782 372795 & 372867
Picturesque meadowland course designed by Peter Alliss.
18 holes, 5800yds, Par 69, SSS 68.
Club membership 600.
Visitors may not play before 10am or after 4pm Fridays, weekends and bank holidays.
Societies telephone or apply in writing.
Green Fees £16 per day (£20 weekends).
Prof Ian Rogers
Designer Peter Alliss
Facilities ▶

Hotel ★★★ 64% Stone House Hotel, Stafford Rd, STONE ☎ 01785 815531 47 ⇄ ↱

Izaak Walton Eccleshall Rd, Cold Norton ST15 0NS
☎ 01785 760900
Opened in 1992, a gently undulating meadowland course with streams and ponds as features.
18 holes, 6281yds, Par 72, SSS 72, Course record 72.
Club membership 400.

Visitors must contact in advance for weekends play.
Societies must telephone in advance.
Green Fees £15 per round (£20 weekends).
Prof Julie Brown
Facilities ⊗)Ⅲ ⊾ ☕ ♀ ⚲ ⌂ ✓ ⟟
Location On B5026 between Stone & Eccleshall

Hotel ★★★ 64% Stone House Hotel, Stafford Rd, STONE ☎ 01785 815531 47 ⇄ ↱

Stone Filleybrooks ST15 0NB ☎ 01785 813103
9-hole parkland course with easy walking and 18 different tees.
9 holes, 6299yds, Par 71, SSS 70, Course record 68.
Club membership 310.

Visitors with member only weekends & bank holidays.
Societies must apply in writing.
Green Fees £20 per day/round.
Facilities ⊗)Ⅲ ⊾ ☕ ♀ ⚲
Location 0.5m W on A34

Hotel ★★★ 64% Stone House Hotel, Stafford Rd, STONE ☎ 01785 815531 47 ⇄ ↱

TAMWORTH Map 07 SK20

Drayton Park Drayton Park B78 3TN
☎ 01827 251139 Fax 01827 284035
Parkland course designed by James Braid. Club established since 1897.
18 holes, 6214yds, Par 71, SSS 71, Course record 62.
Club membership 450.

Visitors with member only weekends. Must contact in advance.
Societies must apply in writing.
Green Fees £29 per day/round.
Prof M W Passmore
Designer James Braid
Facilities ⊗)Ⅲ ⊾ ☕ ♀ ⚲ ⌂ ✓
Location 2m S on A4091, next to Drayton Manor Leisure Park

Hotel ★★★★ 73% The Belfry, WISHAW ☎ 01675 470301 324 ⇄ ↱

Tamworth Municipal Eagle Dr, Amington B77 4EG
☎ 01827 53850
First-class municipal, parkland course and a good test of golf.
18 holes, 6605ydss, Par 73, SSS 72, Course record 63.
Club membership 600.

Visitors must book in advance at weekends.
Societies must contact in advance.
Green Fees not confirmed.
Prof Daryl Scott
Designer Hawtree & Son
Facilities ⊗)Ⅲ ⊾ ☕ ♀ ⚲ ⌂ ⛳ ✓
Location 2.5m E off B5000

Hotel ★★ 62% Angel Croft Hotel, Beacon St, LICHFIELD ☎ 01543 258737 10rm(3 ⇄ 5 ↱) Annexe8 ⇄ ↱

UTTOXETER Map 07 SK03

Uttoxeter Wood Ln ST14 8JR
☎ 01889 565108 & 566552 (Office) Fax 01889 567501
Undulating course with spectacular views adjacent to the racecourse.
18 holes, 5798yds, Par 70, SSS 69, Course record 66.
Club membership 750.

Visitors restricted weekends and competition days.
Societies must apply in writing.
Green Fees £25 per day; £18 per round (£24 per round weekends & bank holidays).
Prof Adam McCandless
Facilities ⊗)Ⅲ ⊾ ☕ ♀ ⚲ ⌂ ✓
Location 1m SE off B5017, follow Racecourse signs town centre

Hotel ★★ 66% Bank House Hotel, Church St, UTTOXETER ☎ 01889 566922 14 ⇄ ↱

WESTON Map 07 SJ92

Ingestre Park ST18 0RE
☎ 01889 270845 Fax 01889 270845
Parkland course set in the grounds of Ingestre Hall, former home of the Earl of Shrewsbury, with mature trees and pleasant views.
18 holes, 6334yds, Par 70, SSS 70, Course record 67.
Club membership 850.

Visitors with member only weekends & bank holidays. Must play before 3.30pm weekdays. Advance booking preferred. Handicap certificate required.
Societies must apply in advance.
Green Fees not confirmed.
Prof Danny Scullion
Designer Hawtree
Facilities ⊗)Ⅲ ⊾ ☕ ♀ ⚲ ⌂ ⚘ 🛺 ✓
Location 2m SE off A51

Hotel ★★★ 64% Tillington Hall Hotel, Eccleshall Rd, STAFFORD ☎ 01785 253531 90 ⇄ ↱

WHISTON Map 07 SK04

Whiston Hall Whiston Hall ST10 2HZ
☎ 01538 266260 Fax 01538 383600
A challenging 18-hole course in scenic countryside, incorporating many natural obstacles and providing a test for all golfing abilities.
18 holes, 5742yds, Par 71, SSS 69.
Club membership 400.

Visitors reasonable dress on the course. Must telephone in advance at weekends.
Societies contact in advance.
Green Fees not confirmed.
Facilities ⊗)Ⅲ ⊾ ☕ ♀ ⚲ ⛳ ✓
& Leisure fishing.
Location Off A52, between Stoke-on-Trent and Ashbourne

Hotel ★★★ 69% George Hotel, Swan Square, Burslem, STOKE-ON-TRENT ☎ 01782 577544 39 ⇄ ↱

SUFFOLK

ALDEBURGH Map 05 TM45

Aldeburgh Saxmundham Rd IP15 5PE
☎ 01728 452890 Fax 01728 452937
A most enjoyable and not unduly difficult seaside course; ideal for golfing holidaymakers. A bracing and fairly open terrain with some trees and heathland.
18 holes, 6330yds, Par 68, SSS 71, Course record 65.
River Course: 9 holes, 4228yds, Par 64, SSS 61.
Club membership 850.

Visitors must contact in advance.
Societies must contact in advance.
Green Fees £35 per day/round (£42 weekends).
Prof Keith Preston
Facilities
Location 1m W on A1094

Hotel ★★★ 70% Wentworth Hotel, Wentworth Rd, ALDEBURGH
☎ 01728 452312 31rm(24 4) Annexe7

BECCLES Map 05 TM49

Beccles The Common NR34 9YN
☎ 01502 712244
Heathland course with natural hazards and particularly exposed to wind.
9 holes, 2779yds, Par 68, SSS 67.
Club membership 160.

Visitors must play with member on Sun.
Societies must telephone in advance.
Green Fees not confirmed.
Facilities
Location NE side of town

Hotel ★★★ 64% Hotel Hatfield, The Esplanade, LOWESTOFT
☎ 01502 565337 33

BUNGAY Map 05 TM38

Bungay & Waveney Valley Outney Common NR35 1DS
☎ 01986 892337 Fax 01986 892222
Heathland course partly comprising Neolithic stone workings, easy walking.
18 holes, 6026yds, Par 69, SSS 69.
Club membership 730.

Visitors should contact in advance. With member only weekends & bank holidays.
Societies must contact in advance.
Green Fees £24 per day; £18 per round.
Prof Nigel Whyte
Facilities
Location 0.5m NW on A143

Hotel ★★★ 64% Hotel Hatfield, The Esplanade, LOWESTOFT
☎ 01502 565337 33

BURY ST EDMUNDS Map 05 TL86

Bury St Edmunds Tut Hill IP28 6LG ☎ 01284 755979
Undulating parkland course with easy walking and attractive short holes.
18 holes, 6678yds, Par 72, SSS 72, Course record 69 or 9 holes, 2217yds, Par 62, SSS 62.
Club membership 850.

Visitors with member only at weekends for 18 hole course.
Societies must apply in writing.
Green Fees not confirmed.
Prof Mark Jillings
Designer Ted Ray
Facilities by prior arrangement
Location 2m NW on B1106 off A45

Hotel ★★★ 70% Angel Hotel, Angel Hill, BURY ST EDMUNDS ☎ 01284 753926 42

The Suffolk Golf & Country Club St John's Hill Plantation, The Street, Fornham All Saints IP28 6JQ
☎ 01284 706777 Fax 10284 706721
Mature parkland course with many water features. Also country club facilities.
18 holes, 6321yds, Par 72, SSS 71.
Club membership 650.

Visitors Weekdays before 8am, between 9.30am and noon and after 1pm. Weekends between 11am and noon and after 1pm.
Societies by arrangement, Mon-Fri.
Green Fees £20 (£25 weekends & bank holidays).
Cards

Prof Steven Hall
Facilities
& Leisure heated indoor swimming pool, sauna, solarium, gymnasium, creche.
Location 2m N off A14

Hotel ★★★ 70% Ravenwood Hall Hotel, Rougham, BURY ST EDMUNDS
01359 270345 7 Annexe7

CRETINGHAM Map 05 TM26

Cretingham IP13 7BA
01728 685275 Fax 01728 685037
Parkland course.
9 holes, 4552yds, Par 66, SSS 64, Course record 61.
Club membership 350.
Visitors booking required for weekends.
Societies must contact in advance.
Green Fees £14 per day; £11 per 18 holes; £7 per 9 holes (£16/£13/£9 weekends & bank holidays).
Cards
Prof Colin Jenkins
Designer J Austin
Facilities
& Leisure hard tennis courts, outdoor swimming pool, pitch & putt.
Location 2m from A1120 at Earl Soham

Hotel ★★ 64% Cedars Hotel, Needham Rd, STOWMARKET 01449 612668 25

FELIXSTOWE Map 05 TM33

Felixstowe Ferry Ferry Rd IP11 9RY 01394 286834
Seaside links course, pleasant views, easy walking. Testing 491-yd, 7th hole. New 9 hole course now open.
Martello Course: 18 holes, 6272yds, Par 72, SSS 70.
Club membership 900.
Visitors may not play weekends on Martello Course.
Societies Tue, Wed & Fri.
Green Fees not confirmed.
Prof Ian MacPherson
Designer Henry Cotton
Facilities
Location NE side of town centre

Hotel ★★ 70% Waverley Hotel, 2 Wolsey Gardens, FELIXSTOWE 01394 282811 19

FLEMPTON Map 05 TL86

Flempton IP28 6EQ 01284 728291
Breckland course.
9 holes, 6240yds, Par 70, SSS 70.
Club membership 300.
Visitors must produce handicap certificate. With member only weekends & bank holidays.
Societies Limited to small societies - must apply in writing.
Green Fees not confirmed.
Prof Mark Jillings
Facilities
Location 0.5m W on A1101

Hotel ★★★ 69% The Priory Hotel, Tollgate, BURY ST EDMUNDS
01284 766181 9 Annexe18

HALESWORTH Map 05 TM37

Halesworth Bramfield Rd IP19 9XA 01986 875567 Fax 01986 874565
A 27-hole professionally designed parkland complex of three 9-hole courses, giving 6 playing options of 3 x 18-hole Par 72 and 3 x Par 36 9-hole.
18 holes, 6580yds, Par 72, SSS 72, Course record 71.
9 holes, 3059yds, Par 36, SSS 36.
Club membership 700.
Visitors visitors welcome at all times except for Sunday before noon on the 18 hole course. Handicap certificate required for 18 hole course.
Societies telephone for booking form.
Green Fees £18 per round (£25 per round weekends). £7.50 per 9 holes.
Prof Philip Heil
Designer J W Johnson
Facilities
Location 0.75m S of town, signposted on left of A144 road to Bramfield

Hotel ★★★ 68% Swan Hotel, Market Place, SOUTHWOLD
01502 722186 24 Annexe18

HAVERHILL Map 05 TL64

Haverhill Coupals Rd CB9 7UW
01440 761951 Fax 01440 761951
An 18 hole course lying across two valleys in pleasant parkland. The front nine with undulating fairways is complimented by a saucer shaped back nine, bisected by the River Stow, presenting a challenge to golfers of all standards.
18 holes, 5898yds, Par 70, SSS 68, Course record 65.
Club membership 600.
Visitors telephone to check for club competitions.
Societies must contact in advance. Tue & Thu only.
Green Fees £19 per day; £16 per 18 holes (£24/£20 weekends & bank holidays).
Prof Simon Mayfield
Facilities
Location 1m SE off A604

Hotel ★★ 70% Four Seasons Hotel, Walden Rd, THAXTED 01371 830129 9rm(8)

HINTLESHAM Map 05 TM04

Hintlesham Hall IP8 3NS
01473 652761 Fax 01473 652750
Magnificent championship length course blending harmoniously with the ancient parkland surrounding this exclusive hotel. The 6630yd parkland course was designed by Hawtree and Son, one of the oldest established firms of golf course architects in the world. The course is fair but challenging for low and high handicappers alike. Hotel offers beautiful accommodation, excellent cuisine and many facilities.
18 holes, 6638yds, Par 72, SSS 72, Course record 67.
Club membership 350.
Visitors must contact in advance.
Societies must telephone in advance.
Green Fees £27 per round.
Cards
Prof Alastair Spink

Designer Hawtree & Sons
Facilities ⊗ 🍽 🍴 ☕ 🍸 ⛳ 🏠 🏌 🚗 🏷 🚙 🏌
& Leisure hard tennis courts, heated outdoor swimming pool, sauna, solarium, gymnasium.
Location In village on A1071

Hotel ★★★★ Hintlesham Hall Hotel, HINTLESHAM ☎ 01473 652334 & 652268 Fax 01473 652463 33 ⇌ ↱

Ipswich Map 05 TM14

Alnesbourne Priory Priory Park IP10 0JT
☎ 01473 727393 Fax 01473 278372
A fabulous outlook facing due south across the River Orwell is one of the many good features of this course set in woodland. All holes run among trees with some fairways requiring straight shots. The 8th green is on saltings by the river.
9 holes, 1700yds, Par 29.
Club membership 30.
Visitors closed on Tuesday. Closed 6 Jan-28 Feb.
Societies Tue only, telephone in advance.
Green Fees £10 weekdays, £11 Saturday, £12 Sunday.
Facilities ⊗ 🍴 ☕ 🍸 ⛳ 🏌 🚗 🏌
& Leisure hard tennis courts, heated outdoor swimming pool, putting green, practice area.
Location 3m SE, off A14

Hotel ★★★ 68% Courtyard by Marriott Ipswich, The Havens, Ransomes Europark, IPSWICH ☎ 01473 272244 60 ⇌ ↱

Fynn Valley IP6 9JA ☎ 01473 785267 Fax 01473 785632
Undulating parkland course plus Par-3 nine-hole and driving range. Many new developments are in hand on this complex.
18 holes, 5873yds, Par 68, SSS 68, Course record 67.
Club membership 700.
Visitors members only Sun until noon.
Societies must apply in advance.
Green Fees £24 per day; £17 per 18 holes (£30/£22 weekends & bank holidays).
Cards [card logos]
Prof Glenn Crane
Designer Tony Tyrrell
Facilities ⊗ 🍽 🍴 ☕ 🍸 ⛳ 🏠 🏌 🏷 🚙 🏌
Location 2m N of Ipswich on B1077

Hotel ★★★ 63% Novotel, Greyfriars Rd, IPSWICH ☎ 01473 232400 101 ⇌ ↱

Ipswich Purdis Heath IP3 8UQ
☎ 01473 728941 Fax 01473 715236
Many golfers are suprised when they hear that Ipswich has, at Purdis Heath, a first-class golf course. In some ways it resembles some of Surrey's better courses; a beautiful heathland/parkland course with two lakes and easy walking.
18 holes, 6405yds, Par 71, SSS 71, Course record 63 or 9 holes, 1930yds, Par 31, SSS 59.
Club membership 850.
Visitors must contact in advance & have a handicap certificate for 18 hole courses.
Societies must contact in advance.
Green Fees not confirmed.
Prof Stephen Whymark
Designer James Braid
Facilities ⊗ 🍽 by prior arrangement 🍴 ☕ 🍸 ⛳ 🏠 🏌
Location E side of town centre off A1156

Hotel ★★★ 73% Marlborough Hotel, Henley Rd, IPSWICH ☎ 01473 257677 22 ⇌ ↱

Rushmere Rushmere Heath IP4 5QQ ☎ 01473 725648
Heathland course with gorse and prevailing winds. Testing 5th hole - dog leg, 419 yards (par 4).
18 holes, 6262yds, Par 70, SSS 68, Course record 66.
Club membership 777.
Visitors not before 2.30pm weekends & bank holidays. Must have a handicap certificate.
Societies weekdays ex Wed by arrangement.
Green Fees £20 per day/round.
Prof N T J McNeill
Facilities ⊗ 🍽 by prior arrangement 🍴 ☕ 🍸 ⛳ 🏠 🏌 🏌
Location 3m E off A12

Hotel ★★★ 73% Marlborough Hotel, Henley Rd, IPSWICH ☎ 01473 257677 22 ⇌ ↱

Lowestoft Map 05 TM59

Rookery Park Carlton Colville NR33 8HJ
☎ 01502 560380 Fax 01502 560380
Parkland course with a 9-hole, Par 3 adjacent.
18 holes, 6779yds, Par 72, SSS 72.
Club membership 1000.
Visitors must have handicap certificate.
Societies by arrangement.
Green Fees not confirmed.
Prof Martin Elsworthy
Designer C D Lawrie
Facilities ⊗ 🍽 ☕ 🍸 ⛳ 🏠 🏌 🏌
Location 3.5m SW on A146

Hotel ★★★ 64% Hotel Hatfield, The Esplanade, LOWESTOFT ☎ 01502 565337 33 ⇌ ↱

Newmarket Map 05 TL66

Links Cambridge Rd CB8 0TG
☎ 01638 663000 Fax 01638 661476
Gently undulating parkland.
18 holes, 6574yds, Par 72, SSS 71, Course record 70.
Club membership 780.
Visitors must have handicap certificate, may not play Sun before 11.30am.
Societies telephone secretary in advance.
Green Fees £28 (£32 weekends & bank holidays).
Prof John Sharkey
Designer Col. Hotchkin
Facilities ⊗ 🍽 by prior arrangement 🍴 ☕ 🍸 ⛳ 🏠 🏌 🏌
Location 1m SW on A1034

Hotel ★★★ 70% Heath Court Hotel, Moulton Rd, NEWMARKET ☎ 01638 667171 41 ⇌ ↱

Newton Map 05 TL94

Newton Green Newton Green CO10 0QN
☎ 01787 377217 & 377501
Flat, 18-hole commonland course.
18 holes, 5960yds, Par 69, SSS 68.
Club membership 640.

Visitors must contact in advance but may not play on Tue or Sat & Sun before 12.30.
Societies apply in advance.
Green Fees £16.50 per 18 holes.
Prof Tim Cooper
Facilities
Location W side of village on A134

Hotel ★★★ 64% The Bull, Hall St, LONG MELFORD ☎ 01787 378494 25

Raydon Map 05 TM03

Brett Vale Noakes Rd IP7 5LR
☎ 01473 310718
Brett Vale course takes you through a nature reserve and on lakeside walks, affording views over Dedham Vale. The excellent fairways demand an accurate tee and good approach shots. 1, 2, 3, 8, 10 and 15 are all affected by crosswinds, but once in the valley it is much more sheltered. Although only 6,000 yards the course is testing and interesting at all levels of golf.
18 holes, 6000yds, Par 70, SSS 68, Course record 65.
Club membership 500.

Visitors must book tee times and wear appropriate clothing.
Societies apply in writing or telephone.
Green Fees £15 per round (£20 weekends).
Cards
Prof Robert Taylor
Facilities
Location B1070 at Raydon, 2m from A12

Hotel ★★★ Maison Talbooth, Stratford Rd, DEDHAM ☎ 01206 322367 10

Southwold Map 05 TM57

Southwold The Common IP18 6TB
☎ 01502 723234 & 723248
Commonland course with 4-acre practice ground and panoramic views of the sea.
9 holes, 6052yds, Par 70, SSS 69, Course record 67.
Club membership 450.

Visitors restricted on competition days (Ladies-Wed, Gents-Sun).
Societies must contact in advance.
Green Fees £18 per round (£22 weekends).
Prof Brian Allen
Facilities
Location From A12 - B1140 to Southwold

Hotel ★★★ 68% Swan Hotel, Market Place, SOUTHWOLD
☎ 01502 722186 24 Annexe18

Stowmarket Map 05 TM05

Stowmarket Lower Rd, Onehouse IP14 3DA
☎ 01449 736473 Fax 01449 736826
Parkland course.
18 holes, 6107yds, Par 69, SSS 69, Course record 66.
Club membership 630.

Visitors must contact in advance.
Societies Thu or Fri, by arrangement.
Green Fees not confirmed.
Facilities by prior arrangement
Location 2.5m SW off B115

Hotel ★★ 64% Cedars Hotel, Needham Rd, STOWMARKET
☎ 01449 612668 25

Thorpeness Map 05 TM45

Thorpeness Golf Club & Hotel IP16 4NH
☎ 01728 452176 Fax 01728 453868
The holes of this moorland course are pleasantly varied with several quite difficult par 4's. Natural hazards abound. The 15th, with its sharp left dog-leg, is one of the best holes. Designed by James Braid.
18 holes, 6271yds, Par 69, SSS 71, Course record 66.
Club membership 270.

Visitors contact in advance.
Societies telephone in advance, deposit required.
Green Fees on application.
Cards
Prof Frank Hill
Designer James Braid
Facilities
& Leisure hard tennis courts.
Location W side of village off B1353

Hotel ★ 60% White Horse Hotel, Station Rd, LEISTON
☎ 01728 830694
10rm(1 7) Annexe3

Waldringfield Map 05 TM24

Waldringfield Heath Newbourne Rd IP12 4PT
☎ 01473 736768
Easy walking heathland course with long drives on 1st, 13th (590yds) and 10th tees.
18 holes, 6141yds, Par 71, SSS 69, Course record 68.
Club membership 600.

Visitors welcome Mon-Fri, weekends & bank holidays after noon.
Societies weekdays by arrangement.
Green Fees not confirmed.
Prof Tony Dobson
Designer Phillip Pilgrem
Facilities by prior arrangement
Location 3m NE of Ipswich off old A12

Hotel ★★★ 73% Seckford Hall Hotel, WOODBRIDGE
☎ 01394 385678 22 Annexe10

WOODBRIDGE Map 05 TM24

Seckford Seckford Hall Rd, Great Bealings IP13 6NT
☎ 01394 388000 Fax 01394 382818
A challenging course interspersed with young tree plantations, numerous bunkers, water hazards and undulating fairways, providing a tough test for all levels of golfer. The testing 18th is almost completely surrounded by water.
18 holes, 5303yds, Par 68, SSS 66, Course record 62.
Club membership 400.

Visitors telephone in advance for tee times.
Societies telephone in advance. Computerised booking system.
Green Fees £15 per 18 holes (£17.50 weekends).
Cards
Prof John Skinner
Designer J Johnson
Facilities
& Leisure heated indoor swimming pool, fishing, sauna, solarium, gymnasium.
Location (3m W of Woodbridge, 0ff A12)

Hotel ★★★ 73% Seckford Hall Hotel, WOODBRIDGE
☎ 01394 385678 22 Annexe10

Ufford Park Hotel Golf & Leisure Yarmouth Rd, Ufford IP12 1QW ☎ 01394 383555 Fax 01394 383582
A challenging new course opened in autumn 1992. The 18-hole Par 71 course is set in ancient parkland has many natural features including 11 water hazards retaind from the original parkland. There is also an extensive hotel and leisure complex beside the course.
18 holes, 6325yds, Par 71, SSS 71, Course record 67.
Club membership 320.

Visitors must book tee time from golf shop 01394 382836
Societies telephone or fax in advance to book tee time.
Green Fees £24 per day; £16 per 18 holes (£30/£20 weekends & bank holidays).
Cards
Prof Stuart Robertson
Designer Phil Pilgrim
Facilities
& Leisure heated indoor swimming pool, sauna, solarium, gymnasium, beautician, physiotheraphist, tuition breaks.
Location yjust off A12, on the B1438)

Hotel ★★★ 70% Ufford Park Hotel Golf & Leisure, Yarmouth Rd, Ufford, WOODBRIDGE
☎ 01394 383555 42 Annexe2

Woodbridge Bromeswell Heath IP12 2PF
☎ 01394 382038 Fax 01394 382392
A beautiful course, one of the best in East Anglia. It is situated on high ground and in different seasons present golfers with a great variety of colour. Some say that of the many good holes the 14th is the best.
18 holes, 6299yds, Par 70, SSS 70, Course record 64.
Forest Course: 9 holes, 6382yds, Par 70, SSS 70.
Club membership 900.

Visitors Main Course: must contact in advance, handicap certificate required, with member only weekends. Forest Course: open all days and no handicap certificate required.
Societies by prior telephone call or in writing.
Green Fees Main Course: £30 per day/round. Forest Course: £15 per day/round.
Prof Adrian Hubert
Designer Davie Grant
Facilities
Location 2.5m NE off A1152

Hotel ★★★ 73% Seckford Hall Hotel, WOODBRIDGE ☎ 01394 385678
22 Annexe10

WORLINGTON Map 05 TL67

Royal Worlington & Newmarket IP28 8SD
☎ 01638 712216 Fax 01638 717787
Inland 'links' course. Favourite 9-hole course of many golf writers.
9 holes, 3105yds, Par 35, SSS 70, Course record 67.
Club membership 325.

Visitors with member only at weekends. Must contact in advance and have a handicap certificate.
Societies must apply in writing.
Green Fees £35 per day; £25 after 2pm.
Prof Malcolm Hawkins
Designer Tom Dunn
Facilities by prior arrangement
Location 0.5m SE

Hotel ★★★ 67% Riverside Hotel, Mill St, MILDENHALL
☎ 01638 717274 20

SURREY

ADDLESTONE Map 04 TQ06

Abbey Moor Green Ln KT15 2XU ☎ 01932 570741
A 9-hole course ideal for low or high handicap players, there are enough hazards to trouble the best without being too punishing to the not so good. The 4th is a drive over water to an angled approach to a green well protected by sand and water, usually with a left to right crosswind.
9 holes, 5150yds, Par 68, SSS 65.
Club membership 300.

Visitors welcome providing they observe smart dress code & course etiquette, tee times should be booked in advance. ▶

Societies apply in writing or by telephone in advance.
Green Fees not confirmed.
Prof Stephen Carter
Facilities
Location Off junc 11 of the M25

Hotel ★★★ 72% Ship Thistle, Monument Green, WEYBRIDGE ☎ 01932 848364 39

New Zealand Woodham Ln KT15 3QD
☎ 01932 345049 Fax 01932 342891
Heathland course set in trees and heather.
18 holes, 6012yds, Par 68, SSS 69, Course record 66.
Club membership 320.
Visitors must contact in advance.
Societies telephone initially.
Green Fees available on application.
Prof Vic Elvidge
Designer Muir Fergusson/Simpson
Facilities
Location 1.5m E of Woking

Hotel ★★★ 72% Ship Thistle, Monument Green, WEYBRIDGE ☎ 01932 848364 39

ASHFORD Map 04 TQ07

Ashford Manor Fordbridge Rd TW15 3RT
☎ 01784 257687 Fax 01784 420355
Tree lined parkland course, looks easy but is difficult.
18 holes, 6352yds, Par 70, SSS 70, Course record 64.
Club membership 700.
Visitors advisable to telephone in advance, handicap certificate required, with member only at weekends but may not play competition days.
Societies welcome weekdays, except Thu am, must contact in advance.
Green Fees £25 per day/round.
Prof Mike Finney
Facilities by prior arrangement
Location 2m E of Staines via A308 Staines by-pass

Hotel ★★★ 70% The Thames Lodge, Thames St, STAINES ☎ 01784 464433 44

BAGSHOT Map 04 SU96

Pennyhill Park Hotel & Country Club London Rd GU19 5ET ☎ 01276 471774 Fax 01276 473217
A nine-hole course set in 11.4 acres of beautiful parkland. It is challenging to even the most experienced golfer.
9 holes, 2095yds, Par 32, SSS 32.
Club membership 100.
Visitors prior booking must be made. telephone in advance.
Green Fees not confirmed.
Facilities
& Leisure hard tennis courts, heated outdoor swimming pool, fishing, sauna.
Hotel ★★★★ Pennyhill Park Hotel, London Rd, BAGSHOT
☎ 01276 471774 22 Annexe67

Windlesham Grove End GU19 5HY
☎ 01276 452220 Fax 01276 452290
A parkland course with many demanding Par 4 holes over 400 yards. Thoughfully designed by Tommy Horton.
18 holes, 6600yds, Par 71, SSS 71, Course record 69.
Club membership 800.
Visitors handicap certificate required, contact in advance.
Societies apply in advance.
Green Fees not confirmed.
Prof Alan Barber
Designer Tommy Horton
Facilities
Location Junct of A30/A322

Hotel ★★★★ Pennyhill Park Hotel, London Rd, BAGSHOT ☎ 01276 471774
22 Annexe67

BANSTEAD Map 04 TQ25

Banstead Downs Burdon Ln, Belmont, Sutton SM2 7DD
☎ 0181 642 2284 Fax 0181 642 5252
A natural downland course set on a site of botanic interest. A challenging 18 holes with narrow fairways and tight lies.
18 holes, 6194yds, Par 69, SSS 69, Course record 64.
Club membership 835.
Visitors must book in advance and have handicap certificate or letter of introduction. With member only weekends.
Societies Thu, by prior arrangement
Green Fees £30 before noon, £20 thereafter.
Prof Robert Dickman
Designer J H Taylor/James Braid
Facilities
Location 1.5m N on A217

Hotel ★★ 64% Driftbridge Hotel, Reigate Rd, EPSOM ☎ 01737 352163 34

Cuddington Banstead Rd SM7 1RD
☎ 0181 393 0952 Fax 0181 786 7025
Parkland course with easy walking and good views.
18 holes, 6436yds, Par 70, SSS 71, Course record 61.
Club membership 694.
Visitors must contact in advance and have a handicap certificate or letter of introduction.
Societies welcome Thu, must apply in advance.
Green Fees £35 per day (£45 per round weekends).
Prof Mark Warner
Designer H S Colt
Facilities
Location N of Banstead station on A2022

Hotel ★★ 64% Driftbridge Hotel, Reigate Rd, EPSOM ☎ 01737 352163 34

BRAMLEY Map 04 TQ04

Bramley GU5 0AL ☎ 01483 892696 Fax 01483 894673
Parkland course, from the high ground picturesque views of the Wey Valley on one side and the Hog's Back. Full on course irrigation system with two reservoirs on the course.
18 holes, 5990yds, Par 69, SSS 69, Course record 63.
Club membership 850.

Visitors may not play Tue am (Ladies Morning) and must play with member at weekends & bank holidays. Must contact in advance.
Societies must telephone the secretary in advance.
Green Fees £33 per day; £27 per round.
Prof Gary Peddie
Designer James Braid
Facilities
Location 3m S of Guildford on A281

Hotel B Forte Posthouse Guildford, Egerton Rd, GUILDFORD ☎ 01483 574444 111

BROOKWOOD Map 04 SU95

West Hill Bagshot Rd GU24 0BH
☎ 01483 474365 Fax 01483 474252
Set in the Surrey landscape of heath, heather and tree lined fairways. An interesting and challenging course with subtle greens and a stream which affects play on seven holes. A premium on the well positioned drive.
18 holes, 6368yds, Par 69, SSS 70, Course record 62.
Club membership 500.
Visitors must contact in advance & have handicap certificate, may not play weekends & bank holidays.
Societies weekdays only (ex Wed). Telephone in advance.
Green Fees £55 per day; £40 per round.
Cards
Prof John A Clements
Designer C Butchart/W Parke
Facilities
Location E side of village on A322

Hotel ★★★★ Pennyhill Park Hotel, London Rd, BAGSHOT ☎ 01276 471774 22 Annexe67

CAMBERLEY Map 04 SU86

Camberley Heath Golf Dr GU15 1JG
☎ 01276 23258 Fax 01276 692505
One of the great 'heath and heather' courses so frequently associated with Surrey. Several very good short holes - especially the 8th. The 10th is a difficult and interesting par 4, as also is the 17th, where the drive must be held well to the left as perdition lurks on the right. A fairway irrigation system has been installed.
18 holes, 6128yds, Par 72, SSS 70, Course record 65.
Club membership 600.

Visitors may not play at weekends. Must contact in advance.
Societies must apply in advance.
Green Fees £56 per day; £36 per round.
Cards
Prof Glen Ralph
Designer Harry S Colt
Facilities by prior arrangement
Location 1.25m SE of town centre off A325

Hotel ★★★★ Pennyhill Park Hotel, London Rd, BAGSHOT ☎ 01276 471774 22 Annexe67

Pine Ridge Golf Centre Old Bisley Rd, Frimley GU16 5NX
☎ 01276 675444 & 20770 Fax 01276 678837
Pay and play heathland course with challenging par 3s, deceptively demanding par 4s and several birdiable par 5s. Good corporate or society packages.
18 holes, 6458yds, Par 72, SSS 71, Course record 67.
Visitors must pre book, no jeans or trainers.
Societies bookable in advance, packages available to suit.
Green Fees not confirmed.
Cards
Prof Andrew Fannon
Facilities
& Leisure ten pin bowling centre for corporate private functions.
Location Just off B3015, near A30

Hotel ★★★ 68% Frimley Hall, Portsmouth Rd, CAMBERLEY ☎ 01276 28321 66

CATERHAM Map 05 TQ35

Happy Valley Rook Ln, Chaldon CR3 5AA
☎ 01883 344555 Fax 01883 344422
Opened in September 1998, this technically challenging course is set in beautiful countryside and features fully irrigated greens and large practice areas.
18 holes, 6900yds, Par 72.
Visitors may play weekdays only, and can book in advance.
Societies apply in writing.
Green Fees £35.
Cards
Designer David Williams
Facilities
Location M25 junct 6 A22

Hotel ★★★★ 77% Coulsdon Manor Hotel, Coulsdon Court Rd, Coulsdon, CROYDON ☎ 0181 668 0414 35

CHERTSEY Map 04 TQ06

Barrow Hills Longcross KT16 0DS ☎ 01344 635770
This parkland course with natural hazards is only open to guests of members.
18 holes, 3090yds, Par 56, SSS 53, Course record 58.
Club membership 355.
Visitors must play with member at all times.
Green Fees not confirmed.
Location 3m W on B386

Hotel ★★★ 70% The Thames Lodge, Thames St, STAINES ☎ 01784 464433 44

Laleham Laleham Reach KT16 8RP
☎ 01932 564211 Fax 01932 564448
Well-bunkered parkland/meadowland course.
18 holes, 6211yds, Par 70, SSS 70.
Club membership 600.
Visitors members guests only at weekends.
Societies must contact in writing.
Green Fees £27 per day; £20 per round.
Prof Hogan Stott
Facilities
Location 1.5m N

Hotel ★★★ 70% The Thames Lodge, Thames St, STAINES
☎ 01784 464433 44

CHIDDINGFOLD Map 04 SU93

Chiddingfold Petworth Rd GU8 4SL
☎ 01428 685888 Fax 01428 685939
With panoramic views across the Surrey Downs, this challenging course offers a unique combination of lakes, mature woodland and wildlife.
18 holes, 5501yds, Par 70, SSS 67.
Club membership 300.
Visitors telephone bookings up to one week in advance.
Societies prior telephone booking required.
Green Fees Mon £10 per round, Tue-Fri £15 per round (£22 per round weekends).
Cards
Prof Paul Creamer
Designer Johnathan Gaunt
Facilities
& Leisure gymnasium.
Location A283

Hotel ★★★★ 71% Lythe Hill Hotel, Petworth Rd, HASLEMERE
☎ 01428 651251 40

CHIPSTEAD Map 04 TQ25

Chipstead How Ln CR5 3LN
☎ 01737 555781 Fax 01737 555404
Hilly parkland course, hard walking, good views. Testing 18th hole.
18 holes, 5491yds, Par 68, SSS 67, Course record 63.
Club membership 650.
Visitors must contact in advance. May not play weekends or Tue mornings.
Societies must apply in writing.
Green Fees £25 per day; £20 per round.
Prof Gary Torbett
Facilities
Location 0.5m N of village

Hotel ★★★★ 70% Selsdon Park Hotel, Addington Rd, Sanderstead, CROYDON
☎ 0181 657 8811 170

CHOBHAM Map 04 SU96

Chobham Chobham Rd, Knaphill GU21 2TZ
☎ 01276 855584 Fax 01276 855663
Designed by Peter Allis and CLive Clark, Chobham course sits among mature oaks and tree nurseries offering tree-lined fairways, together with six man-made lakes.
18 holes, 5821yds, Par 69, SSS 67, Course record 67.
Club membership 750.
Visitors booking in advance essential.
Societies by prior arrangement.
Green Fees not confirmed.
Prof Richard Thomas
Designer Peter Alliss/Clive Clark
Facilities by prior arrangement
Hotel ★★★ 61% Falcon Hotel, 68 Farnborough Rd, FARNBOROUGH
☎ 01252 545378 30

COBHAM Map 04 TQ16

Silvermere Redhill Rd KT11 1EF ☎ 01932 866007
Parkland course with many very tight holes through woodland, 17th has 170-yd carry over the lake. Driving range.
18 holes, 6700yds, Par 73.
Club membership 740.
Visitors may not play at weekends until 1pm. Must contact in advance.
Societies must contact by telephone.
Green Fees not confirmed.
Prof Doug McClelland
Facilities
& Leisure fishing.
Location 2.25m NW off A245

Hotel ★★★★ 65% Woodlands Park Hotel, Woodlands Ln, STOKE D'ABERNON
☎ 01372 843933 59

CRANLEIGH Map 04 TQ03

Fernfell Golf & Country Club Barhatch Ln GU6 7NG
☎ 01483 268855
Scenic woodland/parkland course at the base of the Surrey hills, easy walking. Clubhouse in 400-year-old barn.
18 holes, 5636yds, Par 68, SSS 67, Course record 64.
Club membership 1000.
Visitors welcome weekdays, at weekends may only play after noon. Contact professional in advance 01483 277188
Societies telephone in advance.
Green Fees not confirmed.
Prof Trevor Longmuir
Facilities by prior arrangement
& Leisure hard tennis courts, indoor swimming pool, sauna, solarium, gymnasium.
Location Off A281 Guildford to Horsham road, signposted Cranleigh

Hotel ★★★ 62% Gatton Manor Hotel Golf & Country Club, Standon Ln, OCKLEY
☎ 01306 627555 16

Wildwood Country Club Horsham Rd, Alfold, Cranleigh GU6 8JE ☎ 01403 753255
Parkland with stands of old oaks dominating several holes, a stream fed by a natural spring winds through a series of lakes and ponds. The greens are smooth, undulating and large. The 5th and 16th are the most challenging holes.
Wildwood Countyry Club: 18 holes, 6655yds, Par 72, SSS 73, Course record 65.
Club membership 400.

Visitors welcome subject to availability & booking.
Societies apply in writing or telephone for enquiries.
Green Fees £30 per day; £19 per round (£40/£29 weekends).
Cards
Prof Nicholas Parfrement
Designer Hawtree & Sons
Facilities
& Leisure fishing.
Location Off A281, approx 9m S of Guildford

Hotel ★★★ 62% Gatton Manor Hotel Golf & Country Club, Standon Ln, OCKLEY ☎ 01306 627555 16

DORKING Map 04 TQ14

Betchworth Park Reigate Rd RH4 1NZ ☎ 01306 882052
Parkland course, with hard walking on southern ridge of Boxhill.
18 holes, 6266yds, Par 69, SSS 70, Course record 64.
Club membership 725.

Visitors weekend play Sun pm only. Must contact in advance.
Societies apply in writing.
Green Fees not confirmed.
Prof Tocher
Designer H Colt
Facilities
Location 1m E on A25

Hotel ★★★ 60% The White Horse, High St, DORKING ☎ 01306 881138 36 Annexe32

Dorking Chart Park, Deepdene Av RH5 4BX ☎ 01306 886917
Undulating parkland course, easy slopes, wind-sheltered. Testing holes: 5th 'Tom's Puddle' (par 4); 7th 'Rest and Be Thankful' (par 4); 9th 'Double Decker' (par 4).
9 holes, 5120yds, Par 66, SSS 65, Course record 62.
Club membership 408.

Visitors may not play Wed am and with member only weekends & bank holidays. Contact in advance.
Societies Tue & Thu, telephone in advance.
Green Fees £12 per 18 holes. Twilight £8.
Prof Paul Napier
Designer J Braid/Others
Facilities by prior arrangement
Location 1m S on A24

Hotel ★★★★ 68% The Burford Bridge, Burford Bridge, Box Hill, DORKING ☎ 01306 884561 48

EAST HORSLEY Map 04 TQ05

Drift KT24 5HD ☎ 01483 284641 Fax 01483 284642
Woodland course with secluded fairways and picturesque setting. A challenging course that punishes the wayward shot.
18 holes, 6424yds, Par 73, SSS 72, Course record 70.
Club membership 718.

Visitors book in advance to the pro shop, Mon-Fri only.
Societies telephone in advance.
Green Fees £45 per day; £25 per round.
Cards
Prof Peter Fuller
Designer Sandown
Facilities
Location 1.5m N off B2039

Hotel ★★ 66% Bookham Grange Hotel, Little Bookham Common, Bookham, LEATHERHEAD ☎ 01372 452742 18

EFFINGHAM Map 04 TQ15

Effingham Guildford Rd KT24 5PZ ☎ 01372 452203 Fax 01372 459959
Easy-walking downland course laid out on 27-acres with tree-lined fairways. It is one of the longest of the Surrey courses with wide subtle greens that provide a provocative but by no means exhausting challenge. Fine views.
18 holes, 6524yds, Par 71, SSS 71, Course record 64.
Club membership 800.

Visitors contact in advance. With member only weekends & bank holidays.
Societies Wed, Thu & Fri only and must book in advance.
Green Fees £35 per day; £27.50 per half day.
Prof Steve Hoatson
Designer H S Colt
Facilities
Location W side of village on A246

Hotel ★★ 66% Bookham Grange Hotel, Little Bookham Common, Bookham, LEATHERHEAD ☎ 01372 452742 18

ENTON GREEN Map 04 SU94

West Surrey GU8 5AF ☎ 01483 421275
A good parkland-type course in rolling, well-wooded setting. Some fairways are tight with straight driving at a premium. The 17th is a testing hole with a long hill walk.
18 holes, 6259yds, Par 71, SSS 70, Course record 65.
Club membership 600.

Visitors must contact in advance and have letter of introduction.
Societies must apply in writing. All players to have a handicap.
Green Fees not confirmed.
Prof Alister Tawse
Designer Herbert Fowler
Facilities
Location S side of village

▶

Hotel ★★★ 61% The Bush Hotel, The Borough, FARNHAM ☎ 01252 715237 66

EPSOM Map 04 TQ26

Epsom Longdown Ln South KT17 4JR
☎ 01372 721666 Fax 01372 817183
Traditional downland course with many mature trees and well watered greens..
18 holes, 5701yds, Par 69, SSS 68, Course record 62.
Club membership 800.

Visitors available any day except Tue, Sat & Sun till 12.00 hrs.
Societies must contact in advance.
Green Fees £30 all day; £20 per round.
Prof Ron Goudie
Designer Willie Dunne
Facilities
Location SE side of town centre on B288

Hotel ★★ 64% Driftbridge Hotel, Reigate Rd, EPSOM ☎ 01737 352163 34

Horton Park Country Club Hook Rd KT19 8QG
☎ 0181 393 8400 & 394 2626 Fax 0181 394 1369
Parkland course in picturesque surroundings with a natural lake. An extended 18 hole course is under construction along with a full size par 3 nine hole course, due to open spring 1999. The present course will remain open until the new extended areas are complete.
18 holes, 5100yds, Par 69, SSS 65, Course record 68.
Club membership 534.

Visitors must book for weekends.
Societies must telephone in advance to play at weekends & bank holidays.
Green Fees £17.50 per day; £11 per round (£13 per round weekends & bank holidays).
Cards
Facilities
Hotel ★★ 64% Driftbridge Hotel, Reigate Rd, EPSOM ☎ 01737 352163 34

ESHER Map 04 TQ16

Moore Place Portsmouth Rd KT10 9LN
☎ 01372 463533 Fax 01372 460274
Public course on attractive, undulating parkland laid out some 60 years ago by Harry Vardon. Examples of most of the trees that will survive in the UK are to be found on the course. Testing short holes at 2nd, 3rd and 9th.
9 holes, 2148yds, Par 32, SSS 30, Course record 25.
Club membership 300.
Visitors no restrictions.
Societies must contact in advance.
Green Fees £5.80 (£7.70 weekends & bank holidays).
Prof David Allen
Designer Harry Vardon/David Allen
Facilities
Location SW side of town centre on A244

Hotel ★★★ 72% Ship Thistle, Monument Green, WEYBRIDGE
☎ 01932 848364 39

Sandown Golf Centre Sandown Park, More Ln KT10 8AN
☎ 01372 463340
Flat parkland course in middle of racecourse. Additional facilities include a driving range, and a pitch-and-putt course.
New Course: 9 holes, 2828yds, Par 35, SSS 34.
Par 3: 9 holes, 1193yds, Par 27.
Club membership 650.
Visitors no restrictions.
Societies must apply in writing.
Green Fees not confirmed.
Facilities
Location 1m NW off A307

Hotel ★★ 65% Haven Hotel, Portsmouth Rd, ESHER
☎ 0181 398 0023 16 Annexe4

Thames Ditton & Esher Portsmouth Rd KT10 9AL
☎ 0181 398 1551
Commonland course with public right of way across the course. Although the course is not long, accuracy is essential and wayward shots are normally punished.
18 holes, 5149yds, Par 66, SSS 65, Course record 63.
Club membership 250.
Visitors may not play on Sun mornings. Advisable to telephone for availability.
Societies must contact in advance.
Green Fees not confirmed.
Prof Mark Rodbard
Facilities by prior arrangement
Location 1m NE on A307

Hotel ★★ 65% Haven Hotel, Portsmouth Rd, ESHER
☎ 0181 398 0023 16 Annexe4

FARLEIGH Map 05 TQ36

Farleigh Court Old Farleigh Rd CR6 9PX
☎ 0188362 7711 & 7733 Fax 0188362 7722
Members: 18 holes, 6414yds, Par 72, SSS 71.
Pay & Play: 9 holes, 6562yds, Par 72, SSS 71.
Club membership 450.
Visitors welcome on the Members Course and the Pay & Play Course.
Societies welcome, please and ask for Society Co ordinator.
Green Fees Members Course: £30 (£40 weekends). Pay & Play: £12 (£15 weekends).
Cards
Prof Tom O'Keefe
Designer John Jacobs
Facilities
& Leisure sauna.
Location 1.5m from Selsdon

Hotel ★★★★ 70% Selsdon Park Hotel, Addington Rd, Sanderstead, CROYDON ☎ 0181 657 8811 170

FARNHAM Map 04 SU84

Blacknest Binsted GU34 4QL
☎ 01420 22888 Fax 01420 22001
Privately owned pay and play golf centre catering for all ages and levels of abilities. Facilities include a 15-bay driving range, gymnasium and a challenging, newly-constructed 18-hole course featuring water on 14 holes.
18 holes, 5858yds, Par 70, SSS 69, Course record 65.
Club membership 450.
Visitors welcome at all times but should telephone for tee times especially weekends.
Societies prior arrangements necessary telephone or write.
Green Fees £14 per round (£16.50 weekends). Par 3 course £4.
Cards
Prof Ian Benson
Designer Mr Nicholson
Facilities
& Leisure sauna, solarium, gymnasium, par 3 Academy course.
Location 0.5m S of A31 at Bentley

Hotel ★★★ 60% Farnham House Hotel, Alton Rd, FARNHAM ☎ 01252 716908 20

Farnham The Sands GU10 1PX
☎ 01252 782109 Fax 01252 781185
A mixture of meadowland and heath with quick drying sandy subsoil. Several of the earlier holes have interesting features, the finishing holes rather less.
18 holes, 6325yds, Par 72, SSS 70, Course record 66.
Club membership 700.
Visitors must contact in advance. Must be member of recognised club & have handicap certificate. With member only weekends.
Societies must apply in writing.
Green Fees £37.50 per day; £30 per round.
Prof Grahame Cowlishaw
Facilities by prior arrangement
Location 3m E off A31

Hotel ★★★ 61% The Bush Hotel, The Borough, FARNHAM ☎ 01252 715237 66

Farnham Park Folly Hill, Farnham Park GU9 0AU
☎ 01252 715216
Municipal parkland course in Farnham Park.
9 holes, 1163yds, Par 27, SSS 50, Course record 51.
Club membership 50.
Visitors pay and play everyday.
Societies telephone in advance.
Green Fees £3.90 per 9 holes (£4.40 weekends).
Prof Peter Chapman
Designer Henry Cotton
Facilities
Location N side of town centre on A287

Hotel ★★★ 61% The Bush Hotel, The Borough, FARNHAM ☎ 01252 715237 66

GODALMING Map 04 SU94

Broadwater Park Guildford Rd, Farncombe GU7 3BU
☎ 01483 429955
A Par-3 public course with floodlit driving range.
9 holes, 1287yds, Par 54, SSS 50.
Club membership 160.
Visitors must book for weekends & bank holidays,
Societies telephone in advance
Green Fees not confirmed.
Prof Kevin D Milton
Designer Kevin Milton
Facilities
Location 4m SW of Guildford

Hotel ★★★ 65% Inn on the Lake, Ockford Rd, GODALMING ☎ 01483 415575 21

Hurtmore Hurtmore Rd, Hurtmore GU7 2RN
☎ 01483 426492 Fax 01483 426121
A Peter Alliss/Clive Clark Pay and Play course with seven lakes and 100 bunkers. The 15th hole is the longest at 540yards. Played mainly into the wind there are 10 bunkers to negotiate. The 3rd hole at 440yds stroke Index 1 is a real test. A dogleg right around a lake and 9 bunkers makes this hole worthy of its stroke index.
18 holes, 5514yds, Par 70, SSS 67, Course record 69.
Club membership 200.
Visitors book by telephone up to 6 days in advance.
Societies telephone in advance.
Green Fees £10 per round (£15 weekends).
Cards
Prof Maxine Burton
Designer Peter Alliss/Clive Clark
Facilities
Location 2m NW of Godalming between A3/A3100, access via unclass road

Hotel ★★★ 65% Inn on the Lake, Ockford Rd, GODALMING ☎ 01483 415575 21

Shillinglee Park Chiddingfold GU8 4TA
☎ 01428 653237 & 708158
Manicured parkland course with many natural features including seven ponds. The 4th and 7th are the signature holes requiring tee shots and second shots over ponds, to well-guarded greens.
9 holes, 5032yds, Par 64, SSS 64, Course record 65.
Club membership 400.

Visitors no restrictions but advisable to book starting times.
Societies apply for details.
Green Fees not confirmed.
Prof Roger Mace
Designer Roger Mace
Facilities
Location 5m S of Godalming, off A283

Hotel ★★★ 65% Inn on the Lake, Ockford Rd, GODALMING ☎ 01483 415575 21

GUILDFORD Map 04 SU94

Guildford High Path Rd, Merrow GU1 2HL
☎ 01483 563941 Fax 01483 453228
The course is on typical Surrey downland bordered by attractive woodlands. Situated on chalk, it is acknowledged to be one of the best all-weather courses in the area. The holes provide an interesting variety of play, an invigorating experience.
18 holes, 6090yds, Par 69, SSS 70, Course record 64.
Club membership 700.

Visitors must contact in advance. With member only weekends & bank holidays.
Societies welcome Mon-Fri. Must apply in advance.
Green Fees £35 per day; £25 per round.
Prof P G Hollington
Designer J H Taylor/Hawtree
Facilities
Location E side of town centre off A246

Hotel ★★★ 72% The Manor, Newlands Corner, GUILDFORD
☎ 01483 222624 45

Milford Station Ln, Milford GU8 5HS
☎ 01483 419200 Fax 01483 41999
A Peter Alliss/Clive Clark designed course opened summer 1993. The design has cleverly incorporated a demanding course within an existing woodland and meadow area.
18 holes, 5945yds, Par 69, SSS 68, Course record 67.
Club membership 750.

Visitors telephone 01483 416291 up to 1 week in advance.
Societies telephone in advance.
Green Fees £19.50 weekdays (£35-£25 weekends).
Cards
Prof Bill Irvine
Designer Peter Allis
Facilities
Location 6m SW, leave A3 Milford then A3100 to Enton

Hotel ★★★ 65% Inn on the Lake, Ockford Rd, GODALMING
☎ 01483 415575 21

Roker Park Rokers Farm, Aldershot Rd GU3 3PB
☎ 01483 236677 Fax 01483 232324
A Pay and Play 9-hole parkland course. A challenging course with two Par 5 holes.
9 holes, 3037yds, Par 36, SSS 72.
Club membership 200.

Visitors no restrictions, pay & play, phone for reservations.
Societies prior arrangement with deposit at least 14 days before, minimum 12 persons.
Green Fees £11 per 18 holes; £7 per 9 holes (£14/£8.50 weekends and bank holidays).
Prof Kevin Warn
Designer W V Roker
Facilities
Location A323, 3m from Guildford

Hotel ★★★ 78% The Angel Posting House and Livery, 91 High St, GUILDFORD
☎ 01483 564555 11

HINDHEAD Map 04 SU83

Hindhead Churt Rd GU26 6HX
☎ 01428 604614 Fax 01428 608508
A good example of a Surrey heath-and-heather course, and most picturesque. Players must be prepared for some hard walking. The first nine fairways follow narrow valleys requiring straight hitting; the second nine are much less restricted.
18 holes, 6373yds, Par 70, SSS 70, Course record 63.
Club membership 770.

Visitors must contact in advance and have a handicap certificate.
Societies Wed & Thu only, contact in advance
Green Fees £36 per 18 holes; £28 per 9 holes. (£42/£33 weekends & bank holidays).
Prof Neil Ogilvy
Designer J H Taylor
Facilities
Location 1.5m NW on A287

Hotel ★★★★ 71% Lythe Hill Hotel, Petworth Rd, HASLEMERE
☎ 01428 651251 40

KINGSWOOD Map 04 TQ25

Kingswood Sandy Ln KT20 6NE
☎ 01737 832188
Flat parkland course, easy walking.
18 holes, 6880yds, Par 72, SSS 73.
Club membership 700.

Visitors must contact professional at least 24 hrs in advance. May not play weekends.
Societies must apply in advance.
Green Fees not confirmed.
Prof James Dodds
Designer James Braid
Facilities
& Leisure squash.
Location 5m S of village off A217

Hotel ★★★ 65% Reigate Manor Hotel, Reigate Hill, REIGATE ☎ 01737 240125 50

LEATHERHEAD Map 04 TQ15

Leatherhead Kingston Rd KT22 0EE
☎ 01372 843966 & 843956 Fax 01372 842241
Parkland course with numerous ditches and only two hills, so walking is easy.
18 holes, 6203yds, Par 71, SSS 69, Course record 67.

Visitors telephone pro shop 01372 843956 up to 10 days in advance.
Societies telephone for booking form.
Green Fees not confirmed.
Prof Simon Norman
Facilities
Location 0.25m from junct 9 of M25, on A243

Hotel ★★★★ 65% Woodlands Park Hotel, Woodlands Ln, STOKE D'ABERNON ☎ 01372 843933 59

Pachesham Park Golf Complex Oaklawn Rd KT22 0BT
☎ 01372 843453 Fax 01372 844076
A 9-hole undulating parkland course playing out over 18 holes at 5,618yards.
9 holes, 2805yds, Par 70, SSS 67, Course record 67.
Club membership 495.

Visitors book 2 days in advance by phone. May play weekends after 12.30pm.
Societies apply in advance.
Green Fees £12.50 per 18 holes; £7.50 per 9 holes (£15/£9 weekends & bank holidays).
Cards
Prof Philip Taylor
Designer Phil Taylor
Facilities by prior arrangement
Location On A244, 0.5m from M25 junct 9

Hotel ★★★★ 65% Woodlands Park Hotel, Woodlands Ln, STOKE D'ABERNON ☎ 01372 843933 59

Tyrrells Wood The Drive KT22 8QP
☎ 01372 376025 Fax 01372 360836
Parkland course with easy walking. Snooker.
18 holes, 6282yds, Par 71, SSS 70, Course record 65.
Club membership 700.

Visitors must contact in advance. Restricted weekends.
Societies must apply in advance.
Green Fees £50 per day; £34 per round (£44 per round Sun).
Prof Max Taylor
Designer James Braid
Facilities
& Leisure putting green & limited practice area.
Location 2m SE of town, off A24

Hotel ★★★★ 68% The Burford Bridge, Burford Bridge, Box Hill, DORKING ☎ 01306 884561 48

LIMPSFIELD Map 05 TQ45

Limpsfield Chart Westerham Rd RH8 0SL
☎ 01883 723405
Tight heathland course set in National Trust land, well wooded.
9 holes, 5718yds, Par 70, SSS 68, Course record 64.
Club membership 300.

Visitors with member only or by appointment weekends & not before 3.30pm Thu (Ladies Day).
Societies must apply in advance.
Green Fees £18 per day/round. (£20 weekends & bank holidays).
Facilities by prior arrangement by prior arrangement
& Leisure putting green, practice area.
Location 1m E on A25 from M25 junct 6

Hotel ★★★ 68% Kings Arms Hotel, Market Square, WESTERHAM ☎ 01959 562990 17

LINGFIELD Map 05 TQ34

Lingfield Park Lingfield Rd, Racecourse Rd RH7 6PQ
☎ 01342 834602 Fax 01342 834602
Difficult and challenging, tree-lined parkland course set in 210 acres of beautiful Surrey countryside. Driving range.
18 holes, 6473yds, Par 71, SSS 72, Course record 69.
Club membership 700.

Visitors must be accompanied by member on Sat & Sun. Advisable to telephone first.
Societies must telephone in advance.
Green Fees £27 per round. (£34 after 1pm weekends).
Cards
Prof Christopher Morley
Facilities
Location Entrance next to Lingfield race course

Hotel ★★★ 65% Woodbury House Hotel, Lewes Rd, EAST GRINSTEAD ☎ 01342 313657 14

NEWDIGATE Map 04 TQ14

Rusper Rusper Rd RH5 5BX
☎ 01293 871871 Fax 01293 871456
New course set in mature woodland. The opening two holes give the golfer an encouraging start with the following holes demanding accurate play through the trees. The 5th hole is a challenging Par 5 from the back tee with a gentle dogleg tempting the golfer to take a shortcut.
9 holes, 6218yds, Par 71, SSS 69, Course record 67.
Club membership 270.

Visitors welcome but telephone to reserve time, some restrictions if competitions being played.
Societies telephone in advance for details.
Green Fees £11.50 per 18 holes; £7 per 9 holes (£15.50/£8.50 weekends).
Cards
Prof Janice Arnold
Designer A Blunden
Facilities by prior arrangement
Location Between Newdigate/Rusper, off A24

Hotel ★★★★ 68% The Burford Bridge, Burford Bridge, Box Hill, DORKING ☎ 01306 884561 48

Ockley Map 04 TQ14

Gatton Manor Hotel Golf & Country Club Standon Ln RH5 5PQ ☎ 01306 627555 Fax 01306 627713
Undulating parkland course through woods and over many challenging water holes.
18 holes, 6653yds, Par 72, SSS 72, Course record 68.
Club membership 300.

Visitors may book up to 10 days in advance. Restricted Sun (am). Tee times to be booked through professional 01306 627557
Societies must apply in advance.
Green Fees £36 per day; £21 per round; (£28 per round weekends).
Cards
Prof Rae Sargent
Designer Henry Cotton
Facilities
& Leisure grass tennis courts, fishing, sauna, solarium, gymnasium, bowls.
Location 1.5m SW off A29

Hotel ★★★ 62% Gatton Manor Hotel Golf & Country Club, Standon Ln, OCKLEY ☎ 01306 627555 16

Ottershaw Map 04 TQ06

Foxhills Stonehill Rd KT16 0EL
☎ 01932 872050 Fax 01932 874762
A pair of parkland courses designed in the grand manner and with American course-design in mind. One course is tree-lined, the other, as well as trees, has massive bunkers and artificial lakes which contribute to the interest. Both courses offer testing golf and they finish on the same long 'double green'. Par 3 'Manor' course also available.
Chertsey Course: 18 holes, 6734yds, Par 73, SSS 72.
Longcross Course: 18 holes, 6429yds, Par 72, SSS 71.
Manor Course: 9 holes, 1275yds, Par 27.
Visitors contact sales office to reserve times. Restricted before noon weekends.
Societies welcome Mon-Fri, must apply in advance.
Green Fees under review.
Cards
Prof B Hunt/A Good/R Summerscales
Designer F W Hawtree
Facilities
& Leisure hard tennis courts, outdoor and indoor heated swimming pools, squash, sauna, solarium, gymnasium, health club.
Location 1m NW

Hotel ★★★ 66% The Crown Hotel, 7 London St, CHERTSEY
☎ 01932 564657 Annexe30

Pirbright Map 04 SU95

Goal Farm Gole Rd GU24 0PZ
☎ 01483 473183 & 473205
Beautiful lanscaped parkland 'Pay and Play' course with excellent greens.
9 holes, 1273yds, Par 54, SSS 48.
Club membership 300.
Visitors may not play on Sat before 4pm or Thu mornings.
Societies telephone in advance.
Green Fees £7.50 per 18 holes; £3.75 per 9 holes (£8/£4 weekends and bank holidays).
Designer Bill Cox
Facilities
Location 1.5m NW on B3012

Hotel B Forte Posthouse Farnborough, Lynchford Rd, FARNBOROUGH
☎ 01252 545051 143

Puttenham Map 04 SU94

Puttenham Heath Rd GU3 1AL
☎ 01483 810498 Fax 01483 810988
Picturesque tree-lined heathland course offering testing golf, easy walking.
18 holes, 6214yds, Par 71, SSS 70.
Club membership 650.
Visitors weekdays by prior arrangment tel: 01483 810498, with member only weekends & public holidays.
Societies apply in advance to secretary.
Green Fees £30 per day; £23 per round.
Prof Gary Simmons
Facilities
Location 1m SE on B3000

Hotel ★★★ 61% The Bush Hotel, The Borough, FARNHAM ☎ 01252 715237 66

Redhill Map 04 TQ25

Redhill & Reigate Clarence Rd, Pendelton Rd RH1 6LB
☎ 01737 240777 Fax 01737 242117
Parkland course.
18 holes, 5238yds, Par 67, SSS 66.
Club membership 600.
Visitors may not play before 11am weekends or after 2pm Sun (Jun-Sep). Must contact in advance.
Societies must apply in writing.
Green Fees £12 per round (£18 weekends & bank holidays).
Cards
Prof Warren Pike
Facilities
Location 1m S on A23

Hotel ★★★ 65% Reigate Manor Hotel, Reigate Hill, REIGATE ☎ 01737 240125 50

Reigate Map 04 TQ25

Reigate Heath Flanchford Rd RH2 8QR
☎ 01737 242610 & 226793 Fax 01737 226793
Gorse, heather, pine and birch trees abound on this popular 9-hole heathland course. Sandy soil gives all year round play even in the wettest winters. Clubhouse enjoys panoramic views of the North Downs and Leith Hill.
9 holes, 5658yds, Par 67, SSS 67, Course record 65.
Club membership 550.
Visitors with member only weekends & bank holidays. Must contact in advance.
Societies must apply in writing.
Green Fees £20 per day; £16 morning; £12 afternoon.
Prof Barry Davies
Facilities
Location 1.5m W off A25

Hotel ★★★ 65% Reigate Manor Hotel, Reigate Hill, REIGATE ☎ 01737 240125 50

Reigate Hill Gatton Bottom RH2 0TU
☎ 01737 645577 Fax 01737 642650
Championship standard course opened in 1995 with fully irrigated tees and greens. Feature holes include the 5th which is divided by four bunkers and the par 5 14th involving a tricky second shot across a lake. Very good short holes at 8th and 12th with panoramic views from the tees.
18 holes, 6175yds, Par 72, SSS 70, Course record 75.
Club membership 650.
Visitors must contact in advance to book tee time, may not play weekends until 12 noon.
Societies welcome Mon-Fri but must book in advance.
Green Fees £35 per day; £25 per round. (£35 per round weekends after noon). Twilight golf from 5pm £15..
Cards
Prof Martin Platts
Designer David Williams
Facilities
Location 2m from junct 8 of M25

Hotel ★★★ 63% Bridge House Hotel, Reigate Hill, REIGATE ☎ 01737 246801 & 244821 Fax 01737 223756 39

Shepperton Map 04 TQ06

American Golf at Sunbury Charlton Ln TW17 8QA
☎ 01932 771414 Fax 01932 789300
There is a 9-hole course already in use at Sunbury which at 6210 yards, with two Par 5's and two Par 3's, is one of the longest in the south of England. There is also a new 18-hole course due to open in Autumn 1998.
Sunbury Golf Course: 9 holes, 6210yds, Par 72, SSS 72, Course record 70.
Club membership 300.
Visitors no restrictions.
Societies advance booking necessary.
Green Fees not confirmed.
Prof Alistair Hardaway
Facilities
Hotel ★★★ 64% Shepperton Moat House Hotel, Felix Ln, SHEPPERTON ☎ 01932 241404 156

Tandridge Map 05 TQ35

Tandridge RH8 9NQ
☎ 01883 712274 Fax 01883 730537
A parkland course with two loops of 9 holes from the clubhouse. The first 9 is relatively flat. The second 9 undulates and reveals several outstanding views of the North Downs and the South.
18 holes, 6250yds, Par 70, SSS 70.
Club membership 750.
Visitors must contact in advance. May play Mon, Wed, Thu.
Societies Mon, Wed & Thu, apply in advance.
Green Fees summer; £45 per day or morning round; £35 per afternoon round. Winter £24 per round.
Prof Allan Farquhar
Designer H S Colt
Facilities
Location 2m SE junc 6 M25, 1.5m E of Godstone on A25

Hotel ★★★★ 71% Nutfield Priory, Nutfield, REDHILL ☎ 01737 822066 60

Tilford Map 04 SU84

Hankley Common GU10 2DD
☎ 01252 792493 Fax 01252 795699
A natural heathland course subject to wind. Greens are first rate. The 18th, a long par 4, is most challenging, the green being beyond a deep chasm which traps any but the perfect second shot. The 7th is a spectacular one-shotter.
18 holes, 6418yds, Par 71, SSS 71.
Club membership 700.
Visitors handicap certificate required, restricted to afternoons at weekends.
Societies apply in writing.
Green Fees not confirmed.
Prof Peter Stow
Facilities
Location 0.75m SE

Hotel ★★★ 61% The Bush Hotel, The Borough, FARNHAM ☎ 01252 715237 66

Virginia Water Map 04 TQ06

Wentworth See page 245

Walton-on-Thames Map 04 TQ16

Burhill Burwood Rd KT12 4BL ☎ 01932 227345
A relatively short and easy parkland course with some truly magnificent trees. The 18th is a splendid par 4 requiring a well-placed drive and a long firm second. This course is always in immaculate condition.
18 holes, 6224yds, Par 69, SSS 70, Course record 64.
Club membership 1000.
Visitors may not play Fri-Sun unless introduced by member. Must contact in advance.
Societies apply in writing.
Green Fees not confirmed. ▶

Prof Lee Johnson
Designer Willie Park
Facilities
& Leisure squash.
Location 2m S

Hotel ★★★ 72% Ship Thistle, Monument Green, WEYBRIDGE ☎ 01932 848364 39

WALTON-ON-THE-HILL Map 04 TQ25

WALTON HEATH See page 247

WEST BYFLEET Map 04 TQ06

West Byfleet Sheerwater Rd KT14 6AA
☎ 01932 343433 Fax 01932 340667
An attractive course set against a background of woodland and gorse. The 13th is the famous 'pond' shot with a water hazard and two bunkers fronting the green. No less than six holes of 420 yards or more.
18 holes, 6211yds, Par 70, SSS 70.
Club membership 600.
Visitors must contact professional in advance, only with member at weekends. Restricted Thu (Ladies Day).
Societies must apply in writing.
Green Fees £36.50 per day; £29.50 per round.
Cards
Prof David Regan
Designer C S Butchart
Facilities
Location W side of village on A245

Hotel B Hilton National Cobham, Seven Hills Rd South, COBHAM
☎ 01932 864471 149

WEST CLANDON Map 04 TQ05

Clandon Regis Epsom Rd GU4 7TT ☎ 01483 224888
High quality parkland course with challenging lake holes on the back nine. European Tour specification tees and greens.
18 holes, 6412yds, Par 72, SSS 71.
Visitors a visitor is allowed to play 10 times a year mid-week only.
Societies telephone in advance.
Green Fees not confirmed.
Prof Sean Brady
Facilities
& Leisure sauna.
Location From A246 Guildford/Leatherhead direction

Hotel ★★★ 72% The Manor, Newlands Corner, GUILDFORD ☎ 01483 222624 45

WEST END Map 04 SU96

Windlemere Windlesham Rd GU24 5LS ☎ 01276 858727
A parkland course, undulating in parts with natural water hazards. There is also a floodlit driving range.
9 holes, 2673yds, Par 34, SSS 33, Course record 30.
Visitors no restrictions.
Societies advisable to contact in advance.
Green Fees not confirmed.
Prof David Thomas
Designer Clive Smith
Facilities
Location N side of village at junct of A319/A322

Hotel ★★★★ Pennyhill Park Hotel, London Rd, BAGSHOT
☎ 01276 471774 22 Annexe67

WEYBRIDGE Map 04 TQ06

St George's Hill Golf Club Rd, St George's Hill KT13 0NL ☎ 01932 847758 Fax 01932 821564
Comparable and similar to Wentworth, a feature of this course is the number of long and difficult par 4s. To score well it is necessary to place the drive - and long driving pays handsomely. Walking is hard on this undulating, heavily wooded course with plentiful heather and rhododendrons.
A+B Course: 18 holes, 6569yds, Par 70, SSS 71, Course record 64.
A+C Course: 18 holes, 6097yds, Par 70, SSS 69.
B+C Course: 18 holes, 6210yds, Par 70, SSS 70.
Club membership 600.
Visitors must contact in advance and have a handicap certificate. Visitors may not play at weekends.
Societies must contact in advance.
Green Fees £65 per day; £50 per round. ▶

WENTWORTH CLUB

VIRGINIA WATER ***Surrey*** **☎ 01344 842201**
Fax 01344 842804 **Map O4 TQ06**

John Ingham writes: Among the really famous inland courses in England you have to name Wentworth. The challenge, in terms of sheer yards, is enormous. But the qualities go beyond this, and include the atmosphere, the heathland, the silver birch and fairway-side homes.

The West Course is the one every visitor wishes to play. You can't possibly name the best hole. Bernard Gallacher, the course professional, has his view, but you may select the 7th where the drive rolls downhill and the second shot has to be played high up to a stepped green. The closing holes really sort out the best of them too.

The clubhouse offers facilities not typical of many British golf clubs. The pro shop resembles a plush city store; evening hospitality events are frequent and society meetings here are catered for as at few other centres for sport, and it's all done in five-star style. Probably it is during the World Match-Play championship when Wentworth can be seen at its best. The tents are up, the superstars pile in and out of huge cars and the air is one of luxury and opulence.

One of the attractions of Wentworth is that the great players, including Ben Hogan and Sam Snead, have played here. Gary Player has won marvellously at Wentworth, beating Tony Lema after being seven down in the 36-hole match! Great competitors from the past have stamped their mark here. Arnold Palmer, back in the 1960s, beat Neil Coles in the Match-Play final but then, a generation later, faced young Seve Ballesteros. The Spaniard saved his bacon by pitching in for an eagle three at the last against Palmer, to take the clash into extra holes, where he won.

Visitors weekdays only. Must contact in advance with letter from own club or a current handicap certificate
Societies apply in advance
Green fees (per round) West Course £145; East Course £90 & Edinburgh Course £95 (winter rates cheaper). All major credit cards.
Facilities ⊗ Ⅲ ▙ ☕ 🍷 (David Rennie) 👜 ⌂ ⛳ 🏌 🚗 ⚑ Professional (David Rennie)
Leisure tennis (hard court & grass), outdoor heated swimming pool, gym, private fishing
Location Wentworth Drive, GU25 4LS (west side of Virginia Water on A30 8m from M3 J13)

54 holes. West Course: 18 holes, 6957yds, Par 73, SSS 74, Course record 63
East Course: 18 holes, 6176yds, Par 68, SSS 70, Course record 62
Edinburgh: 18 holes, 6979yds, Par 72, SSS 73, Course record 67

WHERE TO STAY AND EAT NEARBY

HOTELS:

ASCOT

★★★★ ❀ 69% The Royal Berkshire, London Rd, Sunninghill ☎ 01344 23322 63 ⇌ ⚑

★★★★ ❀ 67% The Berystede, Bagshot Rd, Sunninghill. ☎ 01344 2331191 (1 ⚑ 90 ⇌ ⚑)

★★72% Highclere, 19 Kings Road, Sunninghill. ☎ 01344 25220. 11 ⇌ ⚑

BAGSHOT

★★★★❀❀❀ ♣♣ Pennyhill Park, London Rd. ☎ 01276 471774 22 ⇌ ⚑ Annexe 67 ⇌ ⚑.

RESTAURANTS:

BRAY

❀❀❀❀ Waterside Inn, River Cottage, Ferry Rd. ☎ 01628 20691.

Prof A C Rattue
Designer H S Colt
Facilities ⊗
Location 2m S off B374

Hotel ★★★ 72% Ship Thistle, Monument Green, WEYBRIDGE
☎ 01932 848364 39

WOKING Map 04 TQ05

Hoebridge Golf Centre Old Woking Rd GU22 8JH
☎ 01483 722611 Fax 01483 740369
Three public courses set in parkland on Surrey sand belt. 24-bay floodlit driving range.
Main Course: 18 holes, 6536yds, Par 72, SSS 71, Course record 68.
Shey Course: 9 holes, 2294yds, Par 33.
Maybury Course: 18 holes, 2230yds, Par 54.
Club membership 600.

Visitors welcome every day, course and reservation desk open dawn to dusk. Credit card reservations 6 days in advance.
Societies Mon-Fri only, telephone in advance
Green Fees Main course £16 (£18 weekends). Shey Copse £8.30 (£8.80 weekends). Maybury £7.30 all week.
Cards
Prof Tim Powell
Designer John Jacobs
Facilities ⊗
Location On B382 Old Woking to West Byfleet road

Hotel ★★★★ Pennyhill Park Hotel, London Rd, BAGSHOT
☎ 01276 471774 22 Annexe67

Pyrford Warren Ln, Pyrford GU22 8XR
☎ 01483 723555 Fax 01483 729777
Opened in September 1993 this inland links style course was designed by Peter Alliss and Clive Clark. Set between Surrey woodlands, the fairways weave between 23 acres of water courses while the greens and tees are connected by rustic bridges. The signature hole is the Par 5 9th at 595 yards, with a dogleg and final approach over water and a sand shelf.
18 holes, 6230yds, Par 72, SSS 70, Course record 69.
Club membership 600.

Visitors must book in advance.
Societies must contact in advance.
Green Fees £36 per 18 holes (£52 weekends and bank holidays).
Cards
Prof Richard Pilbury
Designer Peter Allis & Clive Clark
Facilities ⊗
Location Off A3 Ripley to Pyrford

Hotel ★★★★ Pennyhill Park Hotel, London Rd, BAGSHOT
☎ 01276 471774 22 Annexe67

Entries with a shaded background identify courses that are considered to be particularly interesting

Woking Pond Rd, Hook Heath GU22 0JZ
☎ 01483 760053 Fax 01483 772441
An 18-hole course on Surrey heathland with few changes from the original course designed in 1892 by Tom Dunn. Bernard Darwin a past Captain and President has written 'the beauty of Woking is that there is something distinctive about every hole...'.
18 holes, 6340yds, Par 70, SSS 70, Course record 65.
Club membership 550.

Visitors must contact secretary at least 7 days prior to playing. No visitors weekends & bank holidays.
Societies telephone intially then confirm in writing, normally 12 months notice.
Green Fees £50 per day/round.
Prof John Thorne
Designer Tom Dunn
Facilities ⊗
Location W of town centre

Hotel ★★★★ Pennyhill Park Hotel, London Rd, BAGSHOT ☎ 01276 471774 22 Annexe67

Worplesdon Heath House Rd GU22 0RA
☎ 01483 472277
The scene of the celebrated mixed-foursomes competition. Accurate driving is essential on this heathland course. The short 10th across a lake from tee to green is a notable hole, and the 18th provides a wonderfully challenging par-4 finish.
18 holes, 6440yds, Par 71, SSS 71, Course record 64.
Club membership 590.

Visitors must play with member at weekends & bank holidays. Must contact in advance and have a handicap certificate.
Societies must contact in writing.
Green Fees £57 per day; £44 per round.
Prof J Christine
Facilities ⊗
Location 6m N of Guildford, off A322

Hotel ★★★★ Pennyhill Park Hotel, London Rd, BAGSHOT ☎ 01276 471774 22 Annexe67

WOLDINGHAM Map 05 TQ35

Duke's Dene Slines New Rd CR3 7HA
☎ 01883 653501 Fax 01883 653502
Located in Halliloo Valley and designed by the American architect Bradford Benz, this pleasant course utilises all the contours and features of the valley.
18 holes, 6393yds, Par 71, SSS 70.
Club membership 744.

Visitors tee times should be booked in advance with pro shop. Weekends available after noon for visitors.
Societies telephone to book.
Green Fees £25 (£30 weekends). Winter £20 (£25 weekends).
Cards
Prof Paul Thornley
Designer Bradford Benz

WALTON HEATH

WALTON-ON-THE-HILL ***Surrey*** **☎ 01737 812380**
Fax 01737 814225 **Map O4 TQ25**

John Ingham writes: Several historic names are etched on the Honours Board at Walton Heath, almost 700 feet above sea level. The rare atmosphere here is justified because these Surrey courses can claim to be the toughest inland examination in Britain. Walton Heath is famous for staging the Ryder Cup and the European Open Championship but older players will remember it best for the Match-Play Championship battles that involved Sir Henry Cotton and Dai Rees as well as huge money matches that brought names such as Bobby Locke and Fred Daly to public prominence.

Once owned by the News of the World newspaper, MP's, Lords and significant members of the press would be invited down to Walton Heath by Sir Emsley Carr, who was one of the first to employ a lady as Secretary and manager of a well-known championship venue.

The courses were designed in 1903 by Herbert Fowler, who used natural hollows and channels for drainage, so the fairways equal the best on any seaside links and quickly dry out, even after a severe storm.

Erratic shots, wide of the prepared surface, are wickedly punished and weekend players are tormented in awful fashion. Nobody escapes undamaged from the gorse and bracken but it is the heather, with those tough stems, that really snarl up any attempt at an over-ambitious recovery shot. So be advised - if you're caught off the fairway, don't attempt anything fancy. Play back on the shortest route to comparative security.

While the Old Course is most frequently played by visitors, the New Course is very challenging and requires all the subtle shots required if you are to get the ball near the hole. And, in the clubhouse, they serve a spectacular lunch.

Visitors limited play weekends. Must contact in advance and have a handicap certificate or letter of introduction

Societies telephone in advance or apply in writing

Green fees On application.

Facilities Professional (Ken Macpherson)

Location Deans Lane, Tadworth KT20 7TP (SE side of village, off B2032)

36 holes. Old Course: 18 holes, 6801yds, Par 72, SSS 73, Course record 65
New Course: 18 holes, 6609 yds, Par 72, SSS 72

WHERE TO STAY AND EAT NEARBY

HOTELS:

DORKING
★★★★ 68% The Burford Bridge, Burford Bridge, Box Hill (2m NE A24)
☎ 01306 884561. 48

REIGATE
★★★ 65% Reigate Manor, Reigate Hill. ☎ 01737 240125. 50 (8 42)

STOKE D'ABERNON
★★★★ 65% Woodlands Park, Woodlands Ln.
☎ 01372 843933. 59 .

RESTAURANTS:

DORKING
Partners & Sons, 2-4 West St.
☎ 01306 882826.

Facilities by prior arrangement by prior arrangement

Hotel ★★★ 68% Kings Arms Hotel, Market Square, WESTERHAM ☎ 01959 562990 17

North Downs Northdown Rd CR3 7AA
☎ 01883 652057 Fax 01883 652832
Downland course, 850 ft above sea-level, with several testing holes and magnificent views.
18 holes, 5843yds, Par 69, SSS 68, Course record 66.
Club membership 700.

Visitors must play with member at weekends and bank holidays. Must contact in advance and have a handicap certificate.
Societies must contact in writing.
Green Fees £25 per day; £20 per round.
Prof M Homewood
Designer Pennink
Facilities
Location 0.75m S

Hotel ★★★ 68% Kings Arms Hotel, Market Square, WESTERHAM ☎ 01959 562990 17

SUSSEX, EAST

BEXHILL — Map 05 TQ70

Cooden Beach Cooden Sea Rd TN39 4TR
☎ 01424 842040 Fax 01424 842040
The course is close by the sea, but is not real links in character. Despite that, it is dry and plays well throughout the year. There are some excellent holes such as the 4th, played to a built-up green, the short 12th, and three good holes to finish. There are added ponds which make the player think more about tee shots and shots to the green.
18 holes, 6470yds, Par 72, SSS 71, Course record 67.
Club membership 730.

Visitors must have a handicap certificate. Restricted at weekends. Book in advance with professional 01424 843938
Societies must contact in advance by telephoning secretary.
Green Fees £29 per day/round (£35 weekends & bank holidays).
Prof Jeffrey Sim
Designer James Braid
Facilities
& Leisure snooker.
Location 2m W on A259

Hotel ★★★ 64% White Friars Hotel, Boreham St, HERSTMONCEUX ☎ 01323 832355 12 Annexe8

Highwoods Ellerslie Ln TN39 4LJ
☎ 01424 212625 Fax 01424 216866
Undulating course.
18 holes, 6218yds, Par 70, SSS 70.
Club membership 820.

Visitors must play with member on Sun. Must contact in advance and have an introduction from own club. Handicap required.
Societies advance notice advised.
Green Fees not confirmed.
Prof M Andrews
Designer J H Taylor
Facilities
Location 1.5m NW

Hotel ★★★ 64% White Friars Hotel, Boreham St, HERSTMONCEUX ☎ 01323 832355 12 Annexe8

BRIGHTON & HOVE — Map 04 TQ30

Brighton & Hove Devils Dyke Rd BN1 8YJ
☎ 01273 556482
Downland course with sea views.
9 holes, 5710yds, Par 68, SSS 68, Course record 65.
Club membership 400.

Visitors must contact in advance, restricted play Wed, Fri & weekends.
Societies must contact secretary in advance.
Green Fees not confirmed.
Cards
Prof Phil Bonsall
Designer James Braid
Facilities
Location 4m NW

Hotel ★★ 61% St Catherines Lodge Hotel, Seafront, Kingsway, HOVE ☎ 01273 778181 50rm(40)

Dyke Devils Dyke, Dyke Rd BN1 8YJ
☎ 01273 857296 Fax 01273 857078
This downland course has some glorious views both towards the sea and inland. The best hole on the course is probably the 17th; it is one of those teasing short holes of just over 200 yards, and is played across a gully to a high green.
18 holes, 6611yds, Par 72, SSS 72, Course record 66.
Club membership 750.

Visitors advisable to contact in advance. May not play before noon on Sun.
Societies apply by telephone or in writing.
Green Fees £38 per day: £28 per round (£40 per round weekends).
Cards
Prof Richard Arnold
Designer Fred Hawtree
Facilities
Location 4m N of Brighton, between A23 & A27

Hotel ★★ 61% St Catherines Lodge Hotel, Seafront, Kingsway, HOVE ☎ 01273 778181 50rm(40)

East Brighton Roedean Rd BN2 5RA
☎ 01273 604838 Fax 01273 680277
Undulating downland course, overlooking the sea. Windy.
18 holes, 6346yds, Par 72, SSS 70, Course record 67.
Club membership 650.

Visitors contact in advance & may only play weekends after 11am.
Societies must contact in advance, handicap certificate required.
Green Fees £24 per day; £18 per round (£32/£22 weekends and bank holidays).
Cards
Prof Robin S Goodway
Designer James Braid
Facilities
Location 2m E of Palace Pier, overlooking marina

Hotel ★★★ 60% The New Madeira Hotel, 19-23 Marine Pde, BRIGHTON
☎ 01273 698331 35

Hollingbury Park Ditchling Rd BN1 7HS
☎ 01273 552010 (sec) & 500086 (res)
Municipal course in hilly situation on the Downs, overlooking the sea.
18 holes, 6500yds, Par 72, SSS 71, Course record 65.
Club membership 300.

Visitors must contact in advance.
Societies telephone the secretary for details.
Green Fees not confirmed.
Prof Graeme Crompton
Facilities
Location 2m N of town centre

Hotel ★★★ 72% Old Ship Hotel, King's Rd, BRIGHTON ☎ 01273 329001 152

Waterhall Waterhall Rd BN1 8YR ☎ 01273 508658
Hilly downland course with hard walking and open to the wind. Private club playing over municipal course.
18 holes, 5773yds, Par 69, SSS 68, Course record 66.
Club membership 300.

Visitors must contact in advance, may not play at start of day.
Societies must contact the secretary in writing or telephone.
Green Fees £17.60 per day; £11.50 per round (£15.50 per round weekends).
Prof Paul Charman
Facilities
Location 2m NE from A27

Hotel ★★ 61% St Catherines Lodge Hotel, Seafront, Kingsway, HOVE
☎ 01273 778181 50rm(40)

West Hove Church Farm, Hangleton BN3 8AN
☎ 01273 419738 & 413494 (pro) Fax 01273 439988
A downland course designed by Hawtree & Sons.
18 holes, 6237yds, Par 70, SSS 70.
Club membership 625.

Visitors tee times by arrangement.
Societies by arrangement.
Green Fees £30 per day; £20 per round (£35/£25 weekends after 12 noon).
Prof Darren Cook
Designer Hawtree & Sons
Facilities
Hotel ★★ 61% St Catherines Lodge Hotel, Seafront, Kingsway, HOVE
☎ 01273 778181 50rm(40)

CROWBOROUGH Map 05 TQ53

Crowborough Beacon Beacon Rd TN6 1UJ
☎ 01892 661511
Standing some 800 feet above sea level, this is a testing heathland course, with panoramic views of the South Downs, Eastbourne and even the sea on a clear day.
18 holes, 6279yds, Par 71, SSS 70, Course record 66.
Club membership 700.

Visitors must contact in advance & have handicap certificate but may only play at weekends & bank holidays after 2.30pm.
Societies telephone or apply in writing to secretary.
Green Fees £40 per day; £25 per round (£30 per round weekends & bank holidays).
Prof D C Newnham
Facilities
Location 1m SW on A26

Hotel ★★★ 76% The Spa Hotel, Mount Ephraim, TUNBRIDGE WELLS ☎ 01892 520331 74

Dewlands Manor Cottage Hill, Rotherfield TN6 3JN
☎ 01892 852266 Fax 01892 853015
A pretty, moderately hilly, Pay and Play meadowland course with water features.
9 holes, 3186yds, Par 36, SSS 70.
Visitors must telephone in advance.
Societies telephone for availability.
Green Fees £24 per 18 holes; £13 per 9 holes (£28/£15 weekends).
Cards
Prof Nick Godin
Designer R M & N M Godin
Facilities
& Leisure indoor teaching, with computer analysis.
Location 0.5m S of Rotherfield

Inn QQQ Plough & Horses Inn, Walshes Rd, CROWBOROUGH ☎ 01892 652614 8

Ditchling Map 05 TQ31

Mid Sussex Spatham Ln BN6 8XJ
☎ 01273 846567 Fax 01273 845767
Mature parkland course with many trees, water hazards, strategically placed bunkers and superbly contoured greens. The 14th hole, a spectacular par 5, demands accurate shotmaking to avoid the various hazards along its length.
18 holes, 6431yds, Par 71, SSS 71, Course record 68.
Club membership 600.
Visitors telephone in advance to book tee times. After 2pm at weekends in summer and after 1pm in winter.
Societies advance booking required.
Green Fees not confirmed.
Prof Chris Connell
Designer David Williams
Facilities
Location 1m E of Ditchling village

Hotel ★★★ 77% Shelleys Hotel, High St, LEWES ☎ 01273 472361 19

Eastbourne Map 05 TV69

Eastbourne Downs East Dean Rd BN20 8ES
☎ 01323 720827 Fax 01323 412506
This downland course has spectacular views over the South Downs and Channel.
18 holes, 6601yds, Par 72, SSS 72, Course record 70.
Club membership 650.
Visitors a handicap certificate is required for weekends. Visitors may not play before 9.15am weekdays and before 11am weekends except by arrangement.
Societies contact secretary in advance for details.
Green Fees £20 per day, £16 per round (£23/£20 weekends).
Prof T Marshall
Designer J H Taylor
Facilities
Location 0.5m W of town centre on A259

Hotel ★★★ 76% Lansdowne Hotel, King Edward's Pde, EASTBOURNE ☎ 01323 725174 122

Royal Eastbourne Paradise Dr BN20 8BP
☎ 01323 729738 Fax 01323 729738
A famous club which celebrated its centenary in 1987. The course plays longer than it measures. Testing holes are the 8th, a par 3 played to a high green and the 16th, a par 5 righthand dogleg.
Devonshire Course: 18 holes, 6109yds, Par 71, SSS 69, Course record 62.
Hartington Course: 9 holes, 4294yds, Par 64, SSS 61.
Club membership 800.
Visitors must contact in advance, may not play weekends except by arrangement. Handicap certificate required for Devonshire course.
Societies must apply in advance.
Green Fees Devonshire £17-£20 per day (£20-£25 weekends). Hartington £12 per day.
Cards
Prof Richard Wooller
Designer Arthur Mayhewe
Facilities
Location 0.5m W of town centre

Hotel ★★★ 76% Lansdowne Hotel, King Edward's Pde, EASTBOURNE ☎ 01323 725174 122

Willingdon Southdown Rd, Willingdon BN20 9AA
☎ 01323 410981 Fax 01323 411510
Unique, hilly downland course set in oyster-shaped amphitheatre.

18 holes, 6118yds, Par 69, SSS 69.
Club membership 570.

Visitors must have handicap, by application, may not play at weekends.
Societies apply in advance.
Green Fees seasonal variations £14-£25 per round (£16-£28 weekends, £12 after 4pm).
Cards
Prof James Debenham
Facilities
Location 0.5m N of town centre off A22

Hotel ★★★ 61% Wish Tower Hotel, King Edward's Pde, EASTBOURNE ☎ 01323 722676 61

FOREST ROW Map 05 TQ43

Ashdown Forest Golf Hotel Chapel Ln RH18 5BB
☎ 01342 824866 Fax 01342 824869
A natural undulating heathland and woodland course cut out of the Ashdown Forest. No sand bunkers, just equally testing heather dunes with the 14th hole regarded as the best. The hotel specialises in catering for golf breaks and societies.
West Course: 18 holes, 5606yds, Par 68, SSS 67.
Club membership 180.

Visitors must contact in advance, bookings up to 6 days in advance.
Societies must telephone in advance.
Green Fees £21 per day; £16 per round (£26/£21 weekends).
Cards
Prof Martyn Landsborough
Facilities
& Leisure hard tennis courts, fishing.
Location 4m S of East Grinstead off A22 & B2110

Royal Ashdown Forest Chapel Ln RH18 5LR
☎ 01342 822018
Undulating heathland course. Long carries off the tees and magnificent views over the Forest. Not a course for the high handicapper.
Old Course: 18 holes, 6477yds, Par 72, SSS 71, Course record 67.
New Course: 18 holes, 5586yds, Par 68, SSS 67.
Club membership 450.

Visitors restricted weekends & Tue. Must have a handicap certificate on Old Course. No restrictions on New Course.
Societies must contact in advance.
Green Fees not confirmed.
Prof Martyn Landsborough
Facilities
Location SE side of village, off B2110

Hotel ★★★ 65% Woodbury House Hotel, Lewes Rd, EAST GRINSTEAD ☎ 01342 313657 14

HAILSHAM Map 05 TQ50

Wellshurst Golf & Country Club North St, Hellingly BN27 4EE ☎ 01435 813456 Fax 01435 812444
There are outstanding views of the South Downs and the Weald Valley from this 18-hole, well-manicured, undulating course. There are varied features and some water hazards. A practice sand bunker, putting green and driving range are available to improve your golf.

18 holes, 5771yds, Par 70, SSS 68.
Club membership 320.

Visitors no restrictions but advisable to book.
Societies telephone in advance to book tee times.
Green Fees £20 per day; £14 per 18 holes (£26/£17.50 weekends & bank holidays).
Cards
Prof Mark Jarvis
Designer The Golf Corporation
Facilities
Location 2.5m N of Hailsham, on A267

Hotel ★★ 65% The Olde Forge, Magham Down, HAILSHAM ☎ 01323 842893 8rm(6)

HASTINGS & ST LEONARDS Map 05 TQ80

Hastings Beauport Park Estate, St Leonards TN38 0TA
☎ 01424 852981
Played over Hastings Public Course. Undulating parkland with stream and fine views.
18 holes, 6248yds, Par 71, SSS 70, Course record 70.
Club membership 400.

Visitors no restrictions.
Societies arrangement by telephone.
Green Fees not confirmed.
Prof Charles Giddins
Facilities
& Leisure hard tennis courts, outdoor swimming pool.
Location 3m N of Hastings on A2100

Hotel ★★★ 72% Beauport Park Hotel, Battle Rd, HASTINGS ☎ 01424 851222 23

HEATHFIELD Map 05 TQ52

Horam Park Chiddingly Rd, Horam TN21 0JJ
☎ 01435 813477 Fax 01435 813677
A pretty woodland course with lakes.
9 holes, 5965yds, Par 70, SSS 68, Course record 64.
Club membership 450.

Visitors contact for tee times.
Societies prior booking required.
Green Fees £19 per day; £15 per 18 holes; £9 per 9 holes (£20/£16/£9.50 weekends).
Cards
Prof Liam Greasley
Facilities
Location Off A267

Hotel ★★★ 68% Boship Farm Hotel, Lower Dicker, HAILSHAM
☎ 01323 844826 Annexe47

HOLTYE Map 05 TQ43

Holtye TN8 7ED ☎ 01342 850635
Undulating forest/heathland course with tree-lined fairways providing testing golf. Difficult tees on back nine.
9 holes, 5289yds, Par 66, SSS 66, Course record 65.
Club membership 500.

Visitors may not play weekend or Thu mornings.
Societies Tue & Fri only, by arrangement.
Green Fees not confirmed.
Prof Kevin Hinton
Facilities
Location N side of village on A264

Hotel ★★★ 65% Woodbury House Hotel, Lewes Rd, EAST GRINSTEAD
☎ 01342 313657 14

LEWES Map 05 TQ41

Lewes Chapel Hill BN7 2BB ☎ 01273 483474 & 473245
Downland course. Fine views.
18 holes, 6213yds, Par 71, SSS 70, Course record 65.
Club membership 660.

Visitors may not play at weekends before 2pm. Bookings taken up to 7 days in advance.
Societies must contact in advance.
Green Fees £18 (£30 weekends & bank holidays).
Prof Paul Dobson
Designer Jack Rowe
Facilities
Location E side of town centre

Hotel ★★★ 68% White Hart Hotel, 55 High St, LEWES ☎ 01273 476694
23rm(19) Annexe29

NEWHAVEN Map 05 TQ40

Peacehaven Brighton Rd BN9 9UH ☎ 01273 512571
Downland course, sometimes windy. Testing holes: 1st (par 3), 4th (par 4), 9th (par 3), 10th (par 3), 18th (par 3).
9 holes, 5305yds, Par 69, SSS 66.
Club membership 270.

Visitors may not play before 11am weekends.
Societies telephone in advance.
Green Fees not confirmed.
Prof Gerry Williams
Designer James Braid
Facilities
Location 0.75m W on A259

Hotel ★★★ 67% The Star Inn, ALFRISTON
☎ 01323 870495 34

RYE Map 05 TQ92

Rye New Lydd Rd, Camber TN31 7QS
☎ 01797 225241
Typical links course with superb greens and views.
Old Course: 18 holes, 6317yds, Par 68, SSS 71, Course record 64.
Jubilee Course: 9 holes, 6141yds, Par 71, SSS 70.
Club membership 1100.

Visitors must be invited/introduced by a member.
Green Fees with member only.
Prof Michael Lee
Designer H S Colt
Facilities
Location 2.75m SE off A259

Hotel ★★★ 62% The George, High St, RYE
☎ 01797 222114 22

SEAFORD Map 05 TV49

Seaford Firle Rd, East Blatchington BN25 2JD
☎ 01323 892442 Fax 01323 89113
The great H. Taylor did not perhaps design as many courses as his friend and rival, James Braid, but Seaford's original design was Taylor's. It is a splendid downland course with magnificent views and some fine holes.
18 holes, 6551yds, Par 69, SSS 71.
Club membership 600.

Visitors must contact in advance.
Societies must contact in advance.
Green Fees £35 per 36 holes; £25 per round.
Prof David Mills
Designer J H Taylor
Facilities
Location Turn inland at war memorial off A259

Hotel ★★★ 67% The Star Inn, ALFRISTON
☎ 01323 870495 34

Seaford Head Southdown Rd BN25 4JS
☎ 01323 890139 & 894843
A links type course situated on the cliff edge giving exception views over the Seven Sisters and coastline. The upper level is reached via a short hole with elevated green - known as the 'Hell Hole' and the 18th Par 5 tee is on the 'Head' being 300 feet above sea level.
18 holes, 5848yds, Par 71, SSS 68.
Club membership 450.

Visitors no restrictions.
Societies write or telephone the Pro's shop.
Green Fees not confirmed.
Prof Tony Lowles
Facilities
Hotel ★★★ 64% Deans Place, Seaford Rd, ALFRISTON ☎ 01323 870248 36

EAST SUSSEX NATIONAL

Uckfield *East Sussex* ☎ 01825 880088
Fax 01825 880066 **Map 05 TQ42**

John Ingham writes: Designed by Bob Cupp on a grand championship scale and opened in 1989, East Sussex National presents two massive courses, one more than 7000 yards long. Both are ideal for big-hitting professionals and already they have staged the European Open here. Boasting a driving range and a Golf Academy, Bob Cupp, once a designer for Jack Nicklaus, decided to use what they call 'bent' grass from tee to green - and the result is an American-type course to test everyone, depending upon which tee you drive from.

Could either course, brand spanking new, compare with the other Sussex classics of Pulborough (West Sussex) and Royal Ashdown Forest, a gem of a place near Forest Row and a course without a single bunker? When first I drove into the vastness of the car park and eyed the huge redbrick clubhouse, I admit it all looked daunting. The experience is not unlike entering a hotel-country club complex in the United States, signing in as one does at the reception area before walking across a suspended corridor towards the huge and well-stocked professional's shop.

The East Sussex National offers the most modern day's golf in the United Kingdom. The greens on both the East and West courses are immaculate and groomed to perfection. Strike the putt solidly and on-line, and it must go in! While it's true that 50,000 spectators can watch you hole out on the last green, it's just as true that on a quiet day out, you can enjoy letting out plenty of shaft without fear of hitting valuable balls into thick woods.

The West course is reserved for members and their guests, but visitors are welcomed on the other course.

Visitors Contact Advance Reservations for details.
Societies must contact Advance Reservations (01825 880231)
Green fees Visitor 18 hole peak rate £55. Telephone for current details. All major credit cards.
Facilities ⊗ 𝍖 ☕ 🍷 🛏 ⛳ ... Professional (Iain Naylor), 3-hole academy course
Leisure hard court tennis, indoor swimming, sauna, solarium.
Location Little Horsted TN22 5ES (2m S on A22)

36 holes. East Course 18 holes, 6760yds, Par72 SSS 72
Course record 65
West Course 18 holes, 6638yds, Par 72, SSS72. Course record 64

WHERE TO STAY AND EAT NEARBY

HOTELS:

UCKFIELD

★★★★ 69% Buxted Park Country House Hotel, Buxted ☎ 01825 732711 44 (2 42)

★★★ 78% Horsted Place, Little Horsted ☎ 01825 750581. 17

HALLAND

★★★ 63% Halland Forge ☎ 01825 840456. Annexe 20 (3 17)

NEWICK

★★★ 75% Newick Park Country Estate ☎ 01825 723633 13 (4 9)

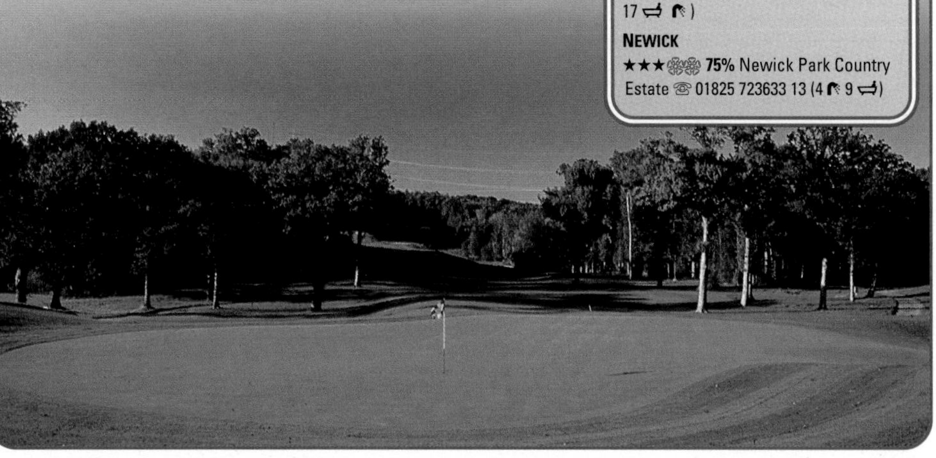

SEDLESCOMBE Map 05 TQ71

Sedlescombe Kent St TN33 0SD
☎ 01424 870898 Fax 01424 870855
This course was established in 1989 and is windswept and challenging. The Par 5 9th holes has a green surrounded by lakes.
18 holes, 6359yds, Par 71, SSS 68.
Club membership 300.

Visitors please telephone and reserve tee times.
Societies please telephone to reserve tee times.
Green Fees not confirmed.
Facilities
Location A21, 4m N of Hastings

Hotel ★★★ 65% Brickwall Hotel, The Green, SEDLESCOMBE ☎ 01424 870253 23

TICEHURST Map 05 TQ63

Dale Hill Hotel & Golf Club TN5 7DQ
☎ 01580 200112 Fax 01580 201249
Picturesque course with woodland, water and gently undulating fairways. Hotel and leisure centre within grounds.
Dale Hill: 18 holes, 6106yds, Par 70, SSS 69.
Ian Woosnam: 18 holes, 6512yds, Par 71, SSS 71.
Club membership 950.

Visitors booking only 7 days in advance.
Societies must contact in advance.
Green Fees Dale Hill: £20 per round, Woosnam: £45 per round (£30/£55 per round weekends & bank holidays).
Cards
Prof Andrew Good
Designer Ian Woosnam
Facilities
& Leisure heated indoor swimming pool, sauna, solarium, gymnasium.
Location N side of village off B2087

Hotel ★★★★ 67% Dale Hill Hotel & Golf Club, TICEHURST ☎ 01580 200112 26

UCKFIELD Map 05 TQ42

EAST SUSSEX NATIONAL See page 253

Piltdown Piltdown TN22 3XB
☎ 01825 722033 Fax 01825 724192
Natural heathland course with much heather and gorse. No bunkers, easy walking, fine views.
18 holes, 6070yds, Par 68, SSS 69, Course record 67.
Club membership 400.

Visitors must telephone pro shop in advance 01825 722389 and have a handicap certificate. Play on Tue, Thu and weekends is restricted.
Societies must contact in writing.
Green Fees £32 per day; £27.50 per round.
Prof John Amos
Facilities by prior arrangement
Location 3m NW off A272

Hotel ★★★ 63% Halland Forge Hotel & Restaurant, HALLAND ☎ 01825 840456 Annexe20

SUSSEX, WEST

ANGMERING Map 04 TQ00

Ham Manor BN16 4JE
☎ 01903 783288 Fax 01903 850886
Two miles from the sea, this parkland course has fine springy turf and provides an interesting test in two loops of nine holes each.
18 holes, 6267yds, Par 70, SSS 70, Course record 64.
Club membership 780.

Visitors must have a handicap certificate. Telephone pro shop in advance 01903 783732.
Societies telephone for details
Green Fees £26 (£40 weekends).
Prof Simon Buckley
Designer Harry Colt
Facilities
Location Off A259

Hotel ★★★ 61% Chatsworth Hotel, Steyne, WORTHING ☎ 01903 236103 107

ARUNDEL Map 04 TQ00

Avisford Park Yapton Ln, Walberton BN18 0LS
☎ 01243 554611 Fax 01243 555580
Newly extended course - now 18-holes - enjoying a country hotel complex setting. The course opens with a real challenge as there is out of bounds water and tree hazards the whole length of this 414yard drive.
18 holes, 5703yds, Par 68, SSS 66.
Club membership 100.
Visitors must contact in advance for weekend play.
Societies apply in writing or telephone.
Green Fees £12 per 18 holes/day (£15 weekends & bank holidays).
Cards
Prof Richard Beach
Facilities
Location Off A27, towards Yapton

Hotel ★★★ 68% Norfolk Arms Hotel, High St, ARUNDEL ☎ 01903 882101 21 Annexe13

BOGNOR REGIS Map 04 SZ99

Bognor Regis Downview Rd, Felpham PO22 8JD
☎ 01243 821929 (Secretary) Fax 01243 860719
This flattish, well tree lined, parkland course has more variety than is to be found on some other South Coast courses. The club is also known far and wide for its enterprise in creating a social atmosphere. The course is open to the prevailing wind.
18 holes, 6238yds, Par 70, SSS 70, Course record 64.
Club membership 700.
Visitors handicap certificate required, must play with member at weekends Apr-Sep. Must contact in advance (pro shop 01243 865209).
Societies phone initially.
Green Fees not confirmed.
Prof Stephen Bassil
Designer James Braid
Facilities by prior arrangement by prior arrangement
Location 0.5m N at Felpham traffic lights on A259

Hotel ★★ 65% Aldwick Hotel, Aldwick Rd, Aldwick, BOGNOR REGIS ☎ 01243 821945 20

BURGESS HILL Map 04 TQ31

Burgess Hill Cuckfield Rd RH15 8RE
☎ 01444 258585 Fax 247318
Opened May 1998, an academy course bordered by a tributary of the River Adur. Facilities available for public use include a floodlit driving range and a large sweeping putting green.
9 holes, 1250yds, Par 27.
Societies contact in advance.
Green Fees £15 (18 holes) £9 (9 holes); offpeak £12 (18 holes) £7.50 (9 holes).
Cards
Prof Giles Downer
Designer Donald Steel
Facilities
Location N of town on B2036

Hotel ★★★ 76% Ockenden Manor, Ockenden Ln, CUCKFIELD ☎ 01444 416111 22

CHICHESTER Map 04 SU80

Chichester Hunston Village PO20 6AX
☎ 01243 533833 Fax 01243 539922
Set amongst lush farmland, the Tower course has four lakes which bring water into play on seven holes. The Florida-style Cathedral course was opened in spring 1994. There is also a 9-hole par 3 and a floodlit driving range.
Tower Course: 18 holes, 6175yds, Par 72, SSS 69, Course record 67.
Cathedral Course: 18 holes, 6461yds, Par 72, SSS 69, Course record 70.
Club membership 500.
Visitors a strict dress code is in operation. Must contact in advance. Tee reservations up to 7 days in advance on 01243 533833.
Societies must contact in advance.
Green Fees Tower: £15 (£19.50 weekends). Cathedral: £20 (£28 weekends). One round of Tower and Cathedral £26 (£36 weekends).
Cards
Prof John Slinger
Designer Philip Saunders
Facilities
& Leisure par 3.
Location 3m S of Chichester, on B2145 at Hunston

Hotel ★★★ 63% The Ship Hotel, North St, CHICHESTER ☎ 01243 778000 34

COPTHORNE Map 05 TQ33

Copthorne Borers Arms Rd RH10 3LL
☎ 01342 712033 & 712058 Fax 01342 717682
Despite it having been in existence since 1892, this club remains one of the lesser known Sussex courses. It is hard to know why because it is most attractive with plenty of trees and much variety
18 holes, 6505yds, Par 71, SSS 71, Course record 67.
Club membership 550.
Visitors advised to contact in advance, may not play weekends before 1pm.
Societies must contact in advance.
Green Fees £36 per day; £28 per round (£30 per round weekends).
Prof Joe Burrell
Designer James Braid
Facilities by prior arrangement by prior arrangement
Location E side of village junc 10 of M23 off A264

Hotel ★★★★ 68% Copthorne London Gatwick, Copthorne Way, COPTHORNE ☎ 01342 714971 227

Effingham Park The Copthorne Effingham Park, Hotel, West Park Rd RH10 3EU ☎ 01342 716528 Fax 716039
Parkland course.
9 holes, 1769yds, Par 30, SSS 57, Course record 28.
Club membership 390.

Visitors restricted at weekends before 11am and not after 4pm Tue, Apr-Oct.
Societies Mon-Fri, and Sat/Sun after 1pm, must write/telephone in advance.
Green Fees £12 per 18 holes: £8.50 per 9 holes (£14/£9.50 weekends & bank holidays). Discounted fees for hotel guests.
Cards
Prof Mark Root
Designer Francisco Escario
Facilities
& Leisure hard tennis courts, heated indoor swimming pool, sauna, solarium, gymnasium.
Location 2m E on B2028

Hotel ★★★★ 63% Copthorne Effingham Park, West Park Rd, COPTHORNE
☎ 01342 714994 122

CRAWLEY Map 04 TQ23

Cottesmore Buchan Hill, Pease Pottage RH11 9AT
☎ 01293 528256 Fax 01293 522819
The course was originally founded in 1974.The Griffin course is undulating with four holes are over water. The newer Phoenix course is shorter and less testing. But both are lined by silver birch, pine and oak, with rhododendrons ablaze in June.
Griffin Course: 18 holes, 6248yds, Par 71, SSS 70.
Phoenix Course: 18 holes, 5514yds, Par 69, SSS 67.
Club membership 1500.
Visitors may only play after 11am at weekends and bank holidays. Must contact in advance.
Societies weekdays, must telephone in advance.
Green Fees Griffin: £32 per day; £25 per round (£42/£31 weekends). Phoenix: £22 per day; £16 per round (£28/£21 weekends).
Cards
Prof Andrew Prior
Designer Michael J Rogerson
Facilities
& Leisure hard tennis courts, heated indoor swimming pool, squash, sauna, solarium, gymnasium.
Location 3m SW 1m W of M23 junc 11

Hotel ★★★★ 66% Holiday Inn London-Gatwick, Langley Dr, CRAWLEY
☎ 01293 529991 223

Ifield Golf & Country Club Rusper Rd, Ifield RH11 0LN
☎ 01293 520222 Fax 01293 612973
Parkland course.
18 holes, 6330yds, Par 70, SSS 70, Course record 65.
Club membership 750.
Visitors must contact professional in advance. Must be guest of member at weekends.
Societies apply in advance.
Green Fees £32 per day; £22 per round weekdays.
Prof Jonathan Earl
Designer Bernard Darwin
Facilities by prior arrangement
& Leisure squash.
Location 1m W side of town centre off A23

Hotel ★★★★ 66% Holiday Inn London-Gatwick, Langley Dr, CRAWLEY
☎ 01293 529991 223

Tilgate Forest Golf Centre Titmus Dr RH10 5EU
☎ 01293 530103
Designed by former Ryder Cup players Neil Coles and Brian Huggett, the course has been carefully cut through a silver birch and pine forest. It is possibly one of th most beautiful public courses in the country. The 17th is a treacherous Par 5 demanding an uphill third shot to a green surrounded by rhododendrons.
18 holes, 6359yds, Par 72, SSS 69 or 9 holes, 1136yds, Par 27.
Visitors may book up to 7 days in advance.
Societies telephone in advance for details.
Green Fees not confirmed.
Prof Sean Trussell
Designer Neil Coles/Brian Huggett
Facilities
Hotel ★★★★ 66% Holiday Inn London-Gatwick, Langley Dr, CRAWLEY
☎ 01293 529991 223

GOODWOOD Map 04 SU80

Goodwood Kennel Hill PO18 0PN
☎ 01243 774968 Fax 01243 781741
Downland course designed by the master architect, James Braid. Many notable holes, particularly the finishing ones: 17 down an avenue of beech trees and 18 along in front of the terrace. Superb views of the downs and the coast.
18 holes, 6434yds, Par 72, SSS 71.
Club membership 930.
Visitors must have handicap certificate
Societies Wed & Thu, telephone secretary in advance.
Green Fees £32 per day (£42 weekends).
Prof Keith MacDonald
Designer J Braid
Facilities
& Leisure snooker.
Location 3m NE of Chichester off A27

Hotel ★★★★ 70% Marriott Goodwood Park, GOODWOOD
☎ 01243 775537 94

HASSOCKS Map 04 TQ31

Hassocks London Rd BN6 9NA
☎ 01273 846630 Fax 01273 846070
Set against the backdrop of the South Downs, Hassocks is an 18 hole par 70 course designed and contoured to blend naturally with the surrounding countryside. A friendly and relaxed course, appealing to golfers of all ages and abilities.
18 holes, 5754yds, Par 70, SSS 68, Course record 73.
Club membership 350.
Visitors phone Pro. shop one week in advance to book.
Societies apply in writing or telephone in advance.
Green Fees £12.50 (£16.25 weekends).
Cards
Prof Charles Ledger
Designer Paul Wright
Facilities
Location On the A273 between Burgess Hill and Hassocks

Hotel ★★★ 63% The Hickstead Hotel, Jobs Ln, Bolney, HICKSTEAD
☎ 01444 248023 50

HAYWARDS HEATH Map 05 TQ32

Haywards Heath High Beech Ln RH16 1SL
☎ 01444 414457 Fax 01444 458319
Pleasant parkland course with several challenging par 4s and 3s.
18 holes, 6204yds, Par 71, SSS 70, Course record 68.
Club membership 770.

Visitors must have a handicap certificate. Must contact in advance.
Societies Wed & Thu only by prior arrangement with the secretary.
Green Fees not confirmed.
Prof Michael Henning
Facilities
Location 1.25m N off B2028

Hotel ★★★ 76% Ockenden Manor, Ockenden Ln, CUCKFIELD
☎ 01444 416111 22

Paxhill Park East Mascalls Ln, Lindfield RH16 2QN
☎ 01444 484467 Fax 01444 482709
A relatively flat parkland course designed by Patrick Tallack. Water hazard on 5th, 13th and 14th holes,
18 holes, 6117yds, Par 70, SSS 69, Course record 67.
Club membership 430.

Visitors welcome but may not play weekend mornings.
Societies must contact in advance.
Green Fees £25 per day; £15 per round (£20 weekend & bank holidays).
Cards
Prof Steve Dunkley
Designer P Tallack
Facilities by prior arrangement
Hotel ★★★ 65% The Birch Hotel, Lewes Rd, HAYWARDS HEATH
☎ 01444 451565 51

HORSHAM Map 04 TQ13

See also **Slinfold**

Horsham Worthing Rd RH13 7AX
☎ 01403 271525 Fax 01403 274528
A short but challenging course with six Par 4s and three Par 3s''s, two of which are played across water. Designed for beginners and intermediates but also challenges better players with a standard scratch of six below par.
9 holes, 4122yds, Par 33, SSS 30, Course record 55.
Club membership 250.

Visitors no restrictions other than not until after 11am on Sat.
Societies apply in advance.
Green Fees £10 per 18 holes; £6 per 9 holes (£10/£7 weekends & bank holidays).
Cards
Prof Neil Burke
Facilities
& Leisure gymnasium.
Location Off A24 rdbt, between Horsham/Southwater, by garage on B2237

Hotel ★★ 67% Ye Olde King's Head Hotel, Carfax, HORSHAM ☎ 01403 253126 42rm(41)

HURSTPIERPOINT Map 04 TQ21

Singing Hills Albourne BN6 9EB
☎ 01273 835353 Fax 01273 835444
Three distinct nines (Lake, River & Valley) can be combined to make a truly varied game. Gently undulating fairways and spectacular waterholes make Singing Hills a test of accurate shotmaking. The opening 2 holes of the Rive Nine have long drives, while the second hole on the Lake course is an Island green where the tee is also protected by two bunkers. The Valley Course demand long, accurate tee shots.
Lake: 9 holes, 3253yds, Par 35, SSS 35.
River: 9 holes, 2826yds, Par 34, SSS 34.
Valley: 9 holes, 3348yds, Par 36, SSS 36.
Club membership 390.

Visitors no restrictions, but strict dress code observed
Societies apply in advance.
Green Fees £28 per day; £18 per 18 holes (£36/£26 weekends & bank holidays)..
Cards
Prof Wallace Street
Designer M R M Sandow
Facilities
Location Off A23, on B2117

Hotel ★★★ 63% The Hickstead Hotel, Jobs Ln, Bolney, HICKSTEAD
☎ 01444 248023 50

LITTLEHAMPTON Map 04 TQ00

Littlehampton Rope Walk, West Beach BN17 5DL
☎ 01903 717170 Fax 726629
A delightful seaside links in an equally delightful setting - and the only links course in the area.
18 holes, 6244yds, Par 70, SSS 70, Course record 62.
Club membership 650.

Visitors contact in advance & must have handicap certificate.
Societies welcome weekdays.
Green Fees £24 per day (£30 weekends & bank holidays).
Prof Guy McQuitty
Facilities
Location 1m W off A259

Hotel ★★★ 78% Bailiffscourt Hotel, CLIMPING ☎ 01903 723511
10 Annexe17

LOWER BEEDING Map 04 TQ22

Brookfield Brookfield Farm Hotel, Plummers Plain RH13 6LU ☎ 01403 891568
This is an unusual golf course in that it has only 7 holes par 3 and 4. However, it has been especially designed as an executive course for beginners and those who find it difficult to play a full 18 holes. It is very popular.
6 holes, 3015yds, Par 57, SSS 53, Course record 53.
Club membership 200.

Visitors no restrictions.
Societies apply in writing or telephone.
Green Fees not confirmed.
Prof Mike Denny
Facilities
& Leisure fishing, sauna.

Farmhouse QQQ Brookfield Farm Hotel, Winterpit Ln, Plummers Plain, LOWER BEEDING
☎ 01403 891568 20

Additional hotel ★★★★ 78% South Lodge Hotel, Brighton Rd, LOWER BEEDING
☎ 01403 891711 Fax 01403 891253 39

MANNINGS HEATH Map 04 TQ22

Mannings Heath Fullers, Hammerpond Rd RH13 6PG
☎ 01403 210228 Fax 01403 270974
The course meanders up hill and down dale over heathland with streams affecting 11 of the holes. Wooded valleys protect the course from strong winds. Famous holes at 12th (the 'Waterfall', par 3), 13th (the 'Valley', par 4).
Waterfall: 18 holes, 6378yds, Par 71, SSS 70, Course record 66.
Kingfisher: 18 holes, 6217yds, Par 70, SSS 70.
Club membership 700.

Visitors may book up to 7 days in advance.
Societies must contact in advance.
Green Fees £32 per 18 holes (£40 weekends & bank holidays). Unlimited golf £42 weekdays £55 weekends.
Cards
Prof Clive Tucker
Designer David Williams
Facilities
& Leisure hard tennis courts, fishing, sauna, chipping practice area.
Location M23 junct 11, take A281 from Horsham or Brighton. Club on N side of village

Hotel ★★★★ 78% South Lodge Hotel, Brighton Rd, LOWER BEEDING
☎ 01403 891711 39

MIDHURST Map 04 SU82

Cowdray Park Petworth Rd GU29 0BB
☎ 01730 813599 Fax 01730 815900
Undulating parkland course with scenic views of surrounding countryside, including Elizabethan ruins. Unusual double green at 8th/16th hole.
18 holes, 6212yds, Par 70, SSS 70, Course record 66.
Club membership 720.

Visitors may play after 9.30am. Advisable to contact in advance.
Societies apply in writing/telephone/e-mail/fax.
Green Fees not confirmed.
Cards
Prof Richard Gough
Designer Jack White
Facilities by prior arrangement
Location 1m E on A272

Hotel ★★★ 73% Spread Eagle Hotel, South St, MIDHURST
☎ 01730 816911 35 Annexe4

PULBOROUGH Map 04 TQ01

West Sussex Golf Club Ln, Wiggonholt RH20 2EN
☎ 01798 872563 Fax 01798 872033
Heathland course.
18 holes, 6221yds, Par 68, SSS 70, Course record 61.
Club membership 850.

Visitors must contact in advance, may not play weekends.
Societies Wed & Thu only, apply in writing.
Green Fees not confirmed.
Prof Tim Packham
Designer Campbell/Hutcheson
Facilities
Location 1.5m E off A283

Hotel ★★★ 69% Roundabout Hotel, Monkmead Ln, WEST CHILTINGTON
☎ 01798 813838 23

PYECOMBE Map 04 TQ21

Pyecombe Clayton Hill BN45 7FF
☎ 01273 845372 Fax 01273 843338
Typical downland course on the inland side of the South Downs. Picturesque with magnificent views.
18 holes, 6278yds, Par 71, SSS 70, Course record 67.
Club membership 700.

Visitors must contact in advance and may only play after 9.15am weekdays and after 2.15pm weekends
Societies telephone secretary in advance.
Green Fees £15 per day (£20 weekends).
Prof C R White
Facilities
Location E side of village on A273

Hotel ★★★ 65% Courtlands Hotel, 21-27 The Drive, HOVE
☎ 01273 731055 43 ⇌ ↱ Annexe12 ⇌ ↱

SELSEY Map 04 SZ89

Selsey Golf Links Ln PO20 9DR ☎ 01243 602203
Fairly difficult seaside course, exposed to wind and has natural ditches.
9 holes, 5834yds, Par 68, SSS 68, Course record 64.
Club membership 360.

Visitors must contact in advance.
Societies must contact in advance in writing
Green Fees £12 per 18 holes (£15 weekends).
Prof Peter Grindley
Designer J H Taylor
Facilities ⊗ ⅢⅠ ⊾ ☕ ♀ ⚲ ⌂ ✓
& Leisure hard tennis courts, bowling, tennis.
Location 1m N off B2145

Hotel ★★★ 63% The Ship Hotel, North St, CHICHESTER ☎ 01243 778000 34 ⇌ ↱

SLINFOLD Map 04 TQ13

Slinfold Park Golf & Country Club Stane St RH13 7RE
☎ 01403 791555
Opened for play in spring 1993, Slinfold course enjoys splendid views among mature trees. The 10th tee is spectacularly located on the centre of one of the two large landscaped lakes. The 166-yard 16th has water running in front of of the tee and everything sloping towards it!
Championship Course: 18 holes, 6407yds, Par 72, SSS 71, Course record 64.
Short Course: 9 holes, 1315yds, Par 28.
Club membership 611.

Visitors subject to booking.
Societies advance booking required, weekends and bank holidays not available.
Green Fees not confirmed.
Prof G McKay
Designer John Fortune
Facilities ⊗ by prior arrangement ⅢⅠ by prior arrangement ⊾ ☕ ♀ ⚲ ⌂ ⚑ ✓ ⚐
Location 4m W on the A29

Hotel ★★★ 72% Random Hall Hotel, Stane St, Slinford, HORSHAM
☎ 01403 790558 15 ⇌ ↱

WEST CHILTINGTON Map 04 TQ01

West Chiltington Broadford Bridge Rd RH20 2YA
☎ 01798 813574 Fax 01798 812631
The Main Course is situated on gently undulating, well-drained greens and offers panoramic views of the Sussex Downs. Three large double greens provide an interesting feature to this new course. Also 9-hole short course and 13-bay driving range.
Windmill: 18 holes, 5888yds, Par 70, SSS 69, Course record 66 or 9 holes, 1360yds, Par 28.

Visitors book tee times in advance.
Societies by prior arrangement.
Green Fees £23 per day; £15 per round (£27.50/£17.50 weekends).
Cards MasterCard VISA Barclays CONNECT DELTA Switch
Prof Clayton Morris
Designer Brian Barnes
Facilities ⊗ ⅢⅠ ⊾ ☕ ♀ ⚲ ⌂ ⚑ ✓ ⚐
Location On N side of village

Hotel ★★★ 69% Roundabout Hotel, Monkmead Ln, WEST CHILTINGTON
☎ 01798 813838 23 ⇌ ↱

WORTHING Map 04 TQ10

Hill Barn Municipal Hill Barn Ln BN14 9QE
☎ 01903 237301
Downland course with views of both Isle of Wight and Brighton.
18 holes, 6224yds, Par 70, SSS 70.
Club membership 1000.

Visitors no restrictions.
Societies must telephone in advance.
Green Fees not confirmed.
Prof A Higgins
Facilities ♀ ⚲ ⌂ ⚑
Location N side of town at junction of A24/A27

Hotel ★★★ 61% Chatsworth Hotel, Steyne, WORTHING ☎ 01903 236103 107 ⇌ ↱

Worthing Links Rd BN14 9QZ
☎ 01903 260801 Fax 694664
The High Course, short and tricky with entrancing views, will provide good entertainment. 'Lower Course' is considered to be one of the best downland courses in the country.
Lower Course: 18 holes, 6530yds, Par 71, SSS 72, Course record 62.
Upper Course: 18 holes, 5243yds, Par 66, SSS 66.
Club membership 1200. ▶

Visitors advisable to contact in advance. Only as guest of member at weekends, but not weekends during GMT.
Societies contact in advance.
Green Fees £30 per day both courses; £25 per round Lower Course, £20 per round Upper Course.
Prof Stephen Rolley
Designer H S Colt
Facilities ⊗
Location N side of town centre off A27

Hotel ★★★ 71% Ardington Hotel, Steyne Gardens, WORTHING ☎ 01903 230451 45

TYNE & WEAR

BACKWORTH Map 12 NZ37

Backworth The Hall NE27 0AH ☎ 0191 268 1048
Parkland course with easy walking, natural hazards and good scenery.
9 holes, 5930yds, Par 71, SSS 69, Course record 64.
Club membership 480.
Visitors visitors may not play Tue (Ladies Day) & weekend mornings. Play limited Sat/Sun during Apr-Sep.
Societies apply in writing to secretary.
Green Fees £16 per day; £12 per round (£16 per round weekends & bank holidays).
Facilities ⊗ by prior arrangement
& Leisure putting green, bowls.
Location W side of town on B1322

Hotel ★★★★ 61% Holiday Inn, Great North Rd, SEATON BURN ☎ 0191 201 9988 150

BIRTLEY Map 12 NZ25

Birtley Birtley Ln DH3 2LR ☎ 0191 410 2207
Parkland course.
9 holes, 5660yds, Par 67, SSS 67, Course record 63.
Club membership 270.
Visitors must play with member at weekends & bank holidays.
Societies apply in writing, must contact 1 month in advance in summer.
Green Fees £12 per round.
Facilities
Hotel B Forte Posthouse Washington, Emerson District 5, WASHINGTON ☎ 0191 416 2264 138

BOLDON Map 12 NZ36

Boldon Dipe Ln, East Boldon NE36 0PQ
☎ 0191 536 5360 & 0191 536 4182 Fax 0191 537 2270
Parkland links course, easy walking, distant sea views, windy.
18 holes, 6362yds, Par 72, SSS 70, Course record 67.
Club membership 700.
Visitors may not play after 3.30pm at weekends & bank holidays.
Societies must contact in advance.
Green Fees £18 (£22 weekends & bank holidays).
Designer Harry Varden
Facilities ⊗
& Leisure snooker.
Location S side of village off A184

Hotel ★★★ 66% Quality Friendly Hotel, Witney Way, BOLDON ☎ 0191 519 1999 82

CHOPWELL Map 12 NZ15

Garesfield NE17 7AP
☎ 01207 561309 Fax 01207 561309
Undulating parkland course with good views and picturesque woodland surroundings.
18 holes, 6603yds, Par 72, SSS 72, Course record 68.
Club membership 770.
Visitors weekends after 4.30pm only, unless with member. Must contact in advance. No visiting parties Mondays or Saturdays.
Societies must contact secretary in advance.
Green Fees £17 per day; £15 per round.
Prof David Race
Designer Harry Fernie
Facilities ⊗
Location From A1 take A694 to Rowlands Gill. Turn right (signed Ryton) to High Spen. Turn left for Chopwell

Hotel ★★★ 66% Chasley Hotel, Newgate St, NEWCASTLE UPON TYNE ☎ 0191 232 5025 93

FELLING Map 12 NZ26

Heworth Gingling Gate, Heworth NE10 8XY
☎ 01632 692137
Fairly flat, parkland course.
18 holes, 6437yds, Par 71, SSS 71.
Club membership 500.
Visitors may not play Sat & before 10am Sun, Apr-Sep.
Societies must apply in writing.
Green Fees not confirmed.
Facilities
Location On A195, 0.5m NW of junc with A1(M)

Hotel B Forte Posthouse Washington, Emerson District 5, WASHINGTON ☎ 0191 416 2264 138

GATESHEAD Map 12 NZ26

Ravensworth Moss Heaps, Wrekenton NE9 7UU
☎ 0191 487 2843
Moorland/parkland course 600 ft above sea-level with fine views. Testing 13th hole (par 3).
18 holes, 5966yds, Par 69, SSS 69.
Club membership 600.
Visitors apply in advance.
Societies apply in writing to secretary.
Green Fees £20 weekdays (£30 weekends & bank holidays), Apr-Sep. £12 weekdays (£20 weekends & bank holidays) Oct-Mar.
Prof Shaun Cowell

Designer J W Fraser
Facilities ⊗ by prior arrangement by prior arrangement
Location 3m SE off A6127

Hotel ★★★ 68% Swallow Hotel, High West St, GATESHEAD ☎ 0191 477 1105 103

Gosforth Map 12 NZ26

Gosforth Broadway East NE3 5ER ☎ 0191 285 3495
Parkland course with natural water hazards, easy walking.
18 holes, 6024yds, Par 69, SSS 68.
Club membership 500.
Visitors must contact in advance. Restricted play on competition days.
Societies telephone in advance.
Green Fees £20 per day.
Prof G Garland
Facilities ⊗
Location N side of town centre off A6125

Hotel ★★★★ 75% Swallow Gosforth Park Hotel, High Gosforth Park, Gosforth, NEWCASTLE UPON TYNE ☎ 0191 236 4111 178

Parklands Gosforth Park Golfing Complex, High Gosforth Park NE3 5HQ ☎ 0191 236 4867
Parklands course is set in pleasant parkland with challenging shots around and sometimes over attractive water hazards. The first 9 holes are easier but the second 9 test even the most experienced golfer.
18 holes, 6060yds, Par 71, SSS 69, Course record 66.
Club membership 750.
Visitors a daily start sheet operates with bookings taken from 4.30pm the previous day during weekdays, and from 8am Fri & Sat for weekends.
Societies by prior arrangement with club secretary.
Green Fees £15 per 18 holes (£18 weekends & bank holidays).
Prof Brian Rumney
Facilities ⊗
Location 3m N, at the end A1 Western by Pass

Hotel ★★★★ 75% Swallow Gosforth Park Hotel, High Gosforth Park, Gosforth, NEWCASTLE UPON TYNE ☎ 0191 236 4111 178

Houghton-le-Spring Map 12 NZ35

Elemore Elemore Ln, Hetton-le-hole DH5 0QB
☎ 0191 553 6720 (Pro) Fax 0191 5536727
A new course.
18 holes, 5947yds, Par 69.
Club membership 400.
Visitors no restrictions.
Societies apply in writing, telephone enquiries welcome.
Green Fees not confirmed.
Designer J Gaunt
Facilities ⊗
Location 4m S of Houghton-Le-Spring on the A182

Hotel ★★ 60% Chilton Lodge Country Pub & Motel, Black Boy Rd, Chilton Moor, Fencehouses, HOUGHTON-LE-SPRING ☎ 0191 385 2694 18

Houghton-le-Spring Copt Hill DH5 8LU
☎ 0191 584 1198 & 584 0048
Hilly, downland course with natural slope hazards.
18 holes, 6443yds, Par 72, SSS 71, Course record 64.
Club membership 600.
Visitors may not play on Sun until 4pm.
Societies must contact secretary in advance.
Green Fees £25 per day; £18 per round (£30/£25 weekends).
Prof Kevin Gow
Facilities ⊗
Location 0.5m E on B1404

Hotel ★★ 60% Chilton Lodge Country Pub & Motel, Black Boy Rd, Chilton Moor, Fencehouses, HOUGHTON-LE-SPRING ☎ 0191 385 2694 18

Newcastle upon Tyne Map 12 NZ26

City of Newcastle Three Mile Bridge NE3 2DR
☎ 0191 285 1775 Fax 0191 2840700
A well-manicured parkland course in the Newcastle suburbs, subject to wind.
18 holes, 6528yds, Par 72, SSS 71, Course record 64.
Club membership 460.
Visitors no restrictions but advisable to telephone first.
Societies telephone in advance
Green Fees £24 per day (£28 weekends & bank holidays).
Prof Steve McKenna
Designer Harry Varden
Facilities ⊗
Location 3m N on B1318

Hotel ★★★ 64% Newcastle Airport Moat House, Woolsington, NEWCASTLE UPON TYNE AIRPORT ☎ 0191 401 9988 100

Newcastle United Ponteland Rd, Cowgate NE5 3JW
☎ 0191 286 9998
Moorland course with natural hazards.
18 holes, 6484yds, Par 72, SSS 71, Course record 68.
Club membership 600.
Visitors must play with member at weekends.
Societies must contact in writing.
Green Fees not confirmed.
Facilities ⊗ by prior arrangement by prior arrangement
Location 1.25m NW of city centre off A6127

Hotel ★★★ 69% Imperial Swallow Hotel, Jesmond Rd, NEWCASTLE UPON TYNE ☎ 0191 281 5511 122

Northumberland High Gosforth Park NE3 5HT
☎ 0191 236 2498 Fax 0191 236 2498
Many golf courses have been sited inside racecourses, although not so many survive today. One which does is the Northumberland Club's course at High Gosforth Park. Naturally the course is flat but there are plenty of mounds and other hazards to make it a fine test of golf. It should be said that not all the holes are within the confines of the racecourse, but both inside and out there are some good holes. This is a Championship course.
18 holes, 6629yds, Par 72, SSS 72, Course record 65.
Club membership 580.
▶

Visitors may not play at weekends or competition days. Must contact in advance.
Societies must apply in writing.
Green Fees £45 per day; £35 per round.
Facilities
Location 4m N of city centre off A1

Hotel ★★★★ 75% Swallow Gosforth Park Hotel, High Gosforth Park, Gosforth, NEWCASTLE UPON TYNE ☎ 0191 236 4111 178

Westerhope Whorlton Grange, Westerhope NE5 1PP
☎ 0191 286 7636
Attractive parkland course with tree-lined fairways, and easy walking. Good open views towards the airport.
18 holes, 6444yds, Par 72, SSS 71, Course record 64.
Club membership 778.
Visitors with member only at weekends. Must contact in advance.
Societies must contact Secretary in advance.
Green Fees not confirmed.
Prof Nigel Brown
Facilities
Location 4.5m NW of city centre off B6324

Hotel ★★★★ 75% Swallow Gosforth Park Hotel, High Gosforth Park, Gosforth, NEWCASTLE UPON TYNE ☎ 0191 236 4111 178

RYTON Map 12 NZ16

Ryton Clara Vale NE40 3TD
☎ 0191 413 3737 Fax 0191 413 1642
Parkland course.
18 holes, 5950yds, Par 70, SSS 69, Course record 68.
Club membership 600.
Visitors with member only at weekends.
Societies apply in advance.
Green Fees £20 per day; £15 per round.
Facilities
Location NW side of town off A695

Hotel ★★★ 71% Gibside Arms Hotel, Front St, WHICKHAM ☎ 0191 488 9292 45

Tyneside Westfield Ln NE40 3QE
☎ 0191 413 2742 Fax 0191 413 2742
Open parkland course, water hazard, hilly, practice area.
18 holes, 6042yds, Par 70, SSS 69, Course record 65.
Club membership 900.
Visitors must contact in advance to play at weekends (after 3pm)
Societies must apply in advance.
Green Fees £25 per day; £20 per round.
Prof Malcolm Gunn
Designer H S Colt
Facilities
Location NW side of town off A695

Hotel ★★★ 71% Gibside Arms Hotel, Front St, WHICKHAM ☎ 0191 488 9292 45

SOUTH SHIELDS Map 12 NZ36

South Shields Cleadon Hills NE34 8EG ☎ 0191 456 8942
A slightly undulating downland course on a limestone base ensuring good conditions underfoot. Open to strong winds, the course is testing but fair. There are fine views of the coastline.
18 holes, 6264yds, Par 71, SSS 70, Course record 64.
Club membership 800.
Visitors must contact in advance.
Societies by arrangement.
Green Fees £20 per day (£25 weekends & bank holidays).
Prof Gary Parsons
Designer McKenzie-Braid
Facilities
Location SE side of town centre off A1300

Hotel ★★★ 64% Sea Hotel, Sea Rd, SOUTH SHIELDS ☎ 0191 427 0999 33

Whitburn Lizard Ln NE34 7AF
☎ 0191 529 4944 Fax 0191 529 4944
Parkland course.
18 holes, 5900yds, Par 69, SSS 68, Course record 64.
Club membership 650.
Visitors restricted weekends & Tue. Contact professional in advance.
Societies must apply in writing to secretary
Green Fees £18 per day (£23 weekends & bank holidays).
Prof David Stephenson
Designer Colt, Alison & Morrison
Facilities
Location 2.5m SE off A183

Hotel ★★★★ 64% Swallow Hotel, Queen's Pde, Seaburn, SUNDERLAND ☎ 0191 529 2041 65

SUNDERLAND Map 12 NZ35

Ryhope Leechmore Way, Ryhope SR2 ODH
☎ 0191 523 7333
A municipal course recently extended to 18 holes.
18 holes, 4601yds, Par 65, SSS 63.
Club membership 350.
Visitors no restrictions.
Societies apply in writing, telephone enquiries welcome.
Green Fees not confirmed.
Facilities
Location 3.5m S of city centre

Hotel ★★★★ 64% Swallow Hotel, Queen's Pde, Seaburn, SUNDERLAND ☎ 0191 529 2041 65

Wearside Coxgreen SR4 9JT
☎ 0191 534 2518 Fax 0191 5342518
Open, undulating parkland course rolling down to the River Wear and beneath the shadow of the famous Penshaw Monument. Built on the lines of an Athenian temple it is a well-known landmark. Two ravines cross the course presenting a variety of challenging holes.
18 holes, 6373yds, Par 71, SSS 74, Course record 63.
Club membership 710.

Visitors may not play before 9.30am, between 12.30-1.30 or after 4pm.
Societies must apply in writing.
Green Fees not confirmed.
Prof Doug Brolls
Facilities
Location 3.5m W off A183

Hotel ★★★★ 64% Swallow Hotel, Queen's Pde, Seaburn, SUNDERLAND
☎ 0191 529 2041 65

TYNEMOUTH Map 12 NZ36

Tynemouth Spital Dene NE30 2ER
☎ 0191 257 4578 Fax 0191 259 5193
Well-drained parkland course, easy walking.
18 holes, 6401yds, Par 70, SSS 71, Course record 64.
Club membership 824.
Visitors must play with member weekends & bank holidays.
Societies must contact in writing.
Green Fees £20 per day; £15 per round.
Prof J P McKenna
Designer Willie Park
Facilities
Location 0.5m W

Hotel ★★★ 63% Grand Hotel, Grand Pde, TYNEMOUTH
☎ 0191 293 6666 40

WALLSEND Map 12 NZ26

Wallsend Rheydt Av, Bigges Main NE28 8SU
☎ 0191 262 1973
Parkland course.
18 holes, 6608yds, Par 72, SSS 72, Course record 66.
Club membership 750.
Visitors may not play before 12.30pm weekends.
Societies must apply in writing.
Green Fees £13 per round (£15 weekends & bank holidays).
Prof Ken Phillips
Facilities
Location NW side of town centre off A193

Hotel ★★★ 69% Imperial Swallow Hotel, Jesmond Rd, NEWCASTLE UPON TYNE
☎ 0191 281 5511 122

WASHINGTON Map 12 NZ25

George Washington Hotel Golf & Country Club Stone Cellar Rd, High Usworth NE37 1PH
☎ 0191 402 9988 Fax 0191 4151166
Championship-standard course. Also a 9-hole (par 3) course, putting green and 21-bay floodlit driving range.
18 holes, 6267yds, Par 73, SSS 71.
Club membership 600.
Visitors must contact in advance. May not play before 10am or between noon & 2pm at weekends.
Societies book in advance.
Green Fees on application.
Cards
Prof Warren Marshall
Facilities
& Leisure heated indoor swimming pool, squash, sauna, solarium, gymnasium.
Hotel ★★★ 67% George Washington County Hotel, Stone Cellar Rd, District 12, High Usworth, WASHINGTON ☎ 0191 402 9988 105

WHICKHAM Map 12 NZ26

Whickham Hollinside Park, Fellside Rd NE16 5BA
☎ 0191 488 1576 Fax 0191 488 1576
Undulating parkland course with attractive panoramic views.
18 holes, 5878yds, Par 68, SSS 68, Course record 61.
Club membership 650.
Visitors must contact Professional in advance.
Societies by arrangement.
Green Fees £20 per day/round (£25 Sun).
Prof Graeme Lisle
Facilities by prior arrangement
& Leisure snooker.
Location 1.5m S

Hotel ★★★ 68% Swallow Hotel, High West St, GATESHEAD ☎ 0191 477 1105 103

WHITLEY BAY Map 12 NZ37

Whitley Bay Claremont Rd NE26 3UF
☎ 0191 252 0180 Fax 0191 297 0030
Downland course close to the sea. A stream runs through the undulating terrain.
18 holes, 6600yds, Par 71, SSS 71, Course record 66.
Club membership 800.

Visitors may not play at weekends.
Societies telephone initially.
Green Fees £30 per day; £22 per round.
Prof Gary Shipley
Facilities
Location NW side of town centre off A1148

Hotel ★★ 52% Holmedale Hotel, 106 Park Av, WHITLEY BAY
☎ 0191 251 3903 & 0191 253 1162 Fax 0191 2 53 0053 18
Additional hotel ★★★ 64% Windsor Hotel, South Pde, WHITLEY BAY
☎ 0191 251 8888 Fax 0191 297 0272 63

WARWICKSHIRE

ATHERSTONE Map 04 SP39

Atherstone The Outwoods, Coleshill Rd CV9 2RL
☎ 01827 713110
Scenic parkland course, established in 1894 and laid out on hilly ground.
18 holes, 6006yds, Par 72, SSS 70, Course record 69.
Club membership 520.
Visitors handicap certificate required. With member only weekends and bank holidays but not Sun. Also with holder of handicap certificate by permission of Club Secretary.
Societies contact in advance.
Green Fees £20 per day/round (£25 bank holidays).
Designer Hawtree
Facilities
Location 0.5m S on B4116

Hotel ★★ 75% Chapel House Hotel, Friar's Gate, ATHERSTONE ☎ 01827 718949 13

BIDFORD-ON-AVON Map 04 SP15

Bidford Grange Stratford Rd B50 4LY
☎ 01789 490319 Fax 01789 778184
Designed by Howard Swan & Paul Tillman, this very long, championship standard course is built to represent a links course and is fully irrigated. There are water hazards on the first 7 holes, and particularly challenging holes on the 16th (223yds,par 3), 8th (600yds, par 5) and an uphill par 4 at the 13th.
18 holes, 7233yds, Par 72, SSS 74, Course record 66.
Club membership 200.
Visitors no restrictions.
Societies apply in writing or phone, minimum 12, maximum 36.
Green Fees £24 per day; £12 per 18 holes, (£30/£15 weekends).
Cards
Facilities
& Leisure fishing.
Location 4m W of Stratford upon Avon, B439

Hotel ★★★ 75% Salford Hall Hotel, ABBOT'S SALFORD
☎ 01386 871300 14 Annexe19

BRANDON Map 04 SP47

City of Coventry-Brandon Wood Brandon Ln, Wolston CV8 3GQ ☎ 01203 543141
Municipal parkland course surrounded by fields and bounded by River Avon on east side. Floodlit driving range.
18 holes, 6610yds, Par 72, SSS 72, Course record 68.
Club membership 500.
Visitors telephone for details.
Societies telephone secretary for details
Green Fees not confirmed.
Prof Chris Gledhill
Facilities
Location Off A45 southbound

Hotel ★★★ 64% The Brandon Hall, Main St, BRANDON ☎ 01203 542571 60

COLESHILL Map 04 SP28

Maxstoke Park Castle Ln B46 2RD
☎ 01675 466743 Fax 01675 466743
Parkland course with easy walking. Numerous trees and a lake form natural hazards.
18 holes, 6442yds, Par 71, SSS 71, Course record 64.
Club membership 720.

Visitors with member only at weekends & bank holidays.
Societies contact in advance.
Green Fees £35 per day; £25 per round.
Prof Neil McEwan
Facilities
Location 3m NE of Coleshill on B4114 turn right for Maxstoke then 1m on right

Hotel ★★ 66% Coleshill Hotel, 152 High St, COLESHILL ☎ 01675 465527 15 Annexe8

HENLEY-IN-ARDEN Map 04 SP16

Henley Golf & Country Club Birmingham Rd B95 5QA
☎ 01564 793715 Fax 01564 795754
Founded in 1994, this improving course is maturing well and provides a good golfing challenge for all handicaps.
18 holes, 6933yds, Par 73, SSS 73.
Club membership 675.

Visitors may book up to 7 days in advance.
Societies apply in writing or telephone in advance.
Green Fees £20 (£25 weekends).
Cards
Prof Somon Edwin
Designer N Selwyn Smith
Facilities
& Leisure hard tennis courts, 9 hole par3.
Location On the left hand side of the Birmingham road, just N of Henley-in Arden

Hotel ★★★ 62% Quality Hotel, Pool Bank, Southcrest, REDDITCH ☎ 01527 541511 58

KENILWORTH Map 04 SP27

Kenilworth Crewe Ln CV8 2EA
☎ 01926 858517 Fax 01926 864453
Parkland course in open hilly situation. Club founded in 1889.
18 holes, 6413yds, Par 73, SSS 71, Course record 62.
Club membership 725.

Visitors must contact in advance.
Societies apply in writing.
Green Fees £28 per day/round (£37 weekends).
Cards
Prof Steve Yates
Designer Hawtree
Facilities
Location 0.5m NE

Hotel ★★ 64% Clarendon House Hotel, Old High St, KENILWORTH ☎ 01926 857668 Cen. Res. 0800 616883 Fax 01926 850669 30

LEA MARSTON Map 04 SP29

Lea Marston Hotel & Leisure Complex Haunch Ln B76 0BY ☎ 01675 470468 Fax 01675 470871
Par 3, 'pay-and-play' course, with water hazards, out of bounds, and large bunkers. The venue for the past two years of the Midlands Professional Par 3 Competition. Golf driving range.
9 holes, 783yds, Par 27, SSS 27, Course record 46.
Club membership 150.

Visitors no restrictions.
Societies must telephone in advance.
Green Fees not confirmed.
Prof Andrew Stokes
Designer J R Blake
Facilities
& Leisure hard tennis courts, heated indoor swimming pool, sauna, solarium, gymnasium.
Hotel ★★★ 72% Lea Marston Hotel & Leisure Complex, Haunch Ln, LEA MARSTON ☎ 01675 470468 49

LEAMINGTON SPA Map 04 SP36

Leamington & County Golf Ln, Whitnash CV31 2QA
☎ 01926 425961 Fax 01926 425961
Undulating parkland course with extensive views.
18 holes, 6488yds, Par 71, SSS 71, Course record 65.
Club membership 802.

Visitors must contact in advance.
Societies telephone in advance.
Green Fees £30 per day; £25 per round (£40 per round weekends).
Prof Iain Grant
Designer H S Colt
Facilities
Location S side of town centre

Hotel ★★★ 60% Manor House Hotel, Avenue Rd, LEAMINGTON SPA ☎ 01926 423251 53

Newbold Comyn Newbold Ter East CV32 4EW
☎ 01926 421157
Municipal parkland course with hilly front nine. The par 4, 9th is a 467-yd testing hole.
18 holes, 6315yds, Par 70, SSS 70, Course record 70.
Club membership 320.

Visitors no restrictions.
Societies apply to professional.
Green Fees £10.50 per round.
Prof Don Knight
Facilities
& Leisure heated indoor swimming pool, gymnasium.
Location 0.75m E of town centre off B4099

Hotel ★★★ 60% Manor House Hotel, Avenue Rd, LEAMINGTON SPA ☎ 01926 423251 53

LEEK WOOTTON Map 04 SP26

The Warwickshire CV35 7QT
☎ 01926 409409 Fax 01926 408409
Opened in 1993, this is an unusual championship standard course. Designed by Karl Litten, the 36 holes are laid out as four interchangeable loops of 9 holes to create six contrasting yet superb courses in a parkland and woodland setting.
South East Course: 18 holes, 7000yds, Par 72, SSS 72, Course record 68.
North West Course: 18 holes, 7400yds, Par 72, SSS 74, Course record 68.
Club membership 880.

Visitors can book up to 7 days in advance.
Societies apply to sales office for details.
Green Fees 18 holes: Nov-Feb £25. Mar, Apr & Oct £30. May-Sep £45.
Cards
Prof J Cook/B Fotheringham
Designer Karl Litten
Facilities
Location On B4115

Hotel ★★★ 67% Chesford Grange Hotel, Chesford Bridge, KENILWORTH
☎ 01926 859331 28 Annexe126

NUNEATON Map 04 SP39

Nuneaton Golf Dr, Whitestone CV11 6QF
☎ 01203 347810 Fax 01203 327563
Undulating moorland and woodland course.
18 holes, 6429yds, Par 71, SSS 71.
Club membership 675.
Visitors must produce evidence of membership of a recognised golf club or society, with member only at weekends.
Societies apply in writing.
Green Fees £30 per day; £25 per round (£18 per round in Winter).
Prof Steven Bainbridge
Facilities
Location 2m SE off B4114

Hotel ★★ 67% Longshoot Toby Hotel, Watling St, NUNEATON
☎ 01203 329711 Annexe47

Oakridge Arley Ln, Ansley Village CV10 9PH
☎ 01676 541389 & 540542 Fax 01676 542709
There are a number of water hazards on the back nine which add to the natural beauty of the countryside. The undulating course is affected by winter cross winds on several holes. Overall it will certainly test golfing skills.
18 holes, 6242yds, Par 71, SSS 70.
Club membership 500.
Visitors contact in advance, with members only at weekends.
Societies apply in writing or telephone in advance.
Green Fees contact for details.
Cards
Prof Ian Sadler
Designer Algy Jayes
Facilities
Location 4m W

Hotel ★★★ 64% Weston Hall, Weston Ln, Weston in Arden, Bulkington, NUNEATON
☎ 01203 640846 38

Purley Chase Pipers Ln, Ridge Ln CV10 0RB
☎ 01203 393118
Meadowland course with tricky water hazards on eight holes and undulating greens. 13-bay driving range.
18 holes, 6772yds, Par 72, SSS 72, Course record 67.
Club membership 750.
Visitors welcome except at weekends.
Societies telephone for provisional booking.
Green Fees not confirmed.
Cards
Prof Gary Carver
Facilities
& Leisure snooker.
Location 2m NW off B4114

Hotel ★★ 67% Longshoot Toby Hotel, Watling St, NUNEATON
☎ 01203 329711 Annexe47

RUGBY Map 04 SP57

Rugby Clifton Rd CV21 3RD ☎ 01788 542306
Parkland course with brook running through the middle and crossed by a viaduct.
18 holes, 5457yds, Par 68, SSS 67, Course record 62.
Club membership 550.
Visitors weekends & bank holidays with member only.
Societies apply in writing.
Green Fees not confirmed.
Prof Andy Peach
Facilities
Location 1m NE on B5414

Hotel ★★★ 59% The Rugby Grosvenor Hotel, Clifton Rd, RUGBY
☎ 01788 535686 21

Whitefields Hotel Golf & Country Club Coventry Rd, Thurlaston CV23 9JR ☎ 01788 815555 Fax 01788 521695
Whitefields has superb natural drainage. There are many water features and the 13th has a stunnning dogleg 442yard Par 4 with a superb view across Draycote Water. The 16th is completely surrounded by water and is particularly difficult.
18 holes, 6223yds, Par 71, SSS 70, Course record 69.
Club membership 400.
Visitors advisable to book unless hotel guest, available 7 days, contact secretary on 01788 815555.
Societies contact secretary in advance.
Green Fees £18-£25 per day (£22-£30 weekends & bank holidays).

Cards
Prof Mark Chamberlain
Designer Reg Mason
Facilities
Location A45 Coventry road, near Dunchurch

Hotel ★★★ 59% Whitefields Hotel Golf & Country Club, Coventry Rd, Thurlaston, RUGBY ☎ 01788 521800 & 522393 Fax 01788 521695 33

STONELEIGH Map 04 SP37

Stoneleigh Deer Park The Clubhouse, The Old Deer Park, Coventry Rd CV8 3DR
☎ 01203 639991 Fax 01203 511533
Parkland course in old deer park with many mature trees. The River Avon meanders through the course and comes into play on 4 holes. Also 9-hole course.
Tantara Course: 18 holes, 6083yds, Par 71, SSS 69.
Avon Course: 9 holes, 1251yds, Par 27.
Club membership 800.
Visitors must contact in advance, no visitors at weekends except by prior arrangement.
Societies by prior arrangement.
Green Fees Tantara £20 per day; £14.50 per round (£30/£22.50 weekends).
Prof Matt McGuire
Designer Ken Harrison
Facilities
Location 3m NE of Kenilworth

Hotel ★★★ 70% De Montfort Hotel, The Square, KENILWORTH ☎ 01926 855944 103

STRATFORD-UPON-AVON Map 04 SP25

Stratford Oaks Bearley Rd, Snitterfield CV37 0EZ
☎ 01789 731980
American styled, parkland course designed by Howard Swan.
18 holes, 6100yds, Par 71, SSS 69, Course record 66.
Club membership 750.
Visitors contact in advance.
Societies telephone in advance.
Green Fees £21 (£27.50 weekends).
Prof Andrew Dunbar
Designer H Swann
Facilities
Location 4m N of Stratford-upon-Avon

Hotel ★★★★ 68% Stratford Manor, Warwick Rd, STRATFORD-UPON-AVON ☎ 01789 731173 104

Stratford-upon-Avon Tiddington Rd CV37 7BA
☎ 01789 205749
Beautiful parkland course. The par 3, 16th is tricky and the par 5, 17th and 18th, provide a tough end.
18 holes, 6311yds, Par 72, SSS 70, Course record 64.
Club membership 750.
Visitors restricted on Wed.
Societies must telephone in advance.
Green Fees not confirmed.
Prof D Sutherland
Facilities
Location 0.75m E on B4086

Hotel ★★★★ 66% The Alveston Manor, Clopton Bridge, STRATFORD-UPON-AVON ☎ 01789 204581 106

Welcombe Hotel Warwick Rd CV37 0NR
☎ 01789 295252 Fax 01789 414666
Wooded parkland course of great character and boasting superb views of the River Avon, Stratford and the Cotswolds. Set within the hotel's 157-acre estate, it has two lakes and water features.
18 holes, 6274yds, Par 70, SSS 70, Course record 64.
Visitors must contact in advance.
Societies booking via Hotel.
Green Fees £40 per round.
Cards
Prof Carl Masons
Designer Thomas Macauley
Facilities
& Leisure hard tennis courts, fishing, solarium, gymnasium, hairdresser, health & beauty salon, snooker.
Location 1.5m NE off A46

Hotel ★★★★ 73% Welcombe Hotel and Golf Course, Warwick Rd, STRATFORD-UPON-AVON ☎ 01789 295252 67

TANWORTH-IN-ARDEN Map 04 SP17

Ladbrook Park Poolhead Ln B94 5ED
☎ 01564 742264 Fax 01564 742909
Parkland course lined with trees.
18 holes, 6427yds, Par 71, SSS 71, Course record 65.
Club membership 700.
Visitors welcome weekdays, with member at weekends. Must contact in advance & have handicap certificate.
Societies apply in advance.
Green Fees £40 per 36 holes, £30 per 18-28 holes.
Prof Richard Mountford
Designer H S Colt
Facilities
Location 2.5m SE of M42 junct 3

Hotel ★★★ Nuthurst Grange Country House Hotel, Nuthurst Grange Ln, HOCKLEY HEATH ☎ 01564 783972 15

UPPER BRAILES Map 04 SP32

Brailes Sutton Ln, Lower Brailes OX15 5BB
☎ 01608 685336
Undulating meadowland on 130 acres of Cotswold countryside. Sutton brook passes through the course and is crossed 5 times.The Par 5 17th offers the most spectacular view of three counties from the tee. There is a prevailing cross wind.
18 holes, 6270yds, Par 71, SSS 70, Course record 72.
Club membership 430.
Visitors advance telephone advisable to 01608 685633.
Societies telephone or write for information to the secretary.
Green Fees £25 per 27/36 holes; £17 per 18 holes (£33/£25 weekends & bank holidays).
Prof Mike Bendall
Designer B A Hull
Facilities

Location 4m E of Shipston-on-Stour, on B4035

Hotel ★★ 63% The Red Lion Hotel, Main St, Long Compton, SHIPSTON ON STOUR
☎ 01608 684221 5

WARWICK Map 04 SP26

Warwick The Racecourse CV34 6HW ☎ 01926 494316
Parkland course with easy walking. Driving range with floodlit bays.
9 holes, 2682yds, Par 34, SSS 66, Course record 67.
Club membership 150.
Visitors must contact in advance. May not play Sun before 12.30pm
Societies contact in advance.
Green Fees £4 per 9 holes (£5 weekends).
Prof Phil Sharp
Designer D G Dunkley
Facilities
Location W side of town centre

Hotel ★★ 62% Warwick Arms Hotel, 17 High St, WARWICK ☎ 01926 492759 35

WEST MIDLANDS

ALDRIDGE Map 07 SK00

Druids Heath Stonnall Rd WS9 8JZ
☎ 01922 455595 (Office) 459523 (Prof)
Testing, undulating heathland course.
18 holes, 6659yds, Par 72, SSS 73.
Club membership 590.
Visitors contact in advance recommended. Weekend play permitted after 2pm.
Societies phone initially.
Green Fees £25 per day (£33 weekends after 2pm).
Prof Glenn Williams
Facilities
& Leisure snooker.
Location NE side of town centre off A454

Hotel ★★★ 70% The Fairlawns at Aldridge, 178 Little Aston Rd, Aldridge, WALSALL
☎ 01922 55122 35

BIRMINGHAM Map 07 SP08

Brandhall Heron Rd, Oldbury, Warley B68 8AQ
☎ 0121 552 2195
Private golf club on municipal parkland course, easy walking, good hazards. Testing holes: 1st-502 yds (par 5); 10th-455 yds dog-leg (par 5).
18 holes, 5734yds, Par 70, SSS 68, Course record 66.
Club membership 300.
Visitors restricted weekends. Telephone for tee times. Access to clubhouse on payment of small entrance fee.
Societies by arrangement, apply in writing
Green Fees not confirmed.
Prof Carl Yates
Facilities
Location 5.5m W of city centre off A4123

Hotel B Forte Posthouse Birmingham Great Barr, Chapel Ln, Great Barr, BIRMINGHAM
☎ 0121 357 7444 192

Cocks Moors Woods Municipal Alcester Rd South, Kings Heath B14 4ER ☎ 0121 444 3584 Fax 0121 441 1305
Although quite short this tree-lined, parkland course has well maintained greens and offers a good test of golf.
18 holes, 5769yds, Par 69, SSS 68.
Club membership 400.
Visitors no restrictions.
Societies must contact in advance.
Green Fees not confirmed.
Prof Steve Ellis
Facilities
& Leisure heated indoor swimming pool, solarium, gymnasium.
Location 5m S of city centre on A435

Hotel B Forte Posthouse Birmingham City, Smallbrook Queensway, BIRMINGHAM
☎ 0121 643 8171 251

Edgbaston Church Rd, Edgbaston B15 3TB
☎ 0121 454 1736 Fax 0121 454 2395
Set in 144 acres of woodland, lake and parkland, two miles from the centre of Birmingham, this delightful course utilises the wealth of natural features to provide a series of testing and adventurous holes set in the traditional double loop that starts directly in front of the Clubhouse, an imposing Georgian mansion.
18 holes, 6106yds, Par 69, SSS 69, Course record 64.
Club membership 880.
Visitors recommended to contact in advance through golf reservations, must have handicap certificate. Most weekends pm.
Societies must apply in writing.
Green Fees £35-£25 (£50-35 weekends).
Prof Andrew H Bownes
Designer H S Colt
Facilities
Location 1m S of city centre on B4217 off A38

Hotel ★★★ 66% Plough & Harrow, 135 Hagley Rd, EDGBASTON
☎ 0121 454 4111 44

Great Barr Chapel Ln, Great Barr B43 7BA
☎ 0121 357 5270
Parkland course with easy walking. Pleasant views of Barr Beacon National Park.
18 holes, 6523yds, Par 72, SSS 71, Course record 67.
Club membership 600.
Visitors restricted at weekends.
Societies must contact in writing.
Green Fees not confirmed.
Prof Richard Spragg
Facilities
Location 6m N of city centre off A 34

Hotel B Forte Posthouse Birmingham Great Barr, Chapel Ln, Great Barr, BIRMINGHAM
☎ 0121 357 7444 192

Handsworth 11 Sunningdale Close, Handsworth Wood B20 1NP ☎ 0121 554 0599
Undulating parkland course with some tight fairways but subject to wind.
18 holes, 6267yds, Par 70, SSS 70, Course record 65.
Club membership 800.

Visitors restricted weekends, bank holidays & Xmas. Must contact in advance and have a handicap certificate.
Societies must contact in advance.
Green Fees not confirmed.
Prof Lee Bashford
Facilities
& Leisure squash.
Location 3.5m NW of city centre off A4040

Hotel ★★★ 67% Birmingham/West Bromwich Moat House, Birmingham Rd, WEST BROMWICH ☎ 0121 609 9988 168

Harborne 40 Tennal Rd, Harborne B32 2JE ☎ 0121 427 3058
Parkland course in hilly situation, with brook running through.
18 holes, 6230yds, Par 70, SSS 70, Course record 65.
Club membership 655.

Visitors must have handicap certificate, contact in advance, may not play weekends except with member, Ladies have priority Tue.
Societies Mon, Wed-Fri apply to secretary, by phone or letter.
Green Fees £35 per day; £30 per round.
Prof Alan Quarterman
Designer Harry Colt
Facilities
Location 3.5 m SW of city centre off A4040

Hotel ★★★ 66% Plough & Harrow, 135 Hagley Rd, EDGBASTON ☎ 0121 454 4111 44

Harborne Church Farm Vicarage Rd, Harborne B17 0SN ☎ 0121 427 1204 Fax 0121 428 3126
Parkland course with water hazards and easy walking. Some holes might prove difficult.
9 holes, 4882yds, Par 66, SSS 64, Course record 64.
Club membership 200.

Visitors must contact in advance.
Societies must telephone in advance.
Green Fees £6 per 18 holes; £3.50 per 9 holes (£7.50/£4 weekends).
Cards
Prof Paul Johnson
Facilities
Location 3.5m SW of city centre off A4040

Hotel ★★★ 66% Plough & Harrow, 135 Hagley Rd, EDGBASTON ☎ 0121 454 4111 44

Hatchford Brook Coventry Rd, Sheldon B26 3PY ☎ 0121 743 9821 Fax 0121 743 3420
Fairly flat, municipal parkland course.
18 holes, 6155yds, Par 69, SSS 69.
Club membership 450.

Visitors are restricted early Sat & Sun.
Societies must contact in advance.
Green Fees £8 per 18 holes (£9 weekends).
Cards
Prof Mark Hampton
Facilities
Location 6m E of city centre on A45

Hotel B Forte Posthouse Birmingham Airport, Coventry Rd, BIRMINGHAM ☎ 0121 782 8141 136

Hilltop Park Ln, Handsworth B21 8LJ ☎ 0121 554 4463 Fax 0121 515 2842
A good test of golf with interesting layout, undulating fairways and large greens, located in the Sandwell Valley conservation area.
18 holes, 6208yds, Par 70, SSS 70.
Club membership 400.

Visitors no restrictions but booking necessary.
Societies telephone Professional in advance.
Green Fees £8.50 per 18 holes; £5.50 per 9 holes (£9/£6 weekends).
Prof Kevin Highfield
Designer Hawtree
Facilities
Location On A41, 1m from junct 1 M5

Hotel ★★★ 67% Birmingham/West Bromwich Moat House, Birmingham Rd, WEST BROMWICH ☎ 0121 609 9988 168

Lickey Hills Rosehill, Rednal B45 8RR ☎ 0121 453 3159 Fax 0121 457 8779
Hilly municipal course overlooking the city.
Lickey Hills: 18 holes, 5835yds, Par 68, SSS 68.
Club membership 300.

Visitors may not play between 9 & 10.30am weekends.
Societies must contact in advance.
Green Fees not confirmed.
Prof Joe Kelly
Facilities
& Leisure tennis courts.
Location 10m SW of city centre on B4096

Hotel ★★ 70% Norwood Hotel, 87-89 Bunbury Rd, Northfield, BIRMINGHAM ☎ 0121 411 2202 18

Moseley Springfield Rd, Kings Heath B14 7DX ☎ 0121 444 2115 Fax 0121 441 4662
Parkland course with a lake, pond and stream to provide natural hazards. The par-3, 4th goes through a cutting in woodland to a tree and garden-lined amphitheatre, and the par-4, 5th entails a drive over a lake to a dog-leg fairway.
18 holes, 6300yds, Par 70, SSS 70, Course record 64.
Club membership 600.

Visitors may only play by prior arrangement.
Societies by prior arrangement.
Green Fees £37 per day.
Prof Gary Edge
Facilities by prior arrangement
Location 4m S of city centre on B4146 off A435

Hotel ★★ 70% Norwood Hotel, 87-89 Bunbury Rd, Northfield, BIRMINGHAM ☎ 0121 411 2202 18

North Worcestershire Frankley Beeches Rd, Northfield B31 5LP ☎ 0121 475 1047 Fax 0121 476 8681
Designed by James Braid and established in 1907, this is a mature parkland course. Tree plantations rather than heavy rough are the main hazards. ▶

18 holes, 5959yds, Par 69, SSS 68, Course record 64.
Club membership 600.
Visitors by prior arrangement with professional. Must play with member at weekends. All visitors must have an official CONGU handicap.
Societies apply in advance in writing or by telephone to the professional tel: 0121 475 5721.
Green Fees £25.50 per day; £18.50 per round weekdays only.
Cards
Prof Finley Clarke
Designer James Braid
Facilities
Location 7m SW of Birmingham city centre, off A38

Hotel ★★ 70% Norwood Hotel, 87-89 Bunbury Rd, Northfield, BIRMINGHAM ☎ 0121 411 2202 18

Warley Lightswood Hill, Warley B67 5ED
☎ 0121 429 2440 Fax 0121 434 4430
Municipal parkland course in Warley Woods. New out of bounds areas and bunkers have tightened the course considerably with further improvement following current tree planting.
9 holes, 5346yds, Par 68, SSS 66.
Club membership 200.
Visitors no restrictions.
Societies but times very limited for large parties.
Green Fees not confirmed.
Prof David Owen
Facilities
Location 4m W of city centre off A456

Hotel ★★★ 66% Plough & Harrow, 135 Hagley Rd, EDGBASTON ☎ 0121 454 4111 44

Coventry — Map 04 SP37

Ansty Golf Centre Brinklow Rd, Ansty CV7 9JH
☎ 01203 621341 Fax 01203 602671
18-hole Pay and Play course of two 9-hole loops. Membership competitions for handicaps. Driving range and putting green.
18 holes, 6079yds, Par 71, SSS 68, Course record 66.
Club membership 400.
Visitors no restrictions.
Societies welcome, telephone in advance.
Green Fees £9 per 18 holes; £5 per 9 holes (£13/£7 weekends).
Prof Phil Tranter
Designer David Morgan
Facilities
Location 3m from city centre via A4600

Hotel ★★★ 62% Ansty Hall, ANSTY ☎ 01203 612222 25 Annexe5

Coventry St Martins Rd, Finham Park CV3 6PJ
☎ 01203 414152 Fax 01203 690131
The scene of several major professional events, this undulating parkland course has a great deal of quality. More than that, it usually plays its length, and thus scoring is never easy, as many professionals have found to their cost.
18 holes, 6601yds, Par 73, SSS 73, Course record 64.
Club membership 500.
Visitors must contact in advance. May not play at weekends and bank holidays.
Societies must apply in writing.
Green Fees £30 per day.
Cards
Prof Philip Weaver
Designer Vardon Bros/Hawtree
Facilities
Location 3m S of city centre on B4133, 2m from jct of A45/A46

Hotel ★★★ 69% Hylands Hotel, Warwick Rd, COVENTRY ☎ 01203 501600 54

Coventry Hearsall Beechwood Av CV5 6DF
☎ 01203 713470
Parkland course with fairly easy walking. A brook provides an interesting hazard.
18 holes, 6005yds, Par 70, SSS 69.
Club membership 650.
Visitors with member only at weekends.
Societies apply in writing to secretary.
Green Fees £24.
Prof Mike Tarn
Facilities
Location 1.5m SW of city centre off A429

Hotel ★★★ 69% Hylands Hotel, Warwick Rd, COVENTRY ☎ 01203 501600 54

GPT The Grange, Copsewood, Binley Rd CV3 1HS
☎ 01203 563127
Flat parkland course with very tight out of bounds on a number of holes, and a river which affects play on five of them. Well-bunkered, with plenty of trees.
9 holes, 6002yds, Par 72, SSS 69.
Club membership 300.
Visitors may not play after 2pm weekdays or before noon on Sun. No visitors Sat.
Societies must contact in advance.
Green Fees not confirmed.
Facilities
Location 2m E of city centre on A428

Hotel ★★★ 60% The Chace Hotel, London Rd, Toll Bar End, COVENTRY ☎ 01203 303398 66

Windmill Village Hotel Golf & Leisure Club Birmingham Rd, Allesley CV5 9AL
☎ 01203 404040 Fax 01203 404042
An attractive 18-hole course over rolling parkland with plenty of trees and two lakes that demand shots over open water. Four challenging Par 5 holes. Good leisure facilities.
18 holes, 5213yds, Par 70, SSS 67, Course record 66.
Club membership 500.
Visitors must contact in advance. Pre-payment required.
Societies telephone for booking form.
Green Fees £9.95 per 18 holes (£12.95 weekends).
Cards
Prof Robert Hunter
Designer Robert Hunter
Facilities
& Leisure hard tennis courts, heated indoor swimming pool, fishing, sauna, solarium, gymnasium, beauty therapist, steam room.

Location On A45 W of Coventry

Hotel ★★★ 74% Brooklands Grange Hotel & Restaurant, Holyhead Rd, COVENTRY ☎ 01203 601601 30

DUDLEY Map 07 SO99

Dudley Turner's Hill, Rowley Regis, Warley B65 9DP
☎ 01384 233877
Fairly hilly parkland course.
18 holes, 5714yds, Par 69, SSS 68.
Club membership 550.
Visitors may not play at weekends.
Societies must contact in advance.
Green Fees £25 per day; £18 per round.
Prof Paul Taylor
Facilities
Location 2m S of town centre off B4171

Hotel ★★★ 62% Himley Country Hotel, School Rd, HIMLEY ☎ 01902 896716 73

Swindon Bridgnorth Rd, Swindon DY3 4PU
☎ 01902 897031 & 895226 Fax 01902 326219
Attractive undulating woodland/parkland course, with spectacular views.
Old Course: 18 holes, 6091yds, Par 71, SSS 69.
New Course: 9 holes, 1135yds, Par 27.
Club membership 700.
Visitors must contact in advance.
Societies must apply in writing.
Green Fees £27 per day; £18 per round (£40/£27 weekends & bank holidays).
Cards
Prof Phil Lester
Facilities
& Leisure fishing.
Location On B4176, 3m from A449 at Himley

Hotel ★★★ 62% Himley Country Hotel, School Rd, HIMLEY ☎ 01902 896716 73

HALESOWEN Map 07 SO98

Corngreaves Hall Corngreaves Rd B64 ☎ 01384 567880
Mature course offering a good challenge to the best golfers with American specification greens and most holes holding a testing start. Magnificent views of the Clent Hills.
9 holes, 2800.
Visitors at anytime by prior arrangement.
Societies apply in writing in advance.
Green Fees not confirmed.
Prof S Joyce/C Yates
Facilities
Hotel ★★★ 62% Talbot Hotel, High St, STOURBRIDGE ☎ 01384 394350 25

Halesowen The Leasowes, Leasowes Ln B62 8QF
☎ 0121 501 3606
Parkland course in convenient position.
18 holes, 5754yds, Par 69, SSS 68, Course record 65.
Club membership 625.
Visitors welcome weekdays, may only play weekends or bank holidays with member.
Societies must apply in writing.
Green Fees £25 per day; £18 per round.
Prof Jon Nicholas
Facilities
Location 1m E junct 3 M5, Leasowes Lane off Manor Lane

Hotel ★★★ 62% Talbot Hotel, High St, STOURBRIDGE ☎ 01384 394350 25

KNOWLE Map 07 SP17

Copt Heath 1220 Warwick Rd B93 9LN
☎ 01564 772650 Fax 01564 771022
Parkland course designed by H. Vardon.
18 holes, 6517yds, Par 71, SSS 71.
Club membership 700.
Visitors must contact in advance and possess official handicap. May not play weekends & bank holidays.
Societies must contact in advance.
Green Fees £40 per day; £35 per round.
Prof Brian J Barton
Designer H Vardon
Facilities
Location On A4141, 0.50m S of junct 5 of M42

Hotel ★★★ 69% St John's Swallow Hotel, 651 Warwick Rd, SOLIHULL ☎ 0121 711 3000 177

MERIDEN Map 04 SP28

Marriott Forest of Arden Golf & Country Club Maxstoke Ln CV7 7HR ☎ 01676 522335 Fax 01676 523711
Two parkland courses, set within the grounds of Packington Estate, with water hazards and offering a fine test of golf. On-site hotel with many leisure facilities.
Arden Course: 18 holes, 6718yds, Par 72, SSS 73, Course record 62.
Aylesford Course: 18 holes, 6525yds, Par 72, SSS 71.
Club membership 800.
Visitors book 10 days in advance, 48 hours in advance for weekends.
Societies by arrangement.
Green Fees Arden Course: £65 per round (£70 weekends). Aylesford: £35 per round (£45 weekends).
Cards
Prof Kim Thomas
Designer Donald Steele
Facilities
& Leisure hard tennis courts, heated indoor swimming pool, fishing, sauna, solarium, gymnasium, health & beauty salon, jacuzzi.
Location 1m SW on B4102

Hotel ★★★★ 70% Marriott Forest of Arden Hotel & Country Club, Maxstoke Ln, MERIDEN ☎ 01676 522335 214

North Warwickshire Hampton Ln CV7 7LL
☎ 01676 522259 Fax 01676 522915
Parkland course with easy walking.
9 holes, 6390yds, Par 72, SSS 70, Course record 65.
Club membership 425.
Visitors must contact in advance.
Societies must apply in writing to secretary.
Green Fees not confirmed.
Prof David Ingram ▶

THE BELFRY

WISHAW *North Warwickshire* ☏ 01675 470301
Fax 01675 470178 Map 07 SP19

John Ingham writes: When professional people are commissioned to turn a piece of farmland into a golf course and hotel complex, they are flattered - and delighted. This happened to Peter Alliss and Dave Thomas, two celebrated tournament competitors. The challenge they were offered: turn an unsympathetic piece of land into a good golf course.The Belfry's first course was opened in 1960.

Since that date the two architects have every reason to be proud. The Belfry, set in 500 acres of Warwickshire countryside, has staged three of the popular Ryder Cup matches, and the two courses - the completely refurbished Brabazon and the Derby - named after two Lords, have received thousands of visitors. These visitors have been entertained with a kindly reception, enhanced by a really excellent hotel. A third course - the PGA National Course opened in Spring 1997. The Belfry is also home to the PGA Training Academy.

Since its establishment, the saplings and newly-created greens have settled down very well and presented a worthwhile face to the world. One of the big challenges of The Belfry are the lakes and many water hazards that gobble up wild shots. Many a famous player, such as Seve Ballesteros, has had balls sinking without trace at the Brabazon's famously testing 18th hole. This monster requires the player to clear the lake twice in its 455-yard drive to reach an uphill, three-tiered, 60-yard long green.

As a public course, The Belfry is open to all-comers every day. This obviously means a great deal of traffic, although there are many other worthwhile courses in the West Midlands such as Hansworth and Little Aston. However, The Belfry is excellently managed and kept in top condition by a team now fully experienced in catering for every golfer. Recently, bunkering and new tees have improved several of the holes and spectator mounding has improved viewing of the golf tournaments.

In its fine parkland setting the club has become well known for its accommodation and fine business facilities and, being so well placed for the NEC, Birmingham and the international airport, it attracts a variety of golfers.

Visitors	must contact in advance. Handicap certificate is required for the Brabazon & PGA courses; 24 or better gentleman, 32 or better Ladies & juniors.
Societies	must telephone in advance
Green fees	Brabazon £75 per round; Derby £35 per round; PGA £60 per round. All major credit cards
Facilities	Professional (P McGovern)
Leisure	hard tennis courts, heated indoor swimming pool, snooker, squash, health spa. Any leisure pursuit arranged.
Location	Sutton Coldfield B76 9PR Lichfield Rd, Wishaw (exit junc 9 M42 4m E)

Brabazon: 18 holes, 7200yds, Par 72, SSS 74.
Derby: 18 holes, 6009yds Par 69, SSS 69
PGA; 18holes, 7072yds Par 72 SSS 74

WHERE TO STAY AND EAT NEARBY

HOTELS:

WISHAW

★★★★ 73%The Belfry, Lichfield Rd. ☏ 01675 470301. 324 320

★★★60% Moxhull Hall, Holly Lane. ☏ 0121-329 2056. 11(3 8) Annexe 9

LEA MARSTON

★★★72% Lea Marston Hotel and Leisure Complex, Haunch Lane. ☏ 01675 47046849 (2 47)

SUTTON COLDFIELD

★★★ 64% Sutton Court, 60-66 Lichfield Rd. ☏ 0121-355 6071, 56 (9 47) Annexe 8

★★★★ New Hall, Walmley Rd. ☏ 0121-378 2442. 62

Facilities
Location 1m SW on B4102

Hotel ★★★ 71% Manor Hotel, Main Rd, MERIDEN ☎ 01676 522735 74

Stonebridge Golf Centre Somers Rd CV7 7PL
☎ 01676 522442 Fax 01676 522447
18 holes, 6240yds, Par 70, SSS 70, Course record 70.
Club membership 360.
Visitors advisable to book in advance, booking up to 7 days in advance.
Societies apply in writing or telephone in advance.
Green Fees £22 per day; £13 per round (£25/£15 weekends and bank holidays).
Cards
Prof Steve Harrison
Facilities
& Leisure fishing.
Hotel ★★★ 71% Manor Hotel, Main Rd, MERIDEN ☎ 01676 522735 74

SEDGLEY Map 07 SO99

Sedgley Golf Centre Sandyfields Rd DY3 3DL
☎ 01902 880503
Public Pay and Play course. Undulating contours and mature trees with extensive views over surrounding countryside.
9 holes, 3147yds, Par 72, SSS 70.
Club membership 150.
Visitors booking advisable for weekends.
Societies must contact in advance.
Green Fees £7.50 per 18 holes; £5.50 per 9 holes (£8/£6 weekends & bank holidays).
Prof Garry Mercer
Designer W G Cox
Facilities
Location 0.5m from town centre off A463

Hotel ★★★ 62% Himley Country Hotel, School Rd, HIMLEY ☎ 01902 896716 73

SOLIHULL Map 07 SP17

Olton Mirfield Rd B91 1JH
☎ 0121 704 1936 & 0121 705 1083 Fax 0121 711 2010
Parkland course with prevailing southwest wind.
18 holes, 6265yds, Par 69, SSS 71, Course record 63.
Club membership 600.
Visitors must contact in advance. No visitors at weekend.
Societies apply in writing.
Green Fees £35 per 36 holes; £30 per 27 holes; £25 per 18 holes.
Prof Mark Daubney
Designer J H Taylor
Facilities
Location Exit M42 junct 5 and take A41 for 1.5m

Hotel ★★★ 69% St John's Swallow Hotel, 651 Warwick Rd, SOLIHULL ☎ 0121 711 3000 177

A comprehensive list of driving ranges is given at the back of this guide. See page 479

Robin Hood St Bernards Rd B92 7DJ ☎ 0121 706 0061
Pleasant parkland course with easy walking and open to good views.Tree lined fairways and varied holes, culminating in two excellent finishing holes. Modern clubhouse.
18 holes, 6635yds, Par 72, SSS 72, Course record 68.
Club membership 650.
Visitors must contact in advance. With member only at weekends.
Societies must contact in advance.
Green Fees £35 per day; £29 per round.
Prof Alan Harvey
Designer H S Colt
Facilities
Location 2m W off B4025

Hotel ★★★ 69% St John's Swallow Hotel, 651 Warwick Rd, SOLIHULL ☎ 0121 711 3000 177

Shirley Stratford Rd, Monkpath B90 4EW
☎ 0121 744 6001
Fairly flat parkland course.
18 holes, 6510yds, Par 72, SSS 71.
Club membership 500.
Visitors may not play bank holidays & with member only at weekends. Handicap certificate is required.
Societies must contact in advance.
Green Fees not confirmed.
Prof C J Wicketts
Facilities
Location 3m SW off A34

Hotel ★★★★ 62% Regency Hotel, Stratford Rd, Shirley, SOLIHULL ☎ 0121 745 6119 112

STOURBRIDGE Map 07 SO98

Hagley Golf & Country Club Wassell Grove, Hagley DY9 9JW ☎ 01562 883701 Fax 01562 887518
Undulating parkland course set beneath the Clent Hills; there are superb views. Testing 15th, par 5, 557 yards.
18 holes, 6353yds, Par 72, SSS 72, Course record 66.
Club membership 700.
Visitors welcome weekdays but restricted Wed (Ladies Day) & with member only at weekends.
Societies Mon-Fri only, must apply in writing.
Green Fees £28 per day; £22 per round.
Prof Iain Clark
Designer Garratt & Co
Facilities
& Leisure squash.
Location 1m E of Hagley off A456. 2m from junct 3 0n M5

Hotel ★★★ 62% Talbot Hotel, High St, STOURBRIDGE ☎ 01384 394350 25

Stourbridge Worcester Ln, Pedmore DY8 2RB
☎ 01384 395566 Fax 01384 444660
Parkland course.
18 holes, 6231yds, Par 70, SSS 69, Course record 67.
Club membership 857.
Visitors contact secretary, no casual visitors weekends. Ladies day Wednesday.

Societies must apply in writing.
Green Fees not confirmed.
Prof M Male
Facilities
Location 2m from town centre

Hotel ★★★ 62% Talbot Hotel, High St, STOURBRIDGE ☎ 01384 394350 25

SUTTON COLDFIELD Map 07 SP19

THE BELFRY See page 273

Boldmere Monmouth Dr B73 6JL
☎ 0121 354 3379 Fax 0121 355 4534
Established municipal course with 10 par 3s and a lake coming into play on the 16th and 18th holes.
18 holes, 4493yds, Par 63, SSS 62, Course record 57.
Club membership 300.
Visitors must contact in advance.
Societies midweek only, apply in writing.
Green Fees £8.50 per 18 holes (£9.50 weekends).
Prof Trevor Short
Facilities
Location Adjacent to Sutton Park

Hotel ★★★ 70% Moor Hall Hotel, Moor Hall Dr, Four Oaks, SUTTON COLDFIELD ☎ 0121 308 3751 74

Little Aston Streetly B74 3AN
☎ 0121 353 2942 Fax 0121 353 2942
Parkland course.
18 holes, 6670yds, Par 72, SSS 73, Course record 64.
Club membership 350.
Visitors must contact in advance & may not play at weekends.
Societies must apply in writing.
Green Fees £50 per day.
Prof John Anderson
Designer H Vardon
Facilities
Location 3.5m NW off A454

Hotel ★★★ 70% Moor Hall Hotel, Moor Hall Dr, Four Oaks, SUTTON COLDFIELD ☎ 0121 308 3751 74

Moor Hall Moor Hall Dr B75 6LN
☎ 0121 308 6130 Fax 0121 308 6130
Parkland course. The 14th is a notable hole.
18 holes, 6249yds, Par 70, SSS 70.
Club membership 600.
Visitors must contact in advance. With member only weekends & bank holidays.
Societies must apply in writing.
Green Fees not confirmed.
Prof Alan Partridge
Facilities
Location 2.5m N of town centre off A453

Hotel ★★★ 70% Moor Hall Hotel, Moor Hall Dr, Four Oaks, SUTTON COLDFIELD ☎ 0121 308 3751 74

Pype Hayes Eachel Hurst Rd, Walmley B76 1EP
☎ 0121 351 1014 Fax 0121 313 0206
Attractive, fairly flat course with excellent greens.
18 holes, 5927yds, Par 71, SSS 69.
Club membership 400.
Visitors phone professional in advance.
Societies contact professional in advance.
Green Fees £8.50 per round; £5.50 per 9 holes (£9.50/£6 weekends).
Cards
Prof James Bayliss
Designer Bobby Jones
Facilities
Location 2.5m S off B4148

Hotel ★★★ 65% Marston Farm Hotel, Bodymoor Heath, SUTTON COLDFIELD ☎ 01827 872133 37

Sutton Coldfield 110 Thornhill Rd, Streetly B74 3ER
☎ 0121 353 9633 Fax 0121 353 5503
A fine natural, heathland course, with tight fairways, gorse, heather and trees; which is surprising as the high-rise buildings of Birmingham are not far away.
18 holes, 6541yds, Par 72, SSS 71, Course record 65.
Club membership 550.
Visitors must contact in advance. Restricted at weekends.
Societies must apply in writing.
Green Fees not confirmed.
Prof Jerry Hayes
Designer D McKenzie
Facilities by prior arrangement by prior arrangement
Location 3m NW on B4138

Hotel ★★★ 70% Moor Hall Hotel, Moor Hall Dr, Four Oaks, SUTTON COLDFIELD ☎ 0121 308 3751 74

Walmley Brooks Rd, Wylde Green B72 1HR
☎ 0121 373 0029 & 377 7272
Pleasant parkland course with many trees. The hazards are not difficult.
18 holes, 6559yds, Par 72, SSS 72, Course record 67.
Club membership 650.
Visitors must contact in advance. May only play weekdays as guest of member.
Societies must contact in advance.
Green Fees £35 per day; £30 per round. ▶

Prof C J Wicketts
Facilities ⊗ ⛳ ☕ ♀ ⛺ ⛓ ⛳
Location 2m S off A5127

Hotel ★★★ 65% Marston Farm Hotel, Bodymoor Heath, SUTTON COLDFIELD ☎ 01827 872133 37 ⇄ ⛳

WALSALL Map 07 SP09

Bloxwich Stafford Rd, Bloxwich WS3 3PQ
☎ 01922 405724 Fax 01922 476593
Undulating parkland course with natural hazards and subject to strong north wind.
18 holes, 6273yds, Par 71, SSS 71, Course record 68.
Club membership 532.

Visitors may not play at weekends.
Societies must contact in advance.
Green Fees £30 per day; £25 per round.
Prof Richard J Dance
Facilities ⊗ ⛳ ☕ ♀ ⛺ ⛓
Location 3m N of town centre on A34

Hotel ★★★ 70% The Fairlawns at Aldridge, 178 Little Aston Rd, Aldridge, WALSALL ☎ 01922 55122 35 ⇄ ⛳

Calderfields Aldridge Rd WS4 2JS
☎ 01922 640540 Fax 01922 638787
Parkland course with lake.
18 holes, 6590yds, Par 73, SSS 72.
Club membership 550.

Visitors no restrictions.
Societies telephone 01922 632243 in advance.
Green Fees not confirmed.
Prof Darren Lewis
Designer Roy Winter
Facilities ⊗ ⛳ ☕ ♀ ⛺ ⛓
& Leisure fishing.
Location On A454

Hotel ★★★ 70% The Fairlawns at Aldridge, 178 Little Aston Rd, Aldridge, WALSALL ☎ 01922 55122 35 ⇄ ⛳

Walsall The Broadway WS1 3EY
☎ 01922 613512 Fax 01922 616460
Well-wooded parkland course with easy walking.
18 holes, 6300yds, Par 70, SSS 70, Course record 65.
Club membership 600.

Visitors must contact in advance. May not play weekends & bank holidays.
Societies must apply in writing.
Green Fees £40 per day; £33 per round.
Prof Richard Lambert
Designer McKenzie
Facilities ⊗ ⛳ ☕ ♀ ⛺ ⛓
Location 1m S of town centre off A34

Hotel ★★★ 65% The Boundary Hotel, Birmingham Rd, WALSALL ☎ 01922 33555 94 ⇄ ⛳

WEST BROMWICH Map 07 SP09

Dartmouth Vale St B71 4DW ☎ 0121 588 2131
Meadowland course with undulating but easy walking. The 617 yd (par 5) first hole is something of a challenge.
9 holes, 6060yds, Par 71, SSS 71, Course record 66.
Club membership 350.

Visitors with member only at weekends. May not play bank holidays or medal weekends.
Societies must apply in writing.
Green Fees £20 per day.
Prof Guy Dean
Facilities ⊗ ⛳ ☕ ♀ ⛺ ⛓
& Leisure snooker.
Location E side of town centre off A4041

Hotel ★★★ 67% Birmingham/West Bromwich Moat House, Birmingham Rd, WEST BROMWICH ☎ 0121 609 9988 168 ⇄ ⛳

Sandwell Park Birmingham Rd B71 4JJ
☎ 0121 553 4637 Fax 0121 525 1651
Undulating wooded heathland course situated in the Sandwell Valley.
18 holes, 6470yds, Par 71, SSS 72, Course record 67.
Club membership 550.

Visitors must contact in advance. May not play at weekends.

Societies must contact in advance.
Green Fees £35 per 36 holes; £30 per 18 holes.
Prof Nigel Wylie
Designer H S Colt
Facilities
Location On A41, 200yds from juct 1 of the M5

Hotel ★★★ 67% Birmingham/West Bromwich Moat House, Birmingham Rd, WEST BROMWICH ☎ 0121 609 9988 168

WOLVERHAMPTON Map 07 SO99

Oxley Park Stafford Rd, Bushbury WV10 6DE
☎ 01902 425892 Fax 01902 712241
Rolling parkland course with trees, bunkers and water hazards.
18 holes, 6222yds, Par 71, SSS 70, Course record 68.
Club membership 550.
Visitors must contact in advance.
Societies must contact in advance.
Green Fees £29 per day; £25 per round.
Prof Les Burlison
Designer H S Colt
Facilities
& Leisure snooker.
Location N of town centre off A449

Hotel ★★ 69% Ely House Hotel, 53 Tettenhall Rd, WOLVERHAMPTON
☎ 01902 311311 18

Penn Penn Common, Penn WV4 5JN ☎ 01902 341142
Heathland course just outside the town.
18 holes, 6462yds, Par 70, SSS 71, Course record 68.
Club membership 650.
Visitors must play with member at weekends.
Societies must contact in advance.
Green Fees £25 per day; £20 per round.
Prof A Briscoe
Facilities
Location SW side of town centre off A449

Hotel ★★★ 63% Goldthorn Hotel, Penn Rd, WOLVERHAMPTON
☎ 01902 429216 66 Annexe27

South Staffordshire Danescourt Rd, Tettenhall WV6 9BQ
☎ 01902 751065 Fax 01902 741753
A parkland course.
18 holes, 6513yds, Par 71, SSS 71.
Club membership 500.
Visitors must contact in advance but may not play weekends & before 2pm Tue.
Societies must apply in writing.
Green Fees not confirmed.
Prof Jim Rhodes
Designer Harry Vardon
Facilities
Location 3m NW off A41

Hotel ★★ 69% Ely House Hotel, 53 Tettenhall Rd, WOLVERHAMPTON
☎ 01902 311311 18

Three Hammers Short Course Old Stafford Rd, Coven WV10 7PP ☎ 01902 790940
Well maintained short course designed by Henry Cotton and providing a unique challenge to golfers of all standards.
18 holes, 1438yds, Par 54, SSS 54, Course record 43.
Visitors no restrictions.
Societies contact for details.
Green Fees not confirmed.
Designer Henry Cotton
Facilities
Location On A449 N of junct 2 M54

Hotel ★★★ 66% Roman Way Hotel, Watling St, Hatherton, CANNOCK
☎ 01543 572121 56

Wergs Keepers Ln, Tettenhall WV6 8UA
☎ 01902 742225 Fax 01902 744748
Open parkland course.
18 holes, 6949yds, Par 72, SSS 73.
Club membership 250.
Visitors are advised to contact in advance.
Societies must contact in advance.
Green Fees £14.50 per day (£18 weekends & bank holidays).
Cards
Designer C W Moseley
Facilities
Location From Wolverhampton take A41 towards Newport for 2.5m then right for 0.5m then right again

Hotel ★★ 69% Ely House Hotel, 53 Tettenhall Rd, WOLVERHAMPTON
☎ 01902 311311 18

WIGHT, ISLE OF

COWES Map 04 SZ49

Cowes Crossfield Av PO31 8HN ☎ 01983 292303
Fairly level, tight parkland course with difficult par 3s and Solent views.
9 holes, 5934yds, Par 70, SSS 68, Course record 66.
Club membership 300.
Visitors restricted Thu & Sun mornings.
Societies Mon-Wed, must contact in advance.
Green Fees £15 per day/round (£18 weekends).
Designer Hamilton-Stutt
Facilities
Location NW side of town

Hotel ★★ 60% The Fountain Hotel, High St, COWES ☎ 01983 292397 20

EAST COWES Map 04 SZ59

Osborne Osborne House Estate PO32 6JX
☎ 01983 295421
Undulating parkland course in the grounds of Osborne House. Quiet and peaceful situation.
9 holes, 6418yds, Par 70, SSS 70, Course record 71.
Club membership 400.

Visitors may not play Tue before 1pm, weekends before noon & bank holidays before 11am.
Societies telephone initially.
Green Fees £16 per day (£19 weekends & bank holidays).
Facilities
Location E side of town centre off A3021

Hotel ★★ 60% The Fountain Hotel, High St, COWES ☎ 01983 292397 20

Freshwater Map 04 SZ38

Freshwater Bay Afton Down PO40 9TZ
☎ 01983 752955
A downland/seaside links with wide fairways and spectacular coastal views of the Solent and Channel.
18 holes, 5474yds, Par 68, SSS 67.
Club membership 450.
Visitors may play daily after 9.30 ex Thu & Sun (10.30).
Societies apply to secretary.
Green Fees £20 per day (£24 weekends & bank holidays).
Designer J H Taylor
Facilities by prior arrangement by prior arrangement
Location 0.5m E of village off A3055

Hotel ★★ 69% Sentry Mead Hotel, Madeira Rd, TOTLAND BAY
☎ 01983 753212 14

Newport Map 04 SZ58

Newport St George's Down, Shide PO30 2JB
☎ 01983 525076
Downland course, fine views.
9 holes, 5710yds, Par 68, SSS 68.
Club membership 350.
Visitors may not play Wed noon-3.30pm or before 3pm Sat & noon Sun.
Societies contact Secretary in advance.
Green Fees not confirmed.
Facilities by prior arrangement
Location 1.5m S off A3020

Hotel ★★ 60% The Fountain Hotel, High St, COWES
☎ 01983 292397 20

Ryde Map 04 SZ59

Ryde Binstead Rd PO33 3NF
☎ 01983 614809 Fax 01983 567418
Downland course with wide views over the Solent.
9 holes, 5287yds, Par 66, SSS 66, Course record 65.
Club membership 500.
Visitors may not play Wed afternoons, Sun mornings or before 10.30am Sat.
Societies must contact in writing.
Green Fees £15 (£20 weekends & bank holidays).
Facilities
Location 1m W on A3054

Hotel ★★ 63% Biskra House Beach Hotel, 17 Saint Thomas's St, RYDE
☎ 01983 567913 9rm(8)

Sandown Map 04 SZ58

Shanklin & Sandown The Fairway, Lake PO36 9PR
☎ 01983 403217 (office) & 404424 (pro) Fax 01983 403217/404424
Heathland course with some hilly holes.
18 holes, 5804yds, Par 70, SSS 68, Course record 64.
Club membership 600.
Visitors must contact in advance & have handicap certificate. May not play before noon Sat or 9.30am Sun.
Societies apply in writing.
Green Fees £22 (£25 weekends).
Prof Peter Hammond
Facilities by prior arrangement by prior arrangement
Location Drive towards Shanklin past Heights Leisure Centre, after 200 yds right into Fairway for 1m

Hotel ★★★ 64% Holliers Hotel, 5 Church Rd, Old Village, SHANKLIN
☎ 01983 862764 30

Ventnor Map 04 SZ57

Ventnor Steephill Down Rd PO38 1BP
☎ 01983 853326
Downland course subject to wind. Fine seascapes.
12 holes, 5767yds, Par 70, SSS 68.
Club membership 297.
Visitors may not play Fri noon-3pm or Sun mornings.
Societies telephone initially.
Green Fees £14 (£16 weekends).
Facilities
Location 1m NW off B3327

Hotel ★★★ 64% Ventnor Towers Hotel, Madeira Rd, VENTNOR
☎ 01983 852277 27

WILTSHIRE

Bishops Cannings Map 04 SU06

North Wilts SN10 2LP
☎ 01380 860627 Fax 01380 860877
High, downland course with fine views.
18 holes, 6322yds, Par 71, SSS 70, Course record 65.
Club membership 800.
Visitors welcome, a handicap certificate is required at weekends.
Societies must book in advance.
Green Fees £25 per day; £19 per round (£25 weekends).
Cards
Prof Graham Laing
Facilities
Location 2m NW

Hotel ★★★ 66% Bear Hotel, Market Place, DEVIZES
☎ 01380 722444 24

Calne Map 03 ST97

Bowood Golf & Country Club Derry Hill SN11 9PQ
☎ 01249 822228 Fax 01249 822218
A long, undulating course designed by Dave Thomas. Set in a Grade I listed Capability Brown park full of mature trees and acres of wildflowers, the course is a real test of golf. A 10-bay driving range and grass teeing area are enhanced by a 3-hole Academy course and putting greens. A recently completed clubhouse extension compliments the quality of the course.
18 holes, 6890yds, Par 72, SSS 73, Course record 67.
Club membership 400.

Visitors welcome except before noon on Sat and Sun. Advisable to book.
Societies booking by telephone.
Green Fees £32 May-Oct 18 holes.
Cards
Prof N Blenkarne
Designer Dave Thomas
Facilities by prior arrangement
Location M4 junct 17 off A4 between Chippenham & Calne

Hotel ★★ 66% Lansdowne Strand Hotel & Restaurant, The Strand, CALNE
☎ 01249 812488 21 Annexe5

Castle Combe Map 03 ST87

Manor House SN14 7JW
☎ 01249 782982 Fax 01249 782992
Opened in 1992 and set in one of the finest locations in England, this 18-hole Peter Alliss/Clive Clark course was designed to marry neatly with the surrounding conservation area. Many mature trees have been used to great effect giving individuality and challenge to every shot. There are spectacular holes at the 17th & 18th with lakes and waterfalls making them memorable.
18 holes, 6340yds, Par 73, SSS 71.
Club membership 450.
Visitors must have a handicap certificate and must contact in advance.
Societies contact in advance.
Green Fees £60 per day; £37.50 per round (£80/£50 weekends & bank holidays).
Cards
Prof Chris Smith
Designer Peter Alliss/Clive Clark

Facilities & Leisure hard tennis courts, heated outdoor swimming pool, fishing, sauna.
Location 5m NW of Chippenham

Hotel ★★★★ Manor House Hotel, CASTLE COMBE
☎ 01249 782206 21 Annexe24

Chapmanslade Map 03 ST84

Thoulstone Park BA13 4AQ
☎ 01373 832825 Fax 01373 832821
A rolling parkland course with natural lakes and mature trees. Hole 7, stroke index 1 has a second shot over a large lake to the green so a straight drive is essential.
18 holes, 6161yds, Par 71, SSS 69.
Club membership 500.
Visitors restricted Sat & Sun mornings. Dress code applies.
Societies telephone in advance.
Green Fees £18 (£24 weekends).
Prof Tony Isaac
Facilities & Leisure putting green.
Location On A36 between Bath/Warminster

Hotel ★★★ 64% Mendip Lodge Hotel, Bath Rd, FROME
☎ 01373 463223 40

Chippenham Map 03 ST97

Chippenham Malmesbury Rd SN15 5LT
☎ 01249 652040 Fax 01249 446681
Easy walking on downland course. Testing holes at 1st and 15th.
18 holes, 5559yds, Par 69, SSS 67, Course record 64.
Club membership 650.
Visitors must contact in advance.
Societies must contact in writing.
Green Fees £20 per day/round (£25 weekends & bank holidays).
Prof Bill Creamer
Facilities
Location M4 junct 17, 1m N off A350

Hotel ★★★★ Manor House Hotel, CASTLE COMBE
☎ 01249 782206 21 Annexe24

CRICKLADE Map 04 SU09

Cricklade Hotel & Country Club Common Hill SN6 6HA
☎ 01793 750751 Fax 01793 751767
A challenging 9-hole course with undulating greens and beautiful views. Par 3 6th (128yds) signature hole from an elevated tee to a green protected by a deep pot bunker.
9 holes, 1830yds, Par 62, SSS 57.
Club membership 170.

Visitors may not play weekends or bank holidays unless accompanied by a member.
Societies apply in writing.
Green Fees £16 per 18 holes, weekdays only.
Cards
Prof Ian Bolt
Designer Ian Bolt/Colin Smith
Facilities
& Leisure hard tennis courts, heated indoor swimming pool, sauna, solarium, gymnasium.
Location On the B4040 out of Cricklade, towards Malmesbury

Hotel ★★★ 66% Stanton House Hotel, The Avenue, Stanton Fitzwarren, SWINDON ☎ 01793 861777 86

ERLESTOKE Map 03 ST95

Erlestoke Sands SN10 5UA
☎ 01380 831069 Fax 01380 831069
The course is set on the lower slopes of Salisbury Plain with distant views to the Cotswolds and Marlborough Downs. The 7th plunges from an elevated three-tiered tee, high in the woods, to a large green with a spectacular backdrop of a meandering river and hills. The course was built to suit every standard of golfer from the novice to the very low handicapper and its two tiers offer lakes and rolling downland.
18 holes, 6406yds, Par 73, SSS 71, Course record 69.
Club membership 706.

Visitors phone for tee booking in advance 01380 830300. Dress rules apply.
Societies must book in advance.
Green Fees £16 per 18 holes (£25 weekends & bank holidays).
Prof Adrian Marsh
Designer Adrian Stiff
Facilities
Location On B3098 Devizes/Westbury road

Hotel ★★★ 66% Bear Hotel, Market Place, DEVIZES ☎ 01380 722444 24

GREAT DURNFORD Map 04 SU13

High Post SP4 6AT
☎ 01722 782356 Fax 01722 782356
An interesting downland course on Wiltshire chalk with good turf and splendid views over the southern area of Salisbury Plain. The par 3, 17th and the two-shot 18th require good judgement.
18 holes, 6297yds, Par 70, SSS 70, Course record 64.
Club membership 580.

Visitors a handicap certificate is required at weekends & bank holidays. Telephone professional in advance 01722 782219.
Societies apply by telephone to manager.
Green Fees not confirmed.
Prof Ian Welding
Facilities
Location 1.75m SE on A345

Hotel ★★★ 68% Rose & Crown Hotel, Harnham Rd, Harnham, SALISBURY ☎ 01722 399955 28

HIGHWORTH Map 04 SU29

Highworth Community Golf Centre Swindon Rd SN6 7SJ
☎ 01793 766014
Public downland course, situated in a high position affording good views.
9 holes, 3120yds, Par 35, SSS 35.
Club membership 150.

Visitors no restrictions.
Societies advisable to contact in advance.
Green Fees not confirmed.
Prof Mark Toombs
Designer T Watt/ B Sandry/D Lang
Facilities
Location Off A361 Swindon to Letchlade road

Hotel ★★★ 63% The Regal Hotel, Oxford Rd, Stratton St Margaret, SWINDON ☎ 01793 831333 91

Wrag Barn Golf & Country Club Shrivenham Rd SN6 7QQ ☎ 01793 861327 Fax 01793 861325
This course, designed by Hawtree, is some 6,500yards long. The Par of 72 can be demanding as it maximises the natural features of gentle contours, trees and water. The Par 3 5th is particularly tricky. A long approach shot has to carry over a stream 5 yards in front of the tree-protected green. The large greenside bunker to the right attracts an alarming number of balls!
18 holes, 6500yds, Par 72.
Club membership 600.

Visitors no restrictions but may not play before noon at weekends.
Societies contact in advance.
Green Fees £22 (£27 weekends & bank holidays).
Prof Barry Loughrey
Designer Hawtree
Facilities
Location On B4000 Shrivenham Road

Hotel ★★★ 66% Stanton House Hotel, The Avenue, Stanton Fitzwarren, SWINDON ☎ 01793 861777 86

KINGSDOWN Map 03 ST86

Kingsdown SN13 8BS
☎ 01225 742530 Fax 01225 743472
Fairly flat, open downland course with very sparse tree cover but surrounding wood.
18 holes, 6445yds, Par 72, SSS 71, Course record 64.
Club membership 650.

Visitors welcome except at weekends. Must contact in advance & have a handicap certificate.
Societies apply by letter.
Green Fees £22.

Prof Andrew Butler
Facilities
Location W side of village

Hotel ★★★★ Lucknam Park, COLERNE
☎ 01225 742777 23 Annexe18

LANDFORD Map 04 SU21

Hamptworth Golf & Country Club Hamptworth Rd, Hamptworth SP5 2DU ☎ 01794 390155 Fax 01794 390022
Hamptworth enjoys ancient woodland and an abundance of wildlife in a beautiful setting on the edge of the New Forest. The 14th is one of its most challenging holes having a narrow fairway guarded by established forest oaks. The 2nd is a dogleg of 543yds and plays differently all year.
18 holes, 6516yds, Par 72, SSS 71, Course record 68.
Club membership 450.
Visitors telephone to check availability.
Societies write or telephone in advance.
Green Fees £25 per day (£25 per round weekends).
Cards
Prof Phil Stevens
Designer Philip Sanders/Brian Pierson
Facilities
& Leisure gymnasium.
Location 1m NW, A36/B3079

Hotel ★★★ 67% Bartley Lodge, Lyndhurst Rd, CADNAM ☎ 01703 812248 31

MARLBOROUGH Map 04 SU16

Marlborough The Common SN8 1DU
☎ 01672 512147 Fax 01672 513164
Downland course with extensive views over the Og valley and Marlborough Downs.
18 holes, 6491yds, Par 72, SSS 71.
Club membership 900.
Visitors restricted at certain times; must have a handicap certificate at weekends. Must contact in advance.
Societies must contact in advance.
Green Fees £32 per day; £22 per round (£40/£30 weekends).
Cards
Prof S Amor
Facilities
Location N side of town centre on A346

Hotel ★★★ 59% The Castle & Ball, High St, MARLBOROUGH
☎ 01672 515201 34

OAKSEY Map 03 ST99

Oaksey Park Golf & Leisure SN16 9SB
☎ 01666 577995 Fax 01666 577174
A testing nine-hole parkland course set on the west side of the Cotswold Water Parks.
9 holes, 3100yds, Par 70, SSS 69, Course record 66.
Club membership 200.
Visitors no restrictions.
Societies telephone for details.
Green Fees £10 per 18 holes; £7 per 9 holes (£14/£9 weekends & bank holidays).
Cards
Designer Chapman & Warren
Facilities
& Leisure fishing, shooting, water sports, horse riding available.
Location On B road connecting A419 & A429, on outskirts of village of Oaksey. S of Cirencester

Hotel ★★★ 69% Stratton House Hotel, Gloucester Rd, CIRENCESTER
☎ 01285 651761 41

OGBOURNE ST GEORGE Map 04 SU27

Ogbourne Downs SN8 1TB ☎ 01672 841327
Downland turf and magnificent greens. Wind and slopes make this one of the most challenging courses in Wiltshire. Extensive views.
18 holes, 6353yds, Par 71, SSS 70, Course record 65.
Club membership 890.
Visitors phone in advance. Handicap certificate required.
Societies must apply for booking form in advance.
Green Fees £20 per day/round (£30 weekends).
Cards
Prof Colin Harraway
Designer J H Taylor
Facilities
Location N side of village on A346

Hotel ★★★ 75% Ivy House Hotel & Garden Restaurant, High St, MARLBOROUGH
☎ 01672 515333 28

SALISBURY Map 04 SU12

Salisbury & South Wilts Netherhampton SP2 8PR
☎ 01722 742645 Fax 01722 742645
Gently undulating and well drained parkland courses in country setting with panoramic views of the cathedral and surrounding country.
Main Course: 18 holes, 6528yds, Par 71, SSS 71, Course record 61.
Bibury Course: 9 holes, 2885yds, Par 33.
Drummond: 18 holes, 6121yds, Par 69, SSS 69, Course record 63.
Club membership 1000.
Visitors must telephone in advance.
Societies telephone initially.
Green Fees telephone for details.
Prof John Cave/Geraldine Teschner
Designer J H Taylor/S Gidman
Facilities
Location 2m W on A3094

Hotel ★★★ 68% Rose & Crown Hotel, Harnham Rd, Harnham, SALISBURY
☎ 01722 399955 28

SWINDON Map 04 SU18

Broome Manor Golf Complex Pipers Way SN3 1RG
☎ 01793 532403 Fax 01793 433255
Two courses and a 34-bay floodlit driving range. Parkland with water hazards, open fairways and short cut rough. Walking is easy on gentle slopes.
18 holes, 6283yds, Par 71, SSS 70, Course record 62 or 9 holes, 2690yds, Par 66, SSS 66.
Club membership 800. ▶

Visitors pre-booking advised for 18 hole course.
Societies must be prebooked.
Green Fees £10.50 per 18 holes; £6.50 per 9 holes.
Cards
Prof Barry Sandry
Designer Hawtree
Facilities
Location 1.75m SE of town centre off B4006

Hotel ★★★ 63% The Regal Hotel, Oxford Rd, Stratton St Margaret, SWINDON
☎ 01793 831333 91

TIDWORTH Map 04 SU24

Tidworth Garrison Bulford Rd SP9 7AF
☎ 01980 842301 Fax 01980 842301
A breezy, dry downland course with lovely turf, fine trees and views over Salisbury Plain and the surrounding area. The 4th and 12th holes are notable. The 564-yard 13th, going down towards the clubhouse, gives the big hitter a chance to let fly.
18 holes, 6101yds, Par 69, SSS 69, Course record 62.
Club membership 700.
Visitors must contact in advance, weekend & bank holiday bookings may not be made until Thursday prior.
Societies Tue & Thu, bookings required 12-18 months in advance.
Green Fees £22 per day.
Prof Terry Gosden
Designer Donald Steel
Facilities
Location W side of village off A338

Hotel ★★★ 62% Ashley Court Hotel, Micheldever Rd, ANDOVER
☎ 01264 357344 9 Annexe26

TOLLARD ROYAL Map 03 ST91

Rushmore Park Golf Club SP5 5QB
☎ 01725 516326 Fax 01725 516466
Peaceful and testing parkland course, founded in 1994, situated on Cranborne Chase with far-reaching views. An undulating course with avenues of trees and well drained greens.
18 holes, 5580yds, Par 71, SSS 67.
Club membership 350.
Visitors booking advisable over weekends.
Societies welcome by appointment.
Green Fees £12 per 18 holes (£15 weekends).
Cards
Prof Sean McDonagh
Designer Tony Crouch
Facilities by prior arrangement
Location 16m SW of Salisbury, entrance off the B3081 between Sixpenny Handley and Tollard Royal

Hotel ★★★ 72% Royal Chase Hotel, Royal Chase Roundabout, SHAFTESBURY
☎ 01747 853355 35

UPAVON Map 04 SU15

Upavon Douglas Av SN9 6BQ
☎ 01980 630787 Fax 01980 630787
Downland course set on sides of infamous valley, with some wind affecting play. Includes a par 5 of 602 yards and finishing hole of 170 yards across a ravine.
18 holes, 6407yds, Par 71, SSS 71, Course record 70.
Club membership 550.
Visitors must contact in advance and may not play before noon at weekends.
Societies telephone in advance.
Green Fees £22 per day; £16 per round.
Cards
Prof Richard Blake
Designer Richard Blake
Facilities by prior arrangement
& Leisure hard tennis courts.
Location 2m E on A342

Hotel ★★★ 66% Bear Hotel, Market Place, DEVIZES ☎ 01380 722444 24

WARMINSTER Map 03 ST84

West Wilts Elm Hill BA12 0AU
☎ 01985 212702 Fax 01985 219809
A hilltop course among the Wiltshire downs on downland turf. Free draining, short, but a very good test of accurate iron play. Excellent greens and clubhouse facilities.
18 holes, 5709yds, Par 70, SSS 68, Course record 62.
Club membership 650.
Visitors must contact in advance. Handicap certificate required.
Societies apply by letter.
Green Fees £28 per day; £18 per round (£36 per day/round weekends & bank holidays).
Cards
Prof Andrew Lamb
Designer J H Taylor
Facilities
Location N side of town centre off A350

Hotel ★★★★ 75% Bishopstrow House, WARMINSTER
☎ 01985 212312 30

WOOTTON BASSETT Map 04 SU08

Brinkworth Longmans Farm, Brinkworth SN15 5DG
☎ 01666 510277
Fairly long and open course with ditches and water hazards on the 2nd and 18th holes. Several testing par 3s with crosswinds and three long and tricky par 5s, notably the 4th, 8th and 14th holes.
18 holes, 5884yds, Par 70, SSS 70.
Club membership 70.
Visitors welcome any time no contact needed.
Societies telephone in advance or apply in writing.
Green Fees not confirmed.
Designer Jullian Sheppard
Facilities
Location Just off B4042 between Malmesbury/Wootton Bassett

Hotel ★★★ 70% Marsh Farm Hotel, Coped Hall, WOOTTON BASSETT
☎ 01793 848044 4 ⇌ ↱ Annexe29 ⇌ ↱

Wiltshire Vastern SN4 7PB
☎ 01793 849999 Fax 01793 849988
A Peter Alliss/Clive Clark design set in rolling Wiltshire downland countryside. A number of lakes add a challenge for both low and high handicappers.
18 holes, 6522yds, Par 72, SSS 71.
Club membership 800.

Visitors must contact in advance.
Societies contact in advance.
Green Fees £40 per day; £30 per round.
Cards
Prof Andy Gray
Designer Peter Allis & Clive Clark
Facilities
Location Leave M4 at junc 16, on A3102

Hotel ★★★ 70% Marsh Farm Hotel, Coped Hall, WOOTTON BASSETT
☎ 01793 848044 4 ⇌ ↱ Annexe29 ⇌ ↱

WORCESTERSHIRE

ALVECHURCH Map 07 SP07

Kings Norton Brockhill Ln, Weatheroak B48 7ED
☎ 01564 826706 & 826789 Fax 01564 826955
An old club with three, 9-hole courses; the Blue, Red and Yellow. Parkland with some exacting water hazards, it has housed important events. There is also a 12-hole, par 3 course.
Red Course: 9 holes, 3372yds, Par 36, SSS 36.
Blue Course: 9 holes, 3382yds, Par 36, SSS 36.
Yellow Course: 9 holes, 3290yds, Par 36, SSS 36.
Club membership 1000.

Visitors must contact in advance. No visitors at weekends
Societies must telephone in advance.
Green Fees £35 per 27 holes; £30 per 18 holes.
Prof Kevin Hayward
Designer F Hawtree
Facilities
Location M42 junct3, off A435

Hotel ★★★ 74% Pine Lodge Hotel, Kidderminster Rd, BROMSGROVE
☎ 01527 576600 114 ⇌ ↱

BEWDLEY Map 07 SO77

Little Lakes Golf and Country Club Lye Head DY12 2UZ
☎ 01299 266385 Fax 01299 266178
A pleasant undulating parkland course extended to 18 holes in April 1995. The course offers some pleasing views and several demanding holes.
18 holes, 5847yds, Par 69, Course record 63.
Club membership 500.

Visitors advisable to telephone in advance.
Societies must telephone in advance.
Green Fees not confirmed.
Prof Mark A Laing
Designer M Laing
Facilities
& Leisure hard tennis courts, outdoor swimming pool, fishing.
Location 2.25m W off A456

Hotel ★★ 64% The George Hotel, Load St, BEWDLEY ☎ 01299 402117 13rm(2 ⇌ 8 ↱)

Wharton Park Longbank DY12 2QW
☎ 01299 405222 & 405163 Fax 01299 405121
18-hole championship-standard course in 140 acres of countryside. Some long Par 5s eg the 9th (594yds) as well as superb par 3 holes at 3rd, 10th, 15th make this a very challenging course.
18 holes, 6603yds, Par 73, SSS 72, Course record 66.
Club membership 500.

Visitors must contact in advance.
Societies prior booking required.
Green Fees £27.50 per day; £20 per round (£25 per round weekends).
Cards
Prof Angus Hoare
Facilities
& Leisure fishing.
Location Off A456 Bewdley bypass

Hotel ★★ 64% The George Hotel, Load St, BEWDLEY
☎ 01299 402117 13rm(2 ⇌ 8 ↱)

BISHAMPTON Map 03 SO95

Vale Golf & Country Club Hill Furze Rd WR10 2LZ
☎ 01386 462781 Fax 01386 462597
Opened in 1991 this course offers an American-style layout, with large greens, trees and bunkers and several water hazards. Its rolling fairways provide a testing round, as well as superb views of the Malvern Hills. Picturesque and peaceful. Also 9-hole course and 20-bay driving range.
International Course: 18 holes, 7114yds, Par 74, SSS 74, Course record 72.
Lenches Course: 9 holes, 2628yds, Par 35, SSS 35.
Club membership 700.

Visitors booking up to one week in advance.
Societies must apply in advance. May only play weekdays on 18 hole course.
Green Fees not confirmed.
Prof Caroline Griffiths
Designer Bob Sandon
Facilities
& Leisure fishing.
Location Signposted off A4538

Hotel ★★ 67% The Chequers Inn, Chequers Ln, FLADBURY ☎ 01386 860276 & 860527 Fax 01386 861286 8 ⇌ ↱

BLAKEDOWN Map 07 SO87

Churchill and Blakedown Churchill Ln DY10 3NB
☎ 01562 700018
Pleasant course on hilltop with extensive views.
9 holes, 6472yds, Par 72, SSS 71, Course record 63.
Club membership 380.

Visitors with member only weekends & bank holidays. Handicap certificate required.
Societies by arrangement through secretary.
Green Fees £17.50 per round.
Prof K Wheeler
Facilities ⊗ ⅏ ♨ ☕ ♀ ⛰ 🏠 ⚲
Location W side of village off A456

Hotel ★★★★ 64% Stone Manor Hotel, Stone, KIDDERMINSTER
☎ 01562 777555 52 ⇌ ♠

BRANSFORD Map 03 SO75

Bank House Hotel Golf & Country Club WR6 5JD
☎ 01886 833551 Fax 01886 832461
The Pine Lakes course is designed as a 'Florida' style course with fairways weaving between water courses, 13 lakes and sculptured mounds with colouful plant displays. The 6,204yd course has doglegs, island greens and tight fairways to challenge all standards of player. The 10th, 16th and 18th (The Devil's Elbow) are particularly tricky.
18 holes, 6204yds, Par 72, SSS 71, Course record 65.
Club membership 350.
Visitors all tee times must be booked, no play before 9.30am.
Societies contact the golf secretary, all tee times must be booked in advance.
Green Fees £25 per day; £15 per round (£25 per round weekends).
Prof Craig George
Designer Bob Sandow
Facilities ⊗ ⅏ ♨ ☕ ♀ ⛰ 🏠 ⚲
& Leisure outdoor swimming pool, sauna, solarium, gymnasium, bowling green.
Location 3m S of Worcester, A4103

Hotel ★★★ 64% Fownes Hotel, City Walls Rd, WORCESTER
☎ 01905 613151 61 ⇌ ♠

BROADWAY Map 04 SP03

Broadway Willersey Hill WR12 7LG
☎ 01386 853683 Fax 01386 858643
At the edge of the Cotswolds this downland course lies at an altitude of 900 ft above sea level, with extensive views. Natural contours and man made hazards mean that drives have to be placed, approaches carefully judged and the greens expertly read.
18 holes, 6216yds, Par 72, SSS 70, Course record 65.
Club membership 850.
Visitors may not play Sat between Apr-Sep before 3pm. Restricted play Sun. Must contact in advance.
Societies Wed-Fri, must contact in advance.
Green Fees £33 per day; £27 per round (£35 weekends & bank holidays).
Prof Martyn Freeman
Designer James Braid
Facilities ⊗ ⅏ ♨ ☕ ♀ ⛰ 🏠 ⚲
Location 1.5m E on A44

Hotel ★★★ 74% Dormy House Hotel, Willersey Hill, BROADWAY
☎ 01386 852711 26 ⇌ ♠ Annexe23 ⇌

BROMSGROVE Map 07 SO97

Blackwell Agmore Rd, Blackwell B60 1PY
☎ 0121 445 1994 Fax 0121 445 4911
Pleasantly undulating parkland with a variety of trees. Laid out in two 9-hole loops.
18 holes, 6230yds, Par 70, SSS 71, Course record 63.
Club membership 385.
Visitors must contact in advance, must have handicap certificate.
Societies must contact in advance.
Green Fees £50 per day.
Prof Nigel Blake
Facilities ⊗ by prior arrangement ⅏ by prior arrangement ♨ ☕ ♀ ⛰ 🏠 ⚲
Location 2m W of Alvechurch

Hotel ★★★ 74% Pine Lodge Hotel, Kidderminster Rd, BROMSGROVE
☎ 01527 576600 114 ⇌ ♠

Bromsgrove Golf Centre Stratford Rd B60 1LD
☎ 01527 575886 Fax 01527 570964
Gently undulating parkland course with large contoured greens, generous tee surfaces and superb views over Worcestershire. Tricky par 3 16th across a lake. Also 41 bay floodlit driving range, floodlit practice bunker and new clubhouse with conference facilities.
18 holes, 5869yds, Par 68, SSS 68.
Club membership 900.
Visitors dress restriction, no T-shirts, jeans, tracksuits etc. 7 day booking facilities available.
Societies packages available, apply in writing or telephone.
Green Fees £12.50 per 18 holes; £7.50 per 9 holes (£16/£9.50 weekends & bank holidays).
Cards
Prof Graeme Long/Mark Davies
Designer Hawtree & Son
Facilities ⊗ ⅏ ♨ ☕ ♀ ⛰ 🏠 ⚲
& Leisure practice bunker.
Location E side of Bromsgrove, 6m W of Alvechurch

Hotel ★★★ 74% Pine Lodge Hotel, Kidderminster Rd, BROMSGROVE
☎ 01527 576600 114 ⇌ ♠

DROITWICH Map 03 SO86

Droitwich Ford Ln WR9 0BQ
☎ 01905 774344 Fax 01905 797 290
Undulating parkland course.
18 holes, 6058yds, Par 70, SSS 69, Course record 62.
Club membership 732.
Visitors with member only weekends & bank holidays.
Societies must apply by telephone and letter.
Green Fees £24 per day/round.
Prof C Thompson
Designer J Braid/G Franks
Facilities ⊗ ⅏ ♨ ☕ ♀ ⛰ 🏠 ⚲
& Leisure snooker.
Location Off A38 Droitwich to Bromsgrove road, midway between Droitwich and M5 junct 5

Hotel ★★★★ 66% Chateau Impney Hotel, DROITWICH ☎ 01905 774411 67 ⇌ ♠

Gaudet Luce Middle Ln, Hadzor WR9 7DP
☎ 01905 796375 Fax 01905 796375
A challenging 18-hole course with two contrasting 9-hole loops. The front nine are long and fairly open, the back nine are tight and compact requiring good positional and approach play. Water features on several holes.
18 holes, 5887yds, Par 70, SSS 68.
Club membership 225.

Visitors welcome, advisable to telephone in advance, proper golfing attire required at all times.
Societies telephone for details.
Green Fees not confirmed.
Prof Mark Laing
Facilities
Location M5 junct 5, left at Tagwell road into Middle Lane, 1st driveway on left to clubhouse

Hotel ★★★★ 66% Chateau Impney Hotel, DROITWICH
☎ 01905 774411 67

Ombersley Bishops Wood Rd, Lineholt, Ombersley WR9 0LE ☎ 01905 620747 Fax 01905 620047
Undulating course in beautiful countryside high above the edge of the Severn Valley. Covered driving range and putting green.
18 holes, 6139yds, Par 72, SSS 69, Course record 67.
Club membership 750.

Visitors suitable dress expected, no jeans, T-shirts etc.
Societies telephone in advance.
Green Fees £11.50 per 18 holes (£15.50 weekends).
Prof Graham Glenister
Designer David Morgan
Facilities
Location 3m W of Droitwich, off A449. At Mitre Oak pub, take A4025 to Stourport, signposted 400yds on left

Hotel ★★★★ 64% Raven Hotel, Victoria Square, DROITWICH
☎ 01905 772224 72

FLADBURY Map 03 SO94

Evesham Craycombe Links, Old Worcester Rd WR10 2QS
☎ 01386 860395
Parkland, heavily wooded, with the River Avon running alongside 5th and 14th holes. Good views. Nine greens played from eighteen different tees.
9 holes, 6415yds, Par 72, SSS 71, Course record 68.
Club membership 383.

Visitors must contact in advance. With members only at weekends.
Societies must apply by letter.
Green Fees not confirmed.
Prof Charles Haynes
Facilities
Location 0.75m N on A4538

Hotel ★★★ 69% The Evesham Hotel, Coopers Ln, Waterside, EVESHAM
☎ 01386 765566 & 0800 716969 (Res) Fax 013 86 765443 40

Additional hotel ★★ 67% The Chequers Inn, Chequers Ln, FLADBURY ☎ 01386 860276 & 860527 Fax 01386 861286 8

HOLLYWOOD Map 07 SP07

Gay Hill Hollywood Ln B47 5PP
☎ 0121 430 8544 & 474 6001 (pro) Fax 0121 436 7796
A meadowland course, some 7m from Birmingham.
18 holes, 6532yds, Par 72, SSS 71, Course record 64.
Club membership 740.

Visitors must contact in advance. May only play at weekends with member.
Societies telephone in advance.
Green Fees £28.50 per day (weekdays).
Prof Andrew Potter
Facilities
Location N side of village

Hotel ★★★★ 62% Regency Hotel, Stratford Rd, Shirley, SOLIHULL
☎ 0121 745 6119 112

KIDDERMINSTER Map 07 SO87

Habberley Low Trimpley DY11 5RG
☎ 01562 745756 Fax 01562 745756
Very hilly, wooded parkland course.
9 holes, 5481yds, Par 69, Course record 62.
Club membership 300.

Visitors may only play weekends with a member.
Societies telephone initially.
Green Fees not confirmed.
Facilities
Location 2m NW ▶

Hotel ★★★★ 64% Stone Manor Hotel, Stone, KIDDERMINSTER ☎ 01562 777555 52

Kidderminster Russell Rd DY10 3HT
☎ 01562 822303 Fax 01562 862041
Parkland course with natural hazards and some easy walking.
18 holes, 6405yds, Par 72, SSS 71, Course record 66.
Club membership 860.

Visitors with member only weekends & bank holidays. Must have a handicap certificate.
Societies Thu only, apply in advance.
Green Fees £35 per day; £25 per round.
Prof Nick Underwood
Facilities
Location 0.5m SE of town centre, signposted off A449

Hotel ★★★★ 64% Stone Manor Hotel, Stone, KIDDERMINSTER ☎ 01562 777555 52

Wyre Forest Zortech Av DY10 4JP
☎ 01299 822682 Fax 01299 879433
Making full use of the existing contours, this interesting and challenging course is bounded by woodland and gives extensive views over the surrounding area. Well drained fairways and greens.
18 holes, 5790yds, Par 70, SSS 68, Course record 68.
Club membership 397.

Visitors preferable to telephone first.
Societies brochure on request, deposit secures date, write or telephone.
Green Fees £9 per 18 holes; £6.50 per 9 holes (£13/£9.50 weekends and bank holidays.
Cards
Prof Simon Price
Facilities
Location Approx half way between Kidderminster/Stourport, on the A451

Hotel ★★★ 68% Stourport Manor, Hartlebury Rd, STOURPORT-ON-SEVERN ☎ 01299 289955 68

MALVERN WELLS — Map 03 SO74

Worcestershire Wood Farm, Hanley Rd WR14 4PP
☎ 01684 575992 & 573905 Fax 01684 575992
Fairly easy walking on windy downland course with trees, ditches and other natural hazards. Outstanding views of Malvern Hills and Severn Valley. 17th hole (par 5) is approached over small lake.
18 holes, 6470yds, Par 71, SSS 71, Course record 65.
Club membership 770.

Visitors only after 10am at weekends or with a member. Must contact in advance. Handicap certificate required.
Societies Thu & Fri only, apply in writing.
Green Fees £28 per day; £22 per round (£33/£25 weekends & bank holidays).
Cards
Prof Richard Lewis
Designer Colt/Braid
Facilities
Location 2m S of Gt Malvern on B4209

Hotel ★★★ 72% The Cottage in the Wood Hotel, Holywell Rd, Malvern Wells, MALVERN ☎ 01684 575859 8 Annexe12

REDDITCH — Map 07 SP06

Abbey Hotel Golf & Country Club Dagnell End Rd B98 9BE ☎ 01527 68006 Fax 01527 584112
Young parkland course opened in 1985, with rolling fairways. A 'Site of Special Scientific Interest', the course includes two fishing lakes and is pleasant to play.
18 holes, 6411yds, Par 71, SSS 71, Course record 69.
Club membership 700.

Visitors must contact in advance.
Societies must apply in writing.
Green Fees £12 per round (£16 weekends).
Cards
Prof S Edwards
Facilities
& Leisure heated indoor swimming pool, fishing, sauna, solarium, gymnasium, massage & beauty facilities.
Location 1.25m N off A441 on B4101

Hotel ★★★ 62% Quality Hotel, Pool Bank, Southcrest, REDDITCH ☎ 01527 541511 58

Pitcheroak Plymouth Rd B97 4PB ☎ 01527 541054
Woodland course, hilly in places.There is also a putting green and a practice ground.
9 holes, 4561yds, Par 65, SSS 62.
Club membership 200.

Visitors no restrictions.
Societies telephone to book.
Green Fees £6.50 per 18 holes; £5 per 9 holes (£7.50/£5.50 weekends).
Cards
Prof David Stewart
Facilities
Location SW side of town centre off A448

Hotel ★★★ 62% Quality Hotel, Pool Bank, Southcrest, REDDITCH ☎ 01527 541511 58

Redditch Lower Grinsty, Green Ln, Callow Hill B97 5PJ
☎ 01527 543079 Fax 01527 543079
Parkland course, the hazards including woods, ditches and large ponds. The par 4, 14th is a testing hole.
18 holes, 6671yds, Par 72, SSS 72, Course record 68.
Club membership 650.

Visitors with member only weekends & bank holidays.
Societies telephone Secretary.
Green Fees £27.50 per day.
Prof Frank Powell
Designer F Pennick
Facilities
Location 2m SW

Hotel ★★★ 62% Quality Hotel, Pool Bank, Southcrest, REDDITCH ☎ 01527 541511 58

TENBURY WELLS — Map 07 SO56

Cadmore Lodge Hotel & Country Club St Michaels, Berrington Green WR15 8TQ
☎ 01584 810044 Fax 01584 810044
A picturesque 9-hole course in a brook valley. Challenging holes include the 1st and 6th over the lake, 8th over the

valley and 9th over hedges.
9 holes, 5132yds, Par 68, SSS 65.
Club membership 200.

Visitors no restrictions but check availability.
Societies telephone in advance.
Green Fees £10 (£14 weekends).
Cards
Facilities
& Leisure hard tennis courts, heated indoor swimming pool, fishing, sauna, gymnasium, bowls.
Location From Tenbury take A4112 to Leominster, after approx 2m turn right for Berrington, 0.75 on left

Hotel ★★ 66% Cadmore Lodge Hotel & Country Club, Berrington Green, St Michaels, TENBURY WELLS ☎ 01584 810044 14

WORCESTER Map 03 SO85

Tolladine Tolladine Rd WR4 9BA ☎ 01905 21074
Parkland course, hilly and very tight, but with excellent views of the surrounding hills and Worcester city.
9 holes, 2813yds, Par 68, SSS 67.
Club membership 350.

Visitors with member only weekend & bank holidays.
Societies must apply in writing.
Green Fees not confirmed.
Prof Clare George
Facilities
Location 1.5m E

Hotel ★★★ 63% The Gifford Hotel, High St, WORCESTER ☎ 01905 726262 95

Worcester Golf & Country Club Boughton Park WR2 4EZ
☎ 01905 422555 Fax 01905 749090
Fine parkland course with many trees, a lake, and views of the Malvern Hills.
18 holes, 6251yds, Par 70, SSS 70, Course record 67.
Club membership 1000.

Visitors Must contact professional in advance. May not play at weekends.
Societies telephone in advance.
Green Fees £25 per day/round.
Prof Colin Colenso
Designer Dr A Mackenzie
Facilities
& Leisure hard and grass tennis courts, squash.
Location 1.5m from city centre on A4103

Hotel ★★★ 63% The Gifford Hotel, High St, WORCESTER ☎ 01905 726262 95

WYTHALL Map 07 SP07

Fulford Heath Tanners Green Ln B47 6BH
☎ 01564 824758
A mature parkland course encompassing two classic par threes. The 11th, a mere 149 yards, shoots from an elevated tee through a channel of trees to a well protected green. The 16th, a 166 yard par 3, elevated green, demands a 140 yard carry over an imposing lake.
18 holes, 6216yds, Par 70, SSS 70, Course record 66.
Club membership 700.

Visitors with member only weekend & bank holidays.
Societies must apply in advance.
Green Fees £32.50 per day.
Prof David Down
Designer Hawtree
Facilities
Location 1m SE off A435

Hotel ★★★ 69% St John's Swallow Hotel, 651 Warwick Rd, SOLIHULL ☎ 0121 711 3000 177

YORKSHIRE, EAST RIDING OF

BEVERLEY Map 08 TA03

Beverley & East Riding The Westwood HU17 8RG
☎ 01482 869519 Fax 01482 868757
Picturesque parkland course with some hard walking and natural hazards - trees and gorse bushes. Also cattle (spring to autumn); horse-riders are an occasional hazard in the early morning.
Westwood: 18 holes, 6127yds, Par 69, SSS 69, Course record 65.
Club membership 530.

Visitors advised to contact pro shop 01482 869519.
Societies telephone 01482 868757, then written confirmation.
Green Fees £16 per day; £12 per round (£21/£16 weekends & bank holidays).
Prof Ian Mackie

Facilities by prior arrangement
Location 1m SW on B1230

Hotel ★★★ 67% Beverley Arms Hotel, North Bar Within, BEVERLEY ☎ 01482 869241 57

BRANDESBURTON Map 08 TA14

Hainsworth Park Burton Holme YO25 8RT
☎ 01964 542362
A parkland course with easy walking.
18 holes, 6048yds, Par 71, SSS 69, Course record 62.
Club membership 500.
Visitors contact in advance.
Societies telephone initially.
Green Fees £18 per day; £14 per round (£22/£18 weekends & bank holidays).
Cards
Prof Paul Binnington
Facilities
& Leisure grass tennis courts, fishing.
Location SW side of village on A165

Hotel ★★ 68% Burton Lodge Hotel, BRANDESBURTON ☎ 01964 542847 8rm(7) Annexe2

BRIDLINGTON Map 08 TA16

Bridlington Belvedere Rd YO15 3NA
☎ 01262 606367 Fax 01262 606367
Clifftop, seaside course, windy at times, with hazards of bunkers, ponds, ditches and trees.
18 holes, 6638yds, Par 72, SSS 72, Course record 66.
Club membership 600.
Visitors must contact in advance, limited at weekends.
Societies telephone bookings in advance.
Green Fees £22 per day; £14 per round (£30 per day/round weekends & bank holidays).
Prof Anthony Howarth
Facilities
Location 1m S off A165

Hotel ★★★ 66% Expanse Hotel, North Marine Dr, BRIDLINGTON ☎ 01262 675347 48

Bridlington Links Flamborough Rd, Marton YO15 1DW
☎ 01262 401584 Fax 01262 401702
Coastal links type course with large greens, numerous water hazards and splendid views towards Flamborough Head. When the wind blows off the sea, the course becomes a challenging test of golf for even the experienced golfer.
Main: 18 holes, 6719yds, Par 72, SSS 72, Course record 70.
Club membership 350.
Visitors telephone to book tee times.
Societies telephone for booking.
Green Fees £18 per day; £12 per round (£22.50/£15 weekends).
Cards
Prof Steve Raybould
Designer Swan
Facilities
Location On the B1255 between Bridlington and Flamborough

Hotel ★★★ 65% Revelstoke Hotel, 1-3 Flamborough Rd, BRIDLINGTON ☎ 01262 672362 25

BROUGH Map 08 SE92

Brough Cave Rd HU15 1HB
☎ 01482 667291 Fax 01482 667291
Parkland course.
18 holes, 6159yds, Par 68, SSS 69, Course record 64.
Club membership 800.
Visitors must have handicap certificate and contact in advance.
Societies apply by letter.
Green Fees £30 per round (£40 weekends).
Cards
Prof Gordon Townhill
Facilities
Location 0.5m N

Hotel B Forte Posthouse Hull, Ferriby High Rd, NORTH FERRIBY ☎ 01482 645212 96

COTTINGHAM Map 08 TA03

Cottingham Woodhill Way HU16 5RZ
☎ 01482 846030 Fax 01482 845932
Gently undulating parkland course incorporating many natural features, including lateral water hazards, several ponds on the approach to greens, and rolling fairways.
18 holes, 6459yds, Par 72, SSS 71, Course record 69.
Club membership 650.
Visitors may book by telephone in advance, times available all day weekdays, after 11am weekends.
Societies deposit required and confirmation in writing.
Green Fees £21 per day; £14 per round (£20 per round weekends).
Prof Chris Gray

Designer Terry Litten
Facilities
& Leisure equestrian centre.
Location 4m from A63/M62 on A164. Turn off to Cottingham on B1233, in 100yds turn left into Woodhill Way

Hotel ★★★ 65% Rowley Manor Hotel, Rowley Rd, LITTLE WEIGHTON 01482 848248 16

DRIFFIELD (GREAT) Map 08 TA05

Driffield Sunderlandwick YO25 9AD
01377 253116 Fax 01377 240599
An easy walking, mature parkland course set within the beautiful Sunderlandwick Estate.
18 holes, 6215yds, Par 70, SSS 69, Course record 67.
Club membership 680.
Visitors must book in advance and adhere to club dress rule.
Societies apply in writing or telephone.
Green Fees £23 per day; £18 per round (£25 per round weekends & bank holidays).
Cards
Facilities
& Leisure fishing.
Location 2m S off A164

Hotel ★★★ 70% Bell Hotel, 46 Market Place, DRIFFIELD 01377 256661 14

FLAMBOROUGH Map 08 TA27

Flamborough Head Lighthouse Rd YO15 1AR
01262 850333 & 850417 Fax 01262 850279
Undulating seaside course.
18 holes, 5976yds, Par 70, SSS 69, Course record 70.
Club membership 500.
Visitors welcome but may not play; before 1pm Sun, Wed between 10.30 & 1.30, Sat between 11.30 & 12.30.
Societies must contact in advance.
Green Fees £16 per day; £13 per round (£19 weekends & bank holidays).
Facilities
Location 2m E off B1259

Hotel ★ 66% Flaneburg Hotel & Restaurant, North Marine Rd, FLAMBOROUGH 01262 850284 14rm(11)

HESSLE Map 08 TA02

Hessle Westfield Rd, Raywell HU16 5YL
01482 650171 & 650190 (Prof)
Well-wooded downland course, easy walking, windy.
18 holes, 6604yds, Par 72, SSS 72, Course record 68.
Visitors not Tue between 9-1 and may not play before 11am on Sat & Sun.
Societies by prior arrangement.
Green Fees £25 per day; £20 per round (£28 per round weekends & bank holidays).
Prof Grahame Fieldsend
Designer D Thomas/P Allis
Facilities
Location 3m SW of Cottingham

Hotel B Forte Posthouse Hull, Ferriby High Rd, NORTH FERRIBY 01482 645212 96

HORNSEA Map 08 TA14

Hornsea Rolston Rd HU18 1XG
01964 532020 Fax 01964 532020
Flat, parkland course with good greens.
18 holes, 6685yds, Par 72, SSS 72, Course record 66.
Club membership 600.
Visitors with member only at weekends & after 3pm. Must contact in advance.
Societies contact Secretary in advance.
Green Fees £26 per day; £19 per round (£30 per round weekends).
Prof Brian Thompson
Facilities
Location 1m S on B1242, follow signs for Hornsea Freeport

Hotel ★★★ 67% Beverley Arms Hotel, North Bar Within, BEVERLEY 01482 869241 57

HULL Map 08 TA02

Ganstead Park Longdales Ln, Coniston HU11 4LB
01482 874754 Fax 01482 874754
Parkland course, easy walking, with water features.
18 holes, 6801yds, Par 72, SSS 73, Course record 67.
Club membership 500.
Visitors contact in advance.
Societies telephone in advance.
Green Fees not confirmed.
Cards
Prof Michael J Smee
Designer P Green
Facilities
Location 6m NE on A165

Hotel ★★★ 66% Quality Royal Hotel, 170 Ferensway, HULL 01482 325087 155

Hull The Hall, 27 Packman Ln HU10 7TJ
01482 658919 Fax 01482 658919
Parkland course.
18 holes, 6242yds, Par 70, SSS 70.
Club membership 840.
Visitors only weekdays. Contact professional 01482 653074.
Societies only on Tue and Thu by prior arrangement.
Green Fees £30 per day; £25 per round.
Prof David Jagger
Designer James Braid
Facilities
Location 5m W of city centre off A164

Hotel ★★★ 71% Willerby Manor Hotel, Well Ln, WILLERBY 01482 652616 51

Springhead Park Willerby Rd HU5 5JE 01482 656309
Municipal parkland course with tight, tree-lined, undulating fairways.
18 holes, 6402yds, Par 71, SSS 71.
Club membership 667.

Visitors welcome ex Sun (tee reserved).
Green Fees not confirmed.
Prof Barry Herrington
Facilities
Location 5m W off A164

Hotel ★★★ 71% Willerby Manor Hotel, Well Ln, WILLERBY ☎ 01482 652616 51

Sutton Park Salthouse Rd HU8 9HF
☎ 01482 374242 Fax 01482 701428
Municipal parkland course.
18 holes, 6251yds, Par 70, SSS 69, Course record 67.
Club membership 300.
Visitors no restrictions.
Societies prior arrangement via club, telephone and confirm in writing.
Green Fees £6.50 per round (£8.50 weekends).
Prof Paul Rushworth
Facilities
Location 3m NE on B1237 off A165

Hotel ★★★ 66% Quality Royal Hotel, 170 Ferensway, HULL
☎ 01482 325087 155

SOUTH CAVE Map 08 SE93

Cave Castle Golf Hotel Church Hill, South Cave HU15 2EU ☎ 01430 421286 Fax 01430 421118
A young but challenging course at the foot of the Wolds with superb views. Tuition, golf clinics and golf breaks are available.
18 holes, 6500yds, Par 73, SSS 71, Course record 71.
Club membership 475.
Visitors must contact in advance, may not play before 11am weekends/bank holidays.
Societies by arrangement with Manager.
Green Fees £12.50 (£18 weekends & bank holidays).
Prof Stephen Mackinder
Designer Mrs N Freling
Facilities
& Leisure fishing.
Location 1m from A63

Hotel ★★ 66% Fox & Coney Inn, Market Place, SOUTH CAVE ☎ 01430 422275 8

WITHERNSEA Map 08 TA32

Withernsea Chesnut Av HU19 2PG ☎ 01964 612078
Exposed seaside links with narrow, undulating fairways, bunkers and small greens.
9 holes, 5907yds, Par 72, SSS 69.
Club membership 300.
Visitors with member only at weekends before 3pm.
Societies apply in writing.
Green Fees £10.
Prof Graham Harrison
Facilities by prior arrangement by prior arrangement by prior arrangement weekends
Location S side of town centre off A1033

Hotel ★★★ 66% Quality Royal Hotel, 170 Ferensway, HULL
☎ 01482 325087 155

YORKSHIRE, NORTH

ALDWARK Map 08 SE46

Aldwark Manor YO6 2NF
☎ 01347 838353 Fax 01347 838867
An easy walking, scenic 18-hole parkland course with holes both sides of the River Ure. The course surrounds the Victorian Aldwark Manor Golf Hotel.
18 holes, 6171yds, Par 71, SSS 70, Course record 69.
Club membership 400.
Visitors must contact in advance, restricted weekends.
Societies must telephone in advance.
Green Fees £25 per day; £20 per round (£30/£25 weekends & bank holidays).
Facilities
& Leisure fishing.
Location 5m SE of Boroughbridge off A1, 12m NW of York off A19)

Hotel ★★★ 70% Aldwark Manor Hotel, Golf & Country Club, ALDWARK
☎ 01347 838146 & 838251 Fax 01347 838867
17 Annexe3rm(2)

BEDALE Map 08 SE28

Bedale Leyburn Rd DL8 1EZ ☎ 01677 422451
Secluded parkland course with many trees.
18 holes, 6610yds, Par 72, SSS 72, Course record 68.
Club membership 600.
Visitors welcome when course is free.
Societies must apply in advance.
Green Fees £18 per day/round (£28 weekends).
Prof Tony Johnson
Facilities
Location 0.25 N of town on A684

Hotel ★★ 62% Motel Leeming, The Great North Rd, Leeming Bar, BEDALE
☎ 01677 422122 40

BENTHAM Map 07 SD66

Bentham Robin Ln LA2 7AG ☎ 01524 262455
Moorland course with glorious views.
9 holes, 5760yds, Par 70, SSS 69, Course record 69.
Club membership 480.
Visitors no restrictions.
Societies must apply in advance.
Green Fees not confirmed.
Facilities
Location N side of High Bentham

Hotel ★★ 67% The Traddock, AUSTWICK
☎ 015242 51224 11

CATTERICK GARRISON Map 08 SE29

Catterick Leyburn Rd DL9 3QE
☎ 01748 833268 Fax 01748 833268
Scenic parkland/moorland course of Championship standard, with good views of the Pennines and Cleveland hills. Testing 1st and 6th holes.

18 holes, 6329yds, Par 71, SSS 70, Course record 68.
Club membership 700.

Visitors tee reservation system in operation telephone professional shop 01748 833671, Tuesday is Ladies day, Thursday Senior priority until 10am.
Societies by arrangement.
Green Fees £20 per day/round (£25 weekends).
Prof Andy Marshall
Designer Arthur Day
Facilities
Location 0.5m W of Catterick Garrison Centre

Hotel ★★ 69% King's Head Hotel, Market Place, RICHMOND ☎ 01748 850220 26 Annexe4

Copmanthorpe Map 08 SE54

Pike Hills Tadcaster Rd YO2 3UW
☎ 01904 700797 Fax 01904 700797
Parkland course surrounding nature reserve. Level terrain.
18 holes, 6146yds, Par 71, SSS 69, Course record 67.
Club membership 750.

Visitors welcome weekdays, with member only weekends & bank holidays.
Societies must apply in advance.
Green Fees £24 per day; £18 per round.
Prof Ian Gradwell
Facilities
Location 3m SW of York on A64

Hotel ★★★★ 64% Swallow Hotel, Tadcaster Rd, YORK ☎ 01904 701000 113

Easingwold Map 08 SE56

Easingwold Stillington Rd YO61 3ET
☎ 01347 821964 (Prof) & 01347 (Sec) Fax 01347 822474
Parkland course with easy walking. Trees are a major feature and on six holes water hazards come into play.
18 holes, 5747mtrs, Par 72, SSS 70, Course record 65.
Club membership 625.

Visitors prior enquiry essential.
Societies prior application in writing essential.
Green Fees £25 per day (£30 weekends).
Prof John Hughes
Designer Hawtree
Facilities
Location 1m Sof Easingwold, 12m N of York

Hotel ★★ 66% George Hotel, Market Place, EASINGWOLD ☎ 01347 821698 15

Filey Map 08 TA18

Filey West Av YO14 9BQ
☎ 01723 513293 Fax 01723 514952
Parkland course with good views, windy. Stream runs through course. Testing 9th and 13th holes.
18 holes, 6112yds, Par 70, SSS 69, Course record 64.
Club membership 900.

Visitors must telephone to reserve tee time.
Societies contact by telephone.
Green Fees £27 per day; £21 per round (£30/£28 weekends).
Prof Gary Hutchinson
Designer Braid
Facilities
Location 0.5m S of Filey

Hotel ★★ 67% Wrangham House Hotel, 10 Stonegate, HUNMANBY ☎ 01723 891333 8 Annexe4

Ganton Map 08 SE97

Ganton YO12 4PA
☎ 01944 710329 Fax 01944 710922
Championship course, heathland, gorse-lined fairways and heavily bunkered; variable winds.
18 holes, 6734yds, Par 73, SSS 74, Course record 65.
Club membership 500.

Visitors by prior arrangement.
Societies prior arrangement in writing.
Green Fees £48 per day/round (£53 weekends & bank holidays).
Cards
Prof Gary Brown
Designer Dunn/Vardon/Braid/Colt
Facilities
Location 11m SW of Scarborough on A64

Hotel ★★★ 62% East Ayton Lodge Country House, Moor Ln, Forge Valley, EAST AYTON ☎ 01723 864227 11 Annexe20

Harrogate Map 08 SE35

Harrogate Forest Ln Head, Starbeck HG2 7TF
☎ 01423 862999 Fax 01423 860073
One of Yorkshire's oldest and best courses was designed in 1897 by 'Sandy' Herd. A perfect example of golf architecture, its greens and fairways offer an interesting but fair challenge. The undulating parkland course once formed part of the ancient Forest of Knaresborough. Excellent clubhouse. ▶

18 holes, 6241yds, Par 69, SSS 70, Course record 64.
Club membership 650.

Visitors advisable to contact professional in advance, weekend play limited.
Societies must contact in writing or intially by telephone.
Green Fees £32 per day; £28 per round (£40 day/round weekends & bank holidays).
Prof Paul Johnson
Designer Sandy Herd
Facilities
Location 2.25m N on A59

Hotel ★★★ 68% The White House, 10 Park Pde, HARROGATE ☎ 01423 501388 11

Oakdale Oakdale HG1 2LN
☎ 01423 567162 & 567188 Fax 01423 536030
A pleasant, undulating parkland course which provides a good test of golf for the low handicap player without intimidating the less proficient. A special feature is an attractive stream which comes in to play on four holes. Excellent views from the clubhouse which has good facilities.
18 holes, 6456yds, Par 71, SSS 71, Course record 61.
Club membership 1034.

Visitors no party bookings weekends.
Societies telephone followed by letter.
Green Fees £27 per round (£32 per round weekends & bank holidays).
Prof Clive Dell
Designer Dr McKenzie
Facilities
Location N side of town centre off A61

Hotel ★★★ 71% Grants Hotel, 3-13 Swan Rd, HARROGATE ☎ 01423 560666 42

Rudding Park HG3 1DJ
☎ 01423 872100 Fax 01423 873011
Opened in Spring 1995, Rudding Park has been designed by Hawtree of Oxford as a parkland course with 5 water features to be operated on a Pay and Play basis.
18 holes, 6871yds, Par 72, SSS 73, Course record 72.

Visitors handicap certificate required, tee reservation available 7 days in advance.
Societies apply by telephone in advance.
Green Fees £27.50 per day; £17.50 per round (£30/£19.50 weekends & bank holidays).
Prof Simon Hotham
Designer Hawtree
Facilities
& Leisure heated outdoor swimming pool, golf academy.
Location 2m SE of Harrogate town centre, off A658 follow brown tourist signs

Hotel ★★★★ 70% Rudding Park House & Hotel, Rudding Park, Follifoot, HARROGATE ☎ 01423 871350 50

HOWDEN — Map 08 SE72

Boothferry Park Spaldington Ln DN14 7NG
☎ 01430 430364
A heavily bunkered meadowland course with several dykes.
18 holes, 6651yds, Par 73, SSS 72, Course record 64.
Club membership 650.

Visitors must contact in advance, tee times bookable.
Societies must contact for booking form.
Green Fees £9 per round (£14 weekends).
Cards
Prof Nigel Bundy
Designer Donald Steel
Facilities
Location 2.5m N of Howden off B1228

Hotel ★★ 68% Clifton Hotel, 1 Clifton Gardens, Boothferry Rd, GOOLE ☎ 01405 761336 9rm(5 3)

KIRKBYMOORSIDE — Map 08 SE68

Kirkbymoorside Manor Vale YO6 6EG
☎ 01751 431525 Fax 01751 433190
Hilly parkland course with narrow fairways, gorse and hawthorn bushes. Beautiful views.
18 holes, 6101yds, Par 69, SSS 69, Course record 65.
Club membership 650.

Visitors are advised to contact in advance, may not play before 9.30 or between 12.30-1.30.
Societies must apply in advance.
Green Fees £18 per day/round (£25 weekends & bank holidays).
Facilities
Location N side of village

Hotel ★★ 72% Appleton Hall Country House Hotel, APPLETON-LE-MOORS ☎ 01751 417227 & 417452 Fax 01751 417540 10

KNARESBOROUGH — Map 08 SE35

Knaresborough Boroughbridge Rd HG5 0QQ
☎ 01423 862690 Fax 01423 869345
Undulating parkland course with mature trees and two water features in attractive rural setting.
18 holes, 6410yds, Par 70, SSS 71, Course record 67.
Club membership 802.

Visitors restricted start times summer weekends.
Societies apply by telephone or letter, no bookings for Sat, Sun or Tue.
Green Fees £28 per day; £22.50 per round (£32.50/£27.50 weekends, no visitors bank holidays unless with member).
Prof Gary J Vickers
Designer Hawtree
Facilities
Location 1.25 N on A6055

Hotel ★★★ 70% Dower House Hotel, Bond End, KNARESBOROUGH ☎ 01423 863302 28 Annexe4rm(3)

MALTON Map 08 SE77

Malton & Norton Welham Park, Norton YO17 9QE
☎ 01653 693882 Fax 01653 697912
Parkland course, consisting of 3 nine hole loops, with panoramic views of the moors. Very testing 1st hole (564 yds dog-leg, left).
Welham Course: 18 holes, 6456yds, Par 72, SSS 71.
Park Course: 18 holes, 6246yds, Par 72, SSS 70.
Derwent Course: 18 holes, 6286yds, Par 72, SSS 70.
Club membership 825.
Visitors anytime except during competitions.
Societies telephone and confirm in writing.
Green Fees £22 per day/round (£28 weekends & bank holidays).
Cards
Prof S Robinson
Facilities
Location 1m S

Hotel ★★★ 70% Burythorpe House Hotel, Burythorpe, MALTON
☎ 01653 658200 11

MASHAM Map 08 SE28

Masham Burnholme, Swinton Rd HG4 4HT
☎ 01765 689379
Flat parkland course crossed by River Burn, which comes into play on several holes.
9 holes, 6068yds, Par 70, SSS 69.
Club membership 327.
Visitors must play with member at weekends & bank holidays.
Societies write or telephone well in advance.
Green Fees £15 per day.
Facilities
Location 1m SW off A6108

Hotel ★ 68% Buck Inn, THORNTON WATLASS
☎ 01677 422461 7rm(5)

MIDDLESBROUGH Map 08 NZ41

Middlesbrough Brass Castle Ln, Marton TS8 9EE
☎ 01642 311515
Undulating parkland course, prevailing winds. Testing 6th, 12th and 15th holes.
18 holes, 6215yds, Par 70, SSS 70, Course record 64.
Club membership 960.
Visitors restricted Tue & Sat.
Societies Wed, Thu & Fri only. Must contact the club in advance.
Green Fees £28 per day (£34 weekends & bank holidays).
Prof Don Jones
Facilities
Location 4m S off A172

Hotel ★★★ 71% Parkmore Hotel, 636 Yarm Rd, Eaglescliffe, STOCKTON-ON-TEES
☎ 01642 786815 55

Middlesbrough Municipal Ladgate Ln TS5 7YZ
☎ 01642 315533 Fax 01642 300726
Parkland course with good views. The front nine holes have wide fairways and large, often well-guarded greens while the back nine demand shots over tree-lined water hazards and narrow entrances to subtly contoured greens. Driving range.
18 holes, 6333yds, Par 71, SSS 70, Course record 67.
Club membership 612.
Visitors book on the day weekdays, 7days in advance for weekends & bank holidays.
Societies apply in writing giving at least 2 weeks in advance.
Green Fees £9.80 per round (£12.25 weekends & bank holidays).
Prof Alan Hope
Designer Shuttleworth
Facilities
Location 2m S of Middlesbrough on the A174

Hotel ★★★ 71% Parkmore Hotel, 636 Yarm Rd, Eaglescliffe, STOCKTON-ON-TEES
☎ 01642 786815 55

NORTHALLERTON Map 08 SE39

Romanby Yafforth Rd DL7 0PE
☎ 01609 779988 Fax 01609 779084
Set in natural undulating terrain with the River Wiske meandering through the course, this fairly new golf venue offers a testing round of golf for all abilities. In addition to the river, two lakes come into play on the 2nd, 5th and 11th holes. 12-bay floodlit driving range.
18 holes, 6663yds, Par 72, SSS 72, Course record 72.
Club membership 500.
Visitors welcome everyday please book tee time in advance.
Societies contact Grant McDonnell for details, tel 01609 778855.
Green Fees £21 per day; £14 per 18 holes (£26/£18 weekends and bank holidays).
Cards
Prof Tim Jenkins
Designer Will Adamson
Facilities
Location On the main Northallerton/Richmond road B6271, 1m W of Northallerton

Hotel ★★ 65% The Golden Lion, High St, NORTHALLERTON
☎ 01609 777411 26rm(21)

PANNAL Map 08 SE35

Pannal Follifoot Rd HG3 1ES
☎ 01423 872628 Fax 01423 870043
Fine championship course. Moorland turf but well-wooded with trees closely involved with play.
18 holes, 6618yds, Par 72, SSS 72, Course record 62.
Club membership 780.
Visitors preferable to contact in advance, weekends limited.
Societies apply in advance.
Green Fees £45 per day; £37 per round (£45 per round weekends).
Prof Murray Burgess
Designer Sandy Herd
Facilities
Location E side of village off A61

Hotel ★★★ 68% The Imperial, Prospect Place, HARROGATE
☎ 01423 565071 85

RAVENSCAR Map 08 NZ90

Raven Hall Hotel Golf Course YO13 0ET
☎ 01723 870353 Fax 01723 870072
Opened by the Earl of Cranbrook in 1898, this 9-hole clifftop course is sloping and with good quality small greens. Because of its clifftop position it is subject to strong winds which make it great fun to play, especially the 6th hole.
9 holes, 1894yds, Par 32, SSS 32.
Club membership 120.
Visitors must contact in advance, busy at weekends, spikes essential, no jeans/T shirts.
Societies telephone in advance.
Green Fees not confirmed.
Facilities
& Leisure hard tennis courts, heated indoor plus outdoor swimming pool, sauna.
Location Situated on cliff top

Hotel ★★★ 63% Raven Hall Hotel, RAVENSCAR ☎ 01723 870353 53

REDCAR Map 08 NZ62

Cleveland Queen St TS10 1BT
☎ 01642 471798 Fax 01642 471798
The oldest golf club in Yorkshire playing over the only links championship course in Yorkshire.
18 holes, 6707yds, Par 72, SSS 72, Course record 67.
Club membership 820.
Visitors advisable to book in advanc.
Societies initially telephone for details.
Green Fees £22 per day; £20 per round (£26/£22 weekends).
Prof Stephen Wynn
Facilities
Location 8m E of Middlesborough

Hotel ★★★ 69% Grinkle Park Hotel, EASINGTON ☎ 01287 640515 20

Wilton Wilton Castle TS10 4QY ☎ 01642 465265
Parkland course with some fine views.
18 holes, 6104yds, Par 70, SSS 69.
Club membership 750.
Visitors telephone professional 01642 452730 to check availability, no visitors Saturday, Ladies competition have priority Tuesday.
Societies must telephone in advance.
Green Fees £18 per 26 or 29 holes (£24 Sunday).
Prof P D Smillie
Facilities
Location 3m W on A174

Hotel ★★★ 69% Grinkle Park Hotel, EASINGTON ☎ 01287 640515 20

RICHMOND Map 07 NZ10

Richmond Bend Hagg DL10 5EX
☎ 01748 823231(Secretary)
Parkland course.
18 holes, 5769yds, Par 70, SSS 68, Course record 64.
Club membership 600.
Visitors may not play before 11.30am on Sun.
Societies must contact in writing or telephone 01748 822457.
Green Fees not confirmed.
Prof Paul Jackson
Designer P Pennink
Facilities
Location 0.75m N

Hotel ★★ 69% King's Head Hotel, Market Place, RICHMOND ☎ 01748 850220 26 Annexe4

RIPON Map 08 SE37

Ripon City Palace Rd HG4 3HH ☎ 01765 603640
Hard-walking on undulating parkland course; two testing par 3's at 5th and 16th.
18 holes, 6120yds, Par 71, SSS 69, Course record 68.
Club membership 675.
Visitors book with professional. Limited play Sat especially Apr-Aug.
Societies contact in writing or telephone.
Green Fees £18 per day (£25 weekends & bank holidays).
Prof S T Davis
Designer H Varden
Facilities
Location 1m NW on A6108

Hotel ★★★ 67% Ripon Spa Hotel, Park St, RIPON ☎ 01765 602172 40

SALTBURN-BY-THE-SEA Map 08 NZ62

Hunley Hall Golf Club Ings Ln, Brotton TS12 2QQ
☎ 01287 676216 Fax 01287 678250
Offering a good test for all golfing abitlities, especially off the white tees on the Morgans course, this newly established course enjoys views of the Heritage Coast.
Morgans: 18 holes, 6918yds, Par 73, SSS 73.
Imperial: 18 holes, 6586yds, Par 72, SSS 72.
Millenium: 18 holes, 5948yds, Par 68, SSS 68.
Club membership 400.
Visitors tee off times must be reserved in advance, times available between 9.30-11.30 and after 1pm.
Societies telephone for information and availability.
Green Fees £18 per day (£25 weekends).
Cards
Prof Andrew Brook
Designer John Morgan
Facilities
Location From A174 take St Margarets Way 0.5m to club

Hotel ★★★ 69% Grinkle Park Hotel, EASINGTON ☎ 01287 640515 20

Saltburn by the Sea Hob Hill, Guisborough Rd TS12 1NJ
☎ 01287 622812
Undulating meadowland course surrounded by woodland. Particularly attractive in autumn. There are fine views of the Cleveland Hills and of Tees Bay.
18 holes, 5846yds, Par 70, SSS 68, Course record 62.
Club membership 900.
Visitors telephone in advance, no visitors on Saturday.
Societies apply in writing.
Green Fees £20 (£25 weekends).
Cards
Prof Mike Nutter
Designer J Braid

Facilities
Location 0.5m out of Saltburn on Guisborough road

Hotel ★★★ 69% Grinkle Park Hotel, EASINGTON
☎ 01287 640515 20

Scarborough Map 08 TA08

Scarborough North Cliff North Cliff Av YO12 6PP
☎ 01723 360786 Fax 01723 362134
Seaside parkland course begining on cliff top overlooking bay and castle. Good views.
18 holes, 6425yds, Par 71, SSS 71, Course record 66.
Club membership 895.
Visitors must be member of a club with handicap certificate. May not play before 10.30am Sun.
Societies prior booking with secretary for parties of 8-40.
Green Fees £25 per day; £18 per round (£28/ £22 weekends & bank holidays).
Prof Simon N Deller
Designer James Braid
Facilities
Location 2m N of town centre off A165

Hotel ★★★ 64% Esplanade Hotel, Belmont Rd, SCARBOROUGH
☎ 01723 360382 73

Scarborough South Cliff Deepdale Av YO11 2UE
☎ 01723 374737
Parkland/seaside course designed by Dr Mackenzie.
18 holes, 6039yds, Par 70, SSS 69, Course record 66.
Club membership 700.
Visitors contact in advance may not play before 9.30am Mon-Fri, 10am Sat and 10.30am Sun.
Societies must contact Secretary in advance.
Green Fees not confirmed.
Prof A R Skingle
Designer McKenzie
Facilities
Location 1m S on A165

Hotel ★★ 62% Bradley Court, Filey Rd, South Cliff, SCARBOROUGH ☎ 01723 360476 40

Selby Map 08 SE63

Selby Brayton Barff YO8 9LD
☎ 01757 228622
Mainly flat, links-type course; prevailing SW wind. Testing holes including the 3rd, 7th and 16th.
18 holes, 6246yds, Par 70, SSS 70.
Club membership 840.
Visitors contact professional on 01757 228785, members and guests only at weekends.
Societies welcome Wed-Fri, must apply in advance.
Green Fees not confirmed.
Prof Andrew Smith
Designer J Taylor & Hawtree
Facilities
Location Off A19 at Brayton

Hotel ★★★ 68% Monk Fryston Hall, MONK FRYSTON
☎ 01977 682369 28

Settle Map 07 SD86

Settle Buckhaw Brow, Giggleswick BD24 0DH
☎ 01729 825288
Picturesque parkland course with stream affecting play on four holes.
9 holes, 5530yds, Par 68, SSS 66, Course record 59.
Club membership 380.
Visitors may not play before 4pm on Sun.
Societies apply in writing or telephone 4 weeks in advance.
Green Fees not confirmed.
Designer Tom Vardon
Facilities
Location 1m N on A65

Hotel ★★★ 67% Falcon Manor Hotel, Skipton Rd, SETTLE
☎ 01729 823814 15 Annexe5

Skipton Map 07 SD95

Skipton Off North West By-Pass BD23 1LL
☎ 01756 795657
Undulating parkland course with some water hazards and panoramic views.
18 holes, 6049yds, Par 70, SSS 69, Course record 67.
Club membership 750.
Visitors welcome by prior arrangement.
Societies must apply in writing.
Green Fees not confirmed.
Prof Peter Robinson
Facilities
Location 1m N on A65

Hotel ★★★ Devonshire Arms Country House Hotel, Bolton Abbey, SKIPTON
☎ 01756 710441 41

Tadcaster Map 08 SE44

Cocksford Cocksford, Stutton LS24 9NG
☎ 01937 834253
Three 9-hole courses; the old 18-hole combination set on undulating meadowland with the famous Cock Beck featuring on 8 of the original 18 holes. Whatever combination you choose the course is relatively short featuring a number of drivable par 4s, but beware danger surrounds many of the greens!
Old Course: 18 holes, 5570yds, Par 71, SSS 69, Course record 65.
Plews Course: 18 holes, 5559yds, Par 70, SSS 68.
Quarry Hills Course: 18 holes, 4951yds, Par 67, SSS 65.
Club membership 450.
Visitors welcome, contact pro shop.
Societies telephone the secretary.
Green Fees not confirmed.
Prof Graham Thompson
Designer Bill Brodigan
Facilities
Location Between York & Leeds, A162 from Tadcaster

Hotel ★★★ 75% Wood Hall Hotel, Trip Ln, Linton, WETHERBY
☎ 01937 587271 37 Annexe6

Scathingwell Scarthingwell LS24 9PF
☎ 01937 557864 (pro) 557878 (club) Fax 01937 557909
Testing water hazards and well placed bunkers and trees provide a challenging test of golf for all handicaps at this scenic parkland course, located 4 miles south of Tadcaster.
18 holes, 6771yds, Par 72, SSS 72.
Visitors dress code must be adhered to.
Societies golf packages available, book one month in advance.
Green Fees £16 per 18 holes (£18 weekends).
Prof Steve Footman
Facilities
Location 4m S of Tadcaster on the A162 Tadcaster/Perrybridge Road, approx 2m from the A1

Hotel B Forte Posthouse Leeds/Selby, SOUTH MILFORD ☎ 01977 682711 95

THIRSK Map 08 SE48

Thirsk & Northallerton Thornton-le-Street YO7 4AB
☎ 01845 522170 & 525115
The course has good views of the nearby Hambleton Hills. Testing course, mainly flat land.
18 holes, 6514yds, Par 72, SSS 71.
Club membership 450.
Visitors must telephone in advance, and have handicap certificate. No play Sun.
Societies must apply in writing.
Green Fees £25 per day; £20 per round.
Prof Robert Garner
Facilities
Location 2m N on A168

Hotel ★★ 62% Three Tuns Hotel, Market Place, THIRSK ☎ 01845 523124 11

WHITBY Map 08 NZ81

Whitby Low Straggleton, Sandsend Rd YO21 3SR
☎ 01947 600660 Fax 01947 600660
Seaside course with 4 holes along cliff tops and over ravines. Good views and fresh sea breeze.
18 holes, 6134yds, Par 71, Course record 66.
Club membership 800.
Visitors may not play on competition days.
Societies must contact in writing.
Green Fees £20 per day (£25 weekends and bank holidays).
Prof Richard Wood
Facilities
Location 1.5m NW on A174

Hotel ★★ 67% White House Hotel, Upgang Ln, West Cliff, WHITBY
☎ 01947 600469 11rm(5 4)

YORK Map 08 SE65

Forest of Galtres Moorlands Rd, Skelton YO3 3RF
☎ 01904 766198 Fax 01904 766198
Level parkland course in the heart of the ancient Forest of Galtres with mature oak trees and interesting water features coming into play on the 5th,6th,14th and 17th holes. Views towards York Minster.
18 holes, 6312yds, Par 72, SSS 70, Course record 67.
Club membership 450.
Visitors telephone to book, may play any time.
Societies booking system, telephone for forms.
Green Fees £21 per day; £16 per round (£25/£21 weekends & bank holidays).
Prof Neil Suckling
Designer Simon Gidman
Facilities
Location 0.5m from the York ring road B1237, just off A19 Thirsk road through the village of Skelton

Hotel ★★ 66% Jacobean Lodge Hotel, Plainville Ln, Wigginton, YORK
☎ 01904 762749 8 Annexe6

Forest Park Stockton-on-the-Forest YO3 9UW
☎ 01904 400425
A parkland/meadowland course, opened in 1991, with natural features including a stream and mature and new trees.
Old Foss Course: 18 holes, 6600yds, Par 71, SSS 72, Course record 73.
The West Course: 9 holes, 6372yds, Par 70, SSS 70.
Club membership 650.
Visitors welcome, subject to tee availability. Advisable to contact club in advance.
Societies by prior arrangement.
Green Fees Old Foss: £22 per day; £16 per round (£28/£21 weekends & bank holidays). West Course: £13 per 18 holes, £8 per 9 holes (£17/£10 weekends & bank holidays).
Cards
Facilities
Location 4m NE of York, 1.5m from end of A64, York bypass

Hotel ★★★ 71% York Pavilion Hotel, 45 Main St, Fulford, YORK
☎ 01904 622099 34

Fulford Heslington Ln YO10 5DY
☎ 01904 413579 Fax 01904 416918
A flat, parkland/moorland course well-known for the superb quality of its turf, particularly the greens, and now famous as the venue for some of the best golf tournaments in the British Isles.
18 holes, 6775yds, Par 72, SSS 72, Course record 62.
Club membership 700.
Visitors must contact in advance.
Societies not Tue am, book with the manager.
Green Fees not confirmed.
Prof Bryan Hessay
Designer Dr Mckenzie
Facilities
Location 2m S of York off A19

Hotel ★★★★ 64% Swallow Hotel, Tadcaster Rd, YORK ☎ 01904 701000 113

Heworth Muncaster House, Muncastergate YO31 9JX
☎ 01904 422389
11-hole parkland course, easy walking. Holes 3 to 9 played twice from different tees.
11 holes, 6141yds, Par 70, SSS 69, Course record 67.
Club membership 550.
Visitors advisable to telephone the professional in advance.
Societies apply in writing.

Green Fees £16 per day; £12 per round (£18/£16 weekends & bank holidays).
Prof Gregg Roberts
Designer B Cheal
Facilities
Location 1.5m NE of city centre on A1036

Hotel ★★★ 73% Dean Court Hotel, Duncombe Place, YORK ☎ 01904 625082 40

Swallow Hall Crockey Hill YO1 4SG
☎ 01904 448889 Fax 01904 448219
A small 18-hole, Par 3 course with 2 par 4s. Attached to a caravan park.
18 holes, 3100yds, Par 56, SSS 56, Course record 58.
Club membership 100.
Visitors no restrictions.
Societies must telephone in advance.
Green Fees £8 per 18 holes; £4 per 9 holes (£9/£4.50 weekends & bank holidays).
Designer Brian Henry
Facilities
& Leisure hard tennis courts.
Location Off A19, signposted to Wheldrake

Hotel ★★★ 71% York Pavilion Hotel, 45 Main St, Fulford, YORK ☎ 01904 622099 34

York Lords Moor Ln, Strensall YO32 5XF
☎ 01904 491840 Fax 01904 491852
A pleasant, well-designed, heathland course with easy walking. The course is of good length but being flat the going does not tire. The course is well bunkered with excellent greens and there are two testing pond holes.
18 holes, 6323yds, Par 70, SSS 70, Course record 66.
Club membership 700.
Visitors with member only weekends, must contact in advance.
Societies more than 16 contact secretary, under 16 contact professional.
Green Fees £32 per 36 holes/£25 per 18 holes (£36 per 36 holes bank holidays).
Prof A B Mason
Designer J H Taylor
Facilities
Location 6m NE, E of Strensall village

Hotel ★★★ 73% Dean Court Hotel, Duncombe Place, YORK ☎ 01904 625082 40

YORKSHIRE, SOUTH

BARNSLEY Map 08 SE30

Barnsley Wakefield Rd, Staincross S75 6JZ
☎ 01226 382856
Undulating municipal parkland course with easy walking apart from last 4 holes. Testing 8th and 18th holes.
18 holes, 5951yds, Par 69, SSS 69, Course record 64.
Club membership 450.
Visitors no restrictions.
Societies by arrangement.
Green Fees not confirmed.
Prof Mike Melling
Facilities
Location 3m N on A61

Hotel ★★★ 68% Ardsley House Hotel, Doncaster Rd, Ardsley, BARNSLEY ☎ 01226 309955 73

Sandhill Middlecliffe Ln, Little Houghton S72 0HW
☎ 01226 753444 Fax 01226 717420
Opened in 1993, the course is reasonably flat with generously wide fairways laid out between and amongst 25 acres of newly planted woodlands. Holes of note are the 4th which is a 311 yard Par 4 to a horseshoe green around a 9-foot deep bunker; the 7th Par 3 to blind reverse Mackenzie Green and the 11th 416 yard Par 4 dogleg where the brave can take on the out of bounds.
18 holes, 6250yds, Par 71, SSS 70, Course record 69.
Club membership 275.
Visitors welcome by prior booking.
Societies telephone for availability, write to confirm.
Green Fees £8.50 (£11 weekends).
Cards
Designer John Royston
Facilities
Location 5m E of Barnsley, off A635

Hotel ★★★ 68% Ardsley House Hotel, Doncaster Rd, Ardsley, BARNSLEY ☎ 01226 309955 73

BAWTRY Map 08 SK69

Austerfield Park Cross Ln, Austerfield DN10 6RF
☎ 01302 710841 Fax 01302 710850
Long moorland course with postage stamp 8th and testing 618-yd 7th. Driving range and Par 3 attached.
18 holes, 6900yds, Par 73, SSS 73, Course record 69.
Club membership 500.
Visitors welcome weekdays, after 10am weekends.
Societies must contact in advance.
Green Fees £18 per day; £14 per round (£22/£17 weekends).
Cards
Prof Peter Rothery
Facilities
Location 2m from Bawtry on A614

Hotel ★★★ 62% The Crown Hotel, High St, BAWTRY ☎ 01302 710341 57

CONISBROUGH Map 08 SK59

Crookhill Park Municipal Carr Ln DN12 2BE
☎ 01709 862979
A naturally sloping parkland course with many holes featuring tight dog-legs and small, undulating greens. The signature hole (11th) involves a fearsome tee shot over a ditch onto a sloping fairway and final shot to an elevated green surrounded by tall trees and deep bunkers.
18 holes, 5849yds, Par 70, SSS 68, Course record 64.
Club membership 350.
Visitors booking system for general play.
Societies bookings taken in advance, deposits taken through booking system.
Green Fees not confirmed.
Prof Richard Swaine
Facilities
Location 1.5m SE on B6094

Hotel ★★★ 64% Danum Hotel, High St, DONCASTER ☎ 01302 342261 66

DONCASTER Map 08 SE50

Doncaster 278 Bawtry Rd, Bessacarr DN4 7PD
☎ 01302 868316
Pleasant undulating heathland course with wooded surroundings. Quick drying, ideal autumn, winter and spring.
18 holes, 6220yds, Par 69, SSS 70, Course record 66.
Club membership 600.

Visitors must contact in advance. Times restricted on Wed & weekends.
Societies must contact in advance.
Green Fees £25 per day; £20 per round (£30/£25 weekends & bank holidays).
Prof Graham Bailey
Designer Mackenzie/Hawtree
Facilities
Location 4m SE on A638

Hotel ★★★ 67% Mount Pleasant Hotel, Great North Rd, ROSSINGTON ☎ 01302 868696 & 868219 Fax 01302 865130 33

Doncaster Town Moor Bawtry Rd, Belle Vue DN4 5HU
☎ 01302 535286 & 533167
Easy walking, but testing, heathland course with good true greens. Friendly club. Notable hole is 11th (par 4), 464 yds. Situated in centre of racecourse.
18 holes, 6072yds, Par 69, SSS 69, Course record 66.
Club membership 520.

Societies must contact in advance.
Green Fees £16 (£18 weekends & bank holidays).
Prof Steven C Poole
Facilities
Location 1.5m E,at racecourse,on A638

Hotel ★★★ 64% Danum Hotel, High St, DONCASTER ☎ 01302 342261 66

Owston Park Owston Ln, Ownston DN6 8EF
☎ 01302 330821
A flat course surrounded by woodland. A lot of mature trees and a few ditches in play. A practice putting green and chipping area.
9 holes, 3042yds, Par 36, SSS 71.

Visitors no restrictions.
Societies telephone in advance.
Green Fees £4.25 per 9 holes (£4.50 weekends).
Cards
Prof Mike Parker
Designer M Parker
Facilities
Location 5m N of Doncaster off A19

Hotel ★★★ 64% Danum Hotel, High St, DONCASTER ☎ 01302 342261 66

Thornhurst Park Holme Ln, Owston DN5 0LR
☎ 01302 337799 Fax 01302 721495
Surrounded by Owston Wood, this scenic parkland course has numerous strategically placed bunkers, and a lake comes into play at the 7th and 8th holes.
18 holes, 6490yds, Par 72, SSS 72, Course record 72.
Club membership 160.

Visitors must wear trousers, shirt with collar and golf shoes, can contact 2 days in advance.
Societies telephone or write in advance.
Green Fees £8 per 18 holes; £4 per 9 holes (£10/£5 weekends & bank holidays).
Cards
Prof Kevin Pearce
Facilities
Location On the A19 between Bentley/Askern, easy access from M62 and A1 (M)

Hotel ★★★ 64% Danum Hotel, High St, DONCASTER ☎ 01302 342261 66

Wheatley Armthorpe Rd DN2 5QB ☎ 01302 831655
Fairly flat well-bunkered, lake-holed, parkland course.
18 holes, 6169yds, Par 70, SSS 69.
Club membership 600.

Societies must contact in advance.
Green Fees not confirmed.
Prof T C Parkinson
Facilities
Location NE side of town centre off A18

Hotel ★★ 69% Regent Hotel, Regent Square, DONCASTER ☎ 01302 364180 50

HATFIELD Map 08 SE60

Kings Wood Thorne Rd DN7 6EP ☎ 01405 741343
A flat course with ditches that come into play on several holes, especially on the testing back nine. Notable holes are the 12th, 16th and par 5 18th.
18 holes, 6002yds, Par 70, SSS 69, Course record 69.
Club membership 100.

Visitors visitors are welcome any time of week, advisable to contact in advance by telephone, especially for weekend play.
Societies apply in writing to the professional, or telephone in advance.
Green Fees £7 per round (£8 weekends).
Cards
Prof Jonathon Drury
Facilities
Location 2m SW of junct 1 of M180, take A614 to Thorne, then Thorne road to Hatfield

Hotel ★★ 69% Belmont Hotel, Horsefair Green, THORNE ☎ 01405 812320 23

HICKLETON Map 08 SE40

Hickleton Lidgett Ln DN5 7BE
☎ 01709 896081 Fax 01709 896081
Undulating parkland course designed by Neil Coles and Brian Huggett.
18 holes, 6434yds, Par 71, SSS 71, Course record 68.
Club membership 625.

Visitors restricted weekdays after 10am & weekends after 2.30pm. Must contact in advance.
Societies must contact in advance.
Green Fees £17 per round (£26 weekends & bank holidays).
Prof Paul Shepherd
Designer Huggett/Coles
Facilities
Location 0.5m W on B6411

Hotel ★★★ 64% Danum Hotel, High St, DONCASTER ☎ 01302 342261 66

HIGH GREEN Map 08 SK39

Tankersley Park S35 4LG ☎ 0114 246 8247
Akin to an inland links, this parkland course is hilly, windy and has good views.
18 holes, 6212yds, Par 69, SSS 70, Course record 64.
Club membership 634.

Visitors must contact in advance.
Societies must apply in writing.
Green Fees £26 per day; £22 per round.
Cards
Prof Ian Kirk
Designer Hawtree
Facilities
Location Off A61/M1 onto A616, Stocksbridge bypass

Hotel ★★★ 68% Tankersley Manor, Church Ln, TANKERSLEY ☎ 01226 744700 40

RAWMARSH Map 08 SK49

Wath Abdy Ln S62 7SJ
☎ 01709 872149 & 878609 (office) Fax 01709 878609
Parkland course, not easy in spite of its length; 17th hole (par 3) is a difficult 244yds with narrow driving area.
18 holes, 5857yds, Par 68, SSS 68.
Club membership 550.

Visitors must play with member at weekends. Must contact in advance and have a handicap certificate.
Societies must contact in writing, may not play at weekends.
Green Fees not confirmed.
Prof Chris Bassett
Facilities
Location 2.5m N off A633

Hotel ★★★ 65% Carlton Park Hotel, 102/104 Moorgate Rd, ROTHERHAM ☎ 01709 849955 75

ROTHERHAM Map 08 SK49

Grange Park Upper Wortley Rd S61 2SJ
☎ 01709 559497
Parkland/meadowland course, with panoramic views especially from the back nine. The golf is testing, particularly at the 1st, 4th and 18th holes (par 4), and 8th, 12th and 15th (par 5).
18 holes, 6421yds, Par 71, SSS 71, Course record 65.
Club membership 214.

Visitors no restrictions.
Societies apply in writing.
Green Fees £8 per round (£9.50 weekends & bank holidays).
Prof Eric Clark
Designer Fred Hawtree
Facilities
Location 3m NW off A629

Hotel ★★★ 68% Tankersley Manor, Church Ln, TANKERSLEY ☎ 01226 744700 40

Phoenix Pavilion Ln, Brinsworth S60 5PA
☎ 01709 363864 & 382624 Fax 01709 363788
Undulating meadowland course with variable wind.
18 holes, 6182yds, Par 71, SSS 69, Course record 65.
Club membership 1100.

Visitors must contact in advance.
Societies must apply in writing.
Green Fees not confirmed.
Prof M Roberts
Designer C K Cotton
Facilities
& Leisure hard tennis courts, squash, fishing, gymnasium.
Location SW side of town centre off A630

Hotel ★★★ 65% Carlton Park Hotel, 102/104 Moorgate Rd, ROTHERHAM ☎ 01709 849955 75

Rotherham Golf Club Ltd Thrybergh Park, Doncaster Rd, Thrybergh S65 4NU
☎ 01709 850812 (Secretary) Fax 01709 855288
Parkland course with easy walking along tree-lined fairways.
18 holes, 6324yds, Par 70, SSS 70, Course record 65.
Club membership 500.

Visitors must contact in advance.
Societies must contact secretary in advance.
Green Fees £28 per day (£35 weekends & bank holidays).
Prof Simon Thornhill
Facilities
Location 3.5m E on A630

Hotel ★★★ 69% Elton Hotel, Main St, Bramley, ROTHERHAM ☎ 01709 545681 13 Annexe16

Sitwell Park Shrogswood Rd S60 4BY
☎ 01709 541046 Fax 01709 703637
Parkland course with easy walking.
18 holes, 6209yds, Par 71, SSS 70, Course record 61.
Club membership 450.

Visitors must contact in advance.
Societies must contact in advance.
Green Fees £28 per day; £24 per round (£32/£28 weekends & bank holidays).
Prof Nic Taylor
Designer A MacKenzie
Facilities
Hotel ★★★★ 66% Hellaby Hall Hotel, Old Hellaby Ln, Hellaby, ROTHERHAM ☎ 01709 702701 52

SHEFFIELD Map 08 SK38

Abbeydale Twentywell Ln, Dore S17 4QA
☎ 0114 236 0763
Parkland course, well-kept and wooded. Testing hole: 12th, par 3.
18 holes, 6419yds, Par 72, SSS 72.
Club membership 750.

Visitors by arrangement.
Societies must apply in writing.
Green Fees not confirmed.
Prof Nigel Perry
Designer Herbert Fowler
Facilities
Location 4m SW of city centre off A621 ▶

Hotel B Forte Posthouse Sheffield, Mancheater Rd, Broomhill, SHEFFIELD
0114 267 0067 135

Beauchief Municipal Abbey Ln S8 0DB
0114 236 7274
Municipal course with natural water hazards. The rolling land looks west to the Pennines and a 12th-century abbey adorns the course.
18 holes, 5452yds, Par 67, SSS 66, Course record 65.
Club membership 450.

Visitors are advised to book in advance in summer.
Societies weekdays only, must apply in writing to: Recreation Department, Tower Lodge, Firth Park Road, Sheffield S5 6WS.
Green Fees not confirmed.
Prof A Highfield
Facilities
Location 4m SW of city centre off A621

Hotel ★★★ 69% Beauchief Hotel, 161 Abbeydale Rd South, SHEFFIELD
0114 262 0500 41

Birley Wood Birley Ln S12 3BP
0114 264 7262
Undulating meadowland course with well-varied features, easy walking and good views. Practice range and green.
18 holes, 5100yds, Par 66, SSS 65, Course record 64.
Club membership 300.

Visitors no restrictions.
Societies apply in advance.
Green Fees not confirmed.
Prof Peter Ball
Facilities
Location 4.5m SE of city centre off A616

Hotel ★★★ 67% Mosborough Hall Hotel, High St, Mosborough, SHEFFIELD
0114 248 4353 23

Concord Park Shiregreen Ln S5 6AE
0114 234 9802 & 257 7378
Hilly municipal parkland course with some fairways wood-flanked, good views, often windy. Seven par 3 holes. Course under development.
18 holes, 4872yds, Par 67, SSS 64, Course record 57.
Club membership 150.

Visitors no restrictions.
Green Fees £6.90.
Prof W Allcroft
Facilities
& Leisure hard tennis courts, heated indoor swimming pool, squash, solarium, gymnasium.
Location 3.5m N of city centre on B6086 off A6135

Hotel B Forte Posthouse Sheffield, Mancheater Rd, Broomhill, SHEFFIELD
0114 267 0067 135

Dore & Totley Bradway Rd, Bradway S17 4QR
0114 236 0492
Flat parkland course.
18 holes, 6265yds, Par 70, SSS 70, Course record 65.
Club membership 580.

Visitors must contact in advance a handicap certificate may be requested, may not play weekends.
Societies must apply in writing.
Green Fees not confirmed.
Facilities
Location 7m S of city centre on B6054 off A61

Hotel B Forte Posthouse Sheffield, Mancheater Rd, Broomhill, SHEFFIELD
0114 267 0067 135

Hallamshire Golf Club Ltd Sandygate S10 4LA
0114 230 2153 Fax 0114 230 2153
Situated on a shelf of land at a height of 850 ft. Magnificent views to the west. Moorland turf, long carries over ravine. Good natural drainage.
18 holes, 6359yds, Par 71, SSS 71, Course record 63.
Club membership 600.

Visitors contact professional in advance. Tees reserved for members 8-9.30 and noon-1.30.
Societies parties of 12+ should book in advance with secretary.
Green Fees £35 per day (£40 weekends & bank holidays).
Prof G R Tickell
Designer Various
Facilities
Location Off A57 at Crosspool onto Sandygate Rd, clubhouse 0.75m on right

Hotel B Forte Posthouse Sheffield, Mancheater Rd, Broomhill, SHEFFIELD
0114 267 0067 135

Hillsborough Worrall Rd S6 4BE
0114 234 9151 (Secretary) & 233 2666 (Pro)
Beautiful moorland/woodland course 500 ft above sea-level, reasonable walking. Challenging first four holes into a prevailing wind and a tight, testing 14th hole.
18 holes, 6216yards, Par 71, SSS 70, Course record 64.
Club membership 650.

Visitors contact professional in advance. May not play Tue (Ladies Day), Thu and weekends before 2pm
Societies must apply in writing to secretary.
Green Fees Apr-Oct: £28 per day; Oct-Mar: £20 per day (£35 per day weekends & bank holidays).
Prof Graham Walker
Facilities
Location 3m NW of city centre off A616

Hotel ★★★ 60% Rutland Hotel, 452 Glossop Rd, Broomhill, SHEFFIELD
0114 266 4411 70 Annexe17

Lees Hall Hemsworth Rd, Norton S8 8LL
0114 255 4402
Parkland/meadowland course with panoramic view of city.
18 holes, 6137yds, Par 71, SSS 69, Course record 63.
Club membership 725.

Visitors restricted Wed.
Societies must apply in writing.
Green Fees not confirmed.
Prof J R Wilkinson
Facilities
Location 3.5m S of city centre off A6102

Hotel B Forte Posthouse Sheffield, Mancheater Rd, Broomhill, SHEFFIELD
0114 267 0067 135

Rother Valley Golf Centre Mansfield Rd, Wales Bar S26 5PQ ☎ 0114 247 3000 Fax 0114 247 6000
The challenging Blue Monster parkland course features a variety of water hazards. Notable holes include the 7th, with its island green fronted by water and dominated by bunkers to the rear. Lookout for the water on the par 5 18th.
18 holes, 6602yds, Par 72, SSS 72, Course record 70.
Club membership 500.

Visitors 2 days in advance booking format.
Societies apply in writing or telephone in advance.
Green Fees £7.50 per round Mon; £11 per round Tue-Fri (£16 weekends). Par 3 £3.50 all week.
Cards
Prof Jason Ripley
Designer Michael Shattock & Mark Roe
Facilities
& Leisure Country Park adjacent with water based sporting activities.
Location Off junct 31 of the M1, follow signs to Rother Valley Country Park

Hotel ★★★ 67% Mosborough Hall Hotel, High St, Mosborough, SHEFFIELD ☎ 0114 248 4353 23

Tinsley Park Municipal Golf High Hazels Park, Darnall S9 4PE ☎ 0114 256 0237
Undulating meadowland course with plenty of trees and rough.
18 holes, 6064yds, Par 71, SSS 69.
Club membership 580.

Visitors no restrictions.
Societies apply in writing to Sheffield City Council, Recreation Dept., Meersbrook Park, Sheffield.
Green Fees £7.50 per round (£8.50 weekends).
Cards
Prof A P Highfield
Facilities by prior arrangement by prior arrangement by prior arrangement
& Leisure hard tennis courts.
Location 4m E of city centre off A630

Hotel ★★★ 67% Mosborough Hall Hotel, High St, Mosborough, SHEFFIELD ☎ 0114 248 4353 23

SILKSTONE Map 08 SE20

Silkstone Field Head, Elmhurst Ln S75 4LD ☎ 01226 790328
Parkland/downland course, fine views over the Pennines. Testing golf.
18 holes, 6069yds, Par 70, SSS 70, Course record 64.
Club membership 508.

Visitors with member only at weekends.
Societies contact in advance.
Green Fees £26 per day/round.
Prof Kevin Guy
Facilities
Location 1m E off A628

Hotel ★★★ 68% Ardsley House Hotel, Doncaster Rd, Ardsley, BARNSLEY ☎ 01226 309955 73

STOCKSBRIDGE Map 08 SK29

Stocksbridge & District 30 Royd Ln, Townend, Deepcar S36 2RZ ☎ 0114 288 2003
Hilly moorland course.
18 holes, 5200yds, Par 65, SSS 65, Course record 60.
Club membership 300.

Visitors contact the professional.
Societies apply to professional.
Green Fees £17 per day; £14 per round (£24 per day weekends).
Prof Timothy Brookes
Designer Dave Thomas
Facilities
Location S side of town centre

Hotel B Forte Posthouse Sheffield, Mancheater Rd, Broomhill, SHEFFIELD ☎ 0114 267 0067 135

THORNE Map 08 SE61

Thorne Kirton Ln DN8 5RJ ☎ 01405 812084 Fax 01405 741899
Picturesque parkland course with 6000 newly planted trees. Water hazards on 11th, 14th & 18th holes.
18 holes, 5366yds, Par 68, SSS 66, Course record 62.
Club membership 300.

Visitors no restrictions.
Societies telephone in advance.
Green Fees £8.75 per round (£9.75 weekends).
Prof Richard Highfield
Designer R D Highfield
Facilities
Location 14m SE of Pontefract off of M18

Hotel ★★ 69% Belmont Hotel, Horsefair Green, THORNE ☎ 01405 812320 23

WORTLEY Map 08 SK39

Wortley Hermit Hill Ln S35 7DF ☎ 0114 288 8469 Fax 0114 288 8469
Well-wooded, undulating parkland course sheltered from prevailing wind.
18 holes, 6028yds, Par 69, SSS 68, Course record 62.
Club membership 510.

Visitors may not play between 11.30am and 1pm. Must contact professional in advance and hold a handicap certificate.
Societies telephone in advance and confirm in writing with deposit.
Green Fees £25 per day (£30 weekends & bank holidays).
Cards
Prof Ian Kirk
Facilities
Location 0.5m NE of village off A629

Hotel B Forte Posthouse Sheffield, Mancheater Rd, Broomhill, SHEFFIELD ☎ 0114 267 0067 135

Entries with a shaded background identify courses that are considered to be particularly interesting

YORKSHIRE, WEST

ALWOODLEY Map 08 SE24

Alwoodley Wigton Ln LS17 8SA
☎ 0113 268 1680 Fax 0113 293 9458
A fine heathland course with length, trees and abundant heather. Many attractive situations - together a severe test of golf.
18 holes, 6686yds, Par 72, SSS 73, Course record 67.
Club membership 452.

Visitors must contact in advance.
Societies must apply in advance.
Green Fees £50 per day/round (£60 weekends & bank holidays).
Prof John Green
Designer Dr Alistair Mackenzie
Facilities
Location 5m N off A61

Hotel ★★★ 65% Harewood Arms Hotel, Harrogate Rd, HAREWOOD
☎ 0113 288 6566 13 Annexe11

BAILDON Map 07 SE13

Baildon Moorgate BD17 5PP ☎ 01274 595162
Moorland course set out in links style with outward front nine looping back to clubhouse. Panoramic views with testing short holes in prevailing winds.
18 holes, 6225yds, Par 70, SSS 70, Course record 64.
Club membership 500.

Visitors contact in advance, restricted Tue & weekends.
Societies large numbers apply in writing, small numbers check with the professional.
Green Fees not confirmed.
Prof Richard Masters
Designer Tom Morris
Facilities
Location 3m N of Bradford, off A6038

Hotel ★★★ 72% Marriott Hollins Hall Hotel and Country Club, Hollins Hill, Baildon, SHIPLEY
☎ 01274 530053 122

BINGLEY Map 07 SE13

Bingley St Ives Golf Club House, St Ives Estate, Harden BD16 1AT ☎ 01274 562436 Fax 01274 511788
Parkland/moorland course.
18 holes, 6485yds, Par 71, SSS 71, Course record 69.
Club membership 450.

Visitors contact professional on 01274 562506, no green fees Sat.
Societies telephone in advance, the professional 01274 562506.
Green Fees £29 per day; £24 per round.
Prof Ray Firth
Designer Alastair Mackenzie
Facilities
Location 0.75m W off B6429

Hotel ★★★ 67% Oakwood Hall Hotel, Lady Ln, BINGLEY
☎ 01274 564123 & 563569
Fax 01274 561477 20

Shipley Beckfoot Ln BD16 1LX
☎ 01274 563212 (Club) & 563674 (Pro) Fax 01274 568652
Well established parkland course, founded in 1922, featuring 6 good par 3's
18 holes, 6215yds, Par 71, SSS 70, Course record 65.
Club membership 600.

Visitors may play Mon, Wed-Fri & Sun, but Tue only after 2.30pm & Sat after 4pm.
Societies initial enquiry by phone to secretary 01274 568652 and or by letter.
Green Fees £27 (£32 weekend & bank holidays).
Prof J R Parry
Designer Colt, Allison, Mackenzie, Braid
Facilities
Location 6m N of Bradford on A650

Hotel ★★★ 67% Oakwood Hall Hotel, Lady Ln, BINGLEY
☎ 01274 564123 & 563569
Fax 01274 561477 20

BRADFORD Map 07 SE13

Bradford Moor Scarr Hall, Pollard Ln BD2 4RW
☎ 01274 771716 & 771718
Moorland course with tricky undulating greens.
9 holes, 5900yds, Par 70, SSS 68, Course record 65.
Club membership 330.
Visitors no visitors at weekends except with member.
Societies can book starting times by application in writing.
Green Fees £6 before 1.30pm, £12 after 1.30pm.
Prof Ron Hughes
Facilities
Location 2m NE of city centre off A658

Hotel ★★ 68% Park Drive Hotel, 12 Park Dr, BRADFORD ☎ 01274 480194 11

Clayton Thornton View Rd, Clayton BD14 6JX
☎ 01274 880047
Moorland course, difficult in windy conditions.
9 holes, 5407yds, Par 68, SSS 67.
Club membership 350.
Visitors may not play before 4pm on Sun.
Societies apply in writing to the Secretary or Captain.
Green Fees not confirmed.
Facilities
Location 2.5m SW of city centre on A647

Hotel ★★★ 64% Novotel, Merrydale Rd, BRADFORD ☎ 01274 683683 127

East Bierley South View Rd, East Bierley BD4 6PP
☎ 01274 681023
Hilly moorland course with narrow fairways. Two par 3 holes over 200 yds.
9 holes, 4700yds, Par 64, SSS 63.
Club membership 300.
Visitors restricted Sat (am), Sun & Mon evening. Must contact in advance.
Societies must apply in writing.
Green Fees £12 per day (£15 weekends & bank holidays).
Facilities
Location 4m SE of city centre off A650

Hotel ★★★ 64% Novotel, Merrydale Rd, BRADFORD ☎ 01274 683683 127

Headley Headley Ln, Thornton BD13 3LX
☎ 01274 833481 Fax 01274 833481
Hilly moorland course, short but very testing, windy, fine views.
9 holes, 5140yds, Par 66, SSS 64, Course record 61.
Club membership 300.
Visitors must contact in advance, may not play weekends & bank holidays.
Societies must contact in advance.
Green Fees £15 per day/round.
Facilities
Location 4m W of city centre off B6145 at Thornton

Hotel ★★ 68% Park Drive Hotel, 12 Park Dr, BRADFORD ☎ 01274 480194 11

Phoenix Park Phoenix Park, Thornbury BD3 7AT
☎ 01274 667573
Very short, tight, moorland course, rather testing.
9 holes, 2491yds, Par 66, SSS 64, Course record 66.
Club membership 260.
Visitors restricted weekends.
Societies must apply in advance.
Green Fees not confirmed.
Facilities
Location E side of city centre on A647

Hotel ★★ 68% Park Drive Hotel, 12 Park Dr, BRADFORD ☎ 01274 480194 11

Queensbury Brighouse Rd, Queensbury BD13 1QF
☎ 01274 882155 & 816864
Undulating woodland/parkland course. Course currently being reconfigured.
9 holes, 5024yds, Par 66, SSS 65, Course record 63.
Club membership 380.
Visitors preferable to telephone in advance, restricted at weekends.
Societies apply in writing.
Green Fees £15 (£30 weekends & bank holidays).
Prof Geoff Howard
Facilities by prior arrangement
Location 4m from Bradford on A647

Hotel ★★ 68% Park Drive Hotel, 12 Park Dr, BRADFORD ☎ 01274 480194 11

South Bradford Pearson Rd, Odsal BD6 1BH
☎ 01274 679195
Hilly course with good greens, trees and ditches. Interesting short 2nd hole (par 3) 200 yds, well-bunkered and played from an elevated tee.
9 holes, 6068yds, Par 70, SSS 68, Course record 65.
Club membership 300.
Visitors must contact professional in advance. Weekends contact for availability. Tuesday Ladies Day.
Societies must apply in writing to the secretary.
Green Fees £14 per day (£22 weekends if available).
Prof Paul Cooke
Facilities
Location 2m S of city centre off A638

Hotel ★★★ 64% Novotel, Merrydale Rd, BRADFORD ☎ 01274 683683 127

West Bowling Newall Hall, Rooley Ln BD5 8LB
☎ 01274 393207 (office) & 728036 (pro)
Fax 01274 393207
Undulating, tree-lined parkland course. Testing hole: 'the Coffin' short par 3, very narrow.
18 holes, 5763yds, Par 68, SSS 67.
Club membership 500.
Visitors must contact in advance, weekend very limited.
Societies must apply in writing.
Green Fees £20 per round (£30 weekends & bank holidays).
Prof Ian A Marshall
Facilities
& Leisure snooker.
Location Corner of M606 & A638 (east)

Hotel ★★★★ 64% Cedar Court Hotel Bradford, Mayo Av, Off Pooley Ln, BRADFORD ☎ 01274 406606 & 406601 Fax 01274 406600 127

West Bradford Chellow Grange Rd BD9 6NP
☎ 01274 542767
Parkland course, windy, especially 3rd, 4th, 5th and 6th holes. Hilly but not hard.
18 holes, 5741yds, Par 69, SSS 68.
Club membership 440.

Visitors restricted Sat. Tuesday is Ladies day, can play if available, advisable to telephone 01274 542102 to reserve a time.
Societies must apply in writing.
Green Fees £18 per day/round.
Prof Nigel M Barber
Designer N
Facilities ⊗ by prior arrangement by prior arrangement
Location W side of city centre off B6144

Hotel ★★★ 72% Marriott Hollins Hall Hotel and Country Club, Hollins Hill, Baildon, SHIPLEY ☎ 01274 530053 122

BRIGHOUSE Map 07 SE12

Willow Valley Golf & Country Club Highmoor Ln, Clifton HD6 4JB ☎ 01274 878624 Fax 01274 852805
A championship length 18-hole course offering a unique golfing experience, featuring island greens, shaped fairways and bunkers, and multiple teeing areas. The 9-hole course offers an exciting challenge to less experienced golfers.
South: 18 holes, 6496yds, Par 72, SSS 69.
North: 9 holes, 4078yds, Par 60, SSS 60.
Club membership 210.

Visitors tee times may be booked by phone on payment of green fee by credit/debit card.
Societies telephone in advence for availability and booking form.
Green Fees South: £35 per day; £20 per 18 holes (£40/£24 weekends and bank holidays). North: £10 for 18 holes; £6 per 9 holes (£12/£6.50 weekends & bank holidays).
Cards
Prof Julian Haworth
Designer Jonathan Gaunt
Facilities ⊗
Location Junct 25 of M62 follow A644 towards Brighouse, at small rdbt turn right, course is 2m on right

Hotel ★★ 70% Healds Hall Hotel, Leeds Rd, Liversedge, DEWSBURY ☎ 01924 409112 25

CLECKHEATON Map 08 SE12

Cleckheaton & District Bradford Rd BD19 6BU
☎ 01274 851266 Fax 01274 871382
Parkland course with gentle hills.
18 holes, 5769yds, Par 71, SSS 68.
Club membership 550.

Visitors parties must arrange in advance, not weekends.
Societies weekdays only; must contact in advance.
Green Fees £26 per day; £24 per round.
Prof Mike Ingham
Facilities
Location 1.5m NW on A638 junc 26 M62

Hotel ★★★ 65% Gomersal Park Hotel, Moor Ln, GOMERSAL ☎ 01274 869386 52

DEWSBURY Map 08 SE22

Hanging Heaton White Cross Rd WF12 7DT
☎ 01924 461606 Fax 01924 430100
Arable land course, easy walking, fine views. Testing 4th hole (par 3).
9 holes, 5400mtrs, Par 69, SSS 67.
Club membership 550.

Visitors must play with member at weekends & bank holidays. Must contact in advance.
Societies must telephone in advance.
Green Fees £12 per day.
Prof S Hartley
Facilities ⊗
Location 0.75m NE off A653

Hotel ★★ 70% Healds Hall Hotel, Leeds Rd, Liversedge, DEWSBURY ☎ 01924 409112 25

ELLAND Map 07 SE12

Elland Hammerstones, Leach Ln HX5 0TA
☎ 01422 372505 & 374886 (pro)
Parkland course.
9 holes, 2815yds, Par 66, SSS 66, Course record 64.
Club membership 450.

Visitors welcome.
Societies must contact in writing.
Green Fees £14 per day/round (£25 weekends & bank holidays).
Prof N Krzywicki
Facilities ⊗
Location 1m SW

Hotel ★★ 70% Rock Inn Hotel & Churchills, Holywell Green, HALIFAX ☎ 01422 379721 18

FENAY BRIDGE Map 08 SE11

Woodsome Hall HD8 0LQ
☎ 01484 602739 Fax 01484 608260
A parkland course with good views and an historic clubhouse.
18 holes, 5807yds, Par 70, SSS 68.
Club membership 800.

Visitors must contact in advance. Jacket and tie required in all rooms.
Societies must apply in writing.
Green Fees £35 per day; £27.50 per round (£40/£35 weekends & bank holidays).
Prof M Higginbotton
Facilities ⊗
Location 1.5m SW off A629

Hotel ★★★ 69% Bagden Hall, Wakefield Rd, Scissett, HUDDERSFIELD ☎ 01484 865330 17

A comprehensive list of driving ranges is given at the back of this guide. See page 479

GARFORTH Map 08 SE43

Garforth LS25 2DS ☎ 0113 286 2021
Parkland course with fine views, easy walking.
18 holes, 6005yds, Par 69, SSS 69.
Club membership 500.
Visitors must contact in advance and have handicap certificate. With member only weekends & bank holidays.
Societies must apply in advance.
Green Fees not confirmed.
Facilities
Location 1m N

Hotel B Hilton National Leeds/Garforth, Wakefield Rd, GARFORTH
☎ 0113 286 6556 144

GUISELEY Map 08 SE14

Bradford (Hawksworth) Hawksworth Ln LS20 8NP
☎ 01943 875570 873719 (Pro) Fax 01943 875570
Moorland course with eight par 4 holes of 360 yds or more. The course is a venue for county championship events.
18 holes, 6259yds, Par 71, SSS 71, Course record 66.
Club membership 600.
Visitors must have a handicap certificate and contact in advance. May not play Sat.
Societies make prior arrangements with manager.
Green Fees £28 per day; £23 per round (£35/£28 weekends and bank holidays).
Prof Sydney Weldon
Designer W H Fowler
Facilities
Location SW side of town centre off A6038

Hotel ★★★ 72% Marriott Hollins Hall Hotel and Country Club, Hollins Hill, Baildon, SHIPLEY
☎ 01274 530053 122

HALIFAX Map 07 SE02

Halifax Bob Hall, Union Ln, Ogden HX2 8XR
☎ 01422 244171 Fax 01422 241459
Hilly moorland course crossed by streams, natural hazards, and offering fine views. Testing 172-yd 17th (par3).
18 holes, 6037yds, Par 70, SSS 70, Course record 63.
Club membership 700.
Visitors contact professional for tee times, 01422 240047. Limited play weekend.
Societies contact manager for dates.
Green Fees £20 per day; £15 per round (£30/£20 weekends).
Prof Michael Allison
Designer A Herd/J Braid
Facilities
Location A629 Halifax/Keighley, 4 miles from Halifax

Hotel ★★★ 74% Holdsworth House Hotel, Holdsworth, HALIFAX
☎ 01422 240024 40

Lightcliffe Knowle Top Rd, Lightcliffe HX3 8SW
☎ 01422 202459
Heathland course.
9 holes, 5388yds, Par 68, SSS 68.
Club membership 545.
Visitors must be a member of a recognised golf club. May not play Sun morning/competition days.
Societies must contact 21 days in advance.
Green Fees £15 per day/round (£20 weekends).
Prof Robert Kershaw
Facilities
Location 3.5m E on A58

Hotel ★★★ 74% Holdsworth House Hotel, Holdsworth, HALIFAX
☎ 01422 240024 40

West End Paddock Ln, Highroad Well HX2 0NT
☎ 01422 341878
Semi-moorland course. Tree lined.
18 holes, 5951yds, Par 69, SSS 69, Course record 62.
Visitors contact in advance.
Societies must apply in writing to Secretary.
Green Fees £25 per day; £20 per round (£30/£25 weekends & bank holidays).
Prof David Rishworth
Facilities
& Leisure snooker.
Location W side of town centre off A646

Hotel ★★★ 74% Holdsworth House Hotel, Holdsworth, HALIFAX
☎ 01422 240024 40

HEBDEN BRIDGE Map 07 SD92

Hebden Bridge Mount Skip, Wadsworth HX7 8PH
☎ 01422 842896 & 842732
Moorland course with splendid views.
9 holes, 5242yds, Par 68, SSS 66, Course record 63.
Club membership 300.
Visitors weekends after 4pm only.
Societies apply in writing.
Green Fees £12 per day (£15 weekends).
Facilities
Location 1.5m E off A6033

Hotel ★★ 66% Hebden Lodge Hotel, 6-10 New Rd, HEBDEN BRIDGE
☎ 01422 845272 15

HOLYWELL GREEN Map 07 SE01

Halifax Bradley Hall HX4 9AN ☎ 01422 374108
Moorland/parkland course, tightened by recent tree planting, easy walking.
18 holes, 6213yds, Par 70, SSS 70, Course record 65.
Club membership 500.
Visitors contact in advance.
Societies must apply in writing.
Green Fees £20 per day (£30 weekends & bank holidays).
Prof Peter Wood
Facilities
Location S on A6112

Hotel ★★ 70% Rock Inn Hotel & Churchills, Holywell Green, HALIFAX
☎ 01422 379721 18

Entries with a shaded background identify courses that are considered to be particularly interesting

HUDDERSFIELD Map 07 SE11

Bagden Hall Hotel & Golf Course Wakefield Rd, Scissett HD8 9LE ☎ 01484 864839 Fax 01484 861001
Well maintained tree-lined course set in idyllic surroundings and offering a challenging test of golf for all levels of handicap. Lake guarded greens require pin-point accuracy.
9 holes, 3002yds, Par 56, SSS 55, Course record 60.
Club membership 150.
Visitors anytime.
Societies company day packages available, telephone Director of golf.
Green Fees £9 per 18 holes (£12 weekends).
Cards
Prof Ian Darren
Designer F O'Donnell/R Brathwaite
Facilities
Hotel ★★★ 69% Bagden Hall, Wakefield Rd, Scissett, HUDDERSFIELD ☎ 01484 865330 17

Bradley Park Off Bradley Rd HD2 1PZ ☎ 01484 223772 Fax 01484 451613
Parkland course, challenging with good mix of long and short holes. Also 14-bay floodlit driving range and 9-hole par 3 course, ideal for beginners. Superb views.
18 holes, 6284yds, Par 70, SSS 70, Course record 65.
Club membership 300.
Visitors may book by phone for weekends and bank holidays from the preceeding Thu.
Societies welcome midweek only, apply in writing to professional.
Green Fees £11 per round (£13 weekends & bank holidays).
Prof Parnell E Reilly
Facilities
& Leisure 9 hole par 3 course.
Location 2.5m from junct 25 of M62

Hotel ★★★ 66% The George Hotel, St George's Square, HUDDERSFIELD ☎ 01484 515444 60

Crosland Heath Felk Stile Rd, Crosland Heath HD4 7AF ☎ 01484 653216
Moorland course with fine views over valley.
18 holes, 5972yds, Par 70, SSS 70.
Club membership 350.
Visitors welcome, but advisable to check with professional.
Societies must telephone in advance.
Green Fees not confirmed.
Prof Chris Gaunt
Facilities
Location SW off A62

Hotel ★★★ 66% The George Hotel, St George's Square, HUDDERSFIELD ☎ 01484 515444 60

Huddersfield Fixby Hall, Lightridge Rd, Fixby HD2 2EP ☎ 01484 426203 Fax 01484 424623
A testing heathland course of championship standard laid out in 1891.
18 holes, 6432yds, Par 71, SSS 71, Course record 64.
Club membership 759.
Visitors must book tee times with professional.
Societies welcome Mon & Wed-Fri, prior arrangement required.
Green Fees £45 per day; £33 per round (£60/£45 weekends).
Prof Paul Carman
Facilities
Location 2m N off A641

Hotel ★★★ 66% The George Hotel, St George's Square, HUDDERSFIELD ☎ 01484 515444 60

Longley Park Maple St, Off Somerset Rd HD5 9AX ☎ 01484 422304
Lowland course, surrounded by mature woodland.
9 holes, 5269yds, Par 66, SSS 66, Course record 61.
Club membership 440.
Visitors by arrangement with professional, must have handicap certificate, restricted Thu & weekends. No catering Mon.
Societies must apply in writing to secretary.
Green Fees £13 per 18 holes weekdays (£16 bank holidays).
Prof John Ambler
Facilities
Location 0.5m SE of town centre off A629

Hotel ★★★ 66% The George Hotel, St George's Square, HUDDERSFIELD ☎ 01484 515444 60

ILKLEY Map 07 SE14

Ben Rhydding High Wood, Ben Rhydding LS29 8SB ☎ 01943 608759
Moorland/parkland course with splendid views over the Wharfe valley.
9 holes, 4711yds, Par 65, SSS 64, Course record 64.
Club membership 260.
Visitors contact in advance. May only play at weekend as guest of member.
Societies advance notice in writing. In view of limited resources requests considered by monthly committee meeting.
Green Fees £10 (£15 weekends & bank holidays).
Facilities
Location SE side of town

Hotel ★★★ 70% Rombalds Hotel & Restaurant, 11 West View, Wells Rd, ILKLEY ☎ 01943 603201 15

Ilkley Nesfield Rd, Myddleton LS29 0BE ☎ 01943 600214
This beautiful parkland course is situated in Wharfedale and the Wharfe is a hazard on each of the first seven holes. In fact, the 3rd is laid out entirely on an island in the middle of the river.
18 holes, 5953yds, Par 69, SSS 70, Course record 66.
Club membership 450.
Visitors advisable to contact in advance.
Societies apply in writing.
Green Fees £35 per day/round (£40 weekends & bank holidays).
Prof John L Hammond
Facilities
& Leisure fishing.
Location W side of town centre off A65

Hotel ★★★ 70% Rombalds Hotel & Restaurant, 11 West View, Wells Rd, ILKLEY ☎ 01943 603201 15

KEIGHLEY Map 07 SE04

Branshaw Branshaw Moor, Oakworth BD22 7ES
☎ 01535 643235 (sec) & 647441 (pro) Fax 01535 647441
Picturesque moorland course with fairly narrow fairways and good greens. Extensive views.
18 holes, 6000yds, Par 69, SSS 69, Course record 64.
Club membership 500.
Visitors welcome most times, restrictions at weekends advisable to ring.
Societies apply in writing to the secretary.
Green Fees £15 per day; £12 per round (£20/£15 weekends).
Prof Mark Tyler
Designer James Braid
Facilities
Location 2m SW on B6149

Hotel ★★ 66% Dalesgate Hotel, 406 Skipton Rd, Utley, KEIGHLEY ☎ 01535 664930 20

Keighley Howden Park, Utley BD20 6DH
☎ 01535 604778 Fax 01535 604778
Parkland course with good views down the Aire Valley.
18 holes, 6149yds, Par 69, SSS 70, Course record 64.
Club membership 600.
Visitors restricted Sat & Sun. Must contact in advance. No catering/bar Mondays, Ladies day on Tuesday.
Societies must apply in advance.
Green Fees not confirmed.
Prof Mike Bradley
Facilities
Location 1m NW of town centre off B6143

Hotel ★★ 66% Dalesgate Hotel, 406 Skipton Rd, Utley, KEIGHLEY ☎ 01535 664930 20

LEEDS Map 08 SE33

Brandon Holywell Ln, Shadwell LS17 8EZ
☎ 0113 273 7471
An 18-hole links type course enjoying varying degrees of rough, water and sand hazards.
18 holes, 4000yds, Par 68.
Visitors pay & play course booking not usually necessary.
Societies telephone or write in advance.
Green Fees not confirmed.
Facilities
Location From Leeds-Wetherby Rd turn left to Shadwell left again up Main St, right at Red Lion Pub

Hotel ★★★ 78% Haley's Hotel & Restaurant, Shire Oak Rd, Headingley, LEEDS ☎ 0113 278 4446 22 Annexe7

Cookridge Hall Golf & Country Club Cookridge Ln LS16 7NL ☎ 0113 2300641 Fax 0113 2857115
American-style course designed by Karl Litten. Expect plenty of water hazards, tees for all standards, and a drivable, yet testing, par 4 18th with an island green.
18 holes, 6779yds, Par 72, SSS 72.
Club membership 600.
Visitors no restrictions.
Societies telephone in advance.
Green Fees £25 per day; £15 per round (£18 per round weekends).
Cards
Prof Mark Pearson
Designer Karl Liiten
Facilities
& Leisure heated indoor swimming pool, sauna, solarium, gymnasium, golf academy,health & fitness club, physio.
Location On Otley Old Road, off A660, 3m N of Leeds

Hotel ★★★ 78% Haley's Hotel & Restaurant, Shire Oak Rd, Headingley, LEEDS ☎ 0113 278 4446 22 Annexe7

Gotts Park Armley Ridge Rd LS12 2QX ☎ 0113 231 1896
Municipal parkland course; hilly and windy with narrow fairways. Some very steep hills to some greens. A challenging course requiring accuracy rather than length from the tees.
18 holes, 4960yds, Par 65, SSS 64, Course record 63.
Club membership 300.
Visitors no restrictions.
Green Fees not confirmed.
Prof John F Simpson
Facilities (evenings)
Location 3m W of city centre off A647

Hotel ★★★★ 69% Queen's Hotel, City Square, LEEDS ☎ 0113 243 1323 190

Headingley Back Church Ln, Adel LS16 8DW
☎ 0113 267 9573 Fax 0113 281 7334
An undulating course with a wealth of natural features offering fine views from higher ground. Its most striking hazard is the famous ravine at the 18th. Leeds's oldest course, founded in 1892.
18 holes, 6298yds, Par 69, SSS 70, Course record 64.
Club membership 675.
Visitors must contact in advance, restricted at weekends.
Societies must telephone in advance and confirm in writing.
Green Fees £35 per day; £30 per round (£40 per day/round weekends & bank holidays).
Prof Steven Foster
Designer Dr Mackenzie
Facilities
Location 5.5m N of city centre off A660

Hotel B Forte Posthouse Bramhope, Leeds Rd, BRAMHOPE ☎ 0113 284 2911 124

Horsforth Layton Rise, Layton Rd, Horsforth LS18 5EX
☎ 0113 258 6819
Moorland/parkland course overlooking airport.
18 holes, 6243yds, Par 71, SSS 70.
Club membership 750.

Visitors restricted Sat & with member only Sun.
Societies must apply in writing.
Green Fees £24 per day; £20 per round (£30 weekends).
Prof Neil Bell
Facilities
Location 6.5m NW of city centre off A65

Hotel B Forte Posthouse Bramhope, Leeds Rd, BRAMHOPE ☎ 0113 284 2911 124

Leeds Elmete Ln LS8 2LJ ☎ 0113 265 8775
Parkland course with pleasant views.
18 holes, 6097yds, Par 69, SSS 69, Course record 63.
Club membership 600.
Visitors with member only weekends, yellow tees only. Must contact in advance.
Societies must apply in writing.
Green Fees not confirmed.
Prof Simon Longster
Facilities
Location 5m NE of city centre on A6120 off A58

Hotel ★★★ 78% Haley's Hotel & Restaurant, Shire Oak Rd, Headingley, LEEDS ☎ 0113 278 4446 22 Annexe7

Leeds Golf Centre Wike Ridge Ln, Shadwell LS17 9JW
☎ 0113 288 6000 Fax 0113 288 6185
Two courses - the 18-hole Wike Ridge, a traditional heathland course designed by Donald Steel. The sand-based greens are constructed to USGA specification and there are an excellent variety of holes with some very challenging Par 5's. The 12-hole Oaks is complemented by a floodlit driving range and other practice facilities. The course is the home of the Leeds Golf Academy.
Wike Ridge Course: 18 holes, 6482yds, Par 72, SSS 71.
Oaks: 12 holes, 1610yds, Par 36.
Club membership 500.
Visitors no restrictions, telephone booking advisable.
Societies tee reservation available in advance.
Green Fees Wike Ridge:£20 per day; £12.50 per 18 holes, £7.50 per 9 holes. (£15 per 18 holes wknds). Oaks:£5 per 12 holes..
Cards
Prof Neil Harvey
Designer Donald Steel
Facilities
Location 5m N,take A58 course on N side of Shadwell

Hotel ★★★ 78% Haley's Hotel & Restaurant, Shire Oak Rd, Headingley, LEEDS ☎ 0113 278 4446 22 Annexe7

Middleton Park Municipal Middleton Park, Middleton LS10 3TN ☎ 0113 270 0449 & 270 9506
Parkland course.
18 holes, 5263yds, Par 68, SSS 66.
Club membership 300.
Visitors may only use the club 6 times in one year.
Green Fees not confirmed.
Prof Jim Pape & Steve Shaw
Facilities
Location 3m S off A653

Hotel ★★★★ 69% Queen's Hotel, City Square, LEEDS ☎ 0113 243 1323 190

Moor Allerton Coal Rd, Wike LS17 7EA
☎ 0113 266 1154 Fax 0113 237 1124
The Moor Allerton Club, established in 1921, has 27 holes set in 220 acres of undulating parkland, with testing water hazards and magnificent views extending across the Vale of York. The Championship Course was designed by Robert Trent Jones, the famous American course architect, and provides a challenge to both high and low handicapped golfers.
Lakes Course: 18 holes, 6470yds, Par 71, SSS 72.
Blackmoor Course: 18 holes, 6673yds, Par 71, SSS 73.
High Course: 18 holes, 6841yds, Par 72, SSS 74.
Club membership 1200.
Visitors contact professional (0113 266 5209).
Societies must apply in advance.
Green Fees 27/36 holes £45, 18 holes £41 (£77/£66 Sat, no casual visitors Sun).
Prof Richard Lane
Designer Robert Trent Jones
Facilities
& Leisure hard tennis courts, sauna, crown green bowls, snooker table.
Location 5.5m N of city centre on A61

Hotel ★★★ 65% Harewood Arms Hotel, Harrogate Rd, HAREWOOD ☎ 0113 288 6566 13 Annexe11

Moortown Harrogate Rd, Alwoodley LS17 7DB
☎ 0113 268 6521 Fax 0113 268 0986
Championship course, tough but fair. Springy moorland turf, natural hazards of heather, gorse and streams, cunningly placed bunkers and immaculate greens. Original home of Ryder Cup in 1929.
18 holes, 6782yds, Par 72, SSS 73, Course record 66.
Club membership 566.
Visitors must contact in advance.
Societies apply in writing in advance.
Green Fees not confirmed.
Prof Bryon Hutchinson
Designer A McKenzie
Facilities
& Leisure practice area.
Location 6m N of city centre on A61

Hotel ★★★ 65% Harewood Arms Hotel, Harrogate Rd, HAREWOOD ☎ 0113 288 6566 13 Annexe11

Oulton Park Rothwell LS26 8EX ☎ 0113 282 3152
27-hole championship-length municipal course. Although municipal, a dress rule is applied. 16-bay driving range.
Main Course: 18 holes, 6450yds, Par 71, SSS 71, Course record 65.
Short Course: 9 holes, 3250yds, Par 35, SSS 35.
Club membership 450.
Visitors must apply 24hrs in advance.
Societies Mon-Fri. Must contact in advance.
Green Fees not confirmed.
Prof Stephen Gromett
Designer Dave Thomas
Facilities
& Leisure heated indoor swimming pool, squash, sauna, solarium, gymnasium.
Location Junc 30 on M62

Hotel ★★★★★ 70% Oulton Hall Hotel, Rothwell Ln, Oulton, LEEDS ☎ 0113 282 1000 152

Roundhay Park Ln LS8 2EJ ☎ 0113 266 2695
Attractive municipal parkland course, natural hazards, easy walking.
9 holes, 5223yds, Par 70, SSS 65, Course record 61.
Club membership 400.

Visitors must contact professional at all times.
Societies telephone or write to the professional.
Green Fees not confirmed.
Prof James Pape
Facilities
Location 4m NE of city centre off A58

Hotel ★★★ 78% Haley's Hotel & Restaurant, Shire Oak Rd, Headingley, LEEDS ☎ 0113 278 4446 22 Annexe7

Sand Moor Alwoodley Ln LS17 7DJ
☎ 0113 268 5180
A beautiful, undulating course overlooking Lord Harewood's estate and the Eccup Reservoir. The course is wooded with some holes adjacent to water. The 12th is perhaps the most difficult where the fairway falls away towards the reservoir.
18 holes, 6429yds, Par 71, SSS 71, Course record 63.
Club membership 553.

Visitors restricted weekends & bank holidays.
Societies must apply in advance.
Green Fees £38 per day; £30 per round (£40 per round Sun & bank holidays).
Prof Peter Tupling
Designer Dr A Mackenzie
Facilities
Location 5m N of city centre off A61

Hotel B Forte Posthouse Bramhope, Leeds Rd, BRAMHOPE ☎ 0113 284 2911 124

South Leeds Gipsy Ln, Beeston LS11 5TU
☎ 0113 277 1676 & 270 2598 (pro)
Parkland course, windy, hard walking, good views.
18 holes, 5769yds, Par 69, SSS 68, Course record 64.
Club membership 500.

Visitors welcome weekdays except competition time, may not play weekends.
Societies must apply in advance.
Green Fees £18 (£26 bank holidays).
Prof Mike Lewis
Facilities
Location 3m S of city centre off A653

Hotel ★★★★ 69% Queen's Hotel, City Square, LEEDS ☎ 0113 243 1323 190

Temple Newsam Temple-Newsam Rd LS15 0LN
☎ 0113 264 5624
Two parkland courses. Testing long 13th (563 yds) on second course.
Lord Irwin: 18 holes, 6460yds, Par 69, SSS 71.
Lady Dorothy: 18 holes, 6276yds, Par 70, SSS 70.
Club membership 520.

Visitors no restrictions.
Societies must apply in advance in writing.
Green Fees £7.50 per round (£9 weekends).
Prof Alan Swaine
Facilities
Location 3.5m E of city centre off A63

Hotel ★★★ 78% Haley's Hotel & Restaurant, Shire Oak Rd, Headingley, LEEDS ☎ 0113 278 4446 22 Annexe7

MARSDEN Map 07 SE01

Marsden Mount Rd, Hemplow HD7 6NN
☎ 01484 844253
Moorland course with good views, natural hazards, windy.
9 holes, 5702yds, Par 68, SSS 68, Course record 63.
Club membership 200.

Visitors must play with member at weekends.
Societies Mon-Fri; must contact in advance.
Green Fees £10 per day.
Prof Nick Krzywicki
Designer Dr McKenzie
Facilities
& Leisure hard tennis courts.
Location S side off A62

Hotel ★★★ 63% Briar Court Hotel, Halifax Rd, Birchencliffe, HUDDERSFIELD ☎ 01484 519902 48

MELTHAM Map 07 SE01

Meltham Thick Hollins Hall HD7 3DQ ☎ 01484 850227
Parkland course with good views. Testing 548 yd, 13th hole (par 5).
18 holes, 6379yds, Par 71, SSS 70, Course record 65.
Club membership 500.

Visitors may not play Sat & Wed (Ladies Day), desirable to contact professional in advance.
Societies must apply in writing.
Green Fees £20 per day (£25 weekends & bank holidays).
Prof Paul Davies
Designer Alex Herd
Facilities
Location SE side of village off B6107

Hotel ★★★ 66% The George Hotel, St George's Square, HUDDERSFIELD ☎ 01484 515444 60

MIRFIELD Map 08 SE21

Dewsbury District Sands Ln WF14 8HJ
☎ 01924 492399 & 496030 Fax 01924 492399
Heathland/parkland course with panoramic views and hard walking. Ponds in middle of 3rd fairway, left of 5th green and 17th green.
18 holes, 6360yds, Par 71, SSS 71.
Club membership 650.

Visitors weekends after 1pm, on non competition days. Telephone in advance.
Societies telephone bookings.
Green Fees £20 per day; £18 per round.
Prof Nigel P Hirst
Designer Old Tom Morris/ Peter Alliss
Facilities
Location 1m S off A644 ▶

Hotel ★★★ 66% The George Hotel, St George's Square, HUDDERSFIELD
☎ 01484 515444 60

MORLEY Map 08 SE22

Howley Hall Scotchman Ln LS27 0NX
☎ 01924 478417 & 473852 Fax 01924 478417
Parkland course with easy walking and good views.
18 holes, 6058yds, Par 71, SSS 69.
Club membership 700.

Visitors standard course only, may not play Sat. Handicap certificate required.
Societies contact for details.
Green Fees £25 per day; £21 per round (£30 day/round Sun & bank holidays).
Prof Gary Watkinson
Facilities
Location 1.5m S on B6123

Hotel ★★ 68% Alder House Hotel, Towngate Rd, Healey Ln, BATLEY
☎ 01924 444777 20

NORMANTON Map 08 SE32

Normanton Snydale Rd WF6 1PN
☎ 01924 892943 Fax 01924 220134
A pleasant, flat course with tight fairways in places and an internal out-of-bounds requiring accuracy.
9 holes, 5288yds, Par 66, SSS 66.
Club membership 400.

Visitors may not play on Sun.
Societies mid-week only, apply in writing or telephone.
Green Fees not confirmed.
Prof Ian Hunt
Facilities
Location 0.5m SE on B6133

Hotel ★★★ 66% Chasley Hotel, Queen St, WAKEFIELD
☎ 01924 372111 64

OSSETT Map 08 SE22

Low Laithes Parkmill Ln, Flushdyke WF5 9AP
☎ 01924 274667 & 266067 Fax 01924 266067
Testing parkland course.
18 holes, 6463yds, Par 72, SSS 71, Course record 65.
Club membership 600.

Visitors may not play before 9.30am and 12.30-1.30 weekdays and before 10am and 12-2 weekends/bank holidays.
Societies by prior arrangement.
Green Fees £23 per day; £19 per round (£32 day/round weekends & bank holidays).
Prof Paul Browning
Designer Dr Mackenzie
Facilities
Location Leave M1 at jct 40 then signposted on Dewsbury road 0.5m from M1

Hotel B Forte Posthouse Northampton/Rugby, CRICK
☎ 01788 822101 88

OTLEY Map 08 SE24

Otley Off West Busk Ln LS21 3NG
☎ 01943 465329 Fax 01943 850387
An expansive course with magnificent views across Wharfedale. It is well-wooded with streams crossing the fairway. The 4th is a fine hole which generally needs two woods to reach the plateau green. The 17th is a good short hole.
18 holes, 6225yds, Par 70, SSS 70, Course record 66.
Club membership 700.

Visitors telephone to check tee time. May not play Tue morning or Sat.
Societies telephone enquiries welcome, bookings in writing.
Green Fees £30 per 36 holes; £24 per 27 holes (£35/£24 weekends).
Prof Steven Tomkinson
Facilities by prior arrangement
Location 1.5m SW off A6038

Hotel B Forte Posthouse Bramhope, Leeds Rd, BRAMHOPE
☎ 0113 284 2911 124

OUTLANE Map 07 SE01

Outlane Slack Ln HD3 3YL
☎ 01422 311789 & 374762
Moorland course.
18 holes, 6015yds, Par 71, SSS 70, Course record 67.
Club membership 600.

Visitors telephone in advance, must be correctly equipped and attired. Limited play Sat, none Sun morning.
Societies apply in writing.
Green Fees £18 per round (£28 weekends & bank holidays). £12.50 per round Sun after 1.30pm.
Prof David Chapman
Facilities
Location S side of village off A640

Hotel ★★★ 69% Old Golf House Hotel, New Hey Rd, Outlane, HUDDERSFIELD
☎ 01422 379311 50

PONTEFRACT Map 08 SE42

Mid Yorkshire Havercroft Ln, Darrington WF8 3BP
☎ 01977 704522 Fax 01977 600823
An 18-hole championship-standard course opened in 1993, and widely considered to be one of the finest new courses in Yorkshire.
18 holes, 6500yds, Par 72, SSS 71, Course record 68.
Club membership 500.

Visitors tee times bookable by telephone, visitors after 12 noon at weekends.
Societies apply in writing to the secretary.
Green Fees £18 per round (£30 weekends).
Cards
Prof Alistair Cobbett
Designer Steve Marnoch
Facilities
Location On the A1, 0.5m south intersection of A1/M62

Hotel ★★★ 71% Wentbridge House Hotel, WENTBRIDGE
☎ 01977 620444 16 Annexe4

Pontefract & District Park Ln WF8 4QS
☎ 01977 792241 Fax 01977 792241
Undulating parkland course, some elevated tees.
18 holes, 6227yds, Par 72, SSS 70.
Club membership 800.

Visitors welcome except Wed & weekends, advisable to contact in advance.
Societies welcome except Wed & weekends.
Green Fees £25 per day/round (£32 weekends & bank holidays).
Prof Nick Newman
Facilities
Location 1.5m W on B6134

Hotel ★★★ 71% Wentbridge House Hotel, WENTBRIDGE
☎ 01977 620444 16 Annexe4

PUDSEY Map 08 SE23

Calverley Woodhall Ln LS28 5QY
☎ 0113 256 9244 Fax 0113 256 9244
Two parkland courses on top of a hill.The course was established 10 years ago and has a few water hazards and some bunkers.
18 holes, 5590yds, Par 68, SSS 67, Course record 64.
Club membership 510.

Visitors Advisable to book 18 hole course in advance and may not play Sun morning. 9 hole course. pay and play at all times.
Societies contact in writing or telephone.
Green Fees £12 (£17 weekends). 9 holes £6.
Prof Derek Johnson
Facilities by prior arrangement
Location Signposted Calverley from A647 Leeds/Bradford road

Hotel ★★ 68% Park Drive Hotel, 12 Park Dr, BRADFORD ☎ 01274 480194 11

Fulneck LS28 8NT ☎ 0113 256 5191
Picturesque parkland course.
9 holes, 5456yds, Par 66, SSS 67, Course record 65.
Club membership 250.

Visitors with member only weekends & bank holidays.
Societies must apply in writing.
Green Fees £14 per day/round.
Facilities by prior arrangement by prior arrangement
Location Pudsey, between Leeds/Bradford

Hotel ★★★ 64% Novotel, Merrydale Rd, BRADFORD
☎ 01274 683683 127

Woodhall Hills Calverley LS28 5UN ☎ 0113 255 4594
Meadowland course, prevailing SW winds, fairly hard walking. Testing holes: 8th, 377 yd (par 4); 14th, 206 yd (par 3).
18 holes, 6001yds, Par 70, SSS 69, Course record 63.
Club membership 570.

Visitors any day advise secretary/professional in advance.
Societies telephone/write in advance.
Green Fees £20.50 per day/round (£25.50 weekends & bank holidays).
Prof Warren Lockett
Facilities
Location 1m NW off A647

Hotel ★★ 68% Park Drive Hotel, 12 Park Dr, BRADFORD ☎ 01274 480194 11

RAWDON Map 08 SE23

Rawdon Golf & Lawn Tennis Club Buckstone Dr LS19 6BD ☎ 0113 250 6040
Undulating parkland course.
9 holes, 5980yds, Par 72, SSS 69.
Club membership 700.

Visitors must contact in advance & have handicap certificate. With member only at weekends.
Societies must contact in advance.
Green Fees not confirmed.
Prof Simon Toot
Facilities
& Leisure hard and grass tennis courts.
Location S side of town off A65

Hotel ★★★ 65% Apperley Manor, Apperley Ln, Apperley Bridge, BRADFORD
☎ 0113 250 5626 13

RIDDLESDEN Map 07 SE04

Riddlesden Howden Rough BD20 5QN ☎ 01535 602148
Undulating moorland course with prevailing west winds, some hard walking and beautiful views. Ten par 3 holes and spectacular 6th and 15th holes played over old quarry sites.
18 holes, 4295yds, Par 63, SSS 61.
Club membership 350.

Visitors restricted before 2pm weekends.
Societies apply by telephone or in writing.
Green Fees £10 per day/round (£15 weekends).
Facilities
Location 1m NW

Hotel ★★ 66% Dalesgate Hotel, 406 Skipton Rd, Utley, KEIGHLEY
☎ 01535 664930 20

SCARCROFT Map 08 SE34

Scarcroft Syke Ln LS14 3BQ ☎ 0113 289 2311
Undulating parkland course with prevailing west wind and easy walking.
18 holes, 6426yds, Par 71, SSS 69.
Club membership 667.

Visitors must contact in advance.
Societies must contact in advance.
Green Fees £32 per day; £26 per round (£40 per round weekends & bank holidays).
Prof Darren Tear
Designer Charles Mackenzie
Facilities
Location 0.5m N of village off A58

Hotel ★★★ 65% Harewood Arms Hotel, Harrogate Rd, HAREWOOD
☎ 0113 288 6566 13 Annexe11

SHIPLEY Map 07 SE13

Northcliffe High Bank Ln BD18 4LJ
☎ 01274 596731 Fax 01274 596731
Parkland course with magnificent views of moors. Testing 1st hole (18th green 100 feet below tee).
18 holes, 6104yds, Par 71, SSS 69, Course record 64.
Club membership 700.
Visitors no restrictions.
Societies book via secretary in advance, weekdays only.
Green Fees not confirmed.
Prof M Hillas
Designer James Braid
Facilities ⊗)Ⅲ ▙ ☕ ♀ ⚠ ⌂ ♈ ↘ ♂
Location 1.25m SW of Shipley, off A650

Hotel ★★★ 72% Marriott Hollins Hall Hotel and Country Club, Hollins Hill, Baildon, SHIPLEY
☎ 01274 530053 122 ⇨ ⚑

SILSDEN Map 07 SE04

Silsden High Brunthwaite BD20 0NH
☎ 01535 652998
Tight downland course which can be windy. Good views of the Aire Valley.
14 holes, 4870yds, Par 65, SSS 64, Course record 61.
Club membership 300.
Visitors may not play before 11am on Sun.
Societies must apply in advance.
Green Fees not confirmed.
Facilities ♀ ⚠
Location 1m E

Hotel ★★ 66% Dalesgate Hotel, 406 Skipton Rd, Utley, KEIGHLEY
☎ 01535 664930 20 ⇨ ⚑

SOWERBY Map 07 SE02

Ryburn The Shaw, Norland HX6 3QP
☎ 01422 831355
Moorland course, easy walking.
9 holes, 4984yds, Par 66, SSS 64, Course record 64.
Club membership 200.
Visitors must contact in advance.
Societies apply in writing.
Green Fees not confirmed.
Facilities ⊗)Ⅲ ▙ ☕ ♀ ⚠
Location 1m S of Sowerby Bridge off A58

Hotel ★★ 69% The Hobbit Hotel, Hob Ln, Norland, Sowerby Bridge, HALIFAX
☎ 01422 832202 17 ⇨ ⚑ Annexe5 ⇨ ⚑

TODMORDEN Map 07 SD92

Todmorden Rive Rocks, Cross Stone Rd OL14 8RD
☎ 01706 812986
Pleasant moorland course.
9 holes, 5382yds, Par 68, SSS 68, Course record 67.
Club membership 240.
Visitors restricted Thu & weekends. Advisable to contact in advance.
Societies must apply in writing.
Green Fees not confirmed.
Facilities ⊗ by prior arrangement)Ⅲ by prior arrangement ▙ ☕ ♀ ⚠
Location NE off A646

Hotel ★★★ 66% Scaitcliffe Hall, Burnley Rd, TODMORDEN
☎ 01706 818888 32 ⇨ ⚑

WAKEFIELD Map 08 SE32

City of Wakefield Lupset Park, Horbury Rd WF2 8QS
☎ 01924 360282
Parkland course.
18 holes, 6319yds, Par 72, SSS 70, Course record 67.
Club membership 600.
Visitors restricted weekends.
Societies must apply in advance to stewardess 01924 367242.
Green Fees £8.50 per round (£10.50 weekends & bank holidays).
Prof Roger Holland
Facilities ⊗)Ⅲ ▙ ☕ ♀ ⚠ ⌂ ♈ ♂
Location 1.5m W of city centre on A642

Hotel B Forte Posthouse Wakefield, Queen's Dr, Ossett, WAKEFIELD
☎ 01924 276388 99 ⇨ ⚑

Painthorpe House Painthorpe Ln, Painthorpe, Crigglestone WF4 3HE ☎ 01924 274527 & 255083
Fax 01924 252022
Undulating meadowland course, easy walking.
9 holes, 4544yds, Par 62, SSS 62, Course record 63.
Club membership 150.
Visitors pay and play Mon-Sat, after 2.30pm on Sun.
Societies must telephone in advance.
Green Fees not confirmed.
Facilities ⊗)Ⅲ ▙ ☕ ♀ ⚠
& Leisure bowling green.
Location 2m S off A636, 0.5m from jct 39 M1

Hotel B Forte Posthouse Wakefield, Queen's Dr, Ossett, WAKEFIELD
☎ 01924 276388 99 ⇨ ⚑

Wakefield Woodthorpe Ln, Sandal WF2 6JH
☎ 01924 258778 (sec) & 255380 (pro) Fax 01924 242752
A well-sheltered meadowland/heath course with easy walking and good views.
18 holes, 6613yds, Par 72, SSS 72, Course record 66.
Club membership 540.
Visitors contact must be made in advance. Visitors Wed, Thu and Fri only.
Societies must apply in writing.
Green Fees £27.50 per day; £22 per round (£30 weekends & bank holidays).
Prof Ian M Wright
Designer McKenzie
Facilities ⊗)Ⅲ ▙ ☕ ♀ ⚠ ⌂ ♂
Location 3m S off A61

Hotel B Forte Posthouse Wakefield, Queen's Dr, Ossett, WAKEFIELD
☎ 01924 276388 99 ⇨ ⚑

WETHERBY Map 08 SE44

Wetherby Linton Ln LS22 4JF
☎ 01937 580089 Fax 01937 581915
Parkland course with fine views.
18 holes, 6235yds, Par 71, SSS 70, Course record 66.
Club membership 650.

Visitors may not play Mon & Tues morning.
Societies apply in writing or telephone in advance.
Green Fees £30 per day; £25 per round (£36 per round/day weekends and bank holidays).
Prof D Padgett
Facilities
& Leisure putting green, practice area.
Location 1m W off A661

Hotel ★★★ 75% Wood Hall Hotel, Trip Ln, Linton, WETHERBY ☎ 01937 587271 37 Annexe6

CHANNEL ISLANDS

ALDERNEY

ALDERNEY Map 16

Alderney Route des Carrieres GY9 3YD ☎ 01481 822835
Undulating seaside course with sea on all sides and offering magnificent views from its high tees and greens. Course designed by Frank Pennink.
9 holes, 5006yds, Par 64, SSS 65, Course record 65.
Club membership 400.

Visitors may not play before 10am at weekends. Advisable to contact in advance.
Societies must contact in advance.
Green Fees not confirmed.
Facilities
Location 1m E of St Annes

Hotel ★★ 72% Inchalla Hotel, St Anne, ALDERNEY ☎ 01481 823220 9

GUERNSEY

L'ANCRESSE VALE Map 16

Royal Guernsey GY3 5BY
☎ 01481 46523 Fax 01481 43960
Not quite as old as its neighbour Royal Jersey, Royal Guernsey is a sporting course which was re-designed after World War II by Mackenzie Ross, who has many fine courses to his credit. It is a pleasant links, well-maintained, and administered by the States of Guernsey in the form of the States Tourist Committee. The 8th hole, a good par 4, requires an accurate second shot to the green set amongst the gorse and thick rough. The 18th, with lively views, needs a strong shot to reach the green well down below. The course is windy, with hard walking. There is a junior section.
18 holes, 6206yds, Par 70, SSS 70, Course record 64.
Club membership 934.

Visitors must have a handicap certificate; may not play on Thu, Sat afternoons & Sun.
Green Fees £34 per day/round.
Cards
Prof Norman Wood
Designer Mackenzie Ross
Facilities
Location 3m N of St Peter Port

Hotel ★★★★ 71% St Pierre Park Hotel, Rohais, ST PETER PORT ☎ 01481 728282 135

ST PETER PORT Map 16

St Pierre Park Golf Club Rohais GY1 1FD
☎ 01481 728282 Fax 01481 712041
Par 3 parkland course with delightful setting, with lakes, streams and many tricky holes.
9 holes, 2610yds, Par 54, SSS 50, Course record 52.
Club membership 200.

Visitors contact in advance.
Societies must contact in advance.
Green Fees not confirmed.
Designer Jacklin
Facilities
& Leisure hard tennis courts, heated indoor swimming pool, sauna, solarium, gymnasium.
Location 1m W off Rohais Rd

Hotel ★★★★ 71% St Pierre Park Hotel, Rohais, ST PETER PORT ☎ 01481 728282 135

JERSEY

GROUVILLE Map 16

Royal Jersey JE3 9BD ☎ 01534 854416
A seaside links, historic because of its age: its centenary was celebrated in 1978. It is also famous for the fact that Britain's greatest golfer, Harry Vardon, was born in a little cottage on the edge of the course and learned his golf here.
18 holes, 6059yds, Par 70, SSS 70, Course record 64.
Club membership 1364.

Visitors restricted to 10am-noon & 2pm-4pm.
Societies welcome Mon-Fri. Must apply in writing.
Green Fees not confirmed.
Prof Tommy Horton
Facilities
Location 4m E of St Helier off coast rd

Hotel ★★★ 67% Old Court House Hotel, GOREY ☎ 01534 854444 58

LA MOYE Map 16

La Moye La Route Orange JE3 8GQ
☎ 01534 43401 Fax 01534 47289
Seaside championship links course (venue for the Jersey Seniors Open) situated in an exposed position on the south western corner of the island overlooking St Ouens Bay. Offers spectacular views, two start points, full course all year - no temporary greens.
18 holes, 6664yds, Par 72, SSS 72, Course record 68.
Club membership 1300.

Visitors must contact course ranger in advance 01534 47166. Visitors may play after 2.30pm weekends and bank holidays.
Societies apply in writing.
Green Fees £40 per round (£45 weekends).
Cards
Prof Mike Deeley
Designer James Braid
Facilities
Location W side of village off A13

Hotel ★★★★ 75% The Atlantic Hotel, La Moye, ST BRELADE ☎ 01534 44101 50

ST CLEMENT Map 16

St Clement Jersey Recreation Grounds JE2 6PN
☎ 01534 21938
Very tight moorland course. Holes cross over fairways, impossible to play to scratch. Suitable for middle to high handicaps.
9 holes, 2244yds, Par 30.
Club membership 500.

Green Fees not confirmed.
Facilities
& Leisure hard tennis courts.
Location E side of St Helier on A5

Hotel ★★★★ Longueville Manor Hotel, ST SAVIOUR ☎ 01534 25501 32

ST OUEN Map 16

Les Mielles Golf & Country Club JE3 7PQ
☎ 01534 482787 Fax 01534 485414
Challenging American-style parkland course with bent grass greens, dwarf rye fairways and picturesque ponds situated in the Island's largest conservation area within St Ouen's Bay.
18 holes, 5633yds, Par 70, SSS 68, Course record 62.
Club membership 1500.

Visitors welcome all times, prior booking recommended.
Societies write in advance to avoid disappointment.
Green Fees not confirmed.
Prof Lee Elstone
Designer J Le Brun/R Whitehead
Facilities
Location Centre of St Ouen's Bay

Hotel ★★★ 67% Mermaid Hotel, ST PETER ☎ 01534 41255 68

ISLE OF MAN

CASTLETOWN Map 06 SC26

Castletown Golf Links Fort Island, Derbyhaven IM9 1VA
☎ 01624 822201 Fax 01624 824633
Set on the Langness Peninsula, this superb Championship course is surrounded on three sides by the sea, and holds many surprises from its Championship tees. The hotel offers many leisure facilities.
18 holes, 6750yds, Par 72, SSS 72, Course record 64.
Club membership 600.

Visitors contact in advance. Sat reserved for hotel residents.
Societies must telephone in advance.
Green Fees £25 per day (£30 weekends & bank holidays).
Cards
Prof Murray Crowe
Designer McKenzie Ross
Facilities
& Leisure heated indoor swimming pool, fishing, sauna, solarium.
Hotel ★★★ 67% Castletown Golf Links Hotel, Fort Island, CASTLETOWN
☎ 01624 822201 58

DOUGLAS Map 06 SC37

Douglas IM2 1AE ☎ 01624 675952
Hilly, parkland and moorland course under the control of Douglas Corporation.
18 holes, 6080yds, Par 69, SSS 68.
Club membership 430.

Visitors no restrictions.
Societies must apply in writing.
Green Fees not confirmed.
Prof K Parry
Facilities
Location 1m W off A1

Hotel ★★★ 71% The Empress Hotel, Central Promenade, DOUGLAS ☎ 01624 661155 102

Mount Murray Hotel & Country Club Mount Murray, Santon IM4 2HT ☎ 01624 661111 Fax 01624 611116
A challenging course with many natural features, lakes, streams etc. Five Par 5's, five Par 3's and the rest Par 4.
18 holes, 6664yds, Par 72, SSS 72.
Club membership 378.

Visitors must contact in advance. Visitors may not play before 9.30am weekends
Societies telephone in advance.
Green Fees £18 (£24 weekends).
Cards
Prof Andrew Dyson
Facilities
& Leisure hard tennis courts, heated indoor swimming pool, squash, sauna, solarium, gymnasium.
Location Located on main road 5m from Douglas towards airport

Hotel ★★★★ 69% Mount Murray Hotel & Country Club, Santon, DOUGLAS ☎ 01624 661111 90

ONCHAN Map 06 SC47

King Edward Bay Golf & Country Club Howstrake, Groudle Rd IM3 2JR ☎ 01624 672709
Club plays over King Edward Bay course. Hilly seaside links course with natural hazards and good views.
18 holes, 5485yds, Par 67, SSS 65, Course record 63.
Club membership 370.

Visitors must have a handicap certificate.
Societies must contact in advance.
Green Fees £10 per day (£14 weekends & bank holidays).
Prof Donald Jones
Designer Tom Morris
Facilities
Location E side of town off A11

Hotel ★★★ 67% Sefton Hotel, Harris Promenade, DOUGLAS ☎ 01624 626011 78

PEEL Map 06 SC28

Peel Rheast Ln IM5 1BG
☎ 01624 842227 Fax 01624 843456
Moorland course, with natural hazards and easy walking. Good views. 11th hole is a par 4, dog-leg.
18 holes, 5850yds, Par 69, SSS 68, Course record 64.
Club membership 856.

Visitors limited availability weekends.
Societies apply in writing.
Green Fees £15 per day (£20 weekends & bank holidays).
Prof Murray Crowe
Designer Robert Braide
Facilities
Location SE side of town centre on A1

Hotel ★★★ 71% The Empress Hotel, Central Promenade, DOUGLAS ☎ 01624 661155 102

PORT ERIN Map 06 SC16

Rowany Rowany Dr IM9 6LN
☎ 01624 834108 or 834072 Fax 01624 834108
Undulating seaside course with testing later holes.
18 holes, 5840yds, Par 70, SSS 69, Course record 66.
Club membership 550.

Visitors must contact in advance.
Societies telephone in advance.
Green Fees £11 per day (£16.50 weekends & bank holidays).
Designer G Lowe
Facilities
& Leisure 18 hole pitch & putt.
Location N side of village off A32

Hotel ★★★ 66% Cherry Orchard Hotel, Bridson St, PORT ERIN ☎ 01624 833811 31

PORT ST MARY Map 06 SC26

Port St Mary Kallow Point Rd
☎ 01624 834932
Slightly hilly course with beautiful scenic views over Port St Mary and the Irish Sea.
9 holes, 5418yds, Par 68, SSS 66, Course record 62.
Club membership 432.

Visitors anytime except between 8-10.30 weekends.
Societies contact for details.
Green Fees £12.
Designer George Duncan
Facilities
& Leisure hard tennis courts.
Hotel ★★★ 66% Cherry Orchard Hotel, Bridson St, PORT ERIN ☎ 01624 833811 31

RAMSEY Map 06 SC49

Ramsey Brookfield IM8 2AH ☎ 01624 812244 Fax 01624 812244
Parkland course, with easy walking. Windy. Good views. Testing holes: 1st, par 5; 18th, par 3.
18 holes, 5960yds, Par 70, SSS 69, Course record 64.
Club membership 1000.

Visitors contact in advance, visitors may not play before 10am weekdays.
Societies must apply in advance.
Green Fees not confirmed.
Prof Calum Wilson
Designer James Braid
Facilities ⊗ Ⅲ ℔ ☕ ♀ ⛰ ⌂ ✓
Location SW side of town

Hotel ★★★ 71% The Empress Hotel, Central Promenade, DOUGLAS
☎ 01624 661155 102 ⇌ ⛲

SCOTLAND

John Ingham writes: According to most historians, Scotland is the birthplace of golf, even though the Chinese, believe it or not, claim hit-and-walk originated in their country, back in the mists of time.

But it is now a sad truth that certain traditional, if old-fashioned courses in Scotland, are taking their position in world golf a little for granted - and they do so at their peril. In simple terms there are links which need, as a matter of some urgency, to be given a rest, notably St Andrews, the monument to the game, now unfairly exposed to a constant stream of golfing tourists, even allowing trollies over the famous 'umps and 'ollows once trod by Jones, Vardon, Tolley, Wethered - you name them.

But contrast St Andrews with the newly-built Loch Lomond which I've played, and like other visitors, was delighted at the privilege of being there. The whole place is immaculate, as indeed is my personal favourite, Gleneagles (King's and Queen's).

Scotland is dotted with superb golfing tests, some which do not require a bank loan prior to the green fee. I'm told to play Royal Dornoch, Machrihanish, Lundin Links, while I know Muirfield inside out as a golf reporter, I've never been put to the test of what Jack Nicklaus thinks is one of the finest, and one that is not hacked to death by nomads.

You can have terrific fun at Turnberry, although it has a couple of mundane opening holes. Royal Troon is a grand spot for an Open Championship, but I wonder how much joy it is in a gale. I know for a fact that Carnoustie can be a nightmare, but Ben Hogan loved it, even though there wasn't a decent hotel in sight, so he stayed private.

Golf Monthly, a magazine old established, ranks four Scottish courses in the top six in the UK. While I don't agree with them, and point out the editor is a Scot (!) it does indicate the colossal strength of Scotland as a place to go. But it has rivals aplenty....in other parts of this golfer's paradise.

SCOTLAND

The directory which follows has been divided into three geographical regions. Counties have not been shown against individual locations as recent legislation has created a number of smaller counties which will be unfamiliar to the visitor. The postal authorities have confirmed that it is no longer necessary to include a county name in addresses, provided a post code is shown. All locations appear in the atlas section at the end of this guide in their appropriate counties.

HIGHLANDS & ISLANDS

This region includes the counties of Aberdeen City, Aberdeenshire, Highland, Moray, Orkney, Shetland and Western Isles which reflect the recent national changes.

ABERDEEN Map 15 NJ90

Auchmill Bonnyview Rd, West Heatheryfold AB16 7FQ
☎ 01224 715214
This course is definitely not for beginners - the fairways are tree-lined and very tight on most holes. Three holes are quite hilly and although the remainder is flat there are nice views over Aberdeen. The course is not recommended for anyone over 22 handicap unless they have plenty of golf balls!
18 holes, 5123metres, Par 68, SSS 67, Course record 67. Club membership 300.
Visitors members have priority Sat & Wed for club competitions.
Societies apply in writing to Leisure and Recreation Dept, Aberdeen District Council.
Green Fees not confirmed.
Designer Neil Coles/Brian Hugget
Facilities ⊗ by prior arrangement ▥ by prior arrangement
Location Outskirts Aberdeen, A96 Aberdeen/Inverness

Hotel ★★★ 67% The Craighaar, Waterton Rd, Bankhead, ABERDEEN ☎ 01224 712275 55

Balnagask St Fitticks Rd AB11 3QT ☎ 01224 876407
Links course. Used by the Nigg Bay Club.
18 holes, 5986yds, Par 70, SSS 69.
Visitors no restrictions.
Societies apply to council tel 01224 276276.
Green Fees not confirmed.
Facilities ⊗
Location 2m E of city centre

Hotel ★★★ 69% Caledonian Thistle, 10 Union Ter, ABERDEEN ☎ 01224 640233 80

Deeside Golf Rd, Bieldside AB15 9DL
☎ 01224 869457 Fax 01224 869457
An interesting riverside course with several tree-lined fairways. A stream comes into play at 9 of the 18 holes on the main course.
18 holes, 5971yds, Par 71, SSS 69, Course record 63. Club membership 800.
Visitors must contact in advance.
Societies apply in writing.
Green Fees £25 per day (£30 weekends & bank holidays).
Prof Frank J Coutts
Facilities ⊗
Location 3m W of city centre off A93

Hotel ★★★★ 70% Ardoe House, Blairs, South Deeside Rd, ABERDEEN ☎ 01224 867355 71

Hazelhead Public Hazelhead AB1 8BD ☎ No telephone
A tree-lined course.
18 holes, 6595yds, Par 70, SSS 70.
Visitors no restrictions.
Societies must contact in advance.
Green Fees not confirmed.
Facilities
Location 4m W of city centre off A944

Hotel ★★★★ 70% Ardoe House, Blairs, South Deeside Rd, ABERDEEN ☎ 01224 867355 71

Kings Links AB24 1RZ ☎ 01224 632269
A typical links course with no tree lines and plenty of bunkers.The 14th hole is tricky - a long par 4 with a raised green and not much fairway round the green. The course is playable all year. Nearby there is a 6-hole course. The Bon Accord Club, Caledonian Club and Northern Club play over this course.
18 holes, 6384yds, Par 72, SSS 71.
Visitors contact starters box on 01224 632269 regarding booking of tee times.
Societies write to the Arts & Recreation Dept, St Nicholas House, Broad Street, Aberdeen.
Green Fees not confirmed.
Facilities
Location 0.75m NE of city centre

Hotel ★★★ 69% Caledonian Thistle, 10 Union Ter, ABERDEEN ☎ 01224 640233 80

Murcar Bridge of Don AB23 8BD
☎ 01224 704354 Fax 01224 704354
Seaside links course, prevailing SW wind, hard-walking. Testing 4th and 14th holes.
Murcar: 18 holes, 6287yds, Par 71, SSS 71, Course record 65. Strabathie: 9 holes, 2680yds, Par 35, SSS 35. Club membership 850.
Visitors must contact in advance.
Societies advance booking required.
Green Fees Murcar: £38 per day; £28 per round (£43 per day/round weekends). Strabathie: £17 per day; £12 per 18 holes (£22 weekends).
Cards
Prof Gary Forbes
Designer Archie Simpson
Facilities ⊗
Location 5m NE of city centre off A92

Hotel ★★★ 67% The Craighaar, Waterton Rd, Bankhead, ABERDEEN ☎ 01224 712275 55

Royal Aberdeen Links Rd, Balgownie, Bridge of Don AB23 8AT ☎ 01224 702571 Fax 01224 826591
Championship links course with undulating dunes. Windy, easy walking.
Balgownie Course: 18 holes, 6372yds, Par 71, SSS 71, Course record 63.

Silverburn Course: 18 holes, 4066yds, Par 64, SSS 60.
Club membership 500.
Visitors times for visitors 10-11.30 and 2-3.30pm weekdays, after 3.30pm weekends. Must contact in advance.
Societies apply in writing.
Green Fees not confirmed.
Cards
Prof Ronnie MacAskill
Designer Baird & Simpson
Facilities
Location 2.5m N of city centre off A92

Hotel ★★★ 69% Caledonian Thistle, 10 Union Ter, ABERDEEN ☎ 01224 640233 80

Westhill Westhill Heights, Westhill, Skene AB32 6RY
☎ 01224 742567
A highland course.
18 holes, 5921yds, Par 69, SSS 69, Course record 65.
Club membership 800.
Visitors must contact in advance.
Societies telephone in advance.
Green Fees not confirmed.
Prof Ronnie McDonald
Facilities
Location 6m NW of city centre off A944

Hotel ★★★ 66% Westhill Hotel, Westhill, ABERDEEN
☎ 01224 740388 37 Annexe13

ABOYNE — Map 15 NO59

Aboyne Formaston Park AB34 5HP
☎ 013398 86328 Fax 013398 87078
Beautiful parkland with outstanding views. Two lochs on course.
18 holes, 5975yds, Par 68, SSS 69, Course record 62.
Club membership 930.
Visitors no restrictions. Advisable to contact in advance.
Societies prior booking essential.
Green Fees not confirmed.
Prof Innes Wright
Facilities
Location E side of village, N of A93

Hotel ★★ 66% Birse Lodge Hotel, 20 Charleston Rd, ABOYNE ☎ 013398 86253 12

ALFORD — Map 15 NJ51

Alford Montgarrie Rd AB33 8AE
☎ 019755 62178 Fax 019755 62178
A flat parkland course in scenic countryside. Divided into sections by a road, a narrow-guage railway and a burn.
18 holes, 5483yds, Par 69, SSS 65, Course record 64.
Club membership 600.
Visitors advisable to contact in advance.
Societies telephone in advance.
Green Fees £19 per day; £13 per round (£27/£21 weekends).
Facilities
Location In the centre of the village on A944

Hotel ★★★ Kildrummy Castle Hotel, KILDRUMMY ☎ 019755 71288 16

ALNESS — Map 14 NH66

Alness Ardross Rd IV17 0QA ☎ 01349 883877
A short, but testing, parkland course with beautiful views over the Cromarty Firth and the Black Isle.
9 holes, 2606yds, Par 66, SSS 64.
Club membership 220.
Visitors telephone in advance for weekend play.
Societies must contact in advance.
Green Fees £8 per day (£10 weekends).
Facilities
& Leisure fishing.
Location 0.5m N off A9

Hotel ★★★ 68% Morangie House Hotel, Morangie Rd, TAIN ☎ 01862 892281 26

ARISAIG — Map 13 NM68

Traigh PH39 4NT ☎ 01687 450337
According to at least one newspaper Traigh is 'probably the most beautifully sited nine-hole golf course in the world'. Whether that is true or not, Traigh lies by the sea alongside sandy beaches with views to Skye and the Inner Hebrides. The feature of the course is a line of grassy hills, originally sand dunes, that rise to some 60 feet. The nine-hole course was completely redesigned in 1995.
9 holes, 2456yds, Par 68, SSS 65, Course record 67.
Club membership 125.
Visitors no restrictions.
Societies contact in advance.
Green Fees £12 per day.
Designer John Salvesen 1994
Facilities
Location 2m N A830

Hotel ★★ 66% Arisaig Hotel, ARISAIG
☎ 01687 450210 13

AUCHENBLAE — Map 15 NO77

Auchenblae AB30 1BU ☎ 01561 320678
Picturesque, small, undulating parkland course offering good views.
9 holes, 2174yds, Par 33, SSS 32, Course record 62.
Club membership 78.
Visitors restricted Wed & Fri evenings.
Societies must telephone in advance.
Green Fees not confirmed.
Facilities
Location 0.5m NE

Hotel ★★ 63% County Hotel & Leisure Club, Arduthie Rd, STONEHAVEN
☎ 01569 764386 14

BALLATER — Map 15 NO39

Ballater Victoria Rd AB35 5QX
☎ 013397 55567 Fax 013397 55057
Moorland course with testing long holes and beautiful scenery.
18 holes, 5638yds, Par 67, SSS 67, Course record 62.
Club membership 750.
Visitors must contact in advance.
Societies prior booking recommended. ▶

Green Fees £27 per day; £18 per round (£31/£21 weekends).
Cards
Prof Bill Yule
Facilities
& Leisure hard tennis courts, fishing, snooker.
Location W side of town

Hotel ★★★ 72% Darroch Learg Hotel, Braemar Rd, BALLATER ☎ 013397 55443 13 Annexe5

BANCHORY — Map 15 NO69

Banchory Kinneskie Rd AB31 5TA
☎ 01330 822365 Fax 01330 822491
Sheltered parkland course situated beside the River Dee, with easy walking and woodland scenery. 12th and 13th holes are testing. Course was reconstructed during 1996 and several new holes introduced.
18 holes, 5775yds, Par 69, SSS 68, Course record 60.
Club membership 975.
Visitors must contact in advance, telephone for details on 01330 822447
Societies must book in advance, no parties Tue & weekends.
Green Fees £26 per day, £19 per round (£26 per day/round weekends).
Prof David Naylor
Facilities
Location A93, 300 yds from W end of High St

Hotel ★★★ 74% Banchory Lodge Hotel, BANCHORY ☎ 01330 822625 22

BANFF — Map 15 NJ66

Duff House Royal The Barnyards AB45 3SX
☎ 01261 812062 Fax 01261 812224
Well-manicured flat parkland, bounded by woodlands and River Deveron. Well bunkered and renowned for its large, two-tier greens.
18 holes, 6161yds, Par 68, SSS 69, Course record 63.
Club membership 1000.
Visitors a handicap certificate is preferred. Some time restrictions.
Societies must apply in writing.
Green Fees £24 per day; £18 per round (£30/£25 weekends).
Cards
Prof Bob Strachan
Designer Dr McKenzie
Facilities
Location 0.5m S on A98

Hotel ★★★ 65% Banff Springs Hotel, Golden Knowes Rd, BANFF ☎ 01261 812881 31

BOAT OF GARTEN — Map 14 NH91

Boat of Garten PH24 3BQ
☎ 01479 831282 Fax 01479 831523
This parkland course was cut out from a silver birch forest though the fairways are adequately wide. There are natural hazards of broom and heather, good views and walking is easy. A round provides great variety.
18 holes, 5866yds, Par 69, SSS 69, Course record 64.
Club membership 600.
Visitors must contact in advance. Handicap certificate required.
Societies must telephone in advance.
Green Fees £26 per day; £21 per round (£31/£26 weekends).
Cards
Designer James Braid
Facilities
& Leisure hard tennis courts.
Location E side of village

Hotel ★★★ 65% Boat Hotel, BOAT OF GARTEN ☎ 01479 831258 32

BONAR BRIDGE — Map 14 NH69

Bonar Bridge-Ardgay Migdale Rd IV24 3EJ
☎ 01863 766375 Fax 01863 766738
Wooded moorland course with picturesque views of hills and loch.
9 holes, 5284yds, Par 68, SSS 67.
Club membership 250.

Visitors no restrictions.
Societies apply in writing.
Green Fees £10 per day.
Facilities
Location 0.5m E

Hotel ★★ 68% Dornoch Castle Hotel, Castle St, DORNOCH
☎ 01862 810216 4 Annexe13

BRAEMAR — Map 15 NO19

Braemar Cluniebank Rd AB35 5XX
☎ 013397 41618
Flat course, set amid beautiful countryside on Royal Deeside, with River Clunie running through several holes. The 2nd hole is one of the most testing in the area.
18 holes, 5000yds, Par 65, SSS 64, Course record 59.
Club membership 450.

Visitors are advised to book 24 hours in advance to play at weekends. Tee reserved until 12.30 on Sat for members only.
Societies must contact secretary in advance 01224 704471.
Green Fees £18 per day; £13 per round (£21/£16 weekends).
Designer Joe Anderson
Facilities
Location 0.5m S

Hotel ★★★ 68% Invercauld Arms, BRAEMAR
☎ 013397 41605 68

BRORA — Map 14 NC90

Brora Golf Rd KW9 6QS
☎ 01408 621417 Fax 01408 622157
Typical seaside links with little rough and fine views. Some testing holes.
18 holes, 6110yds, Par 69, SSS 69, Course record 61.
Club membership 704.

Visitors advisable to book in advance May-Oct.
Societies advisable to book in advance.
Green Fees £25 per day; £20 per round.
Designer James Braid
Facilities
Location E side of village. Follow signs to Beach Car Park

Hotel ★★★ 65% The Links Hotel, Golf Rd, BRORA
☎ 01408 621225 23

BUCKIE — Map 15 NJ46

Buckpool Barhill Rd, Buckpool AB56 1DU
☎ 01542 832236 Fax 01542 832236
Links course with superlative view over Moray Firth, easy walking.
18 holes, 6257yds, Par 70, SSS 70, Course record 64.
Club membership 430.

Visitors apply in advance.
Societies apply in advance.
Green Fees £12 per day; £10 per round (£18/£12 weekends).

Facilities
& Leisure squash.
Location Off A98

Hotel ★★ 65% Mill House Hotel, Tynet, BUCKIE
01542 850233 15

Strathlene Strathlene Rd AB56 2DJ 01542 831798
Windy seaside links course with magnificent view. A special feature of the course is approach shots to raised greens (holes 4,5,6 & 13).
18 holes, 5980yds, Par 69, SSS 69, Course record 65.
Club membership 370.
Visitors booking essential at weekends.
Societies telephone for Mon-Fri & apply in writing for weekends.
Green Fees not confirmed.
Facilities
Location 3m E on A942

Hotel ★★ 65% Mill House Hotel, Tynet, BUCKIE
01542 850233 15
See advertisement on page 317.

CARRBRIDGE Map 14 NH92

Carrbridge Inverness Rd PH23 3AU 01479 841623
Short but challenging part-parkland, part-moorland course with magnificent views of the Cairngorms.
9 holes, 5402yds, Par 71, SSS 68, Course record 64.
Club membership 650.
Visitors during May-Sep, course not open to visitors after 5pm Wed & before 4pm Sun.
Societies small parties welcome, apply in writing.
Green Fees £11-£12 per day (£13 weekends). Evening (after 6.30pm) £6-£8.
Facilities
Location N side of village

Hotel ★★★ 68% Dalrachney Lodge Hotel, CARRBRIDGE 01479 841252 11

CRUDEN BAY Map 15 NK03

Cruden Bay Aulton Rd AB42 0NN
01779 812285 Fax 01779 812945
A typical links course which epitomizes the old fashioned style of rugged links golf. The drives require accuracy with bunkers and protecting greens, blind holes and undulating greens. The 10th provides a panoramic view of half the back nine down at beach level, and to the east can be seen the outline of the spectacular ruin of Slains Castle featured in Bram Stoker's Dracula. The figure eight design of the course is quite unusual.
Main Course: 18 holes, 6395yds, Par 70, SSS 72, Course record 65.
St Olaf Course: 9 holes, 2553yds, Par 64, SSS 65.
Club membership 1100.
Visitors welcome on weekdays, at weekends only when there are no competitions, advisable to contact for details.
Societies weekdays only telephone in advance.
Green Fees Main Course £50 per day; £35 per round (£45 per round weekends): St Olaf £15 per day; £10 per round (£20 per day/round weekends).
Cards
Prof Robbie Stewart
Designer Thomas Simpson
Facilities
Location SW side of village on A975

Hotel ★★ 67% Red House Hotel, Aulton Rd, CRUDEN BAY
01779 812215 6rm(5)

CULLEN Map 15 NJ56

Cullen The Links AB56 4UF 01542 840685
Interesting links on two levels with rocks and ravines offering some challenging holes. Spectacular scenery.
18 holes, 4610yds, Par 63, SSS 62, Course record 58.
Club membership 600.
Visitors no restrictions but during summer club medal matches given preference on Mon/Wed/Sat.
Societies advance applications advisable.
Green Fees £15 per day; £10 per round (£18/£13 weekends).
Designer Tom Morris/Charlie Neaves
Facilities by prior arrangement
Location 0.5m W off A98

Hotel ★★ 64% Cullen Bay Hotel, CULLEN
01542 840432 14
See advertisement on page 321.

DORNOCH Map 14 NH78

The Carnegie Club Skibo Castle IV25 3RQ
01862 894600 Fax 01862 894601
Set within the grounds of an enchanting castle, with the sea on three sides and the hills of Sutherland and Ross-shire all around, this splendid course enjoys a magnificent position. Although not long by modern standards, strong and fickle winds will test even the most experienced golfer. Excellent leisure facilities.
18 holes, 6403yds, Par 71, SSS 71.
Club membership 350.
Visitors weekdays only by written application to the secretary.
Green Fees £130 per round.
Cards
Prof William Milne
Designer J Sutherland/Donald Steel
Facilities
& Leisure hard tennis courts, heated indoor swimming pool, fishing, sauna, solarium, gymnasium.
Location Off A9 3m before Dornoch

Hotel ★★ 68% Dornoch Castle Hotel, Castle St, DORNOCH
01862 810216 4 Annexe13

Royal Dornoch Golf Rd IV25 3LW
01862 810219 Fax 01862 810792
Very challenging seaside championship links, designed by Tom Morris and John Sutherland.
Championship: 18 holes, 6514yds, Par 70, SSS 73, Course record 65.
Struie Course: 18 holes, 5438yds, Par 69, SSS 66.
Club membership 1518.

Visitors must have a handicap of 24 for gentlemen (ladies 35) on Championship Course. Must contact in advance and have a handicap certificate.
Societies must apply in advance.
Green Fees Championship course: £45 per round summer; £30 winter (£55/£36.50 weekends). Struie course £19 per day; £13 per round (£10/£7 winter).
Cards
Prof A Skinner
Designer Tom Morris
Facilities
& Leisure hard tennis courts, fishing.
Location E side of town

Hotel ★★ 68% Dornoch Castle Hotel, Castle St, DORNOCH
☎ 01862 810216 4 Annexe13

DUFFTOWN — Map 15 NJ33

Dufftown Methercluny, Tomintoul Rd AB55 4BS
☎ 01340 820325 Fax 01340 820325
A short and undulating inland course with good views. Highest hole over 1000 ft above sea level.
18 holes, 5308yds, Par 67, SSS 67, Course record 67.
Club membership 250.
Visitors tee reserved Tue & Wed 4.30-6.30 & Sun 7.30-9 & 12.30-2.
Societies apply in writing.
Green Fees not confirmed.
Facilities by prior arrangement by prior arrangement
Location 0.75m SW off B9009

Hotel ★★★ 75% Craigellachie Hotel, CRAIGELLACHIE
☎ 01340 881204 29

DURNESS — Map 14 NC46

Durness Balnakeil IV27 4PG
☎ 01971 511364 Fax 01971 511205
A 9-hole course set in tremendous scenery overlooking Balnakeil Bay. Part links and part inland with water hazards. Off alternative tees for second 9 holes giving surprising variety. Tremendous last hole played across the sea to the green over 100 yards away.
9 holes, 5555yds, Par 70, SSS 69, Course record 72.
Club membership 150.
Visitors restricted 10am-12.30 on Sun during Jun-Sep.
Societies must telephone in advance 01971 511364 (ex Sun).
Green Fees £14 per day.
Designer F Keith
Facilities
& Leisure fishing.
Location 1m W of village overlooking Balnakeil Bay

Guesthouse QQQ Port-Na-Con House, Loch Eribol, by Altnaharra, LAIRG
☎ 01971 511367 3

ELGIN — Map 15 NJ26

Elgin Hardhillock, Birnie Rd, New Elgin IV30 3SX
☎ 01343 542338 Fax 01343 542341
Possibly the finest inland course in the north of Scotland, with undulating greens and compact holes that demand the highest accuracy. There are thirteen par 4's and one par 5 hole on its parkland layout.
18 holes, 6163yds, Par 68, SSS 69.
Club membership 1000.
Visitors must contact in advance, weekend play only by prior arrangement.
Societies telephone secretary for details.
Green Fees £28 per day; £21 per round (£35/£27 weekends).
Prof Ian P Rodger
Designer John Macpherson
Facilities
Location 1m S on A941

Hotel ★★★ 74% Mansion House Hotel, The Haugh, ELGIN
☎ 01343 548811 22

Ellon Map 15 NJ93

McDonald Hospital Rd AB41 9AW
☎ 01358 720576 Fax 01358 720001
Tight, parkland course with streams and a pond.
18 holes, 5986yds, Par 70, SSS 69.
Club membership 710.

Visitors advisable to book in advance
Societies telephone in advance.
Green Fees £14 per round, £20 per day weekdays; (£16-£20/£20-£30 weekends).
Prof Ronnie Urquhart
Facilities
Location 0.25m N on A948

Hotel ★ 65% Meldrum Arms Hotel, The Square, OLDMELDRUM
☎ 01651 872238 7 Annexe4rm

Forres Map 14 NJ05

Forres Muiryshade IV36 0RD
☎ 01309 672250 Fax 01309 672250
An all-year parkland course laid on light, well-drained soil in wooded countryside. Walking is easy despite some hilly holes. A test for the best golfers.
18 holes, 6240yds, Par 70, SSS 70, Course record 64.
Club membership 1000.

Visitors welcome although club competitions take priority. Weekends may be restricted in summer.
Societies advised to telephone 2-3 weeks in advance.
Green Fees £25 per day; £18 per day (£27/£20 weekends).
Cards
Prof Sandy Aird
Designer James Braid/Willie Park
Facilities
Location SE side of town centre off B9010

Hotel ★★ 70% Ramnee Hotel, Victoria Rd, FORRES ☎ 01309 672410 20

Fort Augustus Map 14 NH30

Fort Augustus Markethill PH32 4AU ☎ 01320 366660
Moorland course, with narrow fairways and good views. Bordered by the tree-lined Caledonian Canal to the north and heather clad hills to the south.
9 holes, 5454yds, Par 67, SSS 67, Course record 67.
Club membership 170.

Visitors may not play Sat 1.30-4 & occasional Sun.
Societies telephone in advance.
Green Fees £10 per day.
Facilities
Location 1m SW on A82

Hotel ★★ 67% Lovat Arms Hotel, FORT AUGUSTUS ☎ 01320 366206 & 366204 Fax 01320 366677 23

Fortrose Map 14 NH75

Fortrose & Rosemarkie Ness Rd East IV10 8SE
☎ 01381 620529
Seaside links course, set on a peninsula with sea on three sides. Easy walking, good views. Designed by James Braid; the club was formed in 1888.
18 holes, 5858yds, Par 71, SSS 69, Course record 64.
Club membership 770.

Visitors restricted 8.45-10.15am & 1-2.15 then 4.45-6.30pm.
Societies must telephone in advance.
Green Fees £25 per day; £17 per round (£30/£23 weekends & bank holidays).
Cards
Designer James Braid
Facilities
Location E side of town centre

Fort William Map 14 NN17

Fort William Torlundy PH33 7SN ☎ 01397 704464
Spectacular moorland location looking onto the cliffs of Ben Nevis. Tees and greens are in excellent condition and major drainage improvements to the fairways were implemented in 1995.
18 holes, 6500yds, Par 72, SSS 71, Course record 67.
Club membership 420.

Visitors no restrictions.
Societies must contact in writing.
Green Fees £15 per day/round.
Designer Hamilton Stutt
Facilities
Location 3m NE on A82

Hotel ★★★ 70% Moorings Hotel, Banavie, FORT WILLIAM
☎ 01397 772797 21 Annexe3

Fraserburgh Map 15 NJ96

Fraserburgh AB43 8TL ☎ 01346 516616
Testing seaside course, natural links.
Corbie: 18 holes, 6278yds, Par 70, SSS 70, Course record 66.
Rosehill: 9 holes, 3398yds, Par 70, SSS 72.
Club membership 650.

Visitors no restrictions but advised to check availability.
Societies must contact in advance.
Green Fees Corbie: £14 (£18 weekends). Rosehill £10 (£12 weekends).
Designer James Braid
Facilities
Location 1m SE on B9033

Hotel ★★★ 70% Waterside Inn, Fraserburgh Rd, PETERHEAD
☎ 01779 471121 69 Annexe40

Gairloch Map 14 NG87

Gairloch IV21 2BE ☎ 01445 712407 Fax 01445 712605
Fine seaside links course running along Gairloch Sands with good views over the sea to Skye. In windy conditions each hole is affected.

9 holes, 4514yds, Par 62, SSS 64, Course record 61.
Club membership 250.

Visitors must be competent golfer and member of a recognised club.
Societies apply in writing to secretary.
Green Fees £13.50 per day; £49 per week.
Designer Capt Burgess
Facilities
Location 1m S on A832

Hotel ★★ 64% The Old Inn, Flowerdale, GAIRLOCH
01445 712006 14

GARMOUTH Map 15 NJ36

Garmouth & Kingston Spey St IV32 7NJ
01343 870388 Fax 01343 870388
Seaside course with several parkland holes and tidal waters. Naturally flat and suitable for the elderly.
18 holes, 5874yds, Par 68, SSS 68.
Club membership 500.

Visitors must contact in advance.
Societies advisable to phone in advance.
Green Fees £18 per day; £12 per round (£20/£15 weekends).
Designer George Smith
Facilities by prior arrangement by prior arrangement
& Leisure fishing.
Location In village on B9015

Hotel ★★★ 71% Mansefield House Hotel, Mayne Rd, ELGIN
01343 540883 21

GOLSPIE Map 14 NH89

Golspie Ferry Rd KW10 6ST
01408 633266 Fax 01408 633393
Founded in 1889, Golspie's seaside course offers easy walking and natural hazards including beach heather and whins. Spectacular scenery.
18 holes, 5890yds, Par 68, SSS 68, Course record 64.
Club membership 300.

Visitors contact in advance.
Societies contact in advance.
Green Fees £20 per day; £18 per round (£25 per day weekends & bank holidays).
Cards
Designer James Braid
Facilities
Location 0.5m S off A9

Hotel ★★ 62% Golf Links Hotel, Church St, GOLSPIE
01408 633408 9

GRANTOWN-ON-SPEY Map 14 NJ02

Grantown-on-Spey Golf Course Rd PH26 3HY
01479 872079 (Apr-Oct) Fax 01479 873725
Parkland and woodland course. Part easy walking, remainder hilly. The 7th to 13th really sorts out the golfers.
18 holes, 5710yds, Par 70, SSS 68, Course record 60.
Club membership 720.

Visitors advisable to contact in advance. No visitors before 10am weekends.
Societies clubhouse open Apr-Oct, apply in advance to secretary.
Green Fees £18 per day (£23 weekends) £10 evening round.
Cards
Prof Bill Mitchell
Designer A Brown/W Park/J Braid
Facilities by prior arrangement
Location NE side of town centre

Hotel ★★★ 67% Garth Hotel, Castle Rd, GRANTOWN-ON-SPEY
01479 872836 & 872162
Fax 01479 872116 17

HELMSDALE Map 14 ND01

Helmsdale Golf Rd KW8 6JA 01431 821650
Sheltered, undulating course following the line of the Helmsdale River.
9 holes, 1860yds, Par 62, SSS 61.
Club membership 90.

Visitors no restrictions.
Societies apply in writing.
Green Fees £12 per day; £6 per round; £30 per week.
Facilities
Location NW side of town on A896

Hotel ★★★ 65% The Links Hotel, Golf Rd, BRORA
01408 621225 23

HOPEMAN Map 15 NJ16

Hopeman IV30 2YA
01343 830578 Fax 01343 830152
Links-type course with beautiful views over the Moray Firth. The 12th hole, called the Priescach, is a short hole with a drop of 100 feet from tee to green. It can require anything from a wedge to a wood depending on the wind.
18 holes, 5531yds, Par 67, SSS 67, Course record 63.
Club membership 750.

Visitors must contact in advance, restricted tee times at weekend.
Societies contact in advance.
Green Fees £17 per day; £12 per round (£22/£17 weekends).
Facilities
Location E side of village off B9040

Hotel ★★★ 63% Stotfield Hotel, Stotfield Rd, LOSSIEMOUTH
01343 812011 45

HUNTLY Map 15 NJ53

Huntly Cooper Park AB54 4SH 01466 792643
A parkland course lying between the Rivers Deveron and Bogie.
18 holes, 5399yds, Par 67, SSS 66.
Club membership 850.

Visitors may not play before 8am.
Societies must contact the secretary.
Green Fees £13 per day (£20 weekends).
Facilities
Location N side of Huntly, turn off A96 at bypass roundabout

Hotel ★★★ 64% Castle Hotel, HUNTLY
01466 792696 19

INSCH Map 15 NJ62

Insch Golf Ter AB52 6JY 01464 820363
A challenging 18 hole course, a mixture of flat undulating parkland, with trees, stream and pond.
18 holes, 5500yds, Par 70, SSS 67.
Club membership 400.

Visitors restricted during club competitions and Tee times, ie Mon - Ladies night, Tue - Mens night, Wed - juniors, telephone clubhouse 01464 820363 for information.
Societies apply in writing or telephone, bookings accepted.
Green Fees £12 per day (£18 weekends).
Designer Greens of Scotland
Facilities
Location A96

Hotel ★★ 65% Lodge Hotel, OLD RAYNE
01464 851205 3 Annexe4

INVERALLOCHY Map 15 NK06

Inverallochy Whitelink AB43 5TL
01346 582000
Seaside links course with natural hazards, tricky par 3s and easy walking.
Jnverallochy Golf Club: 18 holes, 5237yds, Par 65, SSS 65, Course record 59.
Club membership 350.

Visitors restricted at weekends and competition days, contact for availability.
Societies apply in writing.
Green Fees not confirmed.
Facilities
Location E side of village off B9107

Hotel ★★★ 70% Waterside Inn, Fraserburgh Rd, PETERHEAD
01779 471121 69 Annexe40

INVERGORDON Map 14 NH76

Invergordon King George St IV18 0BD
01349 852715
Fairly easy but windy 18-hole parkland course, with woodland, wide fairways and good views over Cromarty Firth. Very good greens and a fair challenge, especially if the wind is from the west.
18 holes, 6030yds, Par 69, SSS 69, Course record 66.
Club membership 240.

Visitors visitors advised to avoid Tue & Thu 4.30-6, Mon & Wed 5-6 and Sat 8.30-10 & 1-2pm.
Societies must contact in advance.
Green Fees £20 per day; £15 per round.
Designer A Rae
Facilities
Location W side of town centre on B817

Hotel ★★★ 68% Morangie House Hotel, Morangie Rd, TAIN
01862 892281 26

INVERNESS Map 14 NH64

Inverness Culcabock IV2 3XQ
01463 239882 Fax 01463 239882
Fairly flat parkland course with burn running through it. Windy in winter. The 14th is one of the most difficult Par 4's in the north of Scotland.
18 holes, 6226yds, Par 69, SSS 70.
Club membership 1100.

Visitors restricted at weekends.
Societies must telephone in advance.
Green Fees not confirmed.
Prof Alistair P Thomson
Facilities
Hotel ★★★★ 69% Kingsmills Hotel, Culcabock Rd, INVERNESS
01463 237166 78 Annexe6

Loch Ness Fairways, Castle Heather IV1 2AA
01463 713335 Fax 01463 712695
Challenging parkland course with superb views over Inverness, the Beauly Firth and the Black Isle.
18 holes, 6772yds, Par 73, SSS 72, Course record 69.
Club membership 540.

Visitors please contact in advance, may play at weekends usually after noon.
Societies telephone for details.
Green Fees £20 per day (£25 weekends).
Cards
Prof Martin Piggot
Facilities
Location SW outskirts of Inverness, along new bypass

Hotel ★★ Dunain Park Hotel, INVERNESS
01463 230512 12rm(10)

Torvean Glenurquhart Rd IV3 6JN
01463 711434 (Starter) & 225651 (Secretary)
Fax 01463 225651
Municipal parkland course, easy walking, good views.
18 holes, 5784yds, Par 69, SSS 68, Course record 64.
Club membership 400.

Visitors must contact in advance.
Societies advance bookings through The Highland Council, Town House, Inverness.
Green Fees £12 per round (£14 weekends).
Designer Hamilton
Facilities
Location 1.5m SW on A82

Hotel ★★ Dunain Park Hotel, INVERNESS
☎ 01463 230512 12rm(10)

INVERURIE Map 15 NJ72

Inverurie Blackhall Rd AB51 5JB
☎ 01467 624080 Fax 01467 621051
Parkland course, part of which is through wooded area.
18 holes, 5711yds, Par 69, SSS 68, Course record 64.
Club membership 700.
Visitors book tee time through shop up to 24 hrs in advance 01467 620207.
Societies telephone administrator.
Green Fees £18 per day; £14 per round (£24/£18 weekends).
Facilities
Location W side of town off A96

Hotel ★★★ 69% Strathburn Hotel, Burghmuir Dr, INVERURIE
☎ 01467 624422 25

KEITH Map 15 NJ45

Keith Fife Park AB55 3DY ☎ 01542 882469
Parkland course, with natural hazards over first 9 holes. Testing 7th hole, 232 yds, par 3.
18 holes, 5767yds, Par 69, SSS 68.
Club membership 500.
Visitors no restrictions except competitions.
Societies by arrangement with outings secretary.
Green Fees not confirmed.
Facilities
Location NW side of town centre off A96

Hotel ★★★ 75% Craigellachie Hotel, CRAIGELLACHIE
☎ 01340 881204 29

KEMNAY Map 15 NJ71

Kemnay Monymusk Rd AB51 5RA
☎ 01467 642225 shop & 643746 office Fax 01467 643746
Undulating parkland course with superb views. A stream crosses four holes.
18 holes, 5903yds, Par 70, SSS 69, Course record 69.
Club membership 800.
Visitors telephone shop for booking.
Societies must telephone in advance.
Green Fees not confirmed.
Designer Greens of Scotland
Facilities
Location W side of village on B993

Hotel ★★★ 66% Westhill Hotel, Westhill, ABERDEEN
☎ 01224 740388 37 Annexe13

KINGUSSIE Map 14 NH70

Kingussie Gynack Rd PH21 1LR
☎ 01540 661600 Fax 01540 662066
Hilly upland course with natural hazards and magnificent views. Stands about 1000ft above sea level at its highest point, and the River Gynack comes into play on five holes.
18 holes, 5500yds, Par 66, SSS 68, Course record 63.
Club membership 800.
Visitors advisable to book in advance.
Societies must contact in advance.
Green Fees £18 per day; £15 per round (£22/£17 weekends).
Designer Vardon
Facilities
Location 0.25m N off A86

Hotel ★★ 75% The Scot House Hotel, Newtonmore Rd, KINGUSSIE
☎ 01540 661351 9

KINTORE Map 15 NJ71

Kintore Balbithan Rd AB51 0UR
☎ 01467 632631 Fax 01467 632631
The course covers a large area of ground from the Don Basin, near the clubhouse, to mature woodland at the far perimeter. One of the main attractions is the excellent drainage which results in very few days of lost play.
18 holes, 5997yds, Par 70, SSS 69, Course record 62.
Club membership 700.
Visitors during season booking system is in operation & slots for visitors are available. Other times can be booked 24 hours in advance.
Societies apply in writing or telephone.
Green Fees £15 per day; £11 per round (£20/£16 weekends).
Facilities
Location 1m from village centre on B977

Hotel ★★ 64% Torryburn Hotel, School Rd, KINTORE
☎ 01467 632269 9rm(8)

LEWIS, ISLE OF Map 13 NB43

STORNOWAY Map 13 NB43

Stornoway Lady Lever Park HS2 0XP ☎ 01851 702240
Undulating parkland course set in grounds of Lews Castle with fine views over the Minch to the mainland. A number of very testing par 3's and the 11th hole the 'Dardanelles' one of the most testing par 5's in Europe.
18 holes, 5252yds, Par 68, SSS 67, Course record 62.
Club membership 440.
Visitors no golf on Sun.
Societies apply in writing.
Green Fees £20 per day; £15 per round.
Facilities
Location 0.5m from town centre off A857

Hotel ★★★ 69% Cabarfeidh Hotel, STORNOWAY ☎ 01851 702604 46

LOCHCARRON Map 14 NG83

Lochcarron East End ☎ 01520 722257
Seaside links course with some parkland with an interesting 2nd hole. A short course but great accuracy is required. There are plans to extend to 18-holes on an additional 60 acres.
9 holes, 1750yds, SSS 60.
Club membership 150.
Visitors restricted Fri evening & Sat 2-5pm.
Societies welcome but restricted Fri evening & Sat 2-5pm.
Green Fees £20 per week; £10 per day; £7.50 per 18 holes.
Facilities
Location 1m E

Hotel ★★ 66% Lochcarron Hotel, Main St, LOCHCARRON ☎ 01520 722226 10rm(9)

LOSSIEMOUTH Map 15 NJ27

Moray IV31 6QS
☎ 01343 812018 Fax 01343 815102
Two fine Scottish Championship links courses, known as Old and New (Moray), and situated on the Moray Firth where the weather is unusually mild.
Old Course: 18 holes, 6643yds, Par 71, SSS 73, Course record 65.
New Course: 18 holes, 6005yds, Par 69, SSS 69, Course record 62.
Club membership 1550.
Visitors must contact in advance 01343 813330 Professional.
Societies must contact in advance.
Green Fees not confirmed.
Prof Alistair Thomson
Facilities
Location N side of town

Hotel ★★★ 63% Stotfield Hotel, Stotfield Rd, LOSSIEMOUTH ☎ 01343 812011 45

LYBSTER Map 15 ND23

Lybster Main St KW3 6AE
Picturesque, short heathland course, easy walking.
9 holes, 1896yds, Par 62, SSS 61, Course record 59.
Club membership 140.
Visitors no restrictions.
Societies must contact in advance.
Green Fees £7 per day.
Facilities
Location E side of village

Hotel ★★ 69% Portland Arms, LYBSTER ☎ 01593 721208 19

MACDUFF Map 15 NJ76

Royal Tarlair Buchan St AB44 1TA ☎ 01261 832897
Seaside clifftop course, can be windy. Testing 13th, 'Clivet' (par 3).
18 holes, 5866yds, Par 71, SSS 68, Course record 62.
Club membership 520.
Visitors no restrictions.
Societies apply in writing.
Green Fees £15 per day; £10 per round (£20/£13 weekends).
Facilities
Location 0.75m E off A98

Hotel ★★★ 65% Banff Springs Hotel, Golden Knowes Rd, BANFF ☎ 01261 812881 31

MUIR OF ORD Map 14 NH55

Muir of Ord Great North Rd IV6 7SX
☎ 01463 870825 Fax 01463 870825
Old established (1875), heathland course with tight fairways and easy walking. Testing 13th, 'Castle Hill' (par 3).
18 holes, 5557yds, Par 68, SSS 68, Course record 63.
Club membership 650.
Visitors may not play before 11am weekends without prior agreement and during club competitions.
Societies telephone followed by letter of confirmation.
Green Fees £14.50 per day; £12.50 per round (£18.50/£16.50 weekends). Weekly Mon-Fri £55.
Prof G Leggat
Designer James Braid
Facilities
& Leisure snooker & pool tables.
Location S side of village on A862

Hotel ★★★ 68% Priory Hotel, The Square, BEAULY ☎ 01463 782309 22

NAIRN Map 14 NH85

Nairn Seabank Rd IV12 4HB
☎ 01667 453208 Fax 01667 456328
Championship, seaside links founded in 1887 and created from a wilderness of heather and whin. Designed by Archie Simpson, old Tom Morris and James Braid. Opening holes stretch out along the shoreline with the turn for home at the 10th. Regularly chosen for national championships.

18 holes, 6452yds, Par 71, SSS 73, Course record 65.
Club membership 1150.
Visitors book in advance through secretary, may not play between 8-10.30 am & 12-2.30 pm (Fri & Sat).
Societies subject to availability bookings through secretary's office.
Green Fees £50 per round.
Cards
Prof Robin P Fyfe
Designer A Simpson/Old Tom Morris/James Braid
Facilities
Location 16m E of Inverness on A96

Hotel ★★★★ 67% Golf View Hotel & Leisure Club, Seabank Rd, NAIRN ☎ 01667 452301 47

Nairn Dunbar Lochloy Rd IV12 5AE
☎ 01667 452741 Fax 01667 456897
Links course with sea views and testing gorse-and whin-lined fairways. Testing hole: 'Long Peter' (527 yds).
18 holes, 6712yds, Par 72, SSS 73.
Club membership 700.
Visitors must contact in advance.
Societies must contact in advance.
Green Fees £33 per day; £25 per round (£40/£30 weekends).
Cards
Prof Brian Mason
Facilities
Location E side of town off A96

Hotel ★★ 64% Alton Burn Hotel, Alton Burn Rd, NAIRN ☎ 01667 452051 19rm(14 3) Annexe7

NETHY BRIDGE Map 14 NJ02

Abernethy PH25 3EB ☎ 01479 821305
Picturesque moorland course.
9 holes, 2551yds, Par 33, SSS 33.
Club membership 350.
Visitors contact in advance.
Societies must contact in advance.
Green Fees £12 per day (£16 weekends).
Facilities
Location N side of village on B970

Hotel ★★★ 70% Muckrach Lodge Hotel, DULNAIN BRIDGE ☎ 01479 851257 10 Annexe4

NEWBURGH ON YTHAN Map 15 NJ92

Newburgh on Ythan Newburgh Links AB41 0AW
☎ 01358 789058 Fax 01358 789956
This seaside course was founded in 1888 and is adjacent to a bird sanctuary. Testing 550-yd dog leg (par 5). Extended to 18-hole in 1995.
18 holes, 6162yds, Par 72, SSS 69, Course record 70.
Club membership 400.
Visitors must contact in advance.
Societies apply in advance.
Green Fees £15 per day (£20 weekends).
Facilities
Location E side of village on A975

Hotel ★★ 69% Udny Arms Hotel, Main St, NEWBURGH ☎ 01358 789444 26

NEWMACHAR Map 15 NJ81

Newmachar Swailend AB21 7UU
☎ 01651 863002 Fax 01651 863055
Hawkshill is a championship-standard parkland course designed by Dave Thomas and opened in 1991. Several lakes affect five of the holes and there are well developed birch and Scots pine trees. Swailend is a parkland course designed by Dave Thomas, opened in 1997.
Hawkshill Course: 18 holes, 6623yds, Par 72, SSS 74, Course record 67.
Swailend Course: 18 holes, 6388yds, Par 72, SSS 71.
Club membership 900.
Visitors must contact in advance & have handicap certificate for Hawkshill course.
Societies apply in writing.
Green Fees Hawkshill: £35 per day; £25 per round (£40/£30 weekends). Swailend: £25 per day; £15 per round (£30/£20 weekends).
Cards
Prof Peter Smith
Designer Dave Thomas/Peter Allis
Facilities
Location 2m N of Dyce, off A947

Hotel ★★★ 69% Strathburn Hotel, Burghmuir Dr, INVERURIE ☎ 01467 624422 25

NEWTONMORE Map 14 NN79

Newtonmore Golf Course Rd PH20 1AT
☎ 01540 673328 & 673878 Fax 01540 673878
Inland course beside the River Spey. Beautiful views and easy walking. Testing 17th hole (par 3).
18 holes, 6029yds, Par 70, SSS 69, Course record 68.
Club membership 420.
Visitors contact in advance.
Societies apply in writing to secretary.
Green Fees £16 per day; £13 per round (£21/£15 weekends).
Prof Robert Henderson
Facilities
Location E side of town off A9

Hotel ★★ 75% The Scot House Hotel, Newtonmore Rd, KINGUSSIE ☎ 01540 661351 9

OLDMELDRUM Map 15 NJ82

Old Meldrum Kirk Brae AB51 0DJ
☎ 01651 872648 Fax 01651 873555
Parkland course with tree-lined fairways and superb views. Challenging 196 yard, Par 3, 11th over two ponds to a green surrounded by bunkers.
18 holes, 5988yds, Par 70, SSS 69, Course record 66.
Club membership 700.
Visitors may not play during Club competitions.
Societies apply in writing to secretary
Green Fees £14 (£20 weekends).
Prof John Craven
Facilities
Location E side of village off A947

Hotel ★ 65% Meldrum Arms Hotel, The Square, OLDMELDRUM
☎ 01651 872238 7 Annexe4rm

ORKNEY Map 16

KIRKWALL Map 16 HY41

Orkney Grainbank KW15 1RB ☎ 01856 872457
Open parkland course with few hazards and superb views over Kirkwall and Islands.
18 holes, 5411yds, Par 70, SSS 67, Course record 65.
Club membership 402.

Visitors may not play on competition days.
Societies write or telephone if possible.
Green Fees not confirmed.
Facilities
Location 0.5m W off A965

Hotel ★★★ 64% Ayre Hotel, Ayre Rd, KIRKWALL
☎ 01856 873001 33

STROMNESS Map 16 HY20

Stromness KW16 3DW ☎ 01856 850772
Testing parkland/seaside course with easy walking. Beautiful holiday course with magnificent views of Scapa Flow.
18 holes, 4762yds, Par 65, SSS 63, Course record 61.
Club membership 275.

Visitors no restrictions except during major competitions.
Societies no restrictions.
Green Fees £12 per day/round.
Facilities
& Leisure hard tennis courts, bowling green.
Location S side of town centre off A965

Hotel ★★★ 64% Ayre Hotel, Ayre Rd, KIRKWALL
☎ 01856 873001 33

WESTRAY Map 16 HY44

Westray Rosevale KW17 2DH ☎ 01857 677373
Interesting, picturesque seaside course, easy walking.
9 holes, 2405yds, Par 33.
Club membership 60.

Visitors no restrictions.
Green Fees not confirmed.
Facilities
Location 1m NW of Pierowall off B9066

Hotel ★★★ 64% Ayre Hotel, Ayre Rd, KIRKWALL
☎ 01856 873001 33

PETERCULTER Map 15 NJ80

Peterculter Oldtown, Burnside Rd AB14 0LN
☎ 01224 734994 Fax 01224 735580
The course is a tight Par 68 (from Yellow tees) with a beautiful Par 2 2nd and two Par 5 holes in excess of 500 yards. Surrounded by wonderful scenery and bordered by the River Dee, there is a variety of birds, deer and foxes on the course, which also has superb views up the Dee Valley.
18 holes, 5947yds, Par 68, SSS 68, Course record 68.
Club membership 1035.

Visitors contact 3 days in advance, welcome after 2.30pm weekdays & 4pm weekends.
Societies contact up to 7 days in advance.
Green Fees not confirmed.
Prof Dean Vannet
Designer Greens of Scotland
Facilities
Location On A93

Hotel ★★★ 66% Westhill Hotel, Westhill, ABERDEEN
☎ 01224 740388 37 Annexe13

PETERHEAD Map 15 NK14

Peterhead Craigewan Links, Riverside Dr AB42 1LT
☎ 01779 472149 Fax 01779 480725
The Old Course is a natural links course bounded by the sea and the River Ugie. Varying conditions of play depending on wind and weather. The New Course is more of a parkland course.
Old Course: 18 holes, 6173yds, Par 70, SSS 71, Course record 64.
New Course: 9 holes, 2228yds, Par 31, SSS 31.
Club membership 800.

Visitors welcome any day apart from Saturdays, telephone for details.
Societies apply in writing, not Saturdays.
Green Fees Old Course: £22 per day; £16 per round (£27/£20 weekends). New Course: £9 per day/round.
Prof Donald Slicer
Designer W Park/ L Auchterconie/J Braid
Facilities by prior arrangement by prior arrangement
Location N side of town centre off A952

Hotel ★★★ 70% Waterside Inn, Fraserburgh Rd, PETERHEAD
☎ 01779 471121 69 Annexe40

PORTLETHEN Map 15 NO99

Portlethen Badentoy Rd AB12 4YA
☎ 01224 782575 & 781090 Fax 01224 781090
Set in pleasant parkland, this new course features mature trees and a stream which affects a number of holes.
18 holes, 6707yds, Par 72, SSS 72, Course record 63.
Club membership 1000.

Visitors may not play Sat. Contact in advance.
Societies apply in advance.
Green Fees £21 per day; £14 per round (£30/£21 weekends).

Cards
Prof Muriel Thomson
Designer Cameron Sinclair
Facilities
Location Off A90 S of Aberdeen

Hotel ★★ 63% County Hotel & Leisure Club, Arduthie Rd, STONEHAVEN ☎ 01569 764386 14

REAY — Map 14 NC96

Reay KW14 7RE ☎ 01847 811288
Picturesque seaside links with natural hazards, following the contours of Sandside Bay. Tight and testing.
18 holes, 5884yds, Par 69, SSS 68, Course record 64.
Club membership 325.
Visitors restricted competition days
Societies apply in writing.
Green Fees £15 per day/round.
Facilities
Location 0.5m E off A836

Guesthouse Tigh-na-Clash Guest House, Tigh-na-Clash, MELVICH ☎ 01641 531262 8rm(4)

ROTHES — Map 15 NJ24

Rothes Blackhall AB38 7AN ☎ 01340 831443
A hilly course opened in 1990 on an elevated site overlooking the remains of Rothes castle and the Spey valley. The 2nd fairway and most of the 3rd are sheltered by woodland. The ground alongside the 5th & 6th falls away steeply.
9 holes, 4972yds, Par 68, SSS 65.
Club membership 280.
Visitors course reserved Mon 5-6.30 & Tue 5-7.30.
Societies apply in writing to secretary.
Green Fees not confirmed.
Designer John Souter
Facilities
Location 9m S of Elgin on A941

Hotel ★★★ 76% Rothes Glen Hotel, ROTHES ☎ 01340 831254 16

SHETLAND — Map 16

LERWICK — Map 16 HU44

Shetland PO Box 18 ZE1 0YW ☎ 01595 840369
Challenging moorland course, hard walking. A burn runs the full length of the course and provides a natural hazard. Testing holes include the 3rd (par 4), 5th (par 4).
Dale Course: 18 holes, 5800yds, Par 68, SSS 68, Course record 68.
Club membership 450.
Visitors advisable to contact in advance.
Societies telephone in advance.
Green Fees £12 per day.
Facilities
Location 4m N on A970

Hotel ★★★ 66% Lerwick Hotel, 15 South Rd, LERWICK ☎ 01595 692166 35

WHALSAY, ISLAND OF — Map 16 HU56

Whalsay Skaw Taing ZE2 9AA
☎ 01806 566450 & 566481
The most northerly golf course in Britain, with a large part of it running round the coastline, offering spectacular holes in an exposed but highly scenic setting. There are no cut fairways as yet, these are defined by marker posts, with preferred lies in operation all year round.
18 holes, 6009yds, Par 70, SSS 68, Course record 65.
Club membership 134.
Visitors are advised to telephone, and on arrival on Whalsay call at the shop by the harbour.
Societies telephone in advance.
Green Fees £10 per day; £30 per week.
Facilities
Location N end of Island

Hotel ★★★ 67% Busta House Hotel, BRAE ☎ 01806 522506 20

SKYE, ISLE OF — Map 13 NG53

SCONSER — Map 13 NG53

Isle of Skye IV48 8TD ☎ 01478 650235
Seaside course, often windy, splendid views.
9 holes, 4798yds, Par 66, SSS 64, Course record 64.
Club membership 220.
Visitors contact in advance to avoid competition times.
Societies apply in advance.
Green Fees £12 per day/round.
Facilities
Location 0.5m E of village on A850

Hotel ★★ 72% Rosedale Hotel, PORTREE ☎ 01478 613131 20 Annexe3

SKEABOST BRIDGE — Map 13 NG44

Skeabost Skeabost House Hotel IV51 9NR
☎ 01470 532202
Short woodland and seaside course featuring some very tight fairways and greens.
9 holes, 3056yds, Par 62, SSS 60, Course record 58.
Club membership 80.
Visitors must contact in advance.
Societies contact in advance.
Green Fees not confirmed.
Designer John Stuart
Facilities
& Leisure fishing.
Hotel ★★★ 72% Cuillin Hills Hotel, PORTREE ☎ 01478 612003 16 Annexe9

SOUTH UIST, ISLE OF — Map 13 NF72

ASKERNISH — Map 13 NF72

Askernish Lochboisdale PA81 5SY ☎ No telephone
Golfers play on machair (hard-wearing short grass), close to the Atlantic shore.
9 holes, 5042yds, Par 68, SSS 67, Course record 64.
Club membership 15.

Visitors no restrictions.
Societies welcome.
Green Fees not confirmed.
Designer Tom Morris
Facilities
Location 5m NW of Lochboisdale off A865 via ferry

SPEY BAY Map 15 NJ36

Spey Bay IV32 7PJ ☎ 01343 820424
Seaside links course over gently undulating banks and well-drained ground. Good views along Moray coast. Driving range.
18 holes, 6092yds, Par 70, SSS 69, Course record 66.
Club membership 350.
Visitors telephone for details.
Societies book by telephone.
Green Fees £15 per day; £10 per round (£18/£13 weekends).
Cards
Prof Hamish MacDonald
Designer Ben Sayers
Facilities
& Leisure hard tennis courts.
Location 4.5m N of Fochabers on B9104

Hotel ★★ 65% Mill House Hotel, Tynet, BUCKIE ☎ 01542 850233 15

STONEHAVEN Map 15 NO88

Stonehaven Cowie AB39 3RH
☎ 01569 762124 Fax 01569 765973
Challenging meadowland course overlooking sea with three gullies and splendid views.
18 holes, 5103yds, Par 66, SSS 65, Course record 61.
Club membership 850.
Visitors prefer prior booking, may not play before 4pm Sat.
Societies telephone or fax in advance to W A Donald.
Green Fees £15 per day (£20 weekends).
Designer C Simpson
Facilities
Location 1m N off A92

Hotel ★★ 63% County Hotel & Leisure Club, Arduthie Rd, STONEHAVEN ☎ 01569 764386 14

STRATHPEFFER Map 14 NH45

Strathpeffer Spa IV14 9AS
☎ 01997 421219 & 421011 Fax 01997 421011
Upland course with many natural hazards (few sand bunkers), hard walking and fine views. Testing 3rd hole (par 3) across loch.
18 holes, 4792yds, Par 65, SSS 64, Course record 60.
Club membership 550.
Visitors advisable to contact in advance.
Societies apply in writing.
Green Fees £20 per day; £14 per round.
Cards
Designer Willie Park
Facilities
Location 0.25m N of village off A834

Hotel ★★ 70% Brunstane Lodge Hotel, Golf Rd, STRATHPEFFER ☎ 01997 421261 7rm(6)

TAIN Map 14 NH78

Tain Chapel Rd IV19 1PB
☎ 01862 892314 Fax 01862 892099
Heathland/links course with river affecting 3 holes; easy walking, fine views.
18 holes, 6311yds, Par 70, SSS 70, Course record 66.
Club membership 500.
Visitors no restrictions.
Societies must book in advance.
Green Fees £27 per 36 holes; £21 per round (£31/£25 weekends).
Cards
Designer Tom Morris
Facilities by prior arrangement
Location E side of town centre off B9174

Hotel ★★★ 68% Morangie House Hotel, Morangie Rd, TAIN ☎ 01862 892281 26

TARLAND Map 15 NJ40

Tarland Aberdeen Rd AB34 4TB
☎ 013398 81413
Difficult upland course, but easy walking. Some spectacular holes, mainly 4th (par 4) and 5th (par 3) and fine scenery.
9 holes, 5888yds, Par 67, SSS 68, Course record 65.
Club membership 350.
Visitors must contact in advance.
Societies must telephone in advance.
Green Fees £14 per day (£18 weekends).
Designer Tom Morris
Facilities
Location E side of village off B9119

Hotel ★★ 66% Birse Lodge Hotel, 20 Charleston Rd, ABOYNE ☎ 013398 86253 12

THURSO Map 15 ND16

Thurso Newlands of Geise KW14 7XF
☎ 01847 893807
Parkland course, windy, but with fine views of Dunnet Head and the Orkney Islands.
18 holes, 5828yds, Par 69, SSS 69, Course record 63.
Club membership 301.
Visitors no restrictions.
Societies contact in advance.
Green Fees £15 per day; £50 per week.
Facilities
Location 2m SW on B874

Hotel ★★ 67% Park Hotel, THURSO ☎ 01847 893251 11

TORPHINS Map 15 NJ60

Torphins Bog Rd AB31 4JU ☎ 013398 82115
Heathland/parkland course built on a hill with views of the Cairngorms.
9 holes, 4800yds, Par 64, SSS 64, Course record 63.
Club membership 380.
Visitors must contact in advance. Restricted on competition days (alternate Sat and Sun).
Societies apply in advance.

Green Fees £11 per day (£13 weekends).
Facilities
Location 0.25m W of village off A980

Hotel ★★★ 69% Tor-na-Coille Hotel, BANCHORY
01330 822242 23

TURRIFF Map 15 NJ74

Turriff Rosehall AB53 7HD
01888 562982 Fax 01888 568050
A well-maintained parkland course alongside the River Deveron in picturesque surroundings. 6th and 12th particularly challenging in a testing course.
18 holes, 6107yds, Par 70, SSS 69, Course record 67.
Club membership 894.
Visitors may not play before 10am weekends. Must contact in advance.
Societies apply in writing to the secretary.
Green Fees £20 per day; £16 per round (£27/£21 weekends).
Prof Robin Smith
Facilities
Location 1m W off B9024

Hotel ★★★ 65% Banff Springs Hotel, Golden Knowes Rd, BANFF
01261 812881 31

WICK Map 15 ND35

Wick Reiss KW1 4RW 01955 602726
Typical seaside links course, fairly flat, easy walking. 9 holes straight out and straight back. Normally breezy.
18 holes, 5976yds, Par 69, SSS 69, Course record 63.
Club membership 352.
Visitors no restrictions.
Societies apply in writing or telephone in advance.
Green Fees £15 per day.
Designer James Braid
Facilities
Location 3.5m N off A9

Hotel ★★ 63% Mackay's Hotel, Union St, WICK
01955 602323 26

CENTRAL SCOTLAND

This region includes the counties of Angus, Argyll & Bute, Clackmannanshire, City of Edinburgh, Dundee City, East Lothian, Falkirk, Fife, Inverclyde, Midlothian, Perthshire & Kinross, Stirling and West Lothian which reflect the recent national changes.

ABERDOUR Map 11 NT18

Aberdour Seaside Place KY3 0TX
01383 860080 Fax 01383 860050
Parkland course with lovely views over Firth of Forth.
18 holes, 5460yds, Par 67, SSS 66, Course record 63.
Club membership 800.
Visitors must contact in advance.
Societies telephone secretary in advance.
Green Fees not confirmed.
Prof Gordon McCallum
Facilities
Location S side of village

Hotel ★★ 68% Woodside Hotel, High St, ABERDOUR 01383 860328 20

ABERFELDY Map 14 NN84

Aberfeldy Taybridge Rd PH15 2BH 01887 820535
Founded in 1895, this flat, parkland course is situated by River Tay near the famous Wade Bridge and Black Watch Monument and enjoys some splendid scenery. The new layout will test the keen golfer.
18 holes, 5283yds, Par 68, SSS 66, Course record 67.
Club membership 333.
Visitors are advised to book in advance especially at weekends.
Societies must contact in advance.
Green Fees £22 per day; £14 per round (£25/£16 weekends).
Designer Soutars
Facilities
& Leisure fishing.
Location N side of town centre

Hotel ★★ 67% The Weem, Weem, ABERFELDY
01887 820381 12

ABERFOYLE Map 11 NN50

Aberfoyle Braeval FK8 3UY 01877 382493
Scenic heathland course with mountain views.
18 holes, 5210yds, Par 66, SSS 66.
Club membership 665.
Visitors may not tee off before 10.30am Sat & Sun.
Societies must contact in advance.
Green Fees £16 per day; £12 per round (£24 per day; £16 per round weekends).
Facilities
Location 1m E on A81

Hotel ★★★ 69% Forest Hills Hotel, Kinlochard, ABERFOYLE 01877 7277 17

ABERLADY Map 12 NT47

Kilspindie EH32 0QD
01875 870358 Fax 01875 870358
Seaside course, short but tight and well-bunkered. Testing holes: 2nd, 3rd, 4th and 7th.
18 holes, 5471yds, Par 69, SSS 66, Course record 62.
Club membership 750.
Visitors must contact in advance.
Societies contact secretary in advance.
Green Fees not confirmed.
Prof Graham J Sked
Facilities
Location W side of village off A198

Hotel ★★ 68% Kilspindie House Hotel, Main St, ABERLADY 01875 870682 26

Luffness New EH32 0QA
01620 843114 & 843336 Fax 01620 842933
Links course, National Final Qualifying Course for Open Championship.
18 holes, 6122yds, Par 69, SSS 70, Course record 62.
Club membership 700. ▶

Visitors must contact in advance but may not play at weekends & bank holidays.
Societies telephone for application form.
Green Fees £50 per day; £35 per round.
Designer Tom Morris
Facilities
Location 1m E on A198

Hotel ★★★ Greywalls Hotel, Muirfield, GULLANE
☎ 01620 842144 17 Annexe5

ALLOA Map 11 NS89

Alloa Schawpark, Sauchie FK10 3AX
☎ 01259 722745 & 724476
Undulating, wooded parkland course.
18 holes, 6229yds, Par 69, SSS 71, Course record 63.
Club membership 910.
Visitors 7 day booking system through professional.
Societies apply in writing.
Green Fees not confirmed.
Prof Bill Bennett
Designer James Braid
Facilities
Location 1.5m NE on A908

Hotel ★★★ 75% Gean House, Gean Park, Tullibody Rd, ALLOA
☎ 01259 219275 7

Braehead Cambus FK10 2NT ☎ 01259 725766
Attactive parkland course at the foot of the Ochil Hills, and offering spectacular views.
18 holes, 6086yds, Par 70, SSS 69, Course record 64.
Club membership 800.
Visitors advisable to telephone in advance.
Societies must contact the clubhouse manager in advance tel 01259 725766.
Green Fees £24.50 per day; £18.50 per round (£32.50/£24.50 weekends).
Cards
Prof Paul Brookes
Designer Robert Tait
Facilities
Location 1m W on A907

Hotel ★★★ 75% Gean House, Gean Park, Tullibody Rd, ALLOA
☎ 01259 219275 7

ALVA Map 11 NS89

Alva Beauclerc St FK12 5LD ☎ 01259 760431
A 9-hole course at the foot of the Ochil Hills which gives it its characteristic sloping fairways and fast greens.
9 holes, 2423yds, Par 66, SSS 64, Course record 62.
Club membership 318.
Visitors may not play during medal competitions or Thu evening (Ladies night).
Societies apply in writing or telephone in advance.
Green Fees £12 per day (£15 weekends).
Facilities
Location 7m from Stirling,A91 Stirling/St Andrews rd

Hotel ★★ 66% Harviestoun Country Inn, Dollar Rd, TILLICOULTRY ☎ 01259 752522 10

ALYTH Map 15 NO24

Alyth Pitcrocknie PH11 8HF
☎ 01828 632268 Fax 01828 633491
Windy, heathland course with easy walking.
18 holes, 6205yds, Par 71, SSS 71, Course record 65.
Club membership 1000.
Visitors advance booking advisable, handicap certificate required and dress etiquette must be observed.
Societies must telephone in advance.
Green Fees not confirmed.
Prof Tom Melville
Designer James Braid
Facilities
Location 1m E on B954

Hotel ★★ 62% Angus Hotel, 46 Wellmeadow, BLAIRGOWRIE ☎ 01250 872455 81

Strathmore Golf Centre Leroch PH11 8NZ
☎ 01828 633322 Fax 01828 633533
The Rannaleroch course is set on rolling parkland and heath with splendid views over Strathmore. The course is laid out in two loops of nine which both start and finish at the clubhouse. Among the challenging holes is the 480yard 5th with a 180yard carry over water from a high tee position (a cop out route available!).
Rannaleroch Course: 18 holes, 6454yds, Par 72, SSS 72, Course record 68.
Leitfie Links: 9 holes, 1719yds, Par 29, SSS 29.
Club membership 300.
Visitors no restrictions.
Societies phone enquiry recommended.
Green Fees Rannaleroch: £25 per day; £16 per round (£30/£20 weekends). Leitfie Links: £12 per day; £5 per 9 holes (£15/£6 weekends).
Cards
Designer John Salvesen
Facilities
Location 5m SE of Alyth,off B954 at Meigle onto A926

Hotel ★★★ 75% Old Mansion House Hotel, AUCHTERHOUSE ☎ 01382 320366 6

ANSTRUTHER Map 12 NO50

Anstruther Marsfield, Shore Rd KY10 3DZ
☎ 01333 310956
Seaside links course with some excellent par 3 holes; always in good condition.
9 holes, 4144mtrs, Par 62, SSS 63.
Club membership 700.
Visitors advised to phone in advance.
Societies welcome except Jun-Aug. Must apply in writing.
Green Fees not confirmed.
Facilities
Location SW off A917

Hotel ★★ 63% Smugglers Inn, High St, ANSTRUTHER ☎ 01333 310506 8

Call the AA Hotel Booking Service on 0990 050505 to book at AA recognised hotels and B & Bs in the UK and Ireland, or through our Internet site: http://www.theaa.co.uk/hotels

ARBROATH Map 12 NO64

Arbroath Elliot DD11 2PE ☎ 01241 872069
Municipal seaside links course, with bunkers guarding greens. Played upon by Arbroath Artisan Club.
18 holes, 6185yds, Par 70, SSS 69.
Club membership 550.

Visitors contact professional 01241 875837.
Societies contact professional 01241 875837.
Green Fees not confirmed.
Prof Lindsay Ewart
Designer Braid
Facilities
Location 2m SW on A92

Hotel ★★ 62% Hotel Seaforth, Dundee Rd, ARBROATH ☎ 01241 872232 20

Letham Grange Colliston DD11 4RL
☎ 01241 890373 Fax 01241 890725
Often referred to as the 'Augusta of Scotland', the Old Course provides championship standards in spectacular surroundings with attractive lochs and burns. The New Course is less arduous and shorter using many natural features of the estate.
Old Course: 18 holes, 6632yds, Par 73, SSS 73, Course record 69.
New Course: 18 holes, 5528yds, Par 68, SSS 68, Course record 64.
Club membership 750.

Visitors no visitors weekends before 9.30am, Old Course before 10am Tue & New Course before 10am Fri.
Societies telephone in advance.
Green Fees Old Course: £24 per round (£33 weekends). New Course: £15 per round (£24 weekends).
Cards
Prof Steven Moie
Designer G K Smith/Donald Steel
Facilities
Location 4m N on A933

Hotel ★★★★ 65% Letham Grange Hotel & Golf Course, Colliston, ARBROATH ☎ 01241 890373 19 Annexe22

AUCHTERARDER Map 11 NN91

Auchterarder Orchil Rd PH3 1LS
☎ 01764 662804 (Secretary) Fax 01764 662804
Parkland course with easy walking.
18 holes, 5775yds, Par 69, SSS 68, Course record 62.
Club membership 765.

Visitors must contact professional in advance.
Societies must contact in advance.
Green Fees £26 per day; £18 per round (£34/£24 weekends).
Prof Gavin Baxter
Facilities
Location 0.75m SW on A824

Hotel ★★★★★ The Gleneagles Hotel, AUCHTERARDER ☎ 01764 662231 234

THE GLENEAGLES HOTEL See page 337.

BARRY Map 12 NO53

Panmure Burnside Rd DD7 7RT
☎ 01241 855120 Fax 01241 859737
A nerve-testing, adventurous course set amongst sandhills - its hazards belie the quiet nature of the opening holes. This tight links has been used as a qualifying course for the Open Championship, and features Ben Hogan's favourite hole, the dog-leg 6th, which heralds the toughest stretch, around the turn.
18 holes, 6317yds, Par 70, SSS 71, Course record 62.
Club membership 700.

Visitors may not play Sat. Parties of 5 or more must contact in advance.
Societies must contact secretary in advance.
Green Fees £45 per day; £30 per round.
Cards
Prof Neil Mackintosh
Facilities
Location S side of village off A930

Hotel ★★ 65% Glencoe Hotel, Links Pde, CARNOUSTIE ☎ 01241 853273 7

BATHGATE Map 11 NS96

Bathgate Edinburgh Rd EH48 1BA
☎ 01506 630553 & 652232 Fax 01506 636775
Moorland course. Easy walking. Testing 11th hole, par 3.
18 holes, 6250yds, Par 71, SSS 70, Course record 58.
Club membership 750.

Visitors casual visitors welcome other than on competition days. Handicap certificate advisable.
Societies apply in writing.
Green Fees £21 per day; £16 per round (£32 per day weekends).
Cards
Prof Sandy Strachan
Designer W Park
Facilities
Location E side of town off A89

Hotel ★★★ 67% The Hilcroft Hotel, East Main St, WHITBURN ☎ 01501 740818 31

BLAIR ATHOLL Map 14 NN86

Blair Atholl PH18 5TG ☎ 01796 481407
Parkland course, river runs alongside 3 holes, easy walking.
9 holes, 5710yde, Par 70, SSS 68, Course record 65.
Club membership 400.

Visitors apply in advance to avoid competition times.
Societies apply in writing.
Green Fees £13 per day (£16 weekends).
Designer Morriss
Facilities
Location 0.5m S off B8079

Hotel ★★ 66% Atholl Arms Hotel, BLAIR ATHOLL ☎ 01796 481205 30

BLAIRGOWRIE Map 15 NO14

Blairgowrie Rosemount PH10 6LG
☎ 01250 872622 Fax 01250 875451
Two 18-hole heathland courses, also a 9-hole course.
Rosemount Course: 18 holes, 6588yds, Par 72, SSS 73.
Lansdowne Course: 18 holes, 6802yds, Par 72, SSS 74.
Wee Course: 9 holes, 2327yds, Par 32, SSS 63.
Club membership 1550.

Visitors must contact in advance & have handicap certificate, restricted Wed, Fri & weekends.
Societies must contact in advance.
Green Fees £60 per day for all courses. Rosemount £50 per round; Lansdowne £40 per round; Wee Course £20 per round (£75 per day weekends; £20-£55 per round).
Cards
Prof Charles Dernie
Designer J Braid/P Allis/D Thomas/Old Tom Morris
Facilities
Location (off A93)

Hotel ★★★ Kinloch House Hotel, BLAIRGOWRIE ☎ 01250 884237 21

BONNYRIGG Map 11 NT36

Broomieknowe 36 Golf Course Rd EH19 2HZ
☎ 0131 663 9317 Fax 0131 663 2152
Easy walking mature parkland course laid out by Ben Sayers and extended by James Braid. Elevated site with excellent views.
18 holes, 6150yds, Par 70, SSS 69, Course record 65.

Visitors must contact in advance.
Societies contact for details.
Green Fees £25 two rounds; £17 per round (£20 per round weekends).
Prof Mark Patchett
Designer Ben Sayers/Hawtree
Facilities
Location 0.5m NE off B704

Hotel ★★ 64% Eskbank Hotel, 29 Dalhousie Rd, DALKEITH ☎ 0131 663 3234 16

BRECHIN Map 15 NO56

Brechin Trinity DD9 7PD ☎ 01356 622383
Rolling parkland course, with easy walking and good views of Strathmore Valley and Grampian Mountains.
18 holes, 6092yds, Par 72, SSS 70, Course record 66.
Club membership 620.

Visitors contact Professional on 01356 625270 in advance. Restricted weekends.
Societies must contact club steward in advance.
Green Fees £20 per day; £15 per round (£28/£20 weekends).
Prof Stephen Rennie
Designer James Braid (partly)
Facilities
& Leisure squash.
Location 1m N on B966

Hotel ★★★ 63% Glenesk Hotel, High St, EDZELL ☎ 01356 648319 25rm(24)

BRIDGE OF ALLAN Map 11 NS79

Bridge of Allan Sunnylaw FK9 4LY ☎ 01786 832332
Parkland course, very hilly with good views of Stirling Castle and beyond to the Trossachs. Testing 1st hole, 221 yds (par 3) uphill 6 ft wall 25 yds before green.
9 holes, 4932yds, Par 66, SSS 65, Course record 62.
Club membership 400.

Visitors restricted Sat.
Societies must contact in advance.
Green Fees not confirmed.
Designer Tom Morris
Facilities
Location 0.5m N off A9

Hotel ★★★ 59% Royal Hotel, Henderson St, BRIDGE OF ALLAN ☎ 01786 832284 32

BROXBURN Map 11 NT07

Niddry Castle Castle Rd, Winchburgh EH52 6RQ
☎ 01506 891097
A 9-hole parkland course. While not very long, it requires accurate golf to score well.
9 holes, 5514yds, Par 70, SSS 67.
Club membership 510.

Visitors advisable to contact at weekends, restricted during competition time.
Societies must contact in advance.
Green Fees £12 per round (£17 weekends).
Facilities
Location 9m W of Edinburgh on B9080

THE GLENEAGLES HOTEL

AUCHTERARDER ***Perthshire & Kinross***

☎ 01764 662231 Fax 01764 662134 Map 11 NN91

John Ingham writes: Between Perth and Stirling you'll find those delightful courses, the King's and Queen's designed by James Braid and opened in 1919 to universal acclaim. There is nothing better – anywhere! They represent the best in beautiful, undulating moorland golf set alongside the massive and famous hotel – once the Caledonian Railway Hotel. The splendid Gleneagles Hotel courses are loved by its residents and for very good reasons – they are the stuff of dreams, of springy fairways, heather, bracken and pheasants that dart away when a shot misses the short grass and plunges into the wild life.

The motto there 'High Above the High' is apt as the 395 yard twelfth on the King's, named Tappit Hen (maybe it should be 'tap it in') is more than 600 feet above sea level with magnificent panoramas providing, of course, that mellow Scottish mists allow.

Only visitors to the hotel can play the courses. Years ago I stayed at the Glen with the late Henry Longhurst. 'We'll just have a quick 18 before dinner' he had said and delighted in showing me round the superb course. Since those days Jack Nicklaus has built his type of course there, the Monarch, in an American style. So now all tastes are catered for at this 5-star escape,

Without doubt the Gleneagles experience will impress any golfer and if the weather is fine, there is no better place to be. I used to go there every autumn for the Gleneagles Foursomes and at that time of the year, with the leaves golden, you feel that anything is possible.

Visitors must be resident in the hotel. A handicap certificate is not required but advance booking is essential

Societies must be resident in hotel

Green fees Kings, Queens, Monarchs: resident rate £50 (winter), £80 (summer) per round. Wee: £15 per round.

Facilities (Monarch only) Professional (Greg Schofield). Golf academy

Leisure tennis, squash, swimming, gymnasuim, riding, fishing, shooting

Location Perthshire PH3 1NF (2 miles SW of A823)

63 holes. Kings: 18 holes, 6471yds, Par 68, SSS 71
Queens: 18 holes, 5965 yds, Par 68, SSS 68
Monarch: 18 holes, 6551yds, Par 72,SSS 71
Wee: 9 holes, 1481yds, Par 27

WHERE TO STAY AND EAT NEARBY

HOTELS:

AUCHTERARDER

★★★★★ The Gleneagles Hotel
☎ 01764 662231 234

Hotel ★★★ 60% Forth Bridges Hotel, 1 Ferrymuir Gate, Forth Bridge, SOUTH QUEENSFERRY ☎ 0131 469 9955 108

BURNTISLAND Map 11 NT28

Burntisland Golf House Club Dodhead, Kirkcaldy Rd KY3 9EW ☎ 01592 874093 (Manager) & 873247 (Pro)
This hill course has fine sea views.
18 holes, 5965yds, Par 70, SSS 69, Course record 62.
Club membership 800.

Visitors weekend play restricted. Book by telephoning professional.
Societies apply in writing to manager.
Green Fees not confirmed.
Prof Jacky Montgomery
Designer Willie Park Jnr
Facilities
Location 1m E on B923

Hotel ★★ 65% Inchview Hotel, 69 Kinghorn Rd, BURNTISLAND ☎ 01592 872239 12

BUTE, ISLE OF Map 10 NS05

KINGARTH Map 10 NS05

Bute Kingarth, Rothesay PA20 9HN
☎ 01700 504369
Flat seaside course with good fenced greens.
9 holes, 2497yds, Par 68, SSS 64, Course record 65.
Club membership 210.

Visitors restricted Sat until after 12.30pm.
Societies apply in advance.
Green Fees £8 per day.
Facilities
Location 1m W off A844

Hotel ★★ 77% Ardmory House Hotel & Restaurant, Ardmory Rd, ARDBEG ☎ 01700 502346 5

PORT BANNATYNE Map 10 NS06

Port Bannatyne Bannatyne Mains Rd PA20 0PH
☎ 01700 505223
Seaside hill course with panoramic views. Difficult hole: 4th (par 3).
13 holes, 5085yds, Par 68, SSS 65, Course record 66.
Club membership 200.

Visitors no restrictions.
Societies must telephone in advance.
Green Fees £14 per day.
Facilities by prior arrangement by prior arrangement by prior arrangement by prior arrangement
Location W side of village off A844

Hotel ★★ 77% Ardmory House Hotel & Restaurant, Ardmory Rd, ARDBEG ☎ 01700 502346 5

ROTHESAY Map 10 NS06

Rothesay Canada Hill PA20 9HN
☎ 01700 502244 & 503554 (Pro) Fax 01700 503554
A scenic island course designed by James Braid and Ben Sayers. The course is fairly hilly, with views of the Firth of Clyde, Rothesay Bay or the Kyles of Bute from every hole. Winds are a regular feature which makes the two par 5 holes extremely challenging.
18 holes, 5395yds, Par 69, SSS 66, Course record 62.
Club membership 350.

Visitors pre-booking essential for weekends, telephone professional 01700 503554.
Societies contact in advance, booking essential at weekends.
Green Fees £15 (£24 weekends).
Prof James M Dougal
Designer James Braid & Ben Sayers
Facilities
Hotel ★★ 77% Ardmory House Hotel & Restaurant, Ardmory Rd, ARDBEG ☎ 01700 502346 5

CALLANDER Map 11 NN60

Callander Aveland Rd FK17 8EN
☎ 01877 330090 & 330975 Fax 01877 330062
Challenging parkland course with tight fairways and a number of interesting holes. Designed by Tom Morris Snr and overlooked by the Trossachs.
18 holes, 5151yds, Par 66, SSS 66, Course record 61.
Club membership 750.

Visitors prior booking 24-48 hrs is advised in the playing season. Handicap certificate Wed/Sun.
Societies write or telephone for booking form.
Green Fees £26 per day; £18 per round (£31/£26 weekends).
Prof William Kelly
Designer Morris/Fernie
Facilities
Location E side of town off A84

Hotel ★★★ 71% Roman Camp Country House Hotel, CALLANDER ☎ 01877 330003 14

CARDENDEN Map 11 NT29

Auchterderran Woodend Rd KY5 0NH ☎ 01592 721579
This is a relatively flat course requiring a lot of thought. There are two or three holes to test the best.
9 holes, 5250yds, Par 66, SSS 66, Course record 63.
Club membership 120.

Visitors no visitors between 7-11am & 1-3pm Sat, also some Sun in season.
Societies apply in writing.
Green Fees £7.50 per 18 holes (£10 weekends).
Facilities
Location N end Cardendon, Kirkcaldy/Glenrothes road

Hotel ★★★ 60% Dean Park Hotel, Chapel Level, KIRKCALDY ☎ 01592 261635 20 Annexe12

CARDROSS Map 10 NS37

Cardross Main Rd G82 5LB
☎ 01389 841754 Fax 01389 841754
Undulating parkland course, testing with good views.
18 holes, 6469yds, Par 71, SSS 72, Course record 65.
Club membership 800.
Visitors may not play at weekends unless introduced by member. Contact professional in advance 01359 841350
Societies must contact in writing.
Green Fees £35 per day; £25 per round (half price green fees from Nov-Mar).
Cards
Prof Robert Farrell
Designer James Braid
Facilities
Location In centre of village on A814

Hotel ★★ 61% Commodore Toby Hotel, 112 West Clyde St, HELENSBURGH
☎ 01436 676924 45

CARNOUSTIE Map 12 NO53

CARNOUSTIE GOLF LINKS See page 341.

CARRADALE Map 10 NR83

Carradale PA28 6SG ☎ 01583 431643
Pleasant seaside course built on a promontory overlooking the Isle of Arran. Natural terrain and small greens are the most difficult natural hazards. Described as the most sporting 9-hole course in Scotland. Testing 7th hole (240 yds), par 3. Beware of wild goats in summer.
9 holes, 2392yds, Par 66, SSS 64, Course record 58.
Club membership 320.
Visitors no restrictions
Societies contact in advance.
Green Fees £8 per day.
Facilities
Location S side of village, on B842

Hotel ★★ 67% Seafield Hotel, Kilkerran Rd, CAMPBELTOWN
☎ 01586 554385 3 Annexe6

COLONSAY, ISLE OF Map 10 NR39

SCALASAIG Map 10 NR39

Colonsay PA61 7YP ☎ 01951 200316 Fax 01951 200353
Traditional links course on natural machair (hard wearing short grass), challenging, primitive. Colonsay Hotel, 2 miles away, is the headquarters of the club, offering accommodation and facilities.
18 holes, 4775yds, Par 72, SSS 72.
Club membership 200.
Visitors no restrictions.
Societies apply in writing.
Green Fees not confirmed.
Facilities
Location 2m W on A870

Hotel ★ 75% Colonsay Hotel, SCALASAIG
☎ 01951 200316 10rm(1 7) Annexe1

COMRIE Map 11 NN72

Laggan Braes PH6 2LR ☎ 01764 760055
Scenic highland course with two tricky par 3 holes.
9 holes, 6040yds, Par 70, SSS 70, Course record 62.
Club membership 315.
Visitors apply in advance.
Societies must contact in advance.
Green Fees £10 per day (£16 per day; £12 per round).
Designer Col. Williamson
Facilities
& Leisure fishing.
Location E side of village off A85

Guesthouse QQQ Mossgiel Guest House, Burrell St, COMRIE
☎ 01764 670567 4

COWDENBEATH Map 11 NT19

Cowdenbeath Seco Place KY4 8PD ☎ 01383 511918
A parkland-based 9-hole golf course, due to be extended to 18 holes in June 1998.
Dora Course: 9 holes, 6552yds, Par 72, SSS 71, Course record 68.
Club membership 400.
Visitors no restrictions.
Societies must contact at least 2 weeks in advance.
Green Fees green fees set by Fife Council, season ticket available.
Facilities
Location 6m E of Dunfermline

Hotel ★★ 68% Woodside Hotel, High St, ABERDOUR ☎ 01383 860328 20

CRAIL Map 12 NO60

Crail Golfing Society Balcomie Clubhouse, Fifeness KY10 3XN ☎ 01333 450686 Fax 01333 450416
Perched on the edge of the North Sea on the very point of the golfing county of Fife, the Crail Golfing Society's course at Balcomie is picturesque and sporting. And here again golf history has been made for Crail Golfing Society began its life in 1786. The course is highly thought of by students of the game both for its testing holes and the standard of its greens.
18 holes, 5922yds, Par 69, SSS 69.
Club membership 950.
Visitors must contact in advance, restricted 10am-noon & 2-4.30pm.
Societies must contact in advance, as much notice as possible for weekend play.
Green Fees £30 per day; £20 per round (£38/£25 weekends).
Cards
Prof Graeme Lennie
Designer Tom Morris
Facilities
Location 2m NE off A917 ▶

Hotel ★★ 63% Balcomie Links Hotel, Balcomie Rd, CRAIL ☎ 01333 450237 11

Additional Guesthouse QQQQ The Spindrift, Pittenweem Rd, ANSTRUTHER ☎ 01333 310573 Fax 01333 310573 8

CRIEFF Map 11 NN82

Crieff Ferntower, Perth Rd PH7 3LR
☎ 01764 652909 Fax 01764 655096
This course is what you might call 'up and down' but the turf is beautiful and the highland air fresh and invigorating. There are views from the course over Strathearn. Of the two courses the Ferntower is the more challenging. Both parkland, the Dornock has one water hazard.
Ferntower Course: 18 holes, 6402yds, Par 71, SSS 71, Course record 65.
Dornock Course: 9 holes, 2387yds, Par 32, SSS 63.
Club membership 720.

Visitors must contact professional in advance.
Societies must contact professional in advance.
Green Fees Ferntower: £34 per day, £20 per round (£28 round only weekends). Dornock: £14 per 18 holes; £9 per round daily.
Cards
Prof David Murchie
Designer James Braid
Facilities
Location 0.5m NE on A85

Hotel ★★ 69% Murraypark Hotel, Connaught Ter, CRIEFF ☎ 01764 653731 20

CUPAR Map 11 NO31

Cupar Hilltarvit KY15 5NZ
☎ 01334 653549 Fax 01334 653549
Hilly parkland course with fine views over north east Fife.5th/14th hole is most difficult - uphill and into the prevailing wind.
9 holes, 5500yds, Par 68, SSS 65, Course record 62.
Club membership 450.
Visitors welcome except Sat.
Societies must contact in advance.
Green Fees £12 per round/day (£15 weekends). £50 per week. £25 Family ticket.
Designer Allan Robertson
Facilities
Location 0.75m S off A92

Hotel ★★ 69% Eden House Hotel, 2 Pitscottie Rd, CUPAR ☎ 01334 652510 9 Annexe2

DALKEITH Map 11 NT36

Newbattle Abbey Rd EH22 3AD
☎ 0131 663 2123 & 0131 663 1819 Fax 0131 654 1810
Undulating parkland course on three levels, surrounded by woods.
18 holes, 6005yds, Par 69, SSS 70, Course record 61.
Club membership 700.
Visitors Mon-Fri ex public holidays, before 4pm.
Societies welcome weekdays ex public holidays, before 4pm.
Green Fees £24 per day; £16 per round.
Prof David Torrance
Designer S Colt
Facilities
Location SW side of town off A68

Hotel ★★ 64% Eskbank Hotel, 29 Dalhousie Rd, DALKEITH ☎ 0131 663 3234 16

DALMALLY Map 10 NN12

Dalmally Old Saw Mill PA33 1AE
☎ 01838 200370
A 9-hole flat parkland course bounded by the River Orchy and surrounded by mountains. Many water hazards and bunkers.
9 holes, 2257yds, Par 64, SSS 63, Course record 64.
Club membership 100.
Visitors no visitors on Sun between 9-10 & 1-2.
Societies telephone in advance.
Green Fees £8 per day.
Designer MacFarlane Barrow Co
Facilities by prior arrangement by prior arrangement by arrangement
& Leisure fishing, practice area.
Location On A85, 1.5m W of Dalmally

Hotel ★★ 57% Polfearn Hotel, TAYNUILT ☎ 01866 822251 16rm(3 11)

DOLLAR Map 11 NS99

Dollar Brewlands House FK14 7EA
☎ 01259 742400
Compact hillside course with magnificent views along the Ochil Hills.
18 holes, 5242yds, Par 69, SSS 66, Course record 62.
Club membership 470.
Visitors weekdays course available but restricted Wed ladies day, weekends must contact in advance.
Societies write or telephone in advance.
Green Fees £16 per day; £12 per round (£20 weekends).
Designer Ben Sayers
Facilities
& Leisure snooker.
Location 0.5m N off A91

Hotel ★★★ 59% Royal Hotel, Henderson St, BRIDGE OF ALLAN ☎ 01786 832284 32

CARNOUSTIE GOLF LINKS

CARNOUSTIE *Angus* ☎ 01241 853789
Fax 01241 852720 Map 12 NO53

John Ingham writes: You love it, or hate it - but you respect it. Carnoustie, designed by James Braid, can be a graveyard. Simply standing up to the buffeting is bad enough, but those closing holes, across the Barry Burn (or into it) are a prospect which can gnaw at the mind. The burn twists through the links like an angry serpent and has to be crossed no fewer than seven times.

Back in 1953 they came to see Ben Hogan play in the Open Championship. This little man from Texas had a magic about him, and the huge terrifying links, the dread of any short hitter, certainly promised to be a platform on which to examine the finest golfer of his day, and maybe of any day.

Not since 1860 had any golfer won the Open on his first attempt. Certainly Hogan hadn't come to this awesome place for the money which, in those days, was a pittance. He had come to prove he was the best player in the world. That was pressure!

When Mr Hogan saw the 'Stone Age' course, dating back to the birth of the game, he was shocked because it lacked trees and colour, and looked drab. But he beat the 7200-yard monster course for the 1953 Championship, which was, as they say, something else.

'Winning the British Open at Carnoustie gave me my greatest pleasure' he told the *Fort Worth Star-Telegram.* 'Certainly the other victories were pleasurable, but none gave me the feeling, the desire to perform, that gripped me in Scotland'.

Sadly, Hogan never returned and then the great links was taken from the Open Championship rota. Now, thankfully, they have built a new clubhouse, and an International hotel is being completed. So the R&A has re-instated it for future major events, including the Open

Visitors must contact golf links in advance.Restricted hours. Must have a handicap certificate for Championship course
Societies prior arrangement required either in writing or by telephone
Green fees Championship: £52 per round. Burnside: £28.50 per day; £19 per round; Buddon Links: £22.50 per day; £15 per round.
Combination day tickets: Championship & Burnside £62; Championship & Buddon Links £60; Burnside & Buddon Links £27
Facilities ⛳ ✓
Location Carnoustie DD7 7JE Links Parade (SW side of town, off A930)

54 holes. Championship Course: 18 holes, 6941 yds, Par 72, SSS 75, Course record 64)
Burnside Course: 18 holes, 6020 yds, Par 68, SSS 69
Buddon Links: 18 holes, 5420 yds, Par 66, SSS 66

WHERE TO STAY AND EAT NEARBY

HOTELS:

ARBROATH
★★ 62% Hotel Seaforth, Dundee Rd, ☎ 01241 872232. 20 (14 ⇌ 6 ⇌ ⮣)

CARNOUSTIE
★★ 69% Carlogie House, Carlogie Rd ☎ 01241 853185. 16 (10 ⮣ 1 ⇌ 1 ⇌ ⮣) Annexe 4 ⮣

★★65% Glencoe, Links Pde. ☎ 01241 853273. 7(4 ⮣ 3 ⇌ ⮣)

RESTAURANT:

INVERKEILOR
❀ ❀Gordon's, Homewood House, Main St. ☎ 01241 830364

DRYMEN Map 11 NS48

Buchanan Castle G63 0HY
☎ 01360 660307 Fax 01360 870382
Parkland course, with easy walking and good views.
18 holes, 6086yds, Par 70, SSS 69.
Club membership 830.

Visitors must contact in advance.
Societies must contact in advance.
Green Fees £40 per day; £30 per round.
Prof Keith Baxter
Designer James Braid
Facilities
Location 1m W

Hotel ★★★ 67% Buchanan Arms Hotel, DRYMEN ☎ 01360 660588 52

DUNBAR Map 12 NT67

Dunbar East Links EH42 1LT
☎ 01368 862317 Fax 01368 865202
Another of Scotland's old links. It is said that it was some Dunbar members who first took the game of golf to the North of England. A natural links course on a narrow strip of land, following the contours of the sea shore, there is a wall bordering one side and the shore on the other side making this quite a challenging course for all levels of player. The wind, if blowing from the sea, is a problem.
18 holes, 6406yds, Par 71, SSS 71, Course record 64.
Club membership 1000.

Visitors may not play Thu, between 12.30-2 weekdays, 12-2 weekends or before 9.30am any day.
Societies telephone in advance.
Green Fees £35 per day; £25 per round (£45/£35 weekends).
Prof Derek Small
Designer Tom Morris
Facilities by prior arrangement
Location 0.5m E off A1087

Hotel ★★ 64% Bayswell Hotel, Bayswell Park, DUNBAR ☎ 01368 862225 13

Winterfield North Rd EH42 1AY ☎ 01368 863562
Seaside course with superb views.
18 holes, 5220yds, SSS 64.
Club membership 200.

Green Fees not confirmed.
Facilities
Location W side of town off A1087

Hotel ★★ 64% Bayswell Hotel, Bayswell Park, DUNBAR ☎ 01368 862225 13

DUNBLANE Map 11 NN70

Dunblane New Golf Club Perth Rd FK15 0LJ
☎ 01786 821522 Fax 01786 821522
Well maintained parkland course, with reasonably hard walking. Testing 6th and 9th holes.
18 holes, 5536yds, Par 69, SSS 67.
Club membership 1000.

Visitors may play 9.30am-noon & 2.30-4pm Mon-Fri. Must contact in advance.
Societies welcome Mon, Wed-Fri, contact in advance.
Green Fees £27 per day; £18 per round.
Prof Bob Jamieson
Facilities
Location E side of town on A9

Hotel ★★★ Cromlix House Hotel, Kinbuck, DUNBLANE ☎ 01786 822125 14

DUNDEE Map 11 NO43

Caird Park Mains Loan DD4 9BX ☎ 01382 453606
Municipal parkland course.
18 holes, 5494yds, Par 69, SSS 68, Course record 67.
Club membership 400.

Visitors no restrictions.
Societies must contact in advance 01382 438871.
Green Fees not confirmed.
Prof J Black
Facilities
Location 1.5m N of city centre off A972

Hotel ★★★ 64% The Queen's Hotel, 160 Nethergate, DUNDEE ☎ 01382 322515 47

Camperdown Camperdown House, Camperdown Park DD2 4TF ☎ 01382 623398
Parkland course. Testing 2nd hole.
18 holes, 6548yds, Par 71, SSS 72.
Club membership 600.

Visitors must contact in advance.
Societies must contact in advance.
Green Fees not confirmed.
Facilities
& Leisure hard tennis courts.
Location 3m NW of city centre off A923

Hotel ★★★ 75% Old Mansion House Hotel, AUCHTERHOUSE ☎ 01382 320366 6

Downfield Turnberry Av DD2 3QP
☎ 01382 825595 Fax 01382 813111
A fine inland course of recent Championship rating set in undulating woodland to the north of Dundee. The Gelly burn provides a hazard for several holes.
18 holes, 6822yds, Par 73, SSS 73, Course record 65.
Club membership 750.

Visitors must contact in advance, no visitors at weekends.
Societies must contact in advance.
Green Fees £26-£46 per day; £16-£31 per round.
Prof Kenny Hutton
Designer C K Cotton
Facilities
Location N of city centre off A923

Hotel ★★★ 75% Old Mansion House Hotel, AUCHTERHOUSE ☎ 01382 320366 6

A comprehensive list of driving ranges is given at the back of this guide. See page 479

DUNFERMLINE Map 11 NT08

Canmore Venturefair Av KY12 0PE ☎ 01383 724969
Undulating parkland course affording excellent views.
18 holes, 5474yds, Par 67, SSS 66, Course record 61.
Club membership 710.

Visitors Sat not usually available. Limited Sun. Must contact Professional in advance.
Societies apply in writing to secretary.
Green Fees £20 per day: £15 per round (£35/£25 weekends).
Facilities
Location 1m N on A823

Hotel ★★★ 64% The King Malcolm Thistle Hotel, Queensferry Rd, Wester Pitcorthie, DUNFERMLINE ☎ 01383 722611 48

Dunfermline Pitfirrane, Crossford KY12 8QW
☎ 01383 723534 & 729061
Gently undulating parkland course with interesting contours. Five Par 5's, Five Par 3's. No water hazards.
18 holes, 6237yds, Par 72, SSS 70, Course record 65.
Club membership 690.

Visitors may not play Sat. Contact to check times.
Societies must contact in advance.
Green Fees £30 per day; £20 per round (£35/£25 Sun).
Prof Steve Craig
Designer J R Stutt
Facilities
Location 2m W on A994

Hotel ★★★ 64% The King Malcolm Thistle Hotel, Queensferry Rd, Wester Pitcorthie, DUNFERMLINE ☎ 01383 722611 48

Pitreavie Queensferry Rd KY11 5PR ☎ 01383 722591
Picturesque woodland course with panoramic view of the River Forth Valley. Testing golf.
18 holes, 6086yds, Par 70, SSS 69, Course record 65.
Club membership 700.

Visitors welcome except for competition days.
Societies must write or telephone in advance.
Green Fees not confirmed.
Prof Jim Forrester
Facilities
Location SE side of town on A823

Hotel ★★★ 64% The King Malcolm Thistle Hotel, Queensferry Rd, Wester Pitcorthie, DUNFERMLINE ☎ 01383 722611 48

DUNKELD Map 11 NO04

Dunkeld & Birnam Fungarth PH8 0HU
☎ 01350 727524 Fax 01350 728660
Interesting heathland course with spectacular views of surrounding countryside.
9 holes, 5322yds, Par 68, SSS 66, Course record 64.
Club membership 450.

Visitors must contact in advance.
Societies apply in writing.
Green Fees on application.
Facilities
Location 1m N of village on A923

Hotel ★★★ Kinnaird, Kinnaird Estate, DUNKELD ☎ 01796 482440 9

DUNNING Map 11 NO01

Dunning Rollo Park PH2 0RH ☎ 01764 684747
Parkland course with a series of stone built bridges crossing a burn meandering over a large part of the course.
9 holes, 4836yds, Par 66, SSS 63, Course record 63.
Club membership 580.

Visitors Gents competitions Saturday, Ladies Tue, other than that no restrictions.
Societies must contact in advance in writing.
Green Fees £14 per day; £10 per round (£12 per round weekends).
Facilities
Location 1.5m off A9, 4m N of Auchterarder

Hotel ★★★ 68% Parklands Hotel, St Leonards Bank, PERTH ☎ 01738 622451 14

Whitemoss Whitemoss Rd PH2 0QX
☎ 01738 730300 Fax 01738 730300
Undulating parkland course situated in the scenic Strathearn Valley, ten miles from Perth (off the A9).
18 holes, 5595yds, Par 68, SSS 68, Course record 63.
Club membership 600.

Visitors advisable to telephone in advance, visitors welcome all week, may play 9 holes half price.
Societies please telephone for details.
Green Fees £20 per day; £15 per round.
Designer Whitemoss Leisure
Facilities
& Leisure practice range, chipping bunkers, practice net.
Location Turn off A9 at Whitemoss Road junct, 3m N of Gleneagles

Hotel ★★ 74% Cairn Lodge, Orchil Rd, AUCHTERARDER ☎ 01764 662634 & 662431 Fax 01764 664866 7

DUNOON Map 10 NS17

Cowal Ardenslate Rd PA23 8LT
☎ 01369 705673 Fax 01369 705673
Moorland course. Panoramic views of Clyde Estuary and surrounding hills.
18 holes, 6063yds, Par 70, SSS 70, Course record 63.
Club membership 900.

Visitors advisable to book in advance.
Societies must telephone in advance.
Green Fees £20 per round (£30 weekends).
Prof Russell Weir
Designer James Braid
Facilities
Location 1m N

Hotel ★★ 76% Enmore Hotel, Marine Pde, Kirn, DUNOON ☎ 01369 702230 10

EDINBURGH Map 11 NT27

Baberton 50 Baberton Av, Juniper Green EH14 5DU
☎ 0131 453 4911 Fax 0131 453 4911
Parkland course.
18 holes, 6129yds, Par 69, SSS 70, Course record 64.
Club membership 900.

Visitors may not play at weekends or after 3.30pm weekdays. Contact in advance.

Societies must contact in advance.

Green Fees £28.50 per day; £18.50 per round.

Prof Ken Kelly

Designer Willie Park Jnr

Facilities

Location 5m W of city centre off A70

Hotel ★★★ 70% Bruntsfield Hotel, 69/74 Bruntsfield Place, EDINBURGH ☎ 0131 229 1393 50

Braid Hills Braid Hills Approach EH10 6JZ ☎ 0131 447 6666

Municipal heathland course with good views of Edinburgh and the Firth of Forth.

Course No 1: 18 holes, 6172yds, Par 70, SSS 68, Course record 62.

Course No 2: 18 holes, 4832yds, Par 65, SSS 63.

Visitors may not play on Sat mornings.

Societies telephone Outdoor Recreation Manager 0131 657 4815

Green Fees not confirmed.

Facilities

Location 2.5m S of city centre off A702

Hotel ★★★ 67% Braid Hills Hotel, 134 Braid Rd, Braid Hills, EDINBURGH ☎ 0131 447 8888 68

Bruntsfield Links Golfing Society 32 Barnton Av EH4 6JH ☎ 0131 336 1479 Fax 0131 336 5538

Mature parkland course with magnificent views over the Firth of Forth and to the west. Greens and fairways are generally immaculate. Challenging for all categories of handicap. The course has hosted British Senior and Boys Championships.

18 holes, 6407yds, Par 71, SSS 71, Course record 67.

Club membership 1100.

Visitors must telephone in advance. 0131 336 4050 or 0131 336 1479

Societies apply in writing.

Green Fees £50 per day; £36 per round (£55/£42 weekends).

Prof Brian Mackenzie

Designer Willie Park Jr

Facilities

Location 4m NW of city centre off A90

Hotel ★★★ 60% The Barnton Thistle, Queensferry Rd, Barnton, EDINBURGH ☎ 0131 339 1144 50

Carrick Knowe Carrick Knowe Municipal, Glendevon Park EH12 5UZ ☎ 0131 337 1096

Flat parkland course. Played over by two clubs, Carrick Knowe and Carrick Vale.

18 holes, 6299yds, Par 71, SSS 70.

Club membership 450.

Visitors may be restricted at weekends.

Societies telephone Outdoor Recreation Manager 0131 657 4815.

Green Fees not confirmed.

Facilities

Location 3m W of city centre, S of A8

Hotel B Forte Posthouse Edinburgh, Corstorphine Rd, EDINBURGH ☎ 0131 334 0390 204

Craigentinny Fillyside Rd, Lochend EH7 6RG ☎ 0131 554 7501

To the north east of Edinburgh, Craigentinny course is between Leith and Portobello. It is generally flat although there are some hillocks with gentle slopes. The famous Arthur's Seat dominates the southern skyline.

18 holes, 5418yds, Par 67, SSS 65.

Societies telephone Outdoor Recreation Manager 0131 657 4815

Green Fees not confirmed.

Facilities

Location NE side of city, between Leith & Portobello

Hotel ★★★ 71% The King James Thistle, 107 Leith St, EDINBURGH ☎ 0131 556 0111 143

Craigmillar Park 1 Observatory Rd EH9 3HG ☎ 0131 667 0047

Parkland course, with good views.

18 holes, 5851yds, Par 70, SSS 69, Course record 63.

Club membership 750.

Visitors must contact in advance.

Societies must contact in writing.

Green Fees £25.50 per day; £17.50 per round.

Prof B McGhee

Facilities

Location 2m S of city centre off A7

Hotel ★★ 68% Allison House Hotel, 15/17 Mayfield Gardens, EDINBURGH ☎ 0131 667 8049 23rm(21)

Duddingston Duddingston Rd West EH15 3QD ☎ 0131 661 7688

Parkland, semi-seaside course with burn as a natural hazard. Testing 11th hole. Easy walking and windy.

18 holes, 6647yds, Par 71, SSS 71.

Club membership 700.

Visitors may not play at weekends.

Societies Tue & Thu only. Must contact in advance.

Green Fees £36 per day; £27 per round.

Prof Alastair McLean

Facilities

Location 2.5m SE of city centre off A1

Hotel ★★ 68% Allison House Hotel, 15/17 Mayfield Gardens, EDINBURGH ☎ 0131 667 8049 23rm(21)

Kingsknowe 326 Lanark Rd EH14 2JD ☎ 0131 441 1145

Hilly parkland course with prevailing SW winds.

18 holes, 5979yds, Par 69, SSS 69, Course record 63.

Club membership 800.

Visitors contact in advance and subject to availability of tee times.

Societies apply in writing or telephone secretary.

Green Fees £25 per day; £20 per round (£30 per round weekends).

Prof Andrew Marshall

Designer A Herd/James Braid

Facilities

Location 4m SW of city centre on A70

Hotel ★★★ 70% Bruntsfield Hotel, 69/74 Bruntsfield Place, EDINBURGH ☎ 0131 229 1393 50

Liberton 297 Gilmerton Rd EH16 5UJ
☎ 0131 664 3009 Fax 0131 666 0853
Undulating, wooded parkland course.
18 holes, 5306yds, Par 67, SSS 67, Course record 61.
Club membership 675.
Visitors must contact in advance.
Societies must contact in writing.
Green Fees £30 per day; £17 per round (£25 per round weekends).
Prof Iain Seath
Facilities
Location 3m SE of city centre on A7

Hotel ★★ 64% Eskbank Hotel, 29 Dalhousie Rd, DALKEITH ☎ 0131 663 3234 16

Lothianburn 106A Biggar Rd, Fairmilehead EH10 7DU
☎ 0131 445 2206 & 0131 445 5067
Hillside course with a 'T' shaped wooded-area, situated in the Pentland foothills. Testing in windy conditions. Fine views of Edinburgh and the Lothians.
18 holes, 5568yds, Par 71, SSS 68, Course record 66.
Club membership 850.
Visitors weekends after 3.30pm contact professional, weekdays up to 4pm.
Societies apply to the secretary or telephone in the first instance.
Green Fees £21 per day; £15 per round (£26/£21 weekends).
Prof Kurt Mungall
Designer J Braid
Facilities
Location 4.5m S of city centre on A702

Hotel ★★★ 67% Braid Hills Hotel, 134 Braid Rd, Braid Hills, EDINBURGH
☎ 0131 447 8888 68

Marriott Dalmahoy Hotel Golf & Country Club
Kirknewton EH27 8EB
☎ 0131 333 1845 Fax 0131 333 1433
Two outstanding upland courses, meandering around the lake and across picturesque streams. The West Course is the easier of the two whilst the trickier East Course is a greater challenge, the par 3 15th known as the 'Wee Wrecker' with good reason.
East Course: 18 holes, 6677yds, Par 72, SSS 72, Course record 64.
West Course: 18 holes, 5047yds, Par 68, SSS 68, Course record 60.
Club membership 700.
Visitors welcome Mon-Fri, weekend by application.
Societies telephone or write for information.
Green Fees East: £50. West: £35.
Cards
Prof Brian Anderson/Stuart Callan
Designer James Braid
Facilities
& Leisure hard tennis courts, heated indoor swimming pool, squash, sauna, solarium, gymnasium.
Location 7m W of city centre on A71

Hotel ★★★★ 69% Marriott Dalmahoy Hotel & Country Club, Kirknewton, EDINBURGH
☎ 0131 333 1845
43 Annexe108

Merchants of Edinburgh 10 Craighill Gardens EH10 5PY
☎ 0131 447 1219
Testing hill course.
18 holes, 4889ydss, Par 65, SSS 64, Course record 59.
Club membership 900.
Visitors must play with member at weekends.
Societies must contact in secretary in writing.
Green Fees £15 per day.
Prof Neil Colquhoun
Designer R G Ross
Facilities
Location 2m SW of city centre off A702

Hotel ★★★ 67% Braid Hills Hotel, 134 Braid Rd, Braid Hills, EDINBURGH
☎ 0131 447 8888 68

Mortonhall 231 Braid Rd EH10 6PB
☎ 0131 447 6974 Fax 0131 447 8712
Moorland course with views over Edinburgh.
18 holes, 6557yds, Par 72, SSS 72, Course record 66.
Club membership 525.
Visitors advisable to contact by phone.
Societies may not play at weekends. Must contact in writing.
Green Fees not confirmed.
Prof Douglas Horn
Designer James Braid/F Hawtree
Facilities
Location 3m S of city centre off A702

Hotel ★★★ 67% Braid Hills Hotel, 134 Braid Rd, Braid Hills, EDINBURGH
☎ 0131 447 8888 68

Murrayfield 43 Murrayfield Rd EH12 6EU
☎ 0131 337 3478 Fax 0131 313 0721
Parkland course on the side of Corstorphine Hill, with fine views.
18 holes, 5725yds, Par 70, SSS 69.
Club membership 750.
Visitors contact in advance, may not play at weekends.
Green Fees £30 per day; £25 per round.
Prof J J Fisher
Facilities
Location 2m W of city centre off A8

Hotel B Forte Posthouse Edinburgh, Corstorphine Rd, EDINBURGH
☎ 0131 334 0390 204

Portobello Stanley St EH15 1JJ
☎ 0131 669 4361
Public parkland course, easy walking.
9 holes, 2400yds, Par 32, SSS 32.
Club membership 70.
Visitors may not play Sat 8.30-10am & 12.30-2pm and on competition days.
Societies must contact in advance.
Green Fees not confirmed.
Facilities
Location 3m E of city centre off A1

Hotel ★★★ 64% Kings Manor, 100 Milton Rd East, EDINBURGH ☎ 0131 669 0444 69

Prestonfield Priestfield Rd North EH16 5HS ☎ 0131 667 9665
Parkland course with beautiful views.
18 holes, 6212yds, Par 70, SSS 70, Course record 62.
Club membership 850.

Visitors contact secretary in advance.
Societies must contact secretary.
Green Fees £30 per day; £20 per round (£40/£30 weekends & bank holidays).
Cards
Prof Graham MacDonald
Designer James Braid
Facilities
Location 1.5m S of city centre off A68

Hotel ★★ 64% Eskbank Hotel, 29 Dalhousie Rd, DALKEITH ☎ 0131 663 3234 16

Ravelston 24 Ravelston Dykes Rd EH4 5NZ
☎ 0131 315 2486
Parkland course.
9 holes, 5230yds, Par 66, SSS 65, Course record 64.
Club membership 610.

Visitors must contact in advance but may not play at weekends & bank holidays.
Green Fees £15 per day/round Mon-Fri.
Designer James Braid
Facilities
Location 3m W of city centre off A90

Hotel B Forte Posthouse Edinburgh, Corstorphine Rd, EDINBURGH ☎ 0131 334 0390 204

Royal Burgess 181 Whitehouse Rd, Barnton EH4 6BY
☎ 0131 339 2075 Fax 0131 339 3712
No mention of golf clubs would be complete without mention of the Royal Burgess, which was instituted in 1735, thus being the oldest golfing society in the world. Its course is a pleasant parkland, and one with very much variety. A club which all those interested in the history of the game should visit.
18 holes, 6111yds, Par 71, SSS 69.
Club membership 620.

Visitors must contact in advance. Gentlemen only.
Societies must contact in advance.
Green Fees £47 per day; £37 per round.
Prof George Yuille
Designer Tom Morris
Facilities
Location 5m W of city centre off A90

Hotel ★★★ 60% The Barnton Thistle, Queensferry Rd, Barnton, EDINBURGH ☎ 0131 339 1144 50

Silverknowes Silverknowes, Parkway EH4 5ET
☎ 0131 336 3843
Public links course on coast overlooking the Firth of Forth.
18 holes, 6216yds, Par 71, SSS 70.
Club membership 500.

Visitors restricted Sat & Sun.
Societies must apply in writing to: Leisure Management Unit, Meadowbank Sports Centre, London Road, Edinburgh.
Green Fees not confirmed.
Facilities
Location 4m NW of city centre N of A902

Hotel ★★ 65% Murrayfield Hotel, 18 Corstophine Rd, EDINBURGH ☎ 0131 337 1844 23 Annexe10

Swanston 111 Swanston Rd, Fairmilehead EH10 7DS
☎ 0131 445 2239
Hillside course with steep climb at 12th & 13th holes.
18 holes, 5024yds, Par 66, SSS 65, Course record 63.
Club membership 600.

Visitors contact in advance.
Societies must contact in advance.
Green Fees £22 per day; £15 per round (£25/£20 weekends & bank holidays).
Prof Ian Taylor
Designer Herbert More
Facilities
Location 4m S of city centre off B701

Hotel ★★★ 67% Braid Hills Hotel, 134 Braid Rd, Braid Hills, EDINBURGH ☎ 0131 447 8888 68

Torphin Hill Torphin Rd, Colinton EH13 0PG
☎ 0131 441 1100
Beautiful hillside, heathland course, with fine views of Edinburgh and the Forth Estuary.
18 holes, 4580mtrs, Par 67, SSS 66, Course record 63.
Club membership 550.

Visitors must contact in advance, limited access Sat & Sun.
Societies must contact in advance.
Green Fees £25 per day; £10 per round (£25 per round weekends).
Prof Jamie Browne
Facilities

Location 5m SW of city centre S of A720

Hotel ★★★ 67% Braid Hills Hotel, 134 Braid Rd, Braid Hills, EDINBURGH
☎ 0131 447 8888 68

Turnhouse 154 Turnhouse Rd EH12 0AD
☎ 0131 339 1014
Hilly, parkland/heathland course, good views.
18 holes, 6171yds, Par 69, SSS 70, Course record 64.
Club membership 800.
Visitors may not play at weekends, Wed or Medal Days.
Societies must contact in writing.
Green Fees £24 per day, £16 per round.
Prof John Murray
Designer J Braid
Facilities
Location R6m W of city centre N of A8)

Hotel ★★★ 60% The Barnton Thistle, Queensferry Rd, Barnton, EDINBURGH
☎ 0131 339 1144 50

EDZELL

Map 15 NO66

Edzell High St DD9 7TF
☎ 01356 647283 (Secretary) Fax 01356 648094
This delightful course is situated in the foothills of the Scottish Highlands and provides good golf as well as conveying to everyone who plays there a feeling of peace and quiet. The village of Edzell is one of the most picturesque in Scotland.
18 holes, 6348yds, Par 71, SSS 71, Course record 62.
Club membership 650.
Visitors may not play 4.45-6.15 weekdays & 7.30-10, 12-2 weekends. Not before 2pm on 1st Sat each month.
Societies must contact secretary at least 14 days in advance.
Green Fees £31 per day; £21 per round (£41/£27 weekends).
Prof A J Webster
Designer Bob Simpson
Facilities
Location S side of village on B966

Hotel ★★★ 63% Glenesk Hotel, High St, EDZELL ☎ 01356 648319 25rm(24)

ELIE

Map 12 NO40

Golf House Club KY9 1AS
☎ 01333 330301 Fax 01333 330895
One of Scotland's most delightful holiday courses with panoramic views over the Firth of Forth. Some of the holes out towards the rocky coastline are splendid. This is the course which has produced many good professionals, including the immortal James Braid.
18 holes, 6273yds, Par 70, SSS 70, Course record 62.
Club membership 600.
Visitors advisable to contact in advance, limited availability Sat May-Sep and no visitors Sun May-Sep.
Societies must contact in advance.
Green Fees £40 per day; £32 per round (£55/£45 weekends).
Prof Robin Wilson

Facilities
& Leisure hard tennis courts.
Location W side of village off A917

Hotel ★★★ 73% Old Manor Hotel, Leven Rd, LUNDIN LINKS
☎ 01333 320368 24

ERISKA

Map 10 NM94

Isle of Eriska PA37 1SD
☎ 01631 720371 Fax 01631 720531
This remote and most beautiful 6-hole course, set around the owners hotel, is gradually being upgraded to a testing 9-hole challenge, complete with stunning views.
6 holes, 1588yds, Par 22.
Club membership 40.
Visitors contact in advance.
Green Fees £10 per day ticket.
Cards
Designer H Swan
Facilities
& Leisure hard tennis courts, heated indoor swimming pool, sauna, gymnasium.
Location A828 Connel/Fort William, signposted 4m from North of Benderloch village

Hotel ★★★ Isle of Eriska, ERISKA
☎ 01631 720371 17

FALKIRK

Map 11 NS88

Falkirk 136 Stirling Rd, Camelon FK2 7YP
☎ 01324 611061 Fax 01324 639573/622570
Parkland course with trees, gorse and streams.
18 holes, 6230yds, Par 71, SSS 70, Course record 66.
Club membership 800.
Visitors telephone starter 01324 612219, visiting parties only on Sun. May not play Sat.
Societies telephone 01324 612219 in advance.
Green Fees £20 per day; £15 per round (£30/£25 Sun).
Designer James Braid
Facilities
Location 1.5m W on A9

Hotel ★★★★ 68% Inchyra Grange Hotel, Grange Rd, POLMONT ☎ 01324 711911 109

FALKLAND

Map 11 NO20

Falkland The Myre KY7 7AA ☎ 01337 857404
A flat, well kept course with excellent greens and views of East Lomond Hill and Falkland Palace.
9 holes, 5216yds, Par 68, SSS 65, Course record 62.
Club membership 280.
Visitors parties must make prior arrangements, please check availability at weekends.
Societies must contact in advance.
Green Fees £8 per day (£10 weekends).
Facilities
Location N side of town on A912

Hotel ★★ 66% Lomond Hills Hotel, Parliament Square, FREUCHIE
☎ 01337 857329 & 857498
Fax 01337 858180 25

FAULDHOUSE Map 11 NS96

Greenburn 6 Greenburn Rd EH47 9HG ☎ 01501 770292
Exposed rolling course with sparse tree cover. Water hazards from a pond and a burn.
18 holes, 6045yds, Par 71, SSS 70, Course record 65.
Club membership 900.

Visitors contact in advance for details.
Societies by prior arrangement.
Green Fees £22 per day; £17 per round (£27/£19 weekends).
Prof Malcolm Leighton
Facilities ⊗ ☽ ⛳ ☕ 🍷 🎔 🏠 ✓
Location 3m SW of Whitburn

Hotel ★★★ 67% The Hilcroft Hotel, East Main St, WHITBURN ☎ 01501 740818 31 ⇌ ↱

FORFAR Map 15 NO45

Forfar Cunninghill, Arbroath Rd DD8 2RL
☎ 01307 463773 Fax 01307 468495
Moorland course with wooded, undulating fairways and fine views.
18 holes, 6053yds, Par 69, SSS 70, Course record 61.
Club membership 820.

Visitors may not play before 2.30pm Sat.
Societies must contact in advance.
Green Fees £25 per day; £17.50 per round (£30/£22 weekends & bank holidays).
Prof Peter McNiven
Designer James Braid
Facilities ⊗ ☽ ⛳ ☕ 🍷 🎔 🏠 ✓
Location 1.5m E of Forfar on A932

Hotel ★★★♣ 66% Idvies House Hotel, Letham, FORFAR ☎ 01307 818787 11 ⇌ ↱

GIFFORD Map 12 NT56

Gifford Edinburgh Rd EH41 4QN ☎ 01620 810267
Parkland course, with easy walking.
9 holes, 6243yds, Par 71, SSS 70, Course record 64.
Club membership 400.

Visitors restricted weekends, not after 4pm Sat & noon Sun.
Societies telephone in advance.
Green Fees £15 per day; £10 per round (£10 per round weekends).
Facilities ☕ 🎔 ✓
Location 1m SW off B6355

Hotel ★★ 70% Tweeddale Arms Hotel, GIFFORD ☎ 01620 810240 16 ⇌ ↱

GIGHA ISLAND Map 10 NR64

Gigha PA41 7AA
☎ 01583 505287 01583 505254 Fax 01583 505244
A 9-hole course with scenic views of the Sound of Gigha to the east and to the north the Kilberry Hills. The 9th hole is a good par 3, especially with a strong blow of wind from the west.
9 holes, 5042 yds, Par 66, SSS 65.
Club membership 40.

Visitors no restrictions.
Societies telephone for details.
Green Fees £10 per round.
Facilities ⊗ ☽ ⛳ ☕ 🍷 🛏
Location 0.5m N of Druimeonbeg farm shop

GLENROTHES Map 11 NO20

Glenrothes Golf Course Rd KY6 2LA
☎ 01592 754561
Mature parkland, challenging back nine with burn crossing 4 fairways. Wide fairways offer opportunities for long hitters and birdy chances for those with good short game.
18 holes, 6444yds, Par 71, SSS 71, Course record 67.
Club membership 750.

Visitors no restrictions except for some times at weekends . Bookings for parties can be made in advance.
Societies write to secretary.
Green Fees £16 per day; £10 per round (£20/£14 weekends).
Designer J R Stutt
Facilities ⊗ ☽ ⛳ ☕ 🍷 🎔
Location W side of town off B921

Hotel ★★★ 66% Balgeddie House Hotel, Balgeddie Way, GLENROTHES ☎ 01592 742511 19 ⇌ ↱

GLENSHEE (SPITTAL OF) Map 15 NO16

Dalmunzie Dalmunzie Estate PH10 7QG
☎ 01250 885226 Fax 01250 885225
Well maintained Highland course with difficult walking. Testing short course with small but good greens.
9 holes, 2035yds, Par 30, SSS 30.
Club membership 70.

Visitors restricted Sun 10.30-11.30am.
Societies advance contact preferred.
Green Fees £10 per day; £7 per 9 holes; £40 per week.
Facilities ⊗ ☽ ⛳ ☕ 🍷 🏠 🎾 🛏
& Leisure hard tennis courts, fishing, clay pigeon shooting, mountain bike hire.
Location 2m NW of Spittal of Glenshee

Hotel ★★♣ 67% Dalmunzie House Hotel, SPITTAL OF GLENSHEE ☎ 01250 885224 18rm(16 ⇌ ↱)

GOREBRIDGE Map 11 NT36

Vogrie Vogrie Estate Country Park EH23 4NU
☎ 01875 821716
A 9-hole municipal course located within a country park. The wide fairways are particularly suited to beginners.
9 holes, 2530yds, Par 33.
Visitors book by telephone 24 hrs in advance.
Green Fees £5.40 per 9 holes.
Facilities
Location Off B6372

Hotel ★★★ 64% Johnstounburn House, HUMBIE ☎ 01875 833696
11rm(10) Annexe9

GOUROCK Map 10 NS27

Gourock Cowal View PA19 1HD
☎ 01475 631001 Fax 01475 631001
Moorland course with hills and dells. Testing 8th hole, par 5. Magnificent views over Firth of Clyde.
18 holes, 6512yds, Par 73, SSS 73, Course record 64.
Club membership 720.
Visitors must have handicap certificate or letter of introduction. May not play Sat.
Societies welcome weekdays, must contact in advance.
Green Fees £26 per day; £18 per round (£28/£22 weekends).
Prof Gavin Coyle
Designer J Braid/H Cotton
Facilities
Location SW side of town off A770

Hotel ★★★ 63% Manor Park Hotel, LARGS
☎ 01475 520832 10 Annexe13

GREENOCK Map 10 NS27

Greenock Forsyth St PA16 8RE ☎ 01475 720793
Testing moorland course with panoramic views of Clyde Estuary.
18 holes, 5838yds, Par 69, SSS 69.
Club membership 730.
Visitors may not play Sat. Must contact in advance and have a handicap certificate.
Societies must telephone in advance.
Green Fees not confirmed.
Prof Graham Ross
Designer James Braid
Facilities
Location SW side of town off A770

Hotel ★★★ 63% Manor Park Hotel, LARGS
☎ 01475 520832 10 Annexe13

Greenock Whinhill Beith Rd PA16 9LN
☎ 01475 724694 evenings & weekends only
Picturesque heathland public course.
18 holes, 5504yds, Par 68, SSS 68, Course record 64.
Club membership 200.
Visitors may only use club facilities with member.
Green Fees not confirmed.
Facilities
Location 1.5m SW off B7054

Hotel ★★★ 63% Manor Park Hotel, LARGS
☎ 01475 520832
10 Annexe13

GULLANE Map 12 NT48

Gullane West Links Rd EH31 2BB
☎ 01620 842255 Fax 01620 842327
Gullane is a delightful village and one of Scotland's great golf centres. Gullane club was formed in 1882. There are three Gullane courses and the No 1 is of championship standard. It differs from most Scottish courses in as much as it is of the upland links type and really quite hilly. The first tee is literally in the village. The views from the top of the course are magnificent and stretch far and wide in every direction - in fact, it is said that 14 counties can be seen from the highest spot.
Course No 1: 18 holes, 6466yds, Par 71, SSS 72, Course record 65.
Course No 2: 18 holes, 6244yds, Par 71, SSS 70, Course record 63.
Course No 3: 18 holes, 5252yds, Par 68, SSS 66.
Club membership 1200.
Visitors advance booking recommended.
Societies advance booking advised.
Green Fees not confirmed.
Cards
Prof Jimmy Hume
Designer Willie Park
Facilities
Location At west end of village on A198

Hotel ★★★ Greywalls Hotel, Muirfield, GULLANE
☎ 01620 842144 17 Annexe5

MUIRFIELD (HONOURABLE COMPANY OF EDINBURGH GOLFERS) See page 351.

HADDINGTON Map 12 NT57

Haddington Amisfield Park EH41 4PT
☎ 01620 823627 Fax 01620 826058
Inland course, tree-lined and bunkered, but not hilly.
18 holes, 6317yds, Par 71, SSS 70, Course record 68.
Club membership 650.
Visitors may not play between 7am-10am & noon-2pm at weekends. Must contact in advance.
Societies must contact in advance; deposits required.
Green Fees £25 per day; £17 per round (£30/£22 weekends).
Prof John Sandilands
Facilities
Location E side off A613

Hotel ★★ 70% Tweeddale Arms Hotel, GIFFORD ☎ 01620 810240 16

HELENSBURGH Map 10 NS28

Helensburgh 25 East Abercromby St G84 9JD
☎ 01436 674173 Fax 01436 671170
Sporting moorland course with superb views of Loch Lomond and River Clyde.
18 holes, 6104yds, Par 69, SSS 70, Course record 64.
Club membership 880.
Visitors may not play at weekends.
Societies must contact in writing.
Green Fees £25 per day; £17 per round.
Cards
Prof David Fotheringham
Designer Old Tom Morris
Facilities
Location NE side of town off B832

Hotel ★★ 61% Commodore Toby Hotel, 112 West Clyde St, HELENSBURGH ☎ 01436 676924 45

INNELLAN Map 10 NS17

Innellan Knockamillie Rd PA23 7SG
☎ 01369 830242 & 703327
Situated above the village of Innellan, this undulating hilltop course has extensive views of the Firth of Clyde.
9 holes, 4683yds, Par 64, SSS 64, Course record 63.
Club membership 199.
Visitors welcome but may not play after 5pm on Mondays.
Societies telephone initially.
Green Fees not confirmed.
Facilities
Location 4m S of Dunoon

Hotel ★★ 66% Royal Marine Hotel, Hunters Quay, DUNOON ☎ 01369 705810 25 Annexe10

Entries with a shaded background identify courses that are considered to be particularly interesting

INVERARAY Map 10 NN00

Inveraray Lochgilphead Rd ☎ 01499 302508
Testing parkland course with beautiful views overlooking Loch Fyne.
9 holes, 5790yds, Par 70, SSS 68.
Club membership 160.
Visitors welcome.
Societies write or telephone to the secretary.
Green Fees £10 per day.
Facilities
Location 1m S of Inveraray

ISLAY, ISLE OF Map 10 NR34

PORT ELLEN Map 10 NR34

Machrie Hotel Machrie PA42 7AN
☎ 01496 302310 Fax 01496 302404
Championship links course opened in 1891, where golf's first £100 Open Championship was played in 1901. Fine turf and many blind holes. Par 4.
18 holes, 6226yds, Par 71, SSS 71, Course record 65.
Club membership 340.
Visitors no restrictions.
Societies apply in writing or telephone.
Green Fees £20 per round.
Cards
Designer W Campbell
Facilities
& Leisure fishing.
Location 4m N off A846

Hotel ★★ 58% Lochside Hotel, 19 Shore St, BOWMORE ☎ 01496 810244 8

KENMORE Map 14 NN74

Kenmore PH15 2HN ☎ 01887 830226 Fax 01887 830211
Testing course in mildly undulating natural terrain. Beautiful views in tranquil setting by Loch Tay.
9 holes, 6052yds, Par 70, SSS 69, Course record 69.
Club membership 200.
Visitors advance booking advisable.
Societies telephone in advance.
Green Fees £16 per day; £11 per 18 holes; £8 per 9 holes (£18/£12/£9 weekends).
Cards
Designer Robin Menzies
Facilities
& Leisure fishing.
Location On A827, beside Kenmore Bridge

Hotel ★★ 62% Fortingall Hotel, FORTINGALL ☎ 01887 830367 & 830368 Fax 01887 830367 10

Taymouth Castle PH15 2NT
☎ 01887 830228 Fax 01887 830830
Parkland course set amidst beautiful mountain and loch scenery. Easy walking. Fishing.
18 holes, 6066yds, Par 69, SSS 69, Course record 62.
Club membership 250.
Visitors must book in advance for parties.
Societies must contact in advance.

MUIRFIELD

(Honourable Company of Edinburgh Golfers)

GULLANE *East Lothian* ☎ 01620 842123

Fax 01620 842977 Map 12 NT 48

John Ingham writes: Ask an American superstar to name the best golf course in Great Britain, or maybe even in the entire world, and the likely answer will be Muirfield. It certainly features in the top ten of any meaningful selection.

Purely on shape and balance, the course has everything. Ask competitors in the Open Championship what they think of the last nine holes, and they will tell you it can wreck the stoutest heart. But ask Isoa Aoki of Japan what he thinks, and he will smile and maybe tell of his course record 63 here.

The course was designed by Old Tom Morris in 1891. However, the club was founded in 1744, making it just ten years older than the Royal & Ancient itself but not as old as Royal Blackheath. However, these dates show that Muirfield certainly has seniority and tradition. Quite simply, it is exclusive and entirely excellent. Muirfield has staged some outstanding Open Championships with one, I suspect, standing out in people's minds more than any other.

Back in 1972, Tony Jacklin was Europe's best player and looked set to prove it again at Muirfield when he had appeared to wear down Lee Trevino, the defending champion. At the 71st hole, Trevino seemed to be frittering away strokes as he mis-hit a shot downwind through the dry, fast, green. The next few minutes were truly hair-raising 'I was mad' recalled Trevino. 'My next shot from the bank was strictly a give-up one. And the ball went straight in the hole.' Jacklin had chipped up, well short. Then he missed his putt, turned for the return putt, and missed again. We all did mental arithmetic. Jacklin had blown it and when he bogeyed the last, furious at himself, he suddenly wasn't the winner - Trevino was.

Those of us who were there recall Trevino had holed one bunker shot, and chipped in three times. Muirfield looked on his brilliance with favour and sad Jacklin never won an Open again.

Visitors contact in advance and have handicap certificate

Societies telephone in advance. But restricted to Tue and Thur

Green fees £85 per day; £65 per round

Facilities

Location Duncur Rd, Muirfield, Gullane EH31 2EG (off A198 on NE side of village)

18 holes, 6601 yards, Par 70, SSS 73, Course record 63

WHERE TO STAY AND EAT NEARBY

HOTELS:

ABERLADY

★★ 68% Kilspindie House, Main St. ☎ 01875 870682. 26 (8 18)

GULLANE

★★★ Greywalls, Muirfield. ☎ 01620 842144. 17 (16 1) Annexe 5

NORTH BERWICK

★★★ 64% The Marine, Cromwell Rd. ☎ 01620 892406. 83

★★ 60% Nether Abbey, 20 Dirleton Ave. ☎ 01620 892802. 16 (6 4)

RESTAURANT:

GULLANE

La Potinière, Main St. ☎ 01620 843214.

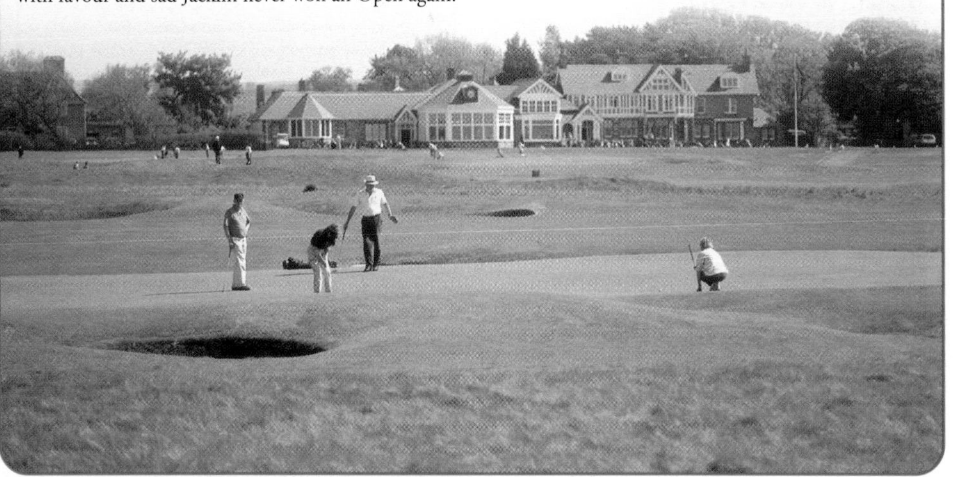

Green Fees £28 per day; £17 round (£38/£21 weekends).
Prof Alex Marshall
Designer James Braid
Facilities ⊗
& Leisure hard tennis courts, fishing.
Location 1m E on A827, 5m W of Aberfeldy

Hotel ★★ 62% Fortingall Hotel, FORTINGALL 01887 830367 & 830368 Fax 01887 830367 10

KILLIN Map 11 NN53

Killin FK21 8TX 01567 820312
Parkland course with good views. Glorious setting.
9 holes, 2600yds, Par 66, SSS 65, Course record 61.
Club membership 250.
Visitors may not play competition days, parties must book in advance.
Societies previous record of courses visited required. Apply in writing or telephone in advance.
Green Fees £15 per day; £12 per round.
Designer John Duncan
Facilities ⊗
Location 1m N on A827

Hotel ★★★ 63% Dall Lodge Country House Hotel, Main St, KILLIN 01567 820217 10

KILMACOLM Map 10 NS36

Kilmacolm Porterfield Rd PA13 4PD
01505 872139 Fax 01505 874007
Moorland course, easy walking, fine views. Testing 7th, 13th and 14th holes.
18 holes, 5961yds, Par 69, SSS 69, Course record 64.
Club membership 850.
Visitors must contact in advance, visitors welcome Tuesday, Wednesday & Thursday.
Societies apply in writing.
Green Fees £30 per 2 rounds; £20 per round.
Prof David Stewart
Designer Willie Campbell
Facilities ⊗
Location SE side of town off A761

Hotel ★★★★ 67% Gleddoch House Hotel, LANGBANK 01475 540711 39

KINCARDINE Map 11 NS98

Tulliallan Alloa Rd FK10 4BB 01259 730396
Partially hilly parkland course with testing 3rd hole (par 4).
18 holes, 5982yds, Par 69, SSS 69.
Club membership 525.
Visitors restricted at weekends.
Societies may not play on Sat; must contact in advance.
Green Fees not confirmed.
Prof Steven Kelly
Facilities
Location 1m NW on A977

Hotel ★★★ 63% Dall Lodge Country House Hotel, Main St, KILLIN 01567 820217 10

KINGHORN Map 11 NT28

Kinghorn Macduff Cres KY3 9RE 01592 890345
Municipal course, 300 ft above sea level with views over Firth of Forth and North Sea. Undulating and quite testing. Facilities shared by Kinghorn Ladies.
18 holes, 5269yds, Par 65, SSS 67.
Club membership 190.
Visitors no restrictions.
Societies must contact in writing.
Green Fees not confirmed.
Facilities ⊗ by prior arrangement by prior arrangement by prior arrangement by prior arrangement
Location S side of town on A921

Hotel ★★★ 60% Dean Park Hotel, Chapel Level, KIRKCALDY 01592 261635 20 Annexe12

KINROSS Map 11 N010

Green Hotel 2 The Muirs KY13 7AS
01577 863407 Fax 01577 863180
Two interesting and picturesque parkland courses, with easy walking.
Red Course: 18 holes, 6256yds, Par 73, SSS 71.
Blue Course: 18 holes, 6438yds, Par 71, SSS 72.
Club membership 600.
Visitors must contact in advance.
Societies must contact in advance.
Green Fees notr comfirmed.
Prof Stuart Geraghty

Designer Sir David Montgomery
Facilities
& Leisure hard tennis courts, heated indoor swimming pool, squash, fishing, sauna, solarium.
Location NE side of town on B996

Hotel ★★★ 73% Green Hotel, 2 The Muirs, KINROSS ☎ 01577 863467 47

KIRKCALDY Map 11 NT29

Dunnikier Park Dunnikier Way KY1 3LP
☎ 01592 261599
Parkland, rolling fairways, not heavily bunkered, views of Firth of Forth.
18 holes, 6036metres, Par 72, SSS 72, Course record 65.
Club membership 660.
Visitors visitors must contact course starter in person.
Societies apply in writing.
Green Fees £16 per day; £10 per round (£20/£14 weekends).
Prof Gregor Whyte
Facilities
Location 2m N on B981

Hotel ★★★ 60% Dean Park Hotel, Chapel Level, KIRKCALDY
☎ 01592 261635 20 Annexe12

Kirkcaldy Balwearie Rd KY2 5LT
☎ 01592 205240 & 203258 (Pro Shop)
Challenging parkland course in rural setting, with beautiful views. On-course watering ensures good conditions all season.
18 holes, 6004yds, Par 71, SSS 69, Course record 65.
Club membership 822.
Visitors may not play Sat. Advised to contact pro-shop 01592 203258.
Societies telephone bookings.
Green Fees £22 per day; £16 per round (£32/£22 Sun).
Prof Anthony Caira
Facilities
Location SW side of town off A910

Hotel ★★★ 60% Dean Park Hotel, Chapel Level, KIRKCALDY
☎ 01592 261635 20 Annexe12

KIRRIEMUIR Map 15 NO35

Kirriemuir Shielhill Rd, Northmuir DD8 4LN
☎ 01575 573317 Fax 01575 573317
Parkland and heathland course set at the foot of the Angus glens, with good view.
18 holes, 5553yds, Par 68, SSS 67, Course record 62.
Club membership 750.
Visitors must play with member at weekends.
Societies must apply in advance, may not play weekends.
Green Fees £22 per day; £16 per round.
Cards
Prof A Caira
Designer James Braid
Facilities
Location 1m N off B955

Hotel ★★★ 73% Castleton House Hotel, Castleton of Eassie, GLAMIS ☎ 01307 840340 6

LADYBANK Map 11 NO30

Ladybank Annsmuir KY15 7RA
☎ 01337 830814 Fax 01337 831505
Picturesque parkland/heathland course, popular with visitors. Qualifying course for the British Open.
18 holes, 6641yds, Par 71, SSS 72, Course record 63.
Club membership 900.
Visitors advance booking essential.
Societies must telephone or write in advance.
Green Fees £38 per day; £28 per round (£35 weekends, no advance booking, very limited).
Cards
Prof Martin Gray
Facilities
Location N side of village off B9129

Hotel ★★ 66% Lomond Hills Hotel, Parliament Square, FREUCHIE
☎ 01337 857329 & 857498
Fax 01337 858180 25

LARBERT Map 11 NS88

Falkirk Tryst 86 Burnhead Rd FK5 4BD
☎ 01324 562054 & 562415
Moorland course, fairly level with trees and broom, well-bunkered. Winds can affect play.
18 holes, 6053yds, Par 70, SSS 69, Course record 62.
Club membership 850.
Visitors must contact in advance no play at weekends.
Societies visitors welcome Mon-Fri must book or telephone.
Green Fees £25 per day; £16 per round.
Prof Steven Dunsmore
Facilities
Location 1m NE off A88/B905

Hotel ★★★★ 68% Inchyra Grange Hotel, Grange Rd, POLMONT
☎ 01324 711911 109

Glenbervie Clubhouse Stirling Rd FK5 4SJ
☎ 01324 562605 Fax 01324 551054
Parkland course with good views.
18 holes, 6423yds, Par 71, SSS 70, Course record 65.
Club membership 600.
Visitors must contact in advance and be accompanied by member.
Societies Tue & Thu only. Apply in writing.
Green Fees not confirmed.
Prof John Chillas
Designer James Braid
Facilities
Location 2m NW on A9

Hotel ★★★★ 68% Inchyra Grange Hotel, Grange Rd, POLMONT
☎ 01324 711911 109

LESLIE Map 11 NO20

Leslie Balsillie Laws KY6 3EZ ☎ 01592 620040
Challenging parkland course.
9 holes, 4686yds, Par 63, SSS 64, Course record 63.
Club membership 230.

Visitors contact secretary in writing.
Societies letter to the Secretary.
Green Fees £8.25 per day (£10.25 weekends).
Designer Tom Morris
Facilities
Location N side of town off A911

Hotel ★★★ 66% Balgeddie House Hotel, Balgeddie Way, GLENROTHES
☎ 01592 742511 19

LEUCHARS Map 12 NO42

St Michaels KY16 0DX
☎ 01334 839365 & 838666 Fax 01334 838666
Parkland course with open views over Fife and Tayside. The undulating course weaves its way through tree plantations. The short Par 4 17th, parallel to the railway and over a pond to a stepped green, poses an interesting challenge.
18 holes, 5802yds, Par 70, SSS 68, Course record 69.
Club membership 550.
Visitors may not play on Sun before noon.
Societies must apply in writing, limited weekends
Green Fees £25 per day; £18 per round.
Facilities
Location NW side of village on A919

Hotel ★★ 69% Eden House Hotel, 2 Pitscottie Rd, CUPAR
☎ 01334 652510 9 Annexe2

LEVEN Map 11 NO30

Leven Links The Promenade KY8 4HS
☎ 01333 428859 & 421390 Fax 01333 428859
Leven has the classic ingredients which make up a golf links in Scotland; undulating fairways with hills and hallows, out of bounds and a 'burn' or stream. A top class championship links course used for British Open final qualifying stages, it has fine views over Largo Bay.
18 holes, 6436yds, Par 71, SSS 70, Course record 62.
Club membership 1000.
Visitors contact in advance. Limited availability Fri pm & Sat, contact for these times no more than 5 days in advance.
Societies apply in advance.
Green Fees £34 per day; £24 per round (£40/£28 weekends).
Designer Tom Morris
Facilities
Hotel ★★★ 59% Caledonian Hotel, 81 High St, LEVEN ☎ 01333 424101 24

Scoonie North Links KY8 4SP ☎ 01333 423437
A pleasant inland links course suitable for all ages.
18 holes, 4979mtrs, SSS 65.
Club membership 150.
Visitors no restrictions.
Societies apply in writing.
Green Fees £16 per day: £10 per round (£20/£14 weekends).
Facilities
Hotel ★★★ 59% Caledonian Hotel, 81 High St, LEVEN
☎ 01333 424101 24

LINLITHGOW Map 11 NS97

Linlithgow Braehead EH49 6QF
☎ 01506 842585 (Secretary) & 844356 (Pro) Fax 01506 84 2764
Slightly hilly parkland course in beautiful setting.
18 holes, 5800yds, Par 70, SSS 68.
Club membership 400.
Visitors may not play Sat. Must book in advance Sun.
Societies must contact in writing.
Green Fees not confirmed.
Prof Steven Rosie
Designer R Simpson of Carnoustie
Facilities
Location 1m S off Bathgate Road off A803

Hotel ★★★★ 68% Inchyra Grange Hotel, Grange Rd, POLMONT ☎ 01324 711911 109

West Lothian Airngath Hill EH49 7RH
☎ 01506 826030 Fax 01506 826030
Hilly parkland course with superb views of River Forth.
18 holes, 6406yds, Par 71, SSS 71, Course record 64.
Club membership 800.
Visitors weekends by arrangement. Advisable to contact in high season.
Societies apply in writing.
Green Fees £22 day ; £17 per round (£30/£22 weekends).
Prof Colin Gillies
Designer Fraser Middleton
Facilities
Location 1m S off A706

Hotel ★★★★ 68% Inchyra Grange Hotel, Grange Rd, POLMONT ☎ 01324 711911 109

LIVINGSTON Map 11 NT06

Deer Park Golf & Country Club Golfcourse Rd EH54 9EG
☎ 01506 431037
Long testing course, fairly flat, championship standard.
18 holes, 6688yds, Par 72, SSS 72, Course record 65.
Club membership 650.
Visitors must book in advance, Sun after 10am.
Societies telephone or write
Green Fees not confirmed.
Prof William Yule
Designer Alliss/Thomas
Facilities
& Leisure heated indoor swimming pool, squash, sauna, solarium, gymnasium.
Location N side of town off A809

Hotel B Hilton National Livingston, Almondview, LIVINGSTON ☎ 01506 431222 120

Pumpherston Drumshoreland Rd, Pumpherston EH53 0LH
☎ 01506 432869
Undulating parkland course with testing 6th hole (par 4), and view of Pentland Hills.
9 holes, 5382yds, Par 66, SSS 66, Course record 64.
Club membership 430.
Visitors must be accompanied by a member.
Societies apply in writing to the secretary.
Green Fees not confirmed.
Facilities
Location 1m E between A71 & A89

Hotel B Hilton National Livingston, Almondview, LIVINGSTON ☎ 01506 431222 120

LOCHGELLY Map 11 NT19

Lochgelly Cartmore Rd KY5 9PB ☎ 01592 780174
Parkland course with easy walking and often windy.
18 holes, 5491yds, Par 68, SSS 67.
Club membership 650.
Visitors no restrictions.
Societies must apply in writing.
Green Fees not confirmed.
Facilities
Location W side of town off A910

Hotel ★★★ 60% Dean Park Hotel, Chapel Level, KIRKCALDY ☎ 01592 261635 20 Annexe12

Lochore Meadows Lochore Meadows Country Park, Crosshill KY5 8BA ☎ 01592 414300 Fax 01592 414345
Lochside course with natural stream running through, and woodland nearby. Country park offers many leisure facilities.
9 holes, 5554yds, Par 72, SSS 71.
Club membership 200.
Visitors no restrictions.
Societies must contact in advance.
Green Fees £7.50 per 18 holes; £4.50 per 9 holes (£10/£6.50 weekends & bank holidays).
Facilities
& Leisure fishing.
Location 2m N off B920

Hotel ★★★ 73% Green Hotel, 2 The Muirs, KINROSS ☎ 01577 863467 47

LOCHGILPHEAD Map 10 NR88

Lochgilphead Blarbuie Rd PA31 8LE ☎ 01546 602340
A varied course with short but interesting holes. Some elevated greens and tees and some tight fairways.
9 holes, 2242yds, Par 64, SSS 63, Course record 54.
Club membership 250.
Visitors restricted during weekend club competitions.
Societies apply in advance, restricted wekends.
Green Fees £10 per day; £30 per week.
Designer Dr I McCamond
Facilities
Location Adjacent to the hospital. Signposted from the village.

Hotel ★★ 64% The Stag Hotel, Argyll St, LOCHGILPHEAD ☎ 01546 602496 17

LONGNIDDRY Map 12 NT47

Longniddry Links Rd EH32 0NL
☎ 01875 852141 & 01875 852228 Fax 01875
Undulating seaside links and partial parkland course. One of the numerous courses which stretch east from Edinburgh right to Dunbar. The inward half is more open than the wooded outward half, but can be difficult in prevailing west wind. No par 5s.
18 holes, 6219yds, Par 68, SSS 70, Course record 63.
Club membership 1000.
Visitors may book tee times up to 7 days in advance, welcome most times except during competitions
Societies Mon-Thu, apply in writing, handicap certificate required.
Green Fees £38 per day; £27 per round (£35 per round weekends).
Cards
Prof John Gray
Designer H S Colt
Facilities
Location N side of village off A198

Hotel ★★ 68% Kilspindie House Hotel, Main St, ABERLADY ☎ 01875 870682 26

LUNDIN LINKS Map 12 NO40

Lundin Golf Rd KY8 6BA
☎ 01333 320202 Fax 01333 329743
The Leven Links and the course of the Lundin Club adjoin each other. The course is part seaside and part inland. The holes are excellent but those which can be described as seaside holes have a very different nature from the inland style ones. The par 3 14th looks seawards across the Firth of Forth towards Edinburgh and the old railway line defines out of bounds at several holes. A number of burns snake across the fairways.
18 holes, 6394yds, Par 71, SSS 71, Course record 63.
Club membership 820.
Visitors visitors welcome weekdays 9-3.30 (3pm Fridays) and Sat after 2.30pm, no vistors Sun. Book well in advance.
Societies book well in advance by telephoning Secretary (mornings).
Green Fees £36 per day; £28 per round. Sat after 2.30pm £36 per round.
Cards
Prof David Webster
Designer James Braid
Facilities
Location W side of village off A915

Hotel ★★★ 73% Old Manor Hotel, Leven Rd, LUNDIN LINKS ☎ 01333 320368 24

Lundin Ladies Woodielea Rd KY8 6AR
☎ 01333 320832
Short, lowland course with Roman stones on the second fairway, and coastal views.
9 holes, 2365yds, Par 68, SSS 67, Course record 67.
Club membership 350.
Visitors contact in advance. Competition days Wed and some weekends.
Societies telephone secretary.
Green Fees not confirmed.
Facilities
Location W side of village off A915

Hotel ★★★ 73% Old Manor Hotel, Leven Rd, LUNDIN LINKS ☎ 01333 320368 24

LUSS Map 10 NS39

LOCH LOMOND See page 357.

MACHRIHANISH Map 10 NR62

Machrihanish PA28 6PT ☎ 01586 810213
Magnificent seaside links of championship status. The 1st hole is the famous drive across the Atlantic. Sandy soil allows for play all year round. Large greens, easy walking, windy. Fishing.
18 holes, 6228yds, Par 70, SSS 71.
Club membership 995.

Visitors no restrictions.
Societies apply in writing.
Green Fees £32 per day; £23 per round (£38 per day Sat).
Prof Ken Campbell
Designer Tom Morris
Facilities
Location 5m W of Campbeltown on B843

Hotel ★★ 67% Seafield Hotel, Kilkerran Rd, CAMPBELTOWN ☎ 01586 554385 3 Annexe6

MARKINCH Map 11 NO20

Balbirnie Park Balbirnie Park KY7 6NR
☎ 01592 612095 Fax 01592 612383
Scenic parkland course with several interesting holes.
18 holes, 6214yds, Par 71, SSS 70, Course record 65.
Club membership 900.

Visitors must contact in advance. Numbers restricted weekends and visitors must play from yellow tees, smart but casual dress code.
Societies booking forms sent out on request by asst secretary.
Green Fees not confirmed.
Prof D F G Scott
Facilities
Location 2m E of Glenrothes

Hotel ★★★★ Balbirnie House, Balbirnie Park, MARKINCH ☎ 01592 610066 30

MILNATHORT Map 11 NO10

Milnathort South St KY13 7XA ☎ 01577 864069
Undulating inland course with lush fairways and excellent greens for most of the year. Strategically placed copses of trees require accurate tee shots. Different tees and greens for each hole will make for more interesting play.
9 holes, 5969yds, Par 71, SSS 69, Course record 65.
Club membership 600.

Visitors must contact in advance.
Societies advisable to book in advance.
Green Fees not confirmed.
Facilities
Location S side of town on A922

Hotel ★★ 64% The Glenfarg Hotel & Restaurant, Main St, GLENFARG
☎ 01577 830241 15rm(14)

MONIFIETH Map 12 NO43

Monifieth Princes St DD5 4AW
☎ 01382 532767 (Medal) & 532967 (Ashludie)
The chief of the two courses at Monifieth is the Medal Course. It has been one of the qualifying venues for the Open Championship on more than one occasion. A seaside links, but divided from the sand dunes by a railway which provides the principal hazard for the first few holes. The 10th hole is outstanding, the 17th is excellent and there is a delightful finishing hole. The Links is to be used as a qualifying course for the 1999 Open which is being held at Carnoustie. The other course here is the Ashludie, and both are played over by a number of clubs who share the links.
Medal Course: 18 holes, 6655yds, Par 71, SSS 72, Course record 63.
Ashludie Course: 18 holes, 5123yds, Par 68, SSS 66.
Club membership 1750.

Visitors must contact in advance. Restricted to after 2pm Sat, 10am Sun & after 9.30pm Mon-Fri.
Societies must contact in advance by telephone or writing to Medal Starter's Box, Princes St, Monifieth.
Green Fees Medal Course: £36 per day, £26 per round (£30 per round weekends). Ashludie Course: £21 per day, £15 per round (£24/£16 weekends).
Prof Ian McLeod
Facilities
Location NE side of town on A930

Hotel ★★ 69% Carlogie House Hotel, Carlogie Rd, CARNOUSTIE
☎ 01241 853185 12 Annexe4

MONTROSE Map 15 NO75

Montrose Links Trust Traill Dr DD10 8SW
☎ 01674 672932 Fax 01674 671800
The links at Montrose like many others in Scotland are on commonland and are shared by three clubs. The Medal course at Montrose - the fifth oldest in the world - is typical of Scottish seaside links, with narrow, undulating fairways and problems from the first hole to the last. The Broomfield course is flatter and easier.
Medal Course: 18 holes, 6470yds, Par 71, SSS 72, Course record 64.
Broomfield Course: 18 holes, 4788yds, Par 66, SSS 63.
Club membership 1300.

Visitors may not play on the Medal Course on Sat before 2.30pm & before 10am on Sun. Must have a handicap certificate for Medal Course. Contact in advance. No restrictions on Broomfield Course.
Societies must contact secretary in advance.
Green Fees Medal: £33 per day; £22 per round (£45/£30 weekends). Broomfield: £10 per round (£14 weekends).
Cards
Prof Kevin Stables ▶

LOCH LOMOND

Luss, Central Scotland Tel: 01436 655540
Fax: 01436 655535

John Ingham writes - Vikings invaded in the ninth century AD. Later came the dreaded English to plunder. If you know the score, follow the Rob Roy Macgregor trail, but don't drand him a cattle thief. The man is legend from the mists of time. Today, instead of swords and crossbows, visitors are greeted not with a hail of arrows, but with views of glens, castles and, if you have the right connections, the chance to visit and play what I regard as the nation's most important new course, Loch Lomond on the bonnie banks.

I arrived in a new Aston Martin, all the way from London and was invited into what used to be the home of the chiefs of Clan Colquhoun. It is now the splendid clubhouse, boasting the Chinese Drawing Room, portraits in oil, beautiful ceilings and it resembles some wondrous film set. Former Scots Guard Captain Neil Hobday, now club manager, ordered coffee.

And the course? I played on the magnificent stretch, more than 7000 yards and found, from the back tee, the 625-yard 6th, on the very edge of the water, to be a real little Loch Lomond monster. But everywhere you look is a scenic wonder, and the course is so well kept, so interesting and inspiring that Nick Faldo went overboard and claimed it to be the finest new course in Europe. Nobody has denied this.

Designed by two Americans, Jay Morrish and the mighty Tom Weiskopf, it altered my view that few Americans are able to build anything other than artificial-lake covered stretches, similar to the ones you find in Arizona. The main problem is that Loch Lomond is very, very exclusive and getting on the course is about as difficult as getting a pass to play Augusta, or Muirfield.

But this international club is there for ever and Scotland, and all golf, is the beneficiary.

Visitor are only permitted to play as a guest of members.

Facilities Professional (Colin Campbell)

Location Rossdhu House, Luss G83 8NT (off A82 north of Glasgow)

18 holes, 7060yds, Par 71, Course record 62.

WHERE TO STAY AND EAT NEARBY

HOTELS:

BALLOCH

★★★★ 80% Cameron House Hotel. ☎ 01389 755565. 96

LUSS

★★★ 70% The Lodge on Loch Lomond. ☎ 01436 860201 29

Designer W Park/Tom Morris
Facilities
Location NE side of town off A92

Hotel ★★★ 64% Park Hotel, 61 John St, MONTROSE
01674 673415 59rm(53)
Additional hotel ★★★ 64% Links Hotel, Mid Links, MONTROSE 01674 671000
Fax 01674 672698 21

MUCKHART Map 11 NO00

Muckhart FK14 7JH 01259 781423
Scenic heathland/downland course.
Muckhart Course: 18 holes, 6034yds, Par 71, SSS 70, Course record 65.
Naemoor Course: 9 holes, 3234yds, Par 35.
Club membership 750.
Visitors telephone to book - steward 01259 781423 or professional 01259 781493.
Societies booking by prior arrangement.
Green Fees Muckhart: £23 per day; £16 per round (£32/£23 weekends). Naemoor: £12 per 18 holes; (£15 weekends).
Prof Keith Salmoni
Facilities
Location SW of village off A91

Hotel ★★★ 66% Gartwhinzean Hotel, POWMILL
01577 840595 23

MULL, ISLE OF Map 10 NM73

CRAIGNURE Map 10 NM73

Craignure Scallastle PA65 6PB
01680 812487 & 812416 Fax 01680 300402
A natural links course designed round the estuary of the Scallastle Burn that flows into the Sound of Mull. Completely re designed in 1978/9. Continual improvements such as 5 new tees in 1998 will soon provide 18 teeing areas for the 9 hole layout.
9 holes, 5378yds, Par 70, SSS 66, Course record 72.
Club membership 100.
Visitors may not play on competition days, contact for fixture list.
Societies write to the secretary 10 days in advance.
Green Fees £11 per day; £40 per week.
Facilities
Location 1.5m N of Craignure A849

Hotel ★★★ 72% Western Isles Hotel, TOBERMORY
01688 302012 26

TOBERMORY Map 13 NM55

Tobermory PA75 6PG
01688 302338 Fax 01688 302140
A beautifully maintained hilltop course with superb views over the Sound of Mull. Testing 3rd hole (par 3). Often described as the best 9 hole course in Scotland.
9 holes, 4890yds, Par 64, SSS 64, Course record 65.
Club membership 150.
Visitors no restrictions except competition days.
Societies preferable to contact in advance.
Green Fees £13 per day.
Designer David Adams
Facilities
Location 0.5m N off A848

Hotel ★★★ 72% Western Isles Hotel, TOBERMORY
01688 302012 26

MUSSELBURGH Map 11 NT37

Musselburgh Monktonhall EH21 6SA
0131 665 2005
Testing parkland course with natural hazards including trees and a burn, easy walking.
18 holes, 6614yds, Par 71, SSS 73, Course record 65.
Club membership 900.
Visitors must contact in advance.
Societies must contact in advance.
Green Fees not confirmed.
Prof Fraser Mann
Designer James Braid
Facilities
Location 1m S on B6415

Hotel ★★ 62% Iona Hotel, Strathearn Place, EDINBURGH
0131 447 6264 & 0131 447 5050
Fax 0131 452 8574 17rm(15)

Musselburgh Old Course 10 Balcarres Rd, Millhill EH21 7SD ☎ 0131 665 5438 (Starter) & 0131 665 6981
A links type course.
9 holes, 2371yds, Par 34, SSS 33.
Club membership 250.

Visitors may not play at weekends.
Societies must contact in advance.
Green Fees not confirmed.
Facilities
Location 1m E of town off A1

Hotel ★★ 62% Iona Hotel, Strathearn Place, EDINBURGH
☎ 0131 447 6264 & 0131 447 5050
Fax 0131 452 8574 17rm(15)

MUTHILL Map 11 NN81

Muthill Peat Rd PH5 2DA
☎ 01764 681523 Fax 01764 656073
Parkland course with fine views. Not too hilly, tight with narrow fairways.
9 holes, 4700yds, Par 66, SSS 63.
Club membership 500.

Visitors no restrictions.
Societies book in advance.
Green Fees £10 per day (£15 weekends).
Facilities
Location W side of village off A822

Hotel ★★ 69% Murraypark Hotel, Connaught Ter, CRIEFF ☎ 01764 653731 20

NORTH BERWICK Map 12 NT58

Glen East Links, Tantallon Ter EH39 4LE
☎ 01620 895288 & 892726 Fax 01620 895288
An interesting course with a good variety of holes. The views of the town, the Firth of Forth and the Bass Rock are breathtaking.
18 holes, 6089yds, Par 69, SSS 69, Course record 64.
Club membership 650.

Visitors booking advisable.
Societies advance booking recommended.
Green Fees £26 per day; £17 per round (£30/£22 weekends).
Cards
Designer McKenzie Ross
Facilities
Location 1m E of B198

Hotel ★★ 60% Nether Abbey Hotel, 20 Dirleton Av, NORTH BERWICK
☎ 01620 892802 16rm(4 6)

North Berwick Beach Rd EH39 4BB
☎ 01620 892135 Fax 01620 893274
Another of East Lothian's famous courses, the links at North Berwick is still popular. A classic championship links, it has many hazards including the beach, streams, bunkers, light rough and low walls. The great hole on the course is the 15th, the famous 'Redan', selected for television's best 18 in the UK. Used by both the Tantallon and Bass Rock Golf Clubs.
18 holes, 6420yds, Par 71, SSS 71, Course record 64.
Club membership 730.

Visitors must contact in advance.
Societies must contact in advance.
Green Fees £45 per day; £30 per round (£60/£45 weekends).
Cards
Prof D Huish
Facilities
Location W side of town on A198

Hotel ★★★ 64% The Marine, Cromwell Rd, NORTH BERWICK
☎ 01620 892406 83

Whitekirk EH39 5PR
☎ 01620 870300 Fax 01620 870330
Scenic coastal course with lush green fairways, gorse covered rocky banks and stunning views. Natural water hazards and strong sea breezes make this well designed course a good test of golf.
18 holes, 6526yds, Par 72, SSS 72.
Club membership 200.

Visitors no restrictions.
Societies apply in writing or telephone.
Green Fees £18 (£25 weekends).
Cards
Prof Chris Patey
Designer Cameron Sinclair
Facilities
Location 3m off the main A1 Edinburgh/Berwick-upon-Tweed road A198 North Berwick

Hotel ★★ 60% Nether Abbey Hotel, 20 Dirleton Av, NORTH BERWICK
☎ 01620 892802 16rm(4 6)

OBAN Map 10 NM83

Glencruitten Glencruitten Rd PA34 4PU
☎ 01631 564604
There is plenty of space and considerable variety of hole on this downland course - popular with holidaymakers. In a beautiful, isolated situation, the course is hilly and testing, particularly the 1st and 12th, par 4's, and 10th and 15th, par 3's.
18 holes, 4452yds, Par 61, SSS 63, Course record 55.
Club membership 600.

Visitors restricted Thu & weekends
Societies must contact in writing.
Green Fees £15 per round/day (£17 weekends).
Cards
Prof Graham Clark
Designer James Braid
Facilities
Location NE side of town centre off A816

Hotel ★★★ 57% Caledonian Hotel, Station Square, OBAN
☎ 01631 563133 70

PENICUIK Map 11 NT25

Glencorse Milton Bridge EH26 0RD
☎ 01968 677189 Fax 01968 674399
Picturesque parkland course with burn affecting ten holes. Testing 5th hole (237 yds) par 3. ▶

18 holes, 5217yds, Par 64, SSS 66, Course record 60.
Club membership 700.
Visitors contact secretary.
Societies contact secretary for details.
Green Fees £24.50 per day; £18.50 per 18 holes.
Prof Cliffe Jones
Designer J R Strutt
Facilities
Location 1.5m N of Penicuik on A701

Hotel ★★ 62% Roslin Glen Hotel, 2 Penicuik Rd, ROSLIN ☎ 0131 440 2029 7

PERTH Map 11 NO12

Craigie Hill Cherrybank PH2 0NE
☎ 01738 620829 & 622644
Slightly hilly, parkland course. Good views over Perth.
18 holes, 5386yds, Par 66, SSS 67, Course record 60.
Club membership 560.
Visitors restricted access Sat. Telephone up to 3 days in advance.
Societies must contact in writing.
Green Fees not confirmed.
Prof Steven Harrier
Designer Fernie/Anderson
Facilities
Location 1m SW of city centre off A952

Hotel ★★★ 58% The Royal George, Tay St, PERTH ☎ 01738 624455 42

King James VI Moncreiffe Island PH2 8NR
☎ 01738 445132 (Secretary) Fax 01738 445132
Parkland course, situated on island in the middle of River Tay. Easy walking.
18 holes, 6038yds, Par 70, SSS 69, Course record 62.
Club membership 650.
Visitors visitors restricted on competition days. Contact professional for bookings.
Societies book by telephone.
Green Fees not confirmed.
Prof Tony Coles
Designer Tom Morris
Facilities
Location SE side of city centre

Hotel ★★★ 63% Queens Hotel, Leonard St, PERTH ☎ 01738 442222 51

Murrayshall Country House Hotel Murrayshall, Scone PH2 7PH ☎ 01738 552784 & 551171 Fax 01738 552595
This course is laid out in 130 acres of parkland with tree-lined fairways, magnificent views of the Grampian Highlands. Hotel and driving range.
18 holes, 6441yds, Par 73, SSS 72.
Club membership 350.
Visitors no restrictions.
Societies telephone in advance.
Green Fees not confirmed.
Cards
Prof Alan Reid
Designer Hamilton Stutt
Facilities
& Leisure hard tennis courts, sauna, gymnasium.
Location E side of village off A94

Hotel ★★★★ 74% Murrayshall Country House Hotel & Golf Course, New Scone, PERTH ☎ 01738 551171 27

North Inch North Inch, off Hay St PH1 5PH
☎ 01738 636481
An enjoyable short and often testing course incorporating mature trees, open parkland with fine views and attractive riverside.
18 holes, 5178yds, Par 65, Course record 60.
Club membership 476.
Visitors advisable to telephone in advance. Due to a flood prevention wall to be built late 97/98 there may be some disruption.
Green Fees not confirmed.
Designer Tom Morris
Facilities
& Leisure squash, gymnasium.
Hotel ★★★ 58% The Royal George, Tay St, PERTH ☎ 01738 624455 42

PITLOCHRY Map 14 NN95

Pitlochry Pitlochry Estate Office PH16 5QY
☎ 01796 472792
A varied and interesting heathland course with fine views and posing many problems. Its SSS permits few errors in its achievement.
18 holes, 5811yds, Par 69, SSS 69, Course record 63.
Club membership 400.
Visitors Sat & Sun may not play before 9.30am.
Societies must contact in advance.
Green Fees not confirmed.

Prof George Hampton
Designer Willy Fernie
Facilities ⊗ 🍴 🍺 ☕ 🍷 👕 🏠 ⛳ 🚜 🏌
Location N side of town off A924

Hotel ★★★ 69% Pine Trees Hotel, Strathview Ter, PITLOCHRY ☎ 01796 472121 19 🛏

POLMONT Map 11 NS97

Grangemouth Polmont Hill FK2 0YE
☎ 01324 503840 Fax 01324 715818
Windy parkland course. Testing holes: 3rd, 4th (par 4's); 5th (par 5); 7th (par 3) 216 yds over reservoir (elevated green); 8th, 9th, 18th (par 4's).
18 holes, 6314yds, Par 71, SSS 71, Course record 70.
Club membership 700.
Visitors must contact in advance.
Societies must contact in writing.
Green Fees not confirmed.
Prof Stuart Campbell
Facilities ⊗ 🍴 🍺 ☕ 🍷 👕 🏠 🏌
Location On unclass rd 0.5m N of M9 junc 4

Hotel ★★★★ 68% Inchyra Grange Hotel, Grange Rd, POLMONT ☎ 01324 711911 109 🛏

Polmont Manuelrigg, Maddiston FK2 0LS
☎ 01324 711277 Fax 01324 712504
Parkland course, hilly with few bunkers. Views of the River Forth and Ochil Hills.
9 holes, 3073yds, Par 72, SSS 69, Course record 66.
Club membership 300.
Visitors no visitors on Sat from Apr-Sep, Mon-Fri must tee of before 5pm.
Societies apply in writing to club secretary.
Green Fees £8 per day (£14 Sun).
Facilities ⊗ 🍴 🍺 ☕ 👕
Location E side of village off A803

Hotel ★★★★ 68% Inchyra Grange Hotel, Grange Rd, POLMONT ☎ 01324 711911 109 🛏

PORT GLASGOW Map 10 NS37

Port Glasgow Devol Rd PA14 5XE
☎ 01475 704181
A moorland course set on a hilltop overlooking the Clyde, with magnificent views to the Cowal hills.
18 holes, 5712yds, Par 68, SSS 68.
Club membership 390.
Visitors may not play on Sat. By prior arrangement or with member Sun.
Societies apply in writing.
Green Fees £20 per day; £15 per round.
Facilities ⊗ 🍴 🍺 ☕ 🍷 👕 🏠
Location 1m S

Hotel ★★★★ 67% Gleddoch House Hotel, LANGBANK ☎ 01475 540711 39 🛏

PRESTONPANS Map 11 NT37

Royal Musselburgh Prestongrange House EH32 9RP
☎ 01875 810276 Fax 01875 810276
Tree-lined parkland course overlooking Firth of Forth.
18 holes, 6237yds, Par 70, SSS 70, Course record 64.
Club membership 970.
Visitors must contact professional in advance, restricted Fri afternoons & weekends.
Societies must contact in advance,
Green Fees not confirmed.
Prof John Henderson
Designer James Braid
Facilities ⊗ 🍴 🍺 ☕ 🍷 👕 🏠 ⛳ 🚜 🚗 🏌
Location W side of town centre off A59

Hotel ★★ 68% Kilspindie House Hotel, Main St, ABERLADY ☎ 01875 870682 26 🛏

RATHO Map 11 NT17

Ratho Park EH28 8NX
☎ 0131 333 2566 333 1752 Fax 0131 333 1752
Flat parkland course.
18 holes, 5900yds, Par 69, SSS 68, Course record 62.
Club membership 850.
Visitors must contact in advance.
Societies must contact in writing.
Green Fees on application.
Prof Alan Pate
Designer James Braid
Facilities ⊗ 🍴 🍺 ☕ 🍷 👕 🏠 🏌
Location 0.75m E, N of A71

Hotel B Forte Posthouse Edinburgh, Corstorphine Rd, EDINBURGH ☎ 0131 334 0390 204 🛏

ST ANDREWS Map 12 NO51

British Golf Museum ☎ 01334 478880 (situated opposite Royal & Ancient Golf Club). The museum which tells the history of golf from its origins to the present day, is of interest to golfers and non-golfers alike. Themed galleries and interactive displays explore the history of the major championships and the lives of the famous players, and trace the development of golfing equipment. An audio-visual theatre shows historic golfing moments.
Open: Etr-mid Oct, daily 9.30am-5.30pm (mid Oct-Etr Thu-Mon 11am-3pm, closed Tue & Wed.
Admission: There is a charge.
☎ for details.

Dukes Course Craigtoun KY16 8NS
☎ 01334 474371 Fax 01334 479456
Blending the characteristics of a links course with an inland course, Dukes offers rolling fairways, undulating greens and a testing woodland section, and magnificent views over St Andrews Bay towards Carnoustie.
18 holes, 6749yds, Par 72, SSS 73.
Club membership 600.
Visitors booking should be in advance to avoid disappointment.
Societies apply in writing or fax in advance.
Green Fees £50 (£55 weekends).
Cards 💳
Prof John Kelly ▶

Designer Peter Thomson
Facilities
& Leisure heated indoor swimming pool, sauna, solarium, gymnasium, tuition available.
Location Follow M90 from Edinburgh onto A91 to Cupar then to St Andrew turning off for Strathkiness

Hotel ★★★★★ 68% The Old Course Hotel, ST ANDREWS ☎ 01334 474371 125

ST ANDREWS LINKS See page 363

ST FILLANS Map 11 NN62

St Fillans South Loch Earn Rd PH6 2NJ ☎ 01764 685312
Fairly flat, beautiful parkland course. Beside the river Earn and set amongst the Perthshire hills. Wonderfully rich in flora, animal and bird life.
9 holes, 5896yds, Par 68, SSS 67, Course record 73.
Club membership 400.

Visitors advisable to contact in advance.
Societies Apr-Oct, apply to starter.
Green Fees not confirmed.
Designer W Auchterlonie
Facilities by prior arrangement
Location E side of village off A85

Hotel ★★★ 69% The Four Seasons Hotel, Loch Earn, ST FILLANS
☎ 01764 685333 12

SALINE Map 11 NT09

Saline Kinneddar Hill KY12 9LT ☎ 01383 852591
Hillside course with panoramic view of the Forth Valley.
9 holes, 5302yds, Par 68, SSS 66, Course record 63.
Club membership 420.

ST ANDREWS LINKS

ST ANDREWS *Fife* ☏ 01334 466666
Fax 01334 477036 Map 12 N051

John Ingham writes: If golf has a mother, then without doubt it is St Andrews, the most famous links in all the world. Sir Winston Churchill is said to have claimed golf was invented by the Devil, and if this is so then the famous Old Course must be the Devil's playground. How can one reconcile these two thoughts; the birthplace and mother of the game - and yet the very Devil of a test?

The great Bobby Jones started by hating St Andrews and shredded his card into a hundred pieces, letting it blow in the wind. But eventually he came to love the place, and earn the affection of all golf. However you view St Andrews, you cannot ignore it. That master shot-maker from America, Sam Snead, took one look and claimed they should plant cattle fodder on the bumpy acres. Gary Player once said it should be towed out to sea, and sunk. But Jack Nicklaus loved it so much that when he won an Open title here, he threw his putter into the air. And he went away, and copied several of the St Andrews features in other courses that now decorate this earth.

St Andrews is much more than an 18-hole test. It is a whole experience and a walk in history. Name the famous players of yesteryear, and they played here, taking divots from the very spot that you can also take divots - merely by paying for a ticket. You too can wander out with your clubs to conquer some holes, maybe, and to be brought to a humbling halt by others.

Jack Nicklaus won his most remarkable victory on this course, thanks to an historic missed putt of just 3 feet 6 inches by Doug Sanders, who had needed a final hole par 4 to win the 1970 Open Championship. The all-time course record is 62, shot by Curtis Strange in the 1987 Dunhill Cup. Surely nobody, not even Tiger Woods, can ever beat that as they've now added many extra yards to several holes.

Visitors must telephone in advance
Societies must book at least a month in advance.
Green fees Old course: £72; New Course £31; Jubilee £29, Eden £21; Strathtyrum £16, Balgove £7 (18 holes).
Facilities
Location St. Andrews KY16 9SF (NW of town off the A91)

Old Course: 18 holes, 6566yds, Par 72, SSS 72
New (West Sands Rd): 18 holes, 6604yds, Par 71, SSS 72
Jubilee (West Sands Rd): 18 holes, 6805yds, Par 72, SSS 73
Eden (Dundee Rd): 18 holes, 6112yds, Par 70, SSS 70
Strathtyrum): 18 holes, 5094yds, Par 69, SSS64
Balgove 9 holes 3060 yds, Par 60

WHERE TO STAY AND EAT NEARBY

HOTELS:
ST ANDREWS

★★★★★ 68% Old Course St Andrews, Old Station Rd. ☏ 01334 474371 125

★★★ 77% St Andrews Golf, 40 The Scores. ☏ 01334 472611. 22 (1 21)

★★★66% Scores, 76 The Scores ☏ 01334 472451 30 (2 28)

★★ 64% Glenfarg, Main St. ☏ 01577 830241 15 (9 6)

RESTAURANTS:
CUPAR

Ostlers Close, Bonnygate ☏ 01334 655574

Visitors advisable to contact in advance and may not play Sat, some restrictions Sun.
Societies contact in advance.
Green Fees £9 per day (£11 Sun).
Facilities ⊗)Ⅲ ⛾ ☕ 🍷 ⛾ ⛾
Location 0.5m E at junc B913/914

Hotel ★★★ 64% The King Malcolm Thistle Hotel, Queensferry Rd, Wester Pitcorthie, DUNFERMLINE ☎ 01383 722611 48 ⛾ ⛾

SOUTHEND Map 10 NR60

Dunaverty PA28 6RW ☎ 01586 830677
Undulating, seaside course.
18 holes, 4799yds, Par 66, SSS 63, Course record 59.
Club membership 400.
Visitors limited Sat, contact in advance.
Societies apply in advance.
Green Fees £19.50 per day; £13 per round.
Facilities ⊗)Ⅲ by prior arrangement ⛾ ☕ ⛾ ⛾ ⛾
& Leisure fishing.
Location 10m S of Campbeltown on B842

Hotel ★★ 67% Seafield Hotel, Kilkerran Rd, CAMPBELTOWN ☎ 01586 554385 3 ⛾ Annexe6 ⛾

SOUTH QUEENSFERRY Map 11 NT17

Dundas Parks Dundas Estate EH30 9PQ
☎ 0131 331 3179
Parkland course situated on the estate of Lady Jane Stewart-Clark, with excellent views. For 18 holes, the 9 are played twice.
9 holes, 6024yds, Par 70, SSS 69, Course record 66.
Club membership 500.
Visitors must contact in advance.
Societies must contact in writing.
Green Fees £10 per day.
Facilities ⛾
Location 0.5m S on A8000

Hotel ★★★ 60% Forth Bridges Hotel, 1 Ferrymuir Gate, Forth Bridge, SOUTH QUEENSFERRY ☎ 0131 469 9955 108 ⛾ ⛾

STIRLING Map 11 NS79

Stirling Queens Rd FK8 3AA
☎ 01786 464098 Fax 01786 450748
Undulating parkland course with magnificent views of Stirling Castle and the Grampian Mountains. Testing 15th, 'Cotton's Fancy', 384 yds (par 4).
18 holes, 6438yds, Par 72, SSS 71, Course record 64.
Club membership 1100.
Visitors may reserve tee off times mid week 9-4.30pm. At weekends tee off times may be reserved on day of play subject to availability.
Societies must apply in writing or telephone.
Green Fees £30 per day; £20 per round.
Cards ⛾ ⛾ ⛾ ⛾ ⛾
Prof Ian Collins
Designer James Braid/Henry Cotton
Facilities ⊗)Ⅲ ⛾ ☕ 🍷 ⛾ ⛾ ⛾ ⛾ ⛾
Location W side of town on B8051

Hotel ★★ 66% Terraces Hotel, 4 Melville Ter, STIRLING ☎ 01786 472268 18 ⛾ ⛾

STRATHTAY Map 14 NN95

Strathtay ☎ 01350 727797
A wooded mainly hilly course with pleasing panoramic views. 5th hole 'Spion Kop' is especially difficult. It is steep, with heavy rough on both sides of the hilly fairway and an unsighted green of the back of the hill which is affected by winds.
9 holes, 4082yds, Par 63, SSS 63, Course record 61.
Club membership 158.
Visitors restricted May-Sep; Sun 12.30-5pm & Mon 6-8pm. Also some Wed & Thu evenings.
Societies by letter or telephone to Secretary T D Lind, Lorne Cottage, Dalguise, Dunkeld, Perthshire PH8 0JX.
Green Fees not confirmed.
Facilities ⛾
Location Eastern end of minor rd to Weem, off A827

Hotel ★★ 67% The Weem, Weem, ABERFELDY ☎ 01887 820381 12 ⛾ ⛾

TARBERT Map 10 NR86

Tarbert PA29 6XX ☎ 01880 820536
Beautiful moorland course. Four fairways crossed by streams.
9 holes, 4460yds, Par 66, SSS 63, Course record 62.
Visitors may not play Sat pm.
Societies apply in writing.
Green Fees not confirmed.
Location N1m W on B8024)

Hotel ★★★ 67% Stonefield Castle Hotel, TARBERT ☎ 01880 820836 33 ⛾ ⛾

TAYPORT Map 12 NO42

Scotscraig Golf Rd DD6 9DZ
☎ 01382 552515 Fax 01382 553130
A rather tight course on downland-type turf with an abundance of gorse. The sheltered position of this Open qualifying course ensures good weather throughout the year.
18 holes, 6550yds, Par 71, SSS 72, Course record 69.
Club membership 850.
Visitors restricted at weekends. Must contact in advance.
Societies advance booking.
Green Fees on application.
Cards ⛾ ⛾
Prof S J Campbell
Designer Tom Morris
Facilities ⊗)Ⅲ ⛾ ☕ 🍷 ⛾ ⛾ ⛾ ⛾ ⛾
Location S side of village off B945

Hotel ★★★ 64% The Queen's Hotel, 160 Nethergate, DUNDEE ☎ 01382 322515 47 ⛾ ⛾

THORNTON Map 11 NT29

Thornton Station Rd KY1 4DW
01592 771111 Fax 01592 774955
A relatively flat, lightly tree-lined, parkland course bounded on three sides by rivers which come into play at holes 14-16.
18 holes, 6177yds, Par 70, SSS 69, Course record 64.
Club membership 700.

Visitors restricted at weekends before 10am & between 12.30-2pm, also Tue 1-1.30 & Thu 9-10. Booking in advance recommended.
Societies apply in advance.
Green Fees £25 per day; £15 per round (£32/£22 weekends).
Facilities
Location 1m E of town off A92

Hotel ★★★ 66% Balgeddie House Hotel, Balgeddie Way, GLENROTHES 01592 742511 19

TIGHNABRUAICH Map 10 NR97

Kyles of Bute PA21 2EE 01700 811603
Moorland course which is hilly and exposed to wind. Good views of the Kyles of Bute.
9 holes, 4778yds, Par 66, SSS 64, Course record 62.
Club membership 150.

Visitors may not play Wed pm or Sun am.
Societies telephone in advance.
Green Fees £8 per day/round (£10 weekends).
Facilities
Location 1.25m S off B8000

Hotel ★★ 77% Kilfinan Hotel, KILFINAN 01700 821201 11

TILLICOULTRY Map 11 NS99

Tillicoultry Alva Rd FK13 6BL 01259 750124
Parkland course at foot of the Ochil Hills entailing some hard walking.
9 holes, 4904metres, Par 68, SSS 66, Course record 61.
Club membership 400.

Visitors must contact in advance.
Societies apply to the secretary.
Green Fees not confirmed.
Facilities
Location A91, 9m E of Stirling

Hotel ★★ 66% Harviestoun Country Inn, Dollar Rd, TILLICOULTRY 01259 752522 10

UPHALL Map 11 NT07

Uphall EH52 6JT 01506 856404 Fax 01506 855358
Windy parkland course, easy walking.
18 holes, 5588yds, Par 69, SSS 67, Course record 62.
Club membership 500.

Visitors restricted weekends.
Societies must contact in advance.
Green Fees £19 per day; £14 per round (£26/£18 weekends).
Prof Gordon Law
Facilities
Location W side of village on A899

Hotel ★★★★ 69% Houstoun House Hotel, UPHALL 01506 853831 27 Annexe47

WEST CALDER Map 11 NT06

Harburn EH55 8RS 01506 871131 & 871256
Moorland, reasonably flat.
18 holes, 5921yds, Par 69, SSS 69, Course record 62.
Club membership 870.

Visitors contact secretary, limited weekends.
Societies must contact in writing.
Green Fees not confirmed.
Prof Stephen Mills
Facilities
Location 2m S on B7008

Hotel ★★★ 67% The Hilcroft Hotel, East Main St, WHITBURN 01501 740818 31

WHITBURN Map 11 NS96

Polkemmet Country Park EH47 0AD 01501 743905
Public parkland course surrounded by mature woodland and rhododendron bushes. 15-bay floodlit driving range.
9 holes, 2969mtrs, Par 37.

Visitors no restrictions.
Green Fees £4-£4.50 per round (£4-£5.25 weekends).
Facilities
Location 2m W off B7066

Hotel ★★★ 67% The Hilcroft Hotel, East Main St, WHITBURN 01501 740818 31

SOUTHERN LOWLANDS & BORDERS

This region includes the counties of City of Glasgow, Dumbarton & Clydebank, Dumfries & Galloway, East Ayrshire, East Dunbartonshire, East Renfrewshire, North Ayrshire, North Lanarkshire, Renfrewshire, Scottish Borders, South Ayrshire and South Lanarkshire which reflect the recent national changes.

AIRDRIE Map 11 NS76

Airdrie Rochsoles ML6 0PQ ☎ 01236 762195
Picturesque parkland course with good views.
18 holes, 6004yds, Par 69, SSS 69, Course record 64.
Club membership 450.

Visitors must contact in advance. With member only weekends & bank holidays.
Societies apply in writing.
Green Fees not confirmed.
Prof A McCloskey
Facilities
Location 1m N on B802

Hotel ★★★★ 64% Westerwood Hotel Golf & Country Club, 1 St Andrews Dr, Westerwood, CUMBERNAULD ☎ 01236 457171 49

Easter Moffat Mansion House, Plains ML6 8NP
☎ 01236 842878
Moorland/parkland course.
18 holes, 6221yds, Par 72, SSS 70, Course record 66.
Club membership 450.

Visitors may only play on weekdays.
Societies must contact in advance.
Green Fees £20 per day; £15 per round.
Prof Graham King
Facilities
Location 2m E on old Edinburgh-Glasgow road

Hotel ★★★★ 64% Westerwood Hotel Golf & Country Club, 1 St Andrews Dr, Westerwood, CUMBERNAULD ☎ 01236 457171 49

ARRAN, ISLE OF Map 10 NR94

BLACKWATERFOOT Map 10 NR82

Shiskine Shore Rd KA27 8AH ☎ 01770 860226
Unique 12-hole links course with gorgeous outlook to the Mull of Kintyre.
12 holes, 2990yds, Par 41, SSS 42.
Club membership 520.

Visitors must contact in advance.
Societies must contact in writing in advance. Jul and Aug no parties.
Green Fees not confirmed.
Designer Fernie of Troon
Facilities
& Leisure hard tennis courts.
Location W side of village off A841

Hotel ★★ Kilmichael Country House Hotel, Glen Cloy, BRODICK ☎ 01770 302219 6 Annexe3

BRODICK Map 10 NS03

Brodick KA27 8DL
☎ 01770 302349 & 302513 Fax 01770 302349
Short seaside course, very flat.
18 holes, 4736yds, Par 65, SSS 65, Course record 64.
Club membership 610.

Visitors must contact in advance but may not play at competition times.
Societies must contact secretary in writing.
Green Fees £18 per day; £13 per round (£25/£16 weekends). £65 per week, £80 per fortnight.
Prof Peter McCalla
Facilities
Location N side of village

Hotel ★★★ 76% Auchrannie Country House Hotel, BRODICK ☎ 01770 302234 28

CORRIE Map 10 NS04

Corrie Sannox KA27 8JD
☎ 01770 810223 Fax 01770 810268
A heathland course on the coast with beautiful mountain scenery. An upward climb to 6th hole, then a descent from the 7th. All these holes are subject to strong winds in bad weather.
9 holes, 1948yds, Par 62, SSS 61, Course record 56.
Club membership 240.

Visitors welcome except Sat pm and first Thu afternoon of the month.
Societies maximum size of party 16, apply in advance.
Green Fees £8 per day.
Facilities
Location 6m N of A841

Hotel ★★★ 76% Auchrannie Country House Hotel, BRODICK ☎ 01770 302234 28

LAMLASH Map 10 NS03

Lamlash KA27 8JU
☎ 01770 600296 & 600196 (Starter) Fax 01770 600296
Undulating heathland course with magnificent views of the mountains and sea.
18 holes, 4640yds, Par 64, SSS 64, Course record 61.
Club membership 400.

Visitors contact in advance.
Societies must contact in writing.
Green Fees £16 per day; £10 per round after 4pm (£20 weekends).
Designer Auchterlonie
Facilities
Location 0.75m N of Lamlash on A841. 3m S of Brodick Ferry Terminal

Hotel ★★★ 76% Auchrannie Country House Hotel, BRODICK ☎ 01770 302234 28

LOCHRANZA Map 10 NR95

Lochranza KA27 8HL
☎ 01770 830273 Fax 01770 830600
This course opened in 1991 is mainly on the level, set amid spectacular scenery where the fairways are grazed by wild red deer, while overhead buzzards and golden eagles may be seen. There are water hazards including the river which is lined by mature trees. The final three holes, nicknamed the Bermuda Triangle, provide an absorbing finish right to the 18th hole - a 530 yard dogleg through trees and over the river. The large greens are played off 18 tees.
9 holes, 5033mtrs, Par 70, SSS 70, Course record 74.

Visitors no restrictions; course closed Nov-mid Apr.
Societies advance booking preferred.
Green Fees £16 per day; £10 per 18 holes.
Designer re laid 1991 I Robertson

Facilities

Hotel ★★ Kilmichael Country House Hotel, Glen Cloy, BRODICK
☎ 01770 302219 6 Annexe3

MACHRIE Map 10 NR83

Machrie Bay KA27 8DZ ☎ 01770 850232
Fairly flat seaside course. Designed at turn of century by William Fernie.
9 holes, 4396yds, Par 66, SSS 66, Course record 56.
Club membership 315.
Visitors no restrictions.
Societies write in advance.
Green Fees £7 per day.
Designer W Fernie
Facilities
& Leisure hard tennis courts, fishing.
Location 9m W of Brodick via String Rd

Hotel ★★ Kilmichael Country House Hotel, Glen Cloy, BRODICK
☎ 01770 302219 6 Annexe3

WHITING BAY Map 10 NS02

Whiting Bay KA27 8QT ☎ 01770 700487
Heathland course.
18 holes, 4405yds, Par 63, SSS 63, Course record 59.
Club membership 350.
Visitors tee reserved 8.45-9.30am, also Sun 11.45-1pm.
Societies apply by telephone and confirm in writing with deposit.
Green Fees £15 per day (£30 weekends).
Facilities
& Leisure pool, snooker.
Location NW side of village off A841

Hotel ★★ Kilmichael Country House Hotel, Glen Cloy, BRODICK
☎ 01770 302219 6 Annexe3

AYR Map 10 NS32

Belleisle Belleisle Park KA7 4DU
☎ 01292 441258 Fax 01292 442632
Parkland course with beautiful sea views. First-class conditions.
Belleisle Course: 18 holes, 6431yds, Par 71, SSS 72.
Seafield Course: 18 holes, 5498yds, Par 68, SSS 66.
Club membership 300.
Visitors advised to contact in advance.
Societies advised to contact in advance, telephone 01292 616255.
Green Fees £18 weekdays (£20 weekends).
Prof David Gemmell
Facilities
Location 2m S on A719

Hotel ★★★ 60% Quality Friendly Hotel, Burns Statue Square, AYR
☎ 01292 263268 70

Dalmilling Westwood Av KA8 0QY ☎ 01292 263893
Meadowland course, with easy walking.
18 holes, 5724yds, Par 69, SSS 68.
Club membership 140.
Visitors must contact in advance.
Societies must contact in advance.
Green Fees £20 per day; £12.50 per round weekdays (£13 weekends)..
Prof Philip Cheyney
Facilities
Location 1.5m E of town centre off A719

Hotel ★★ 66% Carlton Toby Hotel, 187 Ayr Rd, PRESTWICK ☎ 01292 476811 34

BALMORE Map 11 NS57

Balmore Golf Course Rd G64 4AW ☎ 01360 620240
Parkland course with fine views.
18 holes, 5530yds, Par 66, SSS 67, Course record 63.
Club membership 700.
Visitors must contact in advance and be accompanied by member.
Societies apply in writing.
Green Fees not confirmed.
Designer James Braid
Facilities
Location N off A807

Hotel ★★★ 64% Black Bull Thistle, Main St, MILNGAVIE ☎ 0141 956 2291 27

BARASSIE Map 10 NS33

Kilmarnock (Barassie) 29 Hillhouse Rd KA10 6SY
☎ 01292 313920 Fax 01292 313920
The club now has a 27 hole layout. Magnificent seaside links, relatively flat with much heather and small, undulating greens.
18 holes, 6817yds, Par 72, SSS 74, Course record 72.
New 9 hole course: 9 holes, 2888yds, Par 34, SSS 34.
Club membership 600.
Visitors with member only Wed & weekends. May not play Fri am. Contact secretary in advance.
Societies must telephone in advance and confirm in writing.
Green Fees £32.50 per 18 holes.
Prof Gregor Howie
Designer Theodore Moone
Facilities
Location E side of village on B746

Hotel ★★★★ 65% Marine Highland Hotel, TROON ☎ 01292 314444 72

BARRHEAD Map 11 NS45

Fereneze Fereneze Av G78 1HJ
☎ 0141 881 1519 Fax 0141 221 0135
Hilly moorland course, with a good view at the end of a hard climb to the 3rd, then levels out.
18 holes, 5821yds, Par 70, SSS 68.
Club membership 700.

Visitors must contact in advance but may not play at weekends.
Societies apply in writing.
Green Fees £20 per day.
Facilities
Location NW side of town off B774

Hotel ★★★ 69% Dalmeny Park Country House, Lochlibo Rd, BARRHEAD ☎ 0141 881 9211 20

BEARSDEN Map 11 NS57

Bearsden Thorn Rd G61 4BP ☎ 0141 942 2351
Parkland course, with 16 greens and 11 teeing grounds. Easy walking and views over city.
9 holes, 6014yds, Par 68, SSS 69, Course record 67.
Club membership 450.
Visitors must be accompanied by and play with member.
Societies apply by writing.
Green Fees not confirmed.
Facilities
Location 1m W off A809

Hotel ★★★ 64% Black Bull Thistle, Main St, MILNGAVIE ☎ 0141 956 2291 27

Douglas Park Hillfoot G61 2TJ ☎ 0141 942 2220
Parkland course with wide variety of holes.
18 holes, 5957yds, Par 69, SSS 69.
Club membership 900.
Visitors must be accompanied by member and must contact in advance.
Societies Wed & Thu. Must telephone in advance.
Green Fees not confirmed.
Prof David Scott
Facilities
Location E side of town on A81

Hotel ★★★ 64% Black Bull Thistle, Main St, MILNGAVIE ☎ 0141 956 2291 27

Windyhill Baljaffray Rd G61 4QQ
☎ 0141 942 2349 Fax 0141 942 5874
Interesting parkland/moorland course with panoramic views of Glasgow and beyond; testing 12th hole.
18 holes, 6254yds, Par 71, SSS 70, Course record 64.
Club membership 800.
Visitors may not play at weekends. Must contact professional in advance.
Societies must apply in writing.
Green Fees £20 per day.
Prof G Collinson
Designer James Braid
Facilities
& Leisure putting green, practice area.
Location 2m NW off B8050

Hotel ★★★ 64% Black Bull Thistle, Main St, MILNGAVIE ☎ 0141 956 2291 27

BEITH Map 10 NS35

Beith Threepwood Rd KA15 2JR ☎ 01505 503166
Hilly course, with panoramic views over 7 counties.
18 holes, 5616yds, Par 68, SSS 68.
Club membership 420.
Visitors contact for details.
Societies apply in writing to secretary at least 1 month in advance.
Green Fees not confirmed.
Facilities
Location 1.5m NE off A737

Hotel ★★★ 66% Bowfield Hotel & Country Club, Lands of Bowfield, HOWWOOD ☎ 01505 705225 23

BELLSHILL Map 11 NS76

Bellshill Community Rd, Orbiston ML4 2RZ
☎ 01698 745124
Parkland course.
18 holes, 5900yds, Par 69, SSS 69.
Club membership 500.
Visitors apply in writing in advance, may not play on competition Sat & Sun.
Societies apply in writing in advance.
Green Fees £18 (£25 weekends & bank holidays).
Facilities
Location 1m SE off A721

Hotel ★★ 63% Silvertrees Hotel, Silverwells Crescent, BOTHWELL ☎ 01698 852311 7 Annexe19

BIGGAR Map 11 NT03

Biggar The Park, Broughton Rd ML12 6AH
☎ 01899 220319
Flat parkland course, easy walking and fine views.
18 holes, 5600yds, Par 67, SSS 66, Course record 61.
Club membership 340.
Visitors Must contact in advance. Smart casual wear required.
Societies must book in advance, observe dress code.
Green Fees £7.50 per round (£10 weekends & bank holidays).
Designer W Park Jnr
Facilities
& Leisure hard tennis courts.
Location S side of town

Hotel ★★★ 70% Shieldhill Hotel, Quothquan, BIGGAR ☎ 01899 220035 12

BISHOPBRIGGS Map 11 NS67

Bishopbriggs Brackenbrae Rd G64 2DX ☎ 0141 772 1810
Parkland course with views to Campsie Hills.
18 holes, 6041yds, Par 69, SSS 69, Course record 63.
Club membership 600.
Visitors must be accompanied by a member and have introduction from own club.
Societies apply in writing to the Committee one month in advance.
Green Fees not confirmed.
Facilities
Location 0.5m NW off A803

Hotel ★★★ 64% Black Bull Thistle, Main St, MILNGAVIE ☎ 0141 956 2291 27

Cawder Cadder Rd G64 3QD ☎ 0141 772 7101
Two parkland courses; Cawder Course is hilly, with 5th, 9th, 10th, 11th-testing holes. Keir Course is flat.
Cawder Course: 18 holes, 6295yds, Par 70, SSS 71.
Keir Course: 18 holes, 5877yds, Par 68, SSS 68.
Club membership 1150.

Visitors must contact in advance & may play on weekdays only.
Societies must contact in writing.
Green Fees not confirmed.
Facilities
Location 1m NE off A803

Hotel ★★★ 64% Black Bull Thistle, Main St, MILNGAVIE ☎ 0141 956 2291 27

Littlehill Auchinairn Rd G64 1UT ☎ 0141 772 1916
Municipal parkland course.
Littlehills Golf Course: 18 holes, 6240yds, Par 70, SSS 70.

Visitors must contact in advance.
Societies advance bookings required in writing
Green Fees £6.40 per round.
Facilities
Location 3m NE of Glasgow city centre on A803

BISHOPTON Map 10 NS47

Erskine PA7 5PH ☎ 01505 862302
Parkland course.
18 holes, 6287yds, Par 71, SSS 70.
Club membership 700.

Visitors introduced by member or by prior arrangement.
Societies apply in writing.
Green Fees not confirmed.
Prof Peter Thomson
Facilities
Location 0.75 NE off B815

Hotel B Forte Posthouse Glasgow/Erskine, North Barr, ERSKINE ☎ 0141 812 0123 166

BONHILL Map 10 NS37

Vale of Leven North Field Rd G83 9ET ☎ 01389 52351
Hilly moorland course, tricky with many natural hazards - gorse, burns, trees. Overlooks Loch Lomond.
18 holes, 5162yds, Par 67, SSS 66, Course record 61.
Club membership 640.

Visitors may not play Sat.
Societies apply to the secretary.
Green Fees £20 per day; £14 per round (£26/£18 Suns).
Facilities
Location E side of town off A813

Hotel ★★ 65% Dumbuck Hotel, Glasgow Rd, DUMBARTON ☎ 01389 734336 22

BOTHWELL Map 11 NS75

Bothwell Castle Blantyre Rd G71 8PJ
☎ 01698 853177 Fax 01698 854052
Flattish tree lined parkland course in residential area.
18 holes, 6200yds, Par 71, SSS 70, Course record 63.
Club membership 1000.

Visitors may only play Mon-Fri 9.30-10.30am & 2-3pm.
Green Fees not confirmed.
Prof Gordon Niven
Facilities
Location NW of village off B7071

Hotel ★★ 63% Silvertrees Hotel, Silverwells Crescent, BOTHWELL ☎ 01698 852311 7 Annexe19

BRIDGE OF WEIR Map 10 NS36

Ranfurly Castle The Clubhouse, Golf Rd PA11 3HN
☎ 01505 612609 Fax 01505 612609
A highly challenging, 240 acre, picturesque moorland course.
18 holes, 6284yds, Par 70, SSS 71, Course record 65.
Club membership 825.

Visitors golf club members on weekdays only, contact in advance.
Societies Tue only, apply in writing.
Green Fees £40 per day; £30 per round.
Prof Tom Eckford
Designer A Kirkcaldy/W Auchterlomie
Facilities by prior arrangement
Location 5m NW of Johnstone

Hotel ★★★ 66% Bowfield Hotel & Country Club, Lands of Bowfield, HOWWOOD ☎ 01505 705225 23

BURNSIDE Map 11 NS66

Blairbeth Fernbrae Av, Fernhill G73 4SF
☎ 0141 634 3355
Parkland course.
18 holes, 5518yds, Par 70, SSS 68, Course record 64.
Club membership 600.

Visitors must contact in advance & may not play weekends.
Societies apply in advance.
Green Fees on application.
Facilities
Location 2m S of Rutherglen off Burnside road

Hotel ★★★ 66% The Macdonald Thistle, Eastwood Toll, GIFFNOCK ☎ 0141 638 2225 56

Cathkin Braes Cathkin Rd G73 4SE
☎ 0141 634 6605 Fax 0141 634 6605
Moorland course, prevailing westerly wind, small loch hazard at 5th hole.
18 holes, 6208yds, Par 71, SSS 71.
Club membership 890.

Visitors must contact in advance & have handicap certificate but may not play at weekends.
Societies apply in writing.
Green Fees £48 per day; £35 per round.
Prof Stephen Bree
Designer James Braid
Facilities
Location 1m S on B759

Hotel ★★★ 66% The Macdonald Thistle, Eastwood Toll, GIFFNOCK ☎ 0141 638 2225 56

CARLUKE Map 11 NS85

Carluke Mauldslie Rd, Hallcraig ML8 5HG
☎ 01555 771070 & 770574
Parkland course with views over the Clyde Valley. Testing 11th hole, par 3.
18 holes, 5853yds, Par 70, SSS 68, Course record 63.
Club membership 750.

Visitors must contact in advance & may not play weekends and bank holidays.
Societies prior arrangement required.
Green Fees £25 per day; £18 per round.
Prof Richard Forrest
Facilities
Location 1m W off A73

Hotel ★★★ 67% Popinjay Hotel, Lanark Rd, ROSEBANK ☎ 01555 860441 42 Annexe5

CARNWATH Map 11 NS94

Carnwath 1 Main St ML11 8JX ☎ 01555 840251
Picturesque parkland course slightly hilly, with small greens calling for accuracy. Panoramic views.
18 holes, 5953yds, Par 70, SSS 69, Course record 63.
Club membership 470.

Visitors restricted after 5pm, no visitors Sat.
Societies apply in writing or telephone.
Green Fees £20 per day (£30 Sun & bank holidays).
Facilities
Location W side of village on A70

Hotel ★★★ 65% Cartland Bridge Hotel, Glasgow Rd, LANARK ☎ 01555 664426 18

CASTLE DOUGLAS Map 11 NX76

Castle Douglas Abercromby Rd DG7 1BB
☎ 01556 502801 or 502099
Parkland course, one severe hill.
9 holes, 2704yds, Par 68, SSS 66.
Club membership 500.

Visitors welcome except Tue & Thu after 4pm & during competitions. Must contact secretary in advance.
Societies apply by writing to secretary.
Green Fees £12 per day/round.
Facilities
Location W side of town

Hotel ★★ 67% Douglas Arms, King St, CASTLE DOUGLAS ☎ 01556 502231 24

CLARKSTON Map 11 NS55

Cathcart Castle Mearns Rd G76 7YL
☎ 0141 638 9449 Fax 0141 638 9449
Tree-lined parkland course, with undulating terrain.
18 holes, 5832yds, Par 68, SSS 68.
Club membership 995.

Visitors must have a handicap certificate from own club.
Societies Tue & Thu only; must apply in writing.
Green Fees not confirmed.
Prof David Naylor
Facilities
Location 0.75m SW off A726

Hotel ★★★ 66% The Macdonald Thistle, Eastwood Toll, GIFFNOCK ☎ 0141 638 2225 56

CLYDEBANK Map 11 NS56

Clydebank & District Glasgow Rd, Hardgate G81 5QY
☎ 01389 873289 & 878686
An undulating parkland course established in 1905 overlooking Clydebank.
18 holes, 5823yds, Par 68, SSS 68, Course record 64.
Club membership 889.

Visitors round only, weekdays only and no bank holidays. Must tee off before 4.30pm. Apply to professional 01389 878686.
Societies must apply in writing.
Green Fees £15 per round.
Prof David Pirie
Facilities
Location 2m E of Erskine Bridge

Hotel ★★★ 65% Patio Hotel, 1 South Av, Clydebank Business Park, CLYDEBANK ☎ 0141 951 1133 80

Dalmuir Municipal Overtoun Rd, Dalmuir G81 3RE
☎ 0141 952 6372
Hilly, compact parkland course with tough finishing holes.
18 holes, 5349yds, Par 67, SSS 66.

Visitors no restrictions.
Societies contact in advance.
Green Fees prices under review.
Prof Stewart Savage
Facilities
& Leisure bowling, hard tennis court Apr-Sep.
Location 2m NW of town centre

Hotel ★★★ 65% Patio Hotel, 1 South Av, Clydebank Business Park, CLYDEBANK ☎ 0141 951 1133 80

COATBRIDGE Map 11 NS76

Drumpellier Drumpellier Av ML5 1RX
☎ 01236 424139 Fax 01236 428723
Parkland course.
18 holes, 6227yds, Par 71, SSS 70, Course record 60.
Club membership 827.

Visitors must contact in advance, may not play weekends.
Societies apply in advance.
Green Fees £30 per day; £22 per round.
Prof David Ross
Designer W Fernie
Facilities
Location 0.75m W off A89

Hotel ★★★ 67% Bothwell Bridge Hotel, 89 Main St, BOTHWELL ☎ 01698 852246 90

COLDSTREAM Map 12 NT83

Hirsel Kelso Rd TD12 4NJ
☎ 01890 882678 & 882233 Fax 01890 882233
A beautifully situated parkland course set in the Hirsel Estate, with panoramic views of the Cheviot Hills. Each hole offers a different challenge especially the 7th, a 170yd par 3 demanding accuracy of flight and length from the tee to ensure achieving a par.
18 holes, 6092yds, Par 70, SSS 70, Course record 65.
Club membership 680.

Visitors contact for details, no restrictions.
Societies write or telephone the secretary in advance.
Green Fees £18 per day (£25 weekends & bank holidays).
Facilities
Location At W end of Coldstream on A697

Hotel ★★★ 72% Tillmouth Park Hotel, CORNHILL-ON-TWEED
☎ 01890 882255 12 Annexe2

COLVEND Map 11 NX85

Colvend Sandyhills DG5 4PY
☎ 01556 630398 & 610878 (Sec)
Picturesque and challenging course on Solway coast. Superb views.
18 holes, 5220yds, Par 68, SSS 67.
Club membership 490.

Visitors restricted Apr-Sep on Tue, 1st tee reserved for weekly Medal 1-1.30 & 4-6pm and some weekends for open competitions.
Societies must telephone in advance.
Green Fees £18 per day.
Designer Allis & Thomas
Facilities
Location 6m from Dalbeattie on A710 Solway Coast Rd

Hotel ★★ 63% Clonyard House Hotel, COLVEND
☎ 01556 630372 15

CUMBERNAULD Map 11 NS77

Dullatur 1A Glen Douglas Dr G68 0DW
☎ 01236 723230 Fax 01236 727271
Dullatur Carrickstone is a parkland course, with natural hazards and wind. Dullatur Antonine, designed by Dave Thomas, is a modern course opened in 1996.
Carrickstone: 18 holes, 6204yds, Par 70, SSS 70, Course record 68.
Antonine: 18 holes, 5940yds, Par 70, SSS 70, Course record 66.
Club membership 700.

Visitors telephone for availability.
Societies must apply in writing to secretary.
Green Fees £30 per day; £20 per round (£35/£25 weekends).
Cards
Prof Duncan Sinclair
Designer James Braid
Facilities
& Leisure hard tennis courts, sauna, solarium, gymnasium
Location 1.5m N

Hotel ★★★★ 64% Westerwood Hotel Golf & Country Club, 1 St Andrews Dr, Westerwood, CUMBERNAULD ☎ 01236 457171 49

Palacerigg Palacerigg Country Park G67 3HU
☎ 01236 734969 Fax 01236 721461
Well wooded parkland course.
18 holes, 6444yds, Par 72, SSS 71, Course record 65.
Club membership 400.

Visitors anytime except club competitions, advance booking advisable.
Societies apply in writing to the Secretary.
Green Fees £10 per day; £7 per round.
Designer Henry Cotton
Facilities
Location 2m S of Cumbernauld on Palkacerigg road off Lenziemill road B8054

Hotel ★★★★ 64% Westerwood Hotel Golf & Country Club, 1 St Andrews Dr, Westerwood, CUMBERNAULD
☎ 01236 457171 49

Westerwood Hotel Golf & Country Club 1 St Andrews Dr, Westerwood G68 0EW
☎ 01236 457171 Fax 01236 738478
Undulating parkland/woodland course designed by Dave Thomas and Seve Ballesteros. Holes meander through silver birch, firs, heaths and heathers, and the spectacular 15th, 'The Waterfall', has its green set against a 40ft rockface. Buggie track. Hotel facilities.
18 holes, 6616yds, Par 72, SSS 72, Course record 65.
Club membership 1000.

Visitors advised to book in advance.
Societies all bookings through golf coordinator on 01236 457171 ext 215.
Green Fees £22.50 (£27.50 weekends).
Cards
Prof Steven Killin
Designer Seve Ballesteros/Dave Thomas
Facilities
& Leisure hard tennis courts, heated indoor swimming pool, solarium, gymnasium, steam room, snooker room, table tennis, bowling green, aerobics studio.
Location Adjacent to A80, 14m from Glasgow City Centre

Hotel ★★★★ 64% Westerwood Hotel Golf & Country Club, 1 St Andrews Dr, Westerwood, CUMBERNAULD
☎ 01236 457171 49

A comprehensive list of driving ranges is given at the back of this guide. See page 479

CUMMERTREES — Map 11 NY16

Powfoot DG12 5QE
☎ 01461 700276 Fax 01461 700276
The hills of Cumbria, away beyond the Solway Firth, and from time to time a sight of the Isle of Man, make playing at this delightfully compact semi-links seaside course a scenic treat. Lovely holes include the 2nd, the 8th and the 11th, also 9th with World War II bomb crater.
18 holes, 6283yds, Par 71, SSS 70, Course record 63.
Club membership 920.

Visitors contact in advance. May not play 8.45-10 & noon-1.30 weekdays, no visitors Sat or before 2pm Sun.
Societies must book in advance.
Green Fees £30 per day; £23 per round, also 3/5 day ticket available.
Prof Gareth Dick
Designer J Braid
Facilities
Location 0.5m off B724

Hotel ★★ 64% Golf Hotel, Links Av, POWFOOT ☎ 01461 700254 19rm(14)

DUMBARTON — Map 10 NS37

Dumbarton Broadmeadow G82 2BQ
☎ 01389 732830 Fax 01389 765995
Flat parkland course.
18 holes, 5992yds, Par 71, SSS 69, Course record 64.
Club membership 700.

Visitors may play Mon, Thu & Fri only.
Societies must apply in writing to Secretary.
Green Fees £20 per day.
Facilities
Location 0.25m N off A814

Hotel ★★ 65% Dumbuck Hotel, Glasgow Rd, DUMBARTON ☎ 01389 734336 22

DUMFRIES — Map 11 NX97

Dumfries & County Nunfield, Edinburgh Rd DG1 1JX
☎ 01387 253585
Parkland course alongside River Nith, with views over the Queensberry Hills.
18 holes, 5928yds, Par 69, SSS 68.
Club membership 800.

Visitors must contact in advance but may not play most weekends between 9.30-11 & 2-3.30.
Societies apply in writing.
Green Fees £23 (£25 weekends).
Prof Stuart Syme
Designer James Braid
Facilities
Location 1m NE of Dumfries on A701

Hotel ★★★ 65% Station Hotel, 49 Lovers Walk, DUMFRIES ☎ 01387 254316 32
Additional hotel ★★★ 67% Cairndale Hotel & Leisure Club, English St, DUMFRIES ☎ 01387 254111 Fax 01387 250555 76
Additional hotel ★★★ 70% Hetland Hall Hotel, CARRUTHERSTOWN ☎ 01387 840201 Fax 01387 840211 27

Dumfries & Galloway 2 Laurieston Av DG2 7NY
☎ 01387 263848
Parkland course.
18 holes, 5803yds, Par 68, SSS 68.
Club membership 800.

Visitors may not play on competition days.
Societies apply in writing.
Green Fees not confirmed.
Prof Joe Fergusson
Facilities
Location W side of town centre on A75

Hotel ★★★ 67% Cairndale Hotel & Leisure Club, English St, DUMFRIES ☎ 01387 254111 76

DUNS — Map 12 NT75

Duns Longformacus Rd TD11 3NR
☎ 01361 882717 (Sec) & 882194
Interesting upland course, with natural hazards of water and hilly slopes. Views south to the Cheviot Hills. A burn comes into play at 7 of the holes.
18 holes, 6209yds, Par 70, SSS 70.
Club membership 520.

Visitors welcome except competition days and Mon, Tue and Wed after 4pm. Advisable to contact in advance Apr-Oct.
Societies write or telephone the secretary in advance for booking details.
Green Fees £15 per day; £12 per round (£20/£15 weekends).

Designer A H Scott
Facilities
Location 1m W off A6105

Hotel ★★★ 70% Marshall Meadows Country House Hotel, BERWICK-UPON-TWEED ☎ 01289 331133 18

EAGLESHAM Map 11 NS55

Bonnyton Kirktonmoor Rd G76 0QA
☎ 01355 302781 Fax 01355 303151
Dramatic moorland course offering spectacular views beautiful countryside as far as snow-capped Ben Lomond. Tree-lined fairways, plateau greens, natural burns and well situated bunkers and a unique variety of holes offer golfers both challenge and reward.
18 holes, 6255yds, Par 72, SSS 71.
Club membership 960.
Visitors welcome weekdays only (ex Tue), must contact in advance.
Societies must telephone in advance.
Green Fees £31.50 per day, weekdays only.
Prof Kendal McWade
Facilities ⊗
Location 0.25m SW off B764

Hotel ★★★ 64% Bruce Hotel, Cornwall St, EAST KILBRIDE ☎ 01355 229771 78

EAST KILBRIDE Map 11 NS65

East Kilbride Chapelside Rd, Nerston G74 4PF
☎ 01355 247728
Parkland and hill course. Very windy. Testing 7th, 9th and 14th holes.
18 holes, 6419yds, Par 71, SSS 71.
Club membership 850.
Visitors by appointment.
Societies must telephone in advance & submit formal application.
Green Fees not confirmed.
Prof Willy Walker
Facilities ⊗ by prior arrangement
Location 0.5m N off A749

Hotel ★★★ 64% Bruce Hotel, Cornwall St, EAST KILBRIDE ☎ 01355 229771 78

Torrance House Calderglen Country Park, Strathaven Rd G75 0QZ ☎ 013552 48638
A parkland course.
18 holes, 6415yds, Par 72, SSS 69, Course record 71.
Club membership 1000.
Visitors welcome, may book up to six days in advance.
Societies Mon-Fri. Apply in writing to John Dunlop, East Kilbride District Council, Civic Centre, East Kilbride.
Green Fees not confirmed.
Prof John Dunlop
Facilities
Location 1.5m SE of Kilbride on A726

Hotel ★★★ 64% Bruce Hotel, Cornwall St, EAST KILBRIDE ☎ 01355 229771 78

EYEMOUTH Map 12 NT96

Eyemouth Gunsgreen Hill TD14 5SF
☎ 01890 750551 & 750004 (Starter)
This is a seaside course most of it being fairly level. It rises from the 10th to the 12th green at which the golfer enjoys views of most of the course.
18 holes, 6472yds, Par 72, SSS 71, Course record 69.
Club membership 330.
Visitors may not play before 9am Sat or before 10am Sun.
Societies apply in writing or telephone.
Green Fees £22 per day; £15 per day (£30/£20 weekends).
Prof Paul Terras
Designer J R Bain
Facilities ⊗
Location E side of town

Hotel ★★★ 70% Marshall Meadows Country House Hotel, BERWICK-UPON-TWEED ☎ 01289 331133 18

GALASHIELS Map 12 NT43

Galashiels Ladhope Recreation Ground TD1 2NJ
☎ 01896 753724
Hillside course, superb views from the top; 10th hole very steep.
18 holes, 5185yds, Par 67, SSS 66, Course record 61.
Club membership 343. ▶

Visitors must contact the secretary in advance especially for weekends.
Societies arrangements with secretary especially for weekends.
Green Fees £14 per round (£16 weekends).
Designer James Braid
Facilities by prior arrangement by prior arrangement by prior arrangement
Location N side of town centre off A7

Hotel ★★★ 65% Kingsknowes Hotel, Selkirk Rd, GALASHIELS 01896 758375 11

Torwoodlee TD1 2NE 01896 752260
Parkland course with natural hazards designed by Willie Park with a new extension by John Garner, provides a good test for all abilities of play.
18 holes, 6200yds, Par 70, SSS 69, Course record 65.
Club membership 550.
Visitors restricted Thu - ladies day and Sat - mens competitions.
Societies letter to secretary.
Green Fees £25 per day; £18 per round (£30/£25 weekends).
Cards
Prof R Elliot
Designer Willie Park
Facilities
Location 1.75m NW off A7

Hotel ★★★ 65% Kingsknowes Hotel, Selkirk Rd, GALASHIELS 01896 758375 11

GALSTON Map 11 NS53

Loudoun Edinburgh Rd KA4 8PA
01563 821993 & 820551 Fax 01563 822229
Pleasant, fairly flat parkland course with many mature trees.
18 holes, 5773yds, Par 68, SSS 68, Course record 61.
Club membership 750.
Visitors must contact in advance. Must play with member at weekends.
Societies telephone in advance.
Green Fees £30 per day; £18 per round.
Facilities
Location NE side of town on A71

Hotel ★★★ 67% Strathaven Hotel, Hamilton Rd, STRATHAVEN 01357 521778 22

GARTCOSH Map 11 NS66

Mount Ellen G69 8EY
01236 872277 Fax 01236 872249
Downland course with 73 bunkers. Testing hole: 10th ('Bedlay'), 156 yds, par 3.
18 holes, 5525yds, Par 68, SSS 67, Course record 67.
Club membership 500.
Visitors may play Mon-Fri 9am-4pm. Must contact in advance.
Societies must contact in advance.
Green Fees not confirmed.
Prof Gerry Rielly
Facilities
Location 0.75m N off A752

Hotel ★★★★ 65% Copthorne Glasgow, George Square, GLASGOW
0141 332 6711 141

GATEHOUSE-OF-FLEET Map 11 NX55

Gatehouse Laurieston Rd DG7 2PW 01644 450260
Set against a background of rolling hills with scenic views of Fleet Bay and the Solway Firth.
9 holes, 2521yds, Par 66, SSS 66, Course record 60.
Club membership 370.
Visitors restricted Sun before 11.30am.
Societies telephone in advance.
Green Fees £10 per day/round.
Designer Tom Fernie
Facilities
Location 0.25m N of town

Hotel ★★★★ 68% Cally Palace Hotel, GATEHOUSE OF FLEET
01557 814341 56

GIRVAN Map 10 NX19

Brunston Castle Bargany, Dailly KA26 9RH
01465 811471 Fax 01465 811545
Sheltered inland parkland course. A championship design by Donald Steel, the course is bisected by the River Girvan and shaped to incorporate all the natural surroundings. It finishes with the 17th 185 yards over a man made lake. Driving range.
Burns: 18 holes, 6792yds, Par 72, SSS 73, Course record 71.
Club membership 400.
Visitors reserved for members at weekends 8-10 & 12.30-1.30. Must contact in advance.
Societies telephone 01465 811471 to book.
Green Fees not confirmed.
Prof Derek J McKenzie
Designer Donald Steel

Facilities
Location 6m SE of Turnberry, 5m E of Girvan

Hotel ★★★ 76% Malin Court, TURNBERRY
☎ 01655 331457 17

Girvan Golf Course Rd KA26 9HW ☎ 01465 714272
Municipal seaside and parkland course. Testing 17th hole (223-yds) uphill, par 3. Good views.
18 holes, 5098yds, Par 64, SSS 65.
Club membership 175.
Visitors no restrictions.
Societies may not play Jul & Aug.
Green Fees £20 per round, weekdays £12.50 (£13 weekends).
Designer D Kinnell/J Braid
Facilities
Location N side of town off A77

Hotel ★★★ 76% Malin Court, TURNBERRY
☎ 01655 331457 17

GLASGOW Map 11 NS56

Alexandra Alexandra Park, Alexandra Pde G31 8SE
☎ 0141 556 1294
Parkland course, hilly with some woodland. Many bunkers and a barrier of trees between 1st and 9th fairway. Work currently in progress to alter greens and improve course,
9 holes, 2800yds, Par 31, Course record 25.
Club membership 85.
Visitors no restrictions.
Societies telephone 24 hrs in advance or by writing one week in advance.
Green Fees £2.75.
Facilities
Location 2m E of city centre off M8/A8

Cowglen Barrhead Rd G43 1AU
☎ 0141 632 0556 Fax 01505 503000
Undulating and challenging parkland course with good views over the Clyde valley to the Campsie Hills. Club and line selection is most important on many holes due to the strategic placing of copses on the course.
18 holes, 6079yds, Par 69, SSS 69, Course record 63.
Club membership 775.
Visitors play on shorter course. Must contact in advance and have a handicap certificate. No visitors Tue, Fri and weekends.
Societies must be booked in writing through the secretary.
Green Fees £30 per day; £21 per round.
Prof John McTear
Designer David Adams/James Braid
Facilities
Location 4.5m SW of city centre on B762

Hotel ★★★ 66% The Macdonald Thistle, Eastwood Toll, GIFFNOCK ☎ 0141 638 2225 56

Haggs Castle 70 Dumbreck Rd, Dumbreck G41 4SN
☎ 0141 427 1157 Fax 0141 427 1157
Wooded, parkland course where Scottish National Championships and the Glasgow and Scottish Open have been held. Quite difficult.
18 holes, 6464yds, Par 73, SSS 72.
Club membership 900.
Visitors may not play at weekends. Must contact in advance.
Societies apply in writing.
Green Fees not confirmed.
Prof Jim McAlister
Facilities
Location 2.5m SW of city centre on B768

Hotel ★★★ 67% Swallow Hotel, 517 Paisley Rd West, GLASGOW
☎ 0141 427 3146 117

Kirkhill Greenless Rd, Cambuslang G72 8YN
☎ 0141 641 8499 Fax 0141 641 8499
Meadowland course designed by James Braid.
18 holes, 6030yds, Par 70, SSS 70, Course record 63.
Club membership 650.
Visitors must play with member at weekends.
Societies must contact in advance.
Green Fees £25 per day; £20 per round.
Prof Duncan Williamson
Designer J Braid
Facilities
Location 5m SE of city centre off A749

Hotel ★★★ 61% Stuart Hotel, 2 Cornwall Way, EAST KILBRIDE ☎ 013552 21161 39

Knightswood Lincoln Av G13 5QZ ☎ 0141 959 6358
Flat parkland course within easy reach of city. Two dog-legs.
9 holes, 5584yds, Par 68, SSS 67.
Club membership 40.
Visitors reserved tee Wed and Fri am bookings 1 day in advance, no other restrictions.
Societies welcome, must book 1 day in advance.
Green Fees £2.80 per 9 holes; £5.60 per 18 holes.
Facilities
Location 4m W of city centre off A82

Hotel ★★★ 68% Jurys Glasgow Hotel, Great Western Rd, GLASGOW
☎ 0141 334 8161 133

Lethamhill 1240 Cumbernauld Rd, Millerston G33 1AH
☎ 0141 770 6220 Fax 1041 770 0520
Municipal parkland course.
18 holes, 5859yds, Par 70, SSS 69.
Visitors must contact in advance.
Societies must contact in advance.
Green Fees £6.40 per round.
Facilities
Location 3m NE of city centre on A80

Hotel ★★★★ 65% Copthorne Glasgow, George Square, GLASGOW
☎ 0141 332 6711 141

Linn Park Simshill Rd G44 5EP ☎ 0141 633 0377
Municipal parkland course with six par 3's in outward half.
18 holes, 4952yds, Par 65, SSS 65, Course record 61.
Visitors must contact in advance.
Societies advance booking in writing
Green Fees £6.40 per round.
Facilities
Location 4m S of city centre off B766 ▶

Hotel ★★★ 64% Bruce Hotel, Cornwall St, EAST KILBRIDE
☎ 01355 229771 78

Pollok 90 Barrhead Rd G43 1BG
☎ 0141 632 4351 & 632 1080 Fax 0141 649 1398
Parkland course with woods and river.
18 holes, 6254yds, Par 71, SSS 70, Course record 62.
Club membership 620.

Visitors no ladies. Members only until 2pm weekends. Must contact in advance.
Societies must contact in writing.
Green Fees £40 per day; £30 per round.
Designer James Braid
Facilities
Location 4m SW of city centre on A762

Hotel ★★★ 64% The Tinto Firs Thistle, 470 Kilmarnock Rd, GLASGOW
☎ 0141 637 2353 28

Williamwood Clarkston Rd G44 3YR
☎ 0141 637 1783 Fax 0141 637 6688
Undulating parkland course with mature woodlands.
18 holes, 5878yds, Par 67, SSS 69, Course record 61.
Club membership 800.

Visitors apply in writing to secretary, no weekend play.
Societies midweek bookings only, apply in writing to secretary.
Green Fees £35 per day; £25 per round.
Prof Stewart Marshall
Designer James Braid
Facilities
Location 5m S of city centre on B767

Hotel ★★★ 66% The Macdonald Thistle, Eastwood Toll, GIFFNOCK
☎ 0141 638 2225 56

GLENLUCE Map 10 NX15

Wigtownshire County Mains of Park DG8 0NN
☎ 01581 300420
Seaside links course on the shores of Luce Bay, easy walking but affected by winds. The 12th hole, a dogleg with out of bounds to the right,is named after the course's designer, Gordon Cunnigham.
18 holes, 5847yds, Par 70, SSS 68, Course record 67.
Club membership 450.

Visitors may play any day by prior arrangement ex competition days.
Societies must contact in advance.
Green Fees £22 per day ; £17.50 per round (£24/£19.50 weekends); £68 per week.
Designer W Gordon Cunningham
Facilities
Location 1.5m W off A75

Hotel ★★★★ 68% North West Castle Hotel, STRANRAER
☎ 01776 704413 70 Annexe3

GREAT CUMBRAE ISLAND (MILLPORT) Map 10 NS15

Millport Golf Rd KA28 OHB
☎ 01475 530305 (Prof) & 530311 Fax 01475 530306
Pleasantly situated on the west side of Cumbrae looking over Bute to Arran and the Mull of Kintyre. Exposure means conditions may vary according to wind strength and direction. A typical seaside resort course welcoming visitors.
18 holes, 5828yds, Par 68, SSS 69, Course record 64.
Club membership 525.

Visitors advisable to phone and book tee times especially in summer months.
Societies telephone or write in advance.
Green Fees £18.50 per day; £14.50 per round (£24.50/£18.50 weekends & bank holidays).
Prof Kenneth Docherty
Designer James Braid
Facilities
Location Approx 4m from ferry slip

Hotel ★★★ 64% Brisbane House, 14 Greenock Rd, Esplanade, LARGS
☎ 01475 687200 23

GRETNA Map 11 NY36

Gretna Kirtle View DG16 5HD ☎ 01461 338464
A nice parkland course on gentle hills. Opened in 1991, it offers a good test of skill.
9 holes, 3214yds, Par 72, SSS 71, Course record 71.
Club membership 250.

Visitors no restrictions.
Societies telephone in advance.
Green Fees not confirmed.
Designer N Williams
Facilities
Location 0.5m W of Gretna on B721,signposted

Hotel ★★ 67% Solway Lodge Hotel, Annan Rd, GRETNA
☎ 01461 338266 3 Annexe7

HAMILTON Map 11 NS75

Hamilton Carlisle Rd, Ferniegair ML3 7TU
☎ 01698 282872
Beautiful parkland course.
18 holes, 6243yds, Par 70, SSS 71, Course record 62.

Visitors must contact in advance, may not play weekends.
Societies apply in writing.
Green Fees not confirmed.
Prof Maurice Moir
Designer James Braid
Facilities
Location 1.5m SE on A72

Hotel ★★ 63% Silvertrees Hotel, Silverwells Crescent, BOTHWELL
☎ 01698 852311 7 Annexe19

Strathclyde Park Mote Hill ML3 6BY ☎ 01698 429350
Municipal wooded parkland course with views into the Strathclyde Park sailing loch.
9 holes, 3128yds, Par 36, SSS 70, Course record 64.
Club membership 240.

Visitors telephone, same day booking system in operation. May book up to 1 week in advance.
Societies must contact in advance on above telephone number.
Green Fees £2.60 per 9 holes (£3.40 weekends & bank holidays).
Prof William Walker
Facilities
Location N side of town off B7071

Hotel ★★ 63% Silvertrees Hotel, Silverwells Crescent, BOTHWELL ☎ 01698 852311 7 Annexe19

HAWICK Map 12 NT51

Hawick Vertish Hill TD9 0NY ☎ 01450 372293
Hill course with good views.
18 holes, 5929yds, Par 68, SSS 69, Course record 63.
Club membership 600.

Visitors must contact in advance. Course busy Sat until 3pm. 1st tee off time for visitors on Sun 10.30pm.
Societies write or telephone for booking arrangement.
Green Fees £24 per day; £18 per round.
Facilities
Location SW side of town

Hotel ★★ 71% Kirklands Hotel, West Stewart Place, HAWICK ☎ 01450 372263 5 Annexe4

INNERLEITHEN Map 11 NT33

Innerleithen Leithen Water, Leithen Rd EH44 6NL ☎ 01896 830951
Moorland course, with easy walking. Burns and rivers are natural hazards. Testing 5th hole (100 yds) par 3.
9 holes, 6066yds, Par 70, SSS 69, Course record 65.
Club membership 240.

Visitors advisable to check for availability for weekends.
Societies by prior booking.
Green Fees £16 per day; £11 per round (£19/£13 weekends).
Designer Willie Park
Facilities
Location 1.5m N on B709

Hotel ★★★ 71% Peebles Hydro Hotel, PEEBLES ☎ 01721 720602 137

IRVINE Map 10 NS33

Glasgow Gailes KA11 5AE
☎ 0141 942 2011 Fax 0141 942 0770
A lovely seaside links. The turf of the fairways and all the greens is truly glorious and provides tireless play. Established in 1882, and is a qualifying course for the Open Championship.
18 holes, 6513yds, Par 71, SSS 72, Course record 64.
Club membership 1200.

Visitors prior booking through secretary reccomended, no visitors before 2.30pm Sat & Sun.
Societies initial contact by telephone.
Green Fees £52 per day; £42 per round (£47 per round weekends).
Cards
Prof J Steven
Designer W Park Jnr
Facilities by prior arrangement
Location 2m S off A737

Hotel ★★★★ 54% Hospitality Inn, 46 Annick Rd, IRVINE ☎ 01294 274272 127

Irvine Bogside KA12 8SN ☎ 01294 275979
Testing links course; only two short holes.
18 holes, 6400yds, Par 71, SSS 73, Course record 65.
Club membership 450.

Visitors may not play before 3pm Sat & Sun.
Societies are welcome weekdays and pm weekends, telephone in advance.
Green Fees not confirmed.
Prof Keith Erskine
Facilities
Location N side of town off A737

Hotel ★★★★ 54% Hospitality Inn, 46 Annick Rd, IRVINE ☎ 01294 274272 127

Irvine Ravenspark 13 Kidsneuk Ln KA12 8SR
☎ 01294 271293
Parkland course.
18 holes, 6702yds, Par 71, SSS 71, Course record 65.
Club membership 600.

Visitors may not play Sat before 2pm.
Societies not allowed Sat, contact club steward in advance.
Green Fees not confirmed.
Prof Peter Bond
Facilities
Location N side of town on A737

Hotel ★★★ 73% Montgreenan Mansion House Hotel, Montgreenan Estate, KILWINNING ☎ 01294 557733 21

Western Gailes Gailes by Irvine KA11 5AE
☎ 01294 311649 Fax 01294 312312
A magnificent seaside links with glorious turf and wonderful greens. The view is open across the Firth of Clyde to the neighbouring islands. It is a well-balanced course crossed by 3 burns. There are 2 par 5's, the 6th and 14th, and the 11th is a testing 445-yd, par 4, dog-leg.
18 holes, 6639yds, Par 71, SSS 73, Course record 65.

Visitors welcome Mon, Tue (no ladies) Wed, Fri. Must contact in advance and have a handicap certificate.
Societies must contact in advance.
Green Fees £84 per 36 holes; £52 per round.
Facilities
Location 2m S off A737 ▶

Hotel ★★★ 73% Montgreenan Mansion House Hotel, Montgreenan Estate, KILWINNING
☎ 01294 557733 21

JEDBURGH — Map 12 NT62

Jedburgh Dunion Rd TD8 6DQ
☎ 01835 863587
Undulating parkland course, windy, with young trees.
9 holes, 5760yds, Par 68, SSS 67, Course record 62.
Club membership 265.

Visitors restricted at weekends during competitions.
Societies must contact at least one month in advance.
Green Fees £12 per day.
Facilities by prior arrangement by prior arrangement by prior arrangement
Location 1m W on B6358

Hotel ★★ 71% Kirklands Hotel, West Stewart Place, HAWICK
☎ 01450 372263 5 Annexe4

JOHNSTONE — Map 10 NS46

Cochrane Castle Scott Av, Craigston PA5 0HF
☎ 01505 320146 Fax 01505 325338
Fairly hilly parkland course,wooded with two small streams running through it.
18 holes, 6223yds, Par 71, SSS 71, Course record 65.
Club membership 660.

Visitors may not play at weekends. Must contact in writing.
Societies apply in writing.
Green Fees £25 per day; £17 per round.
Prof Jason Boyd
Designer J Hunter
Facilities
Location 1m from Johnstone town centre, off Beith Rd

Hotel ★★★ 65% Lynnhurst Hotel, Park Rd, JOHNSTONE
☎ 01505 324331 21

Elderslie 63 Main Rd, Elderslie PA5 9AZ
☎ 01505 323956 Fax 01505 340346
Parkland course, undulating, with good views.
18 holes, 6175yds, Par 70, SSS 70, Course record 61.
Club membership 940.

Visitors may not play at weekends & bank holidays. Must contact club in advance and preferably have a handicap certificate.
Societies must telephone in advance.
Green Fees £30 per day; £20 per round.
Prof Richard Bowman
Designer J Braid
Facilities
Location E side of town on A737

Hotel ★★★ 65% Lynnhurst Hotel, Park Rd, JOHNSTONE
☎ 01505 324331 21

KELSO — Map 12 NT73

Kelso Racecourse Rd TD5 7SL ☎ 01573 223009
Parkland course. Easy walking.
18 holes, 6046yds, Par 70, SSS 69, Course record 64.
Club membership 500.

Visitors advisable to telephone in advance.
Societies apply in writing.
Green Fees not confirmed.
Designer James Braid
Facilities
Location N side of town centre off B6461

Hotel ★★★ 62% Cross Keys Hotel, 36-37 The Square, KELSO ☎ 01573 223303 24

Roxburghe TD5 8JZ ☎ 01573 450331 Fax 01573 450611
Opened in 1996 and designed by Dave Thomas, this undulating course in set in 200 acres of mature parkland. Deep challenging bunkers, rolling greens and dramatic water hazards, including the River Teviot, provide a good test for all golfing abilities.
18 holes, 6873yds, Par 72, SSS 73.
Club membership 250.

Visitors dress code
Societies please telephone in advance, a number of packages available.
Green Fees £30 midweek; (£40 weekends).
Cards
Prof Gordon Niven
Designer Dave Thomas
Facilities
& Leisure hard tennis courts, fishing, clay pigeon shooting, croquet.

Location 5m E of Jedburgh on A698, 2m W of Kelso on A698

Hotel ★★★ 74% Sunlaws House Hotel & Golf Course, Heiton, KELSO
☎ 01573 450331 16 Annexe6

KILBIRNIE Map 10 NS35

Kilbirnie Place Largs Rd KA25 7AT
☎ 01505 683398
Easy walking parkland course.
18 holes, 5400yds, Par 69, SSS 67.
Club membership 450.

Visitors no restrictions weekdays, no parties on Sun.
Societies must apply in writing in advance.
Green Fees £18 per day; £10 per round.
Facilities
Location 1m W on A760

Hotel ★★★ 70% Priory House Hotel, John St, Broomfields, LARGS
☎ 01475 686460 21

KILMARNOCK Map 10 NS43

Annanhill Irvine Rd KA1 2RT
☎ 01563 521644
Municipal, tree-lined parkland course played over by private clubs.
18 holes, 6269yds, Par 71, SSS 70, Course record 66.
Club membership 394.

Visitors must book at starters office.
Societies apply in writing.
Green Fees on application.
Designer Jack McLean
Facilities by prior arrangement by prior arrangement by prior arrangement by prior arrangement
Location 1m W on A71

Hotel ★★★ 75% Chapeltoun House Hotel, STEWARTON ☎ 01560 482696 8rm(1)
Additional hotel ★★★ 73% Montgreenan Mansion House Hotel, Montgreenan Estate, KILWINNING
☎ 01294 557733 Fax 01294 850397 21

Caprington Ayr Rd KA1 4UW
☎ 01563 523702 & 521915 (Gen Enq)
Municipal parkland course.
18 holes, 5718yds, Par 69, SSS 68.
Club membership 400.

Visitors may not play on Sat.
Societies must contact in advance.
Green Fees £9.50.
Facilities
Location 1.5m S on B7038

Hotel ★★★ 75% Chapeltoun House Hotel, STEWARTON
☎ 01560 482696 8rm(1)

KILSYTH Map 11 NS77

Kilsyth Lennox Tak Ma Doon Rd G65 0RS
☎ 01236 824115 Fax 01236 823089
Hilly moorland course, hard walking. Course and facilities revamped with 18-holes after a serious fire early in 1993.
18 holes, 5912yds, Par 70, SSS 70, Course record 66.
Club membership 500.

Visitors advisable to contact in advance. No restrictions weekdays up to 5pm, may play Sun on application but not Sat.
Societies must contact in advance.
Green Fees not confirmed.
Prof R Abercrombie
Facilities
Location N side of town off A803

Hotel ★★★ 66% Kirkhouse Inn, STRATHBLANE
☎ 01360 770621 15

KIRKCUDBRIGHT Map 11 NX65

Brighouse Bay Borgue DG6 4TS
☎ 01557 870409 Fax 01557 870319
A beautifully situated scenic course on free draining coastal grassland and playable all year. Making use of many natural features - water, gullies and rocks - it provides a testing challenge to golfers of all handicaps. The course is currently being extended to 18 holes and will open in summer 1999.
9 holes, 5426yds, Par 68, SSS 66.
Club membership 170.

Visitors pay as you play - payment at adjacent Leisure Club.
Societies telephone in advance.
Green Fees £10.50 per day.
Designer D Gray ▶

Facilities
& Leisure heated indoor plus outdoor swimming pool, fishing, solarium, gymnasium, mini golf, steam room, adjacent to AA Campsite of the Year 1998.
Location 3m S of Borgue off B727

Hotel ★★ 73% Selkirk Arms Hotel, Old High St, KIRKCUDBRIGHT
01557 330402 15 Annexe1

Kirkcudbright Stirling Crescent DG6 4EZ
01557 330314
Parkland course. Hilly, with hard walking. Good views over the Harbour town of Kirkcudbright and the Dee Estuary.
18 holes, 5739yds, Par 69, SSS 69, Course record 63.
Club membership 500.
Visitors advisable to contact in advance.
Societies contact in advance.
Green Fees £23 per day; £18 per round.
Facilities
Location NE side of town off A711

Hotel ★★ 73% Selkirk Arms Hotel, Old High St, KIRKCUDBRIGHT
01557 330402 15 Annexe1

KIRKINTILLOCH Map 11 NS67

Hayston Campsie Rd G66 1RN
0141 776 1244 & 775 0723 (Sec)
An undulating, tree-lined course with a sandy subsoil.
18 holes, 6042yds, Par 70, SSS 70, Course record 62.
Club membership 800.
Visitors must apply in advance, may not play weekends.
Societies Tue & Thu, apply in writing
Green Fees £30 per day; £20 per round.
Prof Steven Barnett
Designer James Braid
Facilities
Location 1m NW off A803

Hotel ★★★ 66% Kirkhouse Inn, STRATHBLANE
01360 770621 15

Kirkintilloch Campsie Rd G66 1RN
0141 776 1256
Parkland course in rural setting.
18 holes, 5269yds, Par 70, SSS 66.
Club membership 650.
Visitors must be introduced by member.
Societies apply in writing.
Green Fees not confirmed.
Designer James Braid
Facilities
Location 1m NW off A803

Hotel ★★★ 66% Kirkhouse Inn, STRATHBLANE
01360 770621 15

LANARK Map 11 NS84

Lanark The Moor, Whitelees Rd ML11 7RX
01555 663219 & 01555 661456
Chosen as one of the pre-qualifying tests for the Open Championship held at Lanark from 1977 to 1983. The address of the club, 'The Moor', gives some indication as to the kind of golf to be found there. Golf has been played at Lanark for well over a century and the Club dates from 1851.
Old Course: 18 holes, 6423yds, Par 70, SSS 71, Course record 62.
Wee Course: 9 holes, 1489yds, Par 28.
Club membership 880.
Visitors booking advisable, no visitors weekends.
Societies apply in advance.
Green Fees £36 per day; £24 per round. 9 hole course £4 per day.
Prof Alan White
Designer Tom Morris
Facilities
Location E side of town centre off A73

Hotel ★★★ 65% Cartland Bridge Hotel, Glasgow Rd, LANARK
01555 664426 18

LANGBANK Map 10 NS37

Gleddoch Golf and Country Club PA14 6YE
01475 540304
Parkland and heathland course with other sporting facilities available to temporary members. Good views over Firth of Clyde.
18 holes, 5661yds, Par 68, SSS 67.
Club membership 600.
Visitors must contact in advance.
Societies must contact in advance.
Green Fees not confirmed.
Prof Keith Campbell
Facilities
& Leisure grass tennis courts, heated indoor swimming pool, squash, sauna.
Location B789-Old Greenock Road

Hotel ★★★★ 67% Gleddoch House Hotel, LANGBANK 01475 540711 39

LANGHOLM Map 11 NY38

Langholm Whitaside DG13 0JR 013873 80673/81247
Hillside course with fine views, easy to medium walking.
9 holes, 5744yds, Par 70, SSS 68, Course record 63.
Club membership 200.
Visitors restricted Sat & Sun.
Societies apply in writing to secretary.
Green Fees £10 per day/round.
Facilities by prior arrangement by prior arrangement by prior arrangement by prior arrangement
Location E side of village off A7

Hotel ★★ 61% Eskdale Hotel, Market Place, LANGHOLM 013873 80357 & 81178
Fax 013873 80357 15rm(11)

LARGS Map 10 NS25

Largs Irvine Rd KA30 8EU
☎ 01475 673594 Fax 01475 673594
A parkland, tree-lined course with views to the Clyde coast and Arran Isles.
18 holes, 6115yds, Par 70, SSS 71, Course record 63.
Club membership 850.

Visitors may not play competition days. Other times by arrangement.
Societies apply in writing.
Green Fees £35 per day; £25 per round (£35 per round weekends before 4pm).
Prof Robert Collison
Facilities ⊗)‖ ⛳ ☕ ♀ ⛀ 🏠 ♈ ✓
Location 1m S of town centre on A78

Hotel ★★★ 70% Priory House Hotel, John St, Broomfields, LARGS
☎ 01475 686460 21 ⇆ ↗

Routenburn Routenburn Rd KA30 8QA
☎ 01475 673230
Heathland course with fine views over Firth of Clyde.
18 holes, 5675yds, Par 68, SSS 68.
Club membership 500.

Visitors no restrictions.
Societies apply in writing.
Green Fees not confirmed.
Cards VISA
Prof J Grieg McQueen
Designer J Braid
Facilities ⊗)‖ ⛳ ☕ ♀ ⛀ 🏠 ✓
Location 1m N off A78

Hotel ★★★ 63% Manor Park Hotel, LARGS
☎ 01475 520832 10 ⇆ ↗ Annexe13 ⇆ ↗

LARKHALL Map 11 NS75

Larkhall Burnhead Rd ML9 3AB ☎ 01698 889597
Small, inland parkland course.
9 holes, 6234yds, Par 70, SSS 70, Course record 69.
Club membership 250.

Visitors restricted Tue & Sat.
Green Fees not confirmed.
Facilities ♀
Location E side of town on B7019

Hotel ★★★ 67% Popinjay Hotel, Lanark Rd, ROSEBANK
☎ 01555 860441 42 ⇆ ↗ Annexe5 ⇆ ↗

LAUDER Map 12 NT54

Lauder Galashiels Rd TD2 6RS ☎ 01578 722526
Inland course and practice area on gently sloping hill.
9 holes, 3001yds, Par 72, SSS 70, Course record 66.
Club membership 200.

Visitors restricted Wed 4.30-5.30pm and Sun before noon.
Societies telephone in advance.
Green Fees not confirmed.
Facilities ⛀
Location On Galashiels Rd, off A68, 0.5m from Lauder

Hotel ★★ 63% Lauderdale Hotel, 1 Edinburgh Rd, LAUDER ☎ 01578 722231 9 ⇆ ↗

LEADHILLS Map 11 NS81

Leadhills ML12 6XR ☎ no telephone Fax 01659 74324
A testing, hilly course with high winds. At 1500ft above sea level it is the highest golf course in Scotland.
9 holes, 4354yds, Par 66, SSS 64.
Club membership 80.

Visitors no restrictions.
Societies must contact in advance.
Green Fees not confirmed.
Location E side of village off B797

Hotel ★★ 65% Blackaddie House Hotel, Blackaddie Rd, SANQUHAR
☎ 01659 50270 9 ⇆ ↗

LENNOXTOWN Map 11 NS67

Campsie Crow Rd G65 7HX ☎ 01360 310244
Scenic hillside course.
18 holes, 5507yds, Par 70, SSS 68, Course record 69.
Club membership 640.

Visitors contact professional 01360 310920.
Societies wrtten application.
Green Fees £20 per day; £12 per round (£15 per round weekends).
Prof Mark Brennan
Designer W Auchterlonie
Facilities ⊗)‖ ⛳ ☕ ♀ ⛀ 🏠
Location 0.5m N on B822

Hotel ★★★ 66% Kirkhouse Inn, STRATHBLANE
☎ 01360 770621 15 ⇆ ↗

LENZIE Map 11 NS67

Lenzie 19 Crosshill Rd G66 5DA
☎ 0141 776 1535 & 0141 776 6020 Fax 0141 777 7748
Pleasant parkland course.
18 holes, 5984yds, Par 69, SSS 69, Course record 64.
Club membership 890.

Visitors must contact in advance (some Sunday dates available)
Societies apply in writing.
Green Fees £30 per day; £20 per round.
Prof Jim McCallum
Facilities ⊗)‖ ⛳ ☕ ♀ ⛀ 🏠 ↘ ✓
Location N of Glasgow, approx 15 mins from Glasgow city centre, Kirkintilloch turn off M80

Hotel ★★★ 66% Kirkhouse Inn, STRATHBLANE
☎ 01360 770621 15 ⇆ ↗

LESMAHAGOW Map 11 NS83

Holland Bush Acretophead ML11 0JS
☎ 01555 893484 & 893646
Fairly difficult, tree-lined municipal parkland and moorland course. 1st half is relatively flat, while 2nd half is hilly.
18 holes, 6110yds, Par 71, SSS 69, Course record 63.
Club membership 500.

Visitors no restrictions.
Societies contact the professional in advance. ▶

Green Fees £7.50 per round (£8.80 weekends & bank holidays).
Prof Ian Rae
Designer J Lawdon/K Pate
Facilities
Hotel ★★★ 67% Strathaven Hotel, Hamilton Rd, STRATHAVEN ☎ 01357 521778 22

LOCHMABEN Map 11 NY08

Lochmaben Castlehillgate DG11 1NT ☎ 01387 810552
Comfortable-walking parkland course between two lochs with fine old trees and fast greens all year round.
18 holes, 5357yds, Par 67, SSS 66, Course record 61.
Club membership 850.
Visitors advised to contact in advance.
Societies must contact in advance.
Green Fees £20 per day; £16 per round (£25/£20 weekends).
Designer James Braid
Facilities
& Leisure fishing.
Location S side of village off A709

Hotel ★★★ 69% Dryfesdale Hotel, LOCKERBIE ☎ 01576 202427 15rm(9)

LOCHWINNOCH Map 10 NS35

Lochwinnoch Burnfoot Rd PA12 4AN
☎ 01505 842153 & 01505 843029 Fax 01505 843668
Well maintained parkland course incorporating natural burns. Throughout the course the majority of fairways are wide with tricky greens, but always in good condition. Very scenic with lots of bunkers.
18 holes, 6243yds, Par 71, SSS 71, Course record 63.
Club membership 650.
Visitors may not play at weekends and bank holidays unless accompanied by member(check with Pro Shop). Restricted during competition days.
Societies apply in writing to club administrator.
Green Fees £20 per day; £15 per round.
Cards
Prof Gerry Reilly
Facilities
Location W side of town off A760, between Johnstone & Beith, off A737 on Largs road A760

Hotel ★★★ 66% Bowfield Hotel & Country Club, Lands of Bowfield, HOWWOOD ☎ 01505 705225 23

LOCKERBIE Map 11 NY18

Lockerbie Corrie Rd DG11 2ND
☎ 01576 203363 Fax 01576 203363
Parkland course with fine views and featuring the only pond hole in Dumfriesshire.
18 holes, 5614yds, Par 68, SSS 67, Course record 64.
Club membership 620.
Visitors restricted Sun. Advisable to book in advance.
Societies must contact secretary in advance.
Green Fees not confirmed.
Designer James Braid
Facilities
Location E side of town centre off B7068

Hotel ★★★ 69% Dryfesdale Hotel, LOCKERBIE ☎ 01576 202427 15rm(9)

MAUCHLINE Map 11 NS42

Ballochmyle Catrine Rd KA5 6LE
☎ 01290 550469 Fax 01290 553150
Wooded parkland course.
18 holes, 5972yds, Par 70, SSS 69, Course record 64.
Club membership 730.
Visitors no visitors on Mon from Oct-Mar except with member.
Societies apply in writing.
Green Fees not confirmed.
Facilities by prior arrangement
Location 1m SE on B705

Hotel ★ 64% Royal Hotel, 1 Glaisnock St, CUMNOCK ☎ 01290 420822 11rm(6)

MAYBOLE Map 10 NS20

Maybole Municipal Memorial Park KA19 7DX
Hilly parkland course.
9 holes, 2635yds, Par 33, SSS 65, Course record 64.
Club membership 100.
Visitors no restrictions.
Societies must contact in advance.
Green Fees £12 per day; £8.50 per round weekdays (£9 weekends).
Hotel ★★ Ladyburn, MAYBOLE ☎ 01655 740585 8rm(4 3)

MELROSE Map 12 NT53

Melrose Dingleton TD6 9HS
☎ 01896 822855 & 01835 822758
Undulating tree-lined fairways with spendid views. Many bunkers.
9 holes, 5579yds, Par 70, SSS 68, Course record 61.
Club membership 380.
Visitors competitions all Sats and many Suns Apr-Oct, ladies priority Tue, junior priority Wed am in holidays. No visitors to tee off after 4pm Apr-Oct.
Societies apply in writing.
Green Fees £15 per round/day.
Facilities
Location Off A68,S side of town centre on B6359

Hotel ★★★ 67% Burt's Hotel, The Square, MELROSE ☎ 01896 822285 20

MILNGAVIE Map 11 NS57

Clober Craigton Rd G62 7HP ☎ 0141 956 1685
Parkland course. Testing 5th hole, par 3.
18 holes, 5042yds, Par 65, SSS 65, Course record 61.
Club membership 600.
Visitors may not play after 4pm Mon-Fri. Must play with member weekends and bank holidays.
Societies must contact in advance.
Green Fees not confirmed.
Prof A Tak

Facilities
Location NW side of town

Hotel ★★★ 64% Black Bull Thistle, Main St, MILNGAVIE
☎ 0141 956 2291 27

Dougalston Strathblane Rd G62 8HJ
☎ 0141 956 5750 Fax 0141 956 6480
A golf course of tremendous character set in 400 acres dotted with drumlins, lakes and criss-crossed by streams and ditches. One of the toughest tests of golf in the west of Scotland.
18 holes, 6683yds, Par 72, SSS 71.
Club membership 500.
Visitors visitors may only play Mon-Fri, tee times may be booked 3 days in advance.
Societies weekdays only.
Green Fees £14 per round in summer; £10 per round in winter.
Cards
Designer Commander Harris
Facilities
Location NE side of town on A81

Hotel ★★★ 64% Black Bull Thistle, Main St, MILNGAVIE
☎ 0141 956 2291 27

Hilton Park Auldmarroch Estate, Stockiemuir Rd G62 7HB
☎ 0141 956 4657 Fax 0141 956 4657
Moorland courses set amidst magnificent scenery.
Hilton Course: 18 holes, 6054yds, Par 70, SSS 70, Course record 65.
Allander Course: 18 holes, 5374yards, Par 69, SSS 67, Course record 65.
Club membership 1200.
Visitors must contact in advance but may not play at weekends.
Societies apply in advance to secretary.
Green Fees £28 per day; £20 per round.
Prof W McCondichie
Designer James Braid
Facilities
Location 3m NW of Milngavie, on A809

Hotel ★★★ 64% Black Bull Thistle, Main St, MILNGAVIE
☎ 0141 956 2291 27

Milngavie Laighpark G62 8EP
☎ 0141 956 1619 Fax 0141 956 4252
Very scenic moorland course, which plays its full length, challenging SSS, testing 1st hole followed by many others.
18 holes, 5818yds, Par 68, SSS 68, Course record 59.
Club membership 700.
Visitors must contact in advance, may not play weekends.
Societies apply in writing.
Green Fees £30 per day; £20 per round.
Designer The Auchterlonie Brothers
Facilities
Location 1.25m N

Hotel ★★★ 64% Black Bull Thistle, Main St, MILNGAVIE
☎ 0141 956 2291 27

MINTO Map 12 NT52

Minto Denholm TD9 8SH ☎ 01450 870220
Pleasant, undulating parkland course featuring mature trees and panoramic views of Scottish Border country. Short but quite testing.
18 holes, 5460yds, Par 68, SSS 67, Course record 63.
Club membership 670.
Visitors advisable to telephone in advance, and essential for weekends.
Societies telephone or write.
Green Fees £20 per day; £15 per round (£25/£20 weekends & bank holidays).
Facilities
Location 5m from Hawick, 1.25m off A698 at Denholm

Hotel ★★ 71% Kirklands Hotel, West Stewart Place, HAWICK
☎ 01450 372263 5 Annexe4

MOFFAT Map 11 NT00

Moffat Coatshill DG10 9SB ☎ 01683 220020
Scenic moorland course overlooking the town, with panoramic views of southern uplands.
18 holes, 5218yds, Par 69, SSS 67, Course record 60.
Club membership 350.
Visitors advised to contact in advance, no visitors after 12 noon on Wed.
Societies apply in writing to the clubmistress.
Green Fees not confirmed.
Designer Ben Sayers
Facilities
& Leisure games room.
Location From A74 1m on A701 to Moffat, course signposted

Hotel ★★★ 68% Moffat House Hotel, High St, MOFFAT ☎ 01683 220039 20

MONREITH Map 10 NX34

St Medan DG8 8NJ ☎ 01988 700358
Links course with panoramic views of the Solway and Isle of Man.
9 holes, 4608yds, Par 64, SSS 63, Course record 60.
Club membership 300.
Visitors no restrictions.
Societies apply in advance.
Green Fees £45 weekly; £15 per day; £10 per 18 holes; £7 per 9 holes.
Designer James Braid
Facilities
Location 1m SE off A747

Hotel ★★★ 66% Corsemalzie House Hotel, PORT WILLIAM ☎ 01988 860254 14

MOTHERWELL Map 11 NS75

Colville Park New Jerviston House, Jerviston Estate, Merry St ML1 4UG ☎ 01698 265779 (pro) Fax 01698 230418
Parkland course. First nine, tree-lined, second nine, more exposed. Testing 10th hole par 3, 16th hole par 4.
18 holes, 6250yds, Par 71, SSS 70, Course record 63.
Club membership 800.

Visitors must contact in advance in writing.
Societies apply in writing.
Green Fees £20 per day.
Prof Alan Forrest
Designer James Braid
Facilities
Location 1.25m NE on A723 from Motherwell town centre

Hotel ★★ 63% Silvertrees Hotel, Silverwells Crescent, BOTHWELL ☎ 01698 852311 7 Annexe19

MUIRHEAD Map 11 NS66

Crow Wood Garnkirk House, Cumbernauld Rd G69 9JF
☎ 0141 779 4954 Fax 0141 779 9148
Parkland course.
18 holes, 6261yds, Par 71, SSS 71, Course record 62.
Club membership 800.
Visitors must contact in advance but may not play weekends & bank holidays.
Societies apply in advance.
Green Fees £25 per 2 rounds; £20 per round.
Prof Brian Moffat
Designer James Braid
Facilities
Location 0.5m W on A80

Hotel ★★★ 71% Malmaison Hotel, 278 West George St, GLASGOW ☎ 0141 221 6400 73

NEWCASTLETON Map 12 NY48

Newcastleton Holm Hill TD9 0QD ☎ 01387 375257
Hilly course with scenic views over the Liddesdale Valley and Newcastleton.
9 holes, 5748yds, Par 70, SSS 68.
Club membership 100.
Visitors contact the Secretary in advance.
Societies contact by telephone or in writing in advance.
Green Fees £7 per day (£8 weekends).
Designer J Shade
Facilities
& Leisure fishing.
Location W side of village

Hotel ★★ 61% Eskdale Hotel, Market Place, LANGHOLM ☎ 013873 80357 & 81178 Fax 013873 80357 15rm(11)

NEW CUMNOCK Map 11 NS61

New Cumnock Lochhill, Cumnock Rd KA18 4PN
☎ 01290 338848
Parkland course.
9 holes, 5176yds, Par 68, SSS 68, Course record 68.
Club membership 280.
Visitors restricted on Sun competition days.
Societies apply in writing.
Green Fees £7 per day/round.
Designer Willie Fernie
Facilities
& Leisure fishing.
Location 0.75m N on A76

Hotel ★ 64% Royal Hotel, 1 Glaisnock St, CUMNOCK
☎ 01290 420822 11rm(6)

NEW GALLOWAY Map 11 NX67

New Galloway High St DG7 3RN
☎ 01644 420737 Fax 01644 450685
Set on the edge of the Galloway Hills and overlooking Loch Ken, the course has excellent tees and first class greens.
9 holes, 5006yds, Par 68, SSS 67, Course record 63.
Club membership 350.
Visitors restricted on Sun (competition days). All visitors play off yellow markers.
Societies contact secretary in advance.
Green Fees £10 per day.
Designer James Braid
Facilities
Location S side of town on A762

Hotel ★★ 67% Douglas Arms, King St, CASTLE DOUGLAS ☎ 01556 502231 24

NEWTON MEARNS Map 11 NS55

East Renfrewshire Pilmuir G77 6RT
☎ 01355 500258
Undulating moorland with loch; prevailing SW wind.
18 holes, 6097yds, Par 70, SSS 70, Course record 63.
Club membership 900.
Visitors telephone for details.
Societies must contact in advance.
Green Fees £40 per day; £30 per round.
Prof Gordon Clarke
Designer James Braid
Facilities
Location 3m SW on A77

Hotel ★★★ 66% The Macdonald Thistle, Eastwood Toll, GIFFNOCK ☎ 0141 638 2225 56

Eastwood Muirshield, Loganswell G77 6RX
☎ 01355 500280
An undulating moorland course situated in a scenic setting.
18 holes, 5864yds, Par 68, SSS 69, Course record 62.
Club membership 900.
Visitors contact in advance, may only play with member at weekends.
Societies must contact in advance.
Green Fees £30 per day; £24 per round.
Prof Allan McGinness
Designer Theodore Moone
Facilities
Location 2.5m S of Newton Mearns, on A77

Hotel ★★★ 66% The Macdonald Thistle, Eastwood Toll, GIFFNOCK
☎ 0141 638 2225 56

Whitecraigs 72 Ayr Rd G46 6SW
☎ 0141 639 4530 & 0141 639 2140 pro
Beautiful parkland course.
18 holes, 6230yds, Par 70, SSS 70, Course record 65.
Club membership 1078.
Visitors must contact professional in advance and have a handicap certificate. With member only weekends and bank holidays.

Green Fees not confirmed.
Prof Alistair Forrow
Facilities
Location 1.5m NE on A77

Hotel ★★★ 66% The Macdonald Thistle, Eastwood Toll, GIFFNOCK
☎ 0141 638 2225 56

NEWTON STEWART Map 10 NX46

Newton Stewart Kirroughtree Av, Minnigaff DG8 6PF
☎ 01671 402172
Parkland course in picturesque setting. A good test for all standards of golfers with a variety of shots required.
18 holes, 5970yds, Par 69, SSS 70, Course record 66.
Club membership 360.
Visitors must contact in advance.
Societies must contact in advance.
Green Fees £21 per day; £18 per round (£25/£21 weekends & bank holidays).
Facilities
Location 0.5m N of town centre

Hotel ★★ 69% Creebridge House Hotel, NEWTON STEWART ☎ 01671 402121 19

PAISLEY Map 11 NS46

Barshaw Barshaw Park PA1 3TJ ☎ 0141 889 2908
Municipal parkland course.
18 holes, 5703yds, Par 68, SSS 67, Course record 63.
Club membership 100.
Visitors no restrictions.
Societies by prior arrangement with Parks Manager, Dept of Sports & Leisure, Renfrewshire Council, Mirren House, 6 Maxwell St, Paisley PA3 2AB.
Green Fees not confirmed.
Prof John Scott
Facilities
Location 1m E off A737

Hotel ★★★ 69% Glynhill Hotel & Leisure Club, Paisley Rd, RENFREW
☎ 0141 886 5555 & 885 1111 Fax 0141 885 28 38 125

Paisley Braehead PA2 8TZ
☎ 0141 884 3903 Fax 0141 884 3903
Moorland course, windy but with good views. The course has been designed in two loops of nine holes.
18 holes, 6215yds, Par 70, SSS 71.
Club membership 800.
Visitors must contact in advance. Visitors may not play weekends or public holidays.
Societies weekdays only, excluding bank holidays. Contact in advance.
Green Fees £28 per day; £20 per round.
Prof Gordon Stewart
Facilities
Location S side of town off B774

Hotel ★★★ 69% Glynhill Hotel & Leisure Club, Paisley Rd, RENFREW
☎ 0141 886 5555 & 885 1111
Fax 0141 885 2838 125

Ralston Strathmore Av, Ralston PA1 3DT
☎ 0141 882 1349
Parkland course.
18 holes, 6071yds, Par 71, SSS 69, Course record 62.
Club membership 750.
Visitors Mon -Fri only and must be accompanied by member.
Societies written notice required
Green Fees not confirmed.
Prof John Scott
Facilities
Location 2m E off A737

Hotel ★★★ 67% Swallow Hotel, 517 Paisley Rd West, GLASGOW
☎ 0141 427 3146 117

PATNA Map 10 NS41

Doon Valley Hillside Park KA6 7JT
☎ 01292 531607
Established parkland course located on an undulating hillside.
9 holes, 5654yds, Par 70, SSS 68.
Club membership 100.
Visitors mid week tee times available any time, advisable to contact for weekends.
Societies telephone to arrange.
Green Fees £6 per 18 holes (£10 weekends).
Facilities
& Leisure fishing.
Location 10m S of Ayr on the A713

Hotel ★★ Ladyburn, MAYBOLE
☎ 01655 740585 8rm(4 3)

PEEBLES Map 11 NT24

Peebles Kirkland St EH45 8EU ☎ 01721 720197
Parkland course with fine views.
18 holes, 6160yds, Par 70, SSS 70, Course record 63.
Club membership 750.
Visitors advisable to ring for information on availability, no visitors on Sat.
Societies apply by telephone or in writing in advance.
Green Fees £25 per day; £18 per round (£34/£25 weekends).
Prof Craig Imlah
Designer H S Colt
Facilities
Location W side of town centre off A72

Hotel ★★★ 71% Peebles Hydro Hotel, PEEBLES
☎ 01721 720602 137

PORTPATRICK Map 10 NX05

Portpatrick Golf Course Rd DG9 8TB
☎ 01776 810273 Fax 01776 810811
Seaside links-type course, set on cliffs overlooking the Irish Sea, with magnificent views.
Dunskey Course: 18 holes, 5882yds, Par 70, SSS 68, Course record 65.
Dinvin Course: 9 holes, 1504yds, Par 27, SSS 27.
Club membership 750.
Visitors must contact in advance.
Societies must contact in advance. ▶

Green Fees Dunskey: £27 per day; £18 per round (£32/£21 weekends) Dinvin: £12 per day; £8 per 18 holes.
Cards
Designer Charles Hunter
Facilities
Location 300 yds right from war memorial

Hotel ★★★ 69% Fernhill Hotel, PORTPATRICK
☎ 01776 810220 15 Annexe4

PRESTWICK Map 10 NS32

Prestwick 2 Links Rd KA9 1QG
☎ 01292 477404 Fax 01292 477255
Seaside links with natural hazards, tight fairways and difficult fast undulating greens.
18 holes, 6544yds, Par 71, SSS 73.
Club membership 575.
Visitors restricted Thu; may not play at weekends. Must contact in advance and have a handicap certificate.
Societies must contact in writing.
Green Fees £80 per day; £55 per round.
Cards
Prof F C Rennie
Designer Tom Morris
Facilities
Location In town centre off A79

Hotel ★★ 65% Parkstone Hotel, Esplanade, PRESTWICK ☎ 01292 477286 22
Additional hotel ★★ 66% Carlton Toby Hotel, 187 Ayr Rd, PRESTWICK
☎ 01292 476811
Fax 01292 474845 34

Prestwick St Cuthbert East Rd KA9 2SX
☎ 01292 477101 Fax 01292 671730
Parkland course with easy walking, natural hazards and sometimes windy.
18 holes, 6470yds, Par 71, SSS 71, Course record 64.
Club membership 880.
Visitors must contact in advance but may not play at weekends & bank holidays.
Societies Mon-Fri, apply in writing.
Green Fees £30 per day; £22 per round.
Facilities
Location 0.5m E of town centre off A77

Hotel ★★ 62% St Nicholas Hotel, 41 Ayr Rd, PRESTWICK
☎ 01292 479568 17rm(12)

Prestwick St Nicholas Grangemuir Rd KA9 1SN
☎ 01292 477608 Fax 01292 473900
Seaside links course with whins, heather and tight fairways. It provides easy walking and has an unrestricted view of the Firth of Clyde.
18 holes, 5952yds, Par 69, SSS 69, Course record 63.
Club membership 750.
Visitors except Sat, Sun am. Must contact in advance.
Societies must contact in advance.
Green Fees £45 per day; £30 per round (£35 per round Sun).
Designer Charles Hunter
Facilities
Location S side of town off A79

Hotel ★★ 65% Parkstone Hotel, Esplanade, PRESTWICK
☎ 01292 477286 22

RENFREW Map 11 NS46

Renfrew Blythswood Estate, Inchinnan Rd PA4 9EG
☎ 0141 886 6692 Fax 0141 886 1808
Tree-lined parkland course.
18 holes, 6818yds, Par 72, SSS 73.
Club membership 800.
Visitors restricted to Mon, Tue & Thu, apply in advance.
Societies apply in writing in advance.
Green Fees £35 per day; £25 per round.
Prof Stuart Kerr
Designer Commander Harris
Facilities
Location 0.75m W off A8

Hotel ★★★ 69% Glynhill Hotel & Leisure Club, Paisley Rd, RENFREW
☎ 0141 886 5555 & 885 1111 Fax 0141 885 2838 125

RIGSIDE Map 11 NS83

Douglas Water Old School, Ayr Rd ML11 9NP
☎ 01555 880361
A 9-hole course with good variety and some hills and spectacular views. An interesting course with a challenging longest hole of 564 yards but, overall, not too testing for average golfers.
9 holes, 5890yds, Par 72, SSS 69.
Club membership 250.
Visitors no restrictions weekdays or Sun, competitions on Sat normal restrictions.
Societies apply in writing/telephone in advance.
Green Fees £6 weekdays (£10 Sunday & Bank Holidays).

Facilities (prior arrangement)
Location Ayr rd A70

Hotel ★★★ 64% Tinto Hotel, Symington, BIGGAR
01899 308454 29

St Boswells Map 12 NT53

St Boswells Braeheads TD6 0DE 01835 823527
Attractive parkland course by the banks of the River Tweed; easy walking.
9 holes, 5250yds, Par 66.
Club membership 320.
Visitors contact in advance.
Societies booking by writing to secretary.
Green Fees £15 per day; £12 per round (£15 per day/round weekends).
Designer W Park
Facilities by prior arrangement by prior arrangement by prior arrangement
& Leisure fishing.
Location 500yds off A68 east end of village

Hotel ★★★★ 76% Dryburgh Abbey Hotel, ST BOSWELLS
01835 822261 25 Annexe1

Sanquhar Map 11 NS70

Sanquhar Euchen Golf Course, Blackaddie Rd DG4 6JZ
01659 50577
Parkland course, fine views, easy walking. A good test for all standards of golfer.
9 holes, 5594yds, Par 70, SSS 68 or 55 holes.
Club membership 200.
Visitors no restrictions.
Societies must pre-book.
Green Fees £10 per day (£12 weekends).
Facilities by prior arrangement by prior arrangement
& Leisure snooker, pool, carpet bowls.
Location 0.5m SW off A76

Hotel ★★ 65% Blackaddie House Hotel, Blackaddie Rd, SANQUHAR
01659 50270 9

Selkirk Map 12 NT42

Selkirk Selkirk Hill TD7 4NW
01750 20621
Pleasant moorland course set around Selkirk Hill. Unrivalled views.
9 holes, 5620yds, Par 68, SSS 67, Course record 61.
Club membership 364.
Visitors contact in advance, may not play Mon evening, competition/match days.
Societies must telephone in advance.
Green Fees £15 per day.
Facilities by prior arrangement by prior arrangement by prior arrangement
Location 1m S on A7

Hotel ★★★ 67% Burt's Hotel, The Square, MELROSE 01896 822285 20

Shotts Map 11 NS86

Shotts Blairhead ML7 5BJ 01501 820431
Moorland course.
18 holes, 6205yds, Par 70, SSS 70, Course record 63.
Club membership 800.
Visitors visitors by arrangement on Sun.
Societies apply in writing.
Green Fees not confirmed.
Prof Sandy Strachan
Designer James Braid
Facilities
Location 2m from M8 off Benhar Road

Hotel ★★★ 67% The Hilcroft Hotel, East Main St, WHITBURN 01501 740818 31

Skelmorlie Map 10 NS16

Skelmorlie Beithglass PA17 5ES 01475 520152
Parkland/moorland course with magnificent views over Firth of Clyde. Designed by James Braid, the club celebrated its centenary in 1991. The first five holes are played twice.
13 holes, 5056yds, Par 64, SSS 65.
Club membership 385.
Visitors no visitors before 4pm Sat.
Societies apply by telephone.
Green Fees not confirmed.
Designer James Braid
Facilities
& Leisure fishing.
Location E side of village off A78

Hotel ★★★★ 63% Manor Park Hotel, LARGS
01475 520832 10 Annexe13

Southerness Map 11 NX95

Southerness DG2 8AZ
01387 880677 Fax 01387 880644
Natural links, Championship course with panoramic views. Heather and bracken abound.
18 holes, 6566yds, Par 69, SSS 73, Course record 65.
Club membership 830.
Visitors must have handicap certificate and contact in advance.
Societies must contact in advance.
Green Fees £28 per day (£40 per day weekends & bank holidays).
Cards
Designer McKenzie Ross
Facilities
Location 3.5m S of Kirkbean off A710

Hotel ★★ 63% Clonyard House Hotel, COLVEND
01556 630372 15

Stevenston Map 10 NS24

Ardeer Greenhead KA20 4JX
01294 464542 Fax 01294 465316
Parkland course with natural hazards.
18 holes, 6500yds, Par 72, SSS 72, Course record 66.
Club membership 650.
Visitors may not play Sat.
Societies must contact in advance.

Green Fees £22 per day; £12 per round (£30/£20 Sun).
Prof Garrie Thompson
Designer Stutt
Facilities
Location 0.5m N off A78

Hotel ★★★★ 54% Hospitality Inn, 46 Annick Rd, IRVINE ☎ 01294 274272 127

Auchenharvie Moor Park Rd West KA20 3HU
☎ 01294 603103
Long and flat municipal course with narrow greens and a pond affecting the 3rd and 12th holes. Easy walking.
9 holes, 5048yds, Par 65, SSS 64, Course record 67.
Club membership 150.
Visitors municipal course 6 day advance booking system.
Societies apply to professional.
Green Fees not confirmed.
Cards
Prof Bob Rodgers
Facilities
Location Off A738

Hotel ★★★ 73% Montgreenan Mansion House Hotel, Montgreenan Estate, KILWINNING ☎ 01294 557733 21

STRANRAER Map 10 NX06

Stranraer Creachmore by Stranraer DG9 0LF
☎ 01776 870245 Fax 01776 870445
Parkland course with beautiful view of Loch Ryan.
18 holes, 6308yds, Par 70, SSS 72, Course record 66.
Club membership 640.
Visitors must contact in advance. Members times reserved throughout year.
Societies must telephone in advance.
Green Fees £25 per day; £19 per round.
Designer James Braid
Facilities
Location 2.5m NW on A718

Hotel ★★★★ 68% North West Castle Hotel, STRANRAER ☎ 01776 704413 70 Annexe3

STRATHAVEN Map 11 NS64

Strathaven Glasgow Rd ML10 6NL
☎ 01357 520421 Fax 01357 520421
Gently undulating, tree-lined, Championship parkland course with panoramic views over town and Avon valley.
18 holes, 6224yds, Par 71, SSS 71, Course record 63.
Club membership 950.
Visitors welcome weekdays up to 4pm only. Must contact in advance.
Societies apply in writing to general manager.
Green Fees not confirmed.
Prof Matt McCrorie
Designer Willie Fernie/J Stutt
Facilities
& Leisure putting green, practice area.
Location NE side of town on A726

Hotel ★★★ 67% Strathaven Hotel, Hamilton Rd, STRATHAVEN ☎ 01357 521778 22

THORNHILL Map 11 NX89

Thornhill Blacknest DG3 5DW ☎ 01848 330546
Moorland/parkland course with fine views.
18 holes, 6011yds, Par 71, SSS 70.
Club membership 700.
Visitors apply in advance, restricted competition days.
Societies apply in writing.
Green Fees £21 per day (£26 weekends & bank holidays).
Facilities
Location 1m E of town off A76

Hotel ★★ 72% Trigony House Hotel, Closeburn, THORNHILL ☎ 01848 331211 8

TROON Map 10 NS33

ROYAL TROON See page 389

Troon Municipal Harling Dr KA10 6NE
☎ 01292 312464 Fax 01292 312578
Three links courses, two Championship.
Lochgreen Course: 18 holes, 6820yds, Par 74, SSS 73.
Darley Course: 18 holes, 6360yds, Par 71, SSS 63.
Fullarton Course: 18 holes, 4870yds, Par 72, SSS 72.
Club membership 3000.
Visitors no restrictions.
Societies apply in writing.
Green Fees not confirmed.
Prof Gordon McKinlay
Facilities
Location 100yds from railway station

Hotel ★★ 62% Craiglea Hotel, South Beach, TROON ☎ 01292 311366 20rm(10)

TURNBERRY Map 10 NS20

TURNBERRY HOTEL GOLF COURSES See page 391

UDDINGSTON Map 11 NS66

Calderbraes 57 Roundknowe Rd G71 7TS
☎ 01698 813425
Parkland course with good view of Clyde Valley. Testing 4th hole (par 4), hard uphill.
9 holes, 5046yds, Par 66, SSS 67, Course record 65.
Club membership 230.
Visitors weekdays before 5pm.
Societies welcome.
Green Fees £12 per day.
Facilities
Location 1.5m NW off A74

Hotel ★★ 68% Redstones Hotel, 8-10 Glasgow Rd, UDDINGSTON ☎ 01698 813774 & 814843 Fax 01698 815319 18rm(16)

ROYAL TROON

TROON *South Ayrshire* ☎ 01292 311555
Fax 01292 318204 Map 10 NS33

John Ingham writes: When Jack Nicklaus first played Royal Troon in the 1962 Open, he was 22 and hit the ball a long way. At that time Nicklaus told me 'There are only two holes that I might not reach with my second shot. My favourite shot is the drive, which I hit up to 350 yards. Just before I swing,' he said, 'all my concentration is directed on one thing and that is to give the ball as big a hit - and as square a hit - as I physically can.'

While sheer length from the back tees at Royal Troon is a great advantage, bearing in mind the full course measures 7097 yards, where you hit the ball is more important than how far. The reason is that this championship links-type course is peppered with bunkers not visible from the tee.

That particular Open was won by Arnold Palmer, in those days a longish hitter as well. However, Palmer also had a delightful putting touch, essential for Royal Troon greens, which can prove hard to read.

Royal Troon is one of the finest links in the world and in an American list appears at number 36. Created in 1878, it was then mercifully free of jumbo jets from nearby Prestwick and has provided entertaining and testing golf for players from all over the world. Greg Norman holds the record with a 10-under-par round of 64. A round which put him in a tie for the 1989 Open which he lost to Mark Calcavecchia.

In the 1960s I played a round at this grand links with the late Henry Longhurst, a good club single figure man who had once won the German Amateur championship. To my best drives, lashed in the breeze, he would just hiss 'Wrong line' and, sure enough, when we got up the fairway, the ball would be submerged in soft sand. In fact I'm told there are 365 bunkers, one for every day of the year!

The Marine Higland hotel is on the edge of the course and, as there are 22 other courses in the area, this makes a great place for a holiday.

So great is Royal Troon, in fact, that the Royal and Ancient staged the 1997 Open again - for the seventh time since 1923!

Visitors may not play Mon, Tue and Thu only. Must write in advance and have a letter of introduction from own club and a handicap certificate of under 20. Ladies and under 18s may only play on the Portland

Green fees £110 per day

Facilities ⊗))) ⊾ ☕ ♀ ⌂ ⊟ ↑ Professional (B. Anderson)

Location Craigend Rd, Troon KA10 6EP (S side of town on B749)

36 holes. Old Course: 18 holes, 7067yds, Par 73, SSS 74. Course record 64

Portland: 18 holes, 6289yds, Par 71, SSS 70

WHERE TO STAY AND EAT NEARBY

HOTELS:

TROON

★★★ ⚘⚘ Lochgreen House, Monktenhill Rd, Southwood ☎ 01292 313343. 7 ⇄ ↑

★★★★ ⚘ 65% Marine Highland. ☎ 01292 314444, 72 ⇄ ↑

★★★ ⚘⚘ 75% Highgrove House, Old Loans Rd ☎ 01292 312511. 9 (2 ↑ 7 ⇄ ↑)

★★★ ⚘ 73% Piersland House, Craigend Rd. ☎ 01292 314747. 15 (1 ⇄ 14 ⇄ ↑) Annexe 13 ⇄ ↑

Uplawmoor Map 10 NS45

Caldwell G78 4AU
☎ 01505 850366 (Secretary) & 850616 (Pro) Fax 01505 85 0604
Parkland course.
18 holes, 6294yds, Par 71, SSS 70, Course record 63.
Club membership 600.

Visitors must be with member at weekends & bank holidays. Must contact professional in advance.
Societies writing to Secretary.
Green Fees £33 per day; £23 per round.
Prof Stephen Forbes
Facilities
Location 0.5m SW A736

Hotel ★★★ 69% Dalmeny Park Country House, Lochlibo Rd, BARRHEAD
☎ 0141 881 9211 20

West Kilbride Map 10 NS24

West Kilbride 33-35 Fullerton Dr, Seamill KA23 9HT
☎ 01294 823911 Fax 01294 823911
Seaside links course on Firth of Clyde, with fine views of Isle of Arran from every hole.
18 holes, 5974yds, Par 70, SSS 70, Course record 63.
Club membership 840.

Visitors may not play at weekends, must contact in advance.
Societies Tue & Thu only; must contact in advance.
Green Fees £37 per day; £23 per round.
Prof Graham Ross
Designer James Braid
Facilities
Location W side of town off A78

Hotel ★★★ 70% Priory House Hotel, John St, Broomfields, LARGS
☎ 01475 686460 21

West Linton Map 11 NT15

West Linton EH46 7HN ☎ 01968 660256
Moorland course with beautiful views of Pentland Hills.
18 holes, 6132yds, Par 69, SSS 70, Course record 63.
Club membership 800.

Visitors weekdays anytime, weekends not before 1pm.
Societies contact the secretary in writing.
Green Fees £27 per day; £18 per round (£28 per round weekends).
Prof Ian Wright
Designer Millar/Braid/Fraser
Facilities
Location NW side of village off A702

Hotel ★★★ 71% Peebles Hydro Hotel, PEEBLES
☎ 01721 720602 137

Wigtown Map 10 NX45

Wigtown & Bladnoch Lightlands Ter DG8 9EF
☎ 01988 403354
Slightly hilly parkland course with fine views over Wigtown Bay to Galloway Hills.
9 holes, 5462yds, Par 68, SSS 67, Course record 62.
Club membership 150.

Visitors advisable to contact in advance for weekend play. Course closed to visitors during open competitions.
Societies contact secretary in advance.
Green Fees £17 per day; £12 per round.
Designer W Muir
Facilities by prior arrangement by prior arrangement
Location SW on A714

Hotel ★★ 69% Creebridge House Hotel, NEWTON STEWART
☎ 01671 402121 19

Wishaw Map 11 NS75

Wishaw 55 Cleland Rd ML2 7PH
☎ 01698 372869
Parkland course with many tree-lined areas. Bunkers protect 17 of the 18 greens.
18 holes, 6073yds, Par 69, SSS 69, Course record 64.
Club membership 984.

Visitors must contact secretary in advance. May not play Sat but may play alternate Sun.
Societies apply in writing.
Green Fees £21 per day; £13 per round (£26 Sun).
Prof Stuart Adair
Designer James Braid
Facilities
Location NW side of town off A721

Hotel ★★★ 67% Popinjay Hotel, Lanark Rd, ROSEBANK
☎ 01555 860441 42 Annexe5

TURNBERRY HOTEL GOLF COURSES

TURNBERRY *South Ayrshire*

☎ 01655 331000 Fax 01655 331706 Map 10 NS20

John Ingham writes: The hotel is sumptuous, the Ailsa and Arran courses beneath it are total magic. The air reaches down into your inner lung and of all places in Scotland, Turnberry has to be among the finest.

Tunberry is delightfully off the beaten track and, although the courses are principally for residents of the hotel, if you wish to fly in, then Prestwick Airport is only seventeen miles from the first tee. What makes the place so desirable is the warmness of the welcome and, course professional Brian Gunson will tell you, this is literally so on occasions, as the links is on the friendliest of gulf streams.

The Ailsa course has been the venue for the Open in 1977 and 1986 and hosted it again in 1994. It was here in the 1977 Open, that Jack Nicklaus put up such a brave fight against Tom Watson. Then, in 1986, we had a wondrous victory from Greg Norman. He has fond memories of Turnberry, where a few hours after the prize-giving he was able to sit with his wife on the edge of the great links, drinking champagne, and watching the moon roll round the pure white lighthouse out by the 9th green.

Without any doubt, Turnberry is the stuff of dreams and you must go there if you possibly can.

Visitors The golf courses are principally for residents of the hotel, so must contact in advance

Societies contact in advance as courses are for residents of the hotel

Green fees on application.

Facilities ⊗ Ⅲ ⛳ ☕ ♀ 🛏 ⌂ Professional (Brian Gunson)

Leisure tennis (hardcourt), indoor swimming pool, squash, snooker, health spa

Location Turnberry KA26 9LT. On A719 N side of village

36 holes. Ailsa Course: 18 holes, 6440 yds, Par 69, SSS 72, Course record 63 Arran Course: 18 holes, 6014yds, Par 68, SSS 69. Course record 65

WHERE TO STAY AND EAT NEARBY

HOTELS:

MAYBOLE

★★❀ Ladyburn

☎ 01655 740585. 8(7 ⇌ ♠)

TURNBERRY

★★★★★ ❀❀ Turnberry Hotel, Golf Courses & Spa.

☎ 01655 331000. 132 ⇌ ♠

★★★ ❀ 76%Malin Court.

☎ 01655 31457. 17 ⇌ ♠

WALES

John Ingham writes: Those not averse to wearing a daffodil in their lapel each St David's Day will tell you Wales not only boasts some great sporting characters, but also some excellent golf courses which don't cost fortunes to play.

Back in 1960, I drove my black Wolseley across the mountain road to Harlech to report a women's championship for the London Evening Standard. The event was staged across Royal St David's, on the coast just eleven miles from Barmouth and built, in 1893, on low-lying ground beneath the famous castle. It is the grandest seaside links, with dunes, rushes, dog roses.

The Principality has other great courses further south. There's Aberdovey, originally played into sunken flower pots in 1892. Today there's a frightening tee shot along a gorge, between hills. From one tee is an amazing pulpit-like view of the estuary, and Cardigan Bay.

Perhaps the most famous course in Wales is Royal Porthcawl which has opened its doors to championships, and Internationals. Begun in 1891 with nine holes and no clubhouse, it became 'Royal' in 1909 and it takes skill to play, particularly if the off-sea winds and zipping in from the Bristol Channel. Curiously, it often misses the rains on its peninsula as it tends to fall a few mile inland.

By contrast, play at St Pierre, not far from the Severn Bridge near Chepstow, Monmouthshire. The location, parkland with a delightful manor, was found by dear old Bill Graham who bought it, after the war, and with the help of Bill Cox, built it into a splendid and somewhat sumptuous halt for golfers who appreciate more inland parkland fairways.

Today, everyone tells me if I haven't played the Rolls of Monmouth, west of the town on the B4233, a rare treat lies in store Created in 1982, it is considered very upmarket. Play it, they say, before you die.

WALES

The directory which follows has been divided into three geographical regions. Counties have not been shown against individual locations as recent legislation has created a number of smaller counties which will be unfamiliar to the visitor. The postal authorities have confirmed that it is no longer necessary to include a county name in addresses, provided a post code is shown. All locations appear in the atlas at the end of this guide in their appropriate counties.

NORTH WALES

This region includes the counties of Conwy, Denbighshire, Flintshire, Gwynedd, Isle of Anglesey and Wrexham which reflect the recent national changes.

ABERDYFI Map 06 SN69

Aberdovey LL35 0RT
☎ 01654 767493 Fax 01654 767027
A beautiful championship course at the mouth of the Dovey estuary, Aberdovey has all the true characteristics of a seaside links. It has some fine holes among them the 3rd, the 12th, an especially good short hole, and the 11th. There are some striking views to be had from the course.
18 holes, 6445yds, Par 71, SSS 71, Course record 66.
Club membership 1000.

Visitors handicap certificate required, must contact in advance, restrictions at weekends.
Societies prior arrangement essential.
Green Fees £25 per round (£30 weekends).
Cards
Prof John Davies
Facilities
Location 0.5m W on A493

Hotel ★★★ 70% Trefeddian Hotel, ABERDYFI ☎ 01654 767213 46

ABERGELE Map 06 SH97

Abergele Tan-y-Gopa Rd LL22 8DS ☎ 01745 824034 Fax 01745 824034
A beautiful parkland course with views of the Irish Sea and Gwyrch Castle. There are splendid finishing holes, a testing par 5, 16th; a 185 yd, 17th to an elevated green, and a superb par 5 18th with out of bounds just behind the green.
18 holes, 6520yds, Par 72, SSS 71, Course record 66.
Club membership 1250.

Visitors must contact in advance. Limited play weekends.
Societies must contact in advance.
Green Fees Apr-Oct £23 per day (£28 weekends); Nov-Mar £15 per day (£20 weekends).
Prof Iain R Runcie
Designer Hawtree
Facilities
Location 0.5m W off A547/A55

Hotel ★★★ 66% Kinmel Manor Hotel, St Georges Rd, ABERGELE ☎ 01745 832014 42

ABERSOCH Map 06 SH32

Abersoch LL53 7EY ☎ 01758 712622
Seaside links, with five parkland holes.
18 holes, 5819yds, Par 69, SSS 68.
Club membership 650.

Visitors must contact in advance. Competition days Sun & Thu.
Societies must apply in advance.
Green Fees not confirmed.
Prof A D Jones
Designer Harry Vardon
Facilities
Location S side of village

Hotel ★★★ 64% Abersoch Harbour Hotel, ABERSOCH ☎ 01758 712406 9 Annexe5

ANGLESEY, ISLE OF Map 06

Golf Courses on the island of Anglesey are listed below.

AMLWCH Map 06 SH49

Bull Bay LL68 9RY ☎ 01407 830960 Fax 01407 832612
Wales's northernmost course,Bull Bay is a pleasant coastal, heathland course with natural rock, gorse and wind hazards. Views from several tees across Irish Sea to Isle of Man, and across Anglesey to Snowdonia. ▶

18 holes, 6217yds, Par 70, SSS 70, Course record 60.
Club membership 825.

Visitors advisable to contact in advance.
Societies advance booking essential.
Green Fees £20 per day; £15 per round (£25/£20 weekends & bank holidays).
Prof John Burns
Designer W H Fowler
Facilities
Location 1m W of Amlwch on A5025

Hotel ★★ 62% Trecastell Hotel, Bull Bay, AMLWCH
☎ 01407 830651 13rm(11)

BEAUMARIS Map 06 SH67

Baron Hill LL58 8YW ☎ 01248 810231
Undulating course with natural hazards of rock and gorse. Testing 3rd and 4th holes (par 4's). Nole 5/14 plays into the prevailing wind with an elevated tee across two streams. The hole is between two gorse covered mounds.
9 holes, 5062mtrs, Par 68, SSS 69, Course record 62.
Club membership 400.

Visitors ladies have priority on Tue am & club competitions Sun.
Societies apply in writing to secretary.
Green Fees £13 per day; £45 per week.
Facilities
Location 1m SW off A545

Hotel ★★ 67% Bulkeley Hotel, Castle St, BEAUMARIS
☎ 01248 810415 41rm(40)

HOLYHEAD Map 06 SH28

Holyhead Lon Garreg Fawr, Trearddur Bay LL65 2YG
☎ 01407 763279 Fax 01407 763279
Treeless, undulating seaside course which provides a varied and testing game, particularly in a south wind. The fairways are bordered by gorse, heather and rugged outcrops of rock. Accuracy from most tees is paramount as there are 43 fairway and greenside bunkers and lakes. Designed by James Braid. Indoor driving range.
18 holes, 6058yds, Par 70, SSS 70, Course record 64.
Club membership 1120.

Visitors must contact in advance.
Societies must contact in advance.
Green Fees £22 per day; £17 per round (£28/£22 weekends & bank holidays).
Prof Stephen Elliot
Designer James Braid
Facilities
Location 1.25m S on B4545

Hotel ★★★ 71% Trearddur Bay Hotel, TREARDDUR BAY
☎ 01407 860301 31

LLANGEFNI Map 06 SH47

Llangefni (Public) LL77 7LJ
☎ 01248 722193 Fax 01248 750156
Picturesque parkland course designed by Hawtree & Son.
9 holes, 1342yds, Par 28, SSS 28.

Visitors no restrictions.
Green Fees £2.20 9 holes (£3 weekends).
Prof Paul Lovell
Designer Hawtree & Sons
Facilities
Location 1.5m off A5

Hotel ★★★ Tre-Ysgawen Hall, Capel Coch, LLANGEFNI ☎ 01248 750750 20

RHOSNEIGR Map 06 SH37

Anglesey Station Rd LL64 5QX ☎ 01407 811202
Links course, low and fairly level with sand dunes and tidal river.
18 holes, 6300yds, Par 68, SSS 68.
Club membership 400.

Visitors phone in advance, some times are reserved for members. Dress restrictions.
Societies telephone & confirm in writing.
Green Fees not confirmed.
Prof Mark Harrison
Designer H Hilton
Facilities
Location NE side of village on A4080

Hotel ★★★ 71% Trearddur Bay Hotel, TREARDDUR BAY
☎ 01407 860301 31

BALA Map 06 SH93

Bala Penlan LL23 7YD ☎ 01678 520359 & 521361
Mountainous course with natural hazards. All holes except first and last affected by wind.
10 holes, 4962yds, Par 66, SSS 64, Course record 64.
Club membership 200.

Visitors book in advance.
Societies must contact in advance.
Green Fees not confirmed.
Facilities by prior arrangement by prior arrangement by prior arrangement by prior arrangement
Location 0.5m SW off A494

Hotel ★★ 64% Plas Coch Hotel, High St, BALA
☎ 01678 520309 10

BANGOR Map 06 SH57

St Deiniol Penybryn LL57 1PX ☎ 01492 353098
Elevated parkland course with panoramic views of Snowdonia, Menai Straits, and Anglesey.
18 holes, 5068mtrs, Par 68, SSS 67, Course record 61.
Club membership 300.

Visitors must contact in advance.
Societies must contact in advance.
Green Fees £12 per day (£16 weekends).
Designer James Braid
Facilities
Location E side of town centre off A5122

Hotel ★★★ 70% Menai Court Hotel, Craig y Don Rd, BANGOR ☎ 01248 354200 13

Betws-y-Coed Map 06 SH75

Betws-y-Coed LL24 0AL ☎ 01690 710556
Attractive flat meadowland course set between two rivers in Snowdonia National Park.
9 holes, 4996yds, Par 64, SSS 63, Course record 63.
Club membership 350.

Visitors must contact in advance.
Societies must telephone in advance.
Green Fees charges variable.
Facilities
Location NE side of village off A5

Hotel ★★★ 69% The Royal Oak Hotel, Holyhead Rd, BETWS-Y-COED ☎ 01690 710219 27

Bodelwyddan Map 06 SJ07

Kimnel Park LL18 5SR
☎ 01745 833548 Fax 01745 833544
Flat parkland pay and play course that is suitable for beginners.
9 holes, 3100, Par 58, SSS 58.

Visitors no restrictions.
Societies telephone for details.
Green Fees not confirmed.
Prof Peter Stebbings
Designer Peter Stebbings
Facilities
Location y

Hotel ★★★ 64% Oriel House Hotel, Upper Denbigh Rd, ST ASAPH ☎ 01745 582716 19

Brynford Map 07 SJ17

Holywell Brynford CH8 8LQ
☎ 01352 713937 & 710040 Fax 01352 713937
Exposed moorland course, with bracken and gorse flanking undulating fairways. 720 ft above sea level.
18 holes, 6100yds, Par 70, SSS 70, Course record 69.
Club membership 505.

Visitors advisable to book in advance particularly for weekends.
Societies by prior arrangement with the secretary.
Green Fees £15 per day (£20 weekends & bank holidays).
Prof Sean O'Conner
Facilities
Location 1.25m SW off B5121

Hotel ★★ 67% Stamford Gate Hotel, Halkyn Rd, HOLYWELL ☎ 01352 712942 12

Caernarfon Map 06 SH46

Caernarfon Llanfaglan LL54 5RP
☎ 01286 673783 & 678359 Fax 01286 672535
Parkland course with gentle gradients.
18 holes, 5891yds, Par 69, SSS 68, Course record 64.
Club membership 730.

Visitors must contact in advance.
Societies must apply in advance, in writing or by telephone.
Green Fees £22 per day; £17 per round (£26/£22 weekends & bank holidays).
Cards
Prof Aled Owen
Facilities
Location 1.75m SW

Hotel ★★★ 64% Celtic Royal Hotel, Bangor St, CAERNARFON ☎ 01286 674477 110

Caerwys Map 06 SJ17

Caerwys Nine Of Clubs CH7 5AQ ☎ 01352 720692
Following the natural contours of the land and with a south-west aspect, this course could be considered a litle gem. Each approach to every green is different and there are many interesting and challenging holes.
9 holes, 3080yds, Par 60, Course record 61.
Club membership 150.

Visitors no restrictions.
Societies telephone then confirm in writing.
Green Fees not confirmed.
Designer Eleanor Barlow
Facilities
Location 1.5m SW of A55, midway between St Asaph and Holywell

Hotel ★★ 64% Bryn Awel Hotel, Denbigh Rd, MOLD ☎ 01352 758622 7 Annexe10

Chirk Map 07 SJ23

Chirk Golf Club LL14 5AD
☎ 01691 774407 Fax 01691 773878
Overlooked by the National Trust's Chirk Castle, is a championship-standard 18-hole course with a 664 yard, par 5 at the 9th - one of the longest in Europe. Also a 9-hole course, driving range and golf academy.
Manor Course: 18 holes, 7045yds, Par 72, SSS 73, Course record 72.
Club membership 750. ▶

Visitors advisable to contact in advance. May not play in members preferred tee times 7-11 daily.
Societies must telephone for provisonal booking.
Green Fees not confirmed.
Prof Jason Fullard
Facilities
& Leisure squash, fishing.
Location 5m N of Oswestry

Hotel ★★★ 65% Hand Hotel, Church St, CHIRK
☎ 01691 772479 16

COLWYN BAY Map 06 SH87

Old Colwyn Woodland Av, Old Colwyn LL29 9NL
☎ 01492 515581
Hilly, meadowland course with sheep and cattle grazing on it in parts.
9 holes, 5243yds, Par 68, SSS 66, Course record 63.
Club membership 267.
Visitors welcome ex Sat. Contact in advance.
Societies must contact in advance.
Green Fees £10 per day (£15 weekends & bank holidays).
Designer James Braid
Facilities by prior arrangement by prior arrangement by prior arrangement by prior arrangement (weekends/evenings)
Location E side of town centre on B5383

Hotel ★★★ 66% Hopeside Hotel, Princes Dr, West End, COLWYN BAY
☎ 01492 533244 19rm(11 5)

CONWY Map 06 SH77

Conwy (Caernarvonshire) Beacons Way, Morfa LL32 8ER ☎ 01492 592423 Fax 01492 593363
Founded in 1890, Conwy has hosted national and international championships since 1898. Set among sandhills, possessing true links greens and a profusion of gorse on the latter holes, especially the 16th, 17th and 18th. This course provides the visitor with real golfing enjoyment against a background of stunning beauty.
18 holes, 6647yds, Par 72, SSS 72, Course record 69.
Club membership 1050.
Visitors advisable to contact secretary in advance. Limited play weekends.
Societies must contact in advance.
Green Fees £25 per day (£30 weekends & bank holidays).
Prof Peter Lees
Facilities
Location 1m W of town centre on A55

Hotel ★★ 65% Sychnant Pass Country House Hotel, Sychnant Pass Rd, CONWY
☎ 01492 596868 12

CRICCIETH Map 06 SH43

Criccieth Ednyfed Hill LL52 0PH ☎ 01766 522154
Hilly course on Lleyn Peninsula. Good views.
18 holes, 5787yds, Par 69, SSS 68.
Club membership 350.
Visitors must contact in advance.
Societies telephone in advance.
Green Fees not confirmed.
Facilities
Location 1m NE

Hotel ★★★ 68% Bron Eifion Country House Hotel, CRICCIETH
☎ 01766 522385 19

DENBIGH Map 06 SJ06

Bryn Morfydd Hotel Llanrhaedr LL16 4NP
☎ 01745 890280 Fax 01745 890488
In a beautiful setting in the Vale of Clwyd, the original 9-hole Duchess course was designed by Peter Alliss in 1982. In 1992, the 18-hole Dukes course was completed: a parkland course designed to encourage use of finesse in play.
Dukes Course: 18 holes, 5650yds, Par 70, SSS 67, Course record 74.
Duchess Course: 9 holes, 2098yds, Par 27.
Club membership 450.
Visitors must book in advance, good standards of dress apply.
Societies apply in writing.
Green Fees Dukes £12 per 18 holes (£16 weekends); Duchess £5.
Cards
Prof Ivor Jones
Designer Peter Allis/Duncan Muirhead
Facilities
& Leisure heated outdoor swimming pool.
Location On A525 between Denbigh and Ruthin

Denbigh Henllan Rd LL16 5AA
☎ 01745 814159 Fax 814888
Parkland course, giving a testing and varied game. Good views.
18 holes, 5712yds, Par 69, SSS 68, Course record 64.
Club membership 725.
Visitors must contact in advance.
Societies apply in writing.
Green Fees £20 per day (£25 weekends per 18 holes).
Prof Mike Jones
Designer John Stockton
Facilities
Location 1.5m NW on B5382

Hotel ★★★ 62% Talardy Park Hotel, The Roe, ST ASAPH ☎ 01745 584957 18

DOLGELLAU Map 06 SH71

Dolgellau Pencefn Rd LL40 2ES
☎ 01341 422603
Undulating parkland course. Good views of mountains and Mawddach estuary.
9 holes, 4671yds, Par 66, SSS 63, Course record 62.
Club membership 280.
Visitors may not play on Sat.
Societies must contact in advance.
Green Fees £15 per day (£18 weekends & bank holidays).
Facilities
Location 0.5m N

Hotel ★★ 63% Royal Ship Hotel, Queens Square, DOLGELLAU
☎ 01341 422209 24rm(18)

Eyton Map 07 SJ34

Plassey LL13 0SP ☎ 01978 780028
Pleasant 9-hole course set in naturally contoured parkland with water hazards. It is within Plassey Leisure Park and Craft Centre and all park facilities are available to golfers.
9 holes, 2300yds, Par 32, SSS 32.
Club membership 200.

Visitors must contact in advance,
Societies telephone then confirm in writing.
Green Fees not confirmed.
Designer Welsh Golf Union
Facilities
& Leisure heated indoor swimming pool, fishing, sauna, solarium.
Location 2.5m off A483 Chester/Oswestry

Hotel ★★★ 67% Cross Lanes Hotel & Restaurant, Cross Lanes, Bangor Rd, Marchwiel, WREXHAM ☎ 01978 780555 16

Ffestiniog Map 06 SH74

Ffestiniog Y Cefn LL41 4LS ☎ 01766 762637
Moorland course set in Snowdonia National Park.
9 holes, 4570yds, Par 68, SSS 66.
Club membership 150.

Visitors welcome except during competitions.
Societies must telephone in advance.
Green Fees not confirmed.
Facilities
Location 1m E on B4391

Hotel ★★ Hotel Maes y Neuadd, TALSARNAU ☎ 01766 780200 12 Annexe4

Flint Map 07 SJ27

Flint Cornist Park CH6 5HJ
☎ 01244 812974 Fax 01244 811885
Parkland course incorporating woods and streams. Excellent views of Dee estuary and the Welsh hills.
9 holes, 6984yds, Par 69, SSS 69, Course record 65.
Club membership 260.

Visitors must contact in advance, not Sun.
Societies not weekends.
Green Fees £10 per round.
Designer H G Griffith
Facilities
& Leisure hard tennis courts.
Location 1m W

Hotel ★★ 67% Stamford Gate Hotel, Halkyn Rd, HOLYWELL ☎ 01352 712942 12

Harlech Map 06 SH53

Royal St Davids LL46 2UB
☎ 01766 780361 Fax 01766 781110
Championship links, with easy walking and natural hazards.
18 holes, 6427yds, Par 69, SSS 72, Course record 64.
Club membership 700.

Visitors pre booking essential, must hold current handicap certificate.
Societies telephone secretary in advance. Handicap certificates required.
Green Fees Winter: £22 (£27 weekends & bank holidays). Summer: £30 (£35 weekends & bank holidays).
Cards
Prof John Barnett
Facilities
Location W side of town on A496

Hotel ★★ 64% Ty Mawr Hotel, LLANBEDR ☎ 01341 241440 10

Hawarden Map 07 SJ36

Hawarden Groomsdale Ln CH5 3EH
☎ 01244 531447 & 520809
Parkland course with comfortable walking and good views.
18 holes, 5842yds, Par 69, SSS 69.
Club membership 550.

Visitors arrange visit with the professional.
Societies by prior arrangement.
Green Fees not confirmed.
Prof Chris Hope
Facilities
Location W side of town off B5125

Hotel ★★★ 72% The Gateway To Wales Hotel, Welsh Rd, Sealand, Deeside, CHESTER ☎ 01244 830332 39

Llandudno Map 06 SH78

Llandudno (Maesdu) Hospital Rd LL30 1HU
☎ 01492 876450 Fax 01492 871570
Part links, part parkland, this championship course starts and finishes on one side of the main road, the remaining holes, more seaside in nature, being played on the other side. The holes are pleasantly undulating and present a pretty picture when the gorse is in bloom. Often windy, this varied and testing course is not for beginners.
18 holes, 6545yds, Par 72, SSS 72, Course record 66.
Club membership 1045.

Visitors must book in advance.
Societies must apply in advance to secretary.
Green Fees £25 per day (£30 weekends & bank holidays). £18 after 1pm (£22 weekends & bank holidays after 2pm).
Prof Simon Boulden
Facilities
& Leisure snooker room.
Location S side of town centre on A546

Hotel ★★★ 66% Imperial Hotel, The Promenade, LLANDUDNO ☎ 01492 877466 100

Additional hotel ★★ 64% Esplanade Hotel, Glan-y-Mor Pde, Promenade, LLANDUDNO ☎ 0800 318688 (freephone) & 01492 860300 Fax 01492 860418 59

Entries with a shaded background identify courses that are considered to be particularly interesting

North Wales 72 Bryniau Rd, West Shore LL30 2DZ
☎ 01492 875325 Fax 01492 875325
Challenging seaside links with superb views of Anglesey and Snowdonia.
18 holes, 6247yds, Par 71, SSS 71, Course record 65.
Club membership 525.

Visitors must contact in advance.
Societies must contact in advance.
Green Fees £23 per day (£30 weekends & bank holidays).
Cards
Prof Richard Bradbury
Designer Tancred Cummins
Facilities
Location W side of town on A546

Hotel ★★ St Tudno Hotel, Promenade, LLANDUDNO
☎ 01492 874411 20

Rhos-on-Sea Penryhn Bay LL30 3PU
☎ 01492 548115 (Prof)
Seaside course, with easy walking and panoramic views.
18 holes, 6064yds, Par 69, SSS 69, Course record 68.
Club membership 400.

Visitors advised to telephone beforehand to guarantee tee times.
Societies booking essential, telephone in advance.
Green Fees £10 per day (£20 weekends).
Prof Mick Macara
Designer J J Simpson
Facilities
Location 0.5m W of LLandudno, off the A55

Hotel ★★★ 66% Hopeside Hotel, Princes Dr, West End, COLWYN BAY
☎ 01492 533244 19rm(11 5)

LLANFAIRFECHAN Map 06 SH67

Llanfairfechan Llannerch Rd LL33 0ES ☎ 01248 680144
Hillside course with panoramic views of coast.
9 holes, 3119yds, Par 54, SSS 57, Course record 53.
Club membership 159.

Visitors booking necessary at weekends.
Societies apply in writing.
Green Fees £5 per day (£10 weekends & bank holidays).
Facilities
Location W side of town on A55

Hotel ★★ 65% Sychnant Pass Country House Hotel, Sychnant Pass Rd, CONWY
☎ 01492 596868 12

LLANGOLLEN Map 07 SJ24

Vale of Llangollen Holyhead Rd LL20 7PR
☎ 01978 860906 Fax 01978 860906
Parkland course, set in superb scenery by the River Dee.
18 holes, 6656yds, Par 72, SSS 73, Course record 67.
Club membership 760.

Visitors must contact in advance. Restricted club competition days. Handicap certificate required.
Societies apply in writing to the secretary.
Green Fees £25 per day; £20 per round (£30/£25 weekends & bank holidays).
Cards
Prof David Vaughan
Facilities
Location 1.5m E on A5

Hotel ★★★ 69% Bryn Howel Hotel & Restaurant, LLANGOLLEN ☎ 01978 860331 36

MOLD Map 07 SJ26

Old Padeswood Station Rd, Padeswood CH7 4JL
☎ 01244 547401 & 550414 Fax 01244 545082
Meadowland course, undulating in parts.
18 holes, 6685yds, Par 72, SSS 72, Course record 66.
Club membership 600.

Visitors welcome, subject to tee availability.
Societies telephone in advance.
Green Fees £18 per round (£20 weekends & bank holidays).
Prof Tony Davies
Designer Jeffries
Facilities
& Leisure Par 3 9 hole course.
Location 3m SE off A5118

Hotel ★★ 64% Bryn Awel Hotel, Denbigh Rd, MOLD
☎ 01352 758622 7 Annexe10

Padeswood & Buckley The Caia, Station Ln CH7 4JD
☎ 01244 550537 Fax 01244 541600
Gently undulating parkland course, with natural hazards and good views of the Welsh Hills.
18 holes, 5982yds, Par 70, SSS 69, Course record 66.
Club membership 700.

Visitors weekdays only, contact secretary in advance
Societies apply in writing.
Green Fees £20 per round.
Prof David Ashton
Designer Williams Partnership
Facilities
& Leisure snooker.
Location 3m SE off A5118

Hotel ★★ 64% Bryn Awel Hotel, Denbigh Rd, MOLD
☎ 01352 758622 7 Annexe10

Morfa Nefyn Map 06 SH24

Nefyn & District LL53 6DA
☎ 01758 720966 Fax 01758 720476
A 27-hole course played as two separate 18's, Nefyn is a cliff top links where you never lose sight of the sea. A well-maintained course which will be a very tough test for the serious golfer, is still user friendly for the casual visitor. Every hole has a different challenge and the old 13th fairway is approximately 30 yards arcross from sea-to-sea. The course has an added bonus of a pub on the beach roughly halfway round for those whose golf may need some bolstering!
Old Course: 18 holes, 6201yds, Par 71, SSS 71, Course record 67.
New Course: 18 holes, 6548yds, Par 71, SSS 71, Course record 67.
Club membership 800.
Visitors advisable to contact in advance.
Societies apply by telephone.
Green Fees not confirmed.
Prof John Froom
Designer James Braid
Facilities
Location 0.75m NW

Hotel ★★ 78% Plas Bodegroes, Nefyn Rd, PWLLHELI
☎ 01758 612363 9 Annexe2

Northop Map 07 SJ26

Northop Country Park CH7 6WA
☎ 01352 840440 Fax 01352 840445
Designed by former British Ryder Cup captain, John Jacobs, the parkland course gives the impression of having been established for many years. No two holes are the same and designed to allow all year play.
18 holes, 6750yds, Par 72, SSS 73, Course record 69.
Club membership 500.
Visitors advisable to telephone in advance.
Societies apply in writing or by telephone in advance.
Green Fees £28 per round (£35 weekends & bank holidays).
Cards
Prof Matthew Pritchard
Designer John Jacobs
Facilities
& Leisure hard tennis courts, sauna, gymnasium.
Location 150 yds from Connahs Quay turnoff on A55

Hotel ★★★★ 69% St Davids Park Hotel, St Davids Park, EWLOE ☎ 01244 520800 145

Pantymwyn Map 07 SJ16

Mold Cilcain Rd CH7 5EH
☎ 01352 740318 & 741513 Fax 01352 741517
Meadowland course with some hard walking and natural hazards. Fine views.
18 holes, 5528yds, Par 67, SSS 67, Course record 64.
Club membership 600.
Visitors contact in advance.
Societies provisional booking by telephone.
Green Fees £16 per round (£23 weekends & bank holidays).
Prof Neil Coulson
Designer Hawtree
Facilities
Location E side of village

Hotel ★★ 64% Bryn Awel Hotel, Denbigh Rd, MOLD
☎ 01352 758622 7 Annexe10

Penmaenmawr Map 06 SH77

Penmaenmawr Conway Old Rd LL34 6RD
☎ 01492 623330
Hilly course with magnificent views across the bay to Llandudno and Anglesey. Dry-stone wall natural hazards.
9 holes, 5350yds, Par 67, SSS 66, Course record 64.
Club membership 600.
Visitors advisable to contact in advance. May not play Sat.
Societies must contact in advance.
Green Fees £12 weekdays (£18 Sun).
Facilities
Location 1.5m NE off A55

Hotel ★★★ 62% The Castle, High St, CONWY
☎ 01492 592324 29

Porthmadog Map 06 SH53

Porthmadog Morfa Bychan LL49 9UU
☎ 01766 514124 Fax 01766 514638
Seaside links,very interesting but with easy walking and good views.
18 holes, 6363yds, Par 71, SSS 71.
Club membership 900.
Visitors must contact in advance.
Societies apply by telephone initially.
Green Fees £20 per day (£26 weekends & bank holidays).
Prof Peter L Bright
Designer James Braid
Facilities
& Leisure snooker.
Location 1.5m SW

Hotel ★★ 60% Plas Isa Hotel, Porthmadog Rd, CRICCIETH ☎ 01766 522443 14

Prestatyn Map 06 SJ08

Prestatyn Marine Rd East LL19 7HS
☎ 01745 854320 Fax 01745 888353
Very flat seaside links exposed to stiff breeze. Testing holes: 9th, par 4, bounded on 3 sides by water; 10th, par 4; 16th, par 4.
18 holes, 6564yds, Par 72, SSS 72, Course record 66.
Club membership 660.
Visitors welcome except Sat & Tue mornings. Must contact in advance.
Societies prior booking required.
Green Fees £20 per day (£25 weekends & bank holidays).
Prof Malcolm Staton
Designer S Collins
Facilities
Location 0.5m N off A548

Hotel ★★ 61% Hotel Marina, Marine Dr, RHYL
☎ 01745 342371 29

St Melyd The Paddock, Meliden Rd LL19 8NB
☎ 01745 854405
Parkland course with good views of mountains and Irish Sea. Testing 1st hole (423 yds) par 4. 18 tees.
9 holes, 5829yds, Par 68, SSS 68, Course record 65.
Club membership 400.
Visitors must contact in advance.
Societies must telephone in advance.
Green Fees £12 per round (£16 weekends & bank holidays).
Prof Andrew Carr
Facilities
Location 0.5m S on A547

Hotel ★★ 61% Hotel Marina, Marine Dr, RHYL
☎ 01745 342371 29

PWLLHELI Map 06 SH33

Pwllheli Golf Rd LL53 5PS ☎ 01758 701644
Easy walking on flat seaside course with outstanding views of Snowdon, Cader Idris and Cardigan Bay.
18 holes, 6091yds, Par 69, SSS 69, Course record 66.
Club membership 880.
Visitors restricted Tue,Thu & weekends.
Societies must telephone in advance.
Green Fees £22 per day (£27 weekends & bank holidays).
Cards
Prof G D Verity
Designer Tom Morris
Facilities
Location 0.5m SW off A497

Hotel ★★ 78% Plas Bodegroes, Nefyn Rd, PWLLHELI
☎ 01758 612363 9 Annexe2

RHUDDLAN Map 06 SJ07

Rhuddlan Meliden Rd LL18 6LB
☎ 01745 590217 Fax 01745 590472
Attractive, gently undulating parkland course with good views. Well bunkered with trees and water hazards. The 476 yard 8th and 431 yard 11th require both length and accuracy. The clubhouse has been refurbished.
18 holes, 6482yds, Par 71, SSS 71, Course record 66.
Club membership 1060.
Visitors must contact in advance. Sun with member only.
Societies telephone to book reservation.
Green Fees £24 per day; £18 per round (£30 per round Sat).
Prof Andrew Carr
Designer Hawtree & Son
Facilities
Location E side of town on A547

Hotel ★★★ 66% Kinmel Manor Hotel, St Georges Rd, ABERGELE ☎ 01745 832014 42

RHYL Map 06 SJ08

Rhyl Coast Rd LL18 3RE ☎ 01745 353171
Seaside course.
9 holes, 6220yds, Par 70, SSS 70, Course record 65.
Club membership 500.
Visitors must contact in advance. Limited availability at weekends due to club competitions.
Societies must contact in advance.
Green Fees £12 per 18 holes (£15 weekends & bank holidays).
Prof Tim Leah
Designer James Braid
Facilities
Location 1m E on A548

Hotel ★★ 61% Hotel Marina, Marine Dr, RHYL
☎ 01745 342371 29

RUABON Map 07 SJ34

Penycae Ruabon Rd, Penycae LL14 1TP
☎ 01978 810108
An architecturally designed and built 9-hole parkland course offering a challenge for players of all standards. After a lazy Par 4 start the second Par 3 is wooded to one side and guarded by water on the other. The 6th, a 317yds Par 4 makes a very difficult approach to the green. The 7th is another Par 3 , elevated and wooded to one side. The 8th crosses water twice as the river meanders down the fairway.
9 holes, 2140yds, Par 64, SSS 62, Course record 62.
Club membership 200.
Visitors advisable to book in advance.
Societies telephone or write in advance.
Green Fees £7 per 18 holes; £4.50 per 9 holes (£9/£5.50 weekends & bank holidays).
Designer John Day
Facilities by prior arrangement
Location 1m off A5

Hotel ★★★ 65% Hand Hotel, Church St, CHIRK
☎ 01691 772479 16

RUTHIN Map 06 SJ15

Ruthin-Pwllglas Pwllglas LL15 2PE
☎ 01978 790692
Hilly parkland course in elevated position with panoramic views. Stiff climb to 3rd and 9th holes.
10 holes, 5362yds, Par 66, SSS 66.
Club membership 380.
Visitors welcome except for competition days.
Societies apply in writing.
Green Fees £12.50 per round (£18 weekends).
Facilities
Location 2.5m S off A494

Hotel ★★★ 64% Ruthin Castle, RUTHIN
☎ 01824 702664 58

ST ASAPH Map 06 SJ07

Llannerch Park North Wales Golf Range, Llannerch Park LL17 0BD ☎ 01745 730805
9 holes, 1587yds, Par 30.
Visitors pay & play.
Societies telephone in advance.
Green Fees £2.50 per 9 holes.
Designer B Williams
Facilities
Location 1.5m S off A525

Wrexham Map 07 SJ35

Clays Farm Golf Centre Bryn Estyn Rd, Llan-y-Pwll LL13 9UB ☎ 01978 661406 Fax 01978 661417
Gently undulating parkland course in a rural setting with views of the Welsh mountains and noted for the difficulty of its par 3s.
18 holes, 5764yds, Par 69, SSS 69, Course record 68.
Club membership 420.

Visitors must contact in advance.
Societies prior arrangement in writing.
Green Fees not confirmed.
Prof David Larvin
Designer R D Jones
Facilities
Location Off A534

Hotel ★★★ 66% Llwyn Onn Hall Hotel, Cefn Rd, WREXHAM ☎ 01978 261225 13

Wrexham Holt Rd LL13 9SB
☎ 01978 351476 Fax 01978 364268
Inland, sandy course with easy walking. Testing dog-legged 7th hole (par 4), and short 14th hole (par 3) with full carry to green.
18 holes, 6233yds, Par 70, SSS 70, Course record 64.
Club membership 600.

Visitors may not play competition days, and are advised to contact in advance. A handicap certificate is required.
Societies welcome Mon & Wed-Fri. Apply in writing
Green Fees £25 per day/round (£30 weekends & bank holidays).
Prof Roy Young
Designer James Braid
Facilities
Location 2m NE on A534

Hotel ★★★ 66% Llwyn Onn Hall Hotel, Cefn Rd, WREXHAM ☎ 01978 261225 13

MID WALES

This region includes the counties of Ceredigion, Carmarthenshire, Pembrokeshire and Powys which reflect the recent national changes.

Aberystwyth Map 06 SN58

Aberystwyth Brynymor Rd SY23 2HY
☎ 01970 615104 Fax 01970 615104
Undulating meadowland course. Testing holes: 16th (The Loop) par 3; 17th, par 4; 18th, par 3. Good views over Cardigan Bay.
18 holes, 6109yds, Par 71, SSS 71, Course record 67.
Club membership 450.

Visitors must contact in advance.
Societies write or telephone in advance.
Green Fees not confirmed.
Prof Mark Newson
Designer Harry Vardon
Facilities
Location N side of town

Hotel ★★★ 66% Belle Vue Royal Hotel, Marine Ter, ABERYSTWYTH ☎ 01970 617558 36

Ammanford Map 03 SN61

Glynhir Glynhir Rd, Llandybie SA18 2TF
☎ 01269 850472 & 851365 Fax 01269 851365
Parkland course with good views, latter holes close to Upper Loughor River. The 14th is a 394-yd dog leg.
18 holes, 5986yds, Par 69, SSS 70, Course record 66.
Club membership 700.

Visitors no visitors Sun. Contact professional in advance (01269 851010).
Societies welcome weekdays only. Contact in advance.
Green Fees £16 per day (£22 Sat & bank holidays).
Cards 
Prof Duncan Prior
Designer F Hawtree
Facilities by prior arrangement
Location 2m N of Ammanford

Hotel ★★ 68% Mill at Glynhir, Glyn-Hir, Llandybie, AMMANFORD ☎ 01269 850672 11

BORTH Map 06 SN69

Borth & Ynyslas SY24 5JS ☎ 01970 871202
Seaside links, over 100 years old, with strong winds at times although part of the course is sheltered amongst the dunes. Some narrow fairways and plenty of natural hazards.
18 holes, 6116yds, Par 70, SSS 70, Course record 65.
Club membership 625.

Visitors must contact in advance, may play weekends ring to check no competitions in progress.
Societies telephone in advance.
Green Fees not confirmed.
Prof J G Lewis
Facilities by prior arrangement
Location 0.5m N on B4353

Hotel ★★ 67% Four Seasons Hotel, 50-54 Portland St, ABERYSTWYTH
☎ 01970 612120 15rm(14)

BRECON Map 03 SO02

Brecon Newton Park LD3 8PA ☎ 01874 622004
Parkland course, with easy walking. Natural hazards include two rivers on its boundary. Good river and mountain scenery.
9 holes, 5256yds, Par 66, SSS 66, Course record 61.
Club membership 420.

Visitors advisable to contact in advance, limited availability at weekends.
Societies apply in writing.
Green Fees £10 per day.
Designer James Braid
Facilities
Location 0.75m W of town centre on A40

Hotel ★★ 67% Castle of Brecon Hotel, Castle Square, BRECON
☎ 01874 624611 32 Annexe12

Cradoc Penoyre Park, Cradoc LD3 9LP
☎ 01874 623658 Fax 01874 611711
Parkland with wooded areas, lakes and spectacular views over the Brecon Beacons. Challenging golf.
18 holes, 6331yds, Par 72, SSS 72, Course record 65.
Club membership 700.

Visitors must contact secretary in advance.
Societies apply in writing or telephone in advance to secretary.
Green Fees £20 per day (£25 weekends & bank holidays).
Cards
Prof Richard Davies
Designer C K Cotton
Facilities
Location 2m N on B4520

Hotel ★★ 67% Castle of Brecon Hotel, Castle Square, BRECON
☎ 01874 624611 32 Annexe12

BUILTH WELLS Map 03 SO05

Builth Wells Golf Links Rd LD2 3NF
☎ 01982 553296 Fax 01982 551064
Well guarded greens and a stream running thorough the centre of the course add interest to this 18-hole undulating parkland course. The clubhouse is a converted 16th-century Welsh long house.
18 holes, 5386yds, Par 66, SSS 67, Course record 63.
Club membership 380.

Visitors contact secretary.
Societies by prior arrangement.
Green Fees £17 per day; £13 per round (£23/£19 weekends & bank holidays).
Prof Roy Truman
Facilities
Location N of A483

Hotel ★★★ 70% Caer Beris Manor Hotel, BUILTH WELLS
☎ 01982 552601 22

BURRY PORT Map 02 SN40

Ashburnham Cliffe Ter SA16 0HN
☎ 01554 832269 & 833846
This course has a lot of variety. In the main it is of the seaside type although the holes in front of the clubhouse are of an inland character. They are, however, good holes which make a very interesting finish. Course record holder, Sam Torrance.
18 holes, 6916yds, Par 72, SSS 74, Course record 70.
Club membership 730.

Visitors must be bona fide member of affiliated golf club and produce handicap certificate, very limited weekend times.
Societies telephone for initial enquiry.
Green Fees not confirmed.
Prof Robert Ryder
Designer J H Taylor
Facilities
Location 5m W of Llanelli, A484 road

Hotel ★★★ 63% Diplomat Hotel, Felinfoel, LLANELLI
☎ 01554 756156 23 Annexe8

CAERSWS Map 06 SO09

Mid-Wales Golf Centre SY17 5SB ☎ 01686 688303
A 9-hole, Par 3 course with sand bunkers and three ponds.
9 holes, 2554yds, Par 54, SSS 54.
Club membership 95.

Visitors welcome, restricted during competitions on Sun am.
Societies telephone in advance.
Green Fees £6 per 18 holes; £4 per 9 holes (£8/£5 weekends & bank holidays).
Designer Jim Walters
Facilities
Location 0.75m off A470 out of Caersws

Hotel ★★ 65% Elephant & Castle, Broad St, NEWTOWN ☎ 01686 626271 24 Annexe11

CARDIGAN Map 02 SN14

Cardigan Gwbert-on-Sea SA43 1PR
☎ 01239 621775 & 612035 Fax 01239 621775
A links course, very dry in winter, with wide fairways, light rough and gorse. Every hole overlooks the sea.
18 holes, 6426yds, Par 72, SSS 72.
Club membership 600.

Visitors may not play between 1-2pm. Must have a handicap certificate.
Societies must telephone in advance.
Green Fees £17 per day (£22 weekends & bank holidays).
Cards
Prof Colin Parsons
Designer Hawtree
Facilities
& Leisure squash.
Location 3m N off B4548

Hotel ★★★ 66% Cliff Hotel, GWBERT-ON-SEA ☎ 01239 613241 70

CARMARTHEN Map 02 SN42

Carmarthen Blaenycoed Rd SA33 6EH ☎ 01267 281588
Hilltop course with good views.
18 holes, 6245yds, Par 71, SSS 71, Course record 67.
Club membership 700.
Visitors must have a handicap certificate, telephone for times at weekends.
Societies apply in writing minimum of ten days in advance.
Green Fees £18 (£25 weekends & bank holidays). Nov-Mar £15 with meal.
Prof Pat Gillis
Designer J H Taylor
Facilities
Location 4m N of town

Hotel ★★★ 60% The Ivy Bush Royal, Spilman St, CARMARTHEN ☎ 01267 235111 73

Derllys Court Llysonnen Rd SA33 5DT
☎ 01267 211575 Fax 01267 211575
Gently undulating parkland course with challenging par 3s (5th and 8th) and a testing par 5 involving a shot across a lake.
9 holes, 2859yds, Par 35, SSS 66, Course record 33.
Club membership 60.
Visitors welcome at all times.
Societies telephone in advance.
Green Fees £9 per 18 holes; £5 per 9 holes (£10/£6 weekends & bank holidays).
Designer Peter Johnson
Facilities
Location Just off A40 between Carmarthen/St Clears

Hotel ★★★ 60% The Ivy Bush Royal, Spilman St, CARMARTHEN ☎ 01267 235111 73

GWBERT-ON-SEA Map 02 SN15

Cliff Hotel SA43 1PP ☎ 01239 613241 Fax 01239 615391
This is a short course with 2 Par 4's and the remainder are challenging Par 3's. Particularly interesting holes are played across the sea on to a small island.
9 holes, 1545yds, Par 29.
Visitors telephone to book in advance.
Societies telephone in advance.
Green Fees not confirmed.
Facilities
& Leisure heated outdoor swimming pool, squash, fishing, sauna, solarium, gymnasium.
Hotel ★★★ 66% Cliff Hotel, GWBERT-ON-SEA ☎ 01239 613241 70

HAVERFORDWEST Map 02 SM91

Haverfordwest Arnolds Down SA61 2XQ
☎ 01437 764523 Fax 01437 764143
Fairly flat parkland course in attractive surroundings with fine views over the Preseli Hills.
18 holes, 6005yds, Par 70, SSS 69.
Club membership 770.
Visitors restricted at weekends.
Societies apply in writing or telephone for booking form.
Green Fees not confirmed.
Prof Alex Pile
Facilities
Location 1m E on A40

Hotel ★★ 66% Hotel Mariners, Mariners Square, HAVERFORDWEST ☎ 01437 763353 29

HAY-ON-WYE Map 03 SO24

Rhosgoch Rhosgoch, Builth Wells LD2 3JY
☎ 01497 851251
The course is parkland, quite challenging, with beautiful scenery.
9 holes, 4842yds, Par 68, SSS 64, Course record 68.
Club membership 165.
Visitors no restrictions.
Societies please telephone in advance.
Green Fees not confirmed.
Facilities
Location 5m N of Hay-on-Wye

Hotel ★★★ 67% The Swan-at-Hay Hotel, Church St, HAY-ON-WYE
☎ 01497 821188 15 Annexe3

Summerhill Hereford Rd, Clifford HR3 5EW
☎ 01497 820451
Undulating parkland course set deep in the Wye Valley on the Welsh Border overlooking the Black Mountains.
9 holes, 2929yds, Par 70, SSS 67.

Visitors welcome anytime.
Societies contact for information.
Green Fees not confirmed.
Prof Graham Priday
Facilities
Location B4350 Whitney toll bridge road

Hotel ★★★ 67% The Swan-at-Hay Hotel, Church St, HAY-ON-WYE
☎ 01497 821188 15 Annexe3

KIDWELLY Map 02 SN40

Glyn Abbey Trimsaran SA17 4LB ☎ 01554 810278
In the Gwendraeth valley, a new 18-hole parkland course with greens well protected by the planting of 35,000 trees. There is a covered practice area and 9-hole course under construction.
18 holes, 6173yds, Par 70, SSS 69, Course record 68.

Visitors advisable to book for weekends.
Societies must contact in advance.
Green Fees not confirmed.
Designer Hawtrees
Facilities
Location 4.5m E, off B4317

Hotel ★★★ 60% The Ivy Bush Royal, Spilman St, CARMARTHEN ☎ 01267 235111 73

KNIGHTON Map 07 SO27

Knighton Frydd Wood LD7 1DB ☎ 01547 528646
Upland course with hard walking. Fine views over the Welsh/English border.
9 holes, 5338yds, Par 68, SSS 66, Course record 66.
Club membership 150.

Visitors may not play on Sun until after 4.30pm.
Societies must contact in advance.
Green Fees £8 per day (£10 weekends & bank holidays).
Designer Harry Vardon
Facilities
Location 0.5m S off B4355

Hotel ★★★ 61% The Knighton Hotel, Broad St, KNIGHTON ☎ 01547 520530 15

LETTERSTON Map 02 SM92

Priskilly Forest Castlemorris SA62 5EH ☎ 01348 840276
Testing parkland course surrounded by rhododendrons. Beautiful panoramic views. Challenging dog-leg 4th with hazards both sides.
9 holes, 5712yds, Par 70, SSS 68, Course record 76.
Club membership 70.

Visitors advance booking advisable at weekends during summer.
Societies telephone in advance.
Green Fees £10 per day/18 holes; £7 per 9 holes.
Designer J Walters
Facilities
& Leisure fishing.
Location Off B4331 between Letterston and Mathry

Hotel ★★ 63% Abergwaun Hotel, The Market Square, FISHGUARD
☎ 01348 872077 11rm(7)

LLANDRINDOD WELLS Map 03 SO06

Llandrindod Wells LD1 5NY
☎ 01597 822010 & 823873 (sec)
Moorland course, designed by Harry Vardon, with easy walking and panoramic views. One of the highest courses in Wales. (1,100 ft above sea level).
18 holes, 5759yds, Par 68, SSS 67, Course record 65.
Club membership 650.

Visitors no restrictions.
Societies must telephone in advance.
Green Fees not confirmed.
Facilities
Location 1m SE off A483

Hotel ★★★ 66% Hotel Metropole, Temple St, LLANDRINDOD WELLS
☎ 01597 823700 121

LLANDYSSUL Map 02 SN44

Saron Saron SA44 5EL ☎ 01559 370705
Set in 50 acres of mature parkland with large trees and magnificent Teifi Valley views. Numerous water hazards and bunkers.
9 holes, 2400yds, Par 32, Course record 34.

Visitors may play at all times no arrangements required.
Societies telephone for details.
Green Fees £4.50 per 9 holes.
Designer Adas
Facilities
Location Off A484 at Saron

Hotel ★★ 72% Ty Mawr Country Hotel & Restaurant, BRECHFA
☎ 01267 202332 5rm(4)

LLANGATTOCK Map 03 SO21

Old Rectory NP8 1PH ☎ 01873 810373
Sheltered course with easy walking.
9 holes, 2200yds, Par 54, SSS 59, Course record 53.
Club membership 80.

Visitors telephone for information.
Societies telephone for booking.
Green Fees not confirmed.
Cards
Facilities
& Leisure outdoor swimming pool.
Location SW of village

Hotel ★★ 72% Gliffaes Country House Hotel, CRICKHOWELL
☎ 01874 730371 & 0800 146719 (Freephone)
Fax 01874 730463 19 Annexe3

LLANGYBI Map 02 SN65

Cilgwyn SA48 8NN ☎ 01570 493286
Picturesque parkland course in secluded valley, with natural hazards of ponds, stream and woodland.
9 holes, 5309yds, Par 68, SSS 66, Course record 66.
Club membership 300.

Visitors no restrictions, apart from Sun when advisable to telephone.
Societies apply in advance by letter or telephone.
Green Fees £10 per round (£15 weekends & bank holidays).
Facilities
Location 5m N of Lampeter on A485

Hotel ★★★ 70% Falcondale Mansion, LAMPETER ☎ 01570 422910 19

LLANIDLOES Map 06 SN98

St Idloes Penrallt SY18 6LG ☎ 01686 412559
Hill-course, slightly undulating but walking is easy. Good views, partly lined with trees. Sand and grass bunkers.
9 holes, 5540yds, Par 66, SSS 66, Course record 61.
Club membership 339.

Visitors may not play on Sun mornings.
Societies apply in writing to the secretary at least one month in advance.
Green Fees not confirmed.
Facilities ⊗ by prior arrangement by prior arrangement
Location 1m N off B4569

Hotel ★★ 67% Glansevern Arms Hotel, Pant Mawr, LLANGURIG ☎ 0686 440240 7

LLANRHYSTUD Map 06 SN56

Penrhos Golf & Country Club SY23 5AY
☎ 01974 202999 Fax 01974 202100
Beautifully scenic course incorporating lakes and spectacular coastal and inland views. Many leisure facilities.
Penrhos: 18 holes, 6641yds, Par 72, SSS 73, Course record 71.
Academy: 9 holes, 1827yds, Par 31.
Club membership 300.

Visitors must telephone, no jeans allowed on main course.
Societies must telephone in advance.
Green Fees £25 per day; £17 per round (£30/£22 weekends).
Cards
Prof Paul Diamond
Designer Jim Walters
Facilities ⊗
& Leisure hard tennis courts, heated indoor swimming pool, sauna, solarium, gymnasium.
Location Turn off A487 onto B4337 in Llanrhystud. Course 0.25m on left

Hotel ★★★ 68% Conrah Hotel, Ffosrhydygaled, Chancery, ABERYSTWYTH ☎ 01970 617941 11 Annexe9

LLANSTEFFAN Map 02 SN31

Llansteffan SA33 5LU
☎ 01267 241526
A Pay and Play downland course with superb views of the sea and Gower Coast. Quite challenging in a sea breeze!
9 holes, 2165yds, Par 30.

Visitors no restrictions, visitors welcome at all times.
Societies contact in advance for bank holidays.
Green Fees not confirmed.
Facilities
Location S of Carmarthen off B4312

Hotel ★★ 67% Forge Restaurant & Lodge, ST CLEARS ☎ 01994 230300 Annexe18

MACHYNLLETH Map 06 SH70

Machynlleth Ffordd Drenewydd SY20 8UH
☎ 01654 702000
Lowland course with mostly natural hazards.
9 holes, 5726yds, Par 68, SSS 68, Course record 65.
Club membership 250.

Visitors Thur ladies day, Sun morning mens competition.
Societies telephone in advance.
Green Fees £12 per day (£15 weekends & bank holidays).
Facilities
Location 0.5m E off A489

Hotel ★★ 66% Wynnstay Arms Hotel, Maengwyn St, MACHYNLLETH ☎ 01654 702941 23

Milford Haven Map 02 SM90

Milford Haven Woodbine House, Hubberston SA73 3RX
☎ 01646 692368 Fax 01646 697762
Parkland course with excellent greens and views of the Milford Haven waterway.
18 holes, 6030yds, Par 71, SSS 70.
Club membership 520.
Visitors no restrictions, advisable to contact in advance.
Societies telephone to book.
Green Fees £15 per round (£20 weekends & bank holidays).
Cards
Prof D Collins
Facilities
Location 1.5m W

Hotel ★★ 63% Lord Nelson Hotel, Hamilton Ter, MILFORD HAVEN
☎ 01646 695341 32

Newport Map 02 SN03

Newport (Pemb) The Golf Club SA42 0NR ☎ 01239 820244
Seaside links course, with easy walking and good view of the Preselli Hills and Newport Bay.
9 holes, 5815yds, Par 70, Course record 61.
Club membership 350.
Visitors telephone in advance.
Societies must telephone in advance.
Green Fees not confirmed.
Prof Colin Parsons
Facilities
Location 1.25m N

Hotel ★★ 65% Trewern Arms, NEVERN
☎ 01239 820395 9

Newtown Map 06 SO19

St Giles Pool Rd SY16 3AJ ☎ 01686 625844
Inland country course with easy walking. Testing 2nd hole, par 3, and 4th hole, par 4. River Severn skirts four holes.
9 holes, 5936yds, Par 70, SSS 69, Course record 67.
Club membership 350.
Visitors advisable to contact in advance.
Societies must contact in advance.
Green Fees £12.50 per day (£15 weekends & bank holidays).
Prof D P Owen
Facilities
& Leisure fishing.
Location 0.5m NE on A483

Hotel ★★ 65% Elephant & Castle, Broad St, NEWTOWN
☎ 01686 626271 24 Annexe11

Pembroke Dock Map 02 SM90

South Pembrokeshire Military Rd SA72 6SE
☎ 01646 621453
Parkland course overlooking the Cleddau River.
18 holes, 6100yds, Par 71, SSS 70.
Club membership 350.
Visitors must contact in advance, especially during season.
Societies apply in advance.
Green Fees not confirmed.
Facilities
Location SW side of town centre off B4322

Hotel ★★ 61% Old Kings Arms, Main St, PEMBROKE ☎ 01646 683611 21

St David's Map 02 SM72

St David's City Whitesands Bay SA62 6PT
☎ 01437 720312 & 721751
Links course with alternative tees for 18 holes. Panoramic views of St David's Head and Ramsey Island.
9 holes, 6117yds, Par 70, SSS 70, Course record 67.
Club membership 200.
Visitors prior booking with secretary is encouraged but no always necessary, please check for weekends, Ladies Day Fri pm.
Societies book with the secretary in advance.
Green Fees not confirmed.
Facilities
Location 2m W overlooking Whitesands Bay

Hotel ★★★ 75% Warpool Court Hotel, ST DAVID'S ☎ 01437 720300 25

Tenby Map 02 SN10

Tenby The Burrows SA70 7NP
☎ 01834 844447 Fax 01834 844447
The oldest club in Wales,this fine old seaside links, with sea views and natural hazards provides good golf all the year round.
18 holes, 6224yds, Par 69, SSS 71.
Club membership 800.
Visitors subject to competition & tee reservation. Must produce handicap certificate.
Societies must apply in advance.
Green Fees £22 per day (£26 weekends & bank holidays).
Prof Mark Hawkey
Designer James Braid
Facilities

Hotel ★★★ 72% Atlantic Hotel, The Esplanade, TENBY ☎ 01834 842881 & 844176
Fax 01834 842881 ex 256 42

Welshpool Map 07 SJ20

Welshpool Golfa Hill SY21 9AQ ☎ 01938 850249
Undulating, hilly, heathland course with bracing air. Testing holes are 2nd (par 5), 14th (par 3), 17th (par 3) and a memorable 18th.
18 holes, 5708yds, Par 70, SSS 68, Course record 68.
Club membership 400.
Visitors must book in advance, restricted at weekends.
Societies must book in advance.
Green Fees £12.50 per day (£20 weekends & bank holidays).
Designer James Braid
Facilities
Location 3m W off A458

Hotel ★★★ 66% Royal Oak Hotel, WELSHPOOL
☎ 01938 552217 24

SOUTH WALES

This region includes the counties of Blaenau Gwent, Bridgend, Caerphilly, Cardiff, Merthyr Tydfil, Monmouthshire, Neath Port Talbot, Newport, Rhondda Cynon Taff, Swansea, Torfaen and Vale of Glamorgan which reflect the recent national changes.

ABERDARE Map 03 SO00

Aberdare Abernant CF44 0RY
☎ 01685 872797 Fax 01685 872797
Mountain course with parkland features overlooking Cynon Valley.
18 holes, 5875yds, Par 69, SSS 69, Course record 67.
Club membership 550.
Visitors must contact in advance, may only play on Sat and Sun by arrangement with secretary.
Societies apply in writing in advance to the secretary.
Green Fees £14 per day (£18 weekends & bank holidays).
Prof A Palmer
Facilities & Leisure snooker/billiards.
Location 0.75m E

Hotel ★★★ 68% Tregenna Hotel, Park Ter, MERTHYR TYDFIL
☎ 01685 723627 & 382055
Fax 01685 721951 24

ABERGAVENNY Map 03 SO21

Monmouthshire Gypsy Ln, LLanfoist RP7 9HE
☎ 01873 852606 Fax 01873 852606
This parkland course is very picturesque, with the beautifully wooded River Usk running alongside. There are a number of par 3 holes and a testing par 4 at the 15th.
18 holes, 5978yds, Par 70, SSS 69, Course record 65.
Club membership 700.
Visitors must play with member at weekends. Must contact in advance & have handicap certificate.
Societies must contact in writing.
Green Fees £25 per day (£30 weekends & bank holidays).
Prof B Edwards
Designer James Braid
Facilities & Leisure fishing.
Location 2m S off B4269

Hotel ★★ 70% Llanwenarth Arms Hotel, Brecon Rd, ABERGAVENNY
☎ 01873 810550 18

Wernddu Golf Centre Old Ross Rd NP7 8NG
☎ 01873 856223 Fax 01873 852177
A parkland course with magnificent views, wind hazards on several holes in certain conditions and water hazards on four holes. There is a 26 bay floodlit driving range.
18 holes, 5403yds, Par 68, SSS 67, Course record 64.
Club membership 550.
Visitors advisable to book in advance.
Societies telephone in advance.
Green Fees £15 per 18 holes; £10 per 9 holes.
Cards
Prof Alan Ashmead
Designer G Watkins
Facilities & Leisure 9 hole pitch & putt.
Location 1.5m NE on B4521

Hotel ★★★ 58% Angel Hotel, Cross St, ABERGAVENNY ☎ 01873 857121 29

BARGOED Map 03 ST19

Bargoed Heolddu CF81 9GF
☎ 01443 830143 & 836411 (Prof)
Mountain parkland course, challenging par 70 course with pamoramic views.
18 holes, 6049yds, Par 70, SSS 70, Course record 65.
Club membership 600.
Visitors must play with member at weekends.
Societies must contact in advance.
Green Fees £20 per day/round.
Prof C Coombs
Facilities
Location NW side of town

Hotel ★★★ 68% Maes Manor Hotel, BLACKWOOD ☎ 01495 224551 & 220011
Fax 01495 228217 8 Annexe14

BARRY Map 03 ST16

Brynhill Port Rd CF62 8PN ☎ 01446 720277
Meadowland course with some hard walking. Prevailing west wind.
18 holes, 5947yds, Par 70, SSS 68.
Club membership 750.
Visitors must contact in advance. May not play on Sun.
Societies phone secretary for details.
Green Fees not confirmed.
Prof Peter Fountain
Facilities
Location 1.25m N on B4050

Hotel ★★★ 65% Mount Sorrel Hotel, Porthkerry Rd, BARRY ☎ 01446 740069 43

RAF St Athan St Athan CF62 4WA ☎ 01446 797186
This is a very windy course with wind straight off the sea to make all holes interesting. Further interest is added by this being a very tight course with lots of trees.
9 holes, 6452yds, Par 71, SSS 71.
Club membership 450.
Visitors contact in advance, Sun mornings club competitions only.
Societies apply in advance.
Green Fees not confirmed.
Prof Neil Gillette
Facilities
Location Between Barry & Llantwit Major

Hotel ★★ 68% West House Country Hotel & Restaurant, West St, LLANTWIT MAJOR
☎ 01446 792406 & 793726
Fax 01446 796147 21

St Andrews Major Argae Ln, Coldbrook Rd East, Cadoxton CF63 1BL ☎ 01446 722227
A new 9-hole, Pay and Play course with 6 Par 4s and 1 Par 5.
9 holes, 3000yds, Par 70, SSS 68.
Club membership 520.

Visitors must contact in advance.
Societies telephone in advance. Restricted to Tue and Thu.
Green Fees £8 per 9 holes; £13 per 18 holes.
Prof Alan Evans
Facilities ⊗
Location Off Barry new link road

Hotel ★★★ 77% Egerton Grey Country House Hotel, Porthkerry, BARRY
☎ 01446 711666 10

BETTWS NEWYDD Map 03 SO30

Alice Springs NP5 1JY
☎ 01873 880708 Fax 01873 880838
Two 18-hole undulating parkland courses set back to back with magnificent views of the Usk Valley. The Queen's course has testing 7th and 15th holes.
Queens Course: 18 holes, 5390yds, Par 67, SSS 67, Course record 63.
Kings Course: 18 holes, 5896yds, Par 67, SSS 67, Course record 65.
Club membership 350.

Visitors should contact the club in advance for weekend play.
Societies must telephone in advance.
Green Fees not confirmed.
Cards
Prof Paul Williams
Designer Keith R Morgan
Facilities ⊗
Location N of Usk on B4598 towards Abergavenny

Hotel ★★★ 69% Glen-yr-Afon House Hotel, Pontypool Rd, USK
☎ 01291 672302 & 673202
Fax 01291 672597 26

BLACKWOOD Map 03 ST19

Blackwood Cwmgelli NP2 1EL
☎ 01495 222121 (Office) & 223152 (Club)
Heathland course with sand bunkers. Undulating, with hard walking. Testing 2nd hole par 4. Good views.
9 holes, 5332yds, Par 67.
Club membership 310.

Visitors contact club or turn up and pay greens staff, may not play at weekends & bank holidays unless with member.
Societies by prior arrangement for members of a recognised golf club.
Green Fees £13 per round.
Facilities
Location 0.25m N of Blackwood, off A4048

Hotel ★★★ 68% Maes Manor Hotel, BLACKWOOD
☎ 01495 224551 & 220011
Fax 01495 228217 8 Annexe14

Bridgend Map 03 SS97

Coed-Y-Mwstwr The Clubhouse, Coychurch CF35 6AF
☎ 01656 862121
Challenging holes on this 9-hole course include the par 3 3rd (170yds) involving a drive across a lake and the par 4 5th (448yds) which is subject to strong prevailing winds.
9 holes, 5834yds, Par 69, SSS 68, Course record 71.
Club membership 260.

Visitors must have handicap certificate, advisable to contact in advance.
Societies by prior application.
Green Fees £15 per 18 holes; £10 per 9 holes.
Cards
Facilities by prior arrangement
Location 1m out of Coychurch, turn at village garage. 2m W of junct 35 on M4

Hotel ★★★ 75% Coed-Y-Mwstwr Hotel, Coychurch, BRIDGEND ☎ 01656 860621 23

Southerndown Ewenny CF32 0QP
☎ 01656 880476 Fax 01656 880317
Downland championship course with rolling fairways and fast greens. The par-3 5th is played across a valley and the 18th, with its split level fairway, is a demanding finishing hole. Superb views.
18 holes, 6417yds, Par 70, SSS 72, Course record 64.
Club membership 710.

Visitors must contact in advance & have handicap certificate.
Societies by arrangement with secretary.
Green Fees £25 per day (£35 weekends).
Prof D G McMonagle
Designer W Fernie
Facilities
Location 3m SW on B4524

Hotel ★★★ 67% Heronston Hotel, Ewenny, BRIDGEND ☎ 01656 668811 68 Annexe9rm(8)

Caerleon Map 03 ST39

Caerleon NP6 1AY ☎ 01633 420342
Parkland course.
9 holes, 2900yds, Par 34, SSS 34, Course record 29.
Club membership 120.

Visitors contact for details.
Societies telephone.
Green Fees not confirmed.
Prof Alex Campbell
Designer Steel
Facilities
Location 3m from M4 turn off for Caerleon

Hotel ★★★★ 71% Celtic Manor Hotel, Golf & Country Club, Coldra Woods, NEWPORT ☎ 01633 413000 73

Caerphilly Map 03 ST18

Caerphilly Penchapel, Mountain Rd CF83 1HJ
☎ 01222 883481 & 863441 Fax 01222 863441
Undulating mountain course with woodland affording good views especially from 10th hole, 700 ft above sea level.
13 holes, 6032yds, Par 73, SSS 71.
Club membership 700.

Visitors telephone in advance, must produce a current handicap certificate or letter from club secretary, may not play at weekends except with member, no visitors bank holidays.
Societies apply in writing in advance to the secretary.
Green Fees £20 per round Mon-Fri.
Prof Richard Barter
Facilities
Location 0.5m S on A469

Hotel ★★★ 73% Manor Parc Country Hotel & Restaurant, Thornhill Rd, Thornhill, CARDIFF ☎ 01222 693723 12

Mountain Lakes & Castell Heights Blaengwynlais CF83 1NG ☎ 01222 861128 & 886666 Fax 01222 863243
The 9-hole Castell Heights course within the Mountain Lakes complex was established in 1982 on a 45-acre site. In 1988 a further 18-hole course, Mountain Lakes was designed by Bob Sandow to take advantage of 160-acres of mountain heathland, combining both mountain top golf and parkland. Most holes are tree lined and there are 20 'lakes' as hazards. Host of major PGA tournaments.
Mountain Lakes Course: 18 holes, 6046mtrs, Par 74, SSS 73, Course record 69.
Castell Heights Course: 9 holes, 2751mtrs, Par 35, SSS 32, Course record 32.
Club membership 500.

Visitors advisable to check availability, Castell Heights is pay as you play.
Societies written or telephone notice in advance.
Green Fees Mountain Lakes: £15 per round. Castell Heights: £6.50.
Cards
Prof Sion Bebb
Designer Bob Sandown
Facilities
Location Near Black Cock Inn, Caerphilly Mountain

Hotel ★★★ 73% Manor Parc Country Hotel & Restaurant, Thornhill Rd, Thornhill, CARDIFF ☎ 01222 693723 12

Virginia Park Golf Club Virginia Park CF83 3SW
☎ 01222 863919 & 585368
Beside Caerphilly leisure centre, the course is totally flat but with plenty of trees and bunkers and 2 lakes. It is a tight, challenging course with 6 par 4 and 3 par 3 holes. Also a 20-bay flodlit driving range.
9 holes, 2566yds, Par 33.
Club membership 250.

Visitors telephone in advance.
Societies telephone then write to confirm.
Green Fees not confirmed.
Facilities
Location Off Pontyewindy Rd

Hotel ★★★ 73% Manor Parc Country Hotel & Restaurant, Thornhill Rd, Thornhill, CARDIFF ☎ 01222 693723 12

CAERWENT Map 03 ST49

Dewstow NP6 4AH ☎ 01291 430444 Fax 01291 425816
Two picturesque parkland courses with easy walking and spectacular views over the Severn estuary towards Bristol. Testing holes include the Par three 7th, Valley Course, which is approached over water, some 50 feet lower than the tee, and the Par four 15th, Park Course, which has a 50ft totem pole in the middle of the fairway, a unique feature. There is also a 26-bay floodlit driving range.
Valley Course: 18 holes, 6141yds, Par 72, SSS 70, Course record 68.
Park Course: 18 holes, 6176yds, Par 69, SSS 69, Course record 70.
Club membership 850.

Visitors may book two days in advance (six days in advance in winter).
Societies apply in writing or telephone for details.
Green Fees £22 per day; £13 per 18 holes; £8.50 per 9 holes (£16 per round; £10 per 9 holes weekends & bank holidays).
Cards
Prof Gareth Bebb/Kim Dabson
Facilities
Location 0.5m S of A48 at Caerwent

Hotel ★★★★ 68% Marriott St Pierre Hotel & Country Club, St Pierre Park, CHEPSTOW ☎ 01291 625261 148

CARDIFF Map 03 ST17

Cardiff Sherborne Av, Cyncoed CF2 6SJ
☎ 01222 753320 Fax 01222 752134
Parkland course, where trees form natural hazards. Interesting variety of holes, mostly bunkered. A stream flows through course and comes into play on 9 separate holes.
18 holes, 6016yds, Par 70, SSS 70, Course record 66.
Club membership 900.

Visitors contact in advance.
Societies Thu only, pre-booking essential.
Green Fees £30 per day (£35 weekends).
Prof Terry Hanson
Facilities
Location 3m N of city centre

Hotel B Forte Posthouse Cardiff, Pentwyn Rd, Pentwyn, CARDIFF ☎ 01222 731212 142

Cottrell Park Cottrell Park, St Nicholas CF5 6JY
☎ 01446 781781 Fax 01446 781707
Two well designed courses, opened in 1996, set in undulating parkland with mature trees and spectacular views, especially from the par 35 9-hole course. An enjoyable yet testing game of golf for players of all abilities.
Mackintosh: 18 holes, 6407yds, Par 72, SSS 71, Course record 65.
Button: 9 holes, 2807yds, Par 35, SSS 67.
Club membership 925.

Visitors must have a valid handicap certificate, advance bookings up to one week.
Societies welcome on Mon & Tue, apply in writing, min 12-max 60 per person.
Green Fees Mackintosh: 36 holes £33, 27 holes £24.50, 18 holes £20.50. (£43/£32.50/£27 weekends & bank holidays). Button: £10.50 per round (£13.50 weekends & bank holidays).
Cards
Prof Mike Pycroft
Designer MRM Sandow
Facilities
Location M4 junct 33 to Culverhouse Cross A48 to Cowbridge, through St Nicholas on right hand side

Hotel ★★★★ 69% Copthorne Cardiff-Caerdydd, Copthorne Way, Culverhouse Cross, CARDIFF ☎ 01222 599100 135

Llanishen Cwm Lisvane CF4 5UD
☎ 01222 755078 Fax 01222 755078
Mountain course, with hard walking overlooking the Bristol Channel.
18 holes, 5296yds, Par 68, SSS 66, Course record 63.
Club membership 600.

Visitors must play with member at weekends & bank holidays. Must contact in advance.
Societies contact in advance.
Green Fees £24 per round.
Prof Adrian Jones
Facilities
Location 5m N of city centre off A469

Hotel B Forte Posthouse Cardiff, Pentwyn Rd, Pentwyn, CARDIFF ☎ 01222 731212 142

Peterstone Peterstone, Wentloog CF3 8TN
☎ 01633 680009 Fax 01633 680563
Parkland course with abundant water features and several long drives (15th, 601yds).
18 holes, 6555yds, Par 72, SSS 71, Course record 67.
Club membership 714.

Visitors contact in advance suggested.
Societies telephone enquiries welcome.
Green Fees £16.50 (£22.50 weekends).
Cards
Prof Richard Harries
Designer Bob Sandow
Facilities
Location 3m from Castleton off A48

Hotel B Forte Posthouse Cardiff, Pentwyn Rd, Pentwyn, CARDIFF ☎ 01222 731212 142

Radyr Drysgol Rd, Radyr CF4 8BS
☎ 01222 842408 Fax 01222 843914
Hillside, parkland course which can be windy. Good views. Venue for many championships.
18 holes, 6031yds, Par 69, SSS 70, Course record 62.
Club membership 870.

Visitors must play with member at weekends.
Societies must contact in advance.
Green Fees £34 per day.
Prof Robert Butterworth
Facilities
Location M4 junct32, 4.5m NW of city centre off A4119

Hotel ★★★★ 68% The Park Thistle Hotel, Park Place, CARDIFF ☎ 01222 383471 136

St Mellons St Mellons CF3 8XS
☎ 01633 680408 Fax 01633 681219
This parkland course comprises quite a few par-3 holes and provides some testing golf. It is indeed a challenge to the single handicap golfer.
18 holes, 6275yds, Par 70, SSS 70, Course record 63.
Club membership 700.

Visitors must contact in advance. With member only at weekends.
Societies must contact in advance.
Green Fees £28 per round.
Prof Barry Thomas
Facilities
Location 5m NE off A48

Hotel B Forte Posthouse Cardiff, Pentwyn Rd, Pentwyn, CARDIFF ☎ 01222 731212 142

Whitchurch Pantmawr Rd, Whitchurch CF4 6XD
☎ 01222 620985 (Sec) Fax 01222 529860
Well manicured parkland course, slightly undulating, with fine views over the city centre and the Bristol Channel beyond.
18 holes, 6321yds, Par 71, SSS 71, Course record 62.
Club membership 750.

Visitors contact secretary/professional in advance.
Societies Thu only. Must contact in advance.
Green Fees £30 per day (£35 weekends & bank holidays).
Prof Eddie Clark
Designer F Johns
Facilities
Location 4m N of city centre on A470, near junct 32 of M4

Hotel ★★★★ 68% The Park Thistle Hotel, Park Place, CARDIFF ☎ 01222 383471 136

CHEPSTOW Map 03 ST59

ST PIERRE HOTEL See page 413.

Shirenewton Shirenewton NP6 6RL
☎ 01291 641642 Fax 01291 641831
Parkland course with magnificent views over the Severn estuary and extending to the Devon coastline.
18 holes, 6820yds, Par 72.
Club membership 400.

Visitors welcome, advisable to reserve tee times.
Societies contact K Evans for further information.
Green Fees not confirmed.
Prof Mark Kedward
Facilities
Location Junct 22 of M4 off A48

Hotel ★★ 67% Beaufort Hotel, Beaufort Square, CHEPSTOW ☎ 01291 622497 18

Entries with a shaded background identify courses that are considered to be particularly interesting

CLYDACH Map 03 SN60

Inco SA6 5PQ ☎ 01792 844216
Flat meadowland course to be extended to 18 holes.
15 holes, 5994yds, Par 70, SSS 69.
Club membership 300.

Visitors no restrictions.
Societies must contact in advance.
Green Fees not confirmed.
Facilities
Location 0.75m SE on B4291

Hotel ★★ 62% Oak Tree Parc Hotel, Birchgrove Rd, BIRCHGROVE ☎ 01792 817781 10

CREIGIAU (CREIYIAU) Map 03 ST08

Creigiau Llantwit Rd CF4 8NN ☎ 01222 890263
Downland course, with small greens and many interesting water hazards.
18 holes, 6015yds, Par 71, SSS 70, Course record 67.
Club membership 1020.

Visitors must contact in advance. May only play at weekends with member.
Societies Wed only, minimum number 20, must book in advance.
Green Fees £30 per day/round.
Prof Iain Luntz
Facilities
Location 6m NW of Cardiff on A4119

Hotel ★★★★ 71% Miskin Manor Hotel, Groes Faen, Pontyclun, MISKIN ☎ 01443 224204 32 Annexe8

CWMBRAN Map 03 ST29

Green Meadow Golf & Country Club Treherbert Rd, Croesyceiliog NP44 2BZ ☎ 01633 869321 & 860655
Undulating parkland course with panoramic views. The 7th hole is played partly down hill with the front half of the green enclosed with water; the 13th is exposed to winds with large mature trees along righthand side of green.
18 holes, 6029yds, Par 71, SSS 72.
Club membership 400.

Visitors by prior arrangement advised especially at weekends, tel 01633 862626. Correct standard of dress compulsory.
Societies telephone for brochure, Golf Shop 01633 862626.
Green Fees not confirmed.
Prof Dave Woodman
Designer Peter Richardson
Facilities
& Leisure hard tennis courts.
Location 5m N of junct 26 M4, off A4042

Hotel ★★★★ 64% Parkway Hotel, Cwmbran Dr, CWMBRAN ☎ 01633 871199 70

Pontnewydd Maesgwyn Farm, West Pontnewydd NP44 1AB
☎ 01633 482170
Mountainside course, with hard walking. Good views across the Severn Estuary.
10 holes, 5353yds, Par 68, SSS 67, Course record 63.
Club membership 250.

Visitors must play with member weekends & bank holidays.
Green Fees not confirmed.
Facilities
Location N side of town centre

Hotel ★★★★ 64% Parkway Hotel, Cwmbran Dr, CWMBRAN ☎ 01633 871199 70

DINAS POWIS Map 03 ST17

Dinas Powis Old High Walls CF64 4AJ
☎ 01222 512727 Fax 01222 512727
Parkland/downland course with views over the Bristol Channel and the seaside resort of Barry.
18 holes, 5486yds, Par 67, SSS 67, Course record 60.
Club membership 550.
Visitors must contact in advance. No visitors during weekends.
Societies telephone in advance.
Green Fees not confirmed.
Prof Gareth Bennett
Facilities
& Leisure putting green, practice area.
Location NW side of village

Hotel ★★★ 65% Mount Sorrel Hotel, Porthkerry Rd, BARRY ☎ 01446 740069 43

GLYNNEATH Map 03 SN80

Glynneath Pen-y-graig, Pontneathvaughan SA11 5UH
☎ 01639 720452
Attractive hillside golf overlooking the Vale of Neath in the foothills of the Brecon Beacons National Park. Reasonably level farmland/wooded course.
18 holes, 5707yds, Par 69, SSS 68, Course record 65.
Club membership 650.
Visitors restricted starting times at weekend.
Societies must contact in advance.
Green Fees £15 per day (£20 weekends & bank holidays).
Prof Huw Thomas
Designer Cotton/Pennick/Lawri
Facilities
Location 2m NE on B4242

Hotel ★★ 62% Oak Tree Parc Hotel, Birchgrove Rd, BIRCHGROVE ☎ 01792 817781 10

HENSOL Map 03 ST07

Vale of Glamorgan Golf & Country Club Hensol Park CF72 8JY ☎ 01443 222221 Fax 01443 222220
Two courses set in 200 acres of glorious countryside with views over Hensol Park lake and castle. The 18-hole par 72 Lake Course features towering trees, bunkers and water on ten holes. The signature hole, the 12th, has an island green reached via a stone bridge. The club is also home to the Welsh Golf Academy.
Lake: 18 holes, 6507yds, Par 72, SSS 71.
Club membership 1100.
Visitors must have a handicap certificate and may only play with member at weekends.
Societies apply in writing.
Green Fees £30.
Cards
Prof Peter Johnson
Designer Peter Johnson
Facilities
& Leisure fishing, sauna, many facilities in process of being built.
Location 2 mins from junct 34 of M4

Hotel ★★★★ 71% Miskin Manor Hotel, Groes Faen, Pontyclun, MISKIN ☎ 01443 224204 32 Annexe8

LLANWERN Map 03 ST38

Llanwern Tennyson Av NP6 2DY
☎ 01633 412029 Fax 01633 412029
Parkland Course.
18 holes, 6115yds, Par 70, SSS 69, Course record 63.
Club membership 650.
Visitors welcome, but with member only at weekends.
Societies telephone and confirm in writing.
Green Fees £20 per day (£25 weekends).
Prof Stephen Price
Facilities
Location 0.5m S off A455

Hotel ★★★★ 71% Celtic Manor Hotel, Golf & Country Club, Coldra Woods, NEWPORT ☎ 01633 413000 73

MAESTEG Map 03 SS89

Maesteg Mount Pleasant, Neath Rd CF34 9PR
☎ 01656 734106 & 732037
Reasonably flat hill-top course with scenic views.
18 holes, 5929yds, Par 70, SSS 69, Course record 69.
Club membership 720.
Visitors must be a member of a recognised golf club & have a handicap certificate.
Societies apply in writing.
Green Fees £17 per day (£20 weekends & bank holidays).
Prof John Black
Designer James Braid
Facilities
Location 0.5m W off B4282

Hotel ★★★ 66% Aberavon Beach Hotel, PORT TALBOT ☎ 01639 884949 52

MAESYCWMMER Map 03 ST19

Bryn Meadows Golf & Country Hotel The Bryn CF82 7FN
☎ 01495 225590 or 224103 Fax 01495 228272
A heavily wooded parkland course with panoramic views of the Brecon Beacons.
18 holes, 6132yds, Par 72, SSS 69, Course record 68.
Club membership 540.
Visitors may not play Sun mornings. Must contact in advance.
Societies Tue & Thu only.
Green Fees not confirmed.
Prof Bruce Hunter
Designer Mayo/Jeffries
Facilities
& Leisure heated indoor swimming pool, sauna, solarium, gymnasium.
Location On the A4048 Blackwood to Ystrad Mynach rd

ST PIERRE

ST PIERRE PARK, CHEPSTOW *Monmouthshire*
☎ 01291 625261 Fax 01291 629975 Map 03 ST59

John Ingham writes: Just over the Severn Bridge, and a mile down the old Newport road, is St Pierre, the parkland course where huge trees stand in the way of any golf shot not hit on the perfect line!

Set in 400 yards of glorious deer park, with a lake preserved as a wild life sanctuary, a clubhouse which was once a great mansion and the 800-year-old church of St Pierre nearby, you cannot help but be impressed by the place, and the atmosphere.

There are two courses to sample. The Old was designed by C K Cotton in 1962 while the Mathern was created by Bill Graham, a Geordie businessman who snapped up the place after driving past in his car after World War II. He immediately saw the potential as the fast motorway link with London and the south was being created.

The courses have staged several successful tournaments including the old Dunlop Masters which I used to cover for a London newspaper. Competitors would get pretty cross when they found their towering drives achieved nothing because the ball, when they got up to it, was 'snookered' by huge trees, several hundred years old. Among other hazards there was none more fearsome than the lake that guards the short 18th hole - a 'mere' 245 yards across water. Television cameras here filmed Tony Jacklin and Peter Oosterhuis almost holing in one, But they missed Arwyn Griffiths who arrived on the last tee needing a par-3 for an amazing course record 63. Unhappily, Mr Griffiths found the ordeal too much and took a ghastly 11 shots, although he still won the amateur event and was thus able to celebrate at the very excellent 19th hole!

Accommodation is sumptuous within the historic buildings, making it a very special place for a few days away from it all.

While there are stories of spirits walking in the night I suspect they had something to do with the tough Old course which at 6700yards cannily sorts out even the best players while the shorter Mathern, at 5732 yards with a par 68 can also throw up a few nightmare situations if you become stymied behind a whopping oak tree!

Visitors	must contact at least 24 hours in advance. May book 10 days in advance.
Societies	Must make an advance reservation
Green fees	Old Course £55 per round, Mathern Course £40 per round. All credit cards.
Facilities	Professional (Craig Dun).
Leisure	hard tennis courts, indoor swimming pool, sauna, solarium, gymnasium.
Location	Chepstow NP6 6YA (3m SW off A48).

36 holes. Old Course: 18 holes, 6700yds, Par71 SSS 73. Course record 64
Mathern Course: 18 holes, 5732yds, Par 68, SSS 67

WHERE TO STAY AND EAT NEARBY

HOTELS:

CHEPSTOW

★★★★ 68% Marriott St Pierre Hotel & Country Club ☎ 01291 625261 148

★★ 67% The George Hotel, Moor St ☎ 01291 625363. 14

★★68% Castle View, 16 Bridge St ☎ 01291 620349. 9(8 1) Annexe 4

TINTERN

★★ 70% Royal George Hotel ☎ 01291 689205 5 ( ) Annexe 14

WHITEBROOK

★★ 73% The Crown at Whitebrook ☎ 01600 860254 12

Hotel ★★★ 68% Maes Manor Hotel, BLACKWOOD ☎ 01495 224551 & 220011 Fax 01495 228217 8 Annexe14

MARGAM Map 03 SS78

Lakeside Water St SA13 2PA
☎ 01639 899959
A parkland course with bunkers and natural hazards. Eight Par 4's and ten Par 3's.
18 holes, 4390yds, Par 62, SSS 63, Course record 65.
Club membership 250.

Visitors no restrictions.
Societies apply in advance by letter or telephone.
Green Fees £10 per round.
Cards
Prof Mathew Wootton
Designer Matthew Wootton
Facilities
Location Off junct 38 of M4

Hotel ★★★ 66% Aberavon Beach Hotel, PORT TALBOT ☎ 01639 884949 52

MERTHYR TYDFIL Map 03 SO00

Merthyr Tydfil (Cilanws) Cilsanws, Cefn Coed CF48 2NU
☎ 01685 723308
Mountain-top course with good views and water hazards. Requires accuracy off the tee.
18 holes, 5625yds, Par 69, SSS 68, Course record 65.
Club membership 210.

Visitors may not play on Sun.
Societies by prior arrangement.
Green Fees £10 (£15 weekends).
Designer V Price/R Mathias
Facilities by prior arrangement by prior arrangement
Location Off A470 at Cefn Coed

Hotel ★★★ 74% Nant Ddu Lodge Hotel, Cwm Taf, Nant Ddu, MERTHYR TYDFIL ☎ 01685 379111 12 Annexe4

Morlais Castle Pant, Dowlais CF48 2UY
☎ 01685 722822 Fax 01685 722822
Beautiful moorland course overlooking National Park with excellent views of Brecon Beacons and surrounding countryside. The interesting layout of the course makes for a testing game.
18 holes, 6320yds, Par 71, SSS 71.
Club membership 500.

Visitors must contact in advance for weekends.
Societies apply in writing.
Green Fees £14 per day (£16 weekends & bank holidays).
Prof H Jarrett
Facilities
Location 2.5m N off A465. Follow signs for Mountain Railway. Course entrance opposite railway car park

Hotel ★★★ 74% Nant Ddu Lodge Hotel, Cwm Taf, Nant Ddu, MERTHYR TYDFIL ☎ 01685 379111 12 Annexe4

MONMOUTH Map 03 SO51

Monmouth Leasebrook Ln NP5 3SN
☎ 01600 712212
Parkland course in scenic setting. High, undulating land with good views.
18 holes, 5698yds, Par 69, SSS 69, Course record 68.
Club membership 600.

Visitors advisable to contact in advance, bank holidays only with member.
Societies advance notice advisable, write or telephone secretary.
Green Fees £20 per day; £15 per round (£20 per round only weekends).
Facilities
Location 1.5m NE off A40

Hotel ★★ 68% Riverside Hotel, Cinderhill St, MONMOUTH ☎ 01600 715577 & 713236 Fax 01600 712668 17

Rolls of Monmouth The Hendre NP5 4HG
☎ 01600 715353 Fax 01600 713115
A hilly and challenging parkland course encompassing several lakes and ponds and surrounded by woodland. Set within a beautiful private estate complete with listed mansion and panoramic views towards the Black Mountains. The short 4th has a lake beyond the green and both the 17th and 18th holes are magnificent holes with which to end your round.
18 holes, 6733yds, Par 72, SSS 73.
Club membership 131.

Visitors must telephone in advance.
Societies must contact in advance.
Green Fees £32 per day (£37 weekends & bank holidays). Monday special £26 per 18 holes,lunch & coffee.
Cards
Facilities
Location 4m W on B4233

Hotel ★★ 68% Riverside Hotel, Cinderhill St, MONMOUTH ☎ 01600 715577 & 713236 Fax 01600 712668 17

MOUNTAIN ASH Map 03 ST09

Mountain Ash Cefnpennar CF45 4DT
☎ 01443 479459 Fax 01443 479459
Mountain course on heathland with panoramic views of the Brecon Beacons.
18 holes, 5553yds, Par 69, SSS 67, Course record 63.
Club membership 600.

Visitors contact in advance for details.
Societies must contact in writing.
Green Fees £15 per day (£18 weekends).
Prof Marcus Wills
Facilities
Location 1m NW off A4059

Hotel ★★★ 68% Tregenna Hotel, Park Ter, MERTHYR TYDFIL ☎ 01685 723627 & 382055 Fax 01685 721951 24

NANTYGLO Map 03 SO11

West Monmouthshire Golf Rd, Winchestown NP3 4QT
☎ 01495 310233
Established in 1906, this mountain and heathland course was officially designated in 1994 by the Guiness Book of Record as being the highest above sea level, with the 14th tee at a height of 1513ft. The course has plenty of picturesque views, hard walking and natural hazards. Testing 3rd hole, par 5, and 7th hole, par 4.
18 holes, 6013yds, Par 71, SSS 69, Course record 65.
Club membership 350.
Visitors welcome, must be guest of member for play on Sun.
Societies apply in writing or contact golf shop 01495 313052.
Green Fees £15 per day; Mon Special £8.
Facilities
Location 0.25m W off A467

Hotel ★★★ 58% Angel Hotel, Cross St, ABERGAVENNY ☎ 01873 857121 29

NEATH Map 03 SS79

Earlswood Jersey Marine SA10 6JP
☎ 01792 812198
Earlswood is a hillside course offering spectacular scenic views over Swansea Bay. The terrain is gently undulating parkland with natural hazards and is designed to appeal to both the new and the experienced golfer.
18 holes, 5084yds, Par 68, SSS 68.
Visitors no restrictions.
Societies advisable to contact in advance.
Green Fees £8 per 18 holes.
Prof Mike Day
Facilities by prior arrangement by prior arrangement
Location Approx 4m E of Swansea, off A483

Hotel ★★ 65% Castle Hotel, The Parade, NEATH ☎ 01639 641119 & 643581 Fax 01639 641624 28

Neath Cadoxton SA10 8AH
☎ 01639 643615 & 632759
Mountain course, with spectacular views. Testing holes: 10th par 4; 12th par 5; 15th par 4.
18 holes, 6492yds, Par 72, SSS 72, Course record 66.
Club membership 700.
Visitors with member only at weekends & bank holidays.
Societies should either telephone or write in advance.
Green Fees £20 per day.
Prof E M Bennett
Designer James Braid
Facilities
& Leisure snooker.
Location 2m NE off A4230

Hotel ★★ 65% Castle Hotel, The Parade, NEATH ☎ 01639 641119 & 643581 Fax 01639 641624 28

Swansea Bay Jersey Marine SA10 6JP
☎ 01792 812198 & 814153
Fairly level seaside links with part-sand dunes.
18 holes, 6605yds, Par 72, SSS 72.
Club membership 500.
Visitors welcome.
Societies telephone enquiry or letter stating requirements.
Green Fees £16 per day (£22 weekends & bank holidays).
Prof Mike Day
Facilities by prior arrangement
Location 4m W of Swansea off A483

Hotel ★★ 65% Castle Hotel, The Parade, NEATH ☎ 01639 641119 & 643581 Fax 01639 641624 28

NELSON Map 03 ST19

Whitehall The Pavilion CF46 6ST ☎ 01443 740245
Windy hilltop course. Testing 4th hole (225 yds) par 3, and 6th hole (402 yds) par 4. Pleasant views.
9 holes, 5666yds, Par 69, SSS 68, Course record 63.
Club membership 300.
Visitors must be a member of a recognised golf club & have a handicap certificate. Must contact in advance to play at weekends.
Societies must contact in writing 4 weeks in advance.
Green Fees £15 weekdays.
Facilities
Location Turn off A470 to Nelson and take A4054 S

Hotel ★★★ 68% Llechwen Hall Hotel, Llanfabon, PONTYPRIDD ☎ 01443 742050 & 740305 Fax 01443 742189 12

NEWPORT Map 03 ST38

Celtic Manor Golf & Country Club Coldra Woods NP6 2YA ☎ 01633 413000
Roman Road: 18 holes, 7100yds, Par 70, SSS 74, Course record 72.
Coldra Woods: 18 holes, 4094yds, Par 61.
Club membership 400.
Visitors may pay play subject to availability, handicap certificate required for Roman Road course.
Societies telephone with details in advance.
Green Fees not confirmed.
Prof Keith Williams
Designer Robert Trent Jones
Facilities
& Leisure heated indoor swimming pool, sauna, solarium, gymnasium, video golf analysis, beautician, hairdresser.
Location Off junct 24 on M4

Hotel ★★★★ 71% Celtic Manor Hotel, Golf & Country Club, Coldra Woods, NEWPORT ☎ 01633 413000 73

A comprehensive list of driving ranges is given at the back of this guide. See page 479

Newport Great Oak, Rogerstone NP1 9FX
☎ 01633 896794 & 892643 Fax 01633 896676
An undulating parkland course, in an ideal situation on an inland plateau 300ft above sea level with fine views over the surrounding wooded countryside. There are no blind holes, but plenty of natural hazards and bunkers.
18 holes, 6431yds, Par 72, SSS 71, Course record 64.
Club membership 800.

Visitors must contact in advance & have handicap certificate. With member only on Sat.
Societies must contact in writing.
Green Fees £30 per day (£40 Sat).
Prof Paul Mayo
Facilities
Location 1m NW of junct 27 on M4 on B4591 just beyond 'Promotive' Garage

Hotel ★★★★ 71% Celtic Manor Hotel, Golf & Country Club, Coldra Woods, NEWPORT ☎ 01633 413000 73

Parc Church Ln, Coedkernew NP1 9TU
☎ 01633 680933 Fax 01633 681011
A challenging but enjoyable 18-hole course with water hazards and accompanying wildlife. The 38-bay driving range is floodlit until 10pm.
18 holes, 5619yds, Par 70, SSS 68, Course record 71.
Club membership 400.

Visitors must contact in advance 01633 680933.
Societies telephone in advance.
Green Fees £13 per round (£15 weekends).
Prof B Thomas/J Skuse
Designer B Thomas/T F Hicks
Facilities
Location 3m SW of Newport, off A48

Hotel ★★★ 64% Kings Hotel, High St, NEWPORT ☎ 01633 842020 47

Tredegar Park Bassaleg Rd NP9 3PX
☎ 01633 894433 Fax 01633 897152
A parkland course with River Ebbw and streams as natural hazards. The ground is very flat with narrow fairways and small greens. The 17th hole (par 3) is played on to a plateau where many players spoil their medal round.
18 holes, 6095yds, Par 71, SSS 70.
Club membership 750.

Visitors must be a member of a golf club affiliated to a national golf union, please contact in advance.
Societies apply to secretary.
Green Fees £25 per day (£30 weekends & bank holidays).
Prof M L Morgan
Facilities
Location 2m SW off A467 exit 27 of M4

Hotel ★★★ 64% Kings Hotel, High St, NEWPORT ☎ 01633 842020 47

OAKDALE Map 03 ST19

Oakdale Llwynon Ln NP2 0NF ☎ 01495 220044
9 holes, 1344yds, Par 28, Course record 27.

Visitors no restrictions pay & play.
Societies telephone for further information and arrangements.
Green Fees not confirmed.
Prof Clive Coombs
Designer Ian Goodenough
Facilities
Location B4251 E of Blackwood

PENARTH Map 03 ST17

Glamorganshire Lavernock Rd CF64 5UP
☎ 01222 701185 Fax 01222 701185
Parkland course, overlooking the Bristol Channel.
18 holes, 6181yds, Par 70, SSS 70, Course record 64.
Club membership 1000.

Visitors contact professional in advance.
Societies must contact in advance.
Green Fees £28 (£30 weekends & bank holidays).
Cards
Prof Andrew Kerr-Smith
Facilities
& Leisure squash, putting green, practice area.
Location S side of town centre on B4267

Hotel ★ 66% Walton House Hotel, 37 Victoria Rd, PENARTH ☎ 01222 707782 13rm(11)

PENCOED Map 03 SS98

St Mary's Hotel Golf & Country Club St Mary Hill CF35 5EA ☎ 01656 861100 Fax 01656 863400
A parkland course with many American style features. The Par 3 13th called 'Alcatraz' has a well deserved reputation.
St Mary's Course: 18 holes, 5291yds, Par 69, SSS 68, Course record 63.
Sevenoaks Course: 9 holes, 2426yds, Par 35.
Club membership 830.

Visitors must contact in advance and produce a handicap certificate.
Societies telephone Kay Brazell.
Green Fees £14 per round (£16 weekends).
Cards
Prof John Peters
Facilities
& Leisure hard tennis courts.

Hotel ★★★ 72% St Mary's Hotel & Country Club, St Marys Golf Club, PENCOED ☎ 01656 861100 24
See advertisement on page 408.

PENRHYS Map 03 ST09

Rhondda Golf Club House CF43 3PW
☎ 01443 441384
Mountain course with good views.
18 holes, 6205yds, Par 70, SSS 71, Course record 67.
Club membership 600.

Visitors contact secretary for weekend play.
Societies contact for details.
Green Fees £20 per day (£25 weekends & bank holidays).

Prof Rhys Davies
Facilities
Location 0.5m W off B4512

Hotel ★★★ 66% Heritage Park Hotel, Coed Cae Rd, Trehafod, PONTYPRIDD ☎ 01443 687057 44

PONTARDAWE Map 03 SN70

Pontardawe Cefn Llan SA8 4SH
☎ 01792 863118 Fax 01792 830041
Meadowland course situated on plateau 600 ft above sea-level with good views over Bristol Channel and Brecon Beacons.
18 holes, 6038yds, Par 70, SSS 70, Course record 64.
Club membership 500.
Visitors must contact in advance, but may not play on weekends.
Societies apply in writing.
Green Fees £20 per day.
Prof Gary Hopkins
Facilities
Location N side of town centre M4 junc 45 off A4067

Hotel ★★ 62% Oak Tree Parc Hotel, Birchgrove Rd, BIRCHGROVE ☎ 01792 817781 10

PONTLLIW Map 02 SS69

Allt-y-Graban Allt-y-Grabam Rd SA4 1DT
☎ 01792 885757
A challenging parkland course with fine panoramic views, opened in 1993.It is a 9-hole course but with plans for 12 holes. There are 6 par-4 holes and 3 par-3 holes. The 4th is a challenging hole with a blind tee shot into the valley and a dogleg to the left onto an elevated green.
9 holes, 2210yds, Par 66, SSS 66, Course record 63.
Club membership 158.
Visitors no restrictions.
Societies telephone in advance.
Green Fees not confirmed.
Cards
Prof Steven Rees
Designer F G Thomas
Facilities
Location From junct 47 on M4 take A48 towards Pontardulais. Turn left after Glamorgan Arms

Hotel B Hilton National Swansea, Phoenix Way, Swansea Enterprise Park, SWANSEA ☎ 01792 310330 120

PONTYPOOL Map 03 SO20

Pontypool Lasgarn Ln, Trevethin NP4 8TR
☎ 01495 763655
Undulating, mountain course with magnificent views.
18 holes, 6046yds, Par 69, SSS 69.
Club membership 638.
Visitors must have a handicap certificate.
Societies apply in writing or by phone, deposit payable.
Green Fees £20 per day (£24 weekends).
Prof James Howard
Facilities
Location 1.5m N off A4043

Hotel ★★★ 69% Glen-yr-Afon House Hotel, Pontypool Rd, USK ☎ 01291 672302 & 673202 Fax 01291 672597 26

Woodlake Park Golf & Country Club Glascoed NP4 0TE
☎ 01291 673933 Fax 01291 672764
Undulating parkland course with magnificent views over Llandegfedd Reservoir. Superb green constructed to USGA specification. Holes 4, 7 & 16 are Par 3's which are particularly challenging. Holes 6 & 17 are long Par 4's which can be wind affected.
18 holes, 6278yds, Par 71, SSS 72, Course record 68.
Club membership 420.
Visitors book in advance.
Societies telephone or write for society package.
Green Fees £20 per round.
Cards
Prof Adrian Pritchard
Facilities
& Leisure fishing.
Location Overlooking Llandegfedd Reservoir

Hotel ★★★ 69% Glen-yr-Afon House Hotel, Pontypool Rd, USK ☎ 01291 672302 & 673202 Fax 01291 672597 26

PONTYPRIDD Map 03 ST09

Pontypridd Ty Gwyn Rd CF37 4DJ
☎ 01443 409904 Fax 01443 491622
Well-wooded mountain course with springy turf. Good views of the Rhondda Valleys and coast.
18 holes, 5721yds, Par 69, SSS 68.
Club membership 850.
Visitors must play with member on weekends & bank holidays. Must have a handicap certificate.
Societies weekdays only. Must contact in advance.
Green Fees not confirmed.
Prof Wade Walters
Facilities
Location E side of town centre off A470

Hotel ★★★ 66% Heritage Park Hotel, Coed Cae Rd, Trehafod, PONTYPRIDD ☎ 01443 687057 44

PORT TALBOT Map 03 SS78

British Steel Port Talbot Sports & Social Club, Margam SA13 2NF ☎ 01639 814182 & 871111
A 9 hole course with two lakes. All the holes are affected by crosswinds and the 7th, Par 3, is alongside a deep stream, so is very tight.
9 holes, 4726yds, Par 62, SSS 63, Course record 60.
Club membership 250.
Visitors contact in advance, may not play at weekends.
Societies by prior arrangement.
Green Fees not confirmed.
Facilities
& Leisure hard tennis courts.

Hotel ★★★ 66% Aberavon Beach Hotel, PORT TALBOT ☎ 01639 884949 52

PORTHCAWL Map 03 SS87

Royal Porthcawl CF36 3UW
☎ 01656 782251 Fax 01656 771687
This championship-standard heathland/downland links course is always in sight of the sea. With holes facing every point of the compass, the golfer is always tested by the wind and the course has hosted many major tournaments.
18 holes, 6406yds, Par 72, SSS 74.
Club membership 800.

Visitors must contact in advanced & produce handicap certificate limit men 20, ladies 30. Restricted at weekends & bank holidays.
Societies apply in writing.
Green Fees £50 per day (£60 weekends & bank holidays if available).
Cards
Prof Peter Evans
Designer Charles Gibson
Facilities ⊗
Location 1.5m NW of town centre

Hotel ★★★ 61% Seabank Hotel, The Promenade, PORTHCAWL ☎ 01656 782261 61

PYLE Map 03 SS88

Pyle & Kenfig Waun-Y-Mer CF33 4PU
☎ 01656 783093 Fax 01656 772822
Links and downland course, with sand-dunes. Easy walking. Often windy.
18 holes, 6650ydss, Par 71, SSS 73, Course record 68.
Club membership 1010.

Visitors by arrangement midweek, guests of members only at weekends.
Societies for large numbers apply in writing, small numbers telephone booking accepted.
Green Fees £30 per day/round.
Prof Robert Evans
Designer Colt
Facilities ⊗
Location S side of Pyle off A4229. Access via junct 37 on M4

Hotel ★★★ 61% Seabank Hotel, The Promenade, PORTHCAWL ☎ 01656 782261 61

RAGLAN Map 03 SO40

Raglan Parc Parc Lodge, Station Rd NP5 2ER
☎ 01291 690077
New parkland course with well laid greens and a mature back 9 that are already the source of local praise. Several testing holes where a combination of wind and water make golf challenging. Easy walking.
18 holes, 6604yds, Par 72, SSS 73, Course record 67.
Club membership 350.

Visitors advisable to contact in advance.
Societies advance arrangement required.
Green Fees £20 per day (£25 weekends).
Facilities ⊗
Location Off junct of A449/A40

Hotel ★★★ 69% Llansantffraed Court Hotel, Llanvihangel Gobion, ABERGAVENNY ☎ 01873 840678 21

SOUTHGATE Map 02 SS58

Pennard 2 Southgate Rd SA3 2BT
☎ 01792 233131 & 233451 Fax 01792 234797
Undulating, cliff-top seaside links with good coastal views.
18 holes, 6265yds, Par 71, SSS 71, Course record 69.
Club membership 1020.

Visitors advisable to contact Professional in advance.
Societies by prior arrangement, telephone in advance.
Green Fees £24 (£30 weekends & bank holidays).
Prof M V Bennett
Designer James Braid
Facilities ⊗
& Leisure squash.
Location 8m W of Swansea by A4067 and B4436

Hotel ★★ 65% Oxwich Bay Hotel, Oxwich Bay, GOWER ☎ 01792 390329 13

SWANSEA Map 03 SS69

Clyne 120 Owls Lodge Ln, The Mayals, Blackpyl SA3 5DP
☎ 01792 401989 Fax 01792 401078
Challenging moorland course with scenic views of Swansea Bay and The Gower.
18 holes, 6334yds, Par 70, SSS 71, Course record 64.
Club membership 800.

Visitors must be member of a club with handicap certificate and contact in advance.
Societies must contact in advance.
Green Fees £25 (£30 weekends & bank holidays).
Cards
Prof Mark Bevan
Designer H S Colt & Harries
Facilities ⊗
& Leisure snooker.
Location 3.5m SW on B4436 off A4067

Hotel ★★★ 67% Langland Court, Langland Court Rd, LANGLAND ☎ 01792 361545 14 Annexe5

Langland Bay Langland Bay SA3 4QR
☎ 01792 366023 Fax 01792 361082
Parkland course overlooking Gower coast. The par 4, 6th is an uphill dog-leg open to the wind, and the par 3, 16th (151 yds) is aptly named 'Death or Glory'.
18 holes, 5857yds, Par 70, SSS 69.
Club membership 850.

Visitors no restrictions. Tue is Ladies Day.
Societies must telephone in advance.
Green Fees £25 (£30 weekends).
Prof Mark Evans
Designer Henry Cotton
Facilities
Location 6m W on A4067

Hotel ★★★ 67% Langland Court, Langland Court Rd, LANGLAND
01792 361545 14 Annexe5

Morriston 160 Clasemont Rd SA6 6AJ 01792 796528
Pleasant parkland course with a very difficult Par 3 15th hole.
18 holes, 5891yds, Par 68, SSS 68, Course record 64.
Club membership 700.
Visitors may not play Sat. Must contact in advance.
Societies apply in writing.
Green Fees not confirmed.
Prof D A Rees
Facilities
Location 5m N on A48

Hotel ★★ 62% Oak Tree Parc Hotel, Birchgrove Rd, BIRCHGROVE
01792 817781 10

TALBOT GREEN Map 03 ST08

Llantrisant & Pontyclun Llanelry Rd CF7 8HZ
01443 228169
Parkland course.
12 holes, 5712yds, Par 68, SSS 68.
Club membership 600.
Visitors must have handicap certificate.
Societies apply in writing.
Green Fees not confirmed.
Prof Simon Wagstaff
Facilities by prior arrangement by prior arrangement
Location N side of village off A473

Hotel ★★★★ 71% Miskin Manor Hotel, Groes Faen, Pontyclun, MISKIN
01443 224204 32 Annexe8

THREE CROSSES Map 02 SS59

Gower Cefn Goleu SA4 3HS
01792 872480 (Off) 879905 (Pro) Fax 01792 872480
Set in attractive rolling countryside, this Donald Steel designed course provides good strategic hazards, including trees, water and bunkers, outstanding views and a challenging game of golf.
18 holes, 6441yds, Par 71, SSS 72.
Club membership 500.
Visitors tee booking upto 7 days in advance, reservations recommended, some weekend vacancies, dress code and course etiquette must be adhered to.
Societies by prior notice for established golfers.
Green Fees £14 per round (£16 weekends).
Prof Mark Whittingham
Designer Donald Steel
Facilities
Location Sign posted from the village of Three Crosses

Hotel ★★ 74% Beaumont Hotel, 72 Walter Rd, SWANSEA 01792 643956 17

TREDEGAR Map 03 SO10

Tredegar and Rhymney Cwmtysswg, Rhymney NP2 3BQ
01685 840743 & 843400 Fax 01685 842440
Mountain course with lovely views.
9 holes, 5504yds, Par 68, SSS 68, Course record 69.
Club membership 194.
Visitors no restrictions.
Societies must contact in writing.
Green Fees £10 per day.
Facilities
Location 1.75m SW on B4256

Hotel ★★★ 68% Tregenna Hotel, Park Ter, MERTHYR TYDFIL
01685 723627 & 382055
Fax 01685 721951 24

UPPER KILLAY Map 02 SS59

Fairwood Park Blackhills Ln SA2 7JN
01792 203648 Fax 01792 297849
Parkland championship course on the beautiful Gower Peninsula.
18 holes, 6741yds, Par 72, SSS 72, Course record 68.
Club membership 720.
Visitors welcome except when championship or club matches are being held. Must contact in advance.
Societies must contact in advance.
Green Fees £25 per day (£30 weekends & bank holidays).
Prof Gary Hughes
Designer Hawtree
Facilities
Location 1.5m S off A4118

Hotel ★★ 72% Windsor Lodge Hotel, Mount Pleasant, SWANSEA
01792 642158 & 652744
Fax 01792 648996 18

WENVOE Map 03 ST17

Wenvoe Castle CF5 6BE 01222 594371
Parkland course which is hilly for first 9 holes. Pond, situated 280 yds from tee at 10th hole, is a hazard.
18 holes, 6422yds, Par 72, SSS 71, Course record 64.
Club membership 600.
Visitors must be a member of a recognised golf club & have a handicap certificate. Must play with member at weekends.
Societies must contact in writing.
Green Fees £24 per weekday.
Prof Robin Day
Facilities
Location 1m S off A4050

Hotel ★★★ 77% Egerton Grey Country House Hotel, Porthkerry, BARRY
01446 711666 10

Ystalyfera Map 03 SN70

Palleg Lower Cwm-twrch SA9 1QT
☎ no telephone
Heathland course liable to become heavy going after winter rain.
9 holes, 6400yds, Par 72, SSS 72.
Club membership 200.

Visitors restricted Sat (Apr-Sep) & Sun mornings in winter.
Societies must contact two months in advance.
Green Fees not confirmed.
Facilities ♀ (ex Mon)
Location 1.5m N off A4068

Hotel ★★ 62% Oak Tree Parc Hotel, Birchgrove Rd, BIRCHGROVE ☎ 01792 817781 10

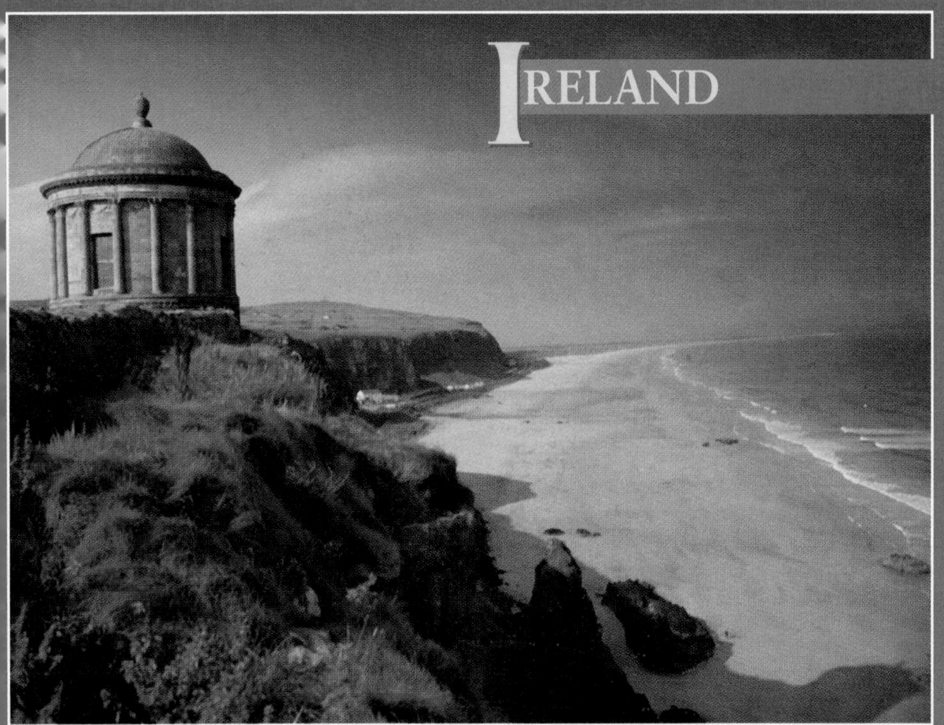

IRELAND

John Ingham writes: Anyone who doesn't love Ireland, doesn't love golf or the blarney that goes with it at the 19th hole. It's here, at the essential pit stop that rounds up the day, that I personally tell the most outrageous lies, exaggerating the utter brilliance of my play.

Frankly, I blame the refreshments provided in hospitable southern Ireland for the fact that not a single Eire golfer has ever won the Open championship. It wasn't the moist climate that prevented Christy O'Connor Snr from winning this major title, and it certainly wasn't the quality of the golf courses to be found, both north and south.

It was northern man, Fred Daly who won in 1947 but I'm not sure he was any better than O'Connor, or Harry Bradshaw (who once tied an Open) or indeed better than the modern set of Irish stars like Darren Clarke, or the fairly new men, Padraig Harrington and Paul McGinley.

The greatest Irish tests of golf are beside the sea. And many of their really great players, amateurs included like Joe Carr, learned how to play the links in sweeping winds. And these are the conditions they usually face at Open championship time. So why don't the Irish win big? I think they may, with Clarke a good bet.

It would be disgraceful to suggest that the first teetotal Irish star will win, and if he does, I'll be the first to buy him a celebration drink. And maybe that says its all. The Irish play the game because they love it, are amused by it. Not for them the grim slog of Nick Faldo, the Englishman. And yet, Ben Hogan, the most frightening serious golfer I ever saw, had Irish blood in him!

So where to go in Ireland? Well, the lists I approve rate Royal Portrush, Newcastle Co Down, Ballybunion (Old), Portmarnock, Connemara, Dingle....but I have a chum who reckons Ballyliffin tops. It's 15 miles north of Derry and to play it costs about £11 in old money, if you arrive on the right day. No I'll tell you the best Irish course - it's Ballybunion, and Tom Watson says so, that's who!

NORTHERN IRELAND

CO ANTRIM

ANTRIM Map 01 D5

Massereene 51 Lough Rd BT41 4DQ
☎ 01849 428096 Fax 01849 487661
The first nine holes are parkland, while the second, adjacent to the shore of Lough Neagh, have more of a links character with sandy ground.
18 holes, 6559yds, Par 72, SSS 71, Course record 66.
Club membership 969.

Visitors must contact in advance.
Societies book in advance.
Green Fees £20 per round (£25 weekends).
Cards
Prof Jim Smyth
Designer F Hawtree
Facilities
Location 1m SW of town

Hotel ★★★★ 70% Galgorm Manor, BALLYMENA ☎ 01266 881001 23

BALLYCASTLE Map 01 D6

Ballycastle Cushendall Rd BT54 6QP
☎ 01265 762536 Fax 01265 769909
An unusual mixture of terrain beside the sea, with magnificent views from all parts. The first five holes are inland type; the middle holes on the Warren are links type and the rest, on high ground, are heath type.
18 holes, 5311mtrs, Par 71, SSS 69, Course record 64.
Club membership 950.

Visitors are welcome during the week.
Societies apply in writing.
Green Fees £18 per round (£25 weekends).
Prof Ian McLaughlin
Facilities
Location Between Portrush & Cushendall (A2)

Hotel ★★ 63% Thornlea Hotel, 6 Coast Rd, CUSHENDALL ☎ 012667 71223 13

BALLYCLARE Map 01 D5

Ballyclare 23 Springdale Rd BT39 9JW
☎ 01960 322696 Fax 01960 322696
Parkland course with lots of trees and shrubs and water hazards provided by the river, streams and lakes.
18 holes, 5745mtrs, Par 71, SSS 71, Course record 67.
Club membership 580.

Visitors must contact in advance.
Societies must contact in advance.
Green Fees £16 (£22 weekends & bank holidays).
Designer T McCauley
Facilities
Location 1.5m N

Hotel ★★★★ 64% Stormont Hotel, 587 Upper Newtonards RD, BELFAST
☎ 01232 658621 109

BALLYGALLY Map 01 D5

Cairndhu 192 Coast Rd BT40 2QG
☎ 01574 583324 Fax 01574 583324
Built on a hilly headland, this course is both testing and scenic, with wonderful coastal views. The 3rd hole has a carry of 180 yds over a headland to the fairway.
18 holes, 5611mtrs, Par 70, SSS 69, Course record 64.
Club membership 905.

Visitors may not play on Sat.
Societies must apply in writing.
Green Fees £15 Mon-Thu; £17 Fri (£24 Sun).
Cards
Prof Robert Walker
Designer Mr Morrison
Facilities
Location 4m N of Larne on coast road

Hotel ★★★ 58% Ballygally Castle Hotel, 274 Coast Rd, BALLYGALLY
☎ 01574 583212 30

BALLYMENA Map 01 D5

Ballymena 128 Raceview Rd BT42 4HY ☎ 01266 861487
Parkland course of level heathland with plenty of bunkers.
18 holes, 5299mtrs, Par 68, SSS 67, Course record 64.
Club membership 895.

Visitors may not play on Tue or Sat.
Societies must contact in advance.
Green Fees not confirmed.
Prof Ken Revie
Facilities
Location 2m E on A42

Hotel ★★★★ 70% Galgorm Manor, BALLYMENA
☎ 01266 881001 23

Galgorm Castle Golf & Country Club Galgorm Rd BT42 1HL ☎ 01266 46161 Fax 01266 651151
18 hole championship course set in 220 acres of mature parkland in the grounds of a historic castle. The course is bordered by two rivers which come into play and includes five lakes. a course of outstanding beauty offering a challenge to both the novice and low handicapped golfer.
18 holes, 6724mtrs, Par 72.
Club membership 400.

Visitors no restrictions.
Societies apply in writing or telephone in advance.
Green Fees £18 (£24 weekends & bank holidays).
Cards
Prof Lesley Callen
Designer Simon Gidman
Facilities
& Leisure fishing.
Location 1m S of Ballymena on A42

Hotel ★★★★ 70% Galgorm Manor, BALLYMENA
☎ 01266 881001 23

CARRICKFERGUS Map 01 D5

Carrickfergus 25 North Rd BT38 8LP
☎ 01960 363713 Fax 01960 363023
Parkland course, fairly level but nevetheless demanding, with a notorious water hazard at the 1st. Well maintained and with nice views.

18 holes, 5759yds, Par 68, SSS 68.
Club membership 850.

Visitors restrictions at weekends.
Societies must contact in advance.
Green Fees not confirmed.
Prof Raymond Stevenson
Facilities ⊗ 〗 ☕ ♀ ⛺
Location 9m NE of Belfast on A2

Hotel ★★★ Chimney Corner Hotel, 630 Antrim Rd, NEWTOWNABBEY
☎ 01232 844925 & 844851
Fax 01232 844352 63

Greenisland 156 Upper Rd, Greenisland BT38 8RW
☎ 01232 862236
A parkland course estling at the foot of Knockagh Hill with scenic views over Belfast Lough.
9 holes, 5536mtrs, Par 71, SSS 68.

Visitors contact club in advance. Play restricted Sat and Thu.
Societies by prior arrangement.
Green Fees £12 per round (£18 weekends & bank holidays).
Facilities ⊗ 〗 ☕ ♀
Hotel ★★★ Chimney Corner Hotel, 630 Antrim Rd, NEWTOWNABBEY
☎ 01232 844925 & 844851
Fax 01232 844352 63

CUSHENDALL Map 01 D6

Cushendall 21 Shore Rd ☎ 012667 71318
Scenic course with spectacular views over the Sea of Moyle and Red Bay to the Mull of Kintyre. The River Dall winds through the course, coming into play in seven of the nine holes.
9 holes, 4386mtrs, Par 66, SSS 63.
Club membership 714.

Visitors Ladies day Thursday, time sheet at weekends.
Societies must contact in writing.
Green Fees £13 per day (£18 weekends).
Designer D Delargy
Facilities ⊗ 〗 ☕ ♀
Hotel ★★ 63% Thornlea Hotel, 6 Coast Rd, CUSHENDALL
☎ 012667 71223 13

LARNE Map 01 D5

Larne 54 Ferris Bay Rd, Islandmagee BT40 3RT
☎ 01960 382228 Fax 01960 382088
An exposed part links, part heathland course offering a good test, particularly on the last three holes along the sea shore.
9 holes, 6686yds, Par 70, SSS 69, Course record 64.
Club membership 430.

Visitors may not play on Sat.
Societies apply in writing or telephone in advance.
Green Fees £8 per day (£15 weekends & bank holidays).
Designer G L Bailie
Facilities ⊗ 〗 ☕ ♀
Location 6m N of Whitehead on Browns Bay rd

Hotel ★★★ 58% Ballygally Castle Hotel, 274 Coast Rd, BALLYGALLY
☎ 01574 583212 30

LISBURN Map 01 D5

Aberdelghy Bell's Ln, Lambeg BT27 4QH
☎ 01846 662738 Fax 01846 603432
This parkland course has no bunkers but the par-3 3rd high on the hill and the 5th hole over the dam provide a challenge. The par-4 6th hole is a long dog leg.
9 holes, 2192mtrs, Par 33, SSS 65.
Club membership 150.

Visitors restricted Sat 8-1pm.
Societies telephone in advance.
Green Fees not confirmed.
Prof Ian Murdoch
Designer Alec Blair
Facilities ☕
Location 1.5m N of Lisburn off A1

Hotel B Forte Posthouse Belfast, Kingsway, Dunmurry, BELFAST
☎ 01232 612101 82

Lisburn Blaris Lodge, 68 Eglantine Rd BT27 5RQ
☎ 01846 677216
Meadowland course, fairly level, with plenty of trees and shrubs. Challenging last three holes.
18 holes, 6647yds, Par 72, SSS 72, Course record 67.
Club membership 1421.

Visitors must play with member at weekends. Must tee off before 3pm weekdays.
Societies must contact in writing.
Green Fees not confirmed.
Prof Blake Campbell
Designer Hawtree
Facilities ⊗ 〗 ♀
Location 2m from town on A1

Hotel ★★★★ 64% Stormont Hotel, 587 Upper Newtonards RD, BELFAST
☎ 01232 658621 109

MAZE Map 01 D5

Down Royal Park Dunygarton Rd BT27 5RT
☎ 01846 621339 Fax 01846 621339
The 9-hole Valley course and the 18-hole Down Royal Park are easy walking, undulating heathland courses. Down Royal's 2nd hole is 628yards and thought to be among the best par 5 holes in Ireland.
Down Royal Park Course: 18 holes, 6824yds, Par 72, Course record 73.
Valley Course: 9 holes, 2500yds, Par 33.
Club membership 40.

Visitors no restrictions, except dress code.
Societies reservations in advance.
Green Fees £14 weekdays (£15 Sat, £17 Sun & bank holidays). Credit cards will be accepted after May 1998.
Facilities ⊗ 〗 ☕ ♀
& Leisure Budget B & B accomodation.
Location Inside Down Royal Race Course

Hotel ★★★ 68% White Gables Hotel, 14 Dromore Rd, HILLSBOROUGH
☎ 01846 682755 31

Newtownabbey Map 01 D5

Ballyearl Golf & Leisure Centre 585 Doagh Rd, Mossley BT36 8RZ ☎ 01232 848287
9 holes, 2520yds, Par 27.
Visitors no restrictions.
Societies telephone in advance.
Green Fees not confirmed.
Prof Jim Robinson
Designer V Lathery
Facilities
& Leisure squash, gymnasium.

Hotel ★★★ Chimney Corner Hotel, 630 Antrim Rd, NEWTOWNABBEY ☎ 01232 844925 & 844851 Fax 01232 844352 63

Mallusk Antrim Rd BT36 ☎ 01232 843799
Attractive 9-hole parkland course featuring 3 small par 4s and several water hazards, notably on the tricky, dog-leg 7th hole.
9 holes, 4444yds, Par 62, SSS 62, Course record 62.
Club membership 150.
Visitors no restrictions.
Societies contact for details.
Green Fees not confirmed.
Designer David Fitzgerald
Facilities
& Leisure hard tennis courts, sauna.

Hotel ★★★ Chimney Corner Hotel, 630 Antrim Rd, NEWTOWNABBEY ☎ 01232 844925 & 844851 Fax 01232 844352 63

Portballintrae Map 01 C6

Bushfoot 50 Bushfoot Rd, Portballintrae BT57 8RR ☎ 01265 731317
A seaside links course with superb views in an area of outstanding beauty. A challenging par-3 7th is ringed by bunkers with out-of-bounds beyond, while the 3rd has a blind approach. Also a putting green and pitch & putt course.
9 holes, 5914yds, Par 70, SSS 67, Course record 68.
Club membership 850.
Visitors must contact in advance.
Societies must contact in advance.
Green Fees £13 per round (£16 weekends & bank holidays).
Facilities
Location Off Ballaghmore rd

Hotel ★★ 65% Beach House Hotel, The Sea Front, PORTBALLINTRAE ☎ 012657 31214 32

Portrush Map 01 C6

Royal Portrush See page 425

Whitehead Map 01 D5

Bentra Municipal Slaughterford Rd BT38 9TG ☎ 01960 378996
A well matured course designed with the experienced golfer and novice in mind with wide fairways and some particularly long holes.
9 holes, 2885mtrs, Par 37, SSS 35.
Green Fees not confirmed.
Facilities

Whitehead McCrae's Brae BT38 9NZ ☎ 01960 353631 Fax 01960 353631
Undulating parkland course with magnificent sea views.
18 holes, 6426yds, Par 72, SSS 71, Course record 67.
Club membership 900.
Visitors may not play on Sat. Must play with member on Sun.
Societies must contact in advance.
Green Fees £13 per day (£19 Sun & bank holidays).
Prof Colin Farr
Designer A B Armstrong
Facilities
& Leisure snooker.
Location 1m from town

Hotel ★★★ Chimney Corner Hotel, 630 Antrim Rd, NEWTOWNABBEY ☎ 01232 844925 & 844851 Fax 01232 844352 63

CO ARMAGH

Armagh Map 01 C5

County Armagh The Demesne, Newry Rd BT60 1EN ☎ 01861 525861 Fax 01861 525861
Mature parkland course with excellent views of Armagh city and its surroundings.
18 holes, 5649mtrs, Par 70, SSS 69, Course record 63.
Club membership 1000.
Visitors time sheet operates at weekends.
Societies must contact in advance.
Green Fees £12 per round (£18 weekends & bank holidays).
Cards
Prof Alan Rankin
Facilities
Location On the Newry road

Hotel ★★★★ 64% Stormont Hotel, 587 Upper Newtonards RD, BELFAST ☎ 01232 658621 109

Lurgan Map 01 D5

Craigavon Golf & Ski Centre Turmoyra Ln, Silverwood BT66 6NG ☎ 01762 326606 Fax 01762 347272
Parkland course with a lake and stream providing water hazards.
18 holes, 6496yds, Par 72, SSS 72.
Club membership 400.
Visitors restricted Sat am.
Societies telephone in advance.
Green Fees £11.50 per day (£14.50 weekends & bank holidays).
Facilities
& Leisure gymnasium, artificial ski slope.
Location 2m N at Silverwood off the M1 ▶

ROYAL PORTRUSH

PORTRUSH *Co Antrim* ☎ 01265 822311

Fax 01265 823139 **Map 01 D4**

John Ingham writes: It was more than thirty years ago that I first saw Royal Portrush, but the memory lingers on. That week in 1960, the great Joe Carr won the British Amateur Championship for his third, and last, time. But everyone there was a winner; the sun shone, and the course glistened as the foaming ocean was almost blown inland on to the briar roses that dotted the rough.

What a splendid seaside paradise this is, I wrote in a London evening newspaper, whose readers were keen to follow players such as Joe Carr and Michael Bonallack. There among the gallery was the late Fred Daly, winner of the 1947 Open and the only Irishman ever to win.

The man who designed this course was Harry S Colt, a name that appears as a creator of many fine courses. This one is considered among the six best in the United Kingdom. It is spectacular, breathtaking, but one of the tightest driving tests known to man because, if you get in the long stuff, you may stay there. On a clear day, you have a fine view of Islay and the Paps of Jura - seen from the 3rd tee. Then there's the Giant's Causeway, from the 5th, as good a downhill dogleg hole as you'll find anywhere.

While the greens have to be 'read' from the start, there are fairways up and down valleys, and holes called Calamity Corner and Purgatory for good reason. The second hole, called Giant's Grave, is 509 yards but there's an even longer one waiting for you at the 17th, while the last hole, a 479-yarder, nearly cost Max Faulkner his 1951 Open title. He hit a crooked drive, and had to bend his second shot with a wooden club. Dressed in primrose-coloured slacks, his colourful plumage and out-going attitude attracted most of the small crowd.

The Open did not return to Portrush and championship golf is the loser because the place is a gem. Founded in 1888, it was also the venue of the first professional golf event held in Ireland, when in 1895, Sandy Herd beat Harry Vardon in the final.

You'll love it.

Visitors must contact in advance, have a letter of introduction from their own club and a handicap certificate. Restricted Wed & Fri pm. Sat & Sun am

Societies must apply in writing.

Green fees Dunluce Links £55 (£65 weekends)
Valley Links £22 per day (£30 weekends)

Facilities Professional (Dai Stevenson)

Location Bushmills Road Portrush BT56 8JQ (0.5m from Portrush on main road to Bushmills)

45 holes. Dunluce Links: 18 holes, 6641 yds, Par 72, SSS 73, course record 66
Valley Links: 18 holes, 6054 yds, Par 70, SSS 70
Skerries Course: 9 holes, 1187 yds

WHERE TO STAY AND EAT NEARBY

HOTELS:

PORTRUSH

★★★ 61% Causeway Coast,
36 Ballyreagh Rd.
☎ 01265 822435. 21

RESTAURANT:

PORTRUSH

Ramore, The Harbour.
☎ 01265 824313.

Hotel ★★★★ 64% Stormont Hotel, 587 Upper Newtonards RD, BELFAST
☎ 01232 658621 109

Lurgan The Demesne BT67 9BN
☎ 01762 322087 Fax 01762 325306
Testing parkland course bordering Lurgan Park Lake with a need for accurate shots. Drains well in wet weather and suits a long straight hitter.
18 holes, 6257yds, Par 70, SSS 70, Course record 66.
Club membership 856.

Visitors may not play Sat, contact in advance.
Societies must contact in advance, not Sat.
Green Fees £15 per round (£20 weekends & bank holidays).
Prof Des Paul
Designer A Pennink
Facilities
Location 0.5m from town centre near Lurgan Park

Hotel ★★★★ 64% Stormont Hotel, 587 Upper Newtonards RD, BELFAST
☎ 01232 658621 109

PORTADOWN Map 01 D5

Portadown 192 Gilford Rd BT63 5LF
☎ 01762 355356
Well wooded parkland course on the banks of the River Bann, which features among the water hazards.
18 holes, 5649mtrs, Par 70, SSS 70, Course record 65.
Club membership 1004.

Visitors may not play on Tue & Sat.
Societies apply in writing.
Green Fees £17 per round (£21 weekends & bank holidays).
Prof Paul Stevenson
Facilities
& Leisure squash.
Location SE via A59

Hotel ★★★★ 64% Stormont Hotel, 587 Upper Newtonards RD, BELFAST
☎ 01232 658621 109

TANDRAGEE Map 01 D5

Tandragee Markethill Rd BT62 2ER
☎ 01762 841272 Fax 01762 840664
Pleasant parkland course, the signature hole is the demanding par 4 11th known as 'The Well Hole', the real strength of Tandragee is in the short holes.
18 holes, 5747mtrs, Par 71, SSS 70, Course record 65.
Club membership 1175.

Visitors contact in advance.
Societies must contact in advance.
Green Fees £15 (£20 weekends & bank holidays).
Prof Paul Stevenson
Designer John Stone
Facilities
& Leisure sauna, gymnasium.
Location On B3 out of Tandragee towards Markethill

Farmhouse Brook Lodge Farmhouse, 79 Old Ballynahinch Rd, Cargacroy, LISBURN
☎ 01846 638454 6rm(4)

CO BELFAST

BELFAST Map 01 D5

See also The Royal Belfast, Hollywood, Co Down.

Balmoral 518 Lisburn Rd BT9 6GX
☎ 01232 381514 Fax 01232 666759
Parkland course, mainly level, with tree-lined fairways and a stream providing a water hazard.
18 holes, 6276yds, Par 69, SSS 70, Course record 64.
Club membership 912.

Visitors may not play Sat or Sun before 2.30pm.
Societies Mon & Thu. Must contact in advance.
Green Fees £20 (£24 Wed; £30 weekends & bank holidays).
Prof Geoff Bleakley
Facilities
Location 2m S next to Kings Hall

Hotel ★★★★ 64% Stormont Hotel, 587 Upper Newtonards RD, BELFAST
☎ 01232 658621 109

Cliftonville 44 Westland Rd BT14 6NH
☎ 01232 744158 & 746595
Parkland course with rivers bisecting two fairways.
9 holes, 6242yds, Par 70, SSS 70, Course record 66.
Club membership 430.

Visitors may not play: after 5pm unless with member, on Sat or on Sun mornings.
Societies must contact in writing.
Green Fees £12 (£15 weekends & bank holidays).
Prof Peter Hanna
Facilities by prior arrangement
Location Between Cavehill Rd & Cliftonville Circus

Hotel ★★★★ 64% Stormont Hotel, 587 Upper Newtonards RD, BELFAST
☎ 01232 658621 109

Dunmurry 91 Dunmurry Ln, Dunmurray BT17 9JS
☎ 01232 610834 Fax 01232 602540
Maturing very nicely, this tricky parkland course has several memorable holes which call for skilful shots.
18 holes, 5832yds, Par 69, SSS 69, Course record 64.
Club membership 900.

Visitors telephone in advance. May only play Sat after 5pm, restricted Fri (Ladies Day).
Societies must contact in writing.
Green Fees £17 per round (£26.50 weekends & bank holidays).
Prof John Dolan
Facilities
Hotel ★★★★ 64% Stormont Hotel, 587 Upper Newtonards RD, BELFAST
☎ 01232 658621 109

Fortwilliam Downview Ave BT15 4EZ
☎ 01232 370770 (Office) & 770980 (Pro)
Parkland course in most attractive surroundings. The course is bisected by a lane.
18 holes, 5789yds, Par 70, SSS 68, Course record 65.
Club membership 1000.

Visitors contact professional in advance.
Societies must contact in advance.

Green Fees not confirmed.
Prof Peter Hanna
Facilities
Location Off Antrim road

Hotel ★★★★ 64% Stormont Hotel, 587 Upper Newtonards RD, BELFAST
☎ 01232 658621 109

Malone 240 Upper Malone Rd, Dunmurry BT17 9LB
☎ 01232 612758 (Office) & 614917 (Pro)
Fax 01232 431394
Two parkland courses, extremely attractive with a large lake, mature trees and flowering shrubs and bordered by the River Lagan. Very well maintained and offering a challenging round.
Main Course: 18 holes, 6189yds, Par 71, SSS 69.
Edenderry: 9 holes, 6320yds, Par 72, SSS 70.
Club membership 1300.
Visitors advisable to contact pro-shop in advance.
Societies apply in writing or fax to club manager. Large group normally Mon & Thu only.
Green Fees £32-£37, Ladies £21/£29; 9 hole course: £16-£21. Ladies £13/£16.
Cards
Prof Michael McGee
Facilities
& Leisure squash, fishing, bowls green.
Location 4.5m S opposite Lady Dixon Park

Hotel ★★★★ 64% Stormont Hotel, 587 Upper Newtonards RD, BELFAST
☎ 01232 658621 109

Mount Ober Golf, Ski & Leisure 24 Ballymaconaghy Rd BT8 4SB ☎ 01232 401811 Fax 01232 705862
Inland parkland course which has recently been refurbished.
18 holes, 5391yds, Par 67, SSS 68, Course record 67.
Club membership 400.
Visitors must contact in advance at weekends & bank holidays, may play Sat after 3.30pm and Sun after 10.30am.
Societies must contact in writing.
Green Fees £11.50 per round (£14 Sun).
Cards
Prof Geoff Loughrey/Steve Rourke
Facilities
Location Off Saintfield Road

Hotel ★★★★ 64% Stormont Hotel, 587 Upper Newtonards RD, BELFAST
☎ 01232 658621 109

Ormeau 50 Park Rd BT7 2FX
☎ 01232 641069 Fax 01232 646250
Parkland.
9 holes, 2653mtrs, Par 68, SSS 65.
Club membership 520.
Visitors welcome weekdays except Tue after 2pm. May play Sat after 5.30pm & Sun by arrangement.
Societies contact in advance.
Green Fees not confirmed.
Prof Bertie Wilson
Facilities
Location S of city centre

Shandon Park 73 Shandon Park BT5 6NY
☎ 01232 401856
Fairly level parkland offering a pleasant challenge.
18 holes, 6261yds, Par 70, SSS 70.
Club membership 1100.
Visitors may not play on competition days. Must contact in advance and have a handicap certificate.
Societies may play Mon & Fri only, applications to club.
Green Fees £22 (£27 weekends).
Prof Barry Wilson
Facilities
Location Off Knock road

Hotel ★★★★ 64% Stormont Hotel, 587 Upper Newtonards RD, BELFAST
☎ 01232 658621 109

DUNDONALD Map 01 D5

Knock Summerfield BT16 2QX
☎ 01232 483251 & 482249 Fax 01232 483251
Parkland course with huge trees, deep bunkers and a river cutting across several fairways. This is a hard but fair course and will test the best of golfers.
18 holes, 6435yds, Par 70, SSS 71, Course record 66.
Club membership 890.
Visitors with member only on Sat, Mon & Thu are Society Days, Tue is Ladies Day, advisable to contact in advance.
Societies must contact in advance.
Green Fees £20 per day (£25 weekends & bank holidays).
Cards
Prof Gordon Fairweather
Designer Colt, Allison & McKenzie
Facilities
Hotel ★★★★ 73% Culloden Hotel, Bangor Rd, HOLYWOOD ☎ 01232 425223 87

NEWTOWNBREDA Map 01 D5

The Belvoir Park 73 Church Rd BT8 4AN
☎ 01232 491693 Fax 01232 646113
This undulating parkland course is not strenuous to walk, but is certainly a test of your golf, with tree-lined fairways and a particularly challenging finish at the final four holes.
18 holes, 6516yds, Par 71, SSS 71, Course record 65.
Club membership 1000.
Visitors must contact in advance, may not play Sat.
Societies must contact in writing.
Green Fees £33 per day (£38 weekends & holidays).
Prof Maurice Kelly
Designer H Holt
Facilities
& Leisure two snooker tables.
Location 3m from city centre off Saintfield/Newcastle rd

Hotel ★★★★ 64% Stormont Hotel, 587 Upper Newtonards RD, BELFAST
☎ 01232 658621 109

CO DOWN

ARDGLASS Map 01 D5

Ardglass Castle Pl BT30 7TP
☎ 01396 841219 Fax 01396 841841
A scenic cliff-top seaside course with spectacular views and some memorable holes.
18 holes, 5498mtrs, Par 70, SSS 69, Course record 65.
Club membership 800.
Visitors must contact in advance.
Societies must contact in advance, welcome weekdays & restricted times Sun.
Green Fees £14 per round (£20 weekends & bank holidays).
Cards
Prof Philip Farrell
Facilities
Location 7m from Downpatrick on the B1

Hotel ★★★★ 62% Slieve Donard Hotel, Downs Rd, NEWCASTLE ☎ 013967 23681 130

ARDMILLAN Map 01 D5

Mahee Island Mahee Island, Comber BT23 6EP
☎ 01238 541234
An undulating parkland course, almost surrounded by water, with magnificent views of Strangford Lough and its islands, with Scrabo Tower in the background. The first professional here was Fred Daly (1933-4) who became British Open Champion in 1947.
9 holes, 5590yds, Par 68, SSS 67, Course record 63.
Club membership 500.
Visitors may not play on Wed after 5pm or Sat before 5pm.
Societies apply in writing.
Green Fees £10 (£15 weekends).
Facilities by prior arrangement by prior arrangement by prior arrangement
& Leisure pool table.
Location Off Comber/Killyleagh road to the left 0.5m from Comber

Hotel ★★★★ 64% Stormont Hotel, 587 Upper Newtonards RD, BELFAST ☎ 01232 658621 109

BALLYNAHINCH Map 01 D5

Spa 20 Grove Rd BT24 8PN
☎ 01238 562365 Fax 01238 564158
Parkland course with tree-lined fairways and scenic views of the Mourne Mountains.
18 holes, 6003mtrs, Par 72, SSS 72, Course record 66.
Club membership 907.
Visitors must contact in advance. No play on Sat.
Societies must contact in advance.
Green Fees £15 per round (£20 weekends & bank holidays).
Designer F Ainsworth
Facilities
& Leisure indoor bowls.
Location 1m S on the Grove Rd

Hotel ★★★★ 62% Slieve Donard Hotel, Downs Rd, NEWCASTLE ☎ 013967 23681 130

BANBRIDGE Map 01 D5

Banbridge 116 Huntly Rd BT32 3UR ☎ 01820 662211
A picturesque course with excellent views of the Movene mountains. The holes are not long, but are tricky.
18 holes, 5003mtrs, Par 69, SSS 67, Course record 62.
Club membership 700.
Visitors may not play Sat or before 11am on Sun. Ladies Day Tue.
Societies must contact in writing.
Green Fees £15 per day (£20 weekends & bank holidays).
Facilities
Location 0.5m along Huntly road

Hotel ★★★★ 62% Slieve Donard Hotel, Downs Rd, NEWCASTLE ☎ 013967 23681 130

BANGOR Map 01 D5

Bangor Broadway BT20 4RH
☎ 01247 270922 Fax 01247 453394
Undulating parkland course in the town. It is well maintained and pleasant and offers a challenging round, particularly at the 5th.
18 holes, 6424yds, Par 71, SSS 71, Course record 62.
Club membership 1147.
Visitors may not play Sat & weekdays 1-2.
Societies must contact in advance, Mon/Wed by telephone, Fri by letter.
Green Fees £17.50 per round (£25 Sun & bank holidays).
Prof Roy Skillen
Designer James Braid
Facilities
Location 1m from town on Donaghadee Road

Hotel ★★★ 63% Royal Hotel, Seafront, BANGOR ☎ 01247 271866 50

Blackwood Golf Centre 150 Crawfordsburn Rd, Clandeboye BT19 1GB
☎ 01247 852706 Fax 01247 853785
The golf centre is a pay and play development with a computerised booking system for the 18-hole championship-standard Hamilton course. The course is built on mature woodland with man-made lakes that come into play on 5 holes. The Temple course is an 18-hole Par 3 course with holes ranging from the 75yd 1st to the 185yd 10th, which has a lake on the right of the green. Banked by gorse with streams crossing throughout, this Par 3 course is no pushover.
Hamilton Course: 18 holes, 6304yds, Par 71, SSS 70.
Temple Course: 18 holes, 2450yds, Par 54.
Visitors pay as you play, computerised booking system for the Hamilton Course, bookable 7 days in advance.
Societies telephone in advance.
Green Fees Hamilton: £14 per 18 holes (£18 weekends & bank holidays). Temple: £7 per 18 holes (£9 weekends).
Cards
Prof Tony White
Designer Simon Gidman
Facilities
Location 2m from Bangor, off A2 to Belfast

Hotel ★★★ 72% Clandeboye Lodge Hotel, 10 Estate Rd, Clandeboye, BANGOR ☎ 01247 852500 43

Carnalea Station Rd BT19 1EZ
☎ 01247 270368 Fax 01247 273989
A scenic course on the shores of Belfast Lough.
18 holes, 5574yds, Par 68, SSS 67, Course record 63.
Club membership 1200.
Visitors restricted Sat.
Societies must contact in advance.
Green Fees £13 (£17 weekends & bank holidays).
Prof Tom Loughran
Facilities
Location 2m W adjacent to railway station

Hotel ★★★ 69% Old Inn, 15 Main St, CRAWFORDSBURN
☎ 01247 853255 33

Clandeboye Tower Rd, Conlig, Newtownards BT23 3PN
☎ 01247 271767 Fax 01247 473711
Parkland/heathland courses. The Dufferin is the championship course and offers a tough challenge demanding extreme accuracy, with its mass of gorse, bracken and strategically placed trees that flank every hole.The slightest error will be punished. The Ava compliments the Dufferin perfectly. Accuracy is also the key with a notable 2nd hole.
Dufferin Course: 18 holes, 6469yds, Par 71, SSS 71.
Ava Course: 18 holes, 5755yds, Par 71, SSS 68.
Club membership 1300.
Visitors must contact in advance.
Societies Mon-Wed, Fri & after 3pm Sat & Sun. Must contact in advance.
Green Fees Dufferin: £25 per round; Ava: £20 per round.
Cards
Prof Peter Gregory
Designer William Robinson
Facilities
Location 2m S on A1

Hotel ★★★ 63% Royal Hotel, Seafront, BANGOR
☎ 01247 271866 50

Helen's Bay Golf Rd, Helen's Bay BT19 1TP
☎ 01247 852815 & 852601 Fax 01247 852815
A parkland course on the shores of Belfast Lough with panoramic views along the Antrim coast. The 4th hole Par 3 is particularly challenging as the green is screened by high trees.
9 holes, 5181mtrs, Par 68, SSS 67.
Club membership 820.
Visitors welcome Sun, Mon, Wed, Thu (before 1.30pm), Fri (after 11.30am during Jul & Aug) & Sat after 6pm. Book in advance with secretary.
Societies welcome Sun, Mon, Wed, Thu (before 1.30pm), Fri & Sat after 6pm. Telephone secretary in advance.
Green Fees not confirmed.
Facilities
Location A2 from Belfast

Hotel ★★★ 69% Old Inn, 15 Main St, CRAWFORDSBURN
☎ 01247 853255 33

CARRYDUFF — Map 01 D5

Rockmount 28 Drumalig Rd, Carryduff BT8 8EQ
☎ 01232 812279 Fax 01232 815851
A demanding 18-hole course set in open parkland with mature trees, several streams, and a tricky lake at the 11th hole. Panoramic views.
18 holes, 6373yds, Par 71, SSS 71, Course record 68.
Club membership 700.
Visitors welcome except for Sat.
Societies welcome except for Wed & Sat, book by telephone.
Green Fees £18 (£22 Sun).
Cards
Designer Robert Patterson
Facilities
Location 10m S of Belfast

Hotel ★★ 65% Balmoral Hotel, Blacks Rd, Dunmurry, BELFAST
☎ 01232 301234 44

CLOUGHEY — Map 01 D5

Kirkistown Castle 142 Main Rd, Cloughey BT22 1JA
☎ 012477 71233 Fax 012477 71699
A seaside semi-links popular with visiting golfers because of its quiet location. The course is exceptionally dry and remains open when others in the area have to close. The Par 4 10th is particularly distinctive with a long drive and a slight dogleg to a raised green with a gorse covered motte waiting for the wayward approach shot.
18 holes, 6167yds, Par 69, SSS 70, Course record 65.
Club membership 931.
Visitors must contact in advance, restricted weekends.
Societies contact in writing or by phone.
Green Fees £13 (£20 weekends & bank holidays).
Cards
Prof Jonathan Peden
Designer James Braid
Facilities
Hotel ★★★ 69% Old Inn, 15 Main St, CRAWFORDSBURN
☎ 01247 853255 33

DONAGHADEE — Map 01 D5

Donaghadee Warren Rd BT21 0PQ
☎ 01247 883624
Undulating seaside course requiring a certain amount of concentration. Splendid views.
18 holes, 5570mtrs, Par 71, SSS 69, Course record 65.
Club membership 1190.
Visitors contact in advance.
Societies telephone in advance.
Green Fees £14 per round (£20 weekends & bank holidays).
Prof Gordon Drew
Facilities
Hotel ★★★ 69% Old Inn, 15 Main St, CRAWFORDSBURN
☎ 01247 853255 33

DOWNPATRICK Map 01 D5

Bright Castle 14 Coniamstown Rd, Bright BT30 8LU
☎ 01396 841319
Parkland course in elevated position with views of the Mountains of Mourne. A good challenge for the energetic golfer.
18 holes, 7300yds, Par 74, SSS 74, Course record 69.
Club membership 60.

Visitors no restrictions.
Societies must contact in advance.
Green Fees not confirmed.
Designer Mr Ennis
Facilities
Location 5m S

Hotel ★★★★ 62% Slieve Donard Hotel, Downs Rd, NEWCASTLE ☎ 013967 23681 130

Downpatrick 43 Saul Rd BT30 6PA
☎ 01396 615947 Fax 01396 617502
This undulating parkland course provides a good challenge.
18 holes, 6100yds, Par 70, SSS 69, Course record 66.
Club membership 800.

Visitors must contact in advance.
Societies must telephone in advance.
Green Fees not confirmed.
Designer Hawtree & Son
Facilities
Location 1.5m from town centre

Hotel ★★ 66% Enniskeen House Hotel, 98 Bryansford Rd, NEWCASTLE ☎ 013967 22392 12

HOLYWOOD Map 01 D5

Holywood Nuns WalK, Demesne Rd
☎ 01232 423135 Fax 01232 425040
Hilly parkland course with some fine views and providing an interesting game.
18 holes, 5480mtrs, Par 69, SSS 68, Course record 64.
Club membership 1100.

Visitors must contact in advance.
Societies must contact in writing.
Green Fees not confirmed.
Prof Michael Bannon
Facilities
Hotel ★★ 75% Rayanne Country House & Restaurant, 60 Desmesne Rd, HOLYWOOD ☎ 01232 425859 6

The Royal Belfast Station Rd, Craigavad BT18 0BP
☎ 01232 428165 Fax 01232 421404
On the shores of Belfast Lough, this attractive course consists of wooded parkland on undulating terrain which provides a pleasant, challenging game.
18 holes, 5963yds, Par 70, SSS 69.
Club membership 1200.

Visitors may not play on Wed or Sat before 4.30pm; must be accompanied by a member or present a letter of introduction from their own golf club. Must contact in advance.
Societies must contact in writing.
Green Fees £30 per round (£40 weekends and bank holidays).
Cards
Prof Chris Spence
Designer H C Colt
Facilities
& Leisure hard tennis courts, squash.
Location 2m E on A2

Hotel ★★★★ 73% Culloden Hotel, Bangor Rd, HOLYWOOD ☎ 01232 425223 87

KILKEEL Map 01 D5

Kilkeel Mourne Park BT34 4LB
☎ 016937 65095 Fax 016937 65095
Picturesquely situated at the foot of the Mourne Mountains. Eleven holes have tree-lined fairways with the remainder in open parkland. The 13th hole is testing and a well positioned tee shot is essential.
18 holes, 6615yds, Par 72, SSS 72, Course record 69.
Club membership 650.

Visitors may not play Sat, possible to play Sun, must contact in advance.
Societies must contact in advance.
Green Fees not confirmed.
Designer Babington/Hackett
Facilities
& Leisure fishing.
Location 3m from Kilkeel on Newry road

Hotel ★★★★ 62% Slieve Donard Hotel, Downs Rd, NEWCASTLE ☎ 013967 23681 130

MAGHERALIN Map 01 D5

Edenmore Edenmore House, 70 Drumnabreeze Rd BT67 0RH ☎ 01846 611310 Fax 01846 613310
Set in mature parkland with gently rolling slopes. The front nine holes provide an interesting contrast to the back nine with more open play involved. Many new paths and features have been recently added.
18 holes, 6244yds, Par 71, SSS 70, Course record 71.
Club membership 350.

Visitors telephone in advance, may not play until after 2pm Sat & with member only Sun.
Societies telephone in advance.
Green Fees £12 per round.
Designer F Ainsworth
Facilities
Hotel B Forte Posthouse Belfast, Kingsway, Dunmurry, BELFAST ☎ 01232 612101 82

NEWCASTLE Map 01 D5

ROYAL COUNTY DOWN See page 431.

ROYAL COUNTY DOWN

NEWCASTLE *Co Down* ☎ 013967 23314
Fax 013967 26281 **Map 01 D5**

Charlie Mulqueen writes: Where the mountains of Mourne sweep down to the sea – that's the location for one of the game's most beautiful and challenging golf courses, Royal Co Down alongside the lovely seaside town of Newcastle. There can be few grander places when the sun shines on the Mournes and on the Irish Sea and on the furze bushes that dot the sides of almost every fairway, turning the whole scene into one of riotous colour in early summer.

The most prestigious Championships, including the British Amateur, men's and ladies', and the Curtis Cup have come to Newcastle where the game began in 1889. Legend has it that Old Tom Morris was commissioned to lay out a course at a cost not exceeding £4. Another of golf's early greats, Harry Vardon, reconstructed the links in 1908, the same year it was made 'Royal' by Edward VII. Slight changes here and there over the decades have served only to make Newcastle a finer and fairer challenge.

Most people's favourite hole at Newcastle is the 9th, a none too difficult par five of less than 500 yards, but it has been suggested that the chief hazards of the hole are the distracting views of the sea and Slieve Donard, the highest of the Mourne Mountains – a breathtaking sight perhaps unrivalled in all of golf. .

However, nobody should run away with the idea that this is anything other than an outstanding test of golf where length, accuracy and a sure touch on the many fiercely undulating greens are all essential attributes. The 13th is such a beautiful hole that it was copied at a course in Cincinatti, Ohio...Newcastle is that kind of place, a jewel among golf courses.

Visitors advisable to contact in advance. May not play Annesley course on Saturdays. May not play on Championship Course Sat, Sun am or Wed after 9am
Societies telephone for availability and confirm in writing.
Green fees not confirmed.
Facilities ⊗ ☕ 🍷 ⌂ Professional (Kevan Whitson)
Location Newcastle BT33 0AN

36 holes. Championship Course 18 holes, 7037yds, Par71 SSS 74. Course record 66
Annesley Links Course 18 holes, 4681yds, Par 66 SSS 63

WHERE TO STAY AND EAT NEARBY

HOTELS:

NEWCASTLE

★★★ 62% Slieve Donard Hotel, Downs Road ☎ 013967 23681 130

★★ 66% Enniskeen Hotel, 98 Bryansford Rd ☎ 013967 22392 12 (3 8 1)

NEWRY Map 01 D5

Newry 11 Forkhill Rd BT35 8LZ
☎ 01693 63871 Fax 01693 63871
Short 18-hole course enjoying panoramic views of the Mourne Mountains and across Newry.
18 holes, 3000mtrs, Par 53, SSS 52, Course record 51.
Club membership 150.
Visitors welcome anytime.
Societies apply in writing or telephone.
Green Fees £5 (£6 weekends).
Cards
Prof Larry Heaney
Designer Michael Heaney
Facilities
& Leisure hard and grass tennis courts, outdoor and indoor heated swimming pools, clay pigeon shooting.
Location 1m from Newry just off the main Dublin road

Hotel ★★ 66% Enniskeen House Hotel, 98 Bryansford Rd, NEWCASTLE
☎ 013967 22392 12

NEWTOWNARDS Map 01 D5

Scrabo 233 Scrabo Rd BT23 4SL
☎ 01247 812355 Fax 01247 822919
Hilly and picturesque, this course offers a good test of golf.
18 holes, 5722mtrs, Par 71, SSS 71, Course record 65.
Club membership 956.
Visitors may not play on Sat or Sun before 11.30am. Contact in advance.
Societies must contact in advance.
Green Fees £15 per round (£20 Sun).
Prof Paul McCrystal
Facilities
Hotel ★★★★ 64% Stormont Hotel, 587 Upper Newtonards RD, BELFAST
☎ 01232 658621 109

WARRENPOINT Map 01 D5

Warrenpoint Lower Dromore Rd BT34 3LN
☎ 016937 53695 Fax 016937 52918
Parkland course with marvellous views and a need for accurate shots.
18 holes, 6108yds, Par 71, SSS 70, Course record 66.
Club membership 1200.
Visitors must contact in advance.
Societies must contact in advance.
Green Fees £20 (£27 weekends & bank holidays).
Cards
Prof Nigel Shaw
Facilities
& Leisure squash.
Location 1m W

Hotel ★★★★ 62% Slieve Donard Hotel, Downs Rd, NEWCASTLE
☎ 013967 23681 130

CO FERMANAGH

ENNISKILLEN Map 01 C5

Ashwoods Golf Centre Sligo Rd BT74 7JY
☎ 01365 325321 & 322908
Only 1 mile from Lough Erne, this course is open meadowland. It has been well planted with many young trees.
14 holes, 1930yds, Par 42.
Visitors no restrictions.
Societies must book in advance.
Green Fees not confirmed.
Prof Pat Trainor
Designer P Loughran
Facilities by prior arrangement by prior arrangement
Location 1.5m W

Hotel ★★★ 70% Killyhevlin Hotel, ENNISKILLEN
☎ 01365 323481 43

Castle Hume Castle Hume BT93 7ED
☎ 01365 327077 Fax 01365 327076
Castle Hulme is a particularly scenic and challenging course. Set in undulating parkland with large rolling greens, rivers, lakes and water hazards all in play on a championship standard course.
18 holes, 6400yds, Par 72, SSS 70, Course record 69.
Club membership 225.
Visitors may play any time subject to advance arrangement.
Societies telephone in advance.
Green Fees £12 per day/round (£15 weekends & bank holidays).
Cards
Designer B Browne
Facilities by prior arrangement
& Leisure fishing.
Location 4m from Enniskillen on the Belleek Rd

Hotel ★★★ 70% Killyhevlin Hotel, ENNISKILLEN
☎ 01365 323481 43

Enniskillen Castlecoole BT74 6HZ
☎ 01365 325250
Meadowland course in Castle Coole estate.
18 holes, 5588mtrs, Par 71, SSS 69, Course record 67.
Club membership 600.
Visitors restricted Tue and weekends.
Societies must contact club steward in advance.
Green Fees not confirmed.
Facilities
Location 1m E

Hotel ★★★ 70% Killyhevlin Hotel, ENNISKILLEN
☎ 01365 323481 43

CO LONDONDERRY

AGHADOWEY Map 01 C6

Brown Trout Golf & Country Inn 209 Agivey Rd BT51 4AD ☎ 01265 868209 Fax 01265 868878

A challenging course with two par 5s. During the course of the 9 holes, players have to negotiate water 7 times and all the fairways are lined with densely packed fir trees.

9 holes, 5510yds, Par 70, SSS 68, Course record 70.
Club membership 250.

Visitors no restrictions.
Societies must contact by telephone, restricted tee-off times Sun.
Green Fees £10 per day (£15 weekends & bank holidays).
Cards
Prof Ken Revie
Designer Bill O'Hara Snr
Facilities
& Leisure fishing, gymnasium.
Location Junc of A54 & B66

Hotel ★★ 67% Brown Trout Golf & Country Inn, 209 Agivey Rd, AGHADOWEY ☎ 01265 868209 17

CASTLEDAWSON Map 01 C5

Moyola Park 15 Curran Rd BT45 8DG ☎ 01648 468468 & 468830 (Prof) Fax 01648 468468

Parkland course with some difficult shots, calling for length and accuracy. The Moyola River provides a water hazard at the 8th. Newly designed par 3, demands good shot placement to a green on an island in the Moyola river, players capabilities will be tested by the undulating green.

18 holes, 6522yds, Par 71, SSS 70, Course record 67.
Club membership 1000.

Visitors contact professional in advance, G.U.I. dress code applies, Ladies day Wednesday, Sat & Sun after 2pm, book in advance to avoid dissappointment.
Societies must contact in advance, preferably in writing
Green Fees £15 (£25 weekends & bank holidays.
Prof Vivian Teague
Designer Don Patterson
Facilities
Location 3m NE of Magherafelt

Hotel ★★★★ 70% Galgorm Manor, BALLYMENA ☎ 01266 881001 23

CASTLEROCK Map 01 C6

Castlerock 65 Circular Rd BT51 4TJ ☎ 01265 848314 Fax 01265 848314

A most exhilarating course with three superb par 4s, four testing short holes and five par 5s. After an uphill start, the hazards are many, including the river and a railway, and both judgement and accuracy are called for. A challenge in calm weather, any trouble from the elements will test your golf to the limits.

Mussenden Course: 18 holes, 6499yds, Par 73, SSS 72, Course record 67.
Bann Course: 9 holes, 2294mtrs, Par 34, SSS 33.
Club membership 1120.

Visitors contact in advance and be members of a recognised club.
Societies must contact in advance.
Green Fees Mussenden: £25 per round (£35 weekends & bank holidays).
Prof Robert Kelly
Designer Ben Sayers
Facilities
Location 6m from Coleraine on A2

Hotel ★★★ 61% Causeway Coast Hotel, 36 Ballyreagh Rd, PORTRUSH ☎ 01265 822435 21

KILREA Map 01 C5

Kilrea Drumagarner Rd

A relatively short undulating inland course with tight fairways and small greens. The opening hole is a long par 3, particularly into the wind.

9 holes, 4514yds, Par 62, SSS 62, Course record 61.
Club membership 300.

Visitors welcome but restricted Tue pm, Wed pm during summer and Sat all year.
Societies contact D P Clarke (Sec), 37 Townhill Rd, Portglenone, Co Antrim BT44 8AD.
Green Fees £10 per day (£12.50 weekends).
Facilities
Hotel ★★ 67% Brown Trout Golf & Country Inn, 209 Agivey Rd, AGHADOWEY ☎ 01265 868209 17

LIMAVADY Map 01 C6

Benone 53 Benone Ave BT49 0LQ ☎ 015047 50555 & 50919

9 holes, 1458yds, Par 27.

Visitors no reservations.
Societies telephone in advance.
Green Fees £4 per day (£4.80 weekends & bank holidays).
Facilities
& Leisure hard tennis courts, heated outdoor swimming pool, bowling green.
Location Between Coleraine/Limavady on A2

Radisson Roe Park Hotel & Golf Resort Roe Park BT49 9LB ☎ 015047 22222 Fax 015047 22313

A parkland course opened in 1992 on an historic Georgian estate. The course surrounds the original buildings and a driving range has been created in the old walled garden. Final holes 15-18 are particularly memorable with water, trees, ▶

out-of-bounds, etc to provide a testing finish.
18 holes, 6318yds, Par 70, SSS 35.
Club membership 500.

Visitors advance booking recommended. Handicap certificate required.
Societies contact in advance.
Green Fees £20 per round all week.
Cards
Prof Seamus Duffy
Designer Frank Ainsworth
Facilities
& Leisure heated indoor swimming pool, fishing, sauna, solarium, gymnasium.
Location Just outside Limavady on A2 Ballykelly/Londonderry road

Hotel ★★★★ 71% Radisson Roe Park Hotel & Golf Resort, LIMAVADY ☎ 015047 22222 64

LONDONDERRY Map 01 C5

City of Derry 49 Victoria Rd BT47 2PU
☎ 01504 46369 Fax 01504 310008
Two parkland courses on undulating parkland with good views and lots of trees. The 9-hole course will particularly suit novices.
Prehen Course: 18 holes, 6406yds, Par 71, SSS 71, Course record 68.
Dunhugh Course: 9 holes, 4708yds, Par 63.
Club membership 732.

Visitors must make a booking to play on Prehen Course at weekends or before 4.30pm on weekdays.
Societies must contact in advance.
Green Fees not confirmed.
Prof Michael Doherty
Facilities
Location 2m S

Hotel ★★★★ 66% Everglades Hotel, Prehen Rd, LONDONDERRY ☎ 01504 346722 65

Foyle International Golf Centre 12 Alder Rd BT48 8DB
☎ 01504 352222 Fax 01504 353967
Scenic parkland course located on the edge of Derry City. Created in 1994 it offers an interesting challenge to golfers of all handicaps, with two lakes and water coming into play on three holes, and numerous well placed bunkers. Good modern clubhouse and a floodlit driving range.
18 holes, 6678yds, Par 72, SSS 71, Course record 70.
Club membership 230.

Visitors welcome any time, no retrictions.
Societies booking up to 12 months in advance with deposit.
Green Fees £11 (£14 weekends & bank holidays). Par 3 £4/£4.50.
Cards
Prof Kieran McLaughlin
Designer Frank Ainsworth
Facilities
& Leisure 9 hole par3.
Location 1m from Foyce Bridge off Cullmore Road

Hotel ★★★ 66% Trinity Hotel, 22-24 Strand Rd, DERRY CITY ☎ 01504 271271 40

PORTSTEWART Map 01 C6

Portstewart 117 Strand Rd BT55 7PG
☎ 01265 832015
Three links courses with spectacular views, offering a testing round on the Strand course in particular.
Strand Course: 18 holes, 6784yds, Par 72, SSS 72.
Old Course: 18 holes, 4733yds, Par 64, SSS 62.
3: 9 holes, 2622yds, Par 32.
Club membership 1460.

Visitors preferred on weekdays.
Societies must contact in advance.
Green Fees not confirmed.
Prof Alan Hunter
Facilities
Hotel ★★★ 61% Causeway Coast Hotel, 36 Ballyreagh Rd, PORTRUSH ☎ 01265 822435 21

CO TYRONE

COOKSTOWN Map 01 C5

Killymoon 200 Killymoon Rd BT80 8TW
☎ 016487 63762 & 62254
Parkland course on elevated, well drained land.
18 holes, 5481mtrs, Par 70, SSS 69, Course record 64.
Club membership 950.

Visitors booking essential through proshop on 016487 63460.
Societies must contact in advance.
Green Fees not confirmed.
Prof Gary Chambers
Facilities
Hotel ★★ 67% Royal Arms Hotel, 51 High St, OMAGH ☎ 01662 243262 19

DUNGANNON Map 01 C5

Dungannon 34 Springfield Ln BT70 1QX
☎ 01868 722098 or 727338 Fax 01868 727338
Parkland course with five par 3s and tree-lined fairways.
18 holes, 5950yds, Par 71, SSS 68, Course record 62.
Club membership 600.

Visitors contact in advance, may not play before 4pm Sat.
Societies apply in writing to secretary.
Green Fees not confirmed.
Designer Sam Bacon
Facilities
Location 0.5m outside town on Donaghmore road

Hotel L The Cohannon Inn, 212 Ballynakilly Rd, DUNGANNON ☎ 01868 724488 50

FINTONA Map 01 C5

Fintona Ecclesville Demesne, 1 Kiln St BT78 2BJ
☎ 01662 841480 & 840777 (office) Fax 01662 841480
Attractive 9-hole parkland course with a notable water hazard - a trout stream that meanders through the course causing many problems for badly executed shots.

9 holes, 5765mtrs, Par 72, SSS 70.
Club membership 380.
Visitors advised to contact in advance at weekends.
Societies apply in writing well in advance, weekends not advisable as competitions played.
Green Fees £15 per day.
Facilities ⊗ by prior arrangement by prior arrangement
Location 8m S of Omagh

Hotel ★★ 69% Mahons Hotel, Mill St, IRVINESTOWN ☎ 013656 21656 18

NEWTOWNSTEWART Map 01 C5

Newtownstewart 38 Golf Course Rd BT78 4HU
☎ 016626 61466 Fax 01662 62506
Parkland course bisected by a stream. Deer and pheasant are present on the course.
18 holes, 5468mtrs, Par 70, SSS 69, Course record 66.
Club membership 700.
Visitors contact in advance.
Societies must contact secretary in advance.
Green Fees £12 (£17 weekends and bank holidays). Weekly £50, monthly £110.
Cards
Facilities ⊗ by prior arrangement by prior arrangement by prior arrangement
& Leisure hard tennis courts.
Location 2m SW on B84

Hotel ★★ 67% Royal Arms Hotel, 51 High St, OMAGH ☎ 01662 243262 19

OMAGH Map 01 C5

Omagh 83a Dublin Rd BT78 1HQ ☎ 01662 243160
Undulating parkland course beside the River Drumnagh, with the river coming into play on 4 of the holes.
18 holes, 5674mtrs, Par 71, SSS 70.
Club membership 850.
Visitors play restricted Sat, no need to contact unless large numbers.
Societies must contact in advance.
Green Fees £10 (£15 weekends & bank holidays).
Facilities
Location On S outskirts of town

Hotel ★★ 67% Royal Arms Hotel, 51 High St, OMAGH ☎ 01662 243262 19

STRABANE Map 01 C5

Strabane Ballycolman Rd ☎ 01504 382271 & 382007
Testing parkland course with the River Mourne running alongside and creating a water hazard.
18 holes, 5537mtrs, Par 69, SSS 69, Course record 62.
Club membership 650.
Visitors by prior arrangement.
Societies must telephone in advance.
Green Fees not confirmed.
Designer Eddie Hackett/P Jones
Facilities ⊗ by prior arrangement by prior arrangement
Hotel ★★ 67% Royal Arms Hotel, 51 High St, OMAGH ☎ 01662 243262 19

REPUBLIC OF IRELAND

CO CARLOW

BORRIS Map 01 C3

Borris Deerpark ☎ 0503 73143
Testing parkland course with tree-lined fairways situated within the McMorrough Kavanagh Estate at the foot of Mount Leinster.
9 holes, 6120mtrs, Par 70, SSS 69, Course record 66.
Club membership 400.
Visitors advisable to contact in advance, weekends very restricted.
Societies applications in writing.
Green Fees IR£12 per round.
Facilities
Hotel ★★★★ Mount Juliet Hotel, THOMASTOWN ☎ 056 24455 32 Annexe21

CARLOW Map 01 C3

Carlow Deerpark ☎ 0503 31695 Fax 0503 40065
Created in 1922 to a design by Tom Simpson, this testing and enjoyable course is set in a wild deer park, with beautiful dry terrain and a varied character. With sandy sub-soil, the course is playable all year round. There are water hazards at the 2nd, 10th and 11th and only two par 5s, both offering genuine birdie opportunities.
18 holes, 5974mtrs, Par 70, SSS 69, Course record 62.
Club membership 1200.
Visitors are welcome, although play is limited on Tue and difficult on Sat & Sun. Must contact in advance.
Societies must book in advance.
Green Fees IR£22 per day (IR£27 per round weekends & bank holidays).
Cards
Prof Andrew Gilbert
Designer Tom Simpson
Facilities ⊗
Location 2m N of Carlow on N9

Hotel ★★★ 67% Dolmen Hotel, Kilkenny Rd, CARLOW ☎ 0503 42002 40

CO CAVAN

BALLYCONNELL Map 01 C4

Slieve Russell Hotel Golf & Country Club
☎ 049 26444 Fax 049 26474
An 18-hole course opened in 1992 and rapidly establishing itself as one of the finest parkland courses in the country. A 9-hole course was recently opened to complement it. On the main course, the 2nd plays across water while the 16th has water surrounding the green. The course finishes with a 519 yard, Par 5 18th. ▶

18 holes, 6650yds, Par 72, SSS 72, Course record 68.
Club membership 770.

Visitors must book in advance for Saturdays.
Societies write or telephone in advance, not allowed Sat.
Green Fees IR£28 per day (IR£36 Sat).
Cards
Prof Liam McCool
Designer Paddy Merrigan
Facilities
& Leisure hard tennis courts, heated indoor swimming pool, squash, sauna, solarium, gymnasium, snooker and pool room.
Location 1.5m E of Ballyconnell

Hotel ★★★★ 67% Slieve Russell Hotel Golf and Country Club, BALLYCONNELL ☎ 049 26444 151

BELTURBET Map 01 C4

Belturbet Erne Hill ☎ 049 22287
Beautifully maintained parkland course with predominantly family membership and popular with summer visitors.
9 holes, 5480yds, Par 68, SSS 65, Course record 64.
Club membership 150.

Visitors must contact in advance.
Societies must contact secretary in advance.
Green Fees IR£10 per day.
Facilities
Hotel ★★★★ 67% Slieve Russell Hotel Golf and Country Club, BALLYCONNELL ☎ 049 26444 151

BLACKLION Map 01 C5

Blacklion Toam ☎ 072 53024
Parkland course established in 1962, with coppices of woodland and mature trees. The lake comes into play on two holes and there are some magnificent views of the lake, islands and surrounding hills. It has been described as one of the best maintained nine-hole courses in Ireland.
9 holes, 5614mtrs, Par 72, SSS 69.
Club membership 250.

Visitors no restrictions.
Societies must contact in advance.
Green Fees IR£8 per day (IR£10 weekends & bank holidays).
Designer Eddie Hackett
Facilities by prior arrangement
& Leisure fishing.
Hotel ★★★ 71% Sligo Park Hotel, Pearse Rd, SLIGO ☎ 071 60291 89

CAVAN Map 01 C4

County Cavan Drumelis ☎ 049 31541 Fax 049 31541
Parkland course.
18 holes, 5519mtrs, Par 70, SSS 69, Course record 66.
Club membership 830.

Visitors welcome but restricted at weekends.
Societies contact for details.
Green Fees not confirmed.
Prof Garan Carroll
Designer Eddie Hackett
Facilities
Location On Killeshandra rd

Hotel ★★★ 64% Kilmore Hotel, Dublin Rd, CAVAN ☎ 049 32288 39

VIRGINIA Map 01 C4

Virginia ☎ 049 47235 & 40223
9 holes, 4139mtrs, Par 64, SSS 62.
Club membership 400.

Visitors may not play Thu & Sun.
Societies must apply in writing to secretary.
Green Fees not confirmed.
Facilities
Location By Lough Ramor

Hotel ★★ 60% Conyngham Arms Hotel, SLANE ☎ 041 24155 16rm(15)

CO CLARE

CLONLARA Map 01 B3

Clonlara Golf & Leisure ☎ 061 354141 Fax 061 354143
A 12-hole parkland course, Par 47, on the banks of the River Shannon with views of Clare Hills. Set in grounds of 63 acres surrounding the 17th century Landscape House, there is also a leisure complex for self-catering holidays.
12 holes, 5187mtrs, Par 71, SSS 69.
Club membership 100.

Visitors players only no accompanying persons.
Societies welcome subject to availability prior notice required.
Green Fees IR£5 Mon-Sat (IR£10 Sun & bank holidays).
Designer Noel Cassidy
Facilities
& Leisure hard tennis courts, fishing, sauna, games room, childrens play area.
Location 7m NE of Limerick

Hotel ★★★★ 71% Castletroy Park Hotel, Dublin Rd, LIMERICK ☎ 061 335566 107

ENNIS Map 01 B3

Ennis Drumbiggle ☎ 065 24074 Fax 065 41848
On rolling hills, this immaculately manicured course presents an excellent challenge to both casual visitors and aspiring scratch golfers, with tree-lined fairways and well protected greens.
18 holes, 5275mtrs, Par 69, SSS 68, Course record 65.
Club membership 1000.

Visitors advisable to contact in advance, course available Mon-Sat at most times.
Societies apply in writing.
Green Fees IR£18 per round.
Cards
Prof Martin Ward
Facilities
Hotel ★★★ 65% Auburn Lodge Hotel, Galway Rd, ENNIS ☎ 065 21247 100

KILKEE Map 01 B3

Kilkee East End ☎ 065 56048
Well established course on the cliffs of Kilkee Bay, with beautiful views.
18 holes, 6500yds, Par 72, SSS 71, Course record 68.
Club membership 390.
Visitors must book in advance.
Societies apply in writing.
Green Fees not confirmed.
Facilities
& Leisure squash, sauna.
Hotel ★★ 60% Halpin's Hotel, Erin St, KILKEE
☎ 065 56032 12

KILRUSH Map 01 B3

Kilrush Parknamoney ☎ 065 51138 Fax 065 52633
Parkland course that was extended to 18 holes in the summer of 1994.
18 holes, 5986yds, Par 70, SSS 70, Course record 68.
Club membership 425.
Visitors welcome, contact in advance.
Societies by prior arrangement.
Green Fees IR£16 per day (IR£18 weekends).
Cards
Facilities
Hotel ★★ 60% Halpin's Hotel, Erin St, KILKEE
☎ 065 56032 12

LAHINCH Map 01 B3

Lahinch ☎ 065 81003 Fax 065 81592
Originally designed by Tom Morris and later modified by Dr Alister MacKenzie, Lahinch has hosted every important Irish amateur fixture and the Home Internationals. The par five 5th - The Klondike - is played along a deep valley and over a huge dune; the par three 6th may be short, but calls for a blind shot over the ridge of a hill to a green hemmed in by hills on three sides.
Old Course: 18 holes, 6696yds, Par 72, SSS 73.
Castle Course: 18 holes, 5594yds, Par 70, SSS 70.
Club membership 1840.
Visitors must contact in advance.
Societies apply in writing
Green Fees Old Course IR£45; Castle Course IR£25.
Cards
Prof R McCavery
Designer Alister MacKenzie
Facilities
Location 2m W of Ennisstymon on N67

Hotel ★★ 70% Sheedy's Spa View Hotel & Orchid Restaurant, LISDOONVARNA
☎ 065 74026 11

MILLTOWN MALBAY Map 01 B3

Spanish Point ☎ 065 84198 Fax 065 84909
A 9-hole links course with 3 elevated greens and 4 elevated tees. The 8th hole is a 75-metre par 3, locally known as 'the Terror'.
9 holes, 4600mtrs, Par 64, SSS 62, Course record 59.
Club membership 250.
Visitors contact in advance. No green fees allowed before 1pm Sun.
Societies apply in writing to the secretary 065 84219
Green Fees IR£10 per day (IR£12 Jun-Sep).
Facilities
Location 2m SW of Miltown Malbay, on N67

Hotel ★★★ 65% West County Conference & Leisure Hotel, Clare Rd, ENNIS
☎ 065 23000 152

NEWMARKET-ON-FERGUS Map 01 B3

Dromoland Castle Golf & Country Club
☎ 061 368444 & 368144 Fax 061 363355/368498
Set in 200 acres of parkland, the course is enhanced by numerous trees and a lake. Three holes are played around the lake which is in front of the castle.
18 holes, 6098yds, Par 71, SSS 72, Course record 67.
Club membership 500.
Visitors must contact in advance.
Societies contact in writing.
Green Fees not confirmed.
Cards
Prof Philip Murphy
Designer Wigginton
Facilities
& Leisure hard tennis courts, fishing, sauna, solarium, gymnasium.
Location 2m N, on main Limerick/Galway rd

Hotel ★★★ 62% Clare Inn Golf and Leisure Hotel, NEWMARKET-ON-FERGUS
☎ 065 230000 161

SCARRIFF Map 01 B3

East Clare Bodyke ☎ 061 921322
Beside Lough Derg, East Clare was opened in June 1992 as a 9-hole course in 148 acre site with natural trees and water on well-drained land. An 18-hole championship course deigned by Arthur Spring is in preparation.
9 holes, 52yds, Par 70, SSS 70 or 32 holes.
Club membership 130.
Visitors no restrictions unless there is a club competition or a society playing.
Societies apply in writing, deposit required.
Green Fees not confirmed.
Facilities
Hotel ★★★ 65% West County Conference & Leisure Hotel, Clare Rd, ENNIS
☎ 065 23000 152

SHANNON AIRPORT Map 01 B3

Shannon ☎ 061 471849 Fax 061 471507
Superb parkland course with tree-lined fairways, strategically placed bunkers, water hazards and excellent greens, offering a challenge to all levels of players - including the many famous golfers who have played here.
18 holes, 6874yds, Par 72, SSS 74, Course record 65.
Club membership 1000.
Visitors must contact in advance & have handicap certificate. Restricted play at certain times.
Societies must contact in writing.
Green Fees IR£22 per day (IR£27 weekends & bank holidays). ▶

Cards
Prof Artie Pyke
Designer John Harris
Facilities
Location 2m from Shannon Airport

Hotel ★★★ 61% Fitzpatrick Bunratty Shamrock Hotel, BUNRATTY
061 361177 115

CO CORK

BANDON — Map 01 B2

Bandon Castlebernard
023 41111 Fax 023 44690
Lovely parkland course in pleasant rural surroundings.
18 holes, 5663mtrs, Par 70, SSS 69, Course record 66.
Club membership 900.
Visitors welcome but may not play during club competitions. Must contact in advance.
Societies must apply in writing or telephone well in advance.
Green Fees IR£15 per day (IR£20 weekends & bank holidays).
Prof Paddy O'Boyle
Facilities
& Leisure hard tennis courts.
Location 2.5km W

Hotel ★★★ 68% Innishannon House Hotel, INISHANNON
021 775121 12 Annexe1

BANTRY — Map 01 B2

Bantry Bay Bantry Bay
027 50579 & 50583 Fax 027 50579
Designed by Christy O'Connor Jnr and extended in 1997 to 18 holes, this challenging and rewarding course is idyllically set at the head of Bantry Bay. Testing holes include the par 5 of 487mtrs and the little par 3 of 127mtrs where accuracy is all-important.
18 holes, 5910mtrs, Par 71, SSS 72, Course record 71.
Club membership 550.
Visitors advance booking recommended. At weekends and bank holidays visitors between 11.30-1.30pm and 3-4.30pm. Catering Mar-Oct only.
Societies must apply in writing.
Green Fees IR£18 per round (IR£20 weekends & bank holidays).
Cards
Prof Finbar London
Designer Christy O'Connor/Eddie Hackett
Facilities
Location 3km N of Bantry town on the N71 Glengarrif road

Hotel ★★★ 58% Westlodge Hotel, BANTRY
027 50360 90

BLARNEY — Map 01 B2

Muskerry Carrigrohane 021 385297
An adventurous game is guaranteed at this course, with its wooded hillsides and the meandering Shournagh River coming into play at a number of holes. The 15th is a notable hole - not long, but very deep - and after that all you need to do to get back to the clubhouse is stay out of the water.
18 holes, 6327yds, Par 71, SSS 71.
Club membership 706.
Visitors may not play Wed afternoon & Thu morning. Some limited opportunities at weekends after 3.30pm. Must contact in advance.
Societies must telephone in advance and then confirm in writing.
Green Fees IR£22 per round (IR£12.50 before 10.30am).
Prof W M Lehane
Designer Dr A MCKenzie
Facilities
Location 2.5m W of Blarney

Hotel ★★★ 68% Blarney Park Hotel, BLARNEY
021 385281 76

CARRIGALINE — Map 01 B2

Fernhill Hotel & Golf Club 021 373103
Parkland course.
18 holes, 5000mtrs, Par 69, SSS 68.
Club membership 200.
Visitors available any time.
Societies telephone in advance.
Green Fees not confirmed.
Facilities
& Leisure hard tennis courts, heated indoor swimming pool, fishing, sauna, solarium, gymnasium.
Location 2m from Ringaskiddy

CASTLETOWNBERE — Map 01 A2

Berehaven Millcove 027 70700
Seaside links founded in 1902.
9 holes, 2398mtrs, Par 68, SSS 66, Course record 63.
Visitors welcome.
Societies telephone in advance.
Green Fees IR£10 per day.
Cards
Facilities
& Leisure hard tennis courts, sauna.
Location 2m E on Glen Garriff Rd

Hotel ★★★ 73% Sea View Hotel, BALLYLICKEY
027 50073 & 50462 Fax 027 51555 17

CHARLEVILLE — Map 01 B2

Charleville 063 81257 & 81515 Fax 063 81274
Wooded parkland course offering not too strenuous walking.
18 holes, 6212yds, Par 71, SSS 69, Course record 65.
Club membership 1000.

Visitors only prebooked at weekends.
Societies contact in advance.
Green Fees IR£15 (IR£17 weekends).
Prof David Keating
Facilities
Hotel ★★★ Longueville House Hotel, MALLOW ☎ 022 47156 & 47306 Fax 022 47459 20

CLONAKILTY Map 01 B2

Dunmore Dunmore, Muckross ☎ 023 33352
A hilly, rocky 9-hole course overlooking the Atlantic.
9 holes, 4464yds, Par 64, SSS 61, Course record 57.
Club membership 250.
Visitors must contact in advance, may not play weekends.
Societies apply in writing.
Green Fees not confirmed.
Designer E Hackett
Facilities
Location 3.5m S of Clonakilty

Hotel ★★ 64% Courtmacsherry, COURTMACSHERRY ☎ 023 46198 13rm(9 1)

CORK Map 01 B2

Cork Little Island ☎ 021 353451 Fax 021 353410
This championship-standard course is always kept in superb condition and is playable all year round. It has many memorable and distinctive features including holes at the water's edge and holes in a disused quarry.
18 holes, 5910mtrs, Par 72, SSS 70.
Club membership 750.
Visitors may not play 12.30-2pm or on Thu (Ladies Day), and only after 2pm Sat & Sun.
Societies must contact in advance.
Green Fees IR£35 (IR£40 weekends).
Cards
Prof Peter Hickey
Designer Alister Mackenzie
Facilities
Location 5m E, on N25

Hotel ★★★★ 65% Jurys Hotel, Western Rd, CORK ☎ 021 276622 185

Fitzpatrick Silver Springs Tivoli ☎ 021 507533
Five Par 4s and 4 Par3s make up this short 9-hole course. The 4th has a 189 metre drive with out of bounds on the righthand side.
9 holes, 1786mtrs, Par 32, Course record 26.
Club membership 70.
Visitors no restrictions.
Societies apply by telephone.
Green Fees not confirmed.
Prof Freddy Twomey
Designer Eddie Hackett
Facilities
& Leisure hard tennis courts, heated indoor swimming pool, squash, sauna, solarium, gymnasium.
Location 1m E of city centre

Hotel ★★★★ 68% Fitzpatrick Silver Springs Hotel, Tivoli, CORK ☎ 021 507533 109

Fota Island Carrigtwohill ☎ 021 883700 Fax 021 883713
Fota Island Golf Club is in the heart of the 780 acre island in Cork Harbour which is recognised as one of Ireland's most outstanding landscapes. The course is gently undulating parkland routed among mature woodlands with occasional views of the harbour. The overall design is very traditional, featuring pot bunkers, a double green and undulating putting surfaces. The 10th and 18th holes are narrow Par 5's that require great accuracy and shotmaking skills. Fota has hosted the Irish Club Professional Championship, the Irish PGA Championship and the Irish Amateur Open.
18 holes, 6500yds, Par 72, SSS 72, Course record 67.
Club membership 400.
Visitors advisable to contact in advance.
Societies contact in advance.
Green Fees IR£32 per round (IR£37 weekends). Extra 18 Holes IR£12 weekdays; IR£15 weekends.
Cards
Prof Kevin Morris
Designer McEvoy/O'Connor
Facilities
Location Off N25 E of Cork City. Take exit for Cobh, course 500m on right

Hotel ★★★ 66% Midleton Park, MIDLETON ☎ 021 631767 40

Mahon Municipal Blackrock ☎ 021 294280
Municipal course which stretches alongside the river estuary, with some holes across water.
18 holes, 4818mtrs, Par 67, SSS 66.
Club membership 380.
Visitors please contact in advance, may not play mornings at weekends.
Societies please telephone in advance.
Green Fees not confirmed.
Designer E Hackett
Facilities
Location 2m from city centre

Hotel ★★★★ 68% Fitzpatrick Silver Springs Hotel, Tivoli, CORK ☎ 021 507533 109

DONERAILE Map 01 B2

Doneraile ☎ 022 24137
Parkland.
9 holes, 5528yds, SSS 66.
Club membership 400.
Visitors no restrictions
Societies welcome.
Green Fees IR£10.
Facilities
Location Off T11

Hotel ★★★ Longueville House Hotel, MALLOW ☎ 022 47156 & 47306 Fax 022 47459 20

DOUGLAS Map 01 B2

Douglas ☎ 021 895297
Level inland course overlooking the city of Cork. Suitable for golfers of all ages and abilities. The course is under re-development for 1999 and therefore the measurements/details given below are due to change.
18 holes, 5383mtrs, Par 70, SSS 68.
Club membership 810. ▶

Visitors advisable to play Mon & Wed-Fri, contact in advance.
Societies must contact in writing, dates allocated early Feb.
Green Fees not confirmed.
Prof Gary Nicholson
Designer Harry Vardon
Facilities

Hotel ★★★★ 65% Jurys Hotel, Western Rd, CORK ☎ 021 276622 185

FERMOY Map 01 B2

Fermoy Corrin Cross ☎ 025 31472
Rather exposed heathland course, bisected by a road.
18 holes, 5586mtrs, Par 70, SSS 69.
Club membership 950.
Visitors contact in advance.
Societies advisable to write in advance.
Green Fees not confirmed.
Facilities
Location 2m SW

Hotel ★★★ Longueville House Hotel, MALLOW ☎ 022 47156 & 47306 Fax 022 47459 20

GLENGARRIFF Map 01 B2

Glengarriff ☎ 027 63150 Fax 027 63575
Founded 1935.
9 holes, 2042mtrs, Par 66, SSS 62.
Club membership 300.
Visitors welcome, details not supplied
Societies apply to club.
Green Fees £12 per day, except Jun, Jul & Aug £12 per 18-holes.
Facilities
Location On N71

Hotel ★★★ 58% Westlodge Hotel, BANTRY ☎ 027 50360 90

KANTURK Map 01 B2

Kanturk Fairyhill ☎ 029 50534
Scenic parkland course set in the heart of the Duhallow region with superb mountain views. It provides a good test of skill for golfers of all standards, with tight fairways requiring accurate driving and precise approach shots to small and tricky greens.
18 holes, 6262yds, Par 72, SSS 70, Course record 70.
Club membership 320.

Visitors Ladies day Wed.
Societies apply in writing or telephone the Secretary.
Green Fees IR£15 per day.
Designer Richard Barry
Facilities
Location 1m from Kanturk on Fairyhill road, 2m off main Mallow/Killarney road from Ballymacquirke Cross

Guesthouse Assolas Country House, KANTURK ☎ 029 50015 6 Annexe3

KINSALE Map 01 B2

Kinsale Farrangalway ☎ 021 774722 Fax 021 773114
In addition to the existing 9-hole (Ringenane) course, a new 18-hole (Farrangalway) course was opened in 1994. Set in unspoilt farmland and surrounded by peacefull rolling countryside, it offers a stiff yet fair challenge to be enjoyed by all standards of golfers. New putting green.
Farrangalway: 18 holes, 6440yds, Par 71, SSS 71, Course record 70.
Ringenane: 9 holes, 5332yds, Par 70, SSS 68, Course record 67.
Club membership 740.
Visitors welcome but may not be able to play at weekends,
Societies apply in writing.
Green Fees Farrangalway: IR£12.50-IR£20 per round (IR£25 weekends). Ringenane; IR£10 per round.
Cards
Prof Ger Broderick
Designer Jack Kenneally
Facilities
Location On main Cork/Kinsale rd

Hotel ★★★ 68% Trident Hotel, Worlds End, KINSALE ☎ 021 772301 58

Old Head ☎ 021 778444 Fax 021 778022
Opened for play in 1997 and designed by Ron Kirby and Joe Carr, the Old Head course is spectacularly situated on a promontory jutting out into the Atlantic. As well as bringing the sea and cliffs into play, you have to contend with strong prevailing winds - a fine test for all serious golfers.
18 holes, 6400yds, Par 72.
Club membership 40.

Visitors tee time must be booked in advance.
Societies pre booking necessary, rates for groups over 24.
Green Fees IR£80 per 36 holes; IR£50 per 18 holes; IR£30 per 9 holes (IR£100/IR£60/IR£40 weekends).
Cards
Designer R Kirby/J Carr/P Merrigan/E Hackett

Facilities
Location From Cork city/airport, follow R600 to Kinsale, then signed to golf course

Hotel ★★★ 64% Acton's Hotel, Pier Rd, KINSALE ☎ 021 772135 56

LITTLE ISLAND Map 01 B2

Harbour Point Clash Rd ☎ 021 353094 Fax 021 354408
A new championship-standard course in rolling countryside on the banks of the River Lee at Cork's scenic harbour. A distinctive and testing course for every standard of golfer.
18 holes, 5883metres, Par 72, SSS 71, Course record 71.
Visitors must contact in advance.
Societies telephone for bookings.
Green Fees IR£12.50-IR£22 per round.
Cards
Prof Brendan McDaid
Designer Patrick Merrigan
Facilities
& Leisure practice area.
Location 5m E of Cork, take Rosslare road E from Cork city & exit at Little Island

Hotel ★★★★ 68% Fitzpatrick Silver Springs Hotel, Tivoli, CORK ☎ 021 507533 109

MACROOM Map 01 B2

Macroom Lackaduve ☎ 026 41072 Fax 026 41391
A particularly scenic parkland course located on undulating ground along the banks of the River Sullane. Bunkers and mature trees make a variable and testing course and the 12th has a 50 yards carry over the river to the green.
18 holes, 5574mtrs, Par 72, SSS 70.
Club membership 600.
Visitors restricted some weekends, contact in advance.
Societies apply in writing.
Green Fees IR£13 (IR£15 weekends & bank holidays).
Designer Jack Kenneally
Facilities
Location Through castle entrance in town square

Hotel ★★ 72% Castle Hotel, Main St, MACROOM ☎ 026 41074 42

MALLOW Map 01 B2

Mallow Ballyellis ☎ 022 21145 Fax 022 42501
Mallow Golf Club was first established in the late 1800's. A well wooded parkland course overlooking the Blackwater Valley, Mallow is straightforward, but no less of a challenge for it. The front nine is by far the longer, but the back nine is demanding in its call for accuracy and the par 3 18th provides a tough finish.
18 holes, 5769metres, Par 72, SSS 71, Course record 67.
Club membership 1400.
Visitors must contact in advance.
Societies apply in advance.
Green Fees IR£20 per round (IR£25 weekends & bank holidays).
Cards
Prof Sean Conway
Designer D W Wishart
Facilities
& Leisure hard tennis courts, squash, sauna, snooker/billiards room, TV room.
Location 1m E of Mallow town

Hotel ★★★ Longueville House Hotel, MALLOW ☎ 022 47156 & 47306 Fax 022 47459 20

MIDLETON Map 01 C2

East Cork Gortacrue ☎ 021 631687
A well wooded course calling for accuracy of shots.
18 holes, 5207mtrs, Par 69, SSS 67, Course record 65.
Club membership 530.
Visitors may not play Sun mornings.
Societies must telephone.
Green Fees IR£15.
Cards
Prof Don MacFarlane
Designer E Hackett
Facilities
& Leisure squash, fishing.
Location On the A626

Hotel ★★★ 66% Midleton Park, MIDLETON ☎ 021 631767 40

MITCHELSTOWN Map 01 B2

Mitchelstown Limerick Rd ☎ 025 27139
Attractive, gently undulating parkland course set in the Golden Vale, noted for the quality of the greens, the magnificent views of the Galtee Mountains and its friendly atmosphere. Ideal for golfers seeking tranquility and a golfing challenge.
18 holes, 5160mtrs, Par 67, SSS 68, Course record 65.
Club membership 400.
Visitors advisable to check in advance.
Societies apply in writing or telephone.
Green Fees IR£10 per day.
Designer David Jones
Facilities
Location 0.75m on Limerick rd from Mitchelstown

Hotel ★★★ Longueville House Hotel, MALLOW ☎ 022 47156 & 47306 Fax 022 47459 20

MONKSTOWN Map 01 B2

Monkstown Parkgariffe, Monkstown ☎ 021 841376
Undulating parkland course with five tough finishing holes.
18 holes, 5441mtrs, Par 70, SSS 68, Course record 66. Club membership 960.

Visitors restricted weekends, must contact in advance.
Societies apply in writing or telephone. Large groups (24+) should book before Xmas.
Green Fees IR£23 Mon-Thu; IR£26 Fri-Sun & bank holidays.
Prof Batt Murphy
Facilities
Location 0.5m SE of Monkstown village

Hotel ★★★★ 65% Jurys Hotel, Western Rd, CORK ☎ 021 276622 185

OVENS Map 01 B2

Lee Valley Golf & Country Club Clashanure
☎ 021 331721 Fax 021 331695
An undulating test of all golfing abilities designed by Ryder Cup star Christy O'Connor Junior. Seven of the 18 holes have water and the unusual feature of two fairy forts which are over 300 years old - can they be blamed for errors on the testing Par 5 8th and 12th holes?! The 508yard, Par 5 8th is already regarded as one of the best holes in Ireland with its spectacular lake a feature from tee to green.
18 holes, 6434mtrs, Par 72, SSS 70, Course record 68. Club membership 400.

Visitors telephone in advance.
Societies telephone in advance.
Green Fees IR£15-£25 per round (IR£20-£27 weekends & bank holidays).
Cards
Prof John Savage
Designer Christy O'Connor
Facilities
Location 8m from Cork on Cork/Killarney road N22

Hotel ★★ 60% Vienna Woods Hotel, Glanmire, CORK ☎ 021 821146 20

SKIBBEREEN Map 01 B2

Skibbereen & West Carbery Licknavar ☎ 028 21227
Slightly hilly course in scenic location.
18 holes, 6004yds, Par 71, SSS 69, Course record 67. Club membership 640.

Visitors advisable to contact in advance.
Societies apply in writing.
Green Fees IR£12 per day (IR£15 May-Sep).
Cards
Facilities
Location 1m W on Baltimore road

Hotel ★★★ 65% Baltimore Harbour Hotel, BALTIMORE ☎ 028 20361 30

YOUGHAL Map 01 C2

Youghal Knockaverry ☎ 024 92787 Fax 024 92641
For many years the host of various Golfing Union championships, Youghal offers a good test of golf and is well maintained for year-round play. There are panoramic views of Youghal Bay and the Blackwater estuary.
18 holes, 5646mtrs, Par 70, SSS 69, Course record 67. Club membership 600.

Visitors may not play Wed (Ladies Day) and should contact in advance for weekends.
Societies must apply in writing a few months in advance.
Green Fees IR£18 per round (IR£20 weekends).
Cards
Prof Liam Burns
Designer Cd. Harris
Facilities
Hotel ★★ 64% Devonshire Arms Hotel and Restaurant, Pearse Square, YOUGHAL ☎ 024 92827 & 92018 Fax 024 92900 10

CO DONEGAL

BALLINTRA Map 01 B5

Donegal Murvagh, Laghy
☎ 073 34054 Fax 073 34377
This massive links course was opened in 1973 and provides a world-class facility in peaceful surroundings. It is a very long course with some memorable holes, including five par 5s, calling for some big hitting. Donegal is the home club of former Curtis Cup captain, Maire O'Donnell.
18 holes, 6243mtrs, Par 73, SSS 73, Course record 68. Club membership 750.

Visitors must contact in advance, limited availability at weekends.
Societies must contact in advance.
Green Fees IR£18 per 18 holes (IR£25 weekends & bank holidays).
Cards
Designer Eddie Hackett
Facilities
Location 6m S of Donegal on Ballyshannon road

Hotel ★★★ 76% Sand House Hotel, ROSSNOWLAGH ☎ 072 51777 46

BALLYBOFEY Map 01 C5

Ballybofey & Stranorlar Stranorlar
☎ 074 31093
A most scenic course incorporating pleasant valleys backed by mountains with three of its holes bordered by a lake. There are three Par 3s on the first nine and two on the second. The most difficult hole is the long uphill Par 4 16th. The only Par 5 is the 7th.
18 holes, 5366mtrs, Par 68, SSS 68, Course record 64.
Club membership 450.

Visitors may play on weekdays. Advisable to book in advance
Green Fees not confirmed.
Facilities
& Leisure squash.
Location 0.25m from Stranorlar

Hotel ★★★ 65% Kee's Hotel, Stranorlar, BALLYBOFEY ☎ 074 31018 36

BALLYLIFFEN Map 01 C6

Ballyliffin Clonmany ☎ 077 76119 Fax 077 76672
The Old course is a links course with rolling fairways, surrounded by rolling hills and bounded on one side by the ocean. Nick Faldo said 'This is the most natural golf links I have ever played.' It has an old-fashioned charm with its uniquely contoured fairways. The new 18-hole course, the Glashedy (opened summer 1995), offers a modern (and arguably 'fairer') championship test.
Old Links: 18 holes, 6384yds, Par 72, SSS 70, Course record 68.
Glashedy Links: 18 holes, 7102yds, Par 71, SSS 74, Course record 70.
Club membership 1034.

Visitors telephone in advance.
Societies telephone in advance.
Green Fees Old Links: IR£17 (IR£20 weekends); Glashedy: IR£25 (IR£30 weekends).
Cards
Designer Tony Craddock/Pat Priddy
Facilities
Guesthouse QQQQ Mount Royd Country Home, CARRIGANS ☎ 074 40163 4

BUNCRANA Map 01 C6

Buncrana Municipal Ballmacarry ☎ 077 62279
A 9-hole course with a very challenging Par-3 3rd with all carry out of bounds on either side.
9 holes, 2125yds, Par 62, SSS 60, Course record 59.
Club membership 100.

Visitors during open competitions only visitors with club handicaps.
Societies write in advance.
Green Fees not confirmed.
Facilities
Guesthouse QQQQ Mount Royd Country Home, CARRIGANS ☎ 074 40163 4

North West Lisfannon, Fahan
☎ 077 61027 Fax 077 63284
A traditional-style links course on gently rolling sandy terrain with some long par 4s. Good judgement is required on the approaches and the course offers a satisfying test coupled with undemanding walking.
18 holes, 5968yds, Par 70, SSS 70, Course record 64.
Club membership 580.

Visitors contact in advance for weekends. Wed - Ladies Day
Societies telephone in advance.
Green Fees IR£15 (IR£20 weekends).
Prof Seamus McBriarty
Facilities
Location 1m S of Buncanna

Guesthouse QQQQ Mount Royd Country Home, CARRIGANS ☎ 074 40163 4

BUNDORAN Map 01 B5

Bundoran ☎ 072 41302 Fax 072 42014
This popular course, acknowledged as one of the best in the country, runs along the high cliffs above Bundoran beach and has a difficult par of 69. Designed by Harry Vardon, it offers a challenging game of golf in beautiful surroundings and has been the venue for a number of Irish golf championships.
18 holes, 5599mtrs, Par 69, SSS 70, Course record 66.
Club membership 560.

Visitors must contact in advance.
Societies must contact in advance.
Green Fees IR£17 (IR£20 weekends & bank holidays).
Prof David T Robinson
Designer Harry Vardon
Facilities
Location Just off Main St, Bundoran on the Sligo/Derry road, 22m N of Sligo

Hotel ★★★ 76% Sand House Hotel, ROSSNOWLAGH ☎ 072 51777 46

CRUIT ISLAND Map 01 B5

Cruit Island Kincasslagh ☎ 075 43296
A links course on a small island. It is perched along the cliffs overlooking the Atlantic. The course is short but always challenging as the wind blows 90% of the time. It is crowned by a magnificent 6th hole which is played across a cove to an island green. With the prevailing wind in your face and the Atlantic waves crashing in front, it is not for the fainthearted.
9 holes, 4833mtrs, Par 68, SSS 66, Course record 62.
Club membership 200.

Visitors restricted Sun & Thu mornings for Club competitions.
Societies apply in writing to secretary.
Green Fees IR£7 per round (IR£10 weekends).
Designer Michael Doherty
Facilities (all day in summer)
Location 8km N of Dungloe

Hotel ★★★ 63% Arnold's Hotel, DUNFANAGHY ☎ 074 36208 & 36142 Fax 074 36352 32

DUNFANAGHY Map 01 C6

Dunfanaghy Kill ☎ 074 36335 Fax 074 36335
Overlooking Sheephaven Bay, the course has a flat central area with three difficult streams to negotiate. At the Port-na-Blagh end there are five marvellous holes, including one across the beach, while at the Horn Head end, the last five holes are a test for any golfer.
18 holes, 5066mtrs, Par 68, SSS 66, Course record 64.
Club membership 395.
Visitors must book in advance, time sheet in operation all year.
Societies must telephone in advance.
Green Fees IR£13 (IR£15 weekends).
Designer Harry Vardon
Facilities
Location On N56

Hotel ★★★ 63% Arnold's Hotel, DUNFANAGHY ☎ 074 36208 & 36142 Fax 074 36352 32

GREENCASTLE Map 01 C6

Greencastle Moville ☎ 077 81013
A typical links course along the shores of Lough Foyle, surrounded by rocky headlands and sandy beaches. In 1992 to celebrate its centenary, the club increased its size from 9 to 18 holes.
18 holes, 5118mtrs, Par 69, SSS 67.
Club membership 600.
Visitors no restrictions.
Societies telephone in advance.
Green Fees not confirmed.
Facilities

Hotel ★★★★ 66% Everglades Hotel, Prehen Rd, LONDONDERRY ☎ 01504 346722 65

GWEEDORE Map 01 B6

Gweedore Derrybeg ☎ 075 31140
This 9-hole links course provides plenty of challenge with two subtle Par 3s and the Par 5 5th/14th at 556yards into the prevailing west wind is a monster.
9 holes, 6201yds, Par 71, SSS 69.
Club membership 175.
Visitors apply in writing for availability of the course, weekend plsy possible if advance permission given.
Societies apply in writing.
Green Fees IR£7 per day (IR£8 weekends & bank holidays).
Facilities

LETTERKENNY Map 01 C5

Letterkenny Barnhill ☎ 074 21150
The fairways are wide and generous, but the rough, when you find it, is short, tough and mean. The flat and untiring terrain on the shores of Lough Swilly provides good holiday golf. Many interesting holes include the intimidating 1st with its high tee through trees and the tricky dog-leg of the 2nd hole. The last 7 holes are on undulating ground, steep climb from 11th green to 12th tee.
18 holes, 6239yds, Par 70, SSS 71, Course record 67.
Club membership 700.
Visitors preferred Mon-Fri, except Wed evenings after 5pm. Advisable to contact in advance for weekends and bank holidays.
Societies apply by writing or telephone.
Green Fees IR£12 per day (IR£15 weekends & bank holidays).
Designer Eddie Hacket
Facilities by prior arrangement by prior arrangement
Location 2m from town on Rathmelton road

Hotel ★★★ 65% Kee's Hotel, Stranorlar, BALLYBOFEY ☎ 074 31018 36

MOVILLE Map 01 C6

Redcastle Redcastle ☎ 077 82073 Fax 077 82214
A testing course enjoying a picturesque setting on the shores of Loch Foyle. The two challenging Par 3 holes should be approached with the necessary respect.
9 holes, 3076yds, Par 36.
Club membership 200.
Visitors welcome except club times advisable to telephone.
Societies enquiries welcome by telephone or in writing.
Green Fees not confirmed.
Facilities
& Leisure hard tennis courts, heated indoor swimming pool, fishing, sauna, gymnasium.
Location Main Londonderry/Moville road

NARIN Map 01 B5

Narin & Portnoo ☎ 075 45107
Seaside links with every hole presenting its own special feature. The Par 4 5th, for instance, demands a perfectly placed drive to get a narrow sight of the narrow entrance to the elevated green. Cross winds from the sea can make some of the Par 4s difficult to reach with two woods.
18 holes, 5322mtrs, Par 69, SSS 68, Course record 63.
Club membership 510.
Visitors weekends by arrangement.
Societies telephone in advance.
Green Fees IR£13 per day (IR£16 weekends & bank holidays).
Facilities
Location 6m from Ardara

Hotel ★★★ 63% Abbey Hotel, The Diamond, DONEGAL ☎ 073 21014 49

PORTSALON Map 01 C6

Portsalon ☎ 074 59459 Fax 074 59459
Another course blessed by nature. The three golden beaches of Ballymastocker Bay lie at one end, while the beauty of Lough Swilly and the Inishowen Peninsula beyond is a distracting but pleasant feature to the west. Situated on the Fanad Peninsula, this lovely links course provides untiring holiday golf at its best.
18 holes, 5880yds, Par 69, SSS 68.
Club membership 400.
Visitors telephone in advance.
Societies telephone in advance.
Green Fees IR£14 (IR£17 weekends & bank holidays).

Facilities ⊗ 🛍 ☕ 🍸 🧥 🏌
Location 20m N of Letterkenny

Hotel ★★★ 71% Fort Royal Hotel, Fort Royal, RATHMULLAN
☎ 074 58100 11 🛁 Annexe4 🛁

RATHMULLAN — Map 01 C6

Otway Saltpans ☎ 074 58319
9 holes, 4234yds, Par 64, SSS 60, Course record 60.
Club membership 92.
Visitors welcome.
Societies contact for details.
Green Fees IR£10 per day.
Facilities 🍸 🧥
Location W shore of Loch Swilly

Hotel ★ 59% Pier Hotel, RATHMULLAN
☎ 074 58178 & 58115 Fax 074 58115 10 🛁

ROSAPENNA — Map 01 C6

Rosapenna Downings ☎ 074 55301 Fax 074 55128
Dramatic links course offering a challenging round. Originally designed by Tom Morris and later modified by James Braid and Harry Vardon, it includes such features as bunkers in mid fairway. The best part of the links runs in the low valley along the ocean.
18 holes, 6271yds, Par 70, SSS 71.
Club membership 200.
Visitors no restrictions.
Societies must contact in advance.
Green Fees not confirmed.
Prof Simon Byrne
Designer Old Tom Morris
Facilities ⊗ 🍴 🛍 ☕ 🍸 🧥 🏠 🏌
& Leisure hard tennis courts.

Hotel ★★★ 63% Arnold's Hotel, DUNFANAGHY
☎ 074 36208 & 36142 Fax 074 36352 32 🛁

CO DUBLIN

BALBRIGGAN — Map 01 D4

Balbriggan Blackhall ☎ 01 8412229 Fax 01 8413927
A parkland course with great variations and good views of the Mourne and Cooley mountains.
18 holes, 5922mtrs, Par 71, SSS 71.
Club membership 650.
Visitors must contact in advance. With member only at weekends.
Societies must apply in writing.
Green Fees IR£16 per round (IR£18 bank holidays).
Designer Paramoir
Facilities ⊗ 🍴 🛍 ☕ 🍸 🧥 🏌
Location 1km S on N1

Hotel ★★★ 64% Boyne Valley Hotel & Country Club, Stameen, Dublin Rd, DROGHEDA
☎ 041 37737 35 🛁

BALLYBOUGHAL — Map 01 D4

Hollywood Lakes
☎ 01 8433406 & 8433407 Fax 01 8433002
A parkland course opened in 1992 with large USGA-type, sand-based greens and tees. There are water features on seven holes. The front nine requires accuracy while the second nine includes a 636yard Par 5.
18 holes, 6246mtrs, Par 72, SSS 72, Course record 67.
Club membership 450.
Visitors welcome Mon-Fri but may only play weekends pm.
Societies telephone then write in advance.
Green Fees IR£17 (IR£22 weekends & public holidays).
Cards VISA
Designer Mel Flanagan
Facilities ⊗ 🍴 🛍 🍸 🧥 🏠 🏌
Location 3m off main Dublin/Belfast road

Hotel ★★★ 69% Marine Hotel, Sutton Cross, DUBLIN 13 ☎ 01 8390000 26 🛁

BRITTAS — Map 01 D4

Slade Valley Lynch Park
☎ 01 4582183 & 4582739 Fax 01 4582784
This is a course for a relaxing game, being fairly easy and in pleasant surroundings.
18 holes, 5388mtrs, Par 69, SSS 68, Course record 65.
Club membership 800.
Visitors must contact in advance.
Societies telephone in advance.
Green Fees IR£15-IR£17 per round.
Prof John Dignam
Designer W Sullivan & D O Brien
Facilities ⊗ 🍴 🛍 ☕ 🍸 🧥 🏠 🏌
Location 9m SW of Dublin on N81

Hotel ★★★ 56% Downshire House Hotel, BLESSINGTON
☎ 045 865199 14 🛁 Annexe11 🛁

CASTLEKNOCK — Map 01 D4

Luttrellstown Castle ☎ 01 8089988 Fax 01 8089989
Set in the grounds of the magnificent 560-acre Luttrellstown Castle estate, this championship course has retained the integrity of a mature and ancient parkland. It is renowned for the quality of its greens and the log-built Clubhouse which provides excellent facilities.
18 holes, 6032mtrs, Par 72, SSS 73, Course record 66.
Club membership 400.
Visitors welcome.
Societies must phone in advance.
Green Fees not confirmed.
Cards MasterCard AMERICAN EXPRESS VISA
Prof Graham Campbell
Designer N Bielenberg
Facilities ⊗ 🍴 🛍 ☕ 🍸 🧥 🏠 🏌
& Leisure hard tennis courts, heated outdoor swimming pool, fishing, sauna, archery, clay pigeon shooting.
Location Porterstown rd

Hotel ★★★ 69% Finnstown Country House Hotel & Golf Course, Newcastle Rd, LUCAN
☎ 01 6280644 25 🛁 Annexe20 🛁

Cloghran Map 01 D4

Forrest Little ☎ 01 8401183
Testing parkland course.
18 holes, 5865mtrs, Par 70, SSS 70.
Visitors preferred weekday mornings.
Green Fees not confirmed.
Prof Tony Judd
Facilities
Location 6m N of Dublin on N1

Hotel ★★★ 69% Marine Hotel, Sutton Cross, DUBLIN 13 ☎ 01 8390000 26

Donabate Map 01 D4

Balcarrick Corballis
☎ 01 8436228 & 8436957 Fax 01 8436957
Splendid 18-hole parkland course located close to the sea. A strong prevailing wind often plays a big part on every hole. Many challenging holes, notably the 7th - nicknamed 'Amen Corner'.
18 holes, 6273mtrs, Par 73, SSS 71.
Club membership 600.
Visitors must contact in advance.
Societies telephone in advance.
Green Fees IR£13 (IR£20 weekends & bank holidays).
Designer Barry Langan
Facilities

Hotel B Forte Posthouse Dublin, Cloghran, DUBLIN ☎ 01 8444211 188

Beaverstown Beaverstown
☎ 01 8436439 & 8436721 Fax 01 8436721
Well wooded course with water hazards at more than half of the holes.
18 holes, 5855mtrs, Par 71, SSS 71, Course record 69.
Club membership 800.
Visitors may not play 12.30-1.30pm daily & must contact in advance to play on Wed, Sat or Sun.
Societies must contact in writing.
Green Fees not confirmed.
Facilities
Location 5m from Dublin Airport

Hotel B Forte Posthouse Dublin, Cloghran, DUBLIN ☎ 01 8444211 188

Corballis Public Corballis ☎ 01 8436583
Well maintained coastal course with excellent greens.
18 holes, 4971yds, Par 65, SSS 64.
Visitors no restrictions.
Societies apply in writing or telephone.
Green Fees IR£9 per round (IR£12 weekends).
Facilities

Hotel B Forte Posthouse Dublin, Cloghran, DUBLIN ☎ 01 8444211 188

Donabate Balcarrick ☎ 01 8436346 & 8436001
Level parkland course.
18 holes, 5704yds, Par 70, SSS 69, Course record 67.
Club membership 900.
Visitors welcome, weekdays & late Sunday afternoon.
Societies must apply in writing.
Green Fees not confirmed.
Prof Hugh Jackson
Facilities

Hotel B Forte Posthouse Dublin, Cloghran, DUBLIN ☎ 01 8444211 188

The Island Corballis
☎ 01 8436104 & 8436205 Fax 01 8436860
Links course on a promontory, with sea inlets separating some of the fairways. Accuracy as well as length of shots are required on some holes and sand hills provide an additional challenge.
18 holes, 6078mtrs, Par 71, SSS 72.
Club membership 800.
Visitors preferred on Mon, Tue & Fri. Telephone for appointment.
Societies must apply in advance.
Green Fees not confirmed.
Prof Kevin Kelliher
Designer Hackett/Hawtree
Facilities

Hotel B Forte Posthouse Dublin, Cloghran, DUBLIN ☎ 01 8444211 188

Dublin Map 01 D4

Carrickmines Carrickmines ☎ 01 2955972
Meadowland course.
9 holes, 6100yds, Par 71, SSS 69.
Club membership 500.
Visitors with member only Sat, Sun & bank holidays.
Societies contact for details.
Green Fees IR£20 per round (IR£23 Sun).
Facilities
Location 7m S of Dublin

Hotel ★★★ 61% Royal Marine Hotel, Marine Rd, DUN LAOGHAIRE ☎ 01 2801911 104

Castle Woodside Dr, Rathfarnham
☎ 01 4904207 Fax 01 4920264
A tight, tree-lined parkland course which is very highly regarded by all who play there.
18 holes, 5732mtrs, Par 70, SSS 68, Course record 63.
Club membership 1200.
Visitors welcome but may not play at weekends & bank holidays.
Societies must apply in writing 6 months in advance.
Green Fees IR£35 per round.
Prof David Kinsella
Designer Barcroft-Pickman & Hood
Facilities

Hotel ★★★★ 70% Jurys Hotel Dublin, Pembroke Rd, Ballsbridge, DUBLIN 4 ☎ 01 6605000 294

Clontarf Donnycarney House, Malahide Rd
☎ 01 8331892 Fax 01 8331933
The nearest golf course to Dublin city, with a historic building as a clubhouse, Clontarf is a parkland type course bordered on one side by a railway line. There are several testing and challenging holes including the 12th, which involves playing over a pond and a quarry.

18 holes, 5459mtrs, Par 69, SSS 68, Course record 67.
Club membership 1100.
Visitors welcome daily but must to contact in advance.
Societies Tue & Fri. Must contact in advance.
Green Fees IR£26 per round (IR£35 weekends & bank holidays).
Prof Joe Craddock
Designer Harry Colt
Facilities
Location 2.5m N via Fairview

Hotel ★★★ 67% Doyle Skylon Hotel, Drumcondra Rd, DUBLIN 9 ☎ 01 8379121 92

Corrstown Corrstown, Kilsallaghan
☎ 01 8640533 & 8640534 Fax 01 8640537
Orchard course plays over pleasant parkland and complimants the 18 hole River Course.
River: 18 holes, 6077mtrs, Par 72, SSS 71.
Orchard: 9 holes, 2792yds, Par 35.
Club membership 900.
Visitors advisable to contact in advance. May play weekends after 2pm.
Societies telephone or write in advance.
Green Fees not confirmed.
Cards
Prof Pat Gittens
Designer Eddie Connaughton
Facilities
Location W of Dublin Airport via St Margarets

Hotel ★★★ 67% Doyle Skylon Hotel, Drumcondra Rd, DUBLIN 9 ☎ 01 8379121 92

Deer Park Hotel & Golf Course Howth ☎ 01 8322624
Claiming to be Irelands largest golf/hotel complex, be warned that its popularity makes it extremely busy at times and only hotel residents can book tee-off times.
St Fintans: 9 holes, 3373yds, Par 37.
Deer Park: 18 holes, 6678yds, Par 72.
Grace O'Malley: 9 holes, 3105yds, Par 35.
Short Course: 12 holes, 1810yds, Par 36.
Club membership 200.
Visitors no restrictions. There may be delays especially Sun mornings.
Societies must contact by telephone.
Green Fees not confirmed.
Facilities
Location On right 0.5m before Howth Harbour

Hotel ★★★ 69% Marine Hotel, Sutton Cross, DUBLIN 13 ☎ 01 8390000 26

Edmonstown Edmondstown Rd, Edmondstown
☎ 01 4931082 Fax 01 4933152
A popular and testing parkland course situated at the foot of the Dublin Mountains in the suburbs of the city. An attractive stream flows in front of the 4th and 6th greens calling for an accurate approach shot.
18 holes, 5393mtrs, Par 70, SSS 70.
Club membership 750.
Visitors must contact in advance as there are daily times reserved for members. Limited times after 3.30pm weekends.
Societies must contact in advance.
Green Fees IR£25 per round (IR£30 weekends & bank holidays).
Cards

Prof Andrew Crofton
Designer McAllister
Facilities

Hotel ★★★ 68% Doyle Montrose Hotel, Stillorgan Rd, DUBLIN ☎ 01 2693311 179

Elm Park Golf & Sports Club Nutley House, Nutley Ln, Dennybrook ☎ 01 2693438
Interesting parkland course requiring a degree of accuracy, particularly as half of the holes involve crossing the stream.
18 holes, 5355mtrs, Par 69, SSS 68, Course record 64.
Club membership 1750.
Visitors must contact in advance.
Societies apply in advance.
Green Fees not confirmed.
Cards
Prof Seamus Green
Facilities
& Leisure hard and grass tennis courts.
Location 3m from city centre

Hotel ★★★★ 70% Jurys Hotel Dublin, Pembroke Rd, Ballsbridge, DUBLIN 4 01 6605000 294

Foxrock Torquay Rd, Foxrock ☎ 01 2895668 & 2893992
A well-treed parkland course.
9 holes, 5667mtrs, Par 70, SSS 69.
Club membership 650.
Visitors welcome but contact in advance, no green fees Tue & weekends.
Societies apply in writing to William Daly.
Green Fees not confirmed.
Prof David Walker
Facilities

Hotel ★★★ 61% Royal Marine Hotel, Marine Rd, DUN LAOGHAIRE ☎ 01 2801911 104

Grange Rathfarnham ☎ 01 4932889
Wooded parkland course which provides both interest and challenge.
18 holes, 5517mtrs, Par 68, SSS 69.
Visitors preferred on weekdays.
Green Fees not confirmed.
Prof W Sullivan
Facilities
Location 6m from city centre

Hotel ★★★ 68% Doyle Montrose Hotel, Stillorgan Rd, DUBLIN ☎ 01 2693311 179

Howth St Fintan's, Carrickbrack Rd, Sutton
☎ 01 8323055 Fax 01 8321793
A moorland course with scenic views of Dublin Bay. It is very hilly and presents a good challenge for the athletic golfer.
18 holes, 5618mtrs, Par 71, SSS 69.
Club membership 1200.
Visitors contact in advance. May not play Wed and weekends.
Societies must contact in advance.
Green Fees not confirmed.
Prof John McGuirk
Designer James Baird
Facilities ⊗ by prior arrangement by prior arrangement

Hotel ★★★ 69% Marine Hotel, Sutton Cross, DUBLIN 13 ☎ 01 8390000 26

Milltown Lower Churchtown Rd
☎ 01 4976090 Fax 01 4976008
Level parkland course on the outskirts of the city.
18 holes, 5638mtrs, Par 71, SSS 69, Course record 64.
Club membership 1400.
Visitors must contact in advance but may not play weekends.
Societies apply in writing.
Green Fees IR£35 Mon-Fri.
Cards
Prof John Harnett
Designer Freddie Davis
Facilities ⊗

Hotel ★★★★ 70% Jurys Hotel Dublin, Pembroke Rd, Ballsbridge, DUBLIN 4
☎ 01 6605000 294

Newlands Clondalkin 22 ☎ 01 4593157
Mature parkland course offering a testing game.
18 holes, 5714mtrs, Par 71, SSS 70.
Club membership 1000.
Visitors must contact in advance and may play Mon, Thu, Fri and Wed mornings only.
Societies must contact in writing.
Green Fees not confirmed.
Prof Karl O'Donnell
Facilities

Hotel ★★★ 67% Doyle Green Isle Hotel, Naas Rd, DUBLIN 22 ☎ 01 4593406 90

The Open Golf Centre Newton House, St Margaret's
☎ 01 8640324 Fax 01 8341400
A 27-hole Pay and Play parkland course that is testing for the low handicap golfer but not too intimidating for high handicapper.
18 holes, 5973yds, Par 71, SSS 69, Course record 66.
9 holes, 2370yds, Par 31.
Visitors no restrictions. Booking essential.
Societies telephone for booking form.
Green Fees IR£8.50 per 18 holes (IR£12.50 weekends & bank holidays).
Cards
Prof Roger Yates
Designer R Yates
Facilities
Location Adjacent to Dublin airport

Hotel ★★★ 69% Marine Hotel, Sutton Cross, DUBLIN 13 ☎ 01 8390000 26

Rathfarnham Newtown ☎ 01 4931201 & 4931561 Fax 01 4931561
Parkland course designed by John Jacobs in 1962.
9 holes, 2921mtrs, Par 36, SSS 70, Course record 69.
Club membership 674.
Visitors must contact in advance but may not play weekends.
Societies restricted to Mon, Wed & Fri.
Green Fees IR£22.50 per round.
Prof Brian O'Hara
Designer John Jacobs
Facilities
Hotel ★★★★ 70% Jurys Hotel Dublin, Pembroke Rd, Ballsbridge, DUBLIN 4
☎ 01 6605000 294

Royal Dublin North Bull Island, Dollymount
☎ 01 8336346 Fax 01 8336504
A popular course with visitors, for its design subtleties, for the condition of the links and the friendly atmosphere. Founded in 1885, the club moved to its present site in 1889 and received its Royal designation in 1891. A notable former club professional was Christie O'Connor, who was appointed in 1959 and immediately made his name. Along with its many notable holes, Royal Dublin has a fine and testing finish. The 18th is a sharply dog-legged par 4, with out of bounds along the right-hand side. The decision to try the long carry over the 'garden' is one many visitors have regretted.
18 holes, 6030mtrs, Par 72, SSS 71, Course record 65.
Club membership 800.
Visitors must contact in advance & have handicap certificate. May not play Wed, Sat until 4pm summer, Sun between 10.30-noon.
Societies must book one year in advance.
Green Fees IR£50 per round (IR£60 weekends & public holidays).
Cards
Prof Leonard Owens
Designer H S Colt
Facilities ⊗
Location 3.5m NE of city centre

Hotel ★★★ 66% Longfield's Hotel, Fitzwilliam St, DUBLIN 2 ☎ 01 6761367 26

St Anne's North Bull Island, Dollymount ☎ 01 8336471
Links course, recently extended from 9 holes to 18.
18 holes, 5652mtrs, Par 70, SSS 69.
Club membership 500.
Visitors telephone for restrictions.
Societies must apply in writing.
Green Fees not confirmed.
Facilities
Hotel ★★★ 66% Longfield's Hotel, Fitzwilliam St, DUBLIN 2 ☎ 01 6761367 26

St Margaret's Golf & Country Club St Margaret's
☎ 01 8640400 Fax 01 8640289
A championship standard course which measures nearly 7,000 yards off the back tees, but flexible teeing offers a fairer challenge to the middle and high handicap golfer. The modern design makes wide use of water hazards and mounding. The Par 5 8th hole is set to become notorious - featuring lakes to the left and right of the tee and a third lake in front of the green. Ryder Cup player,Sam Torrance, has described the 18th as 'possibly the strongest and most exciting in the world'.
18 holes, 6917yds, Par 73, SSS 73, Course record 69.
Club membership 200.

Visitors telephone in advance.
Societies apply in writing or telephone
Green Fees IR£40 per round.
Cards
Designer Craddock/Ruddy
Facilities
Location 9m NW of city centre

Hotel ★★★ 69% Marine Hotel, Sutton Cross, DUBLIN 13 ☎ 01 8390000 26

Stackstown Kellystown Rd, Rathfarnham
☎ 01 4942338 & 4941993
Pleasant course in scenic surroundings.
18 holes, 5925mtrs, Par 72, SSS 72, Course record 70.
Club membership 1042.
Visitors preferred Mon-Fri.
Societies telephone in advance and confirm in writing.
Green Fees not confirmed.
Prof Michael Kavanach
Facilities
& Leisure sauna.
Location 9m S of city centre

Hotel ★★★ 68% Doyle Montrose Hotel, Stillorgan Rd, DUBLIN ☎ 01 2693311 179

Sutton Cush Point, Burrow Rd, Sutton ☎ 01 8324875
Founded in 1890.
9 holes, 5226mtrs, Par 70, SSS 67.
Visitors welcome except for competition days, contact for further details.
Societies by prior arrangement.
Green Fees not confirmed.
Prof Nicky Lynch
Location Approx 7m NE of city

Swords Open Golf Course Balheary Av, Swords
☎ 01 8409819 Fax 01 8409819
Parkland course situated beside the River Broadmeadow in unspoilt countryside, 10 miles from Dublin.
18 holes, 5677mtrs, Par 71, SSS 70.
Club membership 350.
Visitors timesheet bookings available all year, telephone to book.
Societies book well in advance.
Green Fees IR£9 per round (IR£12 weekends and bank holidays).
Designer R Stillwell/T Halpin
Facilities
Hotel ★★★ 67% Doyle Skylon Hotel, Drumcondra Rd, DUBLIN 9 ☎ 01 8379121 92

DUN LAOGHAIRE Map 01 D4

Dun Laoghaire Eglinton Park, Tivoli Rd
☎ 01 2803916 Fax 01 2804868
This is a well wooded parkland course, not long, but requiring accurate club selection and placing of shots. The course was designed by Harry Colt in 1918.
18 holes, 5298mtrs, Par 69, SSS 68, Course record 63.
Club membership 1040.
Visitors may not play Sat until after 5pm. Must contact in advance.
Societies must apply in writing.
Green Fees IR£26 per day.
Prof Owen Mulhall
Designer Harry Colt
Facilities
Location 0.75m from town ventre and ferry port

Hotel ★★★ 61% Royal Marine Hotel, Marine Rd, DUN LAOGHAIRE ☎ 01 2801911 104

KILLINEY Map 01 D4

Killiney Ballinclea Rd ☎ 01 2852823 Fax 01 2852823
The course is on the side of Killiney Hill with picturesque views over south Dublin and the Wicklow Mountains.
9 holes, 5655mtrs, Par 70, SSS 70.
Club membership 450.
Visitors welcome Mon, Wed, Fri & Sun afternoons.
Green Fees IR£20 per round.
Prof P O'Boyle
Facilities

Hotel ★★★ 64% Fitzpatrick Castle Hotel, KILLINEY ☎ 01 2840700 112

KILTERNAN Map 01 D4

Kilternan Golf & Country Club Hotel
☎ 01 2955559 Fax 01 2955670
Interesting and testing course overlooking Dublin Bay.
18 holes, 4952mtrs, Par 68, SSS 68, Course record 68.
Club membership 819.
Visitors may not play before 1.30pm at weekends.
Societies apply in writing/telephone in advance.
Green Fees IR£16 (IR£20 weekends).
Cards
Prof Gary Hendley
Designer Eddie Hackett

Facilities & Leisure hard tennis courts, heated indoor swimming pool, fishing, sauna, solarium, gymnasium, ski club, indoor tennis, sauna & steam bath, jacuzzi, therapy & massage clinic.

Hotel ★★★ 64% Fitzpatrick Castle Hotel, KILLINEY ☎ 01 2840700 112

LUCAN Map 01 D4

Finnstown Fairways Finnstwon Country House Hotel, Newcastle Rd ☎ 01 6280644 Fax 01 6281088
A flat parkland 9-hole course based in grounds originally laid out in the 18th century. Very challenging 6th and 7th holes among many mature trees.
9 holes, 2695yds, Par 66, SSS 66.
Club membership 200.
Visitors time sheet in use, must reserve in advance.
Societies must reserve in advance.
Green Fees IR£15-£19 per day (IR£19 weekends).
Cards
Designer Robert Browne
Facilities
& Leisure hard and grass tennis courts, heated indoor swimming pool, solarium, gymnasium.
Location Off N4, 8 m W of Dublin

Hotel ★★★ 69% Finnstown Country House Hotel & Golf Course, Newcastle Rd, LUCAN ☎ 01 6280644 25 Annexe20

Hermitage Ballydowd ☎ 01 6265049 & 6268491
Part level, part undulating course bordered by the River Liffey and offering some surprises.
18 holes, 6034mtrs, Par 71, SSS 70.
Club membership 1100.
Visitors contact for details
Societies must telephone well in advance.
Green Fees not confirmed.
Prof Ciaran Carroll
Facilities

Hotel ★★★ 69% Finnstown Country House Hotel & Golf Course, Newcastle Rd, LUCAN ☎ 01 6280644 25 Annexe20

Lucan Celbridge Rd ☎ 01 6282106 Fax 01 6282929
Founded in 1897 as a nine hole course and extended to 18 holes in 1988, Lucan involves playing over a lane which bisects the 1st and 7th holes. The first nine is undulating while the back nine is flatter and features water hazards and a 538mtr 5 par 18th hole.
18 holes, 5958mtrs, Par 71, SSS 71.
Club membership 780.
Visitors may play Mon, Tue & Fri.
Societies must apply in writing.
Green Fees IR£20 per round.
Designer Eddie Hackett
Facilities

Hotel ★★★ 59% Lucan Spa Hotel, LUCAN ☎ 01 6280494 65

MALAHIDE Map 01 D4

Malahide Beechwood, The Grange ☎ 01 8461611 Fax 01 8461270
Splendid parkland course with raised greens and water hazards affecting many of the holes, demanding accuracy from tee to green.
Main Course: 18 holes, 5742mtrs, Par 69, SSS 68.
Club membership 1100.
Visitors must contact in advance.
Societies must contact in advance.
Green Fees IR£30 per 18 holes (IR£40 weekends & bank holidays). Mastercard/Amex/Visa accepted.
Prof David Barton
Designer E Hackett
Facilities
& Leisure putting green.
Location 1m from coast road at Portmarnock

Hotel ★★★★ 76% Portmarnock Hotel & Golf Links, Strand Rd, PORTMARNOCK ☎ 01 8460611 103

PORTMARNOCK Map 01 D4

PORTMARNOCK See page 451.

RATHCOOLE Map 01 D4

Beech Park Johnstown ☎ 01 4580522 Fax 01 4588365
Relatively flat parkland with heavily wooded fairways.
18 holes, 5730mtrs, Par 72, SSS 70, Course record 67.
Club membership 750.
Visitors restricted on some days, telephone in advance.
Societies apply in writing.
Facilities
Hotel ★★★ 69% Finnstown Country House Hotel & Golf Course, Newcastle Rd, LUCAN ☎ 01 6280644 25 Annexe20

RUSH Map 01 D4

Rush ☎ 01 8438177
Seaside borders three fairways on this links course. There are 28 bunkers and undulating fairways to add to the challenge of the variable and strong winds that blow at all times and change with the tides. There are no easy holes!
9 holes, 5598mtrs, Par 70, SSS 69.
Club membership 350.
Visitors restricted Wed, Thu, weekends & bankholidays.
Societies apply in writing.
Green Fees not confirmed.
Facilities
Hotel B Forte Posthouse Dublin, Cloghran, DUBLIN ☎ 01 8444211 188

SAGGART Map 01 D4

City West Hotel & Golf Resort
☎ 01 4588566 Fax 01 4588565
18 holes, 6822yds, Par 71, SSS 70, Course record 65.

▶

PORTMARNOCK

PORTMARNOCK *Co Dublin* ☎ 01 8462968
Fax 01 8462601 Map 01 D4

John Ingham writes: The night before our fourball tackled Portmarnock was spent, as I recall, in Dublin. Guinness in that city seems smoother, while the conversation with locals, ranged from why no southern Irish player ever won the Open to how such a small nation can boast so many great writers, wits and actors.

I can thoroughly recommend this preparation, prior to facing one of the world's great golfing challenges - providing you only intend playing eighteen holes in one day! Frankly, you will have to reach into the base of your golf bag to pull out every shot if you want to play to your handicap on this superb links.

An opening birdie, downwind, made me wonder what the fuss was about. Two hours later, with a backswing too fast and the breeze now something near a gale, I decided that a test of 7182 yards off the back tees was too man-size for me. Maybe it would be more enjoyable on a calm, summer evening!

I remember the course not for the way it humiliated me, but for the 1960 Canada Cup where I watched Sam Snead and Arnold Palmer winning with such skillful play. Even so, both took 75 in one round while scores by the mighty Gary Player ranged from 65 to 78.

There are no blind shots, unless you drive into sandhills. This is natural golf with no unfair carries off the tee and the only damage to your card is self-inflicted. True, there are a couple of holes of 560 yards and the 522-yard 16th is frightening as you tee up in a fierce wind.

It's incredible to think that Portmarnock was 'discovered' almost by accident in 1893 by a Mr Pickeman and the course architect, Ross. They had rowed a boat from Sutton to the peninsula where they came across a wilderness of bracken, duneland and natural-looking bunkers made by God. They were inspired to create the course, built a shack for a clubhouse and talked about the only real hazard left - a cow that devoured golf balls.

Today it's so very different - with a modern clubhouse filled with members delighted to belong to such an internationally well-known establishment.

Visitors contact in advance and confirm in writing. Restricted Saturday, Sunday and public holidays. Handicap certificate required
Societies must contact in advance
Green fees Monday-Friday (excluding Wed & public holidays) £IR70/85:
Facilities ⊗ ЭⅢ ⛳ Ψ (all day) ⛟ ⌂ ⛿ ☇ Professional (Joey Purcell)
Location 12m from Dublin. 1m from village down Golf Rd

27 holes Old Course: 18 holes, 7182 yds, Par 72, SSS 75, course record 64
New Course: 9 holes, 3478yds, Par 37

WHERE TO STAY AND EAT NEARBY

HOTELS:
PORTMARNOCK
★★★★ 76% Portmarnock Hotel & Golf Links. ☎ 01 8460611. 103 ⇌

Visitors time sheet in operation, telephone in advance.
Societies apply in writing/telephone in advance.
Green Fees IR£29 per 18 holes (IR£32 weekends).
Cards
Designer Christy O'Connor Jnr
Facilities
& Leisure fishing, sauna, solarium, gymnasium, horse riding, clay pigeon shoot.
Location Naas road, southbound N7

Hotel ★★★ 63% Bewley's Hotel at Newlands Cross, Newlands Cross, Naas Rd, DUBLIN 22 ☎ 01 464 0140 165

SKERRIES Map 01 D4

Skerries Hacketstown ☎ 01 8491567 Fax 01 8491591
Tree-lined parkland course on gently rolling countryside, with sea views from some holes. The 1st and 18th are particularly challenging. The club can be busy on some days, but is always friendly.
18 holes, 6081mtrs, Par 73, SSS 72.
Club membership 800.
Visitors must contact in advance but may not play at weekends.
Societies must contact well in advance in writing.
Green Fees IR£20 per round.
Cards
Prof Jimmy Kinsella
Facilities
Location E of Dublin-Belfast road

Hotel ★★★ 64% Boyne Valley Hotel & Country Club, Stameen, Dublin Rd, DROGHEDA ☎ 041 37737 35

TALLAGHT Map 01 D4

Ballinascorney Ballinascorney
☎ 01 4516430 Fax 01 4516430
Set in the valley of Glenasmole, this very scenic course offers a variety of terrain, where every hole is different with very few parallel holes, many would be considered feature holes.
18 holes, 5466yds, Par 69, SSS 67, Course record 63.
Club membership 500.
Visitors please contact in advance, welcome weekdays and weekends after 4pm.
Societies contact for details.
Green Fees IR£12 (IR£15 weekends & bank holidays).
Designer Eddie Hackett
Facilities
Location 8m SW of Dublin city centre, off the N7

Hotel ★★★ 67% Doyle Green Isle Hotel, Naas Rd, DUBLIN 22 ☎ 01 4593406 90

CO GALWAY

BALLINASLOE Map 01 B4

Ballinasloe Rosglos ☎ 0905 42126 Fax 0905 42538
Well maintained parkland course, recently extended from a par 68 to a par 72.
18 holes, 5865metres, Par 72, SSS 70.
Club membership 840.
Visitors preferably Mon-Sat, contact in advance.
Societies contact in advance.
Green Fees not confirmed.
Facilities

Hotel ★★★ 69% Hayden's Hotel, BALLINASLOE ☎ 0905 42347 48

BALLYCONNEELY Map 01 A4

Connemara ☎ 095 23502 & 23602 Fax 095 23662
This championship links course is situated on the verge of the Atlantic Ocean in a most spectacular setting, with the Twelve Bens Mountains in the background. Established as recently as 1973, it is a tough challenge, due in no small part to its exposed location, with the back 9 the equal of any in the world. The last six holes are exceptionally long and offer a great challenge to golfers of all abilities.
18 holes, 6611mtrs, Par 72, SSS 75, Course record 67.
Club membership 900.
Visitors advisable to book in advance.
Societies telephone in advance.
Green Fees May-Sep: IR£25; Oct-Apr IR£16.
Cards
Prof Hugh O'Neill
Designer Eddie Hackett
Facilities
Location 9m SW of Clifden

Hotel ★★★ 72% Abbeyglen Castle Hotel, Sky Rd, CLIFDEN ☎ 095 21201 36

GALWAY Map 01 B4

Galway Blackrock, Salthill
☎ 091 522033 Fax 091 529783
Designed by Dr Alister MacKenzie, this course is inland by nature, although some of the fairways run close to the ocean. The terrain is of gently sloping hillocks with plenty of trees and furze bushes to catch out the unwary. Although not a long course, it provided a worthy challenge as the venue of the Celtic International Tournament in 1984 and continues to delight the visiting golfer.
18 holes, 6376yds, Par 70, SSS 71, Course record 67.
Club membership 1050.
Visitors preferred on weekdays, except Tue.
Societies must apply in writing.
Green Fees IR£18 per round (£23 weekends).
Prof Don Wallace
Facilities
Location 2m W in Salthill

Hotel ★★★ 59% Lochlurgain Hotel, 22 Monksfield, Upper Salthill, GALWAY ☎ 091 529595 13

Glenlo Abbey Bushypark ☎ 091 526666 Fax 091 527800
A parkland course overlooking the magnificent Lough Corrib but only 10 minutes from the centre of Galway city. Nine fairways but large double green with two flags and four tee postions allows 18 diffent holes. The Par 3, 4th hole is on an island-like green extending into the lough.
9 holes, 6009mtrs, Par 71, SSS 71.
Visitors advisable to contact in advance at peak times.
Societies telephone in advance.
Green Fees IR£20 per 18 holes; IR£18 per 9 holes.
Cards
Prof Gary Todd
Designer Jeff Howes
Facilities
& Leisure fishing, clay pigeon, shooting, lake boating.
Location On N59 Galway/Clifden road 4km from Galway City Centre

Hotel ★★★★ Glenlo Abbey Hotel, Bushypark, GALWAY ☎ 091 526666 45

GORT Map 01 B3

Gort Kilmacduagh Rd, Castlequarter ☎ 091 632244
Replacing the original 9-hole course, this new 18-hole course, opened in June 1996, offers golfers a real challenge. The 564yd 9th and the 516yd 17th are played into a prevailing wind and the par 4 dog-leg 7th will test the best.
18 holes, 6538yds, Par 71, SSS 69.
Club membership 450.
Visitors advisable to telephone in advance.
Societies must contact in advance.
Green Fees IR£12 per day.
Designer Christy O'Connor Jnr
Facilities

Hotel ★★★ 67% Galway Ryan Hotel, Dublin Rd, GALWAY ☎ 091 753181 96

LOUGHREA Map 01 B3

Loughrea Bullaun Rd, Graigue ☎ 091 841049
An excellent parkland course with good greens and extended in 1992 to 18-holes. The course has an unusual feature in that it incorporates a historic souterrain (underground shelter/food store).
9 holes, 5261metres, Par 69, SSS 67, Course record 68.
Club membership 615.
Visitors contact in advance, may not generally play Sun.
Societies written application required. Anytime weekdays, 9-11.30 Sat, no play Sun.
Green Fees not confirmed.
Designer Eddie Hackett
Facilities

Hotel ★★★ 69% Hayden's Hotel, BALLINASLOE ☎ 0905 42347 48

MOUNTBELLEW Map 01 B4

Mountbellew Ballinasloe ☎ 0905 79259
A 9-hole wooded parkland course with 2 quarries and penalty drains to provide hazards.
9 holes, 5143mtrs, Par 69, SSS 66.
Visitors welcome.
Societies by prior arrangement.
Green Fees not confirmed.
Location Of N63 midway between Roscommon/Galway

Hotel ★★★ 69% Hayden's Hotel, BALLINASLOE ☎ 0905 42347 48

ORANMORE Map 01 B3

Athenry Palmerstown ☎ 091 794466 Fax 091 794971
Wooded parkland course, recently extended to 18 holes.
18 holes, 5552metres, Par 70, SSS 70, Course record 68.
Club membership 800.
Visitors advisable to telephone in advance, may not play Sun.
Societies must apply in writing for booking to the secretary.
Green Fees IR£15 weekdays(IR£18 weekends except Sun).
Cards
Prof Declan Cummingham
Designer Eddie Hackett
Facilities
Location 0.5m off Galway to Dublin road

Hotel ★★★ 67% Galway Ryan Hotel, Dublin Rd, GALWAY ☎ 091 753181 96

Galway Bay Golf & Country Club Renville
☎ 091 790500 Fax 091 792510
A championship golf course surrounded on three sides by the Atlantic Ocean and featuring water hazards on a number of holes. Each hole has its own characteristics made more obvious by the everchanging seaside winds. The design of the course highlights and preserves the ancient historic features of the Renville Peninsula. A spectacular setting distractingly beautiful and cleverly designed mix of holes presents a real golfing challenge, demanding total concentration.
18 holes, 6091mtrs, Par 72, SSS 71.
Club membership 400.
Visitors contact in advance.
Societies contact in advance.
Green Fees IR£30 per round (IR£35 weekends & bank holidays).
Cards
Prof Eugene O'Connor
Designer Christy O'Connor Jnr
Facilities
& Leisure sauna.
Location N18 S towards Limerick/Shannon, turn right for Oranmore at rdbt, through village, follow signs

Hotel ★★★ 69% Galway Bay Golf & Country Club Hotel, ORAMORE ☎ 091 790500 92

OUGHTERARD Map 01 B4

Oughterard ☎ 091 552131 Fax 091 552377
Well maintained parkland course with mature trees and shrubs. Some very challenging holes.
18 holes, 6150yds, Par 70, SSS 69, Course record 67.
Club membership 800.
Visitors contact secretary in advance.
Societies must apply in writing.
Green Fees IR£15 per day.

Cards
Prof Michael Ryan
Facilities
Location 1m from town on Galway road

Hotel ★★★ 63% Ross Lake House Hotel, Rosscahill, OUGHTERARD ☎ 091 550109 & 550154 Fax 091 550184 13

PORTUMNA Map 01 B3

Portumna ☎ 0509 41059
Parkland course with mature trees.
18 holes, 5474mtrs, Par 68, SSS 67, Course record 68.
Club membership 650.
Visitors restricted Sun & public holidays.
Societies must contact in writing.
Green Fees IR£12 per round.
Designer E Connaughton
Facilities
Location 2.5m from town on Woodford/Ennis road

Hotel ★★★ 60% County Arms Hotel, BIRR ☎ 0509 20791 24

RENVYLE Map 01 A4

Renvyle House Hotel ☎ 095 43511
Pebble Beach course at Renvyle House is an exceptionally demanding 9 hole course. Exposed to Atlantic winds, crosswinds are a regular feature. A lake comes into play on 3 holes on one of which is a drive over water. On 4 holes pebble beach and the sea demand precision.
9 holes, 2000yds, Par 32.
Visitors must contact in advance.
Societies contact in advance.
Green Fees not confirmed.
Prof Gus Murphy
Facilities
& Leisure hard tennis courts, heated outdoor swimming pool, fishing.

TUAM Map 01 B4

Tuam Barnacurragh ☎ 093 28993 Fax 093 26003
Parkland course with plenty of trees and bunkers.
18 holes, 5513mtrs, Par 72, SSS 70, Course record 72.
Club membership 800.
Visitors preferred Mon-Fri, must contact in advance.
Societies telephone/write in advance.
Green Fees IR£12 per round (IR£14 weekends).
Prof Larry Smyth
Designer Eddie Hackett
Facilities
Location 0.5m from town on Athenry road

Hotel ★★★★ 65% Ardilaun House Hotel, Taylor's Hill, GALWAY ☎ 091 521433 90

CO KERRY

BALLYBUNION Map 01 A3

BALLYBUNION See page 455.

BALLYFERRITER Map 01 A2

Ceann Sibeal ☎ 066 56255 Fax 066 56409
This most westerly golf course in Europe has a magnificent scenic location. It is a traditional links course with beautiful turf, many bunkers, a stream that comes into play on 14 holes and, usually, a prevailing wind.
18 holes, 6700yds, Par 72, SSS 71, Course record 72.
Club membership 432.
Visitors telephone in advance.
Societies must contact in advance.
Green Fees IR£27 per day; IR£21 per round.
Cards
Prof Dermot O'Connor
Designer Hackett/O'Connor Jnr
Facilities
Hotel ★★★ 72% Skellig Hotel, DINGLE ☎ 066 51144 115

CASTLEGREGORY Map 01 A2

Castlegregory Stradbally ☎ 066 39444
A links course sandwiched between the sea and a freshwater lake and mountains on two sides. The 3rd hole is visually superb with a 365yard drive into the wind.
9 holes, 2569mtrs, Par 68, SSS 68, Course record 67.
Club membership 200.
Visitors advisable to contact in advance.
Societies apply in advance.
Green Fees IR£14 per 18 holes.
Designer Dr Arthur Spring
Facilities
& Leisure fishing.
Hotel ★★★ 67% The Brandon Hotel, TRALEE ☎ 066 23333 160

GLENBEIGH Map 01 A2

Dooks ☎ 066 68205 Fax 066 68476
Old-established course on the sea shore between the Kerry mountains and Dingle Bay. Sand dunes are a feature (the name Dooks is a derivation of the Gaelic word for sand bank) and the course offers a fine challenge in a superb Ring of Kerry location.
18 holes, 6010yds, Par 70, SSS 68.
Club membership 750.
Visitors must contact in advance.
Societies contact in advance.
Green Fees IR£20 per round.
Cards
Facilities
Location On N70, between Killorglin and Glenbeigh

BALLYBUNION

BALLYBUNION *Co Kerry*

☎ 068 27146 Fax 068 23787 **Map 01 A3**

John Ingham writes: Since golf is a state of mind over muscle and a great day on the links is exhilarating, it is my view that memorable fairways tend not to be decorated with artificial lakes that are fun only for ducks and golf ball manufacturers.

Some of the best courses look natural, even though they may have been helped along by skilful architects such as Colt, Hawtree or Mackenzie. And in the Emerald Isle, it is entirely appropriate that, back in 1906, a Mr Murphy built Ballybunion on the West Coast of Ireland. Believe me, there are few greater adventures waiting to be tackled and not to play this old course is a crime.

In an American list of the world's top 100 courses, Ballybunion is in there at number eight and the reason is simple: it probably represents the ultimate links on as wild a stretch as you will find. The Atlantic waves crash into the shore and no golfer will ever feel closer to nature as he hunts his ball and flights it through crosswinds and breathtaking views. This course is a star even in a part of Ireland that is wall-to-wall golf courses of the highest calibre. The experience of taking on this classic will be remembered as long as you live.

There are now two courses at Ballybunion, separated only by a 19th hole that has heard all the wondrous stories before, as well as hosting such great names as Tom Watson, five times winner of the Open. Likeable Tom can't speak highly enough of the place and claims that before anyone builds a golf course, they should play Ballybunion.

Visitors must contact in advance.
Societies must book in advance
Green fees Old Course: £IR55 per round; Cashen Course: £IR30 per round. Both courses IR£72.
Facilities Professional (Brian O'Callaghan).
Leisure sauna
Location Sandhill Rd

36 holes. Old Course: 18 holes, 6603 yds, Par 71, SSS 72. Course record 67
Cashen Course: 18 holes, 6216 yds, Par 72

WHERE TO STAY AND EAT NEARBY

HOTELS:

BALLYHEIGE

★★★ 60% The White Sands ☎ 066 33102 81

TRALEE

★★★ 67% The Brandon ☎ 066 23333 160

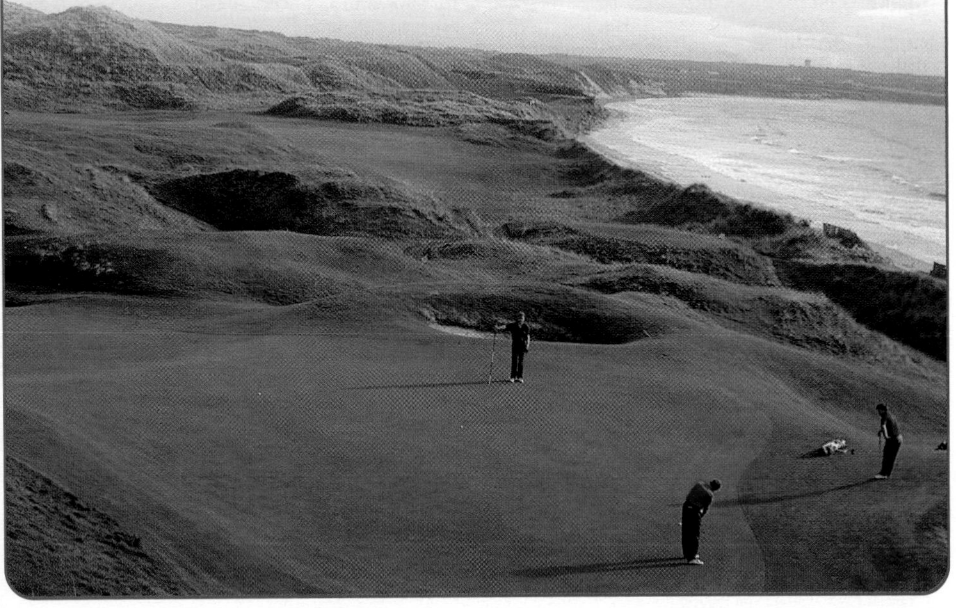

Hotel ★★★ 64% Gleneagle Hotel, KILLARNEY
☎ 064 31870 200

KENMARE Map 01 B2

Kenmare Kilgarvan Rd ☎ 064 41291 Fax 064 42061
Extended to a championship 18-hole course in 1993 this challenging parkland course enjoys a magnificent setting where the cascading waters of the Sheen and Roughty rivers join the Atlantic. Although it can be exacting on a good golfer, it is never unfair to the weak or the novice golfer.
18 holes, 5615yds, Par 71.
Club membership 400.
Visitors enquire for weekends.
Societies contact in advance.
Green Fees not confirmed.
Designer Eddie Hackett
Facilities by prior arrangement

Hotel ★★★★ Park Hotel Kenmare, KENMARE
☎ 064 41200 49

KILLARNEY Map 01 B2

Beaufort Churchtown, Beauford
☎ 064 44440 Fax 064 44752
A championship standard Par 71 parkland course designed by Dr Arthur Spring. This relatively new course is in the centre of south-west Ireland's golfing mecca. Old ruins of an 11th century castle dominate the back nine and the whole course is overlooked by the MacGillycuddy Reeks. The Par 3 8th and Par 4 11th are two of the most memorable holes.
18 holes, 6587yds, Par 71, SSS 72.
Club membership 150.
Visitors booking advisable for weekends.
Societies advance booking essential.
Green Fees IR£25 per round,IR£10 second round (IR£28, IR£12 weekends).
Cards
Designer Arthur Spring
Location 7m W of Killarney, off N72 w

Hotel ★★★ 64% Castlerosse Hotel, KILLARNEY
☎ 064 31144 110

Killarney Golf & Fishing Club Mahony's Point
☎ 064 31034 Fax 064 33065
Both of the courses are parkland with tree-lined fairways, many bunkers and small lakes which provide no mean challenge. Mahoney's Point Course has a particularly testing par 5, 4, 3 finish and both courses call for great skill from the tee. Killarney has been the venue for many important events, including the 1996 Curtis Cup, and is a favourite of many famous golfers
Mahony's Point: 18 holes, 5826mtrs, Par 72, SSS 72, Course record 68.
Killeen: 18 holes, 6006mtrs, Par 72, SSS 73, Course record 65.
Club membership 1300.
Visitors must contact in advance & have a handicap certificate.
Societies must telephone in advance.
Green Fees available on request.
Cards
Prof Tony Coveney
Designer H Longhurst/Sir Guy Campbell
Facilities
& Leisure sauna, gymnasium.
Location On N 72, Ring of Kerry road

Hotel ★★★★ 78% Aghadoe Heights Hotel, KILLARNEY ☎ 064 31766 60

KILLORGLIN Map 01 A2

Killorglin Stealroe ☎ 066 61979 Fax 066 61437
A parkland course designed by Eddie Hackett as a challenging but fair test of golf, surrounded by magnificent views.
18 holes, 6497yds, Par 72, SSS 71, Course record 68.
Club membership 280.
Visitors pre booking of tee time advisable, must be confirmed in writing.
Societies book by telephone, confirm in writing.
Green Fees IR£14 per 18 holes (IR£16 weekends & bank holidays).
Cards
Designer Eddie Hackett
Facilities
& Leisure fishing.
Location 3km from Killorglin, on N70 to Tralee

Hotel ★★★ 67% The Brandon Hotel, TRALEE
☎ 066 23333 160

PARKNASILLA Map 01 A2

Parknasilla ☎ 064 45122 Fax 064 45323
Recently re-designed course with new tees and greens on every hole. The view from the eighth tee is breathtaking with the green on the edge of the sea while the ninth tee is almost surrounded by water.
9 holes, 5400mtrs, Par 70, SSS 69.
Club membership 150.
Visitors may not play on competition days. Must contact in advance.
Societies must contact in advance.
Green Fees IR£15 per day.
Cards
Designer Arthur Spring
Facilities
& Leisure hard tennis courts, heated indoor swimming pool, sauna.
Location 2m E of Sneem village on Ring of Kerry road

Hotel ★★★★ 79% Great Southern Hotel, PARKNASILLA ☎ 064 45122 26 Annexe59

TRALEE Map 01 A2

Tralee West Barrow ☎ 066 36379 Fax 066 36008
The first Arnold Palmer designed course in Europe, the magnificent 18-hole links are set in spectacular scenery on the Barrow peninsula. Perhaps the most memorable hole is the par four 17th which plays from a high tee, across a deep gorge to a green perched high against a backdrop of mountains.

18 holes, 5939mtrs, Par 71, SSS 71, Course record 66.
Club membership 1098.

Visitors may play before 4.20pm on weekdays but only after 10.30am on Wed & 11am-1.30pm on Sat & bank holidays. Must have a handicap certificate and contact in advance.
Societies weekdays only; must contact in writing.
Green Fees IR£45; Early Bird Special IR£35 before 9am weekdays.
Cards
Designer Arnold Palmer
Facilities
Location 8m NW of Tralee on Spa-Fenit road

Hotel ★★★ 67% The Brandon Hotel, TRALEE ☎ 066 23333 160

Waterville Map 01 A2

Waterville House & Golf Links
☎ 066 74102 Fax 066 74482
On the western tip of the Ring of Kerry, this course is highly regarded by many top golfers. The feature holes are the par five 11th, which runs along a rugged valley between towering dunes, and the par three 17th, which features an exceptionally elevated tee. Needless to say, the surroundings are beautiful.
18 holes, 6549yds, Par 72, SSS 72, Course record 71.

Visitors must contact in advance.
Societies must contact secretary/manager in advance.
Green Fees not confirmed.
Prof Liam Higgins
Designer Eddie Hackett
Facilities
& Leisure heated outdoor swimming pool, fishing, sauna.

Hotel ★★★ 62% Derrynane Hotel, CAHERDANIEL ☎ 066 75136 75

CO KILDARE

Athy Map 01 C3

Athy Geraldine ☎ 0507 31729
A meadowland course approaching its centenary year having been founded in 1906.
18 holes, 6159yds, Par 72, SSS 69, Course record 69.
Club membership 475.

Visitors welcome weekdays. Must play with member at weekends.
Societies contact for infromation.
Green Fees IR£13.
Facilities
Location 2m N of Athy

Guesthouse QQQQQ Coursetown Country House, Stradbally Rd, ATHY ☎ 0507 31101 5

Carbury Map 01 C4

Highfield Highfield House ☎ 0405 31021 Fax 0405 31021
A relatively flat parkland course but with interesting undulations, especially by the fast flowing stream which runs through many holes. The 7th doglegs over the lake, the 10th is a great Par 5 with a challenging green, the 14th Par 3 is over rushes onto a plateau green (out of bounds on left) and the 18th Par 3 green is tucked between bunkers and a huge chestnut tree.
18 holes, 5707mtrs, Par 72, SSS 69.
Club membership 400.

Visitors welcome, must contact in advance for weekend play.
Societies telephone or apply in writing.
Green Fees not confirmed.
Designer Alan Duggan
Facilities by prior arrangement
Location 9m from Enfield

Hotel ★★★ 68% Keadeen Hotel, NEWBRIDGE ☎ 045 431666 55

Castledermot Map 01 C3

Kilkea Castle ☎ 0503 45555 Fax 0503 45505
A beautiful course opened in the summer of 1994 in the grounds of a 12th-century castle - visible from all over the course. The River Griese and two lakes create numerous water hazards.
18 holes, 6200mtrs, Par 71, SSS 71.

Visitors welcome contact for details.
Societies welcome, contact for details.
Green Fees on application.
Cards
Facilities
& Leisure hard tennis courts, heated indoor swimming pool, sauna, solarium.

Donadea Map 01 C4

Knockanally Golf & Country Club ☎ 045 69322
Home of the Irish International Professional Matchplay championship, this parkland course is set in a former estate, with a Palladian-style clubhouse.
18 holes, 6485yds, Par 72, SSS 72.
Club membership 500.

Visitors may not play on Sun 8.30am-noon.
Societies must contact in writing or telephone.
Green Fees not confirmed.
Prof Peter Hickey
Facilities
& Leisure fishing.
Location 3m off main Dublin-Galway road

Hotel ★★★ 59% Lucan Spa Hotel, LUCAN ☎ 01 6280494 65

Kildare Map 01 C3

Cill Dara Cill Dara, Little Curragh ☎ 045 521295
Only 1 mile from the famous Curragh racecourse, this 9-hole parkland course is unusual in having links type soil as well as plenty of trees.
9 holes, 5738mtrs, Par 71, SSS 70, Course record 64.
Club membership 450.

Visitors welcome, Wed is Ladies Day and may only play after 4pm Sun.
Societies apply in writing to Mr J Commins, Society Secretary.
Green Fees not confirmed.
Prof Mark O'Boyle
Facilities
Location 1m E of Kildare

Hotel ★★★ 68% Keadeen Hotel, NEWBRIDGE
☎ 045 431666 55

The Curragh Curragh
☎ 045 441238 441714 Fax 045 441714
A particularly challenging course, well wooded and with lovely scenery all around.
18 holes, 6035mtrs, Par 72, SSS 71, Course record 63.
Club membership 900.
Visitors preferred on Mon, Wed, Thu & Fri.
Societies apply in writing.
Green Fees £18 per day (£22 weekends & bank holidays).
Prof Gerry Burke
Facilities
Location Off N7 between Newbridge & Kildare

Hotel ★★★ 68% Keadeen Hotel, NEWBRIDGE
☎ 045 431666 55

KILL Map 01 D4

Killeen ☎ 045 866003
Set in pleasant countryside, the attractive course is characterised by its many lakes. It provides a challenge to test the skills of the moderate enthusiast and the more experienced golfer.
18 holes, 5561mtrs, Par 71, SSS 71.
Visitors please ring for tee-times
Societies must contact in advance.
Green Fees IR£17 per round (IR£20 weekends & bank holidays).
Cards
Designer Pat Ruddy
Facilities
& Leisure putting green, practice area.
Location Off N7 at Kill signposted

Hotel ★★★ 76% Barberstown Castle, STRAFFAN
☎ 01 6288157 22 Annexe4

NAAS Map 01 D4

Bodenstown Sallins ☎ 045 897096
The old course in Bodenstown has ample fairways and large greens, some of which are raised, providing more than a fair test of golf. The Ladyhill course is a little shorter and tighter, but still affords a fair challenge.
Bodenstown: 18 holes, 6132mtrs, Par 71, SSS 71.
Ladyhill: 18 holes, 5428mtrs, Par 71, SSS 68.
Club membership 700.
Visitors may not play on Bodenstown course at weekends.
Societies must contact by telephone.
Green Fees not confirmed.
Designer Richard Mather
Facilities
Location 4m from town near Bodenstown graveyard

Hotel ★★★ 56% Downshire House Hotel, BLESSINGTON
☎ 045 865199 14 Annexe11

Craddockstown Blessington Rd ☎ 045 897610
A gradually maturing parkland course featuring four testing par 3 holes, all over 180 metres in length, sand-based greens, and many trees. Easy walking.
18 holes, 5645yds, Par 71, SSS 69, Course record 67.
Club membership 600.
Visitors should ring in advance to verify tee times available, limited at weekends.
Societies apply in writing.
Green Fees IR£14 per round (IR£18 weekends).
Designer A Spring
Facilities
Location Off the main dual carriageway (N7/N97), head towards Naas, turn left on to Blessington Road

Hotel ★★★ 68% Keadeen Hotel, NEWBRIDGE
☎ 045 431666 55

Naas Kerdiffstown ☎ 045 897509 Fax 045 896109
Scenic parkland course with different tees for the return 9.
18 holes, 5663mtrs, Par 71, SSS 69, Course record 65.
Club membership 800.
Visitors may not play on Sun, Tue or Thu.
Societies must contact in advance.
Green Fees IR£15 per round (IR£20 weekends & bank holidays).
Facilities
Location 1m from town on Sallins-Johnstown road

Hotel ★★★ 56% Downshire House Hotel, BLESSINGTON
☎ 045 865199 14 Annexe11

Woodlands Cooleragh, Coill Dubh
☎ 045 860777 Fax 045 860988
Reconstructed 9-hole course opened in March 1997 offering an interesting challenge with completely new greens, tees and an extra 1000 yards coming into play
9 holes, 6408yds, Par 72, SSS 71.
Club membership 325.
Visitors must contact in advance.
Societies telephone in advance for details.
Green Fees not confirmed.
Designer Tommy Halpin
Facilities
Location Off the Clane/Edenderry road

Hotel ★★★ 68% Keadeen Hotel, NEWBRIDGE
☎ 045 431666 55

STRAFFAN Map 01 D4

Castlewarden
☎ 01 4589254 & 4589838 Fax 01 4588992
Founded in 1990, Castlewarden is maturing into a delightful parkland course with water features and excellent greens.
18 holes, 6502yds, Par 72, SSS 70.
Club membership 765.
Visitors welcome contact for details. Tues Ladies Day.
Societies by prior application.
Green Fees IR£17-IR£20 per 18 holes (IR£20 weekends).
Prof Gerry Egan
Designer Tommy Halpin

Facilities
Location Between Naas/Rathcoole

Hotel ★★★ 62% Ambassador Hotel, KILL
☎ 045 877064 36

The K Club ☎ 01 6017300 Fax 01 6017399
Known as The K-Club, this course is growing in reputation. Designed by Arnold Palmer, its 6,456 metre length is a challenge to even the best golfers. Covering 177 acres of prime Kildare woodland there are 14 man-made lakes as well as the River Liffey to create water hazards. There is the promise of a watery grave at the monster 7th (Par 5, 520 metres) and at the 17th the tee shot is to the green on the water's edge. There is also a practise area and driving range.
18 holes, 6163mtrs, Par 72, SSS 72, Course record 65.
Club membership 520.

Visitors contact in advance to book prefered tee times, restricted at members times.
Societies telephone & write in advance, societies not allowed on weekends & Wed afternoon.
Green Fees IR£120.
Cards
Prof Ernie Jones
Designer Arnold Palmer
Facilities
& Leisure hard tennis courts, heated indoor swimming pool, squash, fishing, sauna, solarium, gymnasium, clay pigeon shooting, archery.
Location From Dublin take N4 and axit R406, entrance to hotel on right in Straffan

Hotel ★★★★★ The Kildare Hotel & Country Club, STRAFFAN
☎ 01 6017200 36 Annexe7

CO KILKENNY

CALLAN Map 01 C3

Callan Geraldine ☎ 056 25136 & 25949
Meadowland.
18 holes, 6377yds, Par 72, SSS 70, Course record 67.
Club membership 500.
Visitors welcome. Must contact in advance.
Societies must apply in writing.
Green Fees IR£11.
Cards
Prof John O'Dwyer
Facilities
& Leisure fishing.
Hotel ★★★ 68% Hotel Kilkenny, College Rd, KILKENNY ☎ 056 62000 80

CASTLECOMER Map 01 C3

Castlecomer Drumgoole ☎ 056 41139
9 holes, 5923mtrs, Par 71, SSS 71, Course record 65.
Club membership 500.
Visitors welcome Mon-Sat book in advance.
Societies welcome Mon-Sat.
Green Fees not confirmed.
Facilities
Location 10m N of Kilkenny

Hotel ★★★ 67% Newpark Hotel, KILKENNY
☎ 056 22122 84

KILKENNY Map 01 C3

Kilkenny Glendine
☎ 056 65400 Fax 056 65400
One of Ireland's most pleasant inland courses, noted for its tricky finishing holes and its par threes. Features of the course are its long 11th and 13th holes and the challenge increases year by year as thousands of trees planted over the last 30 years or so are maturing. As host of the Kilkenny Scratch Cup annually, the course is permanently maintained in championship condition. The Irish Dunlop Tournament and the Irish Professional Matchplay Championship have also been held here.
18 holes, 5857mtrs, Par 71, SSS 70, Course record 64.
Club membership 1000.
Visitors must contact in advance.
Societies must contact in advance.
Green Fees IR£20 per day (IR£22 weekends & bank holidays).
Prof Noel Leahy
Facilities
Location 1m from centre on Castlecomer road

Hotel ★★★ 68% Hotel Kilkenny, College Rd, KILKENNY ☎ 056 62000 80

THOMASTOWN Map 01 C3

MOUNT JULIET GOLF COURSE See page 461.

CO LAOIS

ABBEYLEIX Map 01 C3

Abbeyleix Rathmoyle ☎ 0502 31450
A pleasant, parkland 9 hole course.
9 holes, 5626mtrs, Par 70, SSS 69.
Club membership 300.
Visitors welcome weekdays.
Societies apply in writing.
Green Fees IR£8 per day (IR£10 weekends).
Facilities ⊗ by prior arrangement by prior arrangement

Hotel ★★★ 67% Newpark Hotel, KILKENNY
☎ 056 22122 84

MOUNTRATH Map 01 C3

Mountrath Knockanina ☎ 0502 32558
A picturesque course at the foot of the Slieve Bloom Mountains in central Ireland. The 18 hole course has fine fairways and well bunkered greens, the river Nore flows through the course.
18 holes, 5493mtrs, Par 71, SSS 69, Course record 68.
Club membership 450.
Visitors check for availability at weekends, other days no problem but safer to check.
Societies must contact in advance.
Green Fees not confirmed.
Facilities ⊗ by prior arrangement by prior arrangement
Location 1.5m from town on Dublin-Limerick road

Hotel ★★★ 68% Keadeen Hotel, NEWBRIDGE
☎ 045 431666 55

PORTARLINGTON Map 01 C3

Portarlington Garryhinch ☎ 0502 23115 Fax 0502 23044
Lovely parkland course designed around a pine forest. It is bounded on the 16th and 17th by the River Barrow which makes the back 9 very challenging.
18 holes, 5673mtrs, Par 71, SSS 69.
Club membership 562.
Visitors welcome but restricted Tue-Ladies Day, Sat & Sun societies and club competitions.
Societies must apply in writing.
Green Fees IR£14 (IR£17 weekends).
Designer Eddie Hackett
Facilities ⊗
Location 4m from town on Mountmellick road

Hotel ★★★ 68% Keadeen Hotel, NEWBRIDGE
☎ 045 431666 55

PORTLAOISE Map 01 C3

The Heath ☎ 0502 46533 & 46622 (Pro shop)
One of the oldest clubs in Ireland. The course is set in pretty countryside and offers a good challenge.
18 holes, 5736mtrs, Par 71, SSS 69, Course record 69.
Club membership 800.
Visitors contact in advance, preferred on weekdays.
Societies apply in advance.
Green Fees not confirmed.
Prof Eddie Doyle
Facilities ⊗
Location 3m N on N7

Hotel ★★★ 68% Keadeen Hotel, NEWBRIDGE
☎ 045 431666 55

RATHDOWNEY Map 01 C3

Rathdowney ☎ 0505 46170 Fax 0505 46170
A 18 hole course recently opened. Undulating terrain, 12th & 15th are particularly tough par 4 holes, 6th is a challenging par 5 (550yds) into the prevaling wind. A good test for golfers of all abilities.
18 holes, 5894mtrs, Par 71, SSS 70.
Club membership 320.
Visitors welcome. Ladies have priority on Wed, Sat & Sun mornings are reserved for member & societies.
Societies must apply in writing and pay deposit to confirm booking.
Green Fees IR£10 per day.
Designer Eddie Hackett
Facilities
Location 0.5m SE. Follow signs from town square

Hotel ★★★ 68% Hotel Kilkenny, College Rd, KILKENNY ☎ 056 62000 80

CO LEITRIM

BALLINAMORE Map 01 C4

Ballinamore ☎ 078 44346
A very dry and very testing 9-hole parkland course along the Ballinamore/Ballyconnell Canal.
9 holes, 5680yds, Par 68, SSS 66, Course record 66.
Club membership 100.
Visitors restricted occasionally.
Societies must contact in writing.
Green Fees IR£10 per day.
Designer A Spring
Facilities
& Leisure fishing.

Hotel ★★ 64% Royal Hotel, BOYLE
☎ 079 62016 16

CO LIMERICK

ADARE Map 01 B3

Adare Manor ☎ 061 396204 Fax 061 396800
An 18-hole parkland course, Par 69, in an unusual setting. The course surrounds the ruins of a castle, a friary and an abbey. ▶

MOUNT JULIET

THOMASTOWN *Co Kilkenny*

☎ 056 73000 Fax 056 73019 **Map 01 C3**

Charlie Mulqueen writes: Nick Faldo and David Leadbetter are just two of the game's luminaries to have fallen in love with Mount Juliet, the only Jack Nicklaus designed golf course in Ireland. Faldo, perhaps, is somewhat biased given that he completed a hat-trick of Irish Open successes there in 1993.

Mount Juliet stands as a monument to the architectural ability of Nicklaus. The estate was acquired in the late '80s by Tim Mahony, who gave the Golden Bear a free hand. In return, Nicklaus delivered a 6641 yards, par 72 course of great quality and considerable charm. The hundreds of mature trees help to give the impression that the course has been here for centuries rather than just since 1991 - an occasion marked by a memorable exhibition between Nicklaus and Ireland's own great Christy O'Connor Senior. Since 1993 it has hosted the Murphy's Irish Open.

Mount Juliet's 'signature hole' arrives as early as the third, played from an elevated tee across an awesome lake to an island green. The golfer confronts a lot more water as the round progresses, especially at the perilous 13th, which has certainly proved unlucky for many of the contestants in each of the last three Irish Opens. Nor can even the best relax until they have completed the 470 yards, par four 18th. Again a lake comes into play all the way down the left and very frequently it requires two full woods to reach the long, narrow green. South African David Frost took 10 here in the opening round of the 1993 Irish Open and still hit back to finish third!

When the golf is over, the 1500 acres of the Mount Juliet estate offers many more attractions; horse riding, clay pigeon shooting or archery, fishing in the delightful River Nore or dinner in the superb 18th-century mansion transformed into a luxury hotel. And if the golf hasn't been up to requirements, up you get bright and early the following morning for a lesson on the magnificent David Leadbetter academy. Mount Juliet has it all - it's a must!

Visitors telephone in advance
Societies book in advance by telephone or in writing
Green fees Week days £IR65 (residents £IR35). Weekends £IR70 (residents £IR45)
Facilities ⊗ Professional (Mark Reid) golf academy
Leisure tennis, indoor swimming pool, private fishing, clay target shooting, archery, full leisure centre
Location Dublin/Waterford road (off the N9)

18 holes, 6641yds, Par72 SSS 72
Course record 65

WHERE TO STAY AND EAT NEARBY

HOTELS:

THOMASTOWN

★★★★ Mount Juliet Hotel,
☎ 056 24455. 32 Annexe 21

KILKENNY

★★★ 67% Newpark Hotel
☎ 056 22122. 84 (25 59)

★★★ 68% Hotel Kilkenny, College Rd
☎ 056 62000. 80

18 holes, 5800yds, Par 69, SSS 69.
Club membership 600.
Visitors welcome weekdays, weekends only by arrangement and subject to availability.
Societies by prior arrangement, preferably in writing.
Green Fees IR£15 per day.
Cards
Designer Ben Sayers/Eddie Hacket
Facilities
& Leisure fishing.
Hotel ★★★★ Adare Manor, ADARE ☎ 061 396566 64

LIMERICK Map 01 B3

Castletroy Castletroy
☎ 061 335753 & 335261 Fax 061 335373
Parkland course with out of bounds on the left of the first two holes. The long par five 10th features a narrow entrance to a green guarded by a stream. The par three 13th has a panoramic view of the course and surrounding countryside from the tee and the 18th is a daunting finish, with the drive played towards a valley with the ground rising towards the green which is protected on both sides by bunkers. In recent years the club has hosted the finals of the Irish Mixed Foursomes and the Senior Championships.
18 holes, 5793mtrs, Par 71, SSS 71.
Club membership 1038.
Visitors must contact in advance & have handicap certificate but may not play Sun or 1-2.30pm weekdays.
Societies apply in writing.
Green Fees IR£22 per day/round.
Cards
Facilities
Location 3m from city on Dublin road

Hotel ★★★★ 71% Castletroy Park Hotel, Dublin Rd, LIMERICK ☎ 061 335566 107

Limerick Ballyclough ☎ 061 415146 Fax 061 415146
Tree-lined parkland course which hosted the 1991 Ladies Senior Interprovincial matches. The club are the only Irish winners of the European Cup Winners Team Championship.
18 holes, 5938mtrs, Par 72, SSS 71, Course record 67.
Club membership 1300.
Visitors may not play after 4pm or on Tue & weekends.
Societies must contact in writing.
Green Fees IR£22.50 per round.
Cards
Prof John Cassidy
Designer A McKenzie
Facilities
Location 3m S on Fedamore Road

Hotel ★★★ 72% Jurys Hotel, Ennis Rd, LIMERICK ☎ 061 327777 95

Limerick County Golf & Country Club Ballyneety
☎ 61 351881 Fax 61 351384
Limerick County was designed by Des Smyth and presents beautifully because of the strategic locaton of the main features. It stretches over undulating terrain with one elevated section providing views of the surrounding countryside. It features over 70 bunkers with six lakes and several unique design features.
18 holes, 6712yds, Par 72, SSS 74, Course record 70.
Club membership 300.
Visitors welcome but prebooking essential.
Societies book by telephone or in writing.
Green Fees not confirmed.
Prof Philip Murphy
Designer Des Smyth
Facilities
& Leisure sauna.
Location 5m SE of Limerick on R512

Hotel ★★★ 62% Greenhills Hotel, Caherdavin, LIMERICK ☎ 061 453033 59

NEWCASTLE WEST Map 01 B3

Killeline Cork Rd ☎ 069 61600
Set in 160 acres of gently contoured parkland in the heart of the Golden Vale with views to the Galtee Mountains. Because of its design and many mature trees, accuracy in playing is the key to good scoring.
18 holes, 6007yds, Par 70, SSS 68.
Club membership 400.
Visitors welcome weekdays, by arrangement weekends.
Societies telephone in advance.
Green Fees not confirmed.
Facilities
Location 0.25m off main Limerick/Killarney route

Hotel ★★★ 78% Dunraven Arms Hotel, ADARE ☎ 061 396633 75

Newcastle West Ardagh ☎ 069 76500 Fax 069 76511
A new course set in 150 acres of unspoilt countryside, built to the highest standards on sandy free draining soil. A practice ground and driving range are included. Hazards on the course include lakes, bunkers, streams and trees. A signature hole is likely to be the Par 3 6th playing 185 yards over a lake.
18 holes, 6400yds, Par 71, SSS 72, Course record 67.
Club membership 730.

Visitors advisable to contact in advance, but available most days.
Societies contact in advance.
Green Fees IR£18 per day.
Cards
Designer Dr Arthur Spring
Facilities
Location 2m off N21 between Limerick & Killarney

Hotel ★★★★ Adare Manor, ADARE ☎ 061 396566 64

CO LONGFORD

LONGFORD Map 01 C4

County Longford Glack, Dublin Rd
☎ 043 46310 Fax 043 47082
A lovely 18-hole parkland course with lots of trees.
18 holes, 6044yds, Par 70, SSS 69, Course record 69.
Club membership 819.

Visitors very welcome, but advisable to telephone in advance for Tue and Sun play.
Societies by prior arrangement.
Green Fees not confirmed.
Facilities
Location E of town

Hotel ★★★ 60% Abbey Hotel, Galway Rd, ROSCOMMON ☎ 0903 26240 & 26505 Fax 0903 26021 25

CO LOUTH

ARDEE Map 01 D4

Ardee Townparks ☎ 041 53227
Pleasant parkland course with mature trees and a stream.
18 holes, 6100yds, Par 69, SSS 69.

Visitors may normally play on weekdays (except Wed).
Green Fees not confirmed.
Facilities
Hotel ★★★ 69% Ballymascanlon House Hotel, DUNDALK ☎ 042 71124 55

BALTRAY Map 01 D4

County Louth ☎ 041 22329 Fax 041 22969
Generally held to have the best greens in Ireland, this links course was designed by Tom Simpson to have well guarded and attractive greens without being overly dependant on bunkers. It provides a good test for the modern champion, notably as the annual venue for the East of Ireland Amateur Open.
18 holes, 6613yds, Par 73, SSS 71.
Club membership 1100.

Visitors must contact in advance.
Societies by prior arrangement.
Green Fees IR£40 per day/round (IR£50 weekends).
Cards
Prof Paddy McGuirk
Designer Tom Simpson
Facilities
& Leisure hard tennis courts.
Location 5m NE of Drogheda

Hotel ★★ 60% Conyngham Arms Hotel, SLANE ☎ 041 24155 16rm(15)

DUNDALK Map 01 D4

Ballymascanlon House Hotel
☎ 042 71124 Fax 042 71598
Now a testing 18-hole parkland course with numerous water hazards and two difficult holes through woodland, this very scenic course is set at the edge of the Cooley Mountains.
18 holes, 5548yds, Par 68, SSS 66.

Visitors must telephone in advance to check availability.
Societies booking by telephone or letter.
Green Fees IR£14 per 18 holes (IR£17 weekends & bank holidays).
Cards
Facilities
& Leisure grass tennis courts, heated indoor swimming pool, sauna, gymnasium.
Location 3m N of Dundalk on the Carlingford road

Hotel ★★★ 69% Ballymascanlon House Hotel, DUNDALK ☎ 042 71124 55

Dundalk Blackrock ☎ 042 21731 Fax 042 22022
A tricky course with extensive views.
18 holes, 6115mtrs, Par 72, SSS 72.
Club membership 1000.

Visitors must contact in advance and may not play Tue or Sun.
Societies must apply in writing in advance.
Green Fees not confirmed.
Prof James Cassidy
Facilities
& Leisure sauna.
Location 2.5m S on coast road

Hotel ★★★ 69% Ballymascanlon House Hotel, DUNDALK ☎ 042 71124 55

Killinbeg Killin Park ☎ 042 39303
Opened in 1991 and designed by Eddie Hackett, this undulating 18-hole parkland course has mature woodland and river features.
18 holes, 5293yds, Par 69, SSS 65.
Club membership 100.

Visitors no restrictions.
Societies apply by telephone or in writing in advance.
Green Fees IR£10 (IR£14 weekends & bank holidays).
Designer Eddie Hackett
Facilities by prior arrangement by prior arrangement
Location Bridge-a-Crinn

Hotel ★★★ 69% Ballymascanlon House Hotel, DUNDALK ☎ 042 71124 55

GREENORE Map 01 D4

Greenore ☎ 042 73212 & 73678 Fax 042 73678
Situated amidst beautiful scenery on the shores of Carlingford Lough, the trees here are an unusual feature on a links course. There are quite a number of water facilities, tight fairways and very good greens.
18 holes, 6514mtrs, Par 71, SSS 71.
Club membership 500.

Visitors must contact in advance at weekends. A letter of introduction is desirable, but not essential.
Societies must contact in advance.

Green Fees IR£14 per round (IR£20 weekends & bank holidays).
Facilities
Hotel ★★★ 69% Ballymascanlon House Hotel, DUNDALK ☎ 042 71124 55

TERMONFECKIN Map 01 D4

Seapoint ☎ 041 22333 Fax 014 22331
A very long championship links course of 7,000 yards with a particularly interesting 17th hole.
18 holes, 6339mtrs, Par 72, SSS 71.
Club membership 340.
Visitors phone in advance for restrictions.
Societies telephone in advance.
Green Fees IR£25 (IR£30 weekends & bank holidays).
Cards
Prof David Carroll
Designer Des Smyth
Facilities
Location 4m NE of Drogheda

Hotel ★★ 60% Conyngham Arms Hotel, SLANE ☎ 041 24155 16rm(15)

CO MAYO

BALLINA Map 01 B4

Ballina Mossgrove, Shanaghy
☎ 096 21050 Fax 096 21050
Undulating but mostly flat inland course.
18 holes, 6103yds, Par 71, SSS 69, Course record 69.
Club membership 478.
Visitors welcome but may not play Sun before 3.30pm. Restrictions apply depending on competitions/society visits.
Societies apply in writing or telephone in advance.
Green Fees IR£12 per day (IR£16 weekends & bank holidays).
Cards
Designer E Hackett
Facilities
Location 1m outside town on Bonnocolon Rd

BALLINROBE Map 01 B4

Ballinrobe Cloonagashel ☎ 092 41118 Fax 092 41889
A championship parkland 18 hole course, set in the mature woodlands of a historic estate at Cloonacastle. The layout of the course incorporates seven man made lakes with the river Robe flowing at the back of the 3rd and 5th greens. Ballinrobe is full of charm and character typified by the 19th century period residence now used as the clubhouse.
18 holes, 6043mtrs, Par 73, SSS 72, Course record 69.
Club membership 470.
Visitors welcome daily, telephone to reserve Tee-time.
Societies must telephone or write to Secretary in advance.
Green Fees IR£15-IR£18.
Cards
Prof David Kearney
Designer Eddie Hackett
Facilities
Location Off N84 onto R331 to Claremorris

Hotel ★★★ 65% Breaffy House Hotel, CASTLEBAR ☎ 094 22033 62

BALLYHAUNIS Map 01 B4

Ballyhaunis Coolnaha ☎ 0907 30014 Fax 094 81829
Undulating parkland course with 9 holes, 10 greens and 18 tees.
9 holes, 5413mtrs, Par 70, SSS 68, Course record 68.
Club membership 340.
Visitors welcome all times but must avoid members competitions on Sun & Thu.
Societies must apply in writing or telephone.
Green Fees IR£10 per day.
Facilities by prior arrangement by prior arrangement
Location 3m N on N83

Hotel ★★★ 65% Breaffy House Hotel, CASTLEBAR ☎ 094 22033 62

BELMULLET Map 01 A5

Carne Carne ☎ 097 82292 Fax 097 81477
18 holes, 6119mtrs, Par 72, SSS 72, Course record 72.
Club membership 420.
Visitors welcome, booking essential to guarantee tee-time.
Societies booking advisable.
Green Fees IR£12.50-IR£20 per day.
Designer Eddie Hackett
Facilities
Location 2m from Belmullet

CASTLEBAR Map 01 B4

Castlebar Hawthorn, Rocklands
☎ 094 21649 Fax 094 26088
Mature testing treelined parkland course.
18 holes, 5698mtrs, Par 71, SSS 70, Course record 67.
Club membership 800.
Visitors very welcome weekdays, must contact in advance for weekend play.
Societies must contact in advance.
Green Fees not confirmed.
Facilities
Location 1m from town on Belcarra road

Hotel ★★★ 65% Breaffy House Hotel, CASTLEBAR ☎ 094 22033 62

CLAREMORRIS Map 01 B4

Claremorris Castlemagarrett ☎ 094 71527
A 9-hole parkland course on hilly terrain. A new 18-hole course is due to open in 1998 and will feature plenty of mature trees and numerous water hazards.
18 holes, 6600mtrs, Par 73, SSS 72.
Club membership 300.
Visitors may play weekdays and weekends on request Contact Willie Feeley 094 71868
Societies welcome weekdays, contact 094 62554 for details.

Green Fees IR£12 per 18 holes (IR£15 weekends).
Cards
Designer Tom Craddock
Facilities
Location 1.5m from town, on N17 S of Claremorris

Hotel ★★★ 57% Belmont Hotel, KNOCK
☎ 094 88122 49

KEEL Map 01 A4

Achill Achill Island, Westport ☎ 098 43456
Seaside links in a scenic location on the edge of the Atlantic Ocean.
9 holes, 2723yds, Par 70, SSS 66, Course record 69.
Club membership 170.
Visitors welcome but cannot play on some Sundays
Societies must write or telephone in advance.
Green Fees not confirmed.
Facilities

Hotel ★★★ 65% Hotel Westport, The Demesne, Newport Rd, WESTPORT
☎ 098 25122 129

SWINFORD Map 01 B4

Swinford Brabazon Park ☎ 094 51378
A pleasant parkland course with good views of the beautiful surrounding countryside.
9 holes, 5542mtrs, Par 70, SSS 68.
Club membership 420.
Visitors must contact in advance in peak season.
Societies must apply in writing or telephone in advance.
Green Fees IR£10 per day.
Facilities
& Leisure squash, fishing.
Hotel ★★★ 65% Breaffy House Hotel, CASTLEBAR ☎ 094 22033 62

WESTPORT Map 01 B4

Westport Carrowholly ☎ 098 28262 Fax 098 27217
This is a beautiful course with wonderful views of Clew Bay, with its 365 islands, and the holy mountain called Croagh Patrick, famous for the annual pilgrimage to its summit. Golfers indulge in a different kind of penance on this challenging course with many memorable holes. Perhaps the most exciting is the par five 15th, 580 yards long and featuring a long carry from the tee over an inlet of Clew Bay.
18 holes, 6667yds, Par 73, SSS 71, Course record 65.
Club membership 750.
Visitors must contact in advance.
Societies apply in writing or telephone well in advance.
Green Fees Summer: IR£18 per round; Winter (Nov-Feb) IR£13 per round (IR£23/IR£17 weekends).
Prof Alex Mealia
Designer Fred Hawtree
Facilities
Location 2.5m from town

Hotel ★★★ 65% Hotel Westport, The Demesne, Newport Rd, WESTPORT
☎ 098 25122 129

CO MEATH

BETTYSTOWN Map 01 D4

Laytown & Bettystown ☎ 041 27170 Fax 014 28506
A very competitive and trying links course, home of famous golfer, Des Smyth.
18 holes, 5652mtrs, Par 71, SSS 70.
Club membership 950.
Visitors may not play 1-2pm. Must contact in advance.
Societies must contact in writing.
Green Fees IR£21 per day (IR£26 weekends).
Cards
Prof Robert J Browne
Facilities
& Leisure tennis courts.

Hotel ★★ 60% Conyngham Arms Hotel, SLANE
☎ 041 24155 16rm(15)

DUNSHAUGHLIN Map 01 D4

Black Bush Thomastown ☎ 01 8250021 Fax 01 8250400
Three 9-hole courses, giving three possible 18-hole combinations, set in lovely parkland, with a lake providing a hazard at the 1st. Recently added creeks, trees and bunkers make for challenging and accurate shot-making.
Course 1: 18 holes, 6930yds, Par 73, SSS 72.
Course 2: 9 holes, 3400yds, Par 35, SSS 34.
Club membership 950.
Visitors must contact in advance but cannot play 1-2pm weekdays.
Societies advance booking required.
Green Fees IR£16 per 18 holes (IR£22 weekends); IR£7 per 9 holes (IR£8 weekends).
Cards
Prof Shane O'Grady
Designer Bobby Browne
Facilities
Location 1.5m from village on Dunshaughlin-Ratoath raod

Hotel ★★★ 69% Finnstown Country House Hotel & Golf Course, Newcastle Rd, LUCAN
☎ 01 6280644 25 Annexe20

KELLS Map 01 C4

Headfort ☎ 046 40857 40146 Fax 046 49282
A delightful parkland course which is regarded as one of the best of its kind in Ireland. There are ample opportunities for birdies, but even if these are not achieved, Headfort provides for a most pleasant game.
18 holes, 6007mtrs, Par 72, SSS 71, Course record 67.
Club membership 680.
Visitors restricted Tues Ladies Day. Must contact in advance.
Societies must apply in writing.
Green Fees IR£18 (IR£22 weekends & bank holidays).
Cards
Prof Brendan McGovern
Facilities

Hotel ★★★ 59% Ardboyne Hotel, Dublin Rd, NAVAN ☎ 046 23119 27

KILCOCK Map 01 C4

Kilcock Gallow ☎ 01 6287283 Fax 01 6284294
A parkland course with wide, gently undulating fairways, flat greens and light rough only.
18 holes, 5775mtrs, Par 71, SSS 70, Course record 69.
Club membership 600.

Visitors must contact in advance for weekends, no problem weekdays.
Societies telephone for dates available.
Green Fees IR£11 (IR£13 weekends).
Designer Eddie Hackett
Facilities ⊗)Ⅲ ₺ ☕ ♀ ⛭ ✎ ⛳ ✓
Location 2m from end of M4

Hotel ★★★ 59% Lucan Spa Hotel, LUCAN ☎ 01 6280494 65 ⇌ ⌐

NAVAN Map 01 C4

Royal Tara Bellinter
☎ 046 25508 & 25244 Fax 046 25508
Pleasant parkland course offering plenty of variety. Situated close to the Hill of Tara, the ancient seat of the Kings of Ireland.
New Course: 18 holes, 5757mtrs, Par 71, SSS 70.
Bellinter Nine: 9 holes, 3184yds, Par 35, SSS 35.
Club membership 1000.

Visitors prior arrangement is advisable. Tue is ladies day.
Societies apply in writing or telephone.
Green Fees IR£18 per round (IR£22 weekends & bank holidays).
Prof Adam Whiston
Facilities ⊗)Ⅲ ₺ ☕ ♀ ⛭ ⌂ ↑ ✓
Location 6m from town on N3

Hotel ★★★ 59% Ardboyne Hotel, Dublin Rd, NAVAN ☎ 046 23119 27 ⇌ ⌐

TRIM Map 01 C4

County Meath Newtownmoynagh
☎ 046 31463 Fax 046 37554
Originally a 9-hole course opened in 1971, it was extended to 18-holes in 1990. It is maturing into a very challenging and formidable course with four testing Par 5's. At present new sand-based greens are under construction. Luxurious clubhouse with panoramic views across the course.
18 holes, 6720mtrs, Par 73, SSS 72.
Club membership 900.

Visitors welcome; some restrictions telephone for details.
Societies not Sun, enquiries welcome.
Green Fees IR£15 (IR18 weekends & bank holidays).
Designer Eddie Hackett/Tom Craddock
Facilities ⊗)Ⅲ ₺ ☕ ♀ ⛭ ✓
Location 3m outside Trim on Trim/Longwood rd

Hotel ★★ 60% Conyngham Arms Hotel, SLANE ☎ 041 24155 16rm(15 ⇌ ⌐)

A comprehensive list of driving ranges is given at the back of this guide. See page 479

CO MONAGHAN

CARRICKMACROSS Map 01 C4

Mannan Castle Donaghmoyne
☎ 042 63308 Fax 042 63195
Parkland and picturesque, the course starts with a Par 3, then a dogleg Par 4, next a Par 5 with majestic cypress trees as a back drop to the green. The 4th needs a good tee shot to make the approach shot to the green. The long Par 5 5th requires a straight hitter; the 6th doglegs left and the 7th overlook the whole course. Downhill to the 8th with trouble on the right and straight and long into the 9th.
9 holes, 5900mtr, Par 72, SSS 70.
Club membership 477.

Visitors may play anytime except competition times Sat, Sun & Wed from 2-2.30pm.
Societies apply in writing to the secretary.
Green Fees IR£10 per day.
Designer F Ainsworth
Facilities ₺ ☕ ♀ ⛭
Location 4m N

Hotel ★★★ 69% Ballymascanlon House Hotel, DUNDALK ☎ 042 71124 55 ⇌

Nuremore ☎ 042 61438 & 64016 Fax 042 61853
Picturesque parkland course of championship length incorporating the drumlins and lakes which are a natural feature of the Monaghan countryside. Precision is required on the 10th to drive over a large lake and between a narrow avenue of trees. Signature hole 18th.
18 holes, 6400yds, Par 72, SSS 70, Course record 67.
Club membership 150.

Visitors welcome all times but must contact Maurice Cassidy in advance.
Societies must contact in advance.
Green Fees IR£20 per day (IR£25 weekends & bank holidays).
Cards [MasterCard] [VISA]
Prof Maurice Cassidy
Designer Eddie Hackett
Facilities ⊗)Ⅲ ₺ ☕ ♀ ⛭ ⌂ ↑ ⇌ ✎ ⛳ ✓
& Leisure hard tennis courts, heated indoor swimming pool, squash, fishing, sauna, gymnasium.
Location S on Dublin road N2

Hotel ★★★★ 73% Nuremore Hotel, CARRICKMACROSS ☎ 042 61438 69rm

CASTLEBLAYNEY Map 01 C4

Castleblayney Onomy ☎ 042 46570
Scenic course on Muckno Park estate, adjacent to Muckno Lake and Blayney Castle.
9 holes, 5378yds, Par 68, SSS 66, Course record 68.
Club membership 275.

Visitors no visitors allowed during major weekend competitions.
Societies must contact in advance.
Green Fees IR£8 per day (IR£12 weekends & bank holidays).
Designer Bobby Browne
Facilities ₺ ☕ ♀ ⛭
& Leisure hard tennis courts, fishing.

Hotel ★★★ 69% Ballymascanlon House Hotel, DUNDALK ☎ 042 71124 55

Clones — Map 01 C5

Clones Hilton Park ☎ 047 56017 Fax 042 42333
Parkland course set in Drumlin country. Due to limestone belt, the course is very dry and playable all year round. There is a timesheet in operation on Saturday and Sunday.
9 holes, 5206mtrs, Par 68, SSS 67, Course record 62.
Club membership 329.

Visitors must contact in advance.
Societies apply in writing.
Green Fees IR£10 per day.
Facilities
Location 3m from Clones on Scotshouse rd

Hotel ★★★ 65% Four Seasons Hotel & Leisure Club, Coolshannagh, MONAGHAN ☎ 047 81888 44

Monaghan — Map 01 C5

Rossmore Rossmore Park, Cootehill Rd ☎ 047 81316
An undulating 18-hole parkland course amidst beautiful countryside.
18 holes, 5534mtrs, Par 70, SSS 68, Course record 62.
Club membership 700.

Visitors must contact in advance, tel club house: 047 81316.
Societies must apply in writing.
Green Fees not confirmed.
Designer Des Smyth
Facilities
Location 2m S on Cootehill road

Hotel ★★★ 65% Four Seasons Hotel & Leisure Club, Coolshannagh, MONAGHAN ☎ 047 81888 44

CO OFFALY

Birr — Map 01 C3

Birr The Glenns ☎ 0509 20082
The course has been laid out over undulating parkland utilising the natural contours of the land, which were created during the ice age. The sandy subsoil means that the course is playable all year round.
18 holes, 5700mtrs, Par 70, SSS 70, Course record 62.
Club membership 750.

Visitors contact in advance,
Societies advance contact to secretary.
Green Fees not confirmed.
Facilities
Hotel ★★★ 60% County Arms Hotel, BIRR ☎ 0509 20791 24

Entries with a shaded background identify courses that are considered to be particularly interesting

Edenderry — Map 01 C4

Edenderry ☎ 0405 31072
A most friendly club which offers a relaxing game in pleasant surroundings. In 1992 the course was extended to 18 holes.
18 holes, 6029mtrs, Par 72, SSS 72, Course record 66.
Club membership 700.

Visitors restricted Thu & weekends, ring for times.
Societies may not play on Thu & Sun; must contact the secretary in writing.
Green Fees IR£12 (IR£14 weekends & bank holidays).
Designer Havers/Hackett
Facilities

Tullamore — Map 01 C4

Tullamore Brookfield ☎ 0506 21439 Fax 0506 41806
Well wooded parkland course.
18 holes, 6322yds, Par 70, SSS 70, Course record 65.
Club membership 989.

Visitors must contact in advance, restricted on Tue & at weekends.
Societies must contact in writing.
Green Fees IR£16 (IR£20 weekends & bank holidays).
Prof Donagh McArdle
Designer James Braid/Paddy Merrigam
Facilities
Location 2.5m SW on Kinnity road

Hotel ★★★ 64% Prince Of Wales Hotel, ATHLONE ☎ 0902 72626 73

CO ROSCOMMON

Athlone — Map 01 C4

Athlone Hodson Bay ☎ 0902 92073
A picturesque course with a panoramic view of Lough Ree. Overall, it is a tight, difficult course with some outstanding holes and is noted for its magnificent greens.
18 holes, 5935mtrs, Par 71, SSS 70.
Club membership 1000.

Visitors must contact in advance.
Societies apply in writing.
Green Fees not confirmed.
Prof Martin Quinn
Facilities
Location 4m from town beside Lough Ree

Hotel ★★★ 69% Hodson Bay Hotel, Hodson Bay, ATHLONE ☎ 0902 92444 97

Ballaghaderreen — Map 01 B4

Ballaghaderreen ☎ 0907 60295
Mature 9-hole course with an abundance of trees. Accuracy off the tee is vital for a good score. Small protected greens require a good short-iron plan. The Par 3, 2nd hole at 178 yards has ruined many a good score.
9 holes, 5727yds, Par 70, SSS 66.
Club membership 250. ▶

Visitors no restrictions.
Societies apply in writing or telephone during office hours.
Green Fees IR£10 per day.
Designer Paddy Skerritt
Facilities
Location 2m S of town

Hotel ★★ 64% Royal Hotel, BOYLE ☎ 079 62016 16

BOYLE Map 01 B4

Boyle Roscommon Rd ☎ 079 62594
Situated on a low hill and surrounded by beautiful scenery, this is an undemanding course where, due to the generous fairways and semi-rough, the leisure golfer is likely to finish the round with the same golf ball.
9 holes, 5324yds, Par 67, SSS 66, Course record 65.
Club membership 260.
Visitors no restrictions.
Societies must contact in writing.
Green Fees IR£10 per day.
Designer E Hackett
Facilities
Location 2m from Boyle on the Roscommon road

Hotel ★★ 64% Royal Hotel, BOYLE ☎ 079 62016 16

CARRICK-ON-SHANNON Map 01 C4

Carrick-on-Shannon Woodbrook ☎ 079 67015
A pleasant 9-hole course overlooking the River Shannon.
9 holes, 5571mtrs, Par 70, SSS 68.
Club membership 400.
Visitors contact in advance.
Societies must contact in advance.
Green Fees IR£12 per day.
Designer Eddie Hackett
Facilities
Location 4m W beside N4

Hotel ★★ 64% Royal Hotel, BOYLE ☎ 079 62016 16

CASTLEREA Map 01 B4

Castlerea Clonalis ☎ 0907 20068 & 20705
The clubhouse is virtually at the centre of Castlerea course with 7 tees visible. A pleasant parkland course incorporating part of the River Francis very near the centre of town.
9 holes, 4974mtrs, Par 68, SSS 66, Course record 62.
Club membership 234.
Visitors welcome, but Sunday by arrangement only.
Societies contact for details.
Green Fees IR£10 per day.
Facilities
Location On Dublin/Castlebar road

Hotel ★★★ 60% Abbey Hotel, Galway Rd, ROSCOMMON ☎ 0903 26240 & 26505 Fax 0903 26021 25

ROSCOMMON Map 01 B4

Roscommon Mote Park
☎ 0903 26382 & 26931 Fax 0903 26043
Located on the rolling pastures of the old Mote Park estate, this recently extended 18-hole course successfully blends the old established nine holes with an exciting and equally demanding new 9-hole lay-out. Numerous water hazards, notably on the tricky 13th, multi-tiered greens and an excellent irrigation to give an all-weather surface.
18 holes, 6290mtrs, Par 71, SSS 70, Course record 64.
Club membership 600.
Visitors contact in advance.
Societies apply in writing.
Green Fees IR£15 per day; IR£75 per week.
Facilities
Location 0.5m S of Roscommon town

Hotel ★★★ 60% Abbey Hotel, Galway Rd, ROSCOMMON ☎ 0903 26240 & 26505 Fax 0903 26021 25

STROKESTOWN Map 01 C4

Strokestown Cloonfinlough ☎ 078 33323 & 33084
Picturesque 9-hole course set in parkland with fine views of Cloonfinlough Lake. The three Par 3's are long and quite testing.
9 holes, 2615mtrs, Par 68.
Club membership 250.
Visitors may play any times except during competitions.
Societies apply in writing or telephone at least 2 weeks in advance.
Green Fees not confirmed.
Facilities
& Leisure fishing.
Location 1.5m from Strokestown

Hotel ★★★ 60% Abbey Hotel, Galway Rd, ROSCOMMON ☎ 0903 26240 & 26505 Fax 0903 26021 25

CO SLIGO

BALLYMOTE Map 01 B4

Ballymote Ballinascarrow ☎ 071 83158 & 83089
Although Ballymote was founded in 1940, it has a new course only opened in July 1993. This is a 9-hole parkland course with some trees situated in a spacious with a wonderful view of Ballinascarow Lake. Ideal for family groups.
9 holes, 5302mtrs, Par 68, SSS 67.
Club membership 250.
Visitors welcome except for club competitions.
Societies telephone in advance.
Green Fees IR£7 per day.
Prof Leslie Robinson
Designer Eddie Hacket
Facilities
& Leisure fishing.
Location 1m N

Hotel ★★ 64% Royal Hotel, BOYLE ☎ 079 62016 16

Enniscrone Map 01 B5

Enniscrone ☎ 096 36297 Fax 096 36657
In a magnificent situation with breathtaking views of mountain, sea and rolling countryside, this course offers some unforgettable golf.It was host to the West of Ireland championship and the Ladies Irish Close in 1997. It offers an exciting challenge among its splendid sandhills and a particularly favourite hole is the tenth, with a marvellous view from the elevated tee and the chance of a birdie with an accurate drive.
18 holes, 6620yds, Par 72, SSS 72.
Club membership 750.

Visitors must contact in advance, may not play before 11am or between 1.00 & 4pm on Sun.
Societies must telephone in advance.
Green Fees IR£18 per day (IR£24 per round weekend).
Cards
Prof Charlie McGoldrick
Designer E Hackett
Facilities
Location 0.5m S on Ballina road

Sligo Map 01 B5

County Sligo Rosses Point
☎ 071 77134 or 77186 Fax 071 77460
Now considered to be one of the top links courses in Ireland, County Sligo is host to a number of competitions, including the West of Ireland Championships and Internationals. Set in an elevated position on cliffs above three large beaches, the prevailing winds provide an additional challenge.Tom Watson described it " as a magnificent links, particularly the stretch of holes from the 14th to the 17th."
18 holes, 6037mtrs, Par 71, SSS 72, Course record 66.
Club membership 1069.

Visitors advisable to contact in advance, available most days except Captains or Presidents days.
Societies must contact in writing & pay a deposit.
Green Fees IR£30-IR£40 per day; IR£23-IR£27 per round (IR£40-IR£50/IR£30-IR£35 weekends).
Prof Leslie Robinson
Designer Harry Colt
Facilities
Location Off N15 to Donegal

Hotel ★★★ 65% Tower Hotel, Quay St, SLIGO ☎ 071 44000 58

Strandhill Strandhill ☎ 071 68188 Fax 071 68811
This scenic course is situated between Knocknarea Mountain and the Atlantic, offering golf in its most natural form amid the sand dunes of the West of Ireland. The 1st, 16th and 18th are Par 4 holes over 364 metres in length; the 2nd and 17th are testing Par 3s which vary according to the prevailing wind; the Par 4 13th is a testing dogleg right. This is a course where accuracy will be rewarded.
18 holes, 5516mtrs, Par 69, SSS 68.
Club membership 450.

Visitors must contact in advance.
Societies apply in advance.
Green Fees IR£15 per round (IR£20 weekends & bank holidays).
Facilities
Location 5m from town

Hotel ★★★ 71% Sligo Park Hotel, Pearse Rd, SLIGO ☎ 071 60291 89

Tobercurry Map 01 B4

Tobercurry ☎ 071 85849
A 9-hole parkland course designed by Edward Hackett. The 8th hole, a Par 3, is regarded as being one of the most testing in the west of Ireland.
9 holes, 5490mtrs, Par 70, SSS 69.
Club membership 300.

Visitors restricted on Sun.
Societies telephone in advance on 071 85770.
Green Fees IR£10 per day.
Designer Eddie Hackett
Facilities
Location 0.25m from Tobercurry

CO TIPPERARY

Cahir Map 01 C3

Cahir Park Kilcommon ☎ 052 41474 Fax 052 42717
Parkland course dissected by the River Suir which adds a challenge to the par 4 8th and par 3 16th.
18 holes, 5740mtrs, Par 71, SSS 71.
Club membership 350.

Visitors may play any time except during competitions.
Societies by prior arrangement, apply in writing.
Green Fees IR£15 per round.
Prof Dominic Foran
Designer Eddie Hackett
Facilities by prior arrangement
Location 1m from Cahir on the Clogheen road

Hotel ★★★ 70% Cahir House Hotel, The Square, CAHIR ☎ 52 42727 14

Carrick-on-Suir Map 01 C2

Carrick-on-Suir Garvonne ☎ 051 640047 Fax 051 640558
18 hole parkland course with the backdrop of the Comeragh Mountains on one side and views of the Suir valley on the other.
18 holes, 6061mtrs, Par 73, SSS 71, Course record 69.
Club membership 600.

Visitors may not play on Sun morning
Societies contact for details.
Green Fees not confirmed.
Designer Eddie Hackett
Facilities
Location 2m SW

Hotel ★★★ 73% Minella Hotel, CLONMEL ☎ 052 22388 70

CLONMEL Map 01 C2

Clonmel Lyreanearla, Mountain Rd
☎ 052 24050 & 21138 Fax 052 24050
Set in the scenic, wooded slopes of the Comeragh Mountains, this is a testing course with lots of open space and plenty of interesting features. It provides an enjoyable round in exceptionally tranquil surroundings.
18 holes, 5845mtrs, Par 72, SSS 71.
Club membership 850.

Visitors must contact in advance.
Societies must contact in advance.
Green Fees IR£18 per round (IR£20 weekends).
Prof Robert Hayes
Designer Eddie Hackett
Facilities
Location 3m form Clonmel off N24

Hotel ★★★ 73% Minella Hotel, CLONMEL
☎ 052 22388 70

NENAGH Map 01 B3

Nenagh Beechwood
☎ 067 31476 Fax 067 34808
Interesting gradients call for some careful approach shots. Some magnificent views.
18 holes, 5491mtrs, Par 69, SSS 68, Course record 64.
Club membership 820.

Visitors must contact in advance.
Societies must apply in writing.
Green Fees IR£15 per round.
Prof Gordon Morrison
Designer Eddie Hackett
Facilities
& Leisure putting green, practice area.
Location 3m from town on old Birr rd

Hotel ★★★ 66% Castle Oaks House Hotel, CASTLECONNELL
☎ 061 377666 20

ROSCREA Map 01 C3

Roscrea Golf Club Derryvale ☎ 0505 21130
An 18-hole parkland course.
18 holes, 5750mtrs, Par 71, SSS 70, Course record 69.
Club membership 420.

Visitors on Sun by arrangement.
Societies apply in writing to Hon Secretary.
Green Fees not confirmed.
Facilities
Location N7, Dublin side of Roscrea

Hotel ★★★ 60% County Arms Hotel, BIRR
☎ 0509 20791 24

TEMPLEMORE Map 01 C3

Templemore Manna South ☎ 0504 31400
Parkland course with newly planted trees which offers a pleasant test to visitors without being too difficult. Walking is level too.
9 holes, Par 68, SSS 67, Course record 68.
Club membership 220.

Visitors may not play on Sun during Special Events & Open weeks.
Societies must contact in advance.
Green Fees not confirmed.
Facilities
Location 0.5m S

Hotel ★★★ 60% County Arms Hotel, BIRR
☎ 0509 20791 24

THURLES Map 01 C3

Thurles Turtulla
☎ 0504 21983 & 22466 Fax 0504 24647
Superb parkland course with a difficult finish at the 18th.
18 holes, 5904mtrs, Par 72, SSS 71, Course record 65.
Club membership 920.

Visitors welcome, limited availability at weekends, Tuesday is Ladies day.
Societies apply in writing to Hon Secretary.
Green Fees IR£18 per round.
Prof Sean Hunt
Facilities
& Leisure squash, sauna, gymnasium.
Location 1m from town on Cork road

Hotel ★ 59% Royal Hotel, Bridge St, TIPPERARY TOWN
☎ 062 33244 16

TIPPERARY Map 01 C3

County Tipperary Dundrum House Hotel, Dundrum
☎ 062 71116
The course had been built into a mature Georgian estate using the features of woodland and parkland adorned by the Multeen River. Designed by Philip Walton. The 4th hole is one of the most testing Par 5's in Ireland.
18 holes, 6709yds, Par 72, SSS 72, Course record 70.
Club membership 190.

Visitors booking is advisable especially at weekends.
Societies apply in writing.
Green Fees not confirmed.
Designer Philip Walton
Facilities
& Leisure hard tennis courts, fishing.
Location 7m W of Cashel off N8

Hotel ★ 59% Royal Hotel, Bridge St, TIPPERARY TOWN
☎ 062 33244 16

Tipperary Rathanny ☎ 062 51119
Recently extended to 18-holes, this parkland course has plenty of trees and bunkers and water at three holes to provide additional hazards.
18 holes, 5761mtrs, Par 71, SSS 71, Course record 69.
Club membership 700.

Visitors advisable to contact by phone, weekend play available but limited on Sun.
Societies apply in writing.
Green Fees not confirmed.
Facilities
Location 1m S

Hotel ★ 59% Royal Hotel, Bridge St, TIPPERARY TOWN ☎ 062 33244 16

CO WATERFORD

DUNGARVAN Map 01 C2

Dungarvan Knocknagranagh
☎ 058 41605 & 43310 Fax 058 44113
A championship-standard course beside Dungarvan Bay, with seven lakes and hazards placed to challenge all levels of golfer. The greens are considered to be among the best in Ireland.
18 holes, 6487yds, Par 72, SSS 71, Course record 66.
Club membership 575.

Visitors welcome weekdays, booking advisable weekends.
Societies telephone then write to confim booking.
Green Fees IR£15 per round (IR£20 weekends & bank holidays).
Cards
Prof David Hayes
Designer Moss Fives
Facilities
Location Off N25 between Waterford & Youghal

Hotel ★★★ 56% Lawlors Hotel, DUNGARVAN
☎ 058 41122 & 41056 Fax 058 41000 89

Gold Coast Golf & Leisure Ballinacourty
☎ 058 42249 & 44055 Fax 058 43378
A parkland course bordered by the Atlantic Ocean with unrivalled panoramic views of Dungarvan Bay. The mature tree-lined fairways of the old course are tastefully integrated with the long and challenging newer holes to create a superb course.
18 holes, 6171mtrs, Par 72, SSS 72.
Club membership 450.

Visitors book in advance, times available throughout the week.
Societies apply by telephone in advance.
Green Fees IR£15 (IR£18 weekends).
Cards
Designer Maurice Fives
Facilities
& Leisure hard tennis courts, heated indoor swimming pool, sauna, gymnasium.
Hotel ★★★ 56% Lawlors Hotel, DUNGARVAN
☎ 058 41122 & 41056 Fax 058 41000 89

West Waterford ☎ 058 43216 & 41475 Fax 058 44343
Designed by Eddie Hackett, the course is on 150 acres of rolling parkland by the Brickey River with a backdrop of the Comeragh Mountains, Knockmealdowns and Drum Hills. The first nine holes are laid out on a large plateau featuring a stream which comes into play at the 3rd and 4th holes. The river at the southern boundary affects several later holes.
18 holes, 6004mtrs, Par 72, SSS 74, Course record 70.
Club membership 185.

Visitors pre book for tee times.
Societies telephone or write in advance.
Green Fees IR£20 per 18 holes (IR£25 weekends & bank holidays).
Cards
Designer Eddie Hackett
Facilities
& Leisure hard tennis courts.
Location Approx 3m W of Dungarvan, off N25

Hotel ★★★ 56% Lawlors Hotel, DUNGARVAN
☎ 058 41122 & 41056 Fax 058 41000 89

DUNMORE EAST Map 01 C2

Dunmore East
☎ 051 383151 Fax 051 383151
Challenging golf for low and high handicappers. The 15th hole requires a tee shot that carries 150yards over the sea. The course overlooks the village of Dunmore East and the sea so many holes are affected by crosswinds.
18 holes, 6655yds, Par 72, SSS 70, Course record 69.
Club membership 300.

Visitors welcome, no restrictions.
Societies telephone in advance.
Green Fees IR£10 per day (IR£14 weekends & bank holidays).
Cards
Designer W H Jones
Facilities
Hotel ★★★ 62% Dooley's Hotel, 30 The Quay, WATERFORD
☎ 051 873531 113

LISMORE Map 01 C2

Lismore Ballyin ☎ 058 54026 Fax 058 53338
Picturesque tree-dotted sloping course on the banks of the Blackwater River. Rothwell's is a diffiuclt hole with a sloping green and trees to either side.
9 holes, 5790yds, Par 69, SSS 67, Course record 67.
Club membership 350.

Visitors may not play Sun before noon. Restricted Wed, Thu & weekends.
Societies must apply in writing.
Green Fees not confirmed.
Facilities
Hotel ★★★ 56% Lawlors Hotel, DUNGARVAN
☎ 058 41122 & 41056 Fax 058 41000 89

TRAMORE Map 01 C2

Tramore Newtown Hill
☎ 051 386170 Fax 051 390961
This course has matured nicely over the years to become a true championship test and has been chosen as the venue for the Irish Professional Matchplay Championship and the Irish Amateur Championship. Most of the fairways are lined by evergreen trees, calling for accurate placing of shots, and the course is continuing to develop.
18 holes, 5918mtrs, Par 72, SSS 72, Course record 65.
Club membership 1200.

Visitors pre-booking required.
Societies contact in advance.
Green Fees IR£33 per 36 holes; IR£25 per round (IR£30 weekends & bank holidays).
Cards
Prof Derry Kiely
Designer Capt H C Tippet
Facilities
& Leisure squash.
Location 0.5m from Tramore on Dungaruan coast road

Hotel ★★★ 63% Majestic Hotel, TRAMORE
☎ 051 381761 57

Waterford Map 01 C2

Faithlegg House Dunmore East ☎ 051 382241
Some wicked slopes and borrows on the immaculate greens, a huge 432yard 17th what has a host of problems and a doglegged approach to the two-tier 18th green are just some of the novel features on this course. Set on the banks of the River Suir, the course has been integrated into a landscape textured with mature trees,flowing parkland and five lakes.
18 holes, 6057mtrs, Par 72, SSS 72, Course record 69.
Club membership 65.

Visitors no restrictions.
Societies apply in writing or telephone at least a month in advance.
Green Fees not confirmed.
Prof Ted Higgins
Facilities
Hotel ★★★ 61% Jurys Hotel, Ferrybank, WATERFORD ☎ 051 832111 98

Waterford Newrath ☎ 051 876748 Fax 051 853405
Undulating parkland course in pleasant surroundings.
18 holes, 5722mtrs, Par 71, SSS 70, Course record 66.
Club membership 931.

Visitors must contact in advance.
Societies must apply in writing.
Green Fees not confirmed.
Prof Eamonn Condon
Designer W Park/J Braid
Facilities
Location 1m N

Hotel ★★★ 61% Jurys Hotel, Ferrybank, WATERFORD ☎ 051 832111 98

Waterford Castle The Island, Ballinakill
☎ 051 871633 Fax 051 871634
Parkland course with mature trees, 4 lakes, sandbased tees and greens and good bunkering.
18 holes, 5810mtrs, Par 72, SSS 71, Course record 70.
Club membership 500.

Visitors must contact in advance, pre booking required.
Societies apply in advance.
Green Fees IR£24 per round (IR£27 weekends).
Cards
Designer Den Smyth
Facilities
& Leisure hard tennis courts, heated indoor swimming pool.
Location 2m E of Waterford City, on Island approached by private ferry

Hotel ★★★ 61% Jurys Hotel, Ferrybank, WATERFORD ☎ 051 832111 98

CO WESTMEATH

Athlone Map 01 C4

Glasson Golf & Country Club Glasson
☎ 0902 85120 Fax 0902 85444
An 18-hole championship standard course designed by Christy O'Connor Jnr. There are a number of outstanding holes including the Par 3 15th which has both tee and green situated in Killiure Bay. As Christy said 'Although only 185 yards off the back tee there is no room for error whatsoever'.
18 holes, 6664yds, Par 72, Course record 65.
Club membership 220.

Visitors must book in advance.
Societies book in advance.
Green Fees IR£25 per round (IR£28-£IR30 Fri-Sun).
Cards
Designer Christy O'Connor Jnr
Facilities
Location 6m N of Athlone on N55

Hotel ★★★ 64% Prince Of Wales Hotel, ATHLONE ☎ 0902 72626 73

Delvin Map 01 C4

Delvin Castle Clonyn
☎ 044 64315 & 64733 Fax 044 64733
Situated in the mature parkland of Clonyn Castle, the course is well known for its unique historic setting with a 16th century ruin in the back nine holes and an imposing Victorian castle in the front nine.
18 holes, 5800mtrs, Par 70, SSS 68.
Club membership 400.

Visitors no restrictions. Advance booking recommemded.
Societies apply in writing in advance.
Green Fees IR£10 per round (IR£15 weekends & bank holidays).
Prof David Keenaghan
Designer John Day
Facilities
Location On N52, Dundalk to Mullingar road

Hotel ★★★ 59% Ardboyne Hotel, Dublin Rd, NAVAN ☎ 046 23119 27

Moate Map 01 C4

Moate ☎ 0902 81271
Extended in 1994 to 18 holes, the course is parkland with trees. Although the original 9-holes did not have water hazards the new section has a lake.
18 holes, 5642mtrs, Par 72, SSS 70, Course record 67.
Club membership 550.

Visitors welcome, advisable to telephone in advance.
Societies welcome, prior arrangement not needed.
Green Fees not confirmed.
Designer B Browne
Facilities
Location 1m N

Hotel ★★★ 64% Prince Of Wales Hotel, ATHLONE ☎ 0902 72626 73

Mount Temple Mount Temple Village
☎ 0902 81841 & 81545 Fax 0902 81957
A traditionally built, highly-rated, all year round course with parkland and unique links-type greens and natural undulating fairways. A challenge for all levels of golfers as the wind plays a major part in the scoring on this course.
18 holes, 5950mtrs, Par 71, SSS 71, Course record 73.
Club membership 150.

Visitors welcome but must book for weekends.
Societies telephone in advance.
Green Fees IR£14 per round (IR£16 weekends & bank holidays).
Cards
Designer Michael Dolan
Facilities by prior arrangement
Location 4m off N6 to Mount Temple village, 5m from Athlone

Hotel ★★★ 64% Prince Of Wales Hotel, ATHLONE ☎ 0902 72626 73

MULLINGAR Map 01 C4

Mullingar ☎ 044 48366 Fax 044 41499
The wide rolling fairways between mature trees provide parkland golf at its very best. The course, designed by the great James Braid, offers a tough challenge and annually hosts one of the most important amateur events in the British Isles - the Mullingar Scratch Cup. It has also been the venue of the Irish Professional Championship. One advantage of the layout is that the clubhouse is never far away.
18 holes, 6406yds, Par 72, SSS 71, Course record 63.
Club membership 1000.

Visitors preferred if booked in advance, Sundays are Medal days, Wednesday Ladies day.
Societies apply in writing.
Green Fees not confirmed.
Prof John Burns
Designer James Braid
Facilities
Location 3m S

Hotel ★★★ 64% Prince Of Wales Hotel, ATHLONE ☎ 0902 72626 73

CO WEXFORD

ENNISCORTHY Map 01 D3

Enniscorthy Knockmarshall ☎ 054 33191 Fax 054 34736
A pleasant course suitable for all levels of ability.
18 holes, 6115mtrs, Par 72, SSS 72.
Club membership 900.

Visitors must telephone for booking.
Societies must book in advance.
Green Fees IR£15 per day (IR£18 weekends & bank holidays).
Prof Martin Sludos
Designer Eddie Hackett
Facilities
Location 1m from town on New Ross road

Hotel ★ 56% Murphy-Flood's Hotel, Market Square, ENNISCORTHY ☎ 054 33413 21rm(5 13)

GOREY Map 01 D3

Courtown Kiltennel ☎ 055 25166
A pleasant parkland course which is well wooded and enjoys views across the Irish Sea near Courtown Harbour.
18 holes, 5898mtrs, Par 71, SSS 71, Course record 65.
Club membership 1200.

Visitors must contact in advance.
Societies advisable to contact in advance.
Green Fees not confirmed.
Prof John Coone
Designer Harris & Associates
Facilities
Location 3m from town, off Courtown Road

Hotel ★★★ Marlfield House Hotel, GOREY ☎ 055 21124 19

NEW ROSS Map 01 C3

New Ross Tinneranny ☎ 051 421433 Fax 051 420098
Recently extended to 18-holes, this well kept parkland course has an attractive backdrop of hills and mountains. Straight hitting and careful placing of shots is very important, especially on the 2nd, 6th, 10th and 15th, all of which are challenging holes.
18 holes, 5751yds, Par 71, SSS 70.
Club membership 700.

Visitors welcome, booking required for weekend play.
Societies apply to secretary/manager.
Green Fees IR£14 (IR£16 weekends & bank holidays).
Designer Des Smith
Facilities
Location 3m from town centre

Hotel ★★ 59% The Old Rectory Hotel, Rosbercon, NEW ROSS ☎ 051 421719 12

ROSSLARE Map 01 D2

Rosslare Rosslare Strand ☎ 053 32203 & 32238
This traditional links course is within minutes of the ferry terminal at Rosslare, but its popularity is not confined to visitors from Fishguard or Le Havre. It is a great favourite with the Irish too. Many of the greens are sunken and are always in beautiful condition, but the semi-blind approaches are among features of this course which provide a healthy challenge.
Old Course: 18 holes, 6577yds, Par 72, SSS 71, Course record 68.
New Course: 9 holes, 3153yds, Par 70, SSS 70.
Club membership 1000.

Visitors book in advance.
Societies apply in writing/telephone.
Green Fees Old: IR£22 (IR£30 weekends & bank holidays). New: IR£13 per 18 holes, IR£9 per 9 holes.
Prof Austin Skerritt
Designer Hawtree/Taylor

Facilities ⊗ by prior arrangement by prior arrangement
Location 6m N of Rosslare Ferry Terminal

Hotel ★★★★ 77% Kelly's Resort Hotel, ROSSLARE
053 32114 Annexe99

St Helen's Bay Golf & Country Club St Helens, Kilrane
053 33234 & 33669 Fax 053 33803
A championship-standard golf course designed by Philip Walton. Parkland with water hazards, bunkers and trees incorporated generously.
18 holes, 5813mtrs, Par 72, SSS 72, Course record 69.
Club membership 220.
Visitors contact in advance.
Societies telephone/write in advance.
Green Fees IR£16-IR£20 per 18 holes (IR£20 weekends).
Cards
Designer Philip Walton
Facilities ⊗
& Leisure hard tennis courts, sauna, gymnasium.
Location 5 minutes from the ferryport

Hotel ★★★ 57% Hotel Rosslare, ROSSLARE HARBOUR 053 33110 25

WEXFORD Map 01 D3

Wexford Mulgannon 053 42238
Parkland course with panoramic view of the Wexford coastline and mountains.
18 holes, 6100yds, Par 71, SSS 69.
Club membership 800.
Visitors must contact in advance but may not play Thu & weekends.
Societies must contact in writing.
Green Fees not confirmed.
Prof G Ronayne
Facilities

Hotel ★★★ 72% Talbot Hotel, Trinity St, WEXFORD 053 22566 100

CO WICKLOW

ARKLOW Map 01 D3

Arklow Abbeylands 0402 32492 Fax 0402 32492
Scenic links course.
18 holes, 5404mtrs, Par 68, SSS 67, Course record 66.
Club membership 450.
Visitors may play Mon-Fri and 3hrs Sat 9am-12 noon, must book in advance.
Societies must apply in writing.
Green Fees IR£18 per round.
Designer Hawtree & Taylor
Facilities ⊗
Location 0.5m from town centre

Hotel ★★★ Marlfield House Hotel, GOREY
055 21124 19

BALTINGLASS Map 01 D3

Baltinglass Dublin Rd 0508 81350
On the banks of the River Slaney, the 9-hole course has 4 Par-4s over 400 yards which have to be played twice. Reputed to be one of the hardest 9-hole courses in the Republic.
9 holes, 5554mtrs, Par 68, SSS 69, Course record 68.
Club membership 400.
Visitors advisable to check availability for weekends.
Societies apply in writing.
Green Fees not confirmed.
Facilities ⊗

Rathsallagh 045 403316 Fax 045 403295
Designed by Peter McEvoy and Christy O'Connor Jnr, this is a spectacular course which will test the pro's without intimidating the club golfer. Set in 252 acres of lush parkland with thousands of mature treesn naturalwater hazards and gently rolling landscape.
18 holes, 6916yds, Par 72, SSS 74.
Club membership 220.
Visitors must have appropriate attire & book in advance. Restricted weekends.
Societies telephone in advance.
Green Fees not confirmed.
Designer McEvoy/O'Connor
Facilities ⊗
& Leisure hard tennis courts, heated indoor swimming pool, sauna.
Location 15m SE of Naas

Hotel ★★★ 56% Downshire House Hotel, BLESSINGTON
045 865199 14 Annexe11

BLAINROE Map 01 D3

Blainroe 0404 68168 Fax 0404 69369
Parkland course overlooking the sea on the east coast, offering a challenging round to golfers of all abilities.
18 holes, 6070mtrs, Par 72, SSS 72, Course record 71.
Club membership 868.
Visitors must contact in advance.
Societies must telephone in advance.
Green Fees IR£25 (IR£35 weekends & bank holidays).
Cards
Prof John McDonald
Designer C Hawtree
Facilities ⊗
Location S of Wicklow, on coast road

Hotel ★★★ Tinakilly Country House & Restaurant, RATHNEW
0404 69274 40

BLESSINGTON Map 01 D3

Tulfarris House Hotel & Country Club
045 864574 Fax 045 867561
Designed by Eddie Hachett, this course is on the Blessington lakeshore with the Wicklow Mountains as a backdrop.
9 holes, 2806mtrs, Par 36, SSS 69, Course record 74.
Club membership 150.
Visitors tee booking advisable; may not play Sun 8-12.30pm.

Societies must contact in writing or telephone in advance.
Green Fees IR£10 per round (IR£13.50 weekends & bank holidays).
Prof A Williams
Designer Patrick Merrigan
Facilities
& Leisure hard tennis courts, heated indoor swimming pool, fishing, sauna, gymnasium.
Location Via N81, 2m from Blessington village

Hotel ★★★ 56% Downshire House Hotel, BLESSINGTON ☎ 045 865199 14 Annexe11

BRAY Map 01 D4

Bray Ravenswell Rd ☎ 01 2862484 Fax 01 2862484
A 9-hole parkland course with plenty of trees and bunkers.
9 holes, 5761mtrs, Par 70, SSS 70, Course record 65.
Club membership 500.
Visitors restricted Mon, Sat & Sun.
Societies contact in advance.
Green Fees IR£17 per round.
Prof Michael Walby
Facilities
Hotel ★★★ 64% Fitzpatrick Castle Hotel, KILLINEY ☎ 01 2840700 112

Old Conna Ferndale Rd
☎ 01 2826055 & 2826766 Fax 01 2825611
Parkland course set in wooded terrain with panoramic views of Irish Sea and Wicklow mountains.
18 holes, 6550yds, Par 72, SSS 72, Course record 70.
Club membership 900.
Visitors advisable to contact in advance but may not play weekends. Smart dress essential on course & in clubhouse.
Societies must telephone well in advance.
Green Fees IR£22.50 per round (IR£13.50 before 9.30am).
Prof Paul McDaid
Designer Eddie Hackett
Facilities
Location 2m from Bray

Hotel ★★★ 60% Royal Hotel & Leisure Centre, Main St, BRAY ☎ 01 2862935 91

Woodbrook Dublin Rd ☎ 01 2824799 Fax 01 2821950
Pleasant parkland with magnificent views and bracing sea breezes which has hosted a number of events, including the Irish Close and the Irish Open Championships. A testing finish is provided by an 18th hole with out of bounds on both sides.
18 holes, 6017mtrs, Par 72, SSS 71, Course record 65.
Club membership 1100.
Visitors must contact in advance and have a handicap certificate.
Societies must contact in advance.
Green Fees IR£35 per round (IR£40 weekends).
Cards
Prof Billy Kinsella
Designer Peter McEvoy
Facilities
Location 11m S of Dublin on N11

Hotel ★★★ 60% Royal Hotel & Leisure Centre, Main St, BRAY ☎ 01 2862935 91

BRITTAS BAY Map 01 D3

The European Club ☎ 0404 47415 Fax 0404 47449
A links course that runs through a large dunes system. Since it was opened in 1992 it is rapidly gaining recognition as one of Irelands Best Courses.
18 holes, 6800yds, Par 71, SSS 71.
Club membership 100.
Visitors pre-booking advised especially for weekends, check dress code when booking.
Societies must book in advance.
Green Fees IR£55 per day; IR£35 per round.
Cards
Designer Pat Ruddy
Facilities N
Location 1.5m from Brittas Bay Beach

Hotel ★★★ Tinakilly Country House & Restaurant, RATHNEW ☎ 0404 69274 40

DELGANY Map 01 D3

Delgany ☎ 01 2874536 Fax 01 2873977
An undulating parkland course amidst beautiful scenery.
18 holes, 5474mtrs, Par 69, SSS 68, Course record 61.
Club membership 890.
Visitors may play Mon, Wed (until 10am), Thu & Fri. Contact in advance.
Societies contact in advance.
Green Fees IR£23 per round weekdays (IR£27 weekends).
Cards
Prof Gavin Kavanagh
Designer H Vardon
Facilities
Location 0.75m from village

Hotel ★★★ 60% Royal Hotel & Leisure Centre, Main St, BRAY ☎ 01 2862935 91

GREYSTONES Map 01 D3

Charlesland Golf & Country Club Hotel ☎ 01 2876764
Championship length, Par 72 course with a double dog-leg at the 9th and 18th. Water hazards at the 3rd and 11th.
18 holes, 5907mtrs, Par 72, SSS 72.
Club membership 744.
Visitors must contact in advance.
Societies must apply in advance.
Green Fees not confirmed.
Prof Paul Heeney
Designer Eddie Hackett
Facilities
& Leisure sauna.
Hotel ★★★ Tinakilly Country House & Restaurant, RATHNEW ☎ 0404 69274 40

Greystones ☎ 01 2876624 Fax 01 2873749
A part level and part hilly parkland course.
18 holes, 5401mtrs, Par 69, SSS 68.
Club membership 941.
Visitors may only play Mon, Tue & Fri morning. Must contact in advance.
Societies must contact in writing.
Green Fees not confirmed.

Prof Kevin Daly
Facilities
Hotel ★★★ Tinakilly Country House & Restaurant, RATHNEW 0404 69274 40

KILCOOLE Map 01 D3

DRUIDS GLEN See page 477.

Kilcoole Ballyfillop
01 2872066 2872070 Fax 01 2871803
9 holes, 5506mtrs, Par 70, SSS 69.
Club membership 250.
Visitors restricted Sat & Sun 8-10am.
Societies apply in writing or telephone.
Green Fees IR£12 per 18 holes (IR£15 weekends).
Facilities
Location N11 Kilcoole/Newcastle

Hotel ★★★ 63% Hunter's Hotel, RATHNEW 0404 40106 16

RATHDRUM Map 01 D3

Glenmalure Greenane 0404 46679 Fax 0404 46783
A moorland course with elevated tees and greens. The 3rd, known as the Helicopter Pad, is difficult.
18 holes, 5300yds, Par 71, SSS 67, Course record 71.
Club membership 200.
Visitors no restrictions.
Societies telephone at least 3 days in advance.
Green Fees IR£15 per day (IR£20 weekends & bank holidays).
Designer P Suttle
Facilities
Location 2m W

Hotel ★★★ 64% Woodenbridge Hotel, WOODEN BRIDGE 0402 35146 23

ROUNDWOOD

Roundwood Newtown, Mountkennedy
01 2818488 & 2802555 Fax 01 2843642
Heathland and parkland course with forest and lakes set in beautiful countryside with views of the coast and the Wicklow Mountains.
18 holes, 6685yds, Par 72, SSS 72.
Club membership 100.
Visitors no restrictions
Societies pre booking necessary.
Green Fees IR£20 (IR£25 weekends & holidays).
Facilities
Location 2.5m off N11 at Newtown Mountkennedy on N765

Hotel ★★★ 64% The Glendalough Hotel, GLENDALOUGH 0404 45135 44

SHILLELAGH Map 01 D3

Coollattin Coollattin 055 29125
Plenty of trees provide features on this 18-hole parkland course.
18 holes, 6148yds, Par 70, SSS 68.
Club membership 561.
Visitors may not play weekends. Must contact in advance.
Societies contact for details.
Green Fees IR£15 per round (IR£20 weekends).
Designer Peter McEvoy
Facilities
Hotel ★★★ Marlfield House Hotel, GOREY 055 21124 19

WICKLOW Map 01 D3

Wicklow Dunbur Rd 0404 67379
Partly links, partly meadow, the Wicklow course does not have any trees. It was extended to 18-holes in spring 1994 by adding 11 new holes.
18 holes, 5556mtrs, Par 71.
Club membership 475.
Visitors welcome, no restrictions.
Societies contact for details.
Green Fees not confirmed.
Prof David Daly
Designer Craddock & Ruddy
Facilities
Hotel ★★★ Tinakilly Country House & Restaurant, RATHNEW 0404 69274 40

WOODENBRIDGE Map 01 D3

Woodenbridge Woodenbridge, Arklow
0402 35202 Fax 0402 35202
A level parkland course with undulating fairways and greens, traversed by two lovely meandering rivers.
18 holes, 6344yds, Par 71, SSS 71, Course record 71.
Club membership 550.
Visitors may not play Thu and Sat, prior booking strongly recommended.
Societies Mon, Tue & Fri only, book well in advance.
Green Fees IR£27 per round (IR£35 Sun & bank holidays).
Cards
Designer Paddy Merrigan
Facilities
Location 4m NW of Arklow

Hotel ★★★ 64% Woodenbridge Hotel, WOODEN BRIDGE 0402 35146 23

DRUIDS GLEN

KILCOOLE Co Wicklow

☎ 01 2873600 Fax 01 2873699 Map 01 D3

John Ingham writes: Those who never came face-to-face with Druids, ancient pagan high priests who practised, in full regalia, in dense forests in the fifth century BC, probably missed something. There was evidence of these people in Wales where the good folk talked of them - in hushed tones. Years later, other fanatics came along. They were called golfers and across the water, in Ireland, these two groups have become twinned, like modern cities.

You ask why? Well, a short drive (four wheel type) from Dublin takes you to Druids Glen Golf Club. Built around an old estate inhabited back in the mists of time by Sir Thomas Wentworth, the good chap didn't confuse us by naming it after himself, and the location is a delight.

How does a club come to be named after pagans? It seems the dreaded Druids sailed in and once even tried to repel St Patrick. Today, not in hushed tones, they say a Druids altar remains as proof of their infiltration to the nearby Glen. So, with a wonderful-looking clubhouse and grounds transformed into a scenic delight of fairways and greens, it's there, twenty miles from Dublin, between the Wicklow Hills and the sea.

So the provenance of the place is beyond dispute and now the 18 holes are highlighted by streams, lakes and all manicured into an idyllic setting made available to the professional tour which play the Irish Open there. The experts heaped praise, with Colin Montgomerie, a severe critic of anything less than 5-star, particularly fulsome - after winning the 1997 title!

Off the back tees, the course is more than 7000yards with three holes of more than 500 yards. So a par round of 71 is to talk about and anything less to die for. Water is a hazard, and you are not allowed to recover drowning balls, or to stand on cliff edges.

No expense has been spared to restore the big house and the dining room has an extra touch. It offers views of the sea, and on a clear day, of the Welsh mountains beyond. So those long gone Welsh Druids are not forgotten!

Visitors	advance booking essential
Societies	advance booking essential
Green fees	IR£75 per round
Facilities	
Designer	Tom Cradduck/Pat Ruddy
Location	20m S of Dublin, 3m off the N11 motorway, immediately S of Glen of Downs

18 holes, 6547yds, Par71 SSS 72

WHERE TO STAY AND EAT NEARBY

HOTELS:

RATHNEW

★★★★ Tinakilly Country House & Restaurant ☎ 0404 69274 40

★★★ 63% Hunters Hotel ☎ 0404 40106 13 3

GOLF DRIVING RANGES

ENGLAND

BEDFORDSHIRE

Bedford, Mowsbury Driving Range (01234 216374) 13 bays covered floodlit 9am-9pm

Ivinghoe, John Lambel Driving Range (01296 662720) 30 bays open floodlit 9.30am-9.30pmWD 7.30pmWE

Leighton Buzzard, Aylesbury Vale (01525 240196) 10 bays covered floodlit 8am-9pm (6pm winter)

Luton, Stockwood Park Golf Centre (01582 413704) 20 bays covered floodlit 7am 9.30pmWD6am-8pmWE

Tilsworth, Tilsworth Golf Centre (01525 210721/2) 30 bays covered floodlit 10am-10pm

Wyboston, Wyboston Lakes Range (01480 223004) 14 bays covered floodlit 7am-10pm (9pm winter)

BERKSHIRE

Ascot, Lavender Park Golf Centre (01344 884074/886096) 29 bays floodlit 9am-10.30pmWD 9am-10pmSun

Binfield, Blue Mountain Golf Centre (01344 300200) 33 bays covered floodlit 7.15am-9pmWD 5.30am-9pm Sun

Maidenhead, Bird Hill Golf Range (01628 771030/ 75588) 36 bays covered floodlit 8am-10pm

Wokingham, Downshire Golf Range (01344 422708) 30 bays covered floodlit 7.30am-10pmWD 6am- 10pmWE

BUCKINGHAMSHIRE

Bletchley, Windmill Hill Golf Complex (01908 378623) 23 bays covered floodlit + 5 bays open 8am-9.30pmWD 8am-8pmWE

Colnbrook, Colnbrook Driving Range (01753 682670/685127) 15 bays covered floodlit + 10 bays open 9am-10pmWD 9am-9pmWE

Loudwater, Wycombe Heights Golf Range (01494 812862) 24 bays covered floodlit 10am-10pm (9pmWE)

Wavendon, Wavendon Golf Centre (01908 281811) 36 bays covered floodlit 7am(10amMon)-10pm

CAMBRIDGESHIRE

Hemingford Abbots, Hemingford Golf Centre (01480 492939) 30 bays floodlit 10am-9.30pmWD 9am-8.30pmWE

Thorney, Thorney Golf Centre (01733 270570) 13 bays covered floodlit 8am-dusk

Pidley, Lakeside Lodge (01487 740540) 6 bays covered floodlit + 12 bays open 7am-11pm

Ramsey, Edrich Golf Driving Range (01487 813519) 12 bays covered floodlit + 12 bays open 7am-9pmWD 7am-7pm (summer 9pm)WE

St Neots, Abbotsley Golf & Squash Club (01480 215153) 24 bays floodlit covered 8am-10pm (7am-10pmWE)

CHESHIRE

Hartford, Hartford Golf Range (01606 871162) 30 bays covered floodlit 10am-9pm 10am-7pm Sat

Heaton Mersey, Cranford Golf Driving Range (0161 432 8242) 43 bays covered floodlit 10am-11pm

Knutsford, Mere Golf & Country Club (01565 830219) 6 bays open (floating ball) 8am-7pm (visitors only Mon, Tue & Thu)

Warrington, Drive Time Golf Range (01925 234800) 60 bays covered floodlit 9am-10pm

CORNWALL

Lostwithiel, Lostwithiel Golf & Country Club (01208 873822/873550) 6 bays floodlit 7.30am-9pm

St. Austell, Porthpean (01726 64613) 9 bays covered floodlit 9am-9pm

Redruth, Treleigh, Radnor Golf Centre (01209 211059) 6 bays covered floodlit + 6 bays open 8.30am-8pmWD 8.30am-6pmWE

Truro, Killiow Park (01872 270246) 8 bays indoor floodlit + 4 bays open 9.30am-9pmWD 9am-6pmWE

CUMBRIA

Crosby-on-Eden, Eden (01228 573003) 16 bays floodlit 8am-8.30pmWD 8am-6pmWE

DERBYSHIRE

Chesterfield, Grassmoor Golf Centre (01246 856044) 26 bays floodlit covered 8am-9pmWD 7am-6pmWE

Horsley, Horsley Lodge Golf Range (01332 780838) 10 bays covered floodlit Dawn-10pm

Long Eaton, Trent Lock (0115 9464398/9461184) 24 bays covered floodlit 8am-10pm

DEVON

High Bicklington, Libbaton (01769 560269) 7 bays covered floodlit 8am-10pm (9pm winter)

Ilfracombe, Ilfracombe & Woolacombe Golf Range (01271 866222) 12 bays covered (not floodlit) + 6 open tees 8am-8pm (6pm winter)

Ivybridge, Dinnaton (01752 691288) 6 tee driving net 10am-9pm

Tedburn St. Mary, Fingle Glen Golf Range (01647 61817) 12 bays covered floodlit 9am-9pmWD 9am-8.30pmWE

DORSET

Christchurch, Iford Bridge Golf Range (01202 473817) 14 bays (not floodlit) open 8am-6pm

Wareham, Hyde, East Dorset Golf Centre (01929 472244) 22 bays floodlit (12 indoor) 8am-8pm (7.30am Sun)

Verwood, Crane Valley Golf Range (01202 814088) 10 bays covered + 2 bays open floodlit 7.30am-9pmWD (5pmWE)

Weymouth, Wessex Golf Centre (01305 784737) 20 bays open floodlit 8am-dusk

CO. DURHAM

Chester-le-Street, Roseberry Grange (0191 370 0660) 17 bays covered floodlit 8am-9pmWD 7am-9pm Sat 7pm Sun

Durham, Ramside Hall (0191 386 9514) 16 bays covered floodlit 8am-9.15pm (7pmWE)

Newton Aycliffe, Aycliffe Driving Range (01325 310820) 18 bays covered floodlit 7am-8.30pmWD (8pmWE)

Stockton-on-Tees, Knotty Hill Golf Centre (01740 620320) 14 bays covered floodlit +12 bays open 8am-9pm

ESSEX

Bulphan, Langdon Hills Driving Range (01268 548444) 22 bays covered floodlit 7am-9.30pmWD 9pmWE

Canvey Island, Castle Point (01268 510830) 17 bays covered floodlit 7am-9pmWD 7.30pmWE

Colchester, Colchester Golf Range (01206 230974) 12 bays covered floodlit + 3 open bays 10am-9pmWD 6pmWE

Chelmsford, Regiment Way (01245 361100) 13 bays covered floodlit 7am-9.30pmWD

Earls Colne, Earls Colne (01787 224466) 20 bays covered floodlit 9am-10pmWD 8am-7pmWE

Epping, Nazeing Golf Club (01992 893798) 20 mats open air driving area (buckets of balls available) 7.30am-8pm

Leigh-on-Sea, Leigh Driving Range (01702 710586) 18 bays covered floodlit 9am-9.30pmWD (9pmWE)

Maldon, Woodham Mortimer (01245 222276) 15 bays covered floodlit + 6 open tees 10am-9pm

GLOUCESTERSHIRE

Gloucester, Gloucester Hotel & CC (01452 525653) 12 bays covered floodlit 10am-8.45pm

GREATER LONDON

Addiscombe, Croydon Golf Centre (0181 656 1690) 24 bays covered floodlit 9am-10pmWD (8pmWE)

Arkley, A1 Golf Range (0181 447 1411) 47 bays covered floodlit + 10 open 8am-10pm 7am-10pm WE

Bushey, Bushey Golf Range (0181 950 2215) 27 bays covered floodlit 9am-9.30pm

Carshalton, Oaks Sports Centre (0181 643 8363) 16 bays covered floodlit 9am-10pm

Chadwell Heath, Warren Park (0181 597 1120) 37 bays covered floodlit 9am-10pmWD/Sun 9am-9pm Sat.

Chessington, Chessington Golf Centre (0181 391 0948) 17 bays covered floodlit 8am-10pmWD (7pmWE)

Elstree, Elstree Golf Range (0181 953 6115) 62 bays covered floodlit 7am-10pm

Greenford, Lime Trees Park (0181 842 0442) 20 bays covered floodlit 9am-10pm

Hounslow, Airlinks (0181 561 1418) 36 bays covered floodlit 10am-10pm

Ilford, Barkingside, Fairlop Waters (0181 500 9911) 36 bays covered floodlit 9am-10pm

Kingston, Jack Nicklaus Golf Centre (0181 949 9200) 60 bays covered floodlit 8am-11pmWD (10pmWE)

Northolt, Ealing Golf Range (0181 845 4967) 36 bays covered floodlit + 4 bays open floodlit 9.30am-10pm

Northolt, London Golf Centre (0181 845 3180) 19 bays covered floodlit 9am-10pm

Orpington, Lullingstone Park (01959 533793) 16 bays covered (not floodlit) 7am-darkWD 5am-darkWE

Orpington, Ruxley Park Golf Centre (01689 871490) 28 bays covered floodlit summer 5am-10pm winter 7.30am-10pm

Richmond, Richmond Driving Range (0181 332 9200) 24 bays covered + 5 open floodlit 9.30am-10pm

Ruislip, Ruislip Driving Range (01895 638081) 40 bays covered floodlit 9am-10pm

Twickenham, Twickenham (0181 783 1698) 12 bays covered floodlit 9.30am-10pm

GREATER MANCHESTER

Altrincham, Altrincham (0161 927 7504) 27 bays covered floodlit 9am-9.30pmWD (7pmWE)

Bardsley, Bardsley Park Golf Centre (0161 627 2463) 18 bays covered floodlit 10am-9pmWD 9.30am-5pmWE

Castleton, Castle Hawk Golf Range (01706 659995) 20 bays covered floodlit 9am-7.30pmWD (5pmWE)

Wigan, Up Holland, Beacon Park Driving Range (01695 622700) 24 bays covered floodlit 9am-9pm

HAMPSHIRE

Alton, Worldham Park (01420 543151) 7 bays covered + 7 bays open 9am-8pmWD 8am-7pmWE (till dark winter)

Basingstoke, Basingstoke Golf Centre (01256 350054) 24 bays covered floodlit 8.30amWD/8amWE-9.30pm

Botley, Botley Park Hotel & Country Club (01489 780888) 7 bays open +6 bays covered 8am-8pm

Crondall, Oak Park (01252 8500660) 16 bays floodlit covered summer 7am-8pm winter7am-6pm

Dibden, Dibden Golf Centre (01703 845596) 20 bays covered floodlit 7.45am-8.30pm

Ower, Paulton's Golf Centre (01703 813992) 24 bays covered floodlit 8am-8.30pmWD 7am-6.30pmWE

Liphook, Old Thorns (01428 724555) 5 bays covered 8am-6pm

Portsmouth, Portsmouth Golf Centre (01705 664549) 22 bays covered floodlit 8am-9pmWD 7am-8pmWE

Southampton, Chilworth, Southampton Golf Range (01703 733166) 24 bays covered + 10 bays open floodlit 7.30am-9pmWD (6pmWE)

Tadley, Tadley Driving Range (0118 9815213) 12 bays covered floodlit 8am-9pmWD 7.30am-6pmWE

HEREFORD & WORCESTER

Bishampton, The Vale Driving Range (01386 462781) 20 bays floodlit 7.30am-8pm

Bransford, Bank House Hotel (Pine Lakes) (01886 833551) 20 bays (5 covered) summer 8am-dark winter 8am-4pm (9pm Tue & Thu)

Ombersley, Ombersley Golf Range (01905 620747) 30 bays open summer 6.30am-9pmWD 5.30pm-9pmWE winter daylight hours

Redditch, Abbey Park (01527 63918) 10 bays covered summer 7am-8pm (winter (dusk)

Worcester, Worcester Golf Range (01905 421213) 26 bays covered floodlit 9.30am-9.45pmWD (5.30pmWE/BH)

HERTFORDSHIRE

Berkhamsted, Shooters Golf Centre (01442 872048) 25 bays covered 9.30am-9pm (winter dusk)

Bishop's Stortford, Great Hadham (01279 843558) 15 bays covered floodlit 7.30am-dusk

Graveley, Chesfield Downs (01462 482929) 21 bays covered floodlit 7am-10pm

Hemel Hempstead, Little Hay Golf Range (01442 833798) 23 bays covered floodlit 9am-9pmWD (8pmWE/BH)

Royston, Kingsway (01763 262727/262943) 36 bays covered floodlit 8.30am-10pmWD 7.30am-8pmWE

Royston, Whaddon Golf Centre (01223 207325) 14 bays covered floodlit 8am-9pm

Stevenage, Stevenage Golf Range (01438 880424) 24 bays covered floodlit dawn-10.30pm

Ware, Whitehill Golf Centre (01920 438495) 25 bays covered floodlit + open range 7am-9.30pmMon Wed Thu Fri 10am-9.30pm Tue 7am-duskWE/BH

Welwyn Garden City, Gosling Sports Park (01707 331056) 22bays covered floodlit 10am-10pmMon-Thu 9pm(Fri) 9am-8pmWE

KENT

Ashford, Homelands Bettergolf Centre (01233 661620) 15 bays covered floodlit 8am-10pmMon-Thu (7pm Fri-Sun)

Biddenden, Chart Hills (01580 292148) 35 bays open summer 7.30am-7pm winter 8am-4pm

Chatham, Chatham Golf Centre (01634 848925) 30 bays open floodlit 10am-10pm

Chelmsfield, Chelmsfield Lakes Golf Centre (01689 896266) 40 bays covered floodlit 7am-9.30pmWD 6.30am-9.30pmWE

Dartford, Birchwood Park (01322 660554) 38 bays covered floodlit 7.30am-10pm (5.30pmWE)

Dartford, Swanley, Olympic Golf Centre (01322 669201) 18 bays covered +9 bays open floodlit 10am-10pm

Edenbridge, Edenbridge Golf Range (01732 865202) 16 bays covered floodlit 7am-9pm

Folkestone, Etchinghill Golf Course (01303 863863) 11 bays covered floodlit 8am-8pmWD 7pmWE/BH

Herne Bay, Herne Bay Golf Range (01227 742742) 15 bays covered floodlit 9am-10pm

Maidstone, Langley Park Driving Range (01622 863163) 25 bays covered floodlit 10am-10pmWD 7.30am-duskWE

Orpington, St. Paul's Cray, Ruxley Park Golf Centre (see under Greater London)

Sittingbourne, The Oast Golf Centre (01795 473527) 17 bays covered floodlit 8.30am-9.30pm

Sittingbourne, Upchurch, RiverValley Golf Range (01634 379592) 16 bays covered floodlit 7am-9pmWD 6am-8pmWE

LANCASHIRE

Blackburn, Blackburn Driving Range (01254 581996) 27 bays covered floodlit 9am-9pmWD 7pmWE/BH

Blackpool, Heron's Reach, De Vere Hotel (01253 838866) 18 bays open 7am-10pm

Blackpool, Phoenix Driving Range (01253 854846) 16 bays covered floodlit +9 open 9am-10.30pmWD (winter dusk)

Bolton, Kearsley Golf Range (01204 575726) 10 bays covered floodlit +30 grass tees 11am-10pmWD 11am-5pmWE

Chorley, Euxton Park Golf Centre (01257 261601) 30 bays covered floodlit + grass tees 9.30am-9.30pmWD 8am-7pmWE

Preston, Preston Driving Range (01772 861827) 23 bays covered floodlit 9.30am-9pmWD 9am-6pmWE (Sun only 1.30pm winter)

Tarleton, Leisure Lakes Golf Range (01772 815842) 20 bays covered floodlit 9am-8.30pmWD 6pmWE

Upholland, Beacon Park (01695 622700) 24 bays covered floodlit 9am-9pm

LEICESTERSHIRE

Botcheston, Forest Hill (01455 824800) 20 bays covered floodlit 9am-9pm (10pm summer)

Greetham, Greetham Valley (01780 460666) 16 bays covered floodlit +5 open 8am-9pmWD 7.30am-7pmWE/BH

Leicester, Humberstone Heights (0116 2764674) 30 bays covered floodlit 8.30am-9.30pmWD 7am-7pmWE

Leicester, Whetstone Golf Range (0116 2861424) 20 bays open dawn-dusk

Loughborough, Charnwood Golf Centre (01509 610022) 24 bays covered floodlit 9am-9.30WD 8pm WE summer (7pm winter)

LINCOLNSHIRE

Belton, DeVere Belton Woods (01476 593200) 24 bays covered floodlit 8am-10pm(Summer) 8am-9pm(Winter)

Gainsborough, Gainsborough (01427 613088) 21 bays covered floodlit 7.30am-9pmWD 8am-duskWE

Holbeach, Gedney Hill (01406 330922) 10 bays covered floodlit dawn to dusk

Horncastle, Horncastle (01507 526800) 25 bays covered floodlit 9am-9.30pm

Lincoln, Lincoln Bowls (01522 522059) 20 bays covered floodlit 10am-8.30pm (7.30WE)

Scunthorpe, Messingham, Grange Park (01724 764478) 20 bays covered floodlit 9am-9.30pmWD (8.30pmWE)

Skegness, The Elms Golf Centre (01754 881230) 20 bays covered floodlit 10am-10pm

LONDON SEE ALSO GREATER LONDON

N9 Edmonton, Lea Valley Leisure Centre (0181 345 6666) 20 bays covered floodlit 8am-9.30pmWD (8.30pmWE)

N14 Southgate, Trent Park (0181 367 4653) 24 bays covered floodlit 7.30am-9.30pmWD (9pmWE)

E4 Chingford, Chingford Golf Range (0181 529 2409) 18 bays covered floodlit 9.30am-10pm (Sat 9.30pm)

MERSEYSIDE

Formby, Formby Golf Centre (01704 875952) 14 bays covered floodlit + 7 bays open summer9.30am-9.30pm (winter8.30pm)

Moreton, Wirral Golf & Drive Centre (0151 677 6606) 20 bays covered floodlit +10 bays open 8am-9pm

NORFOLK

Norwich, Bawburgh, Norwich Golf Centre (01603 742323) 14 bays covered floodlit dawn-dusk (9pm winter)

King's Lynn, Eagles Golf Centre (01553 827147) 20 bays covered floodlit 8.30am-8.30pm

King's Lynn, Middleton Hall (01553 841800) 12 bays covered floodlit 7.30am-10pm

Norwich, Sprowston Park (01603 410657) 27 bays covered floodlit 7.30am-9pmWD (7am-7pmWE)

Norwich, Wensum Valley (01603 261012) 8 bays covered floodlit 7.30am-8pm

NORTHAMPTONSHIRE

Daventry, Staverton Park (01327 302000) 16 bays covered floodlit 7.30am-10pm

Northampton, Collingtree Park (01604 700000) 16 bays covered floodlit 7.30am-9pm

Northampton, Delapre Golf Complex (01604 764036) 40 bays covered floodlit 9am-10pm

NOTTINGHAMSHIRE

Newark, John Lee Golf Centre (01636 702161) 24 bays covered floodlit 10am-9pmWD (9am-6pmWE)

Nottingham, Richard Harrod Leisure Centre (0115 961 2949) 26 bays covered floodlit 9.30am-10pm (Mon 12-10pm)

Nottingham, Cotgrave Place Golf Range (0115 933 3344) 10 bays covered floodlit 8am-7pm

Nottingham, Ramsdale Park Golf Centre (0115 965 5600) 22 bays covered floodlit + 1 video training bay 8am-10pmWD

Nottingham, Riverside Golf Centre (0115 986 2179) 24 bays covered floodlit 9.30am-9.30pm

Oxton, Oakmere Park (0115 965 3545) 27 bays covered floodlit 7.30am-8.30pmWD 7am-8.30pmWE

OXFORDSHIRE

Abingdon, Drayton Park (01235 550607) 21 bays covered floodlit 8am-8.15pmWD 7am-6.45pmWE

Oxford, Oxford Golf Centre (01865 721592) 19 bays covered floodlit + 8 bays open 10am-9pmWD 8pmWE.

SHROPSHIRE

Oswestry, Mile End (01691 671246) 12 bays covered floodlit summer 8am-dusk (WE 6pm) winter 8am-6pm

Telford, Telford Hotel Golf & Country Club (01952 586052) 8 bays covered floodlit dawn-10pm

SOMERSET

Congresbury, Mendip Spring (01934 852322) 11 bays covered floodlit 8am-8pm (from 11am Mon & Thu)

Farrington Gurney, Farrington Golf Range (01761 241274) 18 bays covered floodlit +10 open grass 8am-9pm (7.30-8pmWE)

Langport, Long Sutton Golf Range (01458 241017) 12 bays covered floodlit 8am-dusk

Monkton Combe, Combe Grove Manor Golf Range (01225 835533) 20 bays (9 covered) 10am-7.30pmWD 6.30pmWE (winter till dusk)

Taunton, Swingrite Golf Range, Holway (01823 442600) 12 bays covered + 7 bays open floodlit 9am-9pmWD (7pmWE)

Taunton, Oake Manor (01823 461993) 11 bays covered dawn-dusk

Taunton, Taunton Vale, West Monkton (01823 412220) 9 bays covered floodlit 8am-9pm

Tickenham, Tickenham (01275 856626) 24 bays covered floodlit 8.30am-8.30pmWD

Yeovil, Halstock Driving Range (01935 891689) 12 bays covered floodlit 8.30am-dusk (7pm Winter)

STAFFORDSHIRE

Burton-upon-Trent, Craythorne (01283 564329) 13 bays covered floodlit 8am-10.30pm

Litchfield, Seedy Mill Golf Range (01543 417333) 27 bays covered floodlit 7am-10pm

Newcastle-under-Lyme, Keele Golf Centre (01782 717417) 26 bays covered floodlit 9am-9.30pm

SUFFOLK

Halesworth, Halesworth (01986 875567) 10 bays covered floodlit + 8 bays open 8am-dusk

Ipswich, Fynn Valley (01473 785463) 10 bays covered floodlit + 13 bays open 8am-9pmWD (7pmWE)

SURREY

Camberley, Pine Ridge (01276 20770) 36 bays covered floodlit 8am-10pm

Cobham, Silvermere Driving Range (01932 867275) 34 bays covered floodlit 7am-10pmWD (8pmWE)

Esher, Sandown Golf Centre (01372 461234) 33 bays covered floodlit 10am-10pmWD (8.30-8pmWE) closed during race meetings

Farnham, Blacknest Golf Club (01420 22888) 15 bays covered 7.30am-9pm 7am-9pmWE

Godalming, Broadwater Park (01483 429955) 16 bays covered floodlit 8am-10pm

Old Woking, Hoebridge Golf Centre (01483 722611) 25 bays covered floodlit 7.30am-10pmWD dawn-10pmWE

Woking, Windlemere Golf Range (01276 858727) 12 bays covered floodlit 7am-10.30pm

SUSSEX (EAST)

Ditchling, Mid Sussex Golf Course (01273 846567) 20 bays open summer 7.30am-7pm winter 9am-dusk

Eastbourne, Eastbourne Golfing Park (01323 520400) 24 bays covered floodlit 10am-10pm

Hellingly, Wellshurst Golf Range (01435 813456) 8 bays covered floodlit 7.30am-9.30pm

Horam, Horam Park (01435 813477) 16 bays covered floodlit 9am-10.30pm (winter 10pm)

Ticehurst, Dale Hill (01580 200112) 10 open bays 7.30am-7pm

SUSSEX (WEST)

Chichester, Chichester Golf Range (01243 533833) 27 bays covered floodlit 9am-9pm (8am-8pmWE)

Crawley, Pease Pottage Driving Range (01293 521706) 26 bays covered floodlit 8am-10pm

Crawley, Tilgate Driving Centre (01293 530103) 35 bays covered floodlit 7am-10pmWD (6am-8.30pmWE)

Horsham, Horsham Golf Park (01403 271525) 16 bays open 9am-dusk

Pulborough,West Chiltington Driving Range (01798 813574) 8 bays covered floodlit + 8 bays open 7.30am-dusk

Rustington, Rustington Golf Centre (01903 850790) 30 bays covered floodlit +4 bays open 9am-9pm

Slinfold, Slinfold Park (01403 791555) 14 bays covered + 5 bays open floodlit 8am-9pmWD (7pmWE 6pm winter)

TYNE & WEAR

Newcastle-upon-Tyne, Parklands (0191 236 4480) 45 bays two-tier covered floodlit 8am-10.30pm

Washington, Washington Moat House (0191 402 9988) 21 bays covered floodlit 9am-9pm

WARWICKSHIRE

Coventry, Brandon Wood (01203 543141) 11 bays covered + 8 bays open floodlit 9am-9pmWD 9am-duskWE

Lea Marston, Lea Marston Driving Range (01675 470707) 30 bays covered floodlit 8.30am-9.30pmWD

Nuneaton, Purley Chase (01203 395348) 13 bays covered floodlit 7am-9pm (7pmWE)

Stratford-upon-Avon, Stratford Oaks Golf Range (01789 731980) 23 bays covered floodlit 8am-8pm (10pm summer)

Warwick, Warwick Golf Centre (01926 494316) 24 bays covered floodlit 10am-9pmWD 8am-6.30pmWE (winter 4.30pm

WEST MIDLANDS

Bromsgrove, Bromsgrove Golf Centre (01527 575886) 41 bays covered floodlit 9am-10pmWD (8pm WE 6pm winter WE)

Coventry, John Reay Golf Cent(01 203 333920 /333405) 60 bays covered floodlit 9am-10pm 10am10pm

Dudley, Sedgley Driving Range (01902 880503) 16 bays covered floodlit 10am-9pmWD 10am-5pmWE winter

Dudley, Swindon Ridge (01902 896191) 23 bays covered + 5 bays open floodlit 9am-9.30pmWD 10am-6pmWE

Halesowen, Halesowen Golf Range (0121 550 2920) 4 bays covered + 11 bays open 9.30am-8pm (dusk in winter)

Solihull, Four Ashes Golf Centre (01564 779055) 28 bays covered floodlit 10am-10pmWD 10am-6pmWE

Wishaw, The Belfry (01675 470301) 16 bays covered floodlit 7.30am-9.30pm

Wolverhampton, Three Hammers (01902 790940) 23 bays covered floodlit 9.30am-10pmWD 9am-8pmWE

Wolverhampton, Perton Park Golf Range (01902 380103) 12 bays covered + 6 bays open 8am-9pmWD 7.30am-7pmWE (dusk in winter)

WILTSHIRE

Calne, Bowood (01249 822228) 10 bays covered floodlit 7.30am-9.30pm

Westbury, Thoulstone Park (01373 832808) 24 bays covered floodlit 8am-7.30pm (5.30pmSun).

Swindon, Broome Manor Golf Complex (01793 532403) 34 bays covered + 6 bays open floodlit 8am-9.30pmWD 7am-9.30pmWE

Swindon, Wrag Barn Golf Range (01793 766027) 12 bays covered floodlit 8am-7pm 7am-7pm WE

Trowbridge, Wingfield Golf Range (01225 776365) 28 bays covered floodlit 9.30am-9.30pm (8pm Sat 6pm Sun)

YORKSHIRE EAST RIDING

Hull, Hull Golf Centre (01482 492720) 24 bays covered floodlit 9am-9pmWD (8pmWE)

YORKSHIRE (NORTH)

Middlesbrough, Middlesbrough Driving Range (01642 300720) 20 bays covered floodlit 8.30am-10pmWD (6pmWE)

York, York Driving Range (01904 690421) 20 bays floodlit covered 10am-5pm 7pm-10pmWD (8pmSat) closed pmSun

YORKSHIRE (SOUTH)

Bawtry, Austerfield Park (01302 710841) 10 bays covered floodlit 8am-10pm

Barnsley, Sandhill Golf Range (01226 751775) 18 bays covered floodlit 9.30am- 9pmWD (6pmWE)

YORKSHIRE (WEST)

Huddersfield, Bradley Park (01484 223772) 14 bays covered floodlit 9am-9.30pm

Knaresborough, Scotton Golf Range (01423 868943) 12 bays covered + 6 bays open 9.30am-8pm (10am-dusk winter)

Leeds, Leeds Golf Centre (0113 288 6000) 21 bays covered floodlit 7am-9.30pm

Leeds, Oulton Park (0113 282 3152) 16 bays covered + 6 open floodlit 7.30am-9.30pm (Thu 12-9.30pm)

Pontefract, Mid Yorkshire (01977 704522) 28 bays covered floodlit 8am-dusk

CHANNEL ISLANDS

GUERNSEY

L'Ancresse Vale, Royal Guernsey (01481 45070) 12 bays open dawn-dusk

JERSEY

St. Ouens Bays, Les Mielles Golf & Country Club (01534 482787) 25 bays covered + 5 open 7am-dusk

ISLE OF MAN

Douglas, Mount Murray (01624 661111) 20 bays covered + 4 bays open floodlit 10am-10pm

SCOTLAND

HIGHLANDS & ISLANDS

Inverness, Fairways Golf Range (01463 713334) 22 bays covered floodlit 8.30am-10pm

Spey Bays, Spey Bays Hotel (01343 820424) 16 bays covered floodlit 10am-10.30pm

CENTRAL

Bathgate, Whitburn, Polkemmet Country Park (01501 743905) 15 bays covered floodlit 10am-9pmWD 9am-9pmWE

Edinburgh, Port Royal (0131 333 4377) 24 bays covered + 13 bays open floodlit 10am-9pmFri-Mon 9pmTue-Thu

Edinburgh, Lasswade, Melville Golf Centre (0131 663 8038) 22 bays covered + 12 bays open floodlit 9am-10pmWD (8pmWE)

Errol, Middlebank Golf Range (01821 670320) 7 bays covered + 21 bays open floodlit 9am-9pm

Glenrothes, Glenrothes Golf Range (01592 775374) 20 bays covered floodlit 10am-8pmWD 9am-6pmWE

Perth, Murrayshall Country House Hotel (01738 551171) 10 bays covered + 8 open floodlit + indoor facility dawn-dusk

SOUTHERN LOWLANDS & BORDERS

Cumbernauld, Cumbernauld Golf Range (01236 737000) 20 bays covered floodlit 10am-10pm

Cumbernauld, Westerwood (01236 457171) 8 bays open 7.30am-dusk

Glasgow, Bishopbriggs Golf Range (0141 762 4883) 20 bays covered + 4 bays open floodlit 10am-10pm (closed5pm-6pm in winter)

Glasgow, Renfrew, Normandy Golf Range (0141 886 7477) 20 bays covered floodlit 9.30am-9pm (6pmWE)

Glasgow, Uddingston, Nevada-Bobs (0141 641 8899) 25 bays covered floodlit 9.30am-9pmWD 7pmSat (10am-8pmSun) 5.30pmWE winter

Stevenston, Auchenharvie Driving Range (01294 603103) 18 bays covered floodlit 9am-4pm 5pm-9pmWD 8am-5pmWE

WALES

NORTH

Penymynydd, Bannel Golf Range (01244 544639) 10 bays covered floodlit + 3 bays open 10am-8.30pmWD 10am-5.30pmWE

Bodelwyddan, Kinmel Park Golf Complex (01745 833548) 24 bays covered floodlit 9am-9pmWD (8pmWE)

St. Asaph, North Wales Golf Range (01745 730805) 14 bays covered floodlit 10am-9pm (5pmFri-Mon winter)

Wrexham, Clays Farm Golf Centre ((01978 661406/661416) 16 bays covered floodlit 8am-9pmWD 6.30pmWE

CENTRAL

Caersws, Mid-Wales (01686 688303) 12 bays covered floodlit 8.30am-10.30pm (8.30-6.30pmWE winter)

Haverfordwest, Mayfield Golf Range (01437 890308) 12 bays covered floodlit 10am-9pm

Middletown, Welsh Border Golf Range (01743 884247) 10 bays covered floodlit 9am-8.30pm winter dusk (ex 9pm Wed /Thu)

Newport, Parc (01633 680933) 30 bays covered + 8 open floodlit 7.30am-10pmWD (8pmWE)

SOUTH

Abergavenny, Wernddu Golf Centre (01873 856223) 26 bays covered floodlit 7.30am-10pm (8am-9.30pm winter)

Barry, South Wales Golf Range (01446 742434) 16 bays covered floodlit 9am-8pmWD 9am-5pmWE

Bridgend, Pencoed, St. Mary's Driving Range (01656 861599) 15 bays covered floodlit 8am-8pm

Caerleon, Caerleon Driving Range (01633 420342) 12 bays covered floodlit + 3 open 7.30am-8pm

Caerphilly, Mountain Lakes (01222 861128) 20 bays covered floodlit dawn-dusk

Caerwent, Dewstow (01291 430444) 15 bays covered floodlit dawn-dusk

Cwmbran, Green Meadow (01633 862626) 6 bays covered floodlit 8am-10pm

NORTHERN IRELAND

CO ANTRIM

Whitehead, Whitehead Driving Range (01960 353631) 18 bays covered 18 bays open floodlit 10am-9pmWD (6pmWE)

CO ARMAGH

Lurgan, Craigavon Golf Centre (01762 326606) 5 bays covered floodlit 8.30am-9.30pmWD 7pmWE

CO BELFAST

Belfast, Knockbracken Golf Centre (01232 792108) 30 bays covered floodlit + 60 bays open 9am-11pm

Belfast, Newtonabbey, Ballyearl Golf Centre (01232 848287) 27 bays covered floodlit 9am-9pm

CO DOWN

Bangor, Blackwood (01247 852706) 20 bays covered floodlit 8am-10pm

Warrenpoint, Newry & Mourne Golf Centre (016937 73247) 10 bays covered floodlit 10am-10pmWD 10am-8pmWE

CO TYRONE

Omagh, Clanabogan Driving Range (01662 245409) 10 bays covered floodlit 10am-10pm

REPUBLIC OF IRELAND

(From UK dial 00353 and ignore first digit of numbers below)

CO CORK

Little Island, Harbour Point (021 353719) 21 bays covered floodlit 9am-9.30pm (8pmFri-Sun winter)

CO DUBLIN

Dublin, Leopardstown Golf Centre (01 289 5341 / 895671) 40 bays covered floodlit + 50 bays open 8.30am-9.30pmWD 8am-9.15Sat 7.30am-9.15Sun

Dublin, Ward Golf Centre (01 834 8711) 30 bays covered + 20 bays open floodlit 10am-10pm

CO GALWAY

Galway, Galway Range (091 526737 / 26753) 24 bays covered floodlit 10am-10pmWD 10am-9pmWE

CO KILDARE

Celbridge, Celbridge Golf Centre (01 628 8833) 40 bays covered floodlit + 20 bays open 8.30am-10pm 8pm Sat winter

CO LAIOS

Portlaiose, The Heath (0502 46622) 10 bays covered floodlit 10.30am-10.30pm

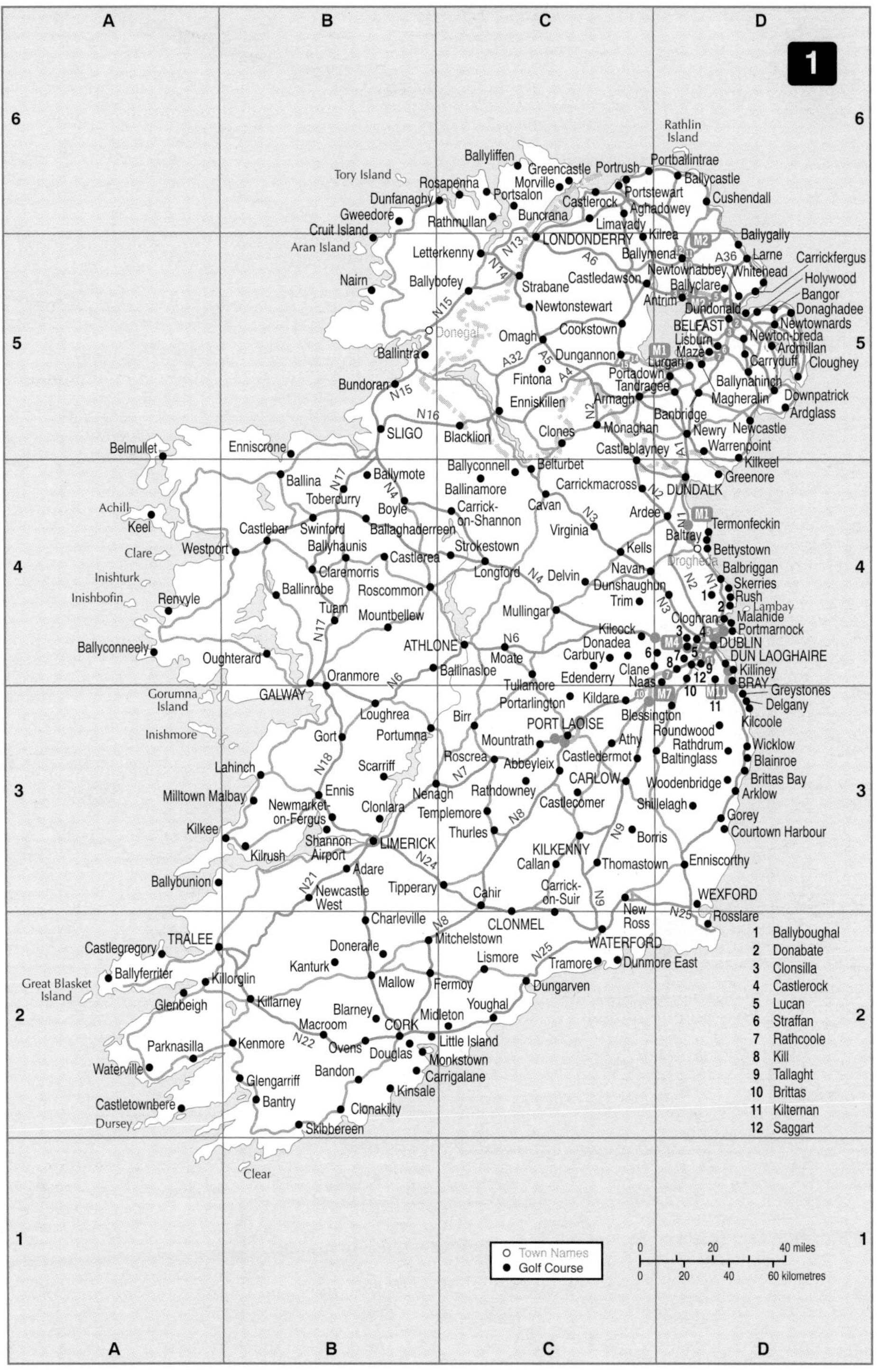
A
B
C
D
1
6
5
4
3
2
1
Rathlin Island
Tory Island
Ballyliffen
Greencastle
Portrush
Portballintrae
Ballycastle
Rosapenna
Morville
Portstewart
Cushendall
Dunfanaghy
Portsalon
Castlerock
Aghadowey
Gweedore
Rathmullan
Buncrana
Limavady
Cruit Island
LONDONDERRY
Kilrea
Ballygally
Aran Island
Letterkenny
Ballymena
A36
Larne
Carrickfergus
Nairn
Ballybofey
Strabane
Castledawson
Newtownabbey
Whitehead
Holywood
Ballyclare
Bangor
Antrim
Dundonald
Donaghadee
Newtonstewart
BELFAST
Newtownards
Donegal
Omagh
Cookstown
Lisburn
Newton-breda
Ballintra
Dungannon
Maze
Ardmillan
Lurgan
Carryduff
Cloughey
Bundoran
Fintona
Portadown
Tandragee
Ballynahinch
Magheralin
Downpatrick
Enniskillen
Armagh
Ardglass
Banbridge
SLIGO
Blacklion
Clones
Monaghan
Newry
Newcastle
Belmullet
Enniscrone
Castleblayney
Warrenpoint
Ballyconnell
Belturbet
Kilkeel
Ballymote
Ballina
Ballinamore
Carrickmacross
Greenore
DUNDALK
Achill
Tobercurry
Boyle
Carrick-on-Shannon
Cavan
Ardee
Termonfeckin
Keel
Castlebar
Swinford
Ballaghaderreen
Virginia
Baltray
Clare
Westport
Ballyhaunis
Strokestown
Kells
Bettystown
Drogheda
Castlerea
Longford
Delvin
Navan
Balbriggan
Inishturk
Claremorris
Dunshaughlin
Skerries
Inishbofin
Renvyle
Ballinrobe
Roscommon
Trim
Rush
Lambay
Tuam
Mullingar
Malahide
Mountbellew
Cloghran
Portmarnock
Kilcock
Ballyconneely
ATHLONE
Donadea
DUBLIN
Moate
Carbury
DUN LAOGHAIRE
Oughterard
Ballinasloe
Clane
Killiney
Oranmore
Edenderry
Naas
BRAY
Tullamore
Gorumna Island
GALWAY
Portarlington
Kildare
Greystones
Delgany
Loughrea
Birr
Blessington
PORT LAOISE
Kilcoole
Inishmore
Gort
Portumna
Roundwood
Mountrath
Athy
Rathdrum
Wicklow
Roscrea
Castledermot
Baltinglass
Lahinch
Scarriff
Abbeyleix
Blainroe
CARLOW
Brittas Bay
Ennis
Rathdowney
Woodenbridge
Milltown Malbay
Nenagh
Arklow
Newmarket-on-Fergus
Clonlara
Templemore
Castlecomer
Shillelagh
Gorey
Kilkee
Thurles
Shannon Airport
LIMERICK
Borris
Courtown Harbour
KILKENNY
Kilrush
Callan
Thomastown
Enniscorthy
Adare
Ballybunion
Tipperary
Newcastle West
Cahir
Carrick-on-Suir
WEXFORD
New Ross
Charleville
CLONMEL
Rosslare
TRALEE
Mitchelstown
WATERFORD
Castlegregory
Doneraile
Lismore
Tramore
Dunmore East
Ballyferriter
Kanturk
Great Blasket Island
Killorglin
Mallow
Fermoy
Dungarvan
Glenbeigh
Killarney
Blarney
Youghal
Macroom
CORK
Midleton
Parknasilla
Kenmore
Ovens
Little Island
Douglas
Waterville
Monkstown
Bandon
Carrigalane
Glengarriff
Kinsale
Bantry
Castletownbere
Clonakilty
Dursey
Skibbereen
Clear
N13
N14
N15
N16
N17
N4
N2
N3
N1
N6
N18
N7
N8
N9
N24
N21
N22
N25
N11
A6
A5
A4
A32
M1
M2
M4
M7
M11
1 Ballyboughal
2 Donabate
3 Clonsilla
4 Castlerock
5 Lucan
6 Straffan
7 Rathcoole
8 Kill
9 Tallaght
10 Brittas
11 Kilternan
12 Saggart
Town Names
Golf Course
0 20 40 miles
0 20 40 60 kilometres

2

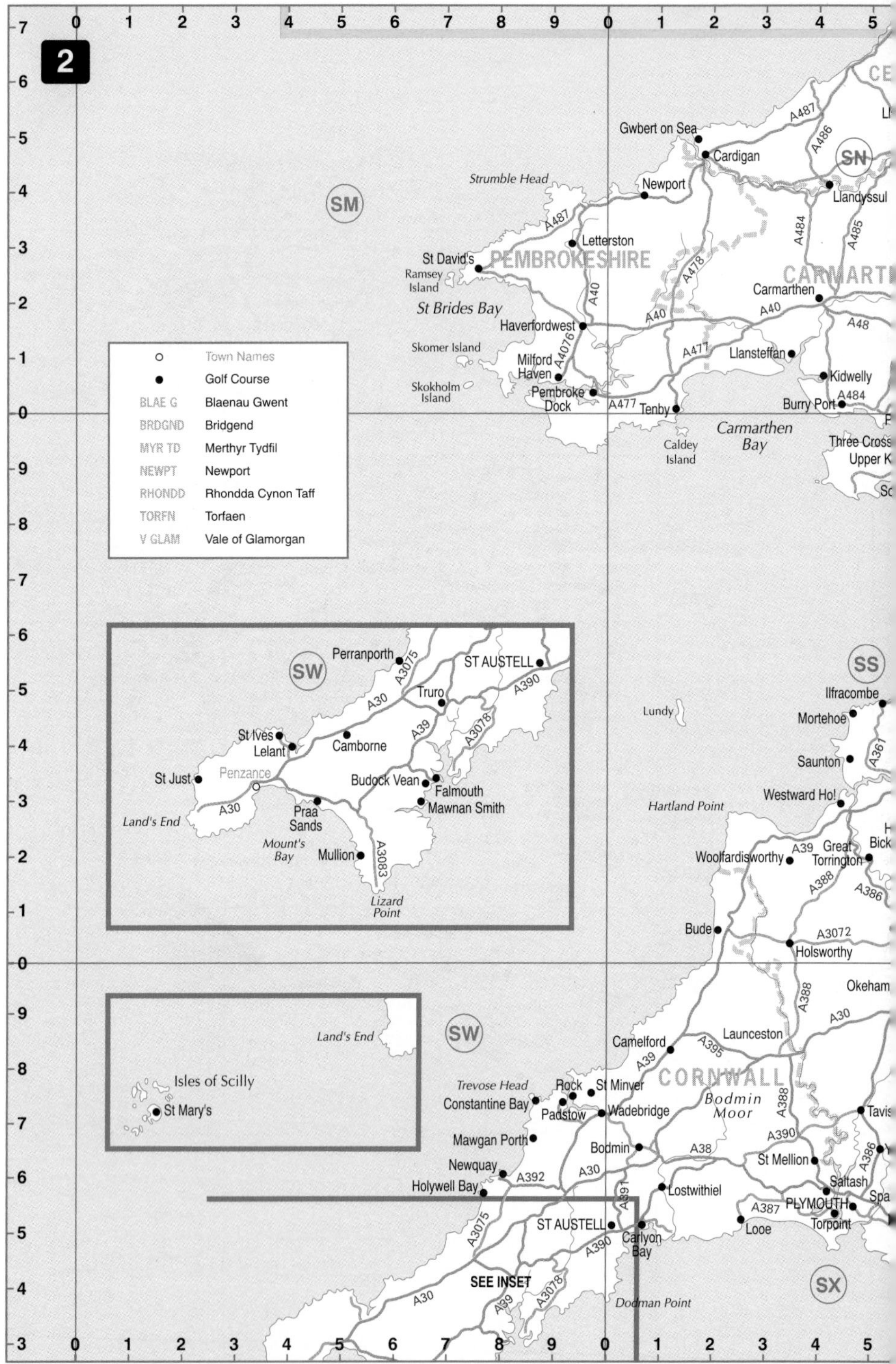
Town Names
Golf Course
BLAE G Blaenau Gwent
BRDGND Bridgend
MYR TD Merthyr Tydfil
NEWPT Newport
RHONDD Rhondda Cynon Taff
TORFN Torfaen
V GLAM Vale of Glamorgan
SM
SN
SW
SS
SX
PEMBROKESHIRE
CARMARTHENSHIRE
CORNWALL
Gwbert on Sea
Cardigan
Newport
Llandyssul
Strumble Head
Letterston
St David's
Ramsey Island
St Brides Bay
Carmarthen
Haverfordwest
Skomer Island
Milford Haven
Llansteffan
Kidwelly
Skokholm Island
Pembroke Dock
Tenby
Burry Port
Carmarthen Bay
Caldey Island
Three Cross
Perranporth
ST AUSTELL
Truro
St Ives
Lelant
Camborne
St Just
Penzance
Budock Vean
Falmouth
Mawnan Smith
Land's End
Praa Sands
Mount's Bay
Mullion
Lizard Point
Lundy
Ilfracombe
Mortehoe
Saunton
Westward Ho!
Hartland Point
Woolfardisworthy
Great Torrington
Bude
Holsworthy
Okeham
Isles of Scilly
St Mary's
Launceston
Camelford
Trevose Head
Rock
St Minver
Constantine Bay
Padstow
Wadebridge
Bodmin Moor
Mawgan Porth
Bodmin
St Mellion
Newquay
Saltash
Holywell Bay
Lostwithiel
PLYMOUTH
Looe
Torpoint
Carlyon Bay
SEE INSET
Dodman Point
A487
A486
A484
A485
A478
A40
A48
A4076
A477
A30
A3075
A390
A39
A3078
A3083
A361
A388
A386
A3072
A395
A38
A392
A387
A391

For continuation pages refer to numbered arrows

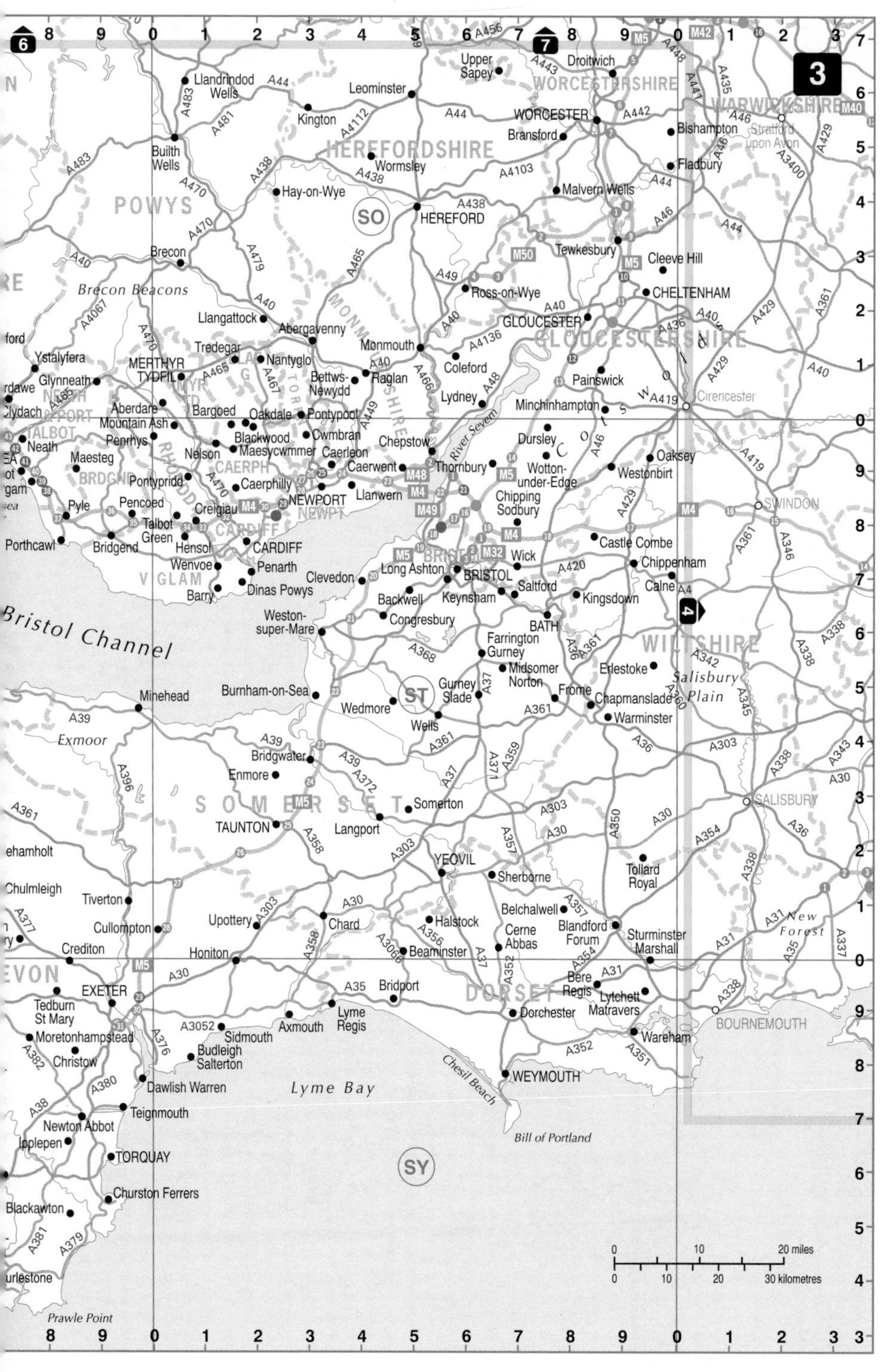

3
6
7
4
WORCESTERSHIRE
WARWICKSHIRE
HEREFORDSHIRE
POWYS
GLOUCESTERSHIRE
SOMERSET
DORSET
WILTSHIRE
DEVON
MONMOUTHSHIRE
V GLAM
CARDIFF
CAERPH
NEWPT
BRISTOL
NEATH PORT TALBOT
BRDGND
RHONDDA
MERTHYR TYDFIL
Upper Sapey
Droitwich
Llandrindod Wells
Leominster
Kington
WORCESTER
Bishampton
Stratford upon Avon
Bransford
Builth Wells
Wormsley
Fladbury
Hay-on-Wye
Malvern Wells
HEREFORD
SO
Brecon
Tewkesbury
Cleeve Hill
Brecon Beacons
Ross-on-Wye
CHELTENHAM
Llangattock
Abergavenny
GLOUCESTER
ford
Ystalyfera
Tredegar
Nantyglo
Monmouth
Coleford
Glynneath
MERTHYR TYDFIL
Bettws-Newydd
Raglan
Painswick
rdawe
Lydney
Cirencester
Clydach
Aberdare
Bargoed
Oakdale
Pontypool
Minchinhampton
Mountain Ash
Blackwood
Cwmbran
Penrhys
Maesycwmmer
Chepstow
Dursley
Neath
Nelson
Caerleon
River Severn
Oaksey
Maesteg
Caerwent
Thornbury
Wotton-under-Edge
Westonbirt
Pontypridd
Caerphilly
Llanwern
NEWPORT
Pyle
Pencoed
Creigiau
Chipping Sodbury
SWINDON
Talbot Green
Hensol
Porthcawl
Bridgend
CARDIFF
Castle Combe
Wenvoe
Penarth
Long Ashton
Wick
Chippenham
Clevedon
BRISTOL
Calne
Barry
Dinas Powys
Saltford
Backwell
Keynsham
Kingsdown
Bristol Channel
Weston-super-Mare
Congresbury
BATH
Farrington Gurney
Midsomer Norton
Erlestoke
Salisbury Plain
Minehead
Burnham-on-Sea
Gurney Slade
Frome
Chapmanslade
Wedmore
ST
Wells
Warminster
Exmoor
Bridgwater
Enmore
Somerton
SALISBURY
TAUNTON
Langport
ehamholt
YEOVIL
Sherborne
Tollard Royal
Chulmleigh
Tiverton
Belchalwell
Halstock
Cullompton
Upottery
Chard
Cerne Abbas
Blandford Forum
New Forest
Sturminster Marshall
Crediton
Honiton
Beaminster
EXETER
Bridport
Bere Regis
Lytchett Matravers
Tedburn St Mary
Lyme Regis
Axmouth
Sidmouth
Dorchester
BOURNEMOUTH
Moretonhampstead
Budleigh Salterton
Wareham
Christow
Chesil Beach
WEYMOUTH
Dawlish Warren
Lyme Bay
Teignmouth
Newton Abbot
Ipplepen
Bill of Portland
TORQUAY
SY
Churston Ferrers
Blackawton
urlestone
Prawle Point
0 10 20 miles
0 10 20 30 kilometres

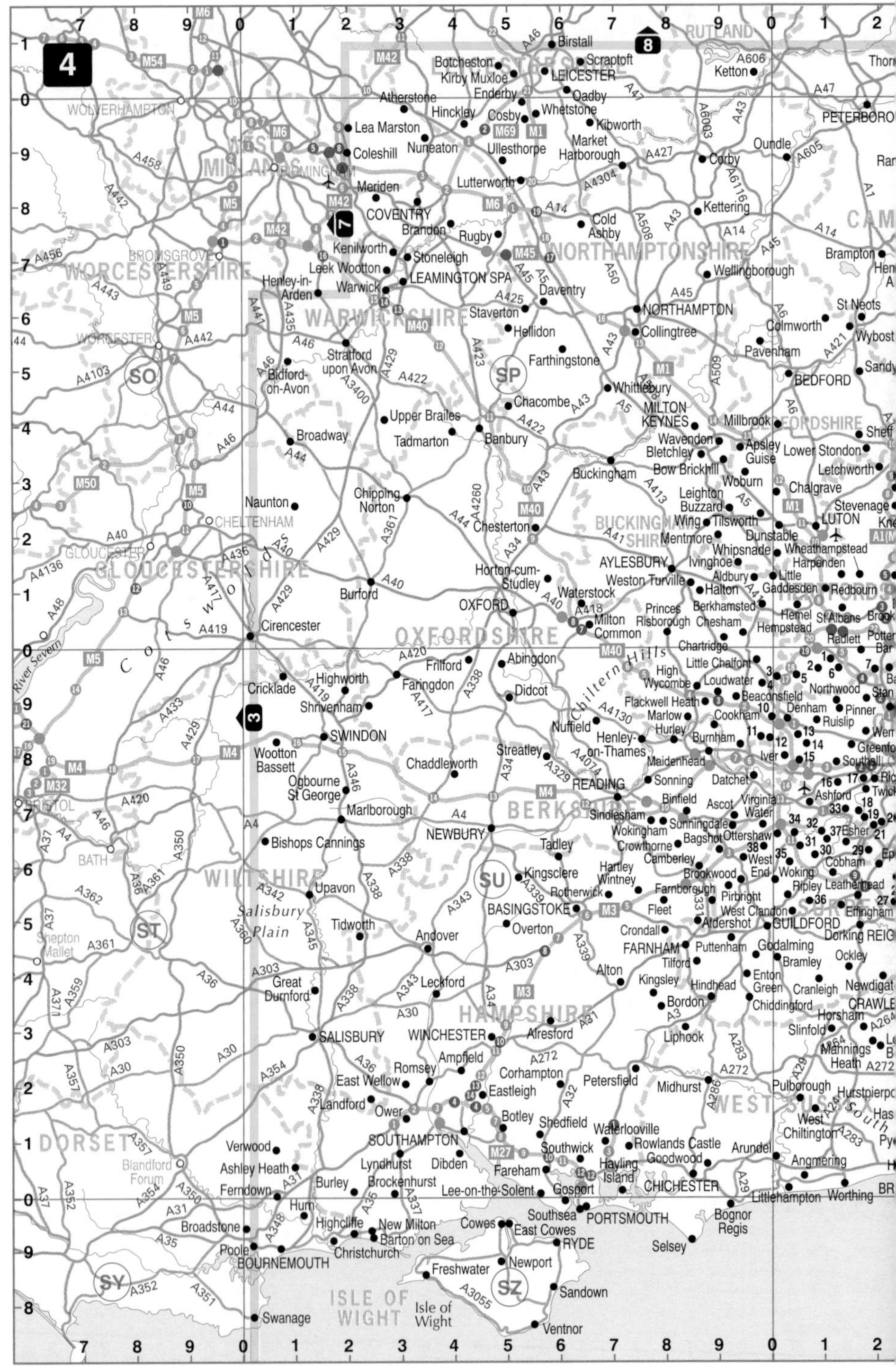

For continuation pages refer to numbered arrows

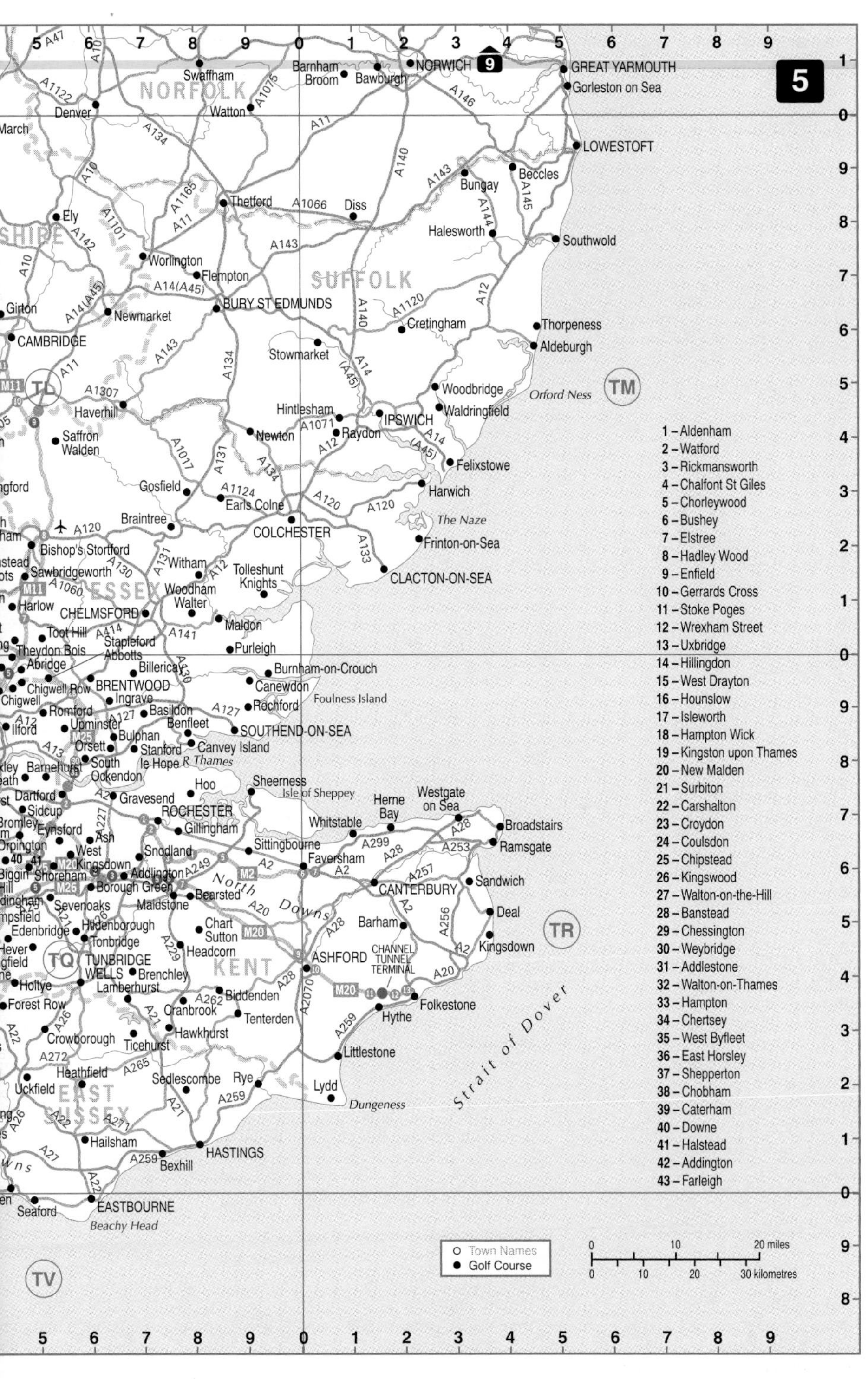

5
NORFOLK
SUFFOLK
ESSEX
KENT
EAST SUSSEX
TL
TM
TQ
TR
TV
NORWICH
GREAT YARMOUTH
Gorleston on Sea
LOWESTOFT
Barnham Broom
Bawburgh
Swaffham
Denver
Watton
March
Beccles
Bungay
Thetford
Diss
Ely
Halesworth
Southwold
Worlington
Flempton
BURY ST EDMUNDS
Girton
Newmarket
CAMBRIDGE
Cretingham
Thorpeness
Aldeburgh
Stowmarket
Woodbridge
Waldringfield
Orford Ness
Haverhill
Hintlesham
IPSWICH
Raydon
Newton
Saffron Walden
Felixstowe
Gosfield
Earls Colne
Harwich
Braintree
COLCHESTER
The Naze
Frinton-on-Sea
Bishop's Stortford
Sawbridgeworth
Witham
Tolleshunt Knights
CLACTON-ON-SEA
Woodham Walter
Harlow
CHELMSFORD
Maldon
Toot Hill
Stapleford Abbotts
Purleigh
Theydon Bois
Abridge
Billericay
Burnham-on-Crouch
Chigwell Row
BRENTWOOD
Canewdon
Chigwell
Ingrave
Foulness Island
Romford
Basildon
Rochford
Ilford
Upminster
Benfleet
SOUTHEND-ON-SEA
Bulphan
Orsett
Stanford le Hope
Canvey Island
R Thames
Barnehurst
South Ockendon
Dartford
Hoo
Sheerness
Isle of Sheppey
Sidcup
Gravesend
ROCHESTER
Herne Bay
Westgate on Sea
Eynsford
Gillingham
Whitstable
Broadstairs
Ash
Sittingbourne
Ramsgate
West Kingsdown
Snodland
Faversham
Addington
Sandwich
Shoreham
Borough Green
North Downs
CANTERBURY
Sevenoaks
Maidstone
Bearsted
Barham
Deal
Edenbridge
Hildenborough
Chart Sutton
Tonbridge
Kingsdown
Hever
Headcorn
ASHFORD
CHANNEL TUNNEL TERMINAL
TUNBRIDGE WELLS
Brenchley
Lamberhurst
Biddenden
Holtye
Forest Row
Cranbrook
Folkestone
Tenterden
Hythe
Crowborough
Hawkhurst
Strait of Dover
Ticehurst
Littlestone
Heathfield
Sedlescombe
Rye
Uckfield
Lydd
Dungeness
Hailsham
HASTINGS
Bexhill
Seaford
EASTBOURNE
Beachy Head
1 – Aldenham
2 – Watford
3 – Rickmansworth
4 – Chalfont St Giles
5 – Chorleywood
6 – Bushey
7 – Elstree
8 – Hadley Wood
9 – Enfield
10 – Gerrards Cross
11 – Stoke Poges
12 – Wrexham Street
13 – Uxbridge
14 – Hillingdon
15 – West Drayton
16 – Hounslow
17 – Isleworth
18 – Hampton Wick
19 – Kingston upon Thames
20 – New Malden
21 – Surbiton
22 – Carshalton
23 – Croydon
24 – Coulsdon
25 – Chipstead
26 – Kingswood
27 – Walton-on-the-Hill
28 – Banstead
29 – Chessington
30 – Weybridge
31 – Addlestone
32 – Walton-on-Thames
33 – Hampton
34 – Chertsey
35 – West Byfleet
36 – East Horsley
37 – Shepperton
38 – Chobham
39 – Caterham
40 – Downe
41 – Halstead
42 – Addington
43 – Farleigh
Town Names
Golf Course
0 10 20 miles
0 10 20 30 kilometres

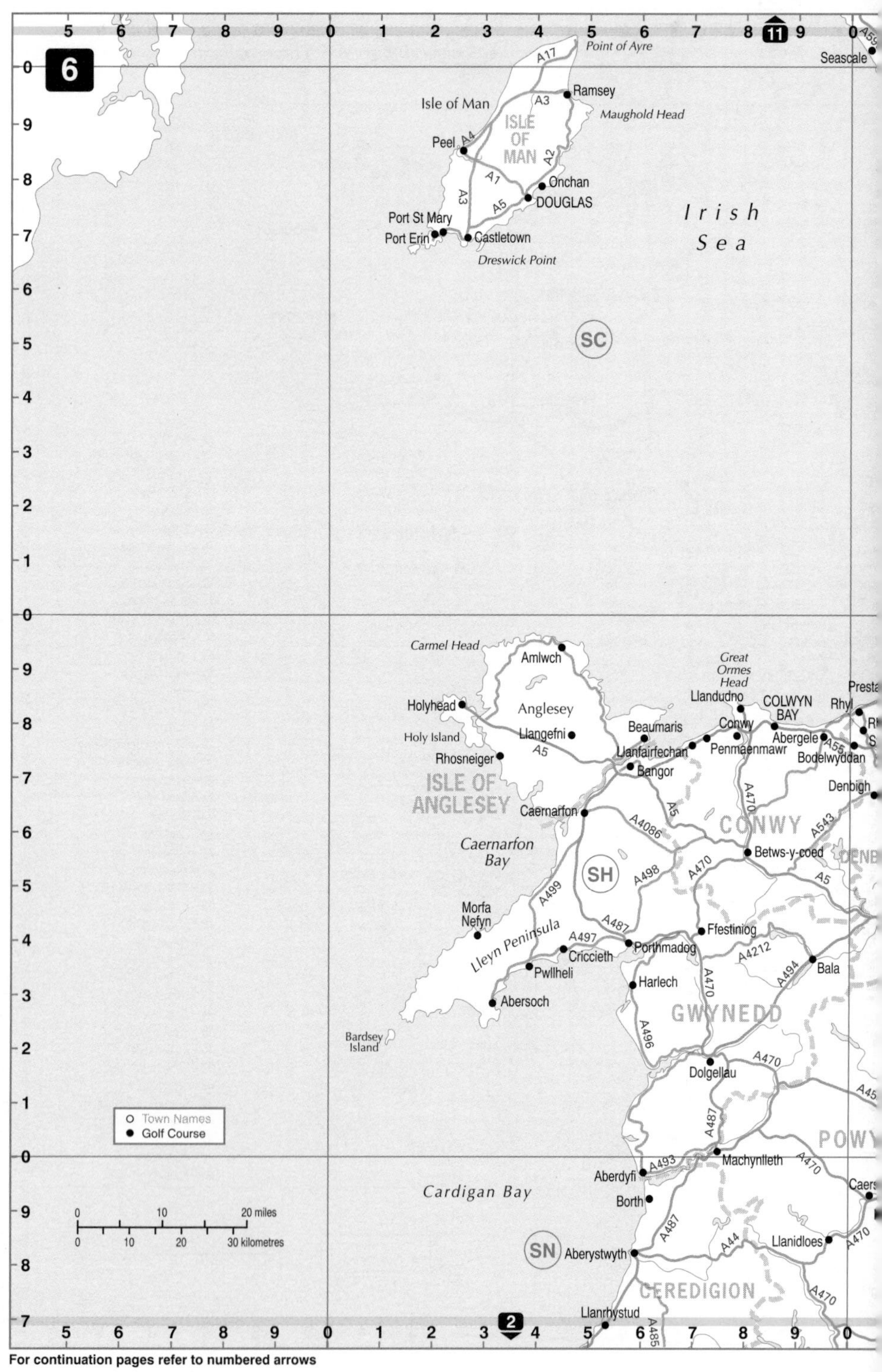

For continuation pages refer to numbered arrows

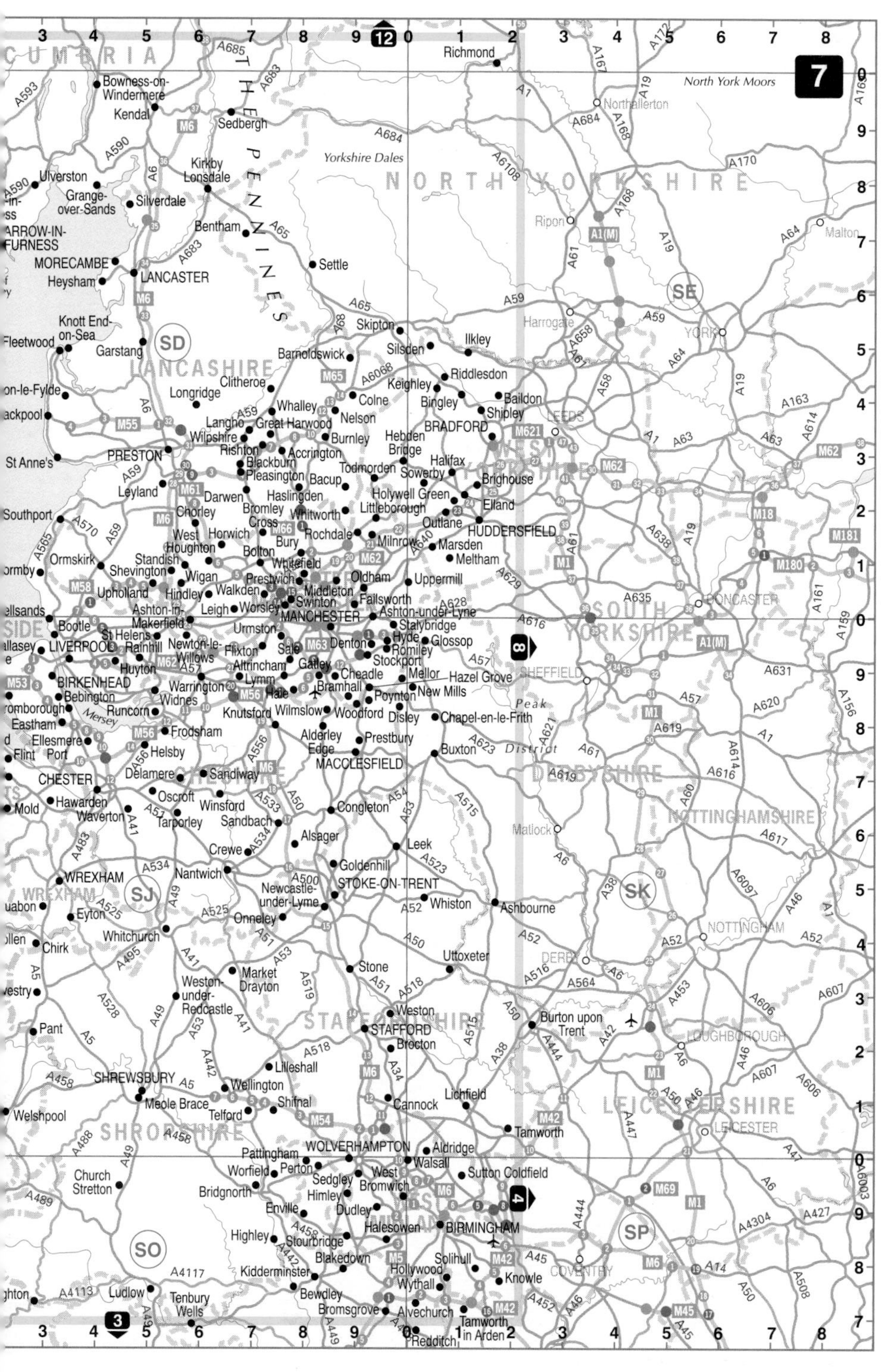

7
CUMBRIA
THE PENNINES
NORTH YORKSHIRE
North York Moors
Yorkshire Dales
LANCASHIRE
WEST YORKSHIRE
SOUTH YORKSHIRE
DERBYSHIRE
NOTTINGHAMSHIRE
STAFFORDSHIRE
SHROPSHIRE
LEICESTERSHIRE
WREXHAM
Peak District
Mersey
SD
SE
SJ
SK
SO
SP
Richmond
Northallerton
Bowness-on-Windermere
Kendal
Sedbergh
Kirkby Lonsdale
Ulverston
Grange-over-Sands
Silverdale
BARROW-IN-FURNESS
MORECAMBE
Heysham
LANCASTER
Bentham
Settle
Ripon
Malton
Harrogate
YORK
Knott End-on-Sea
Fleetwood
Garstang
Skipton
Silsden
Ilkley
Barnoldswick
Riddlesdon
Keighley
Baildon
Shipley
Bingley
Clitheroe
Longridge
Colne
Nelson
Whalley
Langho
Great Harwood
Wilpshire
Burnley
BRADFORD
LEEDS
Blackpool
PRESTON
Rishton
Accrington
Hebden Bridge
Halifax
St Anne's
Blackburn
Pleasington
Todmorden
Sowerby
Brighouse
Leyland
Bacup
Darwen
Haslingden
Holywell Green
Elland
Southport
Chorley
Bromley Cross
Whitworth
Littleborough
Outlane
HUDDERSFIELD
West Houghton
Horwich
Bury
Rochdale
Milnrow
Marsden
Meltham
Ormskirk
Standish
Bolton
Whitefield
Oldham
Uppermill
Shevington
Wigan
Prestwich
Middleton
Upholland
Hindley
Walkden
Swinton
Failsworth
Ashton-in-Makerfield
Leigh
Worsley
MANCHESTER
Ashton-under-Lyne
DONCASTER
Bootle
St Helens
Urmston
Stalybridge
LIVERPOOL
Rainhill
Newton-le-Willows
Flixton
Sale
Denton
Hyde
Glossop
Romiley
Huyton
Altrincham
Gatley
Stockport
BIRKENHEAD
Lymm
Cheadle
Mellor
Hazel Grove
SHEFFIELD
Bebington
Warrington
Hale
Bramhall
Poynton
New Mills
Widnes
Runcorn
Knutsford
Wilmslow
Woodford
Disley
Chapel-en-le-Frith
Eastham
Frodsham
Ellesmere Port
Alderley Edge
Prestbury
Flint
Helsby
Buxton
MACCLESFIELD
CHESTER
Delamere
Sandiway
Hawarden
Oscroft
Winsford
Mold
Waverton
Tarporley
Sandbach
Congleton
Matlock
Alsager
Crewe
Leek
WREXHAM
Nantwich
Goldenhill
Newcastle-under-Lyme
STOKE-ON-TRENT
Whiston
Ashbourne
Eyton
Onneley
Whitchurch
Chirk
NOTTINGHAM
DERBY
Uttoxeter
Stone
Market Drayton
Weston-under-Redcastle
Weston
STAFFORD
Brocton
Burton upon Trent
LOUGHBOROUGH
Pant
Lilleshall
SHREWSBURY
Wellington
Shifnal
Welshpool
Meole Brace
Telford
Cannock
Lichfield
Tamworth
LEICESTER
Pattingham
WOLVERHAMPTON
Aldridge
Walsall
Worfield
Perton
West Bromwich
Sutton Coldfield
Church Stretton
Bridgnorth
Sedgley
Himley
Enville
Dudley
Halesowen
BIRMINGHAM
Highley
Stourbridge
Blakedown
Solihull
COVENTRY
Kidderminster
Hollywood
Wythall
Knowle
Ludlow
Tenbury Wells
Bewdley
Bromsgrove
Alvechurch
Tamworth in Arden
Redditch

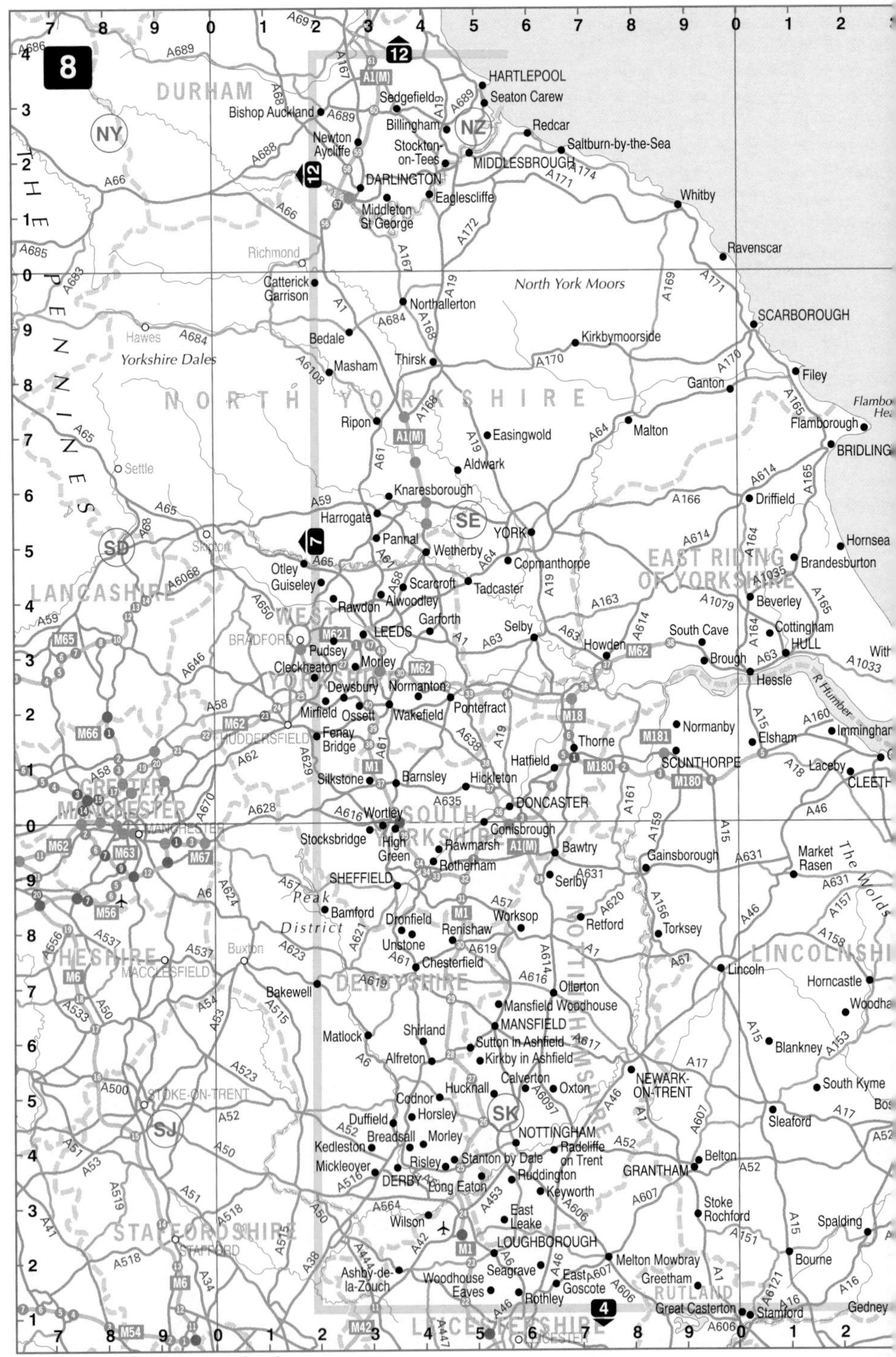

For continuation pages refer to numbered arrows

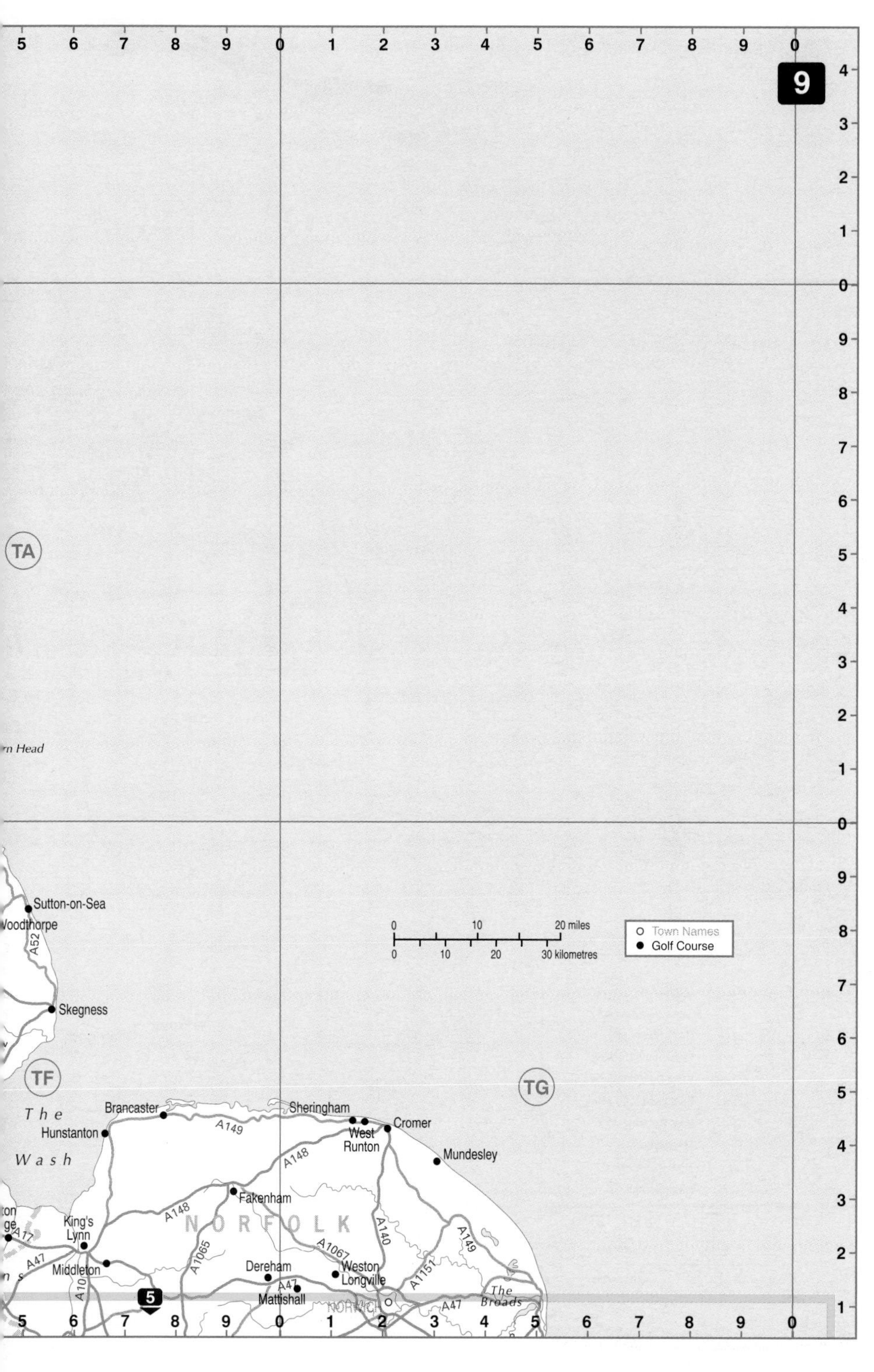
9
TA
TF
TG
rn Head
Sutton-on-Sea
Woodthorpe
A52
Skegness
The Wash
Brancaster
Hunstanton
A149
Sheringham
West Runton
Cromer
Mundesley
A148
Fakenham
NORFOLK
King's Lynn
A17
A47
Middleton
A10
A1065
Dereham
A47
Mattishall
A1067
A140
Weston Longville
NORWICH
A1151
A149
The Broads
0 10 20 miles
0 10 20 30 kilometres
Town Names
Golf Course
5

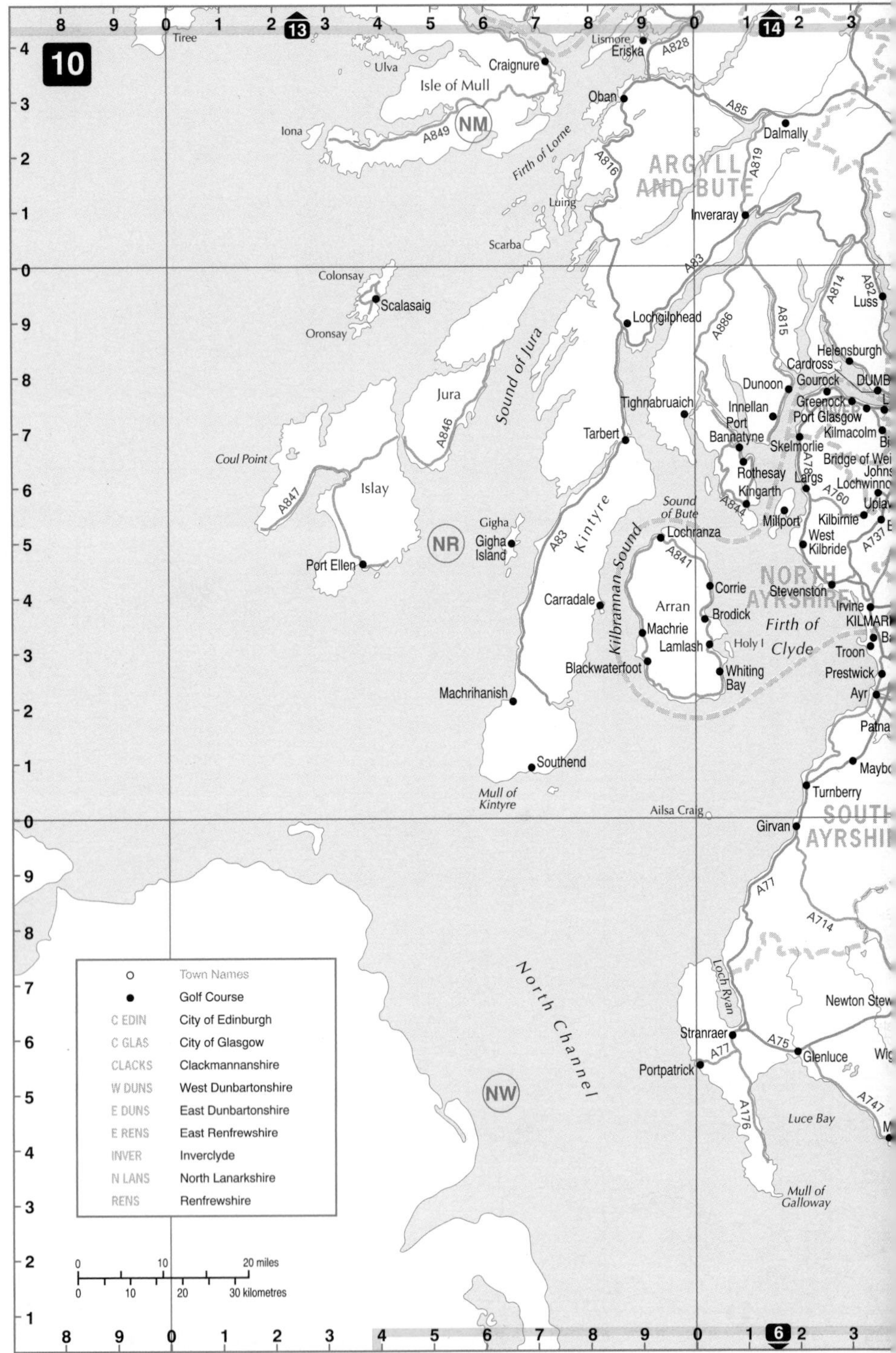

For continuation pages refer to numbered arrows

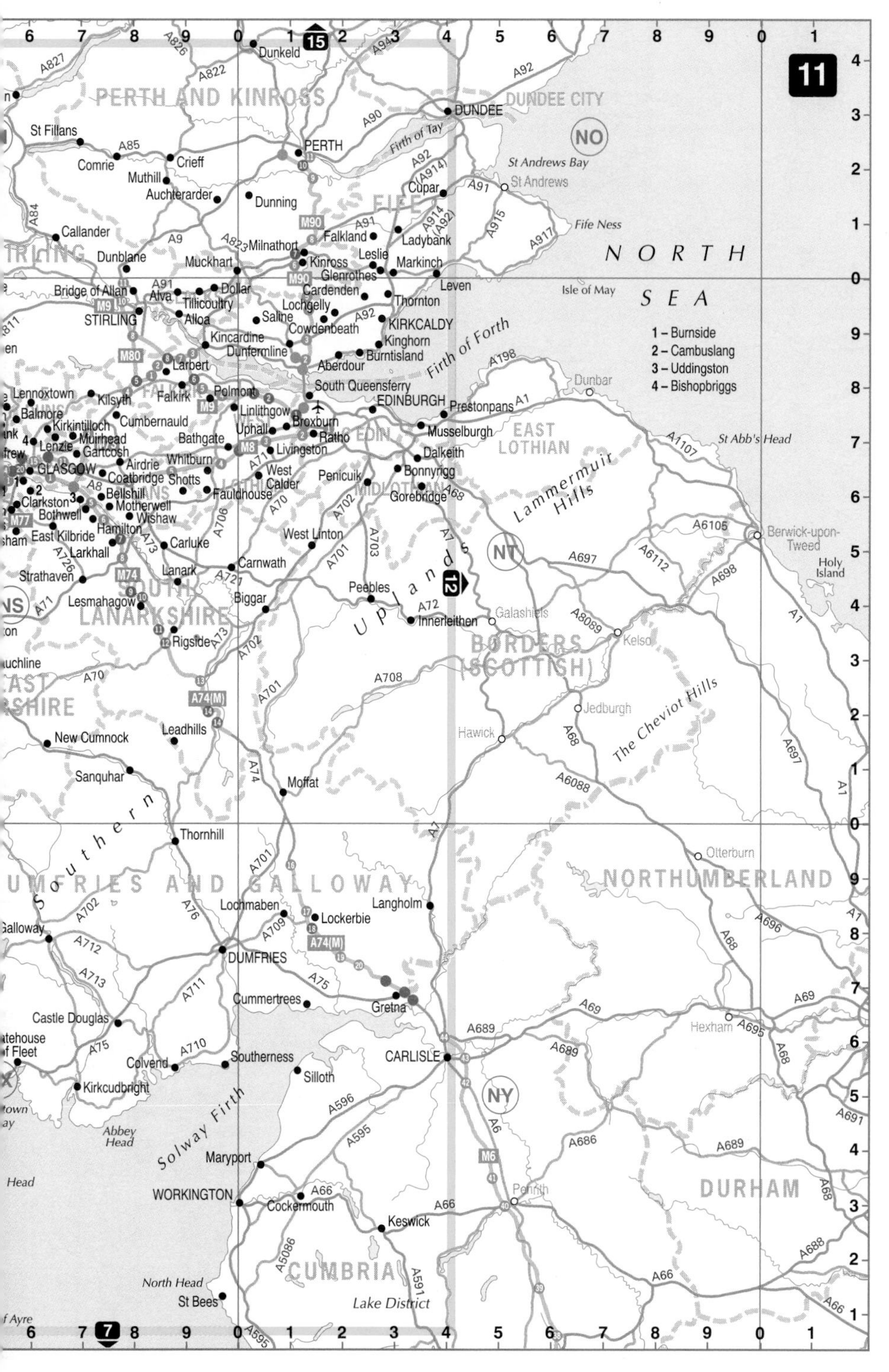
PERTH AND KINROSS
DUNDEE CITY
DUNDEE
PERTH
Firth of Tay
St Andrews Bay
St Andrews
Fife Ness
NORTH SEA
FIFE
STIRLING
EDINBURGH
Firth of Forth
Isle of May
1 – Burnside
2 – Cambuslang
3 – Uddingston
4 – Bishopbriggs
Dunbar
EAST LOTHIAN
St Abb's Head
Lammermuir Hills
GLASGOW
Berwick-upon-Tweed
Holy Island
Peebles
Upland s
Galashiels
Kelso
BORDERS (SCOTTISH)
Jedburgh
Hawick
The Cheviot Hills
SOUTH LANARKSHIRE
Southern
Moffat
Otterburn
NORTHUMBERLAND
DUMFRIES AND GALLOWAY
Lockerbie
Langholm
DUMFRIES
Gretna
CARLISLE
Hexham
Solway Firth
Kirkcudbright
Abbey Head
Maryport
WORKINGTON
Cockermouth
Keswick
Penrith
CUMBRIA
Lake District
DURHAM
St Bees
North Head
NO
NT
NY

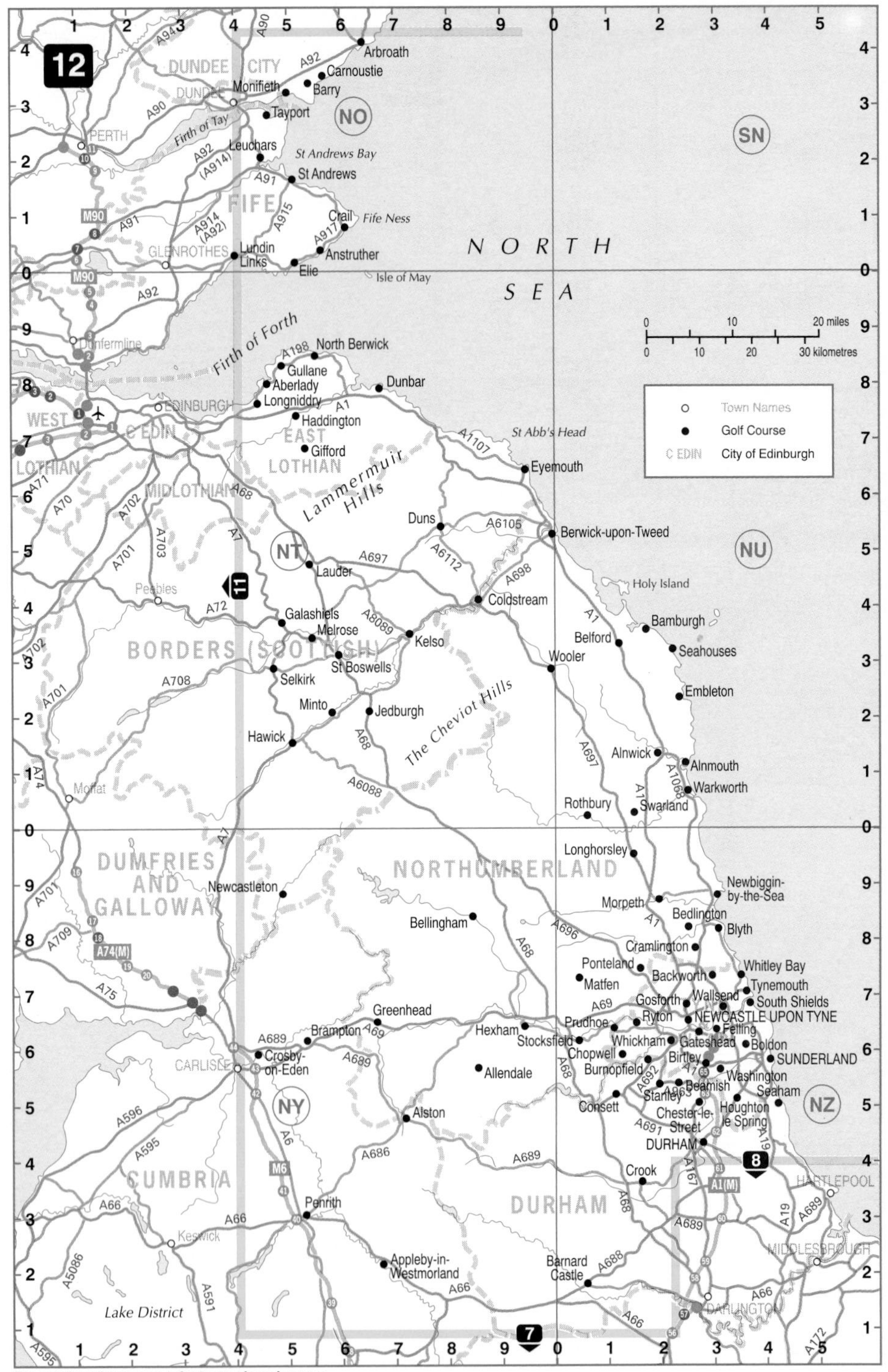

For continuation pages refer to numbered arrows

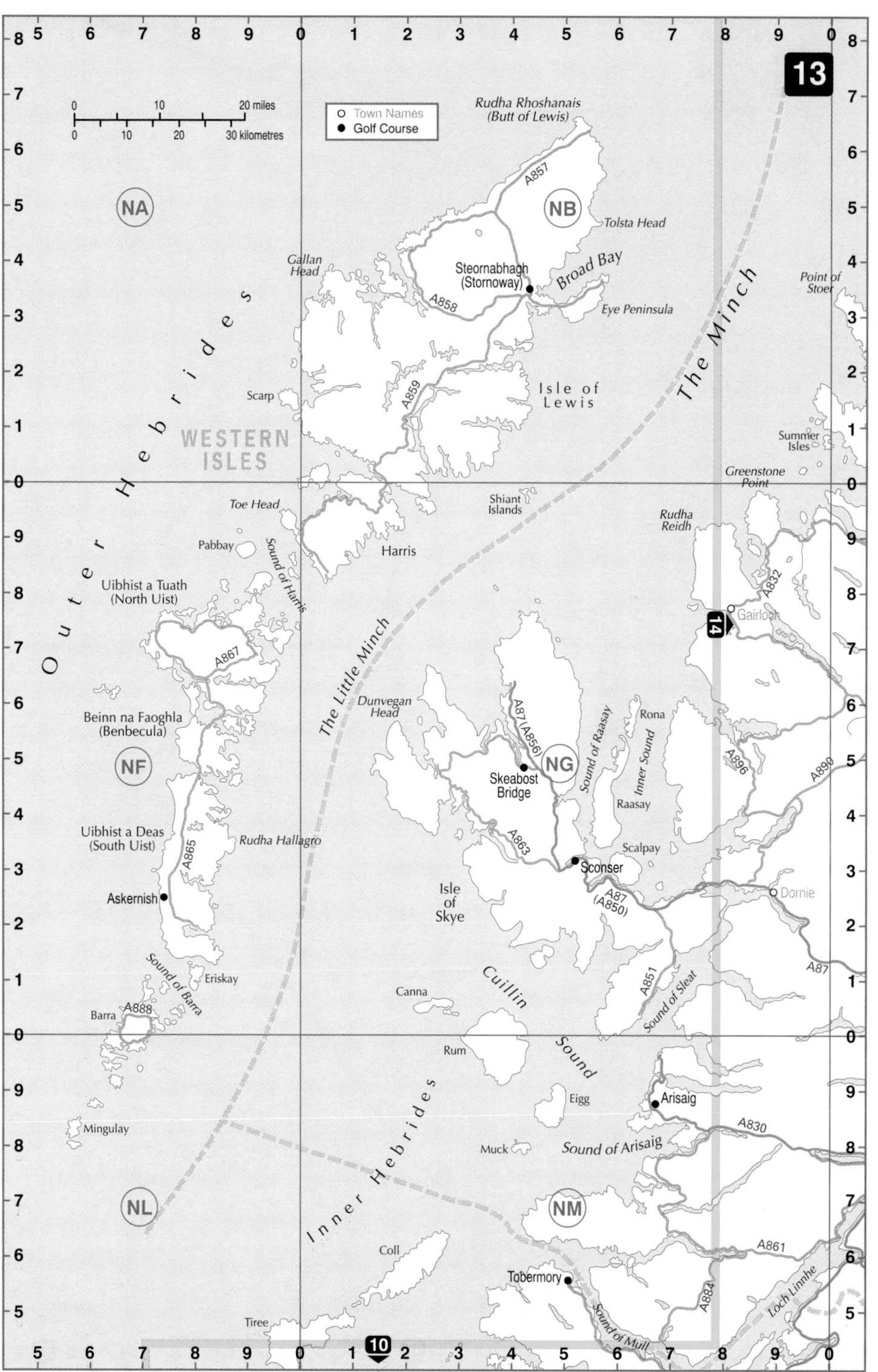
13
Town Names
Golf Course
20 miles
30 kilometres
Rudha Rhoshanais
(Butt of Lewis)
A857
NA
NB
Tolsta Head
Gallan Head
Steornabhagh
(Stornoway)
Broad Bay
A858
Eye Peninsula
The Minch
Point of Stoer
Outer Hebrides
Scarp
A859
Isle of Lewis
WESTERN ISLES
Summer Isles
Greenstone Point
Toe Head
Shiant Islands
Rudha Reidh
Pabbay
Sound of Harris
Harris
Uibhist a Tuath
(North Uist)
A832
Gairloch
14
A867
The Little Minch
Dunvegan Head
A87(A856)
Sound of Raasay
Rona
Beinn na Faoghla
(Benbecula)
Inner Sound
NF
NG
A896
A890
Skeabost Bridge
Raasay
Uibhist a Deas
(South Uist)
A865
Rudha Hallagro
A863
Scalpay
Sconser
Askernish
Isle of Skye
A87
(A850)
Dornie
Sound of Barra
Eriskay
Cuillin
A851
Sound of Sleat
A87
Canna
Barra
A888
Rum
Sound
Arisaig
Eigg
Mingulay
Inner Hebrides
A830
Muck
Sound of Arisaig
NL
NM
Coll
A861
Tobermory
A884
Loch Linnhe
Tiree
Sound of Mull
10

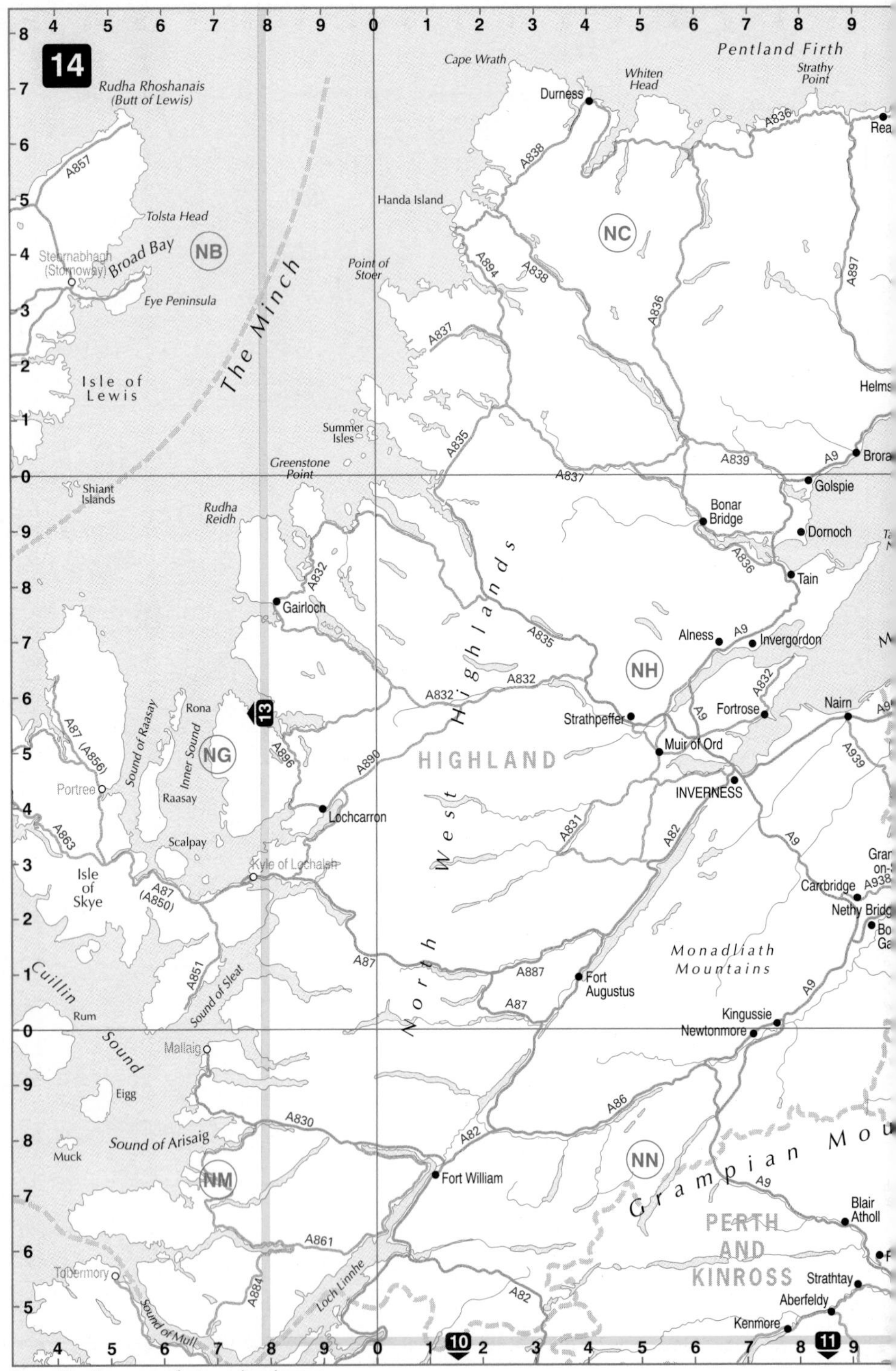

For continuation pages refer to numbered arrows

15
Island of Stroma
Duncansby Head
A836
Noss Head
Wick
A99 (A9)
ND
Lybster
NJ
NK
NO
Fraserburgh
Inverallocky
Cullen
Spey Bay
Garmouth
Buckie
Banff
Macduff
Keith
Rothes
Turriff
Peterhead
Dufftown
Huntly
Cruden Bay
Ellon
Oldmeldrum
Insch
Newburgh on Ythan
ABERDEENSHIRE
Inverurie
Newmachar
Alford
Kemnay
Kintore
ABERDEEN CITY
ABERDEEN
Tarland
Torphins
Peterculter
Aboyne
Ballater
Banchory
Portlethen
Stonehaven
Auchenblae
Edzell
ANGUS
Brechin
Montrose
Kirriemuir
Forfar
Alyth
Lunan Bay
Town Names
Golf Course
20 miles
30 kilometres
12

Orkney Islands

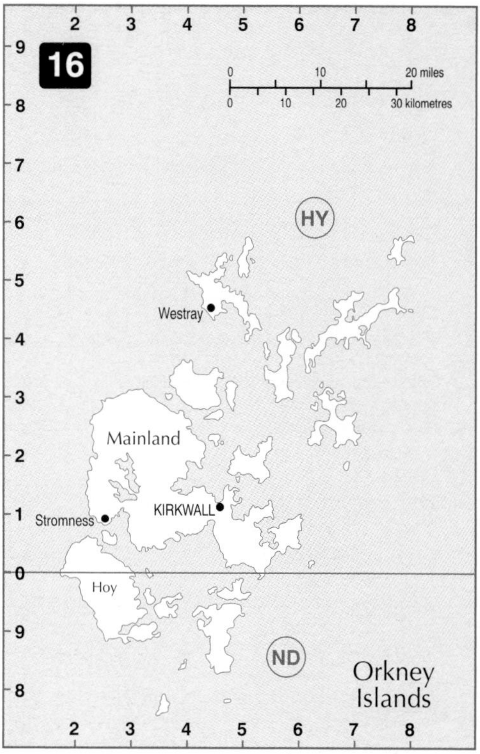

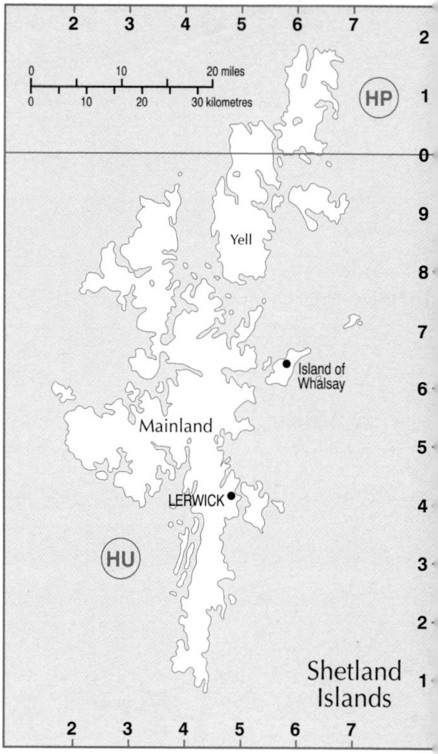

0 10 20 miles
0 10 20 30 kilometres

HY
ND
Westray
Mainland
Stromness
KIRKWALL
Hoy

Shetland Islands

0 10 20 miles
0 10 20 30 kilometres

HP
HU
Yell
Island of Whalsay
Mainland
LERWICK

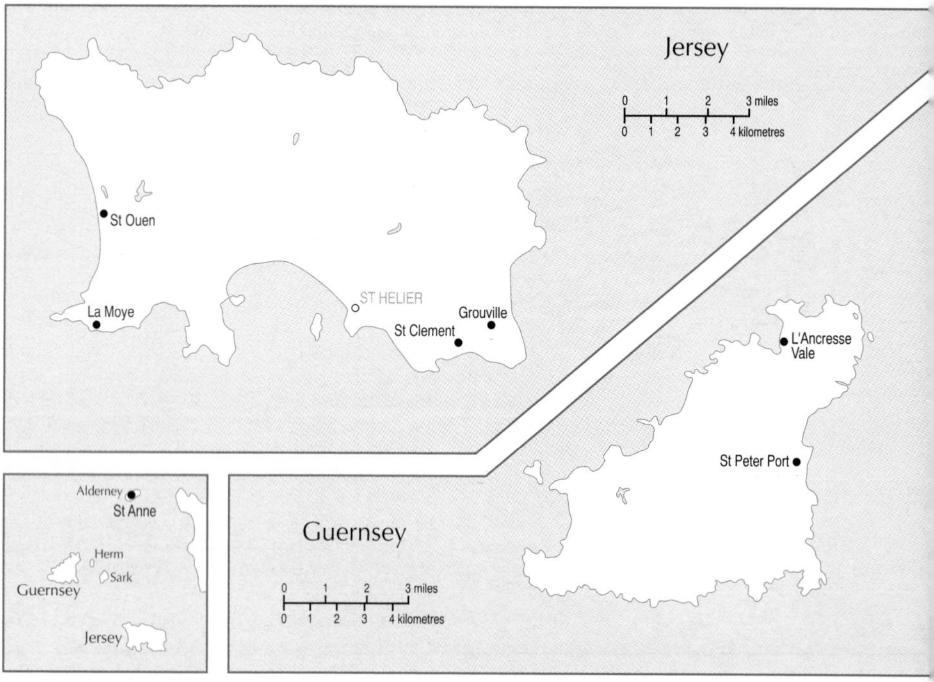

Jersey

0 1 2 3 miles
0 1 2 3 4 kilometres

St Ouen
La Moye
ST HELIER
St Clement
Grouville

Guernsey

0 1 2 3 miles
0 1 2 3 4 kilometres

L'Ancresse Vale
St Peter Port

Alderney
St Anne
Herm
Sark
Guernsey
Jersey

INDEX

A

B

D

E

F

G

H

I

J

K

L

M

N

S

Y